INDIA 2019

A REFERENCE ANNUAL

Compiled by

NEW MEDIA WING

PUBLICATIONS DIVISION

MINISTRY OF INFORMATION AND BROADCASTING

GOVERNMENT OF INDIA

2019 *(Saka 1940)*
63rd Edition

ISBN 978-81-230-3021-0
REF-ENG-OP-153-2018-19

Price : ₹ 350.00

Published by the Director General,
Publications Division,
Ministry of Information and Broadcasting,
Government of India, Soochna Bhawan, CGO Complex,
Lodhi Road, New Delhi-110 003

Website : www.publicationsdivision.nic.in
E-mail : dpd@nic.in

Publications Division
Editor: Roma Chatterjee

New Media Wing
Compilation
K. Satish Nambudiripad
Sayyid Rabeehashmi
Sakshi Singh
Simmi Kumar
Shivanand Pandey

Editorial Coordination : Deepika Kachhal, Shamima Siddiqui
Cover Design : Sisir Kumar Datta
Production : V. K. Meena

Sales Centres : • Soochna Bhavan, C.G.O. Complex, Lodhi Road, **New Delhi**-110003 • Hall No. 196, Old Secretariat, **Delhi**-110054 • 701, C-Wing, 7th Floor, Kendriya Sadan, Belapur, **Navi Mumbai**-400614 • 8, Esplanade East, **Kolkata**-700069 • 'A' Wing, Rajaji Bhawan, Besant Nagar, **Chennai**-600090 • Press Road, Near Govt. Press, **Thiruvananthapuram**-695001 • 204, CGO Towers, M. J. Road, Nampally, Kavadiguda, **Hyderabad**-500080 • 1st Floor, 'F' Wing, Kendriya Sadan, Koramangala, **Bengaluru**-560034 • Bihar State Co-operative Bank Building, Ashoka Rajpath, **Patna**-800004 • Hall No. 1, 2nd Floor, Kendriya Bhawan, Sector-H, Aliganj, **Lucknow**-226024

Typesetter : Quick Prints, Naraina, New Delhi-110 028.
Printed at : MP Printers, (A Unit of DB Corp. Ltd.) Noida, 201305

Contents

सत्यमेव जयते

National Emblem

1 Land and the People

"INDIA is the cradle of the human race, the birthplace of human speech, the mother of history, the grandmother of legend and the great grandmother of tradition. Our most valuable and most instructive materials in the history of man are treasured up in India only."—Mark Twain

India has a unique culture and is one of the oldest and greatest civilizations of the world. It stretches from the snow-capped Himalayas in the north to sun drenched coastal villages of the south and the humid tropical forests on the south-west coast, from the fertile Brahmaputra valley on its east to the Thar desert in the west. It covers an area of 32,87,263 sq. km.[1] It has achieved all-round socio-economic progress during the last so many years of its Independence. India is the seventh largest country in the world and ranks second in population. The country stands apart from the rest of Asia, marked off as it is by mountains and the sea, which give her a distinct geographical entity. Bounded by the Great Himalayas in the north, it stretches southwards and at the Tropic of Cancer tapers off into the Indian Ocean between the Bay of Bengal on the east and the Arabian Sea on the west.

Lying entirely in the northern hemisphere, the mainland extends between latitudes 8°4' and 37°6' north, longitudes 68°7' and 97°25' east and measures about 3,214 km from north to south between the extreme latitudes and about 2,933 km from east to west between the extreme longitudes. It has a land frontier of about 15,200 km. The total length of the coastline of the mainland, Lakshadweep Islands and Andaman and Nicobar Islands is 7,516.6 km.

Geographical Background

Countries having a common border with India are Afghanistan and Pakistan to the north-west, China, Bhutan and Nepal to the north, Myanmar to the far east and Bangladesh to the east. Sri Lanka is separated from India by a narrow channel of sea formed by the Palk Strait and the Gulf of Mannar. The country can be divided into six zones mainly north, south, east, west, central and north-east zone. It has 29 states and seven union territories.

Physical Features

The mainland comprises four regions, namely, the great mountain zone, plains of the Ganga and the Indus, the desert region and the southern peninsula.

The Himalayas comprise three almost parallel ranges interspersed with large plateaus and valleys, some of which, like the Kashmir and Kullu valleys, are fertile, extensive and of great scenic beauty. Some of the highest peaks in

---

[1] Provisional figures

the world are found in these ranges. The high altitudes allow travel only through a few passes, notably the Jelep La and Nathu La on the main Indo-Tibet trade route through the Chumbi valley, north-east of Darjeeling and Shipki La in the Satluj valley, north-east of Kalpa (Kinnaur). The mountain wall extends over a distance of about 2,400 km with a varying depth of 240 to 320 km. In the east, between India and Myanmar and India and Bangladesh, hill ranges are much lower. Garo, Khasi, Jaintia and Naga Hills, running almost east-west, join the chain to Mizo and Rakhine Hills running north-south.

The plains of the Ganga and the Indus, about 2,400 km long and 240 to 320 km broad, are formed by basins of three distinct river systems—the Indus, the Ganga and the Brahmaputra. They are one of the world's greatest stretches of flat alluvium and also one of the most densely populated areas on the earth. Between the Yamuna at Delhi and the Bay of Bengal, nearly 1,600 km away, there is a drop of only 200 metres in elevation.

The desert region can be divided into two parts—the 'great desert' and the 'little desert'. The great desert extends from the edge of the Rann of Kutch beyond the Luni river northward. The whole of the Rajasthan-Sind frontier runs through this. The little desert extends from the Luni between Jaisalmer and Jodhpur up to the northern west. Between the great and the little deserts lies a zone of absolutely sterile country, consisting of rocky land, cut up by limestone ridges.

The Peninsular Plateau is marked off from the plains of the Ganga and the Indus by a mass of mountain and hill ranges varying from 460 to 1,220 metres in height. Prominent among these are the Aravali, Vindhya, Satpura, Maikala and Ajanta. The Peninsula is flanked on the one side by the Eastern Ghats where average elevation is about 610 metres and on the other by the Western Ghats where it is generally from 915 to 1,220 metres, rising in places to over 2,440 metres. Between the Western Ghats and the Arabian Sea lies a narrow coastal strip, while between Eastern Ghats and the Bay of Bengal, there is a broader coastal area. The southern point of the plateau is formed by the Nilgiri Hills where the Eastern and the Western Ghats meet. The Cardamom Hills lying beyond may be regarded as a continuation of the Western Ghats.

Geological Structure

The geological regions broadly follow the physical features and may be grouped into three regions: the Himalayas and their associated group of mountains, the Indo-Gangetic Plain and the Peninsular Shield.

The Himalayan mountain belt to the north and the Naga-Lushai mountain in the east, are the regions of mountain-building movement. Most of this area, now presenting some of the most magnificent mountain scenery in the world, was under marine conditions about 60 crore years ago. In a series of mountain-building movements commencing about seven crore years ago, the sediments and the basement rocks rose to great heights. The weathering and erosive elements worked on these to produce the relief seen today. The Indo-Ganga plains are a great alluvial tract that separate the Himalayas in the north from the Peninsula in the south.

The Peninsula is a region of relative stability and occasional seismic disturbances. Highly metamorphosed rocks of the earliest periods, dating back as far as 380 crore years, occur in this area; the rest being covered by the Gondwana formations, lava flows belonging to the Deccan Trap formation and younger sediments.

River Systems

The river systems of India can be classified into four groups viz., (i) Himalayan rivers, (ii) Deccan rivers, (iii) Coastal rivers and (iv) Rivers of the inland drainage basin. The Himalayan rivers are formed by melting snow and glaciers and therefore, continuously flow throughout the year. During the monsoon months, Himalayas receive very heavy rainfall and rivers swell, causing frequent floods. The Deccan rivers on the other hand are rainfed and therefore fluctuate in volume. Many of these are non-perennial. The Coastal streams, especially on the west coast are short in length and have limited catchment areas. Most of them are non-perennial. The streams of inland drainage basin of western Rajasthan are few and far apart. Most of them are of an ephemeral character.

The main Himalayan river systems are those of the Indus and the Ganga-Brahmaputra-Meghna system. The Indus, which is one of the great rivers of the world, rises near Mansarovar in Tibet and flows through India and thereafter through Pakistan and finally falls into the Arabian sea near Karachi. Its important tributaries flowing in Indian territory are the Sutlej (originating in Tibet), the Beas, the Ravi, the Chenab and the Jhelum. The Ganga-Brahmaputra-Meghna is another important system of which the principal sub-basins are those of Bhagirathi and the Alaknanda, which join at Dev Prayag to form the Ganga. It traverses through Uttarakhand, Uttar Pradesh, Bihar and West Bengal. Below Rajmahal Hills, the Bhagirathi, which used to be the main course in the past, takes off, while the Padma continues eastward and enters Bangladesh. The Yamuna, the Ramganga, the Ghaghra, the Gandak, the Kosi, the Mahananda and the Sone are the important tributaries of the Ganga. Rivers Chambal and Betwa are the important sub-tributaries, which join the Yamuna before it meets the Ganga. The Padma and the Brahmaputra join at Bangladesh and continue to flow as the Padma or Ganga. The Brahmaputra rises in Tibet, where it is known as Tsangpo and runs a long distance till it crosses over into India in Arunachal Pradesh under the name of Dihang. Near Passighat, the Debang and Lohit join the river Brahmaputra and the combined river runs all along the Assam valley. It crosses into Bangladesh downstream of Dhubri.

The principal tributaries of Brahmaputra in India are the Subansiri, Jia Bhareli, Dhansiri, Puthimari, Pagladiya and the Manas. The Brahmaputra in Bangladesh fed by Teesta, etc. finally falls into the Ganga. The Barak river, the head stream of Meghna, rises in the hills in Manipur. The important tributaries of the river are Makku, Trang, Tuivai, Jiri, Sonai, Rukni, Katakhal, Dhaleswari, Langachini, Maduva and Jatinga. Barak continues in Bangladesh till the combined Ganga-Brahmaputra join it near Bhairab Bazar.

In the Deccan region, most of the major river systems flowing generally in the east fall into Bay of Bengal. The major east flowing rivers are Godavari, Krishna, Cauvery and Mahanadi. Narmada and Tapti are major west flowing rivers.

The Godavari in the southern Peninsula has the second largest river basin covering 10 per cent of the area of India. Next to it is the Krishna basin in the region and the Mahanadi is another large basin of the region. The basin of the Narmada in the uplands of the Deccan, flowing to the Arabian Sea and of the Cauvery in the south, falling into the Bay of Bengal are about the same size, though with different character and shape.

There are numerous coastal rivers, which are comparatively small. While only handful of such rivers drain into the sea near the delta of east coast, there are as many as 600 such rivers on the west coast.

A few rivers in Rajasthan do not drain into the sea. They drain into salt lakes and get lost in sand with no outlet to sea. Besides these, there are the desert rivers which flow for some distance and are lost in the desert. These are Luni, Machhu, Rupen, Saraswati, Banas, Ghaggar and others.

The entire country has been divided into 20 river basins/group of river basins comprising 12 major basins and eight composite river basins. The 12 major river basins are : (1) Indus, (2) Ganga-Brahmaputra-Meghna, (3) Godavari, (4) Krishna, (5) Cauvery, (6) Mahanadi, (7) Pennar, (8) Brahmani-Baitarani, (9) Sabarmati, (10) Mahi, (11) Narmada and (12) Tapti. Each of these basins has a drainage area exceeding 20,000 sq. km.

The eight composite river basins combining suitably together all the other remaining medium (drainage area of 2,000 to 20,000 sq.km) and small river systems (drainage area less than 2000 sq.km) for the purpose of planning and management are : (1) Subarnarekha—combining Subarnarekha and other small rivers between Subarnarekha and Baitarani; (2) east flowing rivers between Mahanadi and Pennar; (3) east flowing rivers between Pennar and Kanyakumari; (4) area of Inland drainage in Rajasthan desert; (5) west flowing rivers of Kutch and Saurashtra including Luni; (6) west flowing rivers from Tapi to Tadri; (7) west flowing rivers from Tadri to Kanyakumari and (8) minor rivers draining into Myanmar (Burma) and Bangladesh.

Climate/Seasons

The climate of India may be broadly described as tropical monsoon type. The Indian Meteorological Department (IMD) designates four official seasons: (i) Winter, from December to early April. The year's coldest months are December and January, when temperatures average around 10-15 °C (50-59°F) in the north-west; temperatures rise as one proceeds towards the equator, peaking around

20-25 °C (68-77 °F) in mainland India's south-east, (ii) Summer or pre-monsoon season, lasting from April to June (April to July in north-western India). In western and southern regions, the hottest month is April; for northern regions, May is the hottest month. Temperatures average around 32-40 °C (90-104 °F) in most of the interior, (iii) Monsoon or rainy season, lasting from June to September. The season is dominated by the humid south-west summer monsoon, which slowly sweeps across the country beginning in late May or early June. Monsoon rains begin to recede from North India at the beginning of October. South India typically receives more rainfall, and (iv) Post-monsoon season, lasting from October to December. In north-western India, October and November are usually cloudless.

The Himalayan states, being more temperate, experience two additional seasons: autumn and spring. Traditionally, Indians note six seasons, each about two months long. These are the spring, summer, monsoon, early autumn, late autumn and winter. These are based on the astronomical division of the 12 months into six parts. The ancient Hindu calendar also reflects these seasons in its arrangement of months.

India's climate is affected by two seasonal winds—the north-east monsoon and the south-west monsoon. The north-east monsoon commonly known as winter monsoon blows from land to sea whereas south-west monsoon known as summer monsoon blows from sea to land after crossing the Indian ocean, the Arabian sea and the Bay of Bengal. The south-west monsoon brings most of the rainfall during the year in the country.

Flora

India is rich in flora. Available data place India in the tenth position in the world and fourth in Asia in plant diversity. From about 70 per cent geographical area surveyed so far, over 46,000 species of plants have been described by the Botanical Survey of India (BSI), Kolkata. The vascular flora, which forms the conspicuous vegetation cover, comprises 15,000 species.

With a wide range of climatic conditions from the torrid to the arctic, India has a rich and varied vegetation, which only a few countries of comparable size possess. India can be divided into eight distinct floristic regions, namely, the western Himalayas, the eastern Himalayas, Assam, the Indus plain, the Ganga plain, the Deccan, the Malabar and the Andamans.

The western Himalayan region extends from Kashmir to Kumaon. Its temperate zone is rich in forests of chir, pine, other conifers and broad-leaved temperate trees. Higher up, forests of deodar, blue pine, spruce and silver fir occur. The alpine zone extends from the upper limit of the temperate zone of about 4,750 metres or even higher. The characteristic trees of this zone are high-level silver fir, silver birch and junipers. The eastern Himalayan region extends from Sikkim eastwards and embraces Darjeeling, Kurseong and the adjacent tracts. The temperate zone has forests of oaks, laurels, maples, rhododendrons, alder and birch. Many conifers, junipers and dwarf willows also grow here. The Assam region comprises the Brahmaputra and the Surma valleys with evergreen forests, occasional thick clumps of bamboos and tall grasses. The Indus plain region comprises the plains of Punjab, western Rajasthan and northern Gujarat. It is dry, hot and supports natural vegetation. The Ganga plain region covers the area which is alluvial plain and is under cultivation for wheat, sugarcane and rice. Only small areas support forests of widely differing types. The Deccan region comprises the entire table land of the Indian Peninsula and supports vegetation of various kinds from shrub jungles to mixed deciduous forests. The Malabar region covers the excessively humid belt of mountain country parallel to the west coast of the Peninsula. Besides being rich in forest vegetation, this region produces important commercial crops, such as coconut, betelnut, pepper, coffee, tea, rubber and cashewnut. The Andaman region abounds in evergreen, mangrove, beach and diluvial forests. The Himalayan region extending from Kashmir to Arunachal Pradesh through Sikkim, Meghalaya and Nagaland and the Deccan Peninsula is rich in endemic flora, with a large number of plants which are not found elsewhere.

The flora of the country is being studied by BSI and its nine circle/field offices located all over the country along with certain universities and research institutions.

Ethno-botanical study deals with the utilization of plants and plant products by ethnic races. A scientific study of such plants has been done by BSI. A number of detailed ethno-botanical explorations have been conducted in different tribal areas of the country. More than 800 plant species of ethno-botanical interest have been collected and identified at different centres.

Owing to destruction of forests for agricultural, industrial and urban development, several Indian plants are facing threat of extinction. About 1,336 plant species are considered vulnerable and endangered. About 20 species of higher plants are categorized as possibly extinct, as these have not been sighted during the last six to ten decades. BSI brings out an inventory of endangered plants in the form of a publication titled 'Red Data Book.'

Faunal Resources

India is very rich in terms of biological diversity due to its unique biogeographical location, diversified climate conditions and enormous ecodiversity and geodiversity. India's immense biological diversity encompasses ecosystems, populations, species and their genetic make-up. This diversity can be attributed to the vast variety in physiography and climatic situations resulting in a diversity of ecological habitats ranging from tropical, sub-tropical, temperate, alpine to desert. According to world biogeographic classification, India represents two of the major realms (the Palearctic and Indo-Malayan) and three biomes (Tropical Humid Forests, Tropical Dry/Deciduous Forests and Warm Deserts/ Semi-Deserts). The Wildlife Institute of India has proposed a modified classification which divides the country into ten biogeographic regions: Trans-Himalayan, Himalayan, Indian Desert, Semi-Arid, Western Ghats, Deccan Peninsula, Gangetic Plain, North-East India, Islands and Coasts. In the light of Biodiversity Convention, India holds a unique position with the priority of conservation of natural resources and sustainable development. Infact, within only about 2 per cent of world's total land surface, India is known to have over 7.50 per cent of the species of animals that the world holds and this percentage accounts nearly for 92,037 species so far known, of which insects alone include 61,375 species. It is estimated that about two times that number of species still remain to be discovered in India alone.

Demographic Background

Census

The Census of India 2001, was historic and epoch making, being the first census of the twenty-first century and the third millennium. It reveals benchmark data on the state of abundant human resources available in the country, their demography, culture and economic structure at a juncture, which marks a centennial and millenial transition.

Census 2011 was the 15th census of its kind since 1872. It was held in two phases: House listing and Housing Census (April to September, 2010) and Population Enumeration (February 9 to 28, 2011 with Revisional round during 1st to 5th March,2011). Reference Date was 0.00 hour of March 1, 2011. In snow bound areas, the Population Enumeration was conducted from September 11 to 30, 2010. The Final Population data was released on April 30, 2013.

Population

The population of India as on March 1, 2011 stood at 1,210.9 million (623.2 million males and 587.6 million females). India accounts for a meagre 2.4 per cent of the world surface area of 135.79 million sq.km. Yet, it supports and sustains a whopping per cent of the world population.

The population, which at the turn of the twentieth century was around 238.4 million, increased to reach 1,210.9 million by 2011. As recorded at each decennial census from 1901 the population has grown steadily except for a decrease during 1911-21

Population Density

One of the important indices of population concentration is the density of population. It is defined as the number of persons per sq.km. The population density of India in 2011 was 382 per sq. km-decadal growth 17.72 per cent.

The density of population increased in all states and union territories between 1991 and 2011. Among major states, Bihar is the most thickly populated state with (a population density of) 1,106 persons per sq.km followed by West Bengal 1,028 and Kerala 860.

Sex Ratio

Sex ratio, defined as the number of females per thousand males is an important social indicator to measure the extent of prevailing equality between males and females in a society at a given point of time. The sex ratio in the country has always remained unfavourable to females. It was 972 at the beginning of the twenthieth century and thereafter showed continuous decline until 1941. The sex ratio from 1901-2011 has registered a 10 point increase at census 2011 over 2001; however, child sex ratio has declined to 919 per thousand male.

Literacy

For the purpose of census 2011, a person aged seven and above, who can both read and write with understanding in any language, is treated as literate. A person, who can only read but cannot write, is not literate. In the censuses prior to 1991, children below five years of age were necessarily treated as illiterates.

The results of 2011 census reveal that there has been an increase in literacy in the country. The literacy rate in the country is 73.0 per cent, 80.9 for males and 64.6 for females.

Kerala retained its position by being on top with a 94 per cent literacy rate, closely followed by Lakshadweep (91.9 per cent). Bihar with a literacy rate of 61.8 per cent ranks last in the country. Kerala also occupies the top spot in the country both in male literacy with 96.1 per cent and female literacy with 92.1 per cent. On the contrary, Bihar has recorded the lowest literacy rates both in case of males (71.2 per cent) and females (51.5 per cent).

Note: For details, the Census Report 2011 may be referred to.

2 National Symbols

National Flag

THE National Flag shall be a tricolour panel made up of three rectangular panels or sub-panels of equal width. The colour of the top panel shall be India saffron *(kesari)* and that of the bottom panel India green. The middle panel shall be white, bearing at its centre the design of Ashoka Chakra in navy blue colour with 24 equally spaced spokes. The Ashoka Chakra shall preferably be screen printed or otherwise printed or stenciled or suitably embroidered and shall be completely visible on both sides of the Flag in the centre of the white panel. The National Flag shall be rectangular in shape. The ratio of the length to the height (width) of the Flag shall be 3:2. The design of the National Flag was adopted by the Constitutent Assembly of India on July 22, 1947.

Apart from non-statutory instructions issued by the government from time to time, display of the National Flag is governed by the provisions of the Emblems and Names (Prevention of Improper Use) Act, 1950 (No. 12 of 1950) and the Prevention of Insults to National Honour Act, 1971 (No. 69 of 1971). The Flag Code of India, 2002 is an attempt to bring together all such laws, conventions, practices and instructions for the guidance of all concerned.

The Flag Code of India, 2002 effective from January 26, 2002 superseded the 'Flag Code-India' as it existed then. As per the provisions of the Flag Code of India, 2002, there is no restriction on the display of the National Flag by members of general public, private organizations, educational institutions, etc., except to the extent provided in the Emblems and Names (Prevention of Improper Use) Act, 1950 and the Prevention of Insults to National Honour Act, 1971 and any other law enacted on the subject.

State Emblem

The State Emblem of India is an adaptation of the Lion Capital of Asoka at Sarnath. In the original, the Lion Capital has four lions mounted back to back, on a circular abacus. The frieze of the abacus is adorned with sculptures in high relief of an elephant, a galloping horse, a bull and a lion separated by intervening Dharma Chakras. The abacus rests on a bell shaped lotus.

The profile of the Lion Capital showing three lions mounted on the abacus with a Dharma Chakra in the centre, a bull on the right and a galloping horse on the left, and outlines of Dharma Chakras on the extreme right and left was adopted as the State Emblem of India on January 26, 1950. The bell-shaped lotus was omitted. The motto "*Satyameva Jayate*"-Truth alone Triumphs—written in Devanagari script below the profile of the Lion Capital is part of the State Emblem of India.

In the State Emblem lies the official seal of the Government of India. Its use is regulated by the State Emblem of India (Prohibition of Improper Use) Act, 2005 and The State Emblem of India (Regulation of Use) Rules, 2007 [read with State Emblem of India (Regulation of Use) Amendment Rules, 2010].

National Anthem

The song *Jana-gana-mana,* composed originally in Bangla by Rabindranath Tagore, was adopted in its Hindi version by the Constituent Assembly as the National Anthem of India on January 24, 1950. It was first sung on December 27, 1911 at the Calcutta Session of the Indian National Congress. The complete song consists of five stanzas. The first stanza contains the full version of the National Anthem:

Jana-gana-mana-adhinayaka, jaya he
Bharata-bhagya-vidhata
Panjaba-Sindhu-Gujarata-Maratha
Dravida-Utkala-Banga
Vindhya-Himachala-Yamuna-Ganga
uchchala-jaladhi-taranga
Tava subha name jage, tave
subha asisa mage,
Gahe tava jaya-gatha.
Jana-gana-mangala-dayaka jaya he
Bharata-bhagya-vidhata.
Jaya he, jaya he, jaya he,
Jaya jaya jaya, jaya he!

The playing time of the full version of the National Anthem is approximately 52 seconds. A short version consisting of the first and last lines of the National Anthem (playing time approximately 20 seconds) is also played on certain occasions. The following is Tagore's English rendering of the anthem:

Thou art the ruler of the minds of all people,
Dispenser of India's destiny.

Thy name rouses the hearts of Punjab, Sind,
Gujarat and Maratha,

Of the Dravida and Orissa and Bengal;
It echoes in the hills of the Vindhyas and Himalayas,
mingles in the music of Jamuna and Ganges and is
chanted by the waves of the Indian Sea.
They pray for thy blessings and sing thy praise.
The saving of all people waits in thy hand,
Thou dispenser of India's destiny.
Victory, victory, victory to thee.

National Flag

Published under the direction of Major General Girish Kumar, Surveyor General of India.
Survey of India, Hathibarkala Estate, Post Box No. 37, Dehra Dun- 248001
Department of Science & Technology, Government of India.

2012

POLITICAL MAP OF INDIA SEVENTH EDITION 1:4,000,000

National Song

The song *Vande Mataram,* composed in Sanskrit by Bankimchandra Chatterji, was a source of inspiration to the people in their struggle for freedom. It has an equal status with *Jana-gana-mana.* The first political occasion when it was sung was the 1896 session of the Indian National Congress. The following is the text of its first stanza :

Vande Mataram!

Sujalam, suphalam, malayaja shitalam,
Shasyashyamalam, Mataram!
Shubhrajyotsna pulakitayaminim,
Phullakusumita drumadala shobhinim,
Suhasinim sumadhura bhashinim,
Sukhadam varadam, Mataram!
Vande Mataram,
Vande Mataram!

The English translation of the stanza rendered by Sri Aurobindo in prose[1] is :

I bow to thee, Mother,
richly-watered, richly-fruited,
cool with the winds of the south,
dark with the crops of the harvests,
The Mother!
Her nights rejoicing in the glory of the moonlight,
her lands clothed beautifully with her trees in flowering bloom,
sweet of laughter, sweet of speech,
the Mother, giver of boons, giver of bliss.

National Calendar

The National Calendar based on the *Saka Era,* with *Chaitra* as its first month and a normal year of 365 days was adopted from March 22, 1957 along with the Gregorian calendar for the following official purposes : (i) Gazette of India, (ii) news broadcast by All India Radio, (iii) calendars issued by the Government of India and (iv) Government communications addressed to the public.

Dates of the National Calendar have a permanent correspondence with dates of the Gregorian Calendar, 1 *Chaitra* falling on March 22 normally and on March 21 in leap year.

Relevant Website : www.mha.gov.in

---

1. As published in Volume Eight of Sri Aurobindo Birth Centenary Library, Popular Edition, 1972.

3 Polity

INDIA, a union of states, is a Sovereign Socialist Secular Democratic Republic with a parliamentary system of government. The Republic is governed in terms of the Constitution, which was adopted by Constituent Assembly on November 26, 1949 and came into force on January 26, 1950.

The Constitution which envisages parliamentary form of government is federal in structure with unitary features. The President of India is the constitutional head of executive of the union. Article 74(1) of the Constitution provides that there shall be a Council of Ministers with the Prime Minister as its head to aid and advise the President who shall in exercise of his functions, act in accordance with such advice. The real executive power thus vests in the Council of Ministers with the Prime Minister as its head. The Council of Ministers is collectively responsible to the House of the People (Lok Sabha). Similarly, in states, the Governor is the head of executive, but it is the Council of Ministers with the Chief Minister as its head in whom real executive power vests. The Council of Ministers of a state is collectively responsible to the Legislative Assembly of the state.

The Constitution distributes legislative power between Parliament and State Legislatures and provides for vesting of residual powers in Parliament. The power to amend the Constitution also vests in Parliament. The Constitution has provision for independence of Judiciary, Comptroller and Auditor-General, Public Service Commissions and Chief Election Commission.

Union and its Territory

India comprises 29 states and seven union territories. The states are: Andhra Pradesh, Assam, Arunachal Pradesh, Bihar, Chhattisgarh, Goa, Gujarat, Haryana, Himachal Pradesh, Jammu and Kashmir, Jharkhand, Karnataka, Kerala, Madhya Pradesh, Maharashtra, Manipur, Meghalaya, Mizoram, Nagaland, Odisha, Punjab, Rajasthan, Sikkim, Tamil Nadu, Telangana, Tripura, Uttarakhand, Uttar Pradesh and West Bengal. Union territories are : Andaman and Nicobar Islands, Chandigarh, Dadra and Nagar Haveli, Daman and Diu, National Capital Territory of Delhi, Lakshadweep and Puducherry.

Citizenship

The Constitution of India provides for a single citizenship for the whole of India. Every person who was at the commencement of the Constitution (January 26, 1950) domiciled in the territory of India and: (a) who was born in India; or (b) either of whose parents were born in India; or (c) who has been ordinarily resident in India for not less than five years became a citizen of India.

The Citizenship Act, 1955, deals with matters relating to acquisition, determination and termination of Indian citizenship after the commencement of the Constitution.

Fundamental Rights

The Constitution offers all citizens, individually and collectively, some basic freedoms. These are guaranteed in the Constitution in the form of six broad categories of Fundamental Rights which are justifiable. Articles 12 to 35 contained in Part III of the Constitution deal with Fundamental Rights. These are : (i) Right to equality including equality before law, prohibition of discrimination on grounds of religion, race, caste, sex or place of birth and equality of opportunity in matters of employment; (ii) Right to freedom of speech and expression, assembly, association or union, movement, residence, and right to practice any profession or occupation (some of these rights are subject to security of the state, friendly relations with foreign countries, public order, decency or morality); (iii) Right against exploitation, prohibiting all forms of forced labour, child labour and traffic in human beings; (iv) Right to freedom of conscience and free profession, practice and propagation of religion; (v) Right of any section of citizens to conserve their culture, language or script and right of minorities to establish and administer educational institutions of their choice; and (vi) Right to constitutional remedies for enforcement of Fundamental Rights.

Fundamental Duties

By the 42nd Amendment of the Constitution, adopted in 1976, Fundamental Duties of the citizens have also been enumerated. Article 51 'A' contained in Part IV A of the Constitution deals with Fundamental Duties. These enjoin upon a citizen among other things, to abide by the Constitution, to cherish and follow noble ideals, which inspired India's struggle for freedom, to defend the country and render national service when called upon to do so and to promote harmony and spirit of common brotherhood transcending religious, linguistic and regional or sectional diversities.

Directive Principles of State Policy

The Constitution lays down certain Directive Principles of State Policy, which though not justifiable, are 'fundamental in governance of the country' and it is the duty of the state to apply these principles in making laws. These have been contained in Part IV from Articles 36 to 51 of the Constitution. These lay down that the state shall strive to promote the welfare of people by securing and protecting as effectively as it may a social order in which justice—social, economic and political—shall form the basis in all institutions of national life. The state shall direct its policy in such a manner so as to secure the right of all men and women to an adequate means of livelihood, equal pay for equal work and within limits of its economic capacity and development, to make effective provision for securing the right to work, education and to public assistance in the event of unemployment, old age, sickness and disablement or other cases of undeserved want. The state shall also endeavour to secure to workers a living wage, humane conditions of work, a decent standard of life and full involvement of workers in management of industries.

In the economic sphere, the state is to direct its policy in such a manner as to secure distribution of ownership and control of material resources of community to subserve the common good and to ensure that operation of economic system does not result in concentration of wealth and means of production to common detriment.

Some of the other important directives relate to provision of opportunities and facilities for children to develop in a healthy manner, free and compulsory education for all children upto the age of 14; promotion of education and economic interests of scheduled castes, scheduled tribes and other weaker sections; organisation of village panchayats; separation of judiciary from executive; promulgation of a uniform civil code for whole country; protection of national monuments; promotion of justice on the basis of equal opportunity; provision of free legal aid; protection and improvement of environment and safeguarding of forests and wildlife of the country; and promotion of international peace and security, just and honourable relations between nations, respect for international law, treaty obligations and settlement of international disputes by arbitration.

The Union

Executive

The Union executive consists of the President, the Vice-President and the Council of Ministers with the Prime Minister as the head to aid and advise the President.

President

The President is elected by members of an electoral college consisting of elected members of both Houses of Parliament and Legislative Assemblies of the states in accordance with the system of proportional representation by means of single transferable vote. To secure uniformity among states *inter se* as well as parity between the states, as a whole, and the Union, suitable weightage is given to each vote. The President must be a citizen of India, not less than 35 years of age and qualified for election as a member of the Lok Sabha. His term of office is five years and he is eligible for re-election. His removal from office is to be in accordance with procedure prescribed in Article 61 of the Constitution. He may, by writing under his hand addressed to the Vice-President, resign his office.

The executive power of the Union is vested in the President and is exercised by him either directly or through officers subordinate to him in accordance with the Constitution. The supreme command of defence forces of the Union also vests in him. The President summons, prorogues, addresses, sends messages to Parliament and dissolves the Lok Sabha; promulgates Ordinances at any time, except when both Houses of Parliament are in session; makes recommendations for introducing financial and money bills and gives assent to bills; grants pardons, reprieves, respites or remission of punishment or suspends, remits or commutes sentences in certain cases. When there is a failure of the constitutional machinery in a state, he can assume to himself all or any of the functions of the Government of that state. The President can proclaim emergency in the country if he is satisfied that a grave emergency exists whereby security of India or any part of its territory is threatened whether by war or external aggression or armed rebellion.

Vice-President

The Vice-President is elected by members of an electoral college consisting of members of both Houses of Parliament in accordance with the system of proportional representation by means of single transferable vote. He must be a citizen of India, not less than 35 years of age and eligible for election as a member of the Rajya Sabha. His term of office is five years and he is eligible for re-election. His removal from office is to be in accordance with procedure prescribed in Article 67(b).

The Vice-President is *ex-officio* Chairman of the Rajya Sabha and acts as President when the latter is unable to discharge his functions due to absence, illness or any other cause or till the election of a new President (to be held within six months when a vacancy is caused by death, resignation or removal or otherwise of President). While so acting, he ceases to perform the function of the Chairman of the Rajya Sabha.

Council of Ministers

There is a Council of Ministers, headed by the Prime Minister, to aid and advise the President in exercise of his functions. The Prime Minister is appointed by the President who also appoints other ministers on the advice of Prime Minister. The Council is collectively responsible to the Lok Sabha. It is the duty of the Prime Minister to communicate to the President all decisions of Council of Ministers relating to administration of affairs of the Union and proposals for legislation and information relating to them.

The Council of Ministers comprises ministers who are members of Cabinet, Ministers of State (independent charge), Ministers of State and Deputy Ministers.

Legislature

Legislature of the Union which is called Parliament, consists of the President and two Houses, known as Council of States (Rajya Sabha), and House of the People (Lok Sabha). Each House has to meet within six months of its previous sitting. A joint sitting of two Houses can be held in certain cases.

Rajya Sabha

The Constitution provides that the Rajya Sabha shall consist of 12 members to be nominated by the President from amongst persons having special knowledge or practical experience in respect of such matters as literature, science, art and social service; and not more than 238 representatives of the states and of the union territories. Details of Rajya Sabha members given in Appendices.

Elections to the Rajya Sabha are indirect; members representing states are elected by the elected members of Legislative Assemblies of the states in accordance with the system of proportional representation by means of the single transferable vote, and those representing union territories are chosen in such a manner as Parliament may by law prescribe. The Rajya Sabha is not subject to dissolution; one-third of its members retire every second year.

Relevant Website : www.rajyasabha.in

Lok Sabha

The Lok Sabha is composed of representatives of people chosen by direct election on the basis of adult suffrage. The maximum strength of the House envisaged by the Constitution is now 552 (530 members to represent the states, 20 members to represent the union territories and not more than two members of the Anglo-Indian community to be nominated by the President, if, in his opinion, that community is not adequately represented in the House). The total elective membership of the Lok Sabha is distributed among the states in such a way that the ratio between the number of seats allotted to each state and the population of the state is, as far as practicable, the same for all states. The Lok Sabha at present consists of 543 members. Of these, 530 members are directly elected from the states and 13 from union territories. Following the 84th amendment to the Constitution in 2001, the total number of existing seats as allocated to various states in the Lok Sabha on the basis of the 1971 census shall remain unaltered till the first census to be taken after the year 2026.

The term of the Lok Sabha, unless dissolved earlier is five years from the date appointed for its first meeting. However, while a Proclamation of Emergency is in operation, this period may be extended by Parliament by law for a period not exceeding one year at a time and not extending in any case, beyond a period of six months after the Proclamation is or has ceased to operate. Sixteen Lok Sabhas have been constituted so far. The term of each Lok Sabha and its Speaker(s) is given in table in the following page. The names of members of the 16th Lok Sabha, their constituencies and party affiliations are given in Appendices.

Relevant Website : www.loksabha.in

Qualification for Membership of Parliament

In order to be chosen a member of Parliament, a person must be a citizen of India and not less than 30 years of age in the case of Rajya Sabha and not less than 25 years of age in the case of Lok Sabha. Additional qualifications may be prescribed by Parliament by law.

Lok Sabha and its Speaker(s)

Lok Sabha	Date of First Meeting	Date of Dissolution	Speaker Name	From	To
First Lok Sabha	13 May 1952	4 April 1957[2]	Ganesh Vasudev Mavalankar	15 May 1952	27 February 1956[3]
			M. Ananthasayanam Ayyangar	8 March 1956	10 May 1957
Second Lok Sabha	10 May 1957	31 March 1962[4]	M. Ananthasayanam Ayyangar	11 May 1957	16 April 1962
Third Lok Sabha	16 April 1962	3 March 1967[5]	Sardar Hukam Singh	17 April 1962	16 March 1967
Fourth Lok Sabha	16 March 1967	27 December 1970[6]	Neelam Sanjiva Reddy	17 March 1967	19 July 1969[7]
			Gurdial Singh Dhillon	8 August 1969	19 March 1971
Fifth Lok Sabha	19 March 1971	18 January 1977[8]	Gurdial Singh Dhillon	22 March 1971	1 December 1975[9]
			Bali Ram Bhagat	5 January 1976	25 March 1977
Sixth Lok Sabha	25 March 1977	22 August 1979[10]	Neelam Sanjiva Reddy	26 March 1977	13 July 1977[11]
			K.S. Hegde	21 July 1977	21 January 1985
Seventh Lok Sabha	21 January 1980	31 December 1984[12]	Balram Jakhar	22 January 1980	15 January 1985
Eighth Lok Sabha	15 January 1985	27 November 1989[13]	Balram Jakhar	16 January 1985	18 December 1989
Ninth Lok Sabha	18 December 1989	13 March 1991[14]	Rabi Ray	19 December 1989	9 July 1991
Tenth Lok Sabha	9 July 1991	10 May 1996	Shivraj V. Patil	10 July 1991	22 May 1996
Eleventh Lok Sabha	22 May 1996	4 December 1997[15]	P. A. Sangma	23 May 1996	23 March 1998 (FN)
Twelfth Lok Sabha	23 March 1998	26 April 1999[16]	G.M.C. Balayogi	24 March 1998	20 October 1999 (FN)
Thirteenth Lok Sabha	20 October 1999	6 February 2004[18]	G.M.C. Balayogi	22 October 1999	3 March 2002[17]
			Manohar Gajanan Joshi	10 May 2002	2 June 2004
Fourteenth Lok Sabha	2 June 2004	18 May 2009	Somnath Chatterjee	4 June 2004	1 June 2009
Fifteenth Lok Sabha	1 June 2009	18 May 2014	Meira Kumar	1 June 2009	18 May 2014
Sixteenth Lok Sabha	4 June 2014	-	Sumitra Mahajan	6 June 2014	Till date

1. Under Article 94 of the Constitution, in case of dissolution of the Lok Sabha, the Speaker does not vacate his office until immediately before the first meeting of the House after dissolution.
2. Dissolved thirty eight days before expiry of its term.
3. Died.
4. Dissolved forty days before expiry of its term.
5. Dissolved forty four days before expiry of its term.
6. Dissolved one year and seventy nine days before expiry of its term
7. Resigned.
8. Term of the Lok Sabha which was to expire on 18 March 1976 was extended by one year upto 18 March 1977 by the House of the People (Extension of Duration) Act, 1976. It was extended for a further period of one year upto 18 March 1978 by the House of the People (Extension of Duration) Amendment Act, 1976. However, the House was dissolved after having been in existence for a period of five years, ten months and six days.
9. Resigned.
10. House was dissolved after having been in existence for a period of two years, four months and twenty eight days.
11. Resigned.
12. Dissolved twenty days before expiry of its term.
13. Dissolved forty eight days before expiry of its term.
14. Dissolved after having been in existence for a period of one year, two months and twenty five days.
15. House was dissolved after having been in existence for a period of one year, six months and thirteen days.
16. House was dissolved after having been in existence for a period of one year, one month and four days.
17. Died.
18. Dissolved two hundred fifty three days before expiry of its term.

Functions and Powers of Parliament

The Parliament in India has the cardinal functions of legislation, overseeing of administration, passing of the budget, ventilation of public grievances and discussing various subjects like development plans, national policies and international relations. The distribution of powers between the Union and the states, followed in the Constitution, emphasizes in many ways the general predominance of Parliament in the legislative field. The Parliament can, under certain circumstances, assume legislative power with respect to a subject falling within the sphere exclusively reserved for the states. It can impeach the President and remove the judges of Supreme Court and High Courts, the Chief Election Commissioner and the Comptroller and Auditor General in accordance with the procedure laid down in the Constitution.

All legislation requires consent of both the Houses of Parliament. In the case of money bills, however, the 'will' of the Lok Sabha prevails. Delegated legislation is also subject to review and control by Parliament. Besides the power to legislate, the Constitution vests in Parliament the power to initiate amendment of the Constitution.

Parliamentary Committees

The functions of Parliament are varied in nature. The time at its disposal is limited. It cannot make very detailed scrutiny of all legislative and other matters that come up before it. A good deal of Parliamentary business is, therefore, transacted in the committees. Both Houses of Parliament have a similar committee structure, with few exceptions. Their appointment, terms of office, functions and procedure of conducting business are also more or less similar and are regulated as per rules made by the two Houses under Article 118(1) of the Constitution.

Broadly, Parliamentary Committees are of two kinds—*Standing Committees* and *Ad Hoc Committees*. The former are elected or appointed every year or periodically and their work goes on, more or less, on a continuous basis. The latter are appointed on an *ad hoc* basis as need arises and they cease to exist as soon as they complete the task assigned to them.

Standing Committees : Among the Standing Committees, the three Financial Committees—*Committees on Estimates, Public Accounts* and *Public Undertakings*—constitute a distinct group as they keep an unremitting vigil over Government expenditure and performance. While members of the Rajya Sabha are associated with Committees on Public Accounts and Public Undertakings, the members of the Committee on Estimates are drawn from the Lok Sabha.

The *Estimates Committee* reports on what economies, improvements in organization, efficiency or administrative reform consistent with policy underlying the estimates may be effected. It also examines whether the money is well laid out within limits of the policy implied in the estimates and suggests the form in which estimates shall be presented to the Parliament. The *Public Accounts Committee* scrutinizes appropriation and finance accounts of Government and reports of the Comptroller and Auditor-General. It ensures that public money is spent in accordance with the Parliament's decision and calls attention to cases of waste, extravagance, loss or nugatory expenditure. The *Committee on Public Undertakings* examines reports of the Comptroller and Auditor-General, if any. It also examines whether public undertakings are being run efficiently and managed in accordance with sound business principles and prudent commercial practices.

Besides these three financial committees, the Rules Committee of the Lok Sabha recommended setting-up of *17 Department Related Standing Committees* (DRSCs). Accordingly, 17 Department Related Standing Committees were set up on April 8, 1993. In July, 2004, rules were amended to provide for the constitution of seven more such committees, thus raising the number of DRSCs from 17 to 24. The functions of these committees are : (a) to consider the demands for grants of various ministries/departments of Government of India and make reports to the Houses; (b) to examine such bills as are referred to the committee by the Chairman, Rajya Sabha or the Speaker, Lok Sabha, and make reports thereon; (c) to consider annual reports of ministries/departments and make reports thereon; and (d) to consider policy documents presented to the Houses, if referred to the committee by the Chairman, Rajya Sabha or the Speaker, Lok Sabha, and make reports thereon.

Other *Standing Committees* in each House, divided in terms of their functions, are (i) Committees to Inquire: (a) *Committee on Petitions* examines petitions on bills and on matters of general public interest and also entertains representations on matters concerning subjects in the Union List; and (b) *Committee of Privileges* examines any question of privilege referred to it by the House or Speaker/Chairman; (ii) Committees to Scrutinize : (a) *Committee on Government Assurances* keeps track of all the assurances, promises, undertakings, etc., given by Ministers in the House and pursues them till they are implemented; (b) *Committee on Subordinate Legislation* scrutinizes and reports to the House whether the power to make regulations, rules, sub-rules, bye-laws, etc., conferred by the Constitution or Statutes is being properly exercised by the delegated authorities; and (c) *Committee on Papers Laid on the Table* examines all papers laid on the table of the House by ministers, other than statutory notifications and orders which come within the purview of the Committee on Subordinate Legislation, to see whether there has been compliance with the provisions of the Constitution, Act, rule or regulation under which the paper has been laid; (iii) Committees relating to the day-to-day business of the House: (a) *Business Advisory Committee* recommends allocation of time for items of Government and other business to be brought before the Houses; (b) *Committee on Private Members' Bills and Resolutions of the Lok Sabha* classifies and allocates time to bills introduced by private members, recommends allocation of time for discussion on private members' resolutions and examines Constitution amendment bills before their introduction by private members in the Lok Sabha. The Rajya Sabha does not have such committee. It is the Business Advisory Committee of that House which recommends allocation of time for discussion on stage or stages of private members' bills and resolutions; (c) *Rules Committee* considers matters of procedure and conduct of business in the House and recommends amendments or additions to the rules; and (d) *Committee on Absence of Members from the Sittings of the House of the Lok Sabha* considers all applications from members for leave or absence from sittings of the House. There is no such committee in the Rajya Sabha. Applications from members for leave or absence are considered by the House itself; (iv) *Committee on the Welfare of Scheduled Castes and Scheduled Tribes,* on which members from both Houses serve, considers all matters relating to the welfare of scheduled castes and scheduled tribes which come within the purview of the Union Government and keeps a watch whether constitutional safeguards in respect of these classes are properly implemented; (v) Committees concerned with the provision of facilities to members : (a) *General Purposes Committee* considers and advises Speaker/ Chairman on matters concerning affairs of the House, which do not appropriately fall within the purview of any other Parliamentary Committee; and (b) *House Committee* deals with residential accommodation and other amenities for members; (vi) *Joint Committee on Salaries and Allowances of Members of Parliament*, constituted under the Salary, Allowances and Pension of Members of Parliament Act, 1954, apart from framing rules for regulating payment of salary, allowances and pension to Members of Parliament, also frames rules in respect of amenities like medical, housing, telephone, postal, constituency and secretarial facility; (vii) *Joint Committee on Offices of Profit* examines the composition and character of committees and other bodies appointed by the Central and state governments and union territories administrations and recommends what offices ought to or ought not to disqualify a person from being chosen as a member of either House of Parliament; (viii) The *Library Committee* consisting of members from both Houses, considers matters concerning the Library of Parliament; (ix) On April 29, 1997, a *Committee on Empowerment of Women* with members from both the Houses was constituted, to secure, status, dignity and equality for women in all fields; (x) On March 4, 1997, the *Ethics Committee* of the Rajya Sabha was constituted. The Ethics Committee of the Lok Sabha was constituted on May 16, 2000.

Ad hoc Committees : Such committees may be broadly classified under two heads : (a) committees which are constituted from time to time, either by the two Houses on a motion adopted in that behalf or by Speaker/ Chairman to inquire into and report on specific subjects, *(e.g., Committees on food management in Parliament House Complex, Committee on installation of portraits/statues of National leaders and Parliamentarians in Parliament House Complex, Committee on Security in Parliament Complex, Committee on MPLADS, Committee on Railway convention, etc.)* and (b) Select or Joint Committees on Bills which are appointed to consider and report on a particular bill. These committees are distinguishable from the other *ad hoc* committees as much as they are concerned with bills and the procedure to be followed by them as laid down in the Rules of Procedure and Directions by the Speaker/Chairman.

Leaders of Opposition in Parliament

The Leaders of Opposition in the Rajya Sabha and the Lok Sabha are accorded statutory recognition. Salary and other suitable facilities are extended to them through a separate legislation brought into force on November 1, 1977.

Government Business in Parliament

The Minister of Parliamentary Affairs is entrusted with coordinating, planning and arranging government business in both Houses of Parliament. In discharge of this function, he is assisted by two ministers of state. The minister also keeps close and constant contact with the presiding officers, the leaders as well as chief whips of various parties and groups in both Houses of Parliament.

Consultative Committees

Functioning of Consultative Committees of Members of Parliament for various ministries is one of the functions allocated to the Ministry of Parliamentary Affairs under the Government of India (Allocation of Business) Rules, 1961. The minimum membership of a Consultative Committee is ten and the maximum membership is thirty. The Consultative Committee stands dissolved upon dissolution of every Lok Sabha and are re-constituted upon constitution of each Lok Sabha. 35 Consultative Committees attached to various ministries were constituted for 16th Lok Sabha and 96 meetings were held between June 2016 to May 2017

Youth Parliament Competition

In order to develop democratic ethos in the younger generation the Ministry conducts Youth Parliament Competitions in various categories of schools and colleges/universities. The 'Youth Parliament Scheme' was first introduced in the schools in Delhi in 1966-67. Kendriya Vidyalayas located in and around Delhi were incorporated into the ongoing scheme in 1978. Subsequently, a separate scheme of Youth Parliament for Kendriya Vidyalayas at the national level was launched in 1988. In 1997-98, two new Youth Parliament Schemes at the national level, one for Jawahar Navodaya Vidyalayas and the other for universities/colleges were launched.

All India Whips' Conference

The Ministry of Parliamentary Affairs, organises All India Whips' Conference from time to time with the purpose of establishing suitable links among the whips of various political parties at the centre and the states/union territories who are concerned with the practical working of the legislatures to discuss matters of common interest and to evolve high standards to strengthen the institution of parliamentary democracy. Seventeen All India Whips' Conferences have been organized so far since 1952.

Special Mentions

The Ministry of Parliamentary Affairs takes follow-up action on matters raised under Rule 377 of the Rules of Procedure and Conduct of Business in Lok Sabha and by way of Special Mentions in Rajya Sabha. After 'Question Hour' in Lok Sabha members raise matters of urgent public importance at 12.00 noon. In Rajya Sabha members raises matters of urgent public importance at 11.00 am. Though it is not mandatory, ministers often react to the points made by the members. In the absence of concerned minister, the Minister of Parliamentary Affairs assures the House or the member that their sentiments would be conveyed to the concerned ministers.

Implementation of Assurances

The Ministry culls out from the printed daily proceedings, assurances, promises, undertakings, etc., given by ministers in both the Houses of Parliament, and forward them to the concerned ministries/departments for implementation. Thereafter, periodic review of the stage of implementation is done by the Ministry and the ministries are also reminded to expedite the fulfillment of assurances. On receipt of the Implementation Reports(IRs) from the ministries, after due scrutiny, statements showing action taken by the Government in implementation of the assurances are periodically laid on the Table of the respective House by Minister/Minister of State for Parliamentary Affairs. After the implementation reports are laid, the members as well as the ministries concerned are informed about the laying of the reports.

Goodwill Delegation

The parliamentarians of a country play a significant role in determining the policy of the country and strengthening of relations with other countries. More particularly, it is indeed useful and necessary for a democratic and developing country like India to select some members of Parliament and distinguished personalities and utilize their services in projecting our policies, programme and achievement in different fields with their counterparts and other opinion makers in other countries and secure their support in favour of India.

With these objectives, Ministry of Parliamentary Affairs sponsors Government Goodwill Delegation of Members of Parliament to other countries and receives similar delegations of parliamentarians under the exchange programme from other countries through the Ministry of External Affairs.

Welfare of Members of Parliament

The Ministry of Parliamentary Affairs looks after the welfare of ailing Members of Parliament admitted for treatment in hospitals in Delhi and renders any assistance required by them. In the unfortunate event of passing away of a Member of Parliament in Delhi, the Ministry of Parliamentary Affairs renders all necessary assistance to the bereaved family members in taking the mortal remains of the deceased member for last rites to a place chosen by the family.

Comptroller and Auditor General

The Comptroller and Auditor General (CAG) of India is appointed by the President. The procedure and the grounds for his removal from office are the same as for a Supreme Court judge. He is not eligible for further office under the union or a state government after he ceases to hold his office.

The accounts of the Union and of the states shall be kept in such form as the President may, on the advice of the CAG, prescribe. The reports of the India relating to the accounts of the union shall be submitted to the President, who shall cause them to be laid before each House of Parliament. The reports of the CAG of India relating to the accounts of a state shall be submitted to the Governor of the state, who shall cause them to be laid before the legislature of the state.

The duties, powers and conditions of service of the CAG have been specified by the Comptroller and Auditor General's (Duties, Powers and Conditions of Service) Act, 1971.

Relevant Website : www.cag.gov.in

Attorney-General

The Attorney-General for India is appointed by the President of India. Any person qualified to be a judge of the Supreme Court can be appointed for the post. The duties of the Attorney-General is to give advice to the Government of India upon such legal matters, and to perform such other duties of a legal character, as may from time to time be referred or assigned to him by the President, and to discharge the functions conferred on him by or under the Constitution or any other law for the time being in force. In the performance of his duties the Attorney-General shall have the right of audience in all courts in the territory of India. The Attorney-General shall hold office during the pleasure of the President, and shall receive such remuneration as the President may determine.

Solicitor General of India

The Solicitor General of India is the government's chief legal advisor, and its primary lawyer in the Supreme Court of India. The Solicitor General of India is the secondary law officer of the country, assists the Attorney-General, and is himself assisted by several Additional Solicitors General of India. Like the Attorney-General for India, the Solicitor General and the Additional Solicitors General advise the government and appear on behalf of the Union of India in terms of the Law Officers (Terms and Conditions) Rules, 1972.

However, unlike the post of Attorney-General for India, which is a Constitutional post under Article 76, the posts of the Solicitor General and the Additional Solicitors General are merely statutory. Appointments Committee of the Cabinet appoints the Solicitor General.

Administrative Set-up

The Government of India (Allocation of Business) Rules, 1961 are made by the President of India under Clause (3) of Article 77 of the Constitution for the allocation of business of the Government of India. The ministries/departments of the Government are created by the President on the advice of the Prime Minister under these rules. The business of the government is transacted in the ministries/departments, secretariats and offices as per the distribution of subjects specified in these rules. Each of the ministry(ies) is assigned to a minister by the President on the advice of the Prime Minister. Each department is generally under the charge of a secretary to assist the minister on policy matters and general administration.

Cabinet Secretariat

The Cabinet Secretariat functions directly under the Prime Minister. The administrative head of the Secretariat is the Cabinet Secretary who is also the ex-officio Chairman of the Civil Services Board. The business allocated to Cabinet Secretariat is (i) secretarial assistance to the Cabinet and Cabinet Committees; and (ii) rules of business.

The Cabinet Secretariat is responsible for the administration of the Government of India (Transaction of Business) Rules, 1961 and the Government of India (Allocation of Business) Rules, 1961, facilitating smooth transaction of business in ministries/departments of the government by ensuring adherence to these rules. It assists in decision-making by ensuring inter-ministerial coordination, ironing out differences amongst ministries/departments and evolving consensus through the instrumentality of the standing and *ad hoc* Committees of Secretaries. The Cabinet Secretariat ensures that the President, the Vice-President and ministers are kept informed of the major activities of all ministries/departments by means of monthly summary of their activities. Management of major crisis situations in the country and coordinating activities of various ministries in such a situation is also one of the functions of the Cabinet Secretariat. The Secretaries keep the Cabinet Secretary informed of developments from time to time. The Transaction of Business Rules also require them to keep the Cabinet Secretary informed specially if there are any departures from these rules.

Relevant Website : www.cabsec.gov.in

Ministries/Departments of the Government

The government consists of a number of ministries/departments, their number and character varying from time to time based on factors such as volume of work, priorities attached to certain subjects, etc.

List of the Ministries/Departments[1]

1. **Ministry of Agriculture and Farmers Welfare (Krishi evam Kisan Kalyan Mantralaya)**

---

1. The list of Ministries/Departments is based on the information as given under Allocation of Business Rules, 1961 as amended from time to time and available on Cabinet Secretariat website : http://cabsec.nic.in.

(i) Department of Agriculture, Co-operation and Farmers Welfare *(Krishi, Sahkarita evam Kisan Kalyan Vibhag)*

(ii) Department of Agricultural Research and Education *(Krishi Anusandhan aur Shiksha Vibhag)*

(iii) Department of Animal Husbandry, Dairying and Fisheries *(Pashupalan, Dairy aur Matsyapalan Vibhag)*

2. **Ministry of Ayurveda, Yoga and Naturopathy, Unani, Siddha and Homoeopathy (AYUSH) (Ayurveda, Yoga aur Prakratik Chikitsa, Unani, Siddha aur Homoeopathy) (Ayush Mantralaya)**
3. **Ministry of Chemicals and Fertilizers (Rasayan aur Urvarak Mantralaya)**

(i) Department of Chemicals and Petro-Chemicals *(Rasayan aur Petro-Rasayan Vibhag)*

(ii) Department of Fertilizers *(Urvarak Vibhag)*

(iii) Department of Pharmaceuticals *(Aushadh Vibhag)*

4. **Ministry of Civil Aviation (Nagar Vimanan Mantralaya)**
5. **Ministry of Coal (Koyala Mantralaya)**
6. **Ministry of Commerce and Industry (Vanijya aur Udyog Mantralaya)**

(i) Department of Commerce *(Vanijya Vibhag)*

(ii) Department of Industrial Policy and Promotion *(Audyogik Niti aur Samvardhan Vibhag)*

7. **Ministry of Communications (Sanchar Mantralaya)**

(i) Department of Telecommunications *(Doorsanchar Vibhag)*

(ii) Department of Posts *(Dak Vibhag)*

8. **Ministry of Consumer Affairs, Food and Public Distribution (Upbhokta Mamle, Khadya aur Sarvajanik Vitaran Mantralaya)**

(i) Department of Consumer Affairs *(Upbhokta Mamle Vibhag)*

(ii) Department of Food and Public Distribution *(Khadya aur Sarvajanik Vitaran Vibhag)*

9. **Ministry of Corporate Affairs (Corporate Karya Mantralaya)**
10. **Ministry of Culture (Sanskriti Mantralaya)**
11. **Ministry of Defence (Raksha Mantralaya)**

(i) Department of Defence *(Raksha Vibhag)*

(ii) Department of Defence Production *(Raksha Utpadan Vibhag)*

(iii) Department of Defence Research and Development
(Raksha Anusandhan tatha Vikas Vibhag)

(iv) Department of Ex-servicemen Welfare
(Poorva Senani Kalyan Vibhag)

12. Ministry of Development of North-Eastern Region (Uttar Poorvi Kshetra Vikas Mantralaya)

13. Ministry of Drinking Water and Sanitation (Peya Jal aur Swachhta Mantralaya)

14. Ministry of Earth Sciences (Prithvi Vigyan Mantralaya)

15. Ministry of Electronics and Information Technology (Electroniki aur Soochana Praudyogiki Mantralaya)

16. Ministry of Environment, Forest and Climate Change (Paryavaran,Van aur Jalvayu Parivartan Mantralaya)

17. Ministry of External Affairs (Videsh Mantralaya)

18. Ministry of Finance (Vitta Mantralaya)

(i) Department of Economic Affairs *(Arthik Karya Vibhag)*

(ii) Department of Expenditure *(Vyaya Vibhag)*

(iii) Department of Revenue *(Rajaswa Vibhag)*

(iv) Department of Investment and Public Asset Management (DIPAM) *(Nivesh aur Lok Parisampatti Prabandhan Vibhag)* (DIPAM)

(v) Department of Financial Services *(Vittiya Sewayen Vibhag)*

19. Ministry of Food Processing Industries (Khadya Prasanskaran Udyog Mantralaya)

20. Ministry of Health and Family Welfare (Swasthya aur Parivar Kalyan Mantralaya)

(i) Department of Health and Family Welfare *(Swasthya aur Parivar Kalyan Vibhag)*

(ii) Department of Health Research *(Swasthya Anusandhan Vibhag)*

21. Ministry of Heavy Industries and Public Enterprises (Bhari Udyog aur Lok Udyam Mantralaya)

(i) Department of Heavy Industries *(Bhari Udyog Vibhag)*

(ii) Department of Public Enterprises *(Lok Udyam Vibhag)*

22. Ministry of Home Affairs (Grih Mantralaya)

(i) Department of Internal Security *(Aantarik Suraksha Vibhag)*

(ii) Department of States *(Rajya Vibhag)*

(iii) Department of Official Language *(Raj Bhasha Vibhag)*

(iv) Department of Home *(Grih Vibhag)*

(v) Department of Jammu and Kashmir Affairs *(Jammu tatha Kashmir Vibhag)*

(vi) Department of Border Management *(Seema Prabandhan Vibhag)*

23. Ministry of Housing and Urban Affairs (Awasan aur Shahari Karya Mantralaya)

24. Ministry of Human Resource Development (Manav Sansadhan Vikas Mantralaya)

(i) Department of School Education and Literacy *(School Shiksha aur Saksharta Vibhag)*

(ii) Department of Higher Education *(Uchchatar Shiksha Vibhag)*

25. Ministry of Information and Broadcasting (Soochana aur Prasaran Mantralaya)

26. Ministry of Labour and Employment (Shram aur Rozgar Mantralaya)

27. Ministry of Law and Justice (Vidhi aur Nyaya Mantralaya)

(i) Department of Legal Affairs *(Vidhi Karya Vibhag)*

(ii) Legislative Department *(Vidhayee Vibhag)*

(iii) Department of Justice *(Nyaya Vibhag)*

28. Ministry of Micro, Small and Medium Enterprises (Sukshm, Laghu aur Madhyam Udyam Mantralaya)

29. Ministry of Mines (Khan Mantralaya)

30. Ministry of Minority Affairs (Alpasankhyak Karya Mantralaya)

31. Ministry of New and Renewable Energy (Naveen aur Navikarniya Oorja Mantralaya)

32. Ministry of Panchayati Raj (Panchayati Raj Mantralaya)

33. Ministry of Parliamentary Affairs (Sansadiya Karya Mantralaya)

34. Ministry of Personnel, Public Grievances and Pensions (Karmik, Lok Shikayat tatha Pension Mantralaya)

(i) Department of Personnel and Training
(Karmik aur Prashikshan Vibhag)

(ii) Department of Administrative Reforms and Public Grievances
(Prashasnik Sudhar aur Lok Shikayat Vibhag)

(iii) Department of Pensions and Pensioners' Welfare
(Pension aur Pension Bhogi Kalyan Vibhag)

35. Ministry of Petroleum and Natural Gas (Petroleum aur Prakritik Gas Mantralaya)

36. Ministry of Planning (Yojana Mantralya)

37. Ministry of Power (Vidyut Mantralaya)

38. Ministry of Railways (Rail Mantralaya)

39. Ministry of Road Transport and Highways (Sarak Parivahan aur Raj Marg Mantralaya)

40. Ministry of Rural Development (Gramin Vikas Mantralaya)

(i) Department of Rural Development
(Gramin Vikas Vibhag)

(ii) Department of Land Resources
(Bhumi Sansadhan Vibhag)

41. Ministry of Science and Technology (Vigyan aur Praudyogiki Mantralaya)

(i) Department of Science and Technology
(Vigyan aur Praudyogiki Vibhag)

(ii) Department of Scientific and Industrial Research
(Vigyan aur Audyogik Anusandhan Vibhag)

(iii) Department of Bio-technology *(Biotechnology Vibhag)*

42. Ministry of Shipping (Pot Parivahan Mantralaya)

43. Ministry of Skill Development and Entrepreneurship (Kaushal Vikas aur Udyamita Mantralaya)

44. Ministry of Social Justice and Empowerment (Samajik Nyaya aur Adhikarita Mantralaya)

(i) Department of Social Justice and Empowerment
(Samajik Nyaya aur Adhikarita Vibhag)

(ii) Department of Empowerment of Persons with Disabilities
(Viklangjan Sashaktikaran Vibhag)

45. Ministry of Statistics and Programme Implementation (Sankhyiki aur Karyakram Kiryanvayan Mantralaya)

46. Ministry of Steel (Ispat Mantralaya)

47. Ministry of Textiles (Vastra Mantralaya)

48. Ministry of Tourism (Paryatan Mantralaya)

49. Ministry of Tribal Affairs (Janjatiya Karya Mantralaya)

50. Ministry of Water Resources, River Development and Ganga Rejuvenation (Jal Sansadhan, Nadi Vikas aur Ganga Sanrakshan Mantralaya)

51. Ministry of Women and Child Development (Mahila aur Bal Vikas Mantralaya)

52. Ministry of Youth Affairs and Sports (Yuva Karyakram aur Khel Mantralaya)

(i) Department of Youth Affairs *(Yuva Karyakaram Vibhag)*

(ii) Department of Sports *(Khel Vibhag)*

INDEPENDENT DEPARTMENTS

53. Department of Atomic Energy (Parmanu Oorja Vibhag)

54. Department of Space (Antariksh Vibhag)

APEX/INDEPENDENT OFFICE

55. Cabinet Secretariat (Mantrimandal Sachivalaya)

56. President's Secretariat (Rashtrapati Sachivalaya)

57. Prime Minister's Office (Pradhan Mantri Karyalaya)

58. NITI Aayog (National Institution for Transforming India)

National Authority for Chemical Weapons Convention

The Convention on the Prohibition of the Development, Production, Stockpiling and Use of Chemical Weapons (NACWC) is a multi lateral international treaty which outlaws the production, stockpiling, and use of chemical weapons and their precursors. The CWC came into force with effect from 1997. By March 2016, 192 states have ratified or acceded to the treaty. The Organisation for the Prohibition of Chemical Weapons (OPCW); an intergovernmental organization based in The Hague, Netherlands is the'treaty organisation' for the CWC. The OPCW bagging the Nobel Peace Prize of 2013 is in recognition of the Convention as a very effective Disarmament Treaty.

The National Authority for Chemical Weapons Convention (NACWC) was set up as an office of the Cabinet Secretariat, Government of India to fulfill, on behalf of the Government of India, the obligations under the Chemical Weapons Convention (CWC) and to act as the national focal point for effective liaison with the Organisation for the Prohibition of Chemical Weapons (OPCW) and other state parties on matters relating to the Convention. In 2000, Chemical Weapons Convention Act was passed by the Parliament which came into force in 2005. India is one of the four non-elected Members of the Executive Committee (consisting of 41 members from all over the world) of the OPCW. India has representation in the Advisory Body on Administrative and Finance (ABAF), the Confidentiality Commission, Network Committee on Assistance and Protection, Scientific Advisory Body (SAB) and the newly created Advisory Body on Education and Outreach (ABEO) of the OPCW. India is an active collaborator with OPCW and all other state parties in implementation of the provisions of the Convention.

Project Monitoring Group

Project Monitoring Group (PMG), is an institutional mechanism for resolving a variety of issues including fast tracking of approvals for setting up an expeditious commissioning of large Public, Private and Public-Private Partnership (PPP) project. Project Monitoring Group (PMG) was set up in 2013 under cabinet secretariat. PMG is presently functioning under Prime Minister's Office (PMO) since 2015.

As part of its efforts to ensure timely disposal of applications submitted by investors, PMG is monitoring the development and operation of online digital platforms by various ministries and departments through its web portal e-nivesh monitor (e-nivesh.gov.in). The monitoring mechanism has been developed to track the progress achieved in online processing and disposal of different types of clearances in various central ministries/departments, etc. The portal tracks all digitalized proposals starting from the online submission till clearance by pulling the information from various online central services/ clearance portals of ministries/departments, etc.

Public Grievances

The Directorate of Public Grievances (DPG) was set up in the Cabinet Secretariat in 1988 to entertain grievances from the public after they fail to get satisfactory redress from the ministry/department concerned within a reasonable time. It is thus, an office of the last resort for redress of grievances relating to sectors in its purview. Grievance can be lodged with DPG through post, email or by lodging the complaint online on the portal. The cases received offline are entered in the system and, thereafter, all cases are handled using PGRAMS application.

Each grievance is first scrutinized to see if it relates to a sector in DPG's purview. Those concerning the sectors outside the purview of DPG are forwarded to the Department of Administrative Reforms and Public Grievances for appropriate disposal, under intimation to the complainants. The remaining grievances are then assessed to ascertain whether the issue involved is grave and whether the concerned ministry/department has been given an opportunity to redress the grievance. The grievances of grave nature which are either long pending or where the redress is not forthcoming from concerned service organisation/ministry are taken up for detailed examination. These cases are followed up to a logical and reasonable conclusion. Other cases are transferred to the concerned ministry for appropriate action.

When DPG seeks comments, the department or organization is expected to examine the matter and give a reply within thirty days. After receipt of comments, DPG may, if considered necessary, seek further information to ensure that the grievance is dealt with in a fair and objective manner by the department or organization and confirmation of satisfactory redress of the grievance is also sought from the complainant before closure.

DPG has been progressively computerizing its operations since the early years. The Public Grievance Redress and Monitoring System (PGRAMS), an exclusive automation programme for DPG was adopted in 1999. The PGRAMS is integrated with Centralized Public Grievance Redress and Monitoring System, 'CPGRAMS', the operating system for Public Grievances Portal covering all the ministries/departments of Government of India. With a view to improving further the redress system, a number of measures like launch of Hindi version of PGRAMS to widen its coverage, incorporation of features like e-mail/SMS for better communication with the complainants, press advertisements to increase awareness about DPG in public, etc. were implemented during the year 2016-17.

National Disaster Management Authority

Emergence of an organization is always through an evolutionary process. National Disaster Management Authority (NDMA) has also gone through the same stages. The Government of India, in recognition of the importance of Disaster Management as a national priority, set up a high-powered committee in 1999 and a National Committee after the Gujarat earthquake, for making recommendations on the preparation of disaster management plans and suggesting effective mitigation mechanisms. The Tenth Five-Year Plan document also had, for the first time, a detailed chapter on Disaster Management. The Twelfth Finance Commission was also mandated to review the financial arrangements for disaster management.

In 2005, the government enacted the Disaster Management Act, which envisaged the creation of National Disaster Management Authority, under the Ministry of Home Affairs, headed by the Prime Minister, and State Disaster Management Authorities (SDMAs) headed by respective Chief Ministers, to separhead and implement a holistic and integrated approach to disaster management in the country.

NDMA, as the apex body, is mandated to lay down the policies, plans and guidelines for disaster management to ensure timely and effective response to disasters. Towards this, it has the responsibilities which include:- lay down policies on disaster management ; approve the National Plan; lay down guidelines to be followed by the state authorities in drawing up the State Plan;

lay down guidelines to be followed by the different ministries or departments of the Government of India for the purpose of integrating the measures for prevention of disaster or the mitigation of its effects in their development plans and projects; provide such support to other countries affected by major disasters as may be determined by the central government; take such other measures for the prevention of disaster, or the mitigation, or preparedness and capacity building for dealting with threatening disaster situation or disasters as it may consider necessary; lay down broad policies and guidelines for the functioning of the National Institute of Disaster Management.

Relevant Website : www.ndma.gov.in

Administrative Reforms and Public Grievances

The Department of Administrative Reforms and Public Grievances (DARPG) is the nodal agency of the Government of India for administrative reforms as well as redressal of public grievances relating to the states in general and those pertaining to central government agencies in particular. The Department endeavours to document and disseminate successful good governance practices by way of audio-visual media and publications. It also undertakes activities in the field of international exchange and cooperation to promote public service reforms.

Relevant Website : www.darpg.gov.in

Prime Minister's Award for Excellence in Public Administration

Government of India instituted 'Prime Minister's Award for Excellence in Public Administration' to acknowledge, recognize and reward the extraordinary and innovative work done by officers of the central and state governments. It rewards the outstanding and exemplary performance of civil servants. Since its beginning in 2007 till 2015, 67 awards were conferred in three categories, individual, group, organization. The structure of the Scheme was changed in 2015-16 to focus on excellence in implementation of identified priority programme. A new category of awards one each for Additional Secretary/Joint Secretary level officers and Director/Deputy Secretary, serving in Government of India was also introduced in 2018 to recognize their contribution towards bringing about transformational improvements in processes/systems through simplification, process re-engineering, etc.

Civil Services Day

The Government of India celebrates April, 21 every year as 'Civil Services Day' for the civil servants to rededicate themselves to the cause of citizens and renew their commitment to public service and excellence in work. The first such function was held in Vigyan Bhavan, New Delhi on April 21, 2006. On the occasion, the Prime Minister conferred "Prime Minister's Award for Excellence in Public Administration". This date coincides with the date when the first Home Minister of Independent India Sardar Vallabhbhai Patel addressing the first batch of Indian Administrative Services officers at Metcalf House, New Delhi. It is organised by DARPG annually in New Delhi.

National Conference on e-Governance

DARPG along with the Ministry of Electronics and information Technology, in association with one of the state governments, organizes the National Conference on e-Governance every year since 1997. This provides a platform for the senior officers of the government including IT secretaries of state governments. IT managers of the central government and resource persons, experts, intellectuals from the industry and academic institutions, etc., to discuss, exchange views and experiences relating to various e-Governance initiatives. So far 21 National Conferences on e-Governance have been held. In the Conference the National Awards on e-Governance are given in following categories which include: Excellence in Government Process Re-engineering, Outstanding performance in citizen centric service delivery; Innovations in existing projects of government departments other than PSUs; Best District level initiative through ICT in North East state; Hill states+UTs (excluding Delhi), other states; Use of spatial technology and GIS in e-Governance; Innovative Use of ICT in e-Governance Projects/initiatives by Start-ups; registered with Government; etc.

Each category is given a gold and a silver award. The gold award winning project and its team is given a cash award up to a maximum of ₹ 2 lakh, subject to a ceiling of ₹ 75,000/- per individual and silver winning project and its team is given a cash award up to a maximum of ₹ 1 lakh subject to a ceiling of ₹ 50,000/- per individual.

e-Office Project

e-Office is one of the 31 Mission Mode Projects (MMPs) identified in the erstwhile national e-Governance Plan-2006 NeGP 1.0 and its implementation is being steered by the DAR&PG. The e-Office has been subsumed in the current Digital India Programme (NeGP 2.0). It is being monitored on a regular basis by an apex committee headed by Cabinet Secretary.

Modernisation Scheme

The modernization scheme is being implemented by the DAR&PG from 1987-88 in order to give boost to modernization of offices at branch and section level in various central government offices located in Delhi as an overall process of administrative reforms. As per the scheme, the DARPG extends financial assistance to the extent of 75 per cent of the total cost of the project and the beneficiary has to contribute 25 per cent of the cost.

Redressal Public Grievances

DARPG is responsible for issuing policy guideliness and coordination and monitoring of issues regarding redress of public grievances for the central government. In accordance with the federal principle of governance, the grievances relating to states are forwarded to concerned state government for appropriate action.A mobile app was launched in 2015 which was for android based mobile through which people could lodge and track their public grievance. This has been further developed to make it more user friendly and has now been integrated with the Unified Mobile Application for New-Age Governance (UMANG).

Further, to monitor public grievances on real time and periodically review progress of systemic reforms, an online dashboard has been developed. Systemic reforms and their monitoring metrics, catering to grievance issues are highlighted on the dashboard. This enables Cabinet Secretariat, DARPG and concerned ministries departments to monitor implementation of these reforms. From time to time the version of CPGRAM is being updated taking into account the problems faced by the citizens and the system itself. At present the version 6 of CPGRAMS is in operation from 2018 which provides for one time registration. It also enables the citizen to see all th grievances lodged by him and their status on a single screen.

The Department also coordinates the Citizen Charter and Information and Facilitation Counters (IFCs) initiative of the government of India. With the objective of improving public service delivery and making governments citizen-centric, an assessment improvement framework called "Sevottam" has been developed Support is provided to ministries departments and also to state governments to introduce the Sevottam framework for better service delivery.

Documentation and Dissemination

The Documentation and Dissemination Division of the Department primarily carries out the activities of documentation and dissemination of good governance practices of centre, state/union territory governments with a view to share experience with each other and replicate elsewhere.

Financial Assistance for professional documentation of good governance initiatives:- The objective of the scheme is to provide financial assistance upto ₹ 3.00 lakh to support professional documentation and dissemination of good governance initiatives by the state/UT governments. So far eighty-two projects have been sanctioned. As per the revised scheme of providing financial assistance to the state governments/UT administrations the professional documentation report will now be in e-book form instead of paper documentation and a short documentary film shall also be made by the state/UT govt. with the financial assistance of ₹ 3.00 lakh.

Production of Documentary Films on Best Practices:- The Department is engaged in producing documentary films on best practices across the country. These films are useful for administration and dissemination of success stories which facilitate replication of the same elsewhere. Seventy eight such documentary films have already been produced. These documentary films are available on the website of the Department as well as on YouTube.

Regional Conference :- Regional conferences are organised on specific themes in association with various state/union territory governments with a view to bring national and state level organizations along with other stakeholders including NGOs, intelligentsia, media, etc. on the same platform to share experiences in the formulation and implementation of good governance practices.

Book on Best Practices:- This Division publishes a book containing articles on select award winning good governance practices. These articles are on the initiatives that have been conferred Prime Minister's Award or National e-Governance Awards. This compilation is immensely useful for the administrators as the dissemination of success stories facilitates replication of the same elsewhere also. The Division has already published a series of books on the subject.

Minimum Government - Maximum Governance:- Department of Administrative Reforms and Public Grievances is bringing out a periodical journal "Management in Government" (MIG) since 1969 and now renamed "Minimum Government - Maximum Governance" based on the best practices which were conferred Prime Minister's Award for Excellence in Public Administration and National e-Governance Awards and launched first e-Book in2015. The e-Book "Minimum Government - Maximum Governance" is available on the website of the Department at http://darpg.gov.in/journal-MGMG.

International Exchange and Cooperation

The Department works as the nodal point in respect of matters relating to international cooperation in the field of public administration and governance, which includes organizing programmes as part of projects / bilateral measures taken up in accordance with the Memorandum of Understandings (MoUs) / agreements signed between India and other countries (bilateral or multilateral). The purpose of the international cooperation component is to enable the sharing of information, best practices and personnel across national government. As a part of its international collaborative efforts, the Department of Administrative Reforms and Public Grievances (DARPG) explored the possibility of sharing and exchanging administrative experiences, the Department signed bilateral MOUs with Britain, France, Malaysia, Portugal, Singapore and China and trilateral MoU with South Africa and Brazil (under IBSA). This involves exchange of visits and undertaking programmes/projects and activities particularly in the area of pubic administration and delivery of services, so as to improve upon the current system of governance and instill a greater sense of responsiveness, accountability, transparency, and achieving public service excellence in the context of public service delivery good governance, public service reform, and capacity building and skills upgradation.

Cooperation with Commonwealth Association for Public Administration and Management

The Commonwealth Association for Public Administration and Management (CAPAM), with its headquarters at Ottawa, Canada, is an organization dedicated to strengthening public management and consolidating democracy and good governance in the Commonwealth. It was formed in 1994 as a result of decisions taken at the Commonwealth Heads of Government meetings in Harare in 1991 and in Cyprus in 1993. Since inception, CAPAM has grown to a network of over 1100 members across the Commonwealth countries. The Ministry of Personnel, Public Grievances and Pensions, Government of India became an institutional member of CAPAM in 1997. The membership enables the Government of India to keep pace with the latest developments in the field of public administration, through participation in various programmes of CAPAM viz., international innovations awards programme, international innovations cascading programme, international meetings, seminars and conferences organized by CAPAM, as well as through various publications, journals and study reports. CAPAM recognizes and promotes good governance through its award programmes given under four categories. The international innovations awards celebrate the spirit of innovation in the public service by recognizing organisations that have made significant contributions to improving governance and services in the public sector.

Department of Personnel and Training

The role of the Department of Personnel & Training (DoPT) can be conceptually divided into two parts. In its large nodal role, it acts as the formulator of policy and the watch-dog of the government ensuring that certain accepted standards and norms, as laid down by it, are followed by all ministries/ departments, in the recruitment, regulation of service conditions, posting/ transfers, deputation of personnel as well as other related issues. It also advises all organizations of the central government on issues of personnel management. At a more immediate level, the DoPT has the direct responsibility of being the cadre controlling authority for the IAS and the three secretariat services in the Central Secretariat. The Department also operates the Central Staffing Scheme under which suitable officers from All India Services and Group 'A' Central Services are selected and then placed in posts at the level of Deputy Secretary/ Director and Joint Secretary, on the basis of tenure deputation. The Department also deals with cases of appointment to posts of Chairman, Managing Director, and full-time functional Director/member of the board of management of various public sector undertakings /enterprises, corporations, banks and financial institutions. It also deals with the assignment of Indian experts to various developing countries. It is also responsible for formulation and coordination of training policies for the All India and Central Services and providing support for the capacity building of state government officials

Relevant Website : www.dopt.gov.in

Recruitment Agencies

The two organizations through which the Department ensures recruitment of personnel for the government are the Union Public Service Commission (UPSC) and the Staff Selection Commission (SSC). The former is responsible for conducting examinations for appointment to the higher civil services and civil posts; including recruitment to the All India Services. There is a mandatory provision for consulting the Commission on all matters relating to methods of recruitment, principles to be followed in making promotions and transfers from one service to another and on all disciplinary matters. The SSC is responsible for making recruitment to subordinate staff such as Assistants, Stenographers etc.

Some of the initiatives taken by the DoPT include:

(a) Discontinuation of interview for Gr. B and C posts

Interview has been dispensed with for recruitment by SSC to all Group 'C' and Group 'B' (non-gazetted) from January 2016. This is applicable for recruitment on GoI min./attached/subordinate offices/autonomous bodies/ PSUs. 18 states and all the union territories, namely Andhra Pradesh, Assam, Bihar, Chhattisgarh, Goa, Gujarat, Himachal Pradesh, Jharkhand, Karnataka, Kerala, Madhya Pradesh, Maharashtra, Manipur, Punjab, Rajasthan, Tamil Nadu, Telangana, Uttarakhand, Andaman & Nicobar Islands, Chandigarh, Daman & Diu, Dadra & Nagar Haveli, Delhi, Lakshadweep and Puducherry have adopted the policy of discontinuation of interview in recruitments to lower level posts

(b) Switching from OMR based exam to Computer

To improve transparency and reduce time taken to complete recruitment process, the government has switched over from the traditional OMR (Optical Mark Reader) mode to Computer Based Mode in respect of the various recruitment exams (viz., CGLE, CHSLE, MTS level, etc.) conducted by SSC.

(c) Single Registration and Two Tier System of Examination

At present, candidates seeking government jobs have to appear for different examinations where similar eligibility conditions have been prescribed. Multiple recruitment examinations not only burden the candidates but also results in aviodable expenditure in the conduct of these examinations by various recruitment agencies. Government now proposes to introduce a common eligibility test to shortlist the candidates for vacancies of Group 'B' Non-Gazetted and below through a computer based/online mode test for Tier-1 examination to be conducted by SSC. There will be common registration of candidates through National Career Service (NCS) portal. Final selection will be made through specialised Tier-11 examination to be conducted by individual recruitment agencies.

(d) Self-Certification for Appointment

From June, 2016, the recruiting agencies now issue provisional appointment letters based on the self certification of the candidates. The police verification is to be conducted within six months to confirm the appointment. The idea is to response trust on the citizen and minimise delays due to police verification.

(e) Accelerated filling up of Divyaang Jan Vacancies

Providing equal opportunity to Divyaang Jan, special recruitment drive launched in May, 2015 to fill up 15,694 vacancies of persons with disabilities in central government, of which 13,492 vacancies have already filled up.

(f) Benefit of Reservation to ex-Servicemen

Earlier ex-servicemen were provided one chance to join any civil employment. As per new instructions, they will get chance to join any of the choice post for which he /she had applied before joining the civil employment.

(g) Citizen Centricity in Administration

RTI online portal has been expanded to cover all public authorities registered with the CIC for ease of access to inform by citizens. All public authorities have been aligned.

(h) Placement of Senior Appointment

It has been ensured that appointments and placements to senior positions are based on merit and integrity. Multi-source feedback for empanelment for the posts of Joint Secretary and above has been introduced. The Banks Board Bureau was established for conducting the selection for appointment to board level position in public sector banks. In order to increase the catchment area and to utilise the skill sets of executives working in the private sector/state PSEs, executives from the private (sector/state PSEs have also been made eligible for appointment to board level positions in Central Public Sector Enterprises.

(i) Anti Corruption Strategies

Government of India has been following the policy of "zero tolerance towards corruption". The overall objectives of "maximum governance minimum Government" can only be realized if government and its agencies work in an environment which is citizen centric, transparent and corruption free. In order to achieve these objectives both preventive and punitive actions have been taken.

(j) Intensive Review for Premature Retirement

With a view to weed out ineffective, inefficient and officers of doubtful integrity, intensive review of records of all government employees is carried out under Rule FR 56 J and other corresponding provisions. Measures have been taken to compulsorily retire officers of doubtful integrity against whom frequent complaints and cases have been lodged after thorough scrutiny of the service records.

Administrative Reforms Commission

The second Administrative Reforms Commission (ARC) was constituted in 2005, as a Commission of Inquiry for preparing a detailed blueprint for revamping the public administrative system. It presented 15 reports for consideration: (i) Right to Information: Master Key to Good Governance; (ii) Unlocking Human Capital: Entitlements and Governance - A Case Study; (iii)

Crisis Management: From Despair to Hope; (iv) Ethics in Governance; (v) Public Order : Justice for Each ... Peace for All; (vi) Local Governance; (vii) Capacity Building for Conflict Resolution - Friction to Fusion; (viii) Combating Terrorism; (ix) Social Capital - A Shared Destiny; (x) Refurbishing of Personnel Administration - Scaling New Heights; (xi) Promoting e-Governance - The Smart Way Forward; (xii) Citizen Centric Administration - the Heart of Governance; (xiii) Organisational Structure of Government of India; (xiv) Strengthening Financial Management System; (xv) state and district Administration. The central government considered 14 out of 15 reports and the decisions on the accepted recommendations of 2nd ARC are at various stages of implementation.

Right to Information

The Right to Information Act, 2005 empowers the citizens, promotes transparency and accountability in the working of the government, combat corruption and make the democracy work for people in real sense. The Act aims at creating an informed citizenry which would be better equipped to keep necessary vigil on the instruments of governance and make the government more accountable to the governed.

The Act gives all the citizens the right to seek information held by any authority or body or institution of self government established or constituted by or under the Constitution; or by any other law made by the Parliament or a state legislature; or by notification issued or order made by the central government or a state government. Bodies owned, controlled or substantially financed by the central government or a state government and non-government organizations substantially financed by the central government or a state government also fall within the definition of public authority. The right includes inspection of work, documents and records, taking notes, extracts or certified copies of documents or records, taking certified samples of material held by the public authority or held under the control of the public authority. It also includes information relating to any private body which can be accessed by the public authority under any law for the time being in force. There are some categories of information which each public authority is required to publish *suo moto*.

One has to simply make a request to the Public Information Officer of the office indicating the information sought and the address at which the information is required. The request can be sent either by post or submitted in person in Hindi, English or in the official language of the area and can also be sent through e-mail. If the applicant does not get the information within 30 days or the applicant is not satisfied with the reply given to him, he can make an appeal within 30 days to the appellate authority appointed by the authority who is an officer superior to the Public Information Officer. The appellate authority has to decide the appeal within 30 days of the receipt of appeal. If the applicant is not satisfied even with the decision of the appellate authority, he can file a second appeal with the Central Information Commission or the State Information Commission, as the case may be within 90 days. The Central Information Commission entertains appeals in respect of offices, financial institutions, public sector undertakings, etc. under the central government and the union territories and a State Information Commission deals with the appeals pertaining to offices, financial institutions, public sector undertakings, etc. under the concerned state government.

The Central Information Commission/State Information Commissions are high-powered independent bodies created by the Act, and they can impose penalty on the defaulting Public Information Officers. This comprehensive law covers almost all levels of governance, and are applicable not only to union, state and local governments but also to the recipients of government grants. Access to information under this Act is extensive with minimum exemptions. The Right to Information Act has converted the prevailing culture of secrecy into culture of openness and transparency in the working of the government.

Official Language

Article 343 (1) of the Constitution provides that Hindi in Devanagari script shall be the official language of the Union. Article 343 (2) also provides for continuing the use of English in official work of the Union for a period of 15 years (i.e., upto January 25, 1965) from the date of commencement of the Constitution. Article 343 (3) empowered the Parliament to provide by law for continued use of English for official purposes even after January 25, 1965. The Act also lays down under Section 3 (3) that both Hindi and English shall compulsorily be used for certain specified purpose such as resolutions, general Orders, Rules, Notifications, Administrative and other Reports, Press Communiques; Administrative and other reports and official papers to be laid before a House or the Houses of Parliament; contracts, agreements, licences, permits, tender notices and forms of tender, etc.

With a view to ensuring compliance of the constitutional and legal provisions regarding official language and to promote the use of Hindi for the official purposes of the Union, the Department of Official Language was set up in 1975 as an independent department of the Ministry of Home Affairs. Since then, this Department has been making efforts for accelerating the progressive use of Hindi for the official purposes of the Union. In accordance with the Government of India (Allocation of Business) Rules, 1961, this Department has been entrusted with the following items of work that include:- co-ordination in all matters relating to the progressive use of Hindi as the Official Language of the Union, including administrative terminology, syllabi, textibooks, training courses and equipment (with standardised script) required therefor; matters relating to the Kendriya Hindi Samiti and the Central Translation Bureau, etc.

In 1976, Official Language Rules were framed under the provisions of Section 8 (1) of the Official Languages Act, 1963 as amended in 1967. Salient features of the rules are as under: (i) They apply to all central government offices, including any office of a Commission, Committee or Tribunal appointed by the central government and corporation or company owned or controlled by the central government except Tamil Nadu; (ii) Communications from a central government office to state/union territories or to any person in region 'A' comprising Uttar Pradesh, Uttarakhand, Himachal Pradesh, Madhya Pradesh, Chhattisgarh, Bihar, Jharkhand, Rajasthan, Haryana and union territories of Andaman and Nicobar Islands and Delhi, shall be in Hindi; (iii) Communications from a central government office to states/union territories in region 'B' comprising Punjab, Gujarat, Maharashtra and the union territory of Chandigarh, Daman and Diu and Dadra and Nagar Haveli shall ordinarily be in Hindi and if any communication is issued to any of them in English, it shall be accompanied by a Hindi translation thereof; (iv) Communications from a central government officer to state or union territory in Region 'C' or to any office (not being a central government office) or person in such state shall be in English; and (v) Communications between central government offices in region 'C' to a state or union territory of Region 'A' or Region 'B' or to any office (not being a central government office) or persons in such state may be either in Hindi or English.

Relevant Website : www.rajbhasha.nic.in

Official Language Policy

The features of official language policy are : i) all manuals, codes and other procedural literature relating to central government offices are required to be prepared both in Hindi and English. All forms, headings of registers, name plates, notice boards and various items of stationery, etc. are also required to be in Hindi and English; ii) officers should ensure that documents specified in Section 3 (3) of the Act are issued both in Hindi and English; and iii) the administrative head of each central government office should ensure that the provisions of the Act, the rules and directions issued under Rule 12 shall be properly complied with, and suitable and effective check-points shall be devised for this purpose.

Annual Programme

In compliance with the Official Language Resolution, 1968, an annual programme is prepared by the Department of Official Language in which targets are set for the offices of the central government with regard to originating correspondence, replies in Hindi to letters in Hindi, recruitment of Hindi typists and stenos, websites, inspections and meetings of Hindi Salahakar Samiti and Official Language Implementation Committees, purchase of Hindi books for libraries, and purchase of electronic equipment. A quarterly progress report is submitted by the offices of the central government regarding achievements vis-a-vis the said targets. An Annual Assessment Report is prepared on the basis of these reports, which is laid on the tables of both Houses of the Parliament, and its copies are endorsed to state governments and the ministries/departments of the central government.

Committees/Samitis

The Kendriya Hindi Samiti was constituted in 1967. Chaired by Prime Minister it is the apex policy making body which lays the guidelines for the propagation and progressive use of Hindi as official language of the Union. The Committee of Parliament on official language was constituted in 1976 to periodically review the progress in the use of Hindi as the official language of the Union and to submit a report to the President.

Award Schemes

The Department has Rajbhasha Keerti Puraskar Yojana for awarding the outstanding achievements in the implementation of Official Language Policy of the Union. Under the Rajbhasha Gaurav Hindi Book Writing Scheme, cash awards, shields and certificates are awarded to the working/retired employees of the central government, banks, financial institutions, universities, training institutions and autonomous bodies of the central government for writing original books in Hindi. At zonal level, Zonal Official Language Awards are given annually to the central government offices, public sector undertakings, banks and financial institutions of the central government for outstanding achievements in implementing the Official Language Policy of the Union, and for progressive use of Hindi.

Inter-State Council

The provision for setting up an Inter-State Council is mentioned in Article 263 of the Constitution. In pursuance of the recommendation made by the Sarkaria Commission on Centre-State Relations, the Inter-State Council was set up in 1990. The Inter-State Council (ISC) is a recommendatory body and has been assigned the duties of investigating and discussing such subjects, in which some or all of the states or the union territories and one or more of the states have a common interest, for better coordination of policy and action with respect to that subject. It also deliberates upon such other matters of general interests to the states as may be referred by the Chairman to the Council.

The Prime Minister is the Chairman of the Council. Chief Ministers of all the states and union territories having legislative assemblies, administrators of union territories not having legislative assemblies, governors of states under President's rule and six ministers of cabinet rank in the Union Council of Ministers, nominated by the Chairman of the Council, are members of the Council.

Relevant Website : www.interstatecouncil.nic.in

Zonal Council

Five zonal councils viz., Northern Zonal Council, Central Zonal Council, Eastern Zonal Council, Western Zonal Council and Southern Zonal Council were set up vide Part-III of the States Re-organisation Act, 1956 with the objectives of bringing out national integration; arresting the growth of acute state consciousness, regionalism, linguism and particularistic tendencies; enabling the centre and the states to cooperate and exchange ideas and experiences; and establishing a climate of co-operation amongst the states for successful and speedy execution of development projects.

Composition of Zonal Councils

Zonal Council	Members States/ Union Territories
Northern Zonal Council	Haryana, Punjab, Himachal Pradesh, Rajasthan, Jammu & Kashmir, National Capital Territory of Delhi and the Union Territory of Chandigarh
Central Zonal Council	Uttarakhand, Uttar Pradesh, Chhattisgarh and Madhya Pradesh
Eastern Zonal Council	Bihar, Jharkhand, West Bengal and Odisha
Western Zonal Council	Gujarat, Maharashtra, Goa and the Union Territories of Dadra & Nagar Haveli and Daman and Diu
Southern Zonal Council	Andhra Pradesh, Tamil Nadu, Karnataka, Kerala, Telangana and the Union Territory of Puducherry

Organizational Structure of Zonal Councils

The Union Home Minister is the Chairman of all the zonal councils. The Office of the Vice-Chairman is held by the Chief Minister of the Member State of the respective zonal council by annual rotation, each holding office for a period of one year at a time. Two other ministers of each member state are also members of each Zonal Council. The Chief Secretary of the Member State function as the Secretary of respective Zonal Council by annual rotation and another officer/Development Commissioner and one officer nominated by the Planning Commission for each of the Zonal Councils as Adviser for a period of one year.

The States

The system of government in states closely resembles that of the Union.

Executive

Governor

A state executive consists of Governor and Council of Ministers with Chief Minister as its head. The Governor of a state is appointed by the President for a term of five years office. Only Indian citizens above 35 years of age are eligible for appointment to this office. Executive power of the state is vested in Governor.

The Council of Ministers with the Chief Minister as head, aids and advises Governor in exercise of his functions except in so far as he is by or under the Constitution required to exercise his functions or any of them in his discretion.

In respect of Nagaland, the Governor has special responsibility under Article 371 A of the Constitution with respect to law and order and even though it is necessary for him to consult Council of Ministers in matters relating to law and order, he can exercise his individual judgement as to the action to be taken.

Similarly, in respect of Arunachal Pradesh, the Governor has special responsibility under Article 371 H of the Constitution with respect to law and order. Governor shall, after consulting Council of Ministers, exercise his individual judgement as to the actions to be taken. These are, however, temporary provisions. If the President, on receipt of a report from Governor or otherwise is satisfied that it is no longer necessary for Governor to have special responsibility with respect to law and order, he may so direct by an order.

Likewise, in the Sixth Schedule which applies to tribal areas of Assam, Meghalaya, Tripura and Mizoram as specified in para 20 of that schedule, discretionary powers are given to Governor in matters relating to sharing of royalties between district council and state government. The Sixth Schedule vests additional discretionary powers in Governors of Mizoram and Tripura in almost all their functions (except approving regulations for levy of taxes and money lending by non-tribals by district councils) since December, 1998. In Sikkim, the Governor has been given special responsibility for peace and social and economic advancement of different sections of population.

All Governors while discharging such constitutional functions as appointment of Chief Minister of a state or sending a report to the President about failure of constitutional machinery in a state or in respect of matters relating to assent to a bill passed by legislature, exercise their own judgement.

Council of Ministers

The Chief Minister is appointed by the Governor who also appoints other ministers on the advice of the Chief Minister. The Council of Ministers is collectively responsible to the Legislative Assembly of the state.

Legislature

For every state, there is a legislature which consists of Governor and one House or, two Houses as the case may be. In Andhra Pradesh, Bihar, Jammu and Kashmir, Karnataka, Maharashtra, Telangana and Uttar Pradesh, there are two Houses known as Legislative Council and Legislative Assembly. In the remaining states, there is only one House known as Legislative Assembly. Parliament may, by law, provide for abolition of an existing Legislative Council or for creation of one where it does not exist, if proposal is supported by a resolution of the Legislative Assembly concerned.

Legislative Council

Legislative Council *(Vidhan Parishad)* of a state comprises not more than one-third of total number of members in Legislative Assembly of the state and in no case less than 40 members (Legislative Council of Jammu and Kashmir has 36 members vide Section 50 of the Constitution of Jammu and Kashmir). About one-third of members of the Council are elected by members of Legislative Assembly from amongst persons who are not its members, one-third by electorates consisting of members of municipalities, district boards and other local authorities in the state, one-twelfth by electorate consisting of persons who have been, for at least three years, engaged in teaching in educational institutions within the state not lower in standard than secondary school and a further one-twelfth by registered graduates of more than three years standing. Remaining members are nominated by the Governor from among those who have distinguished themselves in literature, science, art, cooperative movement and social service. Legislative Councils are not subject to dissolution but one-third of their members retire every second year.

Legislative Assembly

Legislative Assembly *(Vidhan Sabha)* of a state consists of not more than 500 and not less than 60 members (Legislative Assembly of Sikkim has 32 members vide Article 371 F of the Constitution) chosen by direct election from territorial constituencies in the state. Demarcation of territorial constituencies is to be done in such a manner that the ratio between population of each constituency and number of seats allotted to it, as far as practicable, is the same throughout the state. Term of an Assembly is five years unless it is dissolved earlier.

Powers and Functions

State legislature has exclusive powers over subjects enumerated in List II of the Seventh Schedule of the Constitution and concurrent powers over those enumerated in List III. Financial powers of legislature include authorization of all expenditure, taxation and borrowing by the state government. Legislative Assembly alone has power to originate money bills. Legislative Council can make only recommendations in respect of changes it considers necessary within a period of 14 days of the receipt of money bills from Assembly. The Assembly can accept or reject these recommendations.

Reservation of Bills

The Governor of a state may reserve any bill for the consideration of the President. Bills relating to subjects like compulsory acquisition of property, measures affecting powers and position of High Courts and imposition of taxes on storage, distribution and sale of water or electricity in inter-state river or river valley development projects should necessarily be so reserved. No bills seeking to impose restrictions on inter-state trade can be introduced in a State legislature without previous sanction of the President.

Control over Executive

State legislatures, apart from exercising the usual power of financial control, use all normal parliamentary devices like questions, discussions, debates, adjournments and no-confidence motions and resolutions to keep a watch over day-to-day work of the executive. They also have their committees on estimates and public accounts to ensure that grants sanctioned by Legislature are properly utilized.

Union Territories

Union territories are administrated by the President acting to such extent, as he thinks fit, through an administrator appointed by him. Administrators of Andaman and Nicobar Islands, Delhi and Puducherry are designated as Lieutenant Governors. The Governor of Punjab is concurrently the administrator of Chandigarh. The administrator of Dadra and Nagar Haveli is concurrently the administrator of Daman and Diu. Lakshadweep has a separate administrator.

The National Capital Territory of Delhi and Union Territory of Puducherry each has a Legislative Assembly and Council of Ministers. The Legislative Assembly of the Union Territory of Puducherry may make laws with respect to matters enumerated in List II or List III in the seventh Schedule of the Constitution in so far as these matters are applicable in relation to the union territory. The Legislative Assembly of National Capital Territory of Delhi has also these powers with the exceptions that entries 1, 2 and 18 of the list II are not within the legislative competence of the Legislative Assembly. Certain categories of bills, however, require the prior approval of the central government for introduction in the Legislative Assembly. Some bills, passed by the Legislative Assembly of the Union Territory of Puducherry and National Capital Territory of Delhi are required to be reserved for consideration and assent of the President.

Local Government

Municipalities

Municipal bodies have a long history in India. The first such Municipal Corporation was set-up in the former Presidency Town of Madras in 1688; and later in Bombay and Kalkata in 1726. The Constitution of India has made detailed provisions for ensuring protection of democracy in Parliament and in the state legislatures. However, the Constitution did not make the local self-government in urban areas a clear-cut constitutional obligation. While the Directive Principles of State Policy refer to Village Panchayats, there is no specific reference to municipalities except the implicity in Entry 5 of the State List, which places the subject of local self-governments as a responsibility of the states.

In order to provide for a common framework for urban local bodies and help to strengthen the functioning of the bodies as effective democratic units of self-government, Parliament enacted the Constitution (74th Amendment) Act, 1992 (known as Nagarpalika Act) relating to municipalities in 1992. It came into effect in 1993. A new Part IX-A relating to the municipalities added to provide for among other things, constitution of three types of municipalities, i.e., *Nagar Panchayats* for areas in transition from a rural area to urban area, Municipal Councils for smaller urban areas and Municipal Corporation for large urban areas, fixed duration of municipalities, appointment of State Election Commission, appointment of State Finance Commission and constitution of metropolitan and district planning committees. All state/union territories administrations have set-up their State Election Commissions and Finance Commissions.

Panchayats

Article 40 of the Constitution which enshrines the Directive Principles of State Policy lays down that the state shall take steps to organize village panchayats and endow them with such powers and authority as may be necessary to enable them to function as units of self-government.

A new Part IX relating to the panchayats was inserted in the Constitution to provide for among other things, Gram Sabha in a village or group of villages; constitution of panchayats at village and other level or levels; direct elections to all seats in panchayats at the village and intermediate level, if any, and to the offices of Chairpersons of panchayats at such levels; reservation of seats for the scheduled castes and scheduled tribes in proportion to their population for membership of panchayats and office of Chairpersons in panchayats at each level; reservation of not less than one-third of the seats for women; fixing tenure of five years for panchayats and holding elections within a period of six months in the event of supersession of any panchayat.

Election Commission

The Election Commission of India (ECI) was constituted in 1950 with its headquarters at New Delhi. It is a permanent independent constitutional body vested with the powers and responsibility of superintendence, direction and control of the entire process of conduct of elections to Parliament and to legislatures of the states and the union territories and elections to the offices of President and Vice-President held under the Constitution.

The Election Commission decides the election schedules for the conduct of elections —both general elections and bye-elections. It prepares, maintains and periodically updates the electoral rolls, supervises the nomination of candidates, registers political parties, monitors the election campaign, including funding and expenditure of candidates. It also facilitates the coverage of the election process by the media, carries out the voter education and awareness measures, organizes the polling stations/ booths where voting takes place, and oversees the counting of votes and the declaration of results. It conducts polling through EVMs (Electronic Voting Machines) and recently, on pilot basis, introduced VVPAT (Voter Verifiable Paper Audit Trail). The Election Commission has also provided for compulsory identification at the time of voting by means of Electors' Photo Identity Cards (EPICs) and distribution of photo slip close to polls.

Elections are conducted according to the constitutional provisions, supplemented by laws made by Parliament. The major laws are the Presidential and Vice-Presidential Elections Act, 1952; the Representation of the People Act, 1950; and the Representation of the People Act, 1951. All political parties are required to get themselves registered with the Election Commission. Based on performance criteria laid down in the Elections Symbols (reservation & allotment) Order 1968, the Commission grants recognition to political parties as national or state parties. It also decides disputes relating to splits/mergers of recognized political parties.

At the state level, the election work is supervised, subject to overall control of the Commission, by the Chief Electoral Officer of the state, who is appointed by the Commission by selection from amongst senior civil servants of the state government. Field administration at the district and sub-divisional levels in India is run by the District Magistrates (Deputy Commissioners/Collectors), Sub-Divisional Magistrates, Revenue Divisional Officers, Tehsildars, etc. The Election Commission utilizes these state government officers, for election work, by designating them as District Election Officers, Electoral Registration Officers, Returning Officers, Assistant Electoral Registration Officers, Assistant Returning Officers, etc. During election time, however, they are available to the Commission, more or less, on a full time basis.

During the last 64 years, the Commission has conducted 16 General Elections to the Lok Sabha and about 365 General Elections to State Legislative Assemblies, thus facilitating peaceful orderly and democratic transfer of power.

Election Commission of India launched the India International Institute of Democracy and Election Management (IIIDEM), an advanced resource centre of learning, research, training and extension for electoral democracy and election management. The Institute presently functions from New Delhi. Courses are conducted in the Institute for ECI's field officials and also for participants from abroad. The Commission is increasingly sharing its expertise and experience with election management bodies of other countries, and providing electoral assistance and training based on bilateral requests and multi-lateral arrangements. ECI has MoUs with 16 countries, besides having MoUs with UNDP, International IDEA and IFES.

Relevant Website : www.eci.gov.in

4 Agriculture

AGRICULTURE plays a vital role in India's economy. 54.6 per cent of the population is engaged in agriculture and allied activities (census 2011) and it contributes 17.4 per cent to the country's Gross Value Added for the year 2016-17 (at current prices). Given the importance of agriculture sector, Government of India took several steps for its sustainable development. Steps have been taken to improve soil fertility on a sustainable basis through the soil health card scheme, to provide improved access to irrigation and enhanced water efficiency through Pradhan Mantri Krishi Sinchai Yojana (PMKSY), to support organic farming through Paramparagat Krishi Vikas Yojana (PKVY) and to support for creation of a unified national agriculture market to boost the income of farmers. Further, to mitigate risk in agriculture sector a new scheme "Pradhan Mantri Fasal Bima Yojana (PMFBY) was been launched for implementation from Kharif 2016.

The Department of Agriculture, Cooperation and Farmers' Welfare (DAC&FW) is one of the three constituent departments of the Ministry of Agriculture and Farmers' Welfare, the other two being Department of Animal Husbandry, Dairying & Fisheries (DAHD&F) and Department of Agricultural Research and Education (DARE).

Relevant Websites : www.agriculture.gov.in   www.agricoop.nic.in
www.dare.nic.in   www.dahd.nic.in

Production

The normal spell of rainfall during monsoon 2016 and the various policy initiatives taken by the Government made it possible to achieve a broad-based record foodgrain production in the year 2016-17. As per the Fourth Advance Estimates for 2016-17, production of rice is estimated at a new record of 110.15 million tonnes. Rice production is 3.50 million tonnes higher than the previous record production of 106.65 million tonnes. The wheat production is higher by 6.10 million tonnes as compared to the wheat production of 92.29 million tonnes in 2015-16. Further, production of coarse cereals is estimated at a new record level of 44.19 million tonnes. It is higher than the previous record production of 43.40 million tonnes achieved during 2010-11 by 0.79 million tonnes and also higher by 5.67 million tonnes as compared to the production of 38.52 million tonnes achieved during 2015- 16.

National Policy for Farmers

Government of India approved the National Policy for Farmers (NPF) in 2007. Many of the provisions of the NPF are being operationalised through various schemes and programmes which are being implemented by different central government departments and ministries. For the operationalisation of the remaining provisions of the Policy, an Action Plan was finalized and circulated to the ministries/departments concerned, as well as to all states/ UTs for necessary follow-up action.

Major Programmes

Pradhan Mantri Krishi Sinchayee Yojana (PMKSY)

The scheme has been approved with an outlay of Rs. 50,000 crore for a period of 5 years (2015-16 to 2019-20). The major objective of PMKSY is to achieve convergence of investments in irrigation at the field level, expand cultivable area under assured irrigation, improve on-farm water use efficiency to reduce wastage of water, enhance the adoption of precision irrigation and other water saving technologies (Per drop, More crop), promote sustainable water conservation practices etc. Cabinet decision was taken in July, 2016 for implementation of PMKSY in a mission mode. The mission is administered by Ministry of Water Resources, River Development and Ganga Rejuvenation with the Per Drop More Crop component being administered by Department of Agriculture, Cooperation and Farmers Welfare (DAC&FW).

Agriculture Credit

Government announces annual target for agriculture credit in the budget every year. Agricultural credit flow has shown consistent progress every year. The target for the year 2016-17 was fixed at ₹ 9,00,000 crore and against this target the achievement was ₹10,65,756 crore. The agriculture credit flow target for 2017- 18 has been fixed at ₹10,00,000 crore. The Department implements the Interest Subvention Scheme under which interest subvention is provided on short-term crop loans upto ₹ 3 lakh for a period of one year which is made available to farmers at subvented interest rate of 7 per cent per annum and in case of timely repayment, the same gets reduced to 4 per cent per annum.

Crop Insurance

In order to protect farmers against crop failure due to natural calamities, pests and diseases, weather conditions, Government of India introduced the National Crop Insurance Programme (NCIP) with component schemes of Modified National Agricultural Scheme (MNAIS), Weather Based Crop Insurance Scheme (WBCIS) and Coconut Palm Insurance Scheme (CPIS). In addition, National Agricultural Insurance Scheme (NAIS) which was withdrawn after implementation of NCIP from rabi 2013-14 and was extended further upto 2015-16. A new scheme "Pradhan Mantri Fasal Bima Yojana (PMFBY) was implemented from kharif 2016 along with restructured pilot Unified Package Insurance Scheme (UPIS) and Weather Based Crop Insurance Scheme (WBCIS).

Commission for Agricultural Costs and Prices

Commission for 'Agricultural Costs and Prices' (CACP), set up with a view to evolve a balanced and integrated price structure, is mandated to advice on the price policy (MSP) of 23 crops. These include seven cereal crops (paddy, wheat, jowar, bajra, maize, ragi and barley), five pulse crops (gram, tur, moong, urad and lentil), seven oilseeds (groundnut, sunflower seed, soyabean, rapeseedmustard, safflower, nigerseed and seasmum), copra (dried coconut), cotton, raw jute and sugarcane. CACP submits its recommendations in the form of Price Policy Reports every year, separately for five groups of commodities namely kharif crops, rabi crops, sugarcane, raw jute and copra.

Determinants of MSP

Cost of production (CoP) is one of the important factors in the determination of MSP of mandated crops. Besides cost, the Commission considers other important factors such as demand and supply, price trend in the domestic and international markets, inter-crop price parity, terms of trade between agricultural and nonagricultural sectors and the likely impact of MSPs on consumers, in addition to ensuring rational utilization of natural resources like land and water. Thus, pricing policy is rooted not in 'cost plus' approach, though cost is an important determinant of MSP.

Indian Council of Agricultural Research

In India, new records are being established in the agriculture sector. India's foodgrain production for the 2016-17 is estimated at record 275.68 million tonnes, which is over 4 per cent higher than the previous record production achieved during 2013-14. In this endeavour, the Indian Council of Agricultural Research (ICAR) has played a vital role by way of technology development, demonstration and transfer in India. The National Agricultural Research System (NARS) of the country has taken up number of activities through Krishi Vigyan Kendras (KVKs) and other programmes for application of farm technologies in farmers'field. Besides, taking up technology assessment, refinement, demonstration and capacity development programmes the other initiatives such as Farmers First, attracting and retaining youth in agriculture (ARYA), climate resilient integrated farming systems (IFS), cluster frontline demonstration (CFLD) of pulses and oilseeds, Cereal Systems Initiatives for South Asia (CSISA), documentation and registration of farmers' varieties under PPV&FRA, pulses seed hubs, KVK Portal, Mera Gaon Mera Gaurav and awareness creations about mega government schemes, etc., were also implemented to espouse the cause of farming community through technology application with their active participation.

Soil and Water Productivity

The National Bureau of Soil Survey and Land Use Planning (NBSS&LUP) developed NBSS BHOOMI Geo-portal to access various thematic information on major physiographic regions, sub-physiographic regions, agro-ecological regions (1992), agro-ecological regions (2015) and agroecological sub-regions of the country. Area/region specific efficient and remunerative crops and cropping sequences were delineated based on soils, landforms, rainfall, temperature, length of growing period and irrigability. The NBSS&LUP developed an android based mobile application on GIS platform to facilitate web-based decision support system (DSS) for land use planning and dissemination of soil health cards information at village and farm level for Gujarat. App will display details of soil map unit information and suggested land use plan for that survey number. The NBSS & LUP has so far prepared Land Resource Inventory (LRI) of 99 blocks. These digitized maps of micronutrients status would be helpful in providing sitespecific variable rate application of micronutrients prescription for sustainable agricultural productivity.

Genetic Resources

In all 21 explorations were undertaken and 1,532 germplasm accessions were collected comprising 1,095 of cultivated plants and 437 wild accessions. The explorations were undertaken two each in Andhra Pradesh, Assam, Chhattisgarh, Maharashtra, Tamil Nadu, Uttar Pradesh, West Bengal and one each in Andaman and Nicobar, Arunachal Pradesh, Karnataka, Nagaland, Odisha, Tripura and Uttarakhand. The population of *momordica cochinchinensis*, collected from the middle Andaman Island, was described as a new subspecies *momordica cochinchinensis subsp. andamanica*, which was subsequently validated through DNA barcoding. During 2017, 411 herbarium specimens were added to the National Herbarium of Cultivated Plants. Out of 28,516 accessions, imported from 39 countries, 2,911 were screened against biotic and 787 against abiotic stresses, and 7,343 were supplied for research use and crop improvement programme within the country. Ten phytosanitory certificates were issued for export of germplasm.

Crop Improvement

Major emphasis was to develop new varieties/hybrids tolerant to various biotic and abiotic stresses with enhanced quality. 209 varieties were developed 117 high-yielding varieties/hybrids of cereals comprising 65 of rice, 14 of wheat, 24 of maize, 5 of finger millet, 3 of pearl millet, 1 each of sorghum, barley, foxtail millet, kodo millet, little millet and proso millet and released for cultivation in different agro-ecological regions of the country. Twenty eight high-yielding varieties of oil seeds, 32 of pulses, 24 of commercial crops (cotton, sugarcane and jute) and eight of forage crops were released for cultivation in different agroecologies.

Livestock

Improvement of indigenous cattle breeds through selection project was conceptualized for the genetic improvement of Gir, Kankrej and Sahiwal cattle in their home tracts. Under network project of buffalo improvement Nli-Ravi, Bhadawari and Swamp breed centres are functioning as conservation and improvement units whereas Jaffarabadi, Pandarpuri and Surti breed centres are concentratng on field progeny testing and maintaining the elite herd for bull production and a breedable herd of 567. All India Coordinated Research

Project (AICRP) on goat improvement covered 13 tribal villages and contributed for a better livelihood security for tribal people as goats are major source of income to poor people in tribal areas and North-Eastern Hill region. Under AICRP on poultry breeding all the 12 centres are workng on the development of locaton specific rural chicken varieties.

Crop Management

A long-term tillage experiment in maize-wheat and rice-wheat system indicated that the wheat crop was not affected by tillage in rice or maize. Enhancing crop yield per unit water use through improved agro-techniques involving sprinklers in summer greengram indicated higher stability in Samrat over IPM 205-7. Sprinkler irrigation resulted in less water use (26.3 per cent) with higher water productivity (43.2 per cent) and net return (28.4) over flood irrigation.

Animal Husbandry, Dairying and Fisheries

Animal Husbandry, Dairying and Fisheries activities, along with agriculture, continue to be an integral part of human life since the process of civilization started. These activities have contributed not only to the food basket and draught animal power but also by maintaining ecological balance. Owing to conducive climate and topography, animal husbandry, dairying and fisheries sectors have played prominent socio-economic role in India. Traditional, cultural and religious beliefs have also contributed in the continuance of these activities. They further also play a significant role in generating gainful employment in the rural sector, particularly among the landless, small and marginal farmers and women, besides providing cheap and nutritious food to millions of people.

Livestock production and agriculture are intrinsically linked, each being dependent on the other, and both crucial for overall food security. Livestock sector is an important subsector of the agriculture of Indian economy. It forms an important livelihood activity for most of the farmers, supporting agriculture in the form of critical inputs, contributing to the health and nutrition of the household, supplementing incomes, offering employment opportunities, and finally being a dependable "bank on hooves" in times of need. It acts as a supplementary and complementary enterprise.

India has vast resource of livestock and poultry, which play a vital role in improving the socio-economic conditions of rural masses. There are about 300 million bovines, 65.07 million sheep, 135.2 million goats and about 10.3 million pigs as per 19th livestock census in the country.

Livestock Production

Livestock production and agriculture are intrinsically linked, each being dependent on the other, and both crucial for overall food security. According to estimates of the Central Statistics Office (CSO), the value of output livestock sector at current prices was about ₹ 5,91,691 crore during 2015-16 which is about 28.5 per cent of the value of output from agricultural and allied sector. At constant prices the value of output from livestock is about 29 per cent of the value of the output from total agriculture and allied sector. India continues to be the largest producer of milk in the world. Several measures have been initiated to increase the productivity of livestock, which has resulted in increasing the milk production significantly from the level of 102.6 million tonnes at the end of the Tenth Plan (2006-07) to 127.9 million tonnes at the end of the Eleventh Plan (2011-12).

Milk Production

Milk production during 2015-16 and 2016-17 was 155.5 million tonnes and 165.4 million tonnes respectively showing an annual growth of 6.37 per cent. The per capita availability of milk was around 355 grams per day in 2016-17.

Egg Production

Poultry production has taken a quantum leap in the last four decades, emerging from an unscientific farming practice to commercial production system with state-of-the art technological interventions. Egg production at the end of the Tenth Plan (2006-07) was 50.70 billion as compared to 66.45 billion at the end of the Eleventh Plan (2011-12). Currently the total poultry population is 729.21 million (as per 19th Livestock Census) and egg production was around 88.14 billion during 2016-17. The per capita availability (2016-17) was around 69 eggs per annum. The poultry meat production is estimated to be 3.46 million tonnes.

Wool Production

Wool production declined marginally at the end of Eleventh Five Year Plan (2011-12) to 44.7 million kg from 45.1 million kg in the end of Tenth Five Year Plan (2006-07). Wool production in the beginning of Twelfth Plan (2012-13) was 46.05 million kgs and increased to 48.1 million kgs in 2014-15 but declined to 43.5 million kgs in 2016-17.

Meat Production

The meat production registered a healthy growth from 2.3 million tonnes at the end of Tenth Five Year Plan (2006-07) to 5.5 million tonnes at the end of the Eleventh Five Year Plan (2011-12). Meat production in the beginning of Twelfth Plan (2012-13) was 5.95 million tonnes which further increased to 7.4 million tonnes in 2016-17.

Fisheries Production

The country has vast potential for fisheries in view of long coastline of about 8,118 kms apart from the inland water resources. During 2016-17, India exported products worth of ₹ 37870.90 crore which is about 0.92 per cent of the National Gross Domestic Product (GDP) and 5.23 per cent to the agriculture GVA (2015-16). India is the second largest producer of fish and also second largest producer of fresh water fish in the world. Fish production increased from 41.57 lakh tonnes (24.47 lakh tonnes for marine and 17.10 lakh tonnes for inland fisheries) in 1991-92 to 107.90 lakh tonnes (35.8 lakh tonnes for marine and 77.69 lakh tonnes for inland fisheries) in 2016-17(Provisional). During the first two quarters of 2017-18 the fish production is estimated at 5.80 million tonnes (P).

National Livestock Mission

For sustainable and continuous growth of livestock sector by emulating the success achieved in dairy and poultry sectors, across species and regions, the National Livestock Mission was launched in 2014-15 with an approved outlay of ₹ 2,800 crore during XII Plan. This Mission is formulated with the objectives of sustainable development of livestock sector, focusing on improving availability of quality feed and fodder, risk coverage, effective extension, improved flow of credit and organisation of livestock farmers / rearers, etc. with the following sub-missions: (i) sub-mission on livestock development; (ii) sub-mission on pig development in north-eastern region; (iii) sub-mission on fodder and feed development; and (iv) sub-mission on skill development, technology transfer and extension.

Livestock Health

With improvement in the quality of livestock through cross-breeding programmes, the susceptibility of these livestock to various diseases including exotic diseases has increased. In order to reduce morbidity and mortality, efforts are being made by the state/union territory governments to provide better health care through polyclinics/veterinary hospitals, dispensaries and first-aid centers including mobile veterinary dispensaries available in the states.

In order to provide referral services, over and above the existing disease diagnostic laboratories in the states, one central and five regional disease diagnostic laboratories have been established which are now fully functional. Further, for control of major livestock and poultry diseases by way of prophylactic vaccination, the required quantity of vaccines are being produced in the country at 27 veterinary vaccine production units including 20 in public sector. While efforts are made to ensure better livestock health in the country, efforts are also being made to prevent ingress of diseases from outside the country, and to maintain standards of veterinary drugs and formulations. At present, the Drugs Controller General of India regulates the quality of veterinary drugs and biologicals.

Livestock Census

The first livestock census was conducted during 1919-1920 and since then it is being conducted quinquennially by all states/UTs of the country. It is the only source, which gives disaggregated information on various species of farm animals and poultry birds. The 19th Livestock Census was conducted in 2012 in the country in participation with animal husbandry departments of the states/ UTs. Breed Survey was also undertaken in 2013 in order to estimate the breedwise number of livestock population on a general principle of 15 per cent sample village across the country.

Indian Fisheries

Presently India is the second largest fish producing and second largest aquaculture nation in the world. India is also a major producer of fish through aquaculture and ranks second in the world after China. The total fish production during 2015-16 (provisional) stood at 10.79 million metric tonne (MMT) with a contribution of 7.21 MMT from inland sector and 3.58 MMT from marine sector.

Fisheries is a sunrise sector with varied resources and potential, engaging over 14.50 million people at the primary level and many more along the value chain. Transformation of the fisheries sector from traditional to commercial scale has led to an increase in fish production.

The historical scenario of Indian fisheries reveals a paradigm shift from marine dominated fisheries to a scenario where inland fisheries emerged as a major contributor to the overall fish production in the country.

Within inland fisheries there is a shift from capture fisheries to aquaculture during the last two and a half decade. Freshwater aquaculture with a share of 34 per cent in inland fisheries in mid-1980s has increased to about 80 per cent in recent years. It has emerged as a major fish producing system. Fish Farmers Development Agencies (FFDA) was set up in various districts for delivering a package of technologies, practices, training and extension and for providing financial assistance to the beneficiaries. Mariculture in the country over the years was confined largely to bivalve molluscs viz., mussels, edible oysters and pearl oysters, and to some extent seaweeds. With a thrust on development of technologies pertaining to sea cage farming during last decade, developmental plans with both forward and back ward linkages are envisaged to allow these activities to become significant contributors to production of seafood in the country.

5 Culture and Tourism

THE mandate of the Ministry of Culture revolves around the functions like preservation and conservation of ancient cultural heritage and promotion of art and culture both tangible and intangible in the country. The Ministry has two attached, six subordinate offices and thirty five autonomous organisations, which are fully funded by the Government. There are seven zonal cultural centres working mainly on folk and traditional arts of different zones. There are also four missions namely National Mission for Manuscripts, National Mission for Monument and Antiquities, National Mission on Libraries, and Gandhi Heritage Sites Mission. Broadly, this Ministry is working on the protection, development and promotion of all types of heritage of culture namely, tangible heritage, intangible heritage and knowledge heritage. In addition, the Ministry also harbours the responsibility of Gandhian heritage and commemoration of important historical events and centenaries of great personalities. In tangible heritage, the Ministry takes care of all the centrally protected monuments of national importance, which is achieved through Archeological Survey of India. Similarly, the Ministry is also promoting a museum movement in the country and majority of the museums are under its administrative control. The Ministry also promotes regional museums through grants-in-aid.

In the field of intangible heritage, the Ministry extends financial support to individuals, group of individuals and cultural organizations engaged in performing visual and literary arts. Similarly, the Ministry through its organizations, is engaged in recognizing excellence in the field of art and culture by way of awards given by institutions like Sahitya Akademi and Sangeet Natak Akademi. The National School of Drama is involved in promoting a vibrant theatre movement of contemporary relevance in the context of our traditions and cultural diversity.

In knowledge heritage, the Ministry is the custodian of all the major libraries in the country. It also extends grant-in-aid for library development and is also responsible for all policy matters regarding library development. Through National Archives of India, Ministry is responsible for maintenance of all archival records of the country. The Ministry is also involved in protection and promotion of Buddhist and Tibetian Culture and is doing this through various institutions located at Sarnath, Varanasi and Leh. This Ministry has a very well-planned capacity-building programme for all those who want to excel in the field of Indian as well as Asian art and culture. Institutions like the School of Archaeology, School of Archives, National Institute of History and Art, Maulana Abul Kalam Azad Institute of Asian Studies are mentionable in this regard. Various courses offered by National School of Drama and Kalakshetra Foundation are also some of the examples of capacity building programmes of the Ministry. The Ministry is also responsible for the implementation of various UNESCO conventions in the field of culture and for entering into Cultural Exchange Agreements with partnering countries. India has Cultural Agreements with 107 countries and agreements relating to Cultural Exchange Programmes have been signed with 69 countries.

Relevant Website : www.indiaculture.nic.in

Lalit Kala Akademi

Lalit Kala Akademi, the National Academy of Art, was set up in 1954. Lalit Kala Akademi is the government's apex cultural body in the field of visual arts in India. It is an autonomous body, which is fully funded by the Ministry of Culture. The Akademi is an institution that has rendered service to the nation in the arts sphere long before the world woke up to the global impact of Indian art. It has established, preserved and documented a permanent collection that reflects the vitality, complexity and unfolding patterns of modern and contemporary art in India. All through the year it presents exhibitions and educational programmes of unparalleled significance; sustains a library, art collection, archives, conservation laboratory and supports scholars and publications of pre-eminent intellectual merit all over the country.

Central to the Akademi's mission is the encouragement of a deeper understanding and enjoyment of modern and contemporary art by a diverse local, national and international audience that it serves. The National Exhibition of Art and the International Triennale - India, are examples of such endeavours.

The Akademi is involved in a wide range of activities promoting Indian art and artists through programmes and strategic partnerships. The Akademi's sincere commitment to the development of art is evident through the strong national and international programmes organized by the headquarters in New Delhi and by the Centres situated at Bhubaneshwar, Chennai, Kolkata, Lucknow, Garhi (New Delhi) and sub centres at Shimla and Patna. Another major art promotional activity of the Akademi is to provide studios to artists who work in various disciplines of art, such as sculpture, graphics, ceramics and paintings. In Delhi, the Akademi administers the Garhi Artists' Studios where approximately 200 artists work regularly. The Akademi has started a regular programme on research and documentation. Scholars are given financial assistance to undertake projects on various contemporary aspects of Indian society and culture.

Relevant Website : www.lalitkala.gov.in

Sangeet Natak Akademi

Sangeet Natak Akademi, India's national academy of music, dance and drama, is a pioneer in the creation of modern India. The ephemeral quality of the arts, and the need for their preservation led to the adapting of a democratic system in which the common man had the opportunity to learn, practice and propagate the arts. In 1945, the Asiatic Society of Bengal submitted a proposal for the creation of a National Cultural Trust consisting of three academies-an academy of dance, drama and music; an academy of letters and an academy of art and architecture. It led to the creation of three national academies after Independence. The national Academy named Sangeet Natak Akademi, was the first of these entities to be established by a resolution of the Ministry of Education. In 1961, the Sangeet Natak Akademi was reconstituted by the Government as a society and registered under the Societies Registration Act, 1860 (as amended in 1957).

The Akademi works towards building up a unified structure of support for the practice of music, dance and drama in India encompassing traditional and modern forms, and urban as well as rural environments. The festivals of music, dance and drama presented or promoted by the Akademi are held all over the country. The great masters of the performing arts have been elected as Fellows of the Akademi. The Sangeet Natak Akademi Awards conferred annually on eminent artists and scholars are considered the most coveted honours in the field of the performing arts. Thousands of institutions across the country, including many in the remote areas, engaged in teaching or promotion of music, dance and theatre, have received financial assistance for their work from the Akademi, as do researchers, authors and publishers in relevant disciplines.

The Akademi has a large archive of audio and video tapes, 16-mm films, photographs and transparencies and remains the single most important resource for researchers in the field of performing arts of India. The Akademi maintains a reference library consisting of books in English, Hindi and some regional languages. The Akademi's publication unit publishes literature on relevant subjects on a small scale.

The Akademi establishes and looks after institutions and projects of national importance in the field of the performing arts. The Jawaharlal Nehru Manipur Dance Academy (JNMDA) in Imphal, the premier institution in the teaching of Manipuri dance and music, established in 1954, is the first of these institutions. In 1959, the Akademi established the National School of Drama and the Asian Theatre Institute; and in 1964, the Kathak Kendra, both being based in Delhi. The Akademi's other projects of national importance are in Kutiyattam theatre of Kerala, commenced in 1991. Kutiyattam was recognized by UNESCO as a masterpiece of oral and intangible heritage of humanity in 2001. The project on Chhau dance of Odisha, Jharkhand and West Bengal began in 1994. The project support to Sattriya music, dance, theatre and allied arts of Assam was started in 2002.

Being the apex body specializing in the performing arts, the Akademi also advises and assists the Government of India in formulating and implementing policies and programmes in the field of the performing arts. It fosters cultural contacts nationally and internationally. The Akademi has held exhibitions and major festivals in foreign countries to foster cultural contact between India and the world.

Relevant Website : www.sangeetnatak.gov.in

National School of Drama

The National School of Drama (NSD)-one of the foremost theatre institutions in the world and the only one of its kind in India was set up by Sangeet Natak Akademi in 1959. Later in 1975, it became an autonomous organization, totally financed by Department of Culture. The objective of the NSD is to train students in all aspects of theatre, including theatre history, production, scene design, costume design, lighting, make-up, etc. The training course at NSD is of three years duration. The eligible applicants for admission to the course are screened through two stages. The Diploma of NSD is recognized by the Association of Indian Universities as equivalent to M.A. Degree for appointment as teachers in colleges/universities and for purposes of registration for Ph.D. The School has a performing wing, a Repertory Company to establish professional theatre and regular experimental work. The NSD has promoted children's theatre. It (renamed as Sanskar Rang Toli) was founded in 1989 and has been actively involved in production of plays for children, organizing summer theatre workshops in the schools of Delhi and also promoting children's theatre through Saturday Club. Since 1998, the School has organized National Theatre Festival for Children christened 'Jashne Bachpan' every year. The first ever National Theatre Festival christened was held from March 18 to April 14, 1999 to commemorate the 50th year of India's Independence has been made an annual feature.

A short-term teaching and training programme titled 'Extension Programme' was started in 1978, under which, the school organizes workshops in collaboration with the local theatre groups/artists and these programmes are invariably held in the local languages. The workshops could be broadly divided under three categories, production oriented workshops, production oriented children's workshops and teaching and training programmes in Theatre. The School has a Regional Research Centre at Bengaluru to cater to the theatrical needs of the four southern states and Puducherry. The School also publishes textbooks on theatre and also arranges for translation of important books on theatre from English into Hindi.

Relevant Website : www.nsd.gov.in

Sahitya Akademi

Sahitya Akademi, India's National Academy of Letters promotes literature in 24 languages of India recognized by it. It organizes programmes, confers Awards and Fellowships on writers in Indian languages and publishes books throughout the year and in 24 recognized languages. Over the past six decades, the Akademi has published over 7000 books in 24 languages. The Akademi publishes original works and also works in translation - fiction, poetry, drama and criticism -covering classical, medieval, pre-modern and contemporary literature. Sahitya Akademi publishes three journals, *Indian Literature* (bi-monthly in English), *Samkaleena Bhartiya Sahitya* (bi-monthly in Hindi) and *Sanskrit Pratibha* (quarterly in Sanskrit). The Akademi is also involved in promoting quality children's literature. The Akademi's head office is situated in New Delhi with offices in Kolkata, Mumbai, Bengaluru and Chennai.

Akademi Awards are most prestigious literary awards in India. Sahitya Akademi Award [the Award carries the prize money of ₹ 1 lakh and citation], awarded to the most outstanding book(s) of literary merit published in the 24 Indian languages recognized by the Akademi. Bhasha Samman [the Award carries the prize money of ₹ 1 lakh and citation] is given to writers / scholars / editors collectors / performers / translators who have made considerable contribution to the propagation and enrichment of languages that have not been recognized by the Akademi in addition to stellar contributions to the research into classical and medieval literature of the country, Translation Prize [the Award carries the prize money of ₹ 50,000 and citation] is given to outstanding translations in all the 24 languages recognized by the Akademi, Bal Sahitya Puraskar [the Award carries the prize money of ₹ 50,000 and citation] is given to outstanding contributions to children's literature in 24 languages and Yuva Puraskar [the Award carries the prize money of ₹ 50,000 and citation] is given to young Indian writers in 24 languages, are the awards instituted by the Akademi.

The Akademi organizes Festival of Letters every year to celebrate Indian writing. Sahitya Akademi promotes Tribal and Oral Literature in the country through its Centre for Tribal and Oral Literature in Delhi and North-East Centre for Oral Literature in Imphal. The Akademi also confers Fellowships on eminent Indian writers and foreign scholars who have served Indian literature.

Monographs on Indian writers (MIL), encyclopaedias, anthologies, archives of Indian literature, national bibliography of Indian literature, encyclopaedia of Indian poetics and histories of Indian literature are some of the major projects undertaken by the Akademi. The Akademi also organizes cultural exchange programmes with different countries and sends and receives several writers' delegations every year besides taking part in literary festivals and book fairs abroad.

Sahitya Akademi Library in New Delhi is one of the very few multilingual libraries which cater solely to literature. With a rich collection of books on literature and literary traditions in 24 recognized Indian languages, this library is one of its kind. In addition to this library, Sahitya Akademi has libraries in its regional offices in Mumbai, Kolkata and Bengaluru. Total number of registered members of Sahitya Akademi library is 13,219; total number of books in the library is 1,72,000 and the library attracts about 150 members every day. For better dissemination of literature in all the twenty four recognized Indian languages, Sahitya Akademi annually participates in about 180 book fairs and exhibitions across the country.

Relevant Website : www.sahitya-akademi.gov.in

Indira Gandhi National Centre for Arts

The Indira Gandhi National Centre for the Arts (IGNCA) is a national level academic research centre encompassing the study and experience of all the arts, classical and folk, written and oral, ancient and modern. Located in the heart of New Delhi, IGNCA is an autonomous trust under the Ministry of Culture. It has a rich collection of resources covering a wide range of disciplines, including archaeology, anthropology, history, philosophy, language and literature, arts and crafts of India, south Asia, south east Asia and west Asia.

The IGNCA has six functional units – Kalanidhi, the multi-form library; Kalakosa, devoted mainly to the study and publication of fundamental texts in Indian languages; Janapada Sampada, the division engaged in lifestyle studies; Kaladarsana; the executive unit which transforms researches and studies emanating from the IGNCA into visible forms through exhibition; Cultural Informatics Lab, which applies technology tools for cultural preservation and propagation; and Sutradhara, the administrative section that acts as a spine supporting and coordinating all the activities.

The IGNCA has a regional centre at Bengaluru. The regional centre for the eastern region office is located in Varanasi. The centre for North East is based in Guwahati. IGNCA has also operationalised six new centres across the country in Ranchi, Puducherry, Vadodara, Thrissur, Goa and Srinagar. IGNCA also manages the National Mission of Manuscripts which has conserved and digitised precious heritage of manuscripts through resource and conservation centres across India.

Relevant Website : www.ignca.gov.in

Centre for Cultural Resources and Training

The Centre for Cultural Resources and Training (CCRT) is one of the premier institutions working in the field of linking education with culture. CCRT was set up in 1979 as an autonomous organization by the Government of India. With headquarters in New Delhi, it has three regional centres at Udaipur, Hyderabad and Guwahati. The broad objectives of CCRT are revitalize the education system by creating an understanding and awareness among students about the plurality of the regional cultures of India and integrating this knowledge with education. The main thrust is on linking education with culture and making students aware of the importance of culture in all development programmes. It conducts a variety of training programmes for in-service teachers drawn from all parts of the country. The training provides an understanding and appreciation of the philosophy, aesthetics and beauty inherent in Indian art and culture and focuses on formulating methodologies for incorporating a cultural component in curriculum teaching. This training also stresses the role of culture in science and technology, housing, agriculture, sports, etc. It creates awareness amongst students and teachers of their role in solving environmental pollution problems and conservation and preservation of the natural and cultural heritage.

CCRT organizes workshops on drama, music, narrative art forms, etc. Teachers are encouraged to develop programmes in which the art form can be profitably utilized to teach educational curriculum. It organizes educational tours to monuments, museums, art galleries, craft centres, zoological parks and gardens, camps on conservation of natural and cultural heritage, camps on learning crafts using low cost locally available resources, lectures and demonstrations by artists and experts on various art forms, demonstrations by artists and craft persons in schools. They emphasize on intellectual and aesthetic development of the students.

Over the years, CCRT has been collecting scripts, colour slides, photographs, audio and video recordings and films. Each year it aims to revive and encourage the art and crafts forms of rural India. It also prepares publications, to provide an understanding and appreciation of aspects of Indian art and culture. CCRT implements the Cultural Talent Search Scholarship Scheme, which provides scholarships to outstanding children in the age group of 10 to 14 years, studying either in recognized schools or belonging to families practicing traditional performing or other arts to develop their talent in various cultural fields particularly in rare art forms. The scholarships continue till the age of 20 years or the first year of a University degree. The Scheme for "Award of Scholarships to Young Artistes (SYA) in Different Cultural Fields" is implemented under which maximum 400 scholarships are provided in the age group of 18 to 25 years in the field of Indian classical music, classical dances, light classical music, theatre, Visual Arts, Folk/ Traditional and Indigenous Arts.

Project Sanskriti is an initiative of Ministry of Culture in developing/ establishing of interpretation centres in educational institutions in Varanasi. CCRT has also instituted Teachers' Award to selected teachers for their outstanding work in education and culture. The award carries a citation, a plaque and a cash price of ₹ 25,000.

Relevant Website : www.ccrtindia.gov.in

Zonal Cultural Centres

Zonal Cultural Centres (ZCCs) aim to arouse awareness of the local culture and to show how these merge into zonal identities and eventually into the rich diversity of India's composite culture. These centres have already established themselves as premier agencies in the field of promotion, preservation and dissemination of culture in the entire country. They promote performing arts by significant contribution in literary and visual arts. The seven Zonal Centres were established under this scheme during 1985-86 at Patiala, Kolkata, Thanjavur, Udaipur, Allahabad, Dimapur and Nagpur. The participation of states in more than one Zonal Cultural Centre according to their cultural linkage is a special feature of the composition of the Zonal Centres. Master craftsmen and artisans from various ZCCs participate in craft fairs. Documentation of various rare folk and tribal art forms is one of the main thrust areas of the ZCCs. Under the National Cultural Exchange Programme (NCEP), exchanges of artists, musicologists, performers and scholars between different regions within the country take place. It has been extremely useful in promoting awareness of different tribal/ folk art forms in different parts of the country. A scheme of theatre rejuvenation provides an opportunity to students, actors artists, directors and writers to perform on a common platform. Guru Shishya Parampara has been introduced to promote new talents. The ZCCs promote craftsmen through Shilpgrams. The ZCCs identify the different performing/ folk art forms in their areas and select one or two talented artists in each of the fields.

Ek Bharat Shreshtha Bharat

Ek Bharat Shreshtha Bharat was announced in 2015 on the occasion of the 140th Birth Anniversary of Sardar Vallabhbhai Patel. The broad objectives of the initiative are:- (i) to celebrate the unity in diversity of our nation and to maintain and strengthen the fabric of traditionally existing emotional bonds between the people of our country; (ii) to promote the spirit of national integration through a deep and structured engagement between all states and union territories through a year-long planned engagement between states; (iii) to showcase the rich heritage and culture, customs and traditions of either state for enabling people to understand and appreciate the diversity that is India, thus fostering a sense of common identity; (iv) to establish long-term engagements; (v) to create an environment which promotes learning between States by sharing best practices and experiences.

The aim of Buddhist Tibetan Institutions (BTI) is to help preserve, promote and propagate the intangible of Buddhist/Tibetan/Himalayan cultural heritage of the country.

Cultural Heritage of the Himalayas

The objective of the scheme is to promote and preserve the cultural heritage of the Himalayas.The scheme was revised in 2011. As per the revised scheme the grant shall be provided for undertaking the activities- (i) study and research on cultural heritage,(ii) preservation of old manuscripts, literature, art & crafts and documentation of cultural activities/ events like music, dance, etc., (iii) dissemination through audio-visual programmes of art and culture and (iv) training in traditional and folk art - in the states falling under the Himalayan Region i.e. Jammu & Kashmir, Himachal Pradesh, Uttarakhand, Sikkim and Arunachal Pradesh. The colleges and universities are also eligible to apply. The quantum of funding has been increased from ₹ 5.00 lakhs to ₹ 10.00 lakhs per year for an organization.

Development of Buddhist/ Tibetan Organization

The objective of the scheme to give financial assistance to the voluntary Buddhist/Tibetan organizations including monasteries engaged in the propagation and scientific development of Buddhist/Tibetan culture and tradition and research in related fields. The scheme was revised in 2011. In the revised scheme new activities like IT upgradation, transport facilities, construction of classrooms, school buildings and training centres, audio-visual recording/documentation of traditional materials have also been included.

Central Institute of Buddhist Studies

The Central Institute of Buddhist Studies (CIBS), Leh Ladakh formerly known as School of Buddhist Philosophy was established at the behest of late Pandit Jawahar Lal Nehru in 1959. The Institute has obtained the Status of Deemed University in January, 2016.

Nava Nalanda Mahavihara

The Nava Nalanda Mahavihara (NNM) was established in 1951 in Nalanda, Bihar by the Government of Bihar. The NNM is an institution of post graduate studies and research in Pali and Buddhism. At present, Nava Nalanda Mahavihara is an autonomous institute under the Ministry of Culture and accorded Deemed University status in 2006.

Central University of Tibetan Studies

The Central University of Tibetan Studies, Sarnath, Varanasi was established in 1967 with a view to educating the youths of Tibet and Indian students of Himalayan border areas. The Institute was declared as a "Deemed to be University" in 1988.

Central Institute of Himalayan Culture Studies

The Central Institute of Himalayan Culture Studies (CIHCS) has been registered as a Society in 2010 under the Societies Registration Act, 1860. The area of operation of the Society shall be all over India. The Institute undertakes under graduate, post graduate and doctoral programmes in Buddhist and Himalayan studies and may also establish and maintain feeder schools. Regular Grants are also provided to six grantee bodies viz., Library of Tibetan Works and Archives, Dharamshala Tibet House, New Delhi, Centre for Buddhist Cultural Studies, Tawang Monastery, Arunachal Pradesh, Namgyal Institute of Tibetology, Sikkim, International Buddhist Confederation, GRL Monastic School, Bomdila, Arunachal Pradesh.

Archaeological Survey of India

The Archaeological Survey of India (ASI) was established in 1861. It functions as an attached office of the Ministry of Culture. The major activities of the Archaeological Survey of India are : survey of archaeological remains and excavations; maintenance and conservation of centrally protected monuments, sites and remains; chemical preservation of monuments and antiquarian remains; architectural survey of monuments; development of epigraphical research and numismatic studies; setting up and re-organization of site museums; expeditions abroad; training in archaeology; publication of technical reports and research works. There are 29 circles, 3 mini circles and five regional directorates through which the Archaeological Survey of India administers the work of preservation and conservation of monuments under its protection.

Under the Ancient Monuments and Archaeological Sites and Remains Act, 1958, the ASI has declared 3,686 monuments/sites to be of national importance in the country which includes twenty one properties that are inscribed on the World Heritage List by UNESCO. Three sites, namely, Champaner-Pavagarh Archaeological Park in Gujarat, Chhatrapati Shivaji Terminus (formerly Victoria Terminus) Station in Mumbai and the Brihadisvara temple complex, Gangaikondacholapuram and the Airavatesvara temple complex, Darasuram as an extension to the Brihadisvara temple complex. Thanjavur (now commonly called as the Great Living Chola Temples) have been inscribed on the World Heritage List of UNESCO in 2004. Nomination dossiers for the Victorian and Art Deco Ensemble of Mumbai have been sent to the World Heritage Centre for inscription on the World Heritage List of UNESCO. The total number of individual structures being maintained by the ASI is over 5,000. Search, study and preservation of cultural heritage lying submerged in inland or territorial waters are among the principal functions of the Underwater Archaeology Wing. It carries out exploration and excavation in Arabian Sea as well as in Bay of Bengal. The Science Branch of the Survey with its headquarters at Dehradun and field laboratories in different parts of the country carries out chemical preservation of monuments, antiquities, manuscripts, paintings, etc.

The Horticulture Branch of the ASI maintains gardens in about 287 centrally protected monuments/sites located in different parts of the country. The branch provides periodic plants to be used in gardens by developing base nurseries at Delhi, Agra, Srirangapatnam and Bhubaneshwar. The Epigraphy Branch at Mysore carries out research work in Sanskrit and Dravidian languages while the one at Nagpur carries out research work in Arabic and Persian.

Relevant Website : www.asi.nic.in

National Mission on Monuments and Antiquities

The National Mission on Monuments and Antiquities (NMMA) was launched in 2007 with the objective to prepare a National database on Built Heritage and Sites (BH&S) and antiquities from different sources and museums during the XIth Five Year Plan for information and dissemination to planners, researchers etc., and better management of such cultural resources. Keeping in view the magnitude of the work involved, and as per recommendations of

National Productivity Council in its 3rd Party Evaluation Report, NMMA has been made a Division of Archaeological Survey of India.

As part of the mandate, NMMA has to prepare two national registers viz., (i) National Register on Built Heritage and Sites and (ii) National Register on Antiquities. About 2.00 lakh data on Built Heritages and Sites has been documented from various secondary sources. NMMA has documented data of approximately 15.00 lakh antiquities so far from different sources.

National Mission for Manuscripts

The National Mission for Manuscripts (NMM) was launched in 2003 with the Indira Gandhi National Centre for Arts (IGNCA) as the nodal agency to reclaim India's inheritance of knowledge contained in the vast treasure of manuscripts. There are Manuscripts Resource Centres (MRC), Manuscripts Conservation Centres (MCC), Manuscripts Partner Centres (MPC) and Manuscripts Conservation Partner Centres (MCPC) all over India to locate, to document, to conserve and to digitize the tangible heritage of India.

Major activities of NMM are documentation of manuscripts through survey, conservation of manuscripts through preventive and curative methods, training courses and workshops on conservation-methods, manuscriptology and paleography workshops for teaching ancient scripts, digitization of manuscripts for archival and easy access to the knowledge-base, dissemination of knowledge contained in the manuscripts through publications, outreach programme to create public awareness of the importance of manuscripts.

National Museum

The National Museum, functions as a subordinate office under the Ministry of Culture since 1960, houses over 2.6 lakh art objects dating from pre-historic era onwards. The main activities of the museum are as follows: exhibitions, reorganization/modernization of galleries, educational activities and outreach programmes, public relations, publications, photo documentation, summer holiday programmes, memorial lectures, museum corner, Photo unit, modelling unit, library, conservation laboratory and workshops.

National Gallery of Modern Art

The National Gallery of Modern Art (NGMA), New Delhi was founded in 1954 to promote and develop contemporary Indian Art. It houses 17,858 works of art, representing about 1,748 contemporary Indian artists. The collection has been built up mainly by purchase and also by gift. The NGMA's important collections include paintings, sculptures, graphic arts and photographs. It organizes exhibitions from its collection and under cultural exchange programme periodically. Several colour reproductions have been brought out. The objective of NGMA is to help people look at the works of modern art with understanding and sensitivity.

Relevant Website : www.ngmaindia.gov.in

Indian Museum

The history and the highlights of the Indian Museum the eighth oldest Museum in the world which houses almost 1.10 lakhs of artefacts telling the oriental history and the heritage of India.

The history of the origin and the growth of the Indian Museum is one of the remarkable events towards the development of heritage and culture of India. Sir William Jones as one of the profoundest scholars devoted his life to the service of India founded Asiatic Society in 1784. Dr. Nathanial Wallich, a Danish Botanist, wrote a letter to the Asiatic Society in which he strongly advocated the formation of a Museum at the premises of the Society. Thus a museum, under the guidance of Dr. Nathanial Wallich was established in 1814 at the cradle of the Asiatic Society. The museum was known in the beginning as the "Asiatic Society Museum" subsequently came to be known as the "Imperial Museum" and later familiarized as the "Indian Museum" which is more familiar by the name "Jadughar" among the visitors. The present building of the Indian Museum was completed in 1875. Though in the beginning Indian Museum was opened with two galleries later on it was transformed into a multipurpose Institution where multi-disciplinary objects have been displayed in its six sections viz, art, archaeology, anthropology, zoology, geology and botany. The Museum which was founded on 1814 at the cradle of the Asiatic Society thus grew into the largest institution of its kind of the country portraying the legacy and pride of the nation. Since 1878, at its present edifice, Indian Museum has been rendering its services to the people of India as an epitome of art and culture of India and is also being highlighted as one of the pioneering national institutions in the Constitution of the Republic of India.

Indian Museum plays a significant role not only preserving the artefacts of the Indian heritage but also acts as a catalyst as an interpretation centre of Indian art heritage to facilitate the audience as a learning centre through its multicultural activities, which is needed to highlight properly to augmenting more and more tourist to the region.

National Council of Science Museums

National Council of Science Museums (NCSM), an autonomous body under the Ministry of Culture, is the largest network of science centres/ museums in the world functioning under a single administrative control. It is primarily engaged in spreading the culture of science in the society especially among students with a motto of 'Communicating Science to Empower People' through its network of Science Centres spread across India. NCSM is the implementing agency for the Science City Scheme for developing new science centres in the country of national, regional and district level. NCSM has its own network of 25 science museums/centres and has also developed and handed over 24 science centres to various State/UT governments. NCSM also provides catalytic support to other organizations by way of developing interactive exhibits and exhibitions using state of the art display technologies and techniques. Through its two-pronged activity one : development of science centres/museums, exhibits, gallery, exhibitions, innovation Hub etc., and other by organising various interactive science programmes and out of school activities, NCSM provides non formal support to the science education to the schools.

The concept of 'Museum on Wheels' was introduced in India in 1965 when Mobile Science Exhibition (MSE) programme started as Mobile Science Museum (MSM) at Ramkrishna Mission School, Kolkata. Today, a fleet of 23 MSE buses, attached to different science centres of NCSM, travel through the parts of rural India and take the message of science and technology to the rural populace. Apart from the exhibition on themes of local relevance the MSE programmes include science shows, hands on workshop for students, night sky observation through telescope, science film shows etc., as value addition. This is one of the most successful programme of NCSM and more than 65 million people, mostly students, have been benefited so far. Last year, this programme has been added in Limca Book of Records for Largest and longest running Informal Science Education Programme in India.

NCSM also facilitates participation of Indian students in International Astronomy Olympiad (Junior category) every year by organising Orientation Cum Selection Camp and Pre Departure Training for selected students. NCSM is also implementing the scheme for setting up of Innovation Hubs in the science centres/institutions to inculcate a culture of innovation, creativity and engagement in science amongst the youth of the country. NCSM has also conceptualised, developed and sent travelling exhibitions to more than 15 countries namely USA, Russia, France, Bulgaria, Nepal, China, Bangladesh, Trinidad & Tobago, Guyana, Bhutan, Indonesia, Malaysia, South Africa, Sri Lanka, Mauritius, Australia and UK. Details, are available on its website.

Relevant Website : www.ncsm.gov.in

Victoria Memorial Hall

The Victoria Memorial Hall, Kolkata (VMH), was founded principally through the efforts of Viceroy Lord Curzon, in 1921 as a period museum in memory of Queen Victoria with particular emphasis on Indo-British history. The VMH was declared an institution of national importance by the Government of India Act of 1935.

It is the premier period museum in India on Indo-British history in the eighteenth, nineteenth and twentieth centuries. It also functions as the premier art gallery, museum, research library, and cultural space in Kolkata. It has been widely hailed as the finest specimen of Indo-British architecture in India, and called the 'Taj of the Raj.' In 2017, the VMH has been recognized by TripAdvisor - the world's largest travel and tourism-related website - as the no. 1 museum in India and the no. 9 museum in Asia. It's rapidly rising global stature as a top tourist destination in India is also indicated by the award of Lonely Planet 'Top Choice' and 'Fodor's Choice' ratings. The VMH is currently by far the most-visited museum in India and one of the top museums in the world in terms of footfall. In 2015 it was also named as the 'Cleanest Monument in India,' for which it bagged the India Today Safaigiri Award.

As a museum, the VMH collection has 28,394 artefacts displayed in nine galleries that encapsulate the history of the country extending over three centuries beginning from 1650 A.D. The collection includes paintings in oil and watercolour, sketches and drawings, aquatints, lithographs, photographs, rare books and manuscripts, stamps and postal stationery, coins and medals, arms and armour, sculptures, costumes, personal relics and other miscellaneous archival documents.

Relevant Website : www.victoriamemorial-cal.org

National Museum Institute of History of Art, Conservation and Museology

It is an autonomous organization, fully funded by the Ministry of Culture, established and declared as a Deemed University in 1989. This is the only Museum University in India and is presently functioning at the first floor of National Museum, New Delhi. The Director General, National Museum is the ex-officio Vice-Chancellor of this University. Main objectives are (a) to provide education and training in the specialized areas of art, history, conservation and museology leading to the award of M.A. and Ph.D. Degrees in these three disciplines, (b) a few short-term courses- Indian art and culture, art appreciation and (Hindi Medium) are also conducted to popularize the Indian culture, (c) to organize seminars/ workshops, conferences and special lectures on museum education, art and culture.

National Research Laboratory for Conservation of Cultural Property

National Research Laboratory for Conservation of Cultural Property (NRLC) was established in 1976, as a subordinate office of the Department of Culture and is recognized by the Department of Science and Technology as a scientific institution of the Government of India. It provides conservation services and technical advise in matters concerning conservation to museums, archives, archaeology departments and other related cultural institutions, imparts training in different aspects of conservation, carries out research in methods and manner of conservation, dissemination of knowledge in conservation and provides services to conservation professional of the country. NRLC with its headquarters at Lucknow, has full fledged Training Institute campus at Jankipuram, Lucknow and a regional centre - Regional Conservation Laboratory at Mysore set up for catering to conservation needs of south India.

Ramakrishna Mission Institute of Culture

The Institute was conceived in 1936 as one of the permanent memorials to Sri Ramakrishna (1836-1886) on the occasion of his first birth centenary. It was formally established in 1938 as a branch centre of the Ramakrishna Mission founded by Swami Vivekananda to propagate the message of Vedanta as propounded by Sri Ramakrishna, whose basic teachings stressed: (i) the equality of all religions; (ii) the potential divinity of man; and (iii) service to man is a way of worshipping God-a new religion for mankind.

Anthropological Survey of India

The Anthropological Survey of India (An.S.I.) is an institution one of its unique kind anywhere the world. It has been mandated to study the bio-cultural attributes of the Indian populations since its establishment, about 65 years before. Over the decades, the An.S.I. grew from strength to strength to acquire an unparalleled blend of holistic perspective to study the human surface of the country. The activities include collection, preservation, maintenance, documentation and study of ethnographic materials as well as ancient human skeletal remains. Of late, the Anthropological Survey of India went about an all round modernization of its infrastructure to usher in the DNA technology to study the phylogenies of Indian populations, the anthropological genetics of diseases and the frontier areas of Anthropology. Over the years, the Survey has generated information from grass-root level through sustained research by its head office, Kolkata, seven regional centres (Port Blair, Shillong, Nagpur, Mysore, Dehradun, Udaipur, Kolkata), one sub-regional centre (Jagadalpur), three field stations Sagar, Ranchi, Visakhpatnam and camp office (New Delhi).

The Survey published various books, monographs, Research Reports and other occasional publications. Survey also publishes its quarterly newsletter and biannual house journal. The survey organizes various conferences, seminar, workshops and exhibition in collaboration with universities and other academic institutions of the country.

Relevant Website : www.ansi.gov.in

National Archives of India

The National Archives of India is the custodian of the non-current records of the Government of India and is holding them in trust for the use of the records creators and the users at large. It is the biggest repository of the non-current records in south east Asia. Archives are the priceless documentary heritage of any nation and as the premier archival institution in the country; the National Archives of India (NAI) plays a key role in guiding and shaping the development of archives both at the national as well as international level. In its unique position as the sole repository of the union government for public records of the country. National Archives of India functions as an attached office of the Ministry of Culture entrusted with the preservation of the documentary heritage of the nation. It is also the nodal agency for the implementation of the Public Records Act, 1993 and public records. It has one regional office at Bhopal and three records centres at Bhubaneswar, Jaipur and Puducherry.

The major activities of the National Archives of India include: making public records accessible to various Government agencies and research scholars;

an online search portal "www. abhilekh-patal.in" now facilitates to access records; rendering technical assistance to individuals and institutions in the field of conservation of records; the Department through its regular diploma courses are being conducted by the School of Archival Studies imparts training in various disciplines of archival sciences. The National Archives of India provides financial assistance to states/union territories, archives, voluntary organizations and other custodial institutions for enhancing documentary heritage of the nation.

E-mail: archives@nic.in

Relevant Website : www.nationalarchives.nic.in

Libraries

National Library

The National Library, Kolkata was originally known as the Imperial Library and was founded in 1891. After independence the name of the Library was changed to National Library. It enjoys the status of an institution of national importance, its functions are : (i) acquisition and conservation of all significant printed material (to the exclusion only of ephemera) as well as of manuscripts of national importance; (ii) collection of printed material concerning the country, no matter where this is published (iii) rendering of bibliographical and documentary services of current and retrospective material, both general and specialized; (iv) acting as referral centre surveying full and accurate knowledge of all sources of bibliographical information and participation in international bibliographical activities and (v) acting as a centre for international book exchange and internal loan.

Relevant Website : www.nationallibrary.gov.in

Central Secretariat Library

The Central Secretariat Library (CSL) originally known as Imperial Secretariat Library, Kolkata was established in 1891. Since 1969 the library has been housed at Shastri Bhawan, New Delhi with a collection of over seven lakh documents mainly on social sciences and humanities. It is a depository of Indian official documents, central government and state government documents. The collection of Area Studies Division is unique in which books have been arranged according to geographical area. It has an extremely rich rare book collection, with a large biographic collection.

It provides all possible readers' services to central government officials and other research scholars visiting the library from all over India. In the recent past, the CSL has digitized the Government of India gazette, committee and commission reports and has also developed the Online Public Access Catalogue (OPAC) system for its collection.

The library has two branches, namely, Hindi and regional languages wing popularly known as Tulsi Sadan Library, Bahawalpur House, New Delhi that houses about 1.9 lakh volumes of Hindi and 13 other constitutionally approved Indian regional language books and a text book library located at R.K. Puram, New Delhi which caters to the need of the wards of Central Government employees of undergraduate level.

Relevant Website : www.csl.nic.in

Other important libraries include: Raja Rammohan Roy Library Foundation, Delhi Public Library, Rampur Raza Library and Khuda Baksh Oriental Public Libirary.

Nehru Memorial Museum and Library

The Nehru Memorial and Museum and Library comprises a Museum on the life and times of Jawaharlal Nehru; the research and publication division; a library that has a pre-eminent position among the social science libraries in the country; the oral history division; the manuscripts division; the centre for contemporary studies; the planetarium; and the Nehru learning centre for children and youth. The Archive is the biggest collections of private papers of individuals and institutions, especially from the freedom struggle. This vast repository of India's modern and contemporary history is used by scholars and academics from all over the world extensively for their research work.

The centre for contemporary studies runs a Fellowship programme (thirty-two Fellows) which is highly regarded in the academic world, it also regularly conducts academic activities such as lectures, conferences, book discussions, panel discussions, conferences/workshops, etc.

The publications division brings out the works of pre-eminent persons from the social sciences, proceeds of conferences, seminars, and also publishes a research series called occasional papers.

The planetarium, the only one in Delhi region, is visited by thousands including school children, college students, teachers, and general public for first-hand knowledge on astronomy and space technology.

Relevant Website : www.nehrumemorial.nic.in

National Mission on Libraries

National Mission on Libraries has been set up by Ministry of Culture, in 2012 in pursuance of National Knowledge Commission recommendations for sustained attention for development of libraries and information science sector.

Its components are: creation of National Virtual Library of India; setting up of NML model libraries; quantitative and qualitative survey of libraries; capacity building. The purpose of National Virtual Library of India is to facilitate a comprehensive database on digital resources on information about India and on information generated in India, in an open access environment.

Performing Arts

The Ministry of Culture administers the following schemes:-

Performing Arts Grants Scheme

This is the flagship scheme of the Ministry in the field of performing arts. Under this scheme, financial assistance is provided to dramatic groups, theatre groups, music ensembles, children's theatre and for all genres of performing arts activities. Under Repertory Grant, financial assistance in favour of a maximum of 1 Guru/Director and 25 Shisyas/Artistes may be provided to a cultural organization for a complete financial year. The existing rate of financial assistance to each Guru/Director is ₹10,000/- per month.

Scheme for Cultural Organizations with National Presence

To promote and support cultural organizations with national presence involved in promotion of art and culture throughout the country, this grant is given to such organizations which has a properly constituted managing body, registered in India having an all India character with national presence in its operation, adequate working strength and have spent ₹ 1 crore or more during 3 of the last 5 years on cultural activities. The quantum of grant under this scheme is ₹ 1 crore to 5 crore. The grant is payable in two installments i.e. 75 per cent and 25 per cent of the approved amount. The complete details regarding the scheme are available on the website of Ministry of Culture www.indiaculture.nic.in/scheme-financial-assistance-cultural-organisations-national-presence.

Scheme of Building Grants

The objective of the scheme is to support voluntary cultural organizations and government-aided cultural organizations to augment their efforts to create cultural space viz, auditorium, appropriately equipped training, rehearsal and performance spaces for artistes etc. and also for purchase of equipment. Studio theatre is also a component under which small, innovative spaces for theatre and other performing arts could be created with 60 per cent government assistance (going up to ₹ 50 lakhs in Metro cities and ₹ 25 lakhs in other places). The complete details regarding the scheme are available on the website of the Ministry www.indiaculture.nic.in/scheme-building-grants-including-studio-theatres.

Tagore Cultural Complexes Scheme

Tagore Cultural Complexes (TCC) is a revived and revamped version of erstwhile Multi Purpose Cultural Complexes Scheme. It was renamed on the 150th Birth Anniversary of Rabindranath Tagore. Under this scheme, financial assistance is provided for the setting up of new cultural complexes of varying scales as also for modernization, renovation and upgradation of existing Tagore auditoria etc., that were built in 1960s and 1970s in various parts of the country to mark Tagore's Birth Centenary. The Scheme is open to state governments, state sponsored bodies, universities, local bodies and other government approved agencies including reputed not-for-profit organizations, etc. The complete details regarding the scheme are available on the website of the Ministry www.indiaculture.nic.in/scheme-tagore-cultural-complexes.

Scheme of Pension to Artistes

Under this Scheme, financial assistance is granted to indigent artistes and traditional scholars who have made significant contribution to art and letters and in their fields, etc., and their income (including income of the spouse) must not exceed ₹ 4,000/- per month and also their age should not be less than 60 years (This does not apply in the case of dependents). Artistes covered under it are considered for financial assistance in the form of monthly allowance under the centre-state quota on sharing basis between centre and state government/ UT administration concerned, with the latter paying a monthly allowance of at least ₹ 500/- per month per beneficiary. The monthly allowance contributed by the central government in such cases shall not exceed ₹ 3,500/- per month per beneficiary. The complete details regarding the scheme are available on www.indiaculture.nic.in/artists-pension-scheme-and-welfare-fund.

Fellowship and Scholarship Scheme

(i) Scheme For The Award of Fellowship to Outstanding Persons in the Field of Culture

Junior/senior fellowships are awarded to outstanding persons in the age group of 25 to 40 years (Jr.) and above 40 years (Sr.) in different cultural fields, for undertaking cultural research.; Junior Fellows and Senior Fellows are granted fellowship @ ₹ 10,000/- p.m. and 20,000/-p.m. respectively for the period of 2 years; online applications are invited and selection is made by an expert committee constituted for this purpose; upto 400 fellowships (200 Junior and 200 Senior) are awarded in a batch year.

(ii) Scheme for Scholarships to Young Artistes in Different Cultural Fields

Under this scheme financial assistance is given to young artistes of outstanding promise in the age group of 18-25 years for advanced training within India in the field of Indian classical music, Indian classical dance, theatre, mime, visual art, folk, traditional and indigenous Arts and Light Classical Music etc. Scholars who are selected are given scholarship @ ₹ 5,000/- p.m. for 2 years. Online applications are invited and selection is made by an expert committee constituted for this purpose. Upto 400 Scholarships are awarded in a batch year.

Production Grant Scheme

The Scheme covers all 'not-for-profit' organizations, NGOs, societies, trusts, universities and individual for supporting the seminars, conference, research, workshops, festivals, exhibitions, symposia, production of dance, drama-theatre, music etc., and small research projects on different aspects of Indian culture. The Organization should have been functioning and registered under the Societies Registration Act (XXI of 1860), Trusts Act, Companies Act or any central or state Act for at least three years for individual applying for financial assistance under the scheme there is no such requirement. Grant is given upto ₹ 5.00 lakhs under the scheme.

Tagore National Fellowship Scheme

The Scheme was introduced in order to invigorate and revitalise the various institutions under the Ministry and other identified cultural institutions in the country, by encouraging scholars/academicians to affiliate themselves with these institutions to work on projects of mutual interest. With a view to infuse fresh knowledge capital into the institutions, the scheme expects these scholars/academicians to select specific resources of the institutions to take up projects and research work that are related to the main objectives of these institutions and to enrich them with a new creative edge and academic excellence. It is open to both Indian nationals and foreign citizens. The proportion of foreigners will not normally exceed one-third of the total fellowships awarded in a year. Tagore fellows are paid an honorarium ₹ 80,000/- p.m. plus contingencies and Tagore Scholars are paid ₹ 50,000/- p.m. as honorarium plus contingencies.

Gandhi Heritage Sites Mission

In April, 2006, Government of India, constituted a Gandhi Heritage Sites Panel with eminent Gandhians. Based on the recommendation of the Panel the "Gandhi Heritage Sites Mission" with a fixed term of 5 years was created in 2013 with a total budget outlay of ₹ 42 crores. The period of Mission has been extended till March, 2020.

The Mission's mandate is to preserve for posterity the 39 core sites as well as some important sites from the master list (consisting of 2000 sites visited by Mahtama Gandhi) and to supervise, guide and assist in conservation initiatives, maintenance or preservation initiatives and the creation of a database of tangible, literary and visual heritage associated with Gandhiji.

Gandhi Smriti and Darshan Samiti

Gandhi Smriti and Darshan Samiti was formed in 1984 by the merger of Gandhi Darshan at Rajghat and Gandhi Smriti, as an autonomous body, and is functioning under the financial support from the Ministry of Culture. The Prime Minister of India is its Chairperson and it has a nominated body of senior Gandhians and representatives of various government departments to guide it in its activities. The basic aim and objective of the Samiti is to propagate the life, mission and thought of Mahatma Gandhi through various socio-educational and cultural programmes. It has two campuses:

Gandhi Smriti is the place where Mahatma Gandhi lived the last 144 days of his life, and where the epic life of Gandhiji ended on January 30, 1948. The

Martyrs Column, the spot where the Mahatma fell to an assassin's bullets stands as the embodiment of all the sufferings and sacrifics that characterised the long struggle of India's Freedom. Photographs, sculptures, paintings, frescos, inscriptions on rocks and relics, exhibitions etc, pertaining to the years Gandhiji stayed there are displayed here. The meagre personal effects of Gandhiji are also carefully preserved. Gandhi Darshan, the second campus is situated adjacent to the Mahatma Gandhi Samadhi at Rajghat. The sprawling thirty-six acre campus came into existence in 1969 to mark the centenary of Mahatma Gandhi. An International Gandhi Darshan Exhibition was housed to commemorate the occasion. At present the Centre provides a comprehensive exhibition on Gandhi, conference halls, camping facilities for major national and international meets, a library, hostel for scholars-in-residence, children's corner, photo unit and a publications division.

Tourism

Ministry of Tourism is the nodal agency to formulate national policies and programmes for the development and promotion of tourism. In the process, the Ministry consults and collaborates with other stakeholders in the sector including various central ministries/ agencies, the state governments/ union territory administrations and the representatives of the private sector. Tourism is a major engine of economic growth and an important source of foreign exchange earnings in many countries including India. It has great capacity to create large scale employment of diverse kind - from the most specialized to the unskilled and hence can play a major role in creation of additional employment opportunities. It can also play an important role in achieving growth with equity. The Ministry of tourism has the main objective of increasing and facilitating tourism in India. Augmenting tourism infrastructure, easing of visa regime, assurance of quality standards in services of tourism service providers, etc., are some of the responsibilities of the Ministry.

The Ministry is according priority for holistic development of tourism destinations into world class destinations using a cluster approach including development of infrastructure, amenities, interpretation centres and skill development by achieving synergy and convergence with other central ministries, state governments and industry stakeholders. As a step in this direction, it has recently launched the 'Adopt A Heritage' project. Heritage sites are being offered for adoption by the public sector, private sector and individuals to become 'Monument Mitras' for developing amenities and facilities at these sites under this programme.

Relevant Website : www.tourism.gov.in

Foreign Tourist Arrivals

Foreign Tourist Arivals (FTAs) during 2017 were 10.18 million with a growth of 15.6 per cent over same period of the previous year. During 2016,

FTAs were 8.8 million with a growth rate of 9.7 per cent over 2015. In 2016, there were 5.77 million arrivals of NRIs, with a growth rate of 9.7 per cent over 2015. ITAs include both FTAs and Arrivals of Non Resident Indians (NRIs).

'Special Tourism Zones'

Creation of 'Special Tourism Zones' anchored on Special Purpose Vehicles (SPVs) is in partnership with the states. Ministry of Tourism has formulated the guidelines for implementation of the new scheme in consultation with the state governments and private sector and is in the process of completing other formalities before launching the scheme.

Foreign Exchange Earnings

Foreign Exchange Earnings through Tourism (FEEs) during 2017 was ₹ 1,80,379 crore with a growth of 17 per cent over same period of previous year. The FEEs from tourism in rupee terms during 2016 was ₹ 1,54,146 crore with a growth rate of 14.0 per cent.

e -Visa facility

Facilitative visa regime is a pre requisite for increasing inbound tourism. The Ministry of Tourism takes the initiative of pursuance with Ministry of Home Affairs and Ministry of External Affairs for achieving the same. December, 2016 the 'e-visa' facility is available under 3 sub - categories i.e. 'e- Tourist Visa', e - Business Visa' and 'e - Medical Visa'. 'E -Visa facility has been extended to the nationals of 163 countries.

24x7 Toll Free Multi-Lingual Tourist Info Line

For providing information relating to Travel and Tourism to the domestic and international tourists/visitors and for assisting them with advice while travelling in India, a 24x7 toll free multi-lingual tourist info line in 10 international languages besides Hindi and English is being run by the Ministry of Tourism. The calls made by tourists (both international and domestic) while in India will be free of charge. This service will be available on the number 1800111363 or on a short code 1363. The international languages handled are Arabic, French, German, Italian, Japanese, Korean, Chinese, Portuguese, Russian and Spanish, in addition to English and Hindi

Niche Products

Welcome cards for distribution at immigration counters to people arriving in India were introduced with few guidelines on how to make their stay more safe and comfortable. The aspect of 'seasonality' in tourism is a challenge. The Ministry of Tourism has taken the initiative of identifying, diversifying, developing and promoting niche products of the country. This is done in order to overcome seasonality and to promote India as a 365 days destination, attract tourists with specific interest, and to ensure repeat visits for the unique products in which India has a comparative advantage. The niche products that have been identified by the Ministry include cruise, adventure, medical, wellness, golf, polo, meetings incentives conferences and expositions (MICE), ecotourism, film tourism and sustainable tourism.

National Medical and Wellness Tourism Board

A National Medical and Wellness Tourism Board has been set up to work as an umbrella organisation to govern and promote medical tourism in India.

Task Force on Adventure Tourism

For development and promotion of adventure tourism, a task force on Adventure Tourism was formed in 2016 to resolve the issues related to adventure tourism which includes safety and security of tourists.

Hospitality Education

Setting in place the framework for supply of trained manpower is a challenge facing the hospitality education. It has been the endeavour of the Ministry to put in place a system of training and professional education, with necessary infrastructure support, capable of generating manpower sufficient to meet the needs of the tourism and hospitality industry, both quantitatively and qualitatively. As of now, there are 42 institutes of Hotel Management (IHMs), comprising 21 Central IHMs and 21 state IHMs, and 10 Food Craft Institutes (FCIs), which have come up with the support of the Ministry. These institutes were set up as autonomous societies with the specific mandate to impart hospitality education / conduct training in hospitality skills. While the IHMs mainly impart degree level hospitality education, the FCIs are concerned with skill level education. National Council for Hotel Management & Catering Technology (NCHMCT) steers and regulates the academic efforts of the IHMs and FCIs.

Indian Institute of Tourism and Travel Management

The Indian Institute of Tourism and Travel Management (IITTM) is an autonomous body under the Ministry with its headquarters at Gwalior. Its centres are at Bhubaneshwar, Nellore, Noida and Goa. IITTM is a pioneer in the field of travel and tourism education and training. It provides specialized training and education for tourism and travel industry.

Indian Culinary Institute

The Ministry of Tourism has set up the Indian Culinary Institute (ICI) at Tirupati, Andhra Pradesh. The first of its kind in India, the Institute has commenced its academic session from August, 2016. The Ministry is also expanding the ICI, by opening its northern chapter at Noida.

Incredible India

The Ministry, as part of its ongoing promotional activities, releases campaigns in the international and domestic markets under the Incredible India brandline, to promote various tourism destinations and products of India to increase foreign tourist arrivals and domestic visits within the country. A series of promotional activities are undertaken in important and potential markets overseas through the India Tourism offices abroad and within India through domestic India Tourism offices, with the objective of showcasing India's tourism potential to foreign and domestic tourists.

International Advertisement Campaign

To promote tourism, the government has also taken many initiatives. An International Advertisement Campaign in electronic and digital media for 2016-17 was launched globally. To begin with the Ministry has launched its campaign on leading television Channels including CNN, BBC, Discovery and TLC , Euro News, History, CNBC, Travel Channel, CBS (USA), Tabi (Japan) and RMC (France) as well as on Google.

The Ministry of Tourism organizes Bharat Parv as part of the Republic Day and Independence Day celebrations with the objective to promote national integrity and to showcase cultural and culinary diversity to the people of our nation.

North East

The North East region of India is being promoted by the Ministry through several media campaigns. The Ministry in partnership with the Discovery Channel has produced documentary series 'Go North East' on the eight states of the region. For creation of tourism infrastructure, the Ministry of Tourism has two major plan schemes viz. Swadesh Darshan - Integrated Development of Theme-Based Tourist Circuits and PRASAD- Pilgrimage Rejuvenation and Spiritual Augmentation Drive for development of tourism infrastructure in the country including historical places and heritage cities.

Swadesh Darshan Scheme

Swadesh Darshan scheme is about developing theme based tourist circuits on the principles of high tourist value, competitiveness and sustainability in an integrated manner by synergizing efforts to focus on needs and concerns of all stakeholders to enrich tourist experience and enhance employment opportunities. Under it thirteen thematic circuits have been identified for development, namely: North-East India Circuit, Buddhist Circuit, Himalayan Circuit, Coastal Circuit, Krishna Circuit, Desert Circuit, Tribal Circuit, Eco Circuit, Wildlife Circuit, Rural Circuit, Spiritual Circuit, Ramayana Circuit and Heritage Circuit.

PRASAD Scheme

Under PRASAD scheme, 25 sites of religious significance have been identified for development namely Amaravati (Andhra Pradesh), Amritsar (Punjab), Ajmer (Rajasthan), Ayodhya (Uttar Pradesh), Badrinath (Uttarakhand), Dwarka (Gujarat), Deoghar (Jharkhand), Belur (West Bengal), Gaya (Bihar) , Guruvayoor (Kerala), Hazratbal (Jammu & Kashmir), Kamakhya (Assam), Kanchipuram (Tamil Nadu), Katra (Jammu & Kashmir), Kedarnath

(Uttarakhand), Mathura (Uttar Pradesh), Patna (Bihar), Puri (Odisha), Srisailam (Andhra Pradesh), Somnath (Gujarat), Tirupati (Andhra Pradesh), Trimbakeshwar (Maharashtra), Ujjain (Madhya Pradesh), Varanasi (Uttar Pradesh) and Vellankani (Tamil Nadu).

Incredible India Mobile App

Incredible India Mobile App was launched to showcase India as a holistic destination, revolving around major experiences, such as spirituality, heritage, adventure, culture, yoga, wellness and more. The mobile app has been designed keeping in mind the preferences of the modern traveller and follows the trends and technologies of international standards. The app has been equipped with features to assist the traveller in each phase of their journey to India.

India Tourism Mart

The first editon of the India Tourism Mart 2018 was organized by the Federation of Associations in the Indian Tourism and Hospitality with the support of the Ministry of Tourism and state governments/union territory administrations in New Delhi. It provided a national platform to different tourism stakeholders for interacting with foreign buyers under one umbrella.

Swachh Paryatan Mobile App

"Swachh Paryatan Mobile App" operated by the Ministry of Tourism for 25 Adarsh Smarak Monuments has been also made available for Windows Phones and iPhone. Earlier it was available for Android Phones only. This mobile app is being monitored by the Project Monitoring Unit of Swachh Bharat Mission in Ministry of Tourism. The Ministry has launched an initiative for providing pre-loaded Sim Cards to foreign tourists arriving in India on e-Visa. This initiative was launched in 2017 in association with Bharat Sanchar Nigam Ltd., (BSNL), wherein BSNL would distribute pre-loaded SIM cards to foreign tourists on e-Visa. This facility will be initially available in the Indira Gandhi International Airport (T3 Terminal), New Delhi and later in the remaining 15 international airports, where e-Visa facility is currently available. This initiative is aimed at providing connectivity to foreign tourists to enable them to stay in touch with their family and friends and also help them to contact with the 24x7 multi lingual toll free helpline of the Ministry for any assistance and guidance during times of distress / medical emergency, etc.

6 Basic Economic Data

THE Ministry of Statistics and Programme Implementation (MoSPI) came into existence as an independent ministry in 1999 after the merger of the Department of Statistics and the Department of Programme Implementation. The Ministry has two wings, one relating to statistics and the other relating to programme implementation. The Statistics Wing redesignated as National Statistics Office (NSO), consists of the Central Statistical Office (CSO) and the National Sample Survey Office (NSSO). The Programme Implementation Wing has three divisions, namely : (i) twenty point programme, (ii) infrastructure and project monitoring, and (iii) Members of Parliament Local Area Development Scheme. Besides these three wings, there is National Statistical Commission (NSC) created through a resolution of Government of India and one autonomous institute, viz., Indian Statistical Institute (ISI) declared as an institute of national importance by an Act of Parliament.

Relevant Website : www.mospi.gov.in

National Statistical Commission

The National Statistical Commission (NSC) was set up in 2005. The setting up of the NSC followed the decision of the Cabinet to accept the recommendation of the Rangarajan Commission, which reviewed the Indian Statistical System in 2001. The NSC was initially constituted in 2006, to serve as a nodal and empowered body for all core statistical activities of the country, to evolve, monitor and enforce statistical priorities and standards and to ensure statistical coordination. It has one part-time Chairperson and four part-time members, each having specialization and experience in specified statistical fields. Besides, Secretary, Planning Commission is an ex-officio member of the Commission. The Chief Statistician of India is the Secretary to the Commission.

Central Statistics Office

The Central Statistics Office (CSO), an attached office of the Ministry, coordinates the statistical activities in the country and evolves statistical standards. Its activities *inter-alia,* include compilation of national accounts, index of industrial production, consumer price indices (urban/rural/ combined), human development statistics, including gender statistics in the states and union territories and dissemination energy statistics, social and environment statistics and preparation of the National Industrial Classification.

The CSO, Ministry of Statistics and Programme Implementation started releasing state/UT-wise as well as All India Consumer Price Indices (CPI) separately for rural, urban and combined (rural plus urban) for the purpose of temporal price comparison with effect from January, 2011 with 2010 as the base year. Accordingly, the annual inflation rates, based on these indices were made available since January, 2012. CSO revised the base year of CPI form 2010-2012 and revised series was launched in 2015. The back series for the revised series of CPI was also made available for the users. All these information may be accessed from the website of this Ministry (www.mopsi.gov.in).

Real Income and Net National Income

The per capita real income i.e., per capita net national income at constant (2011-12) prices, as per the provisional estimates for 2017-18 turned out to be ₹ 86,668 as against the first revised estimate of ₹ 82,229 for 2016-17. This indicates growth in per capita real income of about 5.4 per cent during 2017-18. The per capita income at current prices during 2017-18 is estimated at ₹ 112,835 as compared to ₹ 103,870 for 2016-17, showing a rise of 8.6 per cent.

National Income

According to the provisional estimates of national income, 2017-18, released in May 2018, the GDP at constant (2011-12) prices in 2017-18 is ₹ 130.1 lakh crore as against the first revised estimate of ₹ 121.9 lakh crore for 2016-17, released in January 2018. The growth in real GDP during 2017-18 is estimated at 6.7 per cent as compared to the growth rate of 7.1 per cent in 2016-17.

Services Sector

The share of services in India's Gross Value Added (GVA) at basic prices (at current prices) increased from 49 per cent in 2011-12 to 53.9 per cent in 2017-18 as per Provisional Estimates (PE). On including construction, this share increases and becomes 61.2 per cent in 2017-18. With a 20.8 per cent share, 'financial, real estate, and professional services' as a group is the largest contributor to GVA among the various services sub-sectors, followed by 'trade, hotels, transport, communication and services related to broadcasting' with a 18.5 per cent share and 'public administration, defence and other services' with a share of 14.5 per cent.

In 2017-18, growth of the services sector at constant (2011-12) was observed at 7.9 per cent as compared to 7.5 per cent in 2016-17. This sector's growth is higher than the overall GVA growth of 7.1 per cent and 6.5 per cent at constant prices in 2016-17 and 2017-18 respectively.

Services Trade

In 2016-17 at current prices, services were exported amounting to US$ 163.2 billion compared to US$ 154.5 billion during 2015-16 showing a growth of 5.6 per cent in 2016-17.Whereas, the services were imported amounting to US$ 95.7 billion and US$ 84.8 billion at current prices, during 2016-17 and 2015-16 respectively, showing a growth of 12.9 per cent in 2016-17. This shows a negative growth of (-3.2) per cent on net import of services in 2016-17 as compared to (9.1) per cent in 2015-16. In 2016-17, net import of services financed almost 63.3 per cent of the India's trade deficit on net import of goods.

Annual Survey of Industries

The Annual Survey of Industries (ASI) is the principal source of industrial statistics in india. It provides statistical information to access and evaluate, objectively and realistically, the change in the growth, composition and structure of the organized manufacturing sector comprising activities related to manufacturing processes, repair services, generation, transmission, etc., of electricity, gas and water supply and cold storage.

The ASI extends to the entire country. It covers all factories registered under Sections 2m (i) and 2m (ii) of the Factories Act, 1948, where the manufacturing process is defined under Section 2 (k) of the said Act. Details the survey also covers *bidi* and *cigar* manufacturing establishments registered under the *Bidi* and *Cigar* Workers (Conditions of Employment) Act, 1966. All the electricity undertakings engaged in the generation, transmission and distribution of electricity, not registered with the Central Electricity Authority (CEA) are also covered under ASI.

However defence establishments, oil storage and distribution depots, departmental units such as railway workshops, government mints, sanitary, water supply, gas storage, etc., are excluded from the purview of the survey. The coverage of AS1 has further been extended beyond the purview of the Section 2m (i) and 2m (ii) of the Factories Act, 1948 and the Bidi and Cigar Workers (Conditions of Employment) Act, 1966. To start with, the units with 100 or more employees, not registered under Section 2m (i) and 2m (ii) of the Factories Act, 1948 but registered under any of the seven Acts/Board/ Authority viz.;, Companies Act. 1956, Factories Act. 1948 , Shops and Commercial Establishment Act, Societies Registration Act, Cooperative Societies Act, Khadi and Village Industries Board, Directorate of Industries (District Industries Centre) in the Business Register of Establishments (BRE) are considered. Such units have been included from the BRE of Andhra Pradesh in AS1 2014-15 and from the BREs of Manipur, Chhattisgarh, Himachal Pradesh, Punjab, Uttar Pradesh, Tamil Nadu and Rajasthan in AS1 2015-16.

Index of Industrial Production

Index of Industrial Production (IIP) is released by CSO every month in the form of Quick Estimates with a time-lag of 6 weeks as per the Special Data Dissemination Standard (SDDS) norms of IMF. The base year of all-India IIP was revised from 2004-05 to 2011-12 and the new series was launched in 2017. IIP is compiled using secondary data received from 14 source agencies in various ministries/departments or their attached/subordinate offices. Apart from breakup of the index in three sectors, viz., mining, manufacturing and electricity, the estimates are also simultaneously released as per use-based classification viz., primary goods, intermediate goods, infrastructure construction goods and consumer durables and consumer non-durables. The Quick Estimates are subsequently revised as first Revision after one month from release on receipt of updated production data from the 14 source agencies. Subsequently, the indices are again revised after two months from first Revision. The major source of data for IIP is the Department of Industrial Policy and Promotion that supplies data for 322 out of 407 item groups with a weight of 47.54 pcr cent in overall IIP.

Till July 2018, IIP has been released up to the month of May 2018 as per the actual release calendar. The annual IIP increased by 4.3 per cent in 2017-18 as compared to a growth of 4.6 per cent in 2016-17. During this period electricity sector registered an annual growth of 5.4 per cent as compared to 5.8 per cent during 2016-17. Mining and manufacturing sectors registered annual growths of 2.3 per cent and 5.4 per cent respectively during 2017-18 as compared to 5.3 per cent and 4.4 per cent growths in 2016-17.

As per the use-based categories, primary goods, capital goods, intermediate goods and infrastructure/construction goods registered annual growth rates of 3.7 per cent, 3.7 per cent, 2.3 per cent and 5.6 per cent respectively during 2017-18 as against 4.9 per cent, 3.2 per cent, 3.3 per cent and 3.9 per cent during 2016-17. Consumer durables registered a growth of 0.7 per cent during 2017-18 as compared to 2.9 per cent in 2016-17 while Consumer non-durables registered a growth of 4.3 per cent during 2017-18 as compared to 4.6 per cent in 2016-17.

National Sample Survey Office

The National Sample Survey Office (NSSO), in the Ministry of Statistics and Programme Implementation, is responsible for conduct of large scale sample surveys, in diverse fields, on all India basis. Primary data is collected regularly through nationwide household surveys on various socio-economic subjects, Annual Survey of Industries (ASI) under the Collection of Statistics Act and Enterprise Surveys, as a follow up of the economic census. Besides these surveys, NSSO collects data on rural and urban prices; plays a significant role in the improvement of crop statistics through supervision of the area enumeration and crop estimation surveys of the state agencies. It also maintains a frame of urban areal units for drawing samples for socio-economic surveys in urban areas. The NSSO functions with requisite autonomy, in matters relating to data collection, processing and publication/dissemination of results/data based on its surveys, under overall guidance and supervision of National Statistical Commission (NSC) which appoints working groups/technical committees comprising both official and non-official members on different subjects for finalization of survey instruments for its surveys and methodologies for the same. The Director General (Survey) is responsible for overall coordination and supervision of all activities of NSSO and is assisted by four Additional Director Generals, each one being in-charge of separate divisions responsible for four distinct aspects of such large scale surveys relating to their designing and planning, field work, data processing and coordination.

Price Data Collection

Rural Retail Price Collection (RPC): The data on rural retail prices are collected by Field Operations Divisions (FOD) regularly for compiling the consumer price index (CPI) for agricultural labourers/rural labourers on behalf of the Labour Bureau, Ministry of Labour and Employment. At present, the Labour Bureau compiles and publishes the CPI for agricultural labourers/rural labourers. A commodity basket consisting of 260 commodities was adopted in 1986 with a view to reflect the price changes in respect of the current consumption pattern. The price data for the items in the commodity basket are collected every month from a fixed set of 603 villages/ markets spread over 26 states/UTs using schedules 3.01 (R).The RPC bulletin called the 'Prices and Wages in Rural India' which is published for each quarter, provides price data only at national level and wage data at national and state level for 26 major states.

Twenty Point Programme

The Twenty Point Programme (TPP) initiated since 1975 was restructured in 1982, 1986 and 2006. The thrust of the Programme restructured in 2006 is to eradicate poverty and improve the quality of life of the poor and the under-privileged people all over the country. The programme covers various socio-economic aspects like poverty, employment, education, housing, agriculture, drinking water, afforestation and environment protection, energy to rural areas, welfare of weaker sections of the society, etc.

The Programme originally consisted of 20 points and 66 items being monitored individually by central nodal ministries concerned. Out of the 66 items, 25 were for monthly monitoring, while the rest were to be monitored on annual basis by this Ministry. The monthly information in respect of 21 items was collected from various states/union territories and for the remaining four, the information was collected from the concerned ministries. One of the 66 items viz., 'Sampoorna Grameen Rojgar Yojana (SGRY)' has since been subsumed into another item namely 'National Rural Employment Guarantee Act' with effect from 2008 and has been renamed as Mahatma Gandhi National Rural Employment Guarantee Act from December 2009. Since 2014 the data collection is done on quarterly basis and the monthly monitoring has been changed to quarterly monitoring. At present, out of the remaining 65 items, 19 items are being monitored on quarterly basis. The monitoring mechanism for TPP-2006 has also been widened by including block level monitoring in addition to the existing central, state and district level monitoring.

Monitoring Mechanism

The primary responsibility of implementation and monitoring of the programme lies with the agencies entrusted with the execution of the programme, which in this case are the state governments/union territory administrations and the central nodal ministries. The Ministry of Statistics and Programme Implementation monitors the programmes/schemes covered under TPP-2006 on the basis of performance reports received from state governments/UT administrations and ministries. The Ministry has developed a web based Management Information System to expeditiously collect information from the state governments and the central nodal ministries.

Monitoring Committees at state, district and block level, for monitoring the progress of implementation of all schemes/items covered under the Twenty Point Programme-2006, have been constituted by most of the states/Union Territories as per the provisions of TPP-2006 guidelines.

Monitoring and Impact Assessment

The Ministry has so far undertaken two impact assessment studies. The first study relates to impact of MGNREGA in three selected districts of north--eastern states and the second study was on rehabilitation of disabled persons under Deendayal Disability Rehabilitation Scheme (DDRS) in Delhi, Karnataka, Madhya Pradesh and West Bengal. The Ministry has also undertaken the task of critically examining the reports of evaluation undertaken by Niti Aayog (erstwhile Planning Commission) and by the central nodal ministries of the schemes implemented by them.

Infrastructure Monitoring

The monitoring of important infrastructure sectors in the country is designed to provide an overview of the performance and highlighting slippages, if any, before the decision making authorities. This Ministry monitors the performance of the eleven key infrastructure sectors viz., power, coal, steel, cement, fertilizers, petroleum, road, railways, shipping and ports, civil aviation and telecommunications. The performance of these sectors is analyzed with reference to the present targets for the month and for the cumulative period and the achievements during the corresponding month and cumulative period of the last year. Infrastructure performance is regularly reported through the monthly review report on infrastructure performance.

Members of Parliament Local Area Development Scheme

The Members of Parliament Local Area Development Scheme (MPLADS) was launched in 1993. Initially, Ministry of Rural Development was the Nodal Ministry for this scheme. In October, 1994 this scheme was transferred to the Ministry of Statistics and Programme Implementation. The objective of MPLAD Scheme is to enable MPs to recommend works of developmental nature with emphasizes on creation of durable community assets in the areas of national priorities, viz., drinking water facility; education; electricity facility; health and family welfare; irrigation facility; non-conventional energy severs; railways, roads, pathways and bridges; sanitation and public health, etc., based on the locally felt needs. This Scheme is governed by a set of guidelines. The extant guidelines on the Scheme were revised and published in 2016.

The salient features of the Scheme include:

a) The Scheme is fully funded by the Government of India under which funds are released in the form of grants-in-aid directly to the district authorities.

b) The funds released under the Scheme are non-lapsable, i.e., the entitlement of funds not released in a particular year is carried forward to the subsequent years, subject to eligibility. At present, the annual entitlement per MP/ constituency is ₹ 5 crore.

c) Under it, the role of the Members of Parliament is limited to recommend works. Thereafter, it is the responsibility of the district authority to sanction, execute and complete the works recommended within the stipulated time period.

d) The elected Lok Sabha Members can recommend works in their respective constituencies. The elected members of the Rajya Sabha can recommend works anywhere in the state from which they are elected. Nominated Members of the Parliament can recommend works for implementation, anywhere in the country.

e) MPLADS works can be implemented in areas affected by natural calamities like floods, cyclone, hailstorm, avalanche, cloudburst, pest attack, landslides, tornado, earthquake, drought, tsunami, fire and biological, chemical, radiological hazards, etc.

f) In order to accord special attention to the development of areas inhabited by Scheduled Castes (SCs) and Scheduled Tribes (STs), 15 per cent of MPLADS funds are to be utilized for areas inhabited by SC population and 7.5 per cent for areas inhabited by ST population.

g) If an elected Member of Parliament finds the need, to contribute these funds, to a place outside that state/UT or outside the constituency within the state or both, the MP can recommend eligible works, under these Guidelines upto a maximum of ₹ 25 lakh in a financial year. Such a gesture will promote national unity, harmony, and fraternity among the people, at the grass roots level.

h) The MP can spend a maximum of ₹ 20 lakh per year for giving assistance to Differently Abled Citizens for purchase of tri-cycles (including motorized tri-cycles), battery operated motorized wheel chair and artificial limbs; and aids for visually and hearing impaired.

7 Commerce

THE Department of Commerce comes under the Ministry of Industry and Commerce. The mandate of the Department of Commerce is regulation, development and promotion of India's international trade and commerce through formulation of appropriate international trade and commercial policy and implementation of the various provisions thereof. The basic role of the Department is to accelerated growth of international trade. The Department formulates, implements and monitors the Foreign Trade Policy (FTP) which provides the basic framework of policy and strategy to be followed for promoting exports and trade. Besides, the Department is also entrusted with responsibilities relating to multilateral and bilateral commercial relations, Special Economic Zones, state trading, export promotion and trade facilitation, and development and regulation of certain export oriented industries and commodities.

The long-term vision of the Department is to make India a major player in the world trade by 2020 and assume a role of leadership in the international trade organizations commensurate with India's growing importance. The medium term vision is to double India's exports of goods and services by 2017-18 over the level of 2008-09 with a long-term objective of doubling India's share in global trade.

Relevant Website : www.commerce.gov.in

Global Scenario

The global crisis produced a wide-ranging yet differentiated impact across which included economic slowdown and contraction in world trade. However, the latest number from WTO now points towards healthy prospects for global trade. The estimate for growth in world merchandise trade volume in 2017 was raised to 3.6 per cent. The previous estimate for 2017 was 2.4 per cent. For 2017 trade growth is placed within a range from 3.2 per cent to 3.9 per cent (WTO, 2017). As per the WTO September 2017 press release, Stronger-thanexpected growth is driven by Asia and North America, where import demand is recovering from weak results in 2016. Trade growth should moderate to 3.2 per cent in 2018, within a range from 1.4 to 4.4 per cent, as global GDP growth remains stable. Recovery could be undermined by downside risks, including trade policy measures, monetary tightening, geopolitical tensions and costly natural disasters. India is projected to grow at the rate of 7.4 per cent in 2018 thus becoming the fastest growing economy in the world (IMF, 2018). As per the estimates of the International Monetary Fund (IMF, January

2018), the global economic activity continues to firm up. Global growth, which in 2016 was the weakest since the global financial crisis at 3.2 per cent, is projected at 3.9 per cent in 2018 and 2019. Growth is projected to rise in emerging market and developing economies, supported by improved external factors—a benign global financial environment and a recovery in advanced economies. Growth in China and other parts of emerging Asia remains strong.

Current Focus Areas

Given this positive trajectory of growth, so far as, the export sector is concerned, there are number of critical areas which form the focus of the Department. These include : Foreign Trade Policy 2015-20 has been reviewed and toned up; MEIS incentives for two sub sectors of textiles i.e., readymade garments and made ups increased from 2 to 4 per cent involving additional annual incentives of ₹ 2,743 crore; to provide impetus to the services trade, the SEIS incentives have been increased by 2 per cent for notified services such as business, legal, accounting, architectural, engineering, educational, hospital, hotels and restaurants. The estimated additional annual incentive for the services sector will be ₹ 1,140 crore; the GST rate for transfer/sale of scrips has been reduced to zero from the earlier rate of 12 per cent; and new trust based self-ratification scheme introduced to allow duty free inputs for export production under duty exemption scheme with a self-declaration.

Alignment with GST

Issue of working capital blockage of the exporters due to upfront payment of GST on inputs has been addressed. Under advance authorization, Export Promotion for Capital Goods (EPCG) Scheme, 100 per cent Export Oriented Units (EOU's), exporters have been extended the benefit of sourcing inputs/capital goods from abroad as well as domestic suppliers for exports without upfront payment of GST. Further an e wallet was launched from April 2018 to make these schemes operational. GST has ushered a new regulatory regime for India's exports. It introduced many positive features for domestic firms as well as exporters. Firms now pay less number of taxes (one GST replaces 17 taxes), less amount of tax (average GST rate for industrial products is 18 per cent compared to the pre-GST tax burden of 25-28 per cent), and face less tax on tax incidences. The uniform GST rates across the states further reduce the tax burden and compliance cost. These changes reduce cost and improve competitiveness and hence would be beneficial for exports. GST treats exports as zero rated supply. This is in line with the WTO accepted principles. Initially, the GST law required that all duties must be paid at the time of sourcing of inputs for export production and refund for these to be obtained after the exports. However, the exporters apprehended blockage of working capital. On their request, the GST council decided to allow exemption from payment of GST on inputs sourced using the advance authorizations, EPCG and the 100 per cent EOU schemes.

Government e- Market

Directorate General of Supplies and Disposals (DGS&D) created a dedicated e-market for different goods and services procured/sold by government/PSUs, a technology driven platform to facilitate procurement of goods and services by various ministries and agencies of the government. The portal was launched in 2016 and became fully functional by October, 2016. DGS&D was wound up in October, 2017. Government Marketplace (GeM) - a scalable system and being completely online, transparent, and system driven, makes procurement of goods and services, easy, efficient and fast. GeM covers entire procurement process chain, right from vendor registration, item selection by buyer, supply order generation, and receipt of goods/services by the consignees (s), to online payment to vendor. By 2018 more than 4.44 lakh products and services, about 71,700 sellers and service providers and more than 16,000 buyer organizations are part of GeM. More than 2.36 lakh orders, worth ₹ 4,000 crores have been processed through it.

Trade Facilitation

National Trade Facilitation Committee (NTFC) was set up following ratification by India of the Trade Facilitation Agreement (TFA). Four working groups have been set up to focus on (i) infrastructure, (ii) legal issues, (iii) outreach and (iv) time release study. Further, the National Trade Facilitation Action Plan (NTFAP) drawn out in consultation with the stakeholders, identifying 76 trade facilitation measures with implementation timelines of which 51 are TFA-plus activities. Under TFA category 'B' items, efforts are being made to expedite implementation of these measures within 3 years, in advance of the envisaged 5 years. Comprehensive IT-based system called Export Data Processing and Monitoring System (EDPMS) for monitoring of export of goods and software and facilitating authorised dealer banks to report various returns through a single platform developed by RBI. 24x7 Customs clearance facility has been extended to all Bills of Entry at 19 sea ports and 17 air cargo complexes.

State-of-Art Trade Analytics

A state-of-art trade analytics has been put in place in Directorate General of Foreign Trade (DGFT) for data based policy actions. This initiative envisages processing trade information from Directorate General of Commercial Intelligence and Statistics and other national and international data bases related to India's key export markets and identifying specific actions. Exploring new export markets focus is on increasing India's exports in under and un-tapped markets in high potential regions like Africa, to cover not just trade in goods and investment but also in capacity building, technical assistance and services such as healthcare and education. Sectors like agro processing, manufacturing, mining, textiles, consumer goods, infrastructure development and construction are be focus areas. Greater engagement with Latin America and the Caribbean region, including encouragement of project exports through easy access to credit facilities.

Exploring New Export Products

Focus on increasing exports of products which have become important in the world trade of late, in recognition of the fact that 70 per cent of India's exports involve products whose share in the total world exports is only 30 per cent. Focus will be on promising product groups like medical devices/ equipment, technical textile, electronic component, project goods, defence and hi-tech products in addition to labour intensive and MSME products like agricultural, marine, carpets, leather, Ayush and health, textiles and readymade garments, handloom, handicrafts, coir, jute products, diamond, gold and jewellery. Focus on agricultural exports for increasing farmers' income is to be augmented. It is a stable and 'open' export policy for the long term. Creating cold chain and transport logistics facilities from the farm to the ports and airports. Promoting organic exports through appropriate policy interventions. Setting up credible and up-to-date organic export certification and accreditation programmes.

Web Portals

DGFT has launched an updated website making it more userfriendly and easy to navigate. This website has a large dynamic component whereby the trade community can file applications online for IEC and various other schemes. Indian Trade Portal launched by the Department displays information useful for exports and imports. It contains the trade enquiries uploaded by Indian trade missions, tariff and trade data of India's major trade partners, export market reports, and trade agreements, etc.

Capacity Building

Skilling new entrepreneurs for exports is an important priority. In the last two years, over 50,000 entrepreneurs have been trained under the Niryat Bandhu programme implemented by DGFT, thus complementing the Startup India and Skill India initiatives. Institutional set up under the Department like – Indian Institute of Foreign Trade, Indian Institute of Packaging, Indian Institute of Plantation, Export Promotion Councils, Centres of Excellence, Plantation Research Institutes, etc., – are being leveraged for capacity building, export promotion, research and analysis and long term policy formulation.

Centre for Research in International Trade

Given the growing complexity of the process of globalization and its spillover effects on domestic policymaking, there is a need to significantly deepen existing research capabilities and widen them to encompass new and specialized areas. In this context, a new institution, namely, the Centre for Research in International Trade (CRIT) has been set up. It is expected to fill the gap and will also help in forming enduring coalitions with a large number of developing countries which may have convergence of interests with India and could potentially become India's allies on various trade issues at the global level. CRIT will have 5 centres namely Centre for Trade and Investment law, Centre for Regional Trade, Centre for Training, Centre for Trade Promotion and Centre for WTO Studies. The Council for Trade Development and Promotion was constituted in July 2015. It would ensure a continuous dialogue with state governments and UT's on measures for providing an international trade enabling environment in the states and create a framework for making the states active partners in boosting India's exports. The state governments were requested to develop their export strategy, appoint export commissioners, address infrastructure constraints restricting movement of goods, facilitate refund of VAT/ octroi/state level cess, and address other issues relating to various clearances, etc., and build capacity of new exporters, in order to promote exports.

Integrated Exhibition cum Convention Centre

Modern worldclass Integrated Exhibition cum Convention Centre (IECC) is coming up in New Delhi to create air-conditioned exhibition space of 1.2 lakh sq. mtr. and an iconic state-of-the-art convention centre with 7,000 pax seating capacity. Underground parking space for 4,800 Passenger Car Units (PCU) is also planned. Work has begun and is to completed by September 2019, creating an appropriate venue for all types of major national and international events. It will be a unique symbol of New India, and will reflect India's aspirations to be a global power.

Special Economic Zones

India was one of the first in Asia to recognise the effectiveness of the Export Processing Zone (EPZ) model in promoting exports, with Asia's first EPZ set up in Kandla in 1965. To overcome the shortcomings on account of multiplicity of controls and clearances, absence of world-class infrastructure and an unstable fiscal regime and with a view to attract larger foreign investments in India, the Special Economic Zones (SEZs) Policy was announced in April 2000. This policy intended to make SEZs an engine for economic growth supported by quality infrastructure complemented by an attractive fiscal package, both at the Centre and the state level, with minimum possible regulations. SEZs in India functioned from 2000 to 2006 under the provisions of the Foreign Trade Policy and fiscal incentives were made effective through the provisions of relevant statutes.

The SEZ Act, 2005, supported by SEZ Rules, came into effect in 2006, providing simplification of procedures and single window clearance on matters relating to central and state governments. The main objectives of the SEZ Act are: generation of additional economic activity; promotion of exports of goods and services; promotion of investment from domestic and foreign sources; creation of employment opportunities; and development of infrastructure facilities.

Export Credit

Project exports are being encouraged, especially in the emerging markets with high infrastructure needs, through special lines of credit offered by the Ministry of External Affairs and the Buyers' Credit Scheme of the Department of Commerce through Exim Bank of India and Export Credit Guarantee Corporation of India (ECGC). This will, inter alia, continue to enable Indian businesses to develop long term business relationships, facilitate easier acceptance of India's exports and build visibility for Indian products. In addition, EXIM Bank will undertake a study on the concept of 'revolving credit' for promoting exports in new markets, especially in South Asia, Africa, CIS and Latin America. EXIM Bank will also explore developing strong ties with international lending agencies such as African Development Bank, Inter-American Development Bank, Caribbean Bank, etc. ECGC will be supported to enhance insurance cover to exporters particularly MSME's exploring new or difficult markets. ECGC is a premier export credit agency and its portfolio has nearly 20,000 distinct exporters, 85 per cent of whom are MSMEs. ECGC will get a fresh capital infusion of ₹ 2,000 crores in 3 years, with ₹ 1,000 crores being added to enable it to support a larger number of exporters. ECGC has settled claims of nearly ₹ 7,000 crores in the last 10 years which has provided support to the exporters, and relief to the banking system.

Digitisation and PFMS

Successful implementation of the Public Financial Management System (PFMS) had been rolled out in all PAOS of this office Pay and Accounts Offices of Delhi, Chennai, Kolkata and Mumbai. For digitisation, EAT module and DBT module of PFMS has been implemented for end to end online payments. A part of pre-check as well as payment for bills is also done through electronic mode via PFMS.

Quality Standards

Government is committed to transforming India into a manufacturing and exporting hub. This will require focus on improving product quality. Many Indian products fail quality tests due to traces of pesticides, pathogens, illegal dyes, etc. An endeavour would be made to upgrade quality and infrastructure to help firms to move to higher quality standards and also protect Indian consumers from substandard imports. Setting up more globally accredited testing laboratories, enhancing the capacity of Indian testing laboratories and Mutual Recognition Agreements (MRA) with partner countries would be areas of focus. A roadmap has been developed on measures required to protect consumers, raise the quality of the merchandise produced and enhance India's capacity to export to even the most discerning markets.

Anti Dumping

The role of Directorate General of Anti-Dumping and Allied Duties (DGAD) under the Department is to provide the level playing field to the country's domestic industry from the foreign exporters so that they are able to compete effectively in the domestic market. This measure is taken under the WTO agreement and comes under the Customs Tariff Act, 1975 and Rules made thereunder. In August 2017, the investigation processes of DGAD became ISO 9001:2015 compliant which brought in transparency and accountability in its operations. The Department has developed Standard Operating Procedures (SOPs) for its functions and activities. These SOPs are codified in Quality Manual and procedures.

Medium Term Expenditure Framework, All Schemes Appraised

With the Twelfth Five Year Plan coming to end, for all the existing and new schemes of DOC, a complete and intensive appraisal process was completed for the Medium-Term Expenditure Framework (from 2017-18 to 2019-20) of the 14th Finance Commission. DOC has seven central sector schemes namely; market access initiative, tea development and promotion, integrated coffee development project, sustainable and inclusive development of rubber sector, infusion of capital in ECGC, contribution of grant in aid (corpus) to NEIA Trust and APEDA with a proposed outlay above ₹ 500 crore which is to be continued upto 2019-20. The appraisal process for all the schemes has been completed.

8 Communications and Information Technology

COMMUNICATIONS and information technology in the country are handled by the Ministry of Electronics and Information Technology and Ministry of Communications. The Ministry of Electronics and Technology promotes e-governance and sustainable growth of the electronics, IT and ITeS industries, enhancing India's role in internet governance while the Ministry of Communications looks after the Department of Posts and Department of Telecommunications. Main activities and initiatives of these departments are given here.

Relevant Websites : www.meity.gov.in   www.indiapost.gov.in

Posts

The modern postal system, the most preferred facilitator of communication, was established in India by Lord Clive in 1766 and it was further developed by Warren Hastings in1774. The expansion of its network was made during 1786 to 1793. For the first time, the post offices were regulated through an Act of 1837 on a uniform basis to unite all the post office establishments throughout the then existing three Presidencies into one all-India service. Thereafter, the Post Office Act of 1854 reformed the entire fabric of the postal system and the post offices of India were placed on the present administrative footing on 1st October 1854. This was the time when the first postage stamp valid across the country was issued at an affordable and uniform rate of postage, fixed by weight and not by distance. For the first time the common man could use a facility which included free delivery of letters from door to door—a privilege previously enjoyed only by heads of states and state officials. Since then, the Post Office touched the life of every person of the country. Even though the British established the post office for imperial interests, it along with the railways and telegraph, became one of the greatest engines of social development.

The statute presently governing the postal services in the country is the Indian Post Office Act, 1898. In the mid-19th century, the post office served as facilitator of travel with its conveyance systems and by maintaining the dak bungalows and dak serais. Mail order services were started with the value payable system introduced in 1877, while fund remittances at the doorstep became possible from 1880 through money order services. With the introduction of the Post Office Savings Bank in 1882 banking facilities were accessible to all and by 1884 all government employees were covered by the postal life insurance. Besides providing postal communication facilities, the post office network has also provided facilities for remittance of funds, banking and insurance services since the latter half of the 19th century.

Organization Overview

The Department of Posts comes under the Ministry of Communications. The Postal Service Board, the apex management body of the department, comprises the Chairman and six Members. The six Members of the Board hold portfolios of personnel, operations, technology, postal life insurance, banking and HRD and planning. The Joint Secretary and Financial Advisor to the department is a permanent invitee to the Board. The Chairman of Postal Services Board is also the Secretary of the Department of Posts. Director General and Additional Director General of the Department also participate in the Board's meetings.

Financial Services

Department of Posts is operating Small Savings Schemes on behalf of Ministry of Finance, which frames and modifies rules relating to these schemes and pays remuneration to the Department of Posts. Post Office Savings Bank (POSB) has a customer base of more than 35.62 cr. account holders as on March 31, 2017. Savings bank facility is provided through a network of 1.54 lakh post offices across the country. The post office savings bank operates savings accounts, recurring deposit (RD), time deposit (TD), monthly income scheme (MIS), public provident fund (PPF), national savings certificate (NSC), kisan vikas patra (KVP), senior citizens savings scheme (SCSS) and sukanya samriddhi account. The outstanding balance under all national savings schemes and saving certificates in post office is over ₹ 8,03,243 cr. as on March 31, 2018. (Provisional)

Core Banking

The Core Banking Solution is a part of India Post IT modernization project and aims to bring in various IT solutions with required IT infrastructure in post offices. The project aims to implement core banking in all Departmental Post Offices for small savings schemes during current plan period. The project will bring in facilities of "any time anywhere banking", ATM and internet banking facilities. As on August 10, 2018, 23,557 post offices have converted to CBS. 995 ATMs have been installed in 982 locations across the country.

Mutual Funds

The post office is playing an important role in extending the reach of the capital market of the country and providing the common man easy access to market based investment options. Presently, Mutual Fund products of UTI only are being retailed through over 2000 post offices.

International Money Transfer Service

International money transfer service is a quick and easy way of transferring personal remittances from abroad to beneficiaries in India. As a result of the collaboration of Department of Posts, Government of India with Western Union Financial Services a state-of-the-art international money transfer service is available through the post offices in the country, which enables instantaneous remittance of money from around 195 countries to India. Presently the service is available from 9953 locations across the country.

National Pension Scheme

National pension scheme, earlier known as New Pension System (NPS), for common citizens was introduced by government in 2009. India Post is a point of presence for the national pension system. Subscribers (any Indian citizen) in the age group of 18 to 55 can join NPS and contribute till the age of 60. These pension contributions are invested in various schemes of different pension fund managers appointed by Pension Fund Regulatory and Development Authority (PFRDA).

Social Security Scheme

Jan Suraksha Schemes like the Pradhan Mantri Suraksha Bima Yojana (PMSBY) and Pradhan Mantri Jeevan Jyoti Bima Yojana (PMJJBY) were launched in 2015 in all CBS post offices for all post office savings account holders. Department of Posts has signed Memorandum of Understanding (MoU) with National Insurance Company (NIC) and Life Insurance Corporation of India (LIC) for PMSBY and PMJJBY respectively. Atal Pension Yojna (APY) was launched in all CBS head post offices from 2015.

Core Banking Solution & installation of ATMs

The Core Banking Solution (CBS) is part of the India Post IT Modernization project that aims to bring in various IT solutions with the required infrastructure to the post offices. The project aims to implement Core Banking Solution in all the Departmental Post Offices for Small Savings Schemes during current Plan period. The project will bring in facilities of "any time any where banking". ATM and Internet Banking facilities.

As on 10th August 2018, 23557 Post Offices have been mignated to CBS and 995 ATMs have been installed at various locations across the country

Retailing of Mutual Funds

The post office is playing an important role in extending the reach of the capital market of the country and providing the common man easy access to market based investment options. Presently, Mutual Fund products of UTI MF only are being retailed through over 2,000 post offices.

Jan Suraksha Schemes

Jan Suraksha Schemes viz., Pradhan Mantri Suraksha Bima Yojana (PMSBY) and Pradhan Mantri Jeevan Jyoti Bima Yojana (PMJJBY) in post offices have been launched w.e.f. 07.09.2015 in all CBS post offices for all Post Office Saving Account holders. Department of Posts has signed Memorandum of Understanding (MoU) with National Insurance Company (NIC) and Life Insurance Corporation of India (LIC) for PMSBY & PMJJBY respectively. Atal Pension Yojana (APY) has also been launch in all CBS post offices on 1st December, 2015.

Sukanya Samriddhi Account

Sukanya Samriddhi Account, a new Small Savings Scheme for the welfare of girl child, was launched in 2015. Under the scheme, a legal/ natural guardian can open only one account in the name of one girl child and maximum two accounts in the name of two different girl children up to 10 years from date of birth of the girl child.

India Post Payments Bank

India Post Payments Bank (IPPB) is a Government of India owned bank operating under the Department of Posts. The first phase of the Bank with 650 branches and 3250 post offices as access points was inaugurated in September 2018. Over ten thousand postmen have been roped into the first phase. The aim is to utilise all the post offices in the country as access points and 300,000 postal service workers to provide house to house banking services.

In 2015, the Reserve Bank of India launched its differential banking policy for more focused banking, to boost financial inclusion and promote digital banking. The licence for such bank was provided to India Post in the same year. In 2016, it was registered as a public limited government company for setting up a payments bank. In 2017, Raipur and Ranchi were set up as braches of IPPB.

The Bank offers savings accounts, money transfer and insurances through third parties, bill and utility payments. The Bank - an initiative towards financial inclusion - is envisaged to reach rural and far-flung areas of the country delivering banking services at every doorstep.

Rural Business

Department of Posts has a predominantly rural network of 1,39,067 Post Offices in rural areas out of the total 1,54,965 post offices in the country. The Rural Businesss (RB) Division of the Department of Posts (DoP) has been given the mandate of leveraging the rural network spread across the length and breadth of country to provide accessible and affordable Financial and Postal services to the people in rural areas.

Postal Life Insurance and Rural Postal Life Insurance

Postal Life Insurance (PLI) was introduced on 1st Februray 1884, as a welfare scheme for the benefit of postal employees and later extended to the employees of telegraph department in 1888. It now covers employees of central and state governments, central and state public sector undertakings, universities, government aided educational institutions, nationalized banks and local bodies. PLI also extends the facility of insurance to defence services and para-military forces. Life cover through Postal Life Insurance has been extended to employees of scheduled commercial banks, credit co-operative societies, joint ventures having a minimum 10 per cent stake of central/state govt/PSUs/banks etc., universities/educational institutions affiliated to University Grants

Commission/Central Board of Secondary Education/All India Council of Technical Education/Medical Council of India. Benefits of PLI are now available to professionals such as Doctors, Engineers, Management Consultants, Charted Accountants, Architects, Lawyers, Bankers etc. and to employees of listed companies of NSE (National Stock Exchange) and BSE (Bombay Stock Exchange)

Starting with upper insurance limit of ₹ 4,000/-, maximum sum assured is now ₹ 50 lakhs (Rupees fifty lakhs) for all schemes. There are more than 63.69 lakh policy holders as on March 31, 2018 with a sum of ₹ 1,22,554.08 crore assured. Premim income of Postal Life Insurance for the year 2017-18 was ₹ 7,499. 18 crore. Postal Life Insurance also manages a Group Insurance Scheme for the Extra Departmental Employees (Gramin Dak Sevaks) of the Department of Posts.

Rural Postal Life Insurance

Rural Postal Life Insurance (RPLI) was started in 1995. The prime objective of the scheme is to provide insurance cover to the rural public in general and to benefit weaker sections and women workers of rural areas in particular and also to spread insurance awareness among the rural population.

With liberalization of insurance sector, PLI and RPLI are operating in a very competitive market. PLI and RPLI continue to offer life insurance cover at lower premium rate and higher bonus. Therefore, various schemes of PLI and RPLI are very popular amongst eligible clients and doing well. There are more than 241.1 lakhs RPLI policies as on March 31, 2018 with a sum of ₹ 1,16,17,428.14 crore assured.

PLI offers 6 (six) types of plans: whole life assurance (Surakha), convertible whole life assurance (Suvidha), endowment assurance (Santosh), anticipated endowment assurance (Sumangal), joint life assurance (Yugal Surksha), and children policy (Bal Jiwan Bima).

RPLI also offers 6 (six) types of plans: whole life assurance, convertible whole life assurance (Gram Suvidha), endowment assurance (Gram Santosh), anticipated endowment assurance (Gram Sumangal), 10 years RPLI (Gram Priya) and children policy (Bal Jiwan Bima).

New and Value Added Services

Speed Post

Speed Post was started in 1986 for providing a time-bound and express delivery of letters and parcels weighing upto 35 kg between specified stations in India. It is the flagship product of Department of Posts and the market leader in the domestic express industry with monthly volumes of more than 3 crore articles. The facility for booking is available in almost all the departmental post offices in the country and is delivered across the country. Speed post articles can be tracked online by using a 13 digit speed post article number through the India Post website (www.indiapost.gov.in) or by sending an SMS. Department of Posts also sends free SMS alert when the article is delivered as well as to addressee when the article arrives for delivery subject to the updation of mobile numbers at the time of booking. Insurance facility upto ₹ 1 lakh is also provided as an add-on service for speed post articles.

Leveraging Post Office Network for Setting up Passport Seva Kendra

The Department is associated with the passport services right from its inception as passports are being delivered through speed post. In order to extend passport services on a larger scale and to ensure wider area coverage Department of Posts and Ministry of External Affairs have mutually agreed for leveraging the network of post office as Passport Seva Kendras for benefit of citizens.

Express and Business Parcel

The increasing e-Commerce market has given a boost to the parcel segment where B 2 C parcels are on the rise. At the same time there is a demand to cater to the needs of the C 2 C category parcels also. Accordingly Express Parcel and Business Parcel services were introduced by the Department in 2013.

Express Parcel is a premium parcel service available for retail as well as bulk customers, offering time bound, safe and secure home delivery of parcels. To have minimal transit time these parcels will be given airlift wherever needed. Minimum chargeable weight of Express Parcel is 0.5 kg whereas maximum chargeable weight for retail customers is 20 kg and for contractual customers it is 35 kg.

Business Parcel aims to provide an economical distribution solution to corporate customers by providing surface transmission of the parcels. Minimum chargeable weight of parcels in this category is 2 kg and maximum weight is 35 kg. Service is available for all locations in the country.

Cash on Delivery

Increasing trend for online shopping has tremendous business opportunities for payment services, order processing and fulfillment services, etc. In order to cater to these business opportunities and to provide a fast, safe and economical solution of collection of amount of goods at the time of its delivery and its remittance to sender, Cash on Delivery facility was introduced in 2013 and is available to the contractual customers of Express Parcel, Business Parcel and Speed Post.

Logistics Post

Logistics Post was started to provide distribution solutions to the corporate customers and it has created a niche market in providing express logistics services with a large network in the country. As a part of Supply Chain solution, Full Truck Load (FTL) services, Less Than Truck Load (LTL) services, warehousing services, order processing and fulfillment services and reverse logistics services are being provided by Department of Posts under Logistics Post. There is no upper weight limit for Logistics Post consignment and the minimum chargeable weight is 50 kg if consignments are sent through surface. In case Logistics Post consignments are sent by air, minimum chargeable weight is 25 kg.

Logistics Post Air service has started from 2013 linking following 15 cities: Agartala, Delhi, Mumbai, Kolkata, Nagpur, Bengaluru, Hyderabad, Chennai, Pune, Ahmedabad, Imphal, Guwahati, Patna, Lucknow, Thiruvananthapuam.

Business Posts

A lot of pre-mailing activities like folding, inserting, franking, addressing and pasting, etc., are required to be completed before a mail article is posted. Large organizations were finding it difficult to carry out these pre-mailing activities, Department of Posts introduced 'Business Post' service in 1996 to offer a comprehensive solution to corporate/government organizations/PSUs and other corporate houses for their pre-mailling requirements. Besides bringing in additional revenue, this activity is meeting the need of corporate and bulk mail customers. Business Post services are available in Business Postal Centres at various major post offices across the country. The services include home/office collection, inseartion, sealing, addressing, franking, special handling, etc.

Media Post

India Post offers a unique media concept to help the Indian corporate and the government organizations reach potential customers through Media Post. No other medium can match the sheer expanse of India Post in terms of volume and reach. Media Post offers a range of advertising mediums such as letter boxes, postal stationery, postal premises, etc.

Direct Post

With the increasing commercial activity in the country, the need for direct advertising of products and services by the business organizations is growing. Direct Mail, which can be defined as printed matter usually carrying a sales message or announcement designed to elicit a response from a carefully selected consumer or business market is the most potent medium for direct advertising. In the advanced countries, Direct Mail now constitutes a pre dominant portion of mail traffic handled by postal administrations. Direct mail can be both addressed as well as un-addressed.

Direct Post is the un-addressed component of Direct Mail in India, and would comprise un-addressed postal articles like letters, cards, brochures, questionnaires, pamphlets, samples, promotional items like CDs/floppies and cassettes etc., coupons, posters, mailers or any other form of printed communication that is not prohibited by the Indian Post Office Act 1898 or Indian Post Office Rules 1933.

Retail Post

Post Office is being developed as a one-stop shop to provide a range of utility services to the customers providing convenience and affordability at their door steps. Retail Post leverages the vast network of 1,55,000 post offices and the services under it include collection of electricity bill, telephone bills, taxes, fees, sale of *Rakhi* envelopes, address verification service, sale of application forms of various educational institutions and recruiting agencies, etc.

In order to provide railway tickets through convenient locations, railway reservation tickets of all classes are being sold at the post offices in association with the Ministry of Railways.

Gangajal through Post Offices

India Post has put in place arrangements for supply and distribution of 'Gangajal' sourced from Rishikesh and Gangotri, through post offices across the country from 2016. 'Gangajal' is being made available through Head Post Offices and ePost Office Portal. Arrangements have also been made for door step delivery of 'Gangajal' across the country through Speed Post .

Post Shoppe

The Department of Posts in its endeavour to facilitate customers with pleasant shopping experience has evolved a concept of 'Post Shoppe'. The 'Post Shoppe' is a convenient store format, located in the premises of important post offices, which essentially keeps wide range of collectable philatelic items such as stamps, first day covers, frames, albums and also 'My Stamp' corner where one can get stamps with own photograph. Apart from these, stationery items of general use such as different varieties of covers/envelopes, CD mailers, etc., are also made available at these shops. Besides, 'Post Shoppes' are also a prominent place for items of cultural heritage and traditional items of local importance prepared by artisans. The 'Post Shoppe' have got elegant looks and modern shelf and rack system with open display method creating an attractive look and giving a pleasant shopping experience.

Presently, more than eighty 'Post Shoppe' are functional across the country and these have been well received and appreciated by the customers with increasing footfalls.

Passenger Reservation System

A Memoradum of Understanding was signed between India Post and Ministry of Railways to provide computerised Passenger Reservation System (PRS) terminals in some post offices. Service was initially started in 30 post offices. Now, this number has gone up to around 337. List of Post Offices opening India Post PRS Centre, along with contact details, is available on the web site www.indiapost.gov.in

Since the commencement of service in 2007, service charged being realized by the Department for issuing of reserved tickets have not been upwardly revised.

Sovereign Gold Bond

Department is actively engaged in the premier scheme—Sale of Sovereign Gold Bond (SGB)' introduced in 2015-16 by Ministry of Finance, and operated through RBI. The objective of the scheme is to popularize 'Paper Gold' among . masses and to reach out to the small investors at the grassroot level.

Electronic Indian Postal Order (e-IPO)

Based on the proposal received from Department of Personnel and Training (DoPT), India Post agreed to facilitate acceptance of RTI fees from Indian citizens abroad through e-IPO on ePost Office web portal.

The user may purchase an Indian Postal Order electronically by paying a fee on-line through ePost Office Portal. Payment of fee can be made using debit and credit cards powered by VISA and Master.

Initially this facility was launched in 2013 only for Indian citizens abroad across the globe to seek information from the Central Public Information Officers (CPIOs) under the RTI Act, 2005. Later on, the facility was extended to 176 Indian Missions abroad. EIPO facility was further extended to Indian citizens living in India in 2014 to facilitate them to pay RTI fee online.

e-Post Office

e-Post Office is an e-commerce portal of the Department of Posts which provides selected postal facility through the internet. This portal aims at providing a convenience to the public for availing select postal services from their home/office using their own computer and internet. Customers can buy philatelic stamps and pay PLI/RPLI premium online using credit/debit card through this portal. The customer would need to register on the website for the first time.

e-Post

e-Post is an unregistered hybrid mail provided for both retail as well as corporate customers providing electronic transmission of messages which may include text messages, scanned images, pictures and their delivery in hard copies at the destination through postman/delivery staff. Presently, e-Post booking facility is available in more than 13,000 post offices and are physically delivered through a network of more than 1.54 lakh post offices, etc. to draft, design and send messages as per their business requirements from their office premises by using the internet. Online recharge facility for pre-paid customers is available using credit/debit card.

e-Payment

It is an option for businesses and organizations to collect their bills or other payments through post offices. e-Payment is a many to one solution which allows collection of money (telephone bills, electricity bills, examination fee, taxes university fee, school fee, etc.) on behalf of any organization electronically.

International Relations

India is a member of the Universal Postal Union (UPU) since 1876. This organization of 192 member countries aims to extend, facilitate and improve postal relations among other countries. India, an elected member of the Postal Operations Council (POC) of the UPU is the co-chair of Committee 1 (Supply Chain Integration), and member of the Quality of Service Fund, Board of Trustees (QSF BoT) which works for development of the postal sector in the developing countries.

India is also a member of the Asian-Pacific Postal Union (APPU) along with 31 other member countries. The purpose of the APPU is to extend, facilitate and improve closer postal relations among member countries and to promote cooperation in the field of postal services within the Asia-Pacific region.

Mail Network Optimization Project

Mail Network Optimization Project (MNOP) was undertaken by the Department with the objective of consolidation and optimization of its Mail Network with a view to improve quality of mail operations by streamlining core mail operations. The project covers Speed Post, International Mail, First class mail and second class mail.

MNOP project has been implemented in the entire country comprising 23 postal circles. The benefits to citizen are—improved delivery performance of Speed Post, increased number of Speed Post articles having end-to-end (both booking and delivery) information on Department of Posts website (tracking system).

Dedicated Road Transport Network

Based on the need for providing safe, secure and faster transmission of parcels particularly e-commerce consignments, the Department has set up a dedicated road transport network for transmission of parcels. Under the initiative so far, a total of 42 routes in 17 circles have been made functional connecting 67 cities across the country. Besides, 2 long haul routes have been identified under the plan scheme.

Postman Mobile App

An android based Mobile Application named Postman Mobile App (PMA) designed and developed in-house by the Department at the Centre for Excellence in Postal Technology, (CEPT) Mysuru, has been launched across the country deploying more than 15000 smartphones. The mobile app is being used by the delivery staff for delivering various accountable articles such as Speed Post, Express Parcel, Business Parcel and Regd. Post, including CoD parcels and capturing real time delivery information. The app has the provision of taking the signature of the same prior to the introduction of the application and hence improves overall customer experience and delivery performance. The Department is now in the process of procuring 38000 more smartphones for its delivery staff.

Philately

Philately is the hobby of collecting stamps as well as the study of postal history and other related items. It is a mode of commemorating, celebrating and promoting national heritage, culture, events and personalities. Postage Stamps are pictorial ambassadors. They are a statement of sovereignty of a nation.

After independence, the medium of postage stamps was initially used to highlight the country's achievements in science and technology as well as its socio economic development by depicting themes like Five Year Plans, steel plants, dams, etc. Subsequently, the country's rich cultural and natural heritage came to be showcased and many beautiful stamps were issued in thematic sets on art, architecture, crafts maritime heritage, science, technology, defence, and cinema. Great leaders of national and international standing have also been honoured with commemorative stamps, the most important being Mahatma Gandhi. The Father of the Nation has been honoured with commemorative as well as definitive stamps. Personalities of repute in areas like painting, literature, science, music, social upliftment, etc., have also been portrayed on commemorative stamps.

In keeping with their dual character as a 'Token of Postage' and as 'Cultural Ambassador', there are two categories of stamps viz., definitive and commemorative postage stamps. The definitive postage stamps are meant for day-to-day use as a token of payment of postage on mail articles. These incorporate less complicated design inputs, entailing minimum expenditure in their manufacture, and are printed in large quantities, over longer periods. On the other hand the commemorative postage stamps are designed and printed with greater aesthetic inputs. These are manufactured in limited quantities and generate great interest among philatelists and collectors.

The philatelic activities of the Department include: designing, printing, distribution and sale of commemorative postage stamps through philatelic bureaux and counters, e-post office, etc., designing, printing and distribution of definitive postage stamps and items of postal stationery like envelopes, Inland letter card, postcard, aerogram, registered cover, etc., promotion of philately and conduct and monitoring of Philatelic exhibitions; maintenance of the National Philatelic Museum, Dak Bhawan, New Delhi.

Release of Stamps

A total of 50 issues were released during April, 2017 to March, 2018 commemorating various personalities, events/ occasions. Some of the significant commemorations were —Caves of Meghalaya, Vulnerable Birds, Ramayana, Mahabharata, Indian Cuisine, Nest Stepwells, Hand Fans, Solar System, Headgears of India, Champaran Satyagraha Centenary. Ramayana Stamps were released simultaneously in 40 countries through Indian Missions abroad.

My Stamps

My Stamps are personalized sheets of postage stamps of India Post. Personalization is achieved by printing a thumb nail photograph image of the customer and logos of institutions, or images of artwork, heritage buildings, famous tourist places, historical cities, wildlife, other animals and birds, etc., alongside the selected commemorative postage stamp.

Personalized My Stamp

Personalized My Stamp is a personalized sheet of postage stamps. Alongside these personalized theme stamps, the customers may opt for printing of their own, parents, family, etc., pictures to be printed. Some of the themes of personalized My Stamps are Taj Mahal, Hawa Mahal, Mysore Palace, Indian Army, rose, happy anniversary, Vaishno Devi.

Customized My Stamps

Customized My Stamps is a personalized sheet of postage stamps wherein corporates organizations and institutions can get customized sheets printed from India Post. Alongside these customized themed stamps, the organizations may opt for printing of their logo, images of their organisation/institute printed.

Training Activities

Department of Posts has framed the Postal Training Policy, 2012 in conformity with the National Training Policy, 2012 of Government of India. The key objective of this Policy is "Training for All". Training programmes are available at the entry level (induction training) and there are three Mid-career Training Programmes at specific intervals for all cadres/categories of staff.

The Department has well established training infrastructure. The following training institutes take care of training needs of the Department: Rafi Ahmed Kidwai National Postal Academy (RAKNPA) at Ghaziabad is the apex training institute of the Department recognized by the DoP&T as a Central Training Institute for higher managerial cadres. This imparts induction as well as in-service training to the officers of Indian Postal Service and other managerial cadres of India Post. It also imparts training to managers of foreign postal administrations and officers of various central government departments and PSUs, in areas of common interest. The Academy conducts 'Executive Development Programme' (EDP), 'Management Development Programme' (MDP) and 'Advanced Development Program' (ADP). For the officers of Indian Postal Service.

Postal Training Centres (PTCs) are functioning at Darbhanga, Guwahati, Madurai, Mysore, Saharanpur and Vadodara for training operative staff and inspectorial cadres. Besides, these also organize other specialized training programmes. These six training centres have well equipped computer labs, class-rooms and hostel facilities to take care of the bulk of the training needs of operative staff of the Department.

Public Grievances

Computerised Customer Care Centres

The Department has a well laid out procedure for handling public grievances for its services. A monitoring mechanism to ensure the quality of services and prompt redressal of public grievances is in place.

The Department has upgraded its web-based grievance handling system to interconnect the Customer Care Centres with the objective of systematic handling and quick redressal of public grievances. In 2010, the modified version of Computerized Customer Care Centre (CCCC) software was made operational. New features such as automatic generation of acknowledgement; escalation of unresolved complaints to next higher administrative level for better monitoring and quicker redressal; differentiation of complaints into minor, major or critical; automatic generation of reply to the complainant on completion of inquiry; provision for feedback of complainant; etc., were also incorporated.

Presently 19201 CCCC have been established in the post offices, sorting hubs, speed post centres and divisional/regional/circle headquarters across the country for online exchange of information amongst all the units for speedy redressal of public grievances. The network covers all head post offices in the country with the objective of providing easy and speedy access to information and help required by the customers, apart from the redressal of grievances.

Social Media Cell

Social Media Cell is an independent entity and deals with the twitter and facebook accounts of the Department of Posts. The social media complaints are time bound and are replied within 24 hours. The social media cell monitors the complaints sent to all the circles on daily basis. Till July 2018, the Department received 1,06,096 grievances on Twitter Seva and observed a resolution rate of 99.6 per cent.

India Post Help Centre "1924"

In wake of the initiatives taken up by the Government to bring transparency and accountability, Department of Posts has established "India Post Call Centre" with interactive Voice Response System (IVRS) at Varanasi on June 1, 2018. Till July 2018, the Department received 1,59,586 queries at the Call Centre from its users and prospective users of India Post. This Call Centre aims to assist the general public in the following manner; redressal of public grievances; dissemination of information regarding various initiatives, activities, schemes, programmes and projects undertaken.

Information Technology

Ministry of Electronics and Information Technology (MeitY) deals with policy matters relating to information technology, electronics, internet (other than licensing of ISPs) and cyber security. The aim is to promote e-governance for empowering citizens, promoting the inclusive and sustainable growth of the electronics, IT and ITeS industries, promoting digital transactions and digital payments, enhancing India's role in internet governance, adopting a multipronged approach that includes development of human resources, promoting R&D and innovation, enhancing efficiency through digital services and ensuring a secure cyber space.

With the unveiling of the Digital India programme the role of MeitY has enhanced. The overarching vision of the programme is to transform India into a digitally empowered society and knowledge economy. The programme has three vision areas namely, digital infrastructure as a utility for every citizen, governance and services on demand and digital empowerment of citizens by bridging the digital divide in the country. This transformational programme is designed to build holistic capabilities across infrastructure, manufacturing, skills and delivery platforms which in turn will lead to creation of a self-reliant knowledge economy. Digital infrastructure as a utility includes availability of high speed internet for delivery of services to citizens, digital identity for every citizen, mobile phone and bank account enabling citizen participation in digital and financial space, shareable private space on a public cloud and safe and secure cyber-space.

Governance and services on demand includes seamlessly integrated services across departments or jurisdictions, services availability in real time from online and mobile platforms, digitally transformed services for improving ease of doing business, leveraging GIS for decision support systems and development.

Digital empowerment of citizens includes universal digital literacy, accessible digital resources universally, all documents/ certificates to be available on cloud, availability of digital resources/services in Indian languages and portability of all entitlements through cloud.

The nine pillars of growth viz., broadband highways, universal access to mobile connectivity, public internet access programme, e-governance - reforming government through technology, e-kranti- electronic delivery of services, information for all, electronics manufacturing, IT for jobs and early harvest programmes, are being promoted under Digital India programme. The programme is coordinated by this Ministry with the ministries and departments in the central and state governments partnering it in their respective domain areas.

MeitY functions around the ambit of two major Acts. The Information Technology Act, 2000 which provides legal recognition to the transaction carried out by means of electronic data interchange and other means of electronic communication, commonly referred to as electronic commerce which involves the use of alternatives to paper-based methods of communication and storage of information, to facilitate electronic filing of documents with the government agencies. It gives provisions for the use of electronic records and digital signature with the provision of authentication and security. It also directs the establishment of Cyber Appellate Tribunal. This Act was amended through the Information Technology (Amendment) Act, 2008 which substituted the word "digital signature" with "electronic signature" with major changes in various sections along with insertion of other sections.

To ensure that various benefits and subsidies reach the targeted beneficiaries, the Government made all efforts to leverage the Aadhaar platform. The Aadhaar (Targeted Delivery of Financial and Other Subsidies, Benefits and

Services) Act, 2016 provides for good governance, efficient, transparent and targeted delivery of subsidies, benefits and services, the expenditure for this is incurred from the Consolidated Fund of India, to individuals residing in India through assigning of a unique identity number to such individuals. It covers everything from the enrollment for Aadhaar number, authentication to establishment of UIDAI which has now become a statutory organization.

Digital Identity

Aadhaar provides 12 digit biometric and demographic based identity that is unique, lifelong, online and authenticable. Under the Aadhaar Act 2016, UIDAI is responsible for Aadhaar enrolment and authentication, including operation and management of all stages of Aadhaar life cycle, developing the policy, procedure and system for issuing Aadhaar numbers to individuals and perform authentication and also required to ensure the security of identity information and authentication records of individuals. More than 116 crore Aadhaar numbers have been generated. Aadhaar has been instrumental in the provision of goods and services and is also enhancing and enabling digital transaction and digital payment. Some of major initiatives are:

Aadhaar Enabled Payments : (i) Aadhaar Payment Bridge (APB): A payment can be made to a person's bank account via his/her Aadhaar number, provided it is linked to his/her Aadhaar number. Government of India transfers benefits and subsidies directly to the beneficiaries' bank account through APB. (ii) Aadhaar Enabled Payment System (AEPS): AEPS is the platform in which a person can do basic banking transactions including withdrawal, deposit cash, fund transfer, etc., from his/her bank account at Micro-ATMs using biometric authentication. Bank is chosen by resident as it is a resident present transaction; (iii) Aadhaar Pay: It is merchant version of AEPS. The Application works on a low cost android phone with single finger bio-metric device. It enables merchant to take cashless payment from his customers. It was launched in 2017; (iv) Pay to Aadhaar: It is a facility available on UPI platform integrated in BHIM app. It enables Person-to-Person (P2P) remittance using Aadhaar number of the recipient as financial address. The receiving Aadhaar number should be linked with his/her Aadhaar number. This was also launched in 2017.

Aadhaar Enabled Services: (i) targeted delivery of foodgrains under PDS: Over 18.05 crore ration card holders receive ration post Aadhaar authentication. They are sure that nobody else can claim their rations, reducing pilferage and theft in the process. Aadhaar seeding for de-duplications and other DBT processes has removed over 2.33 crore fake ration cards saving over ₹ 14,000 crore upto March 2017; (ii) PAHAL and Ujjwala Scheme: Over 15.12 crore LPG beneficiaries received LPG subsidy in their bank accounts under the PAHAL scheme. Over 2.5 crore connections were issued to BPL women under Ujjwala Scheme; (iii) ease of opening of bank account using e-KYC: Aadhaar has enabled this by becoming the single document which acts as KYC document for opening a bank account; (iv) e-verification of income tax return: Aadhaar has enabled income tax payer to e-verify their income tax return using Aadhaar OTP authentication, obviating the need for sending the ITR-5 in a physical form to Income Tax Authorities.

e-Governance

With the advent of Digital India as an apex programme various new policy initiatives have been taken up by MeitY such as eKranti, policy on adoption of open source software in e-governance systems, e-mail policy, policy on use of IT resources, policy on collaborative application development by opening the source code of government applications, application development and re-engineering guidelines for cloud ready applications and e-governance competency framework. Major schemes such as e-districts, common service centres and state wide area network (SWAN) have also been working in this direction.

Policy on Adoption of Open Source Software: It encourages the formal adoption and use of Open Source Software (OSS) in government organisations. Accordingly government organisations, while implementing e-governance applications and systems, are to ensure compliance of this policy and decide by comparing both OSS and Closed Source Software (CSS) options with respect to capability, strategic control, scalability, security, life-time costs and support requirements.

Policy on Collaborative Application Development by Opening the Source Code of Government Applications: This policy aims to increase the pace of e-governance application development and rapid roll out/implementation by adopting an open-source code, for high quality e-governance applications. It also intends to encourage innovative e-governance applications and solutions through collaborative development.

Policy on use of IT Resources: This policy governs the usage of IT resources from an end user's perspective. Its objective is to ensure proper access to and usage of government's IT resources and prevent their misuse.

e-mail Policy of Government: This policy lays down the guidelines with respect to use of e-mail services of the government and employees of those state/UT governments that use the e-mail services of GOI and also those state/UT governments that choose to adopt this policy in future. The objective is to ensure secure access and usage of Government of India e-mail services by its users.

Policy on Open Application Programming Interfaces (APIs): The Policy on Open APIs for Government's approach on the use to Open APIs to promote software interoperability for all e-governance applications and systems and provide access to data and services for promoting participation of all stakeholders including citizens.

The e-Governance Competency Framework (e-GCF): Its toolkit contains a set of end-user knowledge areas required for government employees. The objective of the framework is to strengthen the capacity building scheme to identify and define competencies, through a competency-based system which is required for different job roles under e-governance.

In order to transform the quality of services and to provide integrated services the "eKranti" initiative aims to utilize emerging technologies such as cloud and mobile platform and focus on integration of services. The principle of this programme is 'transformation' and not translation, and to provide integrated services and not individual ones. Another important initiative pertains to 'Jeevan Praman' that is, of providing an Aadhaar based digital life certificate for pensioners. Over 88.72 lakh pensioners have registered on the portal and over 77.04 lakh digital life certificates have been successfully processed since its launch.

A 'Digital Locker system' has also been envisaged to serve as a platform to enable citizens to securely share their documents with service providers who can directly access them electronically. 'e-sign' framework has been released, which would allow citizens to digitally sign a document online using Aadhaar authentication.

National Scholarship Portal has been developed as a one-stop solution to implement end-to-end disbursement of the scholarship to the beneficiaries. The process includes student registration, application, approval and disbursement. Over 1.21 crore applictions have been submitted. There are 52 registered schemes from eight ministries/departments.

In order to integrate the delivery of government services (across various departments), an initiative called Mobile Seva has been launched. A portal called 'Vikaspedia' to provide information on health, education, agriculture, energy, social welfare and e-Governance has been developed in more than 15 languages with more languages are being added.

MyGov.in is an innovative platform launched to ensure citizens' engagement in decision making by the Government so that the ultimate goal of "Good Governance" for building India is achieved. This initiative is an opportunity for citizens and well-wishers from across the world to share their views on key issues directly with the Prime Minister of India.

MeitY has developed Rapid Assessment System (RAS) for continuous feedback for e-services delivered by Government of India and state governments. This system has multiple channels for receiving feedback and is backed by analytics. These analytics will help integrated departments for continuous system improvement and better governance.

e-Sampark Database is developed to send messages and emails to public representatives and government employees. This database has 1.90 crore email addreses and over 82 crore mobile numbers. The count of mailers is over 301 crore for 563 campaigns.

e-Taal is a web portal for dissemination of e-transactions statistics of national and state level e-governance projects including mission mode projects. It receives transaction statistics from web based applications periodically on near real time basis. e-Taal presents quick analysis of transaction counts in tabular and graphical form to give quick view of transactions done by various e-governance projects.

Aadhaar-Enabled Biometric Attendance System (AEBS): In order to bring in efficiency in the Government, an Aadhaar enabled Biometric Attendance System was implemented by MeitY.

e-Payment Framework: All payments and receipts to be in electronic mode. The portal payonline.gov.in envisaged as common platform for making physical payments online.

e-Hospital - OPD Registration Framework (ORF) is an initiative to facilitate the patients to take online OPD appointments with government hospitals. This framework also covers patient care, laboratory services and medical record management.

e-Districts: It is one of the Mission Mode Projects(MMPs) under e-Kranti, with the MeitY, as the nodal Ministry, to be implemented by state government or their designated agencies. This MMP aims at electronic delivery of identified high volume citizen centric services, at district and sub-district level, those are not part of any other MMP. It has been launched in 634 districts along with 1012 e-services.

Common Services Centre: This scheme aims at providing ICT enabled front-end service delivery outlets, across rural India covering six lakh villages. These internet enabled centres allow doorstep access to citizens, private and social services for skill development, education, digital literacy, health and financial services. New services namely banking, insurance and pension under Prime Minister Jan Dhan Yojna have made CSCs very vibrant. Digital Sakshartha Abhiyan (DISHA) for undertaking digital literacy has enabled active citizen participation through CSCs. Aadhaar enrolment/update has been enabled through CSCs. In all 3,00,774 Common Services Centres (CSCs) have been registered across the country, among which, 1,96,922 are at Gram Panchayats level till August, 2017.

State Wide Area Network (SWAN): SWAN has been identified as an element of the core infrastructure for supporting the e-governance initiatives and the MeitY has earmarked a significant outlay for supporting this activity. Under the National e-governance action plan, it is proposed to extend connectivity to the block level through NICNET/State Wide Area Network (SWAN). It is operational in 34 states/UTs and average bandwidth utilization is more than 60 per cent. SWAN has been integrated with National Knowledge Network (NKN) in 28 states/UTs.

Capacity Building Scheme II (CB Scheme II): Under the National e-Governance Plan, MeitY, Government of India has approved the Capacity Building Scheme Phase II, to give impetus in building capacities within the government by adapting a harmonized and synchronized approach, to ensure the availability of right skills. The core objective of the Capacity Building Scheme Phase II is to build capacities in central line ministries and state/UT line departments for implementation of various e-Governance initiatives. This is to enhance the abilities of the project teams, to have a holistic understanding on visualizing, conceiving and delivering projects.

GI Cloud: In order to utilize and harness the benefits of Cloud Computing, the government has embarked upon an ambitious and important initiative - "GI Cloud" which has been coined as "MeghRaj". The focus of this initiative is to evolve a strategy and implement various components including governance mechanism to ensure proliferation of Cloud in government. Formulation of the Cloud Policy is one of the primary steps that will facilitate large scale adoption of cloud by government.

National Centre for Geo-Informatics (NCoG) provides GIS based services to government ministries/departments. NCoG is currently involved in rolling out select GIS based decision support system for various organizations. Base map layers for administrative boundaries up to village level, major roads, rivers, rail on the scale of 1:10,000 across India have been completed. GIS based Decision Support System (DSS) platforms developed. So far, 21 applications across various domains are operational.

Promotion of Digital Transactions

Promotion of a digital payments ecosystem is a natural extension of the Digital India programme and has the potential to transform the economy by formalization of financial transactions. Digital payments allow for services to be delivered at a lower cost, afford greater scalability and enable small and micro enterprises to access formal financial services and benefits of e-commerce. A new educational channel "DigiShala" for creating awareness regarding various forms of electronic payment to citizens was launched in 2016. DigiShala is now also available on Dish TV in addition to DD Free Dish. The DigiShala is an education and non-commercial TV channel on DD Free Dish.

The new website www.cashlessindia.gov.in was launched in 2016 to serve as a knowledge repository providing information on different types of digital payment methods, schemes to create awareness among citizens.

The BHIM App was launched in 2016 and within a short span BHIM downloads have crossed 20 million with transactions worth around ₹ 3000 crores. For promotion of BHIM app at merchant end, Aadhaar Pay under new name 'BHIM Aadhaar' was also launched in 2017. A mission has been created under the name 'Digidhan Mission' for creation of ecosystem for promotion of digital payments and transactions.

National Policy on Universal Electronic Accessibility (2013) was formulated to break the barriers faced by differently abled persons by ensuring easy accessibility of electronics and ICT. Electronics and ICT can mitigate the barriers faced by differently abled persons as well as help them to participate independently in day-to-day life. The National Policy on Electronic Accessibility recognizes the need to eliminate discrimination on the basis of disabilities and to facilitate equal access to Electronics and ICT. It recognizes the diversity of differently abled persons and provides for their specific needs.

Cyber Security

Millions of people in the country (both in rural and urban areas) rely on the services and information available in cyber space. As the quantity and value of electronic information has increased, so too have the business models and efforts of criminals and other adversaries who have embraced cyber space as a more convenient and profitable way of carrying out their activities anonymously. Hence, security of cyber space has become an important part of the national agenda.

Considering its vital importance, a National Cyber Security Policy, 2013 was put in place. It is aimed at building a secure and resilient cyber space for citizens, businesses and government, by way of actions to protect information and information infrastructure in cyber space, build capabilities to prevent and respond to cyber threats, reduce vulnerabilities and minimize damage from cyber incidents through a combination of institutional structures, people, processes, technology and cooperation.

National Cyber Co-ordination Centre (NCCC) is being set-up with an aim to generate cyber security situational awareness to anticipate and prepare for cyber attacks. NCCC will aggregate cyber threat related information from various identified sources in the country for near real time threat assessment and situational awareness that will help in analysis and generation of timely alerts and periodic reports. This initiative is expected to help in securing the cyber space and strengthening the cyber security posture in the country by leveraging the expertise of people, deploying standard processes and sharing of resources.

Cyber Swachhta Kendra: Indian Computer Emergency Response Team (CERT-In) has launched a Cyber Swachhta Kendra (Botnet Cleaning and Malware Analysis Centre). This centre is providing detection of malicious programmes and free tools to remove the same for banks as well as common users.

Statutory Organizationss

Controller of Certifying Authorities

Digital Signature Certificates (DSC) are issued by Certifying Authorities (CA) who have been licensed by the Controller of Certifying Authorities

(CCA). The Office of CCA empanels licensed CAs for offering eSign Services for which the legal framework and guidelines are already in place. So far, three of the eight licensed CAs have been empanelled for providing eSign Service. These eSign Service Providers (ESP) are expected to facilitate digital signing for Aadhaar holders only on the basis of their eKYC from UIDAI.

Relevant Website : www.cca.gov.in

Cyber Appellate Tribunal

In accordance with the provision contained under Section 48(1) of the IT Act 2000, the Cyber Regulations Appellate Tribunal (CRAT) was established in 2006. As per the IT Act, any person aggrieved by an order made by the Controller of Certifying Authorities or by an Adjudicating Officer under the Act can appeal before the Cyber Appellate Tribunal (CAT).

Centre for Materials for Electronics Technology

Centre for Materials for Electronics Technology (C-MET) was set up as a registered scientific society in 1990 under the Department of Electronics (now Ministry of Electronics and Information Technology) as a unique concept for development of viable technologies in the area of materials mainly for electronics. C-MET is operating through its laboratories situated at Pune, Hyderabad and Thrissur. The activities at the three labs have specific mandate within the ambit of electronic materials with the concept of bringing out technologies from lab level to pilot plant demonstration ready for Indian industries to take off.

Education and Research Network

Education and Research Network (ERNET): India is an autonomous scientific society of the Ministry. ERNET has made significant contribution for the emergence of networking in the country. In addition to providing connectivity, ERNET has been meeting the needs of academic and research institutions by providing IT consultancy, project management and training.

National e-Governance Division

To meet ever growing demand of e-governance across the nation, National e-Governance Division (NeGD) was established as amalgamation of experts from the private sector and the government. NeGD has been playing a pivotal role in discharging the key tasks including programme management and technical support of various components of the Digital India Programme.

National Informatics Centre

National Informatics Centre (NIC) was established in 1976, and has since emerged as a "prime builder" of e-government/e-governance applications up to the grassroot level as well as a promoter of digital opportunities for sustainable development. NIC, through its ICT network, "NICNET", has institutional linkages with all the ministries/departments of the central government, 36 state governments/union territories, and about 650+ district administrations of India. NIC has been instrumental in steering e-government/e-governance applications in government ministries/departments at the centre, states, districts and blocks, facilitating improvement in government services, wider transparency, promoting decentralized planning and management.

Relevant Website : www.nic.in

Standardization, Testing and Quality Certification

Standardization, Testing, Quality and Certification (STQC) Directorate is an attached office of this Ministry providing quality assurance services in the area of electronics and information technology (IT) through countrywide network of laboratories and centre(s). The services include testing, calibration, IT and e governance, training and certification to public and private organizations.

National Internet Exchange

NIXI is a not for profit organization set up under Section 25 of the Companies Act, 1956 (now Section 8 under Companies Act, 2013) for peering of ISPs among themselves and routing the domestic traffic within the country. NIXI is performing the following three activities: (i) internet exchanges; (ii) IN registry and internationalized domain names (IDNs); (iii) National Internet Registry (NIR).

National Institute of Electronics and Information Technology

National Institute of Electronics and Information Technology (NIELIT) a scientific society of the MeitY, is actively engaged in capacity building and skill development in Information Technology (IT); electronics; communication technologies; hardware; cyber law; cyber security; IPR; GIS; cloud computing; ESDM; e-waste; IoT; e-governance and related verticals. NIELIT offers courses both in the formal as well as the non-formal and is also the preferred agency for many state governments for rolling out IT literacy programmes for its employees and the masses.

Software Technology Parks

Software Technology Parks of India (STPI) was set up in 1991 as an autonomous society under the MeitY. STPI's main objective has been the promotion of software exports from the country. It acts as single-window in providing services to the software exporters. STPI is responsible for implementation of the Software Technology Parks (STP) scheme and the Electronics Hardware Technology Parks (EHTP) scheme.

Media Lab Asia

Media Lab Asia has been promoted by this Ministry as a not-for-profit company. The objective of the company was set to bring the benefits of ICT to the common man. The functional activity includes application areas such as ICT for healthcare, education, livelihood and empowerment of disabled.

National Informatics Centre Services Incorporated

National Informatics Centre Services Inc. (NICSI) was set up by National Informatics Centre (NIC) in 1995 as its extended arm for providing total ICT solutions to the central and state government departments and organizations. Its services include state-of- the-art hardware, software, consulting, technical support, design and development, operations and management, quality check, as well as end-to-end ICT solutions and services.

Telecommunications

Communications sector has assumed the position of an essential infrastructure for socio-economic development in an increasingly knowledge-intensive world. The reach of telecom services to all regions of the country has become an integral part of an innovative and technologically-driven society. As a result of sustainable measures taken by the government over the years, the Indian Telecom Sector has grown exponentially and has become the second largest network in the world, next only to China.

Department of Telecommunications

Department of Telecommunication (DoT) is committed to provide secure, reliable, affordable and high quality converged telecommunication services anytime, anywhere for an accelerated inclusive socio-economic development. The Department is working towards the objective of maximizing public good by making available affordable, reliable and secure voice and data services.

The Telecom Sector in India has witnessed all round growth over the last few years. Along with strong consumer demand, the liberal and reformist policies of the Government of India have been instrumental in the rapid growth of the sector. The government has ensured fair competition among service being available to consumer at affordable prices. Further it has made concerted efforts at encouraging telecom equipment manufacture. The deregulation of Foreign Direct Investment norms has led to an increase in FDI in the sector. India is currently the world's second-largest telecommunications market with a subscriber base of 1.18 billion. India's mobile economy is growing rapidly and currently constitutes more than 98 per cent of all telephone subscriptions. The mobile industry is expected to create a total economics value of ₹14 trillion (US$217.37 billion) by 2020.

Relevant Website : www.dot.gov.in

Tele-density

Tele-density, which denotes the number of telephones per 100 population is an important indicator of telecom penetration in any country. Tele-density in India-was 91.64 per cent at the end of November 2017. The rural tele-density is now 56.58 per cent while that in urban areas it is 167.50 per cent. Amongst the service areas, Himachal Pradesh (153.96 per cent) had the highest tele-density followed by Tamil Nadu (124.38 per cent), Punjab (123.62 per cent), Kerala

(118.58 per cent) and Gujarat (110,00 per cent). On the other hand, it is comparatively low in service areas such as Bihar (60.13 per cent), Assam (68.41 per cent), Madhya Pradesh (69,47 per cent), Uttar Pradesh (69.66 per cent), West Bengal (72.90 per cent) and Odisha (79.58 per cent), Amongst the metros, Delhi tops in tele-density with 259.14 per cent, followed by Kolkata (184.56 per cent) and Mumbai (169.97 per cent).

Internet and Broadband Penetration

The number of Internet subscribers (both broadband and narrowband put together) which was 422.18 million at the end of March, 2017 increased to 429.23 million by the end of September 2017. The number of subscribers accessing internet via wireless phones, etc., was 407.88 million at the end of September 2017. The number of wireline Internet subscribers was 21.35 million during the same period. The number of Broadband subscribers was 350.70 million at the end of November, 2017. There was a net increase of 7.05 million in the Internet subscribers during the period from March to September, 2017.

Research and Development

C-DOT, an autonomous body, is DoT's R&D arm. The organisation is committed to providing a wide range of cost-effective, indigenously developed and state-of-the-art total telecom solution. C-DOT has grown to the level of a national centre for R&D in communication technology in many areas- Satellite communications, IN, ATM, DWDM, NMS. Wireless Broadband, GPON, NGN and Mobile Cellular systems.

DoT has the following PSUs under its administrative control: (a) Bharat Sanchar Nigam Limtied (BSNL); (b) Mahanagar Telephone Nigam Limited (MTNL); (c) ITI Limited; (d) Telecommunications Consultants India Limited (TCIL); (e) Bharat Broadband Network Limited (BBNL); (f) Hemisphere Properties India Limited (HPIL).

Bharat Sanchar Nigam Limited

Bharat Sanchar Nigam Limited (BSNL), fully owned by Government of India, formed in October 2000, provides telecom services across the length and breadth of the country excluding Delhi and Mumbai. BSNL is providing all types of telecom services namely telephone services on landline, WLL and GSM mobile, broadband, internet, leased circuits and long distance telecom services. Rural telephony is one of its focus areas. BSNL also pays special emphasis on development of telecommunication facilities in North-Eastern region and in tribal areas as well as in the LWE affected areas.

Relevant Website : www.bsnl.co.in

Mahanagar Telephone Nigam Limited

Mahanagar Telephone Nigam Limited (MTNL), set up in 1986, is a Navratna PSU and provides telecommunication facilities in India's key metros - Delhi and Mumbai. MTNL is the principal provider of fixed-line telecommunication service in these two metropolitan cities, and for GSM mobile services in four peripheral towns of Noida, Gurgaon, Faridabad and Ghaziabad along with Delhi city and the areas falling under the Mumbai Municipal Corporation, New Mumbai Corporation and Thane Municipal Corporation along with Mumbai city, also come under the jurisdiction of the company. MTNL is providing triple play services i.e., voice, high speed internet and IPTV on its broadband network.

Relevant Website : www.mtnl.net.in

Indian Telephone Industries

Indian Telephone Industries (ITI) Limited was established in 1948, to supply telecom equipment to the then telecom service provider, DoT, ITI started its operations in Bengaluru in 1948, which were further extended to other areas by setting up manufacturing plants at Srinagar in Jammu and Kashmir, Naini, Rae Bareli and Mankapur in Uttar Pradesh, and Palakkad in Kerala. All the manufacturing plants are accreditied with ISO 9001-2000 standards. The establishment of these plants at various locations was aimed not only at the augmentation of manufacturing capacity but also at the development of social infrastructure.

Relevant Website : www.itiltd-india.com

Telecommunications Consultants India Limited

Telecommunications Consultants India Limited (TCIL) was set-up in 1978 with the main objective to provide world class technology in all fields of telecommunications and information technology to excel in its operations in overseas and in the domestic markets by developing proper marketing strategies, to acquire state of the art technology on a continuing basis and to maintain leadership. It has diversified into cyber parks, intelligent buildings, cyber and smart cities and upgradation of legacy networks by focusing on broadband, multimedia convergent service networks, entering new areas of IT and IT-enabled services. It is also developing telecom and IT training infrastructure abroad.

Relevant Website : www.tcil.india.com

Bharat Broadband Network Limited

Bharat Broadband Network Limited (BBNL) a Special Purpose Vehicle (SPV), namely, Bharat Broadband networks Limited (BBNL) was incorporated in 2012 under the Indian Companies Act, 1956 for execution of the Bharat Net for connecting 2.50 lakh (approximately) Gram Panchayats (GPs).

Relevant Website : www.bbnl.nic.in

Hemisphere Properties India Ltd

Hemisphere Properties India Limited (HPIL) is another PSU under DoT. At the time of 25 per cent stake strategic sale in Videsh Sanchar Nigam Limited

(Now Tata Communications Limited), surplus land measuring 773.13 acres was demarcated out of total 1230.13 acres of land at four stations and it was decided that surplus land will not be a part of disinvestment bid and would be managed by a separate realty company.

Vision of Digital India

The vision of Digital India aims to transform the country into a digitally empowered society and knowledge economy. The programme will be implemented in phases till 2018. This programme has been envisaged by Department of Electronics and Information Technology (DeitY). It would also bring in public accountability through mandated delivery of government's services electronically; a Unique ID and e-Pramaan based on authentic and standard based interoperable and integrated government applications and data basis. The source of funding for most of the e-governance projects at present is through budgetary provisions of respective ministries/ departments in the central or state governments. Requirements of funds for individual project(s) for Digital India will be worked out by respective nodal ministries/departments.

Scope of Digital India

The overall scope of this programme is: (a) to prepare India for a knowledge future; (b) on being transformative that is to realize IT (Indian Talent) + IT (Information Technology) = IT (India Tomorrow); (c) making technology central to enabling change; and (d) on being an Umbrella Programme-covering many departments.

The programme weaves together a large number of ideas and thoughts into a single, comprehensive vision, so that each of them is seen as part of a larger goal. Each individual element stands on its own, but is also part of the larger picture.The weaving together makes the Mission transformative in totality.

It will pull together many existing schemes which would be restructured and re-focused and implemented in a synchronized manner. The Common branding of the programmes as Digital India highlights their transformative impact.

Digital India aims to provide the much needed thrust to the nine pillars of growth areas, namely: (1) broadband highways; (2) universal access to mobile connectivity; (3) public internet access programme; (4) e-governance: reforming government through technology; (5) e-Kranti - electronic delivery of services; (6) information for all; (7) electronics manufacturing; (8) IT for Jobs; and (9) early harvest programmes.

Following initiatives have been taken under the Digital India programme. LIMBS (Legal Information and Management Based System) LIMBS is an easy to access, web-based tool for comprehensive, regulatory and proactive monitoring of court cases. It is a web-based platform which provides a common access portal to all users having varying needs and cutting across administration pyramids i.e., access is available right from the file dealer to the top management. LIMBS has use friendly data entry screen for capturing the details of court cases. Progress of court cases can be entered. Various MIS reports help to monitor these cases. E-document vault allows user to enter the important judgement. SMS alerts are used to sensitize the users over important issues.

National Data Sharing and Accessibility Programme

The objective of this policy is to facilitate the access to government owned shareable data and information in both human readable and machine readable forms through a network all over the country in a proactive updatable manner, within the framework of various related policies. Acts and rules of Government of India, thereby permitting wider accessibility and use of public data and information.

e-Office

The main objectives of e-office are:- (a) to improve efficiency, consistency and effectiveness of government responses; (b) to reduce turnaround time and to meet and demands of the citizens charter; (c) to provide for effective resource management to improve the quality of administration; (d) to reduce processing delays; (e) to establish transparency and accountability; and (f) the system will automate movement of files within government offices, etc.

9 Defence

ENHANCING safety and security of the country, providing humanitarian assistance and disaster relief during natural and man-made disasters, modernisation of the Armed Forces and supporting indigenisation and manufacturing of defence equipment through the 'Make -in-India' initiative have been the main features of the Ministry of Defence.

The security situation in Jammu and Kashmir despite a lot of challenges has been brought under control. Relentless operations by the army both, along the Line of Control and in the hinterland have thwarted the designs of giving a fillip to the proxy war being waged against India. Army along with CAPF and JKP continues to put in pressure to bring back normalcy to the Kashmir Valley. Intelligence based operations were launched along Indo-Myanmar border to maintain peace in the region and to effectively neutralise the terrorists. Indian Army continued with the people friendly operations to help the locals.

Second edition of 'Al Nagah' the joint exercise between the Indian and Oman Armies was held at Bakloh, Himachal Pradesh. Both armies shared valuable combat expertise on countering terrorist operations in an international environment. 'Surya Kiran-XI' was held wherein, infantry battalion of Indian Army and Durga Bahsh Battalion of Nepalese Army participated. Eleventh such battalion level exercise between the two countries aimed at training of troops in counter insurgency operations in mountainous terrain. It formally incorporated issues related to humanitarian assistance and disaster relief (HADR) and helped enhance defence co-operation and military relations between the two countries.

Twelfth edition of Indo-Mongolian Joint Military Exercise 'Nomadic Elephant' was held at Vairengte. Mongolian Army was represented by soldiers of the elite Special Forces Task Battalion while Indian Army was represented by a contingent of the Jammu and Kashmir Rifles. The exercise was aimed at training the troops in counter insurgency and counter terrorism operations under the United Nations mandate. As part of the Indo-US defence cooperation, a joint military training, exercise 'Yudh Abhyas-2017' was conducted in USA. The theme of the exercise was to build and develop military relations and inter-operability for conducting counter terrorism, regional security operations and peace keeping operations under UN Charter. The fifth Indo-Sri Lanka Joint Training Exercise 'Mitra Shakti 2017' was conducted in Pune. The exercise focused on counter terrorism operations in semi urban terrain.

First ever tri service exercise 'Indra' between India and Russia was conducted in Russia. Indo-Bangladesh exercise 'Sampriti' was conducted in Vairengte. It was aimed at carrying out operations against terrorists and insurgents on the lines of those in the J&K and NE. Indo-UK Joint Military Exercise. Indo-UK Exercise 'Ajeya Warrior' was conducted in Rajasthan. The training contingent comprised one company each from the Indian and British Army. The aim of the exercise was to build and promote bilateral relations and enhance interoperability while sharing experiences in counter terrorism and counter insurgency operations between the two countries.

As part of first military training being imparted by Indian Army to women officers from abroad, women officers of Afghan Army and Airforce were trained on basic military aspects including physical, weapon training, tactics, communication skills and leadership in chennai.

Ministry of Defence and its Departments

The principal task of the Ministry is to frame policy directions on defence and security related matters and communicate them for implementation to the services headquarters, inter-service organisations, production establishments and research and development organisations. It is required to ensure effective implementation of the government's policy directions and the execution of approved programmes within the allocated resources. The principal functions of the Departments include: dealing with the Integrated Defence Staff (IDS) and three Services and various Inter Service Organisations. It is also responsible for the Defence Budget, establishment matters, defence policy, matters relating to Parliament, defence co-operation with foreign countries and co-ordination of all defence related activities.; the Department of Defence Production deals with matters pertaining to defence production, indigenisation of imported stores, equipment and spares, planning and control of departmental production units of the ordnance factory board and Defence Public Sector Undertakings (DPSUs).; the Department of Defence Research and Development advises the government on scientific aspects of military equipment and logistics and the formulation of research, design and development plans for equipment required by the Services.; and the Department of Ex-Servicemen Welfare deals with all resettlement, welfare and pensionary matters of Ex-Servicemen.

Relevant Websites : www.mod.gov.in www.mod.gov.in/dod
www.ddp.mod.gov.in www.drdo.gov.in
www.desw.gov.in

Army

Global and regional geo-political and geo-strategic issues affect and shape India's security environment. The Indian Army plays a pivotal role in the nation's security construct. External threats to India primarily emanate from the territorial disputes and contested borders with two neighbours. The Indian Army remains resiliently committed in braving the harsh terrain and weather on a daily basis along the national frontiers, to protect the territorial integrity of the nation. Manifestation of sub conventional conflicts is being witnessed in the form of proxy war and insurgency. The Indian Army is at the forefront in combating the internal security challenges in conjunction with other security agencies. The Indian Army is also exploiting its core competencies in training the CAPFs and state police forces towards enhancing their operational employment in combating Left Wing Extremism.

The transportation, logistic and medical infrastructure required for the Army's pan-Indian operational deployment, especially in the remote and border areas, accrue benefits for the local population for humanirarian assistance and disaster relief. The Indian Army also contributes to sand dunes, soil and water conservation. In addition, the Indian Army Training Teams in 10 countries across the world continue to play an important role in training and building the armies of these countries.

Modernisation of the Infantry is being progressed based on five sub system, i.e. lethality, survivability, mobility, situational awareness and sustainability. Artillery would be inducting a variety of gun systems to enhance its long range firepower. Artillery is graduating to an effect based precision targeting capability and has identified key technologies for development. Army Aviation provides the fourth dimensional combat support in terms of reconnaissance, surveillance, direction of artillery fire, support to manoeuvre forces as well as causality evacuation from the battlefield. The Indian Army is committed to enhance its overall effectiveness by revamping its equipment profile and human resource through the tools of technology and innovations. Indian Army is one of the largest troop contributor to UN missions with presence in UN missions.

Relevant Website : www.indianarmy.nic.in

Navy

The raison d'etre of navies is to safeguard the nation's use of seas for its legitimate sovereign purpose, whilst concurrently guarding against inimical use of the sea by others. The full range of operations in which the naval forces may be involved is vast, ranging from high intensity war fighting at one end and humanitarian assistance and disaster relief operations at the other end. This broad continuum of operations can be broken down into distinct roles at each demanding a specific approach to the conduct of operations. Through the discharge of roles, the Indian Navy (IN) acts as the prime enabler and guarantor of the country's maritime sovereignty and myriad use of sea activities. Accordingly, the main roles that IN undertakes are - military, diplomatic, constabulary and benign.

Relevant Website : www.indiannavy.nic.in

Military Role

The primary military objective of the IN is to deter any military adventurism against the country, including intervention in India's affairs and subversive strategies against the national interests and the ability to inflict a crushing defeat on the adversary in the event of hostilities. The ways and means of deterrence by the IN include conventional deterrence by both denial and punishment, by maintaining a robust military capability and posture to convince potential aggressors of high costs and limited gains from any aggression or intervention against India's national interests. India has a long coastline, numerous Island Territories, a vast Maritime Zone, substantial energy infrastructure and other vital assets in the littoral area; besides a large vibrant population, significant portions of which also live in the littoral. Since there are no physical barriers at sea, security of these areas and assets are inherently vulnerable to sea-borne threats, and enhancing their security is a prime objective of the IN in the Military role. The IN has also been designated as the agency responsible for overall Maritime Security including Coastal Security and Offshore Security.

Whilst countering traditional maritime security threats will remain the raison d'etre of the IN, the growths of non-traditional threats in the recent years have necessitated the development of a fresh paradigm for maritime security. There has been a steady rise in non-traditional threats, in occurrence and scale, with the lines at times getting blurred with traditional challenges. This is especially the case where non-traditional threats receive cooperation, support and sponsorship from traditional entities. India is a maritime nation and the economy is critically dependent on the seas for conduct of trade. More than 90 per cent of the trade by volume and 77 per cent by value are transported over the seas. India's reliance on maritime trade for economic growth necessitates due protection of the merchant marine and sea - borne trade.

Over the past years, India's strategic and security interests in the northern IOR and surrounding areas from the Strait of Malacca to the Gulf of Aden have grown. As a responsible nation and benign maritime neighbour, enforcement of international laws, humanitarian assistance and disaster relief in the IOR would continue to remain at the forefront of our international commitments. Towards this end, the IN is being increasingly called upon to address issues pertaining to security and stability in the region. The IN, by virtue of its capability, strategic positioning and presence in the IOR, has been a catalyst for peace and stability in the region. The complex maritime security environment in the IOR requires the IN to maintain a high operational tempo and readiness at all time. Besides a large number of operational deployments, IN has successfully undertaken exercises with numerous navies of friendly foreign countries. In addition, the IN also engages with friendly neighbouring countries to undertake coordinated patrols in common areas of interest. These exercises and patrols have helped strengthening bilateral relationship, cementing the professional ties and streamlining inter-operability issues.

As part of its 'Constabulary Role', the IN is involved in operations like anti-poaching, anti-smuggling, coastal surveillance and anti-piracy. Over the past years, India's strategic and security interests in the northern IOR and surrounding areas from the Strait of Malacca to the Gulf of Aden have grown. As a responsible nation and benign maritime neighbour, enforcement of international laws, humanitarian assistance and disaster relief in the IOR would continue to remain at the forefront of our international commitments. Towards this end, the IN is being increasingly called upon to address issues pertaining to security and stability in the region. The IN, by virtue of its capability, strategic positioning and presence in the IOR, has been a catalyst for peace and stability in the region. The complex maritime security environment in the IOR requires the IN to maintain a high operational tempo and readiness at all times. Besides a large number of operational deployments, IN has successfully undertaken exercises with numerous navies of friendly foreign countries. In addition, the IN also engages with friendly neighbouring countries to undertake coordinated patrols in common areas of interest. These exercises and patrols have helped strengthening bilateral relationship, cementing the professional ties and streamlining inter-operability issues.

Air Force

The Indian Air Force (IAF) has always encouraged development of indigenous defence production capability and capacities. Its quest for operating indigenously built platform and supporting self-reliance has resulted in significant progress on various systems in the IAF. The Defence Procurement Procedure, 2016 assigned highest preference to 'Make' and Buy (Indian-Indigenously Designed and Developed Manufacturer (IDDM)) categories. LCA Mk-1A, Light Combat Helicopter (LCH), AWACS (India) and High Frequency Radio set are some of the cases being progressed through the IDDM route.

Relevant Website : www.indianairforce.nic.in

Make in India

One of the main focus areas of the IAF is to support indigenisation and manufacturing of defence equipment, thus reducing dependence on import of defence equipment. Light Combat Aircraft, Akash Missile, Advance Light Helicopters (ALH) have already been inducted, thus giving impetus to indigenisation. Further, IAF plans to induct more capable and potent LCA Mk-1A in the future. IAF is also actively supporting DoD of LCH, RPAs, Medium Power Radars, Low Level Tracking Radars and other systems. IAF is also closely coordinating with DRDO for development of various types of state-of-art-weapons. Modernisation plan is being pursued to beef up the defence manufacturing base and the eco system. IAF has already identified series of defence equipment that can be manufactured under 'Make' category. MoD has been striving to include the private sector in production of defence equipment. Various projects under 'Strategic Partner' model will give impetus to 'Make in India' initiative. This will not only generate employment, enhance skill level but also assist in harnessing key technologies for growth of aerospace sector in the country.

Digital India Initiative

IAF has established pan IAF captive 3 G WCDMA Mobile Network AFCEL. The network has been fully operational with voice call and data services. In-house initiatives have also seen development of the apps like: Instant Messaging App (AFCHAT); IAF Directory Search App; Conference Scheduler App; Caller-IDApp; Air Force Central Accounts Office (AFCAO) App and Website; Med Watch App.

Women Empowerment

Avani Chaturvedi, Bhawana Kanth and Mohana Singh created history in 2016 by becoming the first women pilots to be commissioned into the fighter stream. These women pilots, now Flying Officers, have been posted to MiG-2 Bison and Hawk units as Sqn Pilots on successful completion of their fighter flying training. A second batch of women cadets also have been selected in fighter stream. Presently, they are completing Stage-II (Fighter) training at Air Force Station Hakimpet and are expected to be commissioned into the Fighter stream after successful completion of their training.

Commissioned Ranks

The following are the commissioned ranks in the three Services; each rank is shown opposite its equivalent in the other Service:

Army	Navy	Air Force
General	Admiral	Air Chief Marshal
Lieutenant General	Vice Admiral	Air Marshal
Major General	Rear Admiral	Air Vice Marshal
Brigadier	Commodore	Air Commodore
Colonel	Captain	Group Captain
Lieutenant Colonel	Commander	Wing Commander
Major	Lieutenant Commander	Squadron Leader
Captain	Lieutenant	Flight Lieutenant
Lieutenant	Sub Lieutenant	Flying Officer

Indian Coast Guard

Indian Coast Guard was constituted in 1977 with following charter of duties: (a) safety and protection of artificial islands, offshore terminals and installations; (b) protection to fishermen including assistance to them at sea while in distress; (c) preserve and protect maritime environment and to prevent and control marine pollution; (d) assisting Customs and other authorities in anti-smuggling operations; (e) safety of life and property at sea and collection of' scientific data; (f) enforcing the provisions of various enactments in the maritime zones.

Relevant Website : www.indiancoastguard.gov.in

Recruitment

The Armed Forces epitomize the ideals of service, sacrifice, patriotism and composite culture of the country. Recruitment to the Armed Forces is voluntary and open to all citizens of India irrespective of caste, class, religion and community provided the laid down physical, medical and educational criteria are met.

Commissioned Officers in the Armed Forces are recruited mainly through UPSC which conducts the following two All India Competitive Examinations:

(a) National Defence Academy (NDA) and Naval Academy (NA): The UPSC holds entrance examination twice a year for entry into the NDA and NA. Candidates on completion of 10+2 examination or while in the 12th standard are eligible to compete. Having cleared UPSC written examination, eligible candidates undergo Service Selection Board (SSB) interview, which lasts for five days. On being medically fit and coming in NDA merit list, successful candidates join the NDA or NA as per their option of service exercised at the time of applying. On completion of the course, they are sent to the respective Service Academies for their pre-commissioning training.

(b) Combined Defence Services Examination (CDSE): CDSE is conducted by the UPSC twice a year. University graduates or those in final year ofgraduation are eligible to appear in the examination. Candidates qualifying in written examination have to undergo SSB interview and medical tests. Candidates whose names appear in the merit list undergo basic military training of 18 months at Indian Military Academy/Air Force Academy and Naval Academy for Permanent Commission and 11 months at Officers Training Academy (OTA) to become Short Service Commissioned Officers (SSCOs). SSCOs can serve for a duration of 10 years extendable to 14 years. However, they can opt for permanent commission after completion of 10 years or seek release after completion of five years of service, which is considered on case to case basis.

Recruitment in Army

Apart from the UPSC entries, Commissioned officers are also recruited in the Army through the following entries:

(a) University Entry Scheme : Pre-Final year students in the notified engineering disciplines are eligible to apply for Permanent Commission in the Technical Arms of the Army as Commissioned Officers under the UES. Eligible candidates are selected through a campus interview by the Screening Teams deputed by the Army Headquarters. These candidates are required to appear before SSB and Medical Board. Successful candidates undergo one year pre-commission training at the Indian Military Academy (IMA), Dehradun. Cadets through this entry are also entitled to one year ante-date seniority on commissioning.

(b) Technical Graduates Course (TGC): Engineering graduates from notified discipline of engineering, post graduates with minimum second division aggregate marks in notified discipline for Army Education Corps and M.Sc. in Agriculture/Dairy for Military Farm are eligible to apply for Permanent Commission through this entry. After the SSB and the Medical Board, the selected candidates are required to undergo one year pre-commissioned training at the IMA, Dehradun. Engineering Graduates through this entry are also entitled to one year ante-date seniority on commissioning.

(c) Short Service Commission (Technical) Entry: The Short Service Commission (Technical) Entry Scheme provides avenue for recruitment to eligible technical graduates/post graduates into Technical Arms. After SSB and medical Board, the selected candidates are required to undergo approximately 49 weeks pre-commission training at OTA, Chennai. On completion of training, they are inducted as Short Service Commissioned Officers. Cadets through this entry are also entitled to one year's ante-date seniority on commissioning.

(d) 10+2 Technical Entry Scheme (TES): Candidates who have qualified 10+2 CBSE/ICSE/State Board Examination with minimum aggregate of 70 per cent marks in Physics, Chemistry and Mathematics are eligible to apply for commission under the 10+2(TES). On being successful in the SSB and being declared fit by the medical board, they undergo one year basic military training at the Officers Training Academy, Gaya and thereafter undergo three years engineering degree course in respective streams before getting Permanent Commission. On being commissioned, they are further put through one year of post commissioning training for the Arm/Service into which they are commissioned.

(e) Short Service Commission (Women): Eligible women candidates are recruited in the Army as Short Service Commission Officers. Commission is granted in Corps of Electronics and Mechanical Engineers, Corps of Engineers, Signals, Army Educational Corps, Military Intelligence Corps, Judge Advocate General's Branch, Army Supply Corps, Army Ordnance Corps and Army Air Defence. Women are offered Short Service Commission in three streams viz. Non-Technical Graduate, Technical and Post Graduate/Specialist for a period of ten years, extendable by additional four years purely on voluntary basis. Recently, Government of India had granted option for permanent commission for officers in Army Education Corps and Judge Advocate General Branch after completion of 10 years of service. The duration of training is 49 weeks at Officers Training Academy, Chennai. For Short Service Commission Women (Technical) Entry, passed or final year/semester students of B.E/B.Tech in notified streams are eligible to apply. Eligible candidates appear for direct SSB interview and Medical Test, thereafter. The applicants for Non-Technical Graduate, however, is required to apply through UPSC and after written examination, come up for SSB interview as is being done for Short Service Commissioned male officers. A total of 20 per cent allotted seats from Non-Technical stream have been reserved for NCC 'C' certificate holders women candidates with minimum 'B' grade and 50 per cent aggregate marks in graduation examination. The applications will be routed through NCC Directorate, Integrated Headquarters of Ministry of Defence (Army), as applicable for male officers. For Judge Advocate General Branch, applications are invited from Law Graduates with minimum 55 per cent, for direct SSB interviews. Widows of Defence Personnel who meet the laid down eligibility criteria are granted four years age relaxation and 5 per cent seats of each course (2.5 each in Tech and Non-Tech) are reserved for them.

Short Service Commission Women (Tech), NCC entry and Judge Advocate General Branch are exempted from written examinations and need to apply directly to Additional Directorate General of Recruiting, Integrated Headquarters of Ministry of Defence (Army). The notification is published along with SSCW (Tech) twice a year.

(f) NCC (Special Entry Scheme): University graduates possessing NCC 'C' Certificate with minimum 'B' grade and 50 per cent aggregate marks in graduation examination are eligible to apply for Short Service Commission through this entry. Those studying in third year are allowed to apply provided they have secured minimum 50 per cent aggregate marks in first two years. Such candidates will need to secure overall aggregate of minimum 50 per cent marks if selected in interview failing which his candidature will be cancelled. Candidates must possess graduation degree at the time of joining OTA or those candidates studying in third year should be able to produce the degree within 12 weeks from date of commencement of training at OTA. Such cadets have to undergo SSB interview followed by a medical board. Candidates meeting the qualitative requirements have to apply through NCC Group Headquarters at the State level. After Screening by respective Group Headquarters, Directorate General of NCC forwards the applications of eligible cadets to the Recruiting Directorate of Integrated Headquarters of Ministry of Defence (Army).

(g) Judge Advocate General Entry: Law graduate with minimum 55 per cent aggregate marks in LLB, age between 21 to 27 years can apply for Judge Advocate General Branch. Eligible candidates are called for direct SSB interview and medical test, thereafter. It is a Short Service Commission Entry wherein suitable candidates can opt for Permanent Commission.

Recruitment of Junior Commissioned Officers and Other Ranks (JCOs and ORs): In the Army, there are eleven Zonal Recruiting Offices, two Gorkha Recruiting Depots, one Independent Recruiting Office and 59 Army Recruiting Offices in addition to 48 Regimental Centers which carry out recruitment through rallies in their respective areas of jurisdiction. Recruitment of JCOs and OR is carried out through Online Application System for Soldier General Duty, Soldier Tradesman, Soldier Technical, Soldier Clerk/Store Keeper Trade and Soldier Nursing Assistant categories. However, for categories like Religious Teacher JCO (RT JCO), Havildar Education, Havildar Auto Cartographer and JCO Catering, application system is being followed. The current recruitment for JCOs and OR comprises screening of aspiring candidates at rally site in the 1.6 km run followed by document checking, physical fitness tests, physical measurements, and medical examination. This is followed by a written examination for the candidates who are found eligible in all respects. Finally, selected candidates are dispatched to respective Training Centers for training. Efforts are made so that each district of the country is covered at least once by recruitment rallies in a recruitment year.

Recruitment in Indian Navy

The Method of Recruitment: The recruitment system of the IN is a streamlined, transparent, expeditious and candidate friendly procedure. There are two modes of induction in the IN, viz. UPSC Entry and Non-UPSC Entry.

(a) UPSC Entry: The UPSC holds an examination, twice a year, for entry into the National Defence Academy (NDA) and Indian Naval Academy (INA) as Permanent Commission (PC) entries. Candidates are eligible to compete on completion of the 10+2 (PCM) Examination or while in the 12th standard. UPSC short lists candidates after written examinations. Thereafter, candidates are sent to the Service Selection Boards located at Bengaluru, Bhopal, Coimbatore and Visakhapatam. Results of qualified candidates are forwarded to UPSC for making the final merit list. Medically fit candidates, who are in the merit list, are intimated for appointment to NDA/INA as cadets. On completion of the NDA/INA training, the Naval Cadets are sent to training ships at Kochi for Naval sea training. For the Graduate Special Entry, the UPSC holds the Combined Defence Services Examination (CDSE), twice a year. Graduates with B Tech degree are also eligible to appear in the examination. Successful candidates join the Indian Naval Academy at Ezhimala, Kerala for the Naval Orientation Course (NOC).

(b) Non-UPSC Entry: The Non-UPSC entries cater for both Permanent Commission (PC) and Short Service Commission (SSC). In this case the applications are invited and short listed at IHQ MoD (Navy). Subsequently the short listed candidates are then sent for Service Selection Boards (SSB) interviews. Thereafter, a merit list, comprising qualified candidates, is prepared as per the availability of vacancies. Recruitment for non-UPSC entries is made through SSBs for the Executive, Engineering including Naval Architects, Electrical Engineering and the Education Branches/cadres of Navy.

(c) 10+2 (Cadet Entry Scheme): This scheme is for permanent commission in the Executive, Engineering and Electrical branches of the IN. Under this scheme, candidates with 10+2 (PCM) qualifications, after selection through the Services Selection Board, are sent to the Indian Naval Academy for the B Tech Course. On successful completion of the course they are granted Permanent Commission in the Executive, Electrical and Engineering branches of the Indian Navy.

(d) University Entry Scheme (UES): The UES has been re-launched as a Short Service Commission Scheme. Seventh and Eighth semester Engineering college students are eligible for induction into the Executive and Technical Branches of the IN. Naval selection teams from the IHQ of MoD (Navy) and Command Headquarters visit AICTE approved engineering colleges, across the country, to short-list the candidates. The short-listed candidates, based on All India Merit, undergo interview at the Services Selection Board. The successful candidates are, thereafter, put through medical tests. Final selection is based on all India merit on the basis of marks obtained in the SSB interviews and availability of vacancies.

(e) Women Officers: Women are being inducted into the Navy, as Short Service Commission (SSC) officers in the Executive (Observer, ATC, Law and Logistic), Education Branch and the Naval Architecture cadre of the Engineering Branch.

(f) Permanent Commission to SSC Officers: The Government has introduced grant of Permanent Commission prospectively to the Short Service Commission officers, for both men and women, of the Executive Branch (Law Cadre), Education Branch and Engineering Branch (Naval Architecture) w.e.f. 2008.

(g) Recruitment through NCC: University graduates possessing Naval Wing NCC 'C' certificate with minimum 'B' grading and 50 per cent marks in the graduation degree examination are inducted in the Navy as regular commissioned officers. These graduates are exempted from appearing in the CDSE conducted by the UPSC and are selected through the SSB interview only. They join the Indian Naval Academy for Naval Orientation Course (NOC) along with the CDSE cadets.

(h) Special Naval Architecture Entry Scheme: The Government has approved the induction of Naval Architect officers into the Engineering Branch of the Indian Navy, as Short Service Commissioned Officers, under a 'Special Naval Architects Entry Scheme' (SNAES). An empowered Naval team visits IIT Kharagpur, IIT Chennai, Cochin University of Science and Technology (CUSAT) and Andhra University, where B Tech (Naval Architecture) courses are conducted, to select candidates through campus interviews. The selected candidates undergo medical examination at the nearest Military Hospital and if found fit, are selected for training.

(i) Recruitment of Sailors: Recruitment into the Navy is carried out on all India basis on state-wise merit of the eligible recruitable male population, as per the number of vacancies available. The number of personnel recruited from a particular state depends on the number of eligible applicants who are able to qualify in the written examination, physical fitness test, and medical examination and their relative position in the merit. There is no quota of vacancies based on caste/creed or religion. Advertisements in all leading National and Regional newspapers and Employment News are published inviting applications from eligible volunteers. Publicity material is also dispatched to a large number of schools/ colleges and all Zilla Sainik Boards. The local administration carries out the publicity drive in rural/ backward areas through local media.

Types of Entries: The various entries, for recruitment of sailors, are as follows (with educational qualifications indicated against each):

(a) Artificer Apprentices (AAs) - 10+2 (PCM).

(b) Senior Secondary Recruits (SSR) - 10+2 (Sc.).

(c) Matric Entry Recruits (MER), for recruitment of Cooks, Stewards and Musicians - Matriculation.

(d) Non Matric Recruits (NMR), for recruitment of Topass Sailors (Safaiwala) - Class VI.

(e) Direct Entry (Outstanding Sportsmen).

Recruitment in Indian Air Force

Selection of Officers

(a) Induction of Officers: Induction to National Defence Academy (NDA) and Combined Defence Service Examination (CDSE) entries are through UPSC. The non-UPSC entries for induction into the officer's cadre are: SSC (Men and Women) Flying, NCC Entry (PC for men), ASC (PC for men), GDOC(Non Tech) (PC for Men), Airmen Entry (PC for Air Warriors), SSS (Technical) (Men and Women) and SSC (Non Tech) (Men and Women).

(b) Recruitment through Service Selection: Recruitment through Service Selection Boards/Air Force Selection Boards is made for the Flying (Pilot), Aeronautical Engineering (Electronics), Aeronautical Engineering (Mechanical), Education, Administration, Logistics, Accounts and meteorology branches for the Air Force.

(c) University Entry Scheme: Final/pre-final year students in engineering disciplines are eligible for induction into the technical branches of Air Force as permanent commissioned officers under the University Entry Scheme.

(d) Recruitment of Women Officers: Eligible women are recruited as Short Service Commissioned Officers in the Flying, Aeronautical Engineering (Electronics), Aeronautical Engineering (Mechanical), Education, Administration, Logistics, Accounts and Meteorology branches of the IAF.

(e) Recruitment through National Cadet Corps (NCC): University graduates possessing NCC 'C' Certificate with minimum 'B' grading and 50 per cent marks in graduation are inducted in Navy and Air Force as Regular Commissioned Officers by way of selection through the Service Selection Boards. For Flying Branch Cadets should have Maths and Physics as main subjects in 10+2 level.

(f) Recruitment of Personnel Below officers Rank (PBORs): The selection of candidates for Personnel below officers Rank (PBORs) is carried out through a centralized selection system on all India basis in which Central Airmen Selection Board (CASB) assisted by 14 Airmen Selection Centres (ASCs) located at different parts of the country, carries out the recruitment.

Training

A large number of training institutions in the Defence Sector work in coordination with one another. While some institutions train personnel from all the 3 services viz. Army, Navy and Air Force, some cater to the training needs of the individual services.

Training of Tri-Services

National Defence College

The National Defence College is a premier training institution of the Ministry of Defence which has established a name for itself as a centre of excellence on matters pertaining to National Security and Strategic Studies. Selected Armed forces officers of the rank of Brigadier/equivalent from Indian and Foreign Armed Forces and Civil Services officers of equivalent status of director and above are nominated for training at the college. The officers undergo an eleven months programme with focus on national Security, covering all dimensions of domestic, regional and international issues to equip future policy makers with background necessary to get a broad understanding of the multifarious economic, political, military scientific and organizational aspects that are essential for planning of national strategy.

Relevant Website : www.ndc.nic.in

College of Defence Management

The College of Defence Management (CDM) is the only tri-service training institution in the country which imparts defence management education to senior officers of the three services, para military forces, officers of the Ministry of Defence and international participants at the conceptual, directional and the functional levels. The College also hosts a number of civilian and foreign delegations on defence management training. To meet the requirements of 'Higher Defence Management' education in the Indian Armed Forces, necessitated by the 'Revolution in Military Affairs', CDM has optimised its existing training infrastructure and yearly trains approximately 500 officers annually. CDM has also developed tailor made capsule courses/ Management Development Programmes (MDPs) for management education at all levels in the Indian Armed Forces. These MDPs are also subscribed by large number of Friendly Foreign countries.

Relevant Website : www.cdm.ap.nic.in

Defence Services Staff College

Defence Services Staff College (DSSC) is an Armed Forces Training Institute (AFTI), which conducts staff course for the selected officers of the three services and also the officers from the central civil services. In addition, defence officers from friendly foreign countries also subscribe to the Staff Course conducted by the college. The officers passing out from DSSC are awarded Master of Science (MSc) in Defence and Stràtegic Studies from Chennai University.

Relevant Website : www.dssc.gov.in

National Defence Academy

National Defence Academy (NDA) is a premier tri-service institution which trains cadets of all three services before inducting them into their respective pre-commissioning training academies. Intake to NDA is organised through UPSC examination which is conducted twice in a year in the month of April and September. Applicants are required to be XII Standard pass and in the age bracket of 16 ½ to 19 ½ years at the time of joining. The three years course at NDA is covered in six semesters and cadets are awarded with BA/ BSc Degree. On conclusion of this training the cadets proceed to their respective Service Academies for further service specific training before being commissioned as officers in the Armed Forces.

Relevant Website : www.nda.nic.in

Indian Military Academy

Founded in 1932, Indian Military Academy (IMA), Dehradun aims at the fullest development of intellectual, moral and physical qualities of persons joining the Army as officers. The various modes of entry into IMA are: (a) on graduation from NDA.; (b) on graduation from Army Cadet College, which is a wing of the IMA itself.; (c) direct entry graduate cadets, who qualify the Union Public Service Commission Exam and get through the Service Selection Board.; (d) for Technical Graduate's Course (TGC).; (e) under university entry scheme (UES) for engineering college students in Final/ Pre-Final year of studies. The IMA also imparts training to Gentlemen Cadets from friendly countries.

Officers Training Academy

Established in 1963, the Officers Training School (OTS) was re-designated as Officers Training Academy (OTA) from 1988 on completion of 25 years of its existence. Its main task, before 1965 was to train Gentlemen Cadets for grant of Emergency Commission. From 1965 onwards, the Academy trains cadets for Short Service Commission. With the entry of women officers in the Army since 1992, around 100 lady officers now get commissioned from OTA every year in Army Service Corps, Judge Advocate General's Department, Corps of Engineers, Signals and Electrical and Mechanical Engineers.

Officers Training Academy

The Academy was commissioned in 2011. The training capacity as of now is around 400 gentlemen cadets. The capacity will be progressively built up to a strength of 750 gentlemen cadets. OTA, Gaya imparts training for the following: (a) 10+2 Technical Entry Scheme; (b) Special Commissioned Officers;

The OTA, Gaya also imparts training to Gentlemen Cadets from friendly countries.

National Cadet Corps

The National Cadet Corps (NCC) was established in 1948 as an Indian military cadet corps. It is a tri-services organisation open to school and college students. It has completed 69 years of its existence. The NCC strives to provide the youth of the country opportunities for all round development with a sense of commitment, dedication, self-discipline and moral values, so that they become responsible citizens and can take their place in all walks of life in the service of the nation. The motto of NCC is "Unity and Discipline". The total sanctioned strength of NCC cadets is 15 lakh. This includes two lakh NCC cadet strength sanctioned in the year 2010 that is being absorbed in five phases @ 40,000 cadets per year. NCC's presence extends to 703 out of 716 districts in the country covering 16,288 institutions.

The enrolment policy of Senior Division/Senior Wing cadets has been changed from 2 years to 3 years. It would result in improvement in training standards and quality output of cadets. NCC has been introduced as an additional/elective subject in Class X and XII. This would make NCC more attractive and cadets would be able to score credit points in their academic results.

Relevant Website : www.nccindia.nic.in

Sainik Schools

The Sainik Schools were established as a joint venture of the central and state government. These are under the overall governance of Sainik Schools Society. At present, there are 26 Sainik Schools located in various parts of the country. The objectives of Sainik Schools include bringing quality public school education within the reach of the common man, all round development of a child's personality and to remove regional imbalance in the officer's cadre of the Armed Forces. The Sainik Schools have shown an upward trend in the number of cadets joining the National Defence Academy in keeping with the primary aim of establishing of Sainik Schools to prepare boys academically, physically and mentally for entry into the National Defence Academy.

Rashtriya Military Schools

There are five Rashtriya Military Schools in the country at Belgaum and Bengaluru in Karnataka, Chail in Himachal Pradesh and Ajmer and Dholpur in Rajasthan. These schools are CBSE affiliated fully residential public schools which function under the aegis of Ministry of Defence. Boys are admitted in class VI and IX based on the results of Common Entrance Test. 70 per cent seats are reserved for wards to JCOs/ORs of Army, Navy and Air Force (including ex-servicemen) and balance 30 per cent for wards of officers of Army, Navy and Air Force (including retired officers) and wards of civilians. A total of 50 seats are reserved for wards of service personnel killed in action. 15 per cent and 7.5 per cent seats are reserved for SC and ST respectively in all categories.

Relevant Website : www.rashtriyamilitaryschools.in

Rashtriya Indian Military College

Rashtriya Indian Military College (RIMC) was established in 1922 with the objective of providing necessary preliminary training for boys of Indian birth or domicile, wishing to become officers in the Armed Forces of India. The institution now serves as a feeder institute to the National Defence Academy. Selection for RIMC is through an All India Entrance Examination comprising a written examination and viva voce. Seats for different States are reserved based on population. The college admits boys in class VIII. 25 cadets are admitted in each term twice a year (January and July) on the basis of All India Entrance Examination without any reservation.

Relevant Website : www.rimc.gov.in

College of Military Engineering

The College of Military Engineering at Pune is a premier technical institution conducting training for personnel of the Corps of Engineers, other Arms and Services, Navy, Air Force, Para Military Forces, Police and Civilians, besides, personnel from friendly foreign countries. CME is affiliated to Jawaharlal Nehru University (JNU) for the award of B.Tech and M. Tech degrees. All India Council for Technical Education (AICTE) also recognizes the graduate and post-graduate courses run by the CME.

Defence Production

Department of Defence Production was set up in 1962 with the objective of developing and promoting the industrial base for production of weapons, equipment, platforms and materials required by armed forces for defence of the country. Over the years, the Department has established wide range of production facilities for various defence equipment through the Ordnance Factories and Defence Public Sector Undertakings (DPSUs). The products manufactured include arms and ammunition, tanks, armoured vehicles, heavy vehicles, fighter aircraft and helicopters, warships, submarines, missiles, ammunition, electronic equipment, earth moving equipment, special alloys and special purpose steels.

The Department promulgated Defence Production Policy which aims at achieving substantive self-reliance in design, development and production of equipment/weapon systems in a scheduled time frame.

Ordnance Factories

The Indian Ordance Factories organisation - a family of 41 ordnance factories under the aegis of its corporate headquarters Ordnance Factory Board, Kolkata - possesses the unique distinction of over 200 year experience in defence production. The organisation is engaged in production, testing, logistics, research, development and marketing of a comprehensive product range in the area of land, sea and air systems. Indian Ordnance Factories is the oldest and largest industrial setup which functions under the Department of Defence Production. The ordnance factories factories form an integrated base for indigenous production of defence hardware and equipment, with the primary objective of self reliance in equipping the armed forces with state-of-the-art battlefield equipment

Ordnance Factory Board (OFB) is working on a number of R&D projects,to provide state-of-the-art battlefield equipment and ammunition to the Services. These include bi-modular charge system for 155mm x 45 calibre 'Dhanush' Gun Armament Upgrade of BMP-II etc. OFB along with DRDO is working on various R&D projects to enhance self-reliance in important arms and ammunitions required by the Forces, 7.62 x 51mm Assault Rifle, Protective Carbine, under Barrel Grenade Launcher Ammunition etc. Besides this, 13 Ordnance Development Centres of OFB are engaged in development of futuristic requirements of the Forces such as 'Futuristic Infantry Combat Vehicle'. 'Air Defence Gun for Army', 'Mounted Gun System', for which OFB has associated with IITs and other Institutions of repute for indigenous development of technologies and products.

Relevant Website : www.ofbindia.gov.in

Defence Undertakings

Hindustan Aeronautics Limited: Hindustan Aeronautics Limited (HAL), established in 1940, is a premier aeronautical Company of Asia. HAL, a *Navratna* DPSU with 20 production Divisions and 11 R&D centers spread across the country in nine geographical locations. HAL's expertise encompasses Design and Development, production, repair, overhaul and upgrade of Aircraft, Helicopters, Aero-engines, Accessories, Avionics and Systems. HAL is providing maintenance support to Indian Defence Services for all the fleet supplied by HAL including fleet such as HS-748, Cheetah / Chetak etc for which OEMs have discontinued their support. The Company also supports non-HAL produced Aircraft and engines like Mirage 2000, An-32, Seaking helicopter modules, Gnome engine, TM-333 2B2 Engine etc. HAL's maintenance support to Indian Army and to Coast Guard is 100 per cent of their fleet and in respect of Indian Air Force and Indian Navy it is 75 per cent and 61 per cent. HAL has positioned itself as a comprehensive solution provider to the Indian Defence Services for aviation requirements that include trainer, fighter, transport aircraft and light helicopters.

Relevant Website : www.hal-india.co.in

Bharat Electronics Limited: Bharat Electronics Limited (BEL) a Navaratna PSU, was established in 1954. BEL has nine manufacturing units across India. The company has core competency in areas of Defence Communications, Radars & Missile Systems, Sonars & Fire Control Systems, Electronic Warfare and Avionics Systems, Network Centric Systems, Electro-Optics, Tank Electronics, Home Land Security etc. Around 88 per cent of turnover comes from these business segments. In the non-defence area, BEL manufactures Electronic Voting Machines (EVMs), Tablet PCs (BEL designed), Doppler Weather Radars, large variety of components like integrated circuits, hybrid micro circuits, semiconductor devices, solar cells, etc. Apart from these, BEL also has presence in the areas of Access Control systems and select non-defence applications.

Relevant Website : www.bel-india.in

BEML Limited: Bharat Earth Movers Limited (BEML), incorporated in 1964, is a Mini-Ratna (Category-I) Public Sector Undertaking, under the Ministry of Defence engaged in the design, development, manufacturing and after-sales -

service of a wide range of products for core sectors of economy such as coal, mining, steel, cement, power, irrigation, construction, road building, Defence, Railway and Metro transportation system and Aerospace. BEML operates in three business segments-mining and construction, defence and aerospace, rail and metro and international business division for export activities.

Relevant Website : www.bemlindia.in

Bharat Dynamics Limited: Bharat Dynamics Limited (BDL) a Mini Ratna Category-I Company was incorporated in 1970 under the Ministry of Defence. A pioneer in the manufacture of Anti-Tank Guided Missiles (ATGM), today, BDL has evolved as a conglomerate manufacturing ATGMs of latest generations, Surface-to-Air weapon systems, strategic weapons, launchers, underwater weapons, decoys and test equipment. Refurbishment and life extension of vintage missiles in line with the requirement of armed forces is also being done to enhance the value with retention of quality.

Relevant Website : www.bdl-india.in

Mazagon Dock Shipbuilders Limited: Mazagon Dock Shipbuilders Limited (MDL) is a leading Defence PSU established as public limited company in 1934. The Company was taken over by the Government of India in 1960 with the aim of building indigenous warships. MDL has built and delivered various types of warships like destroyers, frigates, missile corvettes, missile boats and submarines besides commercial vessels and rigs/platforms for ONGC.

The Company has upgraded and augmented its warship construction facilities in this regard, new facilities of additional production line, module workshop and wet basin have been created as part of the modernization plan. The new assembly workshop has been developed for submarine construction.

Relevant Website : www.mazagondeck.in

Garden Reach Shipbuilders and Engineers Limited: Garden Reach Shipbuilders and Engineers Ltd (GRSE), a Mini Ratna Category-I Company was incorporated as a Defence PSU in 1960. Over the years, GRSE has established well proven capabilities for in-house ship design/ shipbuilding and has made significant contribution to the success of the indigenous warship construction programme. It has emerged as a leading shipyard, building a wide array of vessels, from the state-of-the-art fast attack crafts to world class stealth frigates. Apart from shipbuilding and ship repair, GRSE has also diversified into engineering business with product profile of diesel engines, various deck machinery and pre-fabricated steel bridges,. The Shipyard has modernized its diesel engine plant recently and has tied up with MTU Germany to indigenize manufacturing of marine engines.

Relevant Website : www.grse.in

Goa Shipyard Limited: Goa Shipyard Limited (GSL) is a Mini Ratna Group - I status company and is capable of indigenously designing and building high technology and sophisticated ships to meet the crucial maritime security needs of the country. For over four decades and more, GSL has designed and built wide ranges of sophisticated vessels for defence commercial sectors with special expertise in building modern patrol vessels of steel and alumimum hull. GSL product range includes Offshore Patrol Vessels (OPVs), fast patrol vessels, missile boats, survey vessels, landing craft utility vessels and other auxiliary vessels. It has also successfully ventured into building Glass Reinforced Plastic (GRP) Interceptor boats.

Relevant Website : www.goashipyard.in

Hindustan Shipyard Ltd: Hindustan Shipyard Ltd (HSL) was set up originally in 1941 by Seth Walchand Herachand to promote indigenous shipbuilding industry. The shipyard was transferred to Ministry of Defence in 2010. The shipyard has very good infrastructure and potential of emerging as leading shipyard on the eastern coast. HSL has been entrusted for undertaking construction of various vessels including patrol vessels, repair of submarine, etc. Since inception the shipyard has built 179 ships. HSL is located on the east coast of the country and is nation's premium shipbuilding and ship submarine repair organization.

Relevant Website : www.hslvizag.in

Mishra Dhatu Nigam Ltd: Mishra Dhatu Nigam Limited (MIDHANI) was set up in the early 1970s' initially to manufacture critical materials required in the strategic sectors of India's defence industry. MIDHANI manufactures superalloys, titanium alloys, special steels, magnetic alloys in various forms like cast ingots, forgings, hot rolled and cold rolled rods, wire, sheets and strips, near net shapes, investment castings and industrial fasteners. As part of its CSR activity, it also manufactures bio medical implants for the needy patients.

Relevant Website : www.midhani-india.in

Directorate General of Quality Assurance: Directorate General of Quality Assurance (DGQA) is responsible for quality assurance of all defence stores and equipments, both indigenous as well as.imported for the army, navy (excluding Naval Armaments) and common user items for the air force procured from ordnance factories, public sector undertakings and private sector. It has a vital role to play in defence preparedness of the country. DGQA carries out detailed technical evaluation of weapons and equipment before these are inducted in the Army. There is a paradigm shift in role of DGQA from quality audit to quality management and process audit of the manufacture with a view that a controlled system would give quality product automatically.

Relevant Website : www.dgqadefence.gov.in

Directorate General of Aeronautical Quality Assurance:

Directorate General of Aeronautical Quality Assurance (DGAQA) is the quality assurance (QA) regulatory authority for military aviation stores for IAF, army aviation, naval aviation and indian Coast Guard. It provides QA coverage to military aircraft, helicopter, associated accessories, air armaments, unmanned aerial Vehicles (UAV), missiles, etc. during design, development, production, overhaul, repair, up-gradation and modification at various defence PSUs, ordnance factories, DRDO labs, oil refineries, private trade firms, etc. DGAQA also plays vital role in technical evaluation, field trials, pre-dispatch inspection (PDI) during foreign procurement of military aviation stores.

Relevant Website : www.dgaeroqa.gov.in

Directorate of Standardization

The Directorate of Standardisation (DoS) came into existence in 1962 to contain proliferation of defence inventory of the three services and to reduce it to optimum level by establishing commonality in equipment/components which is progressively achieved through formulation of varied standardisation documents, codification of items and entry control.

Relevant Website : www.ddpdos.gov.in

Directorate of Planning and Coordination

The Directorate of Planning and Coordination, an attached office of Department of Defence Production, was established in 1964. The Directorate is primarily mandated to promote indigenization in defence sector through various enabling policies viz-'Make in India' initiative, liberalization of FDI Policy / Industrial licensing policy, providing level playing field to private sector and giving preference to procurement from indigenous route. The Directorate is responsible to maintain and update the 'Make in India[1] portal on Defence website. The Directorate strives to foster international cooperation in defence sector and boost export of defence equipment to other countries. In addition, the Directorate renders advice from DDP's perspective on capital acquisition proposals of Service Headquarters and also plays significant role in streaming of Defence Procurement Procedure (DDP). The Directorate is also playing key role in the ongoing modernisation of Shipyards.

International Exhibitions in India

To provide a platform for the Indian defence industry to showcase its capabilities, DEO organizes two biennial International exhibitions in India, namely, Aero India and Defexpo India. While Aero India is dedicated to aerospace and aviation industry, focus of Defexpo India is on land and naval systems.

International Exhibitions Abroad

With a view to provide an impetus to export potential to Indian Defence Industry, DEO organizes "India Pavillion" in major defence international exhibitions abroad to develop market for defence products being manufactured by them.

National Institute for Research and Development in Defence Shipbuilding

National Institute for Research and Development in Defence Shipbuilding (NIRDESH) was set up at Kozhikode, Kerala with the objective of achieving self-reliance in shipbuilding. The Institute has been envisaged as a Centre of Excellence for India's futuristic shipbuilding programmes. The thrust areas of NIRDESH would be R&D, ship design, technology development and training along with industry interfacing, training and project management.

Research and Development

Defence Research and Development Organisation (DRDO) is the research and development arm of the Ministry of Defence. It was created in 1958 by merging the units of Defence Science Organisation, which was set up in 1948 to advise and assist the Defence Services on scientific problems and to undertake research in areas related to defence, with the then existing Technical Development Establishments of the three Services. Subsequently, a separate Department of Defence Research and Development (DDRandD) was formed in 1980 to improve administrative efficiency. Starting from a cluster of about 10 laboratories in 1958, DRDO today has 46 laboratories which are spread far and wide; from Tezpur in the east to Mumbai in the west, from Leh in the north to Kochi in the south. DRDO's mandate is to provide assessment and advise on scientific aspects of weapons, platforms and surveillance sensors; to carry out research and to develop cutting-edge technologies leading to production of state-of the-art sensors, weapon systems, platforms and allied equipment for our Defence Services.

In the recent past, the mandate has been widened to support national cyber security architecture which includes testing capabilities, security solutions, networking systems and cyber defence tools. In this process, it has also established national infrastructure, enhanced defence industrial capability and developed committed quality human resources.

DRDO is headed by the Scientific Adviser to Raksha Mantri who is also the Secretary, Department of Defence Research and Development and Director General RandD (DGRandD). Based on the RandD work carried out by the 46 laboratories of DRDO, they are grouped into seven technology clusters namely, Armament and Combat Engineering Systems (ACE), Aeronautical Systems (AERO), Missiles and Strategic Systems (MSS), Naval Systems and Materials (NS and M), Electronics and Communication Systems (ECS), Micro Electronic Devices and Computational Systems (MED and CoS) and Life Sciences (LS).

Human Resources

Being a mission mode organisation, DRDO follows a dynamic system of manpower planning. Authorisation is reviewed after every two years to meet the contingent requirements on account of workload and new projects undertaken by the laboratories. The organisation optimally utilises manpower through dynamic manpower management system. To keep the organisation young and energetic and also to fill deficiencies created on account of retirement and superannuation, scientists are being inducted every year as required bythe laboratories. DRDO follows online receipt of applications under all recruitment and assessment activities thereby discontinuing the offline/ paper application in DRDO. It has a total strength of 25,966 employees, out of which 7,574 are in Defence Research and Development Service (DRDS), 9,643 in Defence Research and Technical Cadre (DRTC) and 8,775 are in Administration and Allied Cadre.

The DRDO ensures training to all cadres of personnel through training institutes, like DIAT, Pune (for technical courses); ITM, Mussoorie (for techno-managerial programmes) and Defence Laboratory, Jodhpur (for technical, administrative and allied cadre). Every year few selected scientists are deputed to undergo ME/ MTech/ PhD at Indian Institute of Technology (IIT), Indian Institute of Science (IISc) and other reputed Indian universities under the sponsorship programme. A Targeted Training Centre has been set up at Dr Raja Ramanna Complex, Bangalore for DRDO scientists. Continuing Education Programme (CEP) are also part of DRDO annual training schedule.

Resettlement of Ex-Servicemen

The Department of Ex-Servicemen Welfare (DESW) formulates various policies and programmes for the welfare and resettlement of Ex-Servicemen (ESM) in the country. The Department has two Divisions viz. Resettlement and Pension, and 3 Attached Offices namely Kendriya Sainik Board Sectt. (KSB Sectt.), Directorate General (Resettlement) (DGR) and Central Organisation, Ex-Servicemen Contributory Health Scheme (CO, ECHS).

Kendriya Sainik Board

Kendriya Sainik Board (KSB) Sectt is the apex body of government of India responsible for implementing government policies for welfare of war-widows/disabled soldiers, ESM and their dependents. It is assisted in its task by 32 Rajya Sainik Boards and 392 Zila Sainik Boards. The Armed Forces Flag Day Fund(AFFDF) is the major source for providing financial assistance to needy war widows/disabled, ESM and their dependents.

Relevant Website : www.ksb.gov.in

Directorate General of Resettlement

Directorate General of Resettlement (DGR) is a tri-service organization which looks after various aspects of resettlement and offers multifarious avenues of Employment, Self Employment and Training to Officers, JCOs/OR and their equivalents in other Services as well as widows and dependents. Nearly 60,000 Armed Forces personnel retire or are released from active service every year, most of them being in the comparatively younger age bracket of 35 to 45 years and need a second career to support their families. These personnel constitute a valuable, disciplined, well-trained, dedicated and talented pool available for nation building.

Relevant Website : www.dgrindia.com

Training Programmes

DGR is entrusted with the responsibility of preparing retiring/retired service personnel for a second career. These resettlement courses are selected with a focus on employability of ESM in Society.

Officers' Training: For training of ESM (Officers), the Resettlement Training Programmes are conducted including 24 Weeks Management Courses at IIMs and other reputed B-Schools, Modular Management courses like Project Finance, Academic Institutions, Supply Chain, Retail, Human Resource, Facility, Export & Import, Event Six Sigma, Jet Transition and Seafaring, etc. at other reputed institutes. Besides, specially designed six week course on Corporate Security and Safety have been in existence for officers looking to venture into self employment fields such as security agencies. 60 per cent course fee is paid by DGR. Widows of officers are also eligible to undergo these courses.

JCOs/ OR and Equivalent Training: For JCOs/ ORs and equivalent, the training courses are conducted for a duration upto one year in diverse fields, such as Security, Fire and Industrial Safety, Computer and IT including 'O' Level, Hospitality, Tourism, Agri based, Business Management, Modular Management, Vocational and Technical, Medical & Healthcare and Library and Information Science, etc. These courses are also run at reputed institutes of accreditation. Cent per cent course fee is paid by DGR. Widows/one dependent of JCOs/OR are also eligible to undergo any course sponsored by DGR. ESM are now also entitled to apply for regular DGR training which are not fully subscribed by retiring personnel. The move of allowing ESM to attend regular DGR courses is aimed to benefit all those ex-servicemen who have not done any resettlement course in the past and are desirous to do these courses to hone their skill. At least two courses are planned every month at all the Regimental Centres to provide variety of courses to the retirees on pension drill.

ESM Training: Under this scheme, funds are allotted to RSBs for conducting vocational training for ESM in their states. The scheme is primarily meant for those ESM who could not avail the facility of resettlement training while in service.

Employment Opportunities

Reservation in Government Jobs: The Central Government has provided for the following reservation for ESM for vacancies in the posts to be filled by direct recruitment: (a) 10 per cent in Group 'C' posts and 20 per cent in Group 'D' posts. In addition 4.5 per cent reservation in each category is meant for disabled soldiers and widows/dependents. (b) 14.5 per cent in Group 'C' and 24.5 per cent Group 'D' posts in PSUs and nationalised banks. (c) 10 per cent posts up to Assistant Commandants in paramilitary forces. (d) cent per cent in Defence Security Corps.

Implementation of Reservation: The Government has designated Directorate General Resettlement as Nodal agency for the monitoring implementation of reservation policy for ESM. Half yearly report for the period ending June 30, 2015 has been compiled based on data received from various organisations.

Jobs in the Corporate/Private Sector: Substantial employment for ESM can be generated in the Private/Corporate sector. In order to generate awareness and urge these sectors to employ ESM, a National Corporate Conclave was conducted by DGR in August 2014 where the competence of the ESM were presented to Corporate Heads and the Raksha Mantri urged them to open the employment opportunities for ESM. DGR has signed a MoU with Confederation of Indian Industries (CII) towards this end.

Schemes for Self Employment

Coal Transportation Schemes and Tipper Attachment: This scheme has been reenergised by issue of new MoU and guidelines in July 2014.

Company Owned Company Operated Retail Outlets: In accordance with the policy guidelines issued by the Ministry of Petroleum and Natural Gas, DGR sponsors officers for management of Retail Outlets of IOCL, BPCL and HPCL all over India under the Company Owned Company Operated (COCO) Schemes.

Gopaljee Dairy and Fresh Farm: The scheme aims at providing self-employment to JCOs/ ORs in the National Capital Region (NCR).

Management of CNG Stations by ESM in NCR: The scope of the scheme has been extended to cover entire NCR to include Noida, Faridabad and Gurugram.

Allotment of Army Surplus Class V 'B' Vehicles: Ex Servicemen and widows of Defence personnel, who died while in service, are eligible to apply for allotment of Army Surplus Class V 'B' Vehicles. 75 ESM were registered with DGR during the year.

Oil Product Agencies Scheme: In accordance with the Policy guidelines issued by the Ministry of Petroleum & Natural Gas/Oil Company, DGR is mandated to issue eligibility certificates for allotment of oil product agencies under the 8 per cent defence quota.

Healthcare

Ex-Servicemen Contributory Health Scheme: Ex-Servicemen Contributory Health Scheme (ECHS) was launched in 2003. The Scheme was expanded in October 2010. ECHS aims to provide quality healthcare to Ex-Servicemen (ESM) and their dependents through a network of ECHS Polyclinics, Service medical facilities and civil empanelled/ Government hospitals spread across the country. The Scheme has been structured on the lines of Central Government Health Scheme (CGHS) and is financed by the Government of India. Endeavour is to ensure cashless treatment by utilising the empanelled hospitals for the veterans and their dependents.

ECHS Polyclinics are designed to provide 'Out Patient Care' that includes consultations, essential investigation and provision of medicines. Specialised consultations, investigations and 'In Patient Care' (Hospitalisation) is provided through spare capacity available in service hospitals, all Government hospitals and also through civil medical facilities empanelled with ECHS.

Central Organisation: At the apex level is the Central Organisation, ECHS located in Delhi, which functions under the Chiefs of Staff Committee through the Adjutant General in the Integrated Headquarters of Ministry of Defence (Army). The Central Organisation is headed by a serving Major General. Executive control of ECHS is vested with Department of Ex-Servicemen Welfare.

ECHS Toll-Free Helpline: ECHS Toll free Helpline has been made available for all ECHS members at 1800-114-115 for resolving queries on membership, treatment and employment. The service is available from Monday to Friday on all working days from 0900-1700 hours.

ECHS Website: All information regarding ECHS, including list of empanelled facilities, forms for membership and latest policies, etc. are available on www.echs.gov.in.

Defence Pensions

Pension to approximately 31 lakh Defence pensioners/family pensioners is disbursed through 21 public sector banks, 3 private sector banks 283 treasuries, 64 Defence Pension Disbursing Offices (DPDOs), 1 post office, 1 Pay and Accounts Offices (PAOs) scattered all over India. For the Armed Forces Pensioners residing in Nepal, disbursement of pension is done through 3 Pension Payment Offices (PPOs).

10 Education

THE essence of human resource development is education, which plays a significant and remedial role in balancing the socio-economic fabric of the country. Since citizens of India are its most valuable resource, the billion-strong nation needs the nurture and care in the form of basic education to achieve a better quality of life. This warrants an all-round development of the citizens, which can be achieved by building strong foundations in education. Good quality education is the foundation of new discoveries, new knowledge, innovation and entrepreneurship that trigger growth and prosperity of the individual as well as that of a nation. For this, we need to make the curriculum and pedagogy relevant to the needs of the society and economy and nurture qualities of problem solving and creative thinking, learning-by-doing, greater engagement with the live context, and confident self-expression from a young age.

To lay emphasis on the educational development of students of weaker sections of the society, a number of innovative initiatives have been taken by the Ministry such as (i) setting up of national monitoring committee on minorities (ii) setting up of national monitoring committee for education of SCs, STs and persons with disabilities (iii) student support initiatives such as National Means-cum-Merit Scholarship Scheme (NMMSS), National Scheme of Incentive to Girls for Secondary Education (NSIGSE), Special Scholarship Scheme for Jammu and Kashmir, scheme of interest subsidy on educational loans (iv) regulations on prevention of discrimination and estasblishment of ombudsman and (v) development of an anti-ragging web portal. Currently, the Ministry of Human Resource Development works through two departments : Department of School Education and Literacy, and Department of Higher Education

Relevant Website : www.mhrd.gov.in

Right of Children to Free and Compulsory Education and Sarva Shiksha Abhiyan

Article 21-A of the Constitution of India and its consequent legislation, the Right of Children to Free and Compulsory Education (RTE) Act, 2009 became operative in the country in 2010. The RTE Act confers the right to elementary education on all children, in the age group of 6-14 years, on the basis of equality of opportunity in a formal school which satisfies certain essential norms and standards. All states and UTs have notified their state RTE Rules. The centrally sponsored scheme of Sarva Shiksha Abhiyan (SSA) supports states and UTs in their efforts to implement the RTE Act. Its interventions include, inter alia, opening of new schools, construction of schools and additional classrooms, constructing toilets and drinking water facilities, provisioning for teachers, in-service training for teachers and academic resource support, free textbooks and uniforms, support for improving learning achievement levels, research, evaluation and monitoring.

Programme Interventions

I. Universal Access: The Sarva Shiksha Abhiyan (SSA) Programme is being implemented since 2001 for universalization of elementary education. It has made significant progress in achieving near universal access and equity.

(a) New Schools: Progress in achieving the goal of universal access under SSA has been consistent over the years. Over the years 2,04,740 primary schools have been sanctioned along with 1,59,415 upper primary schools in a radius of 3 km.

(b) Special Training for mainstreaming out-of-school children: The RTE Act makes a specific provision for Special Training for age-appropriate admission for out-of-school children. A majority of out-of-school children belong to disadvantaged communities - scheduled castes, scheduled tribes, Muslims, migrants, children with special needs, urban deprived children, working children, children in other difficult circumstances, for example, those living in difficult terrain, children from displaced families, and areas affected by civil strife, etc. Special training may be in the form of residential or non-residential courses organized, preferably in the premises of the school, but if such facilities are not available in school, alternate facilities which are safe, secure and accessible may be identified and used.

(c) Residential facilities: SSA has a provision for residential facilities in sparsely populated or hilly and densely forested areas with difficult geographical terrains and in densely populated urban areas. SSA has provided 826 residential institutions with a capacity of around 90,855 children.

(d) Transportation or Escort facilities: These facilities are available for children in remote habitations with sparse populations or in urban areas where availability of land is a problem or children belonging to extremely deprived groups or children with special needs.

(e) Uniforms: SSA provides two sets of uniform to all girls, SC, ST children and Below Poverty Line (BPL) children, wherever (i) state governments have incorporated provision of school uniforms as a child entitlement in their state RTE Rules, and (ii) state governments are not already providing uniforms from the state budgets.

II. Bridging Gender Gaps in Elementary Education

(a) Girls' Education: RTE-SSA provides a clear thrust and special focus on education for girls and children belonging to disadvantaged groups and weaker

sections. The general interventions under SSA apply to all girls and children belonging to disadvantaged and weaker sections; these include ensuring availability of primary and upper primary schools within the habitation as prescribed under the RTE Rules, uniforms, textbooks, etc. Special Training interventions are also largely focused on girls and disadvantaged groups, because it is this category of children who are most deprived of opportunities to pursue their education.

(*b*) *Kasturba Gandhi Balika Vidyalaya (KGBV):* KGBV are residential upper primary schools for girls from SC, ST, OBC Muslim communities and BPL girls. KGBVs are set up in educational backward blocks where schools are at great distances and are a challenge to their security of girls. KGBVs reach out to adolescent girls who are unable to go to regular schools to out of school girls in the 10+ age group who are unable to complete primary school and younger girls of migratory populations in difficult areas of scattered habitations that do not qualify for primary/upper primary schools. KGBVs provide for a minimum reservation of 75 per cent seats for girls from SC/ST/OBC and minorities and 25 per cent to girls from families that live below the poverty line. 3,600 KGBVs are functional in the states and 3,66,756 girls are enrolled in them.

(*c*) *Removal of Gender Bias:* Following the National Curriculum Framework (NCF), 2005 guidelines, states have consciously taken a decision to establish gender as a critical marker of transformation through increasing visual representation of girls and women and facilitating role reversal. Most of the states have incorporated the gender sensitization in their regular School Management Committee (SMC) training modules to deal with issues such as enrolment, retention and completion of education of girls; creating suitable atmosphere for girl students in schools; rapport with female teachers for discussing gender awareness, etc. Trainings of teachers on gender related issues are organized in the states specifically for orientation on gender issues facing adolescent girls in particular.

(*d*) *Digital Gender Atlas for Advancing Girls' Education:* Department of School Education and Literacy has prepared a Digital Gender Atlas for advancing girls' education in the country on its website. The tool, which has been developed with the support of UNICEF, will help identify low performing geographic pockets for girls, particularly from marginalized groups such as scheduled castes, schedule tribes and Muslims, on specific gender related education indicators. In order to plan and execute educational interventions, the purpose of the Gender Atlas is to help identify and ensure equitable education with a focus on vulnerable girls, including girls with disabilities.

(*e*) *Separate Girls' Toilets:* Under SSA, the requirement of school infrastructure facilities including toilets and drinking water are worked out by the state based on need at school/village/block and district level. All new schools sanctioned under SSA are composite schools with facilities like toilets for boys and girls.

III. Inclusive Education

(a) SCs/STs and Muslims

Enrolment of SC children has gone up from 19.06 per cent in 2010-11 to 19.8 per cent in 2015-16 at elementary level which is more than their share in population at 16.60 per cent (as per Census 2011). Enrolment of ST children has marginally gone down from 10.70 per cent in 2010-11 to 10.35 per cent in 2015-16 at elementary level which is more than their share of population at 8.60 per cent (as per census 2011). Enrolment of Muslim children has grown up from 12.50 per cent in 2010-11 to 13.8 per cent in 2015-16 at elementary level which is slightly less than their share in population (14.2 per cent as per Census 2011).

(b) Children with Special Needs

RTE-SSA seeks to ensure that every child with special needs, irrespective of the kind, category and degree of disability, is provided meaningful and quality education. The main components of SSA interventions for such children include identification, functional and formal assessment, appropriate educational placement, preparation of individualized educational plan, provision of aids and appliances, teacher training, resource support, removal of architectural barriers, monitoring and evaluation and a special focus on girls with special needs.

(c) Textbooks for Children

All children are provided free textbooks up to class VIII. In 2016-17 provision was made for providing text books to 8.38 crore children. Concomitantly workbooks and worksheets are being provided by several states, to facilitate activity-based classroom processes and to supplement learning processes.

IV. Sub-Programmes under SSA

(a) The Padhe Bharat Badhe Bharat (PBBB), a sub-programme of the SSA, in classes I and II is focusing on foundational learning in early grades with an emphasis on reading, writing and comprehension and mathematics. States and UTs have been implementing specific interventions like ABL in Tamil Nadu, Nalli Kali in Karnataka, Pragya in Gujarat; steps have been taken to develop specific teacher training modules for teachers teaching students in classes 1 and II. Punjab, Meghalaya, Delhi have introduced programmes for strengthening teaching of maths in classes I and II; in Sikkim schools have set up reading corners for children in the foundational classes through support from community members.

(b) The Rashtriya Aavishkar Abhiyan (RAA), also under the SSA, aims to motivate and engage children of the age group 6-18 years, in science, mathematics and technology by observation, experimentation, inference drawing and model building, through both inside and outside classroom activities. Schools have been adopted for mentoring by institutions of higher education like IIT's, IISER's and NIT's.

(c) Vidyanjali, another sub-programme under SSA, was launched to enhance community and private sector involvement in Government run elementary schools across the country. The aim of the programme is to strengthen implementation of co-scholastic activities in government schools through services of volunteers.

(d) *ShaGun portal - an Initiative to monitor the implementation of SSA:* MHRD has developed a web portal called ShaGun. It aims to capture and showcase innovations and progress in elementary education sector by continuous monitoring. ShaGun will help monitor progress by assessing performance of states and UTs on key parameters and thereby serve as a platform for the central government for effective planning and deliver on the promise of providing quality education to all. ShaGun, which has been coined from the words 'Shala' meaning schools and 'Gunvatta' meaning quality, has been developed with a twin track approach. It has an online monitoring module to measure state-level performance and progress against key educational indicators. It has been developed to collect and report data which will enable the government and administrators to track the efficiency with which SSA funds are being utilized and the results that this is delivering. The SSA ShaGun web portal can be accessed at http://ssashagun.nic.in.

V. Teacher Training

(a) *Availability of Teachers:* To meet the shortage of teachers in elementary schools, 19.49 lakh additional posts have been sanctioned under SSA up to 2016-17. After RTE it is mandatory that only those people may be appointed as teachers who are able to clear TET. CBSE has conducted eleven rounds of Teacher Eligibility Tests (TETs). Apart from these 2.34 lakh part-time instructors have also been sanctioned under SSA.

(b) *In-service Teacher Training:* To upgrade skills of teachers, SSA provides for annual in-service training up to 20 days for all teachers. Support of ₹ 6,000 per teacher per year is provided for two years to untrained teachers, already employed for the NCTE recognized training programme. Apart from this induction training for 30 days is given to freshly trained recruits. All training programmes cover pedagogical issues, including content and methodology, aimed at improving teaching learning transactions in classrooms and learning process in schools. Some of the major focus areas include guiding principles of NCF 2005, CCE, how children learn, subject-specific content or learning difficulties, activity-oriented methods, use of TLMs or learning kits, etc.

(c) *Training of Headmasters:* In order to orient the teachers in managerial skills the heads of the schools are provided training for 10 days in academic financial and human resource management.

(d) *Distance Education Programmes for Teachers:* Capacity building of institutions and personnel at the national, state, district and sub-district levels is being facilitated with assistance of IGNOU and other teacher education institutions in different states. The distance education programme provides technical and academic support in designing, developing, producing and delivering distance learning inputs and materials training of untrained teachers, thus facilitating training of professionally untrained teachers in the states.

VI. Academic Support System

(a) *Academic Support Structures:* 6,759 Block Resource Centres (BRCs) and 76,064 Cluster Resource Centres (CRCs) have been set up across the country as resource centers in each block and cluster, to provide decentralized academic support, training and supervision to teachers and schools.

(b) *School and Teacher Grants:* SSA also provides annual teacher grants of ₹ 500 to all teachers for developing contextual teaching aids. DIETs and BRCs hold regular workshop and training programmes to develop subject and topic related low cost teaching aids. In addition, an annual school grant of ₹ 5000 is provided to each primary and ₹ 7,000 to each upper primary school separately, to meet the cost of school consumables, ₹ 7500 per school is given to each school for maintenance purposes. For new schools, onetime 'Teaching Learning Equipment' grant a ₹ 20,000 per new primary school and ₹ 50,000 per new upper primary school is provided for school equipment and setting up expenses.

(c) *Computer aided learning:* Under SSA, grant up to ₹ 50 lakh is available to each district for strengthening computer aided learning in schools to support enhancement of children's learning. Activities include providing computer equipment or labs to schools, development of curriculum-based e-learning materials in local languages, and training of teachers in computer use. Since inception of the programme, approximately 1,06,753 schools have benefitted from this intervention.

(d) *Learning Enhancement Programmes:* 2 per cent of the total SSA outlay for each district has been made available for 'Learning Enhancement Programmes' that aims specifically at improving the quality of learning processes and learning outcomes.

(e) *Improving student learning outcomes:* The impact of various quality interventions of SSA are reflected in the enhancement of children's learning levels. Being a major thrust area, NCERT launched a programme to measure the achievement level of all children studying in classes III, V and VIII. Improving student learning outcomes has been the key component of SSA.

VII. Infrastructure

RTE-SSA provides flexibility to states in the execution of civil works. Neither designs nor unit costs are centrally prescribed. States are free to evolve building designs based on local site conditions and develop cost estimates based on the state schedule of rates notified by the state governments. School infrastructure provisions, however, is not a standalone activity. The design and quality of school infrastructure has a significant impact on enrolment, attendance and retention of children in schools. Thus 'civil works' under SSA are undertaken to provide all weather building as per provision of RTE Act. RTE-SSA encourages participation by the local community in all civil work activities in order to instil a sense of ownership in them.

RTE-SSA also supports repair of old school buildings, provision of school buildings in respect of building less, dilapidated schools and retrofitting of school buildings to make them hazard resistant.

School Management Committees and Community Participation

SSA has always acknowledged the importance of 'community ownership' pertaining to effective functioning of government schools. As per norms it has been made mandatory for the schools to constitute School Management Committees (SMC) wherein the parents/guardians of students studying in the respective school are the members.

Monitoring Institutes

Institutions, including university departments of education, social science and institutes of national stature have been assigned the work of periodic monitoring of SSA implementation in states and UTs. In large states more than one institute has been assigned the task of monitoring. These monitoring institutes are required to make field visits and report on progress of SSA at the ground level every six months. This cycle is repeated every two years. SSA programme modifies the terms of reference of the monitoring institutes as and when required.

Admissions under Section 12(1) (c) of the RTE Act

Section 12(1) (c) mandates all private unaided schools and special category schools to reserve a minimum of 25 per cent of seats for economically weaker sections. Under the SSA, the Government of India will reimburse the state expenditure towards 25 per cent admissions to private unaided schools, based on per child cost norms notified by the state government, subject to a maximum ceiling of 20 per cent of the size of the SSA annual work plan and budget.

Rashtriya Madhyamik Shiksha Abhiyan

Rashtriya Madhyamik Shiksha Abhiyan (RMSA was launched in 2009 with the objective to enhance access to secondary education and improve its quality. The schemes envisages to enhance the enrolment at secondary stage by providing a secondary school with a reasonable distance of habitation, with an aim to ensure GER of 100 per cent and universal retention by 2020. The other objectives include improving quality of education imparted at secondary level through making all secondary schools conform to prescribed norms, removing gender, socio-economic and disability barriers, etc.

Some of the significant initiatives, under RMSA for improving quality of education are as:-

(*i*) *Shaala Siddhi:* School Standards and Evaluation Framework and its web portal was launched in 2015. It is a comprehensive instrument for school evaluation leading to school improvement. Developed by the National University of Educational Planning and Administration (NUEPA), it aims to enable schools to evaluate their performance in a more focused and strategic manner and facilitate them to make professional judgments for improvement. The programme's objective is to establish an agreed set of standards and benchmarks for each school, by focussing on key performance domains and their core standards.

(ii) Shala Darpan: The "Shaala Darpan Project" to cover all the 1099 Kendriya Vidyalayas was launched in June, 2015. The objective of this project is to provide services based on school management systems to students, parents and communities. Under school information services, the following list of services will be enabled i.e., school profile management, student profile management, employee information, student attendance, leave management, report cards, curriculum tracking custom, SMS alerts for parents / administrators on student and teacher attendance.

(iii) GIS Mapping : To ensure universal access to schools including secondary schools within a reasonable distance of any habitation and without any discrimination, the geographic coordinates of school along with the school information available in UDISE is being uploaded on the school GIS Web enabled platform i.e. http://schoolgis.nic.in. All states have conducted GIS mapping and shared geographical coordinates of schools with the NIC except Jammu and Kashmir.

(iv) National Achievement Survey for Class X: The National Achievement Survey for Class X was undertaken for the first time by MHRD. The survey investigates student achievement in five subjects: English, mathematics, social science, science and modern Indian language. The test has been administered in 33 states and union territories after a scientific and robust process of sample design, test development and translation, with rigorous adherence to technical procedures.

(v) Kala Utsav: Kala Utsav is an initiative of this Ministry to promote arts (music, theatre, dance, visual arts and crafts) in education by nurturing and showcasing the artistic talent of school students at secondary stage in the country, and it is also a platform to bring arts to the centre stage in an inclusive environment.

(vi) Focus on Science and Maths: Rashtriya Avishkar Abhiyan launched in 2015: Under Rashtriya Avishkar Abhiyan, training of 1.04 lakh science and maths teachers, math and science kit, excursion trip to science centres and museum for students, special teaching on science and maths, science exhibition at district level, teaching of Vedic maths, etc., were included under RMSA.

(vii) National Award For Teachers using ICT For Innovation In Education: Under the ICT in schools, to promote computer enabled learning and usage of ICT in teaching in government and government aided secondary and higher secondary schools has provision for instituting a national award for innovative use of ICT to motivate the teachers and teacher educators for innovative use of ICT in teaching-learning.

(*viii*) *Data base of Students and Teachers:*

By 2016, 25,04,73,095 (approx 71.6 per cent) children in the age group of 5 to 18 years were enrolled under Aadhar, as against 20,94,34,376 children (59.8 per cent) at the end of December, 2015.

Vocationalisation of Secondary and Higher Secondary Education

The Centrally sponsored scheme of Vocationalisation of Secondary and Higher Secondary Education was revised in 2014 with a view to align it with the National Skills Qualification Framework (NSQF) into which the NVEQF has been assimilated. The scheme has been subsumed Under Integrated Rashtriya Madhyamik Shiksha Abhiyan. The specific objectives of the scheme are to enhance the employability of youth through demand driven competency based, modular vocational courses; to maintain their competitiveness through provisions of multi-entry multi-exit learning opportunities and vertical mobility/interchange ability in qualifications; to fill the gap between educated and employable; and to reduce the dropout rate at the secondary level and decrease the pressure on academic higher education. The revised scheme while introducing vocational education at the secondary level, seeks to integrate vocational education with general education and provide horizontal and vertical mobility to the students.

Construction and Running of Girls' Hostel

The centrally sponsored scheme of Construction and Running of Girls' Hostel for students of secondary and higher secondary schools was launched in 2008-09 and is being implemented from 2009-10 replacing the earlier NGO driven scheme. The Scheme was subsumed under Rashtriya Madhyamik Shiksha Abhiyan (RMSA). The main objective of the hostel component of RMSA is to improve access and to retain the girl child in secondary and higher secondary classes (IX-XII) so that the girl students are not denied the opportunity to continue their study due to distance to school, parents' financial affordability and other connected social factors. The girl students in the age group of 14-18 years studying in classes IX- to XII belonging to SC, ST, OBC, minority community and BPL families form the target group of the Scheme.

Inclusive Education for Disabled at Secondary Stage

The Scheme of Inclusive Education for Disabled at Secondary stage (IEDSS) was launched in 2009-10 replacing the earlier scheme of Integrated Education for Disabled Children (IEDC). Inclusive Education for Disabled at Secondary Stage (IEDSS) component was subsumed under Rashtriya Madhyamik Shiksha Abhiyan. It provides assistance for the inclusive education of the disabled children in classes IX-XII. The aim of the scheme is to enable all students with disabilities, after completing eight years of elementary schooling, to pursue further four years of secondary schooling (classes IX to XII) in an inclusive and enabling environment. The scheme covers all children passing out of elementary school and studying at the secondary stage in government, local body and government-aided schools, with one or more disabilities as defined under the Persons with Disabilities Act, (1995), and the National Trust Act (1999), namely (i) blindness, (ii) low vision, (iii) leprosy cured, (iv) hearing impairment, (v) loco-motor disabilities, (vi) mental retardation, (vii) mental illness, (viii) autism, (ix) cerebral palsy and may eventually cover speech impairment, learning disabilities, etc.

The components of the scheme include assistance for two major components i.e.-

(a) student-oriented components: (i) assessment of medical / educational needs, (ii) provision of student specific facilities, like assistive devices, therapeutic service, books support services, etc. (iii) development of learning material, iv) purchase of screen reading software. Girls with disability receive special focus and efforts made under the scheme to help them gain access to secondary schools with a provision of monthly stipend of ₹ 200/- for the disabled girls. ₹ 3,000/- per child per annum is provided as Central assistance to be topped by the states by a scholarship of ₹ 600/- per disabled child per annum.

(b) *Other Components:* (i) appointment of special educators, (ii) special pay for general teachers trained in special education -₹ 400/- per month, (iii) construction and equipping of resource rooms, (iv) training of general school teachers to build their capacity to fulfill the needs of children with special needs (v) make schools barrier free.

Centrally Sponsored Scheme for Teacher Education

(A) Strengthening Teacher Education

The centrally sponsored scheme for Teacher Education was initiated in 1987 pursuant to the formulation of the National Policy of Education, 1986. The scheme was revised for the 12th Five Year Plan. It aims to establish DIETs in all districts created up to 2011, thereby increasing their numbers from existing 571 to 646; strengthen existing 106 to 122 Colleges of Teacher Education (CTEs) and up-grade existing government secondary teacher education institutions into CTEs; strengthen existing 32 to 39 Institutes of Advanced Studies in Education (IASEs); up-grade Department of Education in Universities as IASEs; and establish block institutes of teacher education (BITEs) in identified SC/ST/ minority concentration districts.

(B) Quality in Teacher Education

Creation of Separate Cadre: 17-states/ UTs have created separate cadre for teacher educators under the TE- Scheme. States have also been asked to strengthen the cadre of teacher educators in their respective states/UTs.

National Council for Teacher Education (NCTE) Regulations, 2014- Norms and Standards: The NCTE was established with a view to achieving planned and co-ordinated development of the teacher education system throughout the country, the regulation and proper maintenance of norms and standards in the teacher education system, and for matters connected therewith.

Re-organizing/Restructuring of SCERT and Cadre Restructuring for Teacher Educators: Under the CSS-Teacher Education 09 states have re-organized/restructured their SCERT in 2016.

New Activities/Initiatives under CSSTE Scheme

India Teacher Education Portal (Prashikshak): the Department of School Education and Literacy, launched 'India Teacher Education Portal (Prashikshak)' in 2016. This portal is helpful in monitoring of teachers education Institutions and in providing comprehensive information to prospective students and teachers to select the right institute as per choice.

Scheme for Providing Quality Education in Madarsas

Ministry of Human Resource Development, lays emphasis on providing equal opportunities to minorities as far as access to education is concerned. For this purpose, government is implementing the scheme for providing quality education in Madarsas (SPQEM) for the children of minorities. The objectives of the Scheme are: encourage Madarsas and Maktabs to introduce formal subjects i.e., science, mathematics, social studies, Hindi and English by means of providing financial assistance; children studying in Madarsas and Maktabs attain academic proficiency for class I-XII; Madarsas/Maktabs/Dar-ul-Uloom can opt to become accredited study centres with National Institute of Open Schooling (NIOS) for which proper assistance will be provided; children above 14 years in Madarsas/Maktabs/Dar-ul-Uloom are given opportunities to attain vocation training; strengthening of Madarsas Board for Monitoring and Awareness of SPQEM.

The Scheme provides assistance for appointment of teachers for teaching science, mathematics, social studies, languages, computer application and science. Full time graduate teacher is paid salary for 12 months ₹ 6,000/-p.m. and post graduate/B.Ed. ₹ 12,000/-. One time grant of ₹1,00,000/- for science/computer labs/workshops in Madarsas at the secondary/senior secondary level ₹ 5000/- as annual grant for maintenance. One time assistance of up to ₹ 50,000/- for libraries/book banks/teaching learning material followed by an annual grant of ₹ 5,000/-. A grant up to a maximum amount of ₹15,000/- for purchase of science/math kits and other pedagogical equipment. Madarsas which have been in existence at least for three years and registered under central or state government Acts or Madarsas Board or with Waqf Boards or NIOS are eligible to apply for assistance under this programme.

Training is to be arranged in groups for Madarsa teachers appointed under the scheme by SCERTs/DIETs/BRCs. Madarsas with respect to whom expenditure on account of honorarium of the teachers is met by the state government will not be eligible for salary component. Madarsas receiving financial assistance for teacher training, text books, computers, science/maths kits etc., from any other state/central scheme will not be eligible for that component under this scheme.

Infrastructure Development for Minority Institutes

The Scheme facilitates education of minorities by strengthening school infrastructure in minority institutions. It covers the entire country. It is to fund infrastructure development of private aided/unaided minority elementary/secondary/senior secondary schools to the extent of 75 per cent and subject to a maximum of ₹ 50 lakhs per school. Organizations that are recognised by central or state government are eligible to apply, should have been functioning for at least last 3 years and have substantial enrolment of children from minorities. The scheme is implemented through the state governments and all requests for financial assistance are entertained by the state government in the prescribed application form.

National Means-cum-Merit Scholarship Scheme

The centrally sponsored National Means-cum-Merit Scholarship Scheme (NMMSS) was launched in 2008 with the objective to award scholarships to meritorious students of economically weaker sections to arrest their drop out at class VIII and encourage them to continue study at secondary and higher secondary stage up to class XII. One lakh scholarships of ₹ 6,000/- per annum (₹ 500/- per month) per student are awarded to selected students every year for class IX and their continuation up to class XII in a state government, government-aided and local body schools. There is quota of scholarships for different states/UTs. Students whose parental income from all sources is not more than ₹1,50,000/- are eligible to avail the scholarships. There is reservation as per the state government norms. The selection of students for the scholarships is made through an examination conducted by the state governments. Scholarships are disbursed directly by electronic transfer into the bank accounts of students on quarterly basis following DBT mode.

National Scheme of Incentive to Girls

The centrally sponsored National Scheme of Incentive to Girls for Secondary Education (NSIGSE) was also launched in 2008 with the objective to establish an enabling environment to reduce the drop-outs and to promote the enrolment of girl children belonging mainly to SC/ST communities in secondary schools. According to the scheme, a sum of ₹ 3,000/- is deposited in the name of the unmarried eligible girls as fixed deposit on enrolment in class IX, who are entitled to withdraw it along with interest thereon on passing class XI and attaining 18 years of age. The scheme covers (i) all girls belonging to SC/ST communities, who pass VIII and (ii) all girls who pass VIII examination from Kasturba Gandhi Balika Vidyalayas (irrespective of whether they belong to SC/ST) and enrol in class IX in a state government, government-aided and local body schools.

Implementation of Direct Benefit Transfer

Direct Benefit Transfer (DBT) scheme/system was launched from 2013 under which 25 schemes across eight ministries/departments were selected for implementation of DBT system in 43 pilot districts of 16 states/UTs. It envisages direct transfer of funds to beneficiary account through the Aadhaar Payment Bridge (APB). From 2015, DBT Scheme was extended in the entire country. Two scholarship schemes of the Department of School Education and Literacy, viz., National Means-cum-Merit Scholarship Scheme (NMMSS) and National Scheme of Incentive to Girls for Secondary Education (NSIGSE) are covered under it. A National Scholarship Portal (NSP) has been made operational for on-line submission of proposals/list of beneficiaries by the state governments for NMMSS and NSIGSE.

Adult Education

At the time of independence, 86 per cent of India's population was illiterate and as such the main focus of adult education had been on its very bottom tier i.e., imparting of 'Basic literacy'. For accomplishment of this objective, a series of programmes were introduced since the First Plan period, the most prominent, being the National Literacy Mission (NLM), launched in 1988 for the adults in the age group of 15+. The programme of National Literacy Mission was re-vamped in 2009 in alignment with new paradigms of lifelong learning as Saakshar Bharat. Considerable progress has been made in raising the Literacy rate of the country but still the levels remain uneven across different states, districts, social groups and minorities. The overall goal of adult education is to establish a fully literate society through improved quality and standard of adult education and literacy.

The National Literacy Mission Authority (NLMA) is the operating and implementing organization at national level for all the activities envisaged in Adult Education and Skill Development. During the 12th Five Year Plan, NLMA has been striving to raise the literacy rate to 80 per cent and to reduce the gender gap to less than 10 per cent.

Of the 410 districts which qualify for coverage under Saakshar Bharat Programme, the Programme has been sectioned in 404 districts in 26 states and 1 union territory covering about 1.64 lakh Gram Panchayats. During 2016-17 the programme has been continued in these 404 districts. Teaching learning process has commenced in 57.8 lakh Literacy Centres. About 45.73 lakh Volunteer Teachers have been trained by Master Trainers and 2.54 lakh Master Trainers were trained by Resource Persons. In addition about 13.5 thousand Resource Persons have also been trained. Basic Literacy Primers in 13 languages and 26 local dialects have been printed and distributed so far for the learners. Around 8.27 crore learners have been enrolled under basic literacy.

National Award to Teachers

Instituted in 1958, the National Award to Teachers (NAT) is given away by the President of India on 5th September (Teacher's Day) every year to give public recognition to meritorious teachers working in primary, middle and secondary schools. Altogether there are 378 awards out of which 23 are reserved for Sanskrit, Persian and Arabic teachers. Each state/union territory/ organization has an earmarked quota based on the number of teachers. The Scheme also covers teachers of the schools affiliated to Central Board of Secondary Education (CBSE) including teachers of independent affiliated schools situated abroad, Council for Indian School Certificate Examination (CISCE), Sainik School, Kendriya Vidyalaya Sangathan (KVS), Navodaya Vidyalaya Samiti (NVS), Central Tibetan School Administration (CTSA) and schools run by the Atomic Energy Education Society. From the award year 2001, 'Special Awards' have been instituted for teachers promoting inclusive education in schools and the education of children with disabilities in regular schools. The total number of 'Special Awards' are 43. 'Special Awards' are conferred on the teachers of following categories:- teachers with disabilities working in mainstream schools; - special teacher or trained general teachers who have done outstanding work for inclusive education. Each award carries with it a certificate of merit, a cash award of ₹ 50,000/- and a silver medal.

Kendriya Vidyalaya Sangathan

The Scheme of Kendriya Vidyalayas (KVS) (Central Schools) was approved in 1962 to provide uninterrupted education to the wards of transferrable central government employees. Consequently, Central School Organization was started as a unit of the Ministry of Education (now Ministry of Human Resource Development). Initially, 20 regimental schools, then functioning at places having large concentration of defence personnel, were taken over as Central Schools during the academic year 1963-64.

The Kendriya Vidyalaya Sangathan was registered as a society under the Societies Registration Act in 1965. The primary aim of the Sangathan is to provide, establish, endow, maintain, control and manage the Central Schools (Kendriya Vidyalayas) located all over India and abroad. The Government of India wholly finances the Sangathan.

Jawahar Navodaya Vidyalayas

The National Policy on Education, 1986, envisaged setting up of residential Navodaya schools with an aim of providing excellence coupled with equity and social justice. Consequent to this, Navodaya Vidyalaya Samiti was registered as a Society, under the Society Registration Act, of 1860, with the objective to establish Navodaya Vidyalayas to provide good quality modern education - including a strong component of inculcation of values, awareness of the environment, adventure activities and physical education - to the talented children predominantly from the rural areas without regard to their family's socio-economic condition. The opening of a Jawahar Navodaya Vidyalaya is based on the proposal from the concerned state/ UT governments offering about 30 acres of suitable land, free of cost. The state government has also to provide sufficient temporary building and other infrastructures, free of rent, to accommodate 240 students and staff for three to four years or till such time the Samiti constructs its own buildings at the permanent site.

National Council of Educational Research and Training

The National Council of Educational Research and Training (NCERT) provides academic and technical supports for qualitative improvement of school education. The NCERT was established in 1961 as an apex national body to lead qualitative changes in school education. NCERT has been playing an advisory role guiding central and state governments in formulating policies, acts and government programmes. It has played a crucial role in the development of national policies on education (1968-1986) and national curriculum frameworks. The researches undertaken by the Council have led to building new perspective of schooling and also provided inputs for formulation of policies and programmes. NCERT has been designing and offering innovative and need-based courses for teachers, teacher educators and counsellors. The curricular and other learning materials developed by the Council have helped in bringing about quality schooling. NCERT has received recognition both at national and international levels in the area of school education owing to its work done in the last 50 years. It is a unique institution in the country, conducting researches, preparing skilled educational professionals and developing curriculum and curricular materials. The major constituent units of the NCERT are: National Institute of Education (NIE), New Delhi; Central Institute of Education Technology (CIET), New Delhi; Pandit Sunder Lal Sharma Central Institute of Vocational Education (PSSCIVE), Bhopal; five regional institutes of education (RIEs) at Ajmer, Bhopal, Bhubaneswar, Mysore and Umiam (Meghalaya).

National Bal Bhavan

National Bal Bhavan (NBB), established in 1956, is an autonomous institution funded by the Ministry of Human Resource Development. Bal Bhavan as a movement is spread across the length and breadth of the country with 134 affiliated Bal Bhavans and Bal Kendras. In addition there are 48 Bal Bhavan Kendras and a Bal Bhavan at Mandi village in Delhi. National Bal Bhavan aims at enhancing the creative potential of children by providing them various activities, opportunities and common platform to interact, experiment, create and perform according to their age, aptitude and ability. It offers a barrier-free environment with immense possibilities of innovation without any stress or strain. Various creative activities are conducted for children specially from the deprived sections of society on a regular basis at NBB and its affiliated institutes.

Central Board of Secondary Education

The Central Board of Secondary Education is a Board of Education for public and private schools, under the Union Government. Central Board of Secondary Education has asked all schools affiliated to follow only NCERT curriculum.

National Institute of Open Schooling

National Institute of Open Schooling (NIOS) is "Open School" to cater to the needs of a heterogeneous group of learners up to pre-degree level. It was started as a project with in-built flexibilities by the Central Board of Secondary

Education (CBSE) in 1979. In 1986, the National Policy on Education suggested strengthening of Open School System for extending open learning facilities in a phased manner at secondary level all over the country as an independent system with its own curriculum and examination leading to certification. Consequently, the Ministry of Human Resource Development set up the National Open School (NOS) in 1989. In July 2002, the Ministry amended the nomenclature of the organisation from the National Open School to the National Institute of Open Schooling (NIOS) with a mission to provide relevant continuing education at school stage, up to pre-degree level through open learning system to prioritized client groups as an alternative to formal system, in pursuance of the normative national policy documents and in response to the need assessments of the people, and through it to make its share of contribution; to universalisation of education; to greater equity and justice in society, and to the evolution of a learning society.

The NIOS provides opportunities to interested learners by making available the following courses/programmes of study through open and distance learning (ODL) mode: Open Basic Education (OBE) programme for 14+ years age group, adolescents and adults at A, B and C levels that are equivalent to classes III, V and VIII of the formal school system consists of: secondary education course, senior secondary education course, vocational education courses/ programmes, life enrichment programmes.

At the secondary and senior secondary levels, NIOS provides flexibility in the choice of subjects/courses, pace of learning, and transfer of credits from CBSE, some board of school education and state open schools to enable learner's continuation. A learner is extended as many as nine chances to appear in public examinations spread over a period of five years. The credits gained are accumulated till the learner clears required credits for certification. The learning strategies include; learning through printed self-instructional material, audio and video programmes, participating in personal contact programme, and Tutor Marked Assignments. Enrichment is also provided to the learners through the half yearly magazine "Open Learning". The Study Material is made available in English, Hindi and Urdu mediums. The On-Demand Examination System (ODES) is in operation at secondary and senior secondary stage. NIOS offers 28 subjects in eight mediums (Hindi, English, Urdu, Marathi, Telugu, Gujarati, Malayalam and Odia) for secondary examinations and 28 subjects in Hindi, English, Urdu, Bengali and Odia mediums for senior secondary examinations. Besides these, NIOS has provision of offering Vocational subjects in combination with academic subjects at secondary stage and 20 vocational subjects in combination with Academic subjects at senior secondary level.

Mid-Day Meal Scheme

The Mid-Day Meal Scheme covers children of classes I-VI11 studying in government, government-aided schools, special training centres (STC) and madarsas/ maqtabs supported under Sarva Shiksha Abhiyan (SSA). It is the largest school feeding programme in the world, covering 9.78 crore children in

11.40 lakh institutions across the country. Apart from promoting access and retention, the Mid-Day Meal Scheme has also contributed to social and gender equity. It has helped in preventing classroom hunger, promoting school participation and fostering social equality and enhancing gender equality.

Norms for Mid-Day Meal Scheme

(*i*) *Calorific Value of Mid-Day Meals:* The cooked mid day meal consists of 100 grams of wheat/rice, 20 grams of pulses, 50 grams of vegetables and 5 grams of oil/fat and provides 450 calories of energy and 12 grams of protein at primary stage. For upper primary stage children, it consists of 150 grams of wheat/rice, 30 grams of pulses, 75 grams of vegetables and 7.5 gram of oil/fat and provides 700 calories of energy and 20 grams of proteins.

(*ii*) *Cooking cost under MDM Scheme:* The cooking cost covers the expenditure for pulses, vegetables, cooking oils, condiments, fuel, etc. The rate of cooking cost from 2016 is ₹ 4.13 per child per day for primary and ₹ 6.18 per child per day for upper primary. The cooking cost is shared between the centre and the states in the ratio of 60:40. for non-NER states and UTs with legislature, 100 per cent for remaining UTs and 90:10 for NER states and 3 Himalayan states viz., Himachal Pradesh, Jammu and Kashmir and Uttarakhand.

Tithi Bhojan

"Tithi Bhojan" is a concept designed to ensure greater public participation under the Mid-Day Meal Programme being followed in Gujarat. In order to bring in greater community participation, local communities are encouraged to celebrate important family events viz., birth of a child, success in exam, inauguration of new house, etc., by contributing to the mid-day meal served in the local schools. It is voluntarily served by the community/family among school children in several forms like sweets and namkeen along with regular MDM, full meals, supplementary nutritive items like sprouted beans, contribution in kind such as cooking ware, utensils, dinner sets or glasses for drinking water. All the states/UTs have been requested to consider adopting the practice of Tithi Bhojan with this nomenclature or any nomenclature suitable to the state/UT governments. The concept has been adopted by different states with local nomenclatures like '*Sampriti Bhojan*' in Assam, '*Dham*' in Himachal Pradesh, '*Sneh Bhojan*' in Maharashtra, '*Shalegagi Naavu Neevu*' in Karnataka, '*Anna Dhanam*' in Puducherry, '*Priti Bhoj*' in Punjab and '*Utsav Bhoj*' in Rajasthan.

Implementation of Automated Monitoring System

The Department of School Education and Literacy has put in place an automated system of data collection for real time monitoring of MDMS. Such data is being collected from schools with no cost to school headmaster and teachers. Under the automated monitoring system, states/UTs are setting up a suitable system of data collection (i.e. Interactive Voice Response System (IVRS)/SMS/mobile application/web application) from schools on a daily basis and using it for purpose of monitoring and timely follow-up action.

Cent per cent Aadhaar Enrolment of Children

The Department issued notification for enrolment of cent per cent students in all schools. The use of Aadhaar identity document for delivery of services or benefits or subsidies simplify the government delivery processes, brings in transparency and efficiency. Enrolment of children under Aadhaar would enable to eliminate the proxy enrolment and provide the benefits of Mid-Day Meal Scheme to the deserving children in a seamless manner.

Mid-Day Meal Rules

The Mid-Day Meal Rules, (MDM) were notified under the National Food Security Act (NFSA), 2013. All the states/UTs have been advised to disseminate and enforce the MDM Rules 2015 in all eligible schools. The salient features of Mid-Day Meal Rules include: (i) strengthen quality by making testing of food samples mandatory; (ii) enhanced role of school management committees in supervision of MDM in school; (iii) supply of foodgrains at NFSA rates of ₹ 3 per kg for rice and ₹ 2 per kg for wheat instead of BPL rates of ₹ 5.65 and ₹ 4.15 per kg respectively; (iv) food security allowance to be paid by the state government, if MDM is not provided in school on any school day due to non-availability of foodgrains, cooking cost, fuel or absence of cook-cum-helper or any other reason.

Testing of Food Samples

The Mid-Day Meal Guidelines for engagement of accredited labs by the state/UT governments are put in place for testing of the meals served in the schools.

Social Audit

Social audit means the process in which people collectively monitor and evaluate the planning and implementation of a programme or scheme. The social audit was conducted by Society for Social Audit Accountability and Transparency (SSAAT) in two districts viz., Khammam and Chittoor of undivided Andhra Pradesh during 2012-13. Encouraged by the outcome, the Department had issued guidelines in 2014 for conducting of social audit. So far 13 states viz., Bihar, Maharashtra, Odisha, Karnataka, Punjab, Uttar Pradesh, Telangana, Nagaland, Andhra Pradesh, West Bengal, Rajasthan, Mizoram and Tamil Nadu have completed the conduct of social audit.

Higher and Technical Education

There has been phenomenal growth of higher education in India since independence. There were only 20 universities and 500 colleges at the time of independence which have increased by 38 times (i.e., 760) in the case of the universities and 77 times (i.e. 38,498) in the case of colleges. Similarly, there has been tremendous growth in the enrolment also. Moreover, the statistical overview of the higher education system clearly shows that there has been phenomenal growth in institutions (universities, colleges, technical institutions) as well as in intake, enrolment, etc.

National Institutional Ranking Framework

The National Institutional Ranking Framework (NIRF) for educational institutions was launched to meet a felt need for a framework that would enable parents, students, teachers, educational institutions and other stakeholders to rank institutions on the basis of a set of objective parameters and a transparent process. Developed by a team of experts in education and heads of institutions, the portal and the framework is presently available for engineering and management institutions.

Impacting Research Innovation and Technology

To identify the needs of the country in terms of its research and technology requirements, ten goal posts have been identified and research groups are being set up to formulate time-bound plans of action for each. Leading academic institutions like IITs and ISC have been identified to set the process in motion.

Regulator Review

Lots of private institutions have come up in higher education sector with the growing trend of commercialization. They sometimes are not maintaining the laid down standards. UGC's entire functioning continues to be oriented more towards grant giving rather than regulation and enforcement of minimum standards. A UGC Review Committee was constituted in 2014. A similar committee was constituted for the All India Council for Technical Education (AICTE). The Committee is to conduct a review of the present status of AICTE and suggest restructuring and reorganizing of AICTE for attaining even better performance to meet the desired objectives.

Bachelor of Vocational Studies

The UGC has introduced the scheme for B.Voc degree with multiple exits at diploma/ advanced diploma under national skill qualification framework (NSQF). The objectives are: (i) to enhance the employability of youth; (ii) to maintain their competitiveness through provisions of multi-entry multi-exit learning opportunities and vertical mobility; (iii) to fill the gap between educated and employable and (iv) to reduce the dropout rate at the secondary level. Currently, 2035 schools across 25 states are implementing the Scheme.

Skills Assessment Matrix for Vocational Advancement of Youth

A credit framework Skills Assessment Matrix for Vocational Advancement of Youth (SAMVAY) is now in place which allows vertical and lateral mobility within vocational education system and between the current education system. The strength of this framework is the seamless integration of pursuit of academic knowledge and practical vocational skills.

Education Sector Skill Council

Education Sector Skill Council was constituted in 2014, to consider job roles other than academic faculties and teacher qualifications. The functions of the SSC, include setting up of Labour Market Information System (LMIS) to assist planning and delivery of training, identification of skill development needs and preparing a catalogue of skill types, develop skill development plan and maintain skill inventory developing skill competency standards and qualifications.

Yukti - Yogya Kalakriti ki Takneek

Yukti aims at skill development and upgradation of design and technologies enhancing the economic prospects of those engaged in traditional crafts and arts as a means of livelihood. It aims at introducing appropriate designs and technology for innovation and pedagogical methods for introducing skills for upgradation.

SAKSHAM - a Scholarship for Differently-Abled Children

SAKSHAM - Scholarship Scheme for differently-abled children aims at providing encouragement and support to differently-abled children to pursue technical education. Scholarships amounting to ₹ 5 crore per annum as tuition fees and incidentals are to be provided to needy and meritorious students for pursuing technical education at AICTE approved institution. This is to help them to achieve their college goals, despite learning issues, environmental challenges or medical bills.

Ishan Uday-for Students of North East Region

The UGC launched a special scholarship scheme for students of north east region, Ishan Uday from the academic session 2014-15. The Scheme envisages grant of 10,000 scholarships to students from the region whose parental income is below ₹ 4.5 lakh per annum and would be provided scholarship ranging from ₹ 3,500 to ₹ 5,000 per month for studying at undergraduate level in colleges/ universities.

Ishan Vikas - Academic Exposure for North Eastern Students

The programme has been launched with a plan to bring selected college and school students from the north eastern states into close contact with IITs, NITs and IISERs during their vacation periods for academic exposure.

Women Leader

Women appointed as chairpersons, board of governors of apex technical education institutes and in National Institutes of Technology (NITs). For the first time in the history of IITs, two women scientists were nominated on the IIT council.

Pragati

Pragati (scholarship for girl students) - is a scheme of AICTE aimed at providing assistance for advancement of girls participation in technical education. Education is one of the most important means of empowering women with the knowledge, skill and self-confidence necessary to participate fully in the development process. This is an attempt to give every young woman the opportunity to further her education and prepare for a successful future. Salient features of the scheme include: number of scholarships per annum: ₹ 4,000 'One Girl' per family, where the family income is less than ₹ 6 lakh per annum The candidates will be selected on merit at the qualifying examination to pursue technical education from amongst such candidates. Amount of scholarship: tuition fee of ₹ 30,000/- or at actual, whichever is less and ₹ 2,000/- per month for 10 months as incidentals each year. 15 per cent for SC, 7.5 per cent ST and 27 per cent for OBC candidate/applicant are reserved. Out of the total number of scholarships in each scheme, 50 per cent of them are available at each degree / diploma level and also transferrable in the event-of non availability of eligible applicant.

Swami Vivekananda Scholarship for Single Girl Child

The drop-out ratio at various levels of education for girls is much higher than that of boys. Keeping Swami Vivekananda's ideas of women education and to promote girls education, UGC has introduced the Swami Vivekananda Scholarship for Single Girl Child for research in social sciences with an aim to compensate direct costs of higher education especially for such girls who happen to be the only girl child in their family.

Know Your College

Know Your College is a portal developed for helping a prospective student make a valued judgement for selection of college providing the necessary information about the college. Details like collaborations, mobile education, vocational education, community colleges, use of ICT, model curriculum, and a research portal are available. Details about facilities for specially-abled, facilities for girls, placement facilities and entrepreneurship details are also available. Students can lodge online grievances on the portal for redressal. This application allows a student either in the country or outside to submit an online grievance.

Campus Connect

The National Mission on Education through Information and Communication Technology (NMEICT) Scheme aims to leverage the potential of ICT for teaching and learning processes. The Mission has two major components: (a) content generation, (b) providing connectivity along with provision for access devices to the institutions and learners. Under it connectivity to 419 universities/ university level institutions and more than 25,000 colleges and polytechnics in the country has been envisaged to be provided.

National e-Library

The National Digital Library of India is envisaged as a national knowledge asset which will provide ubiquitous digital knowledge source. It will support and enhance education, research and innovation catering to the needs of all types of learner groups over the country.

Swayam - Study Webs of Active -Learning for Young Aspiring Minds

Swayam is a Massive Open Online Courses (MOOCs) initiative on a national platform with a comprehensive academic structure. The integrated platform will offer courses covering engineering, humanities and social sciences etc., to be used by learners at large.

Global Initiative for Academic Network

Global Initiative for Academic Network (GIAN) aims at tapping the talent pool of scientists and entrepreneurs, internationally to encourage their engagement with the institutes of higher education in India so as to augment the country's existing acadèmic resources, accelerate the pace of quality reform, and elevate India's scientific and technological capacity to global excellence.

Research Parks

The objective of the Research Parks is to create a knowledge and innovation ecosystem through collaboration between industry and academia. It will enable, encourage and develop cutting edge technology and innovation that exceeds the global standard.

Growing Aptitude in Numerical Innovations and Training

Growing Aptitude in Numerical Innovations and Training (GANIT) week in schools affiliated to CBSE was organized to commemorate the birth anniversary of Srinivasa Ramanujan and to actively promote interest of students in mathematics.

Copyright

Acquisition of copyright is automatic and it does not require any formality. Copyright comes into existence as soon as a work is created and no formality is required to be completed for acquiring it. However, as per Section 48 of the Act, certificate of registration of copyright and the entries made therein serve as prima facie evidence in a court of law with reference to dispute relating to ownership of copyright. The Copyright Office was established in 1958. It functions under the administrative control of the Department of Higher Education. It is headed by the Registrar of Copyright, who has quasi-judicial powers in handling cases relating to copyright. The main function of the Copyright Office is to undertake registration of copyright. The Register of Copyrights provides information regarding works of copyright to the general public. In addition to registration, facilities like inspection of the Register and taking extracts thereof are also available in the Copyright Office.

As provided under Section 13 of the Copyright Act, 1957, copyright subsists in the following classes or works: (a) original literary, software, musical, and artistic works; (b) cinematographic films; and (c) sound recording. The Copyright Office also registers changes in the particulars of copyright entered in the Register of Copyrights in accordance with Rule 70 of the Copyright Rules, 2013. Section 47 of the Act also provides for inspection of the Register of Copyrights or taking certified copies of the extracts against payment of the prescribed fee. To facilitate this, an index of the works whose particulars have been entered in the Register is also maintained in the Copyright Office. While minor corrections and changes in particulars entered in the Register can be made by the Registrar, only the Copyright Board is empowered to expunge any entries made in the register on an application by the Registrar or any person aggrieved.

Procedure for Registration of Copyright: As per Section 45 of the Copyright Act, 1957 either the author or publisher or owner of copyright or any other person interested in the copyright of a work can make an application in the prescribed format along with prescribed fee to the Registrar of Copyrights for entering particulars of the work in the Register. The Copyright Office provides registration facilities to all types of works and the applications for registration of works can be sent to Copyright Office postally and online.

Modernization of Copyright Office: The e-filing facility was started in 2014 and a new logo of Copyright with newly designed certificate is being used. Digitization of copyright records is under process and about 6.00 lakhs Register of Copyrights have been scanned and will be operative soon.

There is a quasi-judicial body Copyright Board which was constituted in 1958 and had been functioning on a part-time basis. The jurisdiction of the Copyright Board extends to the whole of the country. The Board is entrusted with the task of adjudication of disputes pertaining to copyright registration and assignment of copyright, rectification of registration, grant of compulsory licences in respect of works withheld from public, unpublished Indian works, for benefit of physically disabled persons, production and publication of translations and works for certain specified purposes. The Copyright Board also determines and fixes rate of royalties for statutory licences for cover versions and broadcasting of literary and musical works and sound recordings. It also hears cases in other miscellaneous matters instituted before it under the Act. The Copyright (Amendment) Act, 2012 provides for a three member permanent Copyright Board consisting of a Chairman and two other members.

11 Energy

ENERGY is an essential input for economic development and improving the quality of life. Development of conventional forms of energy for meeting the growing energy needs of society at a reasonable cost is the responsibility of the government. Development and promotion of non-conventional/alternate/new and renewable sources of energy such as solar, wind and bio-energy, etc., are also getting sustained attention. Nuclear energy development is being geared up to contribute significantly to the overall energy availability in the country.

Power

Power development in India commenced at the end of the nineteenth century with the commissioning of electricity supply in Darjeeling during 1897, followed by the commissioning of a hydropower station at Sivasamudram in Karnataka during 1902. In the pre-Independence era, the power supply was mainly in the private sector, that too restricted to the urban areas. With the formation of State Electricity Boards during Five-Year Plans, a significant step was taken in bringing about a systematic growth of power supply industry all over the country. A number of multi-purpose projects came into being, and with the setting up of thermal, hydro and nuclear power stations, power generation started increasing significantly.

The Ministry of Power is primarily responsible for the development of electrical energy in the country. The Ministry is concerned with perspective planning, policy formulation, processing of projects for investment decisions, monitoring of the implementation of power projects, training and manpower development and the administration and enactment of legislation with regard to thermal and hydro power generation, transmission and distribution. In all technical matters, the Ministry of Power is assisted by the Central Electricity Authority (CEA).

The construction and operation of generation and transmission projects in the Central Sector are entrusted to Central Sector Corporations, viz., the National Thermal Power Corporation (NTPC), the National Hydroelectric Power Corporation (NHPC), the North-Eastern Electric Power Corporation (NEEPCO), and the Power Grid Corporation of India Limited (PGCIL). The Power Grid is responsible for all the existing and future transmission projects in the central sector and also for the formation of the National Power Grid. Two joint-venture power corporations, namely, Satluj Jal Vidyut Nigam (SJVN) (formerly known as NJPC) and Tehri Hydro Development Corporation (THDC) are responsible for the execution of the Nathpa Jhakri Power Project in Himachal Pradesh and projects of Tehri Hydro Power Complex in Uttarakhand respectively. Three statutory bodies, i.e., the Damodar Valley Corporation (DVC), the Bhakra-Beas Management Board (BBMB) and Bureau of Energy Efficiency (BEE), are also under the administrative control of the Ministry of Power. Programmes of rural electrification are provided financial assistance by the Rural Electrification Corporation (REC). The Power Finance Corporation (PFC) and Rural Electrification Corporation (REC) provide term-finance to projects in the power sector. The autonomous bodies (societies), namely Central Power Research Institute (CPRI) and the National Power Training Institute (NTPI) are also under the administrative control of the Ministry of Power. A Power Trading Corporation has also been incorporated primarily to support the Mega Power Projects in private sector by acting as a single entity to enter into Power Purchase Agreements (PPAs).

Relevant Website : www.powermin.nic.in

Power Generation

The electricity generation target for the year 2017-18 was fixed at 1229.4 Billion Unit (BU). The actual generation during (April-December, 2017 has 906.2 BU, registering a growth of 3.8 per cent over the generation of 873.1 BU during the corresponding period last year.

Deendayal Upadhyaya Gram Jyoti Yojana

Government of India launched a new scheme namely Deendayal Upadhyaya Gram Jyoti Yojana (DDUGJY) with the following objectives (a) to separate agriculture and non-agriculture feeders for judicious rostering of supply to agricultural and non-agricultural consumers in rural areas; (b) strengthening and augmentation of sub transmission and distribution infrastructure in rural areas; (c) metering in rural areas (feders, distribution transformers and consumers). The erstwhile rural electrification scheme was subsumed in DDUGJY as a separate rural electrification component and the approved outlay of the erstwhile scheme has been carried forward to the DDUGJY.

Saubhagya - Pradhan Mantri Sahaj Bijli Har Ghar Yojana

To achieve universal household electrification in the country by March, 2019, Government launched Saubhagya scheme with total cost of ₹16,320 crore including gross budgetary support of ₹12,320 crore during the entire implementation period. The scope of the Scheme includes: providing electricity connections to all un-electrified households in rural areas. APL households will get electricity connections on payment of ₹ 500 (which is payable is 10 installment in the electricity bill); providing Solar Photo Voltaic (SPV) based standalone system for un-electrified households located in remote and inaccessible villages / habitations, where grid extension is not feasible or cost effective; and providing electricity connections to all remaining economically poor un-electricied households in urban areas.

Integrated Power Development Scheme

In order to provide impetus to strengthening of power distribution sector in urban area, Ministry of Power, launched Integrated Power Development Scheme (IPDS) in 2014 with following components: (i) strengthening of sub-transmission and distribution network in urban areas; (ii) metering of distribution transformers/feeders/consumers in urban areas; (iii) IT enablement of distribution sector and strengthening of distribution network.

UDAY—Ujwal DISCOM Assurance Yojana

UDAY Scheme was launched in 2015 for a sustainable solution to the operational and financial inefficiencies of DISCOMs across the country, through targeted interventions in the form of lower interest costs, reduction of cost of power, increased revenues and improved operational efficiencies.

UDAY is voluntary scheme for participation and 26 states and 1 union territory have joined the scheme. The scheme is being monitored by an inter-ministerial committee and a state level committee. A portal (www.uday.gov.in) has been developed for ease of data entry by states/DISCOMs. This portal provides basic analytics and progress of performance of various states/ DISCOMs in the public domain as a measure of transparency.

Capacity Addition Programme and Achievement during 2017-18

Capacity Addition target of 13171.15 MW including 500 MW of nuclear has been fixed for the year 2017-18. Against this target, a capacity of 4,765 MW has been added till December 2017.

Development of National Grid

National power grid in the country is being developed in a phased manner. All five regional grids, namely northern region, western region, eastern region, northeastern region and southern region have been inter-connected in synchronous mode and total transfer capacity of inter-regional links in June, 2017 is about 75,050 MW.

The updated version of Energy Conservation Building code (ECBC) was launched 2017. The scope of ECBC 2017 includes norms and standards for building design, including norms and standards for building design, including the envelope, lighting, heating, air-conditioning and electrical systems. It sets minimum energy standard for new commercial building having connected load of 100 kw and above or contract demand of 120kw and above.

Pradhan Mantri Ujjwala Yojana

In order to provide clean cooking fuel to poor households especially in rural areas, the Government had launched Pradhan Mantri Ujjwala Yojana to provide deposit free LPG connections to 8 crore women belonging to the Below Poverty Line (BPL) households. The primary objective is to provide access to clean cooking fuel LPG to BPL households thereby protecting their health by reducing the serious health hazards associated with use of conventional cooking fuels such as firewood, coal, cowdung, etc., which causes servere indoor household air pollution. Use of LPG as a cooking fuel frees women from drugery of collecting fire wood, reduce time spent on cooking and prevent deforestation. So far, more than 5.55 crore BPL families have been benefited by this Scheme.

The eligible families are identified through Socio-Economic Caste Census list and in case, name is not found in SECC list , from seven categories i.e., beneficiaries of Pradhan Mantri Awas Yojana (PMAY-Gramin), beneficiaries of Antyodaya Anna Yojana, SC/ST households, most backward classes, forest dwellers, tea/ex-tea garden tribes and residents of islands/ river islands subject to fulfilling other terms and conditions of the Scheme.

PAHAL

Government, as a measure of Good Governance introduced well targeted systems of subsidy delivery to LPG consumers through PAHAL. This initiative was aimed at rationalizing subsidies based on approach to cut subsidy leakages, but not subsidies per se. Applicable subsidy is directly transferred into the bank account of the beneficiaries. So far, more than 22.40 crore LPG consumers have joined the Scheme. PAHAL has entered into Guinness book of World Record being largest Direct Benefit Transfer scheme, so far, more than ₹ 83,653 crore have been transferred into the bank account of consumers.

Petroleum and Natural Gas

The Ministry of Petroleum and Natural Gas is concerned with exploration and production of oil and natural gas (including import of liquefied natural gas), refining, distribution and marketing, import, export and conservation of petroleum products.

Energy is a key driver of economic growth. Efficient, reliable and affordable energy is essential for the sustainable development and inclusive growth of the overall economy. Due to rapid economic expansion, India has become world's fastest growing energy market. India surpassed Russia to become the 3rd largest energy consumer in the world after China and USA during 2015. Oil and gas accounted for around 35 per cent share in India's energy consumption. In fact, India surpassed Japan to become 3rd largest oil consumer in the world after US and China during 2015.

Relevant Website : www.petroleum.nic.in

Production of Crude Oil and Natural Gas

The crude oil production for 2017-18 was at 35.68 million metric tonnes (MMT) as against production of 36.01 MMT in 2016-17, showing a marginal decline of about 0.9 per cent, Natural gas production during 2017-18 at 32.649 billion cubic meters (BCM) registered 2.35 per cent increase over production of 31.8970 BCM in 2016-17.

Refining Capacity

Indian refinery industry has done well in establishing itself as a major player globally. India, which is second largest refiner in Asia after China, is emerging as a refinery hub with refining capacity exceeding demand. The country's refinery capacity has increased to 247.57 MMTPA in April 2018.

Production and Consumption of Petroleum Products

The production of petroleum products was at 254.40 MMT in 2017-18 as against 243.55 MMT achieved in 2016-17, showing an increase of about 4.46 per cent. During 2017-18, the consumption of petroleum products was 204.92 MMT registering a growth of 5:31 per cent as compared to consumption of 194.60 MMT during 2016-17.

Import of Crude Oil

Import of crude oil during 2017-18 was 220.43 MMT valued at ₹ 5,65,951 crore as against import of 213.93 MMT valued at ₹ 4,70,159 crore in 2016-17 which marked an increase of 3.04 per cent in quantity terms and 20.37 per cent in value terms as compared to the import of crude oil during 2016-17.

Imports and Exports of Petroleum Products

During 2017-18 imports of petroleum products were at 35.89 MMT valued at ₹ 86,946 crore which showed decline of 1.09 per cent in quantity terms and 21.49 per cent increase in value terms against 36.29 MMT imports of petroleum products valued at ₹ 71,566 crore during 2016-17. During 2017-18 exports of petroleum products were 66.76 MMT valued at ₹ 2,25,139 crore which shows an increase of 1.91 per cent in quantity terms and 15.52 per cent value terms against the exports of 65.51 MMT valued at ₹ 1,94,893 during 2016-17.

Make in India

To roll out Make in India campaign in oil and gas sector, a policy to provide purchase preference in all public sector undertakings under the Ministry was approved. The policy aims to encourage participation of domestic and overseas players in the domestic oil and gas sector, create employment opportunities, help higher value addition in the products manufactured in the country and services rendered for the oil and gas sector and reduce dependence on imports.

Energy Security

The Government has taken number of key policy initiatives in upstream hydrocarbon sector to augment domestic production of oil and natural gas in the country. With a view to increase domestic production of oil and gas, the discovered Small Field (DSF) Policy was notified for monetization of discovered small fields of ONGC and OIL, which had not been put into production. Under the policy 30 contract areas were awarded for development through International Competitive Bidding (ICB).

Hindustan Petroleum Corporation Limited

Hindustan Petroleum Corporation Limited (HPCL) is a mega Public Sector Undertaking (PSU) with 'Navratna' status. It has two refineries; one in Mumbai (west coast) having a capacity of 6.5 MMTPA and the other in Visakhapatnam (east coast) with a capacity of 8.3 MMTPA. These refineries are producing a wide variety of petroleum products-fuels, lubricants and specialty products. HPCL holds an equity stake of 16.95 per cent in Mangalore Refinery and Petrochemicals Limited, a state-of-art refinery at Mangalore with a capacity of 9.69 MMTPA.

The marketing network of HPCL consist of 13 zonal offices in major cities and 101 regional offices facilitated by a supply and distribution infrastructure comprising terminals, civiation service facilities, LPG bottling plants, lube filling plants, inland relay depots, etc. HPCL has state-of-art information technology infrastructure to support its core business. The data centre is located at Hitech city in Hyderabad.

Relevant Website : www.hindustanpetroleum.com

Gas Authority of India Limited

The setting up of Gas Authority of India Limited (GAIL), formerly known as Gas Authority of India Limited in 1984 heralded a new era of natural gas in the country. Starting as a natural gas transmission company, it is today an integrated energy company in the natural gas value chain with global footprints. Having started as a gas transmission company it grew organically over the years by building a large network of natural gas trunk pipelines covering a length of over 8,700 km. Further, to strengthen position as India's premier integrated gas company, GAIL has set up LNG import infrastructure and will be focusing on areas like city gas distribution, petrochemicals business, diversifying into high margin downstream areas in gas value chain and creating a portfolio of renewable business.

Relevant Website : www.gailonline.com

Pricing of Petroleum Products

The Administered Pricing Mechanisam (APM) or cost plus pricing for petroleum products which was introduced in 1976 was abolished from 2002, consequent to the de-regulation of the oil sector in India. The Government notified that pricing of all petroleum products except PDS kerosene and domestic LPG, would be market determined. In 2006, based on the recommendations of the Rangarajan Committee, the government changed the pricing mechanism for petrol and diesel from import parity to trade parity (trade parity being the weighted average of import parity and export parity prices in the ratio of 80:20) while the pricing of PDS kerosene and domestic LPG continues on import parity basis.

Indian Oil Corporation Limited

Indian Oil Corporation (Indian Oil) is India's flagship national oil company with business interests encompassing the entire hydrocarbon value chain- from refining, pipeline transportation and marketing of petroleum products to exploration and production of crude oil and gas, marketing of natural gas, petrochemicals, renewable energy and now into nuclear energy. The Indian Oil Group of companies own and operate 10 of India's 22 refineries with a combined refining capacity of 213.2 million metric tonnes per annum. Indian Oil's cross-country network of crude oil and product pipeline spans 10,909 km with a capacity of 75.55 MMTPA of crude oil and petroleum products and 96 MMSCMD of gas. This network is the largest in the country and meets the vital energy needs of the consumers in an efficient, economical and environment-friendly manner.

Indian Oil supplies precious petroleum products through an unmatched countrywide network of above 38,000 touch points, which correspond to about 52 per cent of the industry infrastructure. It operates more than 20,000 outlets, the largest and most extensive network of retail outlets. The Corporation's Indane cooking gas reaches the doorsteps of about 65 million households through about 5,934 distributors. These efforts are backed by supplies from 139 terminals and depots, 96 aviation fuel stations and 89 Indane bottling plants. About 6,218 bulk consumer pumps are also operational for the convenience of large consumers, ensuring product and inventory at their doorstep.

Over the years, Indian Oil has grown by expanding its own operations, bringing independent refineries like Chennai Petroleum Corporation Ltd (CPCL) and Bongaigaon Refinery and Petrochemicals Ltd. (BRPL) under its fold, by merging Assam Oil Company (AOC) and IBP Co. Ltd with itself, thus synergizing its refining as well as marketing operations. Having set up subsidiaries in Sri Lanka, Mauritius and the United Arab Emirates, Indian Oil is simultaneously scouting for new business opportunities in the energy markets of Asia and Africa.

Relevant Website : www.iocl.com

Bharat Petroleum Corporation Limited

Bharat Petroleum Corporation Limited (BPCL) is an integrated oil company, in the downstream sector, engaged in refining of crude oil and marketing of petroleum products. It has also diversified into production and marketing of petrochemical feedstock. BPCL has refineries at Mumbai and Kochi with a combined refining capacity of 21.5 MMTPA. Both the refineries are certified under Integrated Management System (IMS) which aims for a unified approach in processes, interfaces, structures and documentation systems by combining the individual management systems under ISO 9001, ISO 14001 and OHSAS 18001 reflecting the continuing commitment towards quality, environment, health and safety.

BPCL has a robust distribution network comprising major storage installations and depots; LPG bottling plants, 1938 km cross-country pipeline and two lubricant blending plants.

Relevant Website : www.bharatpetroleum.com

Oil and Natural Gas Corporation Limited

Oil and Natural Gas Corporation Ltd. (ONGC), engaged in exploration and production of crude oil, natural gas and value added products was incorporated in 1993 under Companies Act, 1956, pursuant to government's decision to transform the statutory commission into a Public Limited Company, through an Act of Parliament [Oil and Natural Gas Commission (Transfer of Undertaking and Repeal, Act, 1993)].

Relevant Website : www.ongcindia.com

ONGC Videsh Limited

ONGC Videsh Limited (OVL), is engaged in exploration and production of oil and gas outside India. OVL was incorporated as Hydrocarbons India Limited in 1965 to perform international exploration and production business. The company was rechristened as ONGC Videsh Limited from 1989. It has participated either directly or through its wholly owned subsidiaries/joint venture companies in 30 projects in 15 countries of which nine projects are operated by OVL, 7 are jointly operated and 14 managed through participating interest. Currently, OVL has oil and gas production from 10 projects in eight countries, namely, Russia (Sakhalin-1 and Imperial Energy), Syria (Al-Furat Petroleum Co.), Vietnam (Block 06.1), Colombia (MECL), Sudan (Greater Nile Petroleum Operating Company), South Sudan (Greater Pioneer Operating Company and Sudd Petroleum Operating Company), Venezuela (San Cristobal) and Brazil (BC-10). There are five projects where hydrocarbons have been discovered and are at various stages of development.

Relevant Website : www.ongcvidesh.com

Bharat Petro Resources Ltd

Bharat Petro Resources Limited (BPRL), formed in 2006, is a wholly owned subsidiary and Exploration and Production (E&P) arm of Bharat Petroleum Corporation Limited (BPCL). While BPCL is engaged in the midstream and downstream segment in India, BPRL carries out upstream activities both in India and overseas. BPRL has participating interest (PI) in 24 blocks spread across 8 countries along with equity stake in 2 Russian entities holding the license to 4 producing assets.

Relevant Website : www.bharatpetroresources.in

Oil India Limited

Oil India Limited (OIL), a Government of India enterprise, is engaged in the business of exploration, production and transportation of crude oil and natural gas. In 1959, Oil India Private Limited was incorporated to expand and develop the newly discovered oil fields of Naharkatiya and Moran in Assam. In 1961, it became a joint venture company between the Indian Government and Burmah Oil Company Limited, UK. In 1981, OIL India Pvt. Ltd. became a wholly-owned Government of India enterprise. In-country operational areas are spread over Assam, Arunachal Pradesh, Mizoram, Bihar, Andhra Pradesh, Puducherry, Andaman and Rajasthan. OIL has presence in nine countries, viz., Venezuela, Libya, Gabon, Iran, Nigeria, Yemen, Sudan, Timor Leste and Egypt, pursuing various activities.

In addition, OIL owns and operates a trunk crude oil pipeline in the north east region of the country for transportation of crude oil to feed Numaligarh, Guwahati and Bongaigaon refineries. OIL also owns and operates a branch line to feed Digboi refinery.

Relevant Website : www.oil-india.com

In response, five states namely Karnataka, Goa, Maharashtra, Gujarat and Bihar have complied with the amended provisions of the IDR Act. This Ministry is regularly following up with remaining States for early implementation of IDR Act.

New and Renewable Energy

Ministry of New and Renewable Energy (MNRE) is the nodal Ministry at the federal level for all matters relating to new and renewable energy. The Ministry has been facilitating the implementation of broad spectrum programmes including harnessing renewable power, renewable energy to rural areas for lighting, cooking and motive power, use of renewable energy in urban, industrial and commercial applications and development of alternate fuels and applications.

Relevant Website : www.nrre.gov.in

Indian Scenario

Over the years, renewable energy sector in the country has emerged as a significant player in the grid connected power generation capacity. It supports the government agenda of sustainable growth, while, emerging as an integral part of the solution to meet the nation's energy needs and an essential player for energy access. It has been realized that renewable energy has to play a much deeper role in achieving energy security in the years ahead and be an integral part of the energy planning process. Renewable energy sector landscape in India has, during the last few years, witnessed tremendous changes in the policy framework with accelerated and ambitious plans to increase the contribution of solar energy. There is a perception that renewable energy can now play a significant role, as also, there is a confidence in the technologies and capacity to do so. Enlarging the scope of the National Solar Mission symbolizes both, and indeed encapsulates the vision and ambition for the future.

Drivers for Development

At present around 69.5 per cent of India's power generation capacity is based on coal. In addition, there is an increasing dependence on imported oil, which is leading to imports of around 33 per cent of India's total energy needs. Despite increase in installed capacity by more than 113 times, India is still not in a position to meet its peak electricity demand as well as energy requirement. The peak power deficit during financial year 2001-02 was 12.2 per cent, approximately 9252 MW, however, at the end of 2014-15, the peak power deficit decreased to the order of 2.4 per cent. As a fallout of this situation, planned and un-planned measures were undertaken by the government and utilities to bridge this demand-supply gap. India faces a challenge to ensure availability of reliable and modern forms of energy for all its citizens. Almost 85 per cent of rural households depend on solid fuel for their cooking needs and only 55 per cent of them have access to electricity. However, even with this low access, most rural households face issues with quality and consistency of energy supply. Lack of rural lighting is leading to large-scale use of kerosene. This usage needs to be reduced, as it leads to increased subsidies and import dependence, and consequent pressure on foreign exchange reserves.

India has taken a voluntary commitment of reducing emission intensity of its GDP by 33-35 per cent from 2005 levels by 2030. In the recently concluded 21st Conference of the Parties to the United Nations Framework Convention on Climate Change (UNFCCC) held at Paris, France, India committed to achieve about 40 per cent cumulative electric power installed capacity from non-fossil fuel based energy resources by 2030 with the help of transfer of technology and low cost international finance including from Green Climate Fund (GCF).

Renewable Energy Potential

India has an estimated renewable energy potential of about 900 GW from commercially exploitable sources viz. Wind - 102 GW (at 80 metre mast height); small hydro - 20 GW; bioenergy - 25 GW; and 750 GW solar power, assuming 3% wasteland is made available. The Ministry had taken up a new initiative in 2014 for implementation of wind resource assessment in uncovered / new areas with an aim to assess the realistic potential at 100 m level in 500 new stations across the country under the National Clean Energy Fund (NCEF). National Institute of Wind Energy has used advanced modelling techniques and revised the estimate the wind power potential at 100 metre at 302 GW.

Renewable energy has a great potential to usher in universal energy access. In a decentralized or standalone mode, renewable energy is an appropriate, scalable and viable solution for providing power to un-electrified or power deficient villages and hamlets. Over 1.2 million households are using solar energy to meet their lighting energy needs and almost similar numbers of the households meet their cooking energy needs from biogas plants. Solar Photovoltaic (PV) power systems are being used for a variety of applications such as rural electrification, railway signalling, microwave repeaters, mobile towers, TV transmission and reception and for providing power to border outposts.

Renewable energy database is updated regularly in the country. The National Institute of Wind Energy (NIWE), formerly known as Centre for Wind Energy Technology, has developed the Wind Atlas of India. NIWE also collects data from Solar Radiation Resource Assessment stations to assess and quantify solar radiation availability and develop Solar Atlas of the country. National Institute of Solar Energy has assessed the State wise solar potential by taking 3 pre cent of the wasteland area to be covered by Solar PV modules. The Indian Institute of Science, Bengaluru has developed Biomass Atlas of India, and the Alternate Hydro Energy Centre, Indian Institute of Technology, Roorkee has assessed small hydro potential in the country.

Renewable Energy for Rural Applications

More than 35,000 biogas plants of the approved models were installed across the country with financial support of the Ministry, taking the cumulative installation to over 49.40 lakh biogas plants in all states and union territories. Under the National Biomass Cookstoves Initiative, several pilot projects have been taken up for deployment of improved biomass cookstoves for demonstration among domestic and large sized community cooking in Anganwadis, mid-day meal schemes in schools, tribal hostels, etc., Projects taken up under Unnat Chulha Abhiyan are now eligible for carbon credits under the CDM mechanism with Sardar Swaran Singh National Institute of Renewable Energy (SSS-NIRE), an autonomous institute of MNRE, located at Jalandhar, Punjab that has been designated as Coordinating and Managing Entity (CME).

National Biogas and Manure Management Programme

The National Biogas and Manure Management Programme (NBMMP) is a central sector scheme which aims to provide biogas plants as an asset for households, communities of households for meeting their clean cooking fuel needs in particular to rural/semi-urban households and organic manure for raising farm yield and productivity and maintaining the soil health. Biogas plants are, thus potential source of helping farmers in adopting organic farming. A biogas plant is a small farm infrastructure asset for farmers and household amenity for others.

The NBMMP was implemented during 2017-18 as per the demand and physical targets received from the states through their designated state nodal agencies/departments, KVIC and BDTCs.

National Solar Mission

26 SPV projects of aggregate 330 MW capacity have been commissioned. Thus, 523 MW solar PV projects and 202.5 MW solar thermal power projects have been commissioned under the bundling scheme. Under the 100 SPV power plants, 78 projects were selected to set up 98 MW capacity projects from 12 states. Against this, 71 projects of total capacity 90.80 MW have been connected to grid.A Payment Security Mechanism involving a revolving fund of ₹ 486

crore has been put in place to ensure timely payments to developers in the event of delays/ defaults in payments by the purchasing state utilities to NVVN.

Solar Cities Programme

Under Development of Solar Cities Programme the Ministry assists municipal corporations and urban local bodies in preparation of a Master Plan for increasing energy efficiency and renewable energy supply in the city.

Coal

The Ministry of Coal (MoC) has the overall responsibility of determining policies and strategies in respect of exploration and development of coal and lignite reserves, sanctioning of important projects of high value and for deciding all related issues. These key functions are exercised through its public sector undertakings, namely Coal India Limited (CIL) and Neyveli Lignite Corporation Limited (NLC) and Singareni Collieries Company Limited (SCCL), a joint sector undertaking of Government of Telangana and Government of India with equity capital in the ratio of 51:49.

Relevant Website : www.coal.nic.in

Coal Reserves

308.802 billion tonnes of coal reserves have been estimated by the Geological Survey of India. The reserves have been found mainly in Jharkhand, Odisha, Chhattisgarh, West Bengal, Madhya pradesh, Telangana and Maharashtra.

Lignite Reserves

The lignite reserves in the country have been estimated at around 44.59 billion tonnes by the Geological Survey of India. The major deposits are located in Tamil Nadu, followed by Rajasthan, Gujarat, Kerala, West Bengal, Jammu and Kashmir and union territory of Puducherry.

Coal Production

The overall production of coal for 2017-18 was projected at 730.10 MT. During the period April to December 2017 the actual production was 461.42 MT compared to 452.97 MT during corresponding period of 2016-17 showing a growth of 1.9 per cent.

Coal India Limited

Coal India Limited (CIL) is a 'Maha Ratna' company under the Ministry of Coal, with headquarters at Kolkata, West Bengal. CIL is the single largest coal producing company in the world and one of the largest corporate employers with a manpower of 3,46,638. CIL operates through 82 mining areas spread over eight provincial states of India. It has 429 mines of which 237 are underground, 166 opencast and 26 mixed mines. CIL is the apex body in coal industry under the administrative control of the Ministry of Coal. Coal India is a holding company with seven wholly owned coal producing subsidiary companies and one mine planning and consultancy company. It encompasses the whole gamut of identification of coal reserves, detailed exploration followed by design and implementation and optimising operations for coal extraction in its mines. The producing companies are: Eastern Coalfields Limited (ECL), Sanctoria, West Bengal; Bharat Coking Coal Limited (BCCL), Dhanbad, Jharkhand; Central Coalfields Limited (CCL), Ranchi, Jharkhand; South Eastern Coalfields Limited (SECL), Bilaspur, Chattisgarh; Western Coalfields Limited (WCL), Nagpur, Maharashtra; Northern Coalfields Limited (NCL), Singrauli, Madhya Pradesh; Mahanadi Coalfields Limtied (MCL), Sambalpur, Odisha. The consultancy company is Central Mine Planning and Design Institute Limited (CMPDIL), Ranchi, Jharkhand.

Relevant Website : www.coalindia.in

Neyveli Lignite Corporation Limited

Neyveli Lignite Corporation Limited (NLC) was registered as a company in November 1956. The mining operations in Mine-I were formally inaugurated in 1957. Neyveli Lignite Corporation has been conferred with 'Navratna' status since 2011. Its registered office at Chennai and corporate office at Neyveli in Tamil Nadu is a pioneer among the public sector undertakings in the energy sector. NLC operates three open cast lignite mines of total capacity of 28.5 million tonnes per annum at Neyveli and one open cast lignite mine of capacity 2.1 million tonnes per annum at Barsingsar, Rajasthan, three thermal power stations with a total installed capacity of 2,490 Mega Watt at Neyveli and one thermal power station at Barsingsar, Rajasthan with an installed capacity of 250 Mega Watt. All the mines of NLC are ISO certified for quality management system, environmental management system and occupational health and safety management system. NLC's growth is sustained and its contribution to India's social and economic development is significant.

Relevant Website : www.nlcindia.com

12 Environment

THE Ministry of Environment, Forest and Climate Change (MoEF&CC) is the nodal agency in the central government for overseeing the implementation of India's environment and forest policies and programmes relating to conservation of the country's natural resources including lakes and rivers, its biodiversity, forests and wildlife, ensuring the welfare of animals and prevention and abatement of pollution. While implementing these policies and programmes, the Ministry is guided by the principle of sustainable development. The Ministry is also the nodal agency for the United Nations Environment Programme (UNEP), International Centre for Integrated Mountain Development (ICIMOD) and the United Nations Conference on Environment and Development (UNCED). The Ministry also coordinates with multilateral bodies such as the Commission on Sustainable Development (CSD), Global Environment Facility (GEF) and regional bodies such as Economic and Social Council for Asia and Pacific (ESCAP) and South Asian Association for Regional Cooperation (SAARC) on matters pertaining to environment.

Relevant Website : www.envfor.nic.in

Botanical Survey of India

Botanical Survey of India (BSI) is the apex research organization under Ministry of Environment, Forest and Climate Change (MoEF&CC), Govt. of India for carrying out taxonomic and floristic studies on wild plant resources of the country. It was established in 1890 with the basic objective to explore the plant resources of country and to identify the plants species with economic virtues. Sir George King, the then Superintendent of the 'Royal Botanic Garden' Calcutta was appointed as first ex-officio Honorary Director of the BSI. After independence the department was reorganized in 1954 by Government of India as a part of scientific development of the country. During the successive plan periods, the functional base of BSI was further expanded to include various new areas such as inventorying of endemic, rare and threatened plant species; evolving conservation strategies; studies on fragile ecosystems and protected areas, like wildlife sanctuaries, national parks and biosphere reserves, multiplication and maintenance of endemic and threatened plant species, wild ornamentals, etc., in Botanic Gardens and Orchidaria; documentation of traditional knowledge associated with plants and development of National Database of herbarium specimens/live collection/ botanical paintings/ illustrations, plant distribution and nomenclature, plant uses, etc.

Zoological Survey of India

The Zoological Survey of India (ZSI), a premier research institution under the Ministry has completed 100 years of services to the Nation, undertaking survey, exploration and research leading to the advancement of our knowledge on the exceptionally rich faunal diversity of the country since its inception in 1916. Over the successive plan periods functions of ZSI have also expanded gradually encompassing areas like the Environmental Impact Assessment with regard to fauna; survey of conservation areas; status survey of endangered species; computerization of digitization of data on faunal resources; Environmental Information System (ENVIS) on faunal diversity; identification and advisory services; National Designated Repository of type and voucher specimens; supporting enforcement of Wildlife (Protection) Act, 1972; establishment of marine aquaria and Museum for awareness on conservation etc., and acts as a custodian of the National Zoological Collections. Headquarters are at Kolkata and 16 Regional centres are located at different parts of the country.

Forest Survey of India

Forest Survey of India (FSI), a national level organization under the Ministry is engaged in the assessment of the country's forest resources on a regular interval. Established in 1981, the Forest Survey of India succeeded the "Preinvestment Survey of Forest Resources" (PISFR), a project initiated in 1965 by Government of India with the sponsorship of FAO and UNDP. The main objective of PISFR was to ascertain the availability of raw material for establishment of wood based industries in selected areas of the country. In its report in 1976, the National Commission on Agriculture (NCA) recommended the creation of a National Forest Survey Organization for collection of reliable data through countrywide comprehensive forest resources survey at regular intervals. Consequently, PISFER was reorganized into FSI in June, 1981. After a critical review of activities, the mandate of FSI was refined in 1986 in order to make it more relevant to the rapidly changing needs and aspirations of the country.

Biodiversity Conservation

The Convention on Biological Diversity (CBD) is one of the key agreements adopted during the Earth Summit held in Rio de Janeiro in 1992. The objective of CBD are: conservation of biological diversity, sustainable use of its components, and fair and equitable sharing of benefits arising out of the use of genetic resources. Pursuant to the ratification of the CBD by India in 1994, several steps were initiated to meet the commitments under the Convention, and to realize the opportunities offered by the Convention. These efforts were aimed at bringing the legislative, administrative and policy regimes in tune with the three-fold objectives of the CBD. India enacted the Biological Diversity (BD) Act in 2002 to give effect to the provision of this Convention. India also prepared a National Biodiversity Action Plan (NBAP) in 2008, and an Addendum to NBAP in 2014 with 20 national targets on biodiversity.

The Nagoya Protocol on access and benefit sharing (ABS) adopted under the aegis of CBD in 2010, is aimed at fair and equitable sharing of benefits arising from the utilization of genetic resources.

Biosphere Reserves

The idea of 'Biosphere Reserves' was intiated by UNESCO in 1973-74 under its Man and Biosphere (MAB) Programme. The MAB, launched in 1970 by UNESCO, is a broad based ecological programme aimed to develop within the natural and social sciences a basis for the rational use and conservation of the resources of the biosphere and for the improvement of the relationship between man and the environment, to predict the consequences of today's actions on tomorrows world and thereby to increase man's ability to manage efficiently the natural resources of the biosphere.

The Indian National Man and Biosphere (MAB) Commitee identifies and recommends potential sites for designation as Biosphere Reserves, following the UNESCO's guidelines and criteria. There are 18 designated Biosphere Reserves (BRs). Out of 18 Biosphere Reserves, 10 Biosphere Reserves have been included in the world Network of Biosphere Reserves of UNESCO.

Implementing organizations are the concerned states/UT government, environment and forest departments/line departments. Lead institutes identified for the Biosphere Reserves conduct research activities on the sanctioned research projects and periodic review and progress reports are evaluated by experts and the evaluation of the completed report is done by the designated committee.

Biodiversity Conservation Scheme Relating to Biosafety

The scheme on Biodiversity Conservation was initiated during 1991-92 during the 8th Plan period, to ensure coordination among various agencies dealing with the issues relating to conservation of biodiversity, and to review, monitor and evolve adequate policy instruments for the same. The main objective is implementation of Cartegena Protocol on Biosafety, UNEP-GEF Supported Capacity building Project on Biosafety (Phase-II) Project and Strengthening of Biosafety Management System.

Cartagena Biosafety Protocol (CPB): It was negotiated under the aegis of the Convention on Biological Diversity (CBD) and adopted in 2000. India is a party to the Protocol. The main objective of the Protocol is to ensure safe transfer. handling and use of living modified organisms (LMOs) resulting from modern biotechnology that may have adverse effect on the conservation and sustainable use biological diversity, taking into account risk to human health.

Forest Protection

This Centrally Sponsored Scheme of intensification of Forest Management Scheme deals within forest fire management, to address the growing concern over adverse effects of forest fire. With this, the present Centrally Sponsored Scheme of Forest Fire Prevention and Management (FPM) was formulated.

Wildlife Conservation

There is a Wildlife Division of the Ministry that has two sub-divisions, namely, Project Elephant Division and Wildlife Division. In addition, there are three autonomous bodies. Wildlife Institute of India (WII) for wildlife research and training. Central Zoo Authority (CZA) for conservation and zoo management and National Tiger Conservation Authority (NTCA). The NTCA has been constituted by converting the Project Tiger Directorate into an autonomous body for tiger conservation. The National Zoological Park in the Capital is also a part of the Wildlife wing of the Ministry of Environment and Forests.

Wildlife Division deals with the policy and law matters and knowledge management for facilitating processes and analysis for evolution of policy and law for conservation of biodiversity and protected area network. This Division of the Ministry provides technical and financial support to the state/Ut governments for wildlife conservation under the Centrally Sponsored Scheme, Integrated Development of Wildlife Habitats and also through Central Sector Scheme- Strengthening of Wildlife Division and Consultancies for Special Tasks, and through grants in aid to the Central Zoo Authority and Wildlife institute of India. Dehradun.

The Government of India provides financial and technical assistance to the state/UT government for activities aimed at wildlife conservation through the Centrally Sponsored Scheme viz., 'Integrated Development of Wildlife Habitats'. The scheme has following three components; support to Protected Areas (national parks, wildlife sanctuaries, conservation reserves and community reserves); protection of wildlife outside protected areas; and recovery programmes for saving critically endangered species and habitats.

Wildlife Crime Control Bureau

Wildlife Crime Control Bureau (WCCB) is a statutory multi-disciplinary body established under the Ministry, to combat organized wildlife crime in the country. The Bureau has its headquarters in New Delhi and five regional offices at Delhi, Kolkata, Mumbai, Chennai and Jabalpur; three sub-regional offices at Guwahati, Amritsar and Cochin; and five border units at Ramanathapuram, Gorakhpur, Motihari, Nathula and Moreh. It is mandated to collect and collate intelligence related to organized wildlife crime activities and to disseminate the same to state and other enforcement agencies for immediate action so as to apprehend the criminals; to establish a centralized wildlife crime data bank; coordinate actions by various agencies in connection with the enforcement of the provisions of the Act; assist foreign authorities and international organization concerned to facilitate co-ordination and universal action for wildlife crime control; capacity building of the wildlife crime enforcement agencies for scientific and professional investigation into wildlife crime and assist state governments to ensure success in prosecutions related to wildlife crimes; and advise the

Government of India on issues relating to wildlife crimes having national and international ramifications, relevant policy and laws. The Wildlife Crime Control Bureau was constituted in 2007.

Central Zoo Authority

The Central Zoo Authority with its headquarters in New Delhi was established in 1992 under the provisions of the Wild Life (Protection) Act, 1972 under the provisions of the Wild Life (Protection) Act, 1972 to oversee the functioning of zoos in the country with the view to enhance their role in conservation. The main objective of the Central Zoo Authority is to enforce minimum standards and norms for upkeep and healthcare of animals in the Indian zoos and to control the mushrooming of ill-conceived, ill planned zoos, to monitor and evaluate the existing zoos and to suggest ways and means for the improvement of zoos in the country so that they can be transferred into potent centres for ex-situ conservation of endangered wild fauna.

National Zoological Park

The National Zoological Park (NZP) was set up in 1959 under this Ministry. The main objective of the Park is to complement and strengthen the national efforts in conservation of the rich biodiversity of the country, particularly the wild fauna. To achieve this objective protocol is adopted which includes: supporting the conservation of endangered species by attempting their coordinated breeding under ex-situ conditions and raise stocks for rehabilitating them in wild as and when it is appropriate and desirable; to inspire amongst zoo visitors empathy for wild animals, an understanding and awareness about the need for conservation of natural resources and maintaing ecological balance; and providing opportunities for scientific studies useful for conservation in general and creation of data base for sharing between the agencies involved in in-situ and ex-situ conservation.

Project Elephant

Project Elephant (PE) was launched by the Government of India in 1991-92 as a centrally sponsored scheme with the objectives: - to protect elephants, their habitat and corridors; to address issues of man-animal conflict; and welfare of domesticated elephants.

Animal Welfare

Animal Welfare General - Animal Board of India

General Animal Welfare covers the welfare of individual animals, mainly domesticated, as also wild animals in captivity, through Animal Welfare Board of India (AWBI). AWBI is a statutory body established with headquarters at Chennai. Its basic mandate is to advise the government on animal welfare issues, and create awareness in animal welfare and to implement the regular schemes of AWBI and also the central sector schemes for the welfare of animals.

Free Mobile Animal Clinic

The Board is providing free, on the spot veterinary treatment to sick and injured animals belonging to poor people through its Mobile Animal Clinic (MAC) programme operating Awareness Rallies Conducted During World Animal Day Week: The Animal Welfare Board of India has organized rallies to create kindness and compassion with the co-ordination of Schools in Chennai and Karuna International, Chennai under Humane Education programme.

Environmental Impact Assessment

Environmental Impact Assessment (EIA), is a planning tool to integrate environmental concerns into the developmental process from the initial stage of planning. It was first used in India as early as 1978 with river valley projects, and was subsequently extended to large public sector projects requiring Public Investment Board (PIB) clearance. These practices were formally codified for the first time in the EIA Notification, 1994. This made the requirement of environmental clearance mandatory for 37 categories of projects/ processes, listed therein. The criterion of investment was the basis for the projects requiring environmental clearance in different sectors.

Control of Pollution

Air Pollution

Rising issue of air pollution is increasingly becoming a serious concern, particularly in metro cities. A large number of cities and towns do not meet the standards for pollutants specifically for particulate matter. In a few cities including Delhi, the ambient particulate matter concentrations are much above the standards i.e., three to four times or even higher. Air quality regulation and actions for abatement of air pollution is undertaken under various provisions of Air (Prevention and Control of Pollution) Act, 1981 and Environment (Protection) Act, (EPA) 1986 which prescribes the mechanism and authorities for handling the issue. The major impact is highlighted with reference to health of people. As per the available data for Delhi and NCR for last five years, Particulate Matter (PM 10 and PM 2.5) concentrations are the major concern for the entire area, however a few violations are observed in NO2 concentrations in Delhi, Meerut and Faridabad. The concentration of SO2 is within the standard limit at all the locations in all the last five years. PM10 are inhalable coarse particles, which are particles with a diameter between 2.5 and 10 micrometers (μm) and PM 2.5 are fine particles with a diameter of 2.5 μm or less.

Generally, for young and healthy people, moderate air pollution levels are unlikely to have any serious short term effects. However, elevated levels and/or long term exposure to air pollution can lead to symptoms and conditions affecting human health. This mainly affects the respiratory and inflammatory systems, but can also lead to more serious conditions such as heart disease. People with lung or heart conditions may be more susceptible to the effects of air pollution.

Measures to Combat Air Pollution

National Ambient Air Quality Standards envisaging 12 pollutants have been notified under the EPA, 1986 along with 115 emission/effluent standards for 104 different sectors of industries, besides 32 general standards. Government is executing a nation-wide programme of ambient air quality monitoring known as National Air Quality Monitoring Programme (NAMP). The network consists of six hundred and ninety-one manual operating stations covering three hundred and three cities/towns in twenty-nine states and four union territories. With reference to vehicular pollution the steps taken include introduction of cleaner/ alternate fuels like gaseous fuel (CNG, LPG, etc.) ethanol blending, universalization of BS-IV by 2017; leapfrogging from BS-IV to BS-VI fuel standards by 1st April, 2020; on going promotion of public transport network of metro, buses, e-rickshaws and promotion of carpooling, streamlining granting of Pollution Under Control Certificate, lane discipline, vehicle maintenance, etc.

National Air Quality Index (AQI) was launched in 2015 starting with 14 cities and then extended to 34. A Graded Response Action Plan for control of air pollution in Delhi and NCR region has been notified. This plan specifies actions required for controlling particulate matter)PM emissions from various sources) and prevent PM 10 and PM 2.5 livels to go beyond 'moderate' national Air Quality Index (AQI) category. The measures are cumulative. Emergency and severe levels include cumulatively all other measures listed in the lower levels and AQI including very poor, poor and moderate. Actions listed in the poor to moderate category need to be implemented though out the year. Central Pollution Control Board (CPCB) has issued a comprehensive set of directions for implementation of 42 measures to mitigate air pollution in major cities including Delhi and NCR. In order to involve people in the efforts, Government launched a campaign called 'Harit Diwali and Swasth Diwali' in 2017 involving over 200 schools in Delhi and over two lakh schools in the country. A mini marathon for 'Swachh Hawa for Swachh and Swasth Bharat' was also organised in 2017.

Noise Pollution

As a follow-up of Section 5.2.8 (IV) of National Environmental Policy (NEP)-2006, ambient noise has been included as a regular parameter for monitoring in specified urban areas. Protocol for National Ambient Noise Monitoring Network Programme has been prepared and circulated to state pollution control boards. Central Pollution Control Board in association with state pollution control boards established Real Time National Ambient Noise Monitoring Network in 7 metropolitan cities and installed 70 noise monitoring system in Mumbai, Delhi, Kolkata, Chennai, Bengaluru, Lucknow and Hyderabad. The steps taken to reduce noise pollution, inter alia, include advisories for noise monitoring on the occasion of Diwali; prohibition of the use of fireworks between 10.00 p.m. and 06.00 a.m.; publicity regarding the ill effects of fire crackers, sensitisation of students through course curriculum besides general awareness building of public at large to avoid bursting of fire-crackers; and issuance of directions under Section 5 of Environment (Protection), Act, 1986 and under section 18 (1) (b) of Air (Prevention and Control of Pollution) Act, 1981.

Scheme of Common Effluent Treatment Plants

The concept of the Common Effluent Treatment Plants (CETPs) arose in order to make a co-operative movement for pollution control. The main objective of the CETPs is to reduce the treatment cost to be borne by an individual member unit to a minimum while protecting the environment to a maximum. Wastewater treatment and water conservation are the prime objectives of the CETP. This concept was envisaged to treat the effluent emanating from the clusters of compatible small-scale industries.

A centrally sponsored scheme has been undertaken by the Government for enabling small scale industries (SSI) to set up new and upgrade the existing common effluent treatment plants to cover all the states in the country. The salient features of the revised scheme include: (a) the central subsidy has been enhanced from 25 per cent to 50 per cent of the project cost; (b) all the three levels of treatment, primary, secondary and tertiary are to be covered for assistance. (c) the management of the Common Effluent Treatment Plants (CETP) is to be entrusted to a Special Purpose Vehicle registered under an appropriate statute.

Hazardous Substance Management

The Hazardous Sustances Management Division (HSMD) is the nodal point within the Ministry for management of solid waste including hazardous substances and chemical emergencies. The main objective of the Division is to promote safe management of solid wastes, management of hazardous substances and wastes including hazardous chemicals, in order to avoid damage to health and environment.

In addition, the Division also administers the Public Liability Insurance Act, 1991 and rules framed thereunder. The activities of the Division are carried out under three main thrust areas viz., hazardous waste management solid waste management and chemical safety.

Chemical Safety

In order to ensure chemical safety, the Ministry notified two sets of Rules under the Environment (Protection) Act, 1986 viz., (i) The Manufacture, Storage and Import of Hazardous Chemicals Rules, 1989 (MSIHC); and (ii) The Chemical Accidents (Emergency, Planning, Preparedness, and Response) Rules (EPPR), 1996. The main objectives of the MISHC rules are to: (a) prevent major accidents arising from industrial activities; and (b)limit the effects of such accidents. The rules endeavour to achieve these objectives by having a quantity-based approach. The MSIHC rules require the occupier to disclose the necessary information to the public in the neighbourhood that is likely to be affected by a major accident at the site. During the process of implementation of MSIHC Rules, 1989, it was felt that a Chemical Crisis Management System has to be established in the country to ensure proper coordination of the activities of the various authorities and to render help to the District Collector who is responsible for the preparation, maintenance and execution of an Off-Site Emergency Plan. Therefore, a set of rules entitled Chemicals Accidents (Emergency Planning, Preparedness and Response) Rules, 1996 was notified with the aim of providing administrative structure at different levels such as national, state, district and local levels for effective planning, preparedness and responses to chemicals accidents and also ensuring availability of information to public likely to be affected by an accident. The Chemical Accidents (EPPR) Rules. 1996 envisage a four-tier crisis management system in the country at the central, state, district and local levels.

Hazardous Waste Management

To address the issue of ensure environmentally sound management of hazardous waste for safety of health and environment during handling of such waste Hazardous Waste (Management, Handling & Transboundary Movement) Rules, 2008 were notified under Environment (Protection) Act, 1986. The Rules lay down procedure towards this process by providing provisions for authorization of hazardous waste generating and units using hazardous waste. It also provides for establishment of Treatment Storage and Disposal Facility (TSDF) for disposal of hazardous wastes. The rules have an important provision on regulation of import/export of hazardous waste in pursuance to our obligation under the Basel Convention on Control of Transboundary Movement of Hazardous waste and its disposal. India is party to the Convention.

The major salient features of Hazardous and Other Wastes (Management and Transboundary Movement) Rules, 2016 include the following:- the ambit of the Rules has been expanded by including 'Other-Waste'.; authorization and registration requirement is replaced with one permission i.e., authorization under the rules for all stakeholders handling the hazardous and other waste; waste management hierarchy in the sequence of priority as prevention, minimization, reuse, recycling, recovery, co-processing; and safe disposal being incorporated; the process of import/export of waste under the rules has been streamlined by simplifying the procedure and by revising the list of waste regulated for import/export; separate schedule has been introduced which comprises waste such as metal scrap, paper waste and various categories of electrical and electronic equipments for re-use purpose exempted from the need of obtaining Ministry's permission; the list of waste prohibited for import has been revised by inclusion of following items: waste edible fats and oils of animals or vegetable origin, household waste, critical care medical equipment, solid plastic wastes, other chemical wastes especially in solvent form.

e-Waste Management

The e-waste rules apply to e-waste generated from IT and telecommunication equipment and consumer electrical and electronics namely television sets (including LCD & LED), refrigerators, washing machines and air-conditioners. These rules empower the concerned state agencies to control, supervise and regulate relevant activities connected with e-waste management such as collection, segregation, dismantling and recycling. Producers are required to set up collection systems and meet the cost involved in the environmentally sound management of e-waste generated from the 'end of life' of their own products. Besides, threshold limits, which are accepted globally have been prescribed for six hazardous substances used in manufacture of electrical and electronics components. Producers are expected to achieve reduction in use of the hazardous substances (RoHS) to the prescribed limit. These rules are the main instrument to ensure environmentally sound management of e-Waste.

Solid Waste Management

Solid Waste Management Rules, 2016

The Ministry revised the rules for management of solid waste in the municipal areas after 16 years. The new rules are now applicable beyond municipal areas and extend to urban agglomerations, census towns, notified industrial townships, areas under the control of Indian Railways, airports, airbase, port and harbour, defence establishments, special economic zones, state and central government organizations, places of pilgrimage, religious and historical importance. The segregation of waste at source has been mandated. Responsibilities of generators have been fixed for segregation of waste in to three streams, wet (biodegradable), dry (plastic, paper, metal, wood, etc.) and domestic hazardous wastes (diapers, napkins, empty containers of cleaning agents, mosquito repellents, etc.) The Rules provide ways for integration of waste pickers/rag pickers. The Rules mandate local bodies to frame their bye-laws to impose 'User Fee', to be paid by the generator to waste collector and for 'Spot Fine' for littering and non-segregation. The concept of partnership as envisaged under Swachh Bharat has been introduced viz., bulk and institutional generators, market associations, event organizers and hotels and restaurants have been directly made responsible for waste segregation and management in partnership with local bodies. All resident welfare and market associations, gated communities and institution with an area >5,000 sq.m. new townships and group housing societies have been made responsible to develop in-house waste handling, and processing arrangements for bio-degradable waste.

Plastic Waste Management Rules, 2016

It is known fact that plastic has multiple uses and the physical and chemical properties lead to their commercial success but inevitably their indiscriminate disposal has become a major threat to the environment. In particular, the plastic carry bags are the biggest contributors of the littered waste and every year, millions of plastic bags end up in the environment vis-a-vis soil, water bodies, water courses, and it takes an average of one thousand years to decompose completely. Therefore, to address the issue of scientific plastic waste management, new regulations namely, the Plastic Waste (Management and Handling) Rules, 2011 were notified in 2011 which included plastic waste management. However, the implementation of these rules was not so effective because their ambit was limited to notified municipal areas whereas today, the plastic has reached our rural areas also. To address these issues and with an objective to set up self-sustainable waste management system, the Ministry notified the Plastic Waste Management Rules, 2016. The Rules provide for: (i) increase in minimum thickness of plastic carry bags from 40 to 50 microns, (ii) first time cover and stipulate minimum thickness of 50 microns for plastic sheets being used for packaging and wrapping commodities to facilitate collection and recycle of plastic waste, (iii) revamped pricing mechanisms for plastic carry bags by introducing plastic waste management fee to be paid by retailers/street vendors willing to provide carry bags as pre-registration charge, (iv) ways and means to promote gainful utilization of plastic waste such as energy recovery, in road construction, etc. (v) introducing user charge and spot fines by local authority.

Construction & Demolition Waste Management, 2016

The Ministry for the first time notified the separate set of rules for management of construction and demolition waste in the country as Construction and Demolition Management Rules, 2016. Prior to these Rules, this was regulated under the Municipal Solid Waste Management Rules, 2000 and was left at the desecration of the urban local bodies. The new rules regulate waste generated from construction, re-modeling, repair and demolition of any civil structure and make a way forward to reuse, recycle such waste in gainful manner. The new rules will apply to everyone who generates construction and demolition waste-building materials, debris, and rubble waste from construction, re-modeling, repair and demolition of any civil structure of individual or organisation or authority. Under the rules every waste generator has been made responsible for collection, segregation of concrete, soil and others and storage of construction and demolition waste generated separately, deposit at collection centre so made by the local body or handover it to the authorised processing facilities, ensure that there is no littering or deposition so as to prevent obstruction to the traffic or the public or drains. The service providers are required to prepare a comprehensive waste management plan covering segregation, storage, collection, reuse, recycling, transportation and disposal of construction and demolition waste generated within their jurisdiction. They are also responsible for removal of all construction and demolition waste.

Fly Ash Utilization

The fast-increasing demand of power coupled with its dependence on coal for about 2/3rd of its energy requirement is leading to generation of large volume of fly ash. The management of fly ash has been a matter of concern in view of requirement of large are of land for its disposal. To address the environmental problems of fly ash disposal, the Ministry issued notification on fly ash utilization in 1999 prescribing the targets for the fly ash utilization for coal/lignite power based thermal power stations with the aim to achieve 100 per cent utilization in phased manner. The notification was amended in 2003, 2009 and recently in 2016. The utilization of fly ash has increased from 6.64 million ton in 1996-97 to a level of 107.77 million ton in 2015-16. Fly ash earlier considered to be "hazardous industrial waste" material, is now considered to be useful and saleable commodity. The objectives of this notification are to protect environment, conserve the top soil, prevent dumping of fly ash from thermal power stations on land and to promote utilization of ash in the manufacture of building materials and construction activity.

International Conventions

Basel Convention

The Basel Convention on the Control of Transboundary Movements of Hazardous Wastes and their Disposal was adopted in 1989 in Basel, Switzerland. The overarching objective of the Basel Convention is to protect human health and the environment against the adverse effets of hazardous wastes. Its scope of application covers a wide range of wastes defined as "hazardous wastes" based on their origin and/or composition and their characteristics, as well as two types of wastes defined as "other wastes" (household waste and incinerator ash).

Rotterdam Convention

The Rotterdam Convention on the prior informed consent procedure for certain Hazardous Chemicals and Pesticides in International Trade came into force in 2004. India acceded to the convention a year later. The Designated National authorities (DNAs) for India are in Ministry of Agriculture and Cooperation. The Official Contact Points (OCPs) are designated in Ministry of Environment, Forest and Climate Change. There are 47 chemicals listed in Annex III to this Convention, which include 33 pesticides and 14 industrial chemicals that have been banned or severely restricted for health or environmental reasons by two or more parties and which the Conference of the Parties (COPs) has decided to subject to the Prior Informed Consent (PIC) procedure.

Stockholm Convention

The Stockholm Convention on persistent Organic Pollutants (POPs) is a global treaty to protect human health and the environment from POPs. The Convention sought initially 12 chemicals, for restriction or elemination of the production and release. Now, the Convention covers 23 chemicals. The Convention came into force in 2004. India ratified the Convention in 2006. As per Article 7 of the Convention, Parties to the Convention were required to develop a National Implementation Plan (NIP) to demonstrate how their obligations to the Convention would be implemented and NIP has been developed through Global Environment Facility (GEF) funding. Ministry of Environment, Forest and Climate Change serves as the focal point for GEF and Stockholm Convention. Designated national authorities are in Ministry of Agriculture and Cooperation and Ministry of Chemicals and Petrochemicals.

Minamata Convention on Mercury

In February 2009, the Governing Council of UNEP adopted Decision 25/5 on the development of a global legally binding instrument on mercury. At the Conference of Plenipotentiaries held in 2013 in Minamata and Kumamoto, Japan, the "Minamata Convention on Mercury", a global treaty to protect human health and the environment from the adverse effects of mercury, was formally adopted.

Strategic Approach to International Chemicals Management

In 2006, over 190 countries including India acceded to the Strategic Approach to International Chemicals Management (SAICM), an international policy framework to foster sound management of chemicals. Initial activities under SAICM included development or updating of national chemicals profiles, strengthening of institutions, and mainstreaming sound management of chemicals in national strateges. Towards this end, India initiated the preparation of the National Chemicals Management Profile to assess India's infrastructure and capacity for management of chemicals.

National River Conservation Plan

The river conservation programme was initiated with the launching of the Ganga Action Plan (GAP) in 1985. The Ganga Action Plan was expanded to cover other rivers under National River Conservation Plan (NRCP) in 1995. The objective of NRCP is to improve the water quality of rivers, which are major water sources in the country, through implementation of pollution abatement works in various towns along identified polluted stretches of rivers on cost sharing basis between the central and state governments. Presently NRCP (excluding Ganga and its tributaries) has covered polluted stretches of 31 rivers in 75 towns spread over 14 states and a treatment capacity of 2445 million litres per day (mld) has been created so far under NRCP (excluding Ganga and its tributaries).

Conservation of Lakes

So far under NLCP/NPCA, a total of 46 projects for conservation of 63 lakes have been sanctioned in 14 states for undertaking works like providing sewerage system and sewage treatment plants, interception and diversion of sewage, desilting, catchment area treatment, storm water management etc. Conservation works for 34 lakes have been completed. Major projects presently under implementation include Dal lake in Jammu & Kashmir, Shivpuri and Sindh Sagar lakes in Madhya Pradesh, twin lakes at Mokokchung in Nagaland (NE region), Annasagar, Pushkar and Pichola lakes in Rajasthan, Ramgarh Tal and Laxmital in Uttar Pradesh.

Conservation of Wetlands

Wetlands are lifeline for a very large number of people and an important source of fresh water to mankind. They provide a host of ecosystem services to humanity, in addition to being host to rich biodiversity. However, due to anthropogenic activities, wetlands are getting degraded. Major pressures on wetlands include fragmentation of hydrological regimes, siltation from degraded catchments, pollution, spread of invasive species and over-harvesting of resources.

To control degradation and conserve wetlands, the National Wetland Conservation Programme (NWCP) was initiated in 1987 and financial assistance is being provided to the state governments for implementing action plans for conservation and management of identified wetlands.

Ramsar Convention

As a commitment for conserving potential wetlands, India became a signatory to the Ramsar Convention in 1982. As per this convention, India is committed for international cooperation and to take national action for conservation and wise use of Wetlands. At present there are 26 Ramsar sites in India.

Wetlands (Conservation and Management) Rules

To implement the objectives of the convention, a regulatory mechanism was put in place through Wetlands (Conservation and Management) Rules in December, 2010 vide GSR-951(E). Central Wetland Regulatory Authority (CWRA) has been constituted under the Wetlands Rules, 2010. 25 wetlands spread over 14 states have already been notified under these Rules.

World Wetland Day

Each year, World Wetland Day is celebrated on 2nd February for increasing awareness and spreading need for conservation and wise use of wetlands all over the world. The World Wetland Day-2017 with the theme 'Wetlands for Disaster Risk Reduction' was celebrated in collaboration with the Government of Madhya Pradesh at Bhoj Wetlands, Bhopal, one of the 26 Ramsar Sites that India has designated under the Ramsar Convention.

National Afforestation and Eco-Development Board

In order to promote afforestation, tree planting, ecological restoration and eco-development activities in the country, the National Afforestation and Eco-Development Board (NAEB) was set up in 1992. Special attention is also given by NAEB to the regeneration of degraded forest areas and lands adjoining forest areas, national parks, sanctuaries and other protected areas as well as the ecologically fragile areas like the Western Himalayas, Aravallis, and Western Ghats etc.

The objective of the NAEB include:- evolve mechanisms for ecological restoration of degraded forest areas and adjoining lands through systematic planning and implementation; restore, through natural regeneration or appropriate intervention, the forest cover in the country for ecological security and to meet the fuelwood, fodder and other needs of the rural communities; sponsor research and extension of findings to disseminate new and proper technologies for the regeneration and development of degraded forest areas and adjoining lands; create general awareness and help foster a people's movement for promoting afforestation and eco-development with the assistance of voluntary agencies, non-governmental organizations, panchayati raj institutions and others and promote participatory and sustainable management of degraded forest areas and adjoining lands.

National Afforestation Programme Scheme

National Afforestation Programme (NAP) is a major afforestation scheme of the NAEB in the Government of India. Launched in 2000-02, the scheme has acquired a pan India ambit over the last nine years of its implementation and was being implemented by 28 states of the country through a twin institutional set up of Forest Development Agencies (FDAs) at the forest division level and Joint Forest Management Committees (JFMCs) at the village level. From 2010-11, State Forest Development Agency (SFDA) were constituted at the state level to smoothen the fund flow to the FDAs. The programme is now implemented through a three tier system of State Forests Development Agency (SFDA) at the state level, Forest Development Agency (FDAs) at the district/forest division level and Joint Forest Management Committees (JFMCs) at the village level. Under Entry Point Activities, community assets are created with a 'care and share' concept. The objectives of the scheme include: protection and conservation of natural resources through active involvement of the people; checking land degradation, deforestation and loss of biodiversity; ecological restoration and environmental conservation and eco-development; evolving village level people's organization which can manage the natural resources in and around villages in a sustainable manner; capability endowment and skill enhancement for improving employability of the rural people.

Eco-Development Forces Scheme

Eco-Development Forces (EDF) Scheme was established in 1980s as a scheme being implemented through Ministry of Defence for ecological restoration of terrains, rendered difficult either due to severe degradation or remote location or difficult law and order situation. It is based on twin objectives of ecological regeneration in difficult areas, and promotion of meaningful employment to ex-servicemen.

Under this scheme, the establishment and operational expenditure on the Eco Task Force (ETF) Battalions raised by Ministry of Defence is reimbursed by Ministry of Environment, Forest and Climate Change while the inputs like sapling, fencing, etc., and also the professional and managerial guidance is provided by the state forest departments.

National Mission for Green India

The National Mission for a Green India (GIM), one of the eight missions under the National Action Plan on Climate Change aims at protecting and enhancing India's diminishing forest cover to counter the perils of climate change. It envisages a holistic view of greening and focuses on multiple ecosystem services along with carbon sequestration and emission reduction as co-benefit.

The Mission embarks on meeting the challenge of climate change adapation and mitigation through sub-missions and a cross-cutting intervention: a) enhancing quality of forest cover and improving eco-system services; b) eco-system restoration and increase in forest cover; c) agroforestry and social forestry; d) promoting alternative fuel energy.

Declaring Eco-Sensitive Areas in Western Ghats

The Western Ghats is a global biodiversity hotspot and a treasure trove of biological diversity harbouring many endemic species of flowering plants, fishes, amphibians, reptiles, birds, mammals and invertebrates. It is also the origin of Godavari, Krishna, Cauvery and a number of other rivers of Peninsular India, upon which much of the economy of the region is dependent. Therefore, there is a need to conserve and protect the unique biodiversity of Western Ghats, while allowing for sustainable and inclusive development of the region. The concept of Ecologically Sensitive Area (ESA) provides a mechanism to conserve biological diversity of an area while allowing for sustainable development to take place.

National Natural Resources Management System

The Scheme "National Natural Resources Management System (NNRMS)" of the Ministry is a part of an umbrella scheme of the erstwhile Planning Commission-Planning Committee-National Natural Resources Management System (PC-NNRMS) and is in operation since, 1985. The prime objective of PCNNRMS is utilization of remote sensing technology for inventorization, assessment and monitoring of country's natural resources.

Forestry Research

Indian Council of Forestry Research and Education

Indian Council of Forestry Research and Education, Dehradun, (ICFRE), an apex body in the national forestry research system, has been undertaking the holistic development of forestry research, education and extension covering all aspects of forestry. The Council deals with solution based forestry research in tune with the emerging issues in the sector, including global concerns such as climate change, conservation of biological diversity, combating desertification and sustainable management and development of resources. Major institutes engaged in forest research include: Forest Research Institute Dehradun; Institute of Forest Genetics and Tree Breeding, Coimbatore; Institute of Wood Science and Technology, Bengaluru; Tropical Forest Research Institute, Jabalpur; Rain Forest Research Institute, Jorhat; Arid Forest Research Institute, Jodhpur; Himalayan Forest Research Institute, Shimla; Institute of Forest Productivity, Ranchi; Institute of Forest Biodiversity, Hyderabad.

Indira Gandhi National Forest Academy

The Academy was constituted in 1987 by upgrading and renaming the erstwhile Indian Forest College, established in 1938. The Academy imparts professional training to the Indian Forest Services (IFS) Probationers and has been accorded the status of "Staff College" for imparting mid-career training for officers of the Indian Forest Service (IFS). The mandate of the Academy is to impart training to IFS Probationers by way of knowledge and skills to the professional foresters and help them to develop competence for managing the country's forest and wildlife resources on a sustainable basis, besides enabling them to act as catalysts for environmental protection, economic development and social change. Its capacity building programmes include training the new entrants to the service, in-service training (Mid Career training programme) to contemporary batches of IFS officers, skills upgradation training to officers inducted into the IFS on promotion from the State Forest Service (SFS). The Academy also provides orientation courses to various other stakeholders like joint training for members of All India Services, Indian Revenue Services Probationers, members of higher judiciary etc.

Wildlife Institute of India

Wildlife Institute of India (WII) was established in 1986 in Dehradun as an autonomous institute of the Ministry. The Institute has emerged as a premier training and research institution in the field of wildlife and protected area management in south and south east Asia. Its primary mandates are to: (i) carry out scientific and applied research on various issues of wildlife and biodiversity conservation, (ii) develop wildlife and biodiversity conservation, (ii) develop wildlife science as a discipline through academic activities, (iii) build capacity in the field of wildlife management and conservation planning, (iv) provide technical inputs to MoEFCC and other international organizations. The Institute has been generating quality information and knowledge products in the field of wildlife science through research and mainstreaming it in capacity building programmes for various target groups and provide advisory support to central and state governments.

Biodiversity Conservation and Rural Livelihood Improvement Project

Wildlife Institute of India (WII) is one of the implementing partners in this project for enhancing capacities of the project implementers and as a knowledge management centre on landscape approach to biodiversity conservation.

National Green Corps Programme

National Green Corps (NGC) were formulated in 2001-02. The phenomenal response that NGC received has made the network more than 1,00,000 Eco clubs across the country in 15 years, making it one of the largest conservation networks. Under NGC programme, 86765 Ecoclubs were supported.

National Environmental Awareness Campaign

The (NEAC) was launched in mid 1986 with the objective of creating environmental awareness at the national level. In this campaign, nominal financial assistance is provided to NGOs, schools, colleges, universities, research institutes, women and youth organisations, army units, government departments, etc., from all over the country for conducting awareness raising and action oriented activities. The theme for 2016-17 was "Swachh Bharat Mission, Ganga Rejuvenation and River Cleaning".

National Nature Camping Programme

National Nature Camping Programme is an initiative of the Ministry in environment education which is aimed at creating greater awareness, understanding and empathy of children with and for the environment. Through this initiative it is hoped that every child who goes through middle school (classes VI-VIII) to get at least one opportunity for a 2-3 day camping experience during these years.

GLOBE

Global Learning and Observation to Benefit the Environment (GLOBE) is a hands on international environmental science and education programme that brings students, teachers and scientists together to study the global environment. MoEFCC and US Government signed an agreement in 2000 to implement the Globe programme in India. Indian Environmental Society, Delhi is an implementing agency for Globe in India.

Centre of Excellence

The Scheme-Centre of Excellence was initiated in the Sixth Five Year Plan. The objective of the scheme is to provide selective support to the universities, reputed institutions including NGOs, professional organizations and other scientific and technological institutions to enable them to develop into advanced centres at the national level in that particular subject area to cater the need of the Ministry. At present there are seven Centre of Excellences functioning under this Ministry. These are Centre for Environment Education, Ahmedabad; CPR Environmental Education Centre, Chennai; Centre for Ecological Sciences, Indian Institute of Science, Bengaluru; Salim Ali Centre for Orhithology and History, Coimbatore; Centre for Environment Management of Degraded Eco systems, Delhi; Madras School of Economics, Chennai; and Foundation for Revitalization of Local Health Traditions, Bengaluru.

National Green Tribunal

The National Green Tribunal (NGT) was set up in 2010 under the NGT Act, 2010, for the purpose of effective and expeditious disposal of cases relating to environmental protection and conservation of forests and other natural resources including enforcement of any legal right relating to environment and giving relief and compensation for damages to persons and property and for matters connected therewith or incidental thereto.

It is a specialized body equipped with the necessary expertise to handle environmental disputes involving multi-disciplinary issues. The Tribunal shall not be bound by the procedure laid down under the Code of Civil Procedure, 1908, but shall be guided by principles of natural justice. The Tribunal is mandated to make an endeavour for disposal of applications or appeals finally within 6 months of filing.

NGT has five places of sitting, i.e, the Principal Bench in Delhi and Zonal Benches in Pune, Kolkata, Bhopal and Chennai. Apart from this the Tribunal holds three circuit Benches at Shimla, Shillong and Jodhpur.

Climate Change

The earth's climate has always changed and evolved. Some of these changes have been due to natural causes but other can be attributed to human activities such as deforestation, emissions from industry and transport etc. which have led to accumulation of gases and aerosols in the atmosphere. These gases are known as Greenhouse Gases (GHGs) because they trap heat and raise air temperatures near the ground, acting like a greenhouse on the surface of the planet. In order to create and strengthen the scientific and analytical capacity for assessment of climate change in the country different studies under Climate Change Action Programme (CCAP) were initiated. Many important bilateral and multilateral meetings and negotiations including Conference of Parties (CoP-22) were held.

National and State Action Plans on Climate Change

India's domestic strategy for addressing climate change is embedded in many of its social and economic development programmes. The National Action Plan on Climate Change (NAPCC) is being implemented through the nodal ministries in specific sectors/ areas. Eight national missions in the area of solar energy, enchanced energy efficiency, sustainable agriculture, sustainable habitat, water, Himalayan eco-system, Green India and strategic knowledge for climate change form the core of NAPCC.

National Adaptation Fund for Climate Change

National Adaptation Fund for Climate Change (NAFCC) is a central sector scheme under implementation in the 12th Five Year Plan with National Bank for Agriculture and Rural Development (NABARD) as National Implementing

Entity (NIE). The overall aim of the fund is to support concrete adaptation activities which are not covered under on-going activities through the schemes of state and central government, that reduce the adverse impact of climate change facing communities, sectors and states.

Climate Change Action Programme

Ministry is implementing a scheme titled 'Climate Change Action Programme' since January, 2014, with an objective to create and strengthen the scientific and analytical capacity for assessment of climate change in the country, putting in place appropriate institutional framework for scientific and policy initiatives and implementation of climate change related actions in the context of sustainable development. The NCAP is a major multi-institutional and multi-agency study. In this initiative, MoEF & CC will collaborate with the Ministry of Earth Sciences, the Indian Space Research Organization, the Ministry of Science and Technology and other associated agencies to enhance understanding of the role of black carbon in climate change through monitoring and assessment of the impacts of Black Carbon using modeling techniques.

Paris Agreement

India ratified the Paris Agreement to the UNFCCC in 2016. The action plan for implementation of Paris Agreement and its components is being developed.

International Negotiations on Climate Change

During the financial year 2016-17, many important bilateral and multilateral meetings and international negotiations on climate change were held.

Ozone Cell

Ozone Layer Protection

Ozone, a tri-atomic molecule of oxygen is formed from oxygen naturally in the upper levels of the earth's atmosphere by high energy ultraviolet (UV) radiation from the sun. The UV radiation breaks down oxygen molecules, releasing free atoms, some of which bond with other oxygen molecule to form ozone. About 90 per cent of ozone formed in this way lies between 10 and 50 kilometers above the earth's surface, called the Stratosphere. The ozone found in the part of the atmosphere is called the ozone layer.

The ozone layer absorbs all the harmful UV-B radiations emanating from the sun. It protects plant and animal life from UV-B radiation. The UV-B radiation has the potential to cause skin cancer, eye cataract, suppress body's immune system, decrease crop yield etc., which led to the adoption of the Vienna Convention for the Protection of the Ozone Layer in 1985 and the Montreal Protocol on Substances that Deplete the Ozone Layer in 1987. The mandate of the Montreal Protocol is to phase out the production and consumption of the

Ozone Depleting Substances (ODSs). India is a party to the Vienna Convention for the Protection of the Ozone Layer and the Montreal Protocol on Substances that Deplete the Ozone Layer and its all amendments/adjustments. The MoEF&CC has set up the Ozone Cell as a National Ozone Unit (NOU) to render necessary services for effective and timely implementation of the protocol and its ODs phase-out programme in India.

Vienna Convention

The Vienna Convention for the Protection of the Ozone Layer and its Montreal Protocol on Substances that Deplete the Ozone Layer are the international treaties specific for the protection of the Stratospheric Ozone (Ozone layer). The Montreal Protocol has been recognized as the most successful international environmental treaty in history. It has been universally ratified and all the 197 UN member countries of the world are the parties to the Vienna Convention and its Montreal Protocol. In the 29 years of operation of the Montreal Protocol, extraordinary international cooperation under this agreement has led to phase-out of production and consumption of several major ODSs such as CFCs, CTC and halons globally from 2010.

United Nations Convention to Combat Desertification

The concern for arresting and reversing land degradation and desertification gets reflected in many of the national policies (for e.g., National Water Policy 2012; National Forest Policy 1988; National Agricultural Policy 2000; Forest (Conservation) Act, 1980; Environment (Protection) Act, 1986, National Environmental Policy, 2006; National Policy for Farmers, 2007; National Rainfed Area Authority (NRAA)-2007 which have enabling provisions for addressing these problems. It is also implicit in the coals of Sustainable Forest Management (SFM), Sustainable Agriculture, Sustainable Land Management (SLM) and the overarching goal of Sustainable development which the country has been pursuing. India became a signatory to the United Nations Convention to Combat Desertification (UNCCD) in 1994. MoEF&CC is the nodal Ministry in the government of India for the UNCCD, and Desertification cell is the nodal point within MoEF&CC to co-ordinate all issues pertaining to the convention.

International Cooperation and Sustainable Development

International Cooperation and Sustainable Development (IC&SD) Division of the Ministry coordinates matters related to international environmental cooperation and sustainable development including Sustainable Development Goals (SDGs).

United Nations Environment Programme

India is a member of UNEP and provides annual financial contribution of USD 100,000 to UNEP Environment Fund. Three of the thirty three members on UNEP's International Resource Panel (IRP) are currently from India. The Ministry is a member of the IRP Steering Committee. IRP supports UNEP's Resource Efficiency/Sustainable consumption and Production (SCP) sub-programme and is carrying out assessments of the world's most critical resource issues with a view to developing practical solutions for government policymakers, industry and society.

Global Environment Facility

India is a founder member of Global Environment Facility (GEF). Set up in 1991, GEF is the designated multilateral funding mechanism of 183 countries to provide incremental finance for addressing global environmental benefits which are also identified national priorities. The GEF mandate is decided as per the guidance provided by the Conference of the parties of the multilateral environmental conventions namely Convention on Biological Diversity (CBD), United Nations Framework Convention on Climate Change (UNFCCC), United Nations Convention to Combat Desertification (UNCCD), Stockholm Convention on PoPs and Minamata Convention on Mercury. The GEF grants are available under five focal areas namely, biodiversity, climate change, land degradation, international waters and chemicals and waste.

13 Finance

THE Ministry of Finance is responsible for administration of finances of the Government. It is concerned with all economic and financial matters affecting the country as a whole including mobilization of resources for development and other purposes. It regulates expenditure of the government including transfer of resources to the states. It is an important ministry within the government concerned with the economy of the country, serving as the Indian treasury department. In particular, it concerns itself with taxation, financial legislation, financial institutions, capital markets, centre and state finances, and the Union Budget. The Ministry is also the cadre controlling authority of the Indian Revenue Service, Indian Economic Service, Indian Cost Accounts Service and Indian Civil Accounts Service.

This Ministry consists of five departments, namely, (i) Economic Affairs, (ii) Expenditure, (iii) Revenue, (iv) Investment and Public Asset Management; and (v) Financial Services.

Relevant Website : www.finmin.nic.in

Department of Economic Affairs

The Department of Economic Affairs is the nodal agency of the government to formulate and monitor country's economic policies and programmes having a bearing on domestic and international aspects of economic management. A principal responsibility of this Department is the preparation and presentation of the Union Budget (including Railway Budget) to the Parliament and budget for the state governments under President's Rule and union territory administrations.Other functions include: formulation and monitoring of macroeconomic policies, including issues relating to fiscal policy and public finance, inflation, public debt management and the functioning of capital market including stock exchanges; production of bank notes and coins of various denominations, postal stationery, postal stamps; and cadre management, career planning and training of the Indian Economic Service (IBS).

The Department, inter alia, monitors current economic trends and advises the Government on all matters having bearing on internal and external aspects of economic management including, prices, credit, fiscal and monetary policy and investment regulations. All the external, financial and technical assistance received by India, except through specialized International Organizations like FAO, ILO, UNIDO and except under International bilateral specific agreement in the field of science and technology, culture and education are also monitored by this Department.

Department of Economic Affairs (DEA) is divided into fourteen functional Divisions, namely: (i) Administration and Coordination Division; (ii) Aid, Accounts and Audit Division; (iii) Bilateral Cooperation Division; (iv) Budget Division; (v) Coin and Currency Division; (vi) Economic Division; (vii) Financial Market Division; (viii) Financial Sector Reforms and Legislation Division; (ix) Financial Stability Division; (x) Infrastructure Policy and Finance Division; (xi) International Economic Relations Division; (xii) Investment Division; (xiii)Multilateral Institutions Division;and (xiv) Statistical and Data Analysis and Monitoring Division. The Department of Economic Affairs is also responsible for preparation and presentation of Union Budget to the Parliament and the Budget for the state governments under President's Rule and union territory administrations. The Directorate of Currency has the administrative control of the Security Printing and Minting Corporation of India Limited (SPMCIL), a wholly owned Government of India Corporation that manages Government of India mints, currency presses, security presses and security paper mill. In addition to formulating and executing policies and programmes relating to designs/security feature of bank notes and coins and issue of commemorative coins, the Directorate of Currency has also been mandated to conduct R and D activities in this area and indigenization of all materials required for production of bank notes and others security products.

Relevant Website : www.dea.gov.in

Annual Budget

The Union Budget (including the Rail Budget) is presented each year on the first working day of February by the Finance Minister of India in Parliament.

Annual Financial Statement

Under Article 112 of the Constitution, a statement of estimated receipts and expenditure of the Government of India has to be laid before Parliament in respect of every financial year. This statement titled "Annual Financial Statement" is the main Budget document. The Annual Financial Statement shows the receipts and payments of government under the three parts in which government accounts are kept: (i) Consolidated Fund, (ii) Contingency Fund and (iii) Public Account. All revenues received by government, loans raised by it, and also its receipts from recoveries of loans granted by it, form the Consolidated Fund. All expenditure of government is incurred from the Consolidated Fund and no amount can be withdrawn from the Fund without authorisation from Parliament. Occasions may arise when government may have to meet urgent unforeseen expenditure pending authorisation from Parliament. The Contingency Fund is an imprest placed at the disposal of the President to incur such expenditure. Parliamentary approval for such expenditure and for withdrawal of an equivalent amount from the Consolidated Fund is subsequently obtained and the amount spent from Contingency Fund is subsequently recouped to the Fund. The corpus of the Fund authorised by the Parliament, at present, is ₹ 500 crore.

Besides the normal receipts and expenditure of Government which relate to the Consolidated Fund, certain other transactions enter Government accounts, in respect of which, Government acts more as a banker, for example, transactions relating to provident funds, small savings collections and other deposits, etc. The moneys thus received are kept in the Public Account and the connected disbursements are also made therefrom. Parliamentary authorisation for such payments from the Public Account is, therefore, not required. In a few cases, a part of the revenue of Government is set apart in separate funds for expenditure on specific objects like road development, primary education including mid-day meal scheme, etc. These amounts are withdrawn from the Consolidated Fund with the approval of Parliament and kept in the Public Account for expenditure on the specific objects. The actual expenditure proposed on the specific objects is, also submitted for vote of Parliament.

Under the Constitution, Budget has to distinguish expenditure on revenue account from other expenditure. Government Budget, therefore, comprises (i) Revenue Budget; and (ii) Capital Budget.

Demands for Grants

The estimates of expenditure from the Consolidated Fund included in the Annual Financial Statement and required to be voted by the Lok Sabha are submitted in the form of Demands for Grants in pursuance of Article 113 of the Constitution. Generally, one Demand for Grant is presented in respect of each ministry or department. However, in respect of large ministries or departments more than one demand is presented. Each demand normally includes the total provisions required for a service, that is, provisions on account of revenue expenditure, capital expenditure, grants to state and union territory governments and also loans and advances relating to the service. In regard to union territories without legislature, a separate Demand is presented for each of the union territories.

Finance Bill

At the time of presentation of the Annual Financial Statement before Parliament, a Finance Bill is also presented in fulfilment of the requirement of Article 110(1)(a) of the Constitution, detailing the imposition, abolition, remission, alteration or regulation of taxes proposed in the Budget. A Finance Bill is a Money Bill as defined in Article 110 of the Constitution. It is accompanied by a Memorandum explaining the provisions included in it.

Appropriation Bills

After the Demands for Grants are voted by the Lok Sabha, Parliament's approval to the withdrawal from the Consolidated Fund of the amounts so voted and of the amount required to meet the expenditure charged on the Consolidated Fund is sought through the Appropriation Bill. Under Article 114(3) of the Constitution, no amount can be withdrawn from the Consolidated Fund without the enactment of such a law by Parliament.

Sources of Revenue

In accordance with the Constitution (Eightieth Amendment) Act, 2000, which has been given retrospective effect from April 1, 1996, all taxes to in the Union List, except the duties and taxes referred to in Articles 268 and 269, respective surcharge on taxes and duties referred to in Article 271 and any cess levied for specific purpose under any law made by Parliament, shall be levied and collected by the Government of India and shall be distributed between the Union and the states in such manner as may be prescribed by the President on the recommendations of the Finance Commission. For the period 2015-2020, the manner of distribution between the Centre and the states has been prescribed in Presidential Orders issued after considering the recommendations of the Fourteenth Finance Commission. The main sources of Union Tax revenue are customs duties, union excise duties, service tax, corporate and income taxes, non—tax revenues largely comprise interest receipts, dividends/profits, fines and miscellaneous receipts collected in the exercise of sovereign functions, regulatory charges and license fees and user charges for publicly provided goods and services.

Public Debt and Other Liabilities

The Public Debt of India is classified into three categories of Union Government liabilities into internal debt, external debt and other liabilities.

Internal debt for Government of India largely consists of fixed tenure and fixed rate government papers (dated securities and treasury bills) which are issued through auctions. These include market loans (dated securities), treasury bills (91, 182 and 364 days) and 14 day treasury bills (issued to state governments only), cash management bills, special securities issued to the Reserve Bank of India (RBI), compensation and other bonds, non-negotiable and non-interest bearing rupee securities issued to international financial institutions and securities issued under market stabilization scheme with a view to reduce dependency on physical gold and reduce imports.

External debt represents loans received from foreign governments and multilateral institutions. The Union Government does not borrow directly from international capital markets. Its foreign currency borrowing takes place from multilateral agencies and bilateral sources, and is a part of official development assistance (ODA). At present, the Government of India does not borrow in the international capital markets.

"Other" liabilities, not a part of public debt, includes other interest bearing obligations of the government, such as post office saving deposits, deposits under small savings schemes, loans raised through post office cash certificates, provident funds and certain other deposits.

The Reserve Bank manages the public debt of the Central and the state governments and also acts as a banker to them under the provisions of the Reserve Bank of India Act, 1934 (Section 20 and 21). It also undertakes similar functions for the state governments by agreement with the Government of the respective state (under Section 21 A).

Reforms in Budget 2018-19

The Budget- 2018-19 contained major reforms, prominent among them are: 'Operation Green' to address the price fluctuations in potato, tomato and onion; creation of two new funds of ₹ 10,000 crore for fisheries and animal husbandry; re-structuring of National Bamboo Mission; higher targets for Ujjwala, Saubhagya and Swachh Mission for free LPG connections, electricity and toilets; outlay on health, education and social protection increased; Eklavya Residential School for tribal students by 2022; fiscal deficit pegged at 3.5 per cent for 2018-19; development of ten prominent sites as iconic tourist destinations; hike in deduction limit for health insurance premium and / or medical expenditure from ₹ 30,000 to ₹ 50,000 under Section 80D; proposed changes in customs duty to promote creation of more jobs and to incentivise domestic value addition and Make in India in sectors such as food processing, electronics, auto components, footwear,furniture,etc.

From the Budget 2017-18 itself new reforms were firmed up for the first time. It contained three major reforms. First, the presentation of the Budget was advanced to 1st February to enable the Parliament to avoid a Vote on Account and pass a single Appropriation Bill for 2017-18, before the close of the current financial year. This enabled the ministries and departments to operationalise all schemes and projects, including the new schemes, right from the commencement of the next financial year. They would be able to fully utilise the available working season before the onset of the monsoon. Second, the merger of the Railways Budget with the General Budget was a historic step. The colonial practice prevalent since 1924 was discontinued. This decision brought the Railways to the centre stage of Government's fiscal policy and facilitated multi modal transport planning between railways, highways and inland waterways. The functional autonomy of Railways will, however, continue. Third, the Plan and non-Plan classification of expenditure has been done away with. This will give a holistic view of allocations for sectors and ministries and would facilitate optimal allocation of resources.

Social Sector Programmes

The flagship programmes continued to receive high priority, viz., Sarva Siksha Abhiyan; Mid-Day Meal Scheme; National Health Mission; Integrated Child Development Services; Swachh Bharat Abhiyan; Mahatma Gandhi National Rural Employment Guarantee Scheme, 100 Smart Cities, etc.

Direct Benefit Transfer

Direct Benefit Transfer (DBT) is a major reform initiative launched by Government of India in 2013 to provide an overarching vision and direction to enable direct cash transfer of benefits under various government schemes and programmes to individuals. Leveraging the gains in the Aadhaar Project, DBT was conceived with the objective of accurately targeting the intended beneficiaries and enhancing efficiency, transparency and accountability in delivery of benefits/services under government schemes. The mandate of DBT was universalized and extended to cover all central sector schemes and centrally sponsored schemes that have any component of cash benefit transfer to individual beneficiaries. Further, the scope of DBT has been further expanded to include in kind transfers to beneficiaries as well as transfers/ honorariums given to various enablers of Government schemes like ASHA, Aanganwadi workers, etc., and not limited to cash transfers to beneficiaries only. DBT has shown promising results in schemes like Pahal (modified DBTL for LPG subsidy), cash subsidy for public distribution system (PDS) in Puducherry, Chandigarh, Daman & Diu, Dadra and Nagar Haveli and Mahatma Gandhi National Rural Employment Guarantee Scheme (MGNREGS) across the country. The large scale implementation of DBT requires placing of new mechanisms, re-engineering of government processes and appropriate distribution of authority, responsibility and financial resources for delivery of public benefits/ services.

Schemes for the Development of Scheduled Castes and Scheduled Tribes

From 2005-06, a separate Statement on the schemes for the welfare of Scheduled Castes (SCs) and Scheduled Tribes (STs) was introduced in the Budget document. From the financial year 2011-12 this statement is focused only on Plan schemes under 'Scheduled Castes Sub Plan' and 'Tribal Sub Plan' exclusively for scheduled castes and scheduled tribes welfare schemes respectively. It shows year-wise budget Estimates and Revised Estimates of current year and Budget Estimates of next financial year.

Economic Growth

India recorded a growth of 7.1 per cent in 2016-17, highest among the major economies in the world, despite the sluggish global economic situation. The growth of Gross Value Added (GVA) for the economy was 7.1 per cent in 2016-17.

The government's systematic focus on economic growth and macro-economic stability and good monsoon make the growth outlook optimistic. The introduction of the Goods and Services Tax (GST) has provided a significant opportunity to improve growth momentum by removing barriers to trade, business and related economic activities.

Public Debt

Public debt includes: (a) internal debt comprising borrowings inside the country like market loans, compensations and other bonds, treasury bills issued to finance state governments, commercial banks and other parties as well as non-negotiable non-interest bearing rupee securities issued to the international financial institutions; and (b) external debt comprising loans from foreign countries, international financial institutions, etc. The "other liabilities" include outstanding against the various small saving schemes, provident funds, securities issued to the oil marketing companies, fertilizer companies and Food Corporation of India, reserve funds and deposits and other items.

Prices and Inflation

Inflation based on Consumer Price Index (Combined), which remained persistently high at around 9-10 per cent during 2012-14, moderated significantly to 5.9 per cent in 2014-15 and further to 4.9 per cent in 2015-16. It averaged 4.5 per cent in 2016-17 and stood at 2.4 per cent in July 2017. It averaged 3.4 per cent in 2017-18 (April-Jan) and stood at 5.1 per cent in January 2018.

Inflation measured in terms of Wholesale Price Index (WPI) icreased to 1.7 per cent in 2016-17. It averaged 2.9 per cent in 2017-18 (April-Jan) and stood at 2.8 per cent in January 2018.

Measures to Control Inflation

The government has taken a number of measures to control inflation. The steps taken, inter alia, include, (i) increased allocation for price stabilization fund to check volatility of prices of essential commodities, in particular of pulses; (ii) approved creation of a dynamic buffer of upto 20 lakh tonnes of pulses for appropriate market intervention; (iii) states/UTs empowered to impose stock limits in respect of pulses, onion, edible oils and edible oil seeds under the Essential Commodities Act and (iv) announced higher Minimum Support Prices so as to incentivize production and thereby enhance availability of food items which may help moderate prices.

Climate Change Finance

India ratified the Paris Agreement in 2016. India's comprehensive NDC target is to lower the emission intensity of GDP by 33 to 35 per cent by 2030 from 2005 levels, to increase the share of non-fossil fuels based power generation capacity to 40 per cent of installed electric power capacity by 2030, and to create an additional (cumulative) carbon sink of 2.5-3 GtCO2e through additional forest and tree cover by 2030. Provision of 'new and additional' financial resources by the developed countries from predominantly public sources and on grant/ concessional basis is extremely important for the achievement of the global climate goals. Provision of finance is embedded in UNFCCC and has also been mentioned in the Paris Agreement for addressing the adaptation and mitigation needs of developing countries. The climate actions will have very significant resource implications especially for a country like India. India's climate actions have so far been largely financed from domestic resources. India already has ambitious climate action plans in place. Preliminary domestic requirements to implement national climate plans add upto more than US$ 2.5 trillion between 2015 and 2030. Substantial scaling up of these plans would require greater resources. Developing countries like India are resource constrained and are already spending enormous amounts on climate change. Implementing climate change mitigation and adaptation actions would require domestic and new and additional funds from developed countries in view of the resource required and the resource gap.

The Green Climate Fund (GCF) is a multilateral fund created to support the efforts of developing countries to respond to the challenge of climate change. GCF launched its initial resource mobilization in 2014, and mobilized resources worth USD 10.3 billion. So far, 43 projects have been approved by the Board of the GCF. India also has one project approved by the Board with NABARD on "Ground water recharge and Solar Micro Irrigation to ensure food security and enhance resilience in vulnerable tribal areas of Odisha" from 16th GCF Board meeting. The project is approved with an outlay of USD 166.29 million including GCF grant support of USD 34.357 million whereas other financial resources would be provided by Government of Odisha and World Bank.

Foreign Exchange Reserves

India's foreign exchange reserves comprise foreign currency assets (FCAs), gold, SDRs and reserve tranche position (RTP) in the IMF. Accretion to foreign exchange reserves is the outcome of absorption of excess of capital flows balance over the current account financing needs and valuation gain/loss. In the recent past, trade deficit witnessed moderation, reflecting the impact of lower crude oil prices, among others. The level of foreign exchange reserves particularly foreign currency assets is largely the outcome of Reserve Bank of India's intervention in the foreign exchange market to stabilise the rupee value. Foreign Exchange Reserves stood at US $ 421.7 billion by February 2018 as against US $ 370 billion at end-March 2017. The current position is at a comfortable level to cushion the exchange rate volatility from any international macroeconomic uncertainty.

Exchange Rate of Rupee

During 2017-18 (April-January), the average monthly exchange rate of rupee (RBI's reference rate) varied between ₹ 65.08 per US dollar in October 2017 and ₹ 63.64 per US dollar in January 2018.

External Debt

External debt stock stood at US$ 495.7 billion at end September 2017 recording an increase of US $ 23.9 billion over the level at end-March 2017. The maturity profile of the external debt indicates dominance of long-term borrowings. At end-September 2017, long-term external debt was US $ 403 billion witnessing an increase of 5 per cent over March-end 2017 level of US $ 383.8 billion. India's foreign exchange reserves provided a cover of 80.7 per cent to the external debt stock at end-September 2017. The external debt management policy of the government emphasizes monitoring of long and short-term debt, raising sovereign loans on concessional terms with longer maturities, regulating external commercial borrowings through various restrictions and rationalizing interest rates on Non-Resident Indian (NRI) deposits. As a result, external debt has remained within manageable limits.

Social Infrastructure, Employment and Human Development

Investment in human capital like education and health are key ingredients for economic development. Much of the impoverishment in the country today can be addressed by enhancing the human capital through investments in nutrition, health, education and by providing appropriate skills for employment. Though India's social policies have focussed on the welfare of the people and also human development, challenges remain in overcoming social and economic barriers to advance the capabilities of the marginalised, women and other weaker sections of the society. With India poised for higher growth anchored on a knowledge economy, there are benefits to be reaped by investing in human capital.

Insolvency And Bankruptcy Code

A Bankruptcy Law Reforms Committee was set up in 2014 for providing an entrepreneur friendly legal bankruptcy framework for meeting global standards for improving the ease of doing business with necessary judicial capacity. Accordingly, the Insolvency and Bankruptcy Code, 2016 (IBC) became operational in 2016. The Code aims to promote entrepreneurship, availability of credit, and balance the interests of all the stakeholders by consolidating and amending the laws relating to reorganization and insolvency resolution of corporate persons, partnership firms and individuals in a time bound manner and for maximization of value of the assets of such persons and matters connected therewith or incidental thereto. It proposes a framework to ensure: early detection of stress in a business; initiation of the insolvency resolution process by debtor, financial creditor or operational creditor; liquidation of unviable businesses; and avoiding destruction of value of failed business. The Ministry of Corporate Affairs is taking further necessary steps for implementation of the Code.

Financial Stability and Development Council

With a view to strengthening and institutionalizing the mechanism for maintaining financial stability, enhancing inter-regulatory coordination and promoting financial sector development, the Financial Stability and Development Council (FSDC) was set up as the apex level forum in 2010. The Council, *inter-alia*, monitors macro prudential supervision of the economy including functioning of large financial conglomerates, and addresses inter-regulatory coordination and financial sector development issues, including issues relating to financial literacy and financial inclusion.

Financial Stability Board

Financial Stability Board (FSB) was established in 2009 under the aegis of G20 by bringing together the national authorities, standard setting bodies and international financial institutions for addressing vulnerabilities and developing and implementing strong regulatory, supervisory and other policies in the interest of financial stability. India is an active member of the FSB having three seats in its Plenary.

Infrastructure Financing

Given the enormity of the investment requirements and the limited availability of public resources for investment in physical infrastructure, it is imperative to explore avenues for increasing investment in infrastructure through various sources. In view of this, government launched the following to mobilize the long term investment in infrastructure in the country:

i.) Bank Financing: Banks continue to be major source of financing infrastructure. RBI has been modifying guidelines for advances to infrastructure including 5/25 scheme, take out financing.

ii.) Institutional Finance: The Government has also set up India Infrastructure Finance Company Limited (IIFCL) with the specific mandate to play a catalytic role in the Infrastructure sector by providing long-term debt for financing infrastructure projects. IIFCL funds viable infrastructure projects through long term debt, refinance to banks and financial institutions for loans granted by them, with tenure exceeding 10 years or any other mode approved by the government.

iii.) Infrastructure Debt Funds (IDFs): Government of India has conceptualized Infrastructure Debt Funds (IDFs) to accelerate and enhance the flow of long term debt into infrastructure projects to help in the migration of project loans for operating assets from banks to the fixed income markets.

iv.) Real Estate Investment Trusts (REITs)/Infrastructure Investment Trust (InvITs): These are trust-based structures that maximize returns through efficient tax pass-through and improved governance structures. Guidelines/Regulations for InvIT and REIT were notified by SEBI in 2014.

Public Private Partnerships

Availability of quality infrastructure is a pre-requisite to achieve broad based and inclusive growth on a sustained basis. Infrastructure is also critical for enhancing productivity and export competitiveness. Given the enormity of the investment requirements and the limited availability of public resources for investment in physical infrastructure, the projected infrastructure investments made it imperative to explore avenues for increasing investments in infrastructure through a combination of public investment and Public Private Partnerships (PPPs). PPPs bridge the deficit in financing of infrastructure projects, and also bring in cost effective new technology for operation and maintenance of created asset, thus, extracting long term value for proposition. India systematically rolled out a PPP programme for the delivery of high-priority public utilities and infrastructure and, over the last decade or so, developed what is perhaps one of the largest Programme in the world.

Information Dissemination

DEA maintains a website dedicated to PPPs, www.pppinindia.gov.in, to provide information related to PPP initiatives in the country. The website serves as a hub of information on PPP initiatives and contains related policy documents, government guidelines issued for mainstreaming PPPs. These include information on the institutional mechanisms for speedy appraisal of PPP infrastructure projects and the schemes for financial support to PPP projects. The website also contains various knowledge products developed in the

PPP cell, sharing PPP best practices to enhance the ability of the public officials as well as private developers to implement PPP projects. www.infrastructureindia.gov.in is a database of infrastructure projects including PPPs being implemented across the sectors in India. It provides key information on the status of infrastructure projects being executed by government as well as the private sector.

G-20

The G20 was formed in 1999, as a forum of Finance Ministers and Central Bank Governors, in recognition of the fact that there was a major shift in the global economic weight from the advanced economies to emerging market economies. The gradually declining role of G8 as world's economic coordinator and the increasing clout of EMEs in global deliberations on economic governance resulted in G20 replacing G8 in 1999. However, G20 rose into true prominence in 2008 when it was elevated from a forum of Finance Ministers and Central Bank Governors to that of the G20 Heads of Nations in order to effectively respond to the global financial crisis of 2007-2010.

BRICS

The BRICS nations or Brazil, Russia, India, China and South Africa form the five key pillars of south-south cooperation and are the representative voice of Emerging Markets and Developing Countries in the global forums such as the G20. The New Development Bank, established by these nations in 2015, marked its first imprints in India by signing a loan agreement for financing of the major district road project in Madhya Pradesh in March 2017. India is working closely with the Bank's management team to develop a robust pipeline of projects cutting across areas such as Smart Cities, renewable energy, urban transport, clean coal technology, solid waste management and urban water supply. The framework of swap lines, conceived as a BRICS Contingent Reserve Arrangement (CRA) with a corpus of US$ 100 billion, stands operationalised in case any member nation requires short-term liquidity support.

United Nations Development Programme

The United Nations Development Programme (UNDP) is the largest channel for development cooperation in the UN . The overall mission of the UNDP is to assist the programme countries through capacity development in Sustainable Human Development (SHD) with priority on poverty alleviation, gender equity, women empowerment and environmental protection. All assistance provided by the UNDP is grant assistance. The UNDP derives its funds from voluntary contributions from various donor countries. India's annual contribution to the UNDP has been to the extent of US$ 4.5 million, which is one of the largest from developing countries. Over and above its annual contribution, India also pays partly for the expenditure of the local office. The country-specific allocation of UNDP resources is made every five years under the Country Cooperation Framework (CCF) which usually synchronizes with India's five- year plans.

Relevant Website : www.undp.org

South Asian Association for Regional Cooperation

The South Asian Association for Regional Cooperation (SAARC), in existence since 1985 (founded in Dhaka), is a regional organisation that aims to promote economic, social, cultural, technical and scientific cooperation in South Asia. Its member states include Afghanistan, Bangladesh, Bhutan, India, Nepal, Maldives, Pakistan and Sri Lanka. Its secretariat is based in Kathmandu, Nepal. It has crafted several regional conventions, agreements and institutions for dealing with issues that affect the citizens of the region. It is a consensus-based forum for the exchange of ideas, development of regional programmes and projects. The Framework for Currency Swap Arrangement for the SAARC countries was formulated with the intention to provide a line of funding for short term foreign exchange requirements or to meet balance of payments crises till longer term arrangements are made or the issue is resolved in the short-term itself. Under the facility, RBI offers swaps of varying sizes to each SAARC member country (Afghanistan, Bangladesh, Bhutan, Maldives, Nepal, Pakistan and Sri Lanka) depending on their two months import requirement and not exceeding US$ 2 billion in total, in USD, Euro or INR. So far, the facility has been availed by Bhutan, Sri Lanka and Maldives.

Relevant Website : www.saarc-sec.org

SAARC Development Fund (SDF)

SDF was established in 2008 by the SAARC countries to improve the livelihood of the people and to accelerate economic growth, social progress and poverty alleviation in the region. The Fund is implementing many SAARC projects and programmes. Project funding in SDF is to be taken up under three windows (Social, Economic and Infrastructure). Of the three windows of SDF, economic and infrastructure windows are being operationalized.

Bilateral Cooperation

Department of Economic Affairs also deals with Bilateral Development Assistance from G-8 countries, namely USA, UK, Japan, Germany, Italy, Canada and Russian Federation as well as the European Union. The Division also deals with the work relating to extension of Lines of Credit to developing countries. It is also the focal point for administering short term foreign training courses of the duration upto four weeks offered by various international agencies/ countries.

Bilateral Official Development Assistance

India has been accepting external assistance from bilateral partners in the form of loans, grants and technical assistance for development of infrastructure, social sector and for enhancement of knowledge/ skills of Indian nationals at both Centre and state level. In terms of the guidelines issued in 2005, bilateral development assistance can be accepted from all G-8 countries, namely USA, UK, Japan, Germany, France, Italy, Canada and the Russian Federation as well as from European Commission. European Union Countries outside the G-8 can also provide bilateral development assistance to India provided they commit a minimum annual development assistance of US$ 25 million.

India-UK Bilateral Development Cooperation Programme

The United Kingdom (UK) has been providing development assistance to India since 1958. Development assistance from UK is received mainly for achieving the SDG's in the areas of health, education, administrative reforms, slum development, etc. The assistance from the UK, through its Department for International Development (DFID), flows to mutually agreed government projects and programmes in the form of financial and technical assistance. Presently, Odisha, Madhya Pradesh and Bihar are the three focus states of DFID.

India-European Union Development Cooperation

The European Union (EU) has been providing development assistance to India in the form of Grants. The priority areas include environment, public health and education. EU implements development cooperation programmes through Country Strategy Paper (CSP). The CSP is based on EU objectives, on the policy agenda of the partner country and on an analysis of the country/ region situation.

European Investment Bank

The European Investment Bank (the BanqueEuropeenned'Investissement) (EIB) is the European Union's financing institution which was established in 1958 under the Treaty of Rome (1957) to provide financing for capital investment. The members of the EIB are the Member States of the European Union, who have all subscribed to the Bank's capital. Outside the European Union, EIB financing operations are conducted principally from the Bank's own resources but also, under mandate, from Union or Member States' budgetary resources. Under these arrangements, the EIB's funds are utilized to finance investments in countries signatory to Co-operation Agreements with the EU.

Indo-German Bilateral Development Cooperation

Germany through their Ministry for Economic Cooperation and Development (BMZ) has been providing both financial and technical assistance to India since 1958. In 2008, the German Ministry for the Environment, Nature Conservation and Nuclear Safety (BMU) also initiated assistance under German Government's 'International Climate Protection Initiative', which is an additional instrument of the German Government over and above and without undermining the existing sources of Official Development Assistance. Priority areas of bilateral cooperation between Germany and India include: Energy, Sustainable Urban Development as well as Environment and Management of Natural Resources.

Indo-French Development Cooperation

The Government of France has been extending development assistance to India since 1968. However, the major drawback of French assistance was that it was tied to supply of goods and services from France. The priority areas for the

French Agency for Development (AFD) financing in India are: (i) energy efficiency and renewable energy; (ii) urban infrastructure (public transport, water, etc.); (iii) the preservation of biodiversity.

Norway

Numerous NGO projects have been cleared with Norway since 2005. Bilateral meetings are periodically held between senior officials of Finance Ministries of India and Norway.

Switzerland

Switzerland has been extending economic and technical assistance to India since 1964 in the form of grants and technical assistance. Switzerland had also provided mix credit comprising 40 per cent grant and 60 per cent loans for power sector project.

U.S. Agency for International Development

The United States of America (USA) bilateral development assistance to India started in 1951. US assistance is mainly administered through the USAID. USAID is presently partnering with the Government of India to strengthen health systems; food security; accelerate transition to low emissions and energy secure economy; reduce greenhouse gas emissions through carbon sequestration by forests.

United States Trade and Development Agency

USTDA promotes economic growth in emerging economies by facilitating the participation of U.S. businesses in the planning and execution of priority development projects in host countries. The Agency's objectives are to help build the infrastructure for trade, match U.S. technological expertise with overseas development needs, and help create lasting business partnerships between the United States and emerging market economies. Since 1992, the U.S. Trade and Development Agency has supported over 100 priority development projects in India with public and private sector sponsors.

Canada

International Development Research Centre (IDRC) extends grant assistance to various governments and non-government organizations for projects in the field of agriculture, health and family welfare, etc.

Credit to Developing Countries

Lines of Credit (LoC) form an important component of India's diplomatic strategy and have been very useful in generating goodwill and building long term partnerships. The Scheme also attempts to promote India's strategic political and economic interest abroad by positioning it as an emerging economic power, investor country and partner for developing countries. The Scheme is also expected to boost Indian export of goods and services to hitherto untapped markets and successfully showcase India's expertise in project planning, design and implementation in diverse areas of socio-economic development such as power, irrigation, agriculture, transport, etc. India has been extending Lines of Credit to Africa and other developing countries under the Indian Development and Economic Assistance Scheme (IDEAS) since 2005-06.

International Monetary Fund

India is a founder member of the International Monetary Fund (IMF) which was established to promote a cooperative and stable global monetary framework. At present, 188 nations are members of the IMF. Since the IMF was established, its purposes have remained unchanged but its operations - which involve surveillance, financial assistance and technical assistance - have developed to meet the changing needs of its member countries in an evolving world economy. The Board of Governors of the IMF consists of one Governor and one Alternate Governor from each member country. For India, the Finance Minister is the ex-officio Governor on the Board of Governors of the IMF. There are three other countries in India's constituency at the IMF, viz. Bangladesh, Bhutan and Sri Lanka. Governor, Reserve Bank of India (RBI) is India's Alternate Governor.

Relevant Website : www.imf.org

World Bank

India has been borrowing from the World Bank through International Bank for Reconstruction and Development (IBRD) and International Development Association (IDA) for various development projects in the areas of poverty reduction, infrastructure, rural development, etc. IDA funds were one of the most concessional external loans for Government of India and were used largely in social sector projects that contribute to the achievement of millennium development goals.

Relevant Website : www.worldbank.org

International Finance Corporation

International Finance Corporation (IFC), a member of the World Bank Group, focuses exclusively on investing in the private sector in developing countries. Established in 1956, IFC has 184 members. India is founding member of IFC. It is an important development partner for India with its operations of financing and advising the private sector in the country. India represents IFC's largest portfolio exposure globally. The IFC's investments in India are spread across important sectors like infrastructure, manufacturing, financial markets, agribusiness, SMEs and renewable energy. Keeping in alignment with the Country Partnership Strategy (CPS) of the World Bank Group in India, IFC focuses on low-income states in India.

New Development Bank

The New Development Bank (NDB) has been instituted with a vision to support and foster infrastructure and sustainable development initiatives in emerging economies. The founding members of the NDB - Brazil, Russia, India,

China and South Africa (BRICS) - brought in capital of USD 1 billion as initial contribution.

Relevant Website : www.ndb.int

Asian Infrastructure Investment Bank

Asian Infrastructure Investment Bank (AIIB) is a Multilateral Development Bank (MDB) set up in 2016 to foster sustainable economic development, create productive assets and improve infrastructure in Asia through financing of infrastructure projects. India is one of the founding Members and the second largest shareholder. India along with 20 other countries signed the Inter-Governmental Memorandum of Understanding (MoU) for establishing the AIIB in Beijing.

Relevant Website : www.aiib.org

International Fund for Agricultural Development

International Fund for Agricultural Development (IFAD) was set up in 1977 as the 13th specialized agency of the UN. It is dedicated to eradicating poverty and hunger in rural areas of developing countries.

Global Environment Facility

The Global Environment Facility (GEF) operates as a mechanism for international cooperation for the purpose of providing new and additional grant and concessional funding to meet the agreed incremental costs of measures to achieve agreed global environmental benefits. GEF provides grants to eligible countries in its focal areas: biodiversity, climate change, land degradation, international waters, chemicals and waste. It also serves as financial mechanism for the Convention on Biological Diversity (CBD), United Nations Framework Convention on Climate Change (UNFCCC), Stockholm Convention on Persistent Organic Pollutants (POPs), UN Convention to Combat Desertification (UNCCD), Minamata Convention on Mercury and supports implementation of the Protocol in countries with economices in transition for the Montreal Protocol on Substances that Deplete the Ozone Layer (MP).

Asian Development Bank

India is a founding member of the Asian Development Bank (ADB) which was established in 1966. ADB has 67 members (including 48 regional and 19 non-regional members), with its headquarters at Manila, Philippines. India is holding 6.331 per cent of shares, totaling 6,72,030 shares in ADB as on 31st December, 2016, with 5.363 per cent voting rights. The Bank is engaged in promoting economic and social progress of its developing member countries (DMCs) in the Asia Pacific Region. The main instruments that it uses to do this are making loans and equity investments, providing technical assistance for the preparation and execution of development projects and programmes and other advisory services, guarantees, grants and policy dialogues. India borrows from ADB within overall external debt management policy pursued by the

Government which focuses on raising funds on concessional terms from less expensive sources with longer maturities. India started borrowing from ADB in 1986.

Relevant Website : www.adb.org

Currency and Coinage

Security Printing and Minting Corporation of India Limited

Security Printing and Minting Corporation of India Ltd. (SPMCIL) is the only PSU under the Department of Economic Affairs. It was formed after corporatisation of nine units, i.e. four mints, four presses (two currency note presses and two security presses) and one paper mill which were earlier functioning under the Ministry. The Company was incorporated in 2006 under the Companies Act, 1956. It is engaged in the manufacturing of security paper, minting of coins, printing of currency and bank notes, non-judicial stamp papers, postage stamps, travel documents, etc. The Company supplies currency/bank notes and coins to RBI, non-judicial stamp papers to various state governments; postal stationery and stamps to postal department; passports, visa stickers and other travel documents to Ministry of External Affairs. Other products include commemorative coins, MICR and Non-MICR cheques etc. SPMCIL has also setup a 50:50 Joint Venture in 2010 with Bhartiya Reserve Bank Note Mudran Pvt. Ltd. (BRBNMPL) in the name of Bank Note Paper Mill India Private Limited (BNPMIPL), a Green-Field project of Bank Note Paper Mill with capacity of 12000 MT per annum having two state of the art technology paper lines of 6000 MT capacity per annum each. The commercial production has started from both the lines.

Relevant Website : www.spmcil.com

New Denomination of Banknotes

New denomination banknote of ₹ 2,000/- introduced on the size, theme, colour and design. This helped in faster remonetisation of the system, subsequent to cancellation of legal tender of specified banknotes.

Cancellation of Legal Tender

The legal tender character of banknotes in the denominations of ₹ 500 and ₹ 1,000 in circulation i.e., 'Specified Bank Notes'(SBN) was cancelled in November, 2016 to curb the problem of black money, Fake Indian Currency Note and various other subversive activities. Replacing high denomination notes required large scale exercise involving 1.3 lakh Bank branches, 1.5 post offices branches, 1 lakh banking correspondents and 2.2 lakh ATMS.

National Investment and Infrastructure Fund

The Government of India has put investment in infrastructure as one of the core elements of its economic programme. India's average investment in infrastructure was 4.7 per cent of GDP during 1992-2010. Moreover, there has been a slowdown in equity inflows into the infrastructure sectors over the past few years, constraining further investment. National Investment and Infrastructure Fund (NIIF) was created with the aim to attract equity investments from both domestic and international sources for infrastructure development in commercially viable projects, both greenfield and brownfield, including stalled projects.

Relevant Website : www.niifindia.in

International Investment Treaties and Framework

India initiated the exercise to negotiate and enter into Bilateral Investment Treaties (BITs)/ Bilateral Investment Promotion and Protection Agreements (BIPAs) with other countries as a part of the comprehensive economic reforms programme which was initiated in 1991. A BIT is essentially an international treaty which increases the comfort level and boosts the confidence of the investors by assuring a minimum standard of treatment and non-discrimination in all matters while providing for an independent forum for dispute settlement through arbitration. In turn, BITs are expected to project India as an attractive foreign direct investment (FDI) destination as well as protect outbound Indian FDI abroad.

Due to considerable socio-economic changes which have taken place since 1993, it was felt that there was a need for closer examination of the entire gamut of issues associated with BITs and also investment chapter of CECAs/CEPAs/ Free Trade Agreements (FTAs). The new Indian Model BIT of 2015 aims to provide appropriate protection to foreign investors in India and Indian investors in the foreign country, in the light of relevant international precedents and practices.

Department of Expenditure

The Department of Expenditure is the nodal Department for overseeing the public financial management system in the central government and matters connected with state finances. It is responsible for the implementation of the recommendations of the Finance Commission and Central Pay Commission, monitoring of audit comments/ observations, preparation of central government accounts. It further assists central ministries/ departments in controlling the costs and prices of public services, reviewing system and procedure to optimize outputs and outcomes of public expenditure. The principal activities of the Department include overseeing the expenditure management in the central ministries/ departments through the interface of the Financial Rules/ regulations/ orders, pre-sanction appraisal of major schemes/ projects, handling bulk of the central budgetary resources transferred to state.

The Personnel and Establishment Division is responsible for administration of various financial rules and regulations like General Financial Rules (GFRs), Delegation of Financial Power Rules (DFPRs), etc., including those relating to personnel matters of central government employees such as regulation of pay and allowances, policy matters on pension, and staffing of government establishments by creation and upgradation of posts, as also cadre reviews.

Relevant Website : www.doe.gov.in

Controller General of Accounts

The Controller General of Accounts (CGA), in the Department of Expenditure, is the Principal Accounting Adviser to Government of India and is responsible for establishing and maintaining a technically sound Management Accounting System. The Office of CGA prepares monthly and annual analysis of expenditure, revenues, borrowings and various fiscal indicators for the Union Government. Under Article 150 of the Constitution, the Annual Appropriation Accounts (Civil) and Union Finance Accounts are submitted to Parliament on the advice of Comptroller and Auditor General of India. Along with these documents, an M.I.S Report titled 'Accounts at a Glance' is prepared and circulated in Parliament. It further formulates policies relating to general principles, form and procedure of accounting for the central and state governments. It administers the process of payments, receipts and accounting in central civil ministries/ departments. Prepares, consolidates and submits the monthly and annual accounts of the central government through a robust financial reporting system aimed at effective implementation of the government fiscal policies. Through its internal audit units in the respective ministries/ departments, it is responsible for maintaining the requisite technical standards of Accounting in the departmentalized accounting offices and for monitoring of financial performance and effectiveness of various programmes, schemes and activities of the civil ministries.

Relevant Website : www.cga.nic.in

Public Financial Management System

The Public Financial Management System (PFMS) is a web-based online software application designed, developed, owned and implemented by the CGA with the aim to provice a sound public financial management system by establishing a comprehensive payment, receipt and accounting network. It has been aimed to achieve (i) "Just in Time"transfer of funds and (ii) complete tracking of realization of funds from its release to its credit into the bank account of intended beneficiaries. PFMS makes a direct and significant contribution to the Digital India initiative by enabling electronic payment and receipts for ministries/departments in Government of India. Integration with financial IT systems of various state governments is one key objective of PFMS which will facilitate complete tracking of funds transferred for scheme implementation and provide more holistic view of finances available for welfare programmes. To achieve these objectives the Treasury Systems of all the states, all the major banks of India and various external MIS Systems have been integrated with PFMS. All the Schemes of GoI and their implementing agencies have been registered on PFMS. It is playing a vital role in making Direct Benefit Transfer (DBT) to weaker section of the society.

Non-Tax Receipt Portal

The objective of the Non Tax Receipts Portal (NTRP), is to provide a one-stop window to citizens/corporates/institutions/other users for making online deposits of Non-Tax receipts (NTR) which are payable to the Government of India. This was inaugurated in 2016. The NTRP portal provides an end to end solution for the complete value chain of non-tax receipts, including online user interface, payment at the payment gateway aggregator, and accounting of the receipts by the government department/ministry. NTRP uses the modality of Payment Gateway Aggregator (PGA). It uses the back-end system of the robust Public Financial Management System where all data is housed and MIS reports are available on the PFMS portal for both accounting and monitoring purposes.

Institute of Government Accounts & Finance

The Institute of Government Accounts & Finance (INGAF) is the training arm of the Controller General of Accounts. It was set up in February, 1992 to train personnel in specific areas of accounting, administrative matters and financial management. In the years following its inception, the Institute has evolved to become an elite training centre in government accounting and public financial management. In addition, the Institute has regional training centres at Chennai, Kolkata, Aizawl and Mumbai.

Central Pension Accounting Office

The Central Pension Accounting Office (CPAO) was established in 1990 for Payment and Accounting of Central (Civil) Pensioners and pension to freedom fighters etc. CPAO is a subordinate office under the Office of the Controller General of Accounts, Ministry of Finance. It has been entrusted with the responsibility of administering the scheme of payment of pension to central government (Civil) pensioners through authorized banks. Its core functions are: issue of Special Seal Authorities(SSAs) authorizing payment of pension in fresh as well as revision of pension cases to the CPPCs (central pension processing centers) of pension disbursing banks; preparation of Budget for the pension grant and accounting thereof; maintenance of data bank of central civil pensioners containing all details indicated in the PPOs and Revision Authorities; handle the grievances of central civil pensioners.

(a) *e-Revision utility for the 7th CPC Pension Revisions:* CPAO has developed e-Revision utility with the facility of sending online digitally signed revision authorities for the revision of 7th CPC pension cases by the PAOs to CPAO. This utility is being used by more than 600 Pay & Accounts Offices of the central civil ministries/departments. CPAO is also issuing digitally signed electronic-Special Seal Authority (e-SSA) to all the 39 CPPCs (Central Pension Processing Centres) of the 24 authority banks for pensions. This service has reduced the paper movement from PAOs to CPAO and from CPAO to banks.

(b) *Online Allotment of Pension Payment Orders (PROS) Number:* From 2016, Central Pension Accounting Office (CPAO) has started facility on online allotment of PPO number on CPAO website for Pay & Accounts Offices to avoid paper based allottment of PPO numbers. This has resulted in less paperwork and the process has been faster than earlier. It has also resulted in saving time and postage cost.

(c) *Electronic-Pension Payment Order (e-PPO) Project*: Paperless movement of digitally signed e-Special Seal Authority (e-SSA) from Central Pension Accounting Office (CPAO) to 39 Central Pension Processing Centres (CPPCs) of 24 authorized banks for pension is in operation and all the CPPCs are getting digitally signed Special Seal Authority (SSA) in fresh as well as the revision pension cases directly into their SFTP servers.

(d) *Web Reponsive Pensioners' Service (WRPS)*: Digital India campaign of Government of India emphasizes that the government services should be made available to the citizens electronically by improving online infrastructure and by increasing internet connectivity or by making the country digitally empowered. Digital India consists of three core components: development of secure and stable digital infrastructure; delivering government services digitally; universal digital literacy.

(e) *Social Media Presence of CPAO:* Official social media accounts of Central Pension Accounting Office on platforms Facebook, Twitter and YouTube have been created to provide better services to the pensioners/family pensioners and to lodge their grievances. This is over and above the latest modes available to the pensioner to contact and communicate with CPAO. Various instructive videos have been made for the better use of the WRPS facility. e-Revision Utility for pensioners and other stakeholders.

Relevant Website : www.cpao.nic.in

National Institute of Financial Management

The National Institute of Financial Management (NIFM) was set up in 1993 as an autonomous body under the Societies Registration Act, to impart training to officers recruited by the Union Public Service Commission through the annual Civil Service Examinations and allocated to the various services responsible for managing senior and top management posts dealing with accounts and finance in the Government of India and to develop as a Centre of Excellence in the areas of financial management and related disciplines, not only in India but also in Asia. The Institute adheres to norms prescribed by the All India Council for Technical Education (AICTE) in respect of faculty qualifications and strength. Currently, the Institute runs five long-term programmes approved by AICTE -Professional Training Course of one year for newly recruited probationers of Accounting services called diploma in public financial management; a one year diploma course in government financial management; a two-year post graduate diploma in management (Financial Management) programme for officers of the central government, the state governments, public sector undertakings and other organizations and a one-year post graduate diploma in management (financial markets) to produce competent researchers, teachers and consultants.

Relevant Website : www.nifm.ac.in

Revision of General Financial Rules

The General Financial Rules (GFRs) are rules and orders dealing with matters involving public finances. General Financial Rules were issued for the first time in 1947 bringing together in one place all existing orders and instructions pertaining to financial matters. These have subsequently been modified and issued as GFRs 1963 and GFRs 2005. The Revised General Financial Rules - 2017 were released in 2017 to enable an improved, efficient and effective framework of fiscal management while providing the necessary flexibility to facilitate timely delivery of services. In the last few years, Government has made many innovative changes in the way it conducts its business. Reforms in Government budgeting like removal of distinction in non-plan and plan expenditure, merger of Railway Budget with General Budget, focusing on outcomes through an improved Outcome Budget document, all needed to be reflected in the GFRs. Increased focus on Public Finance Management System(PFMS), reliance on the Direct Benefit Transfer (DBT) Scheme to ensure efficient delivery of entitlements, introduction of new e-sites like Central Public Procurement Portal, Government e-Marketing (GeM) Portal, Non-Tax Revenue Portal have also necessitated revision of the existing GFRs to keep them in tune with the changing business environment. The objective was to make the GFRs facilitate efficiency while following principles of accountability and procedures of financial discipline and administrative due diligence. New rules on non-tax revenues, user charges, e-receipts portal were added in addition to the manner in which autonomous bodies are run.

Department of Revenue

The Department of Revenue exercises control in respect of revenue matters relating to Direct and Indirect Union taxes through two statutory boards namely, the Central Board of Direct Taxes (CBDT) and the Central Board of Excise and Customs (CBEC). The Department is also entrusted with the administration and enforcement of regulatory measures provided in the enactments concerning Central Sales tax, Stamp duties and other relevant fiscal statutes. Control over production and disposal of opium and its products is vested in this Department.

Relevant Website : www.dor.gov.in

Goods and Services Tax

Legislative Development

The proposal to introduce a national level Goods and Services Tax (GST) was first mooted in 2006-07. The Goods and services Tax Council was constituted in 2016. GST was implemented in the country in July, 2017. Subsuming of various central indirect taxes and levies such as central excise duty, additional excise duties, excise duty levied under the medicinal and toilet preparations (excise duties) Act, 1955, Service Tax, Additional Customs Duty commonly known as countervailing duty, special additional duty of customs, and central surcharges and cesses so far as they relate to the supply of goods and services. Coverage of all goods and services, except alcoholic liquor for human consumption, for the levy of goods and services tax. In case of petroleum and petroleum products, it has been provided that these goods shall not be subject to the levy till a date notified on the recommendation of the GST Council. Compensation to the states for loss of revenue arising on account of implementation of the Goods and Services Tax for a period which may extend to five years.

Indian Stamp Act

The Indian Stamp Act, 1899 is a fiscal statute laying down the law relating to tax levied in the form of stamps on instruments recording transactions. Briefly, the scheme relating to stamp duties, provided for in the Constitution is as follows: (i) Under Article 246, stamp duties on documents specified in Entry 91 of the Union List in Schedule VII of the Constitution (viz., bills of exchange, cheques, promissory notes, bills of lading, letters of credit, policies of insurance, transfer of shares, debentures, proxies and receipts) are levied by the Union but under Article 268, each State, in which they are levied, collects and retains the proceeds (except in the case of Union Territories in which case the proceeds form part of the Consolidated Fund of India). At present duty is levied on all these documents except cheques. (ii) Stamp duties on documents other than those mentioned above are levied and collected by the states by virtue of the Entry 63 in the State List in the 7th Schedule of the Constitution. (iii) Provisions other than those relating to rates of duty fall within the legislative power of both the Union and the states under Entry 44 of the Concurrent List in the Schedule- VII. (iv) The rates of stamp duty in respect of Debenture and Promissory Notes have been rationalized by the central government in September, 2008.

Central Board of Direct Taxes

Direct Taxes

The Central Board of Direct Taxes (CBDT), created by the Central Boards of Revenue Act 1963, is the apex body entrusted with the responsibility of administering direct tax laws in India. It is the cadre controlling authority for the Income Tax Department (ITD). With modern information technology as a key driver, the CBDT has implemented a comprehensive computerization programme in the Income Tax Department. The programme is aimed to establish a taxpayer friendly regime, increase the tax-base, improve supervision and generate more revenue for the Government. The endeavour is to promote voluntary compliance by taxpayers and create a non-intrusive and non-adversarial tax administration.

Relevant Website : www.incometaxindia.gov.in

Revenue Collection

Revenue collection from direct taxes has been growing consistently. As a result of improved tax administration and better tax compliance, direct tax collection has been showing a positive trend over a period of time.

e- Governance Initiatives

(a) Permanent Account Number (PAN)

PAN is a 10 digit alpha-numeric number allotted by the Income Tax Department to taxpayers and to the persons who apply for it under the Income Tax Act, 1961. PAN enables the department to link all transactions of the "person" with the department. The transactions linked through PAN include tax payments, TDS/TCS credits, returns of income/wealth, specified transactions, correspondence, and so on. PAN, thus, acts as an identifier for the "person" with the Income tax department.

(b) Common Business Identification Number (CBIN or BIN)

PAN has now taken on the role of "identifier" beyond the Income tax department as it is now required for various activities like opening of bank account, opening of demat accounts, obtaining registration for Service Tax, Sales Tax / VAT, Excise registration etc. PAN is leveraged to become Common Business Identification Number (CBIN) or simply Business Identification Number (BIN) for providing registration to a number of government departments and services.

(c) One Person One PAN

The Income Tax Act permits one person to have only one PAN. To avoid issuance of duplicate PAN, the data is checked for duplication by using the software having phonetic matching algorithm. In order to leverage the biometric data collected through Aadhaar enrolment it was decided to include Aadhaar Card as a valid Proof of Identity (POI), Proof of Date of Birth (PDOB) and Proof of Address (POA) document for allotment of PAN under Income Tax Rules, 1962. In order to further strengthen the de-duplication process the PAN database is being seeded with Aadhaar number for Individuals and Company Identification Number (CIN) for Corporate Entities.

(d) PAN Service Providers

The services related to PAN such as receiving PAN application forms, verification of the documents submitted, digitizing the PAN application form, uploading the data on the NCC (National Computer Centre), printing PAN cards and dispatching of PAN cards have been outsourced to the PAN Service Providers, M/s UTIITSL and M/s NSDLeGov. The Service Providers through their network of more than 20,000 front offices (PAN centers), receive and process the PAN application submitted by applicants. However, the PAN is generated centrally in the department's database through robust software at National Computer Centre (NCC) of the Income Tax Department and thereafter printed and dispatched through service providers.

(e) PAN Verification Facility

PAN verification facility is provided through CBDT's e-filing server to Government departments through the Internet. One by one PAN verification or Bulk verification of 1,000 PANs in one go through file processing can be done by the users.

PAN can also be verified through "Know Your PAN" facility on Income-tax official web site www.incometaxindia.gov.in where Name, Father's Name and Date of Birth (DOB) /Date of Incorporation (DOI) are known. Service for PAN verification is also provided by income tax PAN Service Providers (UTITSL and NSDLeGov) to agencies such as (i) financial institutions (RBI/Banks) (ii) government agencies (iii) persons required to file Annual Information Return (iv) any other entity required to file Annual Information Return (v) credit card companies/institutions etc.,

(f) Grievances Redressal Machinery

Grievance Redressal Machinery related to PAN is well defined. Whenever a grievance is received related to PAN, appropriate action is taken including forwarding the grievance to field formations with guidance and existing instructions. Grievances are also received through Centralised Public Grievance Redressal and Monitoring System (CPGRAMS). All grievances related to PAN are downloaded from the website of CPGRAMS and after examination, appropriate action is taken by the Directorate and information about redressal action taken in such cases, is uploaded on the website. Further a new mechanism to lodge grievances has been made available to PAN holders and new PAN applicants through eNivaran facility on eFiling portal. Here the complainant can pick specifics of complaint and the authority responsible to redress the matter. The entire process is online and besides functionaries of the department PAN Service Providers M/s UTIITSL and M/s NSDL eGov have been integrated to eNivaran mechanism for resolving the grievances of public.

New Initiatives

(a) Integration with e-Biz portal of DIPP

e-Biz programme is a mission mode project of Department of Industrial Policy and Promotion (DIPP), Ministry of Commerce and Industry to facilitate the investors by providing Single Window clearance like licensing, environment and land clearances, approvals from various ministries and departments for start-up businesses. L1 and L3 integration of PAN and TAN services with e-Biz portal of DIPP has been completed. In L1 integration the applications for PAN and TAN are received through e-Biz portal and forwarded to PAN Service Providers.

(b) Integration with MCA Portal

PAN and TAN processes have been integrated with the process of registration of new companies using a Common Application Form SPICe (INC 32) at MCA portal. PAN and TAN are being allotted in Turn Around Time (TAT) of 4 hours from the time the application data in form 49A and 49B is received from MCA portal. PAN is being printed on Certificate of Incorporation of new companies along with CIN through this process.

(c) Paperless Application using DSC and eSignature

An online paperless procedure for application of PAN using Digital Signature Certificate and Aadhaar based eSignature has been launched at websites of both service providers M/s NSDL and M/s UTIITSL. In this procedure a person having Digital Signature Certificate or eSignature can apply for PAN through online form 49A and upload digitally signed application with scanned copies of Proof of Identity, Proof of Date of Birth, Proof of Address, Photograph and Signature without any need for sending physical documents by post.

(d) Paperless Application using Aadhaar based eKYC

Another paperless procedure for allotment of PAN using Aadhaar data and photograph of applicant has been launched. The process is termed as eKYC process where demographic details and photograph of the applicant are populated directly from Aadhaar database by applicant through an authentication process. The applicant signs the application using Aadhaar based eSignature. The process is entirely paperless and without need for any attachments resulting in faster allotment of PAN.

(e) PAN Card

All new applicants and card reprint requests are now being provided option of receiving digitally signed ePAN card on the lines of eAadhaar letter through email. The initiative has reduced the time of transmission of PAN card through post.

(f) Common Service Centres

Common Service Centres (Village Level Enterprises) have been enrolled with PAN Service Providers M/s UTIITSL and M/s NSDL eGov for receiving PAN applications in far flung corners of the country. The initiative has resulted in outreach of PAN services at village level.

(g) Electronic filing of Income Tax Returns

e-Filing of Income tax returns was introduced for the first time in 2006-07 for corporates. This facility is free of cost to taxpayers. e-returns now account for nearly 98 per cent of total returns filed with the Department. The e-filing website which has over 6.2 crore registered users also provides facility for online filing of various types of forms including audit reports, applications and informational statements by taxpayers. More than 50 forms are available online.

(h) IT enablement of Business Processes

Technology also has an important role in re-engineering business process within the tax administration to empower employees in delivering outcomes in a consistent and efficient manner. Income Tax Business Application (ITBA) was conceptualized with development of new application for computerization of all internal processes of Income Tax Department. The main objective of ITBA is to e-enable all internal business processes so that officers and staff are able to increase their efficiency by bringing information and work at a single place for decision making and reduce drudgery in reporting, correspondence and internal approvals.

(i) Unification of Grievance Redressal Systems- e-Nivaran

e-Nivaran aims to fast track taxpayer's grievance redressal, ensuring early resolution by integrating all the online and physical grievances received by the department and keeping track of it until it reaches its logical conclusion.

(j) National Website of the Income Tax Department http:/incometaxindia.gov.in

A major initiative to enhance taxpayer services was launched by the Income tax Department in 2014 with the unveiling of the new national website (www.incHmctaxindia.gov.in). The same was revamped in 2015 and services incorporated keeping in mind feedback received from various users, trade associations and other stakeholders. The website with New Layout was made available for the users and tax payers in 2015. Several new features and services that have been incorporated to make it more user friendly, informative and useful, are -

Major Citizen Friendly Initiatives

Aayakar Sewa Kendra

The 12 report of 2nd ARC aimed at Citizen Centric Governance with the aid of modern technology. The setting up of ASKs is a step in this direction. Aayakar Sewa Kendra (ASK) is the single window system for implementation of Citizen's Charter of the Income Tax Department and a mechanism for achieving excellence in public service delivery. All communications as well as returns received in ASK mandate timely disposal which can be monitored and reviewed at the highest level. This ensures that a robust architecture of e-Governance is installed and sustained in the Income Tax Department.

Aayakar Setu

The use of smart phone is increasing day by day. With the objective to enhance tax payer services and mobile access experience, a mobile app (available on Android/IOS platform) and responsive version of the Tax Payer Services (TPS) section at the national website called "Aayakar Setu" was launched in 2017. "Aayakar Setu" would facilitate the online payment of the taxes, calculation of taxes, removal of grievances through login to the e-Nivaran module, information about the TPS hierarchy, ASK IT module, Tax Gyaan, TDS/TRACES and other features.

TDS SMS alert Scheme

CBDT has put in place a mechanism for real-time communication to taxpayers (deductees) about information of TDS deduction/deposit by their respective employers or deductors. In order to provide better taxpayer services by providing timely and accurate data to the taxpayers, the scheme for SMS alert to the salaried employees on a quarterly basis has been launched.

Publicity Campaigns

Since, last many years, the Department has shifted its communication strategy to portray itself, not, as a purely enforcement agency but also as a taxpayer facilitator, service provider and major contributor in nation building. This strategy has allowed the Department to communicate effectively with the taxpayers acknowledging their contribution in building a secure, progressive and developed nation.Several publicity campaigns were carried out which included campaigns for awareness of due dates of payment of advance tax, filing of returns, filing of TDS statements and issuance of TDS certificates, filing of annual information return, services of TRPs, vigilance awareness week, income declaration scheme, Pradhan Mantri Garib Kalyan Yojana, demonetization and publication of names of chronic defaulters.

Social Media

The Department has stepped into publicity campaigns through social media channels since 2015 as per the approved Social Media policy. Social Media activities are also being regularly undertaken through the official Twitter account i.e. @IncomeTaxIndia. The twitter account of the Department has more than 1,00,000 followers.

Central Board of Excise and Customs

Central Board of Excise and Customs (CBEC) deals with formulation of policy concerning levy and collection of Customs, Central Excise duties and Service Tax, prevention of smuggling and evasion of duties and all administrative matters relating to Customs, Central Excise and Service Tax formations. The main objectives of CBEC are to collect indirect tax revenues, improve tax payer services, to improve compliance for fair trade and enforcement of border controls and promote efficiency and transparency and develop human resources for such purposes. The CBEC consists of a Chairman and 6 members.

Relevant Website : www.cbic.gov.in

Dispute Settlement and Appeal: The Officers of Customs, Excise and Service Tax have powers to adjudicate cases under the Customs Act, 1962, the Central Excise Act, 1944 and Service Tax laws (Finance Act, 1994). The appellate machinery comprising the Commissioners (Appeals) deals with appeals against the orders passed by the officers lower in rank than Commissioner of Customs and Central Excise. The Customs, Excise and Service Tax Appellate Tribunal, CESTAT (earlier Customs Excise and Gold (Control) Appellate Tribunal) is an independent forum to hear the appeals against orders and decisions passed by the Commissioners of Customs and Excise under the Customs Act, 1962, Central Excise Act, 1944 and a Second appellate forum against orders passed by Commissioner (Appeals).

Customs

The Indian Customs Electronic Data Interchange (EDI) System (ICES) is an EDI based work flow application which enables (i) electronic filing and processing of import and export declarations/manifests (ii) system appraisal of select goods (iii) messaging with custodians and other agencies concerned with cargo clearance. Implemented at 214 locations, ICES cover more than 98 per cent of the country's international trade consignment wise and 90 per cent value wise. With more than 200 crore hits annually, the e-commerce web portal, Indian Customs EDI Gateway (ICEGATE), is the single point of interaction between ICES and Partners in the Customs community and provides such services as registration, e-filing, e-payment, document status and helpdesk as well as data exchange between customs and various regulatory and licensing authorities and facilitation of compliant trade (with concomitant reduction in transaction costs and cargo dwell time) and targeting of non-compliant or risky transactions is achieved through the risk management system. In 2016, Central Board of Excise and Customs (CBEC) launched single window interface for facilitating trade (SWIFT) at all customs EDI locations with six major participating government agencies(PGAs), as a single point interface for clearance of imported goods. SWIFT enables importers to file common electronic 'Integrated Declaration' which compiles the information requirements of customs, FSSAI, plant quarantine, animal quarnatine, drug controller, wild life control bureau and textile committee and replaces nine separate forms earlier required by these agencies.

CBEC-GST Application

GST business processes, namely, Registration, Return, Payment and Refund are provided from the common portal www.gst.gov.in which is managed by GSTN. The CBEC-GST Application is designed, developed and being deployed in a phased manner for providing the corresponding back-end processes. In addition, supplementary business processed like Assessment, Audit, Adjudication etc. are also being hosted on the CBEC-GST Application with user interface available to both trade and departmental users, as the need be.

Enterprise Data Warehouse

CBEC is one of the first government departments to have implemented an Enterprise Date Warehouse, a central repository of clean and consistent, near real time data pertaining to Customs, Central Excise and Service Tax. It employs best-in-class business Intelligence tools for online analytical processing and data mining, and is today the primary source of data and reports required by C.B.E.C. other ministries and external agencies.

Directorate of Enforcement

Directorate of Enforcement was set up at New Delhi in 1956 for enforcement of the provisions of the Foreign Exchange Regulation Act (FERA),

1947. FERA, 1947 was later replaced by Foreign Exchange Regulation Act, 1973. FERA was a Criminal Act, which provided for filing of prosecutions in a court of law, besides adjudication of violations by the Adjudicating Authorities. FERA was repealed in 2000 and replaced with Foreign Exchange Management Act, 1999 (FEMA). Subsequently, the Directorate was also entrusted with the responsibility of implementing the Prevention of Money Laundering Act, 2002 (PMLA), which came into force in 2005. At present, the Directorate of Enforcement enforces two laws viz., the Foreign Exchange Management Act, 1999 (FEMA) and the Prevention of Money Laundering Act, 2002 (PMLA) apart from looking after the residual work initiated under FERA. The Directorate initiates investigations under FEMA for contraventions relating to foreign exchange transactions on the basis of specific intelligence/information and takes appropriate action under FEMA. Complaints are filed before the Adjudicating Authority under the Act. In the event the charge is found substantiated upon adjudication by the competent Adjudicating Authority, penalty up to the maximum of three times of the amount involved in the said contravention can be imposed by the said Authority. Adjudication Authority may also order confiscation of amounts involved in such contravention.

Under the PMLA, the Directorate can initiate investigations only after a Law Enforcement Agency books a case under one of the offences listed in the Schedule to the Act. The Directorate investigates the case to ascertain whether proceeds of crime have been generated from the predicate offence booked by the Law Enforcement Agency, and such proceeds have been laundered. If a *prima-facie* case is made out, the Directorate attaches or seizes the tainted property. The Act also provides for initiating investigations for tracing and immobilizing tainted property arising out of transactions having cross border implications. Such investigations are carried out through Letters of Request with the foreign administrations. The offence of money laundering under PMLA is punishable with imprisonment of not less than three years which may extend to seven years and also with fine. In case of violations pertaining to NDPS Act offences, the imprisonment may extend to 10 years. Upon conviction under PMLA, the attached property is liable to be confiscated.

Relevant Website : www.enforcementdirectorate.gov.in

Financial Intelligence Unit-India

Financial Intelligence Unit-India (FIU-IND) is the central national agency for receiving, processing, analyzing and disseminating information relating to suspect financial transactions. FIU-IND was established by the Government of India in 2004 for coordinating and strengthening collection and sharing of financial intelligence through an effective national, regional and global network to combat money laundering, related crimes and terrorist financing. It is an independent body reporting to the Economic Intelligence Council (EIC) headed by the Finance Minister. For administrative purposes, FIU-IND is under the Department of Revenue, Ministry of Finance. FIU-IND is established as an administrative FIU i.e., as an independent government body that receives analyses and disseminates STR to the appropriate law enforcement or investigation agency. FIU-IND does not investigate cases. The main functions of FIU-IND include domestic co-operation, international co-operation, outreach, compliance and administration of an Information Technology based platform(FINnet) providing end-to-end solution for filing, analysis and dissemination of information, including making request and submission of feedback.

Relevant Website : www.finindia.gov.in

Narcotics Control

The Narcotics Control Division administers the Narcotic Drugs and Psychotropic Substances Act,1985 (61 of 1985), which prohibits ,except for medical and scientific purposes, the manufacture, production, possession, sale, purchase, transport, warehouse, use, consumption, import inter-State, export inter-State, import into India, export from India or transhipment of narcotic drugs and psychotropic substances.

Customs, Excise and Service Tax Appellate Tribunal

Customs, Excise and Service Tax Appellate Tribunal (earlier known as Customs Excise and Gold (Control) Appellate Tribunal) was formed as a quasi-judicial body to hear appeals from the orders and decisions passed by the Commissioner/ Commissioner (Appeals) of Customs, Central Excise and Service Tax under the Customs Act, 1962, Central Excise Act, 1944 and Finance Act, 1994 respectively. The Tribunal is also having appellate jurisdiction on Anti-dumping matters and such matters are heard by special bench headed by the President, CESTAT. The headquarter and Principal Bench of the Tribunal is situated at Delhi. The regional benches are situated at Mumbai, Kolkata, Chennai, Bangalore, Ahmedabad, Chandigarh, Allahabad and Hyderabad having separate territorial jurisdiction. Whereas Delhi and Mumbai have 4 Benches each, Chennai has 2 Benches and all the other places have one Bench each. Each Bench of this Tribunal consists of a judicial member and a Technical Member.

Department of Financial Services

The Department of Financial Services (DFS) is mainly responsible for policy issues relating to Public Sector Banks (PSBs) and Financial Institutions including their functioning, appointment of Chairman, Managing Director and Chief Executive Officers (MD & CEOs), Executive Directors (EDs), Chairman cum Managing Directors (CMDs), legislative matters, international banking relations. Appointment of Governor/Deputy Governor of Reserve Bank of India, matters relating to National Bank for Agriculture and Rural Development (NABARD), Agriculture Finance Corporation, Co-operative Banks, Regional Rural Banks (RRBs) and rural/agriculture Credit. The Department also administers the financial inclusion programme of the government, social security schemes and other targeted schemes aimed at facilitating flow of credit, matters relating to insurance sector and performance of public sector insurance companies, administration of various Insurance Acts. Matters relating to Insurance Regulatory and Development Authority of India (IRDAI) and matters relating to pension reforms including the New Pension System (NPS), etc.

It also covers pension reforms and industrial finance and micro, small and medium enterprise. It startedthe Pradhan Mantri Jan Dhan Yojana. Pension Fund Regulatory and Development Authority (PFRDA) is a statutory body which also works under this Department.

Relevant Website : www.financialservices.gov.in

Reserve Bank of India

The Reserve Bank of India (RBI) is India's central banking institution, which controls the monetary policy of the Indian rupee. It commenced its operations on April 1, 1935 in accordance with the Reserve Bank of India Act, 1934. Following India's independence on 15 August 1947, the RBI was nationalised on 1 January 1949.

The RBI has four zonal offices at Chennai, Delhi, Kolkata and Mumbai. It has 21 regional offices and 11 sub-offices throughout India. Regional offices are located in Ahmedabad, Bengaluru, Bhopal, Bhubaneswar, Chandigarh, Chennai, Delhi, Guwahati, Hyderabad, Jaipur, Jammu, Kanpur, Kochi, Kolkata, Dewas, Lucknow, Mumbai, Nagpur, Patna, Dehradun and Thiruvananthapuram and sub-offices are at Agartala, Aizawal, Dehradun, Gangtok, Imphal, Panaji, Raipur, Ranchi, Shillong, Shimla and Srinagar.

As the central bank of India, RBI is an independent apex monetary authority which regulates banks and provides important financial services like storing of foreign exchange reserves, control of inflation, monetary policy report. A central bank is known by different names in different countries. The functions of a central bank vary from country to country and functions as autonomous or quasi-autonomous body. A central bank is a vital financial apex institution of an economy and the key objects of central banks may differ from country to country, still they perform activities and functions with the goal of maintaining economic stability and growth of an economy.

The RBI plays an important part in the Devlopment Strategy of the country. It is a member bank of the Asian Clearing Union. The general superintendence and direction of the RBI is entrusted with the 21-member central board of directors which has : the governor; four deputy governors; two finance ministry representatives; ten government-nominated directors to represent important elements of India's economy; and four directors to represent local boards headquartered at Mumbai, Kolkata, Chennai and New Delhi.

The central bank executes many functions such as overseeing monetary policy, issuing currency, managing foreign exchange, working as a bank for government and as a banker of scheduled commercial banks. It also works for overall economic growth of the country. The primary objective of RBI is to undertake consolidated supervision of the financial sector comprising commercial banks, financial institutions and non-banking finance companies.

Payment and settlement systems play an important role in improving overall economic efficiency. The Payment and Settlement Systems Act of 2007 (PSS Act) gives the Reserve Bank oversight authority, including regulation and supervision, for the payment and settlement systems in the country. In this role, the RBI focuses on the development and functioning of safe, secure and efficient payment and settlement mechanisms. Two payment systems National Electronic Fund Transfer (NEFT) and Real Time Gross Settlement (RTGS) allow individuals, companies and firms to transfer funds from one bank to another. These facilities can only be used for transferring money within the country. With increasing integration of the Indian economy with the global economy arising from greater trade and capital flows, the foreign exchange market has evolved as a key segment of the Indian financial market and RBI has an important role to play in regulating and managing this segment. It manages forex and gold reserves of the nation.

RBI is the sole body that is authorized to issue currency in India. The bank also destroys the same when they are not fit for circulation. All the money issued by the central bank is its monetary liability, i.e., the central bank is obliged to back the currency with assets of equal value, to enhance public confidence in paper currency. The objectives are to issue bank notes and give public adequate supply of the same, to maintain the currency and credit system of the country to utilize it in its best advantage, and to maintain the reserves. For printing of notes, the Security Printing and Minting Corporation of India Limited (SPMCIL), a wholly owned company of the Government of India, has set up printing presses at Nashik, Maharashtra and Dewas, Madhya Pradesh. The Bharatiya Reserve Bank Note Mudran Private Limited (BRBNMPL), also has set up printing presses in Mysore in Karnataka and Salboni in West Bengal. In all, there are four printing presses. For minting coins, SPMCIL has four mints at Mumbai, Noida (UP), Kolkata and Hyderabad.

In order to curb the fake currency, RBI has launched a website to raise awareness among masses about fake notes in the market www.paisaboltahai.rbi.org.in provides information about identifying fake currency.

Relevant Website : www.rbi.org.in

Regional Rural Banks

The Regional Rural Banks (RRBs) were established under Regional Rural Banks Act, 1976 to create an alternative channel to the cooperative credit structure and to ensure sufficient institutional credit for the rural and agriculture sector. RRBs are jointly owned by Government of India, concerned state government and sponsor banks with the issued capital shared in the proportion of 50 per cent, 15 per cent and 35 per cent, respectively.

Kisan Credit Card

The Kisan Credit Card (KCC) scheme was introduced in 1998-99, as an innovative credit delivery system aiming at adequate and timely credit support from the banking system to the farmers for their cultivation needs including purchase of inputs in a flexible, convenient and cost effective manner. The scheme is being implemented by all cooperative banks, RRBs and public sector commercial banks throughout the country. KCC is one of the most effective tools for delivering agriculture credit. NABARD monitors the scheme in respect of cooperative banks and RRBs and RBI in respect of commercial banks. A new scheme for KCC has been circulated by RBI and NABARD which provides for KCC as an ATM card which can be used at ATM/Point of Sale (POS) terminal.

Rural Infrastructure Development Fund

The Central Government established a fund to be operationalised by NABARD namely, the Rural Infrastructure Development Fund (RIDF), which was set-up within NABARD during 1995-96 by way of deposits from Scheduled Commercial Banks operating within the country from the shortfall in their agricultural/priority sector/weaker sections lending. The fund has since been continued, with its allocation being announced every year in the Union Budget. Over the years, coverage under the RIDF has been broad based, in each tranche, and at present, a wide range of 34 activities are financed under various sectors.

Insurance

Insurance, being an integral part of the financial sector, plays a significant role in India's economy. Apart from protection against mortality, property and casualty risks and providing a safety net for individuals and enterprises in urban and rural areas, this sector encourages savings and provides long-term funds for infrastructure development and other long gestation projects of the country. The development of the insurance sector is necessary to support its continued economic transformation. The public sector insurance companies operating in the sector are: 1. Life Insurance Corporation; 2 National Insurance Company Limited; 3. Oriental Insurance Company Limited; 4. United India Insurance Company Limited; 5. New India Assurance Company Limited; 6. General Insurance Corporation of India Limited and 7 Agriculture Insurance Company of India Limited.

Life Insurance Corporation of India

Life Insurance Corporation of India (LIC) was established by an Act of Parliament called the Life Insurance Corporation of India Act, 1956. It is governed by the Insurance Act, 1938, LIC Act, 1956, LIC Regulations, 1959 and Insurance Regulatory and Development Authority Act, 1999. As on March 31, 2016, LIC has 08 zonal offices, 113 divisional offices, 2,048 branch offices, 73 customer zones, 1,401 satellite offices and 1,240 mini offices in the country. LIC is present in 14 countries abroad through branch offices/joint ventures companies and wholly owned subsidiary.

Relevant Website : www.licindia.in

Reforms in the Insurance Sector

The insurance sector was opened for private participation with the enactment of the Insurance Regulatory and Development Authority Act, 1999. The Insurance Regulatory and Development Authority of India (IRDAI) is functioning from its head office in Hyderabad, Telangana. The core functions of the authority include: (i) licencing of insurers and insurance intermediaries; (ii) financial and regulatory supervision; (iii) regulation of premium rates; and (iv) protection of the interests of the policyholders: With a view to facilitate development of the insurance sector, the authority has issued regulations on protection of the interests of policy holders: obligations towards the rural and social sectors; micro insurance and licensing of agents, corporate agents, brokers, surveyors and third party administrators. IRDAI has also laid down the regulatory framework for registration of insurance companies, maintenance of solvency margin, investments and financial reporting requirements. Since the opening up this sector for private and foreign investment, the number of participants in the insurance industry has gone up from seven insurers to sixty eight insurers as on 31st March 2018 operating in the life, general, and re-insurance segments (including specialized insurers, namely Export Credit Guarantee Corporation and Agricultural Insurance Company (AIC).

One of the key reforms undertaken in this sector is the passing of Insurance Laws (Amendment) Act, 2015 which paved the way for major reform related amendments in the Insurance Act, 1938, the General Insurance Business (Nationalization) Act, 1972 and the Insurance Regulatory and Development Authority (IRDA) Act, 1999. The Insurance Laws (Amendment) Act 2015 seamlessly replaced the Insurance Laws (Amendment) Ordinance, 2014. The amendment Act removed archaic and redundant provisions in the legislations and incorporated certain provisions to provide Insurance Regulatory and Development Authority of India (IRDA) with the flexibility to dischange its functions more effectively and efficiently. It also provided for enhancement of the foreign investment cap in an Indian insurance company from 26 per cent to an explicitly composite limit of 49 per cent with the safeguard of Indian ownership and control. The Insurance Laws (Amendment) Act, 2015 also enabled foreign reinsurers to set up branches in India. It also enable Lloyds of UK and its members to operate in India through setting up of branches for the purpose of reinsurance business or an investors in an Indian Insurance Company within the 49 per cent cap.

Pradhan Mantri Vyay Vandana Yojana

Government launched the Pradhan Mantri Vyay Vandana Yojana (PMVVY) to protect elderly persons aged 60 years and above against a future fall in their interest income due to the uncertain market condition, as also to provide social security in old age. The Scheme is being implemented through LIC of India. It provides an assured return of 8 per cent per annum payable monthly for 10 years. The differential return i.e., the difference between return generated by LIC and the assured return of 8 per cent would be borne by

Government of India as subsidy on annual basis. It was open for subscription for a period of one year i.e., from 4th May, 2017 to 3 rd May, 2018. In pursuance of Budget 2018-19, Government approved the extension of Pradhan Mantri Vyay Vandana Yojana up to 31st March, 2020 and enhanced the limit of maximum purchase price of ₹ 7.5 lakh per family to ₹ 15 lakh per senior citizen.

Aam Aadmi Bima Yojana

For the benefit of the weaker sections of the society, Government of India floated a highly subsidized insurance scheme, viz., Aam Aadmi Bima Yojana (AABY) which is administered through Life Insurance Corporation of India. Under this social security scheme below poverty line (BPL) and marginally above poverty line citizens are covered under 48 identified occupations. The scheme provides death cover of ₹ 30,000/- in case of natural death. In case of death or total disability (including loss of two eyes/two limbs) due to accident, a sum of ₹ 75,000/- and in case of partial permanent disability (loss of one eye/ limb) due to accident, a sum of ₹ 37,500/- is payable to the nominee/ beneficiary. All these benefits are paid for a nominal premium of ₹ 200/- per member per annum, out of which ₹ 100/- is borne by the central government through Social Security Fund maintained through LIC of India, and the balance premium of ₹ 100/- is borne by the member and/or nodal agency and/or central/state government department which acts as the nodal agency. In addition, there is an add on benefit of scholarship at the rate of ₹ 1,200/- per annum per child for two children per family of the insured members studying from 9th to 12th standard (including ITI courses).

Social Security Schemes

Atal Pension Yojana

The Atal Pension Yojana (APY) was launched in May, 2015, to address the longevity risks among the workers in unorganised sector who are not covered under any statutory social security scheme. The APY is focussed on all citizens in the unorganised sector, who join the National Pension System (NPS) administered by the Pension Fund Regulatory and Development Authority (PFRDA).

Any Indian citizen between 18-40 years of age can join through their savings bank account/post office savings account. Minimum pension of ₹ 1,000 or ₹ 2,000 or ₹ 3,000 or ₹ 4,000 or ₹ 5,000 is guaranteed by the Government of India to the subscriber at the age of 60 years, with a minimum monthly contribution (for those joining at age at 18) of 42 or 84 or 126 or 168 or 210, respectively. After the subscriber's demise, the spouse of the subscriber shall be entitled to receive the same pension amount as that of the subscriber until the death of the spouse. After the demise of both the subscriber and the spouse, the nominee of the subscriber shall be entitled to receive the pension wealth, as accumulated till age 60 of the subscriber.

Revisions in APY

In the event of pre-mature death of the subscriber, government has decided to give an option to the spouse of the subscriber to continue contributing to APY account of the subscriber, for the remaining vesting period i.e., till the original subscriber would have attained the age of 60 years. The earlier provision was to hand over lump sum amount to spouse on the premature death (death before 60 years of age) of the subscriber. The spouse of the subscriber shall be entitled to receive the same pension amount as that of the subscriber until the death of the spouse. After the death of both the subscriber and the spouse, the nominee of the subscriber shall be entitled to receive the pension wealth, as accumulated till 60 years of the subscriber.

In order to facilitate subscribers with the convenience and accessibility of his/her APY account, Mobile Application for APY has been launched by PFRDA. This has enabled mobile operations for empowering the subscribers to view Statement of Account and other details of their APY account. All APY subscribers can download NPS Lite mobile applications from google store and install in their mobile phones for real time viewing of APY Accounts. To experience the features, the subscribers need to visit https://npslite-nsdl.com/CRAlite/ website and can explore as per their requirement.

Pradhan Mantri Jeevan Jyoti BimaYojana

Government announced three ambitious social security schemes pertaining to the insurance and pension sectors, namely Pradhan Mantri Jeevan Jyoti BimaYojana (PMJJBY), Pradhan Mantri Suraksha BimaYojana (PMSBY) and the Atal Pension Yojana (APY) to move towards creating a universal social security system, targeted especially for the poor and the under-privileged. PMJJBY is a one year life insurance scheme, renewable from year to year, offering coverage of two lakhs rupees for death due to any reason and is available to people in the age group of 18 to 50 years (life cover up to 55 years of age) having a bank account who give their consent to join and enable auto-debit. It involves convenient bank account linked enrolment with implementation in IT mode, and premium payment through auto-debit from the bank account of the subscriber. Implementation of this scheme enables affordability and targeting in favour of the poor and the under-privileged and would address the situation of low penetration of life insurance in the country.

Pradhan Mantri Suraksha Bima Yojana

The Pradhan Mantri Suraksha Bima Yojana (PMSBY) is a one year personal accident insurance scheme, renewable from year to year, offering coverage for death/disability due to an accident and is available to people in the age group of 18 to 70 years having a bank account who give their consent to join and enable auto-debit. Under the said scheme, risk coverage available will be ₹ 2 lakh for accidental death and permanent total disability and ₹ 1 lakh for permanent partial disability. It involves convenient bank account linked enrolment with implementation in IT mode, and premium payment through auto-debit from the bank account of the subscriber. Implementation of this scheme enables affordability and targeting in favour of the poor and the under-privileged and would address the situation of low penetration of accident insurance in the country.

Pradhan Mantri Jan Dhan Yojana

With a view to increasing banking penetration and promoting financial inclusion and with the main objective of covering all households with at least one bank account per household across the country, a National Mission on financial inclusion named as (PMJDY) was announced in 2014.

Objectives of PMJDY include: (i) universal access to banking facilities for all households across the country through a bank branch or a fixed point business correspondent (BC) within a reasonable distance. (ii) to cover all households with atleast one basic bank account with RuPay Debit card having inbuilt accident insurance cover of ₹ 1 lakh.

Pension Reforms

National Pension System

With a view to providing adequate retirement income, the National Pension System (NPS) was introduced. It has been made mandatory for all new recruits to the Government (except armed forces) with effect from January 1, 2004 and has also been rolled out for all citizens with effect from May 1, 2009 on a voluntary basis. The features of the NPS design are: self-sustainability, portability and scalability. Based on individual choice, it is envisaged as a low cost and efficient pension system backed by sound regulation. As a pure 'defined contribution' product, returns would be totally market driven. The NPS provides various investment options and choices to individuals to switch over from one option to another or from one fund manager to another, subject to certain regulatory restrictions. The NPS architecture is transparent and web enabled. It allows a subscriber to monitor his/ her investments and returns. The facility for seamless portability is designed to enable subscribers to maintain a single pension account (Permanent Retirement Account Number-PRAN) throughout the saving period. Pension Fund Regulatory and Development Authority (PFRDA), set-up as a regulatory body for the pension sector, is engaged in consolidating the initiatives taken so far regarding the full NPS architecture and expanding the reach of NPS distribution network. The process of making NPS available to all citizens entailed the appointment of NPS intermediaries, including institutional entities as Point of Presence (POPs) that serve as pension account opening and collection centres, a Centralized Record Keeping Agency (CRA) and Pension Funds to manage the pension wealth of the investors. The Department of Posts has also been appointed as PoP in addition to other financial institutions which expand the PoP-SP network by more than five times.

A Mobile App for NPS is available for the subscribers in Google Play Store as 'NPS by NSDL e-Gov' and and 'NPS by Karvy-CRA'. Subscribers can access their account through this. The following new features are enabled in Mobile App to facilitate the subscriber's interface with the system: Aadhaar can be linked to NPS account using this app; grievances/queries under NPS can be raised through it; Status of grievance along with resolution details can be viewed; subscriber can reset his/her password using this App; the bilingual version of the App has been developed for convenience of NPS subscribers.

The Retirement Advisers (RAs) are appointed by PFRDA to engage in the activity of providing personalized advice on pension, retirement and NPS thereby extending its outreach. The RAs can be an individual, registered partnership firm, body corporate, or any registered trust or society. The online platform has been developed to facilitate registration of an individual/entity as Retirement Adviser. In order to ease the process of registration of subscribers through Retirement Advisers a hyperlink is provided in welcome screen of RA. This link will re-direct the user to eNPS where he/she can enter RA code and initiate the process of subscriber registration. The Pension Sanchay; a dedicated website (www.pensionsanchay.org.in) is an initiative of PFRDA for increasing financial literacy with special emphasis on concepts of pension and retirement.

Swavalamban Scheme

To encourage the workers in the unorganized sector to save voluntarily for their old age, an initiative called Swavalamban Scheme was launched in 2010. It is a co-contributory pension scheme whereby the central government contributes a sum of ₹ 1,000 per annum in each NPS account opened having a saving of ₹ 1,000 to ₹ 12,000 per annum.

Rural Housing Fund

The Rural Housing Fund was set up in 2008-09 to enable primary lending institutions to access funds for extending housing finance to targeted groups in rural areas at competitive rates.

Pradhan Mantri Mudra Yojana

There are a large number of small business units, estimated at around 5.77 crore in the informal sector, running small manufacturing, trading or service businesses, who find it difficult to access formal systems of credit. The loan requirement of these units is generally below ₹ 10 lakh. While a number of initiatives were taken in the past to improve access to formal credit channels for such units, there was still a significant and large section to which the loan/credit facilities did not percolate. For such units a scheme, namely, Pradhan Mantri Mudra Yojana (PMMY) was launched in 2015, to enable income generating small business enterprises to have access to loans. Accordingly, lending institutions would finance micro entrepeneurs up to ₹ 10 lakh. PMMY is a national mission aimed at increasing the entrepreneurial activity of existing small business and encouraging first generation entrepreneurs.

Micro Units Development and Refinance Agency Limited (MUDRA), is a refinance institution set-up by the government for development of micro units by extending funding support to encourage entrepreneurship in India, mostly from non-corporate small business sector. Under the guidelines of PMMY, MUDRA has launched three innovative products namely Shishu, Kishor, and Tarun, which signifies the stage of growth and funding needs of the micro units or entrepreneur. MUDRA shall refinance through state level institutions, NBFCs, MFIs, regional rural banks, nationalized banks, private banks and other intermediaries. Any Indian citizen who is involved in income generating activity such as manufacturing, processing, trading and service sector and whose credit need is less than ₹ 10 lakh can approach either banks, MFIs, financial institutions or NBFC for availing of MUDRA loans under PMMY. It has been since decided to extend funding support under PMMY for activities allied to agriculture also.

The government has taken various steps towards effective implementation of the Scheme. These, inter alia, include intensive publicity campaigns, simplification of application forms, credit guarantee scheme, refinance from MUDRA Ltd, nomination of Mudra Nodal Officer, weekly video conferences to monitor the progress, etc.

Credit Guarantee Fund for Skill Development

To guarantee the loans and advances upto ₹ 1.5 lakh (term loan) or any other limit as may be decided by the settler, sanctioned and disbursed by the lending institutions without any collateral security and/or third party guarantees to the eligible borrowers pursuing skill development courses as per the Skill Loan Scheme. Any person (Indian national) can avail of skill loan having minimum qualification as per National Skill Qualification Framework (NSQF).

Department of Investment and Public Asset Management

The Department of Disinvestment was set up as a separate Department in 1999 and was later renamed as Ministry of Disinvestment in 2001. From 2004, the Department of Disinvestment is one of the departments under the Ministry of Finance. The Department of Disinvestment has been renamed as Department of investment and Public Asset Management (DIPAM) from 2016. The mandate of the Department includes all matters related to management of Central Government investments in equity including disinvestment of equity in Central Public Sector Undertakings. Decisions on the recommendations of administrative ministries, NITI Aayog, etc., for disinvestment including strategic disinvestment. All matters related to Independent External Monitor(s) for disinvestment and public asset management. Financial policy in regard to the utilization of the proceeds of disinvestment channelized into the National Investment Fund.

Relevant Website : www.dipam.gov.in

Disinvestment Policy

The policy on disinvestment has evolved considerably. The salient features of the Policy include: (a) public sector undertakings are the wealth of the Nation and to ensure this wealth rests in the hands of the people, promote public ownership of CPSEs; (b) while pursuing disinvestment through minority stake sale in listed CPSEs, the Government will retain majority shareholding, i.e. at least 51 per cent of the shareholding and management control of the Public Sector Undertakings; and (c) strategic disinvestment by way of sale of substantial portion of Government shareholding in identified CPSEs upto 50 per cent or more, alongwith transfer of management control.

National Investment Fund

Government constituted the National Investment Fund (NIF) in 2005 into which the proceeds from disinvestment of Central Public Sector Enterprises were to be channelized. The corpus of NIF was to be of a permanent nature and NIF was to be professionally managed to provide sustainable returns to the Government, without depleting the corpus. Selected Public Sector Mutual Funds, namely UTI Asset Management Company Ltd., SBI Funds Management Private Ltd. and LIC Mutual Fund Asset Management Company Ltd. were entrusted with the management of the NIF corpus. As per this Scheme, 75 per cent of the annual income of the NIF was to be used for financing selected social sector schemes which promote education, health and employment. The residual 25 per cent of the annual income of NIF was to be used to meet the capital investment requirements of profitable and revivable PSUs.

In view of the difficult economic situation caused by the global slowdown of 2008-09 and a severe drought in 2009-10, Government approved a change in the policy for utilization of Disinvestment proceeds by granting a one-time exemption to utilize the disinvestment proceeds directly for selected social sector schemes allocated by Department of Expenditure/Planning Commission. In order to align the NIF with the Disinvestment Policy, Government decided that the disinvestment proceeds, with effect from the fiscal year 2013-14, will be credited to the existing NIF which is a public account under the Government Accounts and the funds would remain there until withdrawn/invested for the approved purposes.

It was also simultaneously decided that the NIF would be utilized for the following purposes: subscribing to the shares being issued by the CPSE on rights basis so as to ensure that 51 per cent ownership of the Government in CPSEs is not diluted; preferential allotment of shares of the CPSE to promoters as per SEBI (Issue of Capital and Disclosure Requirements) Regulations, 2009 so that Government shareholding does not go down below 51 per cent in all cases where the CPSEs desire to raise fresh equity to meet their Capex programme, the Government further approved inclusion of the following purposes to be financed from the NIF. Investment by Government in RRBs/ IIFCL/NABRAD/ Exim Bank; equity infusion in various Metro projects; investment in Bhartiya Nabhikiya Vidyut Nigam Limited and Uranium Corporation of India Ltd; investment in Indian Railways towards capital expenditure.

Demonetisation of Banknotes

The Government demonetised 500 and 1,000 banknotes on November 8, 2016. All 500 and 1000 banknotes of the Mahatma Gandhi series ceased to be legal tenders in India from November 9, 2016. New 500 and 2000 banknotes of the Mahatma Gandhi New Series in exchange for the old banknotes were announced. However, the banknote denominations of 100, 50, 20, 10 and 5 of the Mahatma Gandhi series remained legal tender and were unaffected by the policy. The government said that the demonetisation move was an effort to stop counterfeiting of the current banknotes allegedly used for funding terrorism, as well as a crackdown on black money in the country.

14 Corporate Affairs

THE Ministry of Corporate Affairs (MCA) is primarily concerned with administration of the Companies Act 2013, the Companies Act 1956, the Limited Liability Partnership Act, 2008 and other allied Acts and rules and regulations framed there-under mainly for regulating the functioning of the corporate sector. The Ministry is also responsible for administering the Competition Act, 2002 to prevent practices having adverse effect on competition, to promote and sustain competition in markets, to protect the interests of consumers through the commission set up under the Act.

Besides, it exercises supervision over the three professional bodies, namely, Institute of Chartered Accountants of India (ICAI), Institute of Company Secretaries of India (ICSI) and the Institute of Cost Accountants of India (ICAI) which are constituted under three separate Acts of the Parliament for proper and orderly growth of the professions concerned. The Ministry also has the responsibility of carrying out the functions of the Central government relating to administration of Partnership Act, 1931, the Companies (Donations to National Funds) Act, 1951 and Societies Registration Act, 1980.

Relevant Website : www.mca.gov.in

Administrative Structure

The Ministry has a three tier organizational structure with the headquarters at New Delhi, seven offices of Regional Directors (RDs) at Ahmedabad, Chennai, Hyderabad, Kolkata, Mumbai, New Delhi and Shillong, fifteen Registrars of Companies (RoCs), fourteen Official Liquidators (OLs) and nine RoC-cum-OLs in states and union territories.

The jurisdictional Registrars of companies, continue to have jurisdiction over the companies incorporated by the Registrar, CRC under the Companies Act, 2013 for all other provisions of the Act and the rules made thereunder, which may be relevant after incorporation. The Official Liquidators function under the overall administrative control of the Ministry, and are attached to corresponding High Courts. They are mainly responsible for implementing court orders regarding liquidation and final dissolution of the companies.

Central Registration Centre

The project to transform the processing of company incorporation, e-forms was undertaken with one clear objective, i.e., applications for name reservation and incorporation of a company could be processed and completed within D+1 days (D=Date of Payment Confirmation) in line with global best practices. The

MCA rolled out the first phase of Central Registration Centre (CRC) in 2016 for processing name reservation of applicants and second phase of CRC for processing incorporation of company applicants in 2016. The Government Process Reengineering (GPR) exercise is in pursuance of the Ministry's objective of providing greater "Ease of Doing Business" to all the stakeholders and has resulted in faster processing of incorporation related applications, uniformity in application of rules, and eradicating discretion.

The time taken for processing company incorporation applications has been reduced drastically from between 5 to 15 working days in June 2014, to an average of 0.6 working days in March 2017. Similarly, the processing time for name availability applications has been brought down significantly from between 5 to 6 working days in June, 2014, to an average of 0.4 days in March 2017. In addition, more than 90 per cent applications are being approved within one working day. This has resulted in speed, greater transparency, uniformity and eradication of discretion.

Ease of Doing Business

The Ministry has prescribed a Simplified Proforma for Incorporating Companies (SPICe) along with e-MOA (Electronic-Memorandum of Association) and e-AoA (Electronic-Articles of Association) which eliminates the requirement of physically signing the Memorandum of Association (MoA) and Articles of Association (AoA) by the applicant and helps entrepreneurs to start business in India, without much hassles. The fee for filing the incorporation form has been reduced from ₹ 2,000/- to ₹ 500. The integrated form INC-29 has been replaced with SPICe Form. This incorporation form is being processed within 1-2 working days. Electronic integration of MCA21 System with the Central Board of Direct Taxes (CBDT) for issue of PAN and first TAN to an incorporated company using the Simplified Proforma for Incorporating Company Electronically (SPICe) has been undertaken. Stakeholders now submit applications for PAN and TAN at the time of submitting applications for incorporation. The PAN allotted by Income Tax Department is being affixed on the Certificate of Incorporation of the Company from February, 2017. This has resulted in reduction in the number of processes and time taken for starting a business in the country.

SPICe is a more versatile form and leverages on digital technology by eliminating the need for hard copies of physically signed documents being attached to an e-form. Using the integrated e-form SPICe, stakeholders can apply for five services simultaneously viz., company name, company incorporation, DIN of the directors, Permanent Account Number (PAN) and Tax Deduction and Collection Account Number (TAN) for the newly incorporated company. Rule 15 of the Companies Rules, 2014 (Meetings of the Board and its Powers) was amended in 2017 to reduce the threshold to "10 per cent" of the networth/ turnover as the case may be against the earlier threshold of exceeding 10 per cent thereby needing approval of members instead of only board. Common seal under Companies Act, 2013 has been made optional. The requirement for obtaining certificate of commencement of business and requirement for minimum paid up share capital for all companies have been done away with under Companies Act, 2013.

The efforts of the government have paid dividends. According to the Doing Business Report (DBR) of the World Bank, India has jumped 23 positions against its rank of 100 in 2017 to 77 among 190 countries.

The Companies Act, 2013 seeks to bring corporate governance and regulatory practices in India at par with global best practices. The corporate sector has been given more flexibility in regulating its own affairs, subject to full disclosure and accountability of its actions, while minimising Government interference. The Act provides more opportunities for new entrepreneurs and enables wide application of information technology in the conduct of affairs by corporates. Key features of the Act are given here.

Key Features of the Companies Act, 2013

I. Business Friendly Corporate Regulations/Pro-Business Initiatives

- Provision of self-regulation with disclosures/transparency instead of 'Government approval based regime'.
- Automation of corporate records/meetings – statutory recognition to (i) maintenance of documents by companies in electronic form, (ii) 'video-conferencing' as a mode of conducting board meetings, etc.
- Faster mergers and acquisitions including short form of mergers and cross border mergers.
- Summary liquidation: For companies having net assets of ₹ 1 crore or less, Official Liquidators (OLs) are empowered with adjudicatory powers.
- National Company Law Tribunal (NCLT) has been constituted under Section 408 in 2016.
- Concept of 'dormant companies' introduced (companies not engaged in business for two consecutive years can be declared as dormant).
- Concept of One Person Company (OPC) introduced.

II. Good Corporate Governance and Corporate Social Responsibility (CSR)

- Concept of Independent Directors (IDs) included as a statutory requirement u/s 149 (4).
- Provision for constitution of several committees of the Board (Audit Committee, Nomination and Remuneration Committee, Stakeholders Relationship Committee and CSR Committee).

- Woman Director for prescribed class of companies.
- Mandatory provision for constitution of CSR Committee and formulation of CSR Policy, with mandatory disclosure, for prescribed class of companies.

III. Enhancing Accountability of Management

- The term 'Officer in Default' has been reviewed to make it more relevant.
- Terms 'Key Managerial Personnel' (KMP) and 'Promoter' defined to affix responsibility on key functionaries of the company.
- Duties of Directors defined, including to shareholders, employees, the community and environment.
- Cap on number of Directorships: 20 companies, of which 10 can be public companies.

IV. Strengthened Enforcement

- The Central Government to have powers to order investigation, suo-motu, in public interest.
- Statutory recognition of Serious Fraud Investigation Office (SFIO).
- Special Courts have been constituted under Section 435 in 2016.
- Search and seizure of documents, during investigation, without an order from a Magistrate.
- Freezing of assets or disgorgement of illegal gains of company under investigation.

V. Audit Accountability

- Recognition of accounting and auditing standards.
- Stricter disqualification norms for auditors.
- Auditor not to perform specified non-audit services.
- Tenure or rotation of auditors prescribed.
- Internal audit for bigger companies.
- Substantial civil and criminal liability for an auditor in case of non-compliance.
- Tribunal empowered to direct a change of auditor in case of a fraud detected.
- Cost records and cost audit for prescribed class of companies.
- Secretarial audit for prescribed class of companies.

- National Financial Reporting Authority (NFRA) to be constituted.
- Protection of minority shareholders.
- Exit option provided, if there is dissent to change in object clause, or during compromises, etc.
- Valuation mandated during compromise, arrangements, etc.
- Effect of merger on minority shareholding to be disclosed.
- Listed companies to have one Director representing small shareholders.

VI. Investor Protection

- Stringent norms for acceptance of deposits from the public.
- Strengthened role of Investor Education and Protection Fund (IEPF).
- No time bar on claims of dividends from IEPF.
- Class Action Suits recognized.
- Enhanced powers to tribunal for protection of minority rights.

Companies (Amendment) Act, 2015

The Companies Act, 2013 was amended through the Companies (Amendment) Act, 2015 to facilitate business and address certain immediate concerns raised by stakeholders. These amendments along with the relevant rules have been notified and they provide exemptions under various provisions of the Act to (i) private companies, (ii) government companies, (iii) Section 8 companies and (iv) Nidhis.

Insolvency and Bankruptcy Code, 2016 (IBC, 2016)

The Insolvency and Bankruptcy Code, 2016 (Code) became functional from May, 2016. Government of India (Allocation of Business) Rules, 1961 were amended wherein Ministry of Corporate Affairs was entrusted with the responsibility to administer the Code. The Code has been framed with the objective to consolidate and amend the laws relating to reorganization and insolvency resolution of corporate persons, partnership firms and individuals in a time bound manner.

Insolvency and Bankruptcy Board

The Insolvency and Bankruptcy Board of India (IBBI) was established in 2016. The IBBI has the mandate for regulation of insolvency professionals, insolvency professional agencies and information utilities besides exercising other powers and functions as envisaged under the Code.

Special Courts

Under Section 435 of the Companies Act, the Ministry of Corporate Affairs has constituted Special Courts by designating 20 existing Session courts/

Additional Sessions Courts as Special Courts under Section 435 of the Companies Act, 2013 (the Act). These courts are in Jammu and Kashmir, Maharashtra, Goa, Gujarat, Madhya Pradesh, West Bengal, Chhattisgarh, Rajasthan, Punjab, Haryana, Meghalaya, Manipur,Telangana, Andhra Pradesh, Tamil Nadu (Coimbatore), Union Territories of Puducherry, Chandigarh, Andaman and Nicobar Islands, Dadra and Nagar Haveli, Daman and Diu, NCT of Delhi.

National Company Law and Appellate Tribunal

The constitution of National Company Law Tribunal (NCLT) and National Company Law Appellate Tribunal (NCLAT) was done in 2016. These bodies have been constituted for faster resolution of corporate disputes and reducing the multiplicity of agencies thereby promoting 'ease of doing business' in the country. With the constitution of National Company Law Tribunal (NCLT), the Company Law Board (CLB) stands dissolved and cases pending with CLB were transferred to NCLT.

The Insolvency and Bankruptcy Code, 2016 and SICA Repeal Act, 2003 were also put in place in 2016. With this, the Board of Industrial and Financial Reconstruction (BIFR) and Appellate Authority for Industrial and Financial Reconstruction were dissolved and Benches of NCLT were designated to exercise the jurisdiction, powers and authority of Adjudicating Authority conferred by or under part II of the Insolvency and Bankruptcy Code, 2016. Central Government has also notified provision for transfer of proceedings relating to arbitration, compromise, arrangements and reconstruction to the benches of NCLT. The applications pending before High Courts on winding up shall continue to be dealt by the respective High Courts and fresh applications are required to be filed before NCLT. NCLAT has its headquarters at New Delhi. At present the NCLT has its Benches at 10 locations viz., New Delhi, Ahmedabad, Allahabad, Bengaluru, Chandigarh, Chennai, Guwahati, Hyderabad, Kolkata and Mumbai.

The Competition Appellate Tribunal under the provisions of Competition Act was dissolved in 2017 and merged with NCLAT. The appeal against the orders of Competition Commission of India is now with NCLAT.

Companies in the Registry

Total number of companies registered in the country by March, 2017, under the Companies Act, 2013, the Companies Act, 1956 and the previous company Laws, stood at 16,41,333. Of these, 3,01,778 companies were closed; 802 were lying dormant as per Section 455 of Companies Act, 2013; 1,38,206 companies have not filed statutory annual filings consecutively for two years; 5,698 companies are under liquidation; names of 25,264 companies are in the process of being removed under Section 248 of the Companies Act, 2013; and 282 companies were in the process of being re-activated. Taking all these factors into account, there were 11,69,303 active companies in March, 2017.

Corporate Social Responsibility

In India, Corporate Social Responsibility (CSR) for companies has been mandated through legislation through Section 135 of the Companies Act, 2013. Section 135, Schedule VII of the Companies Act, 2013, and the Companies (Corporate Social Responsibility Policy) Rules, 2014 came into force from April, 2014. From time to time the Ministry has made amendments to Companies (CSR Policy) Rules, 2014 and issued clarifications and FAQs by way of circulars, so as to facilitate effective implementation of CSR and ensure its compliance.

Limited Liability Partnerships

In India, about 95 per cent of industrial units are Micro, Small and Medium Enterprises (MSMEs). As per the survey conducted by MSME, over 90 per cent of these are registered as proprietorships, about 2 to 3 per cent as partnerships and less than 2 per cent as companies. The corporate form does not appear to be widely prevalent amongst MSMEs. Analysis of the data collected by the Ministry of MSME suggests that high compliance cost under the Companies Act, 1956 deterred the MSMEs from adopting the corporate form.

The functioning of a proprietorship or a partnership firm is too opaque, making assessment of credit-worthiness by bankers difficult, and therefore, the MSME sector is at a comparative disadvantage vis-à-vis corporate bodies in accessing loan/credit facilities from banks and other financial institutions. A need was felt for a new corporate form that would provide an alternative to the traditional partnership with unlimited personal liability on the one hand, and the statute-based governance structure of the limited liability company on the other. In this context, the Limited Liability Partnership (LLP) Act was enacted in 2008 and came into force from 2009.

LLP is a form of business entity, which allows individual partners to be protected from the joint and several liabilities of partners in a partnership firm. The liability of partners incurred in the normal course of business does not extend to the personal assets of the partners. It is capable of entering into contracts and holding property in its own name. An LLP would be able to fulfil the compliance norms with much greater ease, coupled with limitation of liability. The corporate structure of LLP and the statutory disclosure requirements are expected to enable higher access to credit in the market.

MCA21— e-Governance Project

The Ministry operated an end-to-end e-governance project called MCA21 for end to end service delivery comprising Company and Limited Liability Partnership (LLP) registration, incorporation, registry and other compliance related services. The project was started in March, 2006 on Build, Own, Operate and Transfer (BOOT) Model with the vision was "to introduce a service-oriented approach in the design and delivery of Government services". The project was undertaken on a Mission Mode to bring about a service centric approach in the delivery of public services and administration of the Companies and LLP Act, and it specifically focuses on: (i) speedy incorporation of companies and LLPs, and(ii) providing Ease of Doing Business. The project has been implemented in the Ministry's headquarters, all Regional Directorates and Registrar of Companies offices, to bring about a service centric approach in timely delivery of public services and administration of Companies Act and LLP Act. All services are provided online and the filed documents are available in public domain.

With the help of e-services, the MCA21 System provides to the stakeholders a convenient, easy to use and secure access and delivers all MCA services with improved speed and certainty. It has brought about transparency, speed and efficiency in the functioning of the Ministry. After successfully launching the next generation SAP based platform version 2 of the MCA21 in March, 2016, the project has embarked on to a new phase with the objective of improving it further.

Cost Audit

The companies engaged in the production of goods or providing services as specified in orders issued by the central government under Section 148 of the Companies Act, 2013 are required to include the particulars relating to the utilization of material or labour or to other prescribed items of cost in their books of account. Such companies which are required to maintain cost records, and which have prescribed turnover are also required to get their cost records audited by a cost accountant in practice.

The Companies (Cost Records and Audit) Rules were notified in 2014 specifying the class of companies and the threshold limit, which require to maintain cost records and conduct audit thereof. The aforesaid rules cover 6 regulated sectors and 33 non-regulated sectors which fall under the ambit of Section 148 of the Companies Act, 2013 for maintenance of cost records and conducting of audit thereof subject to the specified threshold limits. The cost records help the compilation of cost database for the own use of such companies for the purpose of cost management, pricing and other related functions. These records are also used by various government agencies like price-fixation authorities, regulatory bodies, WTO implementation and monitoring agencies, Competition Commission of India (CCI), Serious Fraud Investigation Office (SFIO), revenue authorities, and other institutions. The Ministry analyses the cost audit reports and monitors compliance to the Act/Rules by the specified companies.

Investor Education and Protection Fund

The Companies Act provides for establishment of Investor Education and Protection Fund (IEPF) for promoting Investor Awareness and protecting their interests. The amount of dividend, matured deposits, matured debentures, application money, etc., which remained unpaid/unclaimed for a period of seven years from the date they first become due for payment, are transferred to

IEPF. Section 205 C of the Companies Act, 1956 did not allow the refund of such amount to individual once it is transferred to IEPF. Section 125 of Companies Act, 2013 allows refund of unpaid amounts transferred to IEPF. Such refunds are to be made by the Investor Education and Protection Fund Authority under Section 125 of the Act.

IEPF Authority was made functional from 2016. The IEPF Authority is also entrusted with the responsibilities of carrying out investor awareness activities using the amounts transferred to IEPF. Investor Awareness Programmes (IAPs) are organized in association with three professional institutes namely; (a) Institute of Chartered Accounts of India, (b) Institute of Company Secretaries of India and (c) Institute of Cost Accounts of India. In addition, investor awareness activities like Crawler messages on Doordarshan through Prasar Bharati and airing jingles on All India Radio for the period of 90 days to create and increase investor's awareness were taken up.

Indian Corporate Law Service

Ministry of Corporate Affairs is the cadre controlling authority of the Indian Corporate Law service (ICLS). The erstwhile Indian Company Law Service was rechristened in 2008 as the Indian Corporate Law Service.

Serious Fraud Investigation Office

The Serious Fraud Investigation Office (SFIO) was set up in 2003. The Companies Act, 2013, *interalia*, has accorded statutory status to SFIO and its functions and powers have been enhanced substantially with number of enabling provisions in the Act and it was established under Section 211 of the Companies Act, 2013.

The main function of SFIO is to investigate corporate frauds of serious and complex nature. It takes up investigation of frauds characterized by complexity, and having inter-departmental and multi-disciplinary ramifications, substantial involvement of public interest to be judged by size of either monetary appropriation or the number of persons affected and the possibility of investigations leading to, or contributing towards a clear improvement in systems, laws or procedures. Investigations are carried out by a multi disciplinary team which includes experts from the field of accountancy, forensic auditing, taxation, customs and central excise, information technology, capital market, financial transaction (including banking) and enforcement agencies like Central Bureau of Investigation (CBI), Intelligence Bureau (IB) and Enforcement Directorate.

Indian Institute of Corporate Affairs

The Ministry set up the Indian Institute of Corporate Affairs (IICA), a society registered under Societies Registration Act, 1860 to serve as a 'Holistic Think-Tank', and a 'Capacity Building, Service Delivery Institution' to help corporate growth, reforms through synergised knowledge management, partnerships and problem solving in a one-stop-shop mode. The Institute fulfils the training needs of the officers of the Indian Corporate Law Service (ICLS), and other officials working for the Ministry, corporates, PSUs and banks through its network of various schools and centres. National Foundation for Corporate Social Responsibility is also anchored with IICA. It also helps in the continuous improvement of service delivery mechanisms in diverse areas like corporate governance, corporate social responsibility, investor education and protection, business responsibility, finance, competition law, etc.

Relevant Website : www.iica.in

Competition Commission of India

The Competition Commission of India (CCI) was established in 2003 under the Competition Act, 2002, with the objective of eliminating practices having an adverse effect on competition, promoting and sustaining competition, protecting the interest of consumers and ensuring freedom of trade in India. The Competition Act, 2002 was amended twice (Amendment) Act, 2007 and the Government (Amendment) Act, 2009. The provisions of the Competition (Amendment), 2002 relating to anti-competitive agreements and abuse of dominant position were brought into force in 2009 and those relating to combinations from 2011.

By March, 2017, the CCI received 868 matters relating to anti-competitive agreements and abuse of dominance in diverse sectors such as insurance, travel, transport, cement, automobile manufacture, real estate, pharmaceuticals, financial sector, public procurement and entertainment, etc. It passed final orders in 654 cases (about 75.34 per cent). Penalties were also imposed by CCI in some of the serious cases of infringements.

In respect of Regulation of Combinations, the Commission received 498 notices (including 9 suo-motu cases) for combination till March, 2017. Out of them, 482 cases were disposed of within the stipulated time period.

Relevant Website : www.cci.gov.in

15 Food, Civil Supplies and Consumer Affairs

The Ministry of Consumer Affairs, Food and Public Distribution is a ministry with two departments - the Department of Food and Public Distribution and the Department of Consumer Affairs. Department of Consumer Affairs (DCA) one of the two departments under the Ministry was constituted as a separate Department in June 1997 as it was considered necessary to have a separate department to give a fillip to the nascent consumer movement in the country

The Department has been entrusted with the following work: internal trade; the Essential Commodities Act, 1955, etc.; Prevention of Black Marketing and Maintenance of Supply of Essential Commodities Act, 1980; regulation of packaged commodities; training in legal metrology; consumer cooperatives, etc., to name a few.

The Department of Food and Public Distribution, in the Ministry is responsible for management of the food economy of the nation. It undertakes various activities, such as procurement of food items, their storage, movement and delivery to the distributing agencies. The primary policy objective of the Department is to ensure food security for the country through timely and efficient procurement and distribution of foodgrains. This involves procurement of various foodgrains, building up and maintenance of food stocks, their storage, movement and delivery to the distributing agencies and monitoring of production, stock and price levels of foodgrains.

The focus is on incentivizing farmers through fair value of their produce by way of Minimum Support Price mechanism, distribution of Food grains to Below Poverty Line (BPL) families and covering poor households at the risk of hunger under Antyodaya Anna Yojana (AAY), establishing grain banks in food scarce areas and involvement of Panchayati Raj Institutions (PRI) in Public Distribution System (PDS).

Relevant Websites : www.consumeraffairs.nic.in   www.dfpd.nic.in

Consumer Affairs

The mandate of the Department of Consumer Affairs (DCA) is consumer advocacy. India was a pioneer in consumer advocacy with the Consumer Protection Act (CPA), a path breaking legislation at the time, enacted in 1986 and the establishment of a separate government department dedicated to consumer affairs as early as in 1997. Translating this mandate into action entails: enabling consumers to make informed choices; ensuring fair, equitable and consistent outcomes for consumers; and facilitating timely and effective consumer grievance redress.

Consumer Awareness

The Department has been conducting a countrywide multimedia awareness campaign since 2005 on various issues related to consumer rights and responsibilities across diverse subjects. "Jago Grahak Jago" has today become a household axiom. More recently, joint publicity campaigns have been launched in partnership with the related government departments/ organizations that deal with a mass consumer clientele. For instance, on food, with the Food Safety and Standards Authority of India (FSSAI); on financial services with the Reserve Bank of India (RBI); and on medicines with the National Pharmaceutical Pricing Authority (NPPA) through various electronic and print media such as television, radio, newspapers and outdoor advertising. The consumer awareness campaign is implemented through the Directorate of Audio and Visual Publicity (DAVP), the Doordarshan Network (DD) and the All India Radio (AIR) of Ministry of Information and Broadcasting.

Consumer Welfare Fund

The Central Excise and Salt Act, 1944 was amended in 1991 to enable the Central government to create a Consumer Welfare Fund into which unclaimed central excise revenues not refundable to the manufacturers would be credited annually. The Consumer Welfare Fund was created in 1992 with the objective of providing financial assistance to promote and protect the welfare of the consumer, create consumer awareness and strengthen the voluntary consumer movement in the country, particularly in rural areas. The Department of Consumer Affairs operates the fund, set up by the Department of Revenue under the Central Excise and Salt Act, 1944. Under its Rules, since revised in 2014, any agencies/organizations engaged in consumer welfare activities for at least a period of five years and registered under the Companies Act, Societies Registration Act, Cooperative Societies Act or any other law for the time being in force are eligible for financial assistance from the Fund. Asum of ₹ 26.23 crore was available in the Fund in March 2017. An amount of ₹ 11.65 crore was utilized by December 2017 from the Fund.

Commitment to Consumers

The DCA seeks to empower consumers through awareness and education; enhance consumer protection through prevention of unfair trade practices; enable quality assurance and safety through standards and their conformity; and ensure access to an affordable and effective grievance redress mechanism. Consumer markets for goods and services have undergone profound transformation since the enactment of the Consumer Protection Act in 1986. Liberalization, privatization and deregulation; innovations in new technologies and products; the growth of new consumer services; and the rising aspirations of the consumers for better goods and services have been the major drivers of change. The modern marketplace contains a plethora of increasingly complex products and services. The emergence of global supply chains, rise in international trade and the rapid development of e-commerce have led to new delivery systems for goods and services and have provided new opportunities for consumers. Equally, this has rendered the consumer vulnerable to new forms of unfair trade and unethical business practices. Addressing these challenges requires policy coherence; coordinated programme implementation; harmonization of regulatory action and an institutional mechanism by which the interventions of government produce optimal results. Taking the benefits of good governance to the common citizen has been the primary focus of the Department. This is done in partnership with multiple stakeholders - relevant line departments of the government of India, state governments, regulatory agencies, and voluntary consumer organizations.

Consumer Protection Act

A key milestone in consumer advocacy in the country was the enactment of Consumer Protection Act, 1986. This Act provided the legislative framework to better protect the interests of the consumer by creating a formal but quasi-judicial dispute resolution mechanism exclusively for consumers. This progressive legislation established the three tier quasi-judicial consumer dispute redress machinery at the national, state and district levels aimed at providing simple, speedy and affordable redress to consumers.

Bureau of Indian Standards

A new Bureau of Indian Standards (BIS) Act 2016 came into force from 2017. The Act establishes the Bureau of Indian Standards (BIS) as the national Standards Body of India. It has enabling provisions for the Government to bring under compulsory certification regime any goods or article of any scheduled industry, process, system or service which it considers necessary in the public interest or for the protection of human, animal or plant health, safety of the environment, or prevention of unfair trade practices, or national security. Enabling provisions have also been made for making hallmarking of the precious metal articles mandatory. The new Act also allows multiple type of simplified conformity assessment schemes including self-declaration of conformity against a standard which will give simplified options to manufacturers to adhere to the standards and get certificate of conformity. The Act enables the Central government to appoint any authority/agency, in addition to the BIS, to verify the conformity of products and services to a standard and issue certificate of conformity. Further, there is provision for repair or recall, including product liability of the products bearing Standard Mark but not conforming to the relevant Indian Standard. The new Act will further help in ease of doing business in the country, give fillip to "Make In India" campaign and ensure availability of quality products and services to the consumers. Bureau of Indian Standards Rules, were also notified in 2017.

The Bureau of Indian Standards was set up as a statutory organization taking over the assets and liabilities of the Indian Standards Institution (ISI) that came into existence in 1947. The Bureau has its headquarters in New Delhi. It has a network of 05 regional offices, 32 branch offices and 08 laboratories which act as effective link between BIS, government, industry and consumers. The Bureau has made steady progress in the various fields of its key activities namely standards formulation, product certification, management system certification and hallmarking.

Relevant Website : www.bis.gov.in

National Consumer Helpline

National Consumer Helpline (NCH) is a project that operates under the Centre for Consumer Studies at Indian Institute of Public Administration (IIPA). It was set up in 2004 and has customized software which is server based for receiving calls and answering through one PRI line. The Project recognizes the need of consumers for a Telephone Helpline to deal with multitude of problems arising in their day-to-day dealings with business and service providers. Its primary objective is to attend to the telephone calls from consumers and provide information to the callers and register their complaints in the INGRAM portal, to provide advice and counseling to consumers for redressal of their grievances, handle the complaints received online through the INGRAM portal, emails, sms, etc., to assist/guide the consumers in registering their complaints in the appropriate consumer fora, to perform backend operations, etc. National consumer Helpline(NCH) is the core of the Consumer grievance redressal mechanism. It does not work as Call Centre alone. It has partnered with 373 companies that respond online to resolve complaints. This is called convergence mechanism. It also pursues the complaints with the convergence companies, takes feedback from the complainants, does research and analysis of the complaint. NCH provides a National Toll Free No-1800-11-4000. SMS can also be sent to +918130009809 (charges apply) mentioning the name and city. A consumer can call to seek information, advice or guidance for his queries and complaints.

Consumer Grievance Redress

Under the Consumer Protection Act, 1986, a three-tier quasi-judicial mechanism has been set up in the country to adjudicate complaints filed before them and to provide speedy redress to consumers. This includes the National Consumer Disputes Redressal Commission (National Commission) at the apex level with territorial jurisdiction over the whole country and pecuniary jurisdiction to consider consumer disputes/complaints involving claims above ₹ 1.00 crore and with appellate jurisdiction over state/commissions; 35 state consumer disputes redressal commissions (state commissions) with territorial jurisdiction over the state/ UT concerned and financial jurisdiction to entertain consumer complaints involving claims above ₹ 20.00 lakh and up to ₹ 1.00 crore and with appellate jurisdiction over the district fora and 679 District Consumer Disputes Redressal Fora (district forum) with territorial jurisdiction over the district and pecuniary jurisdiction up to ₹ 20.00 lakh.

National Test House

The National Test House (NTH) is a premier test and quality evaluation laboratory for industrial, engineering and consumer products under the administrative control of the Government of India since the year 1912. This century old scientific and technological organization was established originally by the Indian Railway Board as a captive test and quality evaluation laboratory (originally known as Government Test House) at Alipore, Kolkata with a view to examine the quality of the various products meant to be used by the Indian Railways. The first regional laboratory was set up by NTH in Mumbai in 1963 and subsequently at Chennai (1975), Ghaziabad (1977), Jaipur (1994) and Guwahati (1996). The National Test House works in the field of testing, evaluation and quality control of various engineering materials and finished products, calibration of measuring equipment/ instruments and devices. To be precise, the NTH issues test certificates in scientific and engineering fields to certify conformity to national/international specifications or customer standard specifications.

Price Monitoring

The DCA operates a Price Monitoring Cell (PMC) tasked with monitoring prices of select essential commodities. The monitoring is done in respect of both retail and wholesale prices on a daily basis. The Cell monitors the prices of 22 essential commodities, which include cereals, pulses, vegetables, edible oils, sugar, milk, etc., collected form 71 reporting centres across the country through the Civil Supplies Department of states/UTs. These daily commodity prices are available on the Departmental website (www.fea.min.nic.in) and are updated regularly.

The prevailing price situation as well as the other factors that impact prices, both in the domestic and the international markets are analyzed and brought to the notice of the interministerial consultation mechanism for appropriate policy action. Based on the analysis of price data received, specific interventions are undertaken including allowing import of various items of mass consumption at zero or concessional import duties; restriction on exports, when necessary; prescribing stock holding limits under Essential Commodities Act; and allocation of foodgrains at affordable prices under the Targeted Public Distribution System (TPDS). The DCA is working on increasing the number of reporting centres from 71 at present to 100 in a phased manner, enhancing coordination with states/ UTs to make price monitoring more effective, expanding the list of essential commodities currently monitoring keeping in view the changing consumption pattern through periodical market surveys, commodity specific research on consumption pattern through periodical market surveys, commodity specific research studies/ surveys such as demand - supply and consumption pattern analysis of essential food items to facilitate appropriate policy intervention.

Food and Public Distribution

The primary objective of the Department of Food & Public Distribution is to ensure food security for the country through: efficient procurement at Minimum Support Price (MSP), storage and distribution of food grains; ensuring availability of foodgrains sugar and edible oils through appropriate policy instruments; including maintenance of buffer stocks of foodgrains; making foodgrains accessible at reasonable prices, especially to the weaker and vulnerable sections of society under a Targeted Public Distribution System (TPDS);

The main instruments of the Department's food management policy are procurement, storage and movement of foodgrains, public distribution and maintenance of buffer stocks.

Procurement of Foodgrains

Food Corporation of India (FCI), with the help of state government agencies, procures wheat, paddy and coarse grains in various states in order to provide price support to the farmers. Before each Rabi/Kharif crop season, central government announces the Minimum Support Prices (MSP), based on the recommendations of Commission for Agricultural Costs and Prices (CACP), which takes into consideration the cost of various agricultural inputs and the reasonable margin for the farmers for their produce. Details of number of procurement centres to be opened and arrangements like purchase of packaging material and storage space are also kept in line. Sufficient numbers of procurement centres are opened by FCI/state government agencies in mutual consultation before onset of procurement season, keeping in view the procurement potential and geographical spread of the state concerned. Review is made from time to time on the need for additional procurement centres, if any, during the procurement season and required additional procurement centres are also opened. State governments are encouraged to adopt decentralised procurement (DCP) system of procurement so as to maximise procurement, reduce transportation and increase the reach of MSP operations. Under this system, state governments undertake procurement and distribution of foodgrains by themselves. Procured quantities in excess of state's requirement are taken in the Central Pool for distribution elsewhere.

With the substantial increase in production of foodgrains in recent years and with an emphasis on bringing Green Revolution in Eastern-India, the procurement operations have expanded to many states due to which accumulated Central Pool Stock of foodgrains had reached to a record level of 805.16 lakh tonnes in 2012 against the buffer norm of 319 lakh tonnes. Therefore, a balanced policy approach for procurement, distribution and disposal of foodgrains is now being adopted to provide adequate price support to the farmers, to have optimum level of procurement for meeting

TPDS requirement, maintaining buffer stock and to dispose off surpluses without distorting the market in future.

Stock in Central Pool

Foodgrain Stocking Norms (Buffer Norms) were laid down to meet the prescribed minimum stocking norms for food security, to ensure monthly releases of foodgrains for the Targeted Public Distribution System (TPDS), Other Welfare Schemes (OWS), to meet emergency situations arising out of unexpected crop failure, natural disasters, festivals, etc., and to use the foodgrain stock in the Central Pool for market intervention to augment supply so as to help moderate the open market prices.

The stock of foodgrains (rice and wheat) in the Central Pool as in September, 2018 was 590.86 lakh MT (205.77 lakh MT of rice and 385.09 lakh MT of wheat). which is correspondingly higher than required as per the norms.

National Food Security

In order to further strengthen the commitment to food security of the people, Government of India enacted the National Food Security Act, 2013 (NFSA), which came into force from 2013. The Act aims to provide for food and nutritional security in human life cycle approach, by ensuring access to adequate quantity of quality food at affordable prices to people to live with dignity. The Act marks a paradigm shift in approach to food security— from welfare to a rights based one.

The Act provides for coverage of upto 75 per cent of the rural population and upto 50 per cent of the urban population for receiving subsidized foodgrains under Targeted Public Distribution System, thus covering about two-thirds of the population. This coverage for receiving highly subsidized foodgrains is under two categories—households covered under the Antyodaya Anna Yojana (AAY) and the remaining households as priority households. AAY was launched in 2000 to provide focus on food security to the poorest of the poor, and covers 2.5 crore households. Such households are entitled under the Act to receive 35 kg. of foodgrains per households per month, at ₹ 1/2/3 per kg. for coarse grains/wheat/rice. Priority households are entitled to receive 5 kg. of foodgrains per person per month at the above mentioned highly subsidized prices.

The Act also contains provisions for setting up of grievance redressal mechanism at the district and state levels. Separate provisions have also been made for ensuring transparency and accountability.

NFSA is now being implemented in all the states/UTs covering about 80.55 crore beneficiaries, against intended coverage of 81.34 crore people. In Chandigarh, Puducherry and urban areas of Dadra and Nagar Haveli, the Act is being implemented in the cash transfer mode under which food subsidy is being transferred into the bank accounts of beneficiaries who then have a choice to buy foodgrains from open market.

End-to-End Computerisation

Department of Food and Public Distribution is implementing a Plan Scheme on 'End-to-End Computerisation' of TPDS Operations on cost sharing basis with states/UTs with funding requirement of ₹ 884.07 crore, out of which Government of India's share is ₹ 489.37 crore and that of states/UTs is ₹ 394.70 crore. It has become more important after coming into force of the National Food Security Act, under which prices of foodgrains to be distributed through the TPDS are highly subsidised. The scheme has been extended up to 2019. Its key activities include : (a) digitization of beneficiary database to enable correct identification of beneficiaries; removal of bogus cards and better targeting of food subsidies; (b) online allocation of foodgrains to bring transparency in allocation of foodgrains, upto the fair price shops level; and (c) grievance redressal mechanism and transparency portal to introduce transparency and public accountability in the implementation of TPDS through transparency portals, online grievance registration and toll free helpline numbers.

All states/UTs have been requested to seed Aadhaar numbers in ration cards database. Further, action has also been initiated for implementation of FPS automation which involves, installation of Point of Sale (PoS) devices at FPS for authentication of beneficiaries, recording of sales to beneficiaries at the FPS; and uploading of transaction data in central server.

Integrated Management of PDS (IM-PDS)

A new central sector scheme– 'Integrated Management of PDS' (IM-PDS) is to be implemented during FY 2018-19 and 2019-20 for establishing Public Distribution System Network (PDSN) to inter alia implement national level de-duplication of beneficiaries and portability. The Scheme will strengthen better targeting of food subsidy and help the beneficiaries to lift foodgrains from the FPSs of their choice.

According to a notification issued in 2017 (as amended from time to time) under Aadhaar (Targeted Delivery of Financial and Other Subsidies, Benefits and Services) Act, 2016 the individual beneficiaries having ration cards under NFSA need to furnish proof of possession of Aadhaar number or undergo Aadhaar authentication to receive subsidies. Those who do not possess Aadhaar are to make application for Aadhaar enrolment by giving their name, address, mobile number with ration card number and other details with their fair price shop owners or through the web portal provided for the purpose by state/UT governments. The notification further provides that till the Aadhaar is assigned to the beneficiaries the entitlements under

NFSA shall be given to such individuals on production of ration card and either Aadhaar Enrolment ID slip or copy of his/her request made along with any of the following identification documents, namely: (i) voter ID card; or (ii) Permanent Account Number (PAN) Card; or (iii) passport; or (iv) driving license; or (v) certificate of identity having photo issued by the gazetted officer or Tehsildar on an official letter head; or (vi) address card having name and photo issued by Department of Posts; or (vii) Kisan Photo Passbook; or (viii) any other document as specified by the state government or union territory administration.

This Department has also issued instructions to state/UT governments with the direction that in case of failure of biometric authentication due to network/connectivity/linking issue or due to poor biometric of the beneficiary or other technical reasons, the beneficiary is to be provided subsidized foodgrains or cash transfer of food subsidy on the basis of physical production of Aadhaar card by him/her in place of biometric authentication. Further, it has been clarified that no one should be denied foodgrains or deleted from the ration card database only on the ground of non possession of Aadhaar.

Provision has also been made that any member of eligible household listed in the ration card shall be entitled to receive the entire quantity of entitled subsidised food grains or cash transfer of food subsidy under NFSA, if any one member of the household. in the ration card fulfils the identification conditions, in case Aadhaar number is not yet assigned to all such members of the household.

Other Welfare Schemes

Mid-Day Meal Scheme

The Mid-Day Meal Scheme is implemented by the Ministry of Human Resource Development. The Scheme covers students of primary and upper primary classes in the government schools/schools aided by government and the schools run by local bodies. Foodgrains are supplied free of cost at 100 grams for primary stage and at 150 grams for upper primary stage per child per school day where cooked/processed hot meal is being served or 3 kgs per student per month where raw foodgrains are distributed. During 2018-19, 12.12 lakh tonnes of foodgrains comprising 10.25 lakh tonnes of rice and 1.87 lakh tonnes of wheat were allocated under the Scheme.

Wheat Based Nutrition Programme

This Scheme is implemented by the Ministry of Women and Child Development. The foodgrains allotted under it are utilized by the states/UTs under Integrated Child Development Services (ICDS) scheme for providing nutritious/energy food to children in the age group of 0-6 years and expectant/lactating women. During 2018-19, 19.90 lakh tonnes of foodgrains comprising 9.63 lakh tonnes of rice and 10.27 lakh tonnes of wheat were allocated under the Scheme. Also a quantity of 13000 tonnes of maize was allocated under the Scheme.

Scheme for Adolescent Girls

The Ministry of Women and Child Development administers the scheme at the central level. However foodgrains for the Scheme are allotted by the Department of Food and Public Distribution at BPL rates to the Ministry of Women and Child Development. The SABLA scheme was launched in 2010 by merging two schemes namely, Nutrition Programme and Adolescent Girls (NPAG) and Kishori Shakti Yojana (KSY) into a single scheme. The Scheme aims at empowering adolescent girls of 11-18 years by improvement of their nutritional and health status and upgrading various skills useful to them. It also aims at equipping the girls on family welfare, health hygiene, etc., and guiding them on existing public services. The requirement of foodgrains for nutrition is at 100 grams of grains per beneficiary per day for 300 days in a year. During 2017-18, 2.04 lakh tonnes of foodgrains comprising 0.77 lakh tonnes of rice and 1.27 lakh tonnes of wheat were allocated under it.

Supply of Foodgrains to Welfare Institutions

With a view to meeting the requirement of welfare institutions viz., charitable institutions such as beggar homes, nariniketans and other similar welfare institutions not covered under TPDS or under any other welfare schemes, an additional allocation of foodgrains (rice and wheat) not exceeding 5 per cent of the BPL allocation is made to states/UTs at BPL prices.

Supply of Foodgrains for SC/ST/OBC Hostels

This Scheme was introduced in 1994. The residents of the hostels having 2/3rd resident students belonging to SC/ST/OBC are eligible to get 15 kg foodgrains per resident per month. Allocations of foodgrains under it are made by the Department of Food and Public Distribution based on the requests received from the state/UT governments.

Annapurna Scheme

This Scheme is implemented by the Ministry of Rural Development. Indigent senior citizens of 65 years of age or above who are not getting pension under the National Old Age Pension Scheme (NOAPS), are provided 10 kgs. of foodgrains per person per month free of cost under it. Foodgrains are provided by the Department of Food and Public Distribution under the scheme at BPL prices.

Open Market Sale Scheme (Domestic)

In addition to maintaining buffer stocks and for meeting the requirement of the Targeted Public Distribution System (TPDS) and Other Welfare Schemes

(OWS), the FCI sells excess stocks of wheat and rice from the Central Pool at predetermined prices in the open market from time to time under Open Market Sale Scheme (Domestic) through e-tender to enhance the supply especially during the lean season especially in the deficit regions.

Storage of Foodgrains

Capacity of FCI and State Agencies

FCI has its own grid of covered godowns in all states to safely stock the central pool foodgrains. In addition, it hires capacity from Central Warehousing Corporation (CWC) and state agencies like state warehousing corporations as well as private parties.

Sufficient storage capacity is available and against 876.31 lakh MT capacity available, the Central stock of foodgrains stood at 627.13 lakh MT in July 2018.

Augmentation of Storage Capacity

In order to cope with increasing production and procurement of foodgrains, the Department is implementing private entrepreneurs guarantee (PEG) scheme for augmenting the covered storage capacity in the country. Under the PEG scheme, which was launched in 2008, godowns are constructed in PPP mode and the land and construction cost is borne by the selected partners. FCI on its part guarantees 10 year usage of storage capacities to the private investors and 9 years to CWC and SWCs. Locations for construction of godown are identified by the FCI on the basis of recommendations of state level committees to cover the gaps in storage. For consuming areas, the storage gap is assessed on the basis of the 4 months' requirement of PDS and OWS while for procuring states the storage gap has been assessed based on the highest stock levels in the last three years, and keeping in view the potential of procurement. Under the Scheme, a capacity of 141.47 MT was completed in 22 states by July 2018.

As a part of the modernization of storage facilities, modern storage facilities in the form of steel silos are also being created in Public Private Partnership. Each silo will have capacity of 25,000 or 50,000 MT. This will mechanize the existing supply chain and improve operational efficiency.

A Central sector scheme for construction of godowns with focus on augmenting storage capacity is being implemented in North Eastern state. Under it, funds are also provided for construction of storage godowns to improve the supply chain logisties of PDS.

Warehousing Development and Regulatory Authority

For the growth and development of warehousing sector, to bring reforms in the agricultural marketing and to increase credit flow in the farm sector, the government introduced a negotiable warehouse receipt system in the country by enacting the Warehousing (Development and Regulation) Act, 2007 which is in place since 2010. The government constituted the Warehousing Development and Regulatory Authority (WDRA) in 2010 for implementation of the provisions of the Act. The Negotiable Warehouse Receipts (NWRs) issued against stocks of farm produces deposited by the farmers in warehouses would help the farmers in seeking loan from banks. It would help overcoming the situation of distress sale of agricultural commodities by the farmers during peak harvest season. Warehouses need to be registered with the WDRA for issuing NWRs. The warehouses are inspected by the empanelled inspection agencies prior to grant of registration to ensure that basic requirements of scientific and safe storage of agricultural and other commodities are fully met by the warehouses.

The Authority has notified 123 agricultural commodities including cereals, pulses, oilseeds, spices, vegetable oils, edible nuts and other commodities like rubber, tobacco, tea, coffee makhana, etc., and 26 horticultural commodities such as potato, dehydrated onion, garlic, ginger, turmeric, apple and resins for issuance of NWRs.

Central Warehousing Corporation

Central Warehousing Corporation (CWC) is a Public Sector Undertaking (PSU) set up 1957 under this Department to provide scientific storage facilities for agricultural produces, implements and other notified commodities. By August 2018, CWC is operating 431 warehouses with a total storage capacity of 100.28 lakh MT including 44 custom bonded warehouses, 29 container freight stations/inland clearance depots, 3 air cargo complexes and 3 temperature controlled warehouses for providing services to the export/import trade. CWC has 19 associate state warehousing corporations (SWCs) with a total capacity of 352.65 lakh MT.

CWC also has a 100 per cent owned subsidiary company namely, Central Railside Warehouse Company Limited (CRWC) for development of Railside Warehouse Complexes (RWCs). CRWC has 19 RWCs with had a total storage capacity of 3,46,267 MT in August 2018.

Post Harvest Management of Foodgrains

Quality Standard for Foodgrains

The government exercises due control over the quality of foodgrains procured for the central pool. The Quality Control Cells of the Ministry at New Delhi and the field offices at Bengaluru, Bhopal, Bhubaneshwar, Kolkata, Hyderabad, Lucknow, Pune, Guwahati, Chennai and Patna monitor the quality of foodgrains procured, stored and issue for distribution by FCI and state governments and their agencies. During 2017-18, 1170 Food Storage Depots were inspected by the officers of quality control cells.

Indian Grain Storage Management and Research Institute

Indian Grain Storage Management and Research Institute (IGMRI), Hapur and its field stations at Ludhiana (Punjab) and Hyderabad (Andhra Pradesh) are engaged in the training and applied Research and Development (R&D) work relating to grain storage management. The IGMRI also conducts various training courses on storage, inspection of foodgrains, pest control, etc, for the officers of storages agencies and pest control operator, etc.

Central Grain Analysis Laboratory

The Central Grain Analysis Laboratory (CGAL) located in New Delhi assists the Department in monitoring the quality of foodgrains at the time of procurement, storage and distribution by analyzing samples collected by quality control officers. A total of 1548 foodgrain samples for physical parameters, 667 for protein determination, 664 for falling number in wheat samples were analyzed during 2017-18.

Export and Import of Foodgrains

Export Policy of Rice and Wheat

The Government has allowed free export of non-basmati rice by private parties from privately held stocks from 2011. State Trading Enterprises (STEs) including M/s NCCF and NAFED are also permitted to export privately held stocks on non-basmati rice. Export of wheat was also allowed from the same year. Export of non-basmati rice and wheat is permitted through Custom EDI ports. Export is also permitted through the non-EDI Land Custom Stations (LCS) on Indo-Bangladesh and Indo-Nepal Border subject to registration of quantity with DGFT. Export of rice of seed quality and other [rice in husk (paddy or rough) other than seed quality] is permitted under licence.

Export of Wheat and Rice

A quantity of 86.46 lakh MT of non-basmati rice and 2,25,208 lakh MT of wheat was exported under "free export" category during 2017-18.

Status of Export on Government Account

The Government also permits export of wheat and rice to various friendly countries on diplomatic basis/humanitarian aid on the recommendations of the Ministry of External Affairs.

Import of Rice and Wheat

No import of wheat and rice has been made for Central Pool stock during 2017-18. However, a quantity of 16,49,725 MT of wheat and 2,122 MT of non-basmati rice was imported by private traders/millers during 2017-18.

Sugar

Sugar Production

India is the largest consumer and the second largest producer of sugar in the world. The production of sugar during the current sugar season 2017-18 is estimated to be about 322.00 lakh MT.

Sugarcane Pricing Policy

With the amendment of the Sugarcane (Control) Order, 1966 in 2009, the concept of Statutory Minimum Price (SMP) of sugarcane was replaced with the 'Fair and Remunerative Price (FRP)' for 2009-10 and subsequent sugar seasons. The cane price announced by the central government is decided on the basis of the recommendations of the Commission for Agricultural Costs and Prices (CACP) after consulting the state governments and associations of sugar industry. The amended provisions of the Sugarcane (Control) Order, 1966 provides for fixation of FRP of sugarcane having regard to the following factors:- (a) cost of production of sugarcane; (b) return to the growers from alternative crops and the general trend of prices of agricultural commodities; (c) availability of sugar to consumers at a fair price; (d) price at which sugar produced from sugarcane is sold by sugar producers; (e) recovery of sugar from sugarcane; (f) the realization made from sale of by-products viz., molasses, bagasse and press mud or their imputed value; and (g) reasonable margins for the growers of sugarcane on account of risk and profits.

Under the FRP system, the farmers are not required to wait till the end of the season or for any announcement of the profits by sugar mills or the government. The new system also assures margins on account of profit and risk to farmers, irrespective of the fact whether sugar mills generate profit or not and is not dependent on the performance of any individual sugar mill. In order to ensure that higher sugar recoveries are adequately rewarded and considering variations amongst sugar mills, the FRP is linked to a basic recovery rate of sugar, with a premium payable to farmers for higher recoveries of sugar from sugarcane. Accordingly, FRP for 2018-19 sugar season has been fixed at ₹ 275 per qtl. linked to a basic recovery of 10 per cent subject to a premium of ₹ 2.75 per qtl. for every 0.1 percentage point increase above that level.

De-regulation of Sugar Sector

2013-14 was a watershed for the sugar industry. The central government considered the recommendations of the committee headed by Dr. C. Rangarajan on deregulation of sugar sector and decided to discontinue the system of levy obligations on mills for sugar produced after September, 2012 and abolished the regulated release mechanism on open market sale. The deregulation of the sugar sector was undertaken to improve the financial health of sugar mills, enhance cash flows, reduce inventory costs and also result in timely payments of cane price to sugarcane farmers. The recommendations of the committee relating to cane area reservation, minimum distance criteria and adoption of the cane price formula have been left to state governments for adoption and implementation, as considered appropriate by them.

Review of Distribution of Sugar to Antyodaya Anna Yojana Families

Sugar was distributed through the Targeted Public Distribution System (TPDS) by the states/UTs at subsidized prices for which the central government was reimbursing ₹ 18.50 per kg of sugar distributed by the participating state governments /UT administrations. The scheme was covering all BPL population of the country as per 2001 census and all the population of the North Eastern states / special category/ hilly states and island territories. The National Food Security Act, 2013 (NFSA) is now being universally implemented by 36 states/UTs. Under the NFSA, there is no identified category of BPL; however, the Antyodaya Anna Yojana (AAY) beneficiaries are clearly identified. The Sugar Subsidy Scheme has been reviewed and it has been decided that it is imperative to give access to consumption of sugar as a source of energy in diet, for the poorest of the poor section of the society i.e., AAY families. Accordingly, the government has decided that the existing system of sugar distribution through PDS may be continued as per the following:- (i) the existing scheme of supply of subsidized sugar through PDS may be continued for restricted coverage of AAY families only. They will be provided 1 kg of sugar per family per month; (ii) the current level of subsidy at ₹18.50 per kg provided by the central government to states/UTs may be continued for the AAY population. The revised scheme was implemented in 2017. Twelve states participated during 2017-18 and ₹ 300 crore was released as subsidy under it.

Ethanol Blending Petrol Programme

Ethanol is an agro-based product, mainly produced from a by-product of the sugar industry, namely molasses. In years of surplus production of sugarcane, when prices are depressed, the sugar industry is unable to make timely payment of cane price to farmers. The Ethanol Blended Petrol Programme (EBP) seeks to achieve blending of Ethanol with motor sprit with a view to reducing pollution, conserve foreign exchange and increase value addition in the sugar industry enabling them to clear cane price arrears of farmers.

The central government has scaled up blending targets from 5 to 10 per cent under the EBP. The procedure of procurement of ethanol under the EBP has been simplified to streamline the entire ethanol supply chain and remunerative ex-depot price of ethanol has been fixed. To facilitate achieving of new blending targets, a "grid" which networks distilleries to OMC depots and details quantities to be supplied has been worked out.

Sugar Development Fund

Under the Sugar Cess Act, 1982, a cess was collected as excise duty on all sugar produced and sold by any factory within the counrty which has now been abolished through Taxation Laws Amendment Act, 2017. The cess so collected provided funds for Sugar Development Fund (SDF) through budgetary process. The Sugar Development Fund Act, 1982 can be utilized by the Government of India for making loans for facilitating the rehabilitation and modernization, development of sugarcane, bagasse based co-generation power projects, production of anhydrous alcohol or ethanol from alcohol, conversion of existing ethanol plant into zero liquid discharge plant, making grants for any research project aimed at development of sugar industry, defraying expenditure for the purpose of building up and maintenance of buffer stock of sugar, internal transport and freight charges to the sugar factories on export shipments of sugar, financial assistance to sugar factories towards interest on loan given in terms of any scheme approved by the central government from time to time, marketing and promotion service for raw production, interest subvention on scheme for extending soft loan to sugar mills, production subsidy to sugar mills to offset cost of cane and facilitate timely payment of cane price dues to farmers and for defraying any other expenditure for the purpose of this Act.

Production Subsidy

The government has also extended production subsidy at ₹ 4.50 per quintal to sugar mills from 2015 to offset cost of cane and facilitate timely payment of cane price dues of farmers for the sugar season 2015-16. Consequent upon sugar prices reaching substantially higher levels than required for operational viability of the sugar industry, the central government had withdrawn production subsidy scheme since 2016.

Edible Oils

The efficient management of edible oils in the country involves steps to ensure sufficient availability of edible oils to the consumer at reasonable rates. As per the third Advance Estimates for 2017-18 (Nov.-Oct.), estimated oilseeds production is about 306.38 lakh tonnes as compared to 312.76 lakh MT during the previous year.

Vegetable Oil Industry

There are about 100 Vanaspati units and 651 solvent extraction plants/ refineries in the country with an annual capacity to process around 6800 lakh MT of raw material. Due to various reasons, mainly the seasonal availability of raw material, the total capacity utilization of the edible oil industry is around 35 per cent as per estimates given by the Solvent Extractors Association of India.

Ban on Export of Edible Oils

Exports of edible oils has been banned from March 2008 with certain exemptions i.e., coconut oil from all Electronic Data Interchange (EDI) ports and through notified Land Customs Stations (LCS), castor oil, organic edible oils and certain oils produced from minor forest produce. Further, export of edible oil has been permitted in branded consumer packs of upto 5 kg subject to Minimum Export Price of USD 900 per tonnes which was reduced from USD 1100 per tonnes in 2015. Export of rice bran oil in bulk has been allowed from 2015. From 2017, groundnut oil, sesame oil, soyabean oil and maize (corn oil) have been exempted from the ban.

Import Duty on Edible Oils

As there is a continuous demand in excess over the domestic supply of edible oils, its import has been resorted to for more than two decades. In order to maintain uninterrupted supply of edible oils at affordable prices to the consumers and at the same time keeping in mind the interest of the farmers, industry as well as consumers, import duty on crude and refined edible oils was raised to 35 and 45 per cent respectively while import duty on olive oil was increased to 40 per cent. The import duty on crude and palm oil remained at 44 and 54 per cent respectively.

International Cooperation

India is associated with a number of international agencies working in the field of food related matters. These include World Food Programme (WFP), SAARC Food Bank, Food and Agricultural Organisation (FAO), International Grains Council (IGC) and International Sugar Organisation (ISO), etc.

SAARC Food Bank

In pursuance of the decision taken in the 14th SAARC Summit held in New Delhi in 2007, the Heads of States of South Asian Association for Regional Cooperation (SAARC) countries signed the agreement to establish the SAARC Food Bank. The Food Bank will supplement national efforts to provide food security to the people of the region. As per this agreement, SAARC Food Bank is to have a reserve of foodgrains to be maintained by each member states consisting of either wheat or rice, or a combination of both as assessed share of the country.

Food and Agricultural Organisation and Committee on World Food Security

Food and Agricultural Organisation (FAO) is one of the largest specialized agencies in the UN System founded in 1945 with a mandate to raise levels of nutrition and standard of living by improving agricultural productivity and living conditions of rural population. The Committee on World Food Security (CFS) serves as a forum in the United Nations System for review and follow-up of policies concerning world food security, including food production, physical and economic access to food. India is a member of both FAO and CFS. Committee on World Food Security (CFS) monitors the progress of implementation of the WFS Plan of Action.

International Grains Council

India is a member of the International Grains Council (IGC), an inter-governmental forum of exporting and importing countries for cooperation in wheat and coarse grain matters which was previously known as International Wheat Council upto 1995. It administers the Grains Trade Convention, 1995. The IGC Secretariat, based in London since 1949, also services the Food Aid Committee, established under the Food Aid Convention. International Grains Agreement comprises Grains Trade Convention (GTC) and Food Aid Convention (FAC). India is a signatory to the International Grains Agreement (IGA), 1995 and its Grain Trade Convention (GTC), 1995 which is effective from 1995. IGC has two types of members—importing and exporting members. India has been included in the category of exporting member in July, 2003 and represented in the meetings/sessions of the Council held from time to time.

Food Processing Industries

The Ministry of Food Processing Industries was set up in July, 1988 to give an impetus to development of food processing sector in the country. Later this Ministry was made a Department and brought under the Ministry of Agriculture. It was again made a ministry in 2001 and named Ministry of Food Processing Industries.

The Ministry is concerned with formulation and implementation of the policies for the food processing industries within the overall national priorities and objectives. A strong and dynamic food processing sector plays a vital role in diversification and commercialisation of agriculture, enhancing shelf life, ensuring value addition to agricultural produce, generation of employment, enhancing income of farmers and creating markets for export of agro foods. The Ministry acts as a catalyst for bringing in greater investment into this sector, guiding and helping the industry and creating a conducive environment of healthy growth of the food processing industry.

The subjects allocated to the Ministry under Government of India (Allocation of Business) Rules, 1961 are:- (i) industries relating to : (a) processing and refrigeration of certain agricultural products (milk powder, infant milk food, malted milk food, condensed milk, ghee and other dairy products), poultry and eggs, meat and meat products; (b) processing of fish (including canning and freezing); (c) establishment and servicing of development council for fish processing industry; (d) technical assistance and advise to fish processing industry; (e) fruit and vegetable processing industry (including freezing and dehydration); and (f) foodgrains milling industry.

(ii) planning, development and control of, and assistance to, industries relating to bread, oil seeds, meals (edible), breakfast foods, biscuits, confectionery (including cocoa processing and chocolate making), malt extract, protein isolate, high protein food, weaning food and extruded food products (including other ready to eat foods); (iii) beer including non-alcoholic beer; (iv) alcoholic drinks from non-molasses base; (v) specialized packaging for food processing industry, and (vi) aerated water and soft drinks.

www.mofpi.nic.in

Contribution of Food Processing Sector

Over the years agricultural production in India has consistently recorded higher output. India ranks number one in the world in the production of milk, ghee, ginger, bananas, guavas, papayas and mangoes. Further, India ranks second in the world in the production of rice, wheat and several other vegetables and fruits. Abundant supply of raw materials, increase in demand for food products and incentives offered by the Government has impacted food processing sector positively.

Employment in Food Processing Sector

Food processing industry is one of the major employment intensive segments constituting 12.77 per cent of employment generated in all registered factory sector in 2014-15. According to the Annual Survey of Industries (ASI) data for 2014-15, the total number of persons engaged in registered food processing sector was 17.73 lakhs. Unregistered food processing sector supports employment to 47.9 lakh workers as per the NSSO 67th Round, 2010-11.

Fixed Capital in Food Processing Industries

In terms of investment in fixed capital, registered food processing sector is growing annually at an average of 15.60 per cent during six years ending 2014-15. As per the latest ASI 2014-15, the Fixed Capital in FP Industry stood at ₹ 1.92 lakh crore.

FDI in Food Processing Sector

Cent per cent FDI is permitted under the automatic route in food processing industries- manufacturing sector. FDI is allowed through approval route for trading, including through e-commerce in respect of food products manufactured and/or produced in India.

Food Processing and Make in India

Food processing sector has been identified as one of the priority sector under 'Make in India'. With a view to attract investment to this sector, Ministry of Food Processing Industries has been implementing schemes for development of infrastructure for promoting food processing industries.

Mega food parks with common utilities like road, electricity, water supply, sewage facility and common processing facility like pulping, packaging, cold storage, dry storage and logistics are being promoted in areas with strong agricultural resource base. These parks provide fully developed plots and factory sheds to entrepreneurs on long term lease basis where they can set up food processing units in "plug and play model".

Ministry has been disseminating information to potential investors to attract investment to the sector through a dedicated "Investors Portal". The Ministry is also collaborating with Invest India to help the investors in terms of locating joint venture partners, extending hand holding services and expedite regulatory approvals. Ministry is also organizing Road Shows to attract FDI including FDI in retail and promote Make in India Initiative.

National Mission on Food Processing

The Ministry launched a Centrally Sponsored Scheme—National Mission on Food Processing (NMFP) during 12th Plan in 2012. Five ongoing Central Sector Schemes of 11th Plan and four new schemes were merged in the Mission. The CSS-NMFP was implemented through states/UTs. However, the CSS-NMFP was de-linked from the central support in 2015 pursuant to the recommendations of the 14th Finance Commission. Consequently, all nine schemes of the Mission stand discontinued.

Government of India approved a new Central Sector Scheme - Kisan Sampada Yojana - (Scheme for Agro-Marine Processing and Development of Agro-Processing Clusters) in 2017 with an outlay of ₹ 6,000 crore for the period 2016-20 coterminous with the 14th Finance Commission cycle. It is a comprehensive package which will result in creation of modern infrastructure with efficient supply chain management from farm gate to retail outlet. It will not only provide a big boost to the growth of food processing sector in the country but also help in providing better prices to farmers and is considered a big step towards doubling of farmers income, creating huge employment opportunities especially in the rural areas, reducing wastage of agricultural produce, increasing the processing level and enhancing the export of the processed foods.

National Institute of Food Technology, Entrepreneurship and Management

The Ministry established the National Institute of Food Technology, Entrepreneurship and Management at Kundli, in Haryana in May, 2012. NIFTEM has been declared a Deemed University under de novo category. It is running B.Tech., M.Tech. and Ph.D courses and undertakes R&D projects in the area of food technology. Under the Scheme, funds are to be provided to the Institute for creation of academic and administrative infrastructure like foreign students' hostel, sports facilities, hazardous chemical storage, effluent treatment plant, solid waste management system, residential units, etc. Funds will also be provided to promote research activities, expand Village Adoption Programme (VAP) and skill development in the food processing sector. An allocation of ₹ 100 crore has been made to it.

Indian Institute of Food Processing Technology

The Ministry upgraded Indian Institute of Food Processing Technology (IIFPT), Thanjavur, Tamil Nadu to a national level institute in 2008. IIFPT is running B.Tech., M.Tech. and Ph.D courses and undertaking R&D projects in the area of food processing. Under the scheme funds are to be provided to the Institute for creation of infrastructure facilities including purchase of additional land (22.7 acres) for expanding campus and creation of academic and administrative infrastructure like machine fabrication and testing centre, sport complex, auditorium, opening training cum incubation centres and residential units, etc. To enable the Institute to expand its activities, the North East States will include Sikkim and difficult areas will include and programmes to meet the ever expanding need of food processing sector in the country, an allocation of ₹ 75 crore has been made to it.

16 Health and Family Welfare

THE Ministry of Health and Family Welfare is instrumental and responsible for implementation of various programmes on the national scale in the areas of health and family welfare, prevention and control of major communicable and non-communicable diseases as well as promoting research across the country. It is responsible for formulating health and allied policies, providing guidance to states towards implementing health programs, managing centrally sponsored health schemes and programs, medical education, regulation (drugs and devices) and health infrastructure. Expenditure is incurred by the Ministry either directly under central schemes or by way of grants-in-aid to the autonomous/statutory bodies, etc. The Ministry of Health Family Welfare (MoHFW) earlier had two departments - Department of Health & Family Welfare and Department of Health Research.

Department of AIDS Control has been merged with Department of Health & Family Welfare and now be known as National AIDS Control Organization (NACO). In December 2014, Department of AYUSH was made Ministry of Ayurveda, Yoga and Naturopathy, Unani, Siddha and Homeopathy (AYUSH) with focused attention on development of education and research in ayurveda, yoga and naturopathy, Unani, Siddha and homoeopathy systems. Directorate General of Health Services (DGHS) is an attached office which renders technical advice on all medical and public health matters and is involved in the implementation of various health services.

Relevant Websites : www.mohfw.gov.in www.dhr.gov.in
www.naco.gov.in

National Health Policy

The National Health Policy (NHP) was released in 2017 after a gap of 15 years. NHP 2017 addresses the current and emerging challenges necessitated by the changing socio-economic, technological and epidemiological landscape. It envisages providing larger package of assured comprehensive primary healthcare through the health and wellness centres. The policy aims to attain the highest possible level of health and well-being for all at all ages through a preventive and promotive healthcare and universal access to quality health services without anyone having to face financial hardship as a consequence. This would be achieved through increasing access, improving quality and lowering the cost of healthcare delivery. NHP 2017 advocates allocating major proportion (two-thirds or more) of resources to primary care and aims to ensure availability of two beds per 1,000 population distributed in a manner to enable access within golden hour.

Besides this, the highlights of the policy include: (i) Assurance based approach - It advocates progressively incremental assurance based approach with focus on preventive and promotive healthcare; (ii) micronutrient deficiency- There is a focus on reducing micronutrient malnourishment and systematic approach to address heterogeneity in micronutrient adequacy across regions; (iii) Make-in-India initiative- It advocates the need to incentivize local manufacturing to provide customized indigenous products for Indian population in the long run, and (iv) application of digital health- The policy advocates extensive deployment of digital tools for improving the efficiency and outcome of the healthcare system and aims at an integrated health information system which serves the needs of all stake-holders and improves efficiency, transparency, and citizen experience.

One of the mandates of the NHP 2017, is the use of information technology towards healthcare. In line with that the IT initiatives of the Ministry are listed here:

National Health Portal (NHP) is functioning as citizen portal for healthcare providing health related information to citizens and stakeholders in different languages (currently six languages). A voice portal, providing information through a toll-free number 1800-180-1104 and mobile app has also been launched. It serves as a single point access for information on health and diseases including health messages; on regulations, standards, policies, programmes, commissions etc.; directory services - hospitals, blood banks, ambulances.

Hospital Information System (HIS) is being implemented in hospitals for automation of hospital processes to achieve better efficiency and service delivery in public health facilities upto CHC level.

Online Registration System (ORS) is a framework to link various hospitals for online registration, payment of fees and appointment, online diagnostic reports, enquiring availability of blood online, etc. As on date, around 124 hospitals including central hospitals like AIIMS -New Delhi and other AIIMS (Jodhpur; Bihar, Rishikesh, Bhubaneswar, Raipur, Bhopal); RML Hospital; SIC, Safdarjung Hospital; NIMHANS; Agartala Government Medical College; JIPMER, etc., are on board of ORS.

Mera Aspataal (My Hospital) application is an IT based feedback system to collect information on patients' level of satisfaction using a multi-channel approach viz. short message service (SMS), outbound dialing (OBD), web portal, and mobile application. The application automatically contacts the patient (outpatient after the closure of the OPD and the inpatient at the time of discharge) using the above tools to collect information on patients' level of satisfaction.

Mother and Child Tracking System (MCTS) / Reproductive Child Health (RCH) application is an individual-based tracking system across all the states & UTs to facilitate timely delivery of antenatal and postnatal care services and immunization to children with an objective of improving IMR, MMR, & morbidity.

Kilkari application was launched to deliver free weekly audio messages about pregnancy, child birth and care. Assam, Bihar, Chhattisgarh, Delhi, Haryana, Himachal Pradesh, Jharkhand, Madhya Pradesh, Odisha, Rajasthan, Uttar Pradesh and Uttarakhand are covered under it.

Mobile Academy is a free audio training course designed to expand and refresh the knowledge base of ASHAs and improve their communication skills. Launched in 2016, Bihar, Chhattisgarh, Delhi, Haryana, Himachal Pradesh, Jharkhand, Madhya Pradesh, Odisha, Rajasthan, Uttar Pradesh and Uttarakhand are presently covered under it.

TB Patient Monitoring System "Nikshay" for tracking of individuals for treatment-adherence has been implemented across all states for monitoring of TB patients. Also a missed call centre facility with toll free No: 1800-11-6666 for reaching to unreached TB patients has been started, for counselling and treatment support.

Tobacco Cessation Programme is a mobile-based interventional initiative for counseling and helping people to quit tobacco, by giving a missed call to 011-22901701.

m Diabetes Programme is a mobile-based initiative for prevention and care of diabetes by giving a missed call to 011-22901701.

e-CGHS card enables self-printing of CGHS cards from any location.

SUGAM by Central Drugs Standards Control Organisation (CDSCO) enables online submission of applications, their tracking, processing & grant of approvals online mainly for drugs, clinical trials, ethics committee, medical devices, vaccines and cosmetics. Provides a single window for multiple stakeholders (Pharma Industry, Regulators, Citizens) involved in the processes of CDSCO.

Drugs and Vaccine Distribution Management System (DVDMS) (eAushidhi) deals with purchase, inventory management and distribution of various drugs, sutures and surgical items to various district drug warehouse of state/UT, district hospitals, their sub-stores, etc., by automating the workflow of procurement, supply chain, quality control and finance department in state/UT level.

Mobile Apps: various mobile apps have been launched namely—

Indradhanush Immunization for tracking immunication;

India fights Dengue (enables a user to check dengue symptoms, get nearest hospital/blood bank information and share feed-back);

NHP Swasth Bharat (information on disease, lifestyle, first-aid);

NHP Directory Services (information of hospitals and blood banks across the country;

No More Tension (information on stress management related aspects);

Pradhan Mantri Surakshit Matritva Abhiyan (for reporting pregnancy cases across the states).

National Health Mission

Besides the National Health Policy, the efforts of MoHFW are directed towards achieving the global goals, encompassing reproductive health as well as communicable disease viz., AIDS, TB, malaria, leprosy etc. One of the major focus in the health sector has been to increase the funding to healthcare to at-least 2 per cent of the GDP. As a step towards this goal the National Rural Health Mission (NRHM) was launched in 2005 and it morphed into National Health Mission (NHM) with the launch of National Urban Health Mission (NUHM) in 2013. Thereafter, NRHM and NUHM became two sub-missions under the overarching NHM. NHM envisages achievement of universal access to equitable, affordable and quality healthcare services that are accountable and responsive to people's needs. The main programmatic components include health system strengthening in rural and urban areas, Reproductive-Maternal-Neonatal-Child and Adolescent Health (RMNCH+A) interventions and control of communicable and non-communicable diseases.

Mission Indradhanush

Mission Indradhanush was launched in 2014 to cover all those children who have been partially vaccinated or not vaccinated during routine immunization rounds. The objective the schemes is to increase full immunization coverage to at least 90 per cent children by 2020.

Maternal and Neonatal Tetanus Elimination

Maternal and Neonatal Tetanus Elimination (MNTE) is defined as less than one neonatal tetanus case per 1,000 live birth in every district per annum. India has been validated for Maternal and Neonatal tetanus elimination in May 2015. India achieved MNT Elimination through the strengthening of health systems by innovative programmes like Janani Suraksha Yojana (JSY) and Janani Shishu Suraksha Karayakaram (JSSK) to improve institutional delivery and by strengthening Routine Immunization.

New Vaccines

Inactivated Polio Vaccine (IPV): In concurrence with the World Polio End Game strategy, IPV was introduced in November 2015 in six states and expanded throughout the country by June 2016. Till August 2017, around 2.79 crore doses of IPV have been administered to children since its introduction.

Rotavirus Vaccine: This vaccine was launched in March 2016 in Andhra Pradesh, Haryana, Himachal Pradesh and Odisha, to reduce the burden of diarrhea caused by Rotavirus. It has been expanded to five more states namely, Assam, Madhya Pradesh, Rajasthan, Tripura and Tamil Nadu. Approximately 88.73 lakh doses of Rotavirus vaccine have been administered to children since its introduction.

Rubella Vaccine as Measles Rubella (MR) Vaccine: MR vaccination campaign targeting children from 9 months up to 15 years of age, was launched in 2017 in five states viz., Karnataka, Tamil Nadu, Goa, Lakshadweep and Puducherry where subsequent to completion of campaign the MR vaccine was introduced in routine immunization replacing measles containing vaccine 1 & 2 at 9-12 months and 16-24 months of age.

Adult JE vaccine: Japanese Encephalitis vaccination in children was introduced in 2006. However, the vaccine was expanded in adult population of districts with high disease burden in 2015. A total of 35 districts have been identified for adult JE vaccination in Assam, Uttar Pradesh and West Bengal.

Pneumococcal Conjugate Vaccine (PCV): This vaccine is provided to reduce child deaths due to pneumonia - which is a major cause of child mortality. It was launched in 2017 in 3 states i.e. in Himachal Pradesh (12 districts), Uttar Pradesh (6 districts) and Bihar (17 districts) in the first phase.

India New Born Action Plan

This was launched in 2014 with the goal of attaining "Single Digit Neonatal Mortality Rate (NMR) by 2030" and "Single Digit Still Birth rate (SBR) by 2030". Under this, 661 special newborn care units (SNCU) at district level, 2321 newborn stabilization units (NBSU) at first referral units (FRU) level and 18,323 newborn care corners (NBCC) at delivery points are operational.

Ayushman Bharat

Ayushman Bharat - National Health Protection Mission (AB-NHPM) a new centrally sponsored scheme was launched in 2018. This comes under Ayushman Bharat Mission anchored in the MoHFW. The Scheme has the benefit cover of ₹ 5 lakh per family per year. The target beneficiaries are to be more than 10 crore families belonging to poor and vulnerable population based on Socio-Economic Caste Census (SECC) database. With this, AB-NHPM will subsume the on-going centrally sponsored schemes–Rashtriya Swasthya BimaYojana (RSBY) and the Senior Citizen Health Insurance Scheme (SCHIS).

Its salient features are numerous and keeping in mind the poor and the destitute. It has a defined benefit cover of ₹ 5 lakh per family per year. This cover will take care of almost all secondary care and most of tertiary care procedures. To ensure that nobody is left out (especially women, children and the elderly) there will be no cap on family size and age. The benefit cover will also include pre and post-hospitalisation expenses. All pre-existing conditions will be covered from day one of the policy. A defined transport allowance per hospitalization will also be paid to the beneficiary; portable benefits including cashless benefits from any public/private empanelled hospitals across the country.

Being an entitlement based scheme the entitlement is to be decided on the basis of deprivation criteria in the SECC database, female headed households with no adult male member between ages 16 to 59, disabled member and no able bodied adult member in the family, SC/ST households;

and landless households deriving major part of their income from manual casual labour will be automatically covered. The payments for treatment will be done on package rate (to be defined by the government in advance) basis. The package rates will include all the costs associated with treatment. For beneficiaries, it will be a cashless, paper less transaction. Keeping in view the state specific requirements, states/ UTs will have the flexibility to modify these rates within a limited bandwidth.

One of the core principles of AB-NHPM is co-operative federalism and flexibility to states. There is provision to partner the states through co-alliance. This will ensure appropriate integration with the existing health insurance / protection schemes of various central ministries / departments and state governments (at their own cost). State governments will be allowed to expand the Scheme both horizontally and vertically. They can implement through insurance company or directly through trust / society or a mixed model. States would need to have State Health Agency (SHA) to implement it.

In order to ensure that the Scheme reaches the intended beneficiaries and other stakeholders, a comprehensive media and outreach strategy will be developed, which will, inter alia, include print media, electronic media, social media platforms, traditional media, IEC materials and outdoor activities. This will lead to increased access to quality health and medication. In addition, the unmet needs of the population which remained hidden due to lack of financial resources will be catered to.

Relevant Website : www.ayushmanbharat.co.in

Mother's Absolute Affection Programme

"MAA-Mother's Absolute Affection" which is an intensified programme was launched in 2016 in an attempt to bring undiluted focus on promotion of breastfeeding. The goal of the MAA programme is to revitalize efforts towards promotion, protection and support of breastfeeding practices through health systems to enhance breastfeeding rates. The key components of the programme are - awareness generation, promotion of breastfeeding and inter personal counseling at community level, skilled support for breastfeeding at delivery points, monitoring and award/recognition.

Intensified Diarrhoea Control Fortnight

It is a programme to combat diarrhoeal mortality in children with the ultimate aim of zero child deaths due to childhood diarrhea. Intensified Diarrhoea Control Fortnight (IDCF) is being implemented as a campaign in the month of July, since 2014, for control of deaths due to diarrhoea across all states and UTs. Under this, more than 14.7 crore under-5 children have been reached since 2014 by ASHA with prophylactic ORS. Main activities include intensification of advocacy activities, awareness generation activities, diarrhoea management service provision, establishing ORS-zinc demonstration sites, ORS distribution by ASHA through home visitation, detection of undernourished children and their treatment, promotion of infant and young child feeding activities by home visits by ASHA and establishing IYCF corners.

National Deworming Day

To combat Soil Transmitted Helminth (STH) infections, the Ministry has adopted a single day strategy called National Deworming Day (NDD) wherein single dose of albendazole is administered to children from 1-19 years of age group schools and anganwadi centres. Till February 2017, 27.8 crore children were administered albendazole.

Rashtriya Bal Swasthya Karyakram

This initiative launched in 2013 entails provision for Child Health Screening and Early Intervention Services through early detection and management of 4 Ds i.e. defects at birth, diseases, deficiencies, development delays including disability and free management of 30 identified health conditions including surgery at tertiary health facilities. Children between 0-18 years of age are covered in a phased manner across the country.

Rashtriya Kishor Swasthya Karyakram

The Rashtriya Kishor Swasthya Karyakram (RKSK) was launched to provide information, commodities and services to meet the diverse needs of adolescents. The intervention under RKSK are: *Weekly Iron Folic Supplementation:* WIFS is evidence based programmatic response to the prevailing anaemia situation amongst adolescent girls and boys through supervised weekly ingestion of IFA supplementation. *Menstrual Hygiene Scheme:* The scheme aims to ensure that adolescent girls have adequate knowledge and information about menstrual hygiene and the use of sanitary napkins and high quality, safe products are made available to them with knowledge of environmentally safe disposal mechanisms; *Peer Educator Programme:* The Programme aims to ensure that adolescents are benefitted from regular and sustained peer education covering nutrition, sexual and reproductive health, and conditions for NCDs, substance misuse, injuries and violence (including GBV) and mental health. To further equip the peer educators, the Ministry launched "Saathiya Resource Kit" in 2017. Understanding the growing number of mobile based app users, Saathiya Salah App has also been made a part of the "Saathiya Resource Kit". The App is linked to another important piece of cost-effective information platform of a toll-free Saathiya Helpline.

Janani Shishu Suraksha Karyakram

Janani Shishu Suraksha Karyakram (JSSK) scheme entitles all pregnant women delivering in public health institutions to absolutely free and no expense delivery including caesarean section.

Janani Suraksha Yojana

Janani Suraksha Yojana (JSY) is a safe motherhood intervention under the National Health Mission. The objective is to reduce maternal and neonatal mortality by promoting institutional delivery among poor pregnant women.

Family Planning

Mission Parivar Vikas was launched for substantially increasing the access to contraceptives and family planning services in 146 high fertility districts of seven high focus states (Uttar Pradesh, Bihar, Rajasthan, Madhya Pradesh, Chhattisgarh, Jharkhand and Assam) with TFR of 3 and above.

Free Drugs

The initiative has been launched with an objective to put in place systems such as facility wise Essential Drug List (EDL), robust procurement system, IT backed logistics and supply chain management, proper warehousing and necessary drug regulatory and quality assurance mechanisms, standard treatment guidelines, prescription audit and grievance redressal systems etc, to ensure provision of quality free essential drugs.

Free Diagnostic Services

The objective behind the NHM free diagnostic services initiative is to reduce the out-of-pocket expenditure on diagnostics as well as to improve the quality of care. Support is provided to states for providing essential diagnostics free of cost in public health facilities. Operational Guidelines on this initiative have been released on 2nd July, 2015. Five states, namely, Andhra Pradesh, Karnataka, Maharashtra, J&K and Tripura, have already adopted the model as per the national guidelines.

National Ambulance Services

One of the achievements of NRHM is the patient transport ambulances operating under Dial 108/102 ambulance service. Dial 108 is emergency response system, primarily designed to attend to patients of critical care, trauma and accident victims etc. Dial 102 services essentially consist of basic patient transport aimed to cater to the needs of pregnant women and children though other categories are also taking benefit and are not excluded.

National Mobile Medical Unit

Objective of MMU is to take health care to the door step of the public in the rural and underserved areas, especially in under-served areas. 1122 MMU are operational in the country across 335 districts. A whole range of health care services are provided ranging from treatment of minor ailments, communicable and non communicable diseases, reproductive and child health, family planning services and in some cases free of cost diagnostics services to the population in the target area.

National Urban Health Mission

National Urban Health Mission is the initiative to strengthen health systems and service delivery in the urban areas. Under this, 1057 cities/ towns are covered and 4544 existing facilities approved for strengthening as U-PHCs.

Pradhan Mantri Surakshit Matritva Abhiyan

The programme aims to provide assured, comprehensive and quality antenatal care, free of cost, universally to all pregnant women on the 9th of every month. PMSMA guarantees a minimum package of antenatal care services to women in their 2nd/3rd trimesters of pregnancy at designated government health facilities. The programme follows a systematic approach for engagement with private sector which includes motivating private practitioners to volunteer for the campaign; developing strategies for generating awareness and appealing to the private sector to participate in the Abhiyan at government health facilities.

Pradhan Mantri National Dialysis Programme

Support is being provided to all states for provision of free dialysis services for poor. Guidelines for dialysis services in district hospitals in PPP mode have been shared with states/UTs and the programme has been implemented with state support in 384 districts. Under this, every facility will have 6 dialysis machines and will be extended up to 10 machines per facility.

Affordable Medicine and Reliable Implants for Treatment

Affordable Medicines and Reliable Implants for Treatment (AMRIT) outlets have been put in place to provide drugs for cancer and cardiovascular diseases along with cardiac implants. These are provided at 60 to 90 per cent discount on prevailaing market rates.

Kayakalp

Kayakalp awards were launched to promote cleanliness, hygiene and infection control practices in public health facilities. Under this initiative awards and commendation certificates are given to public healthcare facilities that show exemplary performance i.e., meeting standards of protocols of cleanliness, hygiene and infection control.

Organ Transplant

National Organ Transplant Programme was launched for carrying out the activities as per Transplantation of Human Organs and Tissues Act, 1994 training of manpower and promotion of organ donation from deceased persons. Under this, an apex level organization, National Organ and Tissue Transplant Organization (NOTTO) was set-up at Safdarjung Hospital, New Delhi including a National Registry (NOTTR) to provide an online system for procurement and distribution of organs and tissues and to promote deceased organ and tissue donation. Further a 24x7 call centre with toll free helpline number (1800114770) has also been established. Further, operational guidelines for National Organ transplant Programme has been released, policy and criteria for organ allocation in case of kidney, liver, heart and lung and cornea have been approved and SoPs for various vital organs has been approved and uploaded on NOTTO website.

Relevant Website : www.notto.gov.in

Swachh Swasth Sarvatra

Swachh Swasth Sarvatra is a joint initiative of the Ministry of Health and Family Welfare and Ministry of Drinking Water and Sanitation launched in 2016.

Mental Health Care

The Mental Health Care Act, 2017 adopts a rights-based statutory framework for mental health and strengthens equality and equity in provision of mental healthcare services in order to protect the rights of people with mental health problem to ensure that they are able to receive optimum care and are able to live a life of dignity and respect. It strengthens the institutional mechanisms for improving access quality and appropriate mental healthcare services. The Act increases accountability of both government and private sectors in delivery of mental healthcare with representation of persons with mental health problem and their care-givers in statutory authorities such as central and state mental health authority.

The most progressive features of the Act are provision of advance directive, nominated representative, special clause for women and children related to admission, treatment, sanitation and personal hygiene; restriction on use of electro-convulsive therapy and psychosurgery. Decriminalization of suicide is another significant facet of the Act, which will ensure proper management of severe stress as a precursor for suicide attempts.

HIV & AIDS

HIV and AIDS (Provention and Control) Act, 2017, aims to end the epidemic by 2030 in accordance with the sustainable development goals set by the United Nations. A person living with AIDS cannot be treated unfairly at employment, educational establishments, renting a property, standing for public or private office or providing healthcare and insurance services The Act also aims to enhance access to healthcare services by ensuring informed consent and confidentiality for HIV-related testing, treatment and clinical research. Every person in the care and custody of the state shall have right to HIV prevention, testing, treatment and counseling services.

Pradhan Mantri Swasthya Suraksha Yojana

The Pradhan Mantri Swasthya Swasthya Suraksha Yojana (PMSSY) envisages creation of tertiary healthcare capacity in medical education, research and clinical care, in the underserved areas of the country. It aims at correcting regional imbalances in the availability of affordable/reliable tertiary healthcare services and also augmenting facilities for quality medical education in the country. PMSSY has two components- setting up of new AIIMS like institutes in underserved regions of the country: and upgradation of existing Govt Medical Colleges (GMCs). Under PMSSY the pace of construction expedited across all PMSSY projects, achieving, on an average more than 42 per cent increase in capital expenditure, year on year (YOY) basis since 2014-15.

Medical Education

The major step was the passage of Indian Medical Council (Amendment) Act, 2016, a uniform entrance examination for admission to Under Graduate and Post Graduate medical courses in the country viz. National Eligibility-cum-Entrance Test (NEET) has been introduced from the Academic Year 2016-17. It would help curb malpractices in medical admissions especially in private medical colleges, will lead to greater transparency and ensure better standards of Medical Education.

Dental Education

Under Dental Council of India (DCI) framework 12 new dental colleges were established during 2014-16. In last three years, 1670 BDS seats and 943 MDS seats have been added.

Centre for Integrative Medicine and Research

The Centre for Integrative Medicine and Research is a pioneering initiative by AIIMS, New Delhi in quest for convergence of contemporary medicine with India's ancient and traditional medical practices and has been envisioned as a "state-of-the-art" research centre. It has been designed as a perfect platform for rigorous research to establish the efficacy of our traditional methods of healing.

Prevention and Control of Cancer, Diabetes, Cardiovascular Disease & Stroke

Prevention and Control of Cancer, Diabetes, Cardiovascular Disease and Stroke to prevent and control common Non-communicable diseases through behaviour and life style changes. The programmes provisions for screening as well as preventive NCD services to the population.

Revised Tuberculosis Control Programme

The goal of Revised National Tuberculosis Control Programme (RNTCP) is to decrease mortality and morbidity due to TB and cut transmission of infection until TB ceases to be a major public health problem in India. Under Revised National Tuberculosis Control Programme (RNTCP), the government provides support to the state /UT governments for human resource, drugs, diagnostics and consumables.

National AIDS Control Programme

National AIDS Control Programme is a 100 per cent central sector scheme. More than 10 lakh people living with HIV are on ART; one lakh additional patients brought under the ambit of Anti Retro Viral (ARV) treatment in line with 'Test and Treat' Policy launched for covering all patients with ART cover irrespective of CD count or clinical stage.

National Tobacco Control Programme

In 2007- 08, the National Tobacco Control programme (NTCP) was launched in 9 states covering 18 districts. Further, in 2008-09, the programme was up-scaled to cover 12 new states covering 24 districts. Currently the programme is under implementation in 29 states covering 53 districts.

National Mental Health Programme

National Mental Health Programme (NMHP) is being implemented to improve coverage and accessibility of mental health care in the country. For improving reach of mental healthcare, district level activities under it are being supported across all 36 states and UTs. Under it there is provision of regular psychiatric OPD and IPD services at district hospital, free supply of psychotropic drugs, ambulatory support for psychiatric patients, awareness generation activities on mental health in community and camps and outreach clinics in taluka hospitals/community health centres.

National Programme for Healthcare of Elderly

The basic aim of the National Programme for Healthcare of Elderly (NPHCE) programme is to provide separate, specialized and comprehensive health care to the elderly people in the country.

National Programme on Prevention and Management of Burn Injuries

The objective of the programme is to reduce incidence, mortality, morbidity and disability due to burn Injuries, to improve awareness among the general masses and vulnerable groups especially the women, children, industrial and hazardous occupational workers and rehabilitation interventions.

National Oral Health Programme

The programme was initiated in 2014-15 with the objective to reduce the morbidity from oral diseases by strengthening the oral health care delivery in the existing public health facilities of the country. Support under the programme is provided to states for contractual appointment of dental surgeons, dental hygienists, dental assistants, procurement of dental equipment, renovation of the space for dental clinic and consumables required for treatment of dental diseases besides activities like awareness creation about oral diseases, capacity building by training the involved health personnel under the programme.

National Leprosy Eradication Programme

Its objective is to reduce leprosy burden in the country by providing quality leprosy services through general health care - to achieve elimination of leprosy as a public health problem in all states and districts i.e., reduce annual new case detection Ratio to < 1 per 100,000 populations at national level. The programme components include case detection and management, disability prevention and medical rehabilitation, IEC including Behaviour Change Communication (BCC) human resource and capacity building and programme management.

Rashtriya Swasthya Bima Yojana

The objectives of (RSBY) was to provide cashless treatment in any public or private empanelled hospitals for most of the diseases that requires hospitalization, and will give improved access to quality health care to the beneficiaries. This Scheme has been subsumed in the Ayushman Bharat Programme.

Integrated Disease Surveillance Programme

Integrated Disease Surveillance Programme (IDSP) is a centrally sponsored scheme under NHM implemented in all states and UTs. The main objectives and strategies include strengthening /maintaining a decentralized laboratory based IT-enabled disease surveillance system for epidemic prone diseases to monitor disease trends and to detect and respond to outbreaks in early rising phase through trained rapid response teams. Presently, more than 90 per cent districts report weekly data through e-mail/portal (wwwidsp.nic.in). The weekly data are analyzed by SSU/DSU for disease trends. Whenever there is rising trend of illnesses, it is investigated by the RRT to diagnose and control the outbreak.

Food Regulation

The number of food testing labs authorised to undertake tests were increased to 125 and those of referral labs to 16. 19 standards/regulations are operationalized including: Food Safety and Standards (Food for Health Supplements, Nutraceuticals, Foods for Special Dietary Uses, Foods for Special Medical purpose, Functional Foods, and Novel Food) Regulations, 2015; revision of standards of silver leaf (Varakh). Allowing use of Ethylene gas for ripening of fruits; harmonization of food additives with codex; standards for raw pulse; microbiological standards for meat and meat products and milk and milk products; standards for proprietary foods; Food Safety and Standards (Fortification of Food) Regulations, 2016; Food Safety and Standards (Import Regulations), 2017; Food Safety and standards (Food Recall Procedure) Regulations, 2017.

Besides these, manual on quick test for detection of food adulterants at households and labs have been developed. National Milk Quality Survey was initiated. Safe water portal was launched where packaged drinking water under FSSAI or BIS licence number can be tested and validated. Capacity building/ programmes were launched for street food vendors in partnership with Skill India.

Drug Regulation

Medical Device Rules 2017 are notified. These provide for risk-based classification, licensing and regulation of medical devices. National Regulatory Authority (NRA) declared functional with the highest maturity level of 4 in respect of 5 functions and 3 in respect of 4 functions. 344 irrational fixed dose combinations (FDCs) are prohibited. New National List of Essential Medicines (NLEM, 2015) finalized. It now includes 376 medicines. Coronary stents added in NLEM, 2015 and their ceiling prices fixed to provide relief to patients.

Rashtriya Arogya Nidhi

Rashtriya Arogya Nidhi (RAN) was set up in 1997 to provide financial assistance to the patients living below poverty line, who are suffering from major life threatening diseases, to receive medical treatment at Government hospitals. The financial assistance to such patients is released in the form of "one time grant" to the Medical Superintendent of the hospital in which the treatment is being received. Under the scheme central government also provides grant-in-aid to states/union territories (with legislature) to set up State Illness Assistance Fund (SIAF) to the extent of 50 per cent of contribution made by state government/union territories.

Health Minister's Cancer Patient Fund

The scheme Health Minister's Cancer Patient Fund (HMCPF) within RAN was also set up in 2009. In order to utilize the HMCPF, the revolving fund as under RAN, has been established in 27 Regional Cancer Centres (RCCs). Such step ensures and speeds up financial assistance to needy cancer patients and help fulfill the objective of HMCPF under RAN.

Health Minister's Discretionary Grant

Under the scheme of Health Minister's Discretionary Grant (HMDG), financial assistance up to ₹ 1,25,000/- is available to the poor and needy patients to defray a part of expenditure on hospitalization for undergoing major surgical intervention and treatment of major diseases. The patients who are not covered under RAN, due to criterion of below poverty line and whose annual income does not exceed ₹ 1,25,000/- can avail the financial assistance under the scheme.

Global Presence

India is a regular participant and leading speaker at global events viz., World Health Assembly 2017, UN Health Assembly, etc. While India hosted the 2017 BRICS event, MoHFW coordinated the health ministers meet to advocate for continued support of member nations on health issues viz. TB, medical devices and AMR etc. India is the founding member of the Partners in Population & Development (PPD) - an Inter-Governmental Organization, formed during the International Conference on Population and Development (ICPD) in 1994 for promoting South-South Cooperation in the field of Reproductive Health, Population and Development. MoHFW held and inaugurated the Seventh Session of the Conference of the Parties to the WHO Framework Convention on Tobacco Control (FCTC).

Health Research

Indian Council of Medical Research

As one of the oldest medical research bodies in the world, the Indian Council of Medical Research (ICMR) was established in 1911 as the Indian Research Fund Association (IRFA). For over a century, ICMR has spearheaded planning, formulation, coordination, implementation, and promotion of biomedical research both in India and internationally. It has remained the apex and premier medical research organization in the country through its commitments to research, professional development, collaboration, and knowledge dissemination. Across its 32 research institutes as well as through extramural funding of research institutes, medical colleges, and non-governmental organizations, ICMR has made significant scientific contributions to understanding various diseases of national importance such as malaria, Japanese encephalitis, tuberculosis, AIDS, Kala-azar, Filariasis, Leprosy and Poliomyelitis. ICMR has also demonstrated its commitment to current public health concerns including nutrition, reproduction and maternal and child health, occupational and environmental health and health systems research. Its research output and impact has demonstrated considerable and constant growth.

ICMR has also demonstrated its commitment to the future of medical research through its professional development training and capacity building. This includes training programmes, workshops, and short-term research studentships for those preparing for a career in medicine and medical research. It also includes research fellowships and short-term visiting fellowships for upcoming researchers to expand their skills and knowledge early in their career. ICMR also offers Emeritus Scientist positions to enable retired medical scientists and teachers to continue to carry out research on specific topics.

The impact of ICMR spans across the globe with research collaborations spanning every continent. This includes the review and approval of 553 international projects, including 68 funded by ICMR, in the last few years alone. Also, through ICMR's Memoranda of Understandings (MoUs), it has partnered with leading universities from around the world to concentrate efforts on leading health issues such as cancer, diabetes, infectious diseases, and vaccine development. These collaborations facilitate the exchange of scientific information, training, joint projects, and co-authorship of meetings, workshops, seminars, and symposia presentations.

Flagship Programmes

The India TB Research Consortium: ICMR took a lead and initiated a new flagship programme to establish India TB research and development consortium that aims to bring together all major national players (with international collaborators) to address overarching scientific questions to tackle TB in a mission mode.

TB Diagnostic Initiative: Truenat Rif, an indigenous, cost effective, rapid molecular diagnostic kit for TB/MDR-TB has been developed in collaboration with ICMR, DBT and the industry. Feasibility study is currently underway across 100 districts. Active case finding pilot project initiated in five states for bridging gap in last mile delivery of services amongst tribal populations.

e-Health/M-Health and use of Space Technology Tools

With the changing time, ICMR is focusing its efforts on using e-Health/M-Health and promote the use of space technology tools. ICMR has developed-a mobile based disease surveillance system for malaria (MosQuit) using mobile platform. This technology has been developed by RMRC, Dibrugarh in collaboration with CDAC, Pune, which has been deployed in Tengaghat PHC of Assam. ICMR has also developed various e-learning programmes in Health Research as well as prepared databases like TB-Drugs, DDRTB, Food and Nutrition Database, etc. To address the impact of climate change on human health and promote use of space technology tools ICMR has developed an early warning system of JE for Upper Assam, initiated studies on mapping of malaria and mosquito-genic conditions, developed models for predicting filariasis. These efforts will be up-scaled for larger use in the coming year.

Disease Burden Estimation

State-level disease burden estimation launched at the Univ of Washington, USA in collaboration with the Ministry of Health and Family Welfare, to generate state-level disease burden and risk factors estimates to improve health programmes and planning in India.

Preparedness to handle Zika virus outbreak: ICMR-NIV established surveillance at 25 sites in the country for Zika testing. Repeated training and capacity building done for 25 labs + 11 IDSP labs. Four cases of Zika virus were detected through ICMR's surveillance network (3 in Gujarat and 1 in Tamil Nadu). Entomological surveillance for ZV also established.

National Rotavirus surveillance network (NRSN) (2012-2016): The study carried out at 4 Major referral labs, 7 ICMR's Regional labs and 23 hospital sites to see the trend in burden of rotavirus diarrhoea as well as impact of rotavirus vaccine under Universal Immunization Programme.

Relevant Website : www.icmr.nic.in

Ayush

The Ministry of AYUSH was formed in 2014 to ensure the optimal development and propagation of AYUSH systems of health care. Earlier it was known as Department of Indian System of Medicine and Homoeopathy (ISM&H) which was created in 1995 and renamed as Department of Ayurveda, Yoga and Naturopathy, Unani, Siddha and Homoeopathy(AYUSH) in 2003, with focused attention for development of education and research in ayurveda, yoga and naturopathy, unani, siddha and homoeopathy. The latest addition to the AYUSH group of health care systems is sowa-rigpa, the Tibetian health tradition.

Relevant Website : www.ayush.gov.in

Ayush Systems of Healthcare

Ayurveda

'Ayurveda' literally means "Science of Life". Ayurveda is evolved from the various Vedic hymns rooted in the fundamental philosophies about life, disease and health. The Charak Samhita and Sushruta Samhita developed around 2500 BC are the main treaties of Ayurveda fully available today. According to Ayurveda, health is considered as a pre-requisite for achieving the goals of life i.e., Dharma, Artha, Kama and Moksha. Ayurveda takes an integrated view of the physical, mental, spiritual and social aspects of human beings and about the interrelationships between these aspects.

Yoga

Yoga is essentially spiritual and it is an art and science of healthy living which focuses on bringing harmony between body and mind. The word 'Yoga' has two meanings; the first comes from the root 'Yujir' or 'Union', the second is derived from a different root 'yuja' which means 'Samadhi' - the highest state of mind and the absolute knowledge. These two are the most important meanings of the word Yoga according to Panini, the most well-known Sanskrit grammarian.

Yoga is being practiced as part of healthy lifestyle and has become part of our spiritual heritage. In the present era, Yoga is popular world-wide because of its spiritual values, therapeutic credentials, its role in the prevention of diseases, promotion of health and management of lifestyle related disorders. Several clinical studies have lucidly demonstrated the therapeutic potentials of Yoga in the treatment of many lifestyle related or psychosomatic disorders. The specialty of this system is that it can get along with any other systems of health care.

Naturopathy

Naturopathy is a science of health and healing and a drug less therapy based on well founded philosophy. It has its own concept of health and disease and principles of treatment. Naturopathy is a system of medicine that advocates harmonious living with constructive principles of nature on physical, mental, moral and spiritual planes. It has great health promotive and restorative, and disease preventive as well as curative potential.

Unani

The Unani system of medicine originated in Greece and passed through many countries before establishing itself in India during the medieval period. It is based on well-established knowledge and practices relating to the promotion of positive health and prevention of disease. The fusion of traditional knowledge of ancient civilizations like Egypt, Arabia, Iran, China, Syria and India. It emphasizes the use of naturally occurring mostly herbal medicines and some medicines of animals, marine and mineral origin. This system of medicine was documented in Al- Qanoon, a medical classics, by Sheikh Bu-Ali Sina (Avicena) (980-1037) AD), in Al-Havi by Razi (850-923 AD) and in many others books written by the Unani physicians.

Siddha

The Siddha System of medicine is one of the ancient systems of medicine in India having its close links with Dravidian culture. The term Siddha means achievements and Siddhars are those who have achieved perfection in medicine. Eighteen Siddhars are said to have contributed towards the systematic development of this system and recorded their experiences in Tamil language.

Homoeopathy

The physicians from the time of Hippocrates (around 400 B.C.) had observed that certain substances could produce symptoms of a disease in healthy people similar to those of people suffering from the disease. Dr. Christian Friedrich Samuel Hahnemann, a German physician scientifically examined this phenomenon and codified the fundamental principles of Homoeopathy. Homoeopathy was brought into India around 1810 A.D. by European missionaries and received official recognition by a Resolution passed by the Constituent Assembly in 1948 and then by the Parliament.

Sowa-Rigpa

Sowa-Rigpa is among the oldest surviving health traditions of the world with a living history of more than 2500 years. It has been in vogue and practised in Himalayan regions throughout particularly in Leh and Laddakh (J&K), Himachal Pradesh, Arunachal Pradesh, Sikkim, Darjeeling, etc. Sowa-Rigpa is effective in managing chronic diseases like asthma, bronchitis, arthritis, etc. The basic theory of Sowa-Rigpa is explained in terms of (i)the body and the mind as the locus of treatment; (ii)antidote, i.e., the treatment;(iii) the method of treatment through antidote;(iv)medicines that cure the disease and lastly (v) pharmacology. Sowa- Rigpa emphasizes the importance of the five cosmological physical elements in the formation of the human body, the nature of disorders and the remedial measures.

Ayush Healthcare Infrastructure

National AYUSH Mission (NAM) was notified in 2014 which envisages better access to AYUSH services including co-location of AYUSH facilities at Primary Health Centres (PHCs), Community Health Centres (CHCs) and District Hospitals(DHs), upgradation of existing Government AYUSH Hospitals, upgradation of existing government/ panchayat/ government aided AYUSH dispensaries and setting up of upto 50 bedded integrated AYUSH hospitals. It also envisages strengthening of AYUSH educational institutions, facilitate the enforcement of quality control of Ayurveda, Siddha, Unani and Homoeopathy (ASU &H) drugs and sustainable availability of ASU & H raw-materials in the States/UTs during 12th Plan.

Ayush Drug Quality Control

Ministry of AYUSH has a Drug Control Cell to look after and co-ordinate in matters related to Ayurvedic, Siddha , Unani and homoeopathy (ASU&H)

drugs. In addition, the Ministry has taken up amendment of the Drugs and Cosmetics Rules, 1945 for promoting scientific data based shelf life studies and prohibition of the use of prefix and suffix with the names of classical formulations. Under the centrally sponsored initiative of the National AYUSH Mission, grant-in-aid is provided to the states for strengthening of infrastructural, functional and regulatory capacity for manufacturing and testing of drugs and enforcement of the regulatory provisions. Capacity building programmes for the regulatory and scientific staff of the states are regularly organized at the Pharmacopoeial Laboratory of Indian Medicine (PLIM) and the Homoeopathy Pharmacopoeial Laboratory (HPL).

Medical Education in Ayush

The Central Council of Indian Medicine (CCIM) is the statutory body constituted under the Indian Medicine Central Council Act, 1970 which lays down the standards of medical education in Ayurved, Siddha and Unani through its various regulations. Similarly, homoeopathy medical education is being regulated by Central Council of Homoeopathy (CCH) through its various regulations under the Homoeopathy Central Council Act, 1973. For medical education in Yoga and Naturopathy no such governing body exists. Following courses are being offered by the Ayurveda, Siddha, Unani and homoeopathy (ASU&H) colleges. (i) Bachelor of Ayurvedic Medicine and Surgery (B.A.M.S.); (ii) Bachelor of Unani Medicine and Surgery (B.U.M.S.); (iii) Bachelor of Siddha Medicine and Surgery (B.S.M.S.); (iv) Bachelor of Homoeopathy Medicine and Surgery (B.H.M.S.); (v) Post-graduate Ayurveda degree in different specialities (M.D./M.S.-Ayurveda); (vi) Post-graduate Unani degree in different specialities (M.D./M.S.-Unani); (vii) Post-graduate Siddha degree in different specialities (M.D./M.S.-Siddha); (viii) Post-graduate Homoeopathy degree in different specialities (M.D.-Homoeopathy)

Under Graduate Education

There are in all 549 ASU&H (297 Ayurveda, 09 Siddha, 46 Unani and 197 homoeopathy) colleges imparting ASU&H education in the country, out of which 543 ASU&H (295 Ayurveda, 08 Siddha, 45 Unani and 195 Homoeopathy) colleges imparting undergraduate ASU&H education with an admission capacity of 33611 students in India as on 01.01.2016. Out of 543 colleges, 102 ASU&H (57 Ayurveda, 03 Siddha, 10 Unani and 32 Homoeopathy) colleges with 5236 intake capacity (2967 Ayurveda, 160 Siddha, 431 Unani and 1678 Homoeopathy) belong to government sector.

Post Graduate Courses

Out of all medical colleges imparting post graduate ASU&H education, six colleges (02 Ayurveda, 02 homoeopathy, 01 Unani and 01 Siddha) with admission capacity of 225 students (60 Ayurveda, 72 Homoeopathy, 47 Unani and 46 Siddha) were exclusively post graduate institutions.

Autonomous Institutes imparting ASU&H education

(i) *National Institute of Ayurveda, Jaipur:* It offers under-graduate, post-graduate and fellowship programmes in Ayurveda with intake capacity of 92 students in Under-graduate and 104 students in 14 post-graduate courses. It also conducts a Diploma course in Ayurveda Nursing and Pharmacy. The Institute has two hospitals with a bed strength of 300. For the benefits of population belongings to SC and ST, the Institute also organizes regular medical camps in SC and ST inhabited districts of Rajasthan through its mobile clinical unit to provide free medical facility.

(ii) *Institute of Post Graduate Teaching and Research in Ayurveda, Jamnagar:* The Institute offers 10 Post-graduate courses with intake capacity of 50 students and Ph.D. courses. Funded by Government of India it is governed by the Acts & Statute of Gujarat Ayurveda University. The Institute organized various outreach activities in Ayurveda for national programmes and conducted medical camps in rural areas of Gujarat. It has a well-managed hospital with OPD and IPD facilities.

(iii) *National Institute of Homoeopathy, Kolkata:* It offers under-graduate, post-graduate courses in homoeopathy with intake capacity of 93 students in under-graduate and 36 students in 06 post-graduate courses. It has a 100 - bedded hospital attached to it which is being upgraded to a 250 bed hospital. A new hospital building has been constructed by CPWD with additional diagnostic facilities. The academic block has also been augmented from three storey structure to seven.

(iv) *National Institute of Unani Medicine, Bengaluru:* It offers 8 post-graduate level course in Unani with intake capacity of 47 students and has a 180 bedded hospital. The institute regularly organizes academic activities like CME programmes, workshops, seminars and guest lectures. The hospital of the institute provides clinical services to the patients from general and specialty OPDs for skin diseases, GIT and hepato-billiary disorders, neurological disorders, psychiatric and geriatric care.

(v) *National Institute of Siddha, Chennai:* It offers 06 post-graduate courses in Siddha with intake capacity of 46 students, provides medical care and undertakes research to promote and propagate the Siddha system of medicine. A 160 bedded In-patient facility provide medical care in accordance with respective PG Departments. The institute organises two medical camps on every Saturday, one in rural area and the other in semi-urban area to provide free medical facilities to promote the Siddha Medicine as well as community oriented approach to students.

New Autonomous Institutes

(i) *All India Institute of Ayurveda, New Delhi:* It is conceived as an apex institute for Ayurveda with 200 bed referral hospital. The Institute offers post-graduate and Ph.D. courses in Ayurveda with intake capacity of 84 students in 18 post-graduate courses. OPD is already operational in the Institute.

(ii) *North Eastern Institute of Ayurveda & Homeopathy, Shillong:* The project consists of Ayurveda and homoeopathy colleges along with attached hospitals of Ayurveda and Homoeopathy with a capacity of 100 and 50 beds respectively.

Research in AYUSH

The government has set-up five autonomous research councils, namely, Central Council for Research in Ayurvedic Sciences (CCRAS), Central Council for Research in Yoga & Naturopathy (CCRYN), Central Council for Research in Unani Medicines (CCRUM), Central Council for Research in Siddha (CCRS) and Central Council for Research in Homoeopathy (CCRH) with the mandate to under-take research in their respective system.Recently, for the management of diabetes mellitus, the Central Council for Research in Ayurvedic Sciences(CCRAS) has developed a formulation namely, AYUSH-82 from 05 Ayurvedic medicinal plants. The trials of the drug has shown significant reduction in blood sugar level along with clinical improvement. No toxic effects were noted during the trial. CCRAS has initiated action to commercialize AYUSH-82.

In addition to its research work, the 81 institutes under the Council also provide healthcare facilities. The CCRH through its programme namely, Homoeopathy for Healthy Child enrolled 40,000 children with an aim to help them during dentition period and treatment of disease.

National Medicinal Plants Board

National Medicinal Plants Board (NMPB) is an apex national body which co-ordinates all matters relating to medicinal plants sector in the country. The Board was established in 2000 and acts as advisory body to the concerned ministries, departments and Agencies in strategic planning of medicinal plants related initiatives and to plan and provide financial support to programmes relating to conservation, cultivation and also all round development of medicinal plants sector.

AYUSH Services

The National AYUSH Mission (NAM) is a turning point as it inter-alia envisages better access to AYUSH services through increase in number of AYUSH hospitals and dispensaries, ensure availability of AYUSH drugs and trained manpower. It also aims at Improvement in quality of AYUSH Education through enhancement in the number of upgraded educational Institutions, sustained availability of quality raw materials and improved availability of quality Ayurveda, Siddha, Unani and Homoeopathy (ASU &H) drugs through increase in number of pharmacies, setting up of drug laboratories in the states which are responsible for enforcement mechanism of ASU &H drugs.

AYUSH Pharmacopoeial Laboratories

(i) Pharmacopoeial Laboratory for Indian Medicine (PLIM)

Pharmacopoeial Laboratory for Indian Medicine (PLIM) is a subordinate office of Ministry of AYUSH located at Ghaziabad. The laboratory was established in 1970 as a Pharmacopoeial Standards Setting - cum Drugs testing laboratory at national level for Ayurvedic, Siddha and Unani (ASU) Medicine. It acts as an appellate laboratory for testing of Ayurvedic, Siddha and Unani (ASU) drugs under Drugs & Cosmetic Act, 1940. The Pharmacopoeial Laboratory for Indian Medicine was established with the objective to develop and validate Pharmacopoeial standardization of single drug and compound formulations for incorporation in Ayurvedic, Siddha and Unani Pharmacopoeias and analysis of legal drugs samples received from Drugs Control Authorities and Courts.

(ii) Homoeopathic Pharmacopoeial Laboratory (HPL)

Homoeopathic Pharmacopoeia Laboratory, Ghaziabad was set up as a national laboratory for the purpose of laying down standards and testing for identity, purity and quality of homoeopathic medicines. The laboratory also functions as central drug laboratory for the testing of homoeopathic medicines. Standards worked out by the laboratory are published in the Homoeopathic Pharmacopoeia of India (HPI). The Department of Science and Technology has recognized HPL as Science and Technology Institution.

(iii) Pharmacopoeia Commission for Indian Medicines & Homeopathy (PCIM & H)

Development of quality standards on Ayurvedic, Siddha, Unani and Homoeopathic Medicine and their periodic update to the needs of the consumers is the priority of the Ministry of AYUSH. The popularity and demand of ASU&H medicines is increasing rapidly. The Pharmacopoeia Commission for Indian Medicines & Homeopathy (PCIM&H) is an autonomous organization registered under Societies Registration Act, 1860. The main mandate of the commission is publication and revision of the Ayurvedic, Siddha, Unani and Homoeopathy Pharmacopoeia of India at suitable intervals; Publication and revision of the Ayurveda, Siddha and Unani Formularies as well as Homoeopathic Pharmaceutical Codex; nurture and promote awareness of quality in ASU&H drugs/ formulations and drug research on ASU&H products; exchange information and interact with expert committees of the World Health Organization and other international bodies with a view to harmonize and develop the ASU&H Pharmacopoeial standards to make those internationally acceptable; maintain National repository of authentic reference raw materials used in the manufacture of Ayurveda, Siddha, Unani and Homeopathy medicine for the purpose of reference and supply of reference standards to the stake holders at a price; generate and maintain repository of chemical reference marker compounds of the plants or other ingredients used in standardizing Ayurveda, Siddha, Unani and Homeopathy medicine and supply them as reference standards to the stake holders on price, etc.

17 Housing and Urban Affairs

THE Ministry of Housing and Urban Affairs (MoHUA) is entrusted with the responsibility of broad policy formulation and monitoring of programmes regarding urban housing and urban development. It is the nodal Ministry for planning and coordination of urban transport matters at the central level. Urban development is a state subject and the Constitution (Seventy-Fourth) Amendment Act, 1992 enjoins upon the state governments to delegate many functions to urban local bodies. Government of India, however, plays a coordinating and monitoring role and also supports various urban housing programmes, urban livelihood mission and overall urban development through Central and Centrally Sponsored Schemes. The Ministry addresses various issues relevant to urban sector through appropriate policy guidelines, subordinate legislation and sectoral programmes.

Relevant Website : wwwmohua.gov.in

Urbanization in India has become an important and irreversible process, and it is an important determinant of national economic growth and poverty reduction. The process of urbanization has been characterized by a dramatic increase in the number of large cities, although India may be said to be in the midst of transition from a predominantly rural to a quasi-urban society. The 2030 development agenda of the United Nations has emphasized the role of sustainable cities by incorporating Sustainable Development Goal (SDG), i.e., Sustainable Cities and Communities for making cities and human settlements inclusive, safe, resilient and sustainable.As per the Census of India 2011, the population of India is 1,210.50 million, of which 377.10 million (31.2 per cent) is urban and 833.40 million (68.8 per cent) is rural. The urban population is located in 7,933 towns, comprising 4,041 statutory towns and 3,892 census towns. During 2001-2011, in absolute terms, the decadal increase in urban population was 90.99 million vis-à-vis 90.97 million in rural population.At current rate of growth, urban population estimated to reach a staggering 575 million by 2030 and 875 million by 2050.

Pradhan Mantri Awas Yojana- Housing for All (Urban)

Mission Pradhan Mantri Awas Yojana (Urban) for ensuring housing for all in urban areas was launched in 2015 which is to be implemented during 2015-2022. The Mission provides central assistance to all eligible families/ beneficiaries across all statutory towns for houses included under the mission. States/UTs will have the flexibility to include the Planning Areas (to the exclusion of rural areas) as notified with respect to Statutory Towns and such Planning Areas (to the exclusion of rural areas) as notified by development authorities. To address Housing for All in urban area, the Mission has four verticals: (a) *In-situ* Slum Redevelopment (ISSR) with participation of private developers using land as resource for providing housing to eligible slum dwellers; (b) affordable housing through credit-linked subsidy scheme (CLSS now renamed as CLSS for EWS/LIG); (c) affordable Housing in Partnership (AHP) with public and private sectors; (d) subsidy for beneficiary-led individual house construction/ enhancements; size of house for Economically Weaker Section (EWS) is 30 sq. mt., in carpet area but states have flexibility to enhance the size of houses in consultation with the Ministry. EWS family has been defined as family with annual income upto ₹ 3 lakh and LIG with annual income between ₹ 3-6 Lakh.

Progress of the Scheme

35 Memorandum of Agreement (MoA) have been signed with 29 states and 6 UTs; 4,302 cities have been selected in 35 states/UTs for inclusion under the Mission. 7,474 projects for construction of 37,43,631 houses under the mission in 3,361 cities of 35 states/UTs involving Central assistance of ₹ 57,652 crore have been accepted by Government under the Mission.

Smart Cities Mission

The Smart Cities Mission was launched in 2015. The objective of the Mission is to promote cities that provide core infrastructure and give a decent quality of life to its citizens, a clean and sustainable environment and application of 'Smart' solutions. Some of the core infrastructure elements in a Smart City would include adequate water supply, assured electricity supply, sanitation, including solid waste management, efficient urban mobility and public transport, affordable housing, especially for the poor, robust IT connectivity and digitalization, good governance, especially e-Governance and citizen participation, sustainable environment, safety and security of citizens, particularly women, children and the elderly and health and education.

Strategy

The strategic components of the Smart Cities Mission are city improvement (retrofitting), city renewal (redevelopment) and city extension (greenfield development) plus a pan-city initiative in which Smart Solutions are applied covering larger parts of the city. Area-based development would transform existing areas (retrofit and redevelop), including slums, into better planned human settlements, thereby, improving livability of the whole cities. Development of well-planned and fully serviced new areas (greenfield) is to be encouraged around cities in order to accommodate the rapidly expanding population in urban areas.

The Mission will cover 100 cities and its duration will be five years (2015-16 to 2019- 20). The Mission may be continued thereafter in the light of an evaluation to be done by this Ministry and incorporating the learnings into the Mission.

Finances

The Mission will be operated as a Centrally Sponsored Scheme and the Central Government proposes to give financial support to the Mission to the extent of ₹ 48,000 crore over five years i.e., on an average ₹ 100 crore per city per year. An equal amount, on a matching basis, will have to be contributed by the state/ULB; therefore, nearly ₹ 1,00,000 crore of government/ULB funds will be available for Smart Cities development. It is anticipated that substantial funds will be required to implement the Smart City proposal.

Atal Mission for Rejuvenation and Urban Transformation

The Atal Mission for Rejuvenation and Urban Transformation (AMRUT) was launched in 2015. In all, 500 cities have been included in the Mission. All Urban Local Bodies (ULBs) with a population of one lakh or more, all other capital cities of states/ UTs, all Heritage Development and Augmentation Yojana (HRIDAY) cities, identified cities on the stem of the main rivers, from hill states, islands and tourist destinations. Approximately 60 per cent of urban population in the country is covered under AMRUT. It is a centrally sponsored scheme with a total outlay of rupees one lakh crore including a Central Assistance of ₹ 50,000 crore spread over 5 years i.e., from 2015-2016 to 2019-2020. The balance share of ₹ 50,000 crore has to come from states and ULBs.

The thrust areas of the Mission are water supply, sewerage and septage management, storm water drainage, green spaces and park, non-motorized urban transport and capacity building. The Mission focuses on development of basic urban infrastructure in the specified cities with the following expected outcomes: (i) universal coverage for access to potable water for every household; (ii) substantial improvement in coverage and treatment capacities of sewerage; (iii) developing city parks; (iv) reform implementation and capacity building. To mitigate the problem in drinking water sector, the water supply component inter-alia, provides for rehabilitation of old water supply systems including treatment plants and rejuvenation of water bodies, specifically for drinking water supply and recharging of ground water. Recycling/ reuse of waste water, reduction of non-revenue water and exploring possibilities for septage management, are some of the important features.

Heritage City Development

The National Heritage City Development and Augmentation Yojana (HRIDAY), a central sector scheme of the Government of India was launched in 2015 with the aim of bringing together urban planning, economic growth and heritage conservation in an inclusive manner with the objective of preserving the heritage character of each Heritage City. By November 2018 and after a total outlay of ₹ 500 crore, the scheme is being implemented in 12 identified cities namely, Ajmer, Amaravati, Amritsar, Badami, Dwarka, Gaya, Kanchipuram, Mathura, Puri, Varanasi, Velankanni and Warangal.

Urban Transport

A city can be productive if it has a very sound infrastructure and good services. Urban transport is a crucial component of urban infrastructure. It provides access to opportunities, supports urban economic activities, and facilitates social interactions. A good network of roads and an efficient Mass Urban Transport System make significant contributions to improve the working efficiency of a city and its environs. The extent to which the Indian cities can maximize economic performance and reduce poverty will be closely linked to how efficiently their transport system moves people and goods upon which their socio-economic activities depend. The rapidly growing urban population exerts an increasing pressure on the urban transport system resulting in deterioration of the system thus lowering economic productivity. Hence, development of cities through prioritizing urban transport is a step forward in this direction. Global experience has also shown that an efficient shift to public transport can occur only if urban transport is assimilated at the conception stage of land-use and urban planning. This Ministry is the nodal Ministry for planning and coordination of urban transport matters at the central level.However, technical planning of rail transport continues to be with Ministry of Railways. Similarly, road transport is the responsibility of the Ministry of Road Transport and Highways. However, the major responsibility for urban transport infrastructure and service delivery rests with state governments and local bodies.

Deendayal Antyodaya Yojana

Ministry of Housing and Urban Affairs has been implementing a centrally sponsored scheme Deendayal Antyodaya Yojana-National Urban Livelihoods Mission (DAY-NULM) since 2013 for reducing the poverty and vulnerability of urban poor households. The Mission covers all the statutory towns in the country, to be decided by the state as per local need and capability.

Its major components include: (a) social Mobilization and Institutional Development (SM&ID), which envisages mobilisation of urban poor women, differently-abled men and men in vulnerable occupations into thrift and credit-based Self-Help Groups (SHGs) and their federations/ collectives; (b) employment through Skill Training and Placement (EST&P) for skill development of urban poor in market-oriented courses to enable them to earn sustainable livelihoods; (c) self-employment Programme (SEP) provides interest subvention on loans to individuals/groups of urban poor for setting up self-employment ventures/ micro-enterprises; (d) support to urban street vendors to support pro-vendor planning, development of vendors' market, credit enablement, socio-economic survey of street vendors, skill development and micro-enterprises development and convergence with social assistance under various schemes of the Government; (e) innovative and Special Projects (I&SP) to promote pioneering efforts, aimed at catalysing sustainable approaches to urban livelihoods through Public, Private and Community Partnership (PPCP).

Welfare of Street Vendors

The objective of the Street Vendors (Protection of Livelihood and Regulation of Street Vending) Act, 2014 is to protect the rights of urban street vendors and to regulate street vending activities. States/UTs (with legislature) are the appropriate government for framing of rules and schemes under Street Vendors' Act for their respective states/UTs. Ministry being the appropriate Government for UTs (without legislature) has framed rules and schemes under the said Act. So far 28 states/UTs viz., Andhra Pradesh, Assam, Andaman and Nicobar

Islands, Bihar, Chandigarh, Chhattisgarh, Dadra and Nagar Haveli, Diu and Daman, Delhi, Gujarat, Goa, Haryana, Himachal Pradesh, Jharkhand, Karnataka, Lakshadweep, Madhya Pradesh, Odisha, Punjab, Rajasthan, Sikkim, Tamil Nadu, Tripura, Maharashtra, Manipur, Puducherry, Uttarakhand and Uttar Pradesh have notified Rules and 19 states/UTs viz., Andhra Pradesh, Delhi, Jharkhand, Bihar, Madhya Pradesh, Odisha, Rajasthan, Himachal Pradesh, Punjab, Tamil Nadu, Tripura, Chhattisgarh, Maharashtra, Uttar Pradesh, Telangana, Chandigarh, Dadra and Nagar Haveli, Diu and Daman and Andaman Nicobar and Islands have notified the scheme.

Real Estate Act

The Union Cabinet approved the Real Estate (Regulation and Development) Bill in 2015. It became an Act in 2016. It is aimed at establishing the Real Estate Regulatory Authority for regulations and promotion of the real estate and protecting the interest of the consumers. The Act is applicable to 35 states/UTs, except J&K. Out of these, 6 north eastern states have some constitutional issues relating to land belonging to community and autonomous councils and these are under examination. Out of the remaining 29 states/UTs, 26 states/UTs have notified the Real Estate Rules under the Act. 24 states/UTs have notified Real Estate Agreement of Sale Rules along with General Rules and other forms required as per the Act. Other 3 states have drafted the rules but have not yet notified. 8 states/UTs have established permanent Real Estate Regulatory Authority. 21 states/UTs have established interim Real Estate Regulatory Authority. In Gujarat, Tamil Nadu and Andaman and Nicobar Islands, Appellate Tribunal has been set up. 11 states/UTs have appointed interim Appellate Tribunal under the Real Estate Act. 14 states/UTs have made a fully operationalized web portal for enabling online registration of real estate projects and agents.

18 India and the World

THE primary objective of India's engagement with the world is to ensure a peaceful, stable global environment and create the most propitious climate for India's economic growth and development. The rising profile of the country in global affairs and its emergence as a fast growing economy in an otherwise difficult global environment presents a moment of opportunity that can be utilised to diversify India's strategic and economic options. In this context, India's external engagements have sought to simultaneously advance and deepen relations with each bilateral or multilateral partner, in the specific areas where such engagement brings maximum benefit to Indian interests. The common threads that run through the entire gamut of India's international outreach over this period have been put together here.

The Ministry of External Affairs (MEA) also known as the Foreign Ministry, is the government agency responsible for the conduct of foreign relations of the country.

Relevant Website : www.mea.gov.in

Like the previous years 2017-18 saw the continuation of a pragmatic and outcome-oriented foreign policy, aimed at achieving the key goals of ensuring national security and upholding territorial integrity, attaining national economic transformation, and addressing regional and global issues. This approach was reflected in the revitalisation of our traditional ties, in our re-energised strategic and commercial relations, and the continued engagement of our diaspora.

The year witnessed intensive diplomatic engagements. India participated in regional and global discourses, with a constructive approach to all issues. During the year, India became a member of the Wassenaar Arrangement, the Shanghai Cooperation Organisation (SCO) and the Australia Group. The coming into force of the International Solar Alliance, a treaty-based international organisation, marks India's role in addressing the vital issue of climate change. India also participated in various global conferences such as the SCO Summit, the G-20 Summit, the BRICS Summit, the East Asia Summit, and the World Economic Forum at Davos. We hosted the Global Conference on Cyberspace and the Global Entrepreneurship Summit in November 2017, the 3rd edition of the Raisina Dialogue and the ASEAN-India Commemorative Summit in January 2018.

India's immediate neighbourhood continued to receive the highest priority in accordance with the government's "Neighbourhood First" policy. Outgoing visits by Prime Minister to Sri Lanka and Myanmar and by External Affairs Minister (EAM) to Nepal and Bangladesh; incoming visits by Prime Ministers of Sri Lanka, Nepal, Bhutan and Bangladesh; and, Chief Executive of

Afghanistan continued the momentum in our high-level engagement with the neighbourhood. With Afghanistan, the inauguration of a dedicated Air Cargo Corridor in June 2017 between Kabul-Delhi and Kandahar-Delhi provided a fresh impetus to bilateral trade by overcoming regional connectivity constraints. Over 1000 tonnes of cargo has already been transported through the Air Corridor.

Relations with Bangladesh were marked by progress in the areas of civil nuclear energy, space and defence cooperation. A third Line of Credit worth US$ 4.5 billion was announced, that will cover next-generation projects in port construction, railways, power and energy, telecommunications and shipping. Intensive high-level exchanges with Sri Lanka provided a further push towards development projects and greater synergy on issues related to peace and security in the Indian Ocean. India stood by Sri Lanka with prompt assistance during the May 2017 floods. Prime Minister's first bilateral visit to Myanmar gave much needed impetus to the relations and deepened bilateral cooperation. The Line of Credit Agreement for post-2016 earthquake reconstruction projects in Nepal worth US$ 750 million was operationalised. Continued high-level exchanges, including the visit of His Majesty the King of Bhutan in November 2017, have imparted fresh momentum to the multi-faceted bilateral relationship with Bhutan. There has been steady progress in our hydropower cooperation, and the India-Bhutan Trade and Transit Agreement, renewed in November 2016, entered into force in July 2017. These additional trade facilitation measures led to a further enhancement in bilateral trade and investment. The long-standing relationship with Maldives was strengthened through cooperation in the areas of defence and security, institution and capacity building, and assistance in health and education sectors.

Cultural, digital and physical connectivity have emerged as significant themes in Indian diplomacy. With the historic launch of the South Asia Satellite, India demonstrated its commitment to sharing the benefits of our technological capabilities with our regional partners. Lack of connectivity, both within India and in the larger South Asian neighbourhood and beyond, is a constraint on both our capabilities and our competitiveness. Steady progress is being made in our efforts to develop multimodal linkages with Myanmar and Bangladesh. The operationlisation of the Chabahar Port in Iran is expected to deepen connectivity linkages with our partners in Central Asia and on the International North South Transport Corridor. Initiatives to develop connectivity were also taken through groupings such as BIMSTEC and BBIN, aimed at enhancing logistics efficiencies in South Asia and Southeast Asia and to boost economic development. India also ratified the United Nations TIR (Transports Internationaux Routiers) Convention in June 2017.

The Government continued to focus on engagement and deepening of India's ties with all major powers of the world, creating new pathways and mutually beneficial opportunities. In our bilateral engagements with countries such as the USA, Russia, Germany, Japan, Australia and France, the Government focused on the areas of greatest potential in each relationship. India has leveraged the convergence of interests in these partnerships to increase the flow of trade, investment and technologies into the Indian economy. Engagements with global leaders were also held on the sidelines of multilateral engagements such as the UNGA, the G-20 Summit, BRICS Summit, East Asia Summit and the SCO meeting.

India's diplomatic approach and engagement with the wider world is reflective of its confidence as a rising power capable of shaping the global discourse in the emerging multipolar world. The emergence and shared understanding of the significance of Indo-Pacific and reaffirmation of the importance of freedom of navigation, overflight and commerce throughout the region, were some of the highlights of the Prime Minister's highly successful visit to the USA in June 2017. The interaction with the new leadership also reiterated bipartisan support for further strengthening of India-USA relations and a commitment to cooperate in the fight against the global scourge of international terrorism. Celebrating the 70th anniversary of establishment of diplomatic relations, the Prime Minister visited Russia in June 2017 and further strengthened the decades old relationship by signing an agreement for Units V & VI of the Kudankulam Nuclear Power Plant. The annual summit also identified new areas of cooperation between the two countries such as deep sea exploration to building knowledge based economies based on science and technology, innovation, robotics and artificial intelligence, focussing on infrastructure, skill development, agriculture, shipbuilding, railways, aviation and greater connectivity. The 12th India-Japan annual summit in September 2017 witnessed the laying of foundation stone for India's first high-speed rail project in Ahmedabad, Gujarat. It also restated the commitment of both countries towards achieving a "free, open and prosperous Indo-Pacific region where sovereignty and international law are respected." Similarly, India and the EU are also celebrating 55 years of establishing diplomatic relations and witnessed participation of the President of the European Council and the European Commission for the 14th India-EU summit in October 2017. The summit reflected growing convergence between the two on regional and international issues and focused, inter alia, on closer cooperation on counter-terrorism actions and adopted a Joint Statement on Cooperation in Combating Terrorism.

India's diplomatic outreach was also marked by simultaneous engagement with countries to the regions—East, West and South. In pursuance of our "Act East" policy, the Prime Minister attended the 15th ASEAN-India Summit and 12th East Asia Summit (EAS) in Manila in November 2017. There is a strong emphasis on connectivity and stronger integration, and building partnerships to address traditional and non-traditional security threats in the region. Year-long celebrations marked the 25th anniversary of ASEAN-India dialogue partnership. The Government also hosted the landmark ASEAN-India Commemorative Summit in January 2018, with all the ten ASEAN Heads of States participating as Guests of Honour at the Republic Day celebrations.

Prime Minister paid the first ever visit to Israel in July 2017, upgrading the relationship to a strategic level. The two countries signed key agreements to step up cooperation in space, agriculture and water conservation. An MoU was also signed for setting up of India-Israel Industrial Research and Development and Technical Innovation Fund worth US$ 40 million.

In West Asia and the Gulf, the past year saw a visit by Crown Prince of Abu Dhabi to India as the Chief Guest for the Republic Day celebrations in 2017. During the visit, the two countries decided to elevate the ties to the level of Comprehensive Strategic Partnership, marking the Gulf's second largest economy as India's pre-eminent partner in both strategic and economic arenas.

The period under review also saw the inauguration of the first phase of the Chabahar port project in Iran. The maiden consignment of 15,000 tonnes of wheat was shipped to Afghanistan through the Chabahar port in November 2017. Along with the establishment of the India-Afghanistan air-freight corridor, innovative initiatives with regional partners in Central Asia on the International North South Transport Corridor (INSTC), will pave the way for operationalisation of the Chabahar port as an alternate, reliable and robust connectivity hub, and promote trade and transit with the countries in the wider region.

India's outreach to Central Asia saw further progress with the Prime Minister visiting Kazakhstan for the 17th SCO Summit in Astana in June 2017, where India was admitted as a full member of the SCO. Counter-terrorism has emerged as a crucial area of cooperation with the countries in the Central Asia region, with joint working groups on counter-terrorism with Kazakhstan and Uzbekistan. Furthermore, strong relations have been established in textiles, metallurgy, hydrocarbons, mineral processing, IT, food processing, etc.

The Indian Ocean region remains a priority and an important cornerstone of India's diplomatic engagernents. The Indian Ocean Rim Association (IORA) held its 1st IORA Summit in Indonesia in March 2017, where three documents were adopted viz. the IORA Concord laying out the vision of IORA, Declaration on Preventing Violent Extremism and Countering Terrorism, and the Action Plan of IORA for the next 5 years.

India established itself as the first responder in rendering humanitarian and disaster relief. India has shown a willingness and determination to shoulder greater global responsibilities by extending its capacity as a "first responder" to crises beyond its borders. It provided critical relief supplies and medical assistance to the flood ravaged population of Sri Lanka and Bangladesh in the aftermath of Cyclone Mora. Furthermore, the government pledged medical assistance worth US$ 1 million to Yemen and launched 'Operation Insaniyat' for relief of displaced persons in Bangladesh.

The Government has made domestic transformation of the economy intrinsic to its foreign policy strategy. The close association between foreign policy and domestic developmental aspirations has shown significant results in terms of increasing Foreign Direct Investment (FDI) inflows and creating a favourable investment climate. This was proven by the considerable leap in the World Bank's ease of doing business rankings from 142 in 2014 to 100 in 2017. The period also saw fast tracking of international partnerships aimed at promoting and facilitating India's flagship developmental initiatives such as Smart Cities, Skill India, Digital India and Namami Gange etc. A notable achievement was laying the foundation stone of India's first high speed railway project between Mumbai and Ahmedabad in September 2017. India also hosted the 52nd annual meeting of African Development Bank (AfDB) Group.

The emphasis on expanding India's diplomatic footprint to new countries and regions continued this year, with high-level exchanges with a number of countries around the world, many of which had not seen such engagements in recent years. This included our partners in Africa, Latin America and the Caribbean region. At the level of Heads of State and Government, the year witnessed incoming visits by the Prime Ministers of Sri Lanka, Nepal, Bangladesh, Malaysia, Australia, Japan, Latvia, Mauritius, Uganda, Israel and Italy, *inter-alia* and, by the Presidents of Turkey, Belarus, Armenia, Palestine, Afghanistan, Cyprus and Switzerland. Similarly, outgoing visits included those by President to Djibouti and Ethiopia and by Vice President to Poland, Armenia, Uganda, Rwanda and Jakarta. Prime Minister interacted with the new leadership in the USA and France and provided fresh impetus to our existing warm relations with the UAE, Japan, Germany, Spain, Netherlands, Israel, the Philippines, Myanmar, China, Sri Lanka, Portugal, Kazakhstan and Russia. This extensive diplomatic outreach is illustrative of the government's policy of proactive engagements in a fast changing world order so as to preserve and promote our national interests.

On the issue of terrorism, India consistently advocated a policy of zero tolerance. It remained steadfast in its commitment to combat terrorism and supported efforts to expand cooperation to deal with this threat. During the period under review, India proposed a 11-point action plan to G20 leaders in Hamburg and at the BRICS Summit declaration in Xiamen. The plan calls for holding accountable those committing, organising, or supporting terrorist acts. Government continued to work under established frameworks with partner countries like the USA, Russia, Japan and the EU to disrupt financial flows to terrorists and to identify their assets.

A major emphasis of the Government over the years has been on cultural diplomacy by utilising India's cultural heritage and civilisational values and ethos to enhance its standing in the world. The diaspora plays a significant role in this diplomatic outreach, as it is both a component and the target audience. The successful, widespread celebration and participation in the third International Day of Yoga highlights the continued efficacy of India's universal culture. The Indian Council for Cultural Relations (ICCR) organised a number of events across the world to showcase India's rich heritage, including a seminar on Sanskrit in France and a Virat Hindi Kavi Sammelan in the UK. The opening of an Indian Cultural Centre at Tel Aviv was announced during the visit of the Prime Minister to Israel.

The Government has made a concerted effort to engage with the Indian diaspora over the years and extended to them its support and encouragement for contributing to their country of origin. Apart from organising the Pravasi Bhartiya Divas held biennially, the Ministry regularly organises Regional Pravasi Bhartiya Divas outside India to connect with them in specific regions to familiarise them with the policies and programmes of the Government and enable them to contribute to India's development and growth.

The Government's emphasis on providing citizen-centric governance and make its public service delivery functions more efficient continued this year. The e-Tourist Visa (eTV) launched in April 2015 has been further liberalized as e-visa, extending its eligibility from tourism to include business and medical purposes, and expanding its coverage to 161 countries and increasing the duration of stay permitted under the scheme. The process of consular grievance redressal for Indians living abroad has also been improved by making MADAD or the Consular Services Management System available on Mobile Apps and through social media.

Neighbourhood

Afghanistan: India-Afghanistan strategic relationship saw further consolidation with expansion in the multifaceted cooperation in all areas, including political, defence, security, trade and investment, connectivity, development partnership, social and cultural issues, education and capacity building. This was facilitated by exchange of several high-level visits, including visits of President of Afghanistan in October; Chief Executive in September and November 2017; Second Vice President in December and Foreign Minister in September 201 7.

At all the meetings, both sides expressed grave concern at the incidents of terror and violence and noted that terrorism presented the greatest threat to peace, stability and progress of the region and beyond. Success of India's bilateral relationship with Afghanistan can be gauged by the description of India by Afghan leadership as the preferred development partner.

Bangladesh: Continued high-level visits and exchanges, including at the highest political levels between India and Bangladesh helped maintain the momentum of bilateral relations between the two countries. Prime Minister of Bangladesh paid a state visit to India in April 2017 following which tangible progress was made on mutually identified initiatives in multifaceted areas through broadening of cooperation and implementation of the decisions taken during the visit.

Bhutan: India and Bhutan share close and friendly relations characterized by deep mutual trust and understanding. In 2017-18 sustained progress in all areas of cooperation was seen. The momentum of bilateral ties was carried forward by high level visits and meetings of various bilateral mechanism.

Prime Minister of Bhutan visited Guwahati in March 2017 to attend the opening of the 'Namami Brahamputra' river festival as the Guest of Honour.

Its Finance Minister, visited India in 2017 to attend the South Asian Sub regional Economic Cooperation (SASEC) Finance Ministers Meeting in New Delhi.

His Majesty along with Her Majesty, and His Royal Highness Prince visited India in 2017. The visit was the first visit of His Royal Highness the Gyalsey to India. During the visit His Majesty the King of Bhutan had meetings with the President, Vice President, Prime Minister and other dignitaries.

China: The bilateral relations between India and China have progressed under the overall context of Closer Developmental Partnership between the two countries even as both sides managed their differences through dialogue. There have been regular interactions at the summit level. The Brazil, Russia, India, China, and South Africa (BRICS) Summit in China provided opportunities for interactions at ministerial as well as working level between the two countries across political, economic, security and cultural sphere.

Maldives: India's 'Neighbourhood First' policy continued to guide its multifaceted relations with Maldives. The specific focus during the period was on capacity and institution building, besides extending assistance in defence, health and education sectors. Exchange of visits at the level of policymakers added momentum to the close and friendly relationship.

Mauritius: India and Mauritius enjoy close political, economic, cultural and diaspora linkages. With 70 per cent of its population of Indian origin, Mauritius has been a hub for financial services and one of the largest routes for Foreign Direct Investment (FDI) into India. Mauritius is also an important gateway for Indian investments into Africa. There is close bilateral defence partnership, focusing in particular on maritime security.

The India-Mauritius partnership further deepened and diversified across a broad spectrum during this period. The State Visit of Prime Minister of Mauritius to India in May 2017 and the visit by a Parliamentary delegation in June 2017 provided fresh momentum to our bilateral engagement. Indian development assistance projects currently underway in Mauritius added new content to this special partnership.

Myanmar: India's relations with Myanmar in 2017 continued to be special, with culture and people-to-people links being of particular strength and Buddhism providing a special link. Myanmar being the only Association of Southeast Asian Nations (ASEAN) country adjoining India, therefore, remained as our gateway to South East Asia and India's first partner in its 'Act East' Policy.

The highlight of our bilateral relations with Myanmar in 2017 was the first state visit of Prime Minister to Myanmar in 2017. Minister for Petroleum and Natural Gas of India also visited Myanmar in February 2017. In June 2017, the 6th India — Myanmar Joint Trade Committee (JTC) meeting was held in New Delhi. Besides, throughout 2017, India demonstrated strong commitment towards meeting Myanmar's developmental needs through implementation of developmental projects, including training, provision of expertise, Lines of Credit (LOC) and/or grants-in-aid. Bilateral cooperation between the two countries aimed at promotion of inclusive growth and development to contribute to peace, prosperity and stability in the two countries as also in the region.

Nepal: India-Nepal relations derive strength and salience from age-old cultural and religious ties, close people-to-people contacts, multi-faceted economic and development partnership reinforced by open borders and national treatment accorded to each other's citizens. As a part of intensive bilateral engagements, President of Nepal paid a state visit to India in April 2017. Prime Minister of Nepal paid a state visit to India in August 2017. EAM attended the 15th BIMSTEC Ministerial meeting in Kathmandu in August 2017. In keeping with the tradition of regular high-level exchanges, EAM paid another visit to Nepal in February 2017.

The high-level visits and regular meetings of bilateral mechanisms provided an opportunity to review bilateral partnership and to discuss new initiatives for mutual benefit. India and Nepal have comprehensive economic and developmental cooperation. Community driven small development projects like schools, roads, bridges, irrigation facilities, are benefiting people in different districts of Nepal. Under the four Lines of Credit of over US$ 1.65 billion extended by Government of India, a number of infrastructure projects, including post-earthquake reconstruction projects are being implemented there. India offers around 3,000 scholarships to Nepalese students every year, providing opportunities to study in Nepal and in India. More than 250 scholarships are offered annually for government and non-government employees of Nepal for training in technical institutes in India under the Indian Technical and Economic Cooperation (ITEC) programme.

Pakistan: During the period under review, the frequency and intensity of bilateral exchanges between India and Pakistan remained limited. Our efforts to normalise relations with Pakistan continued to be thwarted by Pakistan's support for cross-border infiltration and ceasefire violations along the Line of Control and International Boundary. The government continued its efforts to secure the release of Kulbhushan Jadhav through both diplomatic and legal mechanisms. Repatriation of Uzma and Bijoyeta Bannerjee, Indian women in distress in Pakistan, was facilitated through legal and diplomatic means.

Seychelles: India-Seychelles relationship has embarked on new avenues of cooperation in recent months with robust development partnership, capacity building programmes, maritime security cooperation and cultural exchanges. Blue economy, climate change, renewable energy, tourism and health are the emerging areas of focus and added further substance to the bilateral engagement during the period.

In recognition of the strategic convergence of the two countries in the Indian Ocean region, a bilateral agreement on the development, management, operation and maintenance of facilities on Assumption Island in Seychelles was signed in 2018 in Victoria, Mahe. The agreement is an important step forward in further deepening bilateral defence and security cooperation.

Sri Lanka: India-Sri Lanka relations continued on the high growth trajectory, both in terms of high-level political engagements and economic and people-to-people exchanges during the period. The hallmark of this active phase in the relationship was a more proactive and pragmatic approach to cooperation in the spheres of economic and development partnership, with a strong emphasis on timelines for implementation with regard to bilateral projects.

The landmark visit of Prime Minister to Sri Lanka in May 2017 marked a qualitative transformation in the bilateral engagement. Closer cooperation in bilateral economic projects received a further boost during Sri Lankan Prime Minister's visit in April 2017 with the signing of a MoU for Cooperation in Economic Projects. India-Sri Lanka development partnership further intensified and broadened in scope during this period. India remained as the first responder in Sri Lanka's hour of need on account of natural calamities in 2017 with relief and rehabilitation assistance extended during drought and flood situations.

Indian Ocean Region: India's proactive engagement in the Indian Ocean Region was further intensified during the period. India's approach to the region was directed towards advancing cooperation and using capabilities for larger benefit highlighting the precepts of Security and Growth for All in the Region (SAGAR).

The Indian Ocean Rim Association (IORA) mechanism has a vital role to play in realizing this common aspiration for the region. India considers IORA as an important instrument for promoting cooperation and ensuring stability in the region. The focus during the period was on implementing wide ranging initiatives announced by India during the IORA Leaders' Summit in 2017 in Jakarta.

South-East Asia and Asia-Pacific

Australia: India's relations with Australia entered a more intensive phase due to regular exchange of high-level visits during the year. Australia is increasingly emerging as an important partner in different sectors including development of mineral resources, science and technology, education and skills and water resources management. Recognising importance of relationship between India and Australia, Australia's Foreign Policy White Paper, released by Australian Prime Minister in November 2017 sees India in the front rank of Australia's international partnerships.

Brunei Darussalam: Bilateral relations between India and Brunei Darussalam continued to be close and friendly. The year marks the 25th anniversary of ASEAN-India Dialogue Partnership. 2017 was also the 50th anniversary of ASEAN. These landmark events further increased interactions between the two countries through a number of events in all areas including political, defence, cultural and sports. These landmark events further increased interactions between the two countries through a number of events in all areas including political, defence, cultural and sports.

Cambodia: Bilateral relations with Cambodia progressed in various fields including economic, cultural, people-to-people contact, capacity building and developmental projects. A delegation from Rajya Sabha Secretariat visited Cambodia in June 2017 within the framework of MoU signed between Rajya Sabha Secretariat and the Cambodian Senate in September 2016 to encourage parliamentary exchanges. Indian assistance to Cambodia continued in the field of water resources development, electric transmission line, restoration and conservation of temples and capacity building.

Indonesia: With the visit of Indonesian President to India in December 2016, the bilateral relations with Indonesia took a steep upward trajectory. The year 2017 witnessed many high-level political engagements that have helped in reinvigorating our relationship and has provided the necessary momentum to the bilateral relations.

Lao People's Democratic Republic (PDR): The year saw a continued upward trend in bilateral relations with Lao PDR. Infrastructure projects in areas of irrigation systems, capacity building and human resources and cultural cooperation in restoration of heritage monuments and regular high-level visits were focus of cooperation.

Malaysia: The strategic partnership, established between the two countries in October 2010 and the traditionally close relations, were given a boost with the visit of Prime Minister to Malaysia in 2015. The relations have been elevated to a higher level with the state visit of Prime Minister of Malaysia to India in 2017. The visit coincided with the 60th anniversary of the establishment of India-Malaysia diplomatic relations.

New Zealand: India's relations with New Zealand continued to deepen and expand in various fields such as economic, scientific, cultural, people-to-people contact and coordination on regional and issues of global importance. Sustained high level contacts led to an increasingly multifaceted profile of bilateral engagement as also to a growing level of coordination at regional and multilateral forums.

Philippines: The year 2017 was marked by unprecedented high-level exchanges to the Philippines culminating in the visit of Prime Minister to the Philippines in 2017 to attend the 31st ASEAN and EAS Summits in Manila.

Singapore: During this year, India-Singapore bilateral relations achieved important strides in diverse areas including trade and investment, defence, security, skills, urban planning, and civil aviation.

Thailand: India's relationship with Thailand continued to deepen and strengthened during the year with the exchange of high-level visits and enhanced interactions in trade, investment, defence and security. Both the countries celebrated 70th anniversary of the establishment of diplomatic relations in 2017.

Timor Leste: India participated in the swearing in ceremony of President and 15th anniversary of the restoration of Independence of Timor-Leste held in Dili in 2017.

Vietnam: India and Vietnam celebrated 2017 as the Year of Friendship for commemorating the 45th anniversary of establishment of diplomatic relations and the 10th anniversary of establishment of Strategic Partnership.

Association of Southeast Asian Nations (ASEAN): 2017 was a landmark year, both for ASEAN and for ASEAN-India relations. While ASEAN celebrated fifty years of its existence this year, India celebrated the 25th Anniversary of ASEAN-India Dialogue Partnership, fifteen years of summit level relationship and five years of strategic partnership with ASEAN. Based on the theme of the 25th anniversary celebration of ASEAN-India partnership, 'Shared Values, Common Destiny', India organised commemorative events in India as well as in ASEAN countries encompassing the three pillars of political-security, economic and socio-cultural cooperation.

East Asia

Democratic People's Republic of Korea (DPRK): Since its inception in December 1973, the diplomatic relations between India and DPRK have been cordial. In 2017, DPRK conducted a series of missile and nuclear tests. India deplored the nuclear and ballistic missile programme of the DPRK and remained concerned about the proliferation of nuclear and missile technologies which has adversely impacted India's national security.

Japan: India-Japan relations have undergone a significant and qualitative shift in recent years, propelled by successful and regular high-level visits. Highlight of India-Japan relations in 2017 was Japanese Prime Minister's visit to India in 2017 for the 12th Annual Summit. During the Summit both sides reviewed the recent progress in the multi-faceted cooperation under the framework of the Special Strategic and Global Partnership between the two countries.

Republic of Korea (RoK): India-RoK bilateral relationship, elevated to the level of Special Strategic Partnership during the visit of Prime Minister to RoK in 2015, gathered further momentum. Indian Prime Minister met with RoK President during the G-20 Summit in Hamburg in July 2017. Deepening engagements on the economic side, an MoU between Export-Import (EXIM) Banks of the two countries to establish US$ 9 billion in Korean concessional credit and an agreement between the two governments on US$ 1 billion in Korean Economic Development Cooperation Fund (EDCF) funding for infrastructure development projects in India were signed in June 2017.

Mongolia: India's traditionally friendly and cordial relations with Mongolia have steadily improved over the years, following the Prime Minister's historic visit to Mongolia in May 2015. India-Mongolia relations were upgraded to Strategic Partnership during the visit. India continued to provide technical and economic cooperation to Mongolia in higher education, information and communication technology and human resource development.

Eurasia

2017 marked seventy years of diplomatic relations between India and Russia and twenty five years of diplomatic relations between India and the other countries in Eurasia. The occasions were celebrated through exchange of messages between the dignitaries of the two sides, joint issues of commemorative postal stamps and organization of celebratory avents covering diverse areas of bilateral relations.

Indian Prime Minister had a very successful visit to St. Petersburg in June 2017 for the 18th India-Russia Annual Summit. The visit resulted in the adoption of 'St. Petersburg Declaration' and conclusion of twelve documents related to cooperation in nuclear energy, science and technology, railways, culture, precious stones, engineering, finance, infrastructure, and investment.

15th RIC (Russia India China) Foreign Ministerial meeting was held in New Delhi in 2017 when, on its margins, EAM had bilateral meetings with Russian and Chinse Foreign Ministers. Prime Minister visited Kazakhstan in 2017, to take part in the Heads of State summit of Shanghai Cooperation Organization (SCO). India joined SCO as a full member during the Summit.

During the year multiple business delegations were exchanged and participation in various trade events organized with the countries in the region. The third International Day of Yoga was celebrated enthusiastically across all the countries in Eurasia in June 2017. Track-II Dialogue, exchange of experts and students, pursuit of higher education, university to university tie-ups, cultural and people-to-people exchanges including for availing medical services in India supplemented official talks paving way for productive and meaningful bonds. ITEC courses and Indian Council for Cultural Relations (ICCR) scholarships continued to be popular.

The Gulf and West Asia

Gulf: The growing political engagement with the countries in the region continued during 2017 starting with the successful State Visit of the Crown Prince of Abu Dhabi to India as the Chief Guest at our Republic Day celebrations in January 2017. Among the other key high-level political interactions were the visits to India by Foreign Affairs Ministers of Oman, Yemen, UAE, Iraq and Qatar. On the Indian side, Minister of State (MoS) for External Affairs visited Iraq in 2017. MoS for External Affairs led the Hajj Goodwill Delegation to Jeddah and a delegation for the 3rd Joint Ministerial Commission (JCM) meeting on trade, economic, scientific and technological cooperation in Kuwait both in September 2017.

Iran: 2017 saw an intense engagement with Iran at both political and functional levels. The year saw several important bilateral visits both incoming and outgoing as well as interactions between high level dignitaries in multilateral forums. President of Islamic Republic of Iran visited India in February 2018.

West Asia and North Africa (WANA): The region continues to remain important from energy security, food security and for global peace and security.

Relations with all the countries of WANA region were taken forward in a calibrated manner, through regular holding of institutional dialogue mechanisms and high level exchange of visits. The region was marked by a number of firsts as far as our bilateral relations with Israel, Palestine and Djibouti are concerned. President of India visited Djibouti which was the first ever visit by an Indian President to that country. Prime Minister undertook the first ever historic visit to Israel on the occasion of 25 years of diplomatic relations. Prime Minister of Israel visited India in 2018 as the culmination of the celebrations to mark 25 years of establishment of diplomatic relations. Maghreb region continues to be important for our food security as the region remains primary source of rock phosphate and its derivatives. Somalia, Djibouti and Eritrea are located in the strategically important Horn of Africa region that will be crucial for the security of our maritime trade passing through Red Sea-Gulf of Aden region.

Africa

East and South Africa: During the year 2017-18, our relations with Africa acquired a different quality and content. Continuing with the inclusive and continental approach that began with the hosting of India Africa Forum Summit (IAFS) - III, we further enhanced our political engagement with African countries. In May 2017, we hosted the meeting of African Development Bank (AfDB) in India for the first time. All the countries in the continent have been visited by India at least at the Ministerial level, during the current government's tenure.

India also took initiatives to catalyse collective engagement in Africa with like-minded countries. The initiation of a dialogue with Japan on Asia-Africa Connectivity and launch of Asia Africa Growth Corridor were highlights of the year. Dialogues on Africa were initiated for the first time with Germany (May 2017), France (June 2017) and Russia(November 2017). For the first time, India also attended the Tokyo Internationl Conference on African Development (TICAD)-VI Ministerial Review Meeting in 2017. India also participated in G-20 Conference on Africa and the Compact initiative.

With respect to Africa, another salient feature was enhanced focus on maritime security. Several initiatives under bilateral and multilateral frameworks such as IORA, IBSA and BRICS were taken to further our objectives in this regard. The year saw first ever visit by COSC and CNS to Mozambique and 1st Joint Defence Committee meeting with Madagascar. JDCs and JWG on defence were also held with South Africa and Mozambique. Ship visits to South Africa, Namibia, Tanzania and Madagascar and visits by defence delegations took place in 2017.

On the economic front, our trade with Africa multiplied and diversified. A Regional CII Exim Bank Conclave was held in Kampala. India became the 5th largest investor in Africa with cumulative investment estimated at US$ 54 billion.

African countries overwhelmingly joined the Indo-French initiative International Solar Alliance (ISA). Over half of the countries that have joined ISA so far, are from Africa.

The Electronic Tourist Visa (ETV) Facility was expanded to cover more than 25 countries from Africa. Air connectivity was enhanced with commencement of direct flights of Rwandair (April 2017) and increase in frequency of Ethiopian airlines..Cultural cooperation increased with many countries enthusiastically celebrating Festivals of India, International Yoga Day and Indian festivals.

West Africa: India's relations with countries of West Africa continued on an upward trajectory during 2017. The region (covering twenty five countries of west, north-west, central and south-west Africa) is home to Africa's largest population and fastest growing economies with largest proven reserves of energy resources and minerals. The region is rich in all known minerals. India sources about 18 per cent of its crude oil requirements from this region. India imports over US$ 2 billion worth of gold from Ghana per annum. India also sources ninety per cent of raw cashew from countries in the region including Cote d'lvoire, Guinea Bissau and Senegal. Although the West African region continues to gain strategic importance for India and remains politically stable, it continues to have some hot spots including the Boko Haram insurgency affecting Nigeria and its neighbours (Cameroon, Chad, Niger and Benin), northern Mali, eastern DRC (Democratic Republic of Congo), CAR (Central African Republic) and language crisis in Cameroon (two Anglophone regions asking for more rights and autonomy). There have, however, been better coordination and synergy of efforts amongst the countries of the region to deal with the terrorist menace. There are currently 5,000 plus Indian troops, military observers, and police personnel in the Democratic Republic of Congo under MONUSCO (UN Stabilization Mission in the Democratic Republic of Congo).

As far as economic and commercial relations are concerned, India's bilateral trade with the region currently stands at around US$ 22 billion. Capacity building, skill development and strengthening of physical and social infrastructure have remained at the centre of India's expanding development partnership with the region. For 2017-18, around 1,450 civilian ITEC slots; over 200 defence slots (111 slots to Nigeria) and 300 Indian Council for Cultural Relations (ICCR) scholarships were allocated to West African (WA) countries.

Europe and European Union

Central Europe: India continued with its policy of engaging with the countries of Central Europe to consolidate bilateral relations. On political issues, there was good understanding, both at bilateral and multilateral forums. The growing bilateral trade, business exchanges, educational exchanges and cultural events added to the growing ties with the region. 2017 saw incoming high level visits from Cyprus, Turkey, Switzerland and Latvia. There were outgoing visits of Vice President to Poland and Prime Minister to World Economic Forum and bilateral meeting at Davos, Switzerland. The focus was on disseminating information about progress on the parameters of Ease of Doing Business, creating a unified market through the Goods and Services Tax, liberalization of investment and licensing policies, Insolvency and bankruptcy Code, productive disinvestment measures, launch of digital employment exchanges and government initiatives namely Make in India, start-up/stand-up India, housing for all, urban renewal and rejuvenation, infrastructure including digital infrastructure and Industrial Corridors, Swachh Bharat and Skill India. India and the central European countries continued to extend support to each other in various international fora including the support for each other candidates in international organizations.The 4th India Europe twenty-nine business forum was organized in March 2018.

West Europe: India's engagement with countries in West Europe including Belgium, France, Germany, Italy, Ireland, Portugal, Spain, the Netherlands, the United Kingdom, Andorra and Monaco saw an upswing during fiscal 2016-17. The year was marked with a series of high-level political visits. The 14th India-EU Summit was held 2017. The European Investment Bank also established its South Asian Regional Office in New Delhi. The Prime Minister of Italy visited India in 2017, the first in the last ten years. The visit not only gave a fresh impetus to the bilateral ties, but also sought to revitalize on-going multi-sectoral engagements between the two countries. To commemorate 70 years of establishment of diplomatic ties, Belgian Royals visited India in 2017. The visit was aimed at broad-basing the overall political and economic engagement between the two countries. The Prince of Wales and the Duchess of Cornwall visited India in 2017. The visit was in connection with the Commonwealth Heads of Government Meeting in London. Overall, India's engagement with the countries in Europe West during the year has been deepened with enhanced cooperation in trade, investment, infrastructure, science and technology, research and development, student exchanges, and tourism flows.

The Americas

United States: The India-US bilateral relations continue to witness progress in all key areas of the strategic partnership, including security, defence, economic, energy, technology and people-to-people contact. The assumption of office by the new President in 2017 imparted a fresh mementum to bilateral engagements.

Indian Prime Minister paid an official visit to the US in 2017. The main outcomes reached during the Summit included: further strengthening of counter-terrorism co-operation; establishment of a new consultation mechanism on domestic and international terrorist designations proposals; designation of Hizb-ul-Mujahideen leader Syed Salahuddin as a Specially Designated Global Terrorist: firm message to Pakistan to ensure that its territory is not used to launch terrorist attacks on other countries; etc.

Post-Prime Minister's visit, there were a series of exchanges at political and functional levels in key areas of the strategic partnership including defence and security; counter-terrorism; trade and economic issues; energy; people-to-people contacts; and consultations on regional and international issues. Both countries have agreed to launch a new 2+2 Ministerial Dialogue involving foreign affairs and defence ministries to bring greater synergy in our strategic and defence engagements.

Defence and Security cooperation was a key component of the bilateral strategic engagement. Progress was also made across all areas of defence engagement including defence trade, training and exercises. The Logistic Exchange Memorandum of Agreement (LEMOA) was operationalised.

India-US economic and commercial relations continued to expand during 2017. The US remains India's largest trading partner, goods and services combined. Bilateral trade in goods and services amounted to US$114 billion and the two-way merchandise trade was US$66.7 billion in 2016. During the first ten months of 2017, bilateral merchandise trade stood at US$ 62.26 billion with the balance of trade in favour of India at US$ 19.72 billion.

Cooperation in innovation and entrepreneurship crossed a new milestone with India and the US co-hosting the Global Entrepreneurship Summit in India with the theme of Women First, Prosperity for All. The summit brought together entrepreneurs, investors, and ecosystem supporters from 150 countries.

Canada: India-Canada bilateral relations are underpinned by shared values of democracy and pluralism; expanding economic engagement; regular high-level interactions and extensive people-to-people ties. The relationship received a new momentum with the visit of Prime Minister to Canada in 2015, and the elevation of bilateral relationship to a strategic partnership. The highlight in 2018 was the visit of Prime Minister of Canada to India. During the visit, there were concrete outcomes in the areas of energy, infrastructure, civil nuclear cooperation and skill development.

During 2017-18 there were a series of high-level visits and meetings of bilateral mechanisms namely, India-Canada Security Dialogue, Trade Ministerial Dialogue, Joint Working Group of Agriculture, Joint Committee of Science and Technology and Joint Committee of Civil Nuclear Cooperation.

Canada is home to over 1.4 million Persons of Indian Origin (PIO) who comprise more than 3 per cent of the country's population. There has been a significant increase in number of Indian students in Canada which is now estimated at 1,00,000. Commencement of direct flights between Indian and Canadian cities has contributed to strengthening of people-to-people links. The Department of Posts, India and Canada Post jointly issued commemorative stamps on the theme of Diwali for the first time.

Latin America and Caribbean Countries: India and the Latin America region have continued to be distinct priorities for each other. India attaches importance to its relations with the Latin American and Caribbean (LAC) region and has warm and friendly relations with each of the countries. There are shared common values of democracy and respect for human rights. Our countries also share common membership of many international organizations and work closely together in the UN, G-77, NAM, etc. Latin America and India have a lot in common culturally with a variety of ancestries, ethnic groups and races. The presence of about one million Indian diaspora adds a special dimension to this relationship.

The importance of India's relations with countries of LAC region underscored by Prime Minister during a visit to the region in 2014 (Brazil) continued to gain impetus in further strengthening our relations.

India and LAC countries continued to support each other in international fora. In this context, it will not be out of place to mention that India received the valuable support of LAC countries for the election of Judge Dalveer Bhandari to the International Court of Justice.

Five countries of LAC region, Brazil, Costa Rica, Dominican Republic, Peru and Venezuela, have so far signed the Framework Agreement of the International Solar Alliance, a joint initiative of India and France.

United Nations and International Organizations

The tempo of India's engagement with the United Nations system continued as in the previous years.

India continued with its multilateral engagements at the United Nations and international organisation on all issues of interest including climate change, sustainable development, human rights, and culture. The Universal Periodic Review (UPR) mechanism under the UN Human Rights Council, the UN Oceans Conference, the High Level Political Forum (HLPF) on Sustainable Development of ECOSOC, and the 23rd Conference of Parties of the United Nations Framework Convention on Climate Change (UNFCCC) are among the major meetings participated by India during the period of the Report. At the United Nations Economic and Security Council (ECOSOC) HLPF, India presented its Voluntary National Review (VNR) on the implementation of Sustainable Development Goals (SDGs). India also accepted the Doha Amendment to the Kyoto Protocol under United Nations Framework Convention on Climate Change (UNFCCC). Finally, India was elected to major UN bodies and international organisation including, inter alia, the International Court of justice (ICJ), International Tribunal for the Law of the Sea (ITLOS), International Maritime Organisation (IMO), Executive Board of United Nations Educational, Scientific and Cultural Organisation (UNESCO), and UN Habitat Governing Council.

Disarmament and International Security Affairs

India actively participated in various disarmament, arms control and international security related forums held during the year. A number of civil nuclear cooperation agreements entered into force, namely, with Bangladesh,

Japan and Vietnam. As part of an active engagement with various export control regimes, India became the 42nd member of the Wassenaar Arrangement.

International Solar Alliance

The Founding Conference of the International Solar Alliance (ISA) was held in New Delhi in 2018. It may be recalled that the ISA became an international entity in 2017.

Multilateral Economic Relations

BRICS [Brazil, Russia, India, China and South Africa]: India participated in the Ninth BRICS Summitt in 2017 in Xiamen. The leaders held discussions on economic and finance cooperation, global economic governance, and international peace and security. The outcomes of the Summit included the Xiamen Declaration, in which strong sentiments were expressed by leaders on terrorism.

Twelfth G20 Summit: Indian delegation attended the Twelfth G20 Summit in Hamburg, Germany in 2017. The agenda of the Summit included global growth and trade, sustainable development, climate and energy, partnership with Africa, migration, and health, digitalisation, women's empowerment, and employment.

IBSA (India, Brazil & South Africa): During 2017, two IBSA Foreign Ministers' meetings were held.

SAARC & BIMSTEC

The Bay of Bengal Initiative for Multi-Sectoral Technical and Economic Cooperation (BIMSTEC) is a natural choice to fulfill India's key foreign policy priorities of 'Neighbourhood First' and 'Act East'. India is working with other member states to make BIMSTEC effective and result oriented organization to bring prosperity and development for the region.

In South Asian Association for Regional Cooperation (SAARC), an informal meeting of Council of Ministers was held on the sidelines of 72nd United Nations General Assembly (UNGA) Session in New York in 2017. India participated at official and technical level in other meetings of SAARC including those of its regional centres/specialized bodies and sectoral meetings.

Development Cooperation

Development cooperation is an integral part of India's foreign policy. In recent years, India's development programmes in various countries have expanded substantially, both in geographical reach and sectoral coverage. This inter-alia include grant assistance, Lines Of Credit (LOCs), technical consultancy, disaster relief, humanitarian aid, educational scholarships and a range of capacity-building programmes including short-term civilian and military training courses.

Major developmental projects identified by the host governments as priority areas are under implementation in Afghanistan, Bangladesh, Bhutan,

Nepal, Myanmar, Sri Lanka and Maldives in the areas of infrastructure, hydro-electriciry, power transmission, agriculture, industry, education, health and others. In addition, various projects initiated for development and strengthening of cross-border connectivity with India's neighbours are progressing satisfactorily. Beyond the neighbourhood, bilateral projects in archaeological conservation, information and computer technology (ICT) and small and medium enterprises have been undertaken in South East Asia, Central Asia, Africa and Latin America.

During 2017-I8, 10,918 civilian training slots were offered to 161 partner countries under the ITEC programme. These capacity building courses also included specially designed courses and training programmes in a variety of disciplines, based on specific requests from partner countries. Humanitarian assistance was rendered by India to countries affected by natural disasters. Medical assistance has been provided to Mozambique and Myanmar. Humanitarian assistance in the form of food items was provided to Lesotho, Namibia, Zimbabwe, Bangladesh and Myanmar.

Economic Diplomacy

The MEA through its Economic Diplomacy Division as part of its efforts to give a focused direction to the economic diplomacy dimension of the country's foreign policy undertook a number of initiatives during 2016-17. This Division extends funding to the missions/posts to intensify their economic engagement with the countries of their accreditation under the "Marker Expansion Activities". The funding has been utilized to help promote Indian exports through catalogue shows and buyer-seller meets, engage consultants to prepare market studies, organize business seminars to attract foreign investments, and undertake advocacy work to promote interests of Indian enterprises seeking business opportunities overseas.

States

MEA has a States Division, established in 2014, to foster closer links between Indian missions and posts abroad and states/union territories. The Division successfully endeavoured in promoting external outreach of states through provisional and regional cooperation in the domain of bilateral relations. It facilitated the signing of various Sister City/Sister States and other MoUs between state/union territory governments and foreign entities in 2017. In order to enhance external outreach of states/union territories, it represented MEA at various events in the states, including global investor meets and significant cultural events of states that generate significant international exposure for the states of India. This Division rendered assistance to foreigners in distress and eliminate any negative fallout from these events abroad.

Counter Terrorism

In the wake of various terrorism-related incidents that occurred in different parts of the world in 2017, the issue of terrorism found prominent mention in various high-level bilateral and multilateral meetings. During all such interactions, India strongly condemned terrorism in all its forms and manifestations and reiterated its commitment to combating the menace at a global level.

Global Cyber Issues

Increasing use of Information and Communication Technology (ICT) for the social and economic development of nations has made cyber issues one of the significant subjects of diplomatic discussions around the world. In keeping with its profile the MEA upscaled its Global Cyber Issues cell to create the new Cyber Diplomacy (CD) Division which has been entrusted with the responsibility of projection and safeguarding of Indian interests on the subject in international fora.

Consular, Passport and Visa Services

In recent years, the issuance of passports has emerged as the most noticeable statutory and citizen service rendered by this Ministry. It has made many quantitative and qualitative improvements in the delivery of passport services. Indian Passports [together with other travel documents such as Identity Certificates (IC), Emergency Certificates (EC) for returnees to India, Police Clearance Certificates (PCC) and Line of Control Travel Permits in Jammu and Kashmir] are issued by the Ministry through the Central Passport Organisation and its all India network of 37 Passport Offices, and the Andaman and Nicobar Islands Administration. This network has been vastly expanded by adding 92 Passport Seva Kendras(PSKs) in Public Private Partnership (PPP) mode and 60 Post Office Passport Seva Kendra (POPSKs) in association with Ministry of Communications, as extended arms of Passport Offices. For Indians living abroad, passports, Overseas Citizen of India (OCI) cards, EC and other miscellaneous consular services, apart from attestation of consular documents are being rendered by the 184 Indian Missions/Posts abroad.

During 2017, the Ministry processed approximately 1.17 crore passport and passport related service applications compared to 98.4 lakhs in 2016 marking a growth of nearly 19 per cent.

The Ministry, in association with the Ministry of Communications, has taken an innovative initiative to open Passport Seva Kendras at the Head Post Offices (HPO)/ Post Offices in the country to be known as 'Post Office Passport Seva Kendra' (POPSK). The Ministry has announced opening of 251 POPSKs. Out of these 60 POPSKs became operational till January 2018. Nearly 5 lakh passport applications have been processed at these POPSKs during 2017. With the addition of 251 POPSKs, the total number of PSKs including POPSKs that would be added.

The Ministry integrated its four offices in Mumbai, namely, (i) Passport Office, (ii) Office of the Protector of Emigrants, (iii) Office of the Regional Director of ICCR, and (iv) Branch Secretariat into a single building - the "Videsh Bhavan"-for effective management of its engagement with the State

Government of Maharashtra. The Passport Office at Thane was merged with the Passport Office at Mumbai.

The Ministry of External Affairs celebrated the completion of 50 years of the Passports Act 1967 which was enacted in 1967. To mark the occasion, a Special Commemorative Stamp and First Day Cover were released by the Department of Posts during the Fifth Passport Seva Divas and Passport Officers Conference in 2017.

The pre printed portion of the passport is already in Hindi and English languages. At present, the personal details of the applicant are printed in English language only. The Government has now decided to print personal details on passports in both Hindi and English.

Overseas Indian Affairs

The Government has brought about a transformational change in India's engagement with the Overseas Indian Community. The efforts are geared at strengthening our engagement and outreach with all segments of overseas Indians. The Government has accorded top most priority to their welfare and protection and the institutional framework for support and welfare of overseas Indians has been considerably strengthened. This has been done with an unparalleled focus keeping in the mind the issues and concerns of our migrant workers that are the most vulnerable segment of the Overseas Indian Community.

As part of Government's commitment to strengthen engagement with diaspora, among the major initiatives/programmes launched/hosted during 2017 are Videsh Sampark outreach programme, Know India Programme, Pravasi Bharatiya Divas (PBD) Conferences, Scholarship Programme for diaspora children, Awareness Campaign on Safe and Legal Migration and merger of Ministry's scheme for distressed Indian women married to NRI spouses with Indian Community Welfare Fund.

19 Industry

THE Department of Industrial Policy and Promotion (DIPP), one of the departments under the Ministry of Commerce and Industry, was established in 1995 and was reconstituted 2000 with the merger of the Department of Industrial Development in it. Earlier separate Ministries for Small Scale Industries & Agro and Rural Industries (SSI&A&RI) and Heavy Industries and Public Enterprises (HI&PE) were created in place in 1999. With progressive liberalisation of the Indian economy, initiated in 1991, there has been a consistent shift in the role and functions of this Department. From regulation and administration of the industrial sector, it has been transformed into facilitating investment and technology flows and monitoring industrial development in the liberalised environment.

The role and functions of DIPP, primarily include: (a) formulation and implementation of industrial policy and strategies for industrial development in conformity with the development needs and national objectives; (b) monitoring the industrial growth, in general, and performance of industries specifically assigned to it, in particular, including advice on all industrial and technical matters; (c) formulation of Foreign Direct Investment (FDI) Policy and promotion, approval and facilitation of FDI; (d) formulation of policies relating to Intellectual Property Rights in patents, trademarks, industrial designs and geographical indications of goods and administration of regulations, rules made there under.

The Department monitors the industrial growth and production, in general, and selected industrial sectors, such as cement, paper and pulp, leather, tyre and rubber, light electrical industries, consumer goods, consumer durables, light machine tools, light industrial machinery, light engineering industries etc., in particular. Appropriate interventions are made on the basis of policy inputs generated by monitoring and periodic review of the industrial sector. The Department studies, assesses and forecasts the need for technological development in specific industrial sectors. On this basis, it plans for modernization and technological upgradation of the Indian industry so that, it keeps pace with the international developments in industrial technology on a continuing basis.

In tune with its role as a facilitator of industrial development and investment, the Department plays an active role in investment promotion through dissemination of information on investment climate and opportunities in the country and by advising prospective investors about licensing policy and procedures, foreign collaboration and import of capital goods, etc. The Department is also responsible for Intellectual Property Rights relating to patents, designs, trade marks and Geographical indication of goods and oversees the initiative relating to their promotion and protection.

International cooperation for industrial partnerships is achieved through both bilateral and multilateral arrangements. At bilateral level, in addition to being nodal Department for Indo-Swedish, Indo-Libyan, Indo-Hungarian and Indo-Belarus Joint Commissions, the Department is represented on joint commissions and joint working groups with select countries. Similar initiative is also in place with the European Union.

The Department administers the central legislations: The Explosives Act, 1884, and the Inflammable Substances Act, 1952; the Salt Cess Act, 1953; the Patents Act, 1970, the Trade and Merchandise Marks Act, 1958 and the Designs Act, 2000 and their associated rules, and the Boilers Act, 1923.

Relevant Website : www.dipp.nic.in

Industrial policy of the government seeks to maintain a sustained growth in productivity;to enhance gainful employment;to achieve optimal utilisation of human resources; to attain international competitiveness; and to transform India into a major partner and player in the global arena. Specific steps were taken to boost it further. Industrial licensing has been abolished for most of the industries except for those related to security, strategic and environmental concerns.These are (i) electronic aerospace and defence equipment; (ii) industrial explosives including detonating fuses, safety fuses, gunpowder, cellulose and matches; (iii) specified hazardous chemicals i.e., hydrocyanic acid and its derivatives; phosgene and its derivatives and isocyanates and disocyanates of hydrocarbon, not elsewhere specified (example methyl isocyanate); and (iv) cigars and cigarettes of tobacco and manufactured tobacco substitutes.

Subsequent to the notification of Arms Rules, 2016 "items configured for Military use" are under the purview of Ministry of Home Affairs. Department of Industrial Policy and Promotion (DIPP) has been delegated power for grant of manufacturing license in respect of the category of arms and ammunition and defence items. Presently no item is reserved for exclusive manufacture by MSE Sector. The number of industries reserved for public sector has also been reduced. At present, only atomic energy and railway operations other than construction, operation and maintenance sectors are reserved for public sector. Industries not covered under compulsory licencing and not reserved for public sector are required to file an Industrial Entrepreneurs' Memorandum (IEM) with the Secretariat for Industrial Assistance (SIA), DIPP. There is a paradigm shift in procedural changes, since 2014. A number of initiatives line National Manufacturing Policy, Make in India, Ease of Doing Business and National Intellectual Property Rights policy, etc. have been put in place.

National Manufacturing Policy

In order to bring about a quantitative and qualitative change and to provide necessary impetus to the manufacturing sector, the National Manufacturing Policy (NMP) was notified with the objective of enhancing the share of manufacturing in GDP to 25 per cent and creating 100 million jobs over a decade or so. The Policy is based on the principle of industrial growth in partnership with the states. The policy envisages that central government will create the enabling policy frame work, provide incentives for infrastructure development on a Public Private Partnership (PPP) basis through appropriate financing instruments, and state governments will be encouraged to adopt the instrumentalities provided in it.

National Investment and Manufacturing Zones (NIMZs) are an important instrumentality of the Policy. These zones have been conceived as large integrated industrial townships with state-of-the-art infrastructure; land use on the basis of zoning; clean and energy efficient technology; necessary social infrastructure; skill development facilities, etc., to provide a conducive environment for manufacturing industries.

Manufacturing Clusters

The objective of the National Plan for Manufacturing Clusters is to bring about convergence in the multiple models of development of industrial clusters by the central and state governments so as to affect better cost efficiency and optimal utilization of resources. Following this DIPP has developed Industrial Information System (URL:www.ncog.gov.in/IIS), a web-portal to capture information of all industrial clusters/zones/nodes/parks in existence and those which are in pipeline. The system has been developed in Open Source Software on the GIS layers developed by BISAG.

Foreign Direct Investment Policy

DIPP is the nodal department for formulation of the policy on Foreign Direct Investment (FDI). It is also responsible for maintenance and management of data on inward FDI into India based on the remittances reported by the Reserve Bank of India. With a view to attract higher levels of FDI, a liberal policy has been put in place on FDI under which FDI up to 100 per cent is permitted under the automatic route in most sectors/ activities. Significant changes have been made in the policy regime in recent times to ensure that India remains an increasingly attractive investment destination.

After abolition of the Foreign Investment Promotion Board (FIPB), process for granting FDI approvals has been simplified wherein the work relating to processing of applications for FDI and approval of the government thereon under the extant FDI Policy and FEMA is now handled by the concerned ministries/departments. However, DIPP is a single point interface of the government to facilitate investors for FDI through approval route. In this regard, a new portal (http://www.fifp.gov.in) has been created which is administered by this Department to facilitate clearance of applications which are through approval route. DIPP is the nodal department for approvals in case of single brand retail trading, multi brand retail trading, food product retail trading, non-resident Indian/export oriented units investments. Cases partaining to issue of shares against capital goods/ machinary/pre-operative and pre-incorporation expenses are also processed by DIPP.

Investment Promotion

The Department plays an active role in investment promotion and facilitation through dissemination of information on investment climate and opportunities within the country and by advising prospective investors about investment policies and procedures and opportunities. International co-operation for industrial partnerships is solicited through both bilateral and multilateral arrangements. It also coordinates with apex industry associations like Invest India (National Investment Promotion and Facilitation Agency), Federation of Indian Chambers of Commerce and Industry (FICCI), Confederation of Indian industry (CII), Associated Chambers of Commerce and Industry (ASSOCHAM), etc., in activities relating to promotion of industrial cooperation, both through bilateral and multilateral initiatives, intended to stimulate the flow of foreign direct investment into India.

Ease of Doing Business

In order to improve the business environment in the country, DIPP has taken up a series of measures to simplify and rationalize the regulatory processes (registration and inspection processes) and introduction of information technology as enabler to make governance more efficient and effective. States too have been brought on board in the process to expand the coverage of these efforts. DIPP has been closely working with the state governments and union territory administrations to help them identify constraints in doing business and improving the overall business environment. It launched an online portal to track implementation of reforms on a real-time basis. The same is available on www.eodb.dipp.gov.in.

India ranks 100th in the World Bank's annual Doing Business Report (DBR), 2018 as against 130th rank in DBR, 2017. The ease of doing business index is meant to measure regulations directly affecting businesses and a nation's rank is based on the average of 10 indicators viz., starting a business, dealing with construction permits, getting electricity, registering property, getting credit, protecting minority investors, paying taxes, trading across borders, enforcing contracts and resolving insolvency.

Make in India

The 'Make in India' initiative was launched in 2014 with the objective of facilitating investment, fostering innovation, building best in class manufacturing infrastructure, making it easy to do business and enhancing skill development. Action Plans for 21 key sectors were identified for specific actions under (i) policy initiatives (ii) fiscal incentives (iii) infrastructure creation (iv) ease of doing business (iv) innovation and R&D (vi) skill development areas.

Invest India

Invest India has been set up as a joint venture (not for profit) company between Department of Industrial Policy and Promotion, Federation of Indian Chambers of Commerce & Industry (FICCI), CII, NASSCOM and various state governments. Invest India is the National Investment Promotion and Facilitation

Agency of India and acts as the first point of reference for investors. It is transforming the country's investment climate by simplifying the business environment for investors. Its experts, specializing across different countries, states and sectors, handhold investors through their investment lifecycle – from pre-investment to after-care. This venture provides multiple forms of support such as market entry strategies, deep dive industry analysis, partner search and location assessment policy advocacy with decision makers.

Startup India

Taking into account the long gestation period to establish and operate, DIPP modified the Startup definition. Accordingly, an entity shall be considered as a Startup up to seven years from the date of its incorporation/ registration. However, in the case of Startups in the biotechnology sector, the period shall be up to ten years from the date of incorporation/registration. This will also ensure consistency with the recent enhancement of tax exemption to Startups in the Budget. In order to promote entrepreneurship in the country, the definition of a Startup has also been broadened to include scalability of business model along with high potential of employment generation or wealth creation. To further simplify the process of recognition of a Startup, the requirement of letter of recommendation from an incubator/industry association has also been done away with both for the purpose of recognition as well as availing certificate of eligibility for obtaining tax benefits.

Fund of Funds

For providing fund support for Startups, Government created a 'Fund of Funds for Startups (FFS)' at Small Industries Development Bank of India (SIDBI) with a corpus of ₹ 10,000 crore. The FFS shall contribute to the corpus of Alternate Investment funds (AIFs) for investing in equity and equity linked instruments of various Startups.

Relaxed Norms in Public Procurement

Provision has been introduced in the procurement policy of Ministry of Micro, Small and Medium Enterprises to relax norms pertaining to prior experience/turnover for micro and small enterprises.

Tax Incentives

Income Tax exemption provided to eligible startups for any 3 consecutive assessment years out of 7 years are extended from 3 to 5 years as provisioned earlier. To avail these benefits, a Startup must get a Certificate of Eligibility from the Inter-Ministerial Board (IMB).

Fast-tracking Patent Examination

A Scheme for Startups IPR Protection (SIPP) for facilitating fast track filing of patents, trademarks and designs by Startups has been introduced. It provides for expedited examination of patents filed. This will reduce the time taken in getting patents. The fee for filing of patents for Startups has also been reduced up to 80 per cent.

Self-Certification based Compliance Regime

Compliance norms relating to environmental and labour laws have been eased in order to reduce the regulatory burden on Startups thereby allowing them to focus on their core business and keep compliance costs low. Ministry of Environment, Forest & Climate Change (MoEF&CC) has published a list of 36 white category industries. Startups falling under the 'White category' would be able to self-certify compliance.

Research Parks

Research Parks are being established at IIT Guwahati, Hyderabad, Kanpur, Kharagpur, IISc Bangalore, Gandhinagar, Delhi and Bombay to propel successful innovation through incubation and joint R&D efforts between academia and industry.

Promoting Startups in Biotechnology

With the aim to foster and facilitate bio-entrepreneurship, Bio-clusters, Bio-Incubators, Technology Transfer Offices (TTOs) and Bio-Connect offices are being established in research institutes and universities across India. Seed fund and Equity Funding support is also provided to bio-tech Startups under the initiative.

Mobile App and Startup India Portal

Startup India web portal and mobile app has been developed and operationalized since 2016.

Startup India Hub

Startup India Hub was operationalized in 2016 to resolve queries and handhold Startups. A digital extension to Startup India Hub, an intelligent online hub was operationalized in 2017 which will serve as a platform where all the stakeholders of the Startup ecosystem can collaborate and synergise their efforts. It will facilitate location-wise and sectoral mapping.

Intellectual Property Rights

DIPP is entrusted with the responsibility of formulation of policy in respect of Intellectual Property Rights (IPRs) i.e., patents, designs, trade marks and geographical indication of goods. The Department administers Intellectual Properly Rights (IPRs) Legislations, namely, the Patents Act, 1970, Designs Act, 2000, Trade Marks Act, 1999, Geographical Indications fo Goods (Registration and Protection) Act, 1999, Copyright Act, 1957 (as amended in 2012) and Semi-conductor Integrated Circuits Layout-Design Act, 2000. It also administers establishment matters in respect of the Intellectual Property Appellate Board (IPAB). DIPP undertakes bilateral and multilateral cooperation activities in respect of Intellectual Property Right matters on behalf of the government. It is the nodal department for all matters relating to the World Intellectual Property Organization(WIPO).

Productivity and Quality

DIPP is the nodal department for the promotion of productivity and quality in the industrial sector. The National Productivity Council (NPC) represents India in the Tokyo based Asian Productivity Organization (APO), of which India is a founder member. NPC undertakes productivity augmentation through domain specific consultancy, training, workshops, seminars and conferences to government, public and private sectors, productivity related research, monitoring and evaluation of various government schemes and projects and information dissemination through collaboration with APO.

The Quality Council of India, another autonomous body under this Department, promotes adoption of quality standards relating to Quality Management Systems (ISO 9001 Series), Environment Management Systems (ISO 14001 Series), Food Safety Management Systems (ISO 22000 Series), Product certification and inspection bodies through the accreditation services provided by National Accreditation Board for Certification Bodies (NABCB). Besides NABCB, there are four other boards viz., National Accreditation Board for Education and Training (NABET); National Accreditation Board for Hospitals and Healthcare Providers (NABH); National Accreditation Board for Testing and calibration Laboratories (NABL); and National Board for Quality Promotion (NBQP) which provide accreditation certification on education, health and quality promotion respectively.

Industrial / Economic Corridors

Development of industrial/economic corridors is a very important policy initiative for boosting industrial development, income and employment.

Delhi-Mumbai Industrial Corridor

The Delhi-Mumbai Industrial Corridor (DMIC) project was launched in pursuance of an MoU signed between the Government of India and the Government of Japan in 2006. The DMIC is being developed on either side, along the alignment of the 1504 km long Western Dedicated Rail Freight Corridor between Dadri (UP) and Jawaharlal Nehru Port Trust (JNPT), Navi Mumbai.

Chennai-Bengaluru Industrial Corridor

The Chennai-Bengaluru Industrial Corridor (CBIC) proposes to address the infrastructure bottlenecks through a holistic approach while benefiting from the inherent strengths and competitiveness of each of the CBIC states.

Bengaluru-Mumbai Economic Corridor

The Bengaluru-Mumbai Economic Corridor (BMEC) is intended to facilitate development of a well-planned and resource-efficient industrial base served by world-class sustainable connectivity infrastructure, bringing significant benefits in terms of innovation, manufacturing, job creation and resource security to the two states.

Amritsar-Kolkata Industrial Corridor

In order to give a boost to industrial development in the densely populated states of northern and eastern India, the government is to commence work on creating an Amritsar-Kolkata Industrial Corridor (AKIC). This will be structured around the Eastern Dedicated Freight Corridor (EDFC) as the backbone and also the highway system that exists in this route.

Vizag-Chennai Industrial Corridor

The Visakhapatnam-Chennai Industrial Corridor (VCIC) is a key part of the east Coast Economic Corridor (ECEC), India's first coastal corridor. VCIC is aligned with the Golden Quadrilateral and is poised to play a critical role in driving India's Act East Policy.

National Industrial Corridor Development and Implementation Trust

In view of the success and importance of DMIC project, four more industrial corridors were assurance namely Amritsar - Kolkata Industrial Corridor (AKIC) Bengaluru - Mumbai Economic Corridor (BMEC), Chennai - Bengaluru Industrial Corridor (CBIC) and East Coast Economic corridor with Vizag - Chennai industrial corridor (VCIC) as the initial phase of development. It has been expanded and re-designated as National Industrial Corridor Development and Implementation Trust (NICDIT).

Modified Industrial Infrastructure Upgradation Scheme

Industrial Infrastructure Upgradation Scheme (IIUS) was launched in 2003 with the objective of enhancing industrial competitiveness of domestic industry by providing quality infrastructure through public private partnership in selected functional clusters/locations which have potential to become globally competitive. Modified Industrial Infrastructure Upgradation Scheme (MIIUS) was notified in July 2013. Under MIIUS, projects have been undertaken to upgrade infrastructure in existing industrial parks/ estates/ areas. Greenfield projects can also be undertaken in backward areas and North Eastern Region (NER) under the scheme.

Industrial Performance

The Index of Industrial Production (IIP), measuring industrial performance monitors production in manufacturing, mining and electricity sectors and also to use-based group such as primary, capital, intermediate, infrastructure/ construction goods, consumer durables and consumer non-durables. Central Statistics Office, Ministry of Statistics and Programme Implementation revised the base year of IIP in 2017. The latest series with base year 2011-12 is more representative of the current structure and composition of the industrial sector. As per the new base year, IIP registered growth rate of 4.6 per cent on account of growth in electricity generation, mining and manufacturing.

Performance of Industry

Government has taken numerous steps to boost industrial development, capital formation and employment generation in the country. These, inter-alia, include, 'Make in India', 'Startup India' initiatives and 'Ease of Doing Business'. Steps taken to improve ease of doing business include simplification and rationalization of existing rules and introduction of information technology, setting up of an investor facilitation cell, launch of e-biz portal and liberalizing (FDI) policy and procedures have been simplified and liberalized progressively. Government has taken up a programme of building pentagon of industrial corridors across the country with an objective to provide developed land and quality infrastructure for development of industrial townships.

Performance of Eight Core Industries

The Index of Eight Core Industries (ICI) monitors production of eight core industries i.e., coal, crude oil, natural gas, refinery products, fertilizers, steel, cement and electricity every month. In line with the base year change in IIP, the Office of the Economic Adviser, Department of Industrial Policy and Promotion, revised the base year of Index of Eight Core Industries to 2011-12. These eight industries have combined weight of around 40.27 per cent in Index of Industrial Production (IIP).

Leather Industry

Leather industry plays an important role in the Indian economy in view of its substantial overall output, export earnings and employment potential. The export of leather and leather products from the country has undergone a structural change in the last two decades, share of leather footwear, leather garments, leather goods, and several articles of leather in the total exports has increased substantially as a result of government's policy to encourage export of value added leather products.

Indian Leather Development Programme

Indian Leather Development Programme (ILDP) aims at augmenting raw material base through modernization and technology upgradation of leather units, addressing environmental concerns, human resource development, supporting traditional leather artisans, addressing infrastructure constraints and establishing institutional facilities.

Cement Industry: Cement is one of the most technologically advanced industries in the country. The industry plays a crucial role in the development of housing and infrastructure sector of the economy. Price and distribution control of cement has been removed since 1989 and cement industry was de-licensed in 1991 under Industrial (Development & Regulation) Act, 1951. Since then, this industry has progressed well both in capacity/production and as well as in process technology. India is producing, different varieties of cement like Ordinary Portland Cement (OPC), Portland Pozzolana Cement

(PPC), Portland Blast Furnace Slag Cement (PBFS), Oil Well Cement, White Cement, etc. These different varieties of cement are produced as per Bureau of Indian Standard (BIS) specifications and its quality is comparable with the best in the world. Cement cannot be sold in the country without BIS mark. Indian cement industry has managed to keep pace with global technological advancement. Induction of advanced technology has helped industry immensely to improve its efficiency by conserving energy, fuel and addressing environmental concerns. India is the second largest manufacturer of cement after China in the world.

Ceramic Industry: The Ceramic industry is about 50 years old. It comprises ceramic tiles, sanitary-ware and crockery. Ceramic products are manufactured both in the large and small-scale sector with wide variation in type, size, quality and standard by the national and regional players. India continues to rank No.3 in terms of production and consumption of tiles in the world after China and Brazil. The industry gives direct and indirect employment to over 2 lakh people. With the majority of raw materials necessary for the production of tiles available in the country, the Indian tile industry has kept pace with the times embracing modern technology in designing and manufacturing and is capable of producing world class tiles.

Tyre & Tubes Industry: Tyres play an integral role to ensure mobility including movement of passengers and essential goods across the urban and rural landscape of the country using all types of vehicles ranging from carts, tractors, trucks and buses to the latest generation passenger cars that ply on the modern expressways. All types of tyres required to meet the domestic demand are manufactured in India. These tyres include moped tyre weighing 1.5 kg to off the road tyres for earthmovers which weigh 1.5 tonnes, bias ply tyres to rugged all steel radial truck tyres to high performance passenger car radial and tubeless tyres etc. India is one of the few countries worldwide which has attained self-sufficiency in manufacturing a wide range of tyres for all applications. With the objective of ensuring the safety of human lives and vehicles and also availability of quality products, a Quality (Control) Order for Pneumatic Tyres and Tubes for Automotive Vehicles was notified by the Department in 2009. This prohibits import, sale or distribution of pneumatic tyres and tubes which do not conform to the specified Bureau of Indian Standard and which do not bear the standard mark. Indian Tyre industry consists of 39 companies with 60 tyre manufacturing plants. The large tyre companies are namely, MRF Ltd., Apollo Tyres, JK Tyres, CEAT, Goodyear, Modi Rubber, etc. Three Indian companies (MRF Ltd., Apollo Tyres and J K Tyres) are in the list of top 25 Global Tyre companies.

Rubber Goods Industry: The rubber goods industry excluding tyre and tubes consists of 4550 small and tiny units generating about 5.50 lakhs direct jobs. The rubber industry manufactures a wide range of products like rubber cots and aprons, contraceptives, footwear, rubber hoses, cables, camelback, battery boxes, latex products, conveyor belts, surgical gloves, balloons, rubber moulded goods, etc. The main raw materials used by the rubber goods manufacturing industry are natural rubber, various types of synthetic rubber, carbon black, rubber chemicals, etc.

Cigarette Industry: The cigarette industry is an agro-based labour intensive industry. Cigarette included in the First Schedule to the Industries (Development & Regulations) Act, 1951 requires industrial license.

Paints & Allied Products: The paints and allied Industry which has been exempted from compulsory licensing, mainly consists of paints, enamels, varnishes, pigments, printing inks, etc. These play a vital role in the economy by way of protecting national assets from corrosion. These items are manufactured both in the organized and small scale sector.

Glass Industry: Glass industry comes under the category of delicensed. It covers seven items such as flat glass (including sheet, float, figured, wired, safety, mirror glass), glass fiber and glass wool, hollow glassware, laboratory glassware, table and kitchen glassware, glass bangles and other glassware. There has been growing acceptability of the Indian flat glass products in the global market. The Indian manufacturers had explored new markets. There is considerable scope in demand for glass fibre products particularly due to growth in petrochemical sector and allied products.

Paper Industry: India rules as one of the fastest growing paper market in the world. The growing knowledge base coupled with synergistic contributions from flagship schemes, namely, Sarva Shiksha Abhiyan, (SSA) Rashtriya Madhyamik Shiksha Abhiyan (RMSA), Inclusive Education for the Disabled at Secondary School (IEDSS), adult education, Right to Education and central government scholarship and education loan scheme, assured a robust demand for paper and paper board. The industry was de-licenced in July, 1997. As per the the present policy, FDI up to 100 per cent is allowed on the automatic route for the pulp and paper sector. There are around 850 units which manufacture pulp, paper, paper board and newsprint with an installed capacity of nearly 25 million tonnes out of which 3.5 million tonnes are lying idle. The per capita consumption of paper in India is about 13 kg, which is much lower than world average (58 kg). The Indian paper industry is in a fragmented structure, consisting of small, medium and large paper mills having capacity ranging from 05 to 1500 tonnes per day. These units use wood and agro residues as well as recovered paper as raw material.

Paper & Paperboard Segment: Indigenous paper and paper board segment produces all the main varieties of paper that are in demand in the market viz., writing and printing (38 per cent), packaging grade paper (53 per cent), newsprint (8 per cent) and speciality paper. However, certain speciality paper such as coated paper, security papers and cheque paper, etc., are being imported in the country.

Newsprint: The newsprint sector in the country is governed by the Newsprint Control Order (NCO), 2004. The mills listed under the schedule of this order are exempt from excise duty, subject to actual user condition. At present, there are 124 mills registered under the Schedule to the NCO. However, only 35 are producing newsprint making the operating installed capacity 0.99 million tonnes per annum. 23 mills have closed operations since being listed in the NCO and 89 mills have discontinued the production of newsprint. Nearly half of the newsprint demand in the country is met by imports.

Salt Industry: India continues to hold third position in the production of salt in the world after China and USA with annual production of 260 lakh tonnes and second largest producer of iodized salt, next to China. From an era of shortfall and import at the time of independence, the country has made spectacular progress due to pragmatic policies in short time, sufficiency was achieved (1953) and made a dent in the export market. Since then the country has never looked back.

Explosives: There are 74 factories, in the medium and small scale sector, engaged in the production of explosives. Site Mixed Explosives (SME) has a consolidated licensed capacity of 1656555.5 MT of explosives production.

Light Electrical Industry Sector: The light electrical industry is a diverse sector having a number of distinct products and sub-products. It includes goods like electrical wires and cables, transmission tower, cranes, lifts and escalators, refrigerators, washing machine, air conditioners, storage batteries, dry cell batteries, electrical lamps and tubes etc.

Electrical Wires and Cables: Electrical wires and cable industry is one of the earliest industries established in the country. A wide range of wires and cables are manufactured in the country which includes communication cables such as jelly filled telephone cables, optic fibre cables, local area network cables, switchboard cables, co-axial cables, VSAT cables, electrical cables such as electrical wires, winding wires, automotive/battery cables, UPS cables, flexible wires, low voltage power cables and EHT power cables.

Transmission Towers: Transmission towers support high voltage transmission lines which carry electricity over long distance. These lines typically feed into sub-station so that the electrical voltage can be reduced to a level that can subsequently be used by the customers. There is an increasing trend in India to have larger power stations, particularly mega and ultra-mega power projects. Consequently while there would be fewer but larger power generating stations, the demand for transmission of energy would grow substantially.

Cranes: Cranes and hoists are an important category of material handling equipment required by almost all sectors across the industry. Wide range of cranes are manufactured in the country and these include Electric Overhead Travelling (EOT) cranes, mobile cranes, ladle cranes, hydraulic decks, crab cranes, floating cranes, controller cranes, etc. There is a good potential for growth of this sector in view of increased industrial activities in various fields as well as construction industry.

Lifts and Escalators: The use of lifts and escalators is increasing rapidly due to substantial investments in construction of multi-storied housing complexes, large malls and supermarkets of international standards, modernization of airports and railway stations apart from industrial sectors. A wide range of lifts and escalators are manufactured in India. These include single speed, double speed, gearless, hydraulic, servo and Variable Voltage Variable Frequency (VVVF) elevators.

Refrigerators: In India, refrigerators have the highest aspiration value of all consumer durables with the exception of television. The refrigerator industry has become highly competitive. A number of brands have entered the market and the consumers have wider choices. There are two basic designs adopted in refrigerators presently being manufactured in the country. These are commonly referred to as Direct Cool (DC) and Frost Free (FF). There has been gradual consumer preference shift towards frost free segment. Increasing number of dual income households are shifting the demand from the conventional 180L refrigerators to the larger 220L and higher capacity refrigerators with double doors.

Washing Machines: The washing machine market in the country can be divided into semi-automatic and fully-automatic. With rising incomes and higher aspirations, there is a gradual shift towards higher capacity and fully-automatic washing machines. Controls are changing from purely mechanical to fully electronic as microcontrollers are incorporated into the designs. While providing intelligence, microcontrollers boost reliability, drive down costs and improve energy efficiency.

Air Conditioners: Air Conditioners (AC) are gradually being treated as a necessity in changed socio-economic environment with changing life style. The air-conditioners' market can be classified into three segments: window AC, split AC and central AC. The split ACs are gaining popularity due to limitation of space and increase in number of people living in flats in multi-storied complexes and also because of less noise. Bureau of Energy Efficiency (BEE), a statutory body under the Ministry of Power has introduced energy efficiency based star rating for air conditioners to help consumers buy the best energy efficient products.

Lead Acid Storage Batteries: Lead acid batteries are accumulators of current and power which is discharged over a period of time. They are used in vehicles and also for various industrial uses such as for backup power for UPS application, control rooms, power stations, telecommunications, etc. In addition, it is also used for emergency lights for houses, telephone systems and as power source for mining, etc. A new application of lead acid batteries has emerged today in electric vehicles. The average life of the battery is approximately 2 years, hence these batteries will be needed as replacement throughout the life of the vehicle or the machinery in use. Although there are few large scale manufacturers of the product in India, there are large numbers of very small scale units manufacturing the product in a most unorganized manner. The product manufactured by them normally does not meet the required standards as specified by BIS. In order to ensure safe disposal of lead acid batteries, Ministry of Environment and forest has issued a notification Batteries (Management and Handling) Rules, 2001 under Environment (Protection) Act, 1986.

Dry Cell Batteries: Dry cell batteries are one of the most commonly used items. These are the oldest type of batteries which are still being used. Performance of dry cell batteries has undergone progressive improvements through technological developments. New types of dry cell batteries with longer shelf life and greater dependability and also rechargeable cells have come up. Nickel cadmium batteries and other rechargeable batteries are manufactured in the country to meet the requirement of defence, telecommunications and electronics. The growing popularity of cellular phones, laptops and imported toys could open the market for a new range of batteries that are not produced at present.

Electrical Lamps and Tubes: Wide range of lamps and tubes are being manufactured in the country which include general lighting service lamps such as incandescent bulbs, halogen lamps, gas discharge lamps such as fluorescent tube light, compact fluorescent lamp, high pressure mercury vapour lamps, metal halide lamps, low pressure and high pressure sodium vapour lamps and variety of special lamps. The higher energy cost have led to the development of energy efficient lamps consuming less power and giving output as close to daylight. Compact Fluorescent Lamps (CFL) which consume about 20 per cent of the electricity for the same light output and last up to 8 times longer than the GLS are getting more popular. LEDs have a great potential to provide highly efficient lighting with little environmental pollution in comparison to the incandescent lamps (ICLs) and fluorescent lamps (FTLs, CFLs). Penetration of LEDs in India could significantly reduce lighting load as almost 22-25 per cent of electricity is consumed for lighting, which is also a major contributing factor of peak demand. Due to higher costs, LEDs are not very popular even though its production has started in the country.

Light Engineering Industry Sector: The light Engineering Industry is a diverse industry with the number of distinct sectors. This industry includes mother of all industries like castings and forgings to the highly sophisticated micro-processor based process control equipment and diagnostic medical instruments. This group also includes industries like bearings, steel pipes and tubes, fasteners, etc. The products covered under the engineering industry are largely used as input to the capital goods industry. Hence the demand of this sector in general depends on the demand of the capital goods industry.

Roller Bearing Industry: Roller bearings are essential components in the rotating parts of virtually all machines such as automobiles, electric motors, diesel engines, industrial machinery and machine tools, etc. Bearings are used in diversified fields. Hence, the product range is vast and diversified. The indigenous manufacturers are manufacturing bearings of quality and precision at par with world renowned manufacturers in the diversified range of general purpose where the demand is large to justify indigenous production on economic consideration. Bearings, generally used for special applications that require high technology are still being imported. There is a considerable scope for development of bearings of smaller size and lighter weight with improved performance in harsh operating conditions like high or low temperature.

Ferrous Castings: Ferrous castings are pivotal to the growth and development of engineering industries since these constitute essential intermediates for automobiles, industrial machinery, power plants, chemical and fertilizer plants. Indian foundry industry is the third largest in the world. This industry is now well established in the country and is spread across a wide spectrum consisting of large, medium, small and tiny sector. The salient feature of the foundry industry is its geographical clustering. Typically, each foundry cluster is known for catering to some specific end use markets. For example, the Coimbatore cluster is famous for pump sets castings, the Kolhapur and Belgaum for automotive castings, Rajkot cluster for diesel engine castings and Batala and Jalandhar for machinery parts and agricultural implements.

Process Control Instrument Industry: Process control instruments cover wide range of instruments and systems required for monitoring and measurement of physical, chemical and biological properties. They are used for measurement and control of process variables like pressure, temperature, humidity, liquid level, flow, specific gravity, chemical composition including pH and many forms of spectrometry and spectrophotometry. The process control instruments have become an integral part of the modern industrial activity. This industry is a key industry which provides tools for automation. Their importance is significant in high cost, large and sophisticated process industries like fertilizer, steel, power plant, refineries, petrochemicals, cement and other process industries. The present technology is a microprocessor based centralised control system.

Seamless Steel Pipes and Tubes: Seamless steel pipes and tubes are produced in different sizes. The wide size range makes them suitable for use in number of versatile area of application. The process of manufacture imparts strength and durability to the pipes and thus can be used for corrosion - resisting applications. These pipes are also used for aircraft, missile and anti-friction bearing, ordnance, etc. Ultra-high strength and corrosion-resistant properties make these perfect for oil and gas industry, chemical industry and automobile industry. Oil sector accounts for around 60 per cent of the total requirement of seamless pipes. Bearings and boiler sector contribute around 30 per cent of demand. The industry is able to manufacture tubes up to 14" outer diameter.

Electrical Resistance Welded (ERW) Steel Pipes and Tubes: Based on the customers' requirement, ERW steel pipes and tubes are available in various qualities, wall thickness and diameters of the finished pipes. High performance ERW steel pipes and tubes possess high corrosion resistance, high deformability, high strength and high toughness. These pipes are used in fencing, lining pipes, oil country tubulars, scaffolding, water and gas conveyance, etc. There has been tremendous increase in the production of ERW steel pipes due to higher demand in oil and gas industry, infrastructure and automobile uses. There are a large number of units in the MSME Sector.

Submerged-Arc Welded (SAW) Pipes: There are two types of SAW pipes namely longitudinal and helical welded SAW pipes. Longitudinal SAW pipes are preferred where thickness of pipe is more than 25mm and in high pressure gas pipe line. Helical welded SAW pipes are used for low pressure applications. The cost of helical SAW pipes is less than longitudinal pipes. There is huge demand of SAW pipes in the country due to transportation of oil and gas and transmission of water.

Industrial Fasteners: The fastener industry in India may be classified into two segments: high tensile and mild steel fasteners. These broadly include nuts, bolts, studs, rivets and screws. Mild steel fasteners are primarily manufactured by the unorganized sector while high tensile fasteners requiring superior technology are dominated by companies in the organized sector. Automobile industry accounts for bulk of the total demand of this industry. Consumer durables and railways are the other primary users of the high tensile fasteners. Automobile sector is likely to drive growth in the fastener industry.

Steel Forgings: Forgings are intermediate products used widely by original equipment manufacturers in the production of durable goods. The composition of the Indian forging industry can be categorized into four sectors - large, medium, small and tiny. A major portion of this industry is made up of small and medium units/enterprises (SMEs). The industry was previously labour intensive but with increasing globalization it is becoming more capital intensive. Among the industries that depend on forgings are automotive; agricultural machinery and equipment; valves, fittings, and petrochemical applications; hand tools and hardware; off-highway and railroad equipment; general industrial equipment; ordnance, marine and aerospace. The key driver of demand of forging is the automobile industry. About 65 per cent of the total forging production is used in this sector.

Bicycle Industry: The bicycle industry of India is one of the most established industries. India is the second largest bicycle producer of the world, next only to China. Most of the manufacturing units are located in Punjab and Tamil Nadu with Ludhiana (Punjab) being a major bicycle production hub. The industry is making an endeavour for enhancing export since there is a significant scope for export of bicycles, bicycle spare parts and bicycle accessories. Bicycle companies are now focusing on urban markets and are looking to expand their base in the professional and adventure categories.

Food Processing Machinery: The Indian market for food processing machinery has been growing steadily fuelled by strong domestic demand for processed food and beverage products spurred by increase in income level, increasing number of women joining the work force, rapid urbanization, changing life style and mass media promotion. The most promising areas of growth are fruit and vegetable processing, meat, poultry, dairy and seafood, packaged/convenience food, soft drinks and grain processing. Food processing sector is expected to grow at a healthy pace considering the rapid changes in food habits and consumerist culture developing in the country. The machinery manufacturers have honed their expertise in manufacturing dairy machinery and other core equipment of food processing machinery.

Packaging Machinery Industry: Packaging of consumer products or industrial products is emerging as the USP in the marketing strategies. Developments in packaging technology have not only contributed to improving the aesthetic appeal of the products but also the shelf life. In some cases specialized packaging becomes a technical necessity. Considering the growth prospects in industrial sector and growing consumer awareness of packaging, it is expected that there would be substantial growth in this area. There is a wide range of packaging machinery available in the country covering packaging of vast range of items. Some of the commonly available packing machinery includes machines for coding and on-line printing machines, feeding and labeling machines, strip packaging, form fill and seal machines, carton filling, fully automatic bag making machinery and automatic microprocessor controlled packaging machines.

Water Pollution Control Equipment: Due to growing awareness regarding water pollution and stringent environmental control standards being enforced for various uses including process industries, the water/waste water treatment industry is poised for huge growth. The various categories of water pollution control equipment broadly include waste water treatment plants, drinking water treatment plants and effluent treatment plants. Water/waste water treatment is the process of removing contaminants and it includes physical, chemical and biological processes to remove physical, chemical and biological contaminants. The primary treatment is the first step in the treatment process and involves the removal of pollutants that settles or floats. The common industrial equipments are clarifiers and oil - water separator devices. The secondary treatment is designed to substantially degrade the biological content of the sewage. The common equipments are activated sludge, filters, biological reactors etc. The tertiary treatment is a polishing step to remove contaminants that missed in the primary and secondary treatment and removal of suspended solids, refractory organics and toxic components. Tertiary physical processes are filtration and carbon absorption. Chemical process includes precipitation, oxidation and neutralization. The biological processes involve biodegrading. Organisms such as bacteria, fungi, yeasts and algae are commonly used to break down the organic matters. The cell tissues are then removed from the treated water by physical method.

Air Pollution Control Equipment: Industrialization and urbanization have resulted in a profound deterioration of India's air quality. India's most severe environmental problem, come in several forms, including vehicular emissions and untreated industrial smoke. Air pollution, especially in metropolitan cities and large towns has assumed great significance with the adoption of stringent environmental control standards for various industries. Hence the pollution control equipment industry has acquired importance. Further judicial pronouncements have given a definite direction and urgency for adoption of air pollution control measures. The choice of control method depends on factors such as the nature of pollutant, flow-rate (amount of pollutant emitted), particle size and desired collection efficiency. The air pollution control equipments are broadly classified under the categories such as settling chambers, cyclone and multi -cyclones, bag filters, wet scrubbers, spray tower, venturi scrubber, ionizing scrubber and electrostatic precipitator.

Industrial Gears: Industrial gears comprises mainly gears and gear boxes. Gears are used for two basic purposes: increase or decrease of rotation speed and increase or decrease of power or torque. Gears being an important part of a machine have immense usage within various industries. These industries include automotive industries, coal plants industry, steel plants industry, paper industry, in mining and many more. In these industries they behold a wide area of application. They are used in conveyors, elevators, kilns, separators, cranes and lubrication systems. Gearbox is defined as a metal casing in which a train of gears is sealed. The manufacture of gears and gear boxes involve high precision machining and accurate assembly as mechanical power is to be transmitted noiselessly and with minimum losses. Different types and sizes of gears such as spur gears, helical gears, worm gears, spiral gears and many other kinds are manufactured in the country. The demand for gears and gear boxes predominantly depend on the growth of industrial machinery, machine tools, and consumer and automobile sector. Considering the industrial growth prospects, particularly in automobile sector, the demand for gears and gear boxes is expected to grow at a healthy pace.

Wood-based Industry: Plywood, veneers of all kinds and other wood based products such as particle board, medium density fibre board, etc., form the major segment of this industry in India. The industry comes under the delicenced category.

Watch Industry: The watch industry in the country comprises units both in the organized as well as the small scale sector. The organized sector contributes 40 per cent of the total demand while the rest is met by the unorganized sector. Most of the watches are being manufactured under the electronic system.

Central Public Sector Enterprises

The Ministry of Heavy Industries and Public Enterprises, comprising the Department of Heavy Industry and the Department of Public Enterprises, functions under the charge of Cabinet Minister (Heavy Industries and Public Enterprises). There is a Minister of State for Heavy Industries and Public Enterprises. The Ministry promotes the development and growth of three sectors i.e., capital goods, auto and heavy electrical equipment in the country;

administers 31 Central Public Sector Enterprises (CPSEs); 5 Autonomous Organizations and frames policy guidelines for Central Public Sector Enterprises (CPSEs) and overall administration of CPSEs. In fulfilling its role, the Department coordinates with other ministries, CPSEs and concerned organizations. Some of the important tasks of the Department are listed as follows: coordination of matters of general policy affecting all public sector enterprises; evaluation and monitoring the performance of public sector enterprises, including the Memorandum of Understanding mechanism; matters relating to Permanent Machinery of Arbitration for such enterprises; counselling, training and rehabilitation of employees in CPSUs, rendering advice relating to revival, restructuring or closure of public sector enterprises including the mechanisms; and categorisation of central public sector enterprises including conferring 'Ratna' status.

Relevant Websites : www.dhi.nic.in www.dpe.gov.in

Micro, Small and Medium Enterprises

The Micro, Small and Medium Enterprises (MSME) sector has emerged as a highly vibrant and dynamic sector of the Indian economy over the last five decades. MSMEs not only play crucial role in providing large employment opportunities at comparateively lower capital cost than large industries but also help in industrialization of rural & backward areas, thereby, reducing regional imbalances, assuring more equitable distribution of national income and wealth. MSMEs are complementary to large industries as ancillary units and this sector contributes enormously to the socio-economic development of the country. Ministry of Micro, Small & Medium Entyerprises envisions a vibrant sector by promoting growth and development of the sector, including Khadi, Village and Coir Industries, in cooperation with concerned ministries/ departments, state governments and other stakeholders, through providing support to existing enterprises and encouraging creation of new enterprises.

The Micro, Small and Medium Enterprises Development (MSMED) Act was notified in 2006 to address policy issues affecting MSMEs as well as the coverage and investment ceiling of the sector. The Act provides the first-ever legal framework for recognition of the concept of "enterprise" which comprises both manufacturing and service entities. It defines medium enterprises for the first time and seeks to integrate the three tiers of these enterprises, namely, micro, small and medium. The Act also provides for a statutory consultative mechanism at the national level with balanced representation of all sections of stakeholders, particularly the three classes of enterprises; and with a wide range of advisory function.

In 2007, subsequent to an amendment of the Government of India (Allocation of Business) Rules, 1961, erestwhile Ministry of Small Scale Industries and the Ministry of Agro and Rural Industries were merged to form the Ministry of Micro, Small and Medium Enterprises. This Ministry now designs policies and promotes / facilitates programmes, projects and schemes and monitors their implementation with a view to assisting MSMEs and help them to scale up. The primary responsibility of promotion and development of MSMEs is of the state governments. However, the Government of India, supplements the efforts of the states through various initiatives. The role of the Ministry and its organizations is to assist the states in their efforts to encourage entrepreneurship, employment and livelihood opportunities and enhance the competitiveness of MSMEs in the changed economic scenario.

Relevant Website : www.msme.gov.in

Number of MSMEs

As per the National Sample Survey (NSS) 73rd round, conducted by National Sample Survey Office, in 2015-16, there were 633.88 lakh unincorporated non-agriculture MSMEs, in the country engaged in different economic activities excluding the MSMEs registered under (a) Sections 2 m(i) and 2m(ii) of the Factories Act, 1948, (b) Companies Act, 1956 and (c) Construction activities falling under Section F of National Industrial Classification (NIC) 2008.

Khadi and Village Industries Commission

Khadi and Village Industries Commission (KVIC) established under the Act of Parliament (No. 61 of 1956), and as amended in 1987 and 2006 is a statutory organization under the Ministry of MSME and engaged in promoting and developing Khadi and Village Industries (KVI) for providing employment opportunities in the rural areas, thereby strengthening the rural economy. KVIC has been identified as one of the major organizations in the decentralized sector for generating sustainable non-farm employment opportunities in rural areas at a low per capita investment. KVIC undertakes activities like skill improvement; transfer of technology; research and development; marketing etc. and helps in generating employment/self employment opportunities in rural areas.

Relevant Website : www.kvic.org.in

Coir Board

The Coir Board is a statutory body established under the Coir Industry Act, 1953 for promoting overall development of the coir industry and improvement of the living conditions of the workers engaged in this traditional industry. The functions of the Board for the development of coir industry inter-alia, include undertaking scientific, technological and economic research and development activities; collection of statistics relating to exports and internal consumption of coir and coir products; development of new products and designs; publicity for promotion of exports and internal sales; marketing of coir and coir products in India and abroad; preventing unfair competition among producers and exporters; assisting in the establishment of units for the manufacture of products; promoting cooperative organisations among producers of husk, coir fibre, coir yarn and manufacturers of coir products; ensuring remunerative returns to producers and manufacturers, etc.

Relevant Website : www.kvic.org.in

Textiles

The Indian textiles industry is one of the largest in the world with a large raw material base and manufacturing strength across the value chain. The uniqueness of the industry lies in its strength both in the hand-woven sector as well as in the capital intensive mill sector. The mill sector, with 3400 textile mills having installed capacity of more than 50 million spindles and 842000 rotors is the second largest in the world. Traditional sectors like handloom, handicrafts and small scale power-loom units are the biggest source of employment for millions of people in rural and semi urban area. The textile industry has inherent linkgage with agriculture, culture and traditions of the country making for its versatile spread of products appropriate for both domestic and the export markets. The textile industry contributes to 7 per cent of industry output in value terms of 2 per cent of India's GDP and to 15 per cent of the country's export earnings. With over 45 million people employed directly, this industry is one of the largest sources of employment generation in the country.

In keeping with goal of making India's development inclusive and participative, the government's central focus has been on increasing textile manufacturing by building the best-in-class manufacturing infrastructure, upgradation of technology fostering innovation, enhancing skills and traditional strengths in the textile sector.

Relevant Website : www.texmein.nic.in

India Handloom Brand: Indian handlooms have worldwide recognition through India Handloom Brand (IHB) which guarantees high quality, authentic handloom items made with organic substance. It has partnered with 100 retail stores to sell the exclusive IHB items from their stores. 25 retail stores across India have started operations. 23 garment manufacturers are working with the IHB producers for sourcing the fabrics from IHB registered weavers and have designed and launched a separate range of garments. Leading garment brands have been working with IHB in bringing out a separate range of garment line using handlooms. BIBA, Peter England, ONAYA have already launched a separate range of handloom garments. In order to provide direct marketing platform to handloom weavers/artisans, 21 leading e-commerce companies have been engaged for on-line marketing of handloom products.

Silk

Silk in the Indian subcontinent is a luxury item. In India, about 97 per cent of the raw mulberry silk is produced in the five states of Karnataka, Andhra Pradesh, Tamil Nadu, West Bengal and Jammu and Kashmir. Three other commercially important types of silk fall into the category of non-mulberry silks namely: eri; tasar; and muga.

Cotton

Cotton is one of the most important cash crops in India and the country accounts for around 25 per cent of the total global fibre production. In the raw material consumption basket of the Indian textile industry, the proportion of cotton is around 59 per cent. Cotton sustains the livelihood of an estimated 5.8 million cotton farmers and 40- 50 million people engaged in related activities such as cotton processing and trade.India has the largest area under cotton in the world with around 105 lakh hectares under cotton cultivation which is around 35 per cent of the world area. To support the cotton industry, Government of India announces Minimum Support Price (MSP) for two basic staples groups viz., medium staple and long staple cotton. Cotton Corporation of India (CCI), a Public Sector Undertaking under the Textile Ministry, is the principal agency of Government of India for undertaking MSP operations in the event of prevailing seed cotton (kapas) price touching the MSP level.

Jute

India is the largest producer of jute in the world with an average production of about 80 lakh bales of raw jute annually. The Government of India provides support to the jute growers not only through MSP operation by the Jute Corporation of India but also through direct purchase of jute sacking valued at around ₹ 6000 crore annually for packing foodgrains by invoking provisions under the Jute Packaging Material (Compulsory Use in Packing Commodities) Act, 1987. This is a major support not only to the jute farmers but also to jute mill workers. A software platform "Jute-SMART" (Jute Sacking Supply Management & Requisition Tool) was implemented for procurement of jute sacking from 2016. Through this software, different state government agencies are procuring jute bags of around 27.0 to 30.0 lakh bales (68.0 per cent of the total production of jute goods) annually valued at about. ₹ 7,000 crores. This platform is an excellent example of e-Governance where multiple stakeholders are on the same platform managing the complex transactions relating to procument of jute sacking in a transparent and fair manner for a number of state governments from a number of jute mills involving various intermediaries. Jute - ICARE has been launched for increasing the income of jute farmers by at least 50 per cent through promotion of certified seeds, better agronomic practices and use of microbial retting of the jute plant.

Wool

For the holistic growth of the wool sector, the Ministry formulated a new integrated formulated a new integrated programme i.e. Integrated Wool Development Programme, (IWDP). The programme is to be implemented through Central Wool Development Board in major wool producting states in next three years. A programme for development of Pashmina sector in J&K was announced.

Technical Textiles

Technical textiles are the future of the textiles industry. High tenacity fibers are the lightest and toughest fabrics yet. They have a variety of applications in automobile, aerospace, architecture and building, occupational therapy, sport and apparel industries etc. Eleven Focus Incubation Centres (FICs) have been established on plug and play model, five in COEs and six in IITs (Delhi, Bombay, Kanpur and Kharagpur) in order to help the potential entrepreneurs to enter into technical textiles. 44 demonstration centres in North-East (NE) Region and 9 Demonstration Centers in Rest of India have been set up for promoting usage of agro textiles. Textiles Research Associations (TRA) has developed carbon fibre based space communication system. Low cost modular toilets using jute fibres have been developed.

Impetus to the Powerloom Sector

The powerloom sector is predominantly an unorganised sector and has many micro and small units - with 24.86 lakh powerlooms producing 57 percent of the total cloth in the country. With a view to enhance quality and productivity of the powerloom, the Government launched *IN SITU* upgradation of plain powerlooms as part of PowerTex Indiâ under which plain powerlooms are attached with process control equipment leading to higher productivity, better quality and more than 50 per cent additional value realisation.

New Initiatives

Weavers' Mudra Scheme: Weavers' Mudra Scheme was launched to provide concessional credit to the handloom weavers. Margin Money Assistance to a maximum of ₹ 10,000 per weaver and credit guarantee for a period of 3 years is also provided.

e- Dhaga App: Govt of India launched Enterprise Resource Planning System (ERP) and e-Dhaga mobile App in 2016 to bring efficiency in service delivery to the handloom weavers and help them to access information on 24x7 basis. The App is available in 10 languages-Hindi, English, Assamese, Odiya, Kannada, Tamil, Telugu, Malayalam, Urdu and Bangla.

BunkarMitra Help Line: To provide a single point of contact to handloom weavers for their professional queries "BunkarMitra" -Helpline 18002089988 for handloom weavers was launched in 2017. This service is available from 10:00 AM to 06:00 P.M on all 7 days in a week in seven languages: Hindi, English, Tamil, Telugu, Bengali, Kannada and Assamese.

MoU with Financial Corporations: MoU was signed with National Backward Classes Finance Development Corporation (NBCFDC) and National Schedule Castes Finance Development Corporation (NSFDC) to implement schemes of Government of India for OBC and SC artisans and weavers in 14 identified clusters with necessary forward linkages for income sustainability and enhancement.

Educational facilities to the children of handloom weavers: Memorandums of Understanding was signed with Indira Gandhi National Open University (IGNOU) and National Institute of Open Schooling (NIOS) to provide customized educational service to the weavers for which Ministry provides 75% of the fee in case of SC, ST, BPL and Women weaver families.

Artisan Helpline No 1800 208 4800 was launched in 2017 in seven languages -Hindi, English, Kannada, Assamese, Bengali, Tamil and Telugu.

Hastkala Sahyog Shivirs: Hastkala Sahyog Shivirs for handloom weavers and handicraft artisans are organized across the country. Various activities such as disbursal of MUDRA loan, supply of looms ,accessories and tool kits to weavers and artisans, issue of Pehchan ID Cards, yarn passbooks, enrolment of family member of weavers under IGNOU and NIOS , awareness programmes on GST, GI, Bunkar Mitra helpline and about the schemes of Handlooms and Handicrafts Departments of the Government were organized in the shivirs.

Steel

The Ministry of Steel, is responsible for planning and development of iron and steel industry, development of essential inputs such as iron ore, limestone, dolomite manganese ore, chromites, ferro-alloys, sponge iron etc, and other related functions. Crude steel production has shown a sustained rise since 2013-14 along with capacity.

India is also an important producer of pig iron. Post liberalization, with setting up several units in the private sector, not only imports have drastically reduced but also India has turned out to be a net exporter of pig iron.

Relevant Website : www.steel.gov.in

Global Ranking of Indian Steel

Provisional World Association (world steel) data (Source: World Steel in Figures, 2018) shows that world crude steel production was 1689 mt during 2017, up by 3.8 per cent year over year. China remained the largest crude steel producer in the world and accounted for 72 per cent of Asian and 49 per cent of world crude steel production during 2017 compared to 74 per cent and 50 per cent respectively of 2016. India remained the thrid largest crude steel producer in the world in 2017. But more significantly, at 101.4 mt, India's crude steel production crossed the 100 million tonne mark for the first time, thereby making 2017 a milestone year for the domestic steel industry.

Fertilizers

Department of Fertilizers comes under the ambit of Ministry of Chemicals and Fertilizers. The main objective of the Department is to ensure adequate and timely availability of fertilizers at affordable prices for maximizing agricultural production in the country. The main functions of the Department include planning, promotion and development of the fertilizers industry, planning and monitoring of production, import and distribution of fertilizers and management of financial assistance by way of subsidy/concession for indigenous and imported fertilizers.

The Department has one attached office under it, viz., Fertilizers Industry Coordination Committee (FICC). It also administers 9 Fertilizer Public Sector Undertakings (PSUs).

Agriculture which accounts for about one seventh of the GDP, provides sustenance to nearly two-third of our population, Besides, it provides crucial backward and forward linkages to the rest of economy. Successive five-year Plans have laid emphasis on self-sufficiency and self-reliance in food grain production and concerted efforts in this direction have resulted in substantial increase in agriculture production and productivity. In meeting the domestic requirement of food grains and also generating exportable surpluses, the significant role played by chemical fertilizers is well recognized.

Relevant Website : www.fert.nic.in

Public Sector Undertakings

Fertilizer Corporation of India Limited

Incorporated in 1961, FCI was re-organized along with National Fertilizers Corporation Ltd (NFCL) from 1978 into five companies namely, FCI, NFL, Hindustan Fertilizer Corporation Ltd. (HFCL), Rashtriya Chemicals and Fertilizers Ltd. (RCFL) and Projects and Development India Ltd. (PDIL). Following re-organisation, FCI comprised four units located at Sindri (Jharkhand), Gorakhpur (Uttar Pradesh), Ramagundam (Andhra Pradesh) and Talcher (Odisha), with a total annual capacity of 5.87 lakh MT of nitrogen besides an abandoned project at Korbe (Chhattisgarh).

Relevant Website : www.fertcorpindia.nic.in

Hindustan Fertilizer Corporation Limited

The Hindustan Fertilizer Corporation Limited (HFCL) was incorporated in 1978 as a result of the reorganization of the erstwhile Fertilizer Corporation of India Limited (FCIL), and NFL Group of Companies. The HFCL comprised Barauni Unit (Bihar), Durgapur Unit and Haldia Project (West Bengal) and Namrup Unit (Assam). The Namrup Unit was hived off from 2002 to form a separate entity with the name of Brahmaputra Valley Fertilizer Corporation Ltd (BVFCL).

Rashtriya Chemicals and Fertilizers Limited

Rashtriya Chemicals and Fertilisers Limited (RCF) was incorporated as a separate company in 1978 as a result of reorganization of the erstwhile Fertilizer Corporation of India Limited. At the time of its formation, the company had only one operating unit at Trombay (near Mumbai) and two major projects under implementation viz. Trombay-IV and Trombay-V expansion. The gas based Thal-Vaishet fertilizer complex about 100 kms from Trombay, was later implemented by RCF and it commenced commercial production in 1985.

Relevant Website : www.rcfltd.com

National Fertilizers Limited

National Fertilizers Limited (NFL) was incorporated in 1974 for setting up two nitrogenous plants, at Bathinda (Punjab) and Panipat (Haryana) with

LSHS as fee stock, each having urea production capacity of 5.11 lakh MT per annum. Consequent upon the reorganization of the FCI, the Nangal Unit (including Nangal Expansion Project) of FCI was also transferred to NFL in 1978.

Relevant Website : www.nationalfertilizers.com

Projects and Development India Limited

Projects and Development India Limited (PDIL), an erstwhile division of the Fertilizers Corporation of India was registered as a separate company in 1978. The company has its registered office at Noida, Uttar Pradesh.

Relevant Website : www.pdilin.com

Fertilizers and Chemicals Travancore Limited

Fertilizers and Chemicals Travancore Limited (FACL) was incorporated in 1943. In 1947, FACL started production of ammonium sulphate with an installed capacity of 50,000 MT per annum at Udyogamandal, near Cochin (now Kochi). In 1980, FACL became a PSU and towards the end of 1982, the Government became the major shareholder. From a modest beginning, FACL has grown and diversified into a multi-division, multifunction organization with basic interest in manufacture and marketing of fertilisers and petro-chemicals, engineering consultancy and design and in fabrication and erection of industrial equipment.

Relevant Website : www.fact.co.in

Madras Fertilizers Limited

Madras Fertilizers Limited (MFL) was incorporated in 1906 as a joint venture between GOI and AMOCO India Incorporation of USA (AMOCO) with GOI holding 51 per cent of the equity share capital in 1985, AMOCO disinvested their shares, which were purchased by GOI and NIOC in their respective proportions in 1985. The revised share holding pattern was: GOI 67.55 per cent and NIOC 32.45 per cent.

Relevant Website : www.madrasfert.nic.in

Brahmaputra Valley Fertilizer Corporation Limited

Brahmaputra Valley Fertilizer Corporation Limited (BVFCL) has two operating units at Namrup, Assam. Its corporate office is also situated at Namrup. The other establishments of the company are liaison offices at Noida and Kolkata and marketing offices at Guwahati, Siliguri and Patna.

Relevant Website : www.bvfcl.com

FCI-Aravali Gypsum and Minerals India Limited

FCI-Aravali Gypsum and Minerals India Limited was incorporated under the Companies Act, 1956 as a public sector undertaking in 2003 after being hived off the Jodhpur Mining Organization (JMO) of Fertilizers Corporation of India Limited (FCIL).

Relevant Website : www.fagmil.nic.in

Chemicals and Petrochemicals

The Department of Chemicals and Petrochemicals was under the Ministry of Industry until 1989, when it was brought under the Ministry of Petroleum and Chemicals. In 1991, the Department of Chemicals and Petrochemicals was transferred to the Ministry of Chemicals and Fertilizers. The Department is entrusted with the responsibility of planning, development and regulations of the chemicals, petrochemicals and pharmaceutical industry sector, inducting: drugs and pharmaceuticals, excluding those specifically allotted to other departments; insecticides excluding the aministration of the Insecticides Act, 1968; molasses; alcohol - industrial and potable from the molasses route; all organic and inorganic chemicals not specifically allotted to any other ministry or department; petrochemicals; synthetic rubber; planning, development and control of, and assistance to, all industries dealt with by the Department.

Relevant Website : www.chemicals.nic.in

Chemicals and Petrochemicals Industry

The chemical and petrochemical industry is a knowledge and capital intensive industry. It is an integral constituent of the growing Indian Industry. It includes basic chemicals and its products, petrochemicals, fertilizers, paints, varnishes, gases, soaps, perfumes and toiletry and pharmaceuticals. This industry occupies a pivotal position in meeting basic needs and improving quality of life. The industry is the mainstay of industrial and agricultural development of the country and provides building blocks for several downstream industries, such as textiles, papers, paints, soaps, detergents, pharmaceuticals, varnish, etc.

India produces a large number of fine and speciality Chemicals, which have very specific uses and find wide usage as food additives, pigments, polymer additives and anti-oxidants in the rubber industry, etc. In the chemical sector, 100 per cent FDI is permissible. Manufacture of most of the chemical and petrochemical products is delicensed. The entrepreneurs need to submit an Industrial Entrepreneurs' Memorandum (IEM) to the Department of Industrial Policy and Promotion provided no locational angle is applicable. Only the following items are covered in the compulsory licensing list because of their hazardous nature:- hydrocyanic acid and its derivatives; phosgene and its derivatives; and isocynates and di-isocynates of hydrocarbons.

Department of Chemicals and Petrochemicals is implementing the three schemes under the National Policy on Petrochemicals:- (i) setting up of plastic parks; (ii) setting up of Centres of Ecellence in Polymer Technology; and (iii) national awards for technology innovation in petrochemical and downstream plastic processing industry.

Petroleum Chemical and Petrochemical Investment Regions

The Petroleum Chemical and Petrochemical Investment Regions (PCPIR) Policy, is to promote the petroleum chemical and petrochemical sector in an integrated and environmental friendly manner on a large scale. The policy document put in place in 2007 is also available on the web site of the department. www.chemicals.nic.in

Hindustan Organic Chemicals Limited

Hindustan Organic Chemicals Limited (HOCL) was incorporated in 1960 with the objective of attaining self-reliance in basic organic chemicals. The company has two manufacturing units located at Rasayani (Maharashtra) and Kochi (Kerala). The Rasayani unit (Phenol Complex) commenced production from 1987-88. HOCL is the sole manufacturer of strategically important N_2O_4 (Dinitrogen Tetroxide) in India which is supplied by the company to ISRO for its satellites launching programme. HOCL has a subsidiary company M/s Hindustan Fluorocarbons Limited (HFL) located at Rudraram, Telangana, which manufactures Poly tetra fluro ethylene (PTFE), a high tech engineering plastic, and chloro di-fluoro methane (CFM-22).

Relevant Website : www.hoclindia.com

Hindustan Insecticides Limited

Hindustan Insecticide Limited (HIL) was incorporated in 1954 for manufacture and supply of DDT. In 1957, the company set up a factory at Udyogmandal, Kerala, for manufacture of DDT and in 1977 at Rasayani, Maharashtra, for manufacture of Malathion, an insecticide The third unit of HIL was set up at Bhatinda, Punjab, in 2003. Rasayani and Udyogmandal Plants have both DDT manufacturing and agrochemical manufacturing facilities while Bathinda has only formulations manufacturing and packaging facility.

HIL is the sole supplier of DDT to the National Vector Borne Disease Control Programme (NVBDCP) of the Ministry of Health and Family Welfare, Govt. of India. DDT accounts for almost 50 per cent of the company's turnover. The company exports DDT to some African countries and other products like malathion and mancozeb to countries like Brazil and Argentina. HIL diversified into agro chemicals in the late 1970s to ensure supply of quality pesticides at reasonable prices to the agricultural sector and has a range of technical and formulation grade pesticides. To further consolidate its position, it has also ventured into the seed business. It has got the status of National Level Seed Agency (NLA) from the Union Ministry of Agriculture and is producing and supplying seeds under Govt. sponsored schemes like National Food Security Mission (NFSM), National Mission on Oilseed and Oil Palm (NMOOP) and Mission on Integrated Development of Horticulture (MIDH). In addition, company has diversified into fertilizer segment as well to provide a single stop window for the range of agriculture inputs i.e., pesticides, seeds and fertilizers.

Relevant Website : www.hil.gov.in

Hindustan Flourocarbons Ltd

Hindustan Fluorocarbons Ltd. (HFL), a subsidiary company of Hindustan Organic Chemicals Ltd. (HOCL), was incorporated in 1983. It is located at Rudraram, District Medak, Telangana. The company started production in 1987 and is engaged in the manufacture of Poly Tetra Fluoro Ethylene (PTFE) and of Chloro Di Fluoro Methane (CFM-22). PTFE is extensively used in chemical, mechanical, electrical and electronic industries and has strategic applications in defence and aerospace sectors. CFM-22 is used as a refrigerant and for production of PTFE.

Relevant Website : www.hfl.co.in

Assam Gas Cracker Project - Brahmaputra Cracker & Polymer Limited

The Assam Gas Cracker Project (AGCP) was initiated in pursuance of the Memorandum of Settlement signed between central government, All Assam Students Union (AASU) and All Assam Gana Parished (AAGP) in 1985. This project is of economic significance for Assam and the North East Region. The AGCP was dedicated to the nation in 2016.

Central Institute of Plastics Engineering and Technology

Central Institute of Plastics Engineering & Technology (CIPET), a premier 15 9001:2008 QMS, ISO/IEC - 17025, ISO/IEC-17020 certified Plastics Institute under the aegis of Department of Chemicals & Petrochemicals, was established in 1968. The diversified activities of CIPET include, skill development, technology support to industry, academics and research and development (STAR) in the field of plastics engineeing techology i.e., design, CAD/CAM/ CAE, tooling, plastics processing, testing and quality assurance, etc. The reach of CIPET has been expanded and it is now operating at 30 centres in 18 states across the country. These are 5 High Learning Centres (HLCs) providing undergraduate, postgraduate and doctoral programmes in affiliation with respective state universities, 12 diploma centres focus on diploma and skill oriented programme, 6 Vocational Training Centres (VTCs) provide Vocational Skill Development training programmes aimed at gainful employment to unemployed and underemployed youth, 3 R&D Wings involved in application oriented research in the niche areas of Plastics Engineering and Technology, 3 Specialised Centres provide academic programmes and technology support services relevant to their respective specialized domains and operator level training programmes in plastics processing and recycling technology and 1 polymer data service centre deals with creation of database.

Institute of Pesticide Formulation Technology

Institute of Pesticide Formulation Technology (IPFT) was established in 1991 as an autonomous institution under the Department of Chemicals and Petrochemicals. IPFT is a NABL accredited laboratory for testing of pesticides technical and formulation, pesticide residues in various food matrices and CWC related chemicals. One of the main objectives of the Institute is the development of user and environment friendly pesticide formulation technology. IPFT has established a healthy support with the Pesticide Industries and has been able to successfully transfer more than fifty formulation technologies to Indian and foreign companies.

Pharmaceuticals

The Department of Chemicals and Petrochemials was under the Ministry of Industry until 1989, when it was brought under the Ministry of Petroleum and Chemicals. In 1991, the Department of Chemicals and Petrochemicals was transferredto the Ministry of Chemicals and Fertilizers. The Department is entrusted with the responsibility of planning, development and regulations of the chemicals, petrochemicals and pharmaceutical industry sector.

Relevant Website : www.pharamaceuticals.gov.in

Pharmaceuticals Pricing Policy

The Department notified the National Pharmaceutical Pricing Policy-2012 (NPPP-2012) in 2012 with the objective to put in place a regulatory framework for pricing of drugs to ensure availability of required medicines - "essential medicines" - at reasonable prices, even while providing sufficient opportunity for innovation and competition to support the growth of industry, thereby meeting the goals of employment and shared economic well being for all.

Subsequently, to implement the NPPP-2012, the new Drugs (Prices Control) Order, 2013 was notified in 2013 to control the prices of specified dosages and strengths as under National List of Essential Medicines-2011(NLEM-2011). This was modified to include medicines included in NLEM-2015in 2016 after the same was received from Ministry of Health and Family Welfare that had constituted an Expert Core Committee to review and recommend the revision of National List of Essential Medicines (NLEM-2011) in the context of contemporary knowledge of use of therapeutic products.

Medical Devices

Medical devices industry is a multi-product industry, producing wide range of products. India is growing as a key market for Medical Devices and Diagnostics. Indian Medical Devices industry depends on imports up to an extent of almost 70 per cent. Most hitech innovative products and technology originate from a well-developed eco-system and innovation cycle which needs to be developed in India to promote indigenous industry and to reduce our dependence on imports. In 2014, the government launched the "Make in India" campaign, with the objective of making India a global manufacturing hub; thus, bringing foreign technology and capital into the country.

Pradhan Mantri Bhartiya Janaushadhi Pariyojana

The Jan Aushadhi Scheme was launched in 2008 with the aim of selling affordable generic medicines through dedicated sales outlets i.e., Jan Aushadhi Stores in various districts across the country. Some of the objectives of the scheme include: ensure access to quality medicines; extend coverage of quality generic medicines so as to reduce and thereby redefine the unit cost of treatment per person; create awareness about generic medicines through education and publicity so that quality is not synonymous with only high price ; The first Jan Aushadhi Store was opened at Amritsar in Punjab in 2008. The original target of the campaign was to establish Jan Aushadhi Stores in every district of our country. Recently, "Pradhan Mantri Jan Aushadhi Yojana" (PMJAY) has been renamed as "Pradhan Mantri Bhartiya Janaushadhi Pariyojana" (PMBJP) and "Pradhan Mantri Jan Aushadhi Kendra" (PMJAK) as "Pradhan Mantri Bhartiya Janaushadhi Kendra" (PMBJK).

Indian Drugs and Pharmaceuticals Limited

Indian Drugs and Pharmaceuticals Limited (IDPL) was incorporated in 1961 with the primary objective of creating self-sufficiency in essential life saving drugs and medicines. The company has presently three manufacturing plants, one each at Rishikesh (Uttarakhand), Hyderabad (Andhra Pradesh) and Gurgaon (Haryana). IDPL has two wholly owned subsidiaries, namely, IDPL Ltd., Chennai (Tamil Nadu) and Bihar Drugs and Organic Chemicals Ltd. at Muzaffarpur (Bihar). In addition, IDPL has two joint sector undertakings, promoted in collaboration with the respective state governments. These are Rajasthan Drugs and Pharmaceuticals Ltd. (RDPL), Jaipur, and Orissa Drugs and Chemicals Ltd. (ODCL), Bhubaneshwar. However, the government has decided to de-link RDPL from IDPL and the process of delinking is underway.

Relevant Website : www.idplindia.in

Bengal Chemicals and Pharmaceuticals Limited

Bengal Chemicals and Pharmaceuticals Limited (BCPL) was a sick company in the private sector in the name and style of Bengal Chemicals and Pharmaceuticals Works. A new public sector company in the name and style of Bengal Chemicals and Pharmaceuticals Limited (BCPL) was incorporated in 1961.The company has four manufacturing units-one each at Maniktala at Kolkata, Panihati at North 24 Parganas (West Bengal), one at Mumbai (Maharashtra) and at Kanpur (UP). The company manufactures and markets a wide range of industrial chemicals, a large number of drugs and pharmaceuticals besides cosmetics and home products. In the home products, the well known products include Cantharidine Hair Oil and Lamp Brand Phenol.

Relevant Website : www.bengalchemicals.co.in

Mines and Minerals

Ministry of Mines is responsible for survey and exploration of all minerals, other than natural gas, petroleum and atomic minerals; for mining and metallurgy of non-ferrous metals like aluminium, copper, zinc, lead, gold, nickel, etc. and for administration of the Mines and Minerals (Regulation and Development) Act, 1957 and rules made thereunder in respect of all mines and minerals other than coal, natural gas and petroleum as well as Offshore Areas Mineral (Development and Regulation) Act, 2002 and rules made thereunder.

The Ministry is responsible for legislation for regulation of mines and development of minerals within the territory of India, including mines and minerals underlying the ocean within the territorial waters or the continental shelf, or the exclusive economic zone and other maritime zones of India as may be specified, from time to time by or under any law made by Parliament; regulation of mines and development of minerals other than coal, lignite and sand for stowing and any other mineral declared as prescribed substances for the purpose of the Atomic Energy Act, 1962 (33 of 1962) as declared by law, including questions concerning regulation and development of minerals in various states and the matters connected therewith or incidental thereto; all other metals and minerals not specifically allotted to any other Ministry/ Department, such as aluminium, zinc, copper, gold, diamonds, lead and nickel; planning, development and control of, and assistance to, all industries dealt with by the Ministry; administration and management of Geological Survey of India, Indian Bureau of Mines.

Relevant Website : www.minesgov.in

Mineral Legislation and Reforms

The Central Act to provide for the development and regulation of mines and minerals is the Mines and Minerals (Development and Regulation) Act, 1957, which came into force in 1958. Section 13 of the MMDR Act empowers the central government to formulate rules for regulation of grant of mineral concessions for major minerals; in accordance of which Mineral Concession Rules, 1960 have been framed. Section 18 of MMDR Act, 1957 empowers the Central Government to frame rules for the conservation and systematic development of minerals and for the protection of environment in accordance of which Mineral Conservation and Development Rules, 1988 have been framed. Section 15 of MMDR Act, 1957 empowers state governments to frame rules for regulating the grant of quarry leases, mining leases or other mineral concessions in respect of minor minerals; accordingly all state governments and some union territories have framed their own rules in this regard.

The central government framed the following rules to give effect to the newly amended provision of the said Act and also give boost to the mining sector. The newly framed Rules are listed as The Minerals (Evidence of Mineral Contents) Rules, 2015; The Minerals (Non-exclusive Reconnaissance Permits) Rules, 2015; The Mineral (Auction) Rules, 2015; The Minerals (Mining by Government Companies) Rules, 2015; The Mines and Minerals (Contribution to District Mineral Foundation) Rules, 2015; The National Exploration Trust Rules, 2015; The Minerals (Other than Atomic and Hydrocarbons Energy Mineral Concession) Rules, 2016; The Minerals (Transfer of Mining Lease Granted Otherwise than through Auction for Captive Purpose) Rules, 2016; The Atomic Minerals Concession Rules, 2016; and The Mineral Conservation and Development Rules, 2017.

National Mineral Exploration Trust

The Government notified National Mineral Exploration Trust Rules, 2015 and has also established National Mineral Exploration Trust (NMET) in pursuance of subsection (1) of Section 9C of the Mines and Minerals (Development and Regulation) Amendment Act, 1957, with primary objective to promote regional and detailed mineral exploration in the country to increase overall mineral production and achieve sustainable development of the mineral sector.

Pradhan Mantri Khanij Kshetra Kalyan Yojana

The government launched Pradhan Mantri Khanij Kshetra Kalyan Yojana (PMKKKY) which is to be implemented by the district mineral foundations of the respective districts. PMKKKY will help in creating a congenial mining environment, ameliorate the condition of the affected person and create a win-win situations for the stakeholders. A national portal for DMF is being developed which will help monitor the implementation of projects under the PMKKKY scheme. The monitoring of PMKKKY would be done under "DISHA", the District Development Coordination and Monitoring Committee of Ministry of Rural Development to promote synergy and convergence for greater impact.

National Mineral Exploration Policy

Government unveiled National Mineral Exploration Policy, 2016 (NMEP) which spells out the strategy and outlines the action plan that the Government will adopt to ensure comprehensive exploration of country's mineral resources (non-fuel and non-coal). The NMEP primarily aims at accelerating the exploration activity in the country through enhanced participation of the private sector.

Transparency, Auction, Monitoring and Resource Augmentation

To facilitate and expedite various clearances/approvals required after the mineral block is allocated, an Inter-ministerial Group has been constituted to expedite the requisite clearances to enable the early start of mining activity. The Ministry has developed a Transparency, Auction, Monitoring and Resource Augmentation (TAMRA) portal and mobile application. This will be an interactive platform for all stakeholders to compress the timelines for statutory/ other clearances.

Star Rating of Mines

The Ministry of Mines launched in 2016 Scheme of Star Rating of Mines/ mining leases for implementation of Sustainable Development Framework (SDF). The Star Ratings are to be awarded, based on evaluation of performance of mines on techno, socio-economic and environmental parameters and give objective reporting of their activities. It has been instituted as a two tier system providing self-evaluation templates to be filled in by the mine operator followed by validation through Indian Bureau of Mines.

Mining Surveillance System

To curb the menace of illegal mining, a satellite-based monitoring system namely Mining Surveillance System (MSS), was developed and launched which aims to establish a regime of responsive mineral administration through automatic remote sensing detection technology. The latest satellite image is juxtaposed on geo-referenced mining lease maps to check any illegal mining in the vicinity.

Mineral Resources

The classification of reserves/resources of various minerals based on United Nations Framework Classification (UNFC) was done in April 2010 following which National Mineral Inventory was prepared. The UNFC consists of a three dimensional system with three axes-economic viability; feasibility assessment; and geological assessment.

Bauxite

Total resources of bauxite as per UNFC in the country are placed at 3,897 million tonnes. These resources include 656 million tonnes reserves and 3,240 million tonnes remaining resources. By grades, about 81 per cent resources are of metallurgical grade. The resources of refractory and chemical grades are limited and together account for about 5 per cent. Odisha alone accounts for 51 per cent of country's resources of bauxite followed by Andhra Pradesh (16 per cent), Gujarat (9 per cent), Jharkhand (6 per cent), Maharashtra (5 per cent) and Chhattisgarh and Madhya Pradesh (4 per cent each). Major bauxite resources are concentrated in the east coast of Odisha and Andhra Pradesh.

Chromite

As per UNFC system, total resources of chromite in the country as in 2015 are estimated at 344 million tonnes, comprising 102 million tonnes reserves (30 per cent) and 242 million tonnes remaining resources (70 per cent). About 96 per cent resources of chromite are located in Odisha, mostly in the Sukinda valley in Jajpur and Keonjhar districts. Minor deposits are scattered over Manipur, Nagaland, Karnataka, Jharkhand, Maharashtra, Tamil Nadu and Andhra Pradesh and Telangana. Gradewise, charge-chrome grade accounts for 31 per cent resources followed by ferrochrome grade (18 per cent), beneficiable grade (25 per cent) and refractory grade 14 per cent. Low, others, unclassified and not known grades together account for 13 per cent.

Copper

The total resources of copper ore in the country as in 2015 are estimated at 1511.50 million tonnes with about 12.16 million tonnes of copper metal. Of these 207.77 million tonnes (13.74 per cent) fall under Reserve category containing 2.73 million tonnes of copper metal and the balance 1303.73 million tonnes (86.26 per cent) are 'Remaining Resources' containing 9.42 million tonnes of copper metal. Rajasthan is credited with 813.33 million tonnes ore (54 per cent) containing 4.48 million tonnes of copper metal, Madhya Pradesh 283.43 million tonnes ore (19 per cent), containing 3.42 million tonnes copper, Jharkhand, 295.39 million tonnes ore (20 per cent), containing 3.28 million tonnes of copper metal and the rest 7 per cent are accounted for by other states namely Andhra Pradesh, Gujarat, Haryana, Karnataka, Maharashtra, Meghalaya, Nagaland, Odisha, Sikkim, Tamil Nadu, Telangana, Uttarakhand and West Bengal.

Gold

As per UNFC system, as in 2015, the total resources of gold ore (primary and placer) in the country were estimated at 527.96 million tonnes. Out of these, 17.23 million tonnes were placed under reserves category and the remaining 510.73 million tonnes under remaining resources category. Total resources of gold (primary), in terms of metal, stood at 654.74 tonnes. Out of these, 70.09 tonnes were placed under reserves category and 584.65 tonnes under remaining resources category. The resources include placer-type gold ore in Kerala estimated at 26.12 million tonnes containing 5.86 tonnes gold metal.

The largest resources in terms of gold ore (primary) are located in Bihar (44 per cent) followed by Rajasthan (25 per cent) and Karnataka (21 per cent), West Bengal, and Andhra Pradesh (3 per cent each), Telangana & Madhya Pradesh (2 per cent each). Remaining very small quantity of resources of ore are located in Chhatisgarh, Jharkhand, Kerala, Maharashtra and Tamil Nadu. In terms of metal content, Karnataka remained on top followed by Rajasthan, Bihar, Andhra Pradesh, Jharkhand, etc.

Iron Ore

Hematite and magnetite are the most important iron ores in India. About 59 per cent hematite ore deposits are found in the eastern sector. About 92 per cent magnetite ore deposits occur in southern sector, especially in Karnataka. Of these, hematite is considered to be superior because of its higher grade. Indian deposits of hematite belong to the precambrian iron ore series and the ore is within banded iron ore formations occurring as massive, laminated, friable and also in powdery form.

As per UNFC system, the total resources of hematite as in 2015 are estimated at 22,487 million tonnes of which 5,442 million tonnes (24 per cent) are under 'reserves' category and the balance 17,045 million tonnes (76 per cent) are under 'remaining resources' category. By grades, lumps constitute about 56 per cent followed by fines (21 per cent), lumps with fines (13 per cent) and the remaining 10 per cent are black iron ore, not-known and other grades. Major resources of hematite are located in Odisha - 7,559 million tonnes (34 per cent), Jharkhand - 5,286 million tonnes (24 per cent), Chhattisgarh - 4,858 million tonnes (22 per cent), Karnataka - 2,467 million tonnes (11 per cent) and Goa - 1189 million tonnes (5 per cent). The balance resources of hematite are spread in Andhra Pradesh, Assam, Bihar, Maharashtra, Madhya Pradesh, Meghalaya, Rajasthan and Uttar Pradesh.

Magnetite is another principal iron ore that also occurs in the form of oxide, either in igneous or metamorphosed banded magnetite-silica formation, possibly of sedimentary origin. As per UNFC system, the total resources of magnetite as in 2015 are estimated at 10,789 million tonnes of which 'reserves' constitute a mere 53 million tonnes while 10,736 million tonnes are placed under 'remaining resources'. Classification on the basis of grades shows 20 per cent resources of metallurgical grade while 80 per cent resources belong to unclassified, not-known and other grades. The resources of coal washery and foundry grades constitute meagre proportions. India's 96 per cent magnetite resources are located in four states, namely, Karnataka - 7,802 million tonnes (72 per cent) followed by Andhra Pradesh - 1,392 million tonnes (13 per cent), Rajasthan - 617 million tonnes (6 per cent) and Tamil Nadu - 507 million tonnes (5 per cent). Assam, Bihar, Goa, Jharkhand, Kerala, Maharashtra, Meghalaya and Nagaland together account for the remaining 4 per cent resources.

Lead and Zinc

The total resources of lead and zinc ores as in 2015 as per UNFC system, are estimated at 749.46 million tonnes. Of these, 106.12 million tonnes (14 per cent) fall under 'reserves' while balance 643.34 million tonnes (86 per cent) are classified as 'remaining resources'. The resources of ore containing + 10 per cent Pb and Zn were estimated at 124.33 million tonnes, ore containing 5 to 10 per cent Pb and Zn were 329.88 million tonnes and ore containing less than 5 per cent Pb and Zn were 295.35 million tonnes.

Rajasthan is endowed with the largest resources of lead-zinc ore amounting to 670.34 million tonnes (89.44 per cent), followed by Andhra Pradesh 22.69 million tonnes (3.02 per cent), Madhya Pradesh 14.84 million tonnes (1.98 per cent), Bihar 11.43 million tonnes (1.52 per cent) and Maharashtra 9.27 million tonnes (1.24 per cent). Resources are also established in Gujarat, Meghalaya, Odisha, Sikkim, Tamil Nadu, Uttarakhand and West Bengal.

Manganese Ore

The total resources of manganese ore in the country as in 2015 are placed at 496 million tonnes as per UNFC system. Out of these, 94 million tonnes are categorised as reserves and the balance 402 million tonnes are in the remaining resources category. Gradewise, ferro-manganese grade accounts for 7 per cent, medium grade 11per cent, BF grade 28 per cent and the remaining 54 per cent are of mixed, low, others, unclassified, and not-known grades including 0.17 million tonnes of battery/chemical grade.

Statewise, Odisha tops the total resources with 44 per cent share followed by Karnataka 22 per cent, Madhya Pradesh 12 per cent, Maharashtra and Goa 7 per cent each, Andhra Pradesh 4 per cent and Jharkhand 2 per cent. Rajasthan, Gujarat and West Bengal together shared the remaining about 2 per cent resources.

Nickel

Important occurrence is nickeliferous limonite in the overburden of chromite in Sukinda Valley, Jajpur district, Odisha, where it occurs as oxide. A suitable process is being developed for its utilisation. Nickel also occurs in sulphide form along with copper mineralisation in East Singhbhum district, Jharkhand. In addition, it is found associated with uranium deposits at Jaduguda, Jharkhand and process is being developed for its recovery. Other reported occurrences of nickel are from Karnataka, Kerala and Rajasthan. Polymetallic sea nodules are another source of nickel. As per UNFC, as in 2015, the total resources of nickel ore have been estimated at 189 million tonnes. About 92 per cent resources; i.e., 175 million tonnes are in Odisha. The remaining 8 per cent resources are distributed in Jharkhand (9 million tonnes) and Nagaland (5 million tonnes). Nominal resources are reported from Karnataka (0.23 million tonnes).

Tungsten

The total resources of tungsten ore in the country, as per UNFC system, as in 2015 have been estimated at 87.4 million tonnes containing 142,094 tonnes WO3 content. All these resources are placed under 'remaining resources' category. Resources are mainly distributed in Karnataka (42 per cent), Rajasthan (27 per cent), Andhra Pradesh (17 per cent) and Maharashtra (9 per cent). Remaining 5 per cent resources are in Haryana, Tamil Nadu, Uttarakhand and West Bengal. At Degana, Rajasthan, WO3 value in vein deposits varies from 0.13 to 0.80 per cent while in gravel deposit, it is, on an average 0.04 per cent. In Sirohi deposit, Rajasthan, WO3 content ranges from 0.18 to 0.51 per cent.

Barytes

The total resources of barytes in India as in 2015 as per UNFC system are placed at 86.7 million tonnes constituting 59.2 per cent reserves and 40.8 per cent remaining resources. By grades, 64 per cent resources are of oil-well drilling grade followed by 6 per cent of chemical grade 0.5 per cent of paint grade and 27 per cent constitute low grade. About 2.5 per cent resources are of other, unclassified and not-known categories. Andhra Pradesh alone accounts for 92 per cent of the country's barytes resources followed by Telangana and Rajasthan.

Diamond

Diamond occurrences are reported since prehistoric times in the country. Presently, diamond fields of India are grouped into four regions: 1) South Indian tract of Andhra Pradesh, comprising parts of Anantapur, Cuddapah, Guntur, Krishna, and Kurnool districtsand Mahaboobnagar in Telangana; 2) Central Indian tract of Madhya Pradesh, comprising Panna belt and Chhatarpur districts; 3) Behradin-Kodawali area in Raipur district and Tokapal, Dugapal, etc. areas in Bastar district of Chhattisgarh; and 4) Eastern Indian tract mostly of Odisha, lying between Mahanadi and Godavari valleys.

As per the UNFC system as in 2015 all India resources of diamond are placed at around 31.84 million carats. Out of these, 0.96 million carats are placed under reserves category and 30.87 million carats under remaining resources category. By grades, about 2.38 per cent resources are of gem variety, 2.64 per cent of industrial variety and bulk of the resources (95 per cent) are placed under unclassified category. By states, Madhya Pradesh accounts for about 90.18 per cent resources followed by Andhra Pradesh 5.73 per cent and Chhattisgarh 4.10 per cent.

Dolomite

Dolomite occurrences are widespread in the country. As per UNFC system, as on 1.4.2015 total resources of dolomite are placed at 8,415 million tonnes, out of which 679 million tonnes are placed under reserves category. Major share of about 88 per cent resources was distributed in eight states: namely, Madhya Pradesh (27 per cent), Andhra Pradesh (15 per cent), Chhattisgarh (11 per cent) Odisha (10 per cent), Karnataka and Rajasthan (7 per cent each), Gujarat (6 per cent) and Maharashtra (5 per cent). The remaining 12 per cent resources are distributed in Arunachal Pradesh, Jharkhand, Haryana, Sikkim, Tamil Nadu, Uttarakhand, Uttar Pradesh and West Bengal.

Fire Clay

India possesses substantial reserves of fireclay. The best deposits occur in association with the coal seams in the lower Gondwana coalfields of Andhra Pradesh, Jharkhand, West Bengal, Madhya Pradesh and Neyveli lignite fields in Tamil Nadu. Notable occurrences of fireclay, not associated with coal measures, are reported in Gujarat, Jabalpur region of Madhya Pradesh and Belpahar-Sundergarh areas of Odisha. Reserves and resources of fireclay as per UNFC system of 2015 are estimated at 723 million tonnes. Out of the total resources, Odisha accounts for 24 per cent followed by Madhya Pradesh (18 per cent), Tamil Nadu (16 per cent), Jharkhand (9 per cent) and Rajasthan and Gujarat (8 per cent each). Gradewise, refractory-plastic grade accounts for 37 per cent followed by refractory-unspecified (14 per cent) and refractory-non-plastic/semi-plastic (16 per cent). The remaining 33 per cent are of others, unclassified and not known grades.

Fluorspar

As per the UNFC system, the total resources of fluorite in the country in 2015 are estimated at 18.18 million tonnes. Out of these, 0.29 million tonnes are placed under reserves category. By states, Gujarat accounts for 66 per cent of the total resources having 12 million tonnes, followed by Rajasthan with 5.24 million tonnes (29 per cent), Chhattisgarh 0.55 million tonnes (3 per cent) and Maharashtra 0.39 million tonnes (2 per cent). Gradewise, the resources are classified into marketable grade which accounted for 81 per cent of the total resources, followed by low grade (17 per cent) and unclassified grade (2 per cent).

Gypsum

As per UNFC system, the total resources of mineral gypsum in India in 2015 are estimated at 1,330 million tonnes of which 37 million tonnes have been placed under 'reserves' and 1,293 million tonnes under 'remaining resources' category. Of the total resources, fertilizer/pottery grade accounts for about 80 per cent and cement/paint grade 13 per cent. The unclassified and not-known grades together account for 5 per cent resources. The remaining two percent of resources is shared by surgical plaster and soil reclamation grades. By States, Rajasthan alone accounts for 81 per cent resources and Jammu & Kashmir 14 per cent resources. The remaining 5 per cent resources are in Tamil Nadu, Gujarat, Himachal Pradesh, Karnataka, Uttarakhand, Andhra Pradesh and Madhya Pradesh.

Graphite

Graphite occurrences are reported from various states but the deposits of economic importance are located in Andhra Pradesh, Jharkhand, Karnataka, Kerala, Odisha, Rajasthan and Tamil Nadu. As per the UNFC system, the total resources of graphite in 2015 are placed at about 194.89 million tonnes, comprising 7.96 million tonnes in the reserves category and 186.93 million tonnes under remaining resources category. Arunachal Pradesh accounts for 37 per cent of total resources, followed by Jammu and Kashmir (32 per cent), Odisha (10 per cent), Jharkhand (9 per cent) and Tamil Nadu (4 per cent). However, in terms of reserves, Jharkhand has leading share of about 52 per cent followed by Tamil Nadu 41per cent.

Ilmenite

Ilmenite and rutile along with other heavy minerals are important constituents of beach sand deposits found right from Ratnagiri coast (Maharashtra) in the west to Odisha coast in the east. These minerals are concentrated in Kerala, Tamil Nadu, Odisha and Andhra Pradesh. As per the UNFC system, the total resources of ilmenite in 2015 are estimated at 355.48 million tonnes (including leucoxene), inclusive of indicated, inferred and speculative categories.

Kaolin

China clay resources in the country as per UNFC system in 2015 have been placed at 2,941.25 million tonnes. The reserves constitute only about 8 per cent of the resources at 229.47 million tonnes. The resources are spread over in a number of states of which Kerala holds about 23 per cent, followed by West Bengal 14 per cent, Rajasthan 18 per cent, Odisha 10 per cent and Karnataka 9 per cent. Out of total resources, about 26 per cent or 771 million tonnes fall under ceramic/pottery grade, 4 per cent are classified under chemical, paper filler and cement grades and about 70 per cent or 2,040 million tonnes resources fall under mixed grade, others, unclassified and not-known categories.

Kyanite and Sillimanite

The total resources of kyanite as per UNFC system in the country in 2015 are placed at 105 million tonnes. Statewise, the share of Telangana is 46 per cent of total resources followed by Andhra Pradesh 30 per cent, Karnataka 13 per cent and Jharkhand 7 per cent. Remaining 4 per cent resources are in Kerala, Maharashtra, Rajasthan, Tamil Nadu and West Bengal.

The total resources of sillimanite as per UNFC system in the country in 2015 are placed at 70.2 million tonnes. The resources are located mainly in Tamil Nadu and Odisha (25 per cent each), Uttar Pradesh (16 per cent), Andhra Pradesh (13 per cent), Kerala (10 per cent) and Assam (7 per cent). Remaining 4 per cent resources are in Jharkhand, Karnataka, Madhya Pradesh, Maharashtra, Meghalaya, Rajasthan and West Bengal.

Limestone

The total resources of limestone of all categories and grades as per UNFC system in 2015 are estimated at 203,225 million tonnes. Karnataka is the leading state having 27 per cent of the total resources followed by Andhra Pradesh and Rajasthan (12 per cent each), Gujarat (10 per cent), Meghalaya (9 per cent), Telangana (8 per cent) and Chhattisgarh (5 per cent). The total resources of chalk of all categories and grades as per UNFC system in 2015 are estimated in Gujarat at 6.75 million tonnes of which 5.06 million tonnes (75 per cent) are under reserves category and 1.69 million tonnes are under remaining resources category.

Mica

The most important mica-bearing pegmatites occur in Andhra Pradesh, Bihar, Jharkhand, Maharashtra and Rajasthan. Occurrences of mica pegmatites are also reported from Gujarat, Haryana, Karnataka, Kerala, Odisha, Tamil Nadu and West Bengal. As per UNFC, the total resources of mica in the country in 2015 are estimated at 635,302 tonnes . Andhra Pradesh leads with 40 per cent share in country's total resources followed by Rajasthan (28 per cent) Odisha (16 per cent), Maharashtra (13 per cent), Bihar (2 per cent) and balance (less than 1 per cent) in Jharkhand and Telangana.

Magnesite

The total reserves/resources of magnesite as per UNFC system in 2015 are about 394 million tonnes. Substantial quantities of resources are established in Uttarakhand (59 per cent), followed by Rajasthan (14 per cent) and Tamil Nadu (25 per cent). Resources are also located in Andhra Pradesh, Himachal Pradesh, Jammu and Kashmir, Karnataka and Kerala. Occurrences of magnesite in Tamil Nadu are low in lime and high in silica whereas those of Uttarakhand are high in lime and low in silica.

Phosphate Minerals

The total resources of apatite as per UNFC system in 2015 are placed at 24.04 million tonnes. Of the total resources, the bulk (57 per cent) is located in West Bengal followed by Jharkhand (30 per cent) and Meghalaya (5 per cent). The remaining 8 per cent resources are available in Rajasthan, Andhra Pradesh, Gujarat and Tamil Nadu. The total resources of rock phosphate as per UNFC system in 2015 are placed at 312.68 million tonnes. Of the total resources, 34 per cent are in Jharkhand, 31 per cent in Rajasthan, 19 per cent in Madhya Pradesh, 8 per cent each in Uttar Pradesh and Uttarakhand. Meagre resources are located in Gujarat and Meghalaya.

Other Minerals

Other minerals occurring in significant quantities in India are bentonite (Rajasthan, Gujarat, Tamil Nadu, Jharkhand and Jammu and Kashmir), corundum (Karnataka, Andhra Pradesh, Rajasthan, Tamil Nadu, Telangana and Chhattisgarh), calcite (Andhra Pradesh, Rajasthan, Madhya Pradesh, Tamil Nadu, Haryana, Karnataka, Uttar Pradesh and Gujarat), fuller's earth (Rajasthan, Telangana, Arunachal Pradesh, Assam, Madhya Pradesh and Karnataka), garnet (Tamil Nadu, Orissa, Andhra Pradesh, Rajasthan and Kerala), pyrites (Bihar, Rajasthan, Karnataka, Himachal Pradesh, West Bengal and Andhra Pradesh), steatite (Rajasthan, Uttarakhand, Kerala, Maharashtra, Andhra Pradesh and Madhya Pradesh), wollastonite (Rajasthan and Gujarat), zircon (beach sands of Kerala, Tamil Nadu and Orissa) and quartz and silica minerals and Granite are widespread and occur in nearly all states. Besides, the country has vast marble, slate and sandstone deposits. Marble occurs mainly in Rajasthan, Gujarat and Jammu and Kashmir; slate in Andhra Pradesh and Haryana.

Geological Survey of India

Geological Survey of India (GSI) the premier earth science organization of the country, is the principal provider of basic earth science information to the Government, Industry and the geoscientific sector. Beginning in 1851 as a department engaged primarily in research for coal, GSI in its last 163 years of existence has expanded its activities manifold and has been involved either directly or indirectly in almost all areas of nation building. The vibrant steel, coal, metal, cement and power industries which expanded phenomenally in the post independence era, bear eloquent testimony to GSI's contribution to national development.

GSI is now the custodian of one of the largest and most comprehensive earth science databases developed over the last one and half century. Its Charter of operation laid down by the Government of India details the scope of activities and responsibilities of GSI that encompasses practically the entire gamut of earth science activities. Creation and updation of national geoscientific information and knowledge base through ground, marine and airborne surveys and their dissemination are the primary goals of GSI. The present activity domains of GSI include surface mapping, aerial and remote sensing surveys, offshore surveys, exploration for mineral and energy resources, engineering geology, geotechnical investigations, geoenvironmental studies, geology of water resources, geohazard studies, research and development, training and capacity building and information services etc.

Relevant Website : www.gsi.gov.in

Online Core Business Integrated System and National Aerogeophysical Mapping Programme

GSI launched, in 2017, an Online Core Business Integrated System (OCBIS) which is a state-of-the-art IT enabled system encapsulating all the main activities of GSI using an online digital platform. The workflow of GSI from data acquisition to data storage, analysis and dissemination is digitally captured in this system, besides all the administrative and financial activities of GSI. All available baseline geoscience data of GSI is uploaded on geospatial platform for viewing and extracting free of cost.

Indian Bureau of Mines

Indian Bureau of Mines (IBM) established in March, 1948, is a multi-disciplinary scientific and technical organisation under Ministry of Mines with statutory and developmental responsibilities for conservation and systematic exploitation of mineral resources other than coal, petroleum and natural gas, atomic minerals and minor minerals.

The Indian Bureau of Mines performs regulatory functions under the relevant provisions of the Mines and Mineral (Development and Regulation) Act, 1957 amended in 2015 and rules made there undernamely enforcement of the Mineral Conservation and Development Rules, 2017, Minerals (Other than Atomic and Hydro Carbon Energy Minerals) Concession Rules, 2016 and other new rules and Environmental (Protection) Act, 1986 and Rules made thereunder. It also undertakes scientific, techno-economic, research oriented studies in various aspects of mining geological studies, ore beneficiation and environmental studies.

IBM provides technical consultancy services to the mining industry for the geological appraisal of mineral resources, and the preparation of feasibility report of mining projects, including beneficiation plants. It prepares mineral maps and countrywide inventory of mineral resources of leasehold and freehold areas. It also promotes and monitors community development activities in mining areas. IBM also functions as data bank of mines and minerals and publishes statistical information. It also brings out technical publications/ monographs/bulletins on mineral commodities. It advises the central and state governments on all aspects of mineral industry, trade, legislation etc. IBM has taken many initiatives towards digital India.

The Ministry of Mines has three Public Sector Undertaking (PSUs) under its administrative control. National Aluminium Company Limited (NALCO), Hindustan Copper Limited (HCL) are operating in the field of mining and mineral processing, and Mineral Exploration Corporation Limited (MECL) is operating in the field of mineral exploration.

Relevant Website : www.ibm.nic.in

National Aluminium Company Limited

National Aluminium Company Limited (NALCO) is a Navratna CPSE under Ministry of Mines. It was established in 1981 in the public sector, with its registered office at Bhubaneswar. The Company is a group 'A' CPSE having integrated and diversified operations in mining, metal and power with sales turnover of ₹ 7,933 crore in financial year 2016-17. NALCO is one of the largest integrated Bauxite-Alumina-Aluminium- Power Complex in the country. The Company has a 68.25 lakh TPA Bauxite Mine and 21.00 lakh TPA(normative capacity) Alumina Refinery located at Damanjodi in Koraput dist. of Odisha, and 4.60 lakh TPA Aluminium Smelter and 1200MW Captive Power Plant located at Angul, Odisha. NALCO has bulk shipment facilities at Vizag port for export of Alumina / Aluminium and import of caustic soda and also utilises the facilities at Kolkata and Paradeep ports. The company has registered sales offices in Delhi, Kolkata, Mumbai, Chennai and Bangalore and 11(eleven) stockyards at various locations in the country to facilitate domestic marketing. NALCO is the first Public Sector Company in the country to venture into international market in a big way with London Metal Exchange (LME) registration since 1989. The Company is listed at Bombay Stock Exchange (BSE) since 1992 and National Stock Exchange (NSE) since 1999. Besides, ISO 9001, ISO 14001, OHSAS 18000 and SA 8000 certification; the Company has also adopted ISO 50001 standards for energy management system.

Relevant Website : www.nalcoindia.com

Hindustan Copper Limited

Hindustan Copper Limited (HCL), a Mini Ratna Government of India Enterprise under the administrative control of the Ministry of Mines, was incorporated in 1967 under the Companies Act,1956. It was established as a Govt. of India enterprise to take over all plants, projects, schemes and studies pertaining to the exploration and exploitation of copper deposits, including smelting and refining from National Mineral Development Corporation Ltd. It has the distinction of being the nation's only vertically integrated copper producing company as it manufactures copper right from the stage of mining to beneficiation, smelting, refining and casting of refined copper metal into downstream saleable products.

Relevant Website : www.hindustancopper.com

Mineral Exploration Corporation Limited

Mineral Exploration Corporation Limited (MECL) a Miniratna Company is a premier mineral exploration Public Sector Undertaking of the country with ISO 9001-2008 certification. Since its inception in 1972, it has completed over 1371 projects of detailed mineral exploration and mine development and has added 160 billion tonnes of mineral resources to the National Mineral Inventory. It is the leading organisation both in government and in private sector, possessing entire spectrum of mineral exploration facilities under one roof. Since its inception in 1972, MECL has grown from strength to strength by adopting modern techniques of exploration and it has now emerged as the premier exploration agency in the country.

Relevant Website : www.mecl.gov.in

National Institute of Rock Mechanics

National Institute of Rock Mechanics (NIRM) is the only institution in south Asia exclusively devoted to research in rock mechanics. Over the period of last 25 years, the institute has the privilege to provide its expertise to various central, state government agencies and public sector undertakings in the field of mining, hydroelectric projects, nuclear power projects, oil and gas sector and various infrastructure project authorities including rail, road, airports, hospital etc.

Relevant Website : www.nirm.in

National Institute of Miners' Health

National Institute of Miners' Health, Nagpur (NIMH) is an autonomous institute established under Ministry of Mines, with the objective of promotion of occupational health and prevention of occupational diseases among the persons employed in mining and mineral based industries. The Institute is engaged in research and developmental activities relating to occupational health, work place monitoring etc. The institute has developed the brand image and reputation of providing quality comprehensive technical support services in the field of occupational health and hygiene.

Relevant Website : www.nimh.gov.in

Jawaharlal Nehru Aluminium Research Development and Design Centre

The Jawaharlal Nehru Aluminium Research Development and Design Centre (JNARDDC), Nagpur is a Centre of Excellence set up in 1989 as a joint venture of Ministry of Mines, Government of India and UNDP with a view to provide major R&D support system for the emerging modern aluminium industry in India. The Centre became functional since 1996. The Centre is recognized as scientific and industrial research organization by the Department of Scientific and Industrial Research. It is the only institute of its kind in India pursuing the cause of R&D from bauxite to finished product under one roof.

The Centre caters to R&D needs of both primary and secondary aluminium producers in the basic and applied areas of bauxite, alumina and aluminium, JNARDDC has made key contribution in the areas of beneficiation, characterization, technological evaluation, upgradation of bauxites, reduction of energy consumption and environmental pollution by the effective utilization of aluminium industry residue materials such as red mud, dross and scrap etc. and process modeling for the overall interest of the aluminium industry and the nation as a whole.

Relevant Website : www.jnarddc.gov.in

20 Law and Justice

MINISTRY of Law and Justice is the oldest limb of the Government of India dating back to 1833 when the Charter Act,1833 was enacted by the British Parliament. The said Act vested for the first time legislative power in a single authority, namely the Governor General of Council. By virtue of this authority and the authority vested under him under section 22 of the Indian Councils Act, 1861 the Governor General in Council enacted laws for the country from 1834 to 1920. After the commencement of the Government of India Act, 1919 the legislative power was exercised by the Indian Legislaturae constituted there under. The Government of India Act, 1919 was followed by the Government of India Act, 1935. With the passing of the Indian Independence Act, 1947 India became a Dominion and the Dominion Legislature made laws from 1947 to 1949 under the provisions of section 100 of the Government of India Act, 1935 as adapted by the India (Provisional Constitution) Order, 1947. Under the Constitution of India which came into force on the January 26, 1950 the legislative power is vested in Parliament.

Relevant Website : www.lawmin.gov.in

Ministry of Law and Justice comprises the three Departments namely the Department of Legal Affairs, the Legislative Department and the Department of Justice. The Department of Legal affairs is assigned legal functions including the interpretation of the Constitution and Laws, litigation, legal profession, law reforms, treaties and agreements with foreign countries in the matters of the civil law, legal services including Indian Legal Service, etc. The legislative Department is concerned with the drafting of the principal legislation for the central government.The Department of Justice is concerned with the appointment, resignation and the removal of the Chief Justice of India, the judges of the Supreme Court/High Courts etc.

Relevant Websites : www.legal affairs.gov.in www.doj.gov.in
www.legislative.gov.in

Indian Legal System

The Indian Legal System comprises four components namely the basic values and principles enshrined in the Constitution; rights and obligations conferred by ordinary statues; Organizational set up to enforce these rights and obligations within the Constitutional norms and lastly legal and the judicial personnel. India being a democratic country and there being a representative democracy there is a chain of accountability towards sovereign which lies amongst the people.

Sources of Law

The main sources of law in India are the Constitution, statutes (legislation), customary law and case law. Statutes are enacted by Parliament, state legislatures and union territory legislatures. Besides, there is a vast body of laws known as subordinate legislation in the form of rules, regulations as well as bye-laws made by central/state governments and local authorities like municipal corporations, municipalities, gram panchayats and other local bodies. This subordinate legislation is made under the authority conferred or delegated either by Parliament or state or union territory legislatures concerned. Judicial decisions of superior courts like Supreme Court and High Courts are important sources of law. Decisions of the Supreme Court are binding on all courts within the territory of India. Local customs and conventions which are not against statute, morality, etc., are also recognised and taken into account by courts while administering justice in certain spheres.

Enactment of Law

The Parliament is competent to make laws on matters enumerated in the Union List. State legislatures are competent to make laws on matters enumerated in the State List. Parliament alone has power to make laws on matters not included in the State List or Concurrent List. On matters enumerated in the Concurrent List, laws can be made by both Parliament and the state legislature. But in the event of repugnancy, law made by Parliament shall prevail over law made by state legislature, to the extent of repugnancy, be void unless the latter law having been reserved for consideration of President, has received his assent and in that event shall prevail in that state.

Judiciary

At the apex of the entire judicial system exists the Supreme Court of India with a High Court for each state or group of states and under the High Courts there is a hierarchy of subordinate courts. Panchayat Courts also function in some states under various names like Nyaya Panchayat, Panchayat Adalat, Gram Kachehri, etc., to decide civil and criminal disputes of petty and local nature. Different state laws provide for jurisdiction of these courts.

The highest court in each district is that of District and Sessions Judge. This district court is the principal court of civil jurisdiction and can try all offences including those punishable with death. He is the highest judicial authority in a district. Below him, there are courts of civil jurisdiction, known in different states as Munsifs, Sub-Judges, Civil Judges and the like. Similarly, criminal courts comprise Chief Judicial Magistrate and Judicial Magistrate of First and Second class.

Supreme Court

During the British regime, the King in Council, or Privy Council as it was generally called, was the highest forum to entertain appeals from the judgments and orders passed by the courts in India. On enactment of the Judicial Committee Act, 1833, it came to be called the Judicial Committee of Privy Council. The decisions of the Judicial Committee used to be couched in advisory form, though, in practice, the Crown always accepted its advice, and it was unthinkable that its report will not be given effect to. The Privy Council acted as a channel, through which English concepts came to be assimilated with Indian laws. It served as a bridge between the Indian and the English legal system, over which legal ideas travelled from England to India. It was through this body, that the common law of England was introduced in India under the British regime, as the base of its legal system. During its career as the highest court of appeals from India for the period of about 200 years, Privy Council rendered over 2,500 judgments, and till today these judgments constitute the fountain-source of law on many points in India.

However, there was a rising demand for establishment of Supreme Court in India, since it was felt that appeal to the Privy Council was very costly and beyond the means of common man. More important was the reason that it detracted from the self respect of the Indian people. Government of India Act, 1935 introduced a federal constitution to India, involving distribution of powers between the Centre and the constituent units. The Federal Court of India began functioning from October 01, 1937. To begin with, Federal Court had a very limited jurisdiction, confined to original jurisdiction in disputes between the centre and constituent units or inter se amongst the latter, advisory jurisdiction and appellate jurisdiction on a certificate from the High Court. Appeals from Federal Court could go to the Privy Council, from the judgments rendered in exercise of original jurisdiction, or by leave of the Federal Court or the Privy Council. In cases involving interpretation of Constitution, the parties had to first go to Federal Court in appeal from the High Court, and in other cases appeals from the High Courts lay directly to the Privy Council. It could give advice on such questions of public importance, as were referred to it by the Governor General, in his discretion. The appellate jurisdiction of the Federal Court was enlarged by enactment of Act No. 1 of 1948 and appeals were provided to Federal Court from the judgment of the High Court in the same circumstances, in which appeals could be brought to the Privy Council, without any special leave and also by special leave of the Federal Court in any other case. However, appeals to the Privy Council were still possible by leave of the Federal Court or of the Council.

After achieving independence in August, 1947, there was demand from the Indian polity for enlarging the jurisdiction of Federal Court and granting more powers to it. From 1949 appeals to the Privy Council were abolished altogether and the entire appellate jurisdiction was vested in the Federal Court. On January 26, 1950, Federal Court gave way to the Supreme Court of India under the new Constitution. Supreme Court of India is located on Tilak Marg, New Delhi.

After its inauguration on January 28, 1950, the apex court commenced its sittings in a part of the Parliament House. The Court moved into the present building on August 4, 1958. The original Constitution of 1950 envisaged a Supreme Court with a Chief Justice and 7 puisne Judges - leaving it to Parliament to increase this number. In the early years, all the Judges of the Supreme Court sat together to hear the cases presented before them. As the work of the Court increased and arrears of cases began to cumulate, Parliament increased the number of Judges from 7 in 1950 to 10 in 1956, 13 in 1960, 17 in 1977, 25 in 1986 and 30 in 2009. As the number of the Judges has increased, they sit in smaller Benches of two and three—coming together in larger Benches of 5 and more only when required to do so or to settle a difference of opinion or controversy.

The Supreme Court of India comprises the Chief Justice and 30 other Judges appointed by the President of India. Supreme Court Judges retire upon attaining the age of 65 years. In order to be appointed as a Judge of the Supreme Court, a person must be a citizen of India and must have been, for at least five years, a Judge of a High Court or of two or more such Courts in succession, or an Advocate of a High Court or of two or more such Courts in succession for at least 10 years or he must be, in the opinion of the President, a distinguished jurist. Provisions exist for the appointment of a Judge of a High Court as an ad hoc Judge of the Supreme Court and for retired Judges of the Supreme Court or High Courts to sit and act as Judges of Supreme Court. The Constitution seeks to ensure the independence of Supreme Court Judges in various ways. A Judge of the Supreme Court cannot be removed from office except by an order of the President passed after an address in each House of Parliament supported by a majority of the total membership of that House and by a majority of not less than two-thirds of members present and voting, and presented to the President in the same Session for such removal on the ground of proved misbehaviour or incapacity. A person who has been a Judge of the Supreme Court is debarred from practising in any court of law or before any other authority in India. The proceedings of the Supreme Court are conducted in English only. Supreme Court Rules, 2013 replacing the 1966 Rules, have been framed under Article 145 of the Constitution to regulate the practice and procedure of the Supreme Court. Justice Ranjan Gogoi is the 46th Chief Justice of India.

Relevant Website : www.supremecourtofindia.nic.in

High Courts

High Court stands at the head of the state's judicial administration. There are 24 High Courts in the country, three having jurisdiction over more than one state. Among the union territories, Delhi alone has a High Court of its own. Other six union territories come under the jurisdiction of different state High Courts. Each High Court comprises a Chief Justice and such other Judges as the President may, from time to time, appoint. The Chief Justice of a High Court is appointed by the President in consultation with the Chief Justice of India and the Governor of the state. The procedure for appointing the High Court judges is the same except that the recommendation for the appointment of Judges in the High Court is initiated by the Chief Justice of the High Court concerned.

They hold office up to 62 years of age. To be eligible for appointment as a judge, one must be a citizen of India and should have held a judicial office in India for 10 years or must have practised as an advocate of a High Court or two or more such courts in succession for a similar period.

Jurisdiction and Seat of High Courts

Each High Court has powers of superintendence over all courts and tribunals within its jurisdiction. It can call for returns from such courts, make and issue general rules and prescribed forms to regulate their practices and proceedings and determine the manner and form in which book entries and accounts shall be kept. This table gives the seat and territorial jurisdiction of the high courts.

Name of High Courts, their Principal Seats, Benches and their Jurisdiction

Sl No.	High Court	Principal Seat	Jurisdiction	Permanent Bench and Date from which the Bench began fuctioning
1	Allahabad	Prayagraj	Uttar Pradesh	Lucknow (01.07.1948)
2	Andhra Pradesh	Hyderabad	Andhra Pradesh and Telangana	-
3	Bombay	Mumbai	Maharashtra; Goa; Daman and Diu Dadra and Nagar Haveli	Nagpur (01.05.1960) Panaji (01.07.1948) Aurangabad (27.08.1984)
4	Calcutta	Kolkata	West Bengal and Andaman and Nicobar Islands	Circuit Bench Jalpaiguri (yet to begin functioning)
5	Chhattisgarh	Bilaspur	Chattisgarh	-
6	Delhi	New Delhi	NCT of Delhi	-
7	Gauhati	Guwahati	Assam, Nagaland, Mizoram and Arunachal Pradesh	Kohima (10.02.1990) Aizawl (05.07.1990) Itanagar (12.08.2000)
8	Gujarat	Sola (Ahmedabad)	Gujarat	-
9	Himachal Pradesh	Shimla	Himachal Pradesh	-
10	Jammu and Kashmir	Jammu and Srinagar	Jammu and Kashmir	-
11	Jharkhand	Ranchi	Jharkhand	-
12	Karnataka	Bengaluru	Karnataka	Circuit Benches at Dharwar (07.02.2008) Gulbarga (07.02.2008)
13	Kerala	Kochi	Kerala and Lakshadweep Is.	-

Sl No.	High Court	Principal Seat	Jurisdiction	Permanent Bench and Date from which the Bench began fuctioning
14	Madhya Pradesh	Jabalpur	Madhya Pradesh	Gwalior (01.11.1956) Indore (01.11.1956)
15	Madras	Chennai	Tamil Nadu and Puducherry	Madurai (24.07.2004)
16	Orissa	Cuttack	Odisha	-
17	Patna	Patna	Bihar	-
18	Punjab and Haryana	Chandigarh	Punjab, Haryana and Chandigarh	Chandigarh
19	Rajasthan	Jodhpur	Rajasthan	Jaipur (31.01.1977)
20	Sikkim	Gangtok	Sikkim	-
21	Uttarakhand	Nainital	Uttarakhand	Nainital
22	Manipur	Imphal	Manipur	-
23	Meghalaya	Shillong	Meghalaya	-
24	Tripura	Agartala	Tripura	-

Approved and Working Strength of Supreme Court and High Courts

Statement showing Approved strength, Working Strength and Vacancies of Judges in the Supreme Court of India and the High Courts (As on 01.10.2018)

Sl. No.	Name of the Court	Approved Strength			Working Strength			Vacancies as per Approved Strength		
A	Supreme Court of India	31			25			06		
B.	High Court	Pmt.	Addl.	Total	Pmt.	Addl.	Total	Pmt.	Addl.	Total
1	Allahabad	76	84	160	67	43	104	14	42	56
2	Telengana & Andhra Pradesh*	46	15	61	31	0	31	15	15	30
3	Bombay*	71	23	94	50	20	70	21	03	24
4	Calcutta*	54	18	72	26	07	33	28	11	39
5	Chhattisgarh	17	05	22	09	03	12	08	02	10
6	Delhi*	45	15	60	38	0	38	07	15	22
7	Gauhati	18	06	24	07	11	18	11	-05	06
8	Gujarat	39	13	52	25	06	31	14	07	21
9	Himachal Pradesh*	10	03	13	08	0	08	02	03	05
10	Jammu & Kashmir	13	04	17	11	0	11	02	04	06
11	Jharkhand*	19	06	25	10	07	17	09	-01	08
12	Karnataka*	47	15	62	17	07	24	30	08	38
13	Kerala*	35	12	47	29	08	37	06	04	10

Sl. No.	Name of the Court	Approved Strength			Working Strength			Vacancies as per Approved Strength		
14	Madhya Pradesh	40	13	53	16	17	33	24	-04	20
15	Madras	56	19	75	43	15	58	13	04	17
16	Manipur*	04	01	05	02	0	02	02	01	03
17	Meghalaya	03	01	04	02	0	02	01	01	02
18	Orissa	20	07	27	17	0	17	03	07	10
19	Patna	40	13	53	20	12	32	20	01	21
20	Punjab & Haryana	64	21	85	40	10	50	24	11	35
21	Rajasthan	38	12	50	19	15	34	19	-03	16
22	Sikkim	03	0	03	03	0	03	0	0	0
23	Tripura	04	0	04	02	0	02	02	0	02
24	Uttarakhand	09	02	11	08	01	09	01	01	02
	Total	771	308	1079	495	181	696	276	127	403

**Acting Chief Justice*

Power of Supreme Court and High Courts

Supreme Court has power to issue any person or authority and government within its jurisdiction, direction, order or writs, including writs which are in the nature of for enforcement of Fundamental Rights and for any other purpose. This power may also be exercised by any high court exercising jurisdiction in relation to territories within which the cause of action, wholly or in part arises for exercise of such power, even if the seat of such government or authority or residence of such person is not within those territories.

Subordinate Courts

The structure and functions of subordinate courts are more or less uniform throughout the country. Designations of courts connote their functions. These courts deal with all disputes of civil or criminal nature as per the powers conferred on them. These courts follow two important codes prescribing procedures, i.e., the Code of Civil Procedure, 1908 and the Code of Criminal Procedure, Cr. P.C., 1973 and further strengthened by state level amendments. As per direction of Supreme Court in WP (Civil) 1022/1989 in the All India Judges Association case, a uniform designation has been brought about in the subordinate judiciary's judicial officers all over the country, viz., District or Additional District Judge, Civil Judge (Senior Division) and Civil Judge (Junior Division) on the civil side and on criminal side, Sessions Judge, Additional Sessions Judge, Chief Judicial Magistrate and Judicial Magistrate, etc., as laid down in the Cr.P.C. Appropriate adjustment, if any, has been made in existing posts by indicating their equivalent with any of these categories by all state governments/UT administrations. Under Article 235 of the Constitution of India, the administrative control over the members of subordinate judicial service vests with the concerned High Court. Further in exercise of powers conferred under provision to Article 309 read with Articles 233 and 234 of the Constitution, the state government shall frame rules and regulations in consultation with the High Court exercising jurisdiction in relation to such state. The members of the State Judicial Services are governed by these rules and regulations.

National Mission for Justice Delivery and Legal Reforms

National Mission for Justice Delivery and Legal Reforms was set up in 2011 with the twin objectives of increasing access by reducing delays and arrears in the system and enhancing accountability through structural changes and by setting performance standards and capacities. The Mission has been pursuing a co-ordinated approach for phased liquidation of arrears and pendency in judicial administration, which, *inter-alia,* involves better infrastructure for courts including computerization, increase in strength of subordinate judiciary, policy and legislative measures in the areas prone to excessive litigation, re-engineering of court procedure for quick disposal of cases and emphasis on human resource development. The Mission has taken several steps in each of the strategic areas towards fulfilment of its objectives. All States have formulated their Litigation Policies with a view to reduce the Governmental litigation. State governments have been requested in make an assessment of the impact of the State Litigation Policies on controlling proliferation of litigation by State agencies. Department of Legal Affairs have formulated National Litigation Policy, 2015, which is under active consideration of the Government.

An important aspect of the judicial reforms relates to re-engineering court procedures and court processes for early disposal of cases. Process service has been identified as a major bottleneck for timely delivery of justice. A research note was prepared and circulated to High Courts for improving the process service in civil and criminal matters. A positive response has been received from several High Courts on the suggestions made in the research note. The subject matter of re-engineering of court process and case management is also under active consideration of the National Court Management System (NCMS) of the Supreme Court. Process re-engineering exercise is being carried out under e-Courts Mission Mode Project. For promotion of alternative methods of dispute resolutions, mediation centres are being set up in court complexes at District and Taluka levels. Government agencies are being encouraged to include arbitration/mediation clauses in government contracts. Shortage of judicial officers/judges in district and subordinate courts is one of the main causes for backlog and pendency of cases in courts. The National Mission has regularly pursued this matter with the State Governments and the High Courts. As a result of the concerted efforts of all the stockholders, the sanctioned strength of judicial officers/judges in district and subordinate courts has increased from

17,715 at the end of 2012 to 20,358 as in June, 2015. The mission is now pursuing the matter with the High Courts for filling up the existing vacancies. Emphasis is also being laid on proper training of all court functionaries.

Judicial Infrastructure

The primary responsibility of infrastructure development for the subordinate judiciary rests with the state governments. A centrally sponsored scheme has been in place since 1993-94 to assist the states for the development of judicial infrastructure. It covers the construction of court buildings and residential accommodation of judicial officers. Until 2011, the central and state governments used to contribute an equal share under the scheme but from 2011-12 onwards the central government was contributing 75 per cent of the funds. In the case of states in the north eastern states the central government provides 90 per cent of the funding. Central funding is, however, subject to budgetary allocation for the scheme. Out of Budget allocation of ₹ 562.99 crore for the scheme in the financial year (2015-16), ₹ 542.62 crore has been sanctioned to state/UTs as on 31st December, 2015. Fund sharing pattern of the scheme has now been revised from 75:25 to 60:40 (centre: state) (90:10 for the 8 north-eastern and 3 Himalayan states) with effect from 2015-16.

e-Courts Integrated Mission Mode Project

The e-Courts Integrated Mission Mode Project is one of the e-Governance projects being implemented in High Courts and district/subordinate courts of the country. The project has been conceptualized on the basis of the "National Policy and Action Plan for Implementation of Information and Communication Technology in the Indian Judiciary-2005" by the e-Committee of the Supreme Court of India. The e-Committee was formed in 2004 to draw up an action plan for the ICT enablement of the Judiciary with the Patron in Chief-cum-Adhoc Chairman as the Chief Justice of India.

Out of 14,249, courts to be computerized, at the end of March, 2015 all courts (100 per cent) have been made ready for computerization, out of which LAN has been installed at 13,606 courts (95.49 per cent), hardware at 13426 courts (94.3 per cent) and software is functional at 13,672 courts (95.50 per cent).

Access to Justice for the Marginalised

In partnership with the United Nations Development Programme (UNDP), the Department of Justice (DoJ), Ministry of Law and Justice, is implementing a decade long programme on Access to Justice for Marginalised People (2008-2017). The project extends to the eight UNDAF states of Bihar, Chattisgarh, Jharkhand, Madhya Pradesh, Rajasthan, Uttar Pradesh, Maharashtra and Odisha. This project focuses on strengthening access to justice for the marginalised people by developing strategies that address barriers to accessing justice in legal, social and economic domains. The project is presently in the second phase of implementation. The first phase expanding from 2008 to 2012 made significant contributions.

The second phase of the project extends over five years from 2013 to 2017. In this phase, the project aims to build upon the achievements of previous phase and continues to work on creation of demand for justice and ensuring its supply. Under the project, a technical support team has also been placed with the Department of Justice with the specific purpose of supporting the National Mission for Justice Delivery and Legal Reforms. The second phase of the project will continue to focus both on the demand and supply side. In terms of geographical coverage, the project will focus efforts in 1-2 selected districts in the eight states of Bihar, Chhattisgarh, Jharkhand, Madhya Pradesh, Maharashtra, Odisha, Rajasthan and Uttar Pradesh for better impact. The project will try to ensure sustainability of results achieved in the previous phase.

Legal Affairs

Department of Legal Affairs is the nodal department for reciprocal arrangement with foreign countries for enforcement of arbitral awards pursuant to the New York Convention under section 44(b) of the Arbitration and Concilliation Act, 1996. The department of Legal Affairs is the Central Authority under the Hague Convention of 1965 for service aboard of judicial and extra-judicial documents in civil and commercial matters. Under this obligation, around 9309 requests have been processed since May, 2014 till May, 2017.

Legal Information Management and Briefing System

In line with Digital India mission, this system digitalizes the court case details and brings various stakeholders on a single platform. LIMBS helps to introduce transparency as well as a sense of ownership among various stakeholders during the entire life cycle of a court case. In a very short span, with the help of various ministries and their nodal officers and local admins, LIMBS has captured more than 1.36 L court cases with more than 5500 registered users, more than 14000 advocates, and 1200 courts. Number of Arbitration cases on the portal is 452. More than 200 presentations have been made for concerned officers of the various Ministries/Departments 62 in number.

Way Forward

Department of Legal Affairs has identified some focus areas to encourage the principles of transparency, objectivity and accountability in its dealings with the public in conformity, inter-alia, with the objective of good governance, minimum government, maximum governance and ease of doing business and reducing litigation within the framework and mandate assigned to it. Because of the welfare nature, the size of the government is enormous. New laws and tools are being evolved to meet new situations arising due to growth, development, science and technology, increase in population, paraphernalia and consciousness amongst people about their rights. In this context the following major initiatives/reforms are proposed for vision New India-2022:-

Litigation Assessment

The Department has taken preliminary steps to formulate litigation assessment/legal audit/guidelines to examine a case during its journey arising from a dispute to a full blown litigation and its outcome and subsequent implementation aspect or otherwise. If the litigation assessment is carried out at the stage of policy formulation it would have the following results: (i) a holistic picture will emerge in the proposal; (ii) may prevent litigation to crop up; (iii) will bring down case load on the judicial system and; (iv) reduce consequent burden on the public exchequer.

National Litigation Policy

There are approximately 3.2 crore cases pending in various courts in India. Government is said to be the major litigant and there have been several Law Commission reports suggesting for a Litigation Policy to avoid unwarranted litigation by government and thus bring down load on the court system as well as burden on the public exchequer. Therefore, the draft National Litigation Policy 2017 proposes to put in place a system which prevents, controls and reduces litigation.

Institutionalisation of Arbitration

Delay in conducting the legal procedure and want of timely disposal of investment related cases/application lead to international arbitration involving huge expenditure to the state exchequer. Hence, streamlining the legal and judicial system to ensure speedy resolution of commercial disputes is the need and a necessary requirement. Department of Legal Affairs, constituted a high level committee to review Institutionalization of Arbitration Mechanism in India, under the chairmanship of Hon'ble Justice Shri B. N. Srikrishna. The report of this Committee has been submitted to the Minister for Law and Justice in July, 2017.

Reforms in Legal Profession

Legal fraternity represents the most enlightened and traditionally respected section of the society. In a democratic polity, the role of this dignified profession has always been very important. It is the watchdog of democracy and remains ever vigilant in the matters concerning the rule of law as enshrined and guaranteed by our Constitution. There has been a strong objection on the matter of allowing legal practice in India by foreign lawyers and law firms, inter-alia, on the ground of procedural hurdles faced by Indian Lawyers in case they want to practice in foreign countries. Therefore, the issue is of parity in opportunity to practice on reciprocal basis.

Appellate Tribunal for Foreign Exchange

The Appellate Tribunal for Foreign Exchange was established in 2000 under Section 18 of Foreign Exchange Management Act (FEMA), 1999. Under Section 19 of FEMA, the central government or any person aggrieved by an order made by Special Director (Appeals), or made by an Adjudicating Authority other than referred to in sub-Section (i) of Section 17, may prefer an appeal to the

Appellate Tribunal that may be filed within 45 days from the date of receiving the order by the aggrieved person or the central government.

Section 20 of FEMA provides that the Appellate Tribunal shall consist of a Chairperson and such number of members as the Central Government may deem fit. The jurisdiction of the Appellate Tribunal may be exercised by the Benches. The Bench may be constituted by the Chairperson, with one or more Members as the Chairperson deems fit. The Benches of the Appellate Tribunal shall ordinarily sit in New Delhi and at such other places as the Central Government may, in consultation with the Chairperson, notify and the Chairperson may transfer a Member from one Bench to another. If at any stage it appears that the matter should be heard by a Bench of two Members the Chairperson may transfer the matter to such Bench as he deems fit. A person who is qualified to be a Judge of a High Court or is or has been a Judge of High Court can be appointed as Chairperson of the Tribunal and a person who has been or is qualified to be a District Judge can be appointed as a Member of the Tribunal. Under Section 49 sub-Section (5) clause (b), all appeals which were pending before PERA Board have been transferred and are at the disposal of the Appellate Tribunal constituted under Foreign Exchange Management Act.

Enforcement Agencies

Police

The police force in the country is entrusted with the responsibility of maintenance of public order and prevention and detection of crimes. Public order and police being state subjects under the Constitution, police is maintained and controlled by states. The police force in a state is headed by the Director General of Police/ Inspector General of Police. State is divided into convenient territorial divisions called ranges and each police range is under the administrative control of a Deputy Inspector General of Police. A number of districts constitute the range. District police is further sub-divided into police divisions, circles and police stations. Besides the civil police, states also maintain their own armed police and have separate intelligence branches, crime branches, etc. Police set up in big cities like Delhi, Kolkata, Mumbai, Chennai, Bengaluru, Hyderabad, Ahmedabad, Nagpur, Pune, etc., is directly under a Commissioner of Police who enjoys magisterial powers. All senior police posts in various states are manned by the Indian Police Service (IPS) cadres, recruitment to which is made on All-India basis.

The central government maintains Central Police forces, Intelligence Bureau (IB), Central Bureau of Investigation (CBI), institutions for training of police officers and forensic science institutions to assist the states in gathering intelligence, in maintaining law and order, in investigating special crime cases and in providing training to the senior police officers of the state governments.

Indo-Tibetan Border Police

The ITBP was raised in the wake of Chinese aggression in 1962 with a modest strength of 4 Bns under an integrated 'guerilla-cum-intellgence-cum-fighting Force' self-contained in supplies, communication and intelligence collection. It has evolved with passage of time into a conventional border guarding Force. Today, ITBPF guards 3,488 kms of Indo-China Border and is manning 173 Border Out Posts (BOPs) with altitudes ranging from 9,000 feet to 18,750 feet in the western, middle and eastern sector of the Indo-China Border along the Himalayas from Karakoram Pass in Ladakh to Jachep La in Arunachal Pradesh. 8 ITBPF Bns are deployed in Maoist affected areas of Chhattisgarh. The Force operates through 05 frontier headquarters, 14 sector headquarters, 56 service battalions, 02 DM battalions, 04 specialized battalions and 14 training centres with a total sanctioned strength of 89,432.

ITBP is basically a mountain trained force and most of the officers and men are professionally trained mountaineers and skiers. They have scaled more than 180 Himalayan peaks including Mt. Everest four times including the 2012 expedition. ITBP mountaineers have also successfully climbed peaks in Nepal, Iran, Japan and South America. ITBP skiers have been national champions and have taken part in winter olympics. It has also participated in adventurous White Water Rafting, through turbulent and mighty waters of the Brahamputra, the Indus and the Ganges and has international achievements to its credit in this field.

Relevant Website : www.itbpolice.nic.in

Border Security Force

International borders of India with Pakistan both east and west were being manned by the respective state police forces till Indo-Pak war in September, 1965. Certain inherent shortcomings of this arrangement came to light during the war and it was decided to have one single force under the Union of India for guarding the international borders with Pakistan.

Border Security Force was raised in 1965 with the strength of 25 Battalions and 3 Coys. Over the years, the Force has grown in size and as on date, it has 186 Battalions including 3 NDRF battalions, 5 major training institutions, 11 subsidiary training centres and 03 minor training institutions. The Force Headquarter is in New Delhi. Its field formations includes 2 Special Directorates General (Spl DsG) i.e. Spl DG (Eastern Command) and Spl DG (Western Command), 13 Frontiers and 46 sector headquarters, water wing, air wing and other ancillary units. The sanctioned strength of BSF as on 31.12.2016 is 2,57,363.

BSF's role during peace time is as : (i) to promote a sense of security among the people living in the border areas; (ii) to prevent trans-border crimes, unauthorized entry into or exit from the territory of India; (iii) to prevent smuggling and any other illegal activities on the border; (iv) anti-infiltraton duties; and (v) to collect trans-border intelligence. Its role during war time is as: (i) holding ground in assigned sectors; limited aggressive action against central armed police or irregular forces of the enemy; (iii) maintenance of law and order in enemy territory administered under the army's control; (iv) guarding of prisoners of war camps; (v) acting as guides to the army in border areas; (vi) assistance in control of refugees; (vii) provision of sectors; and (viii) performing special tasks connected with intelligence including raids.

Relevant Website : www.bsf.nic.in

Assam Rifles

The Assam Rifles raised as Catchar Levy in 1835 is the oldest Central Para Military Force in India. The Force was raised primarily to guard the alluvial plains of Assam from the wild and unruly tribes inhabiting the surrounding hill tracts. This was the earliest embodied unit of what eventually developed into the Assam Rifles. Gradually more such units were raised and employed for establishing posts in the interior and thus acted as the strong arm of the civil administration in extending the authority of the Britishers. The Force also helped in opening up these inaccessible and isolated areas and in undertaking development activities; earning many accolades from the administration. The Assam Rifles' contribution towards assimilation of the people of the north-east into the national mainstream is truly monumental. Their long association with the region reflects in the force being fondly called "The Sentinel of the North-East" and "Friends of the Hill People" security in the north-eastern region and guarding the Indo-Myanmar border.

It has its headquarters at Shillong and the Force is completely deployed in the North East for guarding the Indo-Myanmar Border, spread over 1,631 kilometers. It functions under the control of Ministry of Home Affairs. The Force comprises a Directorate General headquarter, three Inspectorate General headquarters, 12 sector headquarters, 46 battalions, one training centre and the administrative elements with a total strength of 63,747 personnel.

Relevant Website : www.assamrifles.gov.in

National Security Guard

Terrorism, both national and international raised its head in the west during the seventies. It manifested in many forms including hijacking of aircraft, taking of hostages, assassination of dignitaries and others. The normal law and order machinery and the defence forces of the West were found wanting to deal with this menace. Specially equipped and trained forces like SAS of UK, Delta Force of USA and GSG-9 of West Germany were raised abroad. The need for creating a special force for executing surgical operations based on tactical intelligence was felt in India when Operation Blue Star was carried out by the army at the Golden Temple, Amritsar in 1984. National Security Guard (NSG) was conceptualised and created after studying and analysing Special Force like SAS in the United Kingdom, GIGN in France, GSG-9 in Germany, Shar-et-matkal in Israel and Delta Force in the USA. Accordingly, NSG was raised in October, 1985 as a Federal Contingency Force under the MHA. It consists of selected and highly motivated personnel from the army as well as the central armed police. 53 per cent of the personnel are drawn from the army while the central armed police like BSF, CRPF and ITBP contribute 47 per cent. NSG has a glorious heritage and is held in high esteem by the nation. Since raising, its commandos have been employed in 114 major successful counter terrorist operations, earning numerous awards and rewards including three Ashok Chakras, two Kirti Chakras, three Shaurya Chakras and 10 PPMG. Nine NSG Commandos have also made the supreme sacrifice in living up to the NSG's motto of Sarvatra Sarvottam Suraksha.

Relevant Website : www.nsg.gov.in

Central Reserve Police Force

The Central Reserve Police Force (CRPF) was formed in July 1939 at Neemuch as the Crown Representative's Police. After independence it was renamed as the Central Reserve Police Force and Sardar Vallabh Bhai Patel, the then Home Minister had visualized a multi-dimensional role for it. The CRPF has innumerable achievements to its credit. It was the CRPF which bore the brunt of the first onslaught of the Chinese aggression at Hot Springs in Ladakh in 1959 when a small CRPF patrol was ambushed and heavily out-numbered by the Chinese army. In the ensuing battle, 10 CRPF men laid down their lives. Every year 21st October is observed as the Police Commemoration Day. The force proved its mettle in 1965 when a small contingent of Second Bn CRPF, successfully fought and repulsed an attack by a Pakistani Brigade on 9th April at Sardar Post in Gujarat, killing 34 Pakistani soldiers and capturing 4 alive. Never in the history of military battles have a handful policemen fought back a full-fledged infantry brigade in such a manner. In this incident six valiant CRPF men also laid down their lives. As a tribute to the saga of our brave men, 9th April is now befittingly celebrated as "Valour Day" in the Force.

The CRPF has also been deployed internationally at Kosovo, Haiti and Sri Lanka. In Sri Lanka, two CRPF Battalions and one company of Mahila Battalion were a part of the Indian Peace Keeping Force. The first major offensive of the LTTE directed against the CRPF, using unconventional warfare was successfully repelled. Now, for the first time in the history of UN, a fully formed women's unit is posted in Liberia as a part of United Nations Peacekeeping Mission. On December 13, 2001 when the terrorists attacked the Parliament House it was the brave CRPF who successfully foiled the attack. In exchange of fire, all the five militants were eliminated. Mahila Ct Kamlesh Kumari who sacrificed her life during the incident was, for her exemplary bravery, awarded the highest peacetime Gallantry Award 'Ashok Chakra' posthumously. When 5 armed terrorists tried to storm the Ram Janambhoomi/Babri Masjid Complex in Ayodhya in July, 2005 and had penetrated the outer security rings, they were confronted by the CRPF posted at the inner security ring. The CRPF Jawans fought bravely and thwarted the evil designs of the terrorists and successfully eliminated all of them on the spot.

From a single battalion in 1939 the Force has now grown to four zones, 20 Adm. Sectors, 2 Ops Sectors, 36 Adm Ranges, 7 Ops Ranges, 228 Bns, 41 group centers, 15 training institutions and 4 composite hospitals. It is the only Central Armed Police Force in the country which has 3 Mahila Battalions. The bulk of the force is deployed in Jammu and Kashmir; left wing extremism affected states and in north-eastern states to tackle terrorist and insurgent activities. It presently has 10 Cobra units, a specially trained force to fight the naxal means. The Cobra battalions have been deployed strategically in the naxal affected areas. CRPF has always been playing a significant role in times of natural disasters. When the destructive Tsunami had caused an unprecedented damage to lives and property or when the J and K earthquake had devastated large areas disrupting life on a massive scale, CRPF played a significant role in the relief, rescue and rehabilitation efforts. We now have two battalions of CRPF designated as Disaster Management battalions and they have been located in Pune and Ahmedabad.

Relevant Website : www.crpf.nic.in

Rapid Action Force

In 1992, 10 Battalions of CRPF were reorganized and converted into 10 battalions of 4 coys each of Rapid Action Force (RAF). The personnel in RAF are trained and equipped to be an effective strike Force in communal riots and similar situations. These Battalions are located at 10 communally sensitive locations across the country to facilitate quick response in case of any such incident. All these Battalions are organized on an unattached pattern and are working under the supervision of an Inspector General.

RAF was raised to deal with communal problems and continues to deal with militancy in J and K and Punjab, insurgency in north-east, overseas deployment for UN Peace Keeping in Haiti, Bosnia and Kosovo, rescue and relief (Odisha super cyclone, Gujarat and JandK earthquake). RAF dealt with mammoth human congregations (Amarnath Yatra, Jagannath Yatra, etc.) combating naxalism in LWE affected states guarding of vital shrines in Ayodhya, Kashi, Mathura, Vaishno Devi and Raghunath Temple, Jammu law and order situation on the issue of revocation of transfer of land to Shri Amarnath Shrine Board, dealt with serious law and order problem due to Gujjar agitation in Rajasthan, dealt effectively with serious stone pelting menace in J and K, and monitored successful completion of elections in various states.

Central Industrial Security Force

Raised in 1969, Central Industrial Security Force (CISF) is providing security cover to 303 units including 59 domestic and international airports and fire protection cover to 87 industrial undertakings. With globalization and liberalization of the economy, CISF is no longer a PSU-centric organization. Instead, it has become a premier multi-skilled security agency of the country, mandated to provide security to major critical infrastructure installations of the country in diverse regions including terrorist and naxal affected areas. CISF is currently providing security cover to 308 units which include atomic power plants, space installations, defence production units, mines, oil fields and refineries, major sea ports, heavy engineering steel plants, fertilizer units, airports, hydro electric/thermal power plants, sensitive government buildings and even heritage monuments (including the Taj Mahal and Red Fort) and also iconic private sector units. The Force is also one of the largest fire protection service providers in the country. It provides fire protection cover to 86 industrial undertakings. CISF has been inducted into Ratnagiri Gas and Thermal Power Station Ltd., Rajiv Gandhi Thermal Power Project, Hissar, Haryana. The specialized task of airport security was assigned to CISF in the wake of hijacking of Indian Airlines plane to Kandhar.

The Force has so far taken over security of all major airports in the country, which includes international airports of Mumbai, Delhi, Chennai and Kolkata. Besides, it has taken over security of 45 government buildings, which include North Block, part of South Block and CGO Complex in Delhi. CISF Act was amended to enable the force to provide security, on payment basis, to private/joint venture industrial undertakings, which are vital for the security and economy of the country. After the Mumbai terrorist attack in November, 2008, the mandate of the force has been broadened to provide direct security cover to private sector also. More than 175 private sector installations have already requested for CISF protection and Infosys Technologies Limited - a multinational information technology services company's headquarter in Bengaluru, became the first private sector company to get the CISF security cover in August 2009. CISF is a cost reimbursement force i.e., it is not a burden on the national exchequer. CISF in October, 2009 started a passenger friendly utility on its official website www.cisf.gov.in for the lost and found articles at all airports where CISF has been deployed.

Relevant Website : www.cisf.gov.in

Sashastra Seema Bal

The 'Sashastra Seema Bal" (SSB) is the newest border guarding force of Union of India entrusted with the guarding of Indo-Nepal and Indo-Bhutan borders. "Sashastra Seema Bal" is guarding Indo-Nepal border since 2001 and was also given the additional responsibility of guarding Indo-Bhutan border in 2004. Sashastra Seema Bal came into existence under the name Special Service Bureau in early 1963 in the wake of Indo-China conflict. Its earlier aim was to build people's morale and inculcate a spirit of resistance in border population in the then NEFA, North Assam, North Bengal, hills of Uttar Pradesh, Himachal Pradesh and Jammu and Kashmir (Ladakh). The area of operation was extended to other border areas in Manipur, Tripura, Jammu, Meghalaya, Sikkim, Rajasthan, Gujarat, Mizoram, South Bengal and Nagaland between 1965-1991.

The role of SSB in earlier setup includes : (i) to inculcate a sense of security and spirit of resistance in border population; (ii) promoting national awareness and security consciousness; and (iii) organizing and preparing border population to resist enemy.

Relevant Website : www.ssb.nic.in

Civil Defence

Civil Defence includes any measures not amounting to actual combat, for affording protection to any person, property, place or thing in India or any part of the territory thereof against any hostile attack whether from air, land, sea or other places or for depriving any such attack of the whole or part of its effect, whether such measures are taken before, during or after the time of such attack, or any measures taken for the purpose of disaster management, before, during, or after any disaster.

The Amendment to the Civil Defence Act, 1968 accorded legal sanction to the additional role of the Civil Defence constituents in the field of disaster mangement. Civil Defence is primarily organized on voluntary basis except for a small nucleus of paid staff and establishment which is augmented during emergencies. Civil Defence volunteers are in various constructive and nation building activities—including providing assistance to the administration in undertaking social and welfare services and in the prevention, mitigation of natural, man made disasters as well as in post-disaster response and relief operations and law and order situations. The training of its organisation is carried out in three tier levels. The training of master trainers and specialized training is conducted at the National Civil Defence College, Nagpur and team/ leadership training is conducted at state civil defence institutes. Training of the volunteers in Civil Defence Organisation is conducted at local/town levels by trained trainers in the form of short-term training programmes. A centrally sponsored scheme was launched at a cost of ₹100 crores in 2009 for revamping the Civil Defence setup in the country during the 11th Plan. The scheme envisages creation of new Civil Defence Training Institutes (CDTIs) in 10 states and renovation of infrastructure of CDTIs in 17 states, in addition 100 multi hazard districts have been selected for creation of civil defence infrastructure. A pilot project has also been launched in 40 selected towns to train and utilize Civil Defence volunteers in internal security tasks.

Home Guards

Home Guards is a voluntary force, first raised in India in December, 1946, to assist the police in controlling civil disturbances and communal riots. Subsequently, the concept of the voluntary citizens force was adopted by several states. In the wake of Chinese aggression in 1962, the Centre advised the states and union territories to merge their existing voluntary organisations into one uniform voluntary force known as Home Guards. The role of Home Guards is to serve as an auxiliary to the police in maintenance of internal security, help the community in any kind of emergency such as an air-raid, fire, cyclone, earthquake, epidemic, etc., help in maintenance of essential services, promote communal harmony and assist the administration in protecting weaker sections, participate in socio-economic and welfare activities and perform civil defence duties. Home Guards are of two types-rural and urban. In border States, Border Wing Home Guard Battalions have also been raised, which serve as an auxiliary to the Border Security Force. The organisation is spread over in all the states and union territories except in Kerala. In seven border states, a total of eighteen (18) Border Wing Home Guards (BWHG) Battalions have also been raised viz., Punjab (6 Bns), Rajasthan (4 Bns), Gujarat (4 Bns) and one each of Bns for Assam, Meghalaya, Tripura and West Bengal to serve as an auxiliary to Border Security Force for preventing infiltration on the international border/coastal areas, guarding of VVIPs and lines of communication in vulnerable areas at the time of external aggression.

Home Guards are raised under the Home Guards Act and rules of the states/union territories. They are recruited from various cross sections of the people such as doctors, engineers, lawyers, private sector organisations, college and university students, agricultural and industrial workers, etc., who give their spare time to the organisation for betterment of the community. All citizens of India, who are in the age group of 18-50, are eligible to become members of Home Guards. Normal tenure of membership in Home Guards is 3 to 5 years. Home Guard personnel are also awarded President's Medal for gallantry, distinguished and meritorious services. A Home Guard, whenever called out for duty/training, is paid duty/training allowance at prescribed rates to meet out-of-pocket expenses. Members of Home Guards in the organisation are trained to assist police in maintenance of law and order, prevention of crime, anti-dacoity measures, border patrolling, prohibition, flood relief, fire-fighting, election duties and social welfare activities. In the event of national emergency, some portion of Civil Defence work is also entrusted to the Home Guards. The Ministry of Home Affairs formulates the policy in respect of role, target, raising, training, equipping, establishment and other important matters of Home Guards Organisation. Expenditure on Home Guards is generally shared between centre and state governments as per existing financial policy.

Fire Services

"Fire Services" is a state subject and has been included as a municipal function in the XII schedule of the Constitution of India in terms of Article 243-W. As such, it is the primary responsibility of the state governments/municipal bodies to enforce the National Building Code and allocate sufficient resources for strengthening and equipping Fire Services to ensure that safety of life and property of citizens within their jurisdiction. The 13th Finance Commission recognizing the need to restructure Fire and Emergency Services across the country has recommended that a portion of the grants provided to the urban local bodies should be spent on revamping of fire services within their respective jurisdiction. Further the Finance Commission has also recommended that all municipal corporations with a population of more than 1 million (2001 census) must put in place a fire hazard response and mitigation plan for their respective areas. Government of India as a supplemental initiative is also implementing a centrally sponsored scheme at a cost of ₹ 200 crores for strengthening of Fire and Emergency Services in the country. The Scheme attempts to fill the existing gaps in fire fighting and rescue capabilities through introduction of modern technology such as advanced fire tender, high pressure pump with mist technology, quick response team vehicle, combi tools for search and rescue and capacity building of various stakeholders.

Personal Law

The people of India are of different religions and faiths. They are governed by different sets of personal laws in respect of matters relating to family affairs, i.e., marriage, divorce, succession, adoption, wills, etc. The subject matter of personal laws is relatable to entry 5 of List III- Concurrent list in the Seventh Schedule to the Constitution of India and hence the Union Legislature, namely Parliament and subject to the provisions of Article 254 of the Constitution. The state legislatures are also competent to make laws in the field.

Marriage

Law relating to marriage and divorce has been codified in different enactments applicable to people of different religions. These are : (1) The Converts Marriage Dissolution Act, 1866; (2) The Divorce Act, 1869; (3) The Indian Christian Marriage Act, 1872; (4) The Kazis Act, 1880; (5) The Anand Marriage Act, 1909; The Indian Succession Act, 1925; (7) The Parsi Marriage and Divorce Act, 1936; (8) The Dissolution of Muslim Marriage Act, 1939; (9) The Special Marriage Act, 1954; (10) The Hindu Marriage Act, 1955; (11) The Foreign Marriage Act, 1969; and (12) The Muslim Women (Protection of Rights on Divorce) Act, 1986.

The Special Marriage Act, 1954 which provides for a special form of marriage and the registration of such marriages extends to the whole of India except the state of Jammu and Kashmir, but also applies to the citizens of India domiciled in Jammu and Kashmir. Persons governed by this Act can specifically register marriage under the said Act even though they are of different religious faiths. The Act also provides that the marriage celebrated under any other form can also be registered under The Special Marriage Act, if it satisfies the requirements of the Act. The Section 4(b) (iii) of the Act, was amended to omit the words "or epilepsy." Sections 36 and 38 have been amended to provide that an application for alimony or the maintenance and education of minor children be disposed off within 60 days from the date of service of notice on the respondent. An attempt has been made to codify customary law which is prevalent among Hindus by enacting the Hindu Marriage Act, 1955. This Act, which extends to the whole of India, except the state of Jammu and Kashmir, applies also to Hindus domiciled in territories to which the Act extends and those who are outside the said territories. It applies to Hindus (in any of its forms or development) and also to Buddhists, Sikhs, Jains and also those who are not Muslims, Christians, Parsis or Jews by religion. However, the Act does not apply to members of any scheduled tribes unless the Central Government by notification in the official Gazette otherwise directs. Provisions as regard to divorce are contained in Section 13 of The Hindu Marriage Act and Section 27 of The Special Marriage Act. Common ground on which divorce can be sought by a husband or a wife under these Acts are: adultery, desertion, cruelty, unsoundness of mind, venereal disease, leprosy, mutual consent and being not heard of as alive for seven years.

As regards the Christians, provisions relating to marriage and divorce are contained in The Indian Christian Marriage Act, 1872 and in Section 10 of The Indian Divorce Act, 1869 respectively. Under that Section the husband can seek divorce on grounds of adultery on the part of his wife and the wife can seek divorce on the ground that the husband has become convert to another religion and has gone through marriage with another woman or has been guilty of : (a) incestuous adultery; (b) bigamy with adultery; (c) marriage with another woman with adultery; (d) rape, sodomy or bestiality; (e) adultery coupled with such cruelty as without adultery would have entitled her to a divorce, (a system of divorce created by the Roman Catholic Church equivalent to judicial separation on grounds of adultery, perverse practices, cruelty) and (f) adultery coupled with desertion without reasonable excuse for two years or more.

In The Divorce Act, 1869 comprehensive amendments were made through The Indian Divorce (Amendment) Act, 2001 to remove discriminatory provisions against women in the matter of divorce and to provide for dissolution of marriage by mutual consent. Further, Section 41 of the 1869 Act was amended by The Marriage Laws (Amendment) Act, 2001 to provide that an application for alimony or the maintenance and education of minor children be disposed off within 60 days from the date of service of notice on the respondent. As regards Muslims, marriages are governed by the Mohammedan Law prevalent in the country. As regards divorce, i.e., a Muslim wife has a much restricted right to dissolve her marriage. Unwritten and traditional law tried to ameliorate her position by permitting her to seek dissolution under the following forms : (a) This is a form of delegated divorce. According to this the husband delegates his right to divorce in a marriage contract which may stipulate, on his taking another wife, the first wife has a right to divorce him; (b) : this is a dissolution of agreement between the parties to marriage on the wife's giving some consideration to the husband for her release from marriage ties. Terms are a matter of bargain and usually take the form of the wife giving up her or a portion of it and (c) : this is divorce by mutual consent.

Further, by The Dissolution of Muslim Marriage Act, 1939, a Muslim wife has been given the right to seek dissolution of her marriage on these grounds; whereabouts of the husband have not been known for a period of four years; husband is not maintaining her for a period of two years; (iii) imprisonment of husband for a period of seven years or more; (iv) failure on the part of husband to perform his marital obligations, without a reasonable cause, for a period of three years; (v) impotency of husband; (vi) two-year long insanity; suffering from leprosy or virulent venereal disease; (viii) marriage took place before she attained the age of 15 years and not consummated; and (x) cruelty.

The Parsi Marriage and Divorce Act, 1936 governs the matrimonial relations of Parsis. The word 'Parsi' is defined in the Act as a Parsi Zoroastrian. A Zoroastrian is a person who professes the Zoroastrian religion. It has a racial significance. Every marriage as well as divorce under this Act is required to be registered in accordance with the procedure prescribed in the Act. The provisions of the Parsi Marriage and Divorce Act, 1936 have been enlarged so as to bring them in line with The Hindu Marriage Act, 1955. Sections 39 and 49 of The Parsi Marriage and Divorce Act, 1936 were amended by The Marriage Laws (Amendment) and education of minor children be disposed off within 60 days from the date of service of notice on the wife or the husband as the case may be. As for the matrimonial laws of Jews, there is no codified law in India. Even today, they are governed by their religious laws. Jews do not regard marriage as a civil contract, but as a relation between two persons involving very sacred duties. Marriage can be dissolved through courts on grounds of adultery or cruelty. Marriages are monogamous.

Adoption

Although there is no general law governing adoption, it is permitted by The Hindu Adoption and Maintenance Act, 1956 amongst Hindus and by custom amongst a few numerically insignificant categories of persons. Since adoption is legal affiliation of a child, it forms the subject matter of personal law. Muslims, Christians and Parsis have no adoption laws and have to approach the court under The Guardians and Wards Act, 1890. Muslims, Christians and Parsis can take a child under the said Act only under foster care. Once a child under foster care attaining the age of majority, that is eighteen years old, he is free to break away all these connections. Besides, such a child does not have the legal right of inheritance. Foreigners, who want to adopt Indian children have to approach the court under the aforesaid Act.

The Hindu law relating to adoption has been amended and codified into the Hindu Adoptions and Maintenance Act, 1956, under which a male or female Hindu having legal capacity, can take a son or a daughter in adoption. In dealing with the question of guardianship of a minor child, as in other spheres of family law, there is no uniform law. Hindu law, Muslim Law and the Guardians and Wards Act, 1890 are three distinct legal systems which are prevalent. A guardian may be a natural guardian, testamentary guardian or a guardian appointed by the court. In deciding the question of guardianship two distinct things have to be taken into account - person of the minor and his property. Often the same person is not entrusted with both. Though The Personal Laws (Amendment) Act, 2010, the Hindu Adoptions and Maintenance Act, 1956 was amended so as to remove the incapacity of married women to take in adoption of a son or a daughter merely on the basis of her marital status and to provide that the mother with the consent of the father and the father with the consent of the mother shall have equal right to give in adoption of their children.

The Hindu Minority and Guardianship Act, 1956 has codified laws of Hindus relating to minority and guardianship. As in the case of uncodified law, it has upheld the superior right of father. It lays down that a child is a minor till the age of 18 years. Prior right of mother is recognised only for the custody of children below five. In case of illegitimate children, the mother has a better claim than the putative father. The act makes no distinction between the person of the minor and his property and therefore guardianship implies control over both. Under the Muslim Law (Shariat), the father enjoys a dominant position. It also makes a distinction between guardianship and custody. For guardianship, which has usually reference to guardianship of property, according to Sunnis, the father is preferred and in his absence his executor. If no executor has been appointed by the father, the guardianship passes on the paternal grandfather to take over responsibility and not that of the executor. Both schools, however, agree that father while alive is the sole guardian. Mother is not recognised as a natural guardian even after the death of the father. As regards rights of a natural guardian, there is no doubt that father's right extends both to the property and person of the child. Even when mother has the custody of minor child father's general right of supervision and control remains. Father can, however, appoint mother as testamentary guardian. Thus, though mother may not be recognised as natural guardian, there is no objection to her being appointed under the father's will.

The Muslim law recognizes that mother's right to custody of minor children is an absolute right. Even the father cannot deprive her of it. Misconduct is the only condition which can deprive the mother of this right. As regards the age at which the right of mother to custody terminates, the Shia school holds that mother's right is only during the period of rearing which ends when the child completes the age of two, whereas Hanafi school extends the period till the minor son has reached the age of seven. In case of girls, Shia law upholds mother's right till the girl reaches the age of seven and Hanafi school till she attains puberty.

The general law relating to guardians and wards is contained in the Guardians and Wards Act, 1890. It clearly lays down that father's right is primary and no other person can be appointed unless the father is found unfit. This Act also provides that the court must take into consideration the welfare of the child while appointing a guardian under the Act. Though The Personal Laws (Amendment) Act, 2010, the Guardians and Wards Act, 1890 was amended so as to include the mother along with the father as a fit person to be appointed as a guardian of a child so that the courts shall not appoint any other person as a guardian of a minor if either of the parents is fit to be the guardian of such minor.

Maintenance

Obligation of a husband to maintain his wife arises out of the status of the marriage. Right to maintenance forms a part of the personal law. Under the

Code of Criminal Procedure, 1973, right of maintenance extends not only to the wife and dependent children, but also to indigent parents and divorced wives. Claims of the wife, etc., however, depends on the husband having sufficient means. Claim of maintenance for all dependent persons was limited to ₹ 500 per month. But, this limit was removed by the Code of Criminal Procedure (Amendment) Act, 2001. Inclusion of the right of maintenance under the Code of Criminal Procedure has the advantage of making the remedy both speedy and cheap. However, divorced wives who have received money payable under the customary personal law are not entitled to claim maintenance under the Code of Criminal Procedure.

Under the Hindu Law, the wife has an absolute right to claim maintenance from her husband. But she loses her right if she deviates from the path of chastity. Her right to maintenance is codified in The Hindu Adoptions and Maintenance Act, 1956. In assessing the amount of maintenance, the court takes into account various factors like position and liabilities of the husband. It also judges whether the wife is justified in living apart from husband. Justifiable reasons are spelt out in the Act. Maintenance (pending the suit) and even expenses of a matrimonial suit will be borne by either, husband or wife, if the other spouse has no independent income for his or her support. The same principle will govern payment of permanent maintenance.

Under the Muslim Law, The Muslim Women (Protection of Rights on Divorce) Act, 1986 protects rights of Muslim women who have been divorced by or have obtained divorce from their husbands and provides for matters connected therewith or incidental thereto. This Act, provides that a divorced Muslim woman shall be entitled to : (a) reasonable and fair provision and maintenance to be made and paid to her within the period by her former husband; (b) where she herself maintains children born to her before or after her former husband for a period of two years from the respective dates of birth of such children; (c) an amount equal to the sum of or dower agreed to be paid to her at the time of her marriage or at any time there after according to the Muslim Law; and (d) all property given to her before or at the time of marriage or after her marriage by her relatives or friends or by husband or any relatives of the husband or his friends.

In addition, the Act also provides that where a divorced Muslim woman is unable to maintain herself after the period the magistrate shall order directing such of her relatives as would been titled to inherit her property on her death according to the Muslim Law and to pay such reasonable and fair maintenance to her as he may determine fit and proper, having regard to the needs of the divorced woman, standard of life enjoyed by her during her marriage and means of such relatives and such maintenance shall be payable by such relatives in proportion to the size of their inheritance of her property and at such periods as he may specify in his order.

Where such divorced woman has children, the magistrate shall order only such children to pay maintenance to her and in the event of any such children being unable to pay such maintenance, the magistrate shall order parents of such divorced woman to pay maintenance to her. In the absence of such relatives or where such relatives are not in a position to maintain her, the magistrate may direct state Wakf Board established under Section 13 of the Wakf Act, 1995 functioning in the area in which the woman resides, to pay such maintenance as determined by him.

The Parsi Marriage and Divorce Act, 1936 recognises the right of wife to maintenance-both alimony and permanent alimony. The maximum amount that can be decreed by the court as alimony during the time a matrimonial suit is pending in court, is one-fifth of the husband's net income. In fixing the quantum as permanent maintenance, the court will determine what is just, bearing in mind the ability of husband to pay, wife's own assets and conduct of the parties. The order will remain in force as long as wife remains chaste and unmarried. The Divorce Act, 1869, governs maintenance rights of a Christian wife. The provisions are the same as those under the Parsi Law and the same considerations are applied in granting maintenance, both alimony and permanent maintenance.

Succession

The Indian Succession Act was enacted in 1925 to consolidate the law applicable to intestate and testamentary succession which was in existence at that time. The Act does not apply to the residents of the union territory of Puducherry. While consolidating the law in respect of succession, two schemes, one relating to succession to property of persons like Indian Christians, Jews and persons married under The Special Marriage Act, 1954 and the other relating to succession rights of Parsis, were adopted.

In the first scheme, applying to those other than Parsis, in the case of a person dying intestate leaving behind a widow and lineal descendants, the widow would be entitled to a fixed share of one-third of property and lineal descendants shall be entitled to the remaining two-thirds. This law was amended subsequently with the objective of improving rights of widows and it was provided that where the intestate dies leaving behind his widows and no lineal descendant and the net value of the estate does not exceed 5,000, the widow would be entitled to the whole of his property. Where the net value of the estate exceeds 5000, she is entitled to charge a sum of 5,000 with interest at four per cent payment and in the residue, she is entitled to her share. The Act imposes no restriction on the power of a person to will away his property.

Under the second scheme, the Act provides for Parsi intestate succession. By The Indian Succession (Amendment) Act, 1991, the Act was amended to provide equal shares for both sons and daughters in their parental properties, irrespective of the fact that it was that of the father or that of the mother. It also enables the Parsis to bequeath their property to religious or charitable purposes, etc., without any restrictions. In effect the amended law provides that where a Parsi dies intestate leaving behind a widow or widower as the case may be and children, the property shall be divided so that the widow or widower and each child receives equal share. Further, where a Parsi dies leaving behind one or both parents in addition to children, or widow/widower and children, the property shall be so divided that the parent or each of the parents shall receive a share equal to half the share of each child.

This Act was amended by The Indian Succession (Amendment) Act, 2002. It was felt that Section 32 of the Principal Act is discriminatory to widows and as such the proviso to Section 32 was omitted to remove discrimination in this regard. Section 213 was also amended by this amending Act to make Christians at par with other communities.

The law relating to testamentary succession among Hindus, Buddhists, Sikhs or Jains, subject to certain restrictions and modifications is carried in Section 57 of the Indian Succession Act, 1925 read within the Third Schedule. The law relating to intestate succession among Hindus is codified in the Hindu Succession Act, 1956. It extends to the whole of India except the State of Jammu and Kashmir. The remarkable features of the Act are the recognition of the right of women to inherit property of an intestate equally with men and abolition of the life estate of female heirs. Further, (vide The Hindu Succession (Amendment) Act, 2005), the Hindu Succession Act, 1956 was amended so as to provide for the equal share to a coparcener daughter in a joint Hindu property.

A vast majority of Muslims in India follow Hanafi doctrines of Sunni law. Courts presume that Muslims are governed by Hanafi law unless it is established to be the contrary. Though there are many features in common between Shia and Sunni schools, yet there are differences in some respects. Sunni law regards Quranic verses of inheritance as an addendum to pre-Islamic customary law and preserves the superior position of male agnates. Unlike Hindu and Christian laws, Muslim law restricts a persons right of testation. A Muslim can bequeath only one-third of his estate. A bequest to a stranger is valid without the consent of heirs if it does not exceed a third of the estate, but a bequest to an heir without the consent of other heirs is invalid. Consent of heirs to a bequest must be secured after the succession has opened and any consent given to a bequest during the life time of the testator can be retracted after his death. Shia law allows Muslims the freedom of bequest within the disposable third.

Anand Marriage (Amendment) Act, 2012

The Anand Marriage Act, 1909 was enacted to remove doubts as to the validity of the marriage rights of the Sikh called "Anand" and it does not provide for the provisions of registration of marriages. The Hindu Marriage Act, 1955 applies to all Hindus, Buddhists, Jains or Sikhs by religion. It also applies to all other persons who are not Muslims, Christians, Parsis or Jews unless they establish that they were not governed by Hindu law, custom or usage prior to the Act. Section 8 of the Hindu Marriage Act, 1955 provides for registration of Hindu marriages and as Sikhs were included in the definition of Hindu, under Section 2 of the Hindu Marriage Act, 1955, a Sikh marriage performed according to the Sikh marriage ceremony called "Anand" or other customary ceremonies could be registered here under the provisions of Section 8 of the Hindu Marriage Act, 1955.

However, vide The Anand Marriage (Amendment), Act, 2012, The Anand Marriage Act, 1909 was amended to provide for registration of Anand marriages commonly known as Anand Karaj.

Election Laws and Electoral Reforms

The Acts in connection with the conduct of elections to Parliament, state legislatures and to the offices of the President and the Vice-President are : (i) The Representation of the People Act, 1950; (ii) The Representation of the People Act, 1951; (iii) The Presidential and Vice-Presidential Elections Act, 1952; (iv) The Delimitation Act, 2002; (v) The Andhra Pradesh Legislative Council Act, 2005; and (vi) The Tamil Nadu Legislative Council Act, 2010. These are administrated by the Legislative Department, Ministry of Law and Justice.

The electoral system of the country, which is also called the first-past-the-post system of elections, has completed sixty six years.

The continuously changing electoral scenario has necessitated reforms of electoral laws on several occasions. In the light of the experience gained during elections, recommendations of the Election Commission, the proposals from different sources including political parties, eminent men in public life and the deliberations in the Legislatures and various public bodies, the successive Governments have taken a number of measures, from time to time, to bring about electoral reforms; though need to effect a comprehensive package of electoral reforms cannot be gainsaid. At present the issue of electoral reforms in its entirety has been referred to the Law Commission of India for its examination and Report. On receipt of the Report of the Law Commission, the matter will be examined in consultation with the stakeholders.

Delimitation of Constituencies

The periodic readjustment of the Lok Sabha and Assembly constituencies is mandatory in a representative system where single-member constituencies are used for electing political representatives. The electoral boundaries are drawn on the basis of the last published census figures and are relatively equal in population. Equally populous constituencies allow voters to have an equally weighted vote in the Legislature. Electoral constituencies that vary greatly in population—a condition called "malapportionment"—violate a central tenet of democracy, namely, that all voters should be able to cast a vote of equal weight. Delimitation and Elections are the two basic pillars of a parliamentary democracy.

The first Delimitation Commission in India was constituted in 1952, the second in 1962 and the third in the year 1973. The third delimitation exercise—based on 1971 census—was completed in the year 1975. The present delimitation, based on 2001 census, has been undertaken after 30 years. The population has increased by almost 87 per cent and the nature of constituencies in the country, by and large, had become malapportioned.

The Government, as part of the National Population Policy strategy, decided to extend the current constitutional freeze on undertaking fresh delimitation up to 2026 as a motivational measure to enable state governments to fearlessly pursue the agenda for population stabilization. It has also been decided, however, to simultaneously undertake readjustment and rationalization of electoral constituencies, including those reserved for the Scheduled Castes and the Scheduled Tribes, based on the population census for the year 1991, without affecting the number of seats allocated to states in the legislative bodies so as to correct the imbalance caused due to uneven growth of population/electorate in different constituencies. The Constitution (Eighty-fourth Amendment) Act, 2001 enacted in 2002 has effected the aforesaid policy decisions of the Government. Pursuant to the enactment of the Constitution (Eighty-fourth Amendment) Act, 2001 which provided for readjustment of electoral constituencies, including those reserved for the Scheduled Castes and the Scheduled tribes. The Delimitation Act, 2002 was enacted. The Delimitation Commission had accordingly been constituted in 2002 under the provisions of the Delimitation Act, 2002 with Shri Justice Kuldip Singh, a retired judge of the Supreme Court as its Chairperson and Shri B.B. Tandon, Election Commissioner in the Election Commission of India and the State Election Commissioner as its members. The main task of the Commission was to readjust the division of territorial constituencies of the seats in the House of the People allocated to each state and the readjustment of the division of territorial constituencies of the total number of seats in the Legislative assembly of each state. Subsequent to that the Constitution (Eighty-seventh Amendment) Act, 2003 was enacted and by that Act the basis of the delimitation of territorial constituencies was changed based on the 2001 census in place of 1991.

Although the rules for delimitation vary across countries, tasks involved in drawing boundaries are generally similar. In India, the drawing of boundaries, generally, entails: (a) allocating seats to the states and districts within a state; creating a database composed of maps, population figures and the details showing geographic/natural/administrative conditions of the area concerned; associating the statutory representatives from the Lok Sabha and State Assemblies; (d) distributing the states and districts into geographic units called the constituencies; (e) having an extensive exercise for public input into delimitation process; (f) summarizing and evaluating the constituencies; and g) passing and publishing the final order. The procedure for delimiting the constituencies in India stands clearly spelt out in The Delimitation Act, 2002.

This legal framework provides for an independent and impartial Delimitation Commission. The final orders of the Commission are not subject to any modification or veto by the Government.

The Delimitation Commission functioned in a transparent manner. The methodology and guidelines were clearly established and published in advance. While framing the constituencies, the Commission—as far as practicable—kept in view the interest of communities such as those sharing a common tribe, race or ethnic background and also those defined geographically or by physical features like mountains, forests, rivers, etc. The Commission drew the boundaries of the constituencies reserved for scheduled castes and scheduled tribes strictly in accordance with the constitutional and statutory provisions. After getting finality of the delimitation exercise, in pursuance of the second proviso to Article 82 and second proviso to clause (3) of Article 170 of the Constitution, a Presidential Order dated February 19, 2008 was issued making new delimitation effective throughout the country. However, Section 10(B) of the Delimitation Act, 2002 deferred the legal effect of the 2007 delimitation order in relation to the state of Jharkhand.

With the issuance of the Presidential Order specifying the date on which the delimitation orders notified by the Delimitation Commission shall take effect, it was necessary to amend the relevant provisions and the First and Second Schedules of the Representation of the People Act, 1950 to reflect the changes made by the delimitation orders notified by the Delimitation Commission. As a consequential requirement, the Representation of the People (Amendment) Act, 2008 amending the Representation of the People Act, 1950 in conformity with the delimitation was enacted and made effective from 2008. By this amendment Act, the First Schedule and the Second Schedule to the Representation of the People Act, 1950 were replaced including other amendments. Further, a new Section 8(A) was inserted in the Representation of the People Act, 1950, which, provided that if the President of India is satisfied that the situation and the conditions prevailing in Arunachal Pradesh, Assam, Manipur or Nagaland are conducive for the conduct of delimitation exercise, he may, by order, rescind the said deferment orders issued under Section 10(A) of The Delimitation Act, 2002 in relation to any of those states and provide for the conduct of delimitation exercise in the states by the Election Commission of India. Further, the Election Commission of India, as per sub-Section (2 of Section 8(A) of The Representation of the People Act, 1950 has now been empowered to undertake fresh delimitation in respect to the aforementioned four states as soon as, may be after the deferment orders in respect to these states are rescinded. A fresh delimitation exercise will be initiated as and when conditions prevailing in these states become conducive to the conduct of delimitation exercise.

After the issuance of the Presidential Order of 2008, the Delimitation Commission had issued eight (8) orders/corrigenda amending its earlier orders in respect of Karnataka, West Bengal, Uttar Pradesh, Tamil Nadu, NCT of Delhi, Bihar and Gujarat.

Reservation of Seats for Women

During the years, a consistent demand has been made for giving adequate representation to women in Parliament and state legislatures. Such a demand finds support in the 73 and 74 Amendments to the Constitution made in 1992. There was a proposal to amend the Constitution and to provide for reservation in Parliament and state legislatures.

Electronic Voting Machines

The use of Electronic Voting Machines (EVMs) was started in the country on experiment basis in 1982. It took more than two decades for the universal use of EVMs and during the General Elections to the Lok Sabha in 2004, EVMs were used in all polling stations across the country. Thereafter EVMs are being used in all the elections of the House of the People and state assemblies. The EVMs were developed at the behest of the Election Commission jointly with two Public Sector Undertakings, Bharat Electronics Limited, Bangalore (BEL) and Electronics Corporation of India Limited, Hyderabad (ECIL) in 1989.

Electors' Photo Identity Cards

The use of electors' photo identity cards by the Election Commission was started in 1993 throughout the country to check bogus voting and impersonation of electors at elections. The electoral roll is the basis for issue of EPICs to the registered electors. The electoral rolls are normally revised every year with 1st January of the year as the qualifying date. Every Indian citizen who attains the age of 18 years or above as on that date is eligible for inclusion in the electoral roll and can apply for the same. Once he is registered in the roll, he would be eligible for getting an EPIC. The scheme of issuing the EPICs is, therefore, a continuous and ongoing process for the completion of which no time limit can be fixed.

However, constant efforts are being made to issue EPIC to all such persons whose names have already been enrolled in the electoral roll, as early as possible. Some of them are: (i) special photography campaigns are organised to make EPIC of all voters; (ii) voters are allowed to give copies of their photographs which are scanned for making EPIC; (iii) booth level officers are appointed by the Commission to collect photographs and make EPIC of all voters; (iv) 25th January has been declared as the National Voters' Day to focus on enrolment of voters and making EPIC; (v) special publicity campaign is undertaken to inform electors of the procedure of preparation of EPIC; and (vi) instruction has been issued that the EPIC number once issued will be valid throughout the elector's life even if address changes.

Voting Rights to the Citizens of India Living Abroad

Section 19 of the Representation of the People Act, 1950 provides that every person who is not less than eighteen years of age on the qualifying date and is ordinarily resident in constituency shall be entitled to be registered in the electoral rolls for that constituency. The meaning of "ordinarily resident" is laid down in Section 20 of the said Act. It has been specified under Chapter-III in the Hand Book for Electoral Registration Officers that a person who has gone out of the country for business or employment should be treated as having moved out of that place. Mere ownership or possession of a building or other immovable property will not bestow on the owner, the residential qualification.

There are a large number of Indian citizens residing outside the country due to various reasons. They have been persistently demanding for conferring them the voting rights.

The Government considered all aspects of the demand and accordingly introduced the Representation of the People (Amendment) Bill, 2006 in Rajya Sabha in 2006 to enable the Indian citizens absenting from their place of ordinarily residence in India owing to their employment, education or otherwise outside India, to get their names registered in the electoral rolls of the concerned constituency of their place of ordinarily residence in India as mentioned in their passport so that they would be in a position to cast their votes in elections to the Lok Sabha and to the state legislatures in case they happen to be in their constituency at the time of polls.

In pursuance of the recommendations of the Standing Committee, the Government have withdrawn, with the leave of the Rajya Sabha, the earlier Bill, namely, The Representation of the People (Amendment) Bill, 2006 introduced on February 27, 2006 in the Rajya Sabha and introduced a fresh Bill, namely, The Representation of the People (Amendment) Bill, 2010 in August, 2010, , to amend the Representation of the People Act, 1950 to : (a) provide that every citizen of India, whose name is not included in the electoral roll and who has not acquired the citizenship of any other country and who is absenting from his place of ordinary residence in India owing to his employment, education, or otherwise outside India, (whether temporarily or not), shall be entitled to have his name registered in the electoral roll in the constituency in which his place of residence in India as mentioned in his passport is located; (b) provide that the Electoral Registration Officer shall make corrections of entries in electoral rolls and inclusion of names in electoral rolls after proper verification; and (c) confer power upon the Central Government to specify, after consulting the Election Commission of India, by rules, the time within which the name of persons referred to in sub-paragraph above shall be registered in the electoral roll and the manner and procedure for registering of such persons in the electoral roll.

The said Bill has been enacted as the Representation of the People (Amendment) Act, 2010. In pursuance of the provisions of the said Act the Central Government, in consultation with the Election Commission prepared and published the Registration of Electors (Amendment) Rules, 2011 on February 3, 2011 and Registration of Electors (Second Amendment) Rules 2011 on February

23, 2011. The Central Government has issued necessary notification bringing the Act into force from February, 2011. The overseas Indians can now furnish the documents self-attested by them and get their name enrolled in the electoral roll of their respective constituency.

Reservation of Seats for Scheduled Castes and Scheduled Tribes

Our Constitution makers were fully conscious of the fact that the Scheduled Castes and Scheduled Tribes had been an oppressed and under-privileged class in our society over the centuries and they deserved a special dispensation so that their condition may be vastly improved. For this purpose, several special provisions were incorporated in our Constitution. One such provision related to the reservation of seats for these communities in Lok Sabha and state legislative assemblies. This provision found place in Articles 330 and 332 of the Constitution. Similarly, they were also sensitive of the difficulties and problems which were likely to be faced by the persons belonging to Anglo Indian community in the country. Consequently, adequate safeguards were provided for them in our Constitution by giving representation to this small section of the society, under Article 331 of the Constitution by way of nomination of two persons of that community in the House of the People by the President.

Likewise, provision for nomination of one member each by the Governor, wherever necessary, belonging to this community in the state legislative assemblies was also incorporated. Initially, the aforesaid provisions were made only for a period of ten years from the commencement of the Constitution. Although several steps have been initiated by the Government from time to time for improving the socio economic status of the Scheduled Castes and Scheduled Tribes, yet they are still far behind other communities. Even in the political field, they are not yet able to come up and get themselves elected to the representative bodies on their own in adequate numbers. Similarly, there are still a small section of Anglo Indians which need representation in the elected bodies. Consequently, the provision initially made for a period of ten years has been extended from time to time. Recently, through the Constitution (One Hundred Ninth Amendment) Bill, 2009 extension of the period for a further ten years has been passed by both the Houses of Parliament and received the assent of the President in January, 2010. The said Bill was enacted as the Constitution (Ninety-fifth Amendment) Act, 2009.

21 Labour, Skill Development and Employment

Labour

THE Ministry of Labour and Employment is one of the important and oldest ministries of the Government of India. The main responsibility entrusted to the Ministry is to protect and safeguard the interests of workers in general and the poor, deprived and disadvantaged sections of the society, in particular. Further, the Ministry aims to create a healthy work environment for higher production and productivity and to develop and coordinate vocational skill training and employment services. To keep itself in tandem with the process of liberalisation, the Ministry's attention is focussed on promotion of welfare of labour and providing social security to the labour force both in organised and unorganised sectors. These objectives are sought to be achieved through implementation of various labour laws, which regulate the terms and conditions of service and employment of workers. Labour being the subject in the Concurrent List under the Constitution of India the state governments are also empowered to enact legislations.

Relevant Website : www.labour.gov.in

New Initiatives

National Career Service Project

The Ministry is implementing the National Career Service (NCS) Project as a Mission Mode Project for transformation of the National Employment Service to provide a variety of employment related services like career counselling, vocational guidance, information on skill development courses, apprenticeship, internships etc. The NCS Portal (www. ncs.gov.in) from 2015. The NCSP is supported by a dedicated helpdesk (multilingual) available from Tuesday to Sunday (8.00 AM to 8.00PM) on 18004251514 for assisting users. It has a rich repository of career content of over 3600 occupations.

The NCS Project has also been enhanced to interlink all employment exchanges with the NCS Portal so that services can be delivered online. The scheme provides for part funding to States for IT upgradation and minor refurbishing of Employment Exchanges and for organizing job fairs.

Pradhan Mantri Rojgar Protsahan Yojana

The Ministry is also implementing "Pradhan Mantri Rojgar Protsahan Yojana" (PMRPY) since 2016-17 with the objective of promoting employment generation with an allocation of ₹ 1,000 crores. Under the scheme, Government of India will pay the Employees Pension Scheme (EPS) contribution of 8.33 per cent for all new employees enrolling in Employees' Provident Fund Organisation (EPFO) for the first three years of their employment. This will incentivise the employers to recruit unemployed persons and also to formalize informal employees. The scheme will be applicable to those having earnings of ₹ 15,000/- per month. A budget provision of ₹ 1000/- crore for this scheme has been made.

Labour Inspection Scheme

A computerized list of inspections is generated randomly based on risk based objective criteria. Serious matters are to be covered under the mandatory inspection list. Complaints based inspections determined centrally after examination based on data and evidence. Mandatory uploading of inspection reports is to be done within 72 hours.

Shram Suvidha Portal

The Ministry has developed a unified web portal 'Shram Suvidha Portal', to bring transparency and accountability in enforcement of labour laws and ease compliance. It caters to four major organisations under the Ministry namely; Office of Chief Labour Commissioner (Central); Directorate General of Mines Safety; Employees' Provident Fund Organisation; and Employees' State Insurance Corporation.

Single Unified Annual Return

Ministry of Labour and Employment has started Single Unified Annual Return for eight Labour Acts. This facilitates filling of simplified Single Online Return by the establishments instead of filing separate Returns, under these Acts. (1) The Payment of Wages Act, 1936; (2) The Minimum Wages Act, 1948; (3) The Contract Labour (Regulation and Abolition) Act, 1970; (4) The Maternity Benefit Act, 1961; (5) The Building and Other Construction Workers (Regulation of Employment and Condition of Service) Act, 1996; (6) The Payment of Bonus Act, 1965; (7) The Inter-State Migrant Workmen (Regulation of Employment and conditions of Service) Act, 1979; and (8) The Industrial Disputes Act, 1947.

Common Registration

Facility for Common Registration under five Central Labour Acts has been developed on e-Biz portal of the Department of Industrial Policy and Promotion. The Acts covered under this include: The Employees Provident Fund and Miscellaneous Provisions Act, 1952; The Employees State Insurance Act, 1948. The Building & Other Construction Workers (RECS) Act, 1996; The Contract Labour (Regulation & Abolition) Act, 1970; and The Inter-State Migrant Workmen (RECS) Act, 1979.

Labour Codes

This Ministry has taken a number of initiatives for bringing transparency and accountability in enforcement of labour laws, with the objective of strengthening the safety, health, social security measures for every worker and bringing ease of compliance for running an establishment to catalyse creation of employment opportunities. These initiatives include governance reforms through use of technology and also legislative reforms by simplifying, rationalising and amalgamating the existing labour laws into four labour codes.

Legislative Initiatives

Draft Small Factory Bill

The Bill provides for regulation of working and service conditions of workers in small manufacturing units employing less than 40 workers. The Bill amalgamates, simplifies and rationalizes the provisions of six Labour Laws at one place for these small factories. The Bill will ease the operation of small factories and thus catalyze the generation of employment through small factories while ensuring, inter- alia social security, safety and health of the workers.

Social Security

Employees' State Insurance Corporation

To provide medical care and cash benefits in case of sickness, maternity and employment injuries, the Employees' State Insurance Act was enacted in 1948. Employees' State Insurance Corporation (ESIC) is implementing the ESI Scheme introduced since 1952. The achievements are as follows:

Health Reforms Agenda of ESIC: A series of Health Reforms Agenda were launched. These include, online availability of Electronic Health Record of ESI Beneficiaries (insured persons and their family members); Abhiyan Indradhanush: ensuring the change of bed sheet according to VIBGYOR pattern during the week i.e. to be changed everyday; medical Helpline No. 1800 11 3839 for emergency and seeking guidance from casualty/emergency of ESIC hospitals; special OPD for senior citizens and differentlyabled persons in ESIC hospitals, in the afternoon.

Some of the other salient features of ESIC 2.0 were up-grading dispensaries to six bedded hospitals in phases, providing of appropriate cancer detection, cardiology/ treatment, yoga facilities at different levels of hospitals, dialysis facilities in all ESIC Model Hospitals on PPP Mode, all possible pathological facilities in hospital premises by outsourcing or by up-grading, Queue Management System in every hospital for helping in registration and pharmacy, behavioral training to para-medical and other staff of the hospitals guiding them to provide due courtesy in dealing with the patients/attendants, feedback system for all indoor patients, proper and attractive signages at the required places in all ESIC Hospitals for guidance and proper communications to the visitors, AYUSH facilities to be extended up to the dispensary level in phases, tele-medicine facilities for the beneficiaries in phases.

Digital India - e-initiatives of ESIC

e-biz Platform:- ESIC was the first organization of Central government, to integrate its services (Registration of Employers through e-biz portal of Department of Industrial Policy and Promotion DIPP) to promote ease of business and curb transaction costs.

e- Pehchan:- A process of establishing the identity of the insured person through Adhaar number has been set up by seeding Adhaar number to the insurance number. This has simplified the identification process of the insured person and his/her dependents at various point of contact during all type of benefit disbursement. The process has enabled to do away with the cumbersome process of making insured persons and their dependents to visit offices to get their biometrics taken for issuance of a pehchan card.

Mobile App for IPs: Our IPs have been provided with a Mobile app "Ask An Appointment" (AAA+) to enable them to book an appointment with the doctors online prior to actually making a visit to the hospital.

Incorporation of Government Directives: Various Government Directives regarding GeM, E-Office etc., either have been incorporated or are in the process of incorporation, adaptation and adoption.

Empowerment to IP: A system is in place to enable the workers to verify their status as covered/uncovered along with their wages/attendance/contri but ion deposited by their employers. ICT division has successfully upgraded the system commensurate with the rapid growth of ESIC in addition to the changing business rules and environment, i.e., a) incorporation of reduced rate of contribution for employers in newly implemented areas. b) incorporating the enhancement in wage ceiling limit from ₹ 15,000/-to ₹ 21,000/- c) the date of payment of ESI contribution has been changed to 15th day after the end of the month.

Unemployment Allowance under Rajiv Gandhi Shramik Kalyan Yojana (RGSKY) has been enhanced from 12 to 24 months. In order to get benefits under RGSKY, the eligibility of contribution condition has also been reduced from three to two years for getting the benefits. In order to encourage employment of disabled person, the employers share of contribution in respect of such disabled employees is paid by the Central government for initial ten years. The employers are exempted from paying their share of contribution up to 10 years in respect of all permanently disabled persons irrespective of their wages working in factories and establishments covered under ESI Act.

ESIC has launched new scheme "One IP-Two Dispensaries" for the benefit of migrant workers. Now, through employer, the insured women/persons can choose two dispensaries, one for self and another for family residing at different locations of the country.

Employees' Provident Fund Organisation

The Employees' Provident Funds (EPF) and Miscellaneous Provisions Act, 1952 provides for Provident Fund, Pension Scheme and Insurance Fund in factories/ establishments employing twenty or more employees in industries mentioned in Schedule-I to the Act. The following three schemes framed are: Employees' Provident Funds Scheme, 1952; Employees' Pension Scheme, 1995 and Employees' Deposit-Linked Insurance Scheme, 1976.

Although for monitoring compliance of covered establishments, the system assisted tool in the form of CCTS Computerized Compliance Tracking System was provided to the field offices of EPFO, no concrete system or procedure for detection of coverable establishment was available to the compliance machinery. It resulted in belated coverage of establishments with consequential legal implications as the establishments were mostly found coverable from retrospective dates but refused to take up past liability related to statutory dues, payment of interest and damages for belated remittance, prosecution cases etc. The Act is applicable on its own volition and these legal actions are attracted for non compliance for whatsoever reason.

The Employees' Provident Funds and Miscellaneous Provisions Act, 1952 provides for Provident Fund, Pension Scheme and Insurance Fund in factories/ establishments employing twenty or more employees in industries mentioned in Schedule to the Act. The Government of India through the Employees' Provident Fund Organization (EPFO) administers the Employees' Provident Fund and Miscellaneous Provisions (EPF&MP) Act, 1952 and the following three schemes framed there under: Employees' Provident Funds Scheme,1952; Employees' Pension Scheme, 1995, and Employees' Deposit-Linked Insurance Scheme, 1976.

Online Registration

The EPFO has launched a portal for Online Registration of Establishments for the employers.

Universal Account Number

The facility of Universal Account Number (UAN) for EPF subscribers was formally launched in 2014. Portability is an inherent feature of the UAN programme. It provides automatic portability of Provident Fund account on change of employment if the employee has activated his UAN by seeding his Know Your Customer details (through the employer).

Pension Reforms

Minimum Pension

During the year one of the long awaited demands for implementation of the minimum pension was given effect to. The Central Government is providing a minimum pension of ₹ 1,000/- per month for member/widow(er)/ disabled/ nominee/dependent parent pensioners, ₹ 750/- per month for orphan pensioners and ₹ 250/- per month for children pensioners.

After implementation of the minimum pension notification the pension for all member/ widow(er)/ disabled/ nominee/ dependent parent pensioners whose original pension were less than ₹ 1,000/- p.m. have been fixed at the minimum of ₹ 1,000/- p.m. Deductions on account of benefits availed by members on the basis of choice exercised at the time of making claims like commutation, return of capital and short service are applied on the minimum pension of ₹ 1,000/- p.m.

Industrial Relations

Twenty-two Central Government Industrial Tribunal (CGIT) -cum-Labour Courts have been set up under the provisions of the Industrial Disputes Act, 1947 for adjudication of industrial disputes in organizations for which the Central Government is the appropriate authority. Through Finance Act,2017, the powers to settle the Appeals arising out of EPF&MP Act,1952 have also been entrusted upon to these Tribunals. These Tribunals are located at Dhanbad (Jharkhand), Mumbai, New Delhi and Chandigarh (two courts each) and one each at Kolkata, Jabalpur, Kanpur, Nagpur, Lucknow, Bengaluru, Jaipur, Chennai, Hyderabad, Bhubaneswar, Ahmedabad, Ernakulam, Asansol and Guwahati. Further, the two Industrial Tribunals at Mumbai and Kolkata also function as National Tribunals.

In order to reduce pendency of cases Lok Adalats are being organized by the CGIT cum-Labour Courts as an Alternate Grievance Redressal System.

Child Labour

Child Labour is an area of great concern and Government of India is committed to address the issue. Considering the magnitude and nature of the problem, it is following a robust multi- generation schemes. It comprises statutory and legislative measures, rescue and rehabilitation, universal elementary education along with social protection and poverty alleviation and employment generation schemes. The objective is to create an environment where families are not compelled to send their children to work. Government has adopted an approach to withdraw and rehabilitate working children from all occupations and processes.

Policy on Child Labour

The National Policy on Child Labour announced in August, 1987, addresses this complex issue in a comprehensive, holistic and integrated manner. The Action Plan under is multi-pronged and mainly consists of: a legislative action plan; project based action in areas of high concentration of child labour; and focus on general development programmes for the benefit of the families of such labour.

Legislative Action Plan

Under the Legislative Action Plan, the Child Labour (Prohibition & Regulation) Act, was enacted in 1986. As per the provisions of the Act, the employment of children below the age of 14 years was prohibited in 18 occupations and 65 processes. Then the Government followed it up with the Child Labour (Prohibition & Regulation) Amendment Act, 2016, which came into force from 2016. The Amendment inter-alia covers the complete prohibition on employment or work of children below 14 years of age in all occupations and processes; linking the age of the prohibition of employment with the age for free and compulsory education under Right to Education Act, 2009; prohibition on employment of adolescents (14 to 18 years of age) in hazardous occupations or processes and making stricter punishment for the employers contravening the provisions of the Act; and project based action plan in the areas of high concentration of child labour. In pursuance of National Child Labour Policy, the National Child Labour Project (NCLP) Scheme was started in 1988 to rehabilitate children rescued from child labour. It is an ongoing Central Sector Scheme and at present sanctioned in 270 districts in the country. Under the Scheme, working children are identified through child labour survey, withdrawn from work and put into the special training centres so as to provide them with an environment to subsequently join mainstream education system. In these special training centres, besides formal education, the children are provided stipend, supplementary nutrition, vocational training and regular health checkups.

As poverty is the primary cause of such a social evil, the educational rehabilitation of such children is further complemented by the economic rehabilitation of the families through the convergence approach so that the children and their families are covered under the benefits of the schemes of various ministries/departments.

Re-alignment of NCLP Scheme with RTE Act

With the enactment of Right to Education (RTE) Act, 2009, there was a need for realignment of the NCLP Scheme with the provisions of RTE Act, 2009. The NCLP Schools could now serve as special training centres for un-enrolled and out of school children in accordance with the provisions of Section 4 of the RTE Act and Rule 5 of the Right of Children for free and compulsory education (RTE) Rules, 2010. The name of "the Child Labour (Prohibition & Regulation) Act, 1986" mentioned at Sl. No. 13 of the list of Central Act provided in Chapter 1 has been replaced with "the Child and Adolescent Labour (Prohibition & Regulation) Act, 1986" from 2016.

Bonded Labour

Rehabilitation of Bonded Labour

With a view to supplementing the efforts of the state governments; a Centrally Sponsored Plan Scheme for rehabilitation of bonded labour was launched in 1978. Under the Scheme, state governments are provided Central assistance on matching grants (50:50) basis for the rehabilitation of bonded labour. The said Plan Scheme was drastically modified in 2000 to provide for 100 per cent assistance for conducting district wise surveys for identification of bonded labour, awareness generation activities, and evaluatory studies. The Rehabilitation grant has also been raised from ₹ 10,000/- per identified bonded labour, to ₹ 20,000/- per identified bonded labour. Further, in the case of North-Eastern states, cent per cent rehabilitation grant is provided in case they fail to provide their matching contribution.

Wages and Bonus

The Minimum Wages Act, 1948

The Minimum Wages Act, 1948 was enacted to safeguard the interests of the workers mostly in the unorganised sector. Under the provision of the Act, both the Central and state governments are the appropriate governments to fix, revise, review and enforce the payment of minimum wages to workers in respect of scheduled employments under their respective jurisdictions. There are 45 scheduled employments in the Central and as many as 1697 in the state sphere. The enforcement of the Minimum Wages Act, 1948 is ensured at two levels. While in the Central sphere, the enforcement is done through the inspecting officers of the Chief Labour Commissioner (Central) commonly designated a Central Industrial Relations Machinery (CIRM), the compliance in the state is ensured through the state enforcement machinery.

In order to protect the minimum wages against inflation, the Central Government has introduced Variable Dearness Allowance (VDA) linked to Consumer Price Index. As regards states UT administrations, 27 of them have made VDA as a component of minimum wages. Both Central and state governments are revising the minimum wages in respect of these scheduled employments from time to time.

In order to have a uniform wage structure and to reduce the disparity in minimum wages across the country, a concept of National Floor Level Minimum Wage (NFLMW) was mooted on the basis of the recommendations of the National Commission on Rural Labour (NCRL) in 1991. NFLMW has been revised from time to time. The Central Government has revised the NFLMW from ₹ 137/- to ₹ 160/- per day from 2015. It, however, needs to be noted that the National Floor Level Minimum Wage, is a non-statutory measure.

Payment of Wages

The Payment of Wages Act, 1936 ensures timely payment of wages and that no unauthorised deductions are made from the wages of the workers. In exercise of the powers conferred by sub-section (6) of Section 1 of the Act, the Central Government, on the basis of figures of the Consumer Expenditure Survey published by National Sample Survey Office, has enhanced the wage ceiling from ₹ 10,000/- to ₹ 18,000/- per month from 2012.

Payment of Wages (Amendment) Act, 2017:- Section 6 of the Payment of Wages Act, 1936 was amended 2017 to enable making payment of wages in cash or by cheque or by crediting in the bank account of the employee. The amendment also enables the appropriate government may, by notification in the Official Gazette, specify the industrial or other establishment, the employer of which shall pay to every person employed in such industrial or other establishment, the wages only by cheque or by crediting the wages in the bank account.

Payment of Bonus

The Payment of Bonus Act, 1965 has been amended to revise the statutory eligibility limit under Section 2 (13) from ₹ 10,000/- to ₹ 21,000/- per month and the calculation ceiling under Section 12 from ₹ 3,500/- to ₹ 7,000/- or the minimum wage for the scheduled employment, as fixed by the appropriate Government, whichever is higher. The changes in the Payment of Bonus Act, 1965 are effective retrospectively from 2014.

Occupational Safety and Health

The provisions on Occupational Safety and Health (OSH) of workers as provided for in the Constitution of India are being implemented through the offices of Directorate General of Mines Safety (DGMS) and the Directorate General of Factory Advice Service and Labour Institutes (DGFASLI). The DGMS enforces the safety and health provisions for the workers in the mining industry through its Inspectors appointed under the Mines Act, 1952. The DGFASLI, through its Inspectorate of Dock Safety enforces safety provisions in the docks and also acts as the coordinating agency at the national level for the Inspectorate of Factories functioning under different state governments.

The Prime Minister's Shram Awards are given to the workers employed in department/public sector undertakings of the Central and state governments and the manufacturing units employing 500 or more workers in the private sector in recognition of their performance, devotion to duty, etc., The Vishwakarma Rashtriya Puraskars (VRP) are given to individual workers or group of workers for their outstanding suggestions leading to improvement in productivity, safety and health as well as the import substitution resulting in the savings of foreign currency. The National Safety Awards (NSA) are given in recognition of good safety performance on the part of the industrial establishments covered under the Factories Act, 1948, the employers covered under the Dock Workers (Safety, Health and Welfare) Act, 1986 and Building and other Construction Workers (Regulation of Employment and Conditions of Service) Act, 1996. The National Safety Award (Mines) are given at the national level in recognition of outstanding safety performance in mines covered under the Mines Act, 1952.

Research and Training

National Board for Workers' Education and Development

The Dattopant Thengadi National Board for Workers' Education and Development was established in 1958 to implement the Workers' Education Programmes at national, regional and unit/village level. The Board undertakes training programmes, which cover workers from organized, unorganized, rural and informal sectors. The main objective of the Board's training programmes is to create awareness among all sections of the working population. Supervisory and managerial cadres are also covered through joint education programmes.

With headquarters at Nagpur, the Board has a network of 50 regional and 8 sub regional directorates spread throughout the country. The six zonal Directorates at Delhi, Guwahati, Kolkata, Chennai, Mumbai and Bhopal monitor the activities of the regional directorates of their respective zone. The Board is tripartite in character and consists of representatives from central organisations of workers/employers, central/state governments and educational institutions.

V.V. Giri National Labour Institute an autonomous body of the Ministry of Labour and Employment, set up in 1974, has grown into a premier institute of labour research and training. Since its inception, the Institute has endeavoured through its research, training, education and publications to reach out to diverse groups concerned with various aspects of labour in the organised and unorganised sectors. The focus of such endeavours is the concern to transfer academic insights and understanding for application to policy formulation and action, so as to ensure a just place for labour in an egalitarian and democratic society.

Skill Development

Skill development and entrepreneurship efforts across the country have been highly fragmented so far. As opposed to developed countries, where the percentage of skilled workforce is between 60 and 90 per cent of the total workforce, India records an abysmal 4.69 per cent of workforce with formal vocational skills. There is a need for speedy reorganization of the ecosystem of skill development and entrepreneurship promotion in the country to suit the needs of the industry and enable decent quality of life to its population. Currently, over 40 Skill Development Programmes (SDPs) are being implemented by over 18 Ministries/Departments of the Government of India. However, there are gaps in the capacity and quality of training infrastructure as well as outputs, insufficient focus on workforce aspirations, lack of certification and common standards and a pointed lack of focus on the unorganized sector. In view of this and recognising the urgency of all concerned stakeholders in this field, a separate ministry was created in 2014, namely, the Ministry of Skill Development and Entrepreneurship. This Ministry is responsible for co-ordination of all skill development efforts, removal of disconnect between demand and supply of skilled manpower, building the vocational and technical training framework, skill up-gradation, building of new skills, and innovative thinking not only for existing jobs but also jobs that are to be created. The Ministry aims to Skill on a large Scale with Speed and high standards in order to achieve its vision of a 'Skilled Inida'.

Relevant Website : www.msde.gov.in

It is aided in these initiatives by its function arms - National Skill Development Agency (NSDA). National Skill Development Corporation (NSDC), National Skill Development Fund (NSDF) and 33 Sector Skill Councils (SSCs) as well as 187 training partners registered with NSDC.

National Skill Development Mission

The National Skill Development Mission was launched in 2015 on the occasion of World Youth Skills Day. It aims to create convergence and expedite cross-sectoral decisions through a high powered decision making framework. It is expected to converge, coordinate, implement and monitor skilling activities on a pan-India basis. The Mission aims to create convergence and expedite cross-sectoral decisions through a high powered decision making framework. It is expected to converge, coordinate, implement and monitor skilling activities on a pan-India basis. It consists of a three tier institutional structure, where the cascading functions of the bodies consist of providing policy directives and guidance, reviewing and monitoring overall progress, and actual implementation in line with Mission objectives. The Mission will also run select sub-missions in high priority areas. At the outset, seven sub-missions have been proposed in the following areas: (i) Institutional Training, (ii) Infrastructure, (iii) Convergence, (iv) Trainers, (v) Overseas Employment, (vi) Sustainable Livelihoods, (vii) Leveraging Public Infrastructure

National Policy on Skill Development and Entrepreneurship

The first National Policy on Skill Development (NPSD) was notified in 2009. The NPSD 2009 laid out the broad framework as well as objectives and outcomes for the skilling landscape in the country. Given the paradigm shift in the skilling ecosystem in the country and the experience gained through implementation of various skill development programmes in the country, there was an imminent need to revisit the earlier policy. Moreover, the 2009 policy itself provided for review every five years to align the policy framework with the emerging trends in the national and international milieu. Accordingly the new National Policy on Skill Development and Entrepreneurship was notified 2015 which replaces the policy of 2009.

The skill component of the policy addresses key issues in the skill landscape: low aspirational value, non-integration with formal education, lack of focus on outcomes, quality of training infrastructure and trainers, among others. The policy aims to align supply with demand, bridge existing skill gaps, promote industry engagement, operationalise a quality assurance framework, leverage technology and promote apprenticeship to tackle the identified issues. It also aims to promote equitable skilling opportunities for socially/ geographically marginalised and disadvantaged groups as well as women.

In the entrepreneurship domain, the policy seeks to promote an entrepreneurial culture through advocacy and integration of entrepreneurship education as a part of formal/skill education, enhance support for entrepreneurs in terms of credit and market linkages, foster innovation-driven and social enterprises and improve ease of doing business. It also suggests ways to further fillip entrepreneurship among women besides endeavouring to meet the entrepreneurial needs of socially/geographically marginalised and disadvantaged groups.

Schemes & Initiatives

Pradhan Mantri Kaushal Vikas Yojana (PMKVY)

PMKVY is the flagship outcome-based skill training scheme of this Ministry. The objective of this skill certification and reward scheme is to enable and mobilize a large number of youth to take up outcome based skill training to become employable and earn their livelihood.

The scheme was launched in 2015. The PMKVY is being implemented by the Centre along with the states.

Pradhan Mantri Kaushal Kendras (PMKK)

This Ministry through National Skill Development Corporation (NSDC), implements Pradhan Mantri Kaushal Kendra (PMKK) Scheme for setting up of model skill centre in every district of the country while ensuring coverage of all the parliamentary constituencies.

The PMKK envisages to: create benchmark institutions that demonstrate aspirational value for competency based skill development training at district level to ensure wider reach of programme focus on elements of quality, sustainability and connect with stakeholders in skills delivery process; transform from a mandate driven footloose model to a sustainable institutional model.

Schemes for Entrepreneurship

Pradhan Mantri Yuva Yojana

This Scheme aims at creating an enabling eco-system for entrepreneurship promotion among youth through entrepreneurship education and training, advocacy, easy access to entrepreneurship support network and promotion of social entrepreneurship. The specific objectives of the scheme are as follows: a) educate and equip potential and early stage entrepreneurs; b) connect entrepreneurs through networks of peers, mentors, incubators, funding and business services; support entrepreneurs through Entrepreneurship Hubs (E-Hubs) and catalyze a culture shift to support aspiring entrepreneurs. The Scheme is being implemented in partnership with both public and private stakeholders.

Udaan

The Special Industry Initiative (SII) for Jammu and Kashmir is funded by Ministry of Home Affairs and implemented by National Skill Development Corporation. The programme is a part of the overall initiative for addressing economic issues in the state and is focused on providing skills and job opportunities to the youth. Simultaneously, the aim is also to provide exposure to corporate India towards the rich talent pool available there.

22 Mass Communication

THE Ministry of Information and Broadcasting, through the mass communication media consisting of radio, television, films, press and print publications, advertising and traditional modes of communication such as dance and drama, plays an effective role in helping people to have access to free flow of information. The Ministry is involved in catering to the entertainment needs of various age groups and focusing attention of the people on issues of national integrity, environmental protection, health care and family welfare, eradication of illiteracy and issues relating to women, children, minority and other disadvantaged sections of the society. The Ministry is divided into four wings i.e., the Information Wing, the Broadcasting Wing, the Films Wing and the Integrated Finance Wing. The Ministry functions through its 21 media units/ attached and subordinate offices, autonomous bodies and PSUs.

The Information Wing handles policy matters of the print and press media and publicity requirements of the Government. This Wing also looks after the general administration of the Ministry.

The Broadcasting Wing handles matters relating to the electronic media and the regulation of the content of private TV channels as well as the programme matters of All India Radio and Doordarshan and operation of cable television and community radio, etc. Electronic Media Monitoring Centre (EMMC), which is a subordinate office, functions under the administrative control of this Division.

The Film Wing handles matters relating to the film sector. It is involved in the production and distribution of documentary films, development and promotional activities relating to the film industry including training, organization of film festivals, import and export regulations, etc. The Integrated Finance Wing looks after the financial aspects of the Ministry.

Relevant Website : www.mib.gov.in

Prasar Bharati

Prasar Bharati (Broadcasting Corporation of India) is the public service broadcaster in the country, with Akashvani (All India Radio) and Doordarshan as its two constituents. It came into existence on November 23, 1997, with a mandate to organize and conduct public broadcasting services to inform, educate and entertain the public and to ensure a balanced development of broadcasting on radio and television.

Objectives

The major objectives of the Prasar Bharati Corporation as laid out in the Prasar Bharati Act, 1990 are as follows : (i) to uphold the unity and integrity of the country and the values enshrined in the Constitution; (ii) to promote national integration; (iii) to safeguard citizen's rights to be informed on all matters of public interest and presenting a fair and balanced flow of information; (iv) to pay special attention to the fields of education and spread of literacy, agriculture, rural development, environment, health and family welfare and science and technology; (v) to create awareness about women's issues and to take special steps to protect the interests of children, the aged and other vulnerable sections of the society; (vi) to provide adequate coverage to the diverse cultures, sports and games and youth affairs; (vii) to promote social justice, safeguard the rights of working classes, minorities and tribal communities; and (viii) to promote research and expand broadcasting facilities and development in broadcast technology.

Prasar Bharati Board

The Corporation, is governed by the Prasar Bharati Board, which comprises a Chairman, an Executive Member (also known as Chief Executive Officer), a Member (Finance), a Member (Personnel), six part-time Members, a representative of the Ministry of Information & Broadcasting and Directors General of All India Radio and Doordarshan as ex-officio Members. The Chairman is a part-time member with a three year tenure subject to an age limit of seventy years. The Executive Member is a whole time member with a five-year tenure subject to an age limit of sixty five years. The Member (Finance) and the Member (Personnel) are whole time members also with a six-year tenure, subject to the age limit of 62 years. The Prasar Bharati Board meets from time to time and deliberates on important policy issues and gives directions to the executive to implement policy guidelines.

Relevant Website : www.prasarbharati.gov.in

All India Radio

After the invention of Radio and the starting of broadcasting in the western countries, broadcasting by private Radio Clubs started in a few cities in India like Mumbai, Kolkata and Chennai.

The first radio programme was broadcast by the Radio Club of Bombay in June, 1923. It was followed by the setting up of a Broadcasting Service that began broadcasting on July 23, 1927 on an experimental basis at Mumbai and Kolkata simultaneously under an agreement between the Government of India and a private company called the Indian Broadcasting Company Ltd. When this company went into liquidation in 1930, Indian State Broadcasting Service under the Department of "Controller of Broadcasts" was constituted and in 1935 Lionel Fielden was appointed the Controller of Broadcasting in India. The Indian State Broadcasting Service was renamed as All India Radio in January 1936. It remained under Department of Communication, Department of I&B, Department of Information and Arts for periods ranging from 1 to 4 years and finally has been under the Ministry of Information and Broadcasting. At the time of partition, India had six radio stations (Delhi, Mumbai, Kolkata, Chennai, Tiruchirapalli and Lucknow) and three radio stations went to Pakistan (Lahore, Peshawar and Dacca, now in Bangladesh).

A 1,000 kw super power medium wave transmitter each was commissioned at Mogra near Kolkata in 1969 and at Rajkot in 1971. Four 500 kw super power short wave transmitters were inaugurated at Bangalore in 1994. This made it one of the biggest transmitting centres in the world. The first ever FM service was started in Madras on July 23, 1977. All AIR stations were provided with 5 channel receiver terminals in 1985. Multitrack recording studio was commissioned at Mumbai in 1994 and in Chennai in 1995.

Infrastructure

All India Radio came to be known as Akashvani from 1957. AIR took over radio stations being run by native states since British days such as Akashvani Mysore, Hyderabad Radio, and Radio Kashmir, etc.

From a meagre 18 transmitters in 1947 AIR acquired 46 by the end of First Plan, 59 by the end of Second Plan, 110 by the end of Third Plan and 433 by the end of 11th Plan and hence forth by March-2018 total number of transmitters went up to 662, consisting of 139 mw, 48 sw and 475 FM transmitters. The number of radio stations went up from six in 1947 to 469 by March, 2018.

Software

AIR has evolved, over the years, a three-tier system of broadcasting namely national, regional, and local. It caters to the information, education, and entertainment needs of the audience through its stations in this country of continental dimension with plural society. They provide news, music, spoken words, and other programmes in 23 languages and 176 dialects to almost the entire population of the country which crossed 1 billion mark recently.

The entertainment channel of AIR named Vividh Bharati was started on October 3, 1957 and since November 1, 1967, commercials were aired on this channel. The first Radio Sangeet Sammelan was organised in 1954, which has since become annual feature. Akashvani Annual Awards to promote excellence in Programme, Engineering, News and Audience Research were instituted in 1974. Doordarshan was separated from AIR on April 1, 1976. The first broadcast by political parties before Elections went on the air in 1977 from different stations of AIR. The North Eastern Service was commissioned on January 3, 1990 at Shillong in the campus of AIR, Shillong. The public service broadcasting initially in the evening transmission for about five and a half hour daily has since been extended to three transmissions. The programmes are beamed through a 50 kw SW transmitter in Hindi and English besides music programmes in different languages/ dialects of all the states of the North East. Phone-in-Programmes were introduced.

Channels and Programmes

The phenomenal growth achieved by All India Radio through eight decades has made it one of the largest media organisations in the world. Now, it has 469 stations and 662 transmitters. To serve the communication needs of the plural society that India is, the network expanded gradually imbibing new technologies and programme production techniques. All India Radio's services are being digitalized.

Objectives

To provide information, education and entertainment, for promoting the welfare and happiness of the masses (*Bahujana Hitaya Bahujana Sukhaya*), All India Radio strives :- (a) to uphold the unity of the country and the democratic values enshrined in the constitution. (b) to present a fair and balanced flow of information of national, regional, local and international interest, including contrasting views, without advocating any opinion or ideology of its own. (c) to produce and transmit varied programmes designed to awaken, inform, enlighten, educate, entertain, and enrich all sections of the people; (d) to produce and transmit programmes relating to developmental activities in all their facets including extension work in agriculture, education, health and family welfare and science and technology; (e) to serve the rural, illiterate and underprivileged population, keeping in the mind the special needs and interest of the young, social and cultural minorities, the tribal population and those residing in border regions, backward or remote areas; (f) to serve the rural population, minority communities, women, children, illiterate as well as other weaker and vulnerable sections of the society; and (g) to promote national integration.

Three-Tier Broadcasting

The three-tier system of broadcasting of AIR caters to the information, education, and entertainment needs of the audiences through its stations in this country of continental dimension and with a plural society. They provide news, music, spoken word and other programmes to almost the entire population of the country, 121.0 crore as per the 2011 census. Its vast reach especially in the rural and tribal areas make it the primary and sometimes the only source of information and entertainment.

In National Service the national programmes, which are heard on the Medium Wave in most parts of the country, cater to the first-tier broadcasting. Recently, it has started airing on Short Wave also. The regional and sub-regional stations provide the second-tier of broadcasting giving the programmes in the regional languages and promoting regional cultural facets. In addition, FM Channels at metros cater to the modern needs of the people primarily the youth. The Vividh Bharati has also been shifted to FM broadcasting system at 40 places. The 86 stations on FM mode set up to cater to the needs and tastes of the audiences of small towns in various parts of the country are the Local Radio stations (LRS). Recently, the community radio has become very popular among different electronic media available in the country. All India Radio has also set-up Community Radio Service at five places in the North Eastern India as the voice of the local tribal population.

Regional Channels

Regional Channels are located mostly in the state capitals and in the major linguistic-cultural regions of every state. Altogether 128 such channels are spread over 29 states and 6 UTs of the country. The public service broadcasting arm of AIR, the Regional Channels put out infotainment programmes with the objective of enriching the lives of their listeners. The Regional Channels, broadcast largely on the Medium Wave frequency, follow a composite programming mix. They also promote art and culture with a major emphasis on Indian classical music. Around 40 per cent of the total broadcast on primary channels comprises music, which includes classical, light, folk, film and the music of various other languages. News and current affairs programmes constitute 20 to 30 per cent of the broadcast time. Radio plays and drama, health and family welfare programmes, programmes for women and children, farm and home programmes aimed at empowering rural masses are the other important segments of the primary channels. These channels being the most accessible of all the AIR channels, strive to reach their audiences in the language most understood by all.

Local Radio Stations

At present 86 Local Radio Stations (LRS) are located across the country. These stations are serving the local population of the area, providing utility services and reaching right into the heart of the community.

FM Rainbow

FM Rainbow channel of All India Radio was launched at a time when radio listening was declining especially in big cities. FM radio filled this gap effectively by ensuring disturbance-free high quality music to its listeners. Even the presentation style of the compere on FM channel was transformed to suit the changing needs of listeners. Interpersonal chatting style of the comperes caught the pulse of youth and allured them to come closer to their radio. In its round-the-clock broadcast, the listeners were served with a recipe of whole new gamut of entertainment. Soon FM radio acquired the status of modern radio because it was speaking in their style and providing them the listening pleasure. The old glory of radio was restored once again at least in terms of listening percentages.

FM Gold

FM Gold channel went on air on September 1, 2001 at Delhi as a niche infotainment channel with 30 per cent of news and current affairs component and 70 per cent of entertainment programming. At present, FM Gold channel is available daily round the clock. FM Gold channel is available at five places four metros i.e., Delhi, Mumbai, Kolkata, Chennai and Ludhiana. This additional channel gave its listeners an option to choose between the two, besides listening to other parallel running AIR and private FM stations in the area. This channel is trying to provide information interlinked with entertainment and brings information updates on traffic, airlines, railways, weather, etc.

DTH Service

DTH Radio Channel is a satellite service meant for the listeners, who own a TV set. The Service is available through the DTH platform of Prasar Bharati with uplinking facilities at Todapur, Delhi. It is not a terrestrial broadcast service and its programmes cannot be tuned in through the ordinary radio receiver sets. It is a 24 hour service broadcast digitally. The programming is planned in such a way that the repetitions are kept at a minimum.

The DTH Service provides 39 different language channels available in every nook and corner of the country. The most significant aspect of this broadcast is its digital quality.

Vividh Bharati

The popular Vividh Bharati Service provides entertainment for 17 hours a day from 41 CBS-VB centres. Beside this, Vividh Bharati Service is also relayed through 65 Local Radio Stations and 100 watt FM transmitters located across the country.

News Services Division

The News Services Division (NSD) of All India Radio has been expanding its presence across various domains with the aim of reaching diverse cross section of people. The News Services Division has substantially increased its presence on the social media and crossed major milestones in reaching out audiences far and wide.

NSD's 46 Regional News Units (RNUs) play a vital role to cater to the information needs of the people. RNUs make bulletins and programmes in 77 regional languages/ dialects to make news region specific and people friendly. The RNUs originate 444 bulletins every day for a total duration of about 33 hours that includes regional, external, DTH services and FM headlines. RNUs also mount 12,720 news- based programmes in a month for a total duration of nearly 1706 hours besides broadcasting special programmes when state assemblies are in session.

FM headlines serve immediate needs of information in Indian languages for listeners during their daily busy schedule in cities and towns. At present 249 headline bulletins in 16 languages are being produced by RNUs.

Units of NSD

To facilitate the news gathering and broadcasting, NSD has various units viz., the Reporting Unit, Talks and Current Affairs Unit, Reference Unit and the Monitoring Unit. With inputs from these units, NSD is able to cover diverse new events and happenings to present a comprehensive view of developments, flagship programmes and new initiatives of the current government like Swatch Bharat Abhiyan, Pradhan Mantri Jan Dhan Yojana, Adarsh, etc. NSD is able to give wide coverage to Prime Minister's and President's visits/tours abroad.

Relevant Websites : www.newsonair.com www.newsonair.nic.in

Mann Ki Baat

For Mann Ki Baat programme, live webcasting is done on website news on air.nic.in. Special window and page is created for the purpose. A special window and page is created for the purpose.

Transcription and Programme Exchange Service

AIR also has a Transcription and Programme Exchange Service which includes units like Central Archives, Sound Archives, Digital Sound Archives, Digital Library, Radio Autobiography, Transcription Unit and Refurbishing Unit.

Central Archives

The Transcription Service was started in April, 1954 and entrusted with the main function of preparing transcription of speeches of all dignitaries with a special reference to the Presidents and Prime Ministers of India. This unit was also performing the duty of the processing of vinyl disc labelled "AIR-TS records" for preservation of recordings for future broadcast. The nomenclature of Service was changed to "Transcription and Programme Exchange Service" from 1959. As the processed records eventually proved to be uneconomical, the processing work had to be closed down in 1967 and new modes of preservation like analogue magnetic tapes, etc., came into use.

Sound Archives

The Sound Archives of All India Radio can be called the National Audio Archives of the nation as it is the treasure house of precious recordings of music and spoken word in different categories. It is the largest audio library of Indian Music recordings. The library preserves a separate collection of Mahatma Gandhi's speeches including his first and the last prayer speeches recorded on May 11, 1947 at Sodepur Ashram, Calcutta and January 29, 1948 at Birla House, Delhi respectively. The only broadcast by Gandhiji from AIR Delhi on November 12, 1947 is also preserved. The library contains recordings of all the Presidents and Prime Ministers of India. Voice recordings of eminent personalities like Rabindra Nath Tagore, Netaji

Subhas Chandra Bose, Dr. B.R. Ambedkar, Sardar Patel, Sarojini Naidu etc., have also been preserved. Apart from this, award-winning radio dramas, features, documentaries and memorial lectures are available in the library.

Digital Sound Archives

Transcription and Programme Exchange Service (T&PES) has taken up a mega project of digitizing all the analogue content. Major steps have been taken in this direction. Resultantly, Akashvani has become one of the major digital libraries in the broadcasting network with internationally accepted norms.

Archives Digital Library

Radio Autobiography

In Radio Autobiography, recordings of eminent personalities from various walks of life are preserved. The Central Archives of All India Radio is a rich repository of priceless recordings of Radio Autobiographies of renowned musicians, public figures, literatures etc. Among such eminent persons recorded are J R D Tata, Ustad Ali Akbar Khan, Harivansh Rai Bachchan and Dr. Verghese Kurien. With the inputs from different AIR stations, the people of eminence are identified.

Programme Exchange Library

The main purpose of this unit is to exchange good quality programmes among the stations as per their requirements. In PEU Library approx. 8000 tapes containing the recordings of music and spoken word programmes are preserved for this purpose. Besides containing both music and spoken word items in different Indian languages, PEU Library is also preserving the language lessons in Bangla, English, Gujarati, Kannada, Malayalam, Marathi, Odiya, Sanskrit, Tamil and Telugu.

Transcription Unit

One of the important functions of transcription unit is to transcribe the recording of speeches delivered by President and Prime Minister and preserve them in the form of volumes for posterity. Tapes containing the recording of speeches along with transcripts are received from various AIR stations. The bound volumes of all transcriptions are prepared and kept in the archives.

Refurbishing Unit

In order to refurbish the vintage music recordings in archives refurbishing unit was installed some years back with the assistance of United Nations Development Programme. Hundreds of hours of recordings of music and voice of Mahatma Gandhi, Pandit Nehru, etc., were refurbished here. As of now this unit takes care of enhancing the audio quality of the recording being released by AIR and Doordarshan archives.

External Services Division

The cardinal role played by international/external broadcasting as an instrument of foreign policy and public diplomacy needs no elaboration. Due to its colonial link with England, broadcasting came almost simultaneously in England and India. Similarly, shortly after BBC started its first foreign language broadcast in Arabic in 1938 on All India Radio entered the domain of external broadcast on October 1, 1939 purely as a tool for propaganda for the Allies during the World War II with a service in Pushto language to counter the German Radio Blitzkrieg in the region and supplement the efforts by the BBC in this part of the world. At the dawn of Independence, ESD had to don a new avatar as the voice of an emerging nation, an old civilization, a tool for diplomacy and also effective propaganda machinery at the time of different crises. Since then the External Services Division of AIR has been a vital link between India and rest of the World, specially with those countries where the interest of India are intertwined because of Indian population staying in those countries.

External Services Division of AIR ranks high among the external radio networks of the world both in its reach and range covering about 100 countries in 27 languages. The AIR, through its external broadcasts, aims to keep the overseas listeners in touch with the ethos of India. The languages in which AIR reaches its foreign audience are English, French, Russian, Swahili, Arabic, Persian, Pushto, Dari, Baluchi, Sinhalese, Nepali, Tibetan, Chinese, Thai, Burmese, and Bhasha Indonesia. The services in Hindi, Tamil, Telugu, Malayalam and Gujarati are directed at overseas Indians, while those in Urdu, Punjabi, Sindhi, Saraiki, Kannada and Bengali are meant for listeners in the Indian sub-continent.

National Academy of Broadcasting and Multimeda

National Academy of Broadcasting and Multimedia (NABM) (Programme) hitherto known as Staff Training Institute (Programme) is the apex training institute of Prasar Bharati. It is responsible for training of in-service Programme and Administrative personnel working at various stations of AIR and Doordarshan.

Audience Research Unit

With the changing mass communication scenario, Audience Research has occupied the centre stage. World over, almost all the big media organizations have been doing in-house audience research in one form or the other or 'Market Research' in marketing parlance as no media organization can afford to put their scarce resource at stake without knowing the potential audience (consumers) and market for their media content.

All India Radio has been the pioneer in this field. It has a wide network of Audience Research Units across the country operational since 1946. It provides programme feedback to programme producers to plan, design, and modify the programmes according to the needs, tastes, and aspiration of the target audience.

Doordarshan

From an experimental service begun at Delhi in September 1959, Doordarshan (DD) over the years has grown tremendously to become one of the leading TV organizations of the world. Over the years, it has not only expanded its network throughout length and breadth of the country but also kept pace with new technological developments in the field of TV broadcasting. Doordarshan is presently operating 34 satellite channels and has a vast network of 67 studios and 1,416 transmitters of varying power providing TV coverage to about 92 per cent population of the country. In addition, it is providing free-to-air DTH service.

Doordarshan is headed by the Director General who is responsible for policy formation, planning and development, infrastructure and technology development, budgetary planning and control, human resource development; overseeing operation and maintenance activities, etc. Four zonal offices located at Delhi, Mumbai, Kolkata and Chennai look after project and maintenance activities in their responsive zone. The various Doordarshan establishments are—Doordarshan Kendras (Studio Centres), High Power Transmitters (LPTs) and Very Low Power Transmitters (VLPTs). Maintenance centres look after clusters of LPTs and VLPTs.

DD National

DD National Channel, a public service broadcaster is the largest terrestrial network in the world. It covers about 92.0 per cent population and 81.0 per cent land area of the country. Being a Public Service Broadcaster the channel continues to make significant contribution to accelerate socio-economic changes, promote national integration, inculcate a sense of unity and fraternity and stimulate scientific temperament among the people. It contributes to dissemination of knowledge/education and information for public awareness about means of population control, family welfare, preservation of environment, ecological balance and measures for women and children welfare. The channel lends a healthy mix of entertainment, information and education. The service is available in terrestrial mode from 05.30 a.m. till midnight. In the satellite mode it is available round-the-clock.

DD News

DD News is the only terrestrial-cum-satellite, multilingual news channel of the country. The news channel has been successfully discharging its responsibility to give balanced, fair and accurate news without sensationalizing as well as by carrying different shades of opinion. DD-News channel was launched in November 2003 by converting DD-Metro into a 24-hours news channel. Its satellite footprint is available across the country. DD News terrestrial reach is 49 per cent area of the country. It is currently producing news content in Hindi, English, Urdu and Sanskrit languages. Over 18 hours of Live transmission include telecast of more than 40 news bulletins in these languages. DD News is having 30 Regional News Units (RNUs) across the country which are broadcasting news bulletins.

DD India

Doordarshan opened its windows to the world by launching its international channel on March 14, 1995. The Channel, initially known as DD-World was renamed DD-India in 2002. The programming offers international viewers an update on the Indian social, cultural, political and economic scene.

DD Bharati

DD Bharati Channel was re-launched in 2012 as a niche channel for art and culture to preserve Indian culture and heritage with authenticity and to present it to the wider public. It is the only Channel dedicated to art and culture in India. DD Bharati has entered into partnerships with various national and international public institutions and NGOs to acquire premiere programmes available in their archives, after making very judicious selection keeping the profile and audience of the channel in view.

DD Urdu

DD Urdu came into existence in 2006 which became 24x7 channel with effect from 2007. The transmission features a mix of repeat and non-repeat, acquired and in-house software, which encapsulates heritage, culture, literature, information, education and social issues specific to the target audience apart from news, live events like Independence Day, Republic Day celebrations, messages of the President and Prime Minister, special programmes on the state leaders. Mandate/the theme that predominantly runs through the transmission relates to modernizing educational and social outlook of the target audience.

DD Sports

Sports Channel of Doordarshan was launched in 1999. The transmission of the channel is round the clock from 2000.

DD Kashir

DD Kashir channel was launched in 2000 with fourteen and a half hours of transmission per day. This was converted into a 24-hour channel a year later.

Doordarshan Commercial Service

Doordarshan Commercial Service (DCS) is an independent wing to co-ordinate all the commercial activities being performed at the headquarters, Doordarshan Kendras, marketing divisions and DCD towards sale of airtime as well as collection of revenue from agencies/clients/ producers. It is responsible for framing of Commercial policies and updating of rate card as per inputs received from Marketing Divisions and regional Kendras, with the approval of Prasar Bharati Board.

DD Archives

Doordarshan Archives reinvented itself in 2003 with a new approach and prepared itself to meet the challenges of Audio Visual Digital World.

Audience Research

The Audience Research unit of Doordarshan with its 19 field units located with Doordarshan Kendras all over the country, is involved in Research studies on various aspects of broadcasting since 1976.

Relevant Website : www.ddindia.gov.in

Electronic Media Monitoring Centre

Protecting the citizens from undesirable content being aired by television channels is a norm followed by almost all leading democracies in the world. In India, Electronic Media Monitoring Centre (EMMC) is entrusted with the task of monitoring the content being aired by TV channels. EMMC is among one of the premier organisations of the world that monitor the broadcasting sector and the content being aired by broadcasters. The Centre is also one of the youngest among the government-owned media units in the country.

It is worth recalling that the need to monitor content arises in response to grievances and complaints coming from different quarters against invasion of raunchy reality shows, talk shows, news, documentaries and soap operas into the television industry.

EMMC records and monitors the content of around 600 channels, beaming over the Indian Territory, so that any violations of codes framed under the Cable Television Network (Regulation) Act, 1995 could be checked. Cable Television Networks (Regulation) Act, 1995 identifies several codes which must be adhered to by all broadcasting entities. The revised up-linking guidelines and downlinking guidelines for channels beamed at Indian viewers also require monitoring of content for possible violations and remedial measures thereto.

Electronic Media Monitoring Centre identifies topical matters of immense public importance and reports them to the Ministry for evaluation and for taking any action, if needed. EMMC also prepares and submits special reports to the Ministry on topics desired by the Government. Setting up examples of success, the EMMC has taken a big leap forward by starting Radio Monitoring since January 1, 2015. The newly started wing of EMMC is currently monitoring Community Radio Stations (CRS) for detection of possible violations. At present, 30 Community Radio Stations from across the country are being monitored to check whether they are airing any content that violates the 'General Agreement between Government of India and Community Radio Stations (GOPA)' and 'Programme and Advertisement

Code of All India Radio'. In a very short span of time, several apparent violations have been detected in the content being broadcast by CRS and submitted before the Ministry by EMMC. These apparent violations not only include obscene and vulgar programmes but several other types of content too which violate general rules laid by the Ministry.

Because of the ever-increasing number of channels, there is a race among channels to attract as many eyeballs as possible, and this trend has resulted in most of the channels treading on a very thin line and often barging into grey area. The somewhat callous attitude of TV channels towards the regulatory guidelines is becoming a matter of concern, particularly when an average Indian family, increasingly finds itself sitting in front of the TV for a time longer than ever before. The change in trend of TV viewing is also due to the fact that television industry has grown immensely over the past few years. Television shows have evolved over the years as more and more TV shows resort to unwarranted content to capture their audience. It has been observed that some of the TV shows affect young viewers and it is becoming a problem. Television influences the lives of young children in a big way. Children are exposed to all sorts of violence and anomalous culture at home. Public Interest obligation is missed by mass media when they air programmes.

Advertisement sector is a key part of Indian television industry. With the rising influence of TV media on people, it has become a catalyst of consumerism. The scope of creativity is enormous in the field of advertising. People like advertisements because they provide information and create awareness about new products in the market. Our decisions, whether to buy a product or not, are often completely influenced by the promotional activities of the companies concerned. Therefore, due to unfair trade practices, deceptive advertisements and widespread adverse impact of the advertisements of unhealthy products like tobacco and liquor, the Government of India has always endeavoured to curb or at least restrict advertisements of such products by bringing in appropriate legislations, orders and directives. As a reaction to the Government's directive to ban advertisements of products that are adverse to health, the major companies of liquor and tobacco have taken the route of "Surrogate Advertisements". These advertisements are bombarded on viewers lest they forget the liquor and tobacco brands as there is a ban on directly advertising them.

The advent of the "Era of Reality Shows", in the Indian TV industry, has generated fairly good TRP for many a TV channels. Nowadays, when every second TV channel is coming with its own version of the "reality programmes based on borrowed ideas and values", it is very much imperative for the Government to ensure that the 'Freedom of Expression' is not misused to play with the young minds of our country. Such shows have a greater impact on children than other regular TV programmes as they interpret real life situations.

Reality shows are meant for adults, and without proper knowledge, understanding, and guidance, children can be misled by such programmes. Some reality shows have children as participants who are under tremendous pressure to perform. Also, children who are left to watch these shows on television can often be baffled at the display and can take them as behaviour expected out of everyone, especially themselves and their peers.

A large number of misleading advertisements make unsubstantiated claims about the impact of certain products. Ministry of I&B has cautioned that advertisements should not dwell on a product's seemingly miraculous properties that cannot be proven. This is in violation of the Advertising Code, particularly rule 7(5) contained in the Cable Television Networks Rules framed under the Cable Television Networks Regulation Act, 1995.

Relevant Website : www.emmc.gov.in

Press and Print Media

Registrar of Newspapers for India

The Office of the Registrar of Newspapers for India (RNI) is an attached office of the Ministry of Information and Broadcasting. Under its Statutory and derivative functions, it verifies and approves titles of newspapers, registers them, checks and establishes circulation claims. It also submits to the Secretary, I & B by 31st December every year the "Press in India Report", highlighting the state of Print Media in the country; the report is subsequently published under the title "Press in India". Under its non-statutory functions, the RNI issues Eligibility Certificates for import of newsprint, to actual users which are registered with RNI as well as Essentiality Certificates for import of printing machinery, etc.

Title Verification

RNI receives applications of the intending publishers for title verification, duly forwarded by the DM concerned and processes them for title verification as per the proviso to Section 6 of the PRB Act. During 2015, RNI scrutinized 15,293 applications for verification of titles, of which 9,272 titles were verified. To facilitate the applicants RNI has started online application filling facility on its website. For further processing by the DM concerned, the applicant is required to take out a printout of the filled application and submit to DM concerned for forwarding to RNI. The applicants are intimated through SMS and e-mail at application receipt stage and title verification stage at RNI to facilitate the applicants and ensure transparency. The status of title applications can be checked on RNI website. Discrepancy letters and title verification letters can also be downloaded from RNI website.

De-Blocking of Titles

After getting the title verified, the publishers are required to get the title registered. If the documents for registration are not received in RNI in 2 years, the title gets de-blocked and is available for verification to any intending applicant.

Registration

After the title verification, publisher is required to submit a declaration duly authenticated by the District Magistrate concerned, along with a copy of the first issue published within specified days after authentication of declaration as per the Act and an affidavit for no-foreign tie-up. After ascertaining that the publication has been printed and published in conformity with the various provisions of the PRB Act and the rules made thereunder, a registration number is allotted to the newspaper/periodical and entries made in the Register of RNI. The Certificate of Registration (CR) is then issued to the publisher.

Annual Statement

As per Section 19D of the PRB Act, an Annual Statement in Form-II prescribed in the Registration of Newspapers (Central) Rules 1956 is required to be submitted by the publishers of newspapers to the Press Registrar on or before the last day of May each year containing various information as prescribed under the rules. It is also obligatory on the part of every publisher to print in the publication, a statement indicating the ownership and other relevant particulars in Form IV in the first issue every year after the last day of February. Annual Statement is the basic document on the basis of which RNI undertakes compilation and analysis of the status of the Press, which is incorporated in its Annual Report, called "Press in India".

Relevant Website : www.rni.nic.in

Press Information Bureau

The Press Information Bureau (PIB) is the nodal agency of the Government of India to disseminate information to the print, electronic and social media on government policies, programmes, initiatives and achievements. It functions as an interface between the government and the media and also provides feedback to the government on the reaction of people as reflected in the media. It has 5 zones comprising 19 regional offices and 17 branch offices, including an Information Centre. PIB disseminates information through different means such as press releases, press notes, feature articles, backgrounds, press briefings, interviews, press conferences and press tours, etc., to cater to the needs of regional media. PIB also uses social media platforms like Twitter, Facebook, Instagram to disseminate information. The information is released in English, Hindi, Urdu along with 13 other regional languages which reaches newspapers and media organizations all over the country. PIB also provides accreditation facility to media persons so as to facilitate access to information from the government sources.

Publicity

Departmental Publicity Officers are attached to various ministries and departments for disseminating information to the media through press releases, press notes, backgrounders etc., and also by arranging press conferences, press tours, media briefings etc. These officers provide the requisite service to their respective ministries and also meet the information needs of media in respect of those ministries.

Prime Minister's Unit

PM's Publicity and Reference Unit is a dedicated unit for the publicity and media support for the Prime Minister's Office and cabinet. The media related compilations prepared by this Unit include daily newspaper clippings highlighting major issues, weekly magazine reports, feedback reports from social media and online media portals and special compendium of press coverage on PM visits.

Social Media

PIB has social media presence on Twitter, Facebook, YouTube and Instagram. The information about various events/activities/programmes of ministries and departments is put out on social media for immediate and wider dissemination. Special infographics, video messages, etc., are created and posted on social media for special events such as budget presentation, Yoga day, Independence Day, etc. Many regional/branch offices of PIB also have their dedicated social media platforms.

Twitter : On twitter, PIB's handle, @pibindia and @pibhindi have nearly 1.35 million+followers and 42,000+followers respectively.

Facebook : PIB's Facebook page, www.facebook.com/pibindia has reached 1,20,000+subscribers.

Instagram : PIB's Instagram gallery, www.instagram.com/pibindia has reached 52,000+subscribers.

Media Interactive Sessions

Media Interactive Sessions are planned in selected state capitals on issues such as socio-economic development, infrastructure, developmental schemes, etc. Under this initiative, important Union Ministries and senior officers of the concerned ministries are invited to participate in the event and interact with the national and local media and highlight the important initiatives taken by the government. 'Vartalap' is a programme organized for small towns/rural journalists to keep them aware/updated about the various central government Flagship Schemes for the welfare of rural populace. Press Tours are conducted by the headquarters/regional and branch offices with a view to showcase the success stories of the various schemes/ projects being run by the government in rural/urban areas throughout the country.

Online Press Accreditation

Press Accreditation is granted to media representatives including members of the foreign media at the headquarters of Press Information Bureau, New Delhi. A fully online system of press accreditation was operationalized in 2010 which is continually updated to keep up with the increasing number of requests for accreditation.

Journalists' Welfare Scheme

A scheme of providing financial assistance to journalists and their families facing acute financial hardship on account of serious ailment is being implemented by PIB which provides for one time ex-gratia relief on urgent basis. The amount of such assistance, upto ₹ 5 lakhs, is extended to the families of deceased journalist or in case of his permanent disability. Assistance upto ₹ 3 lakhs is also extended in case of ailments like cancer, renal failure, heart ailments, etc., and upto ₹ 2 lakhs in case of accidents requirement hospitalization.

Emergency Control Room

The PIB has a News Room/Control Room which is operational round the year to meet challenges emerging out of any eventuality during any time of the day or night. Arrangements for holding press conferences at short notices and simultaneous web-cast through PIB centres across the country are also kept in a state of readiness to handle any sudden development and unexpected situation even after 9.00 P.M. The Control Room functions on 24X7 basis during emergencies and time of crisis.

Feedback, Feature and Photo Services

One of the important functions of PIB is to keep the government informed of public perception about government policies and programmes as reflected in media. The feedback reports include inputs from the national dailies published from the capital, from regional language newspapers as sent by the regional/branch offices, inputs from TV news channels, web media and magazines.

The Bureau also provides inputs regarding media trends on important matters relating to their ministries/departments. The Feature Unit of the Bureau issue features, success stories backgrounders, info-nuggets, photo-features which are also sent to the regional/branch offices for translation and circulation to the local media.

International Film Festival of India

The Press Information Bureau was part of the IFFI 2017 to facilitate dissemination of Festival related information to media at the venue in Goa. It provided favourable and encouraging work environment and facilitated participation of the media persons in the festival.

Relevant Website : www.pib.gov.in

News Agencies

Press Trust of India

India's largest news agency, Press Trust of India (PTI) is a non-profit sharing cooperative owned by the country's newspapers with a mandate to provide efficient and unbiased news to all subscribers. Founded in August, 1947, PTI began functioning from 1949. It offers its news services in English and Hindi languages. Bhasha is the Hindi language news service of the agency. PTI subscribers include 500 newspapers in India and scores abroad. All major TV and radio channels in India and several abroad, including BBC in London, receive its services. PTI now has its own satellite delivery system through a transponder on an INSAT satellite for reaching its services directly to subscribers anywhere in the country. Increasingly more and more subscribers are opting for satellite reception. Photo service is delivered by satellite as well as accessed by dial up.

PTI has also begun satellite transmission by Ku band which offers subscribers the option of receiving news through a cheaper and small size satellite receiver. The Agency is on the Internet too. The agency's news services have been showcased on its website http.//www.ptinews.com. Clients also have the option of taking any of PTI's services through Internet. PTI news is also available through World Space radio broadcast reception. The Photo service is delivered by satellite as well as accessed through dial-up. The agency is now engaged in archiving its photos. It employs more than 400 journalists and 500 stringers to cover almost every district and small town in India. Collectively, they put out more than 2,000 stories and 200 photographs a day.

Its correspondents are also based in leading capitals and important business and administrative centres around the world. It also has exchange arrangements with several foreign news agencies to magnify its global news footprint. Currently, PTI commands 90 per cent of news agency market share in India. Besides the news and photo services, the other services of the agency include mailer packages of feature, science service, economic service and Data India, and screen-based services as News-scan and stock scan. A television wing, PTI-TV, does features and undertakes corporate documentaries on assignment basis. The PTI has arrangements with the Associated Press (AP) and Agency France Press (AFP) for distribution of their news in India. AP's photo and international commercial information are also distributed in the country through PTI.

Relevant Website : www.ptinews.com

United News of India

United News of India (UNI) was incorporated under the Companies Act, 1956 in December, 1959 and started functioning effectively from 1961. In the past five decades, UNI has grown into a major news organisation in India and, with its vibrant presence, provided the much-needed spirit of competition in the vital areas of news gathering and dissemination. It also has a full-fledged Hindi wire service 'UNIVARTA' since 1982 and a Photo Service and a Graphics Service in the same decade. In June 1992, it launched the first ever wire service in Urdu. UNI's Photo Service distributes about 200 pictures every day, including sixty international photographs from EPA, the European Pressphoto Agency and Reuters. Its Graphics Service distributes five or six graphics every day.

Relevant Website : www.uniindia.com

NAM News Network

NAM News Network (NNN) is the internet-based news and photo exchange arrangement of the news agencies belonging to member countries of the nonaligned movement. News and photo contributions of NAM news agencies including Press Trust of India are uploaded onto the NNN website http:/www.namnewsnetwork.org for online access by all. Malaysian news agency Bernama is at present handling the operation of the website from Kuala Lumpur.

Formally launched in April 2006, NNN replaces the Non-aligned News Agencies Pool (NANAP) which had acted as the news exchange mechanism among non-aligned countries for 30 years. With internet a cheap and reliable mode of communication, NNN contributes to sustained flow of information in the 116 member non-aligned world. NANAP, set up in 1976, was the first attempt of the non-aligned movement to provide for exchange of news among its member countries. At a time when communication costs were very high, NANAP provided for sharing of communication channels of member news agencies to ensure a common network for exchange of news among all countries of the non-aligned movement.

Relevant Website : www.namnewsnetwork.org

Press Council of India

The Press Council of India is a statutory quasi-judicial autonomous authority mandated by the Parliament for the twin objective of preserving the freedom of the press and maintaining and improving the standards of newspapers and the news agencies in India exercising equal quasi-judicial functions over the authorities as well the press person. It comprises a Chairman and 28 members. While the Chairman has, by convention, been a sitting or retired judge of the Supreme Court of India, of the 28 members, 20 represent various segments of the Press and eight overseeing the readers' interest, are representatives of the two Houses of Parliament (3 Lok Sabha and 2 Rajya Sabha) and premier literary and legal bodies of the country i.e., University Grants Commission, Bar Council of India and Sahitya Akademi. The Council has its own funds for performance of its functions under the Act that comprises the fee collected from newspapers, other receipts and also grants in-aid by from the central government.

The Press Council has the responsibility to preserve the freedom of the press and to maintain and improve the standards of newspapers and news agencies in the country. There is also an advisory role on the Council in that it can, either *suo-motu* or on a reference made to it by the government under Section 13(2) of the Act, undertake studies and express its opinion in regard to any bill, legislation, law or other matters concerning the press and convey its opinion to the government or the persons concerned. Also, in the matters of public importance concerning its statutory responsibilities, the Council may *suo-moto* take an on-the-spot inquiry.

The Council discharges its functions primarily through adjudications on complaint cases received by it, either against the press for violation of journalistic ethics or by the press for interference with its freedom. Where the Council is satisfied, after inquiry, that a newspaper or a news agency has offended the standards of journalistic ethics or public taste or that an editor or working journalist has committed any professional misconduct, the Council may warn, admonish or censure them or disapprove of their conduct. It is also empowered to make such observations as it may think fit in respect of the conduct of any authority, including Government, for interfering with the freedom of the press so prescribed under Section(4) the decisions of the Council are final and cannot be questioned in any court of law.

Press and Registration Appellate Board

Section 8C of the Press and Registration of Books Act, 1867 entrusts to the Press Council, the Appellate Jurisdiction over the Magisterial Orders of non-authentication of a Declaration under Section 6 or its subsequent cancellation under Section 8B of the said Act. The Board consist of a Chairman and another member to be nominated by the Press Council of India among its members.

National Press Day

The National Press Day is celebrated annually on November 16 as a symbol of a free and responsible press in the country.

Relevant Website : www.presscouncil.nic.in

New Media Wing

Set up in 1945, the Research, Reference and Training Division now renamed as "New Media Wing" functions as information unit for the Ministry of Information & Broadcasting. It provides background, reference and research material for use of the Ministry, its media units and others engaged in mass communication.

Social Media

Since its inception in 2012, Social Media Cell of Ministry of Information and Broadcasting performs various activities to reach out to the last mile. The Ministry is active on all major social media platforms and has built a strong relationship with the audience. Social media interactions in various formats such as Talkathon and Facebook Live are organised regularly to enable direct communication between ministers, senior officers and general public. On Twitter, the official handle of the Ministry, @MIB_India has 929 followers with an average of 6 M impressions per month. The Facebook page of the Ministry,@inbministry has 1.3 M followers. Recently, the Ministry has started a Twitter handle in Hindi, @MIB_Hindi to reach out to the Hindi speaking population on social media space.

India-A Reference Annual

The Division compiles a reference book, 'India-A Reference Annual', on development and progress made by Central ministries/departments, states/union territory administrations and PSUs/autonomous bodies. It is simultaneously published in Hindi titled- 'Bharat'.

Photo Division

Photo Division, an independent media unit meant for the visual support of the varied activities of the Government of India, is a subordinate office of the Ministry of Information and Broadcasting and the biggest production unit of its kind in the country in the field of photography. Photo Division was established in late 1959 as a culmination of the government's decision for establishing a separate department keeping in view the importance of the medium, as the photograph gives the most authentic & truthful record as well as recognize the new medium for right projection, create the archival record under the professional experts. This was done with integrating the photo studios of the Publication Division and the Photo Unit of the Press Information Bureau and D.A.V.P. with a view of eliminating the duplication of the activities. The Division produces photographic visuals of achievements and activities of Government of India for internal and external publicity as well as other purposes. In its 50 years, the Division has a collection of nearly 10 lakhs images in its archive. On the occasion of completion of 50 years of its existence in 2010 the Division introduced National Photography Awards to promote nation's art, culture, development, heritage, history, life, people, society, traditions etc., and to encourage professional and amateur photographers from all corners of the country. The Division has its own official website for the photo publicity of the official assignments. The Division is in the process of selling the photographs through e-commerce gateway.

Synergy with other Media Units

To keep synergy between the other Media Units, the Division has taken up various measures. It has launched its official website to explore the global utility of around 8-10 lakh archival and current images. The Division is in progress of introducing E-commerce feature for the sell/buy of images through the official website. A high capacity server is installed for the on-line/off-line retrieval of archival images. The News Photo Network of the Division has been functioning on complete digital mode to avoid the delay in sending photographs to newspapers and Press Information Bureau. The Division provides facility to DAVP for the supply of life size digital inkjet images for the exhibition purpose.

Relevant Website : www.photodivision.gov.in

Publications Division

Publications Division, a repository of books and journals highlighting subjects of national importance and India's rich cultural heritage, was established in 1941. It has emerged as a premier publishing house of the Government of India, enriching national knowledge repository in : (i) preserving and showcasing India's heritage with quality publications of land and people, history of freedom movement, art and culture, flora and fauna, biographies of the builders of modern India during the freedom movement, leading lights in the field of culture philosophy, science, literature, etc., (ii) chronicling the contemporary with bringing out speeches of the Presidents / Prime Ministers, books on contemporary science, economy, history and other subjects with underlying focus on Indian society and readership, and (iii) bringing out children's literature.

It is among the premier publishing organizations of the Government of India involved in production, sale and distribution of popular books and journals on matters of national importance. The Division publishes books and journals on diverse aspects of Indian panorama, ranging from art and culture, biographies of the Builders of Modern India, cultural leaders of India, life and works of other prominent Indian personalities form different walks of life, India's history and freedom struggle among many other subjects.

The Division has published several books on Gandhian thoughts including the Collected Works of Mahatma Gandhi (CWMG) in 100 volumes, in English and Sampoorna Gandhi Vangmaya in Hindi which is considered to be the most comprehensive and authentic collection of Gandhiji's writings. Publications Division, in collaboration with Gujarat Vidyapith, and under supervision of prominent Gandhian scholars, has also prepared the e-version of the Collected Works of Mahatma Gandhi (e-CWMG), fully searchable master copy, in the form of a well-designed set of DVDs. The print version of CWMG based on the master copy has also been reprinted under guidance of an Experts Panel. Publications Division has also been engaged in restoring and reprinting several heritage publications in partnership with National Gandhi Museum.

Many important Gandhian publications have been brought out to commemorate Gandhiji's 150th birth anniversary in 2019 viz., Indian Women in Satyagraha, Gandhi: an Indian Patriot in South Africa (English), Gandhi in Champaran (Tamil and Kannada editions) and many other Gandhian titles for children and young people in English, Hindi and regional languages.

Journals

Besides books, the Publications Division also publishes 18 monthly journals, which include *Yojana* in English, Hindi and 11 other languages, *Aajkal* (Hindi and Urdu), *Bal Bharati* (Hindi), *Kurukshetra* (English and Hindi) and a weekly journal *Employment News* (English, Hindi and Urdu). Its journals have a large readership and enjoy a high degree of credibility. These journals reflect the initiatives of the Government and the country's progress in different areas covering a wide range of subjects such as economic development, rural reconstruction, community development, literature, culture, children's literature and information on employment and career opportunities. The journals can be subscribed online, details are available on its website.

Employment News/Rozgar Samachar, is a weekly journal, released every Saturday, and is published simultaneously in Hindi, English and Urdu. Launched in 1976, the weekly carries advertisements for job vacancies as advertised by Centre and state governments, public sector undertakings, autonomous bodies, universities, admission notices for professional courses, examination notices and results of organizations like UPSC, SSC and other general recruitment bodies.

Creation of Digital Archives and e-books : Publications Division has undertaken an important task of digitization of its publications with a purpose to preserve and promote the same and is also making e-books of selected saleable titles. The Digital archives is made to preserve the archival value books. Since 2015, the Reference Annual- India and Bharat are digitized and converted into fully searchable and downloadable e-books for use on a variety of electronic devices.

Online sale of books and journals : DPD has also developed a portal to sell its printed journals online through Bharatkosh (www.bharatkosh.gov.in.) payment gateway developed in collaboration with Controller General of Accounts (CGA), Ministry of Finance.

Computerisation of Inventory and other Business operations : The entire business process of Publications Division including inventory management, payment of royalty, sales, accounts, subscribers management, networking with the Sales Emporia have been computerized which enables the websites to sell printed books as well as e books through its Digital Rights Management platform.

The Division has dedicated websites http://www.publications division.nic.in, www.yojana.gov.in for Yojana and http://employmentnews. gov.in for Employment News.

Publications Division also has presence on facebook at https:// www.facebook.com/publications division and twitter.com @DPD_India.

Business and Distribution Network

The sales and distribution of books and periodicals published by Publications Division is undertaken through its headquarters in Soochna Bhawan and offices at Delhi Secretariat, Mumbai, Chennai, Kolkata, Patna, Lucknow, Hyderabad, Thiruvananthapuram.

Relevant Website : www.publicationsdivision.nic.in

Films Division

The story of the Films Division is synchronous with the eventful years of the country since Independence and over the last 67 years, the Division has been motivating the broadest spectrum of the Indian public with a view to enlisting their active participation in nation building activities. The aims and objectives of the Division, focused on national perspectives, are to educate and motivate people in the implementation of national programmes and to project the image of the land and the heritage of the country to Indian and foreign audiences. The Division also aims at fostering the growth of the documentary film movement, which is of immense significance for the country in the information, communication and integration. Films Division produces documentaries, short films, animation films and news magazines. It caters to nearly 4000 cinema theatres all over the country and also to the non-theatrical circuits like units of the Directorate of Field Publicity, Doordarshan, educational institutions, film societies and voluntary organizations. The documentaries and newsreels of state governments are also featured in the Division's release on the theatrical circuit. This Division also sells prints, stock shots, DVDs/VCDs and distribution rights of documentaries and feature films in India and abroad. Apart from production of films, Films Division also gives on hire, its recording theatre, editing rooms and other fine equipment to film makers.

Archival Research Centre

Archival Research Centre (ARC), a multi station research facility by Films Division has been opened on October 26, 2013. The aim of this facility is to share the enormous wealth of visual history and visual documentation that Films Division has accumulated since its conception. The ARC makes the entire archive of Films Division available to the fifteen research stations presently routed to it. The Films Division archive will be available to these fifteen stations for viewing and research purposes.

International Documentary Film Festival

Since 1990, Films Division organises the biennial Mumbai International Film Festival for Documentary, Short and Animation Films (MIFF). It provides a unique opportunity for film makers, producers, distributors, exhibitors and film critics to meet and exchange ideas and concepts.

National Museum of Indian Cinema

The concept of National Museum of Indian Cinema (NMIC) is a unique idea to be pursued for the first time in the history of Indian Cinema. In the last 100 years of Indian Cinema, lot of historical material suitable for the film museum has been destroyed, damaged or not taken care of properly due to lack of restoration and preservation facilities of this kind. The Film Museum will not only provide a store house of information to the laymen but it will also help film makers, film students, enthusiasts and critics to know the development of cinema as a medium of artistic expression not only in the country but in all parts of the world, as there is no Film Museum in India.

FD Zone

FD Zone is a collaborative effort of Films Division with independent film makers to organize regular curated screenings of documentaries, short films and animation films and avant-garde and meaningful cinema. For every screening, an independent film maker curates on voluntary basis a mixture of films of Films Division and independent film makers. The Director, cinematographer or editor, sound recordist and other main members of the crew of the independent films screened in the event are invited for interaction with the audience. The screenings are free and open to all.

Relevant Website : www.filmsdivision.org

National Film Development Corporation Limited

The National Film Development Corporation Limited (NFDC), incorporated in 1975, (100 per cent owned GOI body) was formed by the Government of India with the primary objective of planning and promoting an organized, efficient, and integrated development of the Indian film industry. NFDC was reincorporated in the year 1980, by merging the Film Finance Corporation (FFC) and Indian Motion Picture Export Corporation (IMPEC) with NFDC.

The erstwhile Film Finance Corporation (FFC) was set up in 1964, with the primary objective of extending finance to young talented film makers for film production, whereas, the Indian Motion Picture Export Corporation (MPEC), an autonomous body, was set up to regulate the import and export of Films and canalization of new stock into the country. In recognition of the need for a body that could facilitate the growth of the Indian film industry, the Government of India merged the FFC and IMPEC and NFDC. The NFDC has so far funded/ produced over 200 films. These films, in various Indian languages, have been widely acclaimed and have won many national and international awards. The Corporation has its corporate office at Mumbai along with three regional offices situated at Chennai, Kolkata, and Delhi and a branch office at Thiruvananthapuram.

Relevant Website : www.nfdcindia.com.org

Central Board of Film Certification

Central Board of Film Certification (CBFC) is a statutory body under Ministry of Information and Broadcasting, regulating the public exhibition of films under the provisions of the Cinematograph Act, 1952.

Films can be publicity exhibited in India only after they have been certified by the Central Board of Film Certification. Though the first film in India (*Raja Harishchandra*) was produced in 1913 by Dadasaheb Phalke, the Indian Cinematograph Act was passed and came into effect only in 1920. Censor Boards (*as they were called then*) were placed under police chiefs in cities of Madras, Bombay, Calcutta, Lahore and Rangoon. Regional censors were independent. After Independence autonomy of regional censors was absolished and they were brought under the *Bombay Board of Film Censors*. With implementation of Cinematograph Act, 1952, the board was unified and reconstituted, as the *Central Board of Film Censors*.

Cinematograph (Certification) Rules were revised in 1983 and since then the *Central Board of Film Censors* became known as the Central Board of Film Certification. The Board consists of non-official members and a chairman (all of whom are appointed by central government) and functions with headquarters at Mumbai. It has nine regional offices, one each at Mumbai, Kolkata, Chennai, Bengaluru, Thiruvananthapuram, Hyderabad, New Delhi, Cuttack and Guwahati. The regional offices are assisted in the examination of films by Advisory Panels. The members of the panels are nominated by central government by drawing people from different walks of life for a period of 2 years.

The Certification process is in accordance with the Cinamatograph Act, 1952, the Cinematograph (Certification) Rules, 1983, and the guidelines issued by the central government u/s 5(b). Initially there were only two grading, U and A. In 1983 two more rating were introduced i.e., UA and S. UA means it can be unrestricted public exhibition but with a word of caution that children below 12 years of age will require the parental guidance, the S category is only for special class of persons like doctors, etc.

Relevant Website : www.cbfcindia.gov.in

Directorate of Film Festivals

The Directorate of Film Festivals was set up in 1973 with the prime objective of promoting good cinema. This is undertaken by organizing a range of activities under these broad categories: (a) the International Film Festival of India; (b) the National Film Awards and the Dadasaheb Phalke Award; (c) cultural exchange programme and organizing screening of Indian films through the missions abroad; (d) the selection of Indian Panorama; (e) participation in international film festivals abroad; (f) special film expositions on behalf of the Government of India; and (g) print collection and documentation.

These activities provide a unique platform for exchange of ideas, culture and experiences between India and other countries in the field of cinema. It also provides a powerful platform for Indian cinema and fosters commercial opportunities for Indian films. Within the country, the latest trends in global cinema are made accessible to the general public, film industry and students.

International Film Festival of India

The 49th International Film Festival of India (IFFI), organized jointly by the Ministry of Information and Broadcasting and Government of Goa, successfully concluded on November 28, 2018, after nine days of film screenings, master classes, discussions and other events.

Relevant Website : www.iffigoa.org

National Film Awards

The National Film Awards, the highest awards in the field of cinema continue to underline cinematic excellence. The National Awards along with cinema's highest honour, the Dadasaheb Phalke Award, are presented by the President of India. To commemorate the release of the first Indian Feature Film, Raja Harishchandra on 3rd May 1913, It has been decided to confer the National Film Awards on 3rd May of every year. Accordingly, 64th National Film Awards were given away for 2016.

64th National Film Awards

The Best Feature Film was bagged by 'Kasaav' (Marathi) directed by Sumitra Bhave and Sunil Sukthankar. The award for Best Popular Film Providing Wholesome Entertainment was given to 'Sathamanam Bhavathi' (Telugu) directed by V.V. Reddy. The Best Actor award was presented to Akshay Kumar for the film 'Rustom' (Hindi) and Best Actress to Surbhi C M for the film 'Minnaminungu - the Firefly' (Malayalam). The film 'Fireflies In The Abyss' directed by Chandrashekhar Reddy was adjudged the Best Non-Feature Film. The Best Book on Cinema Award was given to 'Lata : Sur Gatha' written by Yatindra Mishra, whereas G. Dhananjayan was awarded Best Film Critic. The prestigious Dadasaheb Phalke Award for the year 2016 was presented to renowned filmmaker Shri K. Vishwanath for his commendable contribution to Indian Cinema.

Mahatma Gandhi Film Festival

Film Festival on Mahatma Gandhi was organised from April 14-16, 2017 in Motihari, Bihar to commemorate the centenary of the Champaran Satyagraha. The Festival was organised in collaboration with Mahatma Gandhi Central University, Motihari.

Relevant Website : www.dff.nic.in

National Film Archive of India

The importance of preserving cinema as an art and historical document has been recognized all over the world. The task of preserving cinema in all its varied expressions and forms is best entrusted to a national organization having a permanent set-up and the confidence of the film industry and adequate resources and expertise. Thus, the National Film Archive of India (NFAI) was established as a media unit in February, 1964 with the following aims and objectives : to trace, acquire and preserve for posterity the heritage of national cinema and build up a representative collection of world cinema; to classify and document data related to film, undertake and encourage research on cinema and publish and distribute them; to act as a centre for dissemination of films culture in the country and to ensure the cultural presence of Indian cinema abroad. During the 50 years of its existence NFAI has been making rapid strides in achieving its goals.

Film Storage/Preservation

NFAI houses, nearly 27 state-of-the-art, film preservation facilities/ vaults with global standards and specifications. These vaults have the capacity of nearly 2 lakh film reels storage. The film vaults are maintained with following temperatures for black and white films, colour films and nitrate based films:-

Type of films	*Temperatures*	*Relative Humidity*
Nitrate Films	10°—12° C	40 per cent
Black & White films	10°—12° C	40 to 50 per cent
Colour films	2°—4° C	30 per cent

Film Appreciation Course

An important activity under dissemination of film culture is screen education scheme which includes long and short term film appreciation courses, conducted in collaboration with various educational and cultural institutions across India.

Supply of Films

NFAI's activities to disseminate film culture in the country are manifold. Its Distribution Library has about 25 active film club/ members throughout the country. The Archive supplies films for various screening programmes and film festivals across India.

Participation in Film Festivals

NFAI participates in various film festivals in India and abroad, showcasing its collection of classic films at various retrospectives and poster exhibitions on unique themes, curated for the festival.

Relevant Website : www.nfai.gov.in

National Film Heritage Mission

National Film Heritage Mission (NFHM), a prestigious mission of Government of India project was set up in November, 2014 for restoring and preserving the film hertiage of India. This is a part of 12th Five Year Plan which will spill over to 13th Five Year Plan. This initiative will be greatly appreciated by the film industry. This new plan scheme has taken care of digitization/restoration of films available with NFAI.

Objectives of NFHM include: (i) to undertake film condition assessment of the film collection and to ascertain the left over life of the film; (ii) preventive conservation of 1,32,000 film reels; (iii) 2k/4k picture and sound restoration of 1086 landmark feature films and 1152 shorts of Indian Cinema and recording of new picture and sound inter-negatives of each film; (iv) digitization of 1160 feature films and 1660 shorts; (v) construction of archival and preservation facilities for preservation of material restored under NFHM in dust free, low humidity, and low temperature conditions at NFAI campus, Pune; and (vi) training workshops and courses in field of conservation, preservation and archiving in co-ordination with international agencies that are experts in this field.

Children's Film Society of India

Children's Film Society of India (CFSI) which started functioning in 1955 as an autonomous body under Ministry of Information and Broadcasting, is mandated to produce children's film and exhibit and create and nurture a dynamic child's culture in the country with a purpose of stimulating their creativity, compassion and critical thinking. CFSI has produced, exhibited and distributed films, serials, animations and documentaries - that entertain and encourage children to reflect upon the world around them. With an enviable catalogue of over 260 films in 15 different languages, CFSI remains the prime producer of children's films in the country. Several of these films have won prestigious national and international awards.

CFSI films provide a value based edutainment to a large number of children through the art form called cinema. These films are not only bearing entertainment value but there are lots of take away messages in them which include: Dreams aren't impossible when the desire is strong, respect elders, tribal are also the citizens of our country and we must respect them; family is above all and do all to save its each member; hard work not miracles pay you off; social bonding through games; love flora and fauna; don't be ashamed of any physical disability; children also can contribute to nation building, national unity, etc.

Film Production

An opportunity to prospective film-makers to make children's film in any genre or duration in 23 Indian languages, is funded by CFSI. CFSI has annual target of 3 feature+2 short films with total budgetary grant of 10 crores, including NE component. CFSI also undertake dubbing, subtitle and even purchase award winning foreign films.

Participation in National/International Film Festivals

CFSI films participate and win acclaim in various renowned National/ International Film Festivals and have won several prestigious national and international awards.

Relevant Website : www.cfsiindia.org

Directorate of Advertising and Visual Publicity

Directorate of Advertising and Visual Publicity (DAVP), established in 1955, is the nodal multi media advertising agency of the Government of India. Over the past 60 years it has been catering to the communication needs of almost all central ministries/departments, autonomous bodies and PSUs by providing them single window, cost effective service. It informs and educates people, both rural and urban, about the government's policies and programmes and motivates them to participate in developmental activities, through its various vehicles of communication viz., print media advertising, audio visual advertising, printed publicity, exhibitions, outdoor publicity, new media and mass mailing. The organizational set-up of DAVP at the Headquarters consists of several wings like campaign, advertising, outdoor publicity, printed publicity, exhibition, mass mailing, audio visual wing, design studio, administration and accounts wings. It has two regional offices at Bengaluru and Guwahati to coordinate the Directorate's activities in the regions.

DAVP has a network of 32 Field Exhibition Units spread all over the country. The Field Exhibition Units act as a vital communication link between the government and the people. These Units mount multimedia exhibitions on social and developmental themes in far flung areas of the country to disseminate information about the policies and programmes of the central government on key national issues.

Integration of DFP, S&DD and DAVP

Ministry of Information and Broadcasting has integrated the human and financial resources of Directorate of Field Publicity (DFP), Song and Drama Division (S&DD) and DAVP undertaking the integrated publicity/ communication campaigns.

For Regional and Field Units, all regional offices/field units of S &DD and DAVP will be subsumed in the 22 Regional Offices and 147 Field Units of DFP. Accordingly, S&DD and DAVP will have to close their existing regional field units and collocate them in the regional field units closest to them. The Integrated Regional Units will be renamed as Regional Outreach Bureaus (ROBs).

Relevant Website : www.davp.nic.in

Directorate of Field Publicity

Directorate of Field Publicity, (DFP), a media unit is the only Directorate under Government of India engaged in interpersonal communication. DFP undertakes well conceived communication programmes among the target and potential beneficiaries through inter-personal and micro level communication activities like briefings to opinion leaders, interactive sessions with target beneficiaries, group discussions, quiz and other competitions like Healthy Mother & Baby shows, photo exhibitions, rallies, film shows, and public meetings. In this process, DFP gets support from other implementing central and state departments/agencies.

There are 22 regional offices which are mostly located at state capitals and 207 Field Publicity Units which are spread all over the country and mostly located at district headquarters. Each regional office has 6 to 14 Field Units under its jurisdiction. The Field Publicity Units are equipped with vehicles and audio visual equipment for their field level activities. DFP's communication teams organized awareness generation programmes on Government schemes and policies among the masses, mainly in remote, rural and media shadow areas.

DFP has adopted ICT in a big way to facilitate functioning of its Regional Offices and Field Publicity Units in a more effective way. All the Regional Offices and Field Units have been equipped suitably to regularly report on programmes, financial and administrative matters 'online'. DFP has an informative website and 22 of its regions have their respective web pages. The Directorate has been using social media like YouTube, Facebook and Twitter for highlighting its outreach activities and promoting deliverable messages on the programmes and schemes of the government.

Relevant Website : www.dfp.nic.in

Song and Drama Division

The Song and Drama Division was set up in 1954 as a unit of All India Radio and was given the status of an Independent media unit in 1956 with the mandate of development communication. This is the largest organization in the country using performing arts as a medium of communication. The Division uses a wide range of art forms such as drama, ballets, operas, theatrical shows on national themes such as communal harmony, national integration, secularism, promotion of cultural heritage, health, environment, education, etc., through sound and light programmes.

Film and Television Institute of India

The Film and Television Institute of India (FTII) was set up in 1960. Following the addition of Television wing in 1974, the Institute was re-designated as Film and Television Institute of India. The Institute became a Society in October, 1974 under the Registration of Societies Act, 1860. The Society consists of eminent personalities connected with film, television, communication, culture, alumni of institute and ex-officio government members. The Institute is governed by a Governing Council, headed by a Chairman. The academic policies and plans of the Institute are formulated by the Academic Council. The matters involving finance are controlled by the Standing Finance Committee. The Institute consists of two Wings, The Film wing and the TV Wing, and offers courses in both Film and Television. The Three-year Diploma Courses lead to a Post Graduate Diploma in Film Direction, cinematography, Audiography and Film Editing. The Institute also offers a two-year post graduate diploma course in acting, a two-year post graduate course in art direction and production design, and one-year post graduate certificate course.

Film and Television Institute of India provides the latest education and technological experience in the art and technique of film making and television production. In-service training is provided to officers of all grades of the Doordarshan and others. It is equipped with the latest digital and broadcast grade production set-ups viz. Non Linear, beta cam and A/B roll editing setups, digital cameras viz. Sony BVP-500 P, Soft Chroma Keyer, digital special effect generator, silicon graphics 02 workstations with Alias software, modern movie cameras, rerecording equipment etc. which provide an excellent exposure to the faculty and students of Film and Television Institute.

Relevant Website : www.ftiindia.com

Satyajit Ray Film and Television Institute

Satyajit Ray Film and Television Institute (SRFTI), Kolkata was established as an autonomous educational institution and was registered under the West Bengal Societies Registration Act, 1961. Located at Kolkata and named after the legendary film maestro Satyajit Ray, SRFTI is the second national level film training institute to be established by the Government of India. The institute offers three-year post-graduate diploma courses in direction and screenplay writing, cinematography, editing and audiography. Apart from the basic diploma course, the institute also has the provision to conduct short and medium term courses on areas related to film and television. Research and explorative studies in sociology, culture and technology of film and television are the other areas of focus in SRFTI.

SRFTI is run by a Society constituted by the Government of India. The Society runs the Institute through a governing council that is constituted with select members of Society. The Governing Council is the supreme Body for all executive functions of the Institute. It also constitutes different committees/ bodies as deemed necessary viz., Academic Council Standing Finance Committee, etc.

Relevant Website : www.srfti.gov.in

Indian Institute of Mass Communication

The Indian Institute of Mass Communication (IIMC), registered as a society under the Societies Registration Act, 1860 came into existence in 1965. The Institute, was established with the basic objective of undertaking teaching, training and research in the area of mass communication.

The Institute conducts a number of post-graduate diploma courses in print journalism, radio and TV journalism and advertising and public relations. Beginning in 1969, the Institute has organized a Post-Graduate Diploma Course in Development Journalism for middle level working journalists form Asian, African, Latin American and East European countries under the auspices of the Ministry of External Affairs, Government of India since 1969.

A number of specialized short-term courses ranging from one week to twelve weeks are also organized to meet the ever-growing training needs of communication professionals working in various media/publicity outfits of Central/state governments and public sector organizations. The Institute also collaborates with different national and international agencies in conducting training programmes, seminars, workshops. etc. and in undertaking research projects.

The Institute endeavours to contribute towards the creation and strengthening of an information structure suitable not only for India requirements, but also those of other developing countries. It provides its expertise and consultancy services to other institutions/organs of the Central/state governments, public sector organizations, universities and other academic institutions. With the growing popularity of the Institute's training activities and with a view to meeting regional aspirations, the Institute opened a branch at Dhenkanal, Orissa in 1993 for catering to the demands of the eastern region.

At present, the Branch conducts two Post Graduate Diploma Courses—Journalism (English) and Journalism (Odia). The Government of India, through the Ministry of Information and Broadcasting makes financial support to the Institute available. The activities of the Institute are guided by its Executive Council, whose Chairman (Ex Officio) is the Secretary in the Ministry who is also the President of the Institute (Society). The other members of the Council include, *inter-alia,* representatives of the Institute's faculty and eminent personalities from the media. Through its continuous hard work over the last more than four decades of its existence and excellent delivery mechanism, the Institute has achieved the envious position of a "Centre of Excellence" in the area of communication teaching, training and research.

Teaching and Training Programme

The academic and training activities of the Institute can be divided into four programmes : (i.) Post-graduate Diploma programmes for students : These comprise four programmes in Journalism and one in Advertising and Public Relations: 1. Post-graduate Diploma Course in Journalism-English; 2. Post-graduate Diploma Course in Journalism-Hindi; 3. Post-graduate Diploma Course in Journalism-Oriya; 4. Post-graduate Diploma Course in Radio and TV Journalism-English and Hindi; and 5. Post-graduate Diploma Course in Advertising and Public Relations (English and Hindi).

This four month diploma course is highly sought after by mid career level working journalists in Africa, Asia and Latin America and other developing countries. The average intake of participants is 20-25 per batch. The Institute organizes two such courses each year.

Short-term Courses, Workshops, Seminars and Conferences

With a view to contributing towards better understanding of different issues pertaining to mass communication in the context of India and other developing countries and in order to increase awareness about the emerging techniques and sharpening their basic skills, the Institute has been organizing a variety of short- term courses, workshops, seminars and conferences in various areas of communication and media. The Institute runs regular short-term academic programmes for personnel of different media units of the Ministry of Information and Broadcasting. A number of specialized short-term courses, ranging from one week to 12 weeks' duration, are also conducted for meeting the professional training needs of defence officials and those working in various media/publicity organizations of the central/state governments and Public Sector Enterprises.

Relevant Website : www.iimc.nic.in

Broadcast Engineering Consultants India Limited

Broadcast Engineering Consultants India Ltd. (BECIL), a profit making PSE was constituted in 1995 to provide the national broadcasters' expertise to the private broadcasters in the country. At present, BECIL is an established consultancy agency, system integrator and turnkey solution provider in all spheres of Broadcast Engineering. BECIL also undertakes operation and maintenance of various types of broadcast systems. Its clients include government, semi government, overseas and private organisations.

The area of specialisation of BECIL is as follows: establishment of radio and TV transmitting facility including frequency and coverage planning, prediction etc.; setting up state-of-the-art studio facilities for audio and video including ethernet connectivity capable of transmitting live content and data; establishment of cable TV systems and HITs (Head End In The Sky) and wireline broadcasting; turnkey Solution for establishing community radio stations; establishment from concept to commissioning of electronic media monitoring solutions (Radio and TV Terrestrial or Satellite), and security related Surveillance Set ups for GSM, CDMA and VSAT, sales and support for all type of broadcast engineering equipment/system, design and integration of outside broadcast vans (DSNG) with state-of-the- art technology. providing professionals for O&M of broadcast stations, TV studios, satellite earth stations, Electronic Media Monitoring Centre and supply and support for various type of monitoring, interception and encryption, decryption devices for forces and intelligence agencies.

BECIL client list includes Government, Semi Government, Overseas and Private organizations. It has many firsts to its credit like establishment of first teleport in India, first to establish infrastructure, first to set-up multi channel FM transmission in India combining up to 7 FM channels at Bengaluru, first to design and establish HDTV studio set-up for Presidential Secretariat and Lok Sabha TV, to name a few.

Relevant Website : www.becil.com

23 Planning

PLANNING in India derives its objectives and social premises from the Directive Principles of State Policy enshrined in the Constitution. Public and private sectors are viewed as complementary. The private sector covers, besides organized industry, small-scale industries, agriculture, trade and housing, construction and related areas. Individual efforts and private initiatives are considered necessary and desirable in the national endeavour for development with optimum voluntary cooperation.

NITI Aayog

The National Institution for Transforming India (NITI Aayog) came into existence in 2015 replacing the Planning Commission which was established in 1950. The NITI Aayog is the successor to the Planning Commission. The new institution is envisaged to be a catalyst to the developmental process; nurturing an overall enabling environment, through a holistic approach to development going beyond the limited sphere of the public sector and Government of India. This is to be built on the foundation of an empowered role of states as equal partners in national development underlying the principle of cooperative federalism. A knowledge hub of internal as well as external resources; serving as repository of good governance best practices and a think tank offering domain knowledge as well as strategic expertise to all levels of government. A collaborative platform facilitating implementation by monitoring progress, plugging gaps and bringing together the various ministries at the Centre and in states, in the joint pursuit of developmental goals.

Relevant Website : www.niti.gov.in

Objectives

The new institution is envisaged to be a catalyst to the developmental process; nurturing an overall enabling environment, through a holistic approach to development going beyond the limited sphere of the Public Sector and Government of India. This will be built on the foundation of: An empowered role of States as equal partners in national development; operationalizing the principle of Cooperative Federalism.; A knowledge hub of internal as well as external resources; serving as repository of good governance best practices, and a think Tank offering domain knowledge as well as strategic expertise to all levels of government.; A collaborative platform facilitating implementation; by monitoring progress, plugging gaps and bringing together the various Ministries at the Centre and in states, in the joint pursuit of developmental goals.

Founded in 2015, the National Institution for Transformation of India or NITI Aayog has been created to serve as the think tank of the Government of India. The Prime Minister of India serves as the Chair of the institution. The institution plays a leadership role in policymaking in the central government, works closely with state governments, serves as a knowledge hub and monitors progress in the implementation of policies and programmes of the Government of India. The institution provides the central and state governments with relevant strategic and technical advice across the spectrum on key policy elements. These include matters of national and international importance on the economic front, dissemination of best practices from within the country and from other nations, the infusion of new policy ideas and specific issue-based support. Through consultative and other mechanisms, it endeavours to inform of the best practices developed in one or more states or in other parts of the world to all states for possible adoption. It fosters cooperative federalism through structured support and policy guidance to the states on a continuous basis.

The institution designs strategic and long-term policy and programme frameworks and initiatives and monitors their progress and their efficacy regularly. It uses the lessons learnt from monitoring and feedback to make innovative improvements, including necessary mid-course corrections. Also, NITI Aayog actively monitors and evaluates the implementation of programmes and initiatives, including the identification of the needed resources so as to strengthen the prospects of success of the latter. The Aayog publishes policy research papers on contemporary issues, brings out books on best practices, prepares model laws to help states reform their policies and organizes workshops and conferences. For providing directional and policy inputs it serves as a repository of research on good governance and helps disseminate this research to stakeholders.

Composition

The composition of the NITI Aayog is as follows:

Prime Minister of India is the Chairperson. The Governing Council comprises the Chief Ministers of all the states, Chief Ministers of union territories with legislatures, viz., Delhi and Puducherry and Lt. Governors of other union territories. Experts, specialists and practitioners with relevant domain knowledge as special invitees nominated by the Prime Minister. The full time organizational framework will consist of, in addition to the Prime Minister as Chairperson, Vice-Chairperson is to be appointed by the Prime Minister. Full time and part-time members will be maximum of 2, from leading universities, research organizations and other relevant institutions in an ex-officio capacity. Part time members will be on a rotational basis. Ex officio Members will be maximum of 4 members of the Union Council of Ministers to be nominated by the Prime Minister. Chief Executive Officer is to be appointed by the Prime Minister for a fixed tenure, in the rank of Secretary to the Government of India. Secretariat as deemed necessary.

At present the approved constitution of the NITI Aayog is as under:

Chairperson: Shri Narendra Modi, Prime Minister; Vice Chairpersons: Dr. Rajiv Kumar, in the rank of Cabinet Minister; Members: (a) Dr. Bibek Debroy; (b) Dr. V.K. Saraswat; (c) Prof. Ramesh Chand (d) Dr. Vinod K. Paul; Rao Inderjit Singh, MoS for Planning; Amitabh Kant CEO.

Economic Advisory Council to the Prime Minister

Cabinet Secretariat notified the constitution of the Economic Advisory Council to the Prime Minister with the following composition: Dr. Bibek Debroy, Member, NITI Aayog - Chairman; Dr. Surjit Bhalla - Part-time Member; Dr. Rathin Roy - Part-time Member; Dr. Ashima Goyal - Part-time Member; Ms. Shamika Ravi - Part-time Member; Shri Ratan P. Watal, Principal Adviser, NITI Aayog - Member-Secretary.

Third Meeting of the Governing Council

The third meeting of the Governing Council of NITI Aayog was held under the Chairmanship of the Prime Minister in 2017 that was attended by the Minister of Home Affairs, Minister of Railways and Minister of Agriculture and Farmers' Welfare - as ex-officio Members, Minister of Road Transport and Highways, Minister of Social Justice and Empowerment and Minister of Textile as Special Invitees and also by Minister of HRD, Minister of State (I/C), Planning, Vice Chairman, NITI Aayog, permanent Members of NITI Aayog, CEO, NITI Aayog and senior officials of Government of India. In the meeting minutes of the second meeting were confirmed and Action Taken Report upon the decisions taken therein was reviewed.

Atal Innovation Mission

The Atal Innovation Mission (AIM) is a flagship initiative of the Prime Minister, set up by NITI Aayog to promote innovation and entrepreneurship across the length and breadth of the country. AIM is also envisaged as an umbrella innovation organization that would play an instrumental role in alignment of innovation policies between central, state and sectoral innovation schemes incentivizing establishment of an ecosystem of innovation and entrepreneurship at various levels higher secondary schools, science, engineering and higher academic institutions, and SME industry / corporate levels. AIM is setting up Atal Tinkering Labs (ATL) in schools across all 700+ districts across the country. These ATLs are dedicated innovation workspaces of 1000-1500 square feet where latest technologies like 3D printers, robotics, internet of things (IOT), miniaturized electronics 'do it yourself' kits are installed using a grant of ₹ 20 Lakhs from the government so that students from Grade VI to Grade XII can tinker with these technologies and learn to create innovative solutions.

At the university, NGO, SME and Corporate industry levels, AIM is setting up world-class Atal Incubators (AICs) that would trigger and enable successful growth of sustainable startups in every sector / state of the country. AIM is also providing scale up support to existing incubators for scaling up their operations. AIM is providing a grant of upto ₹ 10 crores to successful applicants for setting up Greenfield incubators or scaling up existing ones. The idea is that every one of the 110 named smart cities and the top 5-10 educational / industrial institutions of every state should aspire to have a world class incubator that will provide the youth / startup communities in the universities / industries opportunity to create new startups.

Fourteenth Finance Commission

Appointed every five years the Finance Commission is a constitutional body with the broad mandate to define centre - state federal relations. Its most important task is to recommend division of states' revenues collected by the Centre of the 'divisibility pool' between the Centre and the states and the share to be allocated to each state.

The Fourteenth Finance Commission (FCC) submitted its recommendations to the Government in 2014. Some of its important recommendations include the devolution of a significantly higher share of 42 per cent of the divisible pool to states compared with the 32 per cent share recommended by the 13th Finance Commission.

Erstwhile Planning Commission

The Planning Commission was set up in March, 1950 in pursuance of declared objectives of the Government to promote a rapid rise in the standard of living of the people by efficient exploitation of the resources of the country, increasing production and offering opportunities to all for employment in the service of the community. It was charged with the responsibility of making assessment of all resources of the country augmenting deficient resources, formulating plan for the most effective and balanced utilization of resources and determining priorities. Jawaharlal Nehru was the first chairman of the Planning Commission.

First Plan

Keeping in view the large-scale import of food grains in 1951 and inflationary pressures on the economy, the First Plan (1951-56) accorded the highest priority to agriculture including irrigation and power projects. About 44.6 per cent of the total outlay of ₹ 2,069 crore in the public sector (later raised to ₹ 2,378 crore) was allocated for this purpose. The Plan aimed at increasing the rate of investment from five to about seven per cent of the national income.

Second Plan

The Second Five-Year Plan (1956-57 to 1960-61) sought to promote a pattern of development, which would ultimately lead to the establishment of a socialistic pattern of society in India. Its main aims were (i) an increase of 25 per cent in the national income; (ii) rapid industrialization with particular emphasis on the development of basic and heavy industries; (iii) large expansion of employment opportunities; and (iv) reduction of inequalities in income and wealth and a more even distribution of economic power. The Plan aimed at increasing the rate of investment from about seven percent of the national income to 11 per cent by 1960-61. It laid emphasis on industrialization, increased production of iron and steel, heavy chemicals including nitrogenous fertilizers and development of heavy engineering and machine building industry.

Third Plan

The Third Plan (1961-62 to 1965-66) aimed at securing a marked advance towards self-sustaining growth. Its immediate objectives were to : (i) secure an increase in the national income of over five per cent per annum and at the same time ensure a pattern of investment which could sustain this rate of growth in the subsequent Plan periods; (ii) achieve self-sufficiency in food grains and increase agricultural production to meet the requirements of industry and exports; (iii) expand basic industries like steel, chemicals, fuel and power and establish machine building capacity so that the requirements of further industrialization could be met within a period of about 10 years mainly from the country's own resources; (iv) fully utilize the manpower resources of the country and ensure a substantial expansion in employment opportunities; and establish progressively greater equality of opportunity and bring about reduction in disparities of income and wealth and a more even distribution of economic power. The Plan aimed at increasing the national income by about 30 per cent from ₹ 14,500 crore in 1960-61 to about ₹ 19,000 crore by 1965-66 (at 1960-61 prices) and per capita income by about 17 per cent from 330 to 386 over the same period.

Annual Plans

The situation created by the Indo-Pakistan conflict in 1965, two successive years of severe drought, devaluation of the currency, general rise in prices and erosion of resources available for Plan purposes delayed the finalization of the Fourth Five Year Plan. Instead, between 1966 and 1969, three Annual Plans were formulated within the framework of the draft outline of the Fourth Plan.

Fourth Plan

The Fourth Plan (1969-74) aimed at accelerating the tempo of development of reducing fluctuations in agricultural production as well as the impact of uncertainties of foreign aid. It sought to raise the standard of living through programmes designed to promote equality and social justice. The Plan laid particular emphasis on improving the conditions of the less privileged and weaker sections especially through provision of employment and education. Efforts were directed towards reduction of concentration of wealth, income and economic power to promote equity. The Plan aimed at increasing the net domestic product (at 1968-69 factor cost) from ₹ 29,071 crore in 1969-70 to ₹ 38,306 crore in 1973-74. The average annual compound rate of growth envisaged was 5.7 per cent.

Fifth Plan

The Fifth Plan (1974-79) was formulated against the backdrop of severe inflationary pressures. The major objectives of the plan were to achieve self-reliance and adopt measures for raising the consumption standard of people living below the poverty line. This Plan also gave high priority to bring inflation under control and to achieve stability in the economic situation. It targeted an annual growth rate of 5.5 percent in the national income. Four Annual Plans pertaining to the Fifth Plan period were completed. It was subsequently decided to end the Fifth Plan period with the close of the Annual Plan 1978-79.

Sixth Plan

Removal of poverty was the foremost objective of the Sixth Plan (1980-85). The strategy adopted was to move simultaneously towards strengthening the infrastructure for both agriculture and industry. Stress was laid on tackling interrelated problems through a systematic approach with greater management, efficiency and intensive monitoring in all sectors and active involvement of people in formulating specific schemes of development at the local level and securing their speedy and effective implementation. The actual expenditure in the Sixth Plan stood at ₹ 1,09,291.7 crore (current price) as against the envisaged total public sector outlay of ₹ 97,500 crore (1979-80 prices) accounting for a 12 per cent increase in nominal terms. The average annual growth rate targeted for the Plan was 5.2 per cent.

Seventh Plan

The Seventh Plan (1985-90) emphasized policies and programmes, which aimed at rapid growth in food grains production, increased employment opportunities and productivity within the framework of basic tenets of planning, namely, growth, modernization, self reliance and social justice. Food grains production during the Seventh Plan grew by 3.23 per cent as compared to a long-term growth rate of 2.68 per cent between 1967-68 and 1988-89 and the growth rate of 2.55 per cent in the eighties due to overall favourable weather conditions, implementation of various thrust programmes and concerted efforts of the Government and the farmers. To reduce unemployment and consequently, the incidence of poverty, special programmes like Jawahar Rozgar Yojana were launched in addition to the existing programmes. Due recognition was accorded to the role, small-scale and food processing industries could play in this regard. The total expenditure during the entire Seventh Plan stood at ₹ 2,18,729.62 crore (current prices) as against the envisaged total public sector outlay of ₹ 1,80,000 crore, resulting in a 21.52 per cent increase in nominal terms. During this Plan period, the Gross Domestic Product (GDP) grew at an average rate of 5.8 per cent exceeding the targeted growth rate by 0.8 per cent.

Eighth Annual Plans

The Eighth Five-Year Plan (1990-95) could not take off due to the fast-changing political situation at the Centre. The Eighth five-Year Plan commenced in 1992 and that 1990-91 and 1991-92 were treated as separate Annual Plans. Formulated within the framework of the Approach to the Eighth Five-Year Plan (1990-95), the basic thrust of these Annual Plans was on maximization of employment and social transformation.

Eighth Plan

The Eighth Five-Year Plan (1992-97) was launched immediately after the initiation of structural adjustment policies and macro stabilization policies, which were necessitated by the worsening Balance of Payments positions and the position of inflation during 1990-91. The various structural adjustment policies were introduced gradually so that the economy could be pushed to a higher growth path and improve its strength and thus prevent a crisis in Balance of Payments and inflation in the future. The Eighth Plan took note of some of these policy changes, which were to come about due to these reforms. The Plan aimed at an average annual growth rate of 5.6 per cent and an average industrial growth rate of about 7.5 per cent. These growth targets were planned to be achieved with relative price stability and substantial improvement in the country's Balance of Payments. Some of the salient features of economic performance during the Eighth Five-Year Plan indicate, among other things: (a) a faster economic growth, (b) a faster growth of the manufacturing sector and agriculture and allied sectors, (c) significant growth rates in exports and imports, improvement in trade and current account deficit and a significant reduction in the Central Government's fiscal deficit. However, a shortfall in expenditure in the Central sector due to inadequate mobilization of internal and extra budgetary resources by the PSUs and various departments was witnessed. In the States sector, there as on for the shortfall was lack of mobilization of adequate resources due to deterioration in the balance of current revenues, erosion in the contribution of state electricity boards and state road transport corporations, negative opening balance, mounting non-Plan expenditure and shortfalls in the collection of small savings, etc. The total expenditure during the entire Eighth Plan stood at ₹ 4,95,669 crore by taking 1996-97 (RE) as actual] at current prices as against envisaged total public sector outlay of ₹ 4,34,100 crore (1991-92 prices) resulting in a 14.2 per cent increase in nominal terms. The Eighth Plan envisaged an annual average growth rate of 5.6 per cent. Against this, an average annual growth rate of 6.8 per cent was achieved during this plan period.

Ninth Plan

The Ninth Plan (1997-2002) was launched in the fiftieth year of India's Independence. The Plan aimed at achieving a targeted GDP growth rate of seven per cent per annum and there was emphasis on the seven identified Basic Minimum Services (BMS) with additional Central Assistance earmarked for these services with a view to obtaining a complete coverage of the population in a time-bound manner. These included provision of safe drinking water, availability of primary health service facilities, universalization of primary education, public housing assistance to shelterless poor families, nutritional support to children, connectivity of all villages and habitations and streamlining of the public distribution system with a focus on the poor. The Plan also aimed at pursuing a policy of fiscal consolidation, whereby the focus was on sharp reduction in the revenue deficit of the Government, including the Centre, States and PSUs through a combination of improved revenue collections and control of inessential expenditures, particularly with regard to subsidies and through recovery of user charges and decentralization of planning and implementation through greater reliance on States and Panchayati Raj Institutions.

The specific objectives of the Ninth Plan included : (i) priority to agriculture and rural development with a view to generate adequate productive employment and eradication of poverty; (ii) accelerating the growth rate of the economy with stable prices; (iii) ensuring food and nutritional security for all, particularly the vulnerable sections of society; (iv) providing the basic minimum services of safe drinking water, primary health care facilities, universal primary education, shelter, and connectivity to all in a time-bound manner; (v) containing the growth rate of population; (vi) ensuring mobilization and participation of people at all levels; (vii) empowerment of women and socially disadvantaged groups such as Scheduled Castes, Scheduled Tribes and Other Backward Classes and minorities as agents of socio-economic change and development; (viii) promoting and developing people's participatory institutions like Panchayati Raj Institution, cooperatives and self-help groups; and (ix) strengthening efforts to build self-reliance. The Ninth Plan envisaged an average target growth rate of 6.5 per cent per annum in GDP as against the growth rate of 7 per cent approved earlier in the Approach Paper. The scaling down of the target was necessitated by the changes in the national as well as global economic situation in the first two years of the Ninth Plan. Against this, the achievement in the growth-rate on an average was to be 5.5 per cent per annum.

Tenth Plan

The Tenth Five-Year Plan (2002-07) was approved by the National Development Council (NDC) in December, 2002. The Plan has further developed the NDC mandate objectives, of doubling the per capita income in ten years and achieving a growth rate of eight per cent of GDP per annum. Since economic growth is not the only objective, the Plan aims at harnessing the benefits of growth to improve the quality of life of the people by setting of the following key targets : Reduction in the poverty ratio from 26 per cent to 21 per cent, by 2007; decadal population growth to reduce from 21.3 per cent in 1991-2001 to 16.2 per cent in 2001-11; growth in gainful employment, at least, to keep pace with addition to the labour force; all children to be in school by 2003 and all children to complete five years of schooling by 2007; reducing gender gaps in literacy and wage rates by 50 percent; literacy rate to increase from 65 per cent in 1999-2000, to 75 per cent in 2007; Providing potable drinking water to all villages; increase in forest/tree cover from 19 per cent in 1999-2000, to 25 per cent in 2007; and cleaning of major polluted river stretches.

The Tenth Plan had a number of new features that include, among others, the following: Firstly, the Plan recognised the rapid growth in the labour force. At current rate of growth and labour intensity in production, India faces the possibility of rising unemployment, which could lead to social unrest. The Tenth Plan therefore aims at creating 50 million job opportunities during the period, by placing special emphasis on employment intensive sectors of agriculture, irrigation, agro-forestry, small and medium enterprises, information and communication technology and other services. Secondly, the Plan addresses the issue of poverty and the unacceptably low levels of social indicators. Although these have been the objectives in earlier Plans, in the current Plan there are specific monitorable targets, which will need to be attained along with the growth target.

The Incremental Capital Output Ratio (ICOR) of the economy was expected to come down to about 3.6 as against 4.5 during the Ninth Plan. This decline in ICOR was achieved mainly through better utilization of existing capacities and suitable sectorial allocation of capital and its efficient utilization. The growth target, therefore, would require an investment rate of 28.4 per cent of GDP. This requirement was to be met from domestic savings of 26.8 per cent of GDP and external savings of 1.6 per cent. The bulk of the additional domestic savings will have to come from reduction in Government dis-saving from -4.5 (2001-02) to -0.5 per cent (2006-07) of GDP. The average growth rate in the last four years of the 10th Plan (2003-04 to 2006-07) was little over 8 per cent, making the growth rate 7.7 per cent for the entire 10th Plan period. Though this was below the target of 8 per cent, it is the highest growth rate achieved in any Plan period.

Eleventh Plan

The Eleventh Five Year Plan (2007-12) provided a comprehensive strategy for inclusive development, building on the growing strength of the economy, while also addressing weaknesses that have surfaced. It set a target for 9 per cent growth in the five year period with acceleration during the period to reach 10 per cent by the end of the Plan.

Twelfth Plan

The Twelfth Plan fully recognizes that the objective of development is broad-based improvement in the economic and social conditions of our people. However, rapid growth of GDP is an essential requirement for achieving this objective. The Approach Paper to the Twelfth Plan, had set a target of 9 per cent average growth of GDP over the Plan period (2012 to 2017). That was before the Euro-zone crisis in that year triggered a sharp downturn in global economic prospects, and also before the extent of the slowdown in the domestic economy was known. Twelfth Plan envisaged that the current slowdown in GDP growth can be reversed through strong corrective action, including especially an expansion in investment with a corresponding increase in savings to keep inflationary pressures under control. However, while our full growth potential remains around 9 per cent, acceleration to this level can only occur in a phased manner, especially since the global economy is expected to remain weak for the first half of the Plan period.

Inclusiveness as Poverty Reduction

Distributional concerns have traditionally been viewed as ensuring an adequate flow of benefits to the poor and the most marginalized. This must remain as an important policy focus in the Twelfth Plan. It is worth noting that the record in this dimension of inclusiveness is encouraging. The percentage of the population below the official poverty line has been falling but even as that happens, the numbers below the poverty line remain large. According to the latest official estimates of poverty based on the Tendulkar Committee poverty line, as many as 29.8 per cent of the population, that is 350 million people were below the poverty line in 2009-10.

Life Expectancy

Life expectancy which was only 32 years at the time of independence is now 67 years. In other words, every Indian can expect to live twice as long as was the case at Independence! To summarize, the Twelfth Plan must be guided by a vision of India moving forward in a way that would ensure a broad based improvement in living standards of all sections of the people through a growth process that is faster than the past, more inclusive and also more environmentally sustainable.

Information Technology

The Information Technology sector has made remarkable progress in the last decade. It has transformed the world, enabling innovation and enhancing productivity, connecting people and communities, and improving standards of living and providing opportunities across the globe. While changing the way individuals live, interact, and work, IT has also proven to be a key enabler for enhanced competitiveness and economic and societal modernisation, as well as an important instrument for bridging economic and social divides and reducing poverty. The pace of technological advance is accelerating and electronics and ICT is increasingly becoming a ubiquitous and intrinsic part of people's behaviour and social networks as well as of business practices and government activities and service provision. These transformations will continue to guide human progress forward by further leveraging IT's positive social, political, and economic impact on government, enterprise, and civil society alike.

Vision Document

The Three Year Action Agenda covers the period from 2017-18 to 2019-20, the last years of the Fourteenth Finance Commission. With an increasingly open and liberalized economy and given the new realities of the global economy, it needed to rethink the tools and approaches to conceptualizing the development process. The Action Agenda framework allows to better align the development strategy with the changed reality of India. In preparing the Agenda, the NITI Aayog sought and received inputs from state governments, union territories and ministries of the central government. Extensive consultations were held with groups of scientists, economists, journalists, voluntary organizations, industry associations and experts in education, health, culture, defence, transport and other fields. Many experts also provided useful written inputs.

Global Entrepreneurship Summit 2017

India and United States had co-hosted the Global Entrepreneurship Summit (GES) 2017 in Hyderabad, India. The theme of GES 2017 was Women First, Prosperity for All and aims to create an environment that empowers innovators, particularly women, to take their ideas to the next level. The summit focused on four key industry sectors: energy and infrastructure, healthcare and life sciences, financial technology and digital economy, and media and entertainment

24 Rural Development

INDIA has been a welfare state since independence and the primary objective of all governmental endeavours has been the welfare of its people. The policies and programmes have been designed with the aim of alleviation of rural poverty which has been one of the primary objectives of planned development in India. It was realized that a sustainable strategy of poverty alleviation has to be based on increasing the productive employment opportunities in the process of growth itself. Elimination of poverty, ignorance, diseases and inequality of opportunities and providing a better and higher quality of life were the basic premise upon which all the plans and blue-prints of development were built. Rural development implies both the economic betterment of people as well as greater social transformation. In order to provide the rural people with better prospects for economic development, increased participation of people in the rural development programmes, decentralization of planning, better enforcement of land reforms and greater access to credit are envisaged. Initially, main thrust for development was laid on agriculture, industry, communication, education, health and allied sectors but later on it was realized that accelerated development can be provided only if governmental efforts were adequately supplemented by direct and indirect involvement of people at the grassroot level.

Accordingly, in 1952, an organization known as Community Projects Administration was set up under the Planning Commission to administer the programmes relating to community development. The Community Development Programme, inaugurated in 1952, was an important landmark in the history of rural development. This programme underwent many changes and was handled by different ministries. In October, 1974, the Department of Rural Development came into existence as a part of Ministry of Food and Agriculture. In August, 1979, this Department was elevated to the status of a new Ministry of Rural Reconstruction. That ministry was renamed as Ministry of Rural Development and again converted into a Department under the Ministry of Agriculture and Rural Development. It was later rechristened as Ministry of Agriculture in September, 1985. In 1991 the Department was upgraded as Ministry of Rural Development. Another Department viz., Department of Wasteland Development was created under this ministry in 1992.

The Ministry was again renamed as the Ministry of Rural Development in 1999 with three departments viz., Department of Rural Development, Department of Land Resources and Department of Drinking Water and Sanitation. The Department of Drinking Water and Sanitation was made a separate Ministry from July 2011. Presently, the Ministry of Rural Development consists of two departments, namely, Department of Rural Development and Department of Land Resources.

Relevant Websites : www.rural.nic.in www.dolr.gov.in

Major Programmes for Rural Development

The major programmes being operated by the Ministry of Rural Development are: Mahatma Gandhi National Rural Employment Guarantee Act (MGNREGA) for providing wage employment; National Rural Livelihoods Mission (NRLM) for self employment and skill development; Housing for All: Pradhan Mantri Awaas Yojana - Grameen (PMAY-G) for providing housing to BPL households; Pradhan Mantri Gram Sadak Yojana (PMGSY) for construction of quality roads; National Social Assistance Programme (NSAP) for social pension; Shyama Prasad Mukherjee RURBAN Mission; Integrated Watershed Management Programme (IWMP) for improving the productivity of the land.

Rural Employment

Mahatma Gandhi National Rural Employment Guarantee Act (MGNREGA) has come a long way since its inception, and has become a lifeline to millions. The Act aims at enhancing livelihood security of households in rural areas of the country by providing not less than one hundred days of guaranteed wage employment in a financial year to every household whose adult members volunteer to do unskilled manual work. Social inclusion, gender parity, social security and equitable growth are the founding pillars of Mahatma Gandhi NREGA.

The objectives of the scheme are: providing upto 100 days of unskilled manual work in a financial year to every household in rural areas as per demand resulting in creation of productive assets of prescribed quality and durability; enhance livelihood security of the rural poor by generating wage employment opportunities in works that develop the infrastructure base of the area concerned; strengthening and securing the livelihood resource base of the rural poor; ensure empowerment to women; stimulate the local economy by providing a safety net to rural poor by proactively ensure social inclusion and strengthening grass-root democratic institutions.

The government has been working towards bringing positive changes in the programme with new initiatives. Several steps have been taken to strengthen the overall implementation of MGNREGS within the overall framework of MGNREG Act, 2005. Besides ensuring a high budget allocation of meet the objectives of the Act, measures like electronic fund management system (eFMS), Aadhaar seeding, geo tagging of assets and strengthening of Social Audit System are some steps towards bringing in more transparency and accountability in the programme implementation.

Direct Benefit Transfer

To streamline the fund flow mechanism and bring down delay in payment of wages, the Ministry of Rural Development has implemented National Electronic Fund Management System (NeFMS) in 21 states and 1 union territory. This process reduces the delay in allocation of funds for payment of wages to the states and removes parking of funds at various level. Around 96 per cent of the wages are being paid electronically into the bank/post office accounts of MGNREGA workers through Electronic Fund Management System (eFMS).

Deendayal Antyodaya Yojana—National Rural Livelihoods Mission

National Rural Livelihoods Mission, renamed as Deendayal Antyodaya Yojana—National Rural Livelihoods Mission (DAY-NRLM) was launched in 2011. It seeks to reach out to 8-9 crore rural poor households and organize one woman member from each household into affinity based women SHGs and federations at village level and at higher levels. While doing so, DAY-NRLM ensures adequate coverage of vulnerable sections of the society such that 50 per cent of the beneficiaries are members of the scheduled castes and scheduled tribes, 15 per cent from minority groups and 3 per cent from persons with disability, while keeping in view the overall target of 100 per cent coverage of the rural poor households identified through Socio Economic and Caste Census (SECC) and through participatory processes of identification of poor households and approved by Gram Sabha.

The key components of DAY-NRLM include : (i) *Promoting Institutions of Poor*: Strong quality institutions of poor such as SHGs and their federations are set up on a priority basis. In addition to generic thrift and credit based community institutions and their federations, DAY-NRLM promotes specialized institutions like livelihood collectives, producers' cooperatives/companies for livelihoods promotions. The institutions of poor empower their members and act as medium for transfer of knowledge and technology dissemination, and hubs of production, collectivization and trade; (ii) *Training, Capacity Building and Skill Building*: Systematic and multi-pronged approach has been adopted for providing capacity building to SHGs, their federations, government functionaries, bankers, NGOs and other stakeholders. The capacity building is aimed at providing poor with the knowledge and skills to manage their institutions, link up with markets, manage their existing livelihoods and enhance their credit absorption capacity and credit worthiness. Focus is on developing and engaging community professionals and community resource persons (CRP) in order to provide timely support and bring about reduction in poverty levels; (c) *Community Investment Support Fund* : Community Investment Support Fund is routed to SHGs through federations (primary and secondary level) to support development of suitable livelihoods of members and to initiate collective activities, wherever feasible. A part of the CIF is provided as Vulnerability Reduction Fund (VRF) for supporting the inclusion of very poor communities and making credit accessible to them with or without interest; (d) *National Special Fund Support for Convergence under DAY-NRLP* was provided to help states mainstream convergence as an effective method to reduce poverty and empower rural poor; (e) *Infrastructure creation and Marketing Support*: DAY-NRLM ensures that infrastructure needs for major livelihoods activities of poor are met with. It also provides support for marketing to institutions of poor. The range of activities in marketing support include market research, market intelligence, technology extension, developing backward and forward linkages, building livelihoods collectives and supporting their business plans; (f) *Sensitive support structures*: DAY-NRLM has set up sensitive and dedicated support structures at the national, state, district and sub-district levels. These support structures are staffed with dedicated professionals; (g) *Mahila Kisan Sashaktikaran Pariyojana (MKSP)*: Mahila Kisan Sashaktikaran Pariyojana (MKSP) is a sub-component of NRLM to meet the specific needs of women farmers and achieve socio-economic and technical empowerement of the rural women farmers, predominantly small and marginal farmers; (h) *Aajeevika Grameen Express Yojana*: The Government of India has introduced a new sub-scheme under Deendayal Antyodaya Yojana-National Rural Livelihoods Mission (DAY-NRLM) entitled "Aajeevika Grameen Express Yojana" (AGEY) from the financial year 2017-18. The main objectives of AGEY are: to provide an alternative source of livelihoods to members of SHGs under DAY-NRLM by facilitating them to operate public transport services in backward rural areas, as identified by the states; to provide safe, affordable and community monitored rural transport services to connect remote villages with key services and amenities (including access to markets, education and health) for the overall economic development of the area by making use of the supports available within the framework of DAY-NRLM.

Rural Self Employment Training Institute

It has been decided to set up one Rural Self Employment Training Institute (RSETI) in each district of the country. RSETIs are bank lead initiative with the active support of state government. The Government of India provides one time infrastructure support of ₹ 1 crore besides reimbursing the cost of training rural poor candidates, the state government provides land free of cost or at nominal charges and the banks are responsible for day to day functioning of the RSETI. RSETIs are expected to train 750 rural poor youth each year to take up self employment in the area they reside. RSETIs also provide periodic doses of skill upgradation training for making their initiative viable and sustainable in an increasingly competitive environment. Currently 583 RSETIs are functioning in the country.

Pradhan Mantri Gram Sadak Yojana

Government of India, as the part of poverty reduction strategy, launched the Pradhan Mantri Gram SadakYojana (PMGSY) 2000 as a centrally sponsored scheme to assist the states, though rural roads are in the State List under the

Constitution. The primary objective of Scheme is to provide connectivity by way of an all-weather road (with necessary culverts and cross-drainage structures, which is operable throughout the year), to the eligible unconnected habitations as per core-network with a population of 500 persons (as per 2001 census) and above in plain areas. In respect of 'Special Category States' (North-East, Sikkim, Himachal Pradesh, Jammu and Kashmir and Uttarakhand), the desert areas, the tribal (Schedule V) areas and 88 selected tribal and backward districts, the objective is to connect eligible unconnected habitations as per Core-Network with a population of 250 persons and above (census 2001).

To bring execution of the programme to the desired quality standards, a three tier quality management mechanism has been institutionalized. First-tier of this mechanism is in-house quality control at Programme Implementation Unit (PIU) level. Objective of this tier is process control through mandatory tests on material at field laboratory and workmanship. Second-tier is structured as an independent quality monitoring at state level through State Quality Monitors (SQMs) in which provision of regular inspection of works has been envisaged for ensuring better quality. Under the Third-tier, independent National Quality Monitors (NQMs) are deployed by NRRDA for inspection of road works at random, not only to monitor quality but also to provide guidance by senior professionals to the field functionaries.

Rural Housing

Housing is universally recognized as a basic human need. Reducing rural housing shortage and improving the quality of housing especially for the poor is an important component of the poverty alleviation strategy of the government. The rural housing scheme Indira Awaas Yojana (IAY) implemented by Ministry of Rural Development, aimed at providing houses to families below the poverty line (BPL) in rural areas has since inception provided assistance for construction of 360 lakh houses.

In the context of government's priority for "Housing for All" by 2022, the rural housing scheme IAY has been restructured to Pradhan Mantri Awaas Yojana—Gramin (PMAY-G), which came into effect from the financial year 2016-17. The main features of the scheme include : (a) providing assistance for construction of 1.00 crore houses in rural areas over the period of 3 years from 2016-17 to 2018-19; (b) enhancement of unit assistance from ₹ 70,000 to ₹ 1.20 lakh in plains and from ₹ 75,000 to ₹ 1.30 lakh in hilly states, difficult areas and IAP districts; (c) identification of beneficiaries based on the socio-economic and caste census (SECC 2011) data covering households that are houseless or living in houses with kutcha walls and kutcha roof with two rooms or less after excluding households falling under the automatic exclusion category; (d) setting up of national technical support agency at national level to provide technical support to the implementing agencies and to the beneficiaries in taking up construction of houses and help in achieving the target set under the project.

National Social Assistance Programme

Article 41 of the Constitution of India directs the state to provide public assistance to its citizens in case of unemployment, old age, sickness and disablement and in other cases of undeserved want within the limit of its economic capacity and development. Directive Principles of State Policy enshrined in the Constitution of India enjoin upon the state to undertake within its means a number of welfare measures. It is in accordance with these noble principles that the Government of India introduced National Social Assistance Programme (NSAP) in 1995 as a centrally sponsored scheme under which 100 per cent central assistance is extended to the states/UTs to provide the benefits in accordance with the norms, guidelines and conditions laid down by the central government. NSAP is a social assistance programme for poor households—for the aged, widows, disabled and in the case of death of the breadwinner, thereby aiming at ensuring minimum national standards in addition to the benefits that the states are providing or might provide in further. The intention in providing hundred per cent central assistance is to ensure that social protection to the beneficiaries is available throughout the country. States are free to add on and expand their coverage.

Presently NSAP comprises the following schemes for Below Poverty Line Households (BPL) :

Indira Gandhi National Old Age Pension Scheme (IGNOAPS): Under the scheme, assistance is provided to person of 60 years and above and belonging to family living below poverty line as per the criteria prescribed by Government of India. Central assistance of ₹ 200/- per month is provided to person in the age group of 60-79 years and ₹ 500/- per month to persons of 80 years and above.

Indira Gandhi National Widow Pension Scheme (IGNWPS): Under the scheme central assistance of ₹ 300/- per month is provided to widows in the age-group of 40-79 years and belonging to family living below poverty line as per the criteria prescribed by Government of India. After attaining the age of 80 years, the beneficiary would be shifted to IGNOAPS for getting pension of ₹ 500/- per month.

Indira Gandhi National Disability Pension Scheme (IGNDPS): Under the scheme central assistance of ₹ 300/- per month is provided to persons aged 18-79 years with severe or multiple disabilities and belonging to family living below poverty line as per the criteria prescribed by Government of India. After attaining the age of 80 years, the beneficiary would be shifted to IGNOAPS for getting pension of ₹ 500/- per month.

National Family Benefit Scheme (NFBS): Under the scheme a BPL household is entitled to lump sum amount of money on the death of primary breadwinner aged between 18 and 59 years. The amount of assistance is ₹ 20,000/-.

Annapurna : Under the scheme, 10 kg of foodgrains per month are provided free of cost to those senior citizens who, though eligible under IGNOAPS, are not receiving pension under IGNOAPS.

Deen Dayal Upadhyaya Grameen Kaushalya Yojana

Deen Dayal Upadhyaya Grameen Kaushalya Yojana (DDU-GKY) is the flagship placement linked skill-training programme under the Ministry of Rural Development (MoRD). Announced in 2014, DDU-GKY is a critical component of the National Skill Development Policy, and has an ambitious agenda, to benchmark wage placement-linked skill programmes to global standards and requirements. The ultimate aim is to convert India's demographic surplus into a demographic dividend by developing rural India into a globally preferred source of skilled labour. As a result, the scheme will also benefit more than 55 million poor rural youth who are ready-to-be skilled, by providing sustainable employment. In this way the scheme is expected to play a crucial role in generational poverty alleviation. The scheme is a pioneer in standards-led delivery of skilling, the first to notify standard operating procedures for training, and the first to introduce IT solutions for skilling, including mandatory tablets for trainees, Aadhar-linked biometric information on attendance, and geo-tagged time-stamped record of training centres and classes. DDU-GKY has its roots in the Swarnjayanti Gram Swarozgar Yojana (SGSY). SGSY was formed by the restructuring of the Integrated Rural Development Programme (IRDP) in 1999, with a 15 per cent allocation for special projects. In 2010, SGSY was restructured as the National Rural Livelihoods Mission (NRLM), also known as Aajeevika. The Ministry revised the guidelines in 2013 as Aajeevika Skills with a view to increase the reach of the programme. On Antyodaya Diwas, 25th September 2014, Aajeevika Skills was announced as DDU-GKY with a focus on providing opportunities through skilling for rural poor youth in domestic and global jobs.

Key Features

DDU-GKY follows a 3-tier implementation architecture in PPP mode, with the National Unit responsible for policy, central investments and technical support, SRLMs/State Skills Missions responsible for state investments, implementation and monitoring controls, and Project Implementing Agencies (PIAs), both public and private training partners with a legacy in skill training, responsible for mobilization, training and placements: (i) The focus of this programmes is on the rural youth from poor families, in the age group of 15 to 35 years, belonging to: a) MGNREGA worker household in which household members have together completed 15 days of work; b) RSBY household; c) Antyodaya Anna Yojana card household; d) BPL PDS card households; e) NRLM-SHG household; f) Household covered under auto inclusion parameters of SECC 2011. (ii) Full social inclusion of candidates is ensured by the mandatory coverage of socially disadvantaged groups— 50 per cent allocation to SC/ST groups, 15 per cent to minorities, 33 per cent for women and 3 per cent for persons with disabilities. (iii) Placement in wage employment is mandated for a minimum of 70 per cent of all successful candidates, with a minimum salary of ₹ 6,000/- per month or the minimum wages, whichever is higher. (iv) The programme promotes the economic strategies—Make In India, through pro-active partnership with industry through multi-pronged engagement—champion employer policy, captive employer policy and industrial internship policy.

Saansad Adarsh Gram Yojana

Saansad Adarsh Gram Yojana (SAGY) was launched in 2014 with the aim to develop one village by each Member of Parliament as a model village by 2016 and two more by 2019. The goal of Saansad Adarsh Gram Yojana (SAGY) is to translate the comprehensive and organic vision of Mahatma Gandhi into reality, keeping in view the present context. SAGY lays emphasis on inspiring values of national pride, patriotism, unity, self-confidence to be as important as developing infrastructure. In other words, SAGY attempts to develop the value chain through value change. Till now 702 Gram Panchayats have been identified by Members of Parliament under Phase - I and are taking concrete steps towards their development. This scheme is unique and transformative as it has a holistic approach towards development. It envisages integrated development of the selected village across multiple areas such as agriculture, health, education, sanitation, environment, livelihoods, etc. Far beyond mere infrastructure development, SAGY aims at instilling certain values, such as people's participation, Antyodaya, gender equality, dignity of women, social justice, spirit of community service, cleanliness, eco--friendliness, maintaining ecological balance, peace and harmony, mutual cooperation, self-reliance, local self-government, transparency and accountability in public life, etc., in the villages and their people so that they get transformed into models for others.

Key Features

The distinguishing features of SAGY are as follows: *Village Development Plan*: The Gram Panchayats adopted under SAGY prepared Village Development Plans (VDP) containing prioritized time-bound activities to achieve holistic progress of the village, through convergence of resources. Gram Panchayats have very systematically taken development approach by involving Gram Sabha and they have prepared comprehensive VDP for their development. In order to keep track of the progress of projects listed in the VDP, a Tracking Template has been developed and the progress is monitored online; *Panchayat Darpan:* The Ministry has developed a 35 point impact monitoring tool to gauge the impact of SAGY in the GPs. Progress is measured through outcome indicators broadly covering basic amenities, education, health, sanitation, livelihood, women empowerment, financial inclusion, food security, social security and e-governance. The impact is measured on quarterly (22 indicators), half yearly (7 indicators) and yearly basis (6 indicators).

A campaign, namely, Gram Swaraj Abhiyan was also started. This campaign which, undertaken under "Sabka Sath, Sabka Gaon, Sabka Vikas", is to promote social harmony, spread awareness about pro-poor initiatives of the government, reach out to poor households to enroll them as also to obtain their feedback on various welfare programmes. During this, saturation of eligible households/persons would be made under seven flagship pro-poor programmes namely, Pradhan Mantri Ujjwala Yojana, Saubhagya, Ujala Scheme, Pradhan Mantri Jan Dhan Yojana, Pradhan Mantri Jeevan Jyoti Bima Yojana, Pradhan Mantri Suraksha Bima Yojana and Mission Indradhanush.

Land Reforms

Watershed Management Programme

Land and water are two of the most important natural resources. Population pressures and demands on land and water and the increasing degradation of these resources are affecting the stability and resilience of our ecosystem and environment. The expansion of human settlements and infrastructure and intensification of agriculture and allied activities and their expansion into marginal areas and fragile ecosystems, emphasize the need for integrated planning and management of land and water resources.

A watershed is a topographically delineated area that is drained by a stream system. It includes physical and hydroiogical natural resources. Management of a watershed entails the rational utilization of land and water resources for optimum productivity, with minimum hazards to human settlements. Watershed management is the process of guiding and organizing land use and use of other natural resources in a watershed. Embedded in this approach is the recognition of the inter-relationships between land use, soil and water conservation and the linkages between uplands and downstream areas. Watershed development is a multi-disciplinary field, for sustainable natural resource management. Watershed development activities also contribute towards mitigation and adaptation to global warming.

Watershed Development

Pradhan Mantri Krishi Sinchai Yojana (PMKSY) was launched in 2015-16 by amalgamating ongoing schemes of three ministries viz., Accelerated Irrigation Benefit Programmed (AIBP) and PMKSY (WR) of the Ministry of Water Resources, River Development and Ganga Rejuvenation (MoWR, RD and GR); Integrated Watershed Management Programme (IWMP) of the Ministry of Rural Development, Department of Land Resources (DoLR) and the Micro Irrigation component of On Farm Water Management (OFWM) of National Mission on Sustainable Agriculture (NMSA) of the Ministry of Agriculture and Farmers Welfare, Department of Agriculture, Cooperation and Farmers Welfare (DAC & FW). Under the erstwhile IWMP, 8214 watershed development projects were sanctioned in 28 states (except Goa) during the period 2009-10 to 2014-15 covering an area of about 39.07 million hectares, principally for development of rainfed portions of net cultivated area and culturable wastelands. The activities undertaken inter alia include ridge area treatment, drainage line treatment, soil and moisture conservation, rainwater harvesting, nursery raising, afforestation, horticulture, pasture development, livelihoods for assetless persons, etc. In 2015-16, the IWMP was amalgamated as the Watershed Development Component (WDC) of the Pradhan Mantri Krishi Sinchayee Yojana (PMKSY). No further watershed development projects have been sanctioned from 2015-16 onwards. At present, the principal emphasis is on qualitative and timely implementation and completion of the ongoing watershed development projects.

Natural Land Reforms Modernization

The scheme of National Land Reforms Modernization Programme (NLRMP) has been renamed as Digital India Land Records Modernization Programme (DILRMP) and is being implemented since 2008. Under it, 27 states/UTs have computerized the registration of records (RoR) of land in their respective areas, 19 states/UTs have stopped manual issue of RoRs and 22 states/UTs have uploaded in their websites. Besides, 25 states/UTs have done computerization of Registration and 11 states/UTs have done integration of land records with registration. As regards the training during this period, the NIRD and PR organized 864 training programmes with participation of 22, 032 trainees, including 400 NIRD and PR networking programmes in collaboration with 28 states Institutes of Rural Development in the country.

Panchayati Raj

The mandate of the Ministry of Panchayati Raj (MoPR), which was set up in 2004, is to ensure the compliance of the provisions of Part IX of the Constitution, provisions regarding the District Planning Committees as per Article 243 ZD, and PESA. The Ministry's vision is to attain decentralized and participatory local self-government through Panchayats, or Panchayati Raj Institutions (PRIs). The Ministry's mission is empowerment, enablement and accountability of PRIs to ensure inclusive development with social justice, and efficient delivery of services. The Ministry works to fulfil its mandate in various ways. MoPR fosters knowledge creation and sharing so that the issues to be addressed are clearly articulated, meaningful strategies formulated, and there is sharing within government as well as with non-government agencies and experts. It also provides technical assistance and facilities cross-learning across states. In the light of recent changes in policy and to take advantage of the emerging opportunities, the Ministry has repositioned itself with basic changes in its mandate.

Relevant Website : www.panchayat.gov.in

Constitutional Mandate

Part IX of the Constitution of India provides for setting up of three tiers of Panchayats (only two tiers in case of states of union territories having population less than 2 million): (i) gram panchayats at village level; (ii) district panchayats at district level; and (iii) intermediate panchayats at sub-district level in between gram panchayats and district panchayats. It also provides for gram sabha (general assembly of registered voters who reside in the area of gram panchayat) as a forum for direct participation of villagers in local governance. The Constitution India has fixed five year term for these panchayats and has made provision for the reservation of seats for women and marginalized sections (scheduled castes and scheduled tribes) of Indian society. While reservation of schedule castes (SCs) & scheduled tribes (STs) is in proportion to their share in population, that for women is at least 33.33 per cent. However, many states have increased the reservation of seats and chairperson posts for women in panchayats to 50 per cent. The Constitution of India also stipulates direct elections of all members of panchayats. For conducting these elections, all states are mandated to constitute a state election commission. Also it is compulsory for states to constitute a State election commission. Also it is compulsory for states to constitute a State Finance Commission (SFC) every fifth year for recommending principles for division of financial resources between state and local governments (both urban and rural). SFCs are to make recommendations to the Governor regarding the distribution between the state and panchayats of the net proceeds to taxes, duties, toll and fees, etc. the determination of taxes, dudies, tolls and fees which may be assigned to, or appropriated by, the panchayats, and grants-in-aid to the panchayats from the Consolidated Fund of the State, as well as measures needed to improve the financial position of panchayats.

Within this broad framework, as local government is a state subject, State legislatures have a critical role in determining various aspects of panchayati raj in their states. States are keys as far as devolution of powers to panchayats is concerned. The Constitution envisaged that Panchayats will function as institutions of local government and prepare plans and implement schemes for economic development and social justice, but leaves the precise devolution of powers and authority to panchayats to the states.

Rajiv Gandhi Panchayat Sashaktikaran Abhiyan

To improve the functioning of PRI, the MoPR implemented the Rajiv Gandhi Panchayat Sashaktikaran Abhiyan (RGPSA) in the 12th Five Year Plan period i.e., from 2012-13 upto 2015-16. The RGPSA addressed the major constraints of inadequate devolution of powers, lack of manpower, inadequate infrastructure and limited capacity in the effective functioning of panchayats by providing manpower, infrastructure, training and promotion of devolution of power to panchayats and put in place structures of accountability.

Rashtriya Gram Swaraj Abhiyan

The Rashtriya Gram Swaraj Abhiyan (RGGA) will focus on capacity building of Panchayati Raj Institutions for convergent action to deliver basic services and achieve development goals. Under RGSA comprehensive efforts will be made to support and enhance the capacity building and training facilities for all stakeholders with particular thrust on the aspects of GPDP.

e-Panchayat

e-Panchayat was identified as one of the 27 Mission Mode Projects under the National e-Governance Plan (NeGP) formulated in 2006.

Recommendations of Fourteenth Finance Commission

Under the Fourteenth Finance Commission (FFC) award for the period 2015—2020 grants to the tune of ₹ 2,00,292.20 crore are being devolved to gram panchayats in the country constituted under Part IX of the Constitution constituting an assistance of ₹ 488 per capita per annum at an aggregate level for 26 states to ensure stable flow of resources at regular intervals which will augment resources available with them to discharge their statutorily assigned functions. The FFC has not recommended grants to Non-Part IX areas under Schedule VI in Meghalaya, Mizoram, Tripura and Assam, the areas in the hill districts of Manipur, rural areas of Nagaland and Mizoram.

Drinking Water and Sanitation

The Department of Drinking Water Supply (DDWS) was created in the Ministry of Rural Development in 1999, which was subsequently renamed as the Department of Drinking Water and Sanitation in 2010. Keeping in view the significance of rural water supply and sanitation, the Government of India created and notified the Ministry of Drinking Water and Sanitation as a separate Ministry in 2011. The Ministry of Drinking Water and Sanitation is the nodal Ministry for the overall policy, planning, funding and coordination of the flagship programmes of the Government of India viz., the National Rural Drinking Water Programme (NRDWP) for rural drinking water supply and the Swachh Bharat Mission (Gramin) [SBM(G)] for sanitation in the country.

Relevant Website : www.mdws.gov.in

Swachh Bharat Mission

Swachh Bharat Mission was launched in 2014. The concept of Swachh Bharat Mission is to provide access for every person to sanitation facilities including toilets, solid and liquid waste disposal systems and village cleanliness. The programme is implemented by the Ministry of Drinking Water and Sanitation. An Action Plan has been drawn up for Swachh Bharat to become a reality by 2019, the 150th birth anniversary of Mahatma Gandhi. The Mission aims to increase the access to sanitation from 39 per cent in 2014 to 100 per cent by October, 2019. The Action Plan calls for an Open Defecation Free (ODF) India in five years. To begin with, as part of Swachh Bharat, priority was given to build toilets for boys and girls in all schools of the country. This was completed within one year. To strengthen delivery mechanism in sanitation in rural areas some important measures have been taken up: (a) signing MoU with states, on water and sanitation for implementation of both water and sanitation, with interchangeability of funds between water and sanitation so that idle funds do not lie in states and targets are not starved of funds in either of the two sectors; (b) release to states with 'Just in Time' concept, to be adopted by centre to avoid extra cost of funds to Government of India; (c) enable a system of small loans through agencies like NABARD, SIDBI (or banks through priority sector lending without collateral) to those households for the construction of toilets which are eligible for incentives or need funds to construct better toilets maybe with bathing space; (d) identifying a Swachhagrahi (motivator) for each village equipping him with skills on sanitation and giving him performance linked incentives; and (f) intensive monitoring at the household level shall be taken up through the IMIS of the ministry, as already name of each household has been collected by Ministry of Drinking Water Supply through baseline data.

Swachh Bharat Mission (Gramin)

Intervention in the rural sanitation sector in the country was initially started in 1954 as a part of the First Five Year Plan. The Government introduced a structured scheme in the form of the Central Rural Sanitation Programm (CRSP) in 1986 primarily with the objective of improving the quality of life of the rural people and also to provide privacy and dignity to women. From 1999, a "demand driven" approach under the "Total Sanitation Campaign" (TSC) emphasizing more on Information, Education and Communication (IEC), Human Resource Development (HRD), capacity development activities to increase awareness among the rural people and generation of demand for sanitary facilities was started. The "Nirmal Bharat Abhiyan" (NBA), the successor programme of the TSC, was launched from 2012, aimed at creating Nirmal villages, provided increased incentives through convergence with MNREGS. Though these programmes had their successes, there still remained a large portion of the rural population which did not have access to toilets. To significantly upscale the programme, and bring the focus on the issue of sanitation, the Swachh Bharat Mission (Gramin) was launched in 2014. The focus of the new strategy is to move towards a Swachh Bharat by providing flexibility to state governments (sanitation being a state subject), to decide on their implementation policy and mechanisms, taking into account state specific requirements.

The main objectives of the SBM(G) are : a) bring about an improvement in the general quality of life in the rural areas, by promoting cleanliness, hygiene and eliminating open defecation; b) accelerate sanitation coverage in rural areas to achieve the vision of Swachh Bharat by 2nd October 2019; c) encourage cost effective and appropriate technologies for ecologically safe and sustainable sanitation.

The Ministry is reforming the sanitation sector by shifting metric from building toilets to Open Defecation Free villages. Behaviour change is the primary focus and fundamental tool for achievement of ODF outcomes. The Ministry is doing it by its focused Information , Education and Communication (IEC) programme. It promotes gender sensitive information, behaviour change guidelines and various mass education activities. The Ministry issued gender guidelines in 2017 and menstrual management guidelines in 2015.

Swachhata Pakhwada

Swachhata Pakhwada was started in April 2016 with the objective of bringing a fortnight of intense focus on the issues and practices of Swachhata by engaging GoI ministries and departments in their jurisdiction. An annual calendar is pre-circulated among the ministries to help them plan for the Pakhwada activities.

Namami Gange

Namami Gange Programme is an initiative of Ministry of Water Resources (MOWR), comprising making villages on the bank of river Ganga ODF and interventions dealing with solid and liquid waste management are being implemented by MDWS. All 4470 villages located across 52 districts of Uttarakhand, Uttar Pradesh, Bihar, Jharkhand and West Bengal has since been made ODF by MDWS with active help of state governments. Now the Ministry has taken up 24 villages on the bank of river Ganga to transform them as Ganga Grams in coordination with NMCG.

Swachhta Action Plan

Swachhta Action Plan (SAP), a first of its kind inter-ministerial programme for Swachhta, is a concrete realization of the vision that swachhta is everyone's business. All Union ministries/departments have started to work for its realization in a significant manner with appropriate budget provisions.

Swachh Iconic Places

The Ministry has taken up a multi-stakeholder initiative focusing on cleaning up 100 places across the country that are "iconic" due to their heritage, religious and/or cultural significance. The goal of the Initiative is to improve the cleanliness conditions at these places to a distinctly higher level. This initiative is in partnership with ministries of Urban Development, Tourism and Culture with MDWS being the nodal ministry. So far in first two phases, 20 iconic places has been taken up. All these 20 iconic sites have designated PSUs for financial and technical support.

National Rural Drinking Water Programme

The National Rural Drinking Water Programme (NRDWP) is a centrally sponsored scheme aimed at providing adequate and safe drinking water to the rural population of the country. The NRDWP is a component of Bharat Nirman which focuses on the creation of the infrastructure. This has resulted in the provision of significant additional resources to the sector and for creating an environment for the development of infrastructure and capacities for the successful operation of drinking water supply schemes in rural areas. Rural drinking water supply is a state subject and is also included in the Eleventh Schedule of the Constitution amongst the subjects that may be entrusted to panchayats by the states. Thus the participation of the Panchayati Raj Institutions in the rural drinking water supply sector is an important area of focus.

Government of India's major intervention in water sector started in 1972-73 through the Accelerated Rural Water Supply Programme (ARWSP) for assisting states/UTs to accelerate the coverage of drinking water supply in 'problem villages'. A Technology Mission with stress on water quality, appropriate technology intervention, human resource development support and other related activities was introduced in 1986 which was subsequently renamed as the Rajiv Gandhi National Drinking Water Mission (RGNDWM) in 1991. In 1999-2000, Sector Reform Projects were started to involve the community in planning, implementation and management of drinking water schemes which was in 2002 scaled up as the Swajaldhara programme. The programme was revised in 2009 and named as National Rural Drinking Water Programme (NRDWP).

25 Scientific and Technological Developments

THE Department of Science and Technology (DST) functions as the nodal agency to connect science and technology sector to Government verticals. DST provides the largest extramural research and development support in the country to strengthen national S&T capacity and capability through a competitive mode to scientists cutting across institutions and disciplines. This strategically important function mutually reinforces outcomes of our country's educational, scientific and industrial R&D initiatives and helps transform the S&T landscape of the country.

Department of Science and Technology

Department of Science and Technology, in its endeavour to strengthen national science and technology capacity and capability, kept its pace to implement several planned initiatives to enable Indian S&T community to increase scientific and technological outputs. Some of the important domains in which the Department devotes its attention are: strengthening the pool of scientists and technologists for carrying out globally competitive R&D in cutting edge areas of science; nurturing R&D institutions and building infrastructural facilities for enhancing global ranking of India in scientific research; support for the establishment of multi-stakeholder mechanisms for partnerships for promoting science; deploying technology through national missions; developing capacity of institutions and industry for technology commercialization for solving national challenges; providing S&T inputs to society for its socio-economic benefits; and policy formulation for this sector.

Relevant Website : www.dst.gov.in

Science, Technology and Innovation Policy

The new Science, Technology and Innovation (STI) Policy unveiled in 2013 includes a thrust for innovations in science and technology sector. STI policy reveals an aspiration to gain global competitiveness and link science sector to the developmental agenda of the country. Science, research and innovation system for high technology led path for India (SRISHTI) is the main policy goal. Integration of science, research and innovation systems and emergence of India as one of the top five of six knowledge powers in science are expressed aspirations of the new STI policy. To translate this vision into action, the Department has already established a dedicated Policy Research Cell. Five policy research centres in academic institutions have been established to develop and design new programmes and action plans for implementation in science, technology and innovation sector in the country.

Science and Engineering Research

The research and development in frontier areas of science and engineering has received an overwhelming support with the establishment of the Science and Engineering Research Board (SERB). The multifaceted programmes of the Board have ensured its reach among various S&T stakeholders. Several new initiatives have been launched by the Board recently to reverse the brain drain at different stages of scientific careers such as Early Career Research Awards (ECRA) for young faculty for setting up laboratory facilities for quick launching of research by new faculty, around 300 candidates will be supported annually under ECRA.

Teachers' Associates for Research Excellence (TARE) Mobility Scheme : The Scheme launched in 2016-17 aims to facilitate mobility of faculty members working in a regular capacity in state universities/colleges/academic institutions such as IITs, IISc, IISERs, national labs, etc., located nearer to the institution where the faculty member is working. This would bring in our research stream the latent or dormant scientific manpower with modest investment and improve the potential for research and teaching in two tier institutions. Provision of fellowship amount of ₹ 5,000 per month, contingency grant of ₹ 5 lakh per annum and overhead for a period of 3 years has been made.

Attracting Young Talent

Innovation in science pursuit for inspired research (INSPIRE) is an ongoing initiative for attracting talent for science and research. About 3.67 lakh students in the age group of 10-15 have been provided INSPIRE awards during the last 3 years. Science camps are organised to provide opportunity to class XI students pursuing science to interact with the science icons from India and abroad including Nobel Laureates to experience the joy of innovations. Around 40,000 students have been awarded scholarship for higher education during last three years. INSPIRE faculty awards are provided to post-doctoral researchers in the age group of 27-32 years through contractual and tenure positions for 5 years in basic and applied sciences. Faculty awards have been given to over 700 candidates awarded in the last four years.

Opportunities for Women Scientists

Department of Science and Technology launched several initiatives for women in science under its flagship scheme namely KIRAN (Knowledge Involvement in Research Advancement through Nurturing). Through this unique initiative, DST provides opportunity to women scientists who had break in their career, primarily due to family reasons, to pursue research in physical and mathematical sciences, chemical sciences, life sciences, earth and atmospheric sciences and engineering technology. More than 2,500 women scientists are beneficiaries of this scheme.

Nano Science and Technology

National Mission of Nano Science and Technology - an umbrella programme- was launched in 2007 to promote R&D in this emerging area of research in a comprehensive fashion. The main objectives of this mission are - basic research promotion, research infrastructure development, nano application and technology development, human resource development, international collaboration and orchestrating national dialogues.

Climate Change

National Mission for Sustaining the Himalayan Ecosystem (NMSHE) and National Mission for Strategic Knowledge on Climate Change (NMSKCC) launched under National Action Plan for Climate Change (NAPCC) are under implementation by the Department. As part of deliverables of these national missions, six major research programmes have been initiated. Himalayas Climate Change Portal (http://knowledgeportal-nmshe.in/) was launched to make the knowledge on himalayas readily available for the end users and community

National Initiative for Developing and Harnessing Innovations (NIDHI)

It has evolved as an umbrella scheme for a seamless innovation ecosystem booster. Major links of the innovation to market value chain would be supported and strengthened at various nodes (each node signifying a cluster of 3 neighbouring districts) across the country to attain the mission of nation building through innovation, entrepreneurship and incubation. The specific components of NIDHI are - grand challenge and competitions for scouting innovations; promotion and acceleration of young and aspiring innovators and startups (PRAYAS) - support from idea to prototype; entrepreneur in residence (EIR) - support system to reduce risk; startup-NIDHI through innovation and entrepreneurship development centres (IEDCs) in academic institutions for encouraging students to promote start-ups; start-up centre in collaboration with MHRD - inculcating a spirit of entrepreneurship in national institutions of higher learning; technology business incubator (TBI) - converting innovations to startups; accelerator - fast tracking a start-up through focused intervention; seed support system (SSS) - providing early stage investment; centres of excellence (COE) - a world class facility to help startups go global and/or scale up.

Survey of India

Survey of India (SOI), the national survey and mapping organisation under the Ministry of Science and Technology, was set up in 1767. In its assigned role as the National Principal Mapping Agency, Survey of India bears a special responsibility to ensure that the country's domain is explored and mapped suitably to provide base maps for expeditious and integrated development and ensure that all resources contribute their full measure to the progress, prosperity and security of the country. The primary responsibility of SOI is to maintain topographical map coverage on 1:250K, 1:50K and l:25K scales. The topographical map coverage on l:250K and 1:50K scales covering the entire country has been completed and the map sheets are being updated at regular intervals to depict latest spatial information. Surveys on 1:25K scale were taken up as national requirement keeping in view the priorities indicated by the central/ state governments and other user agencies. It has also been called upon extensively to deploy its expertise in the field of geodetic and geophysical surveys, study of seismicity and seismotectonics, glaciology, participation in Indian Scientific Expedition to Antarctica and projects related to digital cartography and digital photogrammetry, etc., to provide basic data to keep pace with Science and Technology Department.

SOI has undertaken creation of digital cartographic data base of topographical maps on various scales. The digital data is being used by various agencies for planning and GIS applications. It also undertakes large scale surveys for various developmental projects including hydro-electric, irrigation, command area, canal area, cantt. area schemes, etc. The Department is responsible to fix the external boundary of India, their depiction on maps published in the country and also advise on the demarcation of inter-state boundaries. The Survey of India also provides support to other countries e.g., Nigeria, Afghanistan, Kenya, Iraq, Nepal, Sri Lanka, Zimbabwe, Indonesia, Bhutan, Mauritius, etc., in the field of mapping, survey education, transfer of technology, and various other surveying technologies under bilateral arrangements. Under UN mandate, Survey of India also provides support to countries in Asia-Pacific region for capacity building in spatial data infrastructures.

Survey Training Institute, Hyderabad established under UNDP assistance is a premier institution for training in various disciplines of surveying and mapping to the trainees sponsored by the Department, other state/central government organisations and neighbouring countries.

Keeping in view a new National Map Policy announced in May, 2005, Open Series Maps based on UTM projection and WGS-84 datum which is compatible with the coordinate system of GPS, used in all activities of surveying and mapping, are being published for users community. Defence Series Maps based on-Lambert Conformal Conic Projection and WGS-84 datum are being published for defence forces which are declared as classified. SOI is in the forefront of providing tidal information for the Indian Ocean by observing sea level data at various ports of India and other countries. These are crucial for scientific study in fields including climatology modelling, analysis of sea level changes, predicting tsunami, etc. Besides, this is also important input for sea navigation.

Geo-spatial data are being generated at various levels and by various agencies. These are being utilized for various application which need the integration of data from various sources. To enable this data integration, SOI has taken in its hand a herculean task of redefining the vertical datum of geoids by establishing a network of well spread standard ground control points throughout the country. This will enable the state cadastral department besides other agencies and industries engaged in acquiring geo-spatial information to carry out their job in a national reference system.

While Survey of India meets the national needs in cartography, some specialised thematic maps required to meet the needs of the specific users are taken care of by the National Atlas and Thematic Mapping Organisation (NATMO) operating under the Department. It also concentrates in a number of areas to integrate resource maps with other relevant socio-economic data and represent them in spatial forms, useful for developmental planning. NATMO is trying to develop the technology of reverse printing for maps on experimental basis. It is also trying to introduce the technique of using metallic colours in map printing.

Relevant Website : www.surveyofindia.gov.in

Council of Scientific and Industrial Research

The Council of Scientific and Industrial Research, (CSIR) constituted in 1942 is an autonomous body which is known for its cutting edge R&D knowledge base in diverse S&T areas. Having pan-India presence, CSIR has a dynamic network of 38 national laboratories, 39 outreach centres, 3 innovation complexes and 5 units. Its R&D expertise and experience is embodied in about 4000 active scientists supported by about 7000 scientific and technical personnel. It covers a wide spectrum of science and technology—from radio and space physics, oceanography, earth sciences, geophysics, chemicals, drugs, genomics, biotechnology and nanotechnology to mining, aeronautics, instrumentation, environmental engineering and information technology. It provides significant technological intervention in many areas with regard to societal efforts which include environment, health, drinking water, food, housing, energy, leather, farm and non-farm sectors. CSIR is the nation's custodian for measurement standards of mass, distance, time, temperature, current, etc. It has created and is the custodian of Traditional Knowledge Digital Library (TKDL) which is a powerful weapon against unethical commercial exploitation of Indian traditional knowledge. It maintains Microbial Type Culture Collection (MTCC) and Gene Bank. Pioneer of India's intellectual property movement, CSIR today is strengthening its patent portfolio to carve out global niches for the country in select technology domains.

Relevant Website : www.csir.res.in

Atomic Energy

The Department of Atomic Energy (DAE), established in 1954 is engaged in the development of nuclear power technology, applications of radiation technologies in the fields of agriculture, medicine, industry, and basic research. Some of these are : (i) increasing the share of nuclear power through deployment of indigenous and other proven technologies and also developing fast breeder reactors and thorium reactors with associated fuel cycle facilities; (ii) building and operation of research reactors for production of radioisotopes and carrying out radiation technology applications in the field of medicine, agriculture and industry; (iii) developing advanced technologies such as accelerators, lasers and encourage transfer of technology to industry; (iv) support to basic research in nuclear energy and related frontier areas of science, interaction with universities and academic institutions, support to R&D projects having a bearing on DAE's programmes and international cooperation in related areas of research; and (v) contribution to national security. An integrated group of organizations, the department comprises five research centres, three industrial organisations, five public sector undertakings and three service organisations. It has two boards for promoting and funding extramural research in nuclear and allied fields, and mathematics. It also supports seven institutes of international repute, engaged in research in basic sciences, astronomy, astrophysics, cancer research, education, etc., and a society that provides educational facilities to the children of DAE employees.

DAE has wide ranging capabilities in uranium mining and mineral procesing, and is self-suficient inthe production of heavy water, zirconium alloy components and other materials and supplies, for pressurised heavy water reactor. The Nuclear Fuel Complex at Hyderabad manufactures fuel assemblies for pressurised heavy water reactors, boiling water reactors and fast breeder reactor.

Relevant Website : www.dae.nic.in

Heavy Water Board

The Heavy Water Board (HWB) has contributed successfully to the first stage of Nuclear Power Programme by producing heavy water for all pressurised heavy water reactors in a cost effective manner enabling the Department to provide nuclear power at an affordable cost. Presently, the Board is not only self-sufficient in meeting the domestic demand of heavy water, but is also geared up to supply heavy water for the future PHWRs and AHWRs as per the envisioned nuclear power programme of DAE. Over a period of time, HWB has emerged as the largest global producer and a trusted supplier of this strategic material.

HWB has made major progress on its extended mandate in the field of development, demonstration and deployment of technologies for in-core and out of core material inputs for Indian Nuclear Power Programme, required at the front-end as well as back-end of nuclear fuel cycle mainly centering around three broad areas such as solvents for front and back end hydrometallurgical operations of nuclear fuel cycle; demonstrating solvent extraction technology for extraction of various rare materials and producing stable isotopes like ^{10}B for Fast Breeder Reactors and 18_O for societal applications.

Solvent Technology

In the area of solvents, both the industrial facilities at HWP, Baroda and Talcher for production of TBP (Tributyl Phosphate) and D2EHPA have performed very well enabling HWB to meet the entire requirement of NFC, NRB and all other units of DAE.

Boron Enrichment

In consonance with the material input required for second stage of NPP based on FBRs, HWB, with its decades of experience of handling isotope separation process, took up development, demonstration and deployment of indigenous technologies for production of enriched boron. HWB has now acquired comprehensive capability in this area achieving enrichment levels beyond 95 per cent in multiple chemical forms.

Sodium

Sodium is another important input for FBRs, used as coolant in the reactor. Networking with the Indian R&D organizations, HWB has developed indigenous and safer closed electrolytic cell technology for production of nuclear grade sodium. Successively larger size cells are tested with the ultimate intent of an industrial scale set up.

Mineral Exploration and Mining

Atomic Minerals Directorate for Exploration and Research (AMD) continued the accelerated pace of exploration activities by integrated, multi-disciplinary methodology and judicious utilisation of manpower with a focussed approach on augmentation of uranium, thorium and rare metals. This resulted in the augmentation of additional uranium oxide (U_3O_8) reserve of over 15,775 tonnes in Andhra Pradesh, Meghalaya, Rajasthan and Jharkhand.

R&D Support to Power Sector

The research and development support to the Nuclear Power Programme is provided by the research centers of DAE. Numerical models were developed and validated for deflagration, flame acceleration and detonation using experimental data to understand different physical and chemical processes during hydrogen combustion. Fitness-for-Service and assessment of remaining life of hemispherical bottom head of second stage hot tower of HWP, Kota was carried out by finite element analyses and limit load calculations.

Health Safety and Environment

Review of safety of operating stations was carried out on a regular basis. It continued to maintain low radiation exposure in the public domain due to operation of nuclear power stations. At all operating stations of NPCIL certified Environmental Management System (EMS) as per (SO-14001: 2004 and Occupational Health and Safety Management System (OHSMS) as per IS-18001: 2007 are maintained and regular audits (internal, external and management) were carried out for continual improvement.

An online thoron monitoring network was installed and made operational at PRTRF at Trombay to monitor the thoron gas concentration at various locations in the facility. Internal exposure assessment of occupational workers from various facilities of Bhaba Atomic Research Centre (BARC) at Mumbai and Tarapur was carried out by whole body/lung counting and bioassay (urine/fecal) sample analysis. All the plants of Heavy Water Board are certified for ISO Quality Management System, Environmental Management System and OSHA System. The overall safety standards of heavy water plants were far better than similar chemical industries in the country.

Fast Breeder Reactors

For the second stage of the Nuclear Power Generation Programme, the Indira Gandhi Centre for Atomic Research (IGCAR) is pursuing development of sodium cooled fast breeder reactors and associated fuel cycle technologies. Breeder reactors produce more fuel than they consume. The fast reactor programme of IGCAR is supported by its research and development endeavour in a range of disciplines such as reactor engineering, metallurgy, materials science, instrumentation, safety, etc. The Fast Breeder Test Reactor (FBTR), operating at Kalpakkam for over 25 years, also caters to technology development related to fast reactors.

Thorium Based Reactors

Nuclear power employing closed fuel cycle is the only sustainable option for meeting a major part of the world energy demand. World resources of thorium are larger than those of uranium. Thorium, therefore is, widely viewed as the 'fuel of the future'. The Indian Nuclear Power Programme Stage-3 aims at using thorium as fuel for power generation on a commercial scale. In the thorium fuel cycle, thorium 232 is transmuted into the fissile isotope uranium 233 which is a nuclear fuel.

Kalpakkam Mini (Kamini) Reactor

Kamini reactor was operated successfully for neutron radiography of various pyro devices for Department of Space. High temperature fission chambers required for neutron flux measurement of PFBR were successfully tested.

Research Reactors

Dhruva operated at rated power of 100 MWt at a high safety level and availability factor. A number of researchers from across the country utilized the neutron beam facility of the UGC-DAE Consortium for scientific research.

Advanced Technologies

The research centres of DAE are engaged in developing advanced technologies such as accelerators, lasers, advanced materials, robotics, supercomputers, instrumentation and others. BARC, RRCAT, VECC and BRIT are also engaged in the development of radiation technologies and their applications for better crop varieties, techniques for crops protection, radiation based post-harvest technologies, techniques for radio-diagnosis and radiotherapy of diseases particularly cancer, technologies for safe drinking water, better environment and industrial growth.

Electronics & Instrumentation

The Electronics Corporation of India Limited (ECIL) continued to remain engaged in the design, development, manufacture, supply, installation and commissioning of electronic equipment for the atomic energy, defence, aerospace, security, information technology and e-governance sectors.

Robotics

A robot based frameless stereotactic system is developed at BARC for performing neurosurgery which has accuracy and patient comfort level comparable to frame based system. It automates the frameless stereotaxy using a high precision robot (Parallel Mechanism based Robot).

Cryogenics

A cryogenic system consisting of cryogen distribution lines for liquid helium and liquid nitrogen, sub-atmospheric vacuum jacketed lines for helium, warm helium lines between the helium buffer tanks and compressors, and a 500 watt helium liquefier is being set-up for the superconducting electron and heavy-ion linacs at VECC.

Radioisotopes & Radiation Technology

DAE has been playing a significant role in the development and applications of various radioisotopes in healthcare, industry, agriculture and research. India is one of the leading countries in the isotope technology today as a result of the consistent efforts of DAE.

Radioisotopes are produced in the Dhruva Research Reactor at Trombay, accelerator at Kolkata and the various nuclear power plants of NPCIL , a wide variety of radioisotopes for medical, industrial and research applications were produced and supplied by BARC. The Board of Radiation and Isotope Technology (BRIT) produced and supplied a wide range of radioisotope products, and radiation technology equipment for medical and industrial uses.

Homi Bhabha National Institute

The Homi Bhabha National Institute (HBNI) accredited as a deemed university by Ministry of Human Resource and Development (MHRD) completed ten years of its existence. HBNI continued its academic programmes by offering various courses with its eight boards of studies, namely, as chemical sciences, engineering sciences, health sciences, life sciences, mathematical sciences, physical sciences, strategic studies and undergraduate studies.

Training

Selection of trainees under Orientation Course for Engineering Graduates & Science Post-Graduates (OCES) and DAE Graduate Fellowship Schemes

(DGFS) at BARC were pursued with high standards. At IGCAR the training programmes for Trainee Scientific Officers (TSOs) and doctoral programmes in the frontier areas of engineering and basic sciences for the inducted research scholars continued.

Indian Space Programme

Space activities in the country were initiated with the setting up of Indian National Committee for Space Research (INCOSPAR) in 1962. In the same year, work on Thumba Equatorial Rocket Launching Station (TERLS) near Thiruvananthapuram was also started. Indian Space Research Organisation (ISRO) was established in August, 1969. The Government of India constituted the space commission and established the Department of Space (DOS) in 1972 and brought ISRO under DOS in 1972. Space Commission formulates the policies and oversees the implementation of the Indian space programme to promote the development and application of space science and technology for the socio-economic benefit of the country. DOS implements these programmes through, mainly, Indian Space Research Organisation (ISRO), Physical Research Laboratory (PRL), National Atmospheric Research Laboratory (NARL), North Eastern-Space Applications Centre (NE-SAC) and Semi-Conductor Laboratory (SCL). Antrix Corporation, established in 1992 as a government owned company, markets the space products and services.

The period March 2016 - June 2017 witnessed numerous achievements of the Indian Space programme. Twelve launch vehicle missions were successfully accomplished that included seven PSLVs, two GSLV-Mk II and one GSLV-MKIII from Satish Dhawan Space Centre (SHAR), Sriharikota while the ten ISRO satellites, four student satellites and 152 foreign satellites were launched by these missions. India's communication satellites GSAT-18 and GSAT-17 were also successfully launched from French Guiana. The Polar Satellite Launch Vehicle (PSLV) had the unique distinction of launching 104 satellites in a single mission while also demonstrating its capability to place satellites in two different orbits in a single mission.

ISRO also demonstrated new technologies in the launch vehicle programme. The Reusable Launch Vehicle-Technology Demonstrator (RLV-TD) and SCRAMJET Engine Technology Demonstrator had their successful maiden test flights. This apart, the launch of Geosynchronous Satellite Launch Vehicle - Mark II (GSLV- Mk II) became the third consecutively successful launch of GSLV carrying the indigenous Cryogenic Upper Stage (CUS). Mars Orbiter Mission (MOM) spacecraft of India completed two years in its orbit around mars while Astro Sat, India's multi-wavelength observatory, successfully completed one year in orbit.

During 2017 ISRO was also successful in launching GSLV-F09, that could successfully place, the South Asia Satellite (GSAT-9) into GTO, which is a gift from India to SAARC nations. Polar Satellite Launch Vehicle (PSLV) had two successful launches during the year, (i) unique distinction of launching a record number of 104 satellites in a single mission and (ii) launch of 31 satellites. The launch of GSAT-17, a communication satellite was accomplished from French Guiana during June 2017. However, the 41st flight of PSLV carrying India's eighth navigation satellite IRNSS-1H could not place the satellite in the designated orbit and hence was not successful. In 2017, India's Mars Orbiter Mission (MOM) spacecraft completed three years in its orbit around Mars, while AstroSat, India's multi-wavelength observatory, successfully completed two years in orbit. Both these satellites are in good condition and performing satisfactorily.

Relevant Website : www.isro.org

Space Applications

One of the unique characteristics of Indian space programme has been the application-oriented efforts and the benefits that have accrued to the country through these programmes. The social services from INSAT/GSAT systems in various areas of communication in addition to tele-education and telemedicine continued. Remote Sensing applications projects at national, state and local levels made significant progress through a well-established multi-pronged implementation architecture of National Natural Resources Management System (NNRMS) in the country. During the year, Indian Remote Sensing Satellite constellation helped in providing vital inputs in agricultural crops inventory, agricultural drought assessment, forest fire monitoring, effective use of ground-water prospects maps, and varieties of governance applications.

The Disaster Management Support (DMS) Programme of ISRO is continuing to provide space based inputs for the effective management of disasters in the country. The Decision Support Centre (DMSDSC), established at National Remote Sensing Centre (NRSC), is engaged in monitoring of natural disasters such as floods, cyclones, landslides, forest fires, etc. During 2017, India witnessed major floods during June to September affecting more than 104 districts in 8 states, namely, Assam, Gujarat, Manipur, Bihar, Uttar Pradesh, Arunachal Pradesh, Odisha and West Bengal. All the major flood affected states were monitored using satellite data and about 100 maps were disseminated to the concerned states/departments.

During the fire season (February to June), daily near real time fire alerts were provided using satellite data. These inputs were provided in less than 30 minutes from the completion of satellite overpass. The activity was carried out in collaboration with the Forest Survey of India (FSI), covering the entire nation. During 2017, active fire locations information for about 32,546 forest fires were generated and made available to the respective forest departments of the states and FSI. A massive landslide occurred on National Highway, NH 154 (the road between Mandi and Pathankot) near the village of Kotropi, Mandi District, Himachal Pradesh in 2017. The event was monitored using Resourcesat-2 and

Cartosat-2 data. Rainfall as the causative factor for the occurrence of such landslides was recognised.

National Database for Emergency Management (NDEM) continued to provide disaster related inputs for states/UTs with multi-scale geo-spatial database. In addition to these daily data, alerts/warnings from forecasting agencies were also provided as part of NDEM dashboad. IRSO is a signatory of the International Charter for 'Space and Major Disasters', which aims at providing a unified system of space data acquisition and delivery to users affected by disasters. Towards this, ISRO supports the charter and Sentinel Asia by planning satellite data acquisition from various Indian Remote Sensing Satellites and providing the same within a stipulated time period. In 2017, ISRO supported 29 disasters across 22 counties by providing around 140 sets of IRS data.

Space Science and Planetary Research

Mars Orbiter Mission (MOM), which is India's first inter-planetary spacecraft mission, has sucessfully completed three years in its orbit around Mars and still continues to provide vital information on regular basis. The health parameters of spacecraft are normal. Scientific analysis of the data being received from the spacecraft is being done on various aspects of the planet. During the year, an orbit maneuver was also successfully performed on the spacecraft, which removed the danger of long period eclipse till 2021.

AstroSat, India's first multi-wavelength observatory, completed two years in orbit. The satellite is now being operated as an 'Observatory', in which observational time is allocated based on the proposals received from interested researchers and scientists in the country, through IRSO's Announcement of Opportunity (AO).

Capacity Building

The achievements of Indian space programme have been primarily due to the well-established mechanisms of taking up a task and achieving the same with commitment and dedication with professionalism. Recognising the importance of nurturing such unique talents and motivating principles, the Department has always emphasised on the capacity building related aspects. Capacity building encompasses multiples areas of development to ensure that the department achieves its goals, as envisioned. Following are some of the key areas of capacity builiding.

International Cooperation

International cooperation is an integral part of Indian space activities and ISRO continues to lay importance on bilateral and multilateral relations with space agencies and space related bodies with the aim of taking up new scientific and technological challenges, defining international frameworks for exploitation and utilisation of outer space for peaceful purposes, refining space policies and building and strengthening existing ties between the countries. ISRO signed cooperative agreements with the French, UAE, Japanese, US, Vietnamese, Afghanistan and Russian agencies as well the US Geological Survey.

Space Commerce

Antrix Corporation Limited, the commercial arm of the Department of Space, is marketing the Indian space products and services in the global market. Antrix offers a wide range of services from the space based systems through specific commercial contracts with other agencies, including foreign customers. Under commercial contracts with Antrix, 237 international customer satellites have already been successfully launched by PSLV during the period 1999-2018. In 2017 alone, PSLV launched 130 foriegn satellites.

Indian Institute of Space Science and Technology

Towards capacity building in human resources and to meet the growing demands of the Indian Space Programme, the Indian Institute of Space Science and Technology (IIST), a deemed university, was established at Thiruvananthapuram in 2007.

Earth Sciences

Earth system sciences deals with all the five components of the earth system, viz., atmosphere, hydrosphere, cryosphere, lithosphere and biosphere and their complex interaction. The Ministry of Earth Sciences (MoES) holistically addresses all the aspects relating the earth system science for providing weather, climate, ocean, coastal state, hydrological and seismological services. The services include forecasts and warnings for various natural disasters. The services provided are being effectively used by different agencies and state governments for saving human lives and minimizing damages due to natural disasters.

Relevant Website : www.moes.gov.in

Atmospheric and Climate Research

A high resolution global deterministic weather prediction model was commissioned for generating operational weather forecasts at a horizontal resolution of 12 km. With this, MoES has attained the same capability as in USA in using high resolution weather prediction models. Many major improvements have been made in data assimilation for the ingestion of data from the Indian and International satellites in numerical models. Under the Monsoon Mission, operational dynamical model systems have been implemented for extended range and seasonal forecasts. For the first time, forecasts on different time scales during the hot weather season (April to May) including heat waves were issued by the India Meteorological Department.

Improved Weather and Cyclone Predictions

The quality of weather services has shown appreciable improvements during the past three years. Specifically, noticeable improvements were achieved in prediction skills of heavy rainfall and tropical cyclones such as Phailin, Hudhud and Vardah and the heavy rainfall events in Uttarakhand, Jammu and Kashmir and Chennai. For the cyclone, Vardah, which had caused severe damages in the city of Chennai and neighbourhood, accurate predictions were provided almost three days in advance, helping to save thousands of lives. The loss of lives during the last three years due to tropical cyclones has reduced to less than hundred as compared to the thousands during the previous decade.

Agro-Meteorological Advisory Services

The Ministry in collaboration with the Indian Council of Agricultural Research (ICAR) provides the Agromet Advisory Services (AAS) for the benefit of farmers. Farmers make use of these services for planning the operations like sowing, irrigation, application of fertilizer and pesticide, harvest and protection of crops from wather disasters. The services carried out at 130 agro-met zones (cluster of 4-6 districts) now have been successfully extended to the district level and operated across 608 districts of the country. Currently, about 21.69 million farmers are receiving crop specific agro-meteorological advisories in vernacular languages.

Forecasts for Heat and Cold Waves

With global warming, surface air temperatures are expected to further increase and frequency of heat waves may also increase. To provide adequate warnings about heat waves and associated health hazards, MoES for the first time started issuing forecasts for heat waves over the country. A few state governments like Gujarat, Andhra Pradesh, Maharashtra and Odisha have initiated state action plans based on these forecasts during the hot weather season, which could help them to warn people in advance about the occurrence of heat waves and thus saving their lives. MoES has also taken initiative to develop such heat wave action plans with other state governments.

Ocean Services: Technology and Observations

Potential Fishery Zone (PFZ) Advisories

The Indian National Centre for Ocean Information Services (INCOIS) provides PFZ advisories to 2.75 lakh fishermen on a daily basis to help them to easily locate the areas of abundant fish in the ocean.

Ocean Forecasts

Ocean state forecastes (forecasts of waves, currents, sea surface temperature, etc.) to fisher folk, shipping industry, oil and natural gas industry, navy, coast guard and other stakeholders have improved considerably. Oil spill advisories are being provided to facilitate the indication of eco-sensitive zones, potential fishing zones, fishing avoidance zone during the event of oil spill. The ocean state forecasts were also provided before and during the launch day of Re-usable Launch Vehicle Technology Demonstration (RLV-TD) of the Indian Space Research Organisation (ISRO).

The ocean forecast services were extended to two other Indian Ocean Rim countries, namely Sri Lanka and Seychelles on various parameters viz., winds, waves, currents and temperature in map form served under the umbrella of Regional Integrated Multi-Hazard Early Warning System (RIMES) for Afro-Asian Region.

Tsunami Warning System

The Indian Tsunami Warning System established by the Ministry at the Indian Centre for Ocean Information Services (INCOIS), Hyderabad has been recognized as the Regional Tsunami Service Provider (RSTP) for the Indian Ocean region by UNESCO to provide warning to countries of the Indian Ocean. This includes the service of level-2 tsunami advisories for the Indian Ocean. The Indian Tsunami Warning System is equipped to issue warnings within ten minutes of occurrence of earthquakes. The Indian Tsunami Early Warning Centre (ITEWC) kept the watch of all tsunamigenic earthquakes in and around the Indian Ocean and issued appropriate messages in the event of any threats from potential tsunamis.

Ocean Observing System

In 2016, INCOIS deployed 23 ARGO floats in the Indian Ocean having sensors to collect the physical parameters, of which 11 were equipped with both physical and biogeochemical sensors. Over 732 active floats are actively working in the Indian Ocean of which 136 were deployed by India. So far, more than 340856 temperature and salinity profiles, 18993 dissolved oxygen and 7614 chlorophyll profiles were collected by Argo floats in the Indian regions.

Open Cage Culture

Large scale fish production through mariculture is the viable alternative to cope with the ever increasing demand for fish proteins. An open sea cage culture mooring system was designed and developed for commercially important marine finfishes suitable for Indian sea conditions to meet this demand with available marine engineering and biological expertise. The open sea cage culture technology seems to be an ideal alternative livelihood option for the coastal fishers, help generate considerable employment opportunities in the country and to meet the fish food production targets of the nation.

Remotely Operated Vehicles

Indigenously developed 500m depth rated shallow water/polar remotely operated vehile (PROVe) was successfully deployed, in the Andaman coral islands. The vehicle was successfully maneuvered in the undulating reef terrain to record high quality under water visuals of coral reef biodiversity with spectral irradiance.

Polar and Cryosphere Research (PACER)

National Centre for Antarctic and Ocean Research (NCAOR), Goa established a high altitude research station in Himalaya called Himansh (literally meaning, a slice of ice), situated above 13,500 ft (>4000 m) at a remote region in Spiti Himachal Pradesh. This station is equipped with instruments such as, automatic station, water level recorder, steam drill, snow ice corer, ground penetrating radar, differential global positioning system, snow fork, flow tracker, thermister string, radiometer, etc. Water level recorders were installed at five locations along the stretch of 130 km of Chandra river in western Himalaya for hydrological balance/modeling. Glaciers were monitored for mass balance, dynamics, energy balance and hydrology.

Seismology and Geoscience Research (SAGE)

The national seismological network consisting of 82 observatories has been functioning smoothly. Information pertaining to significant earthquake events were transmitted to all concerned state and central government agencies, dealing with relief and rescue operations in the region and also posted on the website. Scientific deep drilling in Koyna which started in 2016 is aimed at setting up of borehole observatory (s) at depth for directly measuring the in-situ physical properties of the rocks, pore-fluid pressure, hydrological parameters, temperature and other parameters of an intra-plate, active fault zone in the near field of earthquakes— before, during and after their occurrence, leading to a better understanding of the mechanics of faulting, physics of reservoir triggered earthquakes and pareparing a predictive model.

Research, Education, Outreach and Training

It comprises the training programmes of the Ministry, R & D in earth and atmospheric sciences programme for extramural support and the outreach and awareness programme. The basic aim of the programme is to nurture the R & D activities being undertaken in various academic and research institutes of the country and to translate the output into operational use by the Ministry.

Biotechnology

Realising the tremendous potential of biotechnology in improving human and animal health and productivity, enhancing agricultural activity and providing safe and clean environment, government set up a multi agency board namely National Biotechnology Board (NBTB) way back in 1982 with participation of DST, UGC, ICMR and CSIR to promote activities in biotechnology. Subsequently, the National Board was upgraded to a fully fledged Department of Biotechnology (DBT) under the Ministry of Science and Technology in 1986. This provided the much needed impetus to biotechnology and the Department conceived programmes and formulated integrated programmes in line with its allocation of business rules.

DBT has infused fresh momentum to the developments in modern biology and biotechnology. The Department, in the past 30 years, has witnessed discerned marturation from a nascent sector to a sunrise industry, making outstanding achievements in the growth and application of and susceptibility of bio-resources and environment and also towards fostering among the major biotech destinations in the world and ranks third in the Asia-Pacific region. India has the second-highest number of US Food and Drug administration (USFDA)-approved plants, after the USA.

The Department has laid impetus on capacity building for carrying out cuttingedge research in the country through fellowships/awards and training programmes. This has helped us nurturing the young talent by imparting them specialised training and rewarding them suitably.

Skill development programmes were initiated to provide high quality hands-on-training (postgraduate diploma/certificate) in tools and techniques used in medical biotechnology, agricultural biotechnology and computational biology so that they are ready for jobs in industries, hospitals, medical colleges, research and development laboratories, diagnostic laboratories etc.

Relevant Website : www.dbtindia.nic.in

Autonomous Institutions

DBT being a visionary in biotech research and promotion established 16 autonomous institutes for pursuing research in various disciplines of biotechnology in the specialized areas of agriculture and allied science, health care, animal sciences, environment, and industry engaged in the theme-based research with the projects sponsored by the national and the international agencies. More than 80 technologies developed under the efforts of autonomous institute and many of them have been commercialized through technology transfer. The autonomous institute of DBT have several research leads including IPR/patents.

National Institute of Immunology (NII), New Delhi continued expansion of scientific programmes in a multi-investigators driven mode to address challenging questions in biology for improvement of healthcare. It also promotes state-of-art teaching and training facilities in advanced biological sciences using an inter-disciplinary approach so as to inculcate the highest level of aptitude and ability in the country's skilled manpower pool.

National Centre for Cell Sciences (NCCS), Pune has taken new initiatives in nurturing young scientific talent and research scholars into its PhD programme dealing with cutting-edge research areas in structural biology, stem cell biology, deciphering the role of RNA in biological control processes and the cellular and molecular basis of memory.

Centre for DNA Fingerprinting and Diagnostics (CDFD), Hyderabad is well equipped with world class state-of-the-art instrumentation and computing infrastructure to facilitate working in frontier areas of research in life sciences. It provides services for agricultural and processed food products for testing purity of samples of agricultural commodity using DNA markers that can distinguish different Basmati varieties and also traits identification and validation. The major areas of research in the institute centred around cell signalling, transcription, structural biology, computational biology and bioinformatics, immunology, genetics and molecular pathogenesis.

Institute of Life Sciences (ILS), Bhubaneshwar is giving focus on infectious disease biology, gene function and regulation and translational research. It has state-of-the-art infrastructural facilities for cutting-edge multidisciplinary research in frontier areas of life sciences.

National Brain Research Centre (NBRC), Manesar is pursuing interdisciplinary research and teaching on epilepsy and brain mapping. The focus of the Institute is on generation of skilled manpower in brain research that would help India to achieve international leadership in this frontier area of science.

National Institute of Plant Genome Research (NIPGR), Delhi is focusing research on understanding of the structure, expression and function of genes along with arrangement of genes on plant genomes and manipulation of plant genes/genomes to breed improved varieties of food and industrial crops for high yields and of better quality products. It is making attempts to translate some of the technologies developed through basic reseach activities for their application in agriculture.

Rajiv Gandhi Centre for Biotechnology (RGCB), Thiruvananthapuram working on research programme on chronic disease biology, tropical disease biology and disease biotechnology.

Institute of Bio-resources and Sustainable Development (IBSD), Imphal is involved in conservation and sustainable utilization of bio-resources for the socio-economic development of the north eastern region. The Institute has taken initiatives in collaborations with other institutions/organizations/universities nationally and internationally relevant to the bio-resources for sharing and sustainable exploitation.

Centre of Innovative and Applied Bio-processing (CIAB), Mohali is giving focus on secondary agriculture and catalyzing research, innovations and knowledge translation for production of secondary agricultural bio-products. The Institute is currently involved in processing of agri-farm and food industry spare biomass through chemical, biological and biotechnological approaches and engaged in transmitting knowledge and leads of bio-resources for productive processing and value additive primary and secondary agriculture bio-products for edible and non-edible usage.

National Institute of Biomedical Genomics (NIBMG), Kalyani is engaged in accelerating genomics for health and disease and discovering genomic evidence that underpins disease and health-related traits. It is pursuing projects on discovery of biological and environmental correlations of pre-term birth and study natural histories of diseases and health related traits.

Regional Centre for Biotechnology (RCB), Faridabad is providing world class education, training and conducts innovative research at the interface of multiple disciplines to create high quality human resource in disciplinary and interdisciplinary areas of biotechnology in a globally competitive research milieu.

Translational Health Science and Technology Institute (THSTI), Faridabad is working on integrated approach in the field of medicine, science, engineering and technology into translational knowledge and making biomedical innovations accessible to public health. The Institute plays a pivotal role in NCR biotech science clusters and targeting at specializing in translational research and related endeavours.

National Institute of Animal Biotechnology (NIAB), Hyderabad has taken initiatives on infectious diseases; brucellosis, theileriosis, babesiosis, newcastle disease virus (NDV), leptospirosis, toxoplasmosis, mastitis, peste des petitsruminants virus (PPR) and foot and mouth disease (FMD) and development of new tools for diagnosing and preventing the diseases.

Institute of Stem Cell Science and Regenerative Medicine (InStem), Bengaluru has successfully attracted outstanding investigators, who have initiated theme driven programmes. A key focus is given to support young investigators through a fellowship programme in stem cell research and applications.

National Agri Food Biotechnology Centre (NABI), Mohali engaged in research programmes and technologies for the biotech cluster at Mohali to make Indian agriculture and food industry more innovation driven, remunerative and sustainable. It is providing sustainable and meaningful answers towards quality nutrition and provides multiple biotechnological and inventive products in agriculture and food sector.

International Centre for Genetic Engineering and Biotechnology (ICGEB), Delhi is endeavouring to bring excellence in genetic engineering with collaborative partnership of scientists from all over the world. The Centre is engaged in conducting training programme on discovery of new drugs against malaria and micro RNAs in plant development and stress management. The broad research areas are malaria, virology, immunology, recombinant gene products, structural and computational biology, plant molecular biology, insect resistance, plant transformation and synthetic biology and bio-fuels.

Industrial and Entrepreneurship Development

Under Industrial and Entrepreneurship Development schemes, the Department supported translational research and public private partnership programme including bio-incubators and biotech parks.

Biotechnology Parks and Incubators

The Department of Biotechnology promotes biotech research and helps to translate research into products and services. One of the means by which development of new commercial products is to be achieved through the setting up the biotechnology parks, where facilities for technology incubation, technology demonstration and pilot plant studies are provided for accelerated commercial development of biotechnology. The Department in partnership with state governments/state government organisations/central government organisations has established biotechnology parks and incubators in diffferent parts of the country to facilitate biotech product development, entrepreneurship, research and innovation.

Bangalore Life Science Cluster for Multi-scale Basic and Applied Research in Biological Sciences (B-Life), Bengaluru promotes research and technology development through generation of ideas, sharing resources and infrastructure amongst the partnering institutes. The cluster partnering institutes are: Institute for Stem Cell Science and Regenerative Medicine (inStem), National Centre for Biological Sciences (NCBS), Centre for Cellular and Molecular Platforms (C-CAMP), and Institute of Bioinformatics and Applied Biotechnology (IBAB). The clusters are engaged in establishment of innovative institutional model for cutting-edge scientific research, where existing centres of excellence are used for the development of new centres with challenging new mandates.

NCR Biotech Science Cluster is established by involving five autonomous institutes of DBT (NII, NIPGR, NBRC, THSTI and RCB). The Cluster is supporting discovery driven research in biology and developments of novel technologies and facilitation of public-private partnerships through biotech business incubators and parks. It creates network with the potential constituent institutions to bring synergistic ecosystem for accelerating discoveries.

Public Sector Undertakings

The Department has promoted new industry academia interface and stimulating strategic research and innovation capabilities of the Indian biotech industry, particularly start-ups and SME's, for creation of affordable products addressing the needs of the largest section of society. As an interface agency Biotechnology Industry Research Assistance Council (BIRAC) has been set up to foster innovation and entrepreneurship, promote affordable innovation in key social sectors, empowerment of start-ups and small and medium enterprises, contribute through partners for capability enhancement and diffusion of innovation, enable commercialization of discovery and ensure global competitiveness of Indian enterprises. BIRAC has initiated partnerships with several national and global partners to collaborate and deliver the salient features of its mandate. Biotech Ignition Grant (BIG) scheme under BIRAC is encouraging scheme for the young investigators for entrepreneurial and managerial development of SME's in biotechnology through incubators.

The Department is also having two PSUs namely Bharat Immunologicals and Biologicals Corporation Limited (BIBCOL) and Biotechnology Industry Research Assistance Council (BIRAC). BIBCOL is a leading biotechnology company based in Uttar Pradesh, currently manufactures and produces a range of pharmaceutical products such as Oral Polio Vaccines (OPV Vaccine), zinc tablet and diarrheal management kit, etc. Its mission is to save the lives of millions of children from avoidable disability, through polio vaccination. BIRAC is a not-for-profit Section 8, Schedule B, public sector enterprise, set up as an interface agency to strengthen and empower the emerging biotech enterprise to undertake strategic research and innovation, addressing nationally relevant product development needs.

BIRAC is a new industry academic interface and implements its mandate through a wide range of impact initiatives, be it providing access to risk capital through targeted funding, technology transfer, IP management and handholding schemes that help bring innovation excellence to the biotech firms and make them globally competitive. In its three years of existence, BIRAC has initiated several schemes, networks and platforms that help to bridge the existing gaps in the industry-academia innovation research and facilitate novel, high quality affordable products development through cutting edge technologies.

26 Transport

A well-knit and coordinated system of transport plays an important role in the sustained economic growth of country. The present transport system of the country comprises several modes of transport including rail, road, coastal shipping, air transport etc. Transport has recorded a substantial growth over the years both in spread of network and in output of the system. The Ministry of Shipping and the Ministry of Road Transport and Highways are responsible for the formation and implementation of policies and programmes for the development of various modes of transport save the railways and the civil aviation.

Railways

The Railways in India provide the principal mode of transportation for freight and passengers. It brings together people from the farthest corners of the country and makes possible the conduct of business, sightseeing, pilgrimage and education. The Indian Railways have been a great integrating force during the last more than 164 years. It has bound the economic life of the country and helped in accelerating the development of industry and agriculture. From a very modest beginning in 1853, when the first train steamed off from Mumbai to Thane, a distance of 34 kms, Indian Railways have grown into a vast network of 7,349 stations spread over a route length of 67,368 km with a fleet of 11,461 locomotives, 53,453 passenger service vehicles, 6,714 other coaching vehicles and 2,77,987 wagons. The growth of Indian Railways in the 165 years of its existence is thus phenomenal. It has played a vital role in the economic industrial and social development of the country. The network runs multi-gauge operations extending over 67,368 route kilometers.

The rolling stock fleet of Indian Railways in services by March, 2017 comprised 39 steam, 6,023 diesel and 5,399 electric locomotives. Currently, the Railways are in the process of inducting new designs of fuel-efficient locomotives of higher horse power, high-speed coaches and modern bogies for freight traffic. Modern signalling like panel inter-locking, route relay inter locking, centralized traffic control, automatic signaling and multi-aspect color light signaling are being progressively introduced. The Indian Railways have made impressive progress regarding indigenous production of rolling stock and variety of other equipment over the years and is now self-sufficient in most of the items.

About 35.32 per cent of the route kilometre and 47.09 per cent of running track kilometre and 48.26 per cent of total track kilometre is electrified. The network is divided into 17 zones. Divisions are the basic operating units. The 17 zones and their respective headquarters are given here:

Zonal Railways	Headquarters
Central	Mumbai
Eastern	Kolkata
East Coast	Bhubaneshwar
East Central	Hajipur
Northern	New Delhi
North Central	Prayagraj
North Eastern	Gorakhpur
Northeast Frontier	Maligaon (Guwahati)
North Western	Jaipur
Southern	Chennai
South Central	Secunderabad
South Eastern	Kolkata
South East Central Railway	Bilaspur
South Western Railway	Hubli
Western	Mumbai
West Central Railway	Jabalpur
Metro Railway	Kolkata

The main objectives of railways planning have been to develop the transport infrastructure to carry the projected quantum of traffic and meet the developmental needs of the economy. Since the inception of the planned era in 1950-51, Indian Railways have implemented nine five-year plans, apart from annual plans in some years. During the Plans, emphasis was laid on a comprehensive programme of system modernization. With capacity being, stretched to its limits, investments of cost-effective technological changes become inescapable in order to meet the ever-increasing demand for rail transport. Along with the major thrust directed towards rehabilitation of assets, technological changes and upgradation of standards were initiated in important areas of track, locomotives, passenger coaches, wagon bogie designs, signalling and telecommunication.

Relevant Website : www.indianrailways.gov.in

Central Public Sector Enterprises

There are thirteen undertakings under the administrative control of the Ministry of Railways, viz., (i) RITES Ltd., (ii) IRCON International Limited, (iii) Indian Railway Finance Corporation Limited (IRFC), (iv) Container Corporation of India Limited (CONCOR), (v) Konkan Railway Corporation Limited (KRCL),

(vi) Mumbai Railway Vikas Corporation Limited (MRVC) (vii) Indian Railway Catering & Tourism Corporation Ltd. (IRCTC), (viii) Railtel Corporation of India Ltd. (Rail Tel), (ix) Rail Vikas Nigam Ltd. (RVNL), (x) Dedicated Freight Corridor Corporation of India Limited (DFCCIL), (xi) Bharat Wagon and Engineering Co. Ltd. (BWEL), (xii) Burn Standard Company Limited (BSCL) and (xiii) Braithwaite and Company Limited (BCL).

Research and Development

The Research Design and Standards Organization (RDSO) at Lucknow is the R&D wing of Indian Railways. It functions as a consultant in technical matters. It also provides consultancy to other organizations connected with railway manufacture and design. RDSO has developed a new design of wider and heavier pre-stressed concrete sleeper RT-8527 for 25 T axle load to achieve higher frame resistance against bucking, higher rubber pad life, and feasibility of reducing de-stressing temperature with likely reduction in rail/weld failures.

Railway Finance

Though a part of the overall financial figures of the Government of India, the Railway Budget was being presented separately to Parliament since 1924-25 owing to the Separation Convention of 1924. The Railways had its own 16 demands for grants, which also used to be considered and passed by the Parliament separately. The main reason behind the Separation Convention was to secure stability for civil estimates as the Railway finance used to be a sizeable part of the general finances. The Government decided to merge the Railway Budget with the general Budget from the 2017-18. The unified budget will bring the affairs of the Railways to centre stage and present a holistic picture of the financial position of the government. This merger would facilitate multimodal transport planning between highways, railways and waterways.

Railways would continue to maintain its distinct entity as a departmentally run commercial undertaking and retain its functional autonomy, delegation of financial powers etc. as per the existing guidelines. Instead of the erstwhile scheme of sixteen demands for grants, the Ministry of Finance introduced one demand for grant for the Ministry of Railways.

Freight Traffic

Rapid progress in industrial and agricultural sectors has generated a higher level of demand for rail transport, particularly in core sectors like coal, iron and steel ores, petroleum products and essential commodities such as food grains, fertilizers, cement, sugar, salt, edible oils etc. Revenue from freight traffic increased from 73.2 million tonnes in 1950-51 to 1106.15 million tonnes in 2016-17. In the same period , IR loaded 1110.95 million tonnes of which 1106.15 million tonnes was revenue-earning and 4.80 million tomes non-revenue-earning, and achieved total net tonne kilometres (NTKMs) of 621 billion as against 656 billion in 2015-16.

Passenger Business

Passenger earnings in 2016-17 were ₹ 46,280.46 crore. This was ₹ 1,997.70 crore (4.51per cent) higher than the earnings in 2015-16. Suburban traffic contributed 5.81 per cent to the total earnings. The remaining 94.19 per cent came from non-suburban passengers. Earnings from Second and sleeper class mail/express passengers comprised 50.20 per cent of the total passenger earnings.

Indian Railways is a commonly used mode of public transportation. During 2016-17, it carried 8,116 million passengers.

Roads

Road transport is a critical infrastructure for economic development of a country. It influences the pace, structure and pattern of development. The Ministry of Road Transport and Highways is the apex body for formulation and administration of the rules, regulations and laws relating to road transport and transport research. It encompasses construction and maintenance of national highways (NHs), administration of Motor Vehicles Act, 1988 and Central Motor Vehicles Rules 1989, National Highways Act,1956 and National Highways Fee (Determination of Rates and Collection) Rules,2008, formulation of broad policies relating to road transport, environmental issues, automotive norms etc. besides making arrangements for movements of vehicular traffic with neighboring countries. The capacity of national highways in term of handling traffic (passenger and goods) needs to be in tandem with the industrial growth. India has a large road network of over 56.03 lakh km. This comprises national highways, expressways, state highways, major district roads, other district roads and village roads. Of this, the length of national highways is nearly 1,29,709 km. The Ministry has been entrusted with the responsibility of developmentand maintenance of national highways (NHs). All roads other than national highways in the states fall within the jurisdiction of respective state governments. In order to assist the state governments in the development of state roads, central government also provides financial assistance out of the Central Road Fund (CRF) and Inter State Connectivity and Economic Importance (ISC & EI) Scheme.

The NHDP was mainly being implemented by National Highways Authority of India (NHAI) and National Highways and Infrastructure Development Corporation Ltd. (NHIDCL), and is spread over seven phases with an estimated expenditure of about ₹ 6,00,000 crore. Some of the major National Highways constructed under this programme include Golden Quadrilateral (GQ) connecting 4 major metropolitan cities viz., Delhi-Mumbai-Chennai-Kolkata, North South & East West Corridors (NS-EW) connecting Srinagar to Kanyakumari and Silchar to Porbandar with a spur from Salem to Cochin, road connectivity of major ports of the country to national highways. The remaining works under NHDP have now been subsumed under the Ministry's new flagship programme - Bharatmala.

Relevant Website : www.morth.nic.in

Development and Maintenance of National Highways

The Government is implementing National Highways Development Project (NHDP), the largest Highways Project ever undertaken in the country since 2000. The NHDP is mainly being implemented by National Highways Authority of India (NHAI) and National Highways & Infrastructure Development Corporation Ltd. (NHIDCL).

Bharatmala Pariyojana

The Ministry has taken up detailed review of NHs network with a view to develop the road connectivity to border areas, development of coastal roads including road connectivity for non-major ports, improvement in the efficiency of national corridors, development of economic corridors, inter corridors and feeder routes along with integration with Sagarmala, etc., under Bharatmala Pariyojana. The Bharatmala Pariyojana envisages development of about 26,000 km length of economic corridors, which along with Golden Quadrilateral (GQ) and North-South and East-West (NS-EW) Corridors are expected to carry majority of the freight traffic on roads. Further, about 8,000 km of inter corridors and about 7,500 km of feeder routes have been identified for improving effectiveness of economic corridors, GQ and NS-EW Corridors. The programme envisages development of Ring Roads / bypasses and elevated corridors to decongest the traffic passing through cities and enhance logistic efficiency; 28 cities have been identified for Ring Roads; 125 choke points and 66 congestion points have been identified for their improvements.

National Highways Authority of India

The National Highways Authority of India (NHAI) was set up in 1995. It is responsible for development, maintenance and management of national highways entrusted to it and for matters related or incidental there to.

National Highways & Infrastructure Development Corporation

The NHIDCL is a fully owned company of the Ministry that exclusively carries out the task of construction/ up-grading/widening of national highways in parts of the country which share international boundaries with neighbouring countries in order to promote regional connectively with neighbouring countries on a sustainable basis.

Indian Academy of Highway Engineers

Indian Academy of Highway Engineers (IAHE) is a registered society under the administrative control of the Ministry. It is a collaborative body of both central and state governments and was set up in 1983 with the objective of fulfilling the long felt need for training of highway engineers in the country, both at the entry level and during the service period.

Major Initiatives

National highways constitute just two per cent of the country's road network but carry 40 per cent of the traffic load. The government is working hard to augment this infrastructure both in terms of length and quality. There are plans to expand the network of national highways so that all parts of the country have an easy access to it. The North East Region, backward and interior areas, border connectivity roads, coastal roads and economically important routes are being given special attention in terms of building road connectivity. The Ministry has eased several norms and polices for aqcuiring land, felling tree, risk balancing, reviving old projects, etc.

National Registry of Vehicle and License Records

In order to usher in transformational improvements in this sector, the Ministry has put in place several policies for citizens. Transport Mission Mode Project has successfully automated RTO operations, set up a consolidated transport database. Along with it, a host of citizen and trade centric applications have also been implemented. The salient aspects of this Mission Mode Project are two flagship applications - Vahan and Sarathi. While Vahan consolidates vehicle registration, taxation, permit, fitness and associated services across the country, Sarathi looks after the driving license, learner licence, driving schools and related activities. This has been implemented in more than 1,000 RTOs across 13 states/UTs with state-specific rules, tax structure, etc.

The database is integrated with Aadhaar for biometric authentication and eKYC, integration with digilocker. This allows use of virtual documents like driving license, registration certificates, permits, etc., as authorized soft copy.

Road Safety

The Government has approved a National Road Safety Policy so as to minimise road accidents. It outlines various measures such as promoting awareness, establishing road safety information data base, identification and rectification of road accident black spots , improving road accident data collection and data base management, training of highway engineers and professionals in road safety engineering, improving vehicular safety standards,encouraging safer road infrastructure including application of intelligent transport, effective trauma care, enforcement of safety laws etc. The important schemes on road safety operated by the Ministry include publicity measures and awareness campaign on road safety, Scheme for Setting up Institutes for Driving Training, Refresher Training of Drivers in Unorganized Sector and Human Resource Development, National Highways Accident Relief Service Scheme (NHARSS), setting up of inspection and certification centres and road safety and pollution testing equipment and programme implementation.

To enhance passenger safety and specially the safety and security of women and children in transit, all the passenger buses and taxis are mandated to be fitted with GPS devices and panic buttons to enable real time tracking and interventions in times of crisis.

e-Tolling

In order to remove traffic bottle neck at toll plazas and ensure seamless movement of vehicles and hassle-free collection of toll, the Government has implemented a nationwide Electronic Toll Collection based on passive Radio Frequency Identification (RFID) conforming to EPC Gen-2, ISO 18000-6C standards. It provides for electronic collection of toll through FASTags. The project was first launched in 2015.

National Green Highways Project

In order to develop eco-friendly highways, the Green Highways (Plantation Transplantation. Beautification and Maintenance) Policy was firmed up in 2016. The Policy aims to develop eco-friendly national highways with the participation of community, farmers, NGOs and private sector. The initial plantation drive on 1,500 km of national highways at a cost of about ₹ 300 crore was launched as part of the Policy.

Shipping

The Ministry of Shipping was formed in 2009 by bifurcating the erstwhile Ministry of Shipping, Road Transport and Highways into two independent ministries. Maritime Transport is a critical infrastructure for the economic development of a country. It influences the pace, structure and pattern of development. The Ministry of Shipping encompasses within its fold shipping and port sectors which also include shipbuilding and ship repair, major ports and inland water transport. It is the apex body for formulation and administration of the rules and regulations and laws relating to shipping. Maritime transport is a critical infrastructure for the social and economic development of a country. It represents the pace, structure and pattern of development of water transport. It has been entrusted with the responsibility to formulate policies and programmes on these subjects and their implementation.

Relevant Website : www.shipmin.gov.in

Maritime Development

India has a long coastline of about 7,517 km, spread on the western and eastern shelves of the mainland and also along the Islands. It is an important natural resource for the country's trade. There are 12 major ports and about 200 non-major ports. Indian shipping industry has over the years played a crucial role in the transport sector of the economy. Approximately 95 per cent of the country's trade by volume and 68 per cent by value is moved through maritime transport. Therefore, shipping and ocean resources, ship design and construction, ports and harbours, issues relating to human resource development, finance, ancillaries and new technologies need to be developed in the light of the emerging scenario. Shipping continues to remain unchallenged as the world's most efficient means of transportation and there is a need to recognize, reward and promote quality within the industry.

Sagarmala Programme

To harness the coastline, 14,500 km of potentially navigable waterways and strategic location on key international maritime trade routes, the Government of India has embarked on the ambitious Sagarmala Programme to promote port-led development in the country. The vision of the Programme is to reduce logistics cost of EXIM and domestic trade with minimal infrastructure investment. This includes: reducing the cost of transporting domestic cargo; lowering logistical cost of bulk commodities by locating future industrial capacities near the coast; improving export competitiveness by developing port proximate discrete manufacturing clusters, etc. The objectives of the Programme include: port modernisation, new port development, port connectivity, coastal community development, etc.

Shipping Industry

Shipping industry is one of the most globalised industries operating in a highly competitive business environment that is far more liberalized than most of the other industries and is, thus, intricately linked to the world economy and trade. Shipping plays an important role in the transport sector of India's economy especially in Exim trade. Approximately 95 per cent of the country's trade in terms of volume and 68 per cent in terms of value is moved by sea.

The salient features of India's shipping policy are the promotion of national shipping to increase self-reliance in the carriage of country's overseas trade and protection of stakeholder's interest in Exim trade.

Ship Building

The Indian shipbuilding industry continued to concentrate on defence, coastal and inland vessels. The fleet expansion plans of Indian Navy and the vessels for the Indian Coast Guard are the two prime segments which were targeted by the Indian shipyards. A shipbuilding subsidy scheme was in existence to promote Indian Shipbuilding industry for Central PSU Shipyards since 1971. The scheme was extended to all Indian shipyards in October 2002. This policy which provided shipbuilding subsidy gave a boost to this Industry.

Ship Repair

The Indian share in the global ship repair market continued to be low as there was very little capacity addition. Indian ship owners continued to rely on overseas repair facilities owing to insufficient capacity and high level of taxation. There are 27 shipyards in the country, 6 under central public sector, 2 under state governments and 19 under private sector.

Ship Recycling

India has 25-30 per cent share in the global ship recycling industry. Ship recycling is carried out mainly at Alang-Sosiya in Gujarat. Started in February, 1983, Alang-Sosiya is the largest ship recycling yard in the world. Approximately 10 km long sea front on the western coast of the Gulf of Cambay adjoining to

Alang-Sosiya village has been developed as a ship recycling yard. It is blessed with high tidal range, long beach with gentle slope and firm ground, facilitating beaching of ships just at the threshold of the plot. It has high recycling potential of more than 450 ships (approximately 4.5 million LDT) per annum. Ship recycling serves the nation by producing about more than 3.5 million ton per annum of re-rollable steel without exploiting the natural resources and provides a green route to generate th secondary steel in place of generation of steel from the ore itself.

Major Ports

Emerging global economy has opened up new avenues in all the sectors in general and maritime sector in particular. Ports provide an inter-face between ocean transport and land based transport and play a vital role in the overall economic development. There are 12 major ports and about 200 non-major ports along India's coastline which is about 7517 km. The 6 major ports–Kolkata, Paradip, Visakhapatnam, Kamarajar (Ennore), Chennai and V.O. Chidamananar are on the east coast and the other major ports viz., Cochin, New Mangalore, Mormugao, Mumbai, Jawaharlal Nehru Port (Sheva, Navi Mumbai) and Deendayal (erstwhile Kandla) are on the west coast. The major ports are under the direct administrative control of the central government and fall in Union List 7th Schedule of Constitution. Ports other than the major ones are under the jurisdiction of the respective maritime state government and fall in the Concurrent List. Of the total traffic handled by all Indian ports, 57 per cent is handled by major ports and 43 by others.

Kolkata Port: Kolkata Port is the only riverine major port in the country having been in existence for about 138 years. It has a vast hinterland comprising the entire Eastern India including West Bengal, Bihar, Jharkhand, U.P., M.P., Assam, North East hill states and the two landlocked neighbouring countries namely, Nepal and Bhutan. The port has twin dock systems viz., Kolkata Dock System on the eastern bank and Haldia Dock Complex on the western bank of river Hooghly.

Paradip Port: Paradip Port is one of the major ports of the country. Government of India took over the management of the port from the state government in 1965. The Government of India declared Paradip Port Trust (PPT) as the eighth major port the country making it the first major port in the east coast commissioned in independent India.

New Mangalore Port: New Mangalore Port was declared the ninth major port in 1974 inaugurated in 1975. The port has 16 berths and one single point mooring with a total capacity of 87.63 MTPA.

Cochin Port: The modern port of Cochin was developed during the period 1920-1940 due to the untiring efforts of Sir Robert Bristow. By 1930-31 it was formally opened for vessels up to 30 feet draught. Cochin was given the status of a major port in 1936. The administration of the port got vested in a Board of

Trustees in 1964 under the Major Port Trusts Act, 1963. Cochin Port is strategically located on the south-west coast of India and at a commanding position at the cross-roads of the east-west ocean trade, it is a natural gateway to the vast industrial and agricultural produce markets of the South-West India. The hinterland of the port includes the whole of Kerala and parts of Tamil Nadu and Karnataka. Cochin with its proximity to the international sea route between Europe and the Far East and Australia can attract a large number of container lines offering immense business opportunities.

Jawaharlal Nehru Port: Constructed in the mid 1980's and commissioned in 1989, Jawaharlal Nehru Port has come a long way by becoming a world-class international container handling port. It is a trendsetter in port development in India through new initiatives like private sector participation. Jawaharlal Nehru Port is an all weather tidal port having 12 berths with a capacity of 89.37 MTPA.

Mumbai Port: Mumbai Port is a fully integrated multi-purpose port handling container, dry bulk, liquid bulk and break bulk cargo. It has extensive wet and dry dock facilities to meet the normal needs of ships using the port. The port has 33 berths with a total capacity of 65.33 MTPA.

Chennai Port: Chennai Port is an all weather artificial harbour with one outer harbour and one inner harbour with a wet dock and a boat basin with round the clock navigation facilities. It was established in 1875. It has 24 berths with a total capacity of 93.44 MTPA.

Mormugao Port: Mormugao Port, situated on the west coast of India, is more than a century old port. It has modern infrastructure capable of handling a wide variety of cargo. It is a natural harbour protected by a breakwater and also by a mole. The Port has excellent infrastructure and a conducive work culture. A deep draft channel with 14.4 mtrs. depth permits large vessels to enter the harbour. The port has 7 berths plus trans-shipment with a total capacity of 50.04 MTPA.

V.O. Chidambarnar Port (Tuticorin): V.O. Chidambaranar Port is located strategically close to the east- west international sea routes on the south eastern coast of India at latitude 8^0 45'N and longitude 78^0 13'E. located in the Gulf of Mannar, with Sri Lanka on the south east and the large land mass of India on the west. The port has 15 berths with a total capacity of 65.90 MTPA.

Deendayal Port (Kandla): Deendayal Port (erstwhile Kandla Port) was established in 1950 as a central government project and Union Government took over Kandla for its development as a major port. It has 28 berths including 3 single buoy moorings including an off-shore terminal at Vadinar with a capacity of 150.26 MTPA.

Visakhapatnam Port: Port of Visakhapatnam, a natural harbour, was opened to commercial shipping in 1933. It is the only Indian port possessing three international accreditations viz., ISO 14001; 2004 (EMS)/OHSAS 18001 and ISO 90001:2000 (QMS). It has mechanized handling facilities for iron ore, iron pellets, alumina, fertilizer raw material, crude oil and POL products, liquid ammonia, phosphoric acid, edible oil, caustic soda and other liquid cargoes. The port has 24 berths with a total capacity of 110.75 MTPA.

Kamarajar Port Limited (Ennore): Kamarajar Port Limited (KPL), the 12th major port under the Ministry of Shipping was commissioned in 2001, primarily as a coal port dedicated to handling thermal coal requirements of Tamil Nadu Electricity Board (TNEB). KPL has the distinction of being the only corporate port amongst the major ports administered by the central government. The port has 8 berths with a total capacity of 57.00 MTPA.

Inland Water Transport

India has one of the longest navigable and inland water networks. However, cargo transport through these inland waterways is, presently less than 1 per cent of the total cargo movement in the country. Inland Waterways Authority of India (IWAI) was constituted in 1986, for the development and regulation of inland waterways for shipping and navigation. 111 inland waterways have been declared as 'National Waterways' under the National Waterways Act, 2016. After declaration of 106 new national waterways, pre-feasibility studies and techno economic studies/Detailed Project Report (DPR) are being carried out which inter- alia cover the potential of navigability, cargo availability, cost of development, etc.

Jai Marg Vikas Project

Jai Marg Vikas Project (JMVP) is being implemented by the IWAI for the capacity augmentation of national waterway I on the Haldia–Varanasi stretch of Ganga-Bhagirathi-Hooghly river system with the technical and financial assistance of the World Bank. The salient features of JMVP include: construction of three multimodal and inter-modal terminals, new navigational lock at Farakka, integrated vessel repair and maintenance facilities, day and night navigational aids, river conservancy work, etc.

Coastal Shipping

Coastal Shipping is fuel efficient, environment friendly and helps in easing traffic congestion on roads. In other large economies like China, USA and Japan the share of waterways is more than that of India. Presently, the share of waterways in transportation of domestic goods is less than its potential.

Cruise Shipping

'Cruise Tourism' is a fast growing component of the leisure industry, worldwide. Through this segment of niche tourism, huge amount of foreign exchange can be earned and income generated onshore by providing the right policy environment and infrastructure. With the steady development of India's economy, growing middle class and increasing disposable income, the overall environment is conducive for the promotion of cruise tourism within the country.

Indian Maritime University

Indian Maritime University (IMU) was set up in 2008 in Chennai with campuses at Chennai, Kolkata and Visakhapatnam as a central university. The existing seven government and government aided maritime training and research institutes viz., Marine Engineering and Research Institute, Kolkata, Marine Engineering and Research Institute, Mumbai, Lal Bahadur Shastri College of Advanced Maritime Studies and Research, Mumbai, T.S. Chanakya, Navi Mumbai, National Maritime Academy, Chennai, Indian Institute of Port Management, Kolkata as well as National Ship Design and Research Centre, Visakhapatnam have been merged with the IMU.

Lighthouses and Lightships

In the vast ocean, a mariner is not sure of his position unless he is guided by some signal from the land/space. Directorate General of Lighthouses and Lightships (DGLL) provides service to enable the mariners to know their position with respect to a fixed point on the land with the help of visual aids to navigation such as lighthouses, light vessels, buoys, beacons and radio aids to navigation like differential global positioning system (DGPS), radar beacons (Racons), vessel traffic service (VTS) and automatic identification system (AIS) etc.

Directorate General of Shipping, Mumbai

The Directorate General of Shipping, an attached office of the Ministry of Shipping, was established in 1949 for administering the Indian Merchant Shipping Act, 1958 on all matters relating to shipping policy and legislation, implementation of various international conventions relating to safety, prevention of pollution and other mandatory regulations of the international maritime organizations, promotion of maritime education and training, examination and certification, supervision of other subordinate offices for their effective functioning etc.

Relevant Website : www.dgshipping.gov.in

Shipping Corporation of India Limited

The Shipping Corporation of India (SCI) was formed in 1961 by amalgamation of Eastern Shipping Corporation and Western Shipping Corporation through 'Shipping Corporation Amalgamation Order 1961. The amalgamation envisaged better co-ordination of policies, greater economy and efficiencies of operations between the two companies. Sailing through for five decades, SCI continues to be the country's premier shipping line, owning a fleet of 70 vessels.

Relevant Website : www.shipindia.com

Cochin Shipyard Limited

Cochin Shipyard Limited (CSL), located in Kochi in Kerala is one of the largest shipyards in the country which can build ships upto 1, 10,000 DWT and repair ships upto 1, 25,000 DWT. The yard has built and delivered over 100 ships including tankers, bulk carriers, port crafts, offshore vessels, tugs and passenger vessels. The company has exported around 45 ships over the last decade and is currently building one of the most prestigious warships of the Indian Navy Indigenous Aircraft Carrier. Apart from the aircraft carrier, the Yard has delivered 20 fast patrol vessels to the Indian Coast Guard. CSL also has a strong presence in ship repair. In the shiprepair segment it has repaired and maintained various types of ships such as merchant vessels, naval crafts, coast guard vessels, dredgers, jack up rigs, etc. It is the only yard which has regularly undertaken dry dock repairs of the aircraft carriers of Indian Navy. CSL had the privilege of receiving INS Viraat for the 13th time - her last refit in 2016-17 and ISO9001 certificate.

Relevant Website : www.cochinshipyard.com

Dredging Corporation of India

Dredging Corporation of India Ltd. (DCIL) was formed in 1976 to provide integrated dredging and related marine services for promoting the country's national and international maritime trade, beach nourishment, reclamation, inland dredging, environmental protection and ultimately to become a global player, in the field of dredging. Located strategically on the eastern seaboard of India at Visakhapatnam, DCI helps ensure continuous availability of the desired depths in the shipping channels of the major and minor ports, navy, fishing harbours and other maritime organizations. It also serves the nation in a variety of ways, be it capital dredging for creation of new harbours, deepening of existing harbours or maintenance dredging for the upkeep of the required depths at various ports.

Relevant Website : www.dredging-india.nic.in

Andaman and Lakshadweep Harbour Works

Andaman and Lakshadweep Harbour Works (ALHW) a subordinate office under Ministry of Shipping was established during 1965 for the service of A&N Islands and Lakshadweep Islands. The ALHW is entrusted with the responsibilities of formulating and implementing the programme of Ministry of Shipping for providing port and harbour facilities in the islands.

Relevant Website : www.andssw1and.nic.in/alhw

Hooghly Dock and Port Engineers Ltd

Hooghly Dock and Port Engineers Limited (HDPEL), Kolkata became a Central Public Sector undertaking in 1984. The Company has two working units in Howrah district of West Bengal, one at Saikia and another at Nazirgunge. The installed capacity in shipbuilding is 1,100 tonnes per annum and in ship-repairs 125 ships per annum. Apart from a dry dock and a jetty, it has six slipways. The yard is capable of constructing various types of ships (including passenger ships) and other vessels such as dredgers, tugs, floating dry docks, fishing trawlers, supply-cum-support vessels, multipurpose harbour, vessels, light house tender vessels, barges, mooring launches, etc., and undertaking repairs of different types of vessels.

Civil Aviation

The Ministry of Civil Aviation is responsible for formulation of national policies and programmes for the development and regulation of the civil aviation sector in the country. It is responsible for the administration of the Aircract Act, 1934, Aircraft Rules, 1937 and various other legislations pertaining to the aviation sector in the country. In addition to primary functions of framing of policies, the Ministry provides guidance to the organisation in the implementation of policy guidelines, monitors and evaluates their activities and also provides their interface with the Parliament. It also supervises implementation by the organizations of special programmes of the Government, particularly those intended for weeker sections of society.

Relevant Website : www.civilaviation.gov.in

National Civil Aviation Policy

For the first time since Independence and Integrated Civil Aviation Policy was notified in June, 2016, which aims at creating an ecosystem that will push the growth of the civil aviation sector, which in turn, would promote tourism, increase employment and lead to a balanced regional growth. The Policy aims to take flying to the masses by making it affordable and convenient, enhance ease of doing business through deregulation, simplified procedures and e-governance and promote the entire aviation sector chain in a harmonized manner covering cargo, MRO, general aviation, aerospace manufacturing and skill development.

Regional Connectivity Scheme

The Regional Connectivity Scheme (RCS)-UDAN was envisaged in National Civil Aviation Policy (NCAP) 2016 with the twin objective of promoting balanced regional growth and making flying affordable for masses. The Scheme, which will be in operation for a period of 10 years, envisages providing connectivity to un-served and underserved airports of the country through revival of existing air strips and airports.

Air Sewa

Air Sewa is an initiative of the Ministry of Civil Aviation launched 2016 to offer people a convenient and hassle-free air travel experience. It works through an interactive web portal (airsewa.gov.in) or a mobile app for both android and iOS platforms that includes a mechanism for grievance redressal, back-office operations for grievance handling flight status/schedule information, airport Information and FAQS, Air Sewa initiative has integrated various stakeholders in aviation sector with whom an air traveler has to interact during the air travel.

FDI Liberalization

Government of India has raised the FDI limit for 49 to 100 per cent in scheduled and non scheduled air transport services, FDI in scheduled airlines upto 49 per cent permitted under automatic route and FDI beyond 49 per cent through Government approval. For NRIs, 100 per cent FDI will continue to he allowed under automatic route.

Directorate General of Civil Aviation

The Directorate General of Civil Aviation (DGCA) is an attached office of the Ministry of Civil Aviation and is headed by Director General (Civil Aviation). The headquarters are located in New Delhi and there are Regional and Sub-regional offices all over the country. DGCA is primarily responsible for regulation of air transport services to/from/within India and for enforcement of civil air regulations, air safety and airworthiness standards. It is also responsible for licensing of pilots, aircraft maintenance engineers and monitoring of flight crew standards; regulation of civil aircraft; investigation of minor air incidents; supervision of training activities of flying/gliding clubsand other such regulatory functions. The regulations are in the forms of the Aircraft Act, 1934, the Aircraft Rules, the Civil Aviation Requirements (CAR), the aeronautical information circulars. It also co-ordinates all regulatory functions with International Civil Aviation Organisation (ICAO).

Relevant Website : www.dgca.nic.in

Bureau of Civil Aviation Security

The Bureau of Civil Aviation Security (BCAS) was initially set up as a cell in the DGCA in 1978, to coordinate, monitor, inspect and train personnel in Civil Aviation Security matters. It was reorganized into an independent Department in 1987. BCAS is the regulator for civil aviation security in the country and is responsible for laying down the standards for pre-embarkation security and anti-sabotage measures in respect of civil flights and ensuring their compliance through regular inspections and security audits. Its main responsibility is to lay down standards and measures in respect of security of civil flights at international and domestic airports in India and Indian aircraft operators at foreign airports. The aim of BCAS is to safeguard civil aviation operations against acts of unlawful interference and it is the regulatory authority for discharging all relevant national and international obligations in respect of aviation security responsibilities which include, inter alia, planning and co-ordination of all aviation security related activities, operational emergencies and crisis management. The BCAS has its headquarters in New Delhi and has nine regional offices at New Delhi, Mumbai, Kolkata, Chennai, Ahmedabad, Amritsar, Guwahati, Hyderabad and Imphal airport.

Relevant Website : www.bcasind.nic.in

Airports Authority of India

Airports Authority of India (AAI) came into being in April 1995. AAI is a Mini Ratna-Category-I PSE involved in building, upgrading, maintaining and managing airports infrastructure across the country. It owns and maintains 125 airports (96-operational and 29 - non-operational) comprising 21-international airport (3 - civil enclaves), 8 - custom airports (4 - civil enclaves), 77 - domestic airports and 19-domestic civil enclaves.

Relevant Website : www.aai.acro

Air Navigation Services

Authority of India (AAI) provides Air Navigation Services (ANS) at all civil airports in the country. AAI manages the designated Indian air space measuring 2.8 million square nautical miles which includes land area measuing 1.05 million square nautical miles and oceanic airspace measuring 1.75 million square nautical miles Air Navigation Services are also provided by the AAI at 11 other airports that are not managed by AAI namely Delhi, Mumbai, Bengaluru, Hyderabad, Cochin, Lengpui, Diu, Latur, Mundra, Nanded and Sathya Sai Puttaparthy airports, which are joint venture airports, state government owned airports and private airports.

GPS Aided Geo Augmented Navigation (GAGAN) is an augmentation system to enhance the accuracy and integrity of GPS signals to meet precision approach requirements in Civil Aviation and it is being implemented jointly by AAI and ISRO. It is fully operational since May 2015 and available on 24 x 7 basis. Presently GAGAN Signal-in-Space is available to users from two geostationary satellites (GSAT-8 and GSAT-10) and third geo-satellite GSAT-15 is in the process of integration with GAGAN system.

Air India

Consequent upon merger of erstwhile Air India Ltd. and Indian Airlines, a new company viz., National Aviation Company of India Limited (NACIL) was incorporated. Consequently post merger, the new entity is known as "Air India" and the appointed date of the merger is 1 April 2007. The "Maharaja" is retained as its mascot. The Registered Office of the Company is in New Delhi. Air India Ltd. is basically a passenger orientated airlines operating to 72 on - line domestic stations (including Alliance Air) and 42 international destinations in 28 countries. It is in transport services sector under the administrative control of the Ministry of Civil Aviation.

Relevant Website : www.airindia.in

Air- India Air Transport Service Limited (*AIATSL*)

AIATSL provides ground handling services at 65 airports. Apart from handling the flights of Air India Limited and its airlines subsidiary companies, ground handling is also provided for 24 foreign scheduled airlines, 4 domestic scheduled airlines, 3 regional airlines, 16 seasional charter airlines, 23 foreign airlines availing perishabale cargo handling.

Air-India Charters Limited (AICL)

AICL operates a low cost airline under the brand name "Air India Express". Launched in 2005 with a fleet of 3 leased B737-800 aircraft, it operated from 3 stations in Kerala to 5 stations in the Gulf. As on 31 March 2016, AICL had a fleet of 17 B737-800 owned and 1 B737-800 leased aircraft. It operated to 12 Indian and 13 foreign on-line stations.

Air-India Engineering Services Limited-Aiesl (AIESL)

AIESL presently provides Maintenance, Repair and Overhaul (MRO) services to a fleet of 135 aircraft of Air India Limited and its subsidiary companies viz. Air India Charters Ltd. and Airline Allied Services Limited and few third party Airlines. MRO services are proposed to be provided to all the airlines and aircraft within the flying distance of 5 hours from the facility.

Airline Allied Services Limited- (AASL)

As in 2016 the Company had 3 ATR-42-320s, 5 ATR-72-600 and 3 CRJ-700s leased aircraft in its fleet. At the end of the year, the network of the Company consisted of 29 stations within the Country. Presently, it operates around 196 flights per week.

Alliance Air operates air services in the North East Region under an MoU with the North Eastern Council (NEC). It also operates flights between Agatti and the mainland under an undertaking of grant of Viability Gap Funding (VGF) by the Lakshadweep Administration. Further, it has charter operations on Portblair/Car Nicobar/Portblair with CRJ aircraft once a week on behalf of the Andaman and Nicobar Administration from July 2014.

Hotel Corporation of India Limited

Subsequent to the sale of 3 units of HCI (Centaur Mumbai Airport, Centaur Juhu Beach, Mumbai and Indo Hokke Hotel Ltd., Rajgir) as a part of disinvestment process as approved by the Government of India, at present, there are three units of HCI viz., Centaur Lake View Hotel (CLVH), Srinagar, Centaur Delhi Airport (CHDA) including Chefair Flight Catering (CFCD), Delhi and Chefair Flight Catering (CFCM), Mumbai.

Relevant Website : www.centaurhotels.com

Pawan Hans Limited

Pawan Hans Limited (PHL) was incorporated in October, 1985 (under the name of 'Helicopter Corporation of India Limited') as a government company under the Companies Act. It was established with the primary objective of providing helicopter support services to the oil sector in offshore exploration, operate in hilly and inaccessible areas and make available charter flights for promotion of travel and tourism. The registered office of Pawan Hans is located in New Delhi, corporate office at Noida and its regional offices are at Mumbai, New Delhi and Guwahati. The Company is providing helicopter services to several state governments namely, Meghalaya, Mizoram, Maharashtra, Tripura, Sikkim, Odisha, Himachal Pradesh and Ministry of Home Affairs. It has provided 04 Dauphin helicopters to Andaman & Nicobar Islands and 02 Dauphin helicopters to Lakshadweep Islands. The Company is also providing helicopter services to NTPC, GAIL, GSPC and Oil India.

Pawan Hans has emerged as one of Asia's largest helicopter operators having a well-balanced own operational fleet of 43 helicopters at present with pan India presence. Pawan Hans has been able to secure long-term contracts with institutional clients mainly in the oil industry and government sector mainly under competitive tender conditions.

It has been providing helicopter support for offshore operation of ONGC for carrying its men and vital supplies round the clock to drilling rigs situated in Bombay off-shore platforms. Pawan Hans operates to ONGC's Rigs (mother platforms and drilling rigs) and production platforms (wells) within a radius of 130 nm. from the main land at Mumbai.

Pawan Hans runs the helicopter services from Phata to the Holy Shrine of Kedarnath during the yatra seasons i.e., May-June and September-October every year. It has also provided helicopter services for the Shri Amarnath Shrine.

Relevant Website : www.pawanhans.co.in

Indira Gandhi Rashtriya Uran Akademi

The Indira Gandhi Rashtriya Uran Akademi (IGRUA) was set up at Fursatganj, Raebareli (Uttar Pradesh) to bring about a quantum improvement in the standards of flying and ground training of commercial pilots in the country. The Akademi is equipped with most modern and sophisticated trainer aircraft along with their associated simulator with 180° view. Up-to-date audio-visual training aids and other facilities for effective ground training. It employs qualified flying and ground instructors, with long experience in the field of aviation and flying training. The aim at IGRUA is not only to train to make a pilot but also to make one an effective systems manager in aeronautics. The flying trainees of the Akademi acquire the standard required for their transit with ease into the cockpits of the airlines. It is an Autonomous Body under the control of the Ministry of Civil Aviation. The Akademi has made remarkable expansion of its existing infrastructure, viz., doubling the capacity of hostel from 72 fully furnished rooms to 144 including a 20 room girls' hostel. Re-carpeting of roads, installation of solar water heating system in hostels, installation of air-conditioning plant having capacity of 60 TR X 3, laying of new water supply lines, renovations of sports complex, a newly constructed swimming pool, recreation centre etc., are the other major infrastructure upgradations carried out in the institutional area.

Relevant Website : www.igrua.gov.in

Airports Economic Regulatory Authority of India

The Airports Economic Regulatory Authority (AERA) is a statutory body constituted under the Airports Economic Regulatory Authority of India Act. 2008 in 2009 with its head office at Delhi.

Rajiv Gandhi National Aviation University

Rajiv Gandhi National Aviation University (RGNAU) is a central university under the administrative control of the Ministry. The university has been established by the Rajiv Gandhi National Aviation University Act, 2013. It is situated at Fursatganj, Raebareli, district Amethi, Uttar Pradesh. The University has been envisaged as the premier institution for higher learning within the aviation milieu aimed at providing cutting edge and critical training and research to enhance the aviation industry within India. It awards diploma, degree and post graduate degrees in the field of civil aviation.

The objective of the University is to facilitate and promote aviation studies, teaching, training and research in conjunction with the industry to achieve excellence in operations and management of all the sub-sectors within the aviation industry.

Relevant Website : www. rgnau.ac.in

27 Water Resources

THE Ministry of Water Resources, River Development and Ganga Rejuvenation lays down policies and programmes for development and regulation of the water resources of the country. It covers sectoral planning, coordination, policy guidelines, technical examination and techno-economic appraisal of projects, providing central assistance to specific projects, facilitation of external assistance and assistance in the resolution of inter-state water disputes, policy formulation, planning and guidance in respect of major, medium and minor irrigation, ground water management, command area development, flood management, dam safety and river development and Ganga rejuvenation (including its tributaries rejuvenation), regulation and development of inter-state rivers, implementation of awards of Tribunals, water quality assessment, bilateral/external assistance and matters relating to rivers common to India and neighbouring countries.

Relevant Website : www.mwr.gov.in

Water Availability

The average annual water availability of any region or country is largely dependent upon hydro-meteorological and geological factors and is generally constant. As per National Commission on Integrated Water Resources Development (NCIWRD) report, the total water availability of the country received through precipitation is about 4000 Billion Cubic Meter (BCM) per annum. After evaporation, 1869 BCM water is available as natural runoff. Due to geological and other factors, the utilizable water availability is limited to 1137 BCM per annum comprising 690 BCM of surface water and 447 BCM of replenishable ground water.

Water availability per person is dependent on population of the country and for India water availability per capita is reducing progressively due to increase in population. The average annual per capita water availability in the years 2001 and 2011 was assessed as 1820 cubic meters and 1545 cubic meters respectively which may reduce further to 1340 and 1140 in the years 2025 and 2050 respectively. Annual per-capita water availability of less than 1700 cubic meters is considered as water stressed condition, whereas annual per-capita water availability below 1000 cubic meters is considered as a water scarcity condition. Due to high temporal and spatial variation of precipitation, the water availability of many region of the country is much below the national average and can be considered as water stressed / water scarce. Total requirement of the country for different uses for high demand scenario for the years 2025 and 2050 has been assessed as 843 BCM and 1180 BCM respectively.

National Water Policy

The National Water Policy, 2012 was adopted by the National Water Resources Council. This Policy has made several recommendations for conservation, development and improved management of water resources in the country. Impertance is on the need for a national water framework law; comprehensive legislation for optimum development of inter-state rivers and river valleys; evolving a system of benchmarks for water uses for different purposes to ensure efficient use of water; setting up of water regulatory authority by each state; and incentivizing recycle and reuse of water. The Policy also lays emphasis on community participation in management of water resources projects and services; incentivizing water saving in irrigation through methods like micro irrigation, automated irrigation operation, etc; undertaking conservation of rivers, river corridors, water bodies and infrastructure in a scientifically planned manner through community participation; and arresting declining ground water levels in over-exploited areas.

National Water Mission

With a view to address Climate Change and the related issues, the National Action Plan on Climate Change (NAPCC) was prepared by the Government, which laid down the principles and identified the approach to be adopted to meet the challenges of impact of climate change through eight national missions. National Water Mission is one of the missions under NAPCC.

The main objective of the National Water Mission is (NWM) "conservation of water, minimizing wastage and ensuring its more equitable distribution both across and within States through integrated water resources development and management". The five identified goals of the Mission are: (a) comprehensive water data base in public domain and assessment of impact of climate change on water resource; (b) promotion of citizen and state action for water conservation, augmentation and preservation; (c) focused attention to vulnerable areas including over-exploited areas; (d) increasing water use efficiency by 20 per cent, and (e) promotion of basin level integrated water resources management. Various strategies for achieving the goals have been identified which lead to integrated planning for sustainable development and efficient management with active participation of the stakeholders.

Main Activities

Comprehensive water data base in public domain: India-WRIS (Water Resource Information System), a portal for providing information on water resources has been developed by Central Water Commission. All the data pertaining to surface water and ground water are made available at India-WRIS. GIS data pertaining to surface water resources and ground water resources are displayed on the site of India-WRIS.

NWM Web Portal

An independent Web Portal of NWM was launched. The portal aims at providing all the information relating to water resources, organisations and their activities on different aspects of water resources at one point.

Assessment of Impact of Climate Change on water resources: NWM has identified eight river basins (Mahanadi, Mahi, Luni, Tapi, Sutlej, Sabarmati, Subarnarekha and western flowing rivers from Tadri to Kanyakumari) for study of impact of climate change in association with research institutes like IITs, NITs, IISc. and NIH under the R & D scheme of the Ministry.

National Mission for Clean Ganga

The Ganga basin is the most populous in the world, with more than 400 million people in India alone. It accounts for 28 per cent of India's water resources, holds about 26 per cent of India's land mass and hosts 43 per cent of the population. The main stem of the river traverses 5 major states namely, Uttarakhand, Uttar Pradesh, Bihar, Jharkhand and West Bengal and travels 2525 kms. The Ganga River basin including all its tributaries cover about a million square kilometres area in 11 states in the country. The Ganga basin exemplifies a typical "hydraulic civilization", where achieving water security to harness the river's productive potential and limit its destructive potential is critical for sustenance and economic growth. Beyond this the river is also a home to some of exotic marine life such as gharials, turtles, Gangetic dolphins and golden mahaseer etc. In addition to its physical resource value, the Ganga is culturally very significant for India. On important religious/spiritual days, millions of people converge on its banks in select cities to pray and bathe in the waters, and for them a clean Ganga holds great value. More than120 million people came to the city of Allahabad for pilgrimage in 2013, making it the largest gathering in the world.

Despite being highly revered and the primary water resource for the heartland of the country, the Ganga river is today seriously polluted and under extreme environmental stress. Rapidly increasing population, rising standards of living and exponential growth of industrialization and urbanization have exposed the mighty Ganga to various forms of degradation. The river suffers from high levels of organic and bacterial pollution, especially in its critical middle stretch, resulting in a wide range of negative impacts, including human health, agriculture, urban services, and the environment. The major source of pollution in the river is untreated domestic and industrial liquid waste thrown in to it. About 70 per cent of the pollution is from untreated domestic sewage, 20 per cent is from toxic industrial waste water and 10 per cent is from non-point sources such as agricultural runoff, open defecation, dumping of solid waste disposal, etc. The threat of global climate change, the effect of glacial melt on Ganga flow and the impacts of infrastructural projects in the upper reaches of the river, raise issues that need a comprehensive response.

There have been previous attempts to clean the river, with mixed results. The Ganga Action Plan (GAP) was launched in 1985 and extended to two phases (GAP I & GAP II) over more than two decades. It focused primarily on urban wastewater and funded a large number of Wastewater Treatment Plants (WWTPs) and related urban waste water infrastructure. Impact data show that, overall, the programme was able to maintain or even improve water quality in spite of significant increases in pollution loadings due to urban and industrial growth. However, there were a number of limitations in its implementation - (1) including insufficient investments, (2) underutilization of created capacity, (3) little ownership of local bodies, (4) long delays, and poor communications - resulting in a public relations failure.

In 2015, the "Namami Gange" - Integrated Ganga Conservation Mission programme was launched. This was at an indicative cost of ₹ 20,000 crores, as an umbrella programme with an aim to integrate previous and currently ongoing projects and new initiatives planned as its part. In 2016, through the River Ganga (Rejuvenation, Protection and Management) Authorities Order 2016, NGRBA has been replaced with a National Ganga Council for Rejuvenation, Protection and Management of River Ganga as an authority. National Mission for Clean Ganga (NMCG) has also been converted in to an authority. National Mission for Clean Ganga.

Jal Kranti Abhiyan

Ministry of Water Resources, River Development & Ganga Rejuvenation launched Jal Kranti Abhiyan(2015-16 to 2017-18) in order to consolidate water conservation and management in the country through a holistic approach involving all stakeholders, making it a mass movement. The objectives of Jal Kranti Abhiyan are as follows: strengthening grass root involvement of all stakeholders including Panchayati Raj Institutions and local bodies in the water security and development schemes (e.g. Participatory Irrigation Management (PIM); encouraging the adoption/utilization of traditional knowledge in water resources conservation and its management; to utilize sector level expertise from different levels in government, NGO's, citizens, etc; and enhancing livelihood security through water security in rural areas.

Pradhan Mantri Krishi Sinchayee Yojana

During 2015-16, Pradhan Mantri Krishi SinchayeeYojana (PMKSY) was launched with an aim to enhance physical access of water on farm and expand cultivable area under assured irrigation, improve on farm water use efficiency, introduce sustainable water conservation practices, etc.

The main objectives of the scheme are include: achieve convergence of investments in irrigation at the field level (preparation of district level and, if required, sub district level water use plans); enhance the physical access of water on the farm and expand cultivable area under assured irrigation (*har khet ko pani*); improve on-farm water use efficiency to reduce wastage and increase availability both in duration and extent; enhance recharge of aquifers and introduce sustainable water conservation practices; promote extension activities relating to water harvesting, water management and crop alignment for farmers and grass root level field functionaries ; and attract greater private investments in precision irrigation.

Major and medium irrigation/ multipurpose irrigation (MMI) projects are being funded under PMKSY-AIBP and Repair, Renovation and Restoration (RRR) of Water Bodies, Surface Minor Irrigation (SMI) projects and Command Area Development & Water Management (CAD&WM) projects are being funded under PMKSY-Har Khet Ko Pani (HKKP).

Accelerated Irrigation Benefit Programme

The Accelerated Irrigation Benefits Programme (AIBP) was launched in 1996-97 to provide Central Assistance to major/medium irrigation projects in the country, with the objective to accelerate implementation of such projects which were beyond resource capability of the states or were in advanced stage of completion. Priority was given to those projects which were started in pre-Fifth and Fifth Plan period and also to those which were benefitting tribal and drought prone areas. From1999-2000 onwards, Central Loan Assistance under AIBP was also extended to minor surface irrigation projects of special category states (Northern Eastern states and hilly states of Himachal Pradesh, Sikkim, Jammu and Kashmir, Uttaranchal and projects benefitting Kalahandi Balangir Koraput districts of Odisha).

Command Area Development and Water Management

The Centrally Sponsored Command Area Development (CAD) Programme was launched in 1974-75 for development of adequate delivery system of irrigation water up to farmers' field with an objective to enhance water use efficiency and production and productivity of crops per unit of land and water for improving socio- economic condition of farmers. The pogramme envisages integration of all activities relating to irrigated agriculture in a coordinated manner with multi- disciplinary team under a Command Area Development Authority.

The Programme was restructured and renamed as Command Area Development and Water Management(CAD&WM) Programme in 2004. The Programme is being implemented pari-passu with Accelerated Irrigation Benefits Programme (AIBP) during the XII Five Year Plan. The programme is under implementationas a sub-component of Har Khet Ko Pani (HKKP) component of Pradhan Mantri Krishi Sinchai Yojana (PMKSY) - from 2015-16 onwards. The ongoing CADWM programme has been restricted to the implementation of CAD works of 99 prioritized AIBP projects from 2016-17 onwards. The activities covered under CAD component are broadly categorized as 'Structural' and 'Non-Structural' interventions as detailed here:

(a) structural intervention: includes survey, planning, design and execution of: (i) on-farm Development (OFD) works; (ii) construction of field, intermediate and link drains; (iii) correction of system deficiencies; and (iv) reclamation of waterlogged areas.

(b) non-structural intervention: includes activities directed at strengthening of Participatory Irrigation Management (PIM): (i) one time functional grant to the registered water users' associations (WUAs); (ii) one time Infrastructure Grant to the registered WUAs; (iii)trainings, demonstration, and adaptive trials with respect to water use efficiency, increased productivity, and sustainable irrigation participatory environment.

To promote water use efficiency in irrigation, financial assistance is provided to the states for development of infrastructure for micro-irrigation to facilitate use of sprinkler / drip irrigation as an alternative to construction of field channels. At least 10 per cent CCA of each project is to be covered under micro-irrigation. Micro-irrigation infrastructure includes components of sump, pump, high-density polyethylene pipelines, and pertinent devices needed for bringing efficiency in water conveyance and field applications (through sprinklers, rain guns, pivots, etc). In case of micro-irrigation, other components such as land levelling, drainage works, etc., would be reduced, or entirely discarded; enabling certain cost savings which is expected to offset the higher cost of micro-irrigation infrastructure.The devices - such as sprinkler/ rain gun/ drip sets, etc. - needed to be installed by individual farmers below farm outlets are not part of the micro-irrigation infrastructure. Farmers are expected to bear the cost of such devices or avail subsidies available in extant scheme of the Ministry of Agriculture.

Participatory Irrigation Management

The National Water Policy stresses participatory approach in water resource management. It has been recognized that participation of beneficiaries will help greatly in the optimal upkeep of irrigation system and effective utilization of irrigation water. The participation of farmers in the management of irrigation would include transfer responsibility for operation and maintenance and also collection of water charges to the Water Users' Association in their respective jurisdiction. One time functional grant at ₹1,200/- per hectare to be shared by the centre, state and farmers in the ratio of 45:45:10 respectively is being paid to outlet level water users associations' as incentive, the interest from which is to be used for maintenance.

Flood Management

Flood Management Schemes

Devastation by floods is a recurrent annual phenomenon in India. Almost every year, some or the other part of the country is affected by floods. These cause enormous damage to life, property - public and private, and disruptions to infrastructure, besides psychological and emotional instability amongst the people. Rashtriya Barh Ayog (RBA) had in 1980, estimated flood-prone area in the country as 40 million hectare (mha) which was revised further to 49.815mha by the Working Group on Flood Management set up by the Planning Commission for the XII Five-Year Plan. In order to protect human life, land and property from flood fury the state governments have been engaged in flood management works for the last 5 decades.

Ganga Flood Control Commission

With the objective to effectively tackle critical and chronic flood problems in the Ganga Basin, Ganga Flood Control Board (GFCB) was set up in 1972. The functions include: to lay down the broad policies and decide priorities in the implementation of various schemes, and to issue necessary directions in respect of formulation of comprehensive plan for flood control in the Ganga basin and approval of schemes.

Ganga Flood Control Commission (GFCC), a subordinate office of this Ministry with its headquarters at Patna, was also created in 1972 to act as the secretariat and executive limb of GFCB and to deal with the floods and its management in Ganga Basin states.

There are 11 states in Ganga Basin, namely, West Bengal, Bihar, Uttar Pradesh, Jharkhand, Himachal Pradesh, Uttarakhand, Haryana, Rajasthan, Madhya Pradesh, Chhattisgarh and NCT Delhi. The river systems of Ganga basin are (1) Gomati, (2) Adhwara Group, (3) Ghaghra, (4) Mahananda, (5) KamlaBalan, (6) Burhi Gandak, (7) Bagmati, (8) Punpun, (9) Kosi, (10) Gandak, (11) Ajoy, (12) Kiul-Harohar, (13) Damodar, (14) Mayurakshi, (15) Yamuna, (16) Ramganga, (17) Tons, (18) Badua-Chandan, (19) Rupnarain-Haldi-Rasulpur, (20) Jalangi, (21) Sone, (22) Tidal rivers and (23) Main Ganga. Most of these rivers are inter-state rivers.

Central Ground Water Board

Ground Water Development

There is considerable variation in ground water potential in different parts of the country. While some areas like Indo-Gangetic Alluvium have huge ground water potential, many hard rock areas have limited ground water resources. Similarly, the development of ground water resources in different areas of the country has not been uniform. Highly intensive development of ground water in certain areas in the country has resulted in over - exploitation leading to decline in ground water levels, whereas in some other areas ground water is still sub-optimally developed, leaving scope for future extraction. CGWB carries out periodic assessment of ground water resources jointly with the state ground water departments.

Aquifier Mapping and Formulation of Aquifier Management Plan

Aquifiers are natural rock formations which can store and economically yield water. In the XII Plan, CGWB has taken up the National Project on Aquifier Management (NAQUIM) to facilitate identification, delineation, characterization and effective management of aquifiers to ensure sustainability of ground water resources. The major activities envisaged under the project include compilation of existing data, data gap analysis, generation of additional data for preparation of aquifier map and formulation of aquifier management plans. Each activity has a number of sub-activities and tasks which are being carried out as per detail protocols for implementation.

Demonstrative Projects on "Artificial Recharge to Groundwater and Rainwater Harvesting

CGWB has implemented demonstrative projects on artificial recharge to groundwater and rain water harvesting in Andhra Pradesh, Arunachal Pradesh, Bihar, Chhattisgarh, Delhi, Gujarat, Himachal Pradesh, Jammu & Kashmir, Jharkhand, Karnataka, Kerala, Madhya Pradesh, Maharashtra, Nagaland, Odisha, Punjab, Rajasthan, Tamil Nadu, Telengana, Uttar Pradesh, West Bengal and UT Chandigarh

Central Ground Water Authority

Central Ground Water Authority (CGWA) has been entrusted with the responsibility of regulating and controlling ground water development and management in the country and issuing necessary directives for the purpose. The Authority performs the following functions: exercise of powers under Section 5 of the Environment (Protection) Act, 1986 for issuing directions and taking such measures in respect of all the matters referred to in sub-section (2) of section 3 of the said Act; to resort to penal provisions contained in Sections 15 to 21 of the said Act; to regulate and control, management and development of ground water in the country and to issue necessary regulatory directions for the purpose.

Rajiv Gandhi National Ground Water Training and Research Institute

The Rajiv Gandhi National Ground Water Training and Research Institute (RGNGWTRI) is the training arm of Central Ground Water Board and is located at Raipur, Chhattisgarh. It caters to the training requirements of Central Ground Water Board and other central and state government organizations, academic institutes, NGOs, etc. RGNGWTRI is implementing a three tier (national level, state and block level) training programme keeping in view the requirements of the National Project on Aquifer Management. RGNGWTRI is also mandated to carry out research in the field of ground water.

Central Water Commission

Central Water Commission (CWC) is headed by a Chairman, with the status of an ex-officio Secretary to the Government of India. The work of the Commission is divided among 3 wings namely, Designs and Research Wing (D&R), Water Planning and Projects Wing (WP&P) and River Management Wing (RM). Each wing comprises a number of units/ organizations and is responsible for the disposal of tasks and duties falling within the scope of functions assigned to it. In order to achieve better management in the water resources sector and have better coordination with the state government departments, CWC has established 13 regional offices. The offices are located at Bengaluru, Bhopal, Bhubaneswar, Chandigarh, Coimbatore, Delhi, Hyderabad, Lucknow, Nagpur,

Patna, Shillong, Siliguri and Gandhi Nagar. National Water Academy, the training institute of CWC, is located at Pune for training of central and state in-service engineers, NGO's, etc.

Relevant Website : www.cwc.gov.in

Functions

CWC is charged with the general responsibility of initiating, coordinating and furthering in consultation with the state governments concerned, schemes for control, conservation and utilization of water resources in the respective state for the purpose of flood management, irrigation, drinking water supply and water power generation. The Commission, if so required, can undertake the construction and execution of any such scheme. The main functions of CWC include: to carry out techno-economic appraisal of irrigation, flood control and multipurpose projects proposed by the state governments; to collect, compile, publish and analyse the hydrological and hydro-meteorological data relating to major rivers in the country, consisting of rainfall, runoff and temperature, etc.; to collect, maintain and publish statistical data relating to water resources and its utilization including quality of water throughout the country; to provide flood forecasting services to all major flood prone inter-state river basins of the country; to undertake construction work of any river valley development scheme on behalf of the Government of India or state government concerned; to impart training to in-service engineers from central and state organizations in various aspects of water resource development; to promote modern data collection techniques such as remote sensing technology for water resources development, flood forecasting and development of related computer software; to carry out morphological studies to assess river behaviour, bank erosion/coastal erosion problems and advise the central and state governments on all such matters.

Hydrological Observations

Central Water Commission is operating a network of 878 hydro-meteorological observation stations throughout the country on all major river basins to observe (i) water level (gauge), (ii) discharge, (iii) water quality, (iv) silt (v) selected meteorological parameters including snow observations at key stations. In addition, it also operates 76 exclusive meteorological observation stations. The data so collected is utilized for planning and development of water resources projects, climate change studies, water availability studies, flood / inflow forecasting, examination of international and inter-state issues, river morphological studies, inland waterway development, reservoir siltation studies and research related activities, etc.

Water Quality Monitoring

Central Water Commission is monitoring water quality at 429 key locations covering all the major river basins of India. It is maintaining a three tier laboratory system for analysis of the physio-chemical parameters of the water. The level-I laboratories are located at 406 field water quality monitoring stations on major rivers of the country where physical parameters such as temperature, colour, odour specific conductivity, electrical conductivity, total dissolved solids, pH and dissolved oxygen of river water are observed. There are 18 level-II laboratories located at selected division offices to analyze 25 physio-chemical characteristics and bacteriological parameters of water. Five level-III/II+ laboratories are functioning at Varanasi, Delhi, Hyderabad, Coimbatore and Guwahati where 41 parameters including heavy metals / toxic parameters and pesticides are analyzed. This data is used by different agencies for planning of water resources project, research purposes, etc. The water quality data being so collected are put in various uses related to planning and development of water resources projects.

Flood Forecasting

There are 221 flood forecasting stations, of which 166 are level forecasting and 55 inflow forecasting stations on major dams/barrages. It covers 19 major river systems in the country including 72 river sub-basins. They pertain to 20 states viz., Andhra Pradesh, Arunachal Pradesh, Assam, Bihar, Chattisgarh, Gujarat, Haryana, Jharkhand, Jammu & Kashmir, Karnataka, Madhya Pradesh, Maharashtra, Odisha, Rajasthan, Tamil Nadu, Telengana, Tripura, Uttaranchal, Uttar Pradesh and West Bengal and one union territory Dadra and Nagar Haveli and National Capital Territory of Delhi. On an average, about 6000 forecasts are being issued during flood season every year by the Central Water Commission. Normally, these forecasts are issued 12 to 48 hours in advance, depending upon the river terrain, the locations of the flood forecasting sites and base stations.The current flood forecasting methodology is being modernised using rainfall- runoff mathematical model like Mike-11 and area inundation modelling.

The Commission is carrying out surveys and investigations for preparation of Detailed Project Reports (DPRs) in the NE region, Sikkim, Uttarakhand, Bihar and J&K on the request of the respective states for development of water resource potential for irrigation, hydropower and other uses. The projects which are presently under investigation are Kalez Khola HE Project (Sikkim), Rukni and Sonai Irrigation Project (Assam),Katakhal Irrigation Project(Assam),Kali Khola HE Project (Sikkim), Tarum Chu HE Project(Sikkim), Suntley HE Project(Sikkim), Twalang HE Project(Mizoram),Ujh Multipurpose Project, 280MW , Kathua(J&K), Bariniun HE Project (J&K).

Morphological Studies

The study of river morphology and implementation of suitable river training work as appropriate have become imperative as large areas of the country are affected by floods every year causing severe damage to life and property in spite of existing flood control measures taken both by central and state governments. Problems are aggregating mainly due to large quantity of silt/ sediment being carried and deposited in its downstream reaches. The special behaviour of the river needs to be thoroughly understood for evolving effective strategies to overcome the problem posed by it. Morphological study of three rivers namely, Ghaghra, Sutluj and Gandak has been completed. Further, morphological studies of 15 rivers namely Ganga, Sharda, Rapti, Kosi, Bagmati, Yamuna, Bramhaputra, Subansiri, Pagladiya, Krishna, Tungbhadra, Mahananda, Mahanadi, Hooghly, and Tapti is under progress.

Design Consultancy

Central Water Commission is actively associated with design of majority of the mega water resources projects in India and neighbouring countries viz., Nepal, Bhutan, Afghanistan, Myanmar, Sri Lanka and African countries by way of design consultancy or in the technical appraisal of the projects. Four design units are functioning to cater to specific requirements and to attend to special design related problems of different regions.

Dam Rehabilitation & Improvement Project

Dam Rehabilitation and Improvement Project (DRIP) is the World Bank assisted project at an estimated cost of ₹ 2,100 crore with the provision of rehabilitation of about 223 large dams in the seven participating states (namely Jharkhand, Karnataka, Kerala, Madhya Pradesh, Odisha, Tamil Nadu and Uttarakhand) along with institutional strengthening component for participating states and Central Water Commission.

National Register of Large Dams

As per the latest information compiled under the National Register of Large Dams (NRLD) maintained by CWC, there are 5701 large dams in the country. Out of this, 5254 large dams have been completed and 447 others are under construction. The NRLD is available on CWC website.

Water Resource Information System

CWC and ISRO jointly developed Water Resources Information System (India-WRIS) in 2010. Subsequently, four versions of the website of India-WRIS have been launched. The ver. 4.1 was launched in 2015 and is available in public domain at 1:250000 scale. The information system contains several GIS layers on water resources projects, thematic layers like major water bodies, land use/land cover, wastelands, land degradation, etc., environmental layers as well as infrastructure and other administrative layers. The information system has all the basic map viewing and navigation capabilities like zoom, overview, bookmark, table of contents, etc. As per provision of Hydro-Meteorological Data Dissemination Policy 2013 (MoWR), all unclassified data of CWC G&D stations has been made available on this website.

Training & Capacity Building

Central Water Commission offers training to water sector professionals every year. These training are organised at National Water Academy (NWA), CWC Headquarter and field offices of CWC. The National Water Academy, CWC is a centre of excellence for imparting training on all facets of Water

Resources Development and Management covering the different areas of planning, design, evaluation, construction, operation and monitoring of water resources projects, and also the application of high-end technology in water sector.

National Water Academy

National Water Academy (NWA) is an institute established under Central Water Commission at Khadakwasla, Pune. The objective of NWA is to function as "Centre of Excellence" in training and capacity building for all stakeholders on various aspects of water resources planning, development and management and to develop institutional capability at the national level for imparting training in new emerging technologies in this sector on continued basis. NWA conducts training programmes on whole gamut of water resources development and management comprising both technical and non-technical areas.

Since its inception in 1988, NWA has contributed immensely in the capacity building and training in this sector for all stakeholders including Cadre Training Programmes for Central Water Engineering Services Officers, capacity building for state and central organizations; programmes under PMKSY; programmes for all other stakeholders like teachers, non-governmental organisations (NGOs), Panchayat Raj Institutions (PRIs), media personnel, youth representatives, etc.

Central Soil and Materials Research Station

Central Soil and Materials Research Station (CSMRS), New Delhi, is a premier organization in the country dealing with the field explorations, laboratory investigations, and basic and applied research in the field of geotechnical engineering and civil engineering materials, particularly for construction of river valley projects and safety evaluation of existing dams. The Research Station primarily functions as an adviser and consultant to various departments of Government of India, state governments and Central Undertakings. The Research Station has excellent facilities and highly qualified officers and has acquired some unique capabilities in the country in the field of geotechnical engineering and construction materials' characterisation. It is involved in the safety evaluation of existing hydraulic structures and quality control of construction for various river valley projects including for projects in neighbouring Bhutan and Nepal.

The sphere of activities of the Station is covered under the following core areas: soil mechanics including studies on expansive soils, studies on dispersive soils, hydraulic fracturing of core materials, and quality control, rockfill, soil dynamics, geosynthetics, numerical modelling and quality control concrete diagnostics and chemistry including diagnostic investigation/health monitoring, material for repair and rehabilitation, petrography, chemical investigation, durability of concrete, chemistry and mineralogy, water quality, alkali aggregate reaction, new material such as polymer, grout, etc.; rock mechanics (I) including foundation rock characterisation, in-situ measurements such as in-situ stresses and deformability, geophysical investigations, numerical modelling.

Farakka Barrage Project

Farakka Barrage Project with headquarters at Farakka in Murshidabad district of West Bengal is a subordinate office under the Ministry of Water Resources, River Development and Ganga Rejuvenation. The Farakka Barrage Project Authority was set up in 1961 with the mandate to execute and thereafter operate and maintain the Farakka Barrage Project Complex comprising Farakka Barrage, Jangipur Barrage, Feeder Canal, Navigation Lock and associated structures.

The Barrage comprises 112 Gates (108 no. main Gates and 4 no. Fish Lock Gates) besides 11 nos. Head Regulator Gates for diversion of approximately 40,000 cusecs (1035 cusecs) of discharge into the feeder canal. The main objective of the Project is to divert adequate quantity of Ganga waters to Bhagirathi-Hoogly river system through 38.38 km long feeder canal for preservation and maintenance of Kolkata Port by improving the regime and navigability of the Bhagirathi-Hoogly river system. Further, with the successful accomplishment of time specific anti-erosion and bank protection works in critical reaches on river Ganga / Padma, FBP authority has been able to ensure the safety of Farakka Barrage besides providing reasonable protection from floods to lives and livelihood of local people in the region.Apart from above, Farakka Barrage Project is facilitating implementation of India-Bangladesh Ganga Water Treaty -1996 on sharing of Ganga water between India and Bangladesh.

Betwa River Board

Betwa River Board (B.R.B) was constituted in 1976 to execute the Rajghat Dam Project and Power House. The project authority started construction of the project under the overall guidance of Betwa River Board Act, 1976. The benefits and cost of the above project are shared equally by Uttar Pradesh and Madhya Pradesh.

Sardar Sarovar Construction Advisory Committee

The Sardar Sarovar Construction Advisory Committee (SSCAC) was constituted by the Government of India in accordance with the directives of the Narmada Water Disputes Tribunal (NWDT) in 1980.

The functions of SSCAC include: scrutinizing the project estimates of dam and powerhouse works and recommend for the administrative approval; examining and recommending on all proposals pertaining to technical features and designs; exploring the requirement of funds for the construction of works and other purposes according to the approved programme; recommending on all sub-estimates and contracts, the cost of which exceeds the powers of project officers.

Tungabhadra Board

The Tungabhadra Board was constituted in 1953. The Board consists of representations from Andhra Pradesh, Karnataka, Telangana and Government of India. In the discharge of its assigned functions, the Board exercises powers of a state government. It makes rules for the conduct of its own business. The governments of Andhra Pradesh, Telangana and Karnataka provide funds in agreed proportions and also depute staff to man the various specified posts, as per an agreed proportion.

Upper Yamuna River Board

Upper Yamuna River Board (UYRB) is a subordinate office under this Ministry. The Board was constituted in 1994 with Himachal Pradesh, Haryana, Uttar Pradesh, Rajasthan and National Capital Territory of Delhi as its measure.

It consists of Member, Central Water Commission and one nominee each from Uttar Pradesh, Uttarakhand, Haryana, Rajasthan, Himachal Pradesh, and National Capital Territory of Delhi. The main function of the Board is to regulate the allocation of available flows amongst the beneficiary states and also monitoring the return flows; monitoring conserving and upgrading the quality of surface and ground water; maintaining hydro-meteorological data for the basin; over viewing plans for watershed management; monitoring and reviewing the progress of all projects upto and including Okhla barrage.

Brahmaputra Board

Brahmaputra Board, an autonomous statutory body was set up and started functioning in 1982. The jurisdiction of Brahmaputra Board includes both Brahmaputra and Barak valley and covers all the states of North Eastern Region, Sikkim and Northern part of West Bengal falling under Brahmaputra basin. The major functions of the Board are to carry out survey and investigation and to prepare Master Plan for control of flood, bank erosion and improvement of drainage congestion, development and utilization of water resources of the Brahmaputra and Barak River system for irrigation, hydro power, navigation and for other beneficial purposes.

Narmada Water Dispute Tribunal Award

The Narmada Water Dispute Tribunal (NWDT) was constituted in 1969 to adjudicate upon the water dispute pertaining to river Narmada. The tribunal has ordered setting up of machinery for implementing its directions and decisions. Accordingly, the Central Government framed the Narmada Water Scheme inter-alia constituting the Narmada Control Authority (NCA).

Krishna River Management Board

Krishna River Management Board (KRMB) was contituted in 2014 with autonomous status under this Ministry. The functions of the Board are: regulation of supply of water from the projects to the respective states having regard to: awards granted by the Tribunals constituted under the Inter-State River Water Disputes Act, 1956; any agreement entered into or arrangement made covering the Andhra Pradesh Government and any other state or union territory; the construction of such remaining on-going or new works connected with the development of the water resource projects relating to the rivers or their tributaries through the successor states as the central government may specify; making an appraisal of any proposal for construction of new projects on Godavari or Krishna rivers and giving technical clearance, after satisfying that such projects do not negatively impact the availability of water as per the awards of the Tribunals constituted under the Inter-State River Water Disputes Act, 1956 for the projects already completed or taken up before the appointed day; and such other functions as the central government may entrust to it on the basis of the principles specified in the Eleventh Schedule.

Polavaram Project Authority

Polavaram Irrigation Project is a multi-purpose irrigation project which is on the river Godavari near Ramayyapeta village of Polavarammandal about 42km upstream of Sir Arthur Cotton Barrage, where river emerges out of last range of the Eastern Ghats and enters the plains in West Godavari District of Andhra Pradesh. It envisages construction of a dam to create ultimate irrigation potential of 2.91 lakh ha. The project also envisages generation of 960MW of hydro power, drinking water supply to a population of 28.50 lakh in 540 villages, diversion of 80TMC of water to Krishna river basin, sharing of 5 TMC and 1.5 TMC water with Odisha and Chhattisgarh, respectively. It creates an irrigation potential of 7.2 lakh acres (2.91 lakh ha) in East Godavari, Visakhapatnam, West Godavari and Krishna districts.

Indo-Bangladesh Water Resources Cooperation

An Indo-Bangladesh Joint Rivers Commission (JRC) is functioning since 1972 with a view to maintain liaison in order to ensure most effective joint efforts in maximizing the benefits from common river systems. A Treaty was signed by the Prime Ministers of India and Bangladesh in 1996 for the sharing of Ganga/ Ganges waters at Farakka during the lean season. As per the Treaty, the Ganga/ Ganges waters is being shared at Farakka (which is the last control structure on river in India) during lean period, from 1st January to 31st May every year, on 10-daily basis as per the formula provided in the Treaty. The validity of Treaty is 30 years.

India Nepal Water Resource Cooperation

The management of floods due to the rivers flowing into India from Nepal has been a concern and the related issues are discussed in the existing Indo-Nepal bilateral mechanisms comprising (i) Joint Ministerial Commission on Water Resources (JMCWR),(ii) Joint Committee on Water Resources (JCWR) and (iii) Joint Standing Technical Committee(JSTC) (iv) Joint Committee on Inundation of Flood Management (JCIFM) (v)Joint Committee on KosiGandakProiects (JCKGP). Government of India has been constantly persuading the Government of Nepal for constructionof storage dams on these rivers for mutual benefit of the two countries.

Indus Waters Treaty

Under the Indus Waters Treaty 1960, India and Pakistan have each created a permanent post of Commissioner for Indus Waters. Each Commissioner is the representative of his government and serves as a regular channel of communication on all matters relating to implementation of the Treaty. The two Commissioners together form the Permanent Indus Commission (PIC).

National Water Development Agency

The National Water Development Agency was set up in 1982 to study the feasibility of the links under peninsular component of national perspective plan. The NWDA is fully funded by Government of India. Its functions were subsequently modified from time to time and the present functions include: (a) to carry out detailed survey and investigations of possible reservoir sites and inter-connecting links in order to establish feasibility of the proposal of peninsular river development and Himalayan river development components forming part of the National Perspective for Water Resources Development; (b) to carry out detailed studies about the quantum of water in various peninsular river systems and Himalayan river systems which can be transferred to other basins/states after meeting the reasonable needs of the basin/states in the foreseeable future; (c) to undertake/construct/repair/renovate/rehabilitate/ implement the projects either on its own or through an appointed agency/ organization/PSU or company and the projects forming part of interlinking of rivers, for completion of projects falling under PMKSY of which projects under Accelerated Irrigation Benefits Programme are also included and similar other projects.

National Institute of Hydrology

The National Institute of Hydrology (NIH), established in 1978 as an autonomous organization under this Ministry, is a premier R&D institute in the country to undertake, aid, promote and coordinate basic, applied and strategic research on all aspects of hydrology and water resources development. The Institute has its headquarters at Roorkee (Uttarakhand). To carry out field related research covering different regions of the country, it has four regional centres located at Belgaum, Jammu, Kakinada and Bhopal, and two centres for Flood Management Studies at Guwahati and Patna.

The objectives of the Institute are: (a) to undertake, aid, promote and coordinate systematic and scientific work on all aspects of hydrology; (b) to cooperate and collaborate with other national and international organizations in the field of hydrology; (c) to establish and maintain a research and reference library in pursuance of the objectives of the society and equip the same with books, reviews, magazines and other relevant publications; and (d) to do all other such things as it may consider necessary, incidental or conducive to the attainment of the objectives for which the Institute has been established. To fulfil these objectives, the Institute has established state-of-art laboratory facilities in nuclear applications in hydrology, water quality, soil water, remote sensing and GIS applications, snow and glacier, numerical groundwater modelling and hydrological instrumentation.

The Institute acts as a centre of excellence for transfer of technology, human resources development and institutional development in specialized areas of hydrology, and conducts user defined, demand-driven research through collaboration with relevant national and international organizations.

National Projects Construction Corporation Limited

National Projects Construction Corporation Limited (NPCC) was established in 1957 as a premier construction company to create necessary infrastructure for economic development of the country. NPCC comply with quality management requirements of ISO 9001-2008 for execution of civil works for thermal and hydro electric projects, river valley projects, industrial structures, project management consultancy services for buildings, housings, roads, bridges and infrastructure projects. In its 59 years of existence the Corporation has successfully associated itself with completion of several national projects from concept to commissioning stage. Some of them are in remote and hazardous location over the country.

Water and Power Consultancy Services

To utilise the expertise of the engineers who had carried out pioneering work and to share the knowledge and experience with other developing countries and in turn earning foreign currency Water and Power Consultancy Services (WAPCOS) was established in 1969. WAPCOS provided opportunities to Indian engineers to work in diverse geographical and climatic regions thereby enhancing India's knowledge and expertise. India came to be recognised for its cost effective technical know-how and dedicated technical manpower. Diplomatic initiatives were facilitated to forge long-term friendships with other developing countries and consultancy services contributed in their own small way in the economic development by earning valuable foreign exchange. Gradually other consultancy organisations established themselves and finally earned name and fame on the strength of the Indian human resources and innovative technology.

Main fields of specialization of the Company cover irrigation, drainage and water management, ground water exploration and minor irrigation, flood control and river morphology, river management, dams and reservoir engineering, water bodies and land conservation, agriculture, watershed management, natural resources management, hydropower, thermal power, pumped storage project, transmission and distribution, rural electrification, non-conventional sources of energy, water supply, sanitation and drainage, environment, ports, harbours and inland waterways, urban and rural areas development, roads and highway engineering, buildings and townships. The Company provides concept to commissioning services for developmental projects in India and abroad.

Consultancy services have made a niche in the innovative as well as conventional fields and have effectively contributed in the development process of the nation. Healthy growth trends all over the world call for requisition of services of consultants for high quality jobs and realization of the need for professional involvement has widened the vistas for consultants to operate.

Immediately after independence, attention was focussed on the construction of water resources and power projects across India. Nearly 4300 large dams (including 695 under construction) have been built and constructed along with canal systems and allied structures. Some of the multipurpose projects like Bhakra Dam, Hirakud Dam, Nagarjuna Dam and Dantewada Dam find mention amongst the world's largest projects. In the first two decades after independence, foreign consultants had to be engaged for the planning and construction of large dams.

North Eastern Regional Institute of Water and Land Management

The North Eastern Regional Institute of Water and Land Management (NERIWALM) was established at Tezpur, Assam by North Eastern Council (NEC), in 1989. The Institute is under the administrative control of this Ministry. The Institute is situated in 3km away from the historically famous town of Tezpur, Sonitpur district of Assam which is located on the north bank of mighty river Brahmaputra at about 180 km from Guwahati. It is connected by road, rail and air with other parts of the country.

The main objective of the Institute is to provide capacity building, undertake research and provide technical services to the line departments in order to improve agricultural production and socio-economic status of the people in north east.

Minor Irrigation and Water Bodies Census

A Centrally Sponsored Scheme, Rationalization of Minor Irrigation Statistics (RMIS) was launched in 1987-88 in the Ministry of Water Resources, with cent per cent assistance to the states/UTs. During the Eleventh Five Year Plan, the RMIS scheme was converted as one of the components of the Central Sector Scheme - Development of Water Resources Information System (DWRIS). In 2017-18, the scheme was renamed as "Irrigation Census" and brought under the umbrella scheme," Prime Minister's Krishi Sinchai Yojana and other Schemes". The main objective of the Irrigation Census scheme is to build up a comprehensive and reliable database in the Minor Irrigation (MI) sector for effective planningand policymaking. Under it, each state/UT has identified a nodal department for compilation of minor irrigation statistics for the entire state/UT.

Data base on Minor Irrigation (MI) schemes plays an important role in policy formulation for water resources available in the country. MI censuses are a rich source of information on India's ground water sector. In the MI Censuses detailed information on various aspects/parameters like irrigation sources (dug well, shallow tube well, medium tube well, deep tube well, surface flow and surface lift schemes),irrigation potential created, potential utilized, ownership,holding size of land by the owner, devices used for lifting water, source of energy, energy conserving devices such as sprinkler and dripirrigation, use of non-conventional energy sources such as solar pumps, windmills etc. is collected.

Detailed database on minor irrigation works in the country has been generated through five censuses carried out under the scheme so far with reference years 1986-87, 1993-94, 2000-01, 2006-07 and 2013-14 respectively.The census reports are available on the website of this Ministry.

28 Welfare

IN 1985-86, the erstwhile Ministry of Welfare was bifurcated into the Department of Women and Child Development and the Department of Welfare. Simultaneously, the Scheduled Castes Development Division, Tribal Development Division and the Minorities and Backward Classes Welfare Division were shifted from the Ministry of Home Affairs and also the Wakf Division from the Ministry of Law to form the then Ministry of Welfare.

Subsequently, the name of the Ministry was changed to the Ministry of Social Justice and Empowerment in May, 1998. Further, in October, 1999, the Tribal Development Division was moved out to form a separate Ministry of Tribal Affairs. In January, 2007 the Minorities Division along with Wakf Unit were moved out of the Ministry and formed a separate Ministry and the Child Development Division was merged with the Ministry of Women and Child Development..

Two departments have been created under the Ministry of Social Justice and Empowerment namely: (i) Department of Social Justice and Empowerment (Samajik Nyaya and Adhikarita Vibhag) (ii) Department of Disability Affairs (Nishaktata Karya Vibhag) since renamed as Department of Empowerment of Persons with Disabilities (Divyangjan).

Relevant Websites : www.socialjustice.nic.in www.disabilityaffairs.gov.in

Welfare of Scheduled Castes and Scheduled Tribes

The Constitution contains several provisions in the nature of safeguards for the Scheduled Castes. The following two Acts specifically aim at curbing (i) untouchability and (ii) atrocities against SCs and STs, and are therefore very important for the Scheduled Castes— (i) The Protection of Civil Rights Act, 1955, and (ii) The Scheduled Castes and the Scheduled Tribes (Prevention of Atrocities) Act, 1989.

Protection of Civil Rights

In pursuance of Article 17 of the Constitution of India, the Untouchability (Offences) Act, 1955 was enacted. Subsequently, it was amended and renamed in 1976 as the Protection of Civil Rights Act, 1955. Rules under this Act, viz., The Protection of Civil Rights Rules, 1977 were notified in 1977. The Act extends to the whole of the country and provides punishment for the practice of untouchability. It is implemented by the respective state governments and union territory administrations.

Scheduled Castes and the Scheduled Tribes (Prevention of Atrocities) Act

The Scheduled Castes and the Scheduled Tribes (Prevention of Atrocities) Act, 1989 (The PoA Act) came into force in 1990. This legislation aims at preventing commission of offences by persons other than scheduled castes and scheduled tribes against scheduled castes and scheduled tribes.

Comprehensive Rules under this Act, titled Scheduled Castes and the Scheduled Tribes (Prevention of Atrocities) Rules, 1995 were notified in 1995, which, *inter-alia*, provide norms for relief and rehabilitation. These Rules had not been amended thereafter.

Scheduled Castes and Scheduled Tribes (Prevention of Atrocities) Amendment Act, 2015 and 2016

Despite the deterrent provisions made in the PoA Act, continuing atrocities against the members of Scheduled Castes (SCs) and Scheduled Tribes (STs) had been a cause of concern. High incidence of occurrences of offences against members of SCs and STs also indicated that the deterrent effect of the PoA Act was not adequately felt by the accused. It was, therefore, considered appropriate to strengthen the Act and make the relevant provisions more effective. Based on the consultation process with all the stakeholders, amendments in the PoA Act were proposed to broadly cover five areas. There have been addition of several new offences and rephrasing of existing ones. The establishment of exclusive special courts for the speedy trial of offences of atrocities against the members of SCs and STs and specification of exclusive special public prosecutor are provided. A new chapter relating to Rights of Victims and Witnesses is inserted. Certain duties and responsibilities are imposed upon the State for making necessary arrangement for protection of victims, their defendants and witnesses.

Relief amount for 47 offences of atrocities is provided for and phasing of payment of relief amount rationalised. Relief amount is enhanced between ₹ 85,000/- to ₹ 8,25,000/- depending upon the nature of the offence. The admissible relief is to be paid within seven days. Investigation and filing of charge sheet is to be done within sixty days.

National Commission for Scheduled Castes

The National Commission for SCs and STs (NCSC) which was set up under Article 383 of the Constitution in 1990 was bifurcated into two Commissions namely, National Commission for Scheduled Castes and National Commission for Scheduled Tribes after the 89th Constitutional (Amendment) Act, 2003. The National Commission for Scheduled Castes is responsible for monitoring the safeguards provided for Scheduled Castes and also to review issues concerning their welfare. Functions of the NCSC as enumerated in the Article 338(5) of the Constitution are– (a) to investigate and monitor all matters relating to the safeguards provided for the scheduled castes under the Constitution or under any other law for the time being in force or under any order of the Government and to evaluate the working of such safeguards; (b) to inquire into specific complaints with respect to the deprivation of rights and safeguards of the scheduled castes; (c) to participate and advise on the planning process of socio-economic development of the scheduled castes and to evaluate the progress of their development under the Union and any state; (d) to present to the President, annually and at such other times as the Commission may deem fit, reports upon the working of those safeguards; (e) to make in such reports, recommendations as to the measures that should be taken by the Union or any state for the effective implementation of those safeguards and other measures for the protection, welfare and socio-economic development of the scheduled castes; and (f) to discharge such other functions in relation to the protection, welfare and development and advancement of the scheduled castes as the President may, subject to the provisions of any law made by Parliament, by rule specify.

Relevant Website : www.ncsc.nic.in

Educational Empowerment

Pre-Matric Scholarship

This is also a centrally sponsored Scheme, which is implemented by the state governments and union territory administrations, which receive 100 per cent central assistance for the total expenditure under the scheme, over and above their respective committed liability. The level of committed liability of respective state governments/union territory administrations for a year is equivalent to the level of actual expenditure incurred by them under the Scheme during the terminal year of the last Five Year Plan. It was started in 1977-78. Initially, it covered only hostellers. Subsequently, in 1991 day scholars were also brought within its purview. Under the Scheme financial assistance is provided for pre-matric education to children of the following target groups, viz., (i) scavengers of dry latrines, (ii) tanners, (iii) flayers and (iv) waste pickers.

Pre-Matric Scholarship for SC Students

The Scheme was introduced in 2012. The Scheme is centrally sponsored and implemented by the state governments and union territory administrations, which provides 100 per cent assistance from Government of India for expenditure under the Scheme, over and above their committed liability. The level of committed liability of a state government/union territory administration for a year will be equivalent to the level of actual expenditure incurred by them under the Scheme during the terminal year of the previous Five Year Plan Period, and will be required to be borne by them by making provision in their own budget.

National Overseas Scholarship for SCs

The Scheme provides for fees charged by institutions as per actual, monthly maintenance allowance, passage visa fee and insurance premium, annual contingency allowance, incidental journey allowance. Only two children of the same parents/ guardians are eligible to get benefit under the Scheme. The second child of the same parents/guardian will be considered only if the slots are still available for that year. The prospective awardees should not be more than 35 years of age. The total number of awards (maximum) to be given each year is 100 and 30 per cent of the awards have been earmarked for women candidates. During 2016- 17 the unfilled slots of 2014-15 and 2015-16 were carried forward to 2016-17. Financial assistance under the Scheme is provided for a maximum period of 4 years for Ph.D and 3 years for Masters programme. The income ceiling from all sources of the employed candidate or his/her parents/guardians should not be more than ₹ 50,000/- per month

Babu Jagjivan Ram Chhatrawas Yojana

The objective of the Scheme is to provide hostel facilities to SC boys and girls studying in middle schools, higher secondary schools, colleges and universities. The state governments/union territory administrations and the central and state universities/institutions are eligible for central assistance, both for fresh construction of hostel buildings and for expansion of the existing hostel facilities while NGOs and deemed universities in the private sector can avail the benefit only for expansion of their existing hostel facilities.

Rajiv Gandhi National Fellowship for SC Students

The Scheme provides financial assistance to scheduled caste students for pursuing research studies leading to M. Phil, Ph.D, and equivalent research degree in universities, research institutions and scientific institutions. University Grants Commission (UGC) is the nodal agency for implementing the Scheme. About 2000 Junior Research Fellowships (JRF) per year are awarded to scheduled caste students. Number of fellowships were increased from 1333 in 2010 to 2000 in 2011. In case of non-availability of adequate number of scheduled caste candidates, the number of fellowships not availed during a year will be carried forward to the next academic session. In case, the number of candidates exceeds the number of available awards, the UGC selects the candidates based on the percentage of marks obtained by the candidates in their post graduation examination. There is no income ceiling prescribed under the Scheme.

Special Central Assistance

Scheduled Castes Sub Plan

Special Central Assistance (SCA) to Scheduled Castes Sub Plan (SCSP) is a central sector Scheme, started in 1980, under which 100 per cent grant is given to the states/UTs, as an additive to their Scheduled Castes Sub Plan (SCSP). The main objective is to give a thrust to family oriented schemes of economic development of SCs below the poverty line.

Scheduled Castes Development Corporations

The centrally sponsored scheme for participating in the equity share of the Scheduled Castes Development Corporations (SCDCs) in the ratio of 49:51 (central/state) was introduced in 1979. At present, SCDCs are functioning in 27 states/UTs. The main functions of such corporations are identification of eligible SC families and motivating them to undertake economic development schemes, sponsoring the schemes to financial institutions for credit support, providing financial assistance in the form of margin money at low rate of interest and subsidy in order to reduce the repayment liability and providing necessary tie up with other poverty alleviation programmes. These Corporations are playing an important role in providing credit and inputs by way of margin money loans and subsidy to the target group.

National Scheduled Castes Finance and Development Corporation

The National Scheduled Castes Finance and Development Corporation (NSFDC) was set up in 1989 under Section 8 of the Companies Act, 2013 (formerly Section 25 of the Companies Act, 1956). The broad objective of NSFDC is to provide financial assistance in the form of concessional loans to scheduled caste families, and skill-cum-entrepreneurial training to the youth of the target group, living below double the poverty line for their economic development.

Venture Capital Fund for Scheduled Castes

Government announced the setting up of a Venture Capital Fund for Scheduled Castes in 2014. This was to promote entrepreneurship among the scheduled castes and to provide concessional finance to them.

Credit Enhancement Guarantee Scheme for Scheduled Castes

In 2014, the government announced that a sum of ₹ 200 crore will be allocated towards credit enhancement facility for young and start-up entrepreneurs, belonging to scheduled castes, who aspire to be part of neo-middle class category with an objective to encourage entrepreneurship in the lower strata of the society resulting in job creation.

Welfare of Persons with Disabilities

In order to give focused attention to different policy issues and meaningful thrust to the activities aimed at welfare and empowerment of the Persons with Disabilities, a separate Department of Disability Affairs was carved out of the Ministry of Social Justice and Empowerment in 2012. The Department acts as a nodal agency for matters pertaining to disability and persons with disabilities including effecting closer coordination among different stakeholders : related central ministries, state/UT governments, NGOs etc., in matters pertaining to disability. According to Census 2011, there are 2.68 crore persons with disabilities in the country (who constitute 2.21 per cent of the total population). Out of the total population of persons with disabilities, about 1.50 crore are men and 1.18 crore are women. These include persons with visual, hearing, speech and locomotor disabilities, mental illness, mental retardation, multiple disabilities and other disabilities.

Constitutional Provisions

The Constitution of India through its Preamble, *inter-alia* seeks to secure to all its citizens; justice, social, economic and political; liberty of thought, expression, belief, faith and worship; equality of status and of opportunity. Part-III of the Constitution provides for a set of six Fundamental Rights to all the citizens (and in a few cases to non-citizens also). These include - Right to Equality; Right to Freedom; Right against Exploitation; Right to Freedom of Religion; Cultural and Educational Rights and Right to Constitutional Remedies. All these rights are also available to the Persons with Disabilities even though no specific mention of such persons appear in this Part of the Constitution.

The Directive Principles of State Policy have been incorporated in Part-IV of the Constitution. Even though non-justiciable, these have been declared as fundamental in the governance of the country. These principles are intended to be the imperative basis of State policy. These are really in the nature of instructions issued to future legislatures and executives for their guidance. Article 41: Right to work, to education and to public assistance in certain cases, provides: "The State shall, within the limits of its economic capacity and development, make effective provision for securing the right to work, to education and to public assistance in case of unemployment, old age, sickness and disablement and in other cases of undeserved want". Besides, Eleventh Schedule to Article 243-G and Twelfth Schedule to Article 243-W, which pertain to the powers and responsibilities of the Panchayats and municipalities respectively with respect to implementation of schemes for economic development and social justice, include welfare and safeguarding the interests of Persons with Disabilities among other weaker sections of the society.

The Department deals with the following legislations governing different aspects of disability and welfare and empowerment of the Persons with Disabilities— The Rehabilitation Council of India Act, 1992; The Persons with Disabilities (Equal Opportunities, Protection of Rights and Full Participation) Act, 1995; and The National Trust for the Welfare of Persons with Autism, Cerebral Palsy, Mental Retardation and Multiple Disabilities Act, 1999.

Department of Empowerment of Persons with Disabilities (DEPwD), has formulated the accessible India Campaign (Sugamya Bharat Abhiyan), as a nation-wide campaign for achieving universal accessibility for PwDs. The campaign targets three separate verticals for achieving universal accessibilities, namely, the built up environment, transportation eco-system and information and communication eco-system. The campaign has ambitious targets with defined timelines and will use IT and social media for spreading awareness about the campaign and seeking commitment/engagement of various stakeholders. The Department has asked various states to identify about 50 to 100 public buildings in big cities and also identify citizen centric public websites, which if made fully accessible would have the highest impact on the lives of PwDs. Once identified "Access Audit" of these buildings and websities will be conducted by professional agencies. As per the audit findings, retrofitting and conversion of buildings, transport and websites would be undertaken by various government departments. This will be supported by the Scheme of Implementation of Persons with Disabilities Act (SIPDA), an umbrella scheme run by the DEPwD for implementing various initiatives for social and economic empowerment of PwDs.

The Department is collaborating with Ministry of Home, Ministry of Health and Family Welfare and Ministry of Tourism for creating "accessible police station", "accessible hospitals" and "accessible tourism" respectively across the country. The Department is also coordinating with the Ministry of Information and Broadcasting for enhancing accessibility of television programmes by incorporating features like captioning, text to speech and audio description. DEPwD is also in the process of creating a mobile app, along with a web portal for crowd sourcing the request regarding inaccessible places. With the app, downloaded on his/her mobile phone, any person would be able to click a photograph or video of an inaccessible public place (like a school, hospital, government office etc.) and upload the same to the Accessible India portal. The portal will process the request for access audit, financial sanction and find retrofitting of the building to make it completely accessible.

Persons with Disability

Section 2 (t) of the Persons with Disabilities (Equal Opportunities, Protection of Rights and Full Participation) Act, 1995, defines a person suffering from not less than 40 per cent of any disability as certified by a medical authority. The disability being blindness (b) low vision (c) leprosy cured (d) hearing impairment (e) loco-motor disability (f) mental illness (g) mental retardation (h) autism (i) cerebral palsy or (j) a combination of any two or more of (g), (h) and (i) (Section 2 (i) of the PwD Act, 1995 read alongwith Section 2(j) of The National Trust for Welfare of Persons with Autism, Cerebral Palsy, Mental Retardation and Multiple Disabilities Act, 1999).

Mental Health Act

Mental illness has been recognized as one of the disabilities under the Persons with Disabilities (Equal Opportunities, Protection of Rights and Full Participation) Act, 1995. The treatment and care of the mentally ill persons are governed by the Mental Health Act, 1987. The Act is administered by the Ministry of Health and Family Welfare.

Persons with Disabilities Act

A comprehensive law, namely, the Persons with Disabilities (Equal Opportunities, Protection of Rights and Full Participation) Act, 1995 was enacted and enforced in 1996. The law deals with both prevention and promotion aspects of the rehabilitation such as education, employment and vocational training, creation of barrier-free environment, provision of rehabilitation services for persons with disabilities, institutional services and supportive social security measures like unemployment allowance and grievance redressal machinery both at the central and state level. National Trust for the Welfare of Persons with Autism, Cerebral Palsy, Mental Retardation and Multiple Disabilities is a statutory body under The National Trust for the Welfare of Persons with Autism,

Cerebral Palsy, Mental Retardation and Multiple Disabilities Act, 1999. The main objectives of the Trust are to enable and empower persons with these disabilities to live independently as fully as possible, to extend support to registered organisations providing need-based services and to evolve procedure for appointment of legal guardians for persons with disabilities requiring such protection.

Chief Commissioner for Persons with Disabilities

The Chief Commissioner is an important statutory functionary, appointed under Section 57 of the Persons with Disabilities (Equal Opportunities, Protection of Rights and Full Participation) Act, 1995. The functions and duties of the Chief commissioner include: coordinating the work of state commissioners for persons with disabilities, monitoring of utilisation of funds disbursed by the central government, taking steps to safeguard rights and facilities made available to persons with disabilities and also to look into complaints with respect to deprivation of rights of persons with disabilities. The Chief Commissioner can also take *suo moto* notice of non-implementation of any rule, law, etc., meant for persons with disabilities and is vested with the powers of a civil court relating to summoning of witness, discovery, requistioning and production of any document, etc.

Rehabilitation Council

The Rehabilitation Council of India is a statutory body set up under the Rehabilitation Council of India Act, 1992. The Council is responsible for regulating the training policies and programmes for various categories of professionals in the area of rehabilitation and special education. Its functions include: (i) standardisation and regulation of training courses at different levels in all the training institutions throughout the country, (ii) recognition of institutions/universities running training courses in the area of rehabilitation of the disabled within and outside the country on a reciprocal basis, (iii) promotion of research in rehabilitation and special education (iv) maintenance of a central rehabilitation register for professionals possessing the recognised rehabilitation qualifications in the area of rehabilitation and (v) encouragement of continuing rehabilitation education programmes in collaboration with organisations working in the area of disability.

Relevant Website : www.rehabcouncil.nic.in

National Institutes

In order to effectively deal with the multi-dimensional problem of the disabled population, the following national institutes/apex level institutes have been set-up in each major area of disability; (i) National Institute for the Visually Handicapped, Dehradun, (ii) National Institute for Orthopaedically Handicapped, Kolkata, (iii) Ali Yavar Jung National Institute for the Hearing Handicapped, Mumbai, (iv) National Institute for the Mentally Handicapped, Secunderabad, (v) National Institute of Rehabilitaion Training and Research, Cuttack, (vi), Institute for the Physically Handicapped, New Delhi, (vii) National

Institute for Empowerment of Persons with Multiple Disabilities, Chennai. These institutes are mainly responsible for conducting innovative researches, organise training programmes for manpower development and deliver services in the country. Artificial Limbs Manufacturing Corporation of India (ALIMCO), Kanpur is a public sector body, engaged in manufacturing of aids and appliances for persons with disabilities. The products manufactured by the Corporation conform to ISI standards approved by the Bureau of Indian Standards. Marketing of products is done through regional marketing centres at Kolkata, Mumbai, Chennai, Bhubaneshwar and Delhi and also through national institutes, voluntary organisations.

Five Composite Regional Centres (CRCs) for the Persons with Disabilities are located at Srinagar, Lucknow, Bhopal, Sundernagar and Guwahati. These centres conduct training programmes to prepare professionals in the field of rehabilitation as well as provide rehabilitation services to the disabled. Four Regional Rehabilitation Centres for Spinal Injuries and other Disabilities at Mohali, Cuttack, Jabalpur and Bareilly are providing services for basic management and follow-up of the spinally injured so as to make the affected persons functionally independent.

Economic Development

The National Handicapped Finance and Development Corporation (NHFDC) is an apex-level financial institution for extending credit facilities to persons with disabilities for their economic development. Funds assistance is disbursed through the channelising agencies authorized by the state governments/UT administrations and non-governmental organisations. It also extends loans for pursuing education at graduate and higher levels. Besides, it assists in the upgradation of technical and entrepreneurial skills to enable beneficiaries to manage their production units efficiently.

Relevant Website : www.nhfdc.nic.in

Assistance to Disabled Persons for Purchase of Appliances

Under the Scheme for Assistance to Disabled Persons for Purchase/Fitting of AIDs and Appliances assistance is given for procuring durable, sophisticated and scientifically manufactured, standard aids and appliances that can promote their physical, social and psychological rehabilitation by reducing the impact of disability and enhance their economic potential. It is implemented through agencies like voluntary organisations, national institutes under the Ministry, ALIMCO, Zilla Panchayats, DRDAs, etc. The implementing agencies are provided grant-in-aid for purchase, fabrication and distribution of aids and appliances. The Scheme also includes under its ambit medical/surgical correction and intervention that may be essential prior to fitment of aids and appliances.

Tribal Affairs

Development of Scheduled Tribes

The Ministry of Tribal Affairs was set up in 1999 after the bifurcation of Ministry of Social Justice and Empowerment with the objective of providing more focused approach on the integrated socio-economic development of the Scheduled Tribes (STs), the most underprivileged of the society, in a coordinated and planned manner. Before the formation of the Ministry, tribal affairs was handled by different ministries at different points in time. It is the nodal Ministry for overall policy, planning and coordination of programmes for development of ST's. To this end , this Ministry has undertaken activities that follow from the subjects allocated under the Government of India (Allocation of Business) Rules, 1961.

Relevant Website : www.tribal.nic.in

Scheduled Areas and Tribal Areas

Scheduled Tribes live in contiguous areas unlike other communities. It is, therefore, much simpler to have an area approach for development activities and also regulatory provisions to protect their interests. In order to protect the interests of scheduled tribes with regard to land alienation and other social factors, provisions of the Fifth Schedule and Sixth Schedule have been enshrined in the Constitution.

The Fifth Schedule under Article 244 (1) of Constitution defines "Scheduled Areas" as such areas as the President may by Order declare to be Scheduled Areas after consultation with the Governor of the state. The Sixth Schedule under Article 244 (2) of the Constitution relates to those areas in the states of Assam, Meghalaya, Tripura and Mizoram which are declared as "Tribal Areas" and provides for district councils and/or regional councils for such areas. These Councils have been conferred with wide ranging legislative, judicial and executive powers. The criteria for declaring any area as a "Scheduled Area" under the Fifth Schedule are: (a) preponderance of tribal population, (b) compactness and reasonable size of the area, (c) a viable administrative entity such as a district, block or taluk, and (d) economic backwardness of the area as compared to neighbouring areas. The specification of "Scheduled Areas" in relation to a state is done by a notified order of the President, after consultation with the state governments concerned. The same applies for altering, increasing, decreasing, incorporating new areas, or rescinding any orders relating to "Scheduled Areas".

The advantages of Scheduled Areas are that: (a) the Governor of a state, which has Scheduled Areas, is empowered to make regulations in respect of the following: (i) prohibit or restrict transfer of land from tribal people; (ii) regulate the business of money lending to the members of scheduled tribes. In making any such regulation, the Governor may repeal or amend any Act of Parliament or of the Legislature of the state which is applicable to the area in question; (ii) The Governor may through public notification direct that any particular Act of Parliament or of the legislature of the state, shall not apply to a Scheduled Area or any part thereof in the state or shall apply to such area subject to such exceptions and modifications as he may specify; (c) the Governor of a state having Scheduled Areas therein, shall annually, or whenever so required by the President of India, make a report to the President regarding the administration of the Scheduled Areas in that state and the executive power of the Union shall extend to the giving of directions to the state as to the administration of the said area; (d) Tribes Advisory Council (TAC) shall be established in states having Scheduled Areas. The role of TAC is to advise the state government on matters pertaining to the welfare and advancement of the scheduled tribes in the state as may be referred to it by the Governor. The TAC will consist of not more than twenty members of whom about 3/4 are to be from ST-MLAs. The TAC may also be established in any state having scheduled tribes but not Scheduled Areas on the direction of the President of India; (e) the Provisions of the Panchayats (Extension to Scheduled Areas) Act, 1996 (PESA), vide which the provisions of Panchayats, contained in Part IX of the Constitution, were extended to Scheduled Areas, also contain special provisions for the benefit of scheduled tribes. The Sixth Schedule under Article 244 of the Constitution identifies autonomous districts in the tribal areas in Assam, Meghalaya, Tripura and Mizoram. It also makes provisions for recognition of autonomous regions within these autonomous districts. These have been specified in Parts I, II, II A and III of the table appended to paragraph 20 of the Sixth Schedule. In other words, areas where provisions of Sixth Schedule are applicable are known as Tribal Areas. The state-wise details of Tribal Areas are as:-

Part-I Assam 1. The North Cachar Hills District; 2. The Karbi-Anglong District; and 3. The Bodo Land Territorial Area Districts; Part II Meghalaya 1. Khasi Hills District; 2. Jaintia Hills District; and 3. The Garo Hills District; Part II Tripura; Tripura Tribal Areas District; and Part III Mizoram 1. The Chakma District 2. The Mara District; and 3. The Lai District

The district or regional councils are empowered to make rules with the approval of the Governor with regard to matters like establishment, construction or management of primary schools, dispensaries, markets, cattle ponds, ferries, fisheries, roads, road transport and waterways in the district. The Autonomous Councils of the North Cachar Hills and Karbi Anglong have been granted additional powers to make laws with respect to other matters like secondary education, agriculture, social security and social insurance, public health and sanitation, minor irrigation, etc., The councils have also been conferred powers under the Civil Procedure Code and Criminal Procedure Code for trial of certain suits and offences, as also the powers of a revenue authority for their area for collection of revenue and taxes and other powers for the regulation and management of natural resources.

Procedure for Declaration as ST

The term scheduled tribes is defined in the Constitution of India under Article 366(25) as such tribes or tribal communities or parts of groups within such tribes or tribal communities as are deemed under Article 342 to be scheduled tribes. Article 342 prescribes the procedure to be followed in the matter of specification of scheduled tribes. In terms of Article 342(1), the President may, with respect to any state or union territory, and where it is a state, after consultation with the Governor thereof, notify tribes or tribal communities or parts thereof as scheduled tribes. This confers on the tribe or part of it a constitutional status invoking the safeguards provided for in the Constitution, to these communities, in their respective states/UTs. Thus, in terms of Article 342(1), only those communities who have been declared as such by the President through an initial public notification will be considered as scheduled tribes. Any further amendment in the list is to be done through an Act of Parliament (Article 342(2)). Parliament may, by law, include in or exclude from the list of scheduled tribes, any tribe or tribal community or parts thereof. The list of scheduled tribes is state-specific. In other words, a community declared as scheduled tribe in one state need not be so in another.

Scheduling and De-Scheduling of Tribes

Thus, the first specification of scheduled tribes in relation to a particular state/ union territory is by a notified order of the President, after consultation with the state governments concerned. The criteria generally adopted for specification of a community as a scheduled tribe are : (a) indications of primitive traits; (b)distinctive culture; (c) shyness of contact with the community at large; and (d) geographical isolation i.e., backwardness.These are not spelt out in the Constitution but have become well established. They take into account the definitions in the 1931 Census, the reports of the first Backward Classes Commission (Kalelkar Committee), 1955, the Advisory Committee on Revision of SC/ ST lists (Lokur Committee), 1965 and the Joint Committee of Parliament on the Scheduled Castes and Scheduled Tribes Orders (Amendment) Bill, 1967 (Chanda Committee), 1969. There are over 700 tribes (with many of them overlapping in more than one state) as notified under Article 342 of the Constitution of India, spread over different states and union territories of the country. It is worth noting that no community has been specified as a scheduled tribe in relation to the states of Haryana and Punjab and the union territories of Chandigarh, Delhi and Puducherry.

Ascertaining ST Status

Where a person claims to belong to a scheduled tribe by birth, it should be verified: (a) that the person and his parents actually belong to the community claimed; (b) that the community is included in the Presidential Order specifying the scheduled tribes in relation to the concerned state; (c) that the person belongs to that state and the area within that state in respect of which the community has been scheduled; (d) he may profess any religion; (e) that he or his parents/ grandparents, etc., should be permanent resident of the state/UT on the date of notification of the Presidential Order applicable in his case; (f) a person who is temporarily away from his permanent place of residence at the time of the notification of the Presidential Order-applicable in his case, say for example to earn a living or seek education, etc., can also be regarded as a scheduled tribe, if his tribe has been specified in that order in relation to his home state/union territory; (g) but he cannot be treated as such in relation to the place of his temporary residence notwithstanding the fact that the name of his tribe has been scheduled in respect of that state where he is temporarily settled, in any Presidential Order; (h) in the case of persons born after the date of notification of the relevant Presidential Order, the place of residence for the purpose of acquiring ST status, is the place of permanent abode of their parents at the time of the notification of the Presidential Order under which they claim to belong to such a tribe. This does not apply to the STs of the Lakshadweep Islands for whom there is a requirement of being born in the union territories in order to be eligible for ST status.

The guiding principle is that no person who is not a scheduled tribe by birth will be deemed to be a member of scheduled tribe merely because he or she has married a person belonging to a scheduled tribe. Similarly, a person who is a member of a scheduled tribe will continue to be a member of that scheduled tribe, even after his or her marriage with a person who does not belong to a scheduled tribe. The candidates belonging to scheduled tribes may get scheduled tribe certificates, in the prescribed form, from any one of the following authorities: District Magistrate/Additional District Magistrate/ Collector/Deputy Commissioner/Additional Deputy Commissioner/Deputy Collector/1st Class Stipendiary Magistrate/City Magistrate/Sub Divisional Magistrate/Taluka Magistrate/Executive Magistrate/Extra Assistant Commissioner [not below the rank of 1st Class Stipendiary Magistrate]; (ii) Chief Presidency Magistrate/Additional Chief Presidency Magistrate/ Presidency Magistrate; (iii) Revenue Officers not below the rank of Tehsildar; (iv) Sub-Divisional Officer of the Area where the candidate and/or his family normally resides; (v) Administrator/ Secretary to the Administrator/ Development Officer (Lakshadweep Islands).

Action is to be taken under the relevant provisions of the Indian Penal Code if any official is found to have issued a Scheduled Tribe certificate carelessly and without proper verification. This will be in addition to other action to which they are liable under the appropriate disciplinary rules applicable to them.

Scheduled Tribe claims on Migration

Migrants from other states/union territories persons belonging to a scheduled tribe who have migrated from one state to another for the purpose of employment, education etc., experience great difficulty in obtaining ST certificates from the state from which they have migrated. In order to remove this difficulty, it has been decided that the prescribed authority of a state government/union territory administration may issue a scheduled tribe certificate to a person who migrated from another state, on the production of the genuine certificate issued to his father/mother by the prescribed authority of the state of the father/mother's origin except where the prescribed authority feels that a detailed enquiry is necessary through the state of origin before issue of the certificate. The certificate will be issued irrespective of whether the tribe in question is scheduled or not in relation to the state/union territory to which the person has migrated to.

National Commission for Scheduled Tribes

National Commission for Scheduled Tribes (NCST) was set up with effect from 19th February, 2004 by amending Article 338 and inserting a new Article 338A in the Constitution, through the Constitution (Eighty-ninth Amendment) Act, 2003. The Chairman and the Vice-Chairman of the Commission have been conferred the rank of Union Cabinet Minister and Minister of State respectively, while the members of the Commission have been given the rank of a Secretary to the Government of India. The main duties of the Commission are to investigate and monitor all matters relating to the safeguards provided for the scheduled tribes and to evaluate the working of such safeguards; and to inquire into specific complaints with respect to the deprivation of rights and safeguards of the scheduled tribes. The Commission is vested with all the powers of a civil court trying a suit while investigating any matter or inquiring into any complaint relating to deprivation of rights and safeguards of the scheduled tribes.

Tribal Sub Plan

The present Tribal Sub Plan (TSP) strategy was initially developed by an Expert Committee set up by the Ministry of Education and Social Welfare in 1972 for rapid socio-economic development of tribal people and was adopted for the first time in the Fifth Five Year Plan. The TSP strategy, with some modifications, continues till this day and the salient features with respect to TSP for states, are: the funds provided under the Tribal Sub Plan of the state have to be at least equal in proportion to the ST population of each state or UT; tribals and tribal areas of a state or union territories are given benefits under the TSP, in addition to what percolates from the overall Plan of a state/UT; the Sub-Plan should; (a) identify the problems and need of tribal people and critical gaps in their development; (b) identify all available resources for TSP; (c) prepare a broad policy framework for development; (d) define a suitable administrative strategy for its implementation; and (e) specify the mechanism for monitoring and evaluation.

The Ministry has issued revised guidelines for inter-state allocation of funds and implementation of programmes / activities under proviso to Article 275(1) of the Constitution and under special central assistance to Tribal Sub Plan (SCA to TSP) in 2016. These guidelines provide focused approach on sectoral allocation and revised inter-state allocation factoring population, area and outcome based performance as parameters. Further, inter-district allocation is also clearly spelt out. Major ST communities are also given priority. Conjunctural use with dovetailing of financial resources from ongoing activities of line department is resorted to ensure larger spatial and higher demographic coverage.

National Scheduled Tribes Finance and Development Corporation

With a view to pay a focused attention and accelerate the pace of economic development of scheduled tribes, the erstwhile National Scheduled Castes and Scheduled Tribes Financial Development Corporation was bifurcated and

National Scheduled Tribes Finance and Development Corporation (NSTFDC) was set up in 2001 under the Ministry of Tribal Affairs. The NSTFDC has been granted license under Section 25 of the Companies Act (A Company not for profit). In order to achieve the mandate set for the NSTFDC, (for undertaking self-employment ventures/activities) financial assistance is extended by NSTFDC to the scheduled tribes, who are having annual family income upto double the poverty line. NSTFDC also provides financial assistance as grant for skill and entrepreneurial development of the target group. The financial assistance is channelized through government owned agencies nominated by the respective ministries/state governments and union territory administrations. NSTFDC also provides financial assistance for procurement and marketing minor forest produce so as to avoid the distress sale of produce/ products by the scheduled tribes.

Eligibility Criteria

The beneficiary (ies) should belong to ST community and annual family income of the beneficiary (ies) should not exceed double the poverty line (DPL) income limit (presently DPL is ₹ 39,500/- per annum for the rural areas and ₹ 54,500/- per annum for the urban areas). In the case of Self Help Groups (SHGs), all the members of the SHG should belong to the ST community having annual family income upto Double the Poverty Line (DPL). Similarly for cooperative society, loan is extended to the eligible STs through cooperative society having minimum 80 per cent or more STs as members.

Term loan is provided for income generating activities. Marketing support assistance is provided for financial support for meeting the working capital requirement of the central/state government owned agencies and national level federations for undertaking procurement and/or marketing of minor forest produce/agricultural produce collected/ grown by the STs and /or related product/services. Marketing support assistance extended to the beneficiaries through the SCAs, the interest is at par with rates of interest for long term loan and the assistance is extended to the central/ state/UT owned organizations, national level federations directly involved in procurement, the interest rate is 7 per cent per annum. Assistance by way of grant is also given.

Special Schemes

Adivasi Mahila Sashaktikaran Yojana (AMSY) is an exclusive Scheme for the economic development of ST women, at a highly concessional rate of interest. Under it NSTFDC provides term loan for scheme(s)/ project(s) costing upto ₹ 50,000/- per individual unit/profit centre. Financial assistance up to 99 per cent of the cost of the scheme(s)/project(s) is provided by the NSTFDC.

Micro-credit scheme is meant to provide financial assistance for undertaking small self-employment ventures/activities by the eligible STs through existing profit making SHGs. SCAs shall provide eligible amount of subsidy or margin money as per their scheme(s) for the target group and remaining amount may be provided as term loan by NSTFDC.

Tribal Cooperative Marketing Development Federation

The Tribal Cooperative Marketing Development Federation of India Limited (TRIFED), was set up in 1987 as a national level apex body under the Multi State Cooperative Societies Act, 1984 (MSCS Act, 1984) After the enactment of the Multi-State Cooperative Societies Act, 2002 (MSCS Act, 2002) TRIFED is deemed to be registered under the latter Act and is also listed in the Second Schedule to the Act as a National Cooperative Society.

The bye-laws of TRIFED were revised in April, 2003 in tune with the new Multi State Cooperative Societies Act, 2002 read with the Multi State Cooperative Societies Rules, 2002. Under its revised mandate TRIFED has stopped bulk procurement in Minor Forest Produce (MFP) and surplus Agricultural Produce (SAP) from tribals. TRIFED now functions as a 'market developer' for tribal products and as 'service provider' to its member federations.

Relevant Website : www.trifed.in

Forest Rights of STs

The Scheduled Tribes and Other Traditional Forest Dwellers (Recognition of Forest Rights) Act, 2006 seeks to recognize and vest the forest rights and occupation in forest land in forest dwelling scheduled tribes and other traditional forest dwellers who have been residing in such forests for generations but chose rights on ancestral lands and their habitat were not adequately recognized in the consolidation of state forests during the colonial period as well as in independent India resulting in historical injustice to them. The Act has been notified for operation from 2007.

Rules, for implementing the provisions of the Act, were notified in 2008 and they envisage the constitution of various Committees under the Act, viz, the sub divisional level committee, district level committee and the state level monitoring committee, by the state governments. All the states have been requested to nominate the nodal officer for implementing the provisions of the Act. The state governments were also requested to take necessary steps to ensure that awareness is created about the objectives, provisions and procedures of the Act and the Rules through various measures including awareness programmes and printed material such as posters in the regional languages; ensure the translation and publication of the Act and the Rules in all the regional languages and arrange to distribute to all gram sabhas, forest right committees and all departments of the government including panchayati raj, rural development, tribal and social welfare and forest departments; undertake the orientation of officials, civilian representative and non-governmental organizations in the state, who can then be called upon to assist as resource persons in the awareness programmes; and sensitize the sub-divisional and district level committees on the objectives, provisions and procedures of the Act and the Rules.

As per the Act, the responsibility for recognition and vesting of forest rights and distribution of land rights rests with the state government. All the state governments have been directed that the entire process of vesting of forest rights as per the Scheduled Tribes and Other Traditional Forest Dwellers (Recognition of Forest Rights) Act, 2006 should be completed at the earliest. Web-based MIS for online monitoring of the implementation of the Act has been made operational from 2008 for testing purposes on website http://www.tribal.gov.in.

Vanbandhu Kalyan Yojana

The central government launched an approach, namely, Vanbandhu Kalyan Yojana (VKY) with a view to translate the available resource into overall development of tribal population with an outcome-based orientation. The VKY has been adopted as a strategic process. It aims at creating enabling environment for need based and outcome oriented holistic development of tribal people. This process envisages to ensure that all the intended benefits of goods and services under various programmes / schemes of central as well as state governments actually reach the target groups by convergence of resources through appropriate institutional mechanism.

Umbrella Scheme for Education of ST Children

The Ministry is re-engineering its educational schemes with the objective of providing adequate educational infrastructure for STs and incentive for education for ST children through scholarships. This is intended to be achieved through convergence of schemes of line ministries along with simplification of process for availing scholarships and also through technological aids in improving learning activities. As needs vary from state to state, the proposed new scheme is expected to give flexibility to each state/UT. In the proposed Umbrella Scheme, the following schemes have been merged: (a) establishing and strengthening of ashram schools; (b) establishing and strengthening of hostels; (c) vocational training in tribal areas; (d) pre-matric and post-matric scholarship.

Overseas Scholarships

The Scheme of National Overseas Scholarships (NOS) for ST students has been revised. The Scheme is providing scholarship to students selected for pursuing higher studies abroad for post-graduation, Ph. D and post-doctoral research programmes. It has been revised to make it more beneficial for ST students.

To expand the scope of field of study, the number of awards has been increased from existing 15 to 20. In order to make the Scheme more inclusive, out of total 20 awards, 3 have been earmarked for Particularly Vulnerable Tribal Groups (PVTGs) and 30 per cent awards for girl candidates. Now with the inclusion of more subjects into it and reorganizing field of study by grouping various subjects under broadbased fields, more ST students would be benefitted as the number of subjects has increased from 35 to 52. Earlier the eligibility criteria was 60 per cent marks, now it has been reduced to 55 per cent so as to enable a larger number of ST students to become eligible to apply for the scholarhips. The maximum income celling has been increased to ₹ 6 lakhs per annum. However, all other parameters being same, preference is given to students with lower income. Similarly, financial assistance, equipment allowance and includental journey expenses have been increased to 10 per cent keeping in view the inflation rates.

Welfare of Other Backward Classes

The Second Backward Classes Commission (commonly known as Mandal Commission), constituted under Article 340, submitted its report in 1980. In the light of this report, the Government of India provided 27 per cent reservation in central government posts for persons belonging to the socially and economically backward classes, (also referred to as "Other Backward Classes" or OBCs). The Government in 1993 reserved 27 per cent of vacancies in civil posts and services under the Central Government, to be filled through direct recruitment in favour of the Other Backward Classes (OBCs). With the amendment of Article 15 of the Constitution in 2006 and the enactment of the Central Educational Institutions (Reservation in Admissions) Act in 2007, listing of other backward classes has become relevant for admission in central educational institutions also. Under this Act, OBC students are entitled to 27 per cent reservation in central educational institutions in a phased manner, over a period of three years commencing from the academic session 2008-09. The National Commission for Backward Classes (NCBC) was set up in 1993 as per the provision of the National Commission for Backward Classes Act, 1993.

Relevant Website : www.ncbc.nic.in

Pre-Matric Scholarship for OBCs

In this scheme, the expenditure is shared between centre and state in 50:50 ratio. The aim of this Scheme is to motivate children of OBCs studying at pre-matric stage. The income ceiling for eligibility should not exceed ₹ 2,50,500/- per annum.

Post-Matric Scholarship for OBCs

The objective of the Scheme is to provide financial assistance to the OBC students studying at post-matriculation or post-secondary stage to enable them complete their education. The income ceiling of parents/guardians for eligibility is ₹ 1.00 lakh per annum (including self income, if employed.

Construction of Hostels for OBC Boys and Girls

This Scheme aims at providing hostel facilities to students belonging to socially and educationally backward classes, especially from rural areas, to enable them to pursue secondary and higher education. The funding pattern as per the guidelines are: (i) the cost of construction for boys hostels is shared between the centre and the state in 60:40 ratio. For the girls hostels the ratio is 90:10; (ii) in case of union territories, the central assistance is 100 per cent and for north eastern states. it is 90 per cent; (iii) for central universities / institutes, the central government share is 90 per cent and the remaining 10 per cent is borne by the central university institute for both boys and girls; (iv) the private universities/ institutions and NGOs can avail central assistance up to 45 per cent of the cost. The remaining 55 per cent shall be borne by state and university/ institution/NGO in 45:10 ratio; (v) the amount of grant will be released in 3 installments in 50:45:5 ratio, of which 5 per cent grant will be released after completion of the work and occupation of the rooms by the OBC boys and girls. The construction work of the hostel has to be completed within eighteen months from award of work order or two years from the release of central assistance, whichever is earlier. In no case the time will be extended beyond 2 years. Any cost escallation due to delay in project will be borne by the state/ institute.

National Fellowship for OBC Students

Assistance for Skill Development

The aim of the Scheme is to involve the voluntary sector to improve educational and socio-economic conditions of the target group i.e., Other Backward Classes (OBCs)/De-notified, Nomadic and Semi-Nomadic Tribes (DNTs)/Economically Backward Classes (EBCs) with a view to upgrade skill to enable them to start income generating activities on their own or get gainfully employed in some sector or the other.

It aims at providing financial assistance to the OBC students in obtaining quality higher education leading to degrees such as M.Phil and Ph.D in universities, research institutions and scientific institutions. The Scheme is designed to provide a total number of 300 junior research fellowships per year from 2014-15 onwards and 300 senior research fellowships from 2016-17 to Other Backward Class (OBC) students. The UGC is the nodal agency for implementing it and notifies the scheme through advertisements in the media at a suitable date. The Scheme covers all universities/institutions recognized by the University Grants Commission. The rate of fellowship for JRF level is ₹ 25000 per month and for SRF level, it is ₹ 28000 per month.

Dr. Ambedkar Scheme of Interest Subsidy on Educational Loans

The objective of the Scheme is to award interest subsidy to meritorious students belonging to the Other Backward Classes (OBCs) and EconomicallyBackward Classes (EBCs) so as to provide them better opportunities for higher education abroad and enhance their employability. For the eligibility of OBC candidates, total income from all sources of the employed candidates, or his/her parents/guardians in case of unemployed candidate, shall not exceed present creamy layer criteria. For the eligibility of EBC candidates, total income from all sources of the employed candidate or his/her parents/guardians in case of unemployed candidate, shall not exceed ₹ 2.50 lakh per annum. Out of the total outlay for a year, a minimum of 50 per cent amount is earmarked for interest subsidy to the girl students.

Post-Matric Scholarship to the EBC Students

This is a centrally sponsored Scheme being implemented through the state governments and UT administrations. The objective of the Scheme is to provide financial assistance to the EBC students studying at post-matriculation or post-secondary stage. The income ceiling of parents/guardians for eligibility is ₹ 1.00 lakh per annum (including self income, if employed).

Dr. Ambedkar Scholarship for DNTs

This is a centrally sponsored Scheme launched in 2014-15 for the welfare of those DNT students who are not covered under SC, ST or OBC. The income ceiling for eligibility is ₹ 2.00 lakh per annum. It is implemented through state governments/UT administrations. The expenditure is shared between centre and state in 75:25 ratio.

Nanaji Deshmukh Scheme of Construction of Hostels

This is a centrally sponsored Scheme launched from 2014-15 being implemented through state governments/UT administrations/central universities. The Scheme aims at providing hostel facilities to those DNT students who are not covered under SC, ST or OBC, to enable them to pursue secondary and higher education. The income ceiling for eligibility is ₹ 2.00 lakh per annum. The central government will provide a maximum of 500 seats per annum throughout the country. The cost norm under the scheme is ₹ 3.00 lakh per seat for the hostel (which is shared between centre and state in 75:25 ratio) and ₹ 5,000/- per seat for furniture. The construction work of the hostel has to be completed within eighteen months from award of work order or two years from the release of central assistance, whichever is earlier. In no case the time will be extended beyond 2 years. Any cost escalation due to delay in project will be borne by the state / institute.

National Backward Classes Finance and Development Corporation

National Backward Classes Finance and Development Corporation (NBCFDC) was incorporated in 1992 as a Company not for profit with an objective to promote economic and developmental activities for the benefit of backward classes and to assist the poorer sections of these classes in skill development and self employment ventures. It is a Government of India Undertaking under the aegis of Ministry of Social Justice and Empowerment. The Corporation extends various types of loans to the target group i.e., members of backward classes. The members of backward classes having annual family income of less than double the poverty line (i.e. ₹ 98,000/- in rural areas and ₹ 1,20,000/- in urban areas) are eligible to obtain loan under NBCFDC schemes through SCAs. Besides other developmental activities, the Corporation is promoting, marketing facilities for the artisans of the target group by providing opportunities to participate in the country's leading fairs like India International Trade Fair, Dilli Haat, Surajkund Crafts Mela as well as in the exhibitions/fairs organized in their respective states.

NBCFDC helps traditional artisans by way of providing them platform to exhibit their products in these exhibitions to establish marketing linkages. The stalls are allotted free of cost to all the beneficiary artisans. NBCFDC also motivates the State Channelizing Agencies (SCAs) to organize or participate in exhibitions to showcase the schemes of the Corporation and also to exhibit the diverse products and services for which NBCFDC has provided financial assistance to the members of backward classes in different parts of the country through SCAs.

Social Defence

In the areas of Social Defence the Ministry is committed towards welfare of older persons and rehabilitation of drug addicts. The programmes for the targeted groups are given here.

National Policy for Older Persons

The existing National Policy on Older Persons (NPOP) was announced in 1999 to reaffirm the commitment to ensure the well-being of the older persons. The Policy envisaged state support to ensure financial and food security, health care, shelter and other needs of older persons, equitable share in development, protection against abuse and exploitation, and availability of services to improve the quality of their lives. The primary objectives were: to encourage individuals to make provision for their own as well as their spouse's old age; to encourage families to take care of their older family members; to enable and support voluntary and non-governmental organizations to supplement the care provided by the family; to provide adequate healthcare facility to the elderly; to promote research and training facilities to train geriatric care givers and organizers of services for the elderly; etc.

National Council for Older Persons

The government has reconstituted National Council for Older Persons (NCOP) to advise and aid the government on developing policies and programmes for older persons. It provides feedback to the government on the implementation of the national policy on older persons and the specific initiatives for older persons. The NCOP is the highest body to advise and coordinate with the government in the formulation and implementation of policy and programmes for the welfare of the aged. Under Integrated Programme for Older Persons, financial assistance upto 90 per cent of the project cost is provided to NGOs for establishing and maintaining old age homes, day care centres, mobile medicare units and to provide non-institutional services to older persons. In order to have a definite structure as well as regional representation, the Council has been reconstituted and renamed as National Council of Senior Citizens (NCSrC) in 2012.

Drugs and Psychotropic Substances

The Narcotic Drugs and Psychotropic Substances Act, 1985, was enacted, *inter alia,* to curb drug abuse. Section 71 of the Act provides that the Government may, in its discretion, establish as many centres as it thinks fit for identification, treatment, education, after-care, rehabilitation, social reintegration of addicts and for supply, subject to such conditions and in such manner as may be prescribed, by the concerned government of any narcotic drugs and psychotropic substances to the addicts registered with the government and to others where such supply is a medical necessity. Accordingly the Department has been supporting Integrated Rehabilitation Centre for Addicts (IRCAs) under the Scheme of Prevention of Alcoholism and Substance (Drugs) Abuse being run by voluntary organizations.

Narcotic Drugs and Psychotropic Substances Policy

Ministry of Finance in consultation with all stakeholders including the Department of Social Justice and Empowerment has brought the Narcotic Drugs and Psychotropic Substances Policy (NDPS Policy) which aims to: (a) spell out the policy towards narcotic drugs and psychotropic substances; (b) serve as a guide to various ministries and organisations in the government and to the state governments as well as international organisations, NGOs, etc., and (c) re-assert India's commitment to combat the drug menace in a holistic manner.

Minorities

The Ministry of Minority Affairs was established in 2006. It has been mandated for formulation of policies, schemes and programmes for welfare and socio-economic development of 6 (six) notified minority communities namely, Muslims, Christians, Sikhs, Buddhists, Parsis and Jains, which constitute more than 19 per cent of India's population. From October 2016, the mandate of the Ministry has been expanded to manage Haj Pilgrimage as well.

Relevant Websites : www.ncm.nic.in www.minorityaffairs.gov.in

15-Point Programme for Minorities

The Prime Minister's 15-Point programme for the Welfare of Minorities was announced in 2006. The objectives of the programme are: (a) enhancing opportunities for education, (b) ensuring an equitable share for minorities in economic activities and employment, through existing and new schemes, enhanced credit support for self-employment and recruitment to state and central government jobs, (c) improving the conditions of living of minorities by ensuring an appropriate share for them in infrastructure development schemes, (d) prevention and control of communal disharmony and violence. An important aim of the new programme is to ensure that the benefits of various government schemes for the underprivileged reach the disadvantaged sections of the minority communities. In order to ensure that the benefits of these schemes flow equitably to the minorities, the new programme envisages location of a certain proportion of development projects in minority concentration areas. It also provides that, wherever possible, 15 per cent of physical targets and financial outlays under various schemes should be earmarked for the target groups.

Scholarship Schemes for Minority Students

This Ministry is implementing three scholarship schemes for the educational empowerment ot students belonging to the notified minority communities:- (i) pre-matric scholarship; (ii) post-matric scholarship; and (iii) merit-cum-means based scholarship.

To improve transparency in scholarship schemes, a new and revamped version of National Scholarship Portal was launched for various ministries Central government including Ministry of Minority Affairs for extending scholarships during 2016-17. All the above three scholarship schemes of this Ministry are on NSP 2.0 portal. The scholarships are transferred in the bank accounts of students in Direct Benefit Transfer (DBT) mode. Wherever Aadhaar numbers are available, the bank accounts of students are being limited and transferred to such accounts.

(i) Pre-Matric Scholarship Scheme: The pre-matric scholarship scheme was approved in 2008. It is a central sector scheme with 100 per cent central funding. The students who secure 50 per cent marks in the previous examination and whose parents'/guardians' annual income does not exceed ₹ 1.00 lakh, are eligible. Under the Scheme, 30 lakh fresh scholarships are proposed to be awarded every year in addition to the renewals. 30 per cent of scholarships have been earmarked for girl students. The scholarship of ₹ 1000/- to ₹ 10,700/- is awarded to every selected student. An outlay of ₹ 5000/- crore has been provided in the XII Five Year Plan to award 414.50 lakh scholarships fresh and renewals during the Plan period (2012-17).

(ii) Post-Matric Scholarship Scheme: The scheme of post-matric scholarship was launched in 2007. It is a central sector scheme awarded for studies in India in a government higher secondary school/college including residential government higher secondary school/college and eligible private institues selected and notified in a transparent manner by the state government/union territory administration concerned. Students who secure 50 per cent marks in the previous year's final examination and whose parents'/guardians' annual income does not exceed ₹ 2.00 lakh are eligible for award of scholarship. Under the Scheme, 5 lakh fresh scholarships are proposed to be awarded every year in addition to the renewals. 30 per cent of scholarships have been earmarked for girl students. In case sufficient numbers of girl students are not available then eligible boy students are given these scholarships.

(iii) Merit-cum-Means based Scholarship: The merit-cum means based scholarship scheme is a central sector scheme launched in 2007 wherein 100 per cent scholarship expenditure is being borne by the central govemment. Scholarships are awarded for pursuing professional and technical courses, at undergraduate and post-graduate levels, in institutions recognized by appropriate authority. Under the scheme, 60,000 fresh scholarships are proposed to be awarded every year in addition to the renewals. 30 per cent of these scholarships are earmarked for girl students, which may be utilized by eligible boy students, if adequate

numbers of eligible girl students are not available. 85 institutes for professional and technical courses have been listed in the scheme. Eligible students from the minority communities admitted to these institutions are reimbursed full course fee. A course fee of ₹ 20,000 per annum is reimbursed to students studying in other institutions. Besides, a student is also eligible for maintenance allowance of up to ₹ 10,000/- p.a. To be eligible, a student should have secured admission in any technical or professional institution, recognized by an appropriate authority. In case of students admitted without a competitive examination, they should have secured not less than 50 per cent marks. The annual income of the family from all sources should not exceed ₹ 2.50 lakh.

Maulana Azad National Fellowship

The Maulana AzadNational Fellowship (MANF) scheme for minority students was launched in 2009 as a Central Sector Scheme (CSS). It is implemented through University Grants Commission (UGC) and cent per cent central assistance is provided under the Scheme. The objective of the Scheme is to provide five year fellowships in the form of financial assistance to students from minority communities, notified by the central government to pursue higher studies such as M.Phil and Ph.D courses. The fellowship and covers all universities/institutions recognized by the UGC. The Fellowship is awarded to research scholars pursuing regular and full time M.Phil and Ph.D courses. In order to qualify for the award of JRF/SRF, the UGC norms would be applicable at pre-M.Phil and pre-Ph.D stage, respectively, including the minimum score of 55 per cent at post graduate level 30 per cent of the fellowships have been earmarked for female candidates. In case there is shortage of female candidates, the fellowship can be passed on to male candidates of the same minority community.

Naya Savera - Free Coaching and Allied Scheme

The "Free Coaching and Allied Scheme for the candidates belonging to miniority communities was launched in 2007 by this Ministry.

Nai Udaan

The objective of the Scheme is to provide financial support to the minority candidates clearing prelims conducted by Union Public Service Commission, Staff Selection Commission and State Public Service Commissions to adquately equip them to compete for appointment to Civil Services in the Union and the state governments and to increase the representation of the minority in the civil services by giving direct financial support to candidates.

Padho Pardes

The objective of the Scheme is to award interest subsidy to meritorious students belonging to economically weaker sections of notified minority communities so as to provide them better opportunities for higher education abroad and enhance their employability. The interest subsidy under the Scheme shall be available to the eligible students only once, either for masters or Ph.D levels.

Nai Roshni

This Ministry implements an exclusive scheme 'Nai Roshni' for leadership development of minority women with an aim to empower and instill confidence in them by providing knowledge, tools and techniques for interacting with government systems, banks and intermediaries at all levels. It is implemented through empanelled non-governmental organizations.

National Commission for Minorities

The Minorities Commission which was set up in 1978 became a statutory body with the enactment of the National Commission for Minorities Act, 1992 after which it was renamed as the National Commission for Minorities. The first statutory National Commission was set up in 1993. The NCM Act, 1992 was amended in 1995 which provided for a Vice Chairperson in the Commission. With the 1995 amendment, the Commission's composition was expanded to 7 members (including a Chairperson and a Vice Chairperson). The provision under Section 3(2) of the Act stipulates that five members including the Chairpersons shall be from amongst the minority communities.

Relevant Website : www.ncm.nic.in

State Commission for Minorities

Thirteen state governments, namely, Andhra Pradesh, Assam, Bihar, Chhattisgarh, Government of NCT of Delhi, Jharkhand, Karnataka, Maharashtra, Madhya Pradesh, Rajasthan, Uttar Pradesh, Tamil Nadu and West Bengal have set up statutory commissions for minorities. Manipur and Uttarakhand have set up non-statutory commissions.

National Commission for Religious and Linguistic Minorities

Commissioner for Linguistic Minorities

The Office of the Commissioner for Linguistic Minorities (CLM) was established in 1957. in pursuance of the provision of Article 350-B of the Constitution which envisages investigation by CLM of all matters relating to the safeguards provided for the linguistic minorities in the country under the Constitution and reporting to the President upon these matters at such intervals as the President may direct. The President may want that all such reports be laid before each House of the Parliament and sent to the government administration of states/UTs concerned. The CLM organization has its headquarters at Delhi with three zonal offices at Belgaum, Chennai and Kolkata. Ths CLM interacts with states/UTs on all the matters pertaining to the issues concerning implemantation of the Constitutional and nationally agreed safeguards provided to lingustic minoritiers.

Constitutional Safeguards for Linguistic Minorities

Under the Constitution of India, certain safeguards have been granted to the religious and linguistic minorities. Article 29 and 30 seek to protect the interests of minorities and recognize their right to conserve their distinct language, script or culture and to establish and administer educational institutions of their choice. Article 347 makes provision for Presidential direction for official recognition of any language spoken by a substantial proportion to the populations of a state or any part thereof for such purpose as the President may specify. Article 350 gives the right to submit representation for redressal of grievances to any authority of the Union or a state in any of the languages used in the Union/states. Article 360A provides for instruction in the mother tongue at the primary stage of education to children belonging to linguistic minority groups. Article 350B provides for a Special Officer designated as Commissioner for Linguistic Minorities to investigate all matters relating to the safeguards provided for linguistic minorities under the Constitution.

Central Wakf Council

A Wakf is a permanent dedication of movable or immovable properties for purposes recognised by the Muslim Law as religious, pious or charitable. Apart from these religious aspects, the Wakfs are also instruments of social and economic upliftment. Administration of central legislation for Wakfs is the responsibility of the Ministry of Social Justice and Empowerment. For the purpose of advising the central government on matters relating to working of the state Wakf Boards and the proper administration of the Wakfs in the country, the Central Wakf Council was established as a statutory body in 1964, under Section 8A of the Wakf Act, 1954 (now read as Sub-Sec(1) of the Section 9 of Wakf Act, 1995). The present Council was reconstituted in 2005. The Union Minister in charge of Wakf is the Chairperson of the Council. The Central Wakf Council is also playing a vital role in the development of the society by way of implementing development of urban Wakf properties and educational development programmes.

Relevant Website : www.centralwakfcouncil.org

Durgah Khawaja Saheb Act

It is an Act to make provision for the proper administration of Dargah and Endowment of the Dargah Khwaja Moin-ud-din Chishty (R.A.). Under this central Act, the administration, control and management of the Dargah Endowment has been vested in a representative committee known as the Dargah Committee appointed by the central government. The Dargah of Khwaja Moin-ud-din Chishti at Ajmer in Rajasthan is a Waqf of international fame. It is being administered under the Dargah Khwaja Saheb Act, 1955. With the help of the Government of India, the Ministry of Urban Development and with the active involvement of the government of Rajasthan through local administration, the Dargah Committee is implementing a scheme of providing lodging facilities for lakhs of pilgrims who visit the holy Dargah during the annual Urs. The facility was earlier named "Vishram Sthali" and has been renamed "Gharib Nawaz Mehmankhana". The infrastructure is meant to provide facilities/ amenities to the zaireen of Dargah Khwaja Sahab.

Women and Child Development

The development of women and children is of paramount importance and sets the pace for overall development. A separate Ministry of Women and Child Development came into existence from 2006 with the prime intention of addressing gaps in state action for women and children and for promoting inter-ministerial and inter-sectoral convergence to create gender equitable and child centred legislation, policies and programmes. The Ministry has the main responsibility to advance the rights and concerns of women and children and to promote their survival, protection, development and participation in a holistic manner. The Ministry has a vision of empowered women living with dignity and contributing as equal partners in development in an environment free from violence and discrimination and well nurtured children with full opportunities for growth and development in a safe and protective environment. Its mission for children is to ensure development, care and protection through cross-cutting policies and programmes, spread awareness about their rights, facilitate access to learning, nutrition, institutional and legislative support for enabling them to grow and develop to their full potential.

Relevant Website : www.wcd.nic.in

Acts relating to Women and Children

The Ministry is in charge of the administration of the following Acts relating to women and children: (a) The Immoral Traffic (Prevention) Act, 1956 (as amended in 1986), (b) The Indecent Representation of Women (Prevention) Act, 1986 (60 of 1986), (c) The Dowry Prohibition Act, 1961 as amended in 1986, (d) The Commission of Sati (Prevention) Act, 1987 (3 of 1988), (e) The Prohibition of Child Marriage Act, 2006 (notified in January, 2007), (f) Protection of Women from Domestic Violence Act, 2005, (g) National Commission for Women Act, 1990, (h) Infant Milk Substitutes, Feeding Bottles and Infant food (Regulation of Production, Supply and Distribution) Act, 1992 (41 of 1992),(i) Commission for Protection of Child Rights Act, 2005, and (j) Juvenile Justice (Care and Protection of Children) Act 2000, (k) The Protection of Children from Sexual Offences (POCSO) Act and POCSO Rules, 2012 and (l) Sexual Harassment of Women at Workplace (Prevention, Prohibition and Redressal), 2012. The Juvenile Justice (Care and Protection of Children), Amendment Bill was passed in Parliament in August, 2011. The Ministry's mandate primarily includes formulation of plans, policies and programmes for women and children; enactment and amendment of legislations related to them; and overall guidance and coordination of efforts of governmental and non-governmental organizations working in the field of women and child development. The Ministry's schemes and programmes play a supplementary and complementary role to the development programmes of the Ministry.

Beti Bachao Beti Padhao

Beti Bachao Beti Padhao is one the flagship programmes of the Government, launched in 2015 to address the declining Child Sex Ratio (CSR) and address other related issues of disempowerment of women. CSR is the number of girls against 1000 boys in the age group of 0-6 years. It is a tri-ministerial, convergent effort of Ministries of Women and Child Development, Health and Family Welfare and Human Resource Development with focus on the following: awareness and advocacy campaign; multi-sectoral action in select 161 districts (low on CSR); enabling girls' education; effective enforcement of pre-conception and pre natal diagnostic techniques (PC&PNDT) Act.

The specific objectives of the Scheme include preventing gender biased sex selective elimination; ensuring survival and protection of the girl child and ensuring education and participation of the girl child.s The multi-sectoral, action in districts lays special focus on effective implementation and monitoring of PC&PNDT Act, promotion of early registration of pregnancy, institutional deliveries and registration of births by the Ministry of Health and Family Welfare; making schools girl-friendly: enrolment of girls in schools, retention of girls in secondary schools, availability of functional toilets by the Ministry of Human Resource Development; awareness generation, advocacy, community mobilization and training of stakeholders, local champions, rewards to institutions and frontline workers by the Ministry of Women and Child Development. It is envisaged to bring an improvement in sex ratio at birth (SRB) in the short term while child sex ratio (CSR) with manifestation of over-all development such as improved health and nutrition, gender parity in education, better sanitation, opportunities and removal of asymmetries between the genders is endeavoured in the long term. In a short span of time, the clarion call of Beti Bachao Beti Padhao is resonating across the country. This programme has been successful in establishing improvement in CSR as a national agenda. It has stirred national consciousness with the political leadership and government, both at the central and states/UTs level owning the initiative. Several innovative interventions have been demonstrated on ground in the selected districts.

This has resulted in building around the increased issue of awareness, sensitization and conscious declining CSR in the public domain. Encouraging results are emerging with improving trends seen in sex ratio at birth, institutional deliveries, ANC Registrations and girls enrolment in School at Secondary levels in majority of the selected districts.

Social Media Presence:

BBBP Facebook Page:

https: //www.facebook.com/WCD.BetiBachaoBetiPadhao

YouTube channel on BBBP (for films! audio-video spots):

www.youwbe.com/user/BetiBachaoBetiPadhao

Vand aspedia:http: / /vikaspedia.in/social-welfare/women-and-child development/child-development-i /girl-child-welfare/beti-bachao-beti padhao

BBBP Mobile Application:

https:/ /apps.mgov.gov.in/descp.doappid=792

Pradhan Mantri Matru Vandana Yojana

Government announced pan India implementation of maternity benefit programme to eligible pregnant women and lactating mothers. The programme was named Pradhan Mantri Matru Vandana Yojana (PMMVY).

It is a centrally sponsored Scheme under which the grant-in-aid is PMMVY released to states/UTs in cost sharing ratio between the centre and the states and UTs with legislature as 60:40, for north-eastern states and Himalayan states it will be 90:10 and 100 per cent for union territories without legislature.

PMMVY envisages providing cash incentive amounting to ₹ 5,000/- directly to the bank/post office account of PW and LM in DBT mode during pregnancy and lactation in response to individual fulfilling specific conditions.

Poshan Abhiyaan

Poshan Abhiyaan is a flagship programme of Ministry of Women and Child Development which ensures convergence with various programmes i.e., Anganwadi Services. Pradhan Mantri Matru Vandana Yojana (PMMVY). Scheme for Adolescent Girls (SAG) of MWCD Janani Suraksha Yojana (JSY), National Health Mission (NHM). Swachh Bharat Mission. Public Distribution System (PDS). It focuses to lay emphasis on the first 1000 days of the child, which includes the nine months of pregnancy, six months of exclusive breastfeeding and the period from 6 months to 2 years to ensure focused interventions on addressing undermutrition. Besides increasing the birth weight. It will help reduce both Infant Mortality Rate (IMR) and Maternal Mortaility Rate (MMR). Additional one year of sustained intervention (till the age of 3 years) would ensure that the gains of the first 1000 days are consolidated. Attention is also given on children in the age group of 3-6 years for their overall development through the platform of the Anganwadi Services.

One Stop Centres

Women who suffer violence face huge problems in getting justice as they have to register FIRs and engage lawyers to fight court cases. In many cases the medical evidence gets destroyed due to lack of knowledge or pressure from perpetrators. As a result, very often women suffer violence but do not complain. In order to assist such women, a new initiative to establish One Stop Centres (OSC) was conceived and is being implemented across the country since April 2015. A woman who has suffered violence can get medical, police, legal and psychological counselling assistance at these centres. These also have a place for them to temporarily stay in case their condition so warrants. The OSC, popularly known by the name of Sakhi will be integrated with 181 and other existing helplines. The first centre was inaugurated at Raipur, Chhattisgarh in 2015. So far 138 such centres have been operational in 31 states/UTs., catering to the needs of the women affected by violence. Over 4000 women have been assisted in these centres, which have come up in the last six months or so. At least one such centre will be established in each district by the end of 2018-19.

The scheme is implemented through the state/UT government. The management committee headed by District Collector is responsible for the day to day operation of the OSC.

Universalisation of Women Helpline

The Scheme of Universalisation of Women Helpline is being implemented since 2015, intended to provide 24 hour emergency and non-emergency response to women affected by violence through referral (linking with appropriate authority such as police, One Stop Centre, hospital) and information about women related government schemes / programmes across the country through a single uniform number (181). Women Helpline will be integrated with One Stop Centre Scheme and women in need of redressal services will be referred here. The Scheme envisages that the states/UT s will utilise or augment their existing women helplines through a dedicated single national number.Department of Telecommunication, has allocated short code 181 to all states/UT s. So far, women helplines have been operational in 22 states/UTs i.e., Andhra Pradesh, Arunachal Pradesh, Chhattisgarh, Chandigarh (UT). Delhi, Madhya Pradesh, Gujarat, Kerala, Uttarakhand, Mizoram. Jharkhand, Bihar, Punjab, Maharashtra, Odhisa, Uttar Pradesh, Meghalaya, Haryana, Nagaland, West Bengal, Sikkim and Meghalaya.

Panic Button on Mobile Phones

To provide emergency response to women in distress, MWCD had taken up the installation of physical panic button on mobile phones. Based on extensive stakeholder consultations initiated by the Ministry the 'Panic Button and Global Positioning System in Mobile Phone Handsets Rules, 2016' have been notified by the Department of Telecommunications. Under these rules, all new feature phones will have the facility of panic button configured to the numeric key 5 or 9 and all smart phones will have it configured to three times short pressing of the on-off button. Further, all new mobile phones will be required to have the facility of identifying the location through satellite based OPS. An Emergency Response Support System (ERSS) is also being set up under Nirbhaya Fund in collaboration with MHA, which will integrate all emergency numbers to 112 with state-of-art technology to respond to distress signals sent from panic button.

Mahila Police Volunteers

The broad mandate of Mahila Police Volunteers (MPVs) is to report to authorities/police the incidences of violence against women such as domestic violence, child marriage, dowry harassment and violence faced by women in public spaces. Haryana has become the first state to operationalise the Mahila Police Volunteers scheme. It was launched jointly by the WCD Ministry and Haryana government in 2016 for the districts of Karnal and Mahendragarh in the state. Other states are expected to follow the same soon.

Reservation for Women in Police Force

The WCD Ministry has been working along with the Ministry of Home Affairs to improve overall police responsiveness to gender sensitive cases and to bring visibility to more women and strengthen gender sensitivity in police force. An advisory has been issued to all state governments to increase representation of women in police to 33 per cent of the total strength. As a result, reservation has been extended in 14 states/union territories. So far 8 states viz., Bihar, Gujarat, Odisha, Nagaland, Rajasthan, Jharkhand, Madhya Pradesh, Telangana and 6 UTs namely Chandigarh, Daman and Diu, Lakhadweep and Dadra and Nagar Haveli, NCT Delhi, Puducherry have aleady extended such reservation.

Inclusion of Acid Attack as Disability

Taking note of the long lasting damage or disfigurement on the life of a person attacked with acid as well as constant medical attention, MWCD requested Ministry of Social Justice and Empowerment to include acid attack induced damage or disfigurement within the list of specified disabilities. The recently enacted Rights of Persons with Disabilities Act, 2016 notified in 2016, included acid attack as a kind of disability. Acid attack victims can now avail disability benefits.

Guidelines for Matrimonial Websites

In view of the increasing number of crimes committed against women on the account of information shared in matrimonial websites, it was decided to look into the issue and put in place a regulatory framework in order to check this misuse. The Ministry has already carried out extensive work for the preparation of the due diligence guidelines for the matrimonial websites and prepared a concept paper detailing extent of the problem, existing safeguards, existing legal remedies, etc., which has been circulated to stakeholders concerned.

NRI Matrimonial Disputes

Due to increase in Indian Diaspora and consequent overseas marriages, women whether residing in India or abroad, are facing issues related to desertion, domestic violence, exparte divorce and custody of children, etc. As the issues involve inter-country jurisdiction, women engaged in such cases face legal hurdles due to lack of information regarding procedures when the other party is residing abroad. To spread information MWCD has prepared Standard Operating Procedures (SoPs) for women involved in NRI matrimonial disputes. These SoPs narrate the step wise correct legal recourse to be undertaken by women to facilitate speedy access to justice. These are also intended to serve as an effective reference manual for court and police officials across the country who are investigating such disputes or representing such women's interest in courts.

Gender Budgeting Initiatives

Gender Budgeting (GB) is a powerful tool for achieving gender mainstreaming so as to ensure that benefits of development reach women as much as men. It is not an accounting exercise alone but an ongoing process of keeping a gender perspective at various steps of budget planning, allocation, implementation, impact/outcome assessment, review and audit. To institutionalize such budgeting in the country, the setting up of Gender Budgeting Cells (GBCs) in all ministries/departments was mandated by the Ministry of Finance in 2007. The MWCD as the nodal agency for gender budgeting is undertaking several initiatives for taking it forward at the national and state levels. 57 central ministries and departments have set up GBCs which are expected to serve as a focal point for coordinating gender budgeting initiatives, both intra and inter-ministerial. 21 states and union territories have designated Gender Budgeting nodal centres.

Gender Champions

The initiative of Gender Champions is being implemented through educational institutions to sensitize young students and create awareness on laws, legislations, legal rights and life skills education. The Gender Champion guidelines developed by MWCD are being operationalized in collaboration with the Ministry of Human Resource Development. A Training Module for Gender Champions has been developed for adoption by educational institutes.

Mandatory Mention of Widows' Name on Death Certificates

To ensure that a widow is facilitated to get all her entitlements after the death of her husband, WCD Ministry is working with the office of Registrar General of India as well as the state governments to ensure that the name of the widow is compulsorily mentioned in the death certificate of her husband.

Shelter Home for Widows

It is the largest ever such facility being established or funded by the government, the Home, which will have a capacity to house 1000 women, is being constructed on 1.424 hectare of land at an estimated cost of ₹ 57 crore (including cost of the land) at Vrindavan. The design of the Home has been prepared in consultation with HelpAge India and is old age friendly.

Training for Women Heads of Panchayats

Although 33 per cent posts of heads of Gram Panchayats have been reserved for women, they are unable to exercise real authority for betterment of villages due to lack of training and continued dominance/interference by their husbands, etc. In order to empower these women at grass root level, WCD has initiated a massive programme to train over 2 lakh women heads of Panchayats. The training was started from 2016 onwards in partnership with Ministry of Rural Development. The training modules cover all aspects of village level management including basic knowledge of government schemes, social issues and their resolution, management of panchayat finances, village infrastructure, etc. This Scheme is being implemented in collaboration with Ministry of Panchayati Raj.

Extending Maternity Leave Duration

The WCD Ministry has been working to extend the maternity leave period for working women to seven months to enable them to provide exclusive breastfeeding to children for six months after child birth and complementary foods thereafter to help reduce incidence of malnutrition. Ministry of Labour and Employment carried out suitable amendments in the Act, which are as follows: (i) enhancement of maternity leave under Maternity Benefit Act, 1961 from existing 12 weeks to 26 weeks; (ii) extension of maternity benefit to adopting mothers and commissioning mothers; (iii) establishment of crèche facility within the office/factory premises.

The Act is now called the Maternity Benefit (Amendment) Act, 2017.

Sexual Harassment of Women at Workplace

To ensure safety and security of women at workplaces, the Ministry of Women and Child Development is working towards the effective implementation of the Sexual Harassment of Women at Workplace (Prevention, Prohibition and Redressal) Act, 2013. In this regard, advisories and monitoring framework have been issued to state governments/central ministries/departments to ensure the effective implementation of the sexual harassment Act, expeditious inquiry into the complaint and to prevent further victimisation of the complainant. In addition, MWCD has also prepared and released a Handbook on the Act which provides information about the provisions of the Act in an easy-to-use practical manner.

Village Convergence and Facilitation Service

Village Convergence and Facilitation Service (VCFS) is an initiative launched in 2015 aimed at creating awareness through community engagement. Dedicated village coordinators are selected to facilitate convergence on women's issues and work in close coordination with the gram panchayat and its sub-committees. In this manner, issues pertaining to education, health, nutrition, legal rights, safety and security of women are addressed and access to schemes/programmes being implemented by the government such as Beti Bachao Beti Padhao, Jan Dhan Yojana, One Stop Centre, Women Helpline, etc., are provided. VCFS has been extended from 100 gender critical districts to cover 303 districts across the country.

Rashtriya Mahila Kosh

Rashtriya Mahila Kosh (RMK) is a society, registered under the Societies Registration Act, 1860 and an apex micro-finance organization established in 1993. The main objective of RMK is to provide micro-credit to poor women through intermediary organizations (IMO), which includes Section 25 companies, NGOs among others for various livelihood support and income generating activities at concessional terms in a client-friendly procedure to bring about their socio-economic development. The target beneficiaries are entrepreneurs from different economic activities ranging from traditional and modern handicraft to small business such as petty shop, etc. The loans are sanctioned through various schemes of RMK viz., main loan scheme, loan promotion scheme, etc.

Women of India Exhibitions/Festivals

The Initiative was started in 2014 to link women organic farmers and entrepreneurs directly to the market. Three such exhibitions/ festivals have already been held in Delhi, many more such exhibitions/festivals are being organised in locations outside Delhi. Such events are being held to provide a platform so that women entrepreneurs and farmers especially from rural India get an opportunity to exhibit and sell their products. Such exhibitions/festivals empower women through knowledge sharing and creating entrepreneurial opportunities to make societal balance through financial inclusion.

Mahila e-Haat

The Ministry of Women and Child Development launched "Mahila e-Haat", a unique direct online digital marketing platform for women entrepreneurs/SHOs/NGOs in 2016. This can become a game changer initiative as it can become a catalyst in strengthening women entrepreneurship and financial inclusion. The USP of Mahila e-haat is facilitating direct contact between the vendor and buyer. It is easy to access as the entire business of e-Haat can be handled through a mobile.

National Policy for Women

The Draft National Policy for Women, 2016, is in its last stages of finalization. It has been revised after 15 years and is expected to guide government action on women's issues over the next 15-20 years. The policy addresses women's issues on a life-cycle continuum and encompasses a wide spectrum of issues from education, health, economic participation, decision making, violence, creation of an enabling environment, etc.

New Passport Rules

In a major move, on insistence of the Ministry of WCD, the Ministry of External Affairs issued new Passport Rules (https://www.mea.gov.in/pressreleases.html) in 2016 for the benefit of single/divorced mothers and their children including adopted/adoptable children. Now, as per the revised Rules, submission of father's name is not mandatory and a person can obtain passport only by specifying his/her mother's name. Further, a person does not need to submit her/his marriage/ divorce certificates.

Legislation on Trafficking

Ministry of Women and Child Development has drafted a comprehensive legislation on Trafficking - Trafficking of Persons (Prevention, Protection and Rehabilitation) Bill, 2017 with a view to fill the existing gaps and cover all aspects of trafficking by including various offences pertaining to trafficking prevention, protection and rehabilitation of victims. The draft Bill also proposes to tackle trafficking by creating a strong legal, economic and social environment for the victims by putting in place dedicated institutional mechanisms at district, state and national level.

Children's Issues

Missing/Trafficked/Runaway Children

Khoya-Paya Portal: In order to bring citizen participation for protecting children, a new citizen based portal Khoya-Paya was launched in 2015 which enables posting of information of missing and sighted children. It also provides facility for matching the two databases - missing and sighted children. Between June 2015 and March, 2017, 7671 missing/sighted children cases were closed on the portal. The railway stations are to have NGOs/Child Help Groups/ Childline Units working with them for restoration of children to their parents/ guardians or their rehabilitation in the absence of parents/guardians.

Awareness campaign via posters in railway coaches was launched in 2015. One lakh posters have been put in trains in the first phase.

Expansion of Childline: This Childline is a nation-wide initiative for rescuing and assisting children in distress conditions. Over the years, Childline (1098 helpline number) has been extended to 412 locations from 316 cities and will be expanded to another 100 cities soon.

POCSO e-Box

Children are often unable to complain about sexual abuse because it is usually done by someone known to them. In order to provide them with a safe and anonymous mode of making a complaint, an internet based facility, e-Box, has been provided. Here, a child or anyone on his/her behalf can file a complaint with minimal details. As soon as the complaint is filed, a trained counsellor immediately contacts the child and provides assistance. The counsellor also registers a formal complaint on behalf of the child wherever required. POCSO e-box launched in 2016, has received and handled 300 complaints.

Juvenile Justice

The Juvenile Justice (Care and Protection of Children) Model Rules, 2016 (JJ Model Rules, 2016) was notified thereby repealing the Juvenile Justice (Care and Protection of Children) Rules, 2007 (JJ Rules, 2007). The JJ Model Rules, 2016 are based on the philosophy that children need to be reformed and reintegrated into society. The Rules are appreciative of the developmental needs of children and therefore the best interest of the child is the primary consideration. Child friendly procedures are incorporated across the board. The JJ Model Rules, 2016 prescribe detailed child friendly procedures for the police, Juvenile Justice Board and children's court. Some of these procedures include: no child to be sent to jail or lock-up, no child to be handcuffed, a child to be provided appropriate medical assistance, parent/guardian to be informed about legal aid, etc. The Juvenile Justice Board and the Children's Court are required to put the child at ease and to encourage him/her to state the facts and circumstances without any fear, after understanding the questions put across in a language understood by the child.

Various new forms have been added in the JJ Model Rules, 2016 to review the progress of children in Juvenile Justice System and to ensure adequate rehabilitation and restoration services for them. Some of the new forms are case monitoring sheet, detailed individual child care plan, application for registration of child care institutions, certificate for registration, quarterly report by Juvenile Justice Board/ Child Welfare Committee, etc. Further, monitoring provisions have been strengthened.

Comprehensive Adoption Reforms

Government has notified Juvenile Justice Act, 2015 and Chapter VIII of the Act provisions for adoption of orphaned, abandoned and surrendered children and also adoption of children by relatives. The Act has adequate safeguards for the children to ensure their best interest and it provides for reporting of all adoptions in the country including relative adoptions. Further, all adoptions under the Act have to proceed as per the Adoption Regulations framed by Central Adoption. Central Adoption Resource Agency has been reconstituted as Central Adoption Resource Authority (CARA) under this Act.

The Adoption Regulations were notified in 2017 and in supersession of Guidelines Governing Adoption of Children, 2015. Registering online with Central Adoptions Resource Authority (CARA) is mandatory to adopt a child from anywhere in India. Central Adoption Resource Information and Guidance System (CARINGS) is the only official portal of CARA for legal adoption process. Under Section 80 and 81 of the Juvenile Justice (Care and Protection of Children) Act, 2015 any person or agency who indulges in illegal adoption shall be punished. By adopting a child illegally, one may unintentionally become part of a child trafficking network. Adoption is a socio-legal process and there is no role of touts/middlemen in it as they may mislead people to adopt a child illegally. The Adoption Regulations contain the provisions for in-country and inter-country adoptions of OAS (orphaned, abandoned and surrendered) children. Procedures related to adoption by relatives both within the country and abroad have been defined in the Regulations. Adoption of step-children has been brought in. There are 32 schedules annexed to the Regulations including model adoption applications to be filed in the court and this would considerably address delays prevalent in obtaining the court order.

National Nutrition Mission

National Nutrition Mission (NNM) is proposed to achieve improvement in nutritional status of children (O-6years), adolescent girls and pregnant women and lactating mothers in a time bound manner over a period of three years with the objectives of preventing and reducing under-nutrition in children (0-3 years); reducing the prevalence of anaemia among young children (6-59 months); reducing the prevalence of anaemia among women and adolescent girls (15-49 years) and reducing low birth weight.

Anganwadi Services

The Integrated Child Development Services (ICDS) Scheme now known as Anganwadi Services Scheme was launched in 1975 with the objective to improve the nutritional and health status of children in the age-group 0-6 years; lay the foundation for proper psychological, physical and social development of the child; reduce the incidence of mortality, morbidity, malnutrition and school dropouts; achieve effective co-ordination of policy and implementation amongst the various departments to promote child development; and enhance the capability of the mothers to look after the normal health and nutritional needs of the children through proper nutrition and health education. The beneficiaries of the scheme are children below six years of age, pregnant and lactating mothers. It is self selecting and is open to all the beneficiaries without any pre-condition.

These objectives are achieved by providing a package of six services by AWWs/ AWHs under the ICDS scheme, viz., supplementary nutrition, pre-school non-formal education, nutrition and health education, immunization, health check-up; and referral services. The concept of providing a package of services is based primarily on the consideration that the overall impact will be much larger if the different services develop in an integrated manner as the efficacy of a particular service depends upon the support it receives from related services. These services are provided through 14 lakhs sanctioned Anganwadis spread across the country. Sections 4, 5, 6 and 7 of the National Food Security Act are applicable to the ICDS as these Sections make a provision for providing nutritious food to the children including malnourished children and pregnant and lactating mothers. As per the provisions of the Act, the Rules for providing SNP under the ICDS were notified in 2017.

Improving Anganwadi Infrastructure

The Government is committed to repositioning the Anganwadi Centre (AWC) as a vibrant early childhood development centre to become the first village outpost for health, nutrition and early learning. Towards this end, several steps have been taken for improvement and strengthening of ICDS scheme covering programmatic, management and institutional areas.

Supplementary Nutrition

In pursuance of the provisions contained in the National Food Security Act (NFSA), 2013, the Ministry has notified the (under the Integrated Child Development Scheme Rules, 2017) in 2017 to regulate the entitlement specified under provisions of said Act for every pregnant woman and lactating mother till 6 months after child birth, and every child in the age group of 6 months to 6 years (including those suffering from malnutrition) for 300 days in a year, as per the nutritional standards specified in Schedule II of the said Act. In case of non-supply of the entitled quantities of foodgrains or meals to entitled persons, such persons shall be entitled to receive such food security allowance from the concerned state government, within such time and manner as may be prescribed by the central government.

ICDS System

MWCD implementing International Development Association (IDA) assisted in 162 high burden districts of 8states inthe country covering 3.68

lakh Anganwadi Centres with the following project development objective: (i) to strengthen the Integrated Child Development Services (ICDS) policy framework, systems and capacities, and facilitate community engagement, to ensure greater focus on children under three years of age; (ii) to strengthen convergent actions for improved nutrition outcomes. One of the key activities in ICDS System's Strengthening and Nutrition Improvement Project (ISSNIP) is Information and Communication Technology enabled Real Time Monitoring (ICT-RTM) of ICDS. It intends to leverage ICT to set up a real time monitoring system for improving the service delivery mechanism and ensuring better supervision of ICDS Scheme by deploying a mobile solution driven by a customized ICDS-Common Application Software (ICDS-CAS) at the Anganwadi Centres in selected states. A memorandum of co-operation was signed with Bill and Melinda Gates Foundation (BMGF) to support the design, development and deployment of Common Application Software (CAS) to drive the IT enabled Real Time Monitoring of ICDS and Support System. Accordingly, a customised Common Application software (ICDS-CAS) has been developed.

Scheme for Adolescent Girls

Scheme for Adolescent Girls (SAG) was introduced in 2010-11 and is operational in 205 selected districts across the country. It aims at all-round on pilot basis development of adolescent girls of 11-18 years.The Scheme is being implemented through the state governments/UTs with the cost sharing ratio between the centre and the states and UTs (with legislatures) in the ratio of 50:50 for nutrition and 60:40 for rest of the components. For eight north eastern states (Arunachal Pradesh, Assam, Manipur, Meghalaya, Mizoram, Nagaland, Tripura and Sikkim) and three special category Himalayan states (H.P., JandK and Uttrakhand), the share of centre and state is in the ratio of 90:10. Union territories (without legislatures) are funded 100 per cent of the financial norms or the actual expenditure incurred whichever is less. Anganwadi Centre (AWC) is the focal point for the delivery of the services. The Scheme has two major components- nutrition and non-nutrition.

Under the nutrition component, the out-of-school adolescent girls (11-l4years) attending AWCs and all girls (14-18 years) are provided supplementary nutrition in the form of takehome ration/hot cooked meal. Each adolescent girl is given 600 calories and 18-20 grams of protein and micronutrients (which is approx. 1/3 of recommended dietary allowance) per day for 300 days in a year. The nutrition provided is as per the norms for pregnant and lactating mothers. While the nutrition component aims at improving the health and nutrition status of the adolescent girls, the non-nutrition component, addresses the development needs. In the non-nutrition component, out-of-school adolescent girls of 11-18 years are being provided IFA supplementation, health check-up, and referral services, nutrition and health education, Adolescent Reproductive Sexual Health (ARSH) counselling/ guidance on family welfare, life skill education, guidance on accessing public services and vocational training (only 16-18 year old adolescent girls). The Scheme also aims at mainstreaming out-of-school girls to school system.

Junk Food Guidelines

Junk Food Guidelines have been developed and forwarded to MHRD and MoHFW for implementation. MHRD has requested all CBSE affiliated schools to follow them. MHRD has been requested to issue an advisory to all the states/ UTs accordingly. It has also been suggested in the guidelines that vendors/ street vendors should not be permitted to sell these foods during school timings in a vicinity of 200 meters from any school. The guidelines also provide a list of suitable food items to be offered in the school canteen.

Major Initiatives of Food and Nutrition Board

Food and Nutrition Board (FNB) under MWCD is in process of setting up of 4 food testing Laboratories viz., central laboratory at Faridabad and 3 regional food testing laboratories at Mumbai, Chennai and Kolkata for analyzing the food and nutritional supplements for food safety and quality to ensure nutritional and feeding norms for supplementary nutrition in ICDS Scheme.

MWCD, taking note of the widely prevalent deficiencies of iron, vitamin-A, iodine and other micronutrients in the population, particularly among women and children, has taken the initiative towards addressing this issue through fortification of foods. In this regard, a comprehensive regulation on fortification of Foods namely 'Food Safety and Standards (Fortification of Foods) Regulations, 2016 was operationalized which sets the standards for fortification of major staple foods namely, wheat flour, rice, milk, edible oil and salt. A logo has also been launched.

National Plan of Action for Children

The National Plan of Action for Children (NPAC), 2016 is based on the principles embedded in the National Policy for Children, 2013. The Action Plan has four key priority areas: survival, health and nutrition; education and development; protection; and participation. The NPAC seeks to ensure convergence of ongoing programmes and initiation of new programmes so as to focus on objectives through well-defined strategies and activities to achieve desired level of outcome for children.

Miscellaneous Issues

Direct Benefit Transfer

Government of India adopted Direct Benefit Transfer (DBT) using Aadhaar as the identifier of beneficiaries for delivery of services, benefits or subsidies of various central sector and centrally sponsored schemes to individuals as well as groups where money is spent from the Consolidated Fund of India. In pursuance of directions of the government for implementation of DBT in its schemes, MWCD has identified 15 schemes/components for its implementation.

For transfer of maternity benefits under Pradhan Mantri Matru Vandana Yojana, the Ministry has launched https://pmmvy-cas.nic.in/ portal for direct transfer of incentives in the account of the beneficiary. This portal is also local government director code (LGD) embedded and hence records the location.

Engagement on Social Media

The Ministry is active on social media platforms of Facebook, Twitter and YouTube with followers numbering in lakhs. Social media is being used as a medium to spread awareness among the general public on issues concerning women and children, aiding positive attitude and behaviour change. This medium is also being leveraged to disseminate information on the various schemes and programmes of the government so as to increase citizen engagement. In line with the agenda of the government to use the power and reach of social media to reach out to citizens, the Ministry has started# HelpMeWCD where women and children can send in their grievances. The Ministry is also running a grievance redressal cell which registers and responds to direct complaints via email from women and children across the country.

29 Youth Affairs and Sports

THE Ministry of Youth Affairs and Sports functioned under the overall guidance of the Minister of State (Independent Charge) for Youth Affairs and Sports during the year. In April, 2008, two separate Departments, namely, Department of Youth Affairs and Department of Sports, were created under the Ministry.

The youth represent the most dynamic and vibrant segment of the population. India is one of the youngest nations in the world, with about 65 per cent of the population under 35 years of age. The youth in the age group of 15-29 years comprise 27.5 per cent of the population. It is estimated that by the year 2020, the population of India would have a median age of 28 years only. This 'demographic dividend' offers a great opportunity. In order to capture this demographic dividend, it is essential that the economy has the ability to support the increase in the labour force and the youth have the appropriate education, skills, health awareness and other enablers to productively contribute to the economy. The Government of India makes significant investment on programmes for the youth, through various ministries/departments.

Relevant Website : www.yas.nic.in

National Youth Policy

The National Youth Policy, 2014 (NYP-2014) was launched in 2014, replacing the erstwhile National Youth Policy, 2003. NYP-2014 has been finalised after extensive consultations with all the stakeholders. The Policy defines 'youth' as persons in the age-group of 15-29 years.

Schemes for Youth

The Department of Youth Affairs was operating a number of schemes for development and empowerment of youth. Some of the schemes had annual outlay of less than ₹ 10 crores. In order to improve the effectiveness of these schemes, it was considered necessary to merge these schemes into a single scheme, which can act as the flagship scheme of the Department. This would help in achieving better synergies between the schemes and thereby, improve their effectiveness and help in achieving better outcomes with the available resources.

The Department undertook a comprehensive exercise to re-structure/consolidate all the schemes which are now being operated by Department of Youth Affairs into 3 flagship schemes as follows:

S. No.	Names of Old Schemes	Names of New Schemes
1.	Nehru Yuva Kendra Sangathan (NYKS)	Merged into a new 'umbrella' Scheme called "Rashtriya Yuva Sashaktikaran Karyakram (RYSK)".
2.	National Youth Corps (NYC)	
3.	National Programme for Youth & Adolescent Development (NPYAD)	
4.	International Cooperation	
5.	Youth Hostels (YH)	
6.	Assistance to Scouting & Guiding Organisations	
7.	National Discipline Scheme (NDS)	
8.	National Young Leaders Programme (NYLP)	
9.	National Service Scheme (NSS)	National Service Scheme (NSS)
10.	Rajiv Gandhi National Institute of Youth Development (RGNIYD)	Rajiv Gandhi National Institute of Youth Development (RGNIYD)

Rashtriya Yuva Sashaktikaran Karyakram

Nehru Yuva Kendra Sangathan

Nehru Yuva Kendra Sangathan (NYKS), launched in 1972, is one of the largest youth organisations in the world. NYKS currently has about 8.7 million youth enrolled through 3.04 lakh youth clubs/mahila mandals. NYKS has presence in 623 districts through Nehru Yuva Kendras (NYKs). The objective of the programme is to develop the personality and leadership qualities of the youth and to engage them in nation-building activities. The areas of focus of the NYKS activities include literacy and education, health and family welfare, sanitation and cleanliness, environment conservation, awareness on social issues, women empowerment, rural development, skill development and self-employment, entrepreneurship development, civic education, disaster relief and rehabilitation, etc. The youth associated with Nehru Yuva Kendras are not only socially aware and motivated but are also inclined towards social development work through voluntary efforts.

National Youth Corps

The Scheme of National Youth Corps (NYC) was launched in 2010-11 and the same is being implemented through NYKS. The main objectives of the Scheme are as follows: to set up a group of disciplined and dedicated youth who have the inclination and spirit to engage in the task of nation-building; to facilitate the realization of inclusive growth (both social and economic); to act as group modulators and peer group educators; and to act as role models for the younger cohort, especially towards enhancement of public ethics, probity and dignity of labour.

Under it, youth in the age-group of 18-25 years are engaged as volunteers to serve upto maximum 2 years in nation-building activities. The minimum qualification for NYC volunteers is Class-X passed and they were initially paid an honorarium of ₹ 2,500/- per month, but the same was increased to ₹ 5,000/- per month from 2016. The selection of NYC volunteers is done by a selection committee, headed by District Collector/Deputy Commissioner of the concerned district. The volunteers are given 15-day induction training at the time of joining and 7-day refresher training in the second year of their tenure. Normally, 2 NYC volunteers are deployed in every block. They act as an extended arm of NYKS in the block and play an active role in implementation of various programmes and initiatives of NYKS.

National Service Scheme

National Service Scheme (NSS) was introduced in 1969 with the primary objective of developing the personality and character of the youth through voluntary community service. Education through Service is the purpose of the NSS. The ideological orientation of the NSS is inspired by the ideals of Mahatma Gandhi. Very appropriately, the motto of NSS is "not me, but you". An NSS volunteer places the 'community' before 'self'. NSS aims at developing the following qualities/ competencies among the volunteers: to understand the community in which the NSS volunteers work and to understand themselves in relation to their community; to identify the needs and problems of the community and involve themselves in problem-solving exercise; to develop among themselves a sense of social and civic responsibility; to utilize their knowledge in finding practical solutions to individual and community problems; to gain skills in mobilizing community participation; and to practise national integration and social harmony.

Rajiv Gandhi National Institute of Youth Development

Rajiv Gandhi National Institute of Youth Development (RGNIYD), Sriperumbudur, Tamil Nadu, is an 'Institute of National Importance' under the Ministry of Youth Affairs and Sports. The RGNIYD was set up in 1993 as a society under the Societies Registration Act, 1975 and was conferred the status of 'Deemed to be University' under 'de-novo' category in 2008, by the Ministry of Human Resources Development. The Institute functions as a vital resource centre with its multi-faceted functions of offering academic programmes at post graduate level encompassing various dimensions of youth development, engaging in seminal research in the vital areas of youth development and conducting training/capacity building programmes in youth development, besides the extension and outreach initiatives across the country.

National Programme for Youth and Adolescent Development

National Programme for Youth and Adolescent Development (NPYAD) scheme was introduced in 2008. Under it, financial assistance is provided to government/non-government organisations for taking up youth and adolescent activities. The assistance under NPYAD is provided under 5 major components, namely: (a) youth leadership and personality development training; (b) promotion of national integration; (c) promotion of adventure; Tenzing Norgay National Adventure Awards; (d) development and empowerment of adolescents; (e) technical and resource development.

National Youth Festival

Under promotion of national integration, of NPYAD, a National Youth Festival is organised in January every year to commemorate the birth anniversary of Swami Vivekananda (12th January), which is celebrated as National Youth Day. The Festival is organised in one of the states willing and equipped to host it. The expenditure is shared between the Centre and the host state. The programmes organised include various cultural programmes (both competitive and non-competitive), youth convention, suvichar, exhibitions, adventure programmes, etc. About 5,000 youth from various states/ UTs of the country participate in the Festival.

Youth Hostels

Youth Hostels are built to promote youth travel and to enable the young people to experience the rich cultural heritage of the country. The construction of the youth hostels is a joint venture of the central and state governments. While the central government bears the cost of construction, the state governments provide fully developed land free-of-cost, with water supply, electricity connection and approach roads. Youth hostels are located in areas of historical and cultural value, in educational centres, in tourist destinations, etc. Such hostels provide good accommodation for the youth at reasonable rates. Out of 83 currently operational hostels, 11 have been transferred to Nehru Yuva Kendra Sangathan, Sports Authority of India, concerned state governments, for optimum use for youth and sports development and the remaining 72 hostels are under direct control of the Ministry.

Assistance to Scouting and Guiding Organisation

The Department provides assistance to the scouting and guiding organisations, with a view to promote the scouts and guides movement in the country. This is an international movement aimed at building character, confidence, idealism and spirit of patriotism and service among young boys and girls. Scouting and guiding also seeks to promote balanced physical and mental development among the boys and girls. The financial assistance is provided to scouting and guiding organisations for various programmes such as organization of training camps, skill development programmes, holding of jamborees, etc. The activities, inter alia, include programmes related to adult literacy, environment conservation, community service, health awareness and promotion of hygiene and sanitation.

Sports

Sports and games have always been seen as an integral component in all round development of human personality. Apart from being means of entertainment and physical fitness, sports have also played a great role in generation of spirit of healthy competition and bonding within the community. Achievements in sports have always been a source of national pride and prestige. With modern sports being highly competitive, the use of modern infrastructure, equipment and advanced scientific support has changed the scenario of sports at the international level. Keeping in line with the growing demands for advanced infrastructure, equipment and scientific support, Government of India has taken several initiatives and is providing the necessary assistance to sportspersons by way of training and exposure in international competitions backed up with scientific and equipment support.

National Sports Policy

National Sports Policy, 2001 envisages mainly broadbasing and promotion of excellence in sports. The salient features of this Policy are: (i) broadbasing of sports and achievement of excellence; (ii) upgradation and development of infrastructure; (iii) support to national sports federations and other appropriate bodies; (iv) strengthening of scientific and coaching support to sports; (v) incentives to promote sports; (vi) enhanced participation of women, scheduled tribes and rural youth; (vii) involvement of corporate sector in sports promotion; and (viii) promotion of sports mindedness among the public at large.

Sports Authority of India

The Sports Authority of India (SAI) was established in 1984 as a registered society primarily to ensure effective maintenance and optimum utilization of the sports infrastructure that was built in Delhi during ASIAD, 1982. It is now the nodal agency in the country for broadbasing sports and for training of sportspersons to achieve excellence in national and international sports. The Society for National Institute of Physical Education and Sports (SNIPES) was merged with SAI in 1987. Subsequently Netaji Subhash National Institute of Sports (NSNIS), Patiala and its allied centres at Bengaluru, Kolkata and Gandhinagar, and Lakshmibai National College of Physical Education at Thiruvananthapuram came under SAI. It has now regional centres at Bengaluru, Gandhinagar, Kolkata, Sonepat, Bhopal, Imphal, Chandigarh and Lucknow. SAI also operates a High Altitude Training Center (HATC) at Shillaroo (HP). SAI operates various schemes at sub-junior, junior and senior levels, namely, National Sports Talent Contest (NSTC), Army Boys Sports Company (ABSC), SAI Training Centres (STC) and Special Area Games to achieve excellence at national and international level. SAI has also set up centres of excellence for elite sportspersons at each of its regional centres and one at the National Institute of Sports, Patiala. With a view to promote sports on single discipline basis, National Sports Academies have been set up by SAI, in collaboration with the National Sports Federations to attract sports talent in the respective sports discipline in the age group of 14-25 years. The Scheme envisages modern training centres having state of the art sports facilities, equipment, requisite sports science infrastructure as well as qualified personnel to meet the daily requirement of the trainees.

For optimum utilization of its five stadia which were renovated at substantial cost for Commonwealth Games, 2010, Sports Authority of India introduced 'Come and Play Scheme' in 2011. The designated areas in the SAI stadia viz., Jawaharlal Nehru Stadium, Dr. Karni Singh Shooting Ranges, Dr. SPM Swimming Pool Complex, Major Dhyan Chand Hockey Stadium and Indira Gandhi Indoor Stadium (Gymnastics, Wrestling and Cycling Velodrome) were thrown open in 2011 for both imparting professional training to establish sportspersons and also to beginners with the objective of encouraging participation in sports and for optimum utilization of stadia.

After the successful launch of the Scheme in Delhi, SAI launched the 'Come and Play Scheme' in all its centres spread across the country from 2011 with the objective of encouraging the local youth to use the sports facilities available at these centres and to impart coaching, primarily to the beginners, to encourage participation in sports.

Lakshmibai National Institute of Physical Education

The Institute was established initially as a college in 1957, the centenary year of the first war of Independence. The University is located at Gwalior, where Rani Lakshmibai of Jhansi had laid down her life for the country's freedom struggle. In recognition of the services rendered in the field of physical education and sports by the Institute, it was upgraded to a "Deemed University" in 1995. The Lakshmibai National Institute of Physical Education (LNIPE) is fully funded by the Government of India. The Institute offers the following full time courses: (1) Bachelor of Physical Education (BPE) (4 year degree course), (2) Master of Physical Education (MPE) (2 year course), (3) M. Phil in Physical Education (1 year course) and (4) Ph.D in Physical Education. Apart from these, following certificate, diploma and post-graduate courses are also being conducted by the Institute: (a) adventure sports, (b) special sports, (c) youth affairs, (d) information technology, (e) sports coaching, (f) yoga and alternate therapies, (g) sports management, and (h) sports journalism. The Institute also conducts in-service training programmes in physical education for ex-army personnel, refresher/orientation course for physical education teachers in universities, colleges and schools. The Institute attracts students from abroad also. A North East Campus of LNIPE has also been established at Guwahati (Assam) and is functioning since 2010-11.

National Sports University

In recognition of the talent and contribution of the sportspersons of the North Eastern states in general and Manipur in particular, the Government of India decided to set up a National Sports University in Manipur. The Manipur government has provided land measuring 325.90 acres in west Imphal District for setting up of this University. It will be first of its kind, to promote sports education in the areas of sports sciences, sports technology, sports management and sports coaching besides functioning as the national training centre for select sports disciplines by adopting best international practices. The University will impart Bachelor's, Master's and Doctoral programmes in sports coaching, sports sciences and physical education in various disciplines. Specialised degree programmes in various sports education and coaching disciplines are envisaged in the future. From the academic session 2018-19, M.Sc. (Sports Coaching) and MA (Sports Psychology) have been introduced.

Khelo India

The Ministry of Youth Affairs and Sports was implementing a centrally sponsored scheme called the Panchayat Yuva Krida aur Khel Abhiyan (PYKKA) from 2008-09 to 2013-14.The scheme aimed at creation of basic sports infrastructure at village and block / Panchayat levels through development and maintenance of playgrounds and mass participation in sports through conduct of annual sports competitions. Separately, an Urban Sports Infrastructure Scheme (USIS) was also introduced in 2010-11 and continued up to 2015-16. The PYKKA scheme provided for mid-term review. Accordingly, the scheme was reviewed and revamped as the Rajiv Gandhi Khel Abhiyan (RGKA), implemented during 2014-15 to 2015-16-which envisaged construction of block level sports complex comprising both indoor and outdoor playing facilities through convergence with other schemes of the Government; and conduct of competitions block upwards. A new umbrella Scheme "Khelo India" was launched during 2016-17 after merger of existing scheme Rajiv Gandhi Khel Abhiyan (RGKA), Urban Sports Infrastructure Scheme (USIS) and National Sports Talent Search System Programme (NSTSSP).

The revamped Khelo India has been evolved after a lot of deliberations with all stakeholders, including departments of sports of states and UTs. The Scheme is being implemented as a central sector scheme. The revamped Khelo India has twelve components, which aim at achieving the twin objectives of the National Sports Policy 2001- broadbasing of sports and achieving excellence in sports, which in turn will infuse sports culture in the country and enable it to derive benefits that sports offers, namely, holistic development of children and youth, community development, gender equity, healthy nation, national pride and economic opportunities related to sport development.

Its 12 verticals are: play field development, community coaching development, state level Khelo India centres, annual sports competitions, talent search and development, utilization and creation / upgradation of sports infrastructure, support to national / regional / state sports academies, physical fitness of school-going children, sports for women, promotion of sports among persons with disabilities, sports for peace and development and promotion of rural and indigenous/tribal games.

Promotion of Excellence in Sports

Scheme of Assistance to National Sports Federations

Under this Scheme, the Government of India provides assistance to National Sports Federations (NSFs) for conducting national championships and international tournaments, participation in international tournaments abroad, organizing coaching camps, procuring sports equipment, engagement of foreign coaches, etc.

Scheme of Human Resources Development in Sports

The Scheme of Human Resource Development in Sports, was launched in the 2013-14 after thorough revision of the "Scheme of Talent Search and Training". The main focus of the Scheme is to give emphasis on the academic and intellectual side of sports management by awarding Fellowships to deserving candidates for specialized studies at Masters' and Doctoral level, The Scheme also extends financial assistance for training / seminars / conferences / workshops and short-term courses for coaches technical and support staff at national and international level.

National Sports Development Fund

The National Sports Development Fund (NSDF) was instituted with a view to mobilizing resources from the government as well as non-governmental sources, including the private/corporate sector and non-resident Indians, for promotion of sports and games in the country. To make contributions to the fund attractive, 100 per cent exemption from income tax is available on all contributions. The funds available under NSDF are used for promotion of sports in general and specific sports disciplines and individual sportspersons for achieving excellence at the national and international level in particular; imparting special training and coaching in relevant sport disciplines to sportspersons, coaches and sports specialists; to construct and maintain infrastructure as may be required for promotion of excellence in sports; to supply equipment to governmental and non-governmental organizations and individuals with a view to promoting excellence in sports; to identify problems and take up research and development studies for providing support to excellence in sports, etc.

Incentive Schemes for Sportspersons

Various schemes to give incentives to sportspersons to take up sports are also implemented by the Ministry.

Rajiv Gandhi Khel Ratna Award

The Scheme was launched in 1991-92 with the objective of honouring sportspersons to enhance their general status and to give them greater dignity and place of honour in society. Under it, an amount of ₹ 7.5 lakh is given as award for the most spectacular and outstanding performance by a sportsperson over a period of four years immediately preceding the year in which award is to be given.

For 2018, this award has been conferred upon Ms.Saikhom Mirabai Chanu for weightlifting and Shri Virat Kohli for cricket.

Arjuna Award

The award was instituted in 1961. To be eligible for the award, a sportsperson should have not only good performance consistently for the previous four years at the international level with excellence for the year for which award is recommended, but should have also shown qualities of leadership, sportsmanship and a sense of discipline. The awardee is given a statuette, a certificate, ceremonial dress and a cash award of rupees five lakh. For 2018, 20 sportspersons were given the award in various disciplines.

Dhyan Chand Award for Life Time Achievement

This award was instituted in 2002. It is given to honour those sportspersons who have contributed to sports by their performance and continue to contribute to promotion of sports even after their retirement from active sporting career. The awardee is given a statuette, a certificate, ceremonial dress and a cash award of rupees five lakh. For 2018, this award was given to four sportspersons.

Dronacharya Award

This award was instituted in 1985 to honour eminent coaches who have successfully trained sportspersons or teams and enabled them to achieve outstanding results in international competitions. The awardee is given a statuette of Guru Dronacharya, a certificate, ceremonial dress and a cash award of five lakhs. For 2018, eight persons received the honour in various disciplines.

Maulana Abul Kalam Azad Trophy

This trophy was instituted in 1956-57. The top overall performing university in the inter-university tournaments is given the Maulana Abul Kalam Azad (MAKA) Trophy, which is a rolling trophy. A small replica of the MAKA Trophy is also awarded for retention by the university. For 2018, the Trophy was bagged by Guru Nanak Dev University, Amritsar.

Rashtriya Khel Protsahan Puraskar

With a view to recognizing the contribution made to sports development by entities other than sportspersons and coaches, Government has instituted a new award titled 'Rashtriya Khel Protsahan Puraskar' from 2009, which has four categories, namely, identification and nurturing of budding / young talent, encouragement to sports through corporate social responsibility, employment of sportspersons and sports welfare measures and sports for development. The award consists of a citation and a trophy in each of the above mentioned categories. There is no cash award.

For 2018, awards were given for three categories - identification and nurturing of budding / young talent, encouragement to sports through corporate social responsibility, employment of sportspersons and sports welfare measures and sports for development.

Special Awards to winners in International Sports Events and their Coaches

This Scheme was introduced in 1986 to encourage and motivate outstanding sportspersons for higher achievements and to attract the younger generation to take up sports as a career. Under it, special awards are given to sportspersons and their coaches for winning medals in recognized international sports events held in a year at the following rates:

(a) Category : Open Category Sports

S. No.	Name of Event	Amount of Award Money (in Rupees) Gold Medal	Silver Medal	Bronze Medal
1	Olympic Games (Summer & Winter)	75 lakh	50 lakh	30 lakh
2	Asian Games	30 lakh	20 lakh	10 lakh
3	Commonwealth Games	30 lakh	20 lakh	10 lakh
4	World Championships or World Cup (conducted in Four Year Cycle)/All England Championship of Badminton	40 lakh	25 lakh	15 lakh
5	World Championships/ World Cup (held once in two years)	20 lakh	14 lakh	8 lakh
6	World Championships/World Cup (held annually)	10 lakh	7 lakh	4 lakh
7	Asian Championships (Held once in 4 years)	15 lakh	10 lakh	5 lakh
8	Asian Championships (held once in 2 years)	7.5 lakh	5 lakh	2.5 lakh
9	Asian Championships (held annually)	3.75 lakh	2.5 lakh	1.25 lakh
10	Commonwealth Championships (held once in 4 years)	15 lakh	10 lakh	5 lakh
11	Commonwealth Championships (held once in 2 years)	7.5 lakh	5 lakh	2.5 lakh
12	Commonwealth Championships (held once in 1 year)	3.75 lakh	2.5 lakh	1.25 lakh
13	World University Games	3.75 lakh	2.5 lakh	1.25 lakh

(b) Category :- Para - Sports

S. No.	Name of Event	Amount of Award Money (in Rupees)		
		Gold Medal	Silver Medal	Bronze Medal
1	Paralympic Games (Summer & Winter)	75 lakh	50 lakh	30 lakh
2	Para Asian Games	30 lakh	20 lakh	10 lakh
3	Commonwealth Games (Para Athletes)	30 lakh	20 lakh	10 lakh
4	IPC World Cup/ Championship (held biennially)	20 lakh	14 lakh	8 lakh
5	IPC World Cup/ Championship (held biennially)	10 lakh	7 lakh	4 lakh

(c) Category:- Blind-Sports

S. No.	Name of Event	Amount of Award Money (in Rupees)		
		Gold Medal	Silver Medal	Bronze Medal
1	IBSA World Championship	10 lakh	7 lakh	4 lakh

(d) Category:- Sports for Deaf

S. No.	Name of Event	Amount of Award Money (in Rupees)		
		Gold Medal	Silver Medal	Bronze Medal
1	Deaflympics	15 lakh	10 lakh	5 lakh

(e) Category:- Special Olympics-Sports

S. No.	Name of Event	Amount of Award Money (in Rupees)		
		Gold Medal	Silver Medal	Bronze Medal
1	Special Olympics (Summer/Winter)	5 lakh	3 lakh	1 lakh

(f) Category: - Blind Cricket World Cup

S. No.	Name of Event	Amount of Award Money (in Rupees)
1	Blind Cricket World Cup (held in 4 years)	5 lakh

Cash award is also given to coaches who have trained the medal winners for at least 180 days immediately preceding the tournament. Award money to a coach is 50 per cent of the award money given to the sportsperson coached. In case, there is more than one coach, the award money is distributed among them equally.

Scheme of Pension to Meritorious Sportspersons

This Scheme was launched in 1994. As per the Scheme, those sportspersons, who are Indian citizens and have won gold, silver and bronze medals in Olympic Games, World Cup / World Championships, Asian Games, Commonwealth Games, Para-Olympics and Para-Asian Games, have attained the age of 30 years and have retired from active sports career are eligible for pension for life. Rates of pension have been doubled from April 2018. Enhanced rates of pension are as under:

S. No.	Category of Meritorious Sportspersons	Rate of Pension (₹/per month)
1	Medallists at the Olympic Games / Para Olympic Games	20,000
2	Gold medallists at the World Cup/World Championship* in Olympic and Asian Games disciplines	16,000
3	Silver and Bronze medallists at the World Cup in Olympic and Asian Games disciplines	14,000
4	Gold medallists of the Asian/Commonwealth Games/Para Asian Games	14,000
5	Silver and Bronze medallists of the Asian/Commonwealth Games/ Para Asian Games	12,000

* *World Cup/World Championship held once in four years only shall be considered.*

Pandit Deendayal Upadhyay National Welfare Fund

The name of National Welfare Fund for sportspersons was changed to Padit Deendayal Upadhyay National Welfare Fund for sportspersons from 2017. This Fund was set up in 1982 with a view to assisting outstanding sportspersons of yesteryears, living in indigent circumstances who had won glory for the country in sports. Assistance is given in the form of lumpsum financial assistance, to sportspersons or their families in case of sustaining a fatal injury during training for, or participation in, an international competition; sportsperson sustaining injury other than a fatal injury, families of sportspersons living in indigent circumstances, for medical treatment of sportspersons, and for sports promoters (referees, coaches and umpires) living in indigent circumstances. Assistance is provided to those whose monthly income from all sources is less than ₹ 2,00,000/- per annum.

Scheme of Assistance for Anti-Doping Activities

Doping is the deliberate or inadvertent use by sportspersons of a substance or method banned by Medical Commission of International Olympic Committee / World Anti Doping Agency (WADA). In pursuit of gold and glory, large numbers of sportspersons all over the world are tempted to use performance enhancing substances in an effort to gain a competitive edge over others. India is no exception to this malaise. Recognizing the urgent need for embarking upon a concerted effort to check doping in collaboration with the global anti doping community, the Government of India became one of the members of the Foundation Board of WADA, set up with the initiative of the International Olympic Committee.

National Anti Doping Agency

National Anti Doping Agency (NADA), set up in 2009, is the national organization responsible for promoting, coordinating, and monitoring the doping control programme in sports in the country. The Anti Doping rules of NADA are compliant with the Anti Doping Code of WADA.

National Dope Testing Laboratory

The National Dope Testing Laboratory (NDTL) is an autonomous body under this Ministry. It is accredited by National Accreditation Board for Testing and Calibration Laboratories (NABL) for ISO:IEC 17025 (2003) and World Anti-Doping Agency (WADA) (September, 2008) for testing of urine and blood samples from human sports. NDTL is one of the 33 WADA accredited laboratories in the world and one among seven in Asia. It has state- of-the-art facilities for both routine and research activities. NDTL was registered in 2008 under Registration of Society Act, 1860. Apart from human dope testing, NDTL has diversified in the area of horse dope testing and proficiency testing programme.

30 States and Union Territories

Andhra Pradesh

Area :	1,60,200 sq. km	*Population*	: 4.9 crore (as per prov. census 2011)
Capital :	Hyderabad	*Principal Languages*	: Telugu, Urdu, Hindi, Banjara

THE earliest mention of the Andhras is said to be in *Aitereya Brahmana* (2000 BC). It indicates that the Andhras, originally an Aryan race living in north India migrated to south of the Vindhyas and later mixed with non-Aryans. Regular history of *Andhra Desa,* according to historians, begins with 236 BC, the year of Ashoka's death. During the following centuries, *Satavahanas, Sakas, Ikshvakus,* Eastern *Chalukyas,* and *Kakatiyas* ruled the Telugu country. Other dynasties that ruled over the area in succession were the kingdoms of Vijayanagar and Qutub Shahi followed by Mir Qumruddin and his successors, known as the Nizams. Gradually, from the 17th century onwards, the British annexed territories of the Nizam and constituted the single province of Madras. After Independence, Telugu-speaking areas were separated from the composite Madras Presidency and a new Andhra State came into being on 1st October 1953. With the passing of the States Reorganisation Act, 1956, there was a merger of Hyderabad State and Andhra State, and consequently Andhra Pradesh came into being on 1 November 1956.

Andhra Pradesh is situated on the country's southeastern coast. It is the eighth largest state in the country covering an area of 160,205 sq. km. According to 2011 census, the state is tenth largest by population, with 49,386,799 inhabitants.

The state has the second longest coastline of 974 km (605 mi) among all the states of India, second only to Gujarat. It borders Telangana in the north west, Chhattisgarh in the north, Odisha in the north-east, Karnataka in the west, Tamil Nadu in the south and water body of Bay of Bengal in the east. A small enclave of 30 sq.km of a district of Puducherry, lies in the Godavari delta to the north east of the state.

Andhra Pradesh Reorganisation Act, 2014

Andhra Pradesh Reorganisation Act, 2014 commonly called Telangana Act is an Act of Indian Parliament proclaiming the bifurcation of the Andhra Pradesh into two states, Telangana and residuary Andhra Pradesh. The Act consists of all aspects of division of assets and liabilities, finalize the boundaries of the proposed new states and status of Hyderabad.

Agriculture

Agriculture is the main occupation of about 62 per cent of the people in the state. Rice is a major food crop and staple food contributing about 77 per cent of the foodgrain production. Other important crops are jowar, bajra, maize, ragi, small millets, pulses, castor, tobacco, cotton and sugarcane. Forests cover 23 per cent of the state's area. Important forest products are teak, eucalyptus, cashew, casuarina, bamboo, softwood, etc.

Irrigation

Numerous projects have been taken up under *Jalayagnam* programme. The programme aims at completing the ongoing and new projects in a record time to provide immediate irrigation to water starved areas on top priority by mobilizing funds from all possible sources.

Power

Important power projects in the state are the Nagarjunasagar and Neelam Sanjiva Reddy Sagar (Srisailam Hydel Project), Upper Sileru, Lower Sileru, Tungabhadra Hydel Projects and Nellore, Ramagundam, Kothagudem, Vijayawada and Mudanur Thermal Power Projects. Vijayawada Thermal Power Station with an installed capacity of 1,260 MW and Kothagudem Thermal Power Station with an installed capacity of 1,220 MW are the main sources of thermal power generation. The 1,000 MW coal-based Simhadri Thermal Power Station aims at supplying the entire energy generated to the state.

Industries

The state government is extending various incentives for SSI and tiny sector and large and medium scale industries. The state government has been promoting the manufacturing sector in a big way by providing concessions in power tariff, allotting land and relaxing labour laws in Special Economic Zones (SEZs).

Mines and Geology

Andhra Pradesh is well known globally for its variety of rocks and minerals and is called Ratna Garbha. The state has the largest deposits of quality chrysotile asbestos in the country. Other important minerals found in the state are copper ore, manganese, mica, coal and limestone. The Singareni Coal Mines supply coal to the entire south India. The state produces about 100 to 110 million tonnes of industrial minerals and 200 million cubic metres of stone and building material. AP stands first in barytes and limestone production in the country.

Information Technology

Andhra Pradesh has been forging ahead in the sphere of Information Technology. It is ahead of other states in exploiting the opportunities to the hilt. The state government has introduced many schemes to utilize the maximum number of skilled human resources in the IT Sector.

Transport

Roads : The total R&B network in the state is 69,051 km of which, the national highways passing through the state constitute 4,472 km and the state highways constitute 10,519 km. Major district roads constitute 32,170 km and rural roads 21,714 km. The density with reference to R&B network in the state is 0.23 km per one sq.km. and 0.86 km per 1000 persons.

Railways : Of the railways route covering 5,107 km in Andhra Pradesh, 4,633 km is broad-gauge, 437 km is metre-gauge and 37 km is narrow gauge.

Aviation : Important airports in the state are located at Shamshabad, Tirupathi and Visakhapatnam. International flights are operated from Shamshabad.

Ports : There is one major port at Visakhapatnam under the Central Government and 13 non-major ports under state government. Ports offer tremendous potential for development and for the growth of a wide spectrum of maritime activities such as international shipping, coastal shipping, ship repairs, fishing, captive ports for specific industries, all weather ports, tourism and sports, etc.

Tourist Centres

Andhra Pradesh Tourism Development Corporation continues to strive for promotion of new tourism products such as eco-tourism, beach-tourism and cruise-tourism. The Corporation currently runs a chain of 52 hotels with 1043 rooms and 2222 beds in prime locations fostering homely ambience. An impressive fleet of 144 buses cater to varied tour packages connecting important tourism locations within and outside the state.

Charminar, Salarjung Museum, Golconda Fort in Hyderabad, Thousand Pillar Temple and Fort in Warangal, Sri Lakshmi Narasimha Swamy Temple at Yadagirigutta, Buddha Stupa at Nagarjunakonda, Nagarjuna Sagar, Sri Venkateswara Temple at Tirumala-Tirupathi, Sri Mallikarjunaswamy Temple at Srisailam, Kanaka Durga Temple at Vijayawada, Sri Satyanarayana Swamy Temple at Annavaram, Sri Varaha Narasimha Swamy Temple at Simhachalam, Sri Sita Rama Temple at Bhadrachalam, Araku Valley, Horsley Hills, Nelapattu, etc., are the major tourist attractions of the state.

Relevant Website : www.ap.gov.in

Government

Governor	: E.S.L. Narasimhan	*Chief Secretary*	: Anil Chandra Punetha
Chief Minister	: N. Chandra Babu Naidu	*Jurisdiction of High Court*	: Andhra Pradesh and Telangana

Arunachal Pradesh

Area	: 83,743 sq. km	*Population*	: 13.84 lakh (as per prov. census 2011)
Capital	: Itanagar	*Principal Languages*	: Nyishi, Adi, Bengali, Nepali, Hindi, Mohpa, Assamese, Wancho, Tangsa, Mishmi, Mishing, Nocte, etc.

History and Geography

Arunachal Pradesh became a full-fledged state on February 20, 1987. Till 1972, it was known as the North-East Frontier Agency (NEFA). It gained the Union Territory status on 20 January 1972 and renamed as Arunachal Pradesh. On August 15, 1975, an elected Legislative Assembly was constituted and the first Council of Ministers assumed office. The first general election to the Assembly was held in February 1978. Administratively, the state is divided into sixteen districts. The capital of the state is Itanagar in Papum Pare district. Itanagar is named after Ita fort, meaning fort of bricks, built in the 14th century AD. Arunachal Pradesh finds mention in the literature of *Kalika Purana* and *Mahabharata*. This place is the Prabhu Mountains of the *Puranas*.

The widely scattered archaeological remains at different places in Arunachal Pradesh bear testimony to its rich cultural heritage.

Agriculture and Horticulture

Agriculture is the mainstay of the people of the state and mainly depends on *jhum* cultivation. Encouragement is being given to the cultivation of cash crops like potatoes and horticulture crops like apples, oranges and pineapples.

Industries and Minerals

For conservation and exploration of the vast minerals the Arunachal Pradesh Mineral Development and Trading Corporation Limited (APMDTCL) was set up in 1991.

Festivals

Some of the important festivals of the state are *Mopin* and *Solung* of the Adis, *Lossar* of the Monpas, *Boori-boot* of the Hill Miris, *Sherdukpens*, *Dree* of the Apatanis, *Si-Donyi* of the Tagins, *Reh* of the ldu-Mishmis, *Nyokum* of the Nyishis, etc. Animal sacrifice is a common ritual in most festivals.

Tourist Centres

Places of tourist interest are Tawang, Dirang, Bomdila, Tipi, Itanagar, Malinithan, Likabali, Pasighat, Along, Tezu, Miao, Roing, Daporijo Namdapha, Bhismaknagar, Parshuram Kund and Khonsa.

Relevant Website : www.arunachalpradesh.gov.in

Government

Governor	: Brig. Dr. B.D. Mishra (Retd.)	Chief Secretary	: Satya Gopal
Chief Minister	: Pema Khandu	Jurisdiction of High Court	: Falls under Guwahati High Court

Assam

Area	: 78,438 sq. km	Population	: 3.12 crore (census 2011)
Capital	: Dispur	Principal Language	: Asamiya, Bodo

History and Geography

Assam is situated in the north-east corner of the country between 89° 42' E to 96° E longitude and 24° 8' N to 28° 2' N latitude. For centuries, people and communities have been attracted to the fertile environs of Assam and its abundant natural resources. Streams of people have met and mingled, cultures and customs have merged and in this process a rich and composite culture has been evolved.

The state also known as a "Land of Red River and Blue Hills", is one of the most attractive and beautiful states of the country. The mighty river Brahmaputra flows through it, serving as a lifeline for its people settled on both sides of its banks. The word 'Assam' is believed to have derived from the Sanskrit word Asoma meaning peerless or unparalleled. Another academic interpretation claims that the word came from the Ahoms, who ruled the land for about six hundred years prior to its annexation by the British. The influence of several races like Austric, Mongolian, Dravidian and Aryan that came to this land long long ago; have contributed to its rich composite culture.

Assam was known as Pragjyotisha or the place of eastern astronomy during the epic period and later named as Kamrupa. The earlier epigraphic reference to the kingdom of Kamrupa is found in the Allahabad pillar inscription of King Samudragupta. Kamrupa is mentioned as a *pratyanta* or frontier state outside the Gupta Empire, but with friendly and subordinate relation to it. Hiuen Tsang, the Chinese scholar pilgrim who visited Kamrupa in about 743 AD on an invitation of its monarch, Kumar Bhaskar Varman, left a record of the kingdom he called Kamolupa. Kamrupa also figured in the writings of the Arabian historian Alberuni in the eleventh century. Thus, from the epic period down to the twelfth century AD, the eastern frontier kingdom was known as Pragjyotisha and Kamrupa and kings called themselves ' Lords of Pragjyotisha'.

The advent of the Ahoms across the eastern hills in 1228 AD was the turning point in Assam history. They ruled Assam nearly for six centuries. The Burmese entered through the eastern borders and over-ran the territory at a time when court intrigues and dissensions were sapping the vitality of the Ahom royalty. It became a British protectorate in 1826 when the Burmese ceded Assam to the British under the provision of the Treaty of Yandaboo.

Assam covers an area of 78,438 sq. km, which represents 2.39 per cent of the total land area of the country. International boundaries that extend up to nearly 3,200 km, surround the state. Assam - the gateway to the north-eastern states is surrounded by Bhutan and Arunachal Pradesh on the north, Manipur, Nagaland and Arunachal Pradesh on the east and Meghalaya, Tripura and Mizoram on the south and Bangladesh, Meghalaya and West Bengal on the west.

Physiography

A significant geographical aspect of Assam is that it contains three of six physiographic divisions of India—the Northern Himalayas (eastern Hills) the Northern Plains (Brahmaputra Plain), and Deccan Plateau (Karbi Anglong). As the Brahmaputra flows in Assam the climate here is cold and there is widespread rainfall. The hills of Karbi Anglong, North Cachar and those in and close to Guwahati (also Khasi-Garo Hills) now eroded and dissected are originally parts of the South Indian Plateau system. In the south, the Barak originating in the Barail Range (Assam-Nagaland border) flows through the Cachar district with a 25-30 miles (40-50 km) wide valley and enters Bangladesh with the name Surma river. The almond shaped valley is built mostly by aggregation work of the Brahmaputra and its tributaries. Most of the prominent towns and cities of Assam are situated in this valley whose length and breadth are 725 kms and 80-100 kms respectively. Running through a narrow passage at the Meghalaya plateau and Bhutan-Arunachal-Himalayas, the valley finally opens out into the North Bengal Plains.

The second natural division of Assam is the Barak or Surma valley which is surrounded by north Cachar, Manipur and Mizoram. This valley is dominated by the Barak river. It flows through the valley and finally empties itself to the old bed of Brahmaputra in Bangladesh. This valley has hills and 'Beels' or lakes in plenty. Flood is a common feature lending the quality of fertility to the valley.

The two valleys are separated by long range of hills. The Karbi Hills and the N.C. Hills are located in the south of the Brahmaputra valley. Karbi Hills are a part of the Meghalaya plateau. These hills are dotted with plain areas. The average height of this plateau is 600 metres with occasional peaks like Chenghehision (1,359 m) and Dunbukso (1,361 m). Greenery is the hallmark of these hills, slowly reaching their full height towards the middle of the Dima Hasao district, merging with the Barail range, which is the highest hill range in Assam. The elevation of the Barail range varies from 1,000 to 1,200 metres above sea level. The south side of the Barail range is very steep. It attains a maximum height of 1,953 metres in Mahadeo peak to the east of Haflong. This valley is full of dense forest and rare wildlife.

Economy

The state finances have improved considerably. Over the years with industry and businesses picking up.

Agriculture

Assam is endowed with abundant fertile land and water resources with a total geographical area of 78,438 sq. km. The mighty river Brahmaputra and the Barak with their 121 small and tiny tributaries and branches flow through the two valleys keeping the state fertile and cool all along.

Assam has achieved 40 per cent increase in the contribution of agriculture to state GDP. Rice production has increased to 54.40 lakh MT. Likewise, production of foodgrains has also increased from 41.72 lakh MT to 57.22 lakh MT.

Forest & Wildlife

Assam has a total 29,282 sq. km. area of forest and tree cover which covers 37.33 per cent of total geographical area of the state. It has 13,870 sq. km of Reserved Forests; 3103 sq. km. of Proposed Reserved Forests; 5,850 sq. km of Unclassed State forests; and 3,925 sq. km of Protected Area Network. (Source: FSI Data-2009 and "Assam 2011", page-152).

About 180 species of mammals are found in the state which includes globally threatened species such as Golden Langoor, Hoolock Gibbon, Pigmy Hog, Hispid Hare, White-winged Wood Duck, Tiger, Clouded Leopard, Elephant, Swamp Deer, Gangetic Dolphin, etc. More than 800 species of birds and about 195 species of reptiles are found in the state. Strong enforcement of wildlife conservation measures have resulted increase in the tiger population of the state. The tiger population has risen to 167 in 2014 from 143 during 2010-11. The rhino population in Assam stands at 2,624 as per 2015 census. Efforts are also being taken to provide sustainable livelihood to the forest communities.

Industry

Today's Assam embarks on the new charter in the path of development, laying emphasis on new capital formation through the creation of ecologically compliant assets in a sustainable manner. Loans are extended for small industries and service sector under PMRY scheme (till 2008) and under PMEGP. Under these schemes, 2,76,022 unemployed youths have been offered self-employment opportunities between 2001 and 2014.

Power

The state's power generation in 2014-15 was 1,894.7 MU as against 935 MU in 2001. Number of consumers accordingly has increased to 33 lakh as compared to 9 lakh in 2001. Similarly, per capita availability of electricity has also increased to 232 units as against 83 units in 2001. This has become possible due to timely execution of renovation and modernization works in all areas of power generation, distribution and transmission.

Transport & Communication

The state government has been placing great priority on expanding and improving the rural road network and construction of RCC bridges by replacing old timber bridges. Since 2001, more than 23,000 km of all-weather roads and about 3800 RCC bridges have been constructed. Moreover, construction of about 5,000 km all-weather roads including construction of 1,250 numbers of RCC bridges is in progress.

Festivals

Assam, being an inseparable part of this great country, shares all the religious festivals observed elsewhere. The state also has an exclusive range of festivals which have enriched the cultural mosaic of the land. *Bihu* is by far the most important festival of Assam. While *Rongali Bihu* or *Bohag Bihu*, coinciding with the Assamese New Year, is the principal *Bihu*, the harvest festival, known as the *Bhogali Bihu* or *Magh Bihu* is also equally important. There is a third *Bihu* called the *Kangali Bihu* or *Kati Bihu*, which is solemnly observed to prey of love and yearning, sometimes having distinct erotic overtones, with characteristically catchy and earthy tunes. The Bodos, the largest tribal group, perform *Kherai* puja as a festival, which assumes the shape of a fair in most places. The *Kherai puja* is accompanied by shamanistic dance performed by female artists who get into a trance, other with vigorous movements of the head, tossing and swinging the dishevelled hair. *Bathow* is another important puja of the Bodos.

Tourism

Over the years, Assam, the "Gateway of the North-East" has emerged as a popular tourist destination. The natural beauty and bounty, the environment, rich topography, the unique flora and fauna, the biodiversity, virgin forest, proud hills and green valleys all contribute in making Assam a major hub for wildlife and echo-tourism. Assam is located about 79.5 m above sea level. The five national parks, nineteen wildlife sanctuaries and three bird sanctuaries are treasure houses of rare flora and fauna.

Important places of tourism are Kamakhya Temple, Umananda (Peacock Island)Temple, Navagraha (temple of nine planets), Basistha Ashram, Doul Govinda Temple, State Zoo, State Museum, Madan Kamdev Temple—a magnificent archeological place of interest, Saraighat Bridge, Srimata Sankaradeva Kalakshetra Science Museum, Kaziranga National Park, etc.

Relevant Website : www.assam.gov.in

Government

Governor	:	Prof. Jagdish Mukhi	*Chief Secretary*	:	Alok Kumar
Chief Minister	:	Sarbananda Sonowal			
			Jurisdiction of High Court	:	Guwahati High Court

Bihar

Area	:	94,163 sq km	*Population*	:	10.41 crore (2011 census)
Capital	:	Patna	*Principal Language*	:	Hindi

History and Geography

The name Bihar is derived from the Sanskrit word Vihara which means "abode". The word Vihar is itself derived from the word Brahmavihara meaning "Brahma abidings" of "Sublime attitudes. "The state finds mention in the *Vedas, Puranas,* ancient epics, etc., and was the main scene of activities of Buddha and 24 Jain Trithankars. Taking off from its origin, Bihar or ancient Magadha has been the cradle of Indian civilization and the centre of Indian culture and education since time immermorial. From Magadha arose India's first greatest empire, the Maurya Empire, as well as one of the world's greatest pacifist religions, Buddhism. It has also been the home to Jainism. It was in Bihar that the ancient universities of India Nalanda and Vikramshila were built to convey the educational riches of the state.

Great rulers of the state before the Christian era were Bimbisar, Udayin, who founded the city of Pataliputra, Chandragupta Maurya and Emperor Ashoka, the Sungas and the Kanvas. Then came the Kushan rulers followed by Chandragupta Vikramaditya of the Gupta dynasty. Muslim rulers made inroads into the territory during the medieval period. The first conqueror of Bihar was Mohammed- bin-Bakhtiar Khalji. The Tughluqs and then the Mughals followed the Khaljis.

One of the major states of the Indian Union, Bihar is bound on the north by Nepal, on the east by West Bengal, on the west by Uttar Pradesh and on the south by Jharkhand. Bihar has a number of rivers, the most important of which is the Ganga. The other rivers are the Sone, Punpun, Falgu, Karmanasa, Durgawati, Kosi, Gandak, Ghaghara, etc.

Agriculture

Bihar has a total geographical area of about 93.60 lakh hectares, out of which only 55.54 lakh hectares is the net cultivated area with a gross cultivated area of 72.95 lakh hectares. The principal food crops are paddy, wheat, maize and pulses. Main cash crops are sugarcane, potato, tobacco, oilseeds, onion, chillies, jute and mesta. Bihar has a notified forest area of 6.22 lakh hectare, which is 6.65 per cent of its geographical area. About 30.64 thousand hectares net area and 44.33 thousand hectare gross area had received irrigation from different sources.

Irrigation

Bihar has an irrigation potential of 28.73 lakh hectares created through major and medium irrigation schemes and 6.63 lakh hectares through minor irrigation schemes.

Festivals

Festivals are the nerves of any Indian society, spread in each and every part of its body system. Bihar is no exception. All most all the important festivals celebrated at the national level like Durga Puja, Deepawali, Janmastami, Holi, Id, Christmas, etc., have a strong bond with Bihar's cultural and social life. Besides, there are certain peculiar and important festivals which define the social fabric of this of this state include *Chhath Pooja*, also called *Chhathi Dala Chhath and Surya Shashthi*, 'Sama Chakeba', the *Harihar Mela* of Sonepur, etc.

Tourism

A state with so much of history and knowledge has its share of places of tourist interest. Bihar attracts hordes of tourists not just of the country but abroad as well. Prominent places of interest include–Patna, Bodh Gaya, Gaya, Rajgir, Sitamarhi — the birth place of Sita, Barabar Caves, Kesaria Stupa, 100 feet tall Dev Sun Temple of Aurangabad, Jain temples, Buddlist Stupas to name the prominent ones.

Relevant Website : www.gov.bih.nic.in

Government

Governor	: Lalji Tandon	*Chief Secretary*	: Deepak Kumar
Chief Minister	: Shri Nitish Kumar	*Jurisdiction of High Court*	: Patna High Court

Chhattisgarh

Area	: 1,35,192 sq km	*Population*	: 2.56 crore (census 2011)
Capital	: Raipur	*Principal Language*	: Hindi

History and Geography

Chhattisgarh, carved out of Madhya Pradesh came into being in November 2000 as the 26th state of the Union. It fulfils the long-cherished demand of the people. In ancient times the region was known as Dakshin-Kausal. This finds mention in *Ramayana* and *Mahabharata* also. Between the sixth and twelfth centuries Sarabhpurias, Panduavanshi, Somvanshi, Kalchuri and Nagvanshi rulers dominated this region. Kalchuris ruled in Chhattisgarh from 980 to 1791 AD. With the advent of the British in 1845, Raipur gained prominence instead of capital Ratanpur. In 1904 Sambalpur was transferred to Odisha and estates of Sarguja were transferred from Bengal to Chhattisgarh.

Chhattisgarh is bounded by southern Jharkhand and Odisha in the east, Madhya Pradesh and Maharashtra in the west, Uttar Pradesh and western Jharkhand in the north and Andhra Pradesh in the south. Area-wise, Chhattisgarh is the ninth largest state and population-wise it is seventeenth populous state of the nation.

Agriculture

Total geographical area of the state is 137.90 lakh ha. out of which arable land is about 47.70 lakh ha. Area under kharif crop is around 47.60 lakh ha. and rabi is 16.61 lakh ha.

The main kharif crop of this region is paddy which is about 76 per cent of total kharif crops. Apart from it other main crops grown here are maize, soyabean, groundnut, urdbean and pigeon pea. Similarly main rabi crops grown here are wheat, gram, lathyrus, mustard and linseed.

The agro climate zones of Chhattisgarh are three viz., Northern Hill Zone, Chhattisgarh Plain and Plateau of Baster. The average annual rainfall of this area is about 1307.3 mm.

Irrigation and Power

When the state came into being, the total irrigation capacity was 13.28 lakh hectares which has 23 per cent of total sown area which has now increased to 18.44 lakh hectares which is 33.15 per cent of total sown area.

Mineral Resources

Chhattisgarh has the perfect geological set up to host a number of economically crucial minerals. Large deposits of coal, iron ore, limestone, bauxite and dolomite are found in various parts of the state. Districts of north Chhattisgarh such as Surguja, Raigarh, Koriya and Bilaspur are known for huge coal deposits.

Industry

The economy is largely natural resource driven and it leverages the state's rich mineral resources. The key sectors where Chhattisgarh has a competitive advantage include cement, mining, steel, aluminium and power. One of the most mineral-rich states in India, Chhattisgarh provides a lucrative opportunity for cement production at the most competitive prices.

Transport

Roads: The total length of the roads in the state under PWD is 31803 km. The length of national highway is 2226 km; state highways 5240 km 10,539.80 km; main district roads; and 13798 km other district and rural roads. The length of roads in Chhattisgarh has increased from 17.75 km to 21.40 km per 100 km.

Railways : Raipur, Bilaspur, Durg, Rajnandgaon, Raigarh and Korba are important railway stations.

Tourist Centres

Chhattisgarh, situated in the heart of India, is endowed with a rich cultural heritage and attractive natural diversity. The state is full of ancient monuments, rare wildlife species, carved temples, Buddhist sites, palaces, waterfalls, caves, rock paintings and geographical formations.

Relevant Website : www.cgstate.gov.in

Government

Governor	:	Anandiben Patel	*Chief Secretary*	:	Vivek Kumar Dhand
Chief Minister	:	Bhupesh Baghel	*Jurisdiction of High Court*	:	Chhattisgarh High Court

Goa

Area	:	3,702 sq km	*Population*	:	14.59 lakh (prov. census 2011)
Capital	:	Panaji	*Principal Languages*	:	Konkani (Official Language); other languages: Marathi, Hindi, English, Kannada

History and Geography

Goa, known in the bygone days as Gomanchala, Gopakapattam, Gopakapuri, Govapuri, Gomantak, etc., abounds in a rich historical heritage. Early history of Goa is obscure. In the first century of the Christian era, it was a part of the Satavahana empire, followed by the Kadamba, the Rashtrakutas of Malkhed, the Chalukyas and the Silharas. The empire of the Yadavas by the end of the 14th century was displaced by the Khiljis of Delhi and thus Muslim rule came to Goa. After the discovery of the sea route to India by Vasco-da-Gama in 1498, many Portuguese expeditions came to India. In 1510, Alfonso de Albuquerque with the help of the emperor of Vijayanagar attacked and captured Goa. With the arrival of the Jesuit priest Francis Xavier in 1542, proselytisation began in Goa. However, the Portuguese continued to rule over the territory except for an interlude during the latter half of the 17th century when Shivaji conquered a few areas in and around Goa.

Even after India's independence, Goa continued to be in the hands of the Portuguese. However, they could not fulfil the aspirations of the Goan people and ultimately on 19 December 1961, Goa was liberated and made a composite Union Territory with Daman and Diu. In May 1987, Goa was conferred statehood and Daman and Diu was made a separate Union Territory. It is situated on the western coast of the Indian peninsula. On its north runs the

Terekhol river which separates Goa from Maharashtra and on the south lies north Canara district of Karnataka. On the east lie the Western Ghats and in the west the Arabian Sea. Panaji, Margao, Vasco, Mapusa and Ponda are the main towns of Goa.

Agriculture

The total cultivated area of the state is 160,320 hectares while the total production is 108,333 tonnes. A subsidy of upto 90 per cent is also provided for construction of polyhouses and green houses. Similar subsidies are provided for drip irrigation and for construction of biogas plants.

Water Resources

The Water Resources Department apart from supplying raw water for irrigation has also augmented raw water supply to the PWD. Assonora Water Works has been augmented with a 25 MLD raw water from Chapora river at Sal and 10 MLD from Amthane tank.

Industries

All schemes under the State Industrial Policy as well as the State Biotech Policy will continue to be in force and are to be popularized further. To provide encouragement to artisans of Goan handicrafts, it is proposed to develop Goa Haat-cum-shilpagram, new emporia in Goa and outside Goa and develop e-portal for the sale of handicraft items across the globe.

Transport

Roads: Of the motorable roads, national highway constitutes 264 km, state highways 279.4 km and other roads MDR/RR/4501.18 km.

Railways : Goa is linked with Mumbai, Mangalore and Thiruvananthapuram through the Konkan Railway, which has introduced several fast trains on these lines. Vasco da Gama is connected with Bengaluru and Belgaum on the South Central Railway, presently for goods traffic only.

Aviation : Mumbai, Delhi, Thiruvananthapuram, Cochin, Chennai, Agati and Bengaluru are linked with Dabolim through regular airline services.

Ports : Mormugao is the major port in the state which handles cargo vessels. Minor ports are located at Panaji, Tiracol, Chapora, Betul and Talpona, out of which Panaji is the main operative port. One off-shore berth at Panaji has also been commissioned.

Tourist Centres

Important tourist centres are Colva, Calangute, Vagator, Baga, Harmal, Anjuna and Miramar beaches; Basilica of Bom Jesus and St. Cathedral churches at Old Goa; Kavlem, Mardol, Mangeshi, Bandora Temples; Aguada, Terekhol, Chapora and Cabo de Rama Forts; Dudhsagar and Harvalem waterfalls and Mayem lake resort. The state has rich wildlife sanctuaries, viz., Bondla, Cotigao, Molem and Dr Salim Ali Bird Sanctuary at Chorao covering an area of 354 sq km.

Forest

Goa has a good forest cover of 34 per cent against the national requirement of 33 per cent and nearly 62 per cent of tree cover.

Health

Goa became the first state in the country to launch diabetic registry. The new district hospitals at Margao, Mapusa and the new 170 bedded ID hospital at Ponda are important hospitals.

Relevant Website : www.goa.gov.in

Government

Governor	: Mridula Sinha	*Chief Secretary*	: Dharmendra Sharma
Chief Minister	: Manohar Parrikar	*Jurisdiction of High Court*	: Goa Bench of Bombay High Court

Gujarat

Area	: 1,96,024 sq km	*Population*	: 60,439,692 (prov. census 2011)
Capital	: Gandhinagar	*Principal Language*	: Gujarati

History and Geography

The history of Gujarat goes back to 2000 BC. It is believed that Lord Krishna left Mathura to settle in the west coast of Saurashtra which later came to be known as Dwarka. Later it witnessed various kingdoms as Mauryas, Guptas and others. It was during the rule of Chalukyas (Solankis) that Gujarat witnessed progress and prosperity. In spite of the plundering of Mahmud Ghazni, the Chalukya kings were able to maintain general prosperity and well-being. After this glorious respite, Gujarat faced troubled times under the Muslims, Marathas and the British rule. Before independence, the present territories of Gujarat used to be in two parts - the British and the Princely territories. With the reorganization of the states, the Union of the States of Saurashtra and the Union Territory of Kachchh along with the former British Gujarat became a part of the biggest bilingual State of Bombay. Gujarat officially formed as a state in May 1960. It is situated on the west coast of India. The state is bounded by the Arabian Sea on the west, Pakistan and Rajasthan in the north and north-east respectively, Madhya Pradesh in the south-east and Maharashtra in the south.

Agriculture

In order to boost agricultural growth and to further improve it, the state government celebrated 2014-15 as *krishi vikas varsh*. 'Krishi Mahotsav' is being organized every year to make farmers aware of modern technologies and methods of scientific farming. Gujarat is the major producer of cotton, groundnut and tobacco and provides inputs for important industries like textiles, oil and soap. Other important cash crops are paddy, wheat and bajra.

Electricity

Gujarat has become the first state in the country to come with a solar policy in 2009, with a view to give boost to the solar energy sector. Installed capacity of this project is about 400 MW.

Roads

Road network plays a crucial role in the development of the state. As a novel approach, the state government has involved private sector in the building of a sound road network. With a view to meet up the needs of increasing population, BRTS facility has been started in Ahmedabad for speedy commuting.

Ports

During the last decade, Gujarat has acquired a status of an important maritime state of the country. Nearly 80 per cent of the total traffic on the non-major ports and about 48 per cent of the total traffic on all the ports of the country is being recorded on the ports of Gujarat, which is a matter of pride for the state. There are 41 minor and intermediate and one major port—Kandla Port.

Festivals

Tarnetar fair is held at village Tarnetar of Surendranagar district in the honour of Lord Shiva. This fair is held every year in the month of *Bhadrapada* (August/September). *Madhavrai fair* at Madhavpur near Porbandar is held on the ninth day of the bright half of the month of *Chaitra* (March/April). *Ambaji fair* dedicated to *Amba* mother goddess is held in Banaskantha district. The biggest annual fair, *Janmashtami,* the birthday of Lord Krishna, is celebrated at Dwarka and Dakor with great enthusiasm. *Navratri* - world's longest dance festival, *Jagannath Rath Yatra* famous chariot festival, *Modhera Dance Festival-Utrardh Mhotsav* in the backdrop of famous Sun Temple in north Gujarat, *Rann Utsav*—basking in moonlit nights in the vast stretches of Rann of Kutchh and other festivals are *Makar-Sankranti, Dang Darbar, Shamlaji fair,* and *Bhavnath fair.*

Tourist Centres

Religious spots like Dwarka, Somnath, Palitana, Pavagadh, Ambaji, Bhadreshwar, Shamlaji, Taronga and Girnar; Porbandar, birth place of Mahatma Gandhi, monuments of architectural and archaeological surprises like Patan, Siddhpur, Ghurali, Dabhoi; Vadnagar, Modhera, Lothal and Ahmedabad; beaches like Ahmadpur-Mandvi, Chorvad, Ubharat, and Tithal; the hill station Saputara, lion sanctuary of Gir forest and wild ass sanctuary in small desert of Kachchh area are major tourist attractions in the state. Moreover Sabarmati Riverfront: Displays development level and tourism potential. Sursagar lake in Vadodara, centre of tourists' attraction, Nal Sarovar Bird Sanctuary—Home for migrant birds from across the globe.

Relevant Website : www.gujaratindia.com

Government

Governor	: Om Parkash Kohli	*Chief Secretary*	: J.N. Singh
Chief Minister	: Vijay Rupani	*Jurisdiction of High Court*	: Gujarat High Court

Haryana

Area	: 44,212 sq km	*Population*	: 2.54 crore (2011 census)
Capital	: Chandigarh	*Principal Language*	: Hindi

History and Geography

Haryana has a proud history dating back to the Vedic Age. The state was home to the legendary Bharata dynasty, after which the country was named Bharat. The land of Haryana has been the cradle of Indian culture and civilization. Archaeological findings by Guy E. Pilgrim in 1915 established that 15 million years ago, the early man lived in the Shivaliks. *Vamana Purana* states that King Kuru ploughed the field of Kurukshetra with a golden plough, drawn by the Nandi of Lord Shiva, and reclaimed an area of seven 'kosas'.

Replete with myths, legends and Vedic references, Haryana's past is steeped in glory. It was on the soil of Haryana that Saint Ved Vyas wrote *Mahabharata*. It was here that Lord Krishna preached the gospel of duty to Arjuna about 5,000 years ago. It was here that the epic battle of Mahabharata was fought. Being the gateway to north India, the region has been the battleground of many a war. The Huns, the Turks and the Tughlaqs invaded India and decisive battles were fought on this land. At the end of the 14th century, Taimur led an army through this area to Delhi. Later, the Mughals defeated the Lodhis in the historic battle of Panipat in 1526. Another decisive battle was fought in 1556 at this very site, establishing the supremacy of the Mughals up to the advent of the British rule, and the rise of Delhi as the imperial capital of India.

An adjunct to Delhi, Haryana practically remained anonymous until the uprising in 1857. After the British crushed the rebellion, they deprived the Nawabs of Jhajjar and Bahadurgarh, the Raja of Ballabhgarh and Rao Tula Ram of Rewari in Haryana region, of their territories. These were either merged with British territories or handed over to the rulers of Patiala, Nabha and Jind, making Haryana a part of the Punjab province. With the reorganization of Punjab in November 1956, Haryana was born as a full-fledged state.

Strategically located, Haryana is bounded by Uttar Pradesh in the east, Punjab in the west, Himachal Pradesh in the north, and Rajasthan in the south. The National Capital of Delhi juts into Haryana. With just 1.37 per cent of the total geographical area and less than two per cent of India's population,

Haryana has carved a place of distinction for itself. Ranked among the most prosperous states in the country, Haryana has the second highest per capita income in India, after Goa.

Agriculture

Agriculture is the mainstay of more than 65 per cent population in Haryana with the second largest contribution to the food bowl of the country. Under the diversification of crops, more and more area is being brought under cash crops like sugarcane, cotton and oilseeds, vegetable and fruits. Sustainable agriculture is being promoted through the propagation of resource conserving technologies and organic farming.

Irrigation

The 1,429-strong network of canals constitutes the bedrock of the irrigation system in Haryana with 6.83 lakh tubewells and pumpsets playing no mean role. The major irrigation projects in the state are Western Yamuna Canal System, Bhakra Canal System and Gurgaon Canal System. Giving practical shape to the lift irrigation system for the first time in India, Haryana has raised water from lower levels to higher and drier slopes through the Jawaharlal Nehru Canal, Project. The state is among the beneficiaries of the multipurpose Sutlej-Beas project, sharing benefits with Punjab and Rajasthan.

Power

The first state in the country to have achieved hundred per cent rural electrification way back in 1970, Haryana is well on way to becoming power surplus from a power deficit state.

Education

Haryana is emerging as an education hub and shaping into a modern-day Takshila and Nalanda. Making elementary education available at reachable distance to all children and opening a large number of institutes of higher learning, offering global standard education, the state is moving fast on the road to becoming a modern hub of education. According to 2011 census, the literacy rate in Haryana is 76.64 per cent against the all-India literacy rate of 74.04 per cent. Haryana's female literacy rate is 66.77 per cent and male literacy rate is 85.38 per cent. The rural population is served by primary schools within a radius of 1.01 km, middle schools within a radius of 1.17 km, high schools within a radius of 1.45 km, and senior secondary schools within a radius of 2.10 km.

Industry

The investment and industry-friendly policies pursued by the state government have made Haryana the cynosure of all investing eyes and put the state on threshold of industrial revolution. Haryana today is the largest producer of passenger cars, tractors, motorcycles, bicycles, refrigerators, scientific instruments, etc. Besides, it is the largest exporter of basmati rice.

Panipat handlooms and carpets are known all over the world besides its tasty *panchranga* pickle.

Health

Healthcare has been made both affordable and reachable by setting up a state-wide network of district and sub-divisional hospitals. These are being beefed up with staff and equipment and deficiencies in referral services are being removed. The state-wide network of health centres includes 56 hospitals, 109 community health centres, 467 primary health centres, 2,630 sub-centres, 15 district TB centres, 639 ayurvedic, homeopathy and unani centres, 90 urban RCH centres are functioning.

Information Technology

Out of the 85 proposals for setting up IT/cyber parks in the state, recommended by the committee constituted for the purpose, 35 companies have been granted licences by the town and country planning department.

Transport

Road and rail transport are the main carriers of passenger traffic in Haryana with aviation too playing a small role. It is one state where all villages are linked with metalled roads. The length of the roads in the state is more than 35,303 km.

Railways also play an important role in carrying both interstate and intrastate passengers. Kalka, Ambala, Kurukshetra, Panipat, Rohtak, Jind, Hisar and Jakhal are important railway stations. There is a railway workshop at Jagadhari. Aviation too plays its role. There are civil aerodromes at Pinjore, Karnal, Hisar, Bhiwani and Narnaul.

Tourist Centres

A pioneer in highway tourism, Haryana has set up a vast network of 43 tourist complexes all over the state. Having 846-roomed accommodation in them, Haryana tourism attracts 70 lakh tourists every year. The state government has adopted a multi-pronged strategy to promote tourism. Besides, tourist facilities have been set up at the district headquarters, and in important towns, to cater to the needs of tourists and local people. Some of the important tourist complexes are Surajkund and Baddhkal Lake near Delhi; Sultanpur Birds Sanctuary (Sultanpur); Sohna and Damdama in Gurgaon; and the fascinating pocket of pines in the Morni Hills. The other important resorts are Ethnic India (Rai Sonipat), Blue Jay (Samalkha), Skylark (Panipat), Karna Lake and Oasis (Uchana), Parakeet (Pipli), Kingfisher (Ambala), Magpie (Faridabad), Dabchick (Hodal), Shama (Gurgaon), Jungle Babbler (Dharuhera), Gaurriyya (Bahadurgarh), Myna (Rohtak), Blue Bird (Hisar), Red Bishop (Panchkula), and Pinjore Gardens (Pinjore).

Relevant Website : www.haryana.gov.in

Government

Governor	:	Satyadeo Narain Arya	*Chief Secretary*	:	Depinder Singh Dhesi
Chief Minister	:	Manohar Lal Khattar	*Jurisdiction of High Court*	:	Punjab and Haryana High Court

Himachal Pradesh

Area	:	55,673 sq km	*Population*	:	68.65 lakh (census 2011)
Capital	:	Shimla	*Principal Languages*	:	Hindi and Pahari

History and Geography

Himachal Pradesh, a beautiful land is situated in the lap of the western Himalayas, located between 30°.22' and 33°. 12' North latitude and between 75°.47' and 79°. 4[1] East longitude. This wonderful land inhabited by people of various castes and religions groups, is also called as "Dev Bhumi: the abode of gods and goddesses". Himachal drives its name from the Himalayas, literally means "land of snowy mountains". The territory of this state can be divided into three zones, Outer Himalayas or the Shivaliks, Inner Himalayas or Mid-Mountains and the Greater Himalayas or Alpine Zone. The entire state is punctuated with stone as well as wood temples. The rich culture and traditions have made Himachal a unique world in itself. The shadowy valleys, rugged crags, glaciers, gigantic pines, roaring rivers and exquisite flora and fauna compose the symphony that is forever vibrant Himachal.

Himachal Pradesh has a very eventful career. On 15th April 1948, the Pradesh was born as a result of the integration of some thirty erstwhile Princely Hill States; twenty six Shimla Hill States and four Punjab Hill States. At the time of its inception, the total area of Himachal Pradesh was 27,018 sq. km. with a population of 9, 35,000. On the recommendations of Punjab Boundary Commission, the Government of India, while reorganizing Punjab into two separate states of Punjab and Haryana decided to integrate the Punjab hill areas of the districts of Kangra, Shimla, Kullu and Lahaul-Spiti, Nalagarh area of Ambala district, parts of Una tehsil of Hoshiarpur district, and of Pathankot tehsil of Gurdaspur district with Himachal Pradesh. The integration came about on November 1, 1966 and Himachal's territorial area increased to 55,673 sq.km. The new state was inaugurated in Shimla in 1971. With this, emergence of Himachal Pradesh as the eighteenth state of the Indian Union.

Agriculture

Agriculture provides direct employment to about 70 per cent of the main working population of the state. Income from agriculture and allied sectors accounts for nearly 22.1 per cent of the total state domestic product. Out of the total geographical area of 55, 673 sq. km., area of operational holding is about 9.79 lakh hectares.

The agro-climatic conditions in the state are congenial for the production of cash crops like seed potato, off-season vegetables and ginger. In order to increase the production of food grains, emphasis has been laid on distribution of seeds of high yielding varieties to the farmers. "Mukhya Mantri Jaivik Kheti Purskar Yojna" has been started to boost the morale of the farmers. Himachal Pradesh has bagged "Krishi Karmanya Puraskar" on national level for the consecutive years in 2014-2015 and 2015-2016. For the welfare of farmers, 2,061 bank branches in the state are implementing Kisan Credit Card Scheme. "Mukhya Mantri Khet Sanrakshan Yojna" was launched to protect the farms from wild animals by providing solar fencing. Subsidy on anti-hail nets has been increased from 50 per cent to 80 per cent.

Horticulture

Himachal Pradesh is called the "Fruit Bowl" of the country. Horticulture plays an important role in the agrarian economy. Over 2.27 lakh hectare area has been brought under fruit cultivation and fruit production has reached 10.28 lakh MT. The state has favourable climatic conditions to produce a variety of fruits such as apple, pear, peach, plum, apricot, mango, litchi, guava, strawberry and citrus fruits. For protection of horticulture crops from hailstorms, 15, 51,813 sq. meter area has been brought under anti-hail nets. The Horticulture Technology Mission is being implemented for the integrated development of horticulture. This Mission is based on the "End To End Approach" taking into account the entire gamut of horticulture development with all backward and forward linkages in a holistic manner. To ensure remunerative prices in apple, mango and citrus fruits produce to the farmers, state government has starting marketing intervention scheme.

Roads

Being a hilly state, the roads are very important and main mode of communication for the people. There were only 288 km of roads in the state at time of its formation in the year in 1948. The state government has constructed 36,256 km of motorable road till December, 2016.

"Pradhan Mantri Gram Sadak Yojna" has shown remarkable progress in the state. "Mukhya Mantri Gram Sadak Yojna" has also been implemented to provide last mile connectivity to villages/habitations.

Hydro-Power Generation

Hydel-power potential is the key to prosperity of the state and out of the total available potential of 27,436 MW, the state has harnessed 10,351 MW power so far. Cent per cent electrification had been achieved in the state.

Irrigation and Water Supply

Water is an essential amenity for the development of any state. Irrigation facility for the agriculture and horticulture is being provided in the state. Out of the total 3.35 lakh hectare area that can be provided assured irrigation facility,

2.69 lakh hectare area has been brought under irrigation schemes. Water treatment plants are being provided in all the drinking water supply schemes.

Forestry

Forest in Himachal Pradesh covers an area of 37, 033 sq. km which comes to 66.52 per cent of the total geographical area of the state. The strategy of government in forestry management is conservation along with rational utilization and side by side expanding its base. Forest plantation is being carried out under productive forestry scheme and soil conservation schemes. A new scheme "Sub-Mission on Agro Forestry" was launched with the objective to increase tree plantation in an integrated manner along with crops and livestock to improve employment opportunities of small farmers. Wildlife and nature conservation schemes aim at improving the habitat and facilitating provisions of areas (sanctuaries and national parks) so as to accord protection to the various species of birds and animals facing extinction.

Tourism

The state is endowed with all the basic resources necessary for thriving tourism activity like geographical and cultural diversity, clean and peaceful environment and beautiful streams, sacred shrines, historic monuments and hospitable people. Tourism industry has been given very high priority and the government has developed appropriate infrastructure for its development which includes public utility services, roads, communication network, airports, transport facilities, clean toilets at bus stands, restaurants and petrol pumps, water supply and other civic amenties. Besides there are 2,604 hotels having about 70869 of bed facility, about 787 home stay units are there in the state.

Tourism contributes 6.8 per cent to state GDP and it is set to increase. Incentive of revised rates of electicity duty has been given to the new tourism industry. Package tours are being developed and focus is kept on the adventure, religious heritage, winter sports, trekking and outdoor activities.

Relevant Website : www.himachal.nic.in

Government

Governor	:	Dev Vrat	*Chief Secretary*	:	B.K. Agarwal
Chief Minister	:	Jai Ram Thakur	*Jurisdiction of High Court*	:	Himachal Pradesh

Jammu and Kashmir

Area	:	*2,22,236 sq km	*Population*	:	1.25 crore (2011 census)
Capital	:	Srinagar (Summer) Jammu (Winter)	*Principal Languages*	:	Urdu, Dogri, Kashmiri, Pahari, Punjabi, Ladakhi, Balti, Gojri and Dadri

* includes 78,114 sq km under illegal occupation of Pakistan, 5,180 sq km illegally handed over by Pakistan to China and 37,555 sq km under illegal occupation of China. The population figures exclude population of areas under unlawful occupation of Pakistan and China where census could not be taken.

History and Geography

According to the most popular legend that is also recorded in *Rajtarangani* and *Nilmat Purana*, two most authoritative books, Kashmir was once a large lake and it was Kashyap Rishi who drained off the water, making it a beautiful abode. But geologists have their own theory, which says that geographical changes made way for the outflow of water by subsidence of the mountain at Khadianayar, Baramulla and thus emerged the Valley of Kashmir, the paradise on earth. Ashoka introduced Buddhism to Kashmir in the 3rd century B.C. which was later strengthened by Kanishka. Huns got the control of the valley in the early 6th century. The valley regained freedom in 530 AD but soon came under the rule of the Ujjain empire. After the decline of the Vikramaditya dynasty, the valley had its own rulers. There was a synthesis of Hindu and Buddhist cultures. Lalitaditya (697-738 AD) extended his rule up to Bengal in the east, Konkan in the south, Turkistan in the north-west and Tibet in the north-east. Considered as the most famous Hindu ruler, he was known for constructing beautiful buildings. Islam came to Kashmir during 13th and 14th centuries AD. Zain-ul-Abedin (1420-70) was the most famous Muslim ruler, who came to Kashmir when the Hindu King Sinha Dev fled before the Tatar invasion. Later Chaks over-ran Haider Shah, son of Zain-ul-Abedin. They continued to rule till 1586 when Akbar conquered Kashmir. In 1752, Kashmir passed on from the control of the Mughal emperor to Ahmed Shah Abdali of Afghanistan. The valley was ruled by the Pathans for 67 years.

Name of Jammu figures in the *Mahabharata*. The finds of Harappan remains and artefacts of Mauryan, Kushan and Gupta periods at Akhnoor have added new dimensions to its ancient character. The land of Jammu was divided into 22 hill principalities. Raja Maldev, one of the Dogra rulers, conquered many territories to consolidate his kingdom. Raja Ranjit Dev ruled over Jammu from 1733 to 1782. His successors were weak and thus Maharaja Ranjit Singh annexed the territory to Punjab. He later handed over Jammu to Raja Gulab Singh, a scion of the old Dogra ruling family, who had grown powerful among Ranjit Singh's governors and had annexed almost the whole of Jammu region. The state was governed by Dogra rulers till 1947 when Maharaja Hari Singh signed the *Instrument of Accession* in favour of the Indian Union on 26 October 1947.

Transport

Roads : The state is connected to the rest of the country through just one highway (NH 1A), 400 km stretch (approx.) maintained by Border Roads Organization (BRO). As railway network is still in infancy stage, this has rendered the state totally dependent on road connectivity which provides links to the remote areas of the state. The Jammu-Srinagar National Highway (NH1A) is considered to be the most expensive road for maintenance in the world.

Railways : Because of the difficult terrain railway network has not developed as in other parts of the country. At present Jammu is the rail head of the state and the line has been extended upto district Udhampur only (53 km). In July 2014, the first Katra-Udhampur train was flagged off.

Aviation : There are three major airports in the state providing aerial transport among three regions of the state and the country. Out of the three, Srinagar airport has been upgraded as international airport (named as Sheikh-ul-Alam Airport), while the facilities at Jammu and Leh airports have also been upgraded. One more airport at Kargil headquarters is connected by Dakota service.

Agriculture

Agriculture constitutes an important sector of the state economy as around 70 per cent of the population derive greater part of their income directly or indirectly from this sector. Economy continues to be predominantly agrarian as 49 per cent (2011) of the total working force with 42 per cent as cultivators and 7 per cent as agriculture labourers depend directly on agriculture for their livelihood. Agriculture has a significant contribution in the export of rare produce like saffron, honey and basmati and remains an important source of raw material demanded by many industries.

Irrigation

Irrigation is an essential input of agriculture and is practiced in all parts of the world where rainfall does not provide enough ground moisture. A major constraint to the development of agriculture is the fact that only 50 per cent of the ultimate irrigation potential of the state has been harnessed. The ultimate irrigation potential has been assessed at 1,358 thousand hectare, which includes 250 thousand hectare to be developed through major and medium irrigation and 1,108 thousand hectare through minor irrigation.

Horticulture

Jammu and Kashmir is well known for its horticulture produce both in India and abroad. The state offers good scope for cultivation of all types of horticulture crops covering a variety of temperate fruits like apple, pear, peach, plum, apricot, almonds, cherry and sub-tropical fruits like mango, guava, citrus, litchi, etc. Apart from this, well-known spices like *saffron* and *zeera* are cultivated in some parts of the state.

Industry

To usher in new era of industrialization comprehensive industrial policy came into being in 2004 to be lasted till 2015 under which planned incentives are being taken to raise the state which is predominantly known as consumer state for most of its requirements to a level of self sufficiency and in the near future to a producer state.

Handloom

It is also labour intensive cottage industry having considerable potential for generation of employment opportunities. To give boost to this industry the state government is laying focus on product design and diversification, providing credit facilities, enhancing weavers' productivity through upgradation of skills and use of efficient looms, market access to handloom products.

Tourism

Jammu and Kashmir is an important tourist destination and has been a place of attraction for tourists since centuries. The lush green forests, sweet springs, perennial rivers, picturesque alpine scenery and pleasant climate of Kashmir valley—the paradise on earth—has remained an internationally acclaimed tourist destination, whereas Jammu region—the land of temples is attracting a large number of pilgrim tourists and the important destination has been the Shri Mata Vaishno Devi Shrine. Ladakh region—the moon land has been a much sought after destination especially for the foreign tourists and is famous for adventure tourism.

Power

The estimated hydro power potential is 20,000 megawatts (MWs), of which 16,480 MWs were identified.

Fairs and Festivals

The fairs and festivals are a reflection of diverse cultural and social heritage of the state. All Hindu, Muslim and Sikh fairs and festivals are celebrated with full vigour and enthusiasm regardless of the religion. Like all parts of India, Jammu and Kashmir also celebrates Diwali, Holi, Eid-ul-Fitr, Eid-ul-Azha, Milad-un-Nabi.

Relevant Website : www.jammukashmir.nic.in

Government

Governor	: Satya Pal Malik	*Chief Secretary*	: B.V.R. Subrahmanyam
Chief Minister	:	*Jurisdiction of High Court*	: Jammu, Kashmir & Ladakh

Jharkhand

Area	: 79,716 sq km	*Population*	: 3,29,88,134 (as per 2011 census)
Capital	: Ranchi	*Principal Language*	: Hindi

History and Geography

Jharkhand which came into being in November 2000 as the 28th state of the Union is the homeland of the tribals who had dreamt of a separate state for a long time. According to legend, Raja Jai Singh Deo of Odisha had declared himself the ruler of Jharkhand in the 13th century. It largely comprises forest tracks of Chhotanagpur plateau and Santhal Pargana and has distinct cultural traditions. In post-Independence era, the Jharkhand Mukti Morcha started a regular agitation which impelled the Government to establish the Jharkhand Area Autonomous Council in 1995 and finally a full-fledged state.

Jharkhand is bounded by West Bengal in the east, Uttar Pradesh and Chhattisgarh in the west, Bihar in the north and Odisha in the south.

Agriculture

The state has an area of 79,714 sq km of which 18,423 sq km is forest land. Agriculture and allied activities are the major source of Jharkhand's economy. The total cultivable land is only 38 lakh hectare.

Irrigation and Power

Damodar, Maurakshi, Barakar, North Koyel, South Koyel, Sankh, Subarnarekha, Kharkai, and Ajay are major water resources in the state. The net sown area is 1.8 million hectare of which 8 per cent is irrigated. The installed capacity of power in the state is 2,590 MW.

Industry and Minerals

Some of Jharkhand's major industries are Bokaro Steel Plant in the public sector, Tata Iron and Steel Company (TISCO) in Jamshedpur in the private sector. Other important industries are Tata Engineering and Locomotive Company (TELCO), Timken India Limited (Jamshedpur), Bharat Coking Coal Limited (Dhanbad), Khilari Cement Factory (Palamu), Indian Aluminum (Muri), ACC Cement (Chaibasa), Central Coalfields Limited (Ranchi), Usha Martin, Usha Beltron, Uranium Corporation (I) Limited (Jadugora), Hindustan Copper Limited (Mussabani), Tin Plate Company of India Limited (Jamshedpur), Indian Explosive Limited (Gomia), Hindalco Bauxite (Lohardaga), etc.

The state is rich in mineral resources. The important available minerals are coal, iron ore, limestone, copper ore, bauxite, pyrite, china clay, kyanite, fine clay, dolomite, graphite, bentonite, soap stone, quartz sand and silica sand. The nascent state has the enormous potential for exploitation of coal, mica and other minerals particularly in Singhbhum, Bokaro, Hazaribagh, Ranchi, Koderma and Dhanbad.

Transport

Roads : The total length of roads is 4,311 km. This includes 1,500 km national highways and 2,711 km state highways.

Railways : The state has a well-developed railway system. Ranchi, Bokaro, Dhanbad, Jamshedpur are some of the major railway stations.

Aviation : Ranchi is connected with Delhi, Patna and Mumbai. Cities which have air strips are Jamshedpur, Bokaro, Giridih, Deoghar, Hazaribagh, Daltonganj and Noamundi.

Tourist Centres

There are many scenic attractions in the state, namely, Ichagarh Bird Sanctuary, Udhwa Sanctuary-Sahibganj (Pataura Lake), Chachro Crocodile Breeding Centre–Koderma (Tilaya Dam), Chandrapura Bird Sanctuary, Jawaharlal Nehru Zoological Garden (Bokaro), Tenughat Bird Sanctuary, Dalma WildLife Sanctuary (Jamshedpur), Tata Steel Zoological Park (Jamshedpur), Palkote Wildlife Sanctuary (Gumla), Bhagwan Birsa Zoological Gardens (Ranchi), Birsa Deer Sanctuary (Kalmati Ranchi), Betla National Park (Palamau), Ranchi Aquarium (Ranchi), Hazaribagh National Park, Tatoloi Hot Water Stream (Dumka) and Saranda Forest.

Apart from this, Jharkhand has some famous temples like, Jharkhand Dham, Langta Baba Temple/Majar, Bindhvashini Temple, Masanjore Dam, etc.

Relevant Website : www.jharkhand.gov.in

Government

Governor	: Draupadi Murmu	*Chief Secretary*	: Sudhir Tripathy
Chief Minister	: Raghubar Das	*Jurisdiction of High Court*	: Jharkhand

Karnataka

Area	: 1,91,791 sq km	*Population*	: 6.11 crore (prov. census 2011)
Capital	: Bengaluru	*Principal Language*	: Kannada

History and Geography

Karnataka has a recorded history of more than 2,000 years. Apart from its subjection to the rule of Nandas, Mauryas and the Satavahanas, Karnataka came to have indigenous dynasties like the Kadambas of Banavasi and the Gangas from the middle of the 4th century AD. The world renowned Gomateshwara monolith at Shravanabelagola was installed by a Ganga minister Chavundaraya. The colossal rock cut image of Sri Gomateshwara is the most magnificent among all Jaina works of art. Numerous visitors arrive at Shravanabelagola to gaze at this and other monuments. The Chalukyas of Badami (500-735 AD) reigned over a wider area, from Narmada to the Kaveri from the days of Pulikeshi II (609-642 AD) who even defeated the mighty Harshavardhana of Kanauj. This dynasty created fine, everlasting and the most beautiful monuments at Badami, Aihole and Pattadakal, both structural and rock-cut. Aihole has been one of the cradles of temple architecture in the country. The Rashtrakutas (753-973 AD) of Malkhed who succeeded them heaped tributes on the rulers of Kanauj successively in the so-called 'Age of Imperial Kanauj'. Kannada literature developed during this period. Outstanding Jain scholars of India lived in their court. The Chalukyas of Kalyana (973 to 1189 AD) and their feudatories, the Hoysalas of Halebidu built exquisite temples, encouraged literature and various fine arts. Noted jurist Vijnaneshwara (work: *Mitakshara*) lived at Kalyana. The great religious leader Basaveshwara was a minister at Kalyana. Vijayanagar empire (1336-1646) patronised and fostered indigenous traditions and encouraged arts, religion and literature in Sanskrit, Kannada, Telugu and Tamil. Overseas trade flourished. The Bahamani Sultans (Capital: Gulbarga, later Bidar) and the Bijapur Adilshahis raised fine Indo-Saracenic buildings and encouraged Urdu and Persian literature. Advent of the Portuguese resulted in the introduction of new crops (tobacco, maize, chillies, groundnut, potato, etc.). After the fall of the Peshwa (1818) and Tipu (1799), Karnataka came under British rule. Christian missionaries introduced English education and printing during the 19th century. Revolution in transport, communication and industries was ushered in. The urban middle-class emerged. Mysore dynasty initiated and helped industrialisation and cultural growth.

Freedom movement was followed by the movement for the unification of Karnataka. After Independence, the Mysore state was created in 1953, wherein all the Kannada dominant areas under different dispensations were unified and the enlarged Mysore state carved in 1956 and was renamed Karnataka in 1973.

Karnataka is situated between $11^{\circ}31'$ and $18^{\circ}14'$ north latitudes and $74^{\circ}12'$ and $78^{\circ}10'$ east longitudes. It is bounded by Goa and Maharashtra on the north; Telangana and Andhra Pradesh on the east; Tamil Nadu on the south east and Kerala on the south.

Forestry and Wildlife

The forest department manages about 20.15 per cent of the geographical area of the state. Forests have been classified as reserved forests, protected forests, unclassified forests, villages forests, and private forests. There are 5 national parks and 23 wildlife sanctuaries. To overcome shortage of fuel wood, fodder and timber, degraded forests and waste lands are being developed. Emphasis is also being laid on the conservation, protection and development of the fragile ecosystem of the Western Ghats. Several wildlife protection schemes such as Project Tiger and Project Elephant are being implemented with the central assistance. The concept of Joint Forest Planning and

Management applied to the two externally aided projects viz., Western Ghats Forestry and Environment Project (DFID) and Forestry and Environment Project for Eastern Plains (JBIS) has resulted in village forest planning and management through establishment of Village Forest Committees.

Agriculture

The state has 66 per cent rural population and 55.60 per cent of workers are agricultural labourers. The state has 60 per cent (114 lakh ha) cultivable land and 72 per cent of the cultivable area is rainfed; only 28 per cent is under irrigation. The state has 10 agro climatic zones. The red soil constitutes major soil type, followed by black soil. The net sown area of the state constituted 51.7 per cent of the total land.

Dairy

Karnataka is one of the major milk producers and the Karnataka Milk Federation has 21 dairy processing plants with a capacity of 26.45 lakh litres a day and 42 chilling centres having 14.60 lakh litres of chilling capacity.

Horticulture

Horticulture crops are grown in an area of 16.80 lakhs hectare and the produces amount to 101 lakh tonnes. The Union Government earmarked ₹ 171.29 crore for Karnataka under National Horticulture Mission.

Power Generation

Karnataka was the pioneer in establishing hydroelectric projects in the country. It has 7222.91 power generation installed capacity and 31,229 million units of electricity was generated.

Biotechnology

Karnataka state and Bengaluru city in particular have become the largest bio-clusters in the country.

Transport

Roads : Total road length has increased from 83,749 km to 2,15,849 km.

Ports : The state has a maritime coastline of 155 nautical mile (300 kilometres) and has only one major port at Mangalore, i.e., New Mangalore Port and studded with ten minor ports—Karwar, Belekeri, Tadria, Honnavar, Bhatkala, Kundapur, Hangarkatta, Malpe, Padubidri and Old Mangalore. Out of ten ports, Karwar is the only all weather port while the other nine are the riverine anchorage lighterage ports.

Aviation : The Civil Aviation Sector has seen tremendous growth with international air passenger traffic growth of 50 per cent and domestic air passenger growth at 44 per cent.

Tourism

Karnataka "One State Many Worlds" is becoming a hub of tourist attraction of south India. The IT and BT Centre in Bengaluru has received more tourists in the recent past. The state is known for its heritage monuments and eco-tourism destinations. The Golden Chariot named after the famous Stone Chariot in Hampi, a world heritage site, in southern India will travel through timeless historical heritage sites, resplendent palaces, wildlife and golden beaches. Its 7 nights/8 days colourful journey begins every Monday from Bengaluru and traverses through Mysore, visiting Srirangapatna, Mysore Palace, the Nagarhole National Park (Kabini) and continuing to the historical sites of Shravanabelagola, Belur—the 11th century cradle of Hoysala architecture and a world heritage site, Halebidu, Hampi and thereafter entering into the triangular heritage sites of Badami, Pattadakal, Aihole and finally the Golden Beaches of Goa before ending in Bengaluru.

Relevant Website : www.karnataka.gov.in

Government

Governor	: Vajubhai Vala	*Chief Secretary*	: T.M. Vijaya Bhaskar
Chief Minister	: H.D. Kumaraswamy	*Jurisdiction of High Court*	: Karnataka

Kerala

Area	: 38,852 sq km	*Population*	: 3,34 crore (as per census 2011)
Capital	: Thiruvananthapuram	*Principal Language*	: Malayalam

History and Geography

Kerala is in the extreme south-west of the Indian subcontinent. When independent India amalgamated small states together Travancore and Cochin states were integrated to form Travancore-Cochin state in July 1949. However, Malabar remained under the Madras province. Under the States Re-organisation Act, 1956, Travancore-Cochin state and Malabar were united to form Kerala state in November, 1956.

In between the high Western Ghats on the east and the Arabian Sea on the west, the width of the state varies from 35 km to 120 km. According to the geographical features, the state can be divided into hills, valleys, midland plains and coastal belt. 44 rivers (41 west flowing and 3 east flowing) cut across the state with their innumerable tributaries and branches. The backwaters form an attractive and economically valuable feature of Kerala.

Agriculture

Kerala, the land of lush green paddy fields, cool coconut groves, fragrant spice garden, dubbed as "God's Own Country" is nestled in the southern tip of India. Fertile soil and warm humid tropical climate make Kerala an ideal place for cultivation of a wide variety of crops which included coconut, rice, rubber, banana, spices, fruits, vegetables, cashew nut, tubers, coffee, tea, medicinal plants, arecanut, etc.

Industry

To transform Kerala into a vibrant entrepreneurial society with faster, inclusive and sutainable economic growth in order to achieve global standards in every domain, the government has taken steps to implement investor friendly industrial policy to enable constructive investment in all sectors.

Irrigation

The surface irrigation constitutes major chunk of irrigation infrastructure. There are 18 dams intended for irrigation. Irrigation development is mainly centered on the developement of surface water resources mainly on the major and medium irrigation projects. In each Plan, priority in allocation was given for the development of major and medium irrigation projects. Rice is the major crop benefited through irrigation infrastructure. With the fast changes taking place in the farm front with notable reduction in the area under rice cultivation, even the distribution system already developed for gravity irrigation to service rice cultivation now require realignment.

Drinking Water

Demand for water is increasing due to multitude of human activities in the country. The primary responsibility of providing drinking water facilities in the country rests with the respective state governments. In urban and rural areas of the state, 29 per cent and 71 per cent of the population were covered.

Power

Power sector plays a vital role in all developmental activities in Kerala. Obviously power crisis is the prime obstacle to start new initiatives in the industrial field. Kerala is a power deficit state which imports 60 per cent of power from other states. A major achievement is that it has achieved full electrification in all villages.

Transport

Transport sector plays a pivotal role in the overall development of the country which enables social, cultural and trade development between countries. Transport infrastructure consists of fixed installations, roads, railways, airways, waterways, canals, pipelines and terminals. Kerala holds a good transport system. The roads are maintained by National Highway Authority, public works department, local bodies, Department of Irrigation, Kerala State Electricity Board, Department of Forest, railways, etc.

Port Sector : Kerala lies in the south west corner of the Indian peninsula. It has a coastal length of 585 km and has an average width of about 60 km with one major port at Kochi and 17 minor ports. The geographical location of the state is very close to international shipping route. There are 17 minor ports, out of which 3 are considered as intermediate ports based on berthing, cargo handling and storage facilities available in them. These have contributed much to the development of industry, trade, commerce and agriculture in the country.

Railways : Railways are essentially the cause for industrial upsurge in the nation and it still remained the largest employment provider for the huge population of the country. The total railway route in Kerala has a length of 1257 km and covers 13 railway routes.

Air Transport : Kerala has three airports at Thiruvananthapuram, Kochi and Kozhikode, handling both international and domestic flights. Thiruvananthapuram and Kozhikode airports are owned by Government of India and Kochi airport is owned by Kochi International Airport Ltd., a company set up by Government of Kerala with public private participation.

Festivals

Kerala is the home of many colourful festivals. *Onam* is the most typical of festivals which coincides with the harvest season. It is now celebrated on astronomical New Year Day. Navarathri is celebrated as Saraswathi Pooja. Maha Shivarathri is celebrated on the banks of Periyar river as a spectacular festival which is compared to Kumbhamela. The 41-day festival, which coincides with Makaravilakku in Sabarimala Ayyappan Temple, attracts lakhs of people from India and abroad. The Vallamkali or boat race is typical of Kerala. All the boat festivals have a religious origin except Nehru Trophy Boat Race conducted in the Punnamada Lake. Thrissur celebrates *Pooram* festival in April - May every year with an impressive procession of caparisoned elephants and display of unparalleled pyrotechnics. Main Christian festivals are Christmas and Easter. Mormon Convention held every year on the Pumba riverbed is the biggest gathering of Christians in Asia. The Muslims celebrate *Milade Shareef, Ramzan Id-ul-Fitr* and *Bakrid*.

Tourism

Kerala, located on the south western tip of India, enjoys unique geographical features that have made it one of the most sought after tourist destinations in the world. Fondly referred to as "God's Own Country", Kerala was selected by the National Geographic Traveller as one of the 50 destinations of a lifetime and one of the thirteen paradises in the world. Its unique eco-tourism initiatives, culture and traditions coupled with its varied demography has made Kerala one of the most popular tourist destinations in the world. An equable climate, serene beaches, tranquil stretches of back waters; lush hill stations and exotic wildlife are the major attractions of this land. A unique advantage of Kerala is that most of the destinations here are only a two-four hour drive from the other.

Relevant Website : www.kerala.gov.in

Government

Governor	: Justice (Retd.) P. Sathasivam	*Chief Secretary*	: Tom Jose
Chief Minister	: Pinarayi Vijayan	*Jurisdiction of High Court*	: Kerala and Lakshadweep

Madhya Pardesh

Area	: 3,08,252 sq km	Population	: 7.27 crore (prov. census 2011)
Capital	: Bhopal	Principal Language	: Hindi

History and Geography

Madhya Pradesh is the second largest Indian state in size with an area of 3,08,000 sq.km. Geographically it occupies a pivotal position in the country. King Ashoka, first of all, ruled over Ujjain. A sizeable portion of Central India was part of the Gupta empire (300-500 A.D.). The Muslims here in the beginning of 11th century. First of all, Mahmud Ghazni came over here and then Mohammad Gouri, who incorporated some parts of Central India into the ruling territory of Delhi. This part was also part of the Mughal empire. During the period between the beginning of the influence of Marathas and the death of Madhoji Scindia in 1794, Marathas were on the ascendant in Central India but later on the small states started coming into existence. These small states became the cause of perpetuation of British power in the country.

Queen Ahilyabai Holkar of Indore, the Gond Maharani Kamalapati and Queen Durgawati, etc., were women rulers whose names have left an indelible imprint on Indian history for their outstanding rule. Madhya Pradesh came into being in November 1956. It was reorganised in November 2000 to create a new Chhattisgarh state. The successive state, now, is bounded in north by Uttar Pradesh, east by Chhattisgarh, south by Maharashtra and west by Gujarat and Rajasthan.

Economy

Madhya Pradesh has gone from strength to strength in economic growth that has emerged as a study of success all over the country. Its GSDP has gone up from more ₹ 1 lakh crore to a whopping ₹ 5 lakh crore over the decade.

Agriculture

Madhya Pradesh has posted country's highest agricultural growth rate which had averaged above 20 per cent over last four years. The state leads the country in production of pulses, oilseeds, soyabean, gram, pea, garlic, guava and medicinal and aromatic herbs. Horticulture is being promoted in a big way.

Irrigation

Top priority has been given to irrigation following which the area under irrigation has increased from mere 7.5 lakh hectare ten years back to 40 lakh hectare now. Narmada-Kshipra Link Project has been implemented. Three major, five medium and over 700 minor irrigation projects have been completed over last five years, thereby increasing the canal irrigation capacity by over 2.5. times.

Power

Madhya Pradesh has witnessed a total turn-around in power sector. Power availability has increased from just 4500 MW twelve years ago to 17,169 MW now. Country's largest 130 MW solar energy plant has been established in Neemuch.

Industry

In order to promote micro, small and medium industries, a separate MSME department has been set up. Following implementation of MSME Promotion Policy of State Government 50,000 units were registered under industry based memorandum. With an investment of over ₹ 5 thousand crore these units have provided jobs to over 2 lakh people.

Department of Happiness

A Department of Happiness has been set up in the state as part of efforts to create an enabling atmosphere for people to live a happy and blissful life. The concept of happiness that Madhya Pradesh aspires to pursue is primarily based on time tested Indian wisdom besides taking into account the indices that determine national growth as also the experiences of other countries in our strategies and action plans.

Transport

Roads : The total length of roads in the state is 58,423 km. The length of national highway in the state is 4,709 km while state highway extends to 10,501 km.

Railways : The main rail route linking northern with southern India passes through the state. Main junctions are Bhopal, Bina, Gwalior, Indore, Itarsi, Jabalpur, Katni, Ratlam and Ujjain. The divisional railways headquarters are at Bhopal, Ratlam and Jabalpur.

Festivals

A number of festivals are celebrated in the state. An important tribal festival is *Bhagoriya* marked by traditional gaiety and enthusiasm. *Shivratri* is celebrated in Khajuraho, Bhojpur, Pachmarhi and Ujjain and has its own local flavour while *Ramnavami* festival at Chitrakoot and Orchha has a unique sense of devotion imbued with tradition. Festivals of Orchha, Malwa, Pachmarhi bring to the fore repertoire of culture and art of the people. Tansen Music Festival, Gwalior; Ustad Allauddin Khan Music Festival Maihar; Kalidas Samaroh, Ujjain; and Festival of Dances at Khajuraho was some of the well-known art festivals of Madhya Pradesh. An annual Narmada Festival has been started from this year at Bedhaghat in Jabalpur, famous for its marble rocks. A Shivpuri festival has been started at Shivpuri. Betwa festival has also been started at Vidisha.

Tourist Centres

Perfectly preserved medieval cities, refreshing and enchanting wildlife sanctuaries and some of the holiest and most revered pilgrim centres offer to the tourist the most fulfilling experience. Tranquil beauty of Pachmarhi, glittering splendour of marble rocks and roaring sound of Dhuandhar Fall at Bedaghat, Kanha National Park, with its unique Barasingha, and Bandhavgarh National Park with its prehistoric caves and wildlife are some of the major attractions of the state. Gwalior, Mandu, Datia, Chanderi, Jabalpur, Orchha, Raisen, Sanchi, Vidisha, Udaygiri, Bhimbetika, Indore and Bhopal are the places well-known for their historical monuments. Maheshwar, Omkareshwar, Ujjain, Chitrakoot and Amarkantak are major centres of pilgrimage. Unique temples of Khajuraho are famous all over the world. The temples of Orchha, Bhojpur and Udaypur attract large number of tourists as well as pilgrims. Archaeological treasures are preserved in the museums at Satna, Sanchi, Vidisha, Gwalior, Indore, Mandsaur, Ujjain, Rajgarh, Bhopal, Jabalpur, Rewa and many other places. Omkareshwar, Maheshwar and Amarkantak have been declared holy cities for their integrated development in accordance with their religious significance.

Relevant Website : www.mp.nic.in

Government

Governor	: Anandiben Patel	*Chief Secretary*	: Sudhi Ranjan Mohanty
Chief Minister	: Kamal Nath	*Jurisdiction of High Court*	: Madhya Pradesh

Maharashtra

Area	: 3,07,713 sq km	*Population*	: 11.24 crore (census 2011)
Capital	: Mumbai	*Principal Language*	: Marathi

History and Geography

The first well-known rulers of Maharashtra were the Satavahanas (230 BC to 225 AD), who were practically the founders of Maharashtra, and have left a plethora of literary, epigraphic, artistic, and archaeological evidence. Then came the Vakatakas, who established a pan-Indian empire. Under them, this area witnessed an all-sided development in the fields of learning, arts and religion. Some of the Ajanta Caves and Fresco Paintings reached their pinnacle during their rule. After the Vakatakas and after a brief interlude of the Kalachuri dynasty, the most important rulers were the Chalukyas followed by the Rashtrakutas and the Yadavas apart from the Shilaharas on the coast. The Yadavas, with Marathi as their court language extended their authority over large parts of the Deccan.

While the Bahamani rule brought a degree of cohesion to the land and its culture, a uniquely homogeneous evolution of Maharashtra as an entity became a reality under the able leadership of Shivaji. A new sense of Swaraj and nationalism was evolved by Shivaji. His noble and glorious power stalled the Mughal advances into this part of India. The Peshwas established the Maratha supremacy from the Deccan Plateau to some areas in northern India.

Maharashtra was in the forefront during freedom struggle and it was here that the Indian National Congress was born. A galaxy of leaders from Mumbai and other cities of the state led the Congress movement under the guidance of Tilak and then Mahatma Gandhi. Maharashtra was the home of Gandhiji's movement, while Sevagram was the capital of nationalistic India during the Gandhian era.

The administrative evolution of Maharashtra is the outcome of the linguistic reorganisation of the states of India, effected in May, 1960. The state was formed by bringing together all contiguous Marathi-speaking areas, which previously belonged to four different administrative hegemonies. They were the districts between Daman and Goa that formed part of the original British Bombay Province; five districts of the Nizam's dominion of Hyderabad; eight districts in the south of the Central provinces (Madhya Pradesh) and a sizeable number of petty native-ruled state enclaves lying enclosed within the above areas, were later merged with adjoining districts. Located in the north centre of Peninsular India, with the command of the Arabian Sea through its Port of Mumbai, Maharashtra has a remarkable physical homogeneity, enforced by its underlying geology. The dominant physical trait of the state is its plateau character. Maharashtra is a plateau of plateaus, its western upturned rims rising to form the Sahyadri Range parallel to the sea-coast and its slopes gently descending towards the east and south-east. Satpura ranges cover the northern part, while Ajanta and Satmala ranges run through central part. Arabian Sea guards the western boundary of the state, while Gujarat and Madhya Pradesh are on the northern side. Chhattisgarh and Telangana cover the eastern boundary of the state. Karnataka and Andhra Pradesh are on its southern side.

Agriculture

About 65 per cent of the total workers in the state depend on agriculture and allied activities. Principal crops are rice, jowar, bajra, wheat, tur, moong, urad, gram and other pulses. The state is a major producer of oilseeds. Groundnut, sunflower, soyabean are major oilseed crops. Important cash crops are cotton, sugarcane, turmeric and vegetables.

Industry

The state has been identified as the country's powerhouse and Mumbai, its capital as the centre point of India's financial and commercial markets. Industrial sector occupies a prominent position in the economy of Maharashtra. Food products, breweries, tobacco and related products, textiles and textile products, paper and paper products, printing and publishing, rubber, plastic, chemical and chemical products, machinery, electrical machinery, apparatus and appliances, and transport equipment and parts contribute substantially to the industrial production.

Transport

Roads : Total length of roads in the state is 2.43 lakh km consisting of 4,376 km of national highways, 34,157 km of state highways, 50,256 km of major district roads, 46,817 km of other district roads, and 1,06,601 km of village roads.

Railways : Maharashtra has 5,983 km of railway routes which is 9.2 per cent of total railway route in the country.

Aviation : There are 3 international and 5 domestic airports in the state. To reduce congestion in Mumbai International Airport, an additional airport is coming up at Navi Mumbai.

Ports : Mumbai is a major port. There are 2 major and 48 notified minor ports in the state.

Tourist Centres

Some important tourist centres are Ajanta, Ellora, Elephanta, Kanheri and Karla caves, Mahabaleshwar, Matheran and Panchgani, Jowhar, Malshej Ghat, Amboli, Chikhaldara, Panhala hill stations and religious places at Pandharpur, Nashik, Shirdi, Nanded, Aundha Nagnath, Trimbakeshwar, Tuljapur, Ganapatipule, Bhimashankar, Harihareshwar, Shegaon, Kolhapur, Jejuri and Ambajogai.

Relevant Website : www.maharashtra.gov.in

Government

Governor	:	Chennamaneni Vidyasagar Rao	*Chief Secretary*	:	D.K. Jain
Chief Minister	:	Devendra Fadnavis	*Jurisdiction of High Court*	:	Maharashtra, Goa, Daman and Diu, Dadra and Nagar Haveli

Manipur

Area	:	22,327 sq km	*Population*	:	28.56 lakh (2011 census)
Capital	:	Imphal	*Principal Language*	:	Manipuri

History and Geography

Manipur has a long and glorious history from before the beginning of the Christian era. The political history of Manipur could be traced back to 33

A.D. with the coronation of Nongda Lairen Pakhangba. After Pakhangba a number of kings ruled over the kingdom of Manipur. The independence and sovereignty remained uninterrupted until the Burmese invasion and occupation for around seven years in the first quarter of the 19th century (1819-1826). Then, Manipur came under British rule in 1891. Manipur regained its independence in 1947 and merged into Indian Union in 1950. Thus, it became a Part C State under the purview of Chief Commissioner. During 1950-51, an advisory form of Government was introduced and in 1957 this was replaced by a Territorial Council of 30 elected and 2 nominated members. Later, in 1963 a Territorial Assembly of 30 elected and 3 nominated members was set up under the Government of Union Territories Act, 1963. The status of administrator was raised from that of a Chief Commissioner to that of a Lt. Governor in December, 1969. Manipur became a full-fledged state in 1972 with a Legislative Assembly of 60 members of whom 19 are reserved for Scheduled Tribes and one for Scheduled Castes. The state is represented in the Lok Sabha by two members and by one member in the Rajya Sabha.

The state is situated in the extreme north-eastern border of the country. It is bound on the east by upper Myanmar, on the north by Nagaland, on the west by Cachar district of Assam and on the south by Chin hills of Myanmar and Mizoram. Manipur has a total border line of about 854 km of which about 352 km are international boundary line with Myanmar on the east and south-east. This state is in a geographically unique position, since it virtually is the meeting point between India and South-East Asia. Manipur lies between 23.80^0 N and 25.68^0 N latitude and between 93.03^0 E and 94.78^0 E longitude.

The state has a total area of 22,327 sq. km. There is a small oval shaped plain in the central part. This central plain known as Imphal Valley is at a height of about 790 metres above Mean Sea Level (MSL). This valley is surrounded by hills on all sides. The hill covers about 9/10 of the total area of the state. The hill ranges are higher on the north and gradually diminish in height towards the south. The valley itself slopes down towards the south.

Agriculture

Agriculture and allied activities are the only mainstay of the state's economy where about 70 per cent of the population depends on it. The state has two topographical zones — valley and hills. The valley is known as the 'Rice Bowl' of the state. The valley has sub-tropical to tropical to sub-temperate climates. The hills have sub-temperate to temperate climate with an average altitude of 3000 metres above MSL. It has distinct winter, warm, humid and rainy summer. The average rainfall during the last ten years has been recorded 1482.20 mm, with heavy precipitation during the month of June, July and August. The growth of agriculture in the state has been quite uneven for the reason that its production still depends on seasonal rainfall.

Forest

In terms of forest canopy density classes, it has 701 sq. km of very dense forests, 5474 sq. km. moderately dense forests and 11,105 sq. km open forests.

Irrigation

Major and medium irrigation projects had been introduced in the state. So far 8 (eight) major and medium irrigation and multipurpose projects have been taken up of which 5 projects viz. Loktak Lift Irrigation Project, Khoupum Dam Project, Imphal Barrage Project, Sekmai Barrage Project and Singda Multipurpose Project have been completed.

Commerce and Industries

The handloom industry is by far the largest and most important cottage industry. It improves the socio-economic conditions of handloom weavers and has attained high degree of excellence. As per the 3rd National Handloom Census of Weavers and Allied Workers 2010, Manipur topped in distribution of handloom workers. There are 218,753 handloom workers (200,607 weavers, 18, 146 workers) which is 4th position among the top states of the country, 1,90,634 looms which is 3rd position and consuming 186,703 kg of yarn KVIC/ private owners. Manipur is, therefore, among the top four states of the country promoting and nurturing the handloom industry for generating employment to a large section of the state's population.

Power

Power supply in Manipur is fully dependent on the Central Generating Stations situated in the North Eastern Region (NER). As the generating stations in the NER are mainly of hydel in nature, during lean period there is a shortfall in generation and therefore the available share of Manipur reduces drastically.

Transport

Roads: Road transport is the only means of communication in the state and there are no inland waterways, railways or ropeways. All development activities depend entirely on the road transport facilities. Three national highways : i) NH-39, ii) NH-53 and iii) NH-150 criss-cross the state connecting all districts. Imphal, the capital is connected by NH-39 with Nagaland on the north and Myanmar on the east, on the west with Assam by NH-53 and Mizoram on the south by NH-150.

Aviation : Imphal airport is the second largest airport in the north eastern region, which is connected to Agartala, Aizwal, Dimapur, Guwahati, Kolkata, Pune, Silchar, Bengaluru and New Delhi.

Railways: The state was included in the railway map of India with the opening of a rail head at Jiribam in 1990. It is 225 km from Imphal. Dimapur (Nagaland), 215 km from Imphal is the nearest rail-head. The Jiribam - Tupul - Imphal railway line has been declared as a national project. Construction of the line is in good progress and is targeted for completion by 2014 (upto Tupul) and 2016 (upto Imphal).

Festivals

A year in Manipur represents a cycle of festivals. Hardly a month passes by without a festival which to the Manipuris is a symbol of their social, cultural and religious aspirations. Important festivals of the state are *Lai Haraoba, Rasa Leela, Cheiraoba, Ningol Chak-Kouba, Rath-Jatra, Idul Fitr, Imoinu Iratpa, Gaan-Ngai, Lui-Ngai-Ni, Idul Zuha, Yaoshang (Holi), Durga Puja, Mera Houchongba, Diwali, Kut, Christmas*, etc.

Tourist Centres

Manipur is not only the gateway of the north eastern region but is also a fascinating destination for discerning tourists. Blessed with a salubrious climate, natural beauty and scenic splendour, the state extends to the tourists a warm welcome. Some important tourist centres in the state are Kangla, Shree Shree Govindajee Temple, Khwalramband Bazar (Ima Keithel), War Cemeteries, Shaheed Minar, Nupi Lan (Women's War) Memorial Complex, Khonghampat Orchidarium, INA Memorial (Moirang), Loktak Lake, Keibul Lamjao National Park, Sendra, Moreh, Siroy Hills, Dzuko Valley, State Museum, Kaina Tourist Home, Khongjom War Memorial Complex, India Peace Memorial (Red Hill), etc.

Relevant Website : www.manipur.gov.in

Government

Governor	: Dr. Najma A. Heptulla	*Chief Secretary*	: Rajani Ranjan Rashmi
Chief Minister	: N. Biren Singh	*Jurisdiction of High Court*	: Manipur

Meghalaya

Area	: 22,429 sq km	*Population*	: 29.67 lakh (prov. 2011 census)
Capital	: Shillong	*Principal Languages*	: Khasi, Garo & English

History and Geography

Meghalaya was created as an autonomous state within the state of Assam in 1970. The full-fledged state of Meghalaya came into existence in 1972. It is bound on the north and east by Assam and on the south and west by Bangladesh. Meghalaya literally means the 'Abode of Clouds' and is essentially a hilly state. It is predominately inhabited by the tribal Khasis, Jaintias and Garos population. The Khasi Hills and Jaintia Hills which form the central and eastern part of the state form an imposing plateau with rolling grassland, hills and river valleys. The southern face of the plateau is marked by deep gorges and abrupt slopes, at the foot of which, a narrow strip of plain runs along the international border with Bangladesh.

Carved from the erstwhile state of Assam, Meghalaya became a full fledged State on January 21, 1972. Bounded on the north and east by Assam and on the south and west by Bangladesh, Meghalaya is spread over an area of 22, 429 square kilometers, and lies between 24^0 57′ and 26^0 10 north latitude and 89^0 46′ and 92^0 53′ east longitudes.

Agriculture

Meghalaya is basically an agricultural state with about 81 per cent of its total population depending entirely on it for their livelihood. The hilly terrain and land conditions of the state do not offer much scope in bringing additional area under wet condition, but the state has a vast potential for developing horticulture. The agro-climatic variations offer much scope for cultivation of temperate as well as tropical fruits and vegetables. Besides the major food crops of rice and maize, the state is also renowned for its horticultural crops like orange. lemon, pineapple, guava, litchi, banana, jackfruits and temperate fruits such as plum, pear, peach, etc. Potato, ginger, turmeric, black pepper, arecanut, tezpata, betel, short- staple cotton, jute, mesta, mustard and rapeseed etc., are some of the important cash crops. Apart from these, the state has achieved success in the cultivation of non-traditional crops like tea, cashew nut, oilseeds, tomato, mushroom, wheat, etc.

Forest

The total forest area is 9,49,56,000 hectares which includes reserved forest, protected forest, national park and unclassed forest. The principal timber species are sal, teak, titachap, gomari, bol, pine, birch and makri-sal. The principal forest products include timber, bamboo, reed, broomstick, cane, ipecac, medicinal herbs and plants, cinnamon and thatch grass. Azaleas and rhododendrons grow wild in the forests of Khasi Hills and Jaintia Hills forest and many kinds of wild and rare orchids are also found in many parts of the state. Pitcher plants, the insect-eating plants of botanical wonder is found in plenty in the Jaintia Hills, West Khasi Hills and South Garo Hills and it is said that such a plant is found nowhere else in the world. Many rare and interesting plants like wild citrus and pygmy lily are also found.

Wildlife

The state is also rich in wildlife. There are elephants, tigers, bears, wild-boars, leopards, golden cats, leopard cats and jungle cats, deers of various kinds, binturongs, slow loris, monkeys of different types including capped-langurs, golden langurs and hoolock, flying squirrels and giant squirrels. There are also many rare and interesting birds including the hornbills, partridges, pheasants, teals, snipes, geese, ducks and quails. The state has two national parks, viz, Nokrek and Balpakram and two wildlife sanctuaries, viz, Nongkhyllem and Siju.

Industry

The most important non-agro based industry is cement. Because of its rich limestone deposits, the state has a number of cement plants operating in different parts. The number of small scale industrial units covering service industry, bakeries, furniture making, iron and steel fabrication, tyre retreading etc., are increasing. The Meghalaya Industrial Development Corporation encourages private entrepreneurs to register themselves so that they may benefit from support and training to set up industries in small and tiny sectors by way of financing and equity participation.

Places of Interest

Meghalaya is dotted with a number of lovely tourist spots. Shillong, the capital city, has a number of beautiful spots. They are the Ward's Lake, the Phan Nonglait Park, the expensive Polo Grounds, the Elephant Falls, the Shillong Peak over looking the city. Umiam, lies 17 km away from Shillong and has been developed into a popular tourist centre in the state. Shillong Peak, an ideal picnic spot rises 1960 metres above the sea level and is 10 km from the city. Sohra, 56 km from Shillong, is noted for its heavy rainfall. It is 1,300 metres above sea-level. Mawsynram, is situated on the South West of Shillong by the side of Shillong-Mawphlang-Balat road. It closely rivals Sohra in annual rainfall. Jakrem, 64 km from Shillong, is a popular health resort with hot springs of sulphur water which is believed to have medicinal properties. Ranikor, 140 km from Shillong. It is also a place of scenic beauty. Dawki, 96 km from Shillong. It is an excellent picnic spot with silver streams and deep waters with magnificient views of the Khasi Hills on one side and Bangladesh on the other.

Transport

Being a hilly state, with 4/5th of the population living in the rural areas, the necessity of proper road network is of utmost importance. The state is not served by railways and river transportation is not feasible. Hence roads are the only means of bulk transportation here.

Roads: Six national highways pass through the state. The state has 9350 km of road length with road density of 41.69 km per 100 sq.kms.

Aviation: The only airport in the state at Umroi, 35 km from Shillong is functional.

Natural Features

The Khasi Hills and Jaintia Hills which form the central and eastern part of Meghalaya is an imposing plateau with rolling grasslands, hills and river valleys. The southern face of the plateau is marked by deep gorges and abrupt slopes. At the foot of these slopes, a narrow strip of plain land runs along the international border with Bangladesh.

The Garo hills which form the western part of Meghalaya is lower in elevation. The greater part of Garo Hills range in height from 450 m to 600 m and drop steeply to the Brahmaputra valley on the north and to the plains of Bangladesh on the south, Nokrek Peak (1412m) east of Tura town, is the highest peak in western Meghalaya.

A number of rivers, none of them navigable, reign this mountainous state. In the Garo hills, the Manda, the Damring and the Janjiram flow towards the north while the Ringge and the Ganol flow in the westerly direction. Those that flow to the south are the Simsang, which is the biggest river in Garo hills and the Bhogai.

Relevant Website : www.meghalaya.gov.in

Government

Governor	: Tathagata Roy	*Chief Secretary*	: Kuljit Singh Kropha
Chief Minister	: Conrad Kongkal Sangma	*Jurisdiction of High Court*	: High Court of Meghalaya

Mizoram

Area	: 21,081 sq km	*Population*	: 10.97 lakh (Prov. 2011 census)
Capital	: Aizawl	*Principal Languages*	: Mizo, English and Lushai

History and Geography

Mizoram is a mountainous region which became the 23rd state of the Indian Union in February 1987. It was one of the districts of Assam till 1972 when it became a Union Territory. After being annexed by the British in 1891, for the first few years, Lushai hills in the north remained under Assam while the southern half remained under Bengal. Both these parts were amalgamated in 1898 into one district called Lushai Hills District under the Chief Commissioner of Assam. With the implementation of North-Eastern Reorganization Act in 1972, Mizoram became a Union Territory and as a sequel to the signing of the historic memorandum of settlement between the Government of India and the Mizo National Front in 1986, it was granted statehood in 1987. Sandwiched between Myanmar in the east and the south and Bangladesh in the west, the state occupies an area of great strategic importance in the north-eastern corner of India. Mizoram has a great natural beauty and an endless variety of landscape rich in flora and fauna.

The Mizos came under the influence of the British Missionaries in the 19th century. Now most of the Mizos are Christians. Mizo language has no script of its own. The missionaries introduced the Roman script for the Mizo language and formal education.

Agriculture

About 60 per cent of the people of the state are engaged in agricultural and allied activities. The main pattern of the agriculture followed is *jhum* or shifting cultivation. Of the total 21 per cent is put on paddy/seasonal crops. About 63 per cent of the total crop area is under *jhum* cultivation. To replace the destructive and unproductive *jhum* cultivation with sustainable means of occupation, the state government has launched an innovative programme called the New Land Use Policy covering all the districts. The area under Jhum cultivation has decreased from 44,947 hectare at the beginning of 11th Plan to 20,064 hectare during 2014-15 which account for above 55.36 per cent reduction. The significant reduction in *jhum* area is mainly due to the implementation of NLUP, oil palm development programme, sugarcane cultivation programme, RKVY, and RAD.

Horticulture

Owing to the fact that more than 60 per cent of the population depends on land based activities for their livelihoods, horticulture plays a vital role and occupies very important place in the economy of Mizoram. Because of its advantageous agro-climatic condition, hilly terrain nature of the landscape and well distributed rainfall during monsoon season horticulture is a sustainable land based activities for development of the economy. Out of the estimated total of 21 lakh hectare of land 6.30 lakh hectare is available for cultivation of horticulture crops. The main horticulture crops are mandarin orange, banana, passion fruit, grapes, hatkora, pineapple, papaya, etc. and flowers like anthurium, bird of paradise, orchid, chrysanthemum, rose and other subsidiary seasonal flowers. Spices like ginger, turmeric, black pepper, bird's eye chillies are also grown. A multi-purpose packaging house has been set up at the Horticulture Centre, Chite in collaboration with M/s Argos (Agri Projects) Ltd., Israel.

Floriculture was a growing occupation in Mizoram. Cultivation of anthurium was introduced in 2002 and today anthurium cut flowers are exported outside the state and overseas market. Commercial cultivation of rose under hi-tech green house was introduced in 2006 and about 10,000 rose cut flowers are being harvested everyday.

Forest

Mizoram has one of the highest forest cover among the states of India. India State of Forest Report-2015 indicated that about 91.47 per cent of the state's total geographical area is under forests cover. Tropical semi evergreen, tropical moist deciduous, subtropical broadleaved hill and subtropical pine forests are the common vegetation types found. Bamboo resources covers around 31per cent (about 6446 sq.km) of its geographical area and as many as 35 species of bamboo have been identified in the state of which Melocanna baccifera (mautak) contributes about 77 per cent of the total bamboo coverage.

Jhum cultivation, or slash-and-burn practice, was a historic tradition and a threat to its forest cover. This practice is reduced in recent decades from a government supported initiative particularly New Land Use Policy of the state.

The popular and effective Green Mizoram Programme has been continuing with stress on the survival of the trees planted under which mass afforestation and maintenance activities have been taken up every year. 4700 hectares of plantation have also been created under the National Afforestation Programme.

Irrigation

Due to hilly nature of the state, all irrigation projects are confined to minor irrigation. As per estimation of Mizoram Remote Sensing Application Centre, the total Wet Rice Cultivation potential area is 74,644 ha. So far, 439 minor irrigation projects covering 18,228 ha command area have been completed. 25 new minor irrigation projects are proposed to be cover during 2016-17 which will cover an area of 1,117.90 ha. and create an irrigation potential of 1656 ha. The proposed projects will benefit 791 of farmers covering different parts of the state.

Industry

Due to its topographical and geographical disadvantages coupled with underdeveloped infrastructure and transport bottleneck, growth in industry is very modest. However, with the opening up of border trade with Myanmar and Bangladesh, the 'Look/Act East Policy' of the Government of India and the peaceful condition of the state, industrialization is gaining momentum.

Small industries dominate the industrial scenario acquiring prominent place in the socio-economic development of the state. With the objectives of promoting industries in rural areas, the state government has been running two commonly facility centre and one Regional Industrial Development Corporation (RIDC) with an intake of 35 trainers.

Scientific cultivation of tea has also been taken up. Establishment of apparel training and design centre, gems cutting and polishing are in the pipeline to encourage setting up of Export Oriented Units (EOUs). Of the cottage industries, handloom and handicraft are given high priority and the two sectors are nourishing to meet consumers' demand in the state and in neighbouring states of Maghalaya, Nagaland, etc.

Power

As per the 18th Power Survey of India, the bulk power requirement of Mizoram is 201 MW and the allocated share is 103.09 MW (real time power availability is normally 60 MW). Per capita consumption is 280 kWh. The present peak demand is 102 MW but the state generates only about 15 MW from the installed capacity of 29.35 MW. The rest of the requirement has to be imported from various sources like Loktak, Ranganadi, etc from central sector utilities like NEEPCO, NHPC, NTPC, etc.

Transport

Road: Road serves as the most important means of communication, transportation of goods and passengers within the state, inter-state and with international borders. Total road length in the state is 6349.60 km and road density is 300012 km/100 sq km approximately. There are six national highways passing through the length and breadth of Mizoram. NH 54 connects Aizawl with the rest of the country through Silchar, Assam. Aizawl is also accessible by road from Shillong and Guwahati.

Railways: Broad gauge rail link has been established in Bairabi, Mizoram near Assam border.

Aviation: The airport at Lengpui is connected by flights to and from Kolkata, Imphal and Guwahati. Internal helicopter service also connects Aizawl with Lunglei, Lawngtlai, Saiha, Chawngte, Serchhip, Champhai, Kolasib, Khawzawl, Mamit and Hnahthial.

Festivals

Being predominantly an agricultural community all the activities of the Mizo centre around jhum cultivation. 'Kut' is the Mizo term for festival. Among the various cultural festivals, only three, viz., Chapchar Kut, Mim Kut and Thalfavang Kut are being observed now a days.

Tourist Centres

Mizoram is a place with flora and fauna rich landscape and pleasant climate. Aizawl, the capital city is located at 3715 ft above sea level, is a religious and cultural centre. Champhai is a beautiful resort on the Myanmar border. Tam Dil, a natural lake with virgin forest, is 76km from Aizawl and 10 km from tourist resort of Saitual. Vantawng Falls, 5 km from the town of Thenzawl is the highest and most beautiful waterfall in the state. 2 km from Vantawng one can find a quaint and beautiful fall known as Tuirihiau. Thenzawl is also the main centre for handlooms. Phawngpui is the highest peak at an elevation of 2157 m and a trekkers delight. Just 30 km from Aizawl is beautiful Reiek Peak. A typical Mizo village which is a recreation of an old Mizo village is located at Falkawn, 24 km from Aizawl. Hmuifang Tlang about 50 km and Sialsuk Tlang about 66 km from Aizawl respectively are popular tourist destination. The Department of Tourism has opened tourist lodges in all the bigger towns all over the state and highway restaurants and travellers inns in other township. There is also a recreational centre at Beraw Tlang, Aizawl and Alpine Picnic Hut at district park near Zobawk. Reiek Tlang, where the Tourism Department created a typical Mizo village, modern Mizo village, resort.

Relevant Website : www.mizoram.gov.in

Government

Governor	: Kummanam Rajasekharan	*Chief Secretary*	: Arvind Ray
Chief Minister	: Zoramthanga	*Jurisdiction of High Court*	: Falls under the jurisdiction of Guwahati High Court. There is a Bench at Aizawl.

Nagaland

Area	: 16,579 sq km	*Population*	: 19.79 lakh (Prov. census 2011)
Capital	: Kohima	*Principal Languages*	: English, Hindi and 16 tribal dialects, Nagamese

History and Geography

Nagaland became the 16th state of the Indian Union in 1963. It is bordered by Myanmar on the east, Arunachal on the north, Assam on the west and Manipur on the south. It lies between the parallels of 98 degree and 96 degree east longitude and 26.6 degree and 27.4 degree latitude north of the equator.

The Naga people belong to the Indo-Mongoloid group of people living in a contiguous areas of the north-eastern hills of India and the upper portion of western Myanmar. The major recognised tribes of Nagaland are Angami, Ao, Chakhesang, Chang, Khiamniungan, Kuki, Konyak, Kachari, Lotha, Phom, Pochury, Rengma, Sangtam, Sumi, Yimchungrii and Zeliang. The Naga languages differ from tribe to tribe and sometimes even from one village to another. They are, however, under the Tibeto-Burman family.

In the 12th and 13th centuries, gradual contacts with the Ahoms of present day Assam was established but this did not have any significant impact on the traditional Naga way of life. However, in the 19th century the British appeared on the scene and ultimately the area was brought under British administration. After Independence this territory was made a centrally administered area in 1957, administered by the Governor of Assam. It was known as the Naga Hills Tuensang Area. This failed to quell popular aspirations and polilical unrest began. Hence, in 1961, the area was renamed as Nagaland and given the status of state of the Indian Union, which was formally inaugurated in December 1963.

Agriculture

Nagaland is basically a land of agriculture with about 70 per cent of the population depending on agriculture. The contribution of this sector is very significant. Rice is the staple food. It occupies about 70 per cent of the total area under cultivation and constitutes about 75 per cent of the total food production in the state. The major land use pattern is slash and burn cultivation locally known as *jhum*. Total cultivable area is 7,21,924 hectares.

Forest

Out of the total land area of 16,579 sq.km, forest area occupies approximately 8,62,9.30 sq.km. There are Rangapahar wildlife sanctuaries in Dimapur district, Fakim wildlife sanctuaries in Tuensang district and Singphan wildlife sanctuaries in Mon district, Intanki National Park in Peren district and Zoological Park in Dimapur district.

Power

The state has an installed generation capacity of 27.84 MW only from small hydro electric power projects against the requirement of 95 MW. The main source of power is from the Central Sector Power allocation.

Irrigation

The state has so far been constructing minor irrigations to divert small hill streams to the valleys and terraced field for rice cultivation covering an area of 82,150 hectares.

Transport

The state is connected to the rest of the country with airport and railway stations at Dimapur and National Highway-39 which passes through the state from Dimapur via Kohima to Manipur. This NH-39 is soon to be an international route under the Look East Policy of the central government. The rest of the state is connected only with roads covering about 24,709 km, this includes the NH-61 and state highways. The state is also inter-connected with postal services in all district headquarters, telephone line and mobile services.

Tourism

With the opening of the state to the international tourists by relaxing the Restricted Area Permit (RAP), a good number of foreign tourists as well as domestic tourists visit Nagaland every year.

The Hornbill festival conceived by the Tourist Department and held in the first week of December is an annual event where all tribes of the state come together to celebrate, exhibit and sell their traditional wares, foodstuffs and crafts. Three traditional festivals, namely *Sekrenyi* at Touphema in Kohima district (Feb), *Monyu* at Pongo in Longleng sub-division (April) and *Moatsu* at Chuchuyimlang in Mokokchung district (May) have been identified as festival destinations.

Music and dances are an intrinsic part of Naga life. Folk songs and ballads eulogizing bravery, beauty, love, generosity, etc, are transmitted from generation to generation. Likewise dancing is an important part of every festive occasion. Feasting, singing, dancing and merry-making invariably accompany festivals. Name of the tribes and their festivals are Angami-Sekrenyi, Ao-Moatsu, Chakhesang-Sukhrunye and Tsukhenye, Chang-Naknyulem, Khiamniungan-Tsokum, Kuki-Mimkut, Konyak-Aoleang Monyu, Kachari-Bushu, Lotha-Tokhu Emong, Phom-Monyu, Pochury-Yemshe, Rengma-Ngada, Sumi-Tuluni, Sangtam-Amongmong, Yimchungru-Metemneo, and Zeliang-Meileingi/Hega Langsimngi/Chegagadi.

Industries

Under the 'Year of Entrepreneur 2010' Entrepreneur Awareness Programme was held in all the (11) eleven districts of Nagaland. The state has set up 17 Citronella Demonstration Farms (i.e. 'Economic Plant') all over the state. The Nagaland Handloom and Handicrafts Development Cooperation Ltd, Dimapur is the state owned corporation, which is responsible for the promotion and marketing of handloom and handicraft products. An Industrial Growth Centre has been established at Ganeshnagar, Dimapur to facilitate entrepreneurs and educated unemployed youth to promote industries.

Relevant Website : www.nagaland.gov.in

Government

Governor	: P. B. Acharya	*Chief Secretary*	: Tenjen Toy
Chief Minister	: Neiphiu Rio	*Jurisdiction of High Court*	: Falls under Guwahati High Court.

Odisha

Area	: 1,55,707 sq km	*Population*	: 41,947.358 (2011 census)
Capital	: Bhubaneswar	*Principal Language*	: Odia

History and Geography

The history of Odisha dates back to antiquity, its most famous old names being Kalinga, Utkal and Odra. By the time of Mahavir and Buddha, the Kalinga region on the entire east coast acquired recognition and fame. Mauryan Emperor, Ashoka's invasion of Kalinga was an epoch-making event of ancient times of far reaching consequences. Kalinga was conquered but the conquest changed the heart of the conqueror. The transformation of Ashoka changed the course of religion and cultural history not only of India but also of the whole of Asia. The next great era of Odishan history commenced during the reign of Mahameghavahana Kharavela who ruled in the 1st half of the second century B.C. During Kharavela's reign the empire of Kalinga extended upto the river Ganga in the north and the river Godavari in the south. Subsequently the great dynasties such as the Shailodvabas, Bhoumakaras, Somavamsis, Gangas were not only great empire builders, but also promoters of art, literature and culture. The world famous Sun Temple at Konark was built in the thirteenth century by Narasimha Deva, the famous Jagannath temple at Puri in the twelfth century by Anangabhima Deva and the Lingaraj temple, Bhubaneshwar in the eleventh century by Jajati-II. Odisha was ruled successively by five Muslim kings till 1592 from mid-16th century, when Akbar annexed it into the Mughal empire with the decline of the mughal empire, Marathas occupied Odisha. They continued to hold it till the British took over the province in 1803.

Modern Odisha was born in 1936. The state, the land of Lord Jagannath, situated on the shores of Bay of Bengal is surrounded by West Bengal on the north-east, Jharkhand on the north, Chhattisgarh and Telangana on the west and Andhra Pradesh on the south. Its diverse landscape comprises coastal plains, mountainous terrain, plateaus, verdant river valleys and slopes dotted with watersheds, springs, lakes and forest cover of varying density.

Agriculture

Agriculture continues to be the backbone of the state's economy. Majority of the population is dependant on it as the National Sample Survey Organisation (NSSO) survey of 2012-13 indicates that farm income has doubled as compared to the survey of 2002-03. State government has intensified the efforts to enhance farmers' income with sustainable agricultural practices by promoting efficient extension and production technology, post harvest solutions, effective value addition and remunerative market options.

The state government provides health insurance coverage of ₹ 1.00 lakh to 5 members of every farming community under "Biju Krushak Kalyan Yojana". The state has emerged as the largest producer of sweet potato in the country contributing 30 per cent of total national production and third largest state in production of cashew. Odisha has also emerged as a leading supplier of mango graft in the country by enhancing production from 23.85 lakh to 54.56 lakh. In last five years 19 new cold stores with capacity 85200 MT have been established. A special programme for augmentation of production, processing and marketing of tomato, onion and potato has been initiated during 2018-19.

Irrigation

Odisha is primarily an agrarian economy. The cropped area is about 87.46 lakh hectares out of which 18.79 lakh hectares are irrigated. The weather favours a lot of crops, prominent being rice, pulses, oil seeds, jute, roselle, sugarcane, coconut and turmeric are important crops. The state government has launched number of short gestation projects like mega lift irrigation projects, deep bore well, construction programme and check dam construction programme to meet the irrigation needs of the farmers. The target is to bring an additional 10 lakh hectare of cultivable land under irrigation cover by the end of 2019. Under Parvati Giri Mega Lift Irrigation work of 171 mega lift schemes including upper indravati lift canal system have been taken up.

Industry

Most large-scale industries in the state are mineral based, while 25 per cent of the iron ore reserves in the country. Odisha has been receiving heavy investments in the industrial sector in recent years. Odisha emerged as a 'Leader' in Ease of Doing Business in the country and is consistently ranked amongst the top 3 states in terms of attracting live manufacturing investments in the country. The state also has one of the highest rates of implementation of industrial projects in the country. Government has taken significant steps in terms of introducing industry-friendly policy and regulatory framework to facilitate inclusiveness, encourage innovation and achieve sustainable industrial development.

Transport

Roads: Government is implementing different schemes for providing better road connectivity and building infrastructure in rural areas. During 2017-18, about 8,000 kilometers of rural roads and 145 bridges on rural roads are targeted to be completed under different schemes such as Biju Setu Yojana, Rural Infrastructure Development Fund, Pradhan Mantri Grama Sadak Yojana and Mukhya Mantri Sadak Yojana. Government has achieved many milestones on road connectivity. On an average, Works Department has improved about 2.1 kilometers of road every day and has completed 20 major bridges every year. 343 bridges, 9 road over bridges, 3 fly overs have been completed and 13,090 kilometers of roads have been improved since 2000.

Railways: Government is committed to improve railway density in the state. MoUs with Ministry of Railways for two new projects namely 130 kilometers Jeypore-Malkangiri and 38 kilometers Nabarangpur-Jeypore to bring rail connectivity for the first time to Malkanagiri and Nabarangpur districts have been signed. Government has also offered sharing of 50 per cent of land and construction cost for 32 kilometers of Puri-Konark Railway project.

Ports: Paradeep Port declared 8th major port of the country 1966 by Government of India. It is the only major port in Odisha and the first major port ont he East Coast commissioned in Independent India. With 480 kms of coastline Odisha has 13 potential sites for minor ports development. These are located at Gopalpur, Behuda Muhan and Palur in Ganjam district, Baliharchandi and Astaranga in Puri district, Jatadhar Muhan in Jagatsinghpur district, Inchri, Chandipur, Bahabalpur, Kirtania and Bichitrapur (Talasari) in Balasore district and Dhamra and Chudamani in Bhadrak district. Government of Odisha is making effort to develop a river port on Mahanadi river near Paradip to boost coastal shipping. Inland Waster Transport (TWT) has vast potential but a small network in Odisha. The passenger launch services are used in remote areas where other modes of transport are generally lacking. Inland water transport services are provided by the state government.

Aviation: Government has taken proactive steps for implementation of RCS-UDAN Scheme in Utkela and Jeypore Airstrips. Jharsuguda airport is fully developed now.

Power

Energy is the driving force of economic growth either in the form of finite resources such as coal, oil and gas or in renewable forms such as hydroelectric wind solar and biomas or its converted form of electricity. To provide 24x7 quality and uniterrupted power at an affordable rate to the people, Government has developed a comprehensive strategy to augment generation.

Tourism

Odisha is a veritable tourists' paradise; which offers a plethora of opportunities to cater to various tastes and choices in varied forms. The silver beaches of Chandipur, the blue sea of Gopalpur, the exotic and golden beaches of Konark and Puri, red crabs of Talasari beach, attract tourists throughtout the year. Chilika, the largest brackish water inland lake in Asia nestles in the heart of coastal Odisha. Chilika lake an ecological wonder, is the largest brackish water lagoon in Asia, an important wetland situated in Odisha on the eastern coast of India. Declared a Ramsar site, it is famous for its rich diversity of local and migratory birds. Bhitarkanika is the second largest mangrove eco-system with an area of 672 sqkms of wildlife sanctuary of which 175 sqkm was declared a national park in 1998, situated in the district of Kendrapara, on the eastern coast of India. Bhitarkanika is one of the most spectacular wildlife sanctuaries and national parks in the country, home to virgin mangrove forests and wetlands. Its rich biodiversity harbours 71 species of mangrove and associated species, 35 species of reptiles, 297 species of birds including international winter migrants from central Asia and Europe and 26 species of mammals including spotted deer, sambar, fishing cats, porcupines and otters, etc.

Relevant Website : www.odisha.gov.in

Government

Governor	: Prof. Ganeshi Lal	*Chief Secretary*	: Aditya Prasad Padhi
Chief Minister	: Naveen Patnaik	*Jurisdiction of High Court*	: State of Odisha

Punjab

Area	: *50,362 sq km*	*Population*	: *2,77,43,338*
Capital	: Chandigarh	*Principal Language*	: Punjabi

History and Geography

Ancient Punjab formed part of the vast Indo-Iranian region. In later years it saw the rise and fall of the Mauryas, Bactrians, Greeks, Sakas, Kushans and Guptas. Medieval Punjab saw a supremacy of the Muslims. Ghaznavi was followed by the Ghoris, the slaves, the Khiljis, the Tughlaks, the Lodhis and the Mughals. Fifteenth and sixteenth centuries marked a period of watershed in the history of Punjab. Through teachings of Guru Nanak, Bhakti movement received a great impetus. Sikhism began as a socio religious movement, which was more interested in fighting evils in religion and society. It was Guru Gobind Singh, the tenth Guru, who transformed the Sikhs into the Khalsa. They rose to challenge tyranny and after centuries of servitude, established a Punjabi Raj based on secularism and patriotism. Maharaja Ranjit Singh, in the works of a Persian writer, changed Punjab from Madam-Kada to Bagh-Bahist (from the abode of sorrow to the garden of paradise). But soon after his death the entire edifice collapsed due to internal intrigues and British machinations. After two abortive Anglo-Sikh wars, Punjab was finally annexed to the British Empire in 1849.

The fight against the British rule had begun long before Mahatma Gandhi's arrival on the scene. The revolt found expression through the movement of a revivalist or reformist character. First it was the Namdhari sect, which believed in self-discipline and self-rule. Later, it was Lala Lajpat Rai who played a leading role in the freedom movement. Punjab was in the vanguard of India's freedom struggle on all fronts in India and abroad. Punjab's hardships did not end with Independence. It had to face the misery of partition with large-scale blood shed and migration. Besides their rehabilitation, there was the task of re-organization of the state.

Eight princely states of East Punjab were grouped together to form a single state called PEPSU—Patiala and the East Punjab States Union—with Patiala as its capital. PEPSU state was merged with Punjab in 1956 with its capital at Chandigarh. Later in 1966, Haryana was carved out of Punjab. Situated in the north-western corner of the country, Punjab is bound on the west by Pakistan, on the north by Jammu and Kashmir, on the north-east by Himachal Pradesh and on the south by Haryana and Rajasthan.

The state ranks seventh as gross producer of wheat in the world and it generates third largest marketable surplus after Canada and Australia which is about one tenth of the global trade in wheat. In case of rice, its marketable surplus is second only to Thailand. This has become possible due to the excellent conditions with respect to creation of infrastructure, adoption of appropriate technologies, good extension services and government incentives and enabling state policies. The state government has continued to give greater thrust on development of agriculture. The record productivity of cotton i.e., 756 kg lint per ha was achieved during 2016-17. Area under cotton rose from 2.53 lakh hac to 3.5 lakh hac during 2017-18.

Horticulture is a high value segment of agriculture. In Punjab, with only 4 per cent of total cropped area, horticulture crops are contributing approx. 10.50 per cent GDP to the total agriculture produce.

Irrigation

Since both surface as well as ground water resources in the state have already been fully utilised as such the increase in agricultural production solely depends on the improved efficiency of water use. State is focusing on significant improvements in the economy of water use and in the operational efficiency by modernisation of existing canal system which is centuries old. During the year 2016-17 the work of lining of watercourses in a length of 4758 km was carried out and an area of 210375 hectare brought under better irrigation facilities by the Punjab Water Resources Management and Development Corporation. An area of 6700 hectare was brought under irrigation by installation of deep tube well sand laying under ground pipelines.

Power

Punjab has already achieved status of power surplus state with commissioning of three new thermal power plants at Rajpura (1400 MW), Talwandi Sabo (1980 MW) and Goindwal Sahib (540 MW) thus totalling to 3920 MW. With this, now the gross installed capacity is 13960 MW including its own installed capacity and share from NRSE projects, BBMB and other Cenral Sector projects. On green energy front, PSPCL has installed capacity/ share from central sector projects of 1253 MW which include solar projects of capacity 830 MW and rest from non solar projects including biomass and mini/ micro hydel projects.

Roads

The total road network length is 71742 km, consisting of 2630 km national highways 1133 km state highways, 1826 km major district roads and 5119 km of other district roads(ODRs) and 61034 km rural link roads. Out of the link roads PWD B&R looks after 31696 km and Punjab Mandi Board looks after 29338 km of link roads.

Aviation

Punjab has two international airports at Amritsar (Rajasansi) and Mohali. First phase of the terminal building at Mohali airport is complete and awaiting commissioning.

Fairs and Festivals

Besides festivals of Dussehra, Diwali, Holi, other important festivals/ fairs/melas are Maghi Mela at Mukatsar, Rural Sports at Kila Raipur, Basant at Patiala, Holla Mohalla at Anandpur Sahib, Baisakhi at Talwandi Sabo, Urs at Rauza Sharif at Sirhind, Chappar Mela at Chappar, Skeikh Farid Aagman Purb at Faridkot, Ram Tirath Mela at Village Ram Tirath, Shaheedi Jor Mela at Sirhind, Harballab Sangeet Sammelan Baba Sodal at Jalandhar. In addition to these, three heritage festivals at Amritsar, Patiala, Kapurthala are also celebrated every year and are very popular among the tourists.

Government

Governor	: V.P. Singh Badnore	*Chief Secretary*	: Karan Avtar Singh
Chief Minister	: Capt. Amarinder Singh	*Jurisdiction of High Court*	: Punjab, Haryana & Chandigarh

Rajasthan

Area	: 3,42,239 sq km	*Population*	: 6.86 crore
Capital	: Jaipur	*Principal Languages*	: Hindi and Rajasthani

History and Geography

Rajasthan is the largest state in India area-wise. Prior to independence it was known as Rajputana or Rajputs—a martial community who ruled over this area for centuries. The history of Rajasthan dates back to the pre-historic times. Around 3,000 and 1,000 BC, it had a culture akin to that of the Indus Valley civilization. It were the Chauhans who dominated Rajput affairs from seventh century and by 12th century they had become an imperial power. After the Chauhans, it were the Guhilots of Mewar who controlled the destiny of the warring tribes. Besides Mewar, the other historically prominent states were

Marwar, Jaipur, Bundi, Kota, Bharatpur and Alwar. Other states were only offshoots of these. All these states accepted the British Treaty of Subordinate Alliance in 1818 protecting the interest of the princes. This naturally left the people discontented.

After the revolt of 1857, the people united themselves under the leadership of Mahatma Gandhi to contribute to the freedom movement with the introduction of provincial autonomy in 1935 in British India agitation for civil liberties and political rights became stronger in Rajasthan. The process of uniting scattered states commenced from 1948 to 1956 when the States Reorganization Act was promulgated, first came Matsya Union (1948) consisting of a fraction of states, slowly and gradually other states merged with this Union. By 1949, major states like Bikaner, Jaipur, Jodhpur. and Jaisalmer joined this Union making it the United State of Greater Rajasthan. Ultimately in 1958, the present state of Rajasthan formally came into being, with Ajmer state, the Abu Road Taluka and Sunel Tappa joining it.

The entire western flank of the state borders with Pakistan, while Punjab in north, Haryana in north-east, Uttar Pradesh in east and Madhya Pradesh in south-east and Gujarat lies in south-west of the state.

Agriculture

Estimated total sown area in the state is 241.21 lakh hectare. Principal crops in the state are wheat, barley, jowar, millet, maize, gram, oilseeds, kharif pulses and cotton. Cultivation of vegetable and citrus fruits such as orange and malta have also picked up over last few years. Red chilies, mustard, cumin seeds and methi are commercial crops.

Industry

Endowed with a rich culture, Rajasthan is also rich in minerals and is fast emerging on the industrial scenario of the country. Some of the important central undertaking are Hindustan Zinc Smelter Plant at Devari (Udaipur), Chanderia (Chittorgarh), Hindustan Copper Plant at Khetri Nagar (Jhunjhunu), Hindustan Salt Ltd. at Sambhar (Jaipur), HMT Ltd. at Ajmer and Precision Instruments Factory at Kota. Major industries are textiles and woollens, engineering goods, electronic items, automobile, food processing, gems and jewellery, cement, marble slabs and tiles, glass and ceramics, oxygen, zink, fertilizers, railway wagons, ball bearings, water and electricity metres, sulphuric acid, handicraft items, television sets, synthetic yarn, insulators, stainless steel, re-rolling, steel-foundry and insulting bricks. Besides precious and semi-precious stones, caustic soda, calcium carbide, nylon and tyers, etc. are other important industries.

Rajasthan has rich deposits of zinc concentrates, emerald, garnet, gypsum, silver, asbestos, felspar and mica. The state also abounds in exports, so Exports Promotion Industrial Park of the state has been established and made operational at Sitapura (Jaipur), Boranada (Jodhpur). Inland Container Depots have been established at Jaipur, Bhilwara, Jodhpur, and Bhiwadi (Alwar) to promote the exporters. Special Economic Zone for gems and jewellery at Sitapura (Jaipur) and Special Economic Zone for handicraft at Boranada (Jodhpur) have been established and Multipurpose Special Economic Zone "Mahendra World City" has been established in PPP model at Jaipur.

Minerals

The state is one of the leading mineral producing states in the country. The state has a glorious heritage in the field of mining and is second only to Jharkhand as regards to mineral wealth. It is referred to as museum of minerals; having resources of both metallic and non-metallic minerals including building stones and also resources of radioactive minerals, lignite, petroleum and natural gas. Important minerals with which the name of state is associated are non-ferrous metals such as lead-zinc, copper, ferromagnesian metals such as tungsten, a number of industrial minerals and different varieties of dimensional and decorative stones. There are 79 varieties of minerals available out of which 57 are produced commercially. Presently it is the sole producer of lead-zinc, wollastonite, calcite and selenite and leading producer of silver, gypsum, marble, ochre, ball clay, rock phosphate, cadmium and feldspar in the country. Different varieties of marble, granite, sandstone and Kota stone of the state has a large demand not only in the country but also world over. With the discovery of oil and natural gas in western Rajasthan the state has become the second highest producer of crude oil after Bombay High.

More than 85 per cent of the country's potash, lead-zinc, silver and wollastonite resources are located in the state. The state possess substantial share of the total resources of potash (94 per cent), lead-zinc ore (89 per cent), wollastonite (88 per cent), silver ore (87 per cent), gypsum (82 per cent), fuller's earth (74 per cent), diatomite (72 per cent), feldspar (66 per cent), marble (64 per cent), asbestos (61 per cent), copper ore (50 per cent), calcite (50 per cent), talc-soapstone-steatite (49 per cent), granite (42 per cent), ball clay (38 per cent), rock phosphate (30 per cent), fluorite (29 per cent), tungsten ore (27 per cent), laterite (26 per cent), gold ore (primary) (23 per cent), mica (21 per cent) and china clay (16 per cent).

Power

The installed power capacity in the state was 15,986.87 MW in which 5,357.35 MW produced from state owned projects, 853.44 MW from collaboration projects, 2,803.47 MW from the allocation from central power generating stations, 3,916.61 MW from wind, solar and biomass projects and 3,056.00 MW from private sector projects.

Mahatma Gandhi National Rural Employment Guarantee Scheme

In first phase Mahatma Gandhi National Rural Employment Guarantee Scheme was initiated in six districts—Banswara, Dungarpur, Jhalawar, Karouli, Sirohi and Udaipur. In second phase this scheme was initiated in other six districts Barmer, Chittorgarh, Jaisalmer, Jalore, Sawai Madhopur and Tonk. In third phase this scheme was launched in rest of the districts of the state.

Transport

Roads : The estimated total length of roads is 2,07,019 km.

Railways : Jodhpur, Jaipur, Bikaner, Sawai Madhopur, Kota, Bharatpur and Udaipur are main railway junctions of the state. Total length of railway line is 5,871.65 km (4801.18 km broad gaze, 983.71 km gaze and 86.76 km narrow gaze) in the state.

Jaipur Metro : Jaipur Metro is a rapid transit system in Jaipur city. In June 2015, it began commercial service between Chandpole and Mansarovar. It is India's sixth metro rail system after those in Kolkata, Delhi NCR, Bengaluru, Gurugram and Mumbai. It is the first metro in the country to run on double storey elevated road and track. The construction work is on for the next phase.

Aviation : All eminent cities are regular connected with Jaipur airport under domestic air services in which Delhi, Mumbai, Ahemdabad, Kolkata, Chennai, Hyderabad, Bengaluru, Pune and Guwahati are important domestic air services. International air services are also available for Dubai, Mascutt and Sharjah from Jaipur airport.

Festivals

Rajasthan is a land of festivals and fairs, besides the national festivals of Holi, Deepawali, Vijayadashmi, Christmas, etc., auspicious days related to deities of gods and goddesses, saintly figures, folk heroes and heroines are celebrated. Important fairs are Teej, Gangaur, Holi-Dhulandi, Kite and Rajasthan Divas (Jaipur), annual Urs of Ajmer Sherif and Galiakot Pushkar Fair (Ajmer), Ramdevji Cattle Fair (Nagaur), Camel Festival (Bikaner), Desert Festival (Jaisalmer), Beneshwar Fair (Dungarpur), Braj-Holi Festival (Bharatpur), Kailadevi Fair, Shri Mahaveer Fair (Karouli), Ranakpur Festival, Godwar Festival (Pali), Mewar Festival (Udaipur), Summer and Winter Festivals in Mount Abu (Sirohi), Kajli Teej and Bundi Festival (Bundi), Dussehra Festival and Adventure Festival (Kota), Matsya Festival (Alwar), Marwar Festival (Jodhpur), Chandrabhaga Fair (Jhalawar), Jambheshwar Fair and Koloyat Fair (Nokha Bikaner) and Khatu Shyamji Fair (Khatu-Sikar), etc.

Tourists Centres

Jaipur, Jodhpur, Udaipur, Bikaner, Mount Abu (Sirohi), Ranthambore National Park (Tiger Reserve)-(Sawai Madhopur), Sariska Tiger National Park (Alwar), Keoladeo National Park (Bharatpur), Ajmer, Jaisalmer, Pali, Bundi, Kota, Jhalawar, Shekhawati (Sikar) and Chittorgarh are important places of tourists interest in the state.

Relevant Website : www.rajasthan.gov.in

Government

Governor	: Kalyan Singh	*Chief Secretary*	: Devendra Bhushan Gupta
Chief Minister	: Ashok Gehlot	*Jurisdiction of High Court*	: Rajasthan

Sikkim

Area	: 7,096 sq km	*Population*	: 6.11 lakh (provisional census 2011)
Capital	: Gangtok	*Principal Languages*	: Lepcha, Bhutia, Nepali, Limboo, Sikkimese

History and Geography

The early history of Sikkim starts in the 13th century with the signing of a blood-brotherhood treaty between the Lepcha Chieftain Thekong Tek and Bhutia Chieftain Khye-Bumsa at Kabi Lungtsok in North Sikkim. This follows the historic visit of three revered Lamas to Yuksam in 1641 in West Sikkim where they consecrated Phuntsog Namgyal, a sixth generation descendant of Khye-Bumsa as the first Chogyal of Sikkim, thus heralding the beginning of the Namgyal dynasty in Sikkim. With the march of history, events in Sikkim saw the process of democratisation and became an integral part of the Indian Union in 1975. Sikkim, the land blessed by Guru Padmasambhava during his sojourn to Tibet in 8th century, are inhabited by people from different communities and live in total harmony. Sikkim is perhaps the most peaceful state of the Indian Union to promote communal harmony, a feat which is much to be expected in a plural society like India.

The world's third highest mountain, Khangchendzonga, is regarded as the guardian deity of Sikkim. Sikkim is one of the 18 biodiversity hotspots in the world. More than 5000 species of angiosperms are found in the state, nearly one third of the total species of angiosperms are found in the country. There are over 4,500 species of flowering plants, 362 species of ferns and allies, over 550 species of wild orchids, atleast 36 species of rhododendrons besides many variations and wild natural hybrids, 11 species of oaks, 30 species of primulas, 28 bamboos, over 700 species of butterflies, probably thrice as many moths, at least 48 species of freshwater fish, around 50 species of amphibians, over 80 reptiles, 600 species of birds and around 150 species of mammals in the state.

Rare and globally threatened snow leopard, Tibetan argali sheep, red panda, as well as highest altitude domesticated bovid, the yak, black-necked crane and fairrieanum orchid are some of the important species found here.

Tourism

Situated in the eastern Himalayas, Sikkim is one of the most beautiful states of the Indian Union. It is home to the third highest mountain in the world, Mt. Khangchendzonga which is also worshipped as the guardian deity. It is adorned with snowy mountains, luxuriant forests with exotic flora and fauna, pristine waterfalls, sacred lakes, holy caves, medicinal hot-springs, cascading rivers and gentle streams making it a tourist destination for all seasons. An interlace of mixed culture of various communities residing here, the state celebrates festivals and activities of each other with grand fervour. There are tours for everyone, from those seeking solitude for meditation to the adventurous or those seeking leisure holiday. For the more adventurous there is trekking in the mountains, river rafting, bird watching, mountain biking, rock climbing, paragliding and angling as well as the mountain flights for experiencing the snow clad mountains.

Agriculture

In the agriculture sector, the state has made immense breakthrough with the introduction of crops like baby corn, sweet corn, etc., bringing manifold increase in income to the farming community. Focus is on crops which can grow under moisture stress conditions and which have high global demands of the likes of buckwheat, millet and such other cereals.

Horticulture

The production of fruits has increased from 5250 tonnes to 22240 recording to growth of 323 per cent. Vegetable production has increased from 22130 tonnes to 78820 tonnes registering 256 per cent growth. In floriculture a record growth of 200 ha with production of over 230 lakh numbers of cut flowers and planting materials.

Irrigation and Power

The Department of Irrigation and Flood Control has covered 3866.68 hectares of agricultural land in Eleventh Five Year Plan.

Power

The total hydro power potential of Sikkim as assessed by Central Water Commission, is around 8,000 MW. With the view to harness the immense hydro power potential of the state, the Government of Sikkim in the year 2004 constituted the Hydro Committee to examine the various aspects related to hydro power development and make recommendations for early implementation of the hydro power projects.

Transport

Roads : Gangtok is connected by roads with Darjeeling district of West Bengal and also with all the district headquarters within Sikkim. The total road length of the state is 3,672.32 km and 216 bridges, which includes 873.40 km road maintained by the Border Roads Organisation.

Railways and Aviation : The closest railway stations are Siliguri (113 km) and New Jalpaiguri (125 km) connecting Kolkata, Delhi and other important cities and Bagdogra airport. The state has its first airport at Pakyong in East Sikkim. There is a regular helicopter service between Gangtok and Bagdogra.

Information Technology

The state government has made encouraging steps to improve the lives of common people through several IT-oriented projects. To meet the objectives various initiatives have been taken like the establishment of 45 community service centres and state-wide area network all across even in remote areas as a step to bring IT to the grassroot level of people. This has greatly increased the government's interface with the public and enhanced the quality of some state services. CSC in Sherethang which is an achievement for the state government and its citizens, is declared as the highest cyber cafe in the world by the Limca Book of Records.

Relevant Website : www.sikkim.gov.in

Government

Governor	: Ganga Prasad	*Chief Secretary*	: Dr A.K. Srivastava
Chief Minister	: Pawan Kumar Chamling	*Jurisdiction of High Court*	: Sikkim

Tamil Nadu

Area	: 1,30,060 sq km	*Population*	: 7.21 crore (census 2011)
Capital	: Chennai	*Principal Language*	: Tamil

History and Geography

Tamil Nadu has a hoary antiquity. Though early *Sangam* classics throw historical references it is only from the Pallavas we pass to recorded history. South India had remained under the hegemony of the Cholas, the Cheras and the Pandyas for centuries. The Pallavas held supremacy from about the second quarter of the fourth century AD. They were the originators of the famous Dravidian style of temple architecture. The last Pallava ruler was Aparajita in whose reign the later Cholas under Vijayalaya and Aditya asserted themselves by about the 10th century. At the end of the 11th century, Tamil Nadu was ruled by several dynasties like the Chalukyas, Cholas and Pandyas. In the two centuries that followed, the imperial Cholas gained paramountcy over South India.

Muslims gradually strengthened their position, which led to the establishment of the Bahamani Sultanate, by the middle of the 14th century. At the same time, the Vijayanagar Kingdom quickly consolidated itself and extended its sway over the whole of South India and at the close of the century, Vijayanagar became the supreme power in South. However, it crumbled at the battle of Talikota in 1564 to the confederate forces of the Deccan Sultans.

Even during the period of the tumultuous confusion that followed the battle of Talikota, European commercial interest had appeared as rivals in the area of South India. The Portuguese, the Dutch, the French and the English came in quick succession and established trading centres known as 'Factories'. East India Company which had established their factory at Masulipatnam, now in Andhra Pradesh, in 1611 gradually annexed territories by encouraging enmity among the native rulers. Tamil Nadu was one of the first of British settlements in India. The state is the successor to the old Madras Presidency which in 1901 covered the bulk of the southern peninsula. The composite Madras state was later reorganised and the present Tamil Nadu was formed.

Tamil Nadu is bound on north by Andhra Pradesh and Karnataka, on west by Kerala, on east by the Bay of Bengal and on south by the Indian Ocean.

Agriculture

The Mettur Dam was opened in 2011 bringing an additional paddy area of 1,80,000 acres. Around 1,22,230 farmers are benefited. To reduce the burden of the farmers, 4 per cent VAT exemption to agricultural inputs and farm machineries. 63.40 lakh farmers are benefited.

Tourism

As a veritable treasure trove of art and culture, the state has always been a great attraction to offer to the tourists. It is the consummate expression of art and culture of past period than elsewhere in the country. The state possesses the glorious sculptures, frescoes and murals adorning walls and pillars, giant temple towers (gopurams). Tamil Nadu has multifarious tourist attractions which include 1076 km of pristine coastline, more than 30,000 temples and places of worship date back beyond the beginning of the Christian era, waterfalls, wildlife sanctuaries, hill stations, dam sites, arts, exotic culture, beautifully made handicrafts and handlooms, heritage, cuisine, business opportunities, etc.

To facilitate the visiting tourists, Tamil Nadu Tourism is making a concerted effort in improving the basic infrastructure and services in a big way in all important tourist centres. Alternate demand through promotion of medical tourism, educational tourism, adventure tourism, rural tourism and business tourism also enabled a quantum leap in tourist arrivals.

Geology and Mining

Minerals form the basic resources for several important industries and contribute substantially to the Gross State Domestic Product and Industrial Growth. Minerals are considered to be the backbone for the economic growth and deemed to be the wealth of the country. The developmental activities of the state and its economic prosperity are reflected by the availability of mineral, wealth and its prudent exploitation.

The state is endowed with several industrial minerals like lignite, limestone, garnet sand, silica sand, quartz and feldspar, graphite, oil and natural gas, magnesite, iron ore, etc., and also common use minor mineral deposits including world famous black granite and multi colour granite deposits which enabled in setting up of cement, refractory, glass, ceramic and granite polishing industries.

Transport

Roads: The length of road network under the control of Highway Department is 62,294 km.

Railways : (1) Total length of route km is 3846 km.

(2) Running Track km as on March 2015 : 4943 km

The major stations are: Chennai Central, Tiruchirappalli, Madurai, Tirunelveli, Nagarkoil, Coimbatore , Erode, Salem, Jolarpettai, Katpadi and Arakkonam.

Ports: Major ports are Chennai, Ennore and Thoothukudi. There are 23 declared minor ports including 7 government. Minor ports namely Cuddalore, Nagapattinam, Rameswaram, Pamban, Colachel, Kanneyakumari and Valinokkam. There are 16 declared captive minor ports including Kattupalli, Ennore Minor Port, PY-3 Oilfield and Thirukkadaiyur which are operational and others are at various stages of obtaining statutory clearances and development.

Relevant Website : www.tn.gov.in

Government

Governor	: Banwarilal Purohit	*Chief Secretary*	: Dr. Girija Vaidyanathan
Chief Minister	: Edappadi K. Palaniswami	*Jurisdiction of High Court*	: Madras High Court

Telangana

Area	: 114840 sq. km	*Population*	: 3,51,93,978 (as per 2011 census)
Capital	: Hyderabad	*Principal Languages*	: Telugu and Urdu

In 2014 Telangana was formed as 29th state of India with Hyderabad as its capital. Earlier Telangana was part of Andhra State as per the linguistic re-organisation of states in 1956. Telangana state has 10 districts including Hyderabad, Adilabad, Khammam, Karimnagar, Mahbubnagar, Medak, Nalgonda, Nizamabad, Rangareddy and Warangal.

History of Telangana

The name Telangana refers to the word Trilinga Desa, earned due to the presence of three ancient Shiva temples at Kaleswaram, Srisailam and Draksharamam. A more historical reason is that during the reign of Nizams the region was known as Telugu Angana to differentiate it from the areas where Marathi was spoken. The region has been ruled by great dynasties such as Sathavahanas, Kakatiyas, Chalukyas, Mughals, Qutubshahis, Asafjahis. The Kakatiyas contributions to architecture are considered very impressive. Among Kakatiyas, Prataparudra was a great ruler who ruled till AD 1323. The Satavahanas ruled Telangana region for about 400 years right from the 2nd century BC to beyond the 2nd century AD.

There have been several movements to revoke the merger of Telangana and Andhra, major ones occurred in 1969, 1972 and 2009. The movement for a new state of Telangana gained momentum over the decades. In 2009 the

Government of India announced the process of formation of the Telangana. Violent protests led by people in the Coastal Andhra and Rayalaseema regions occurred immediately after the announcement, and the decision was put on hold in December, 2009. The movement continued in Hyderabad and other districts of Telangana. There have been large scale strikes, protests and demonstrations coupled with many suicides also demanding separate statehood.

In July, 2013 the process of formation of a separate state gained momentum. After various stages, the Bill was placed in the Parliament and in February, 2014 Andhra Pradesh Reorganization Bill was passed by the Parliament for the formation of Telangana state comprising ten districts from north-western Andhra Pradesh.

Geography

Telangana is situated on the Deccan plateau in the central stretch of the eastern seaboard of the Indian Peninsula. It covers 114,800 sq km (44,300 sq miles). The region is drained by two major rivers, with about 79 per cent of the Godavari river catchment area and about 69 per cent of the Krishna river catchment area, but most of the land is arid due to higher elevation of most of the state compared to rivers. Telangana is also drained by several minor rivers such as the Bhima, the Manjeera and the Musi. The state is surrounded by Maharashtra on north and north-west; Karnataka on the west; Chhattisgarh on the north-east and Odisha lies on its west.

Agriculture

Rice is the major food crop of the state. Other important crops are tobacco, mango, cotton and sugarcane. The major kharif coarse cereals maize, jowar, bajra, ragi are produced in the state. Out of the total geographical area 40.5 per cent is under net area sown, 23.9 per cent is under forests, 10.5 per cent is under current fallow lands, 7.7 per cent is under non-agricultural uses and 5.4 per cent is under barren and uncultivable land. Net cropped area is 46.54 lakh hectares. Agriculture production depends upon the distribution of rainfall. The influence of south-west monsoon is predominant.

Arts and Crafts

Handicrafts have been an integral part of the state. The region offers many astounding handicrafts like bidri crafts, banjara needle crafts, dokra metal crafts, nirmal arts, bronze castings, lacquerware, etc. Be it an intricate needle craft or the surprising bronze castings, metal craft or the classic stone craft, Telangana has a wide assortment of handicrafts.

Festivals

'Bathukamma' is a colourful and vibrant festival and this unique festival of flowers stands as a symbol of cultural identity. "Bonalu" is an annual Hindu festival celebrated in the state in which Goddess Mahakali is worshipped.

Dussehra, Samakka Saarakka Jaathara, Peerla Panduga, Ramzan are also largely celebrated in Telangana.

Relevant Website : www.telangana.gov.in

Government

Governor	: E.S.L. Narasimhan	*Chief Secretary*	: Shailendra Kumar Joshi
Chief Minister	: Kalvakuntla Chandrashekar Rao	*Jurisdiction of High Court*	: Hyderabad High Court

Tripura

Area	: 10,486 sq km	*Population*	: 36.74 lakh (prov. census 2011)
Capital	: Agartala	*Principal Languages*	: Bengali and Kokborok

History

Tripura has its unique tribal culture and a fascinating folklore. The history of Tripura can be learnt from *Rajmala* chronicles of King Tripura and writings of historians. There are references of Tripura even in the *Mahabharata* and the *Puranas*. According to *Rajmala*, the rulers were known by the surname *Fa* meaning *father*. There is a reference to rulers of Bengal helping Tripura kings in the 14th century. Kings of Tripura had to face frequent Mughal invasions with varying successes. They defeated the Sultans of Bengal in several battles. Nineteenth century marked the beginning of the modern era in Tripura when King Maharaja Bir Chandra Kishore Manikya Bahadur modelled his administrative set-up on the British India pattern and brought in various reforms. His successors ruled Tripura till 15 October 1949 when the state merged with the Indian Union. Initially, a part 'C' State, it became a centrally administered territory with the Re-organisation of States in 1956. In 1972, Tripura attained the status of a full-fledged state.

Tripura is strategically situated between the river valleys of Myanmar and Bangladesh. Encircled almost on three sides by Bangladesh, it is linked with Assam and Mizoram in the north-east.

Agriculture

The economy of Tripura is primarily dependent on agriculture. 24 per cent land is being utilized by this sector, and 51 per cent population is dependent on agriculture for their livelihood.

Irrigation

Tripura is predominantly a hilly state having geographical area of 10,49,169 hectare. Amid the undulating terrain the recently assessed land under cultivation is 2,55,241 hectares. Irrigable land is 1,17,00 hectares.

Tourism

Tripura is a small but picturesque state in the north eastern region of the country. The area is about 10,491,69 sq km. to its north, south and south east it has an international boundary with Bangladesh while to its east; it shares a common boundary with two states of Assam and Mizoram. There are 19 ethnic tribes, Bengali, Manipuri and others, inhabiting this panoramic tiny state.

The scenic beauty of Tripura, its rich and varied culture, archaeology and architecture, its handloom and handicraft which is exquisite in colour, excellent in design and craftsmanship, its verdant forests, and lakes, its excellent bracing climatic conditions, its enhancing and abounding floral treasures and panoramic view points and above all its very hospitable ethnic population are so attractive that anyone who visits the state once cannot resist his temptation to come oftener.

Relevant Website : www.tripura.gov.in

Government

Governor	: Kaptan Singh Solanki	*Chief Secretary*	: Dr. L. K. Gupta
Chief Minister	: Biplab Kumar Deb	*Jurisdiction of High Court*	: High Court of Tripura

Uttarakhand

Area	: 53,483 sq km	*Population*	: 1.01 crore (census 2011)
Capital	: Dehradun	*Principal Languages*	: Hindi, English, Garhwali, Kumauni

History

Uttarakhand finds mention in the ancient Hindu scriptures as Kedarkhand, Manaskhand and Himavant. The Kushanas, Kunindas, Kanishka, Samudra Gupta, Pauravas, Katuris, Palas, Chandras and Panwars and the British have ruled it in turns. It is often called the Land of the Gods *(Dev Bhoomi)* because of its various holy places and abundant shrines. The hilly regions of Uttarakhand offer pristine landscapes to the tourists. Uttarakhand was earlier a part of the United Province of Agra and Awadh which came into existence in 1902. In 1935, the name of state was shortened to the United Province. In January 1950, the United Province was renamed as Uttar Pradesh and Uttaranchal remained a part of Uttar Pradesh before it was carved out in 2000. It is incepted as the 27th state of India.

Located in the foothills of the Himalayas, the state has international boundaries with China (Tibet) in the north and Nepal in the east. On its north-west lies Himachal Pradesh while on the south is Uttar Pradesh.

Agriculture

About 90 per cent of the population depends on agriculture. The total cultivated area in the state is 7,67,459 hectare.

Industry and Minerals

The state is rich in mineral deposits like limestone, marble, rock phosphate, dolomite, magnesite, copper graphite, gypsum, etc.

Irrigation and Energy

Agricultural land under irrigation is 5,61,733 hectare. The state has excellent potential for hydropower generation. There are a number of hydroelectric projects on the rivers Yamuna, Bhagirathi, Bhilangana, Alaknanda, Mandakini, Saryu, Gauri, Kosi and Kali generating electricity.

Transport

Roads : The total length of metalled roads is 33,914 km. The length of PWD roads is 25,665 km. The length of roads built by local bodies is 2,674 km.

Railways : The main railway stations are Dehradun, Haridwar, Roorkee, Kotdwar, Kashipur, Udhamsingh Nagar, Haldwani, Ramnagar and Kathgodam.

Aviation : There are air strips at Jolly Grant (Dehradun) and Pantnagar (Udham Singh Nagar). Air strips at Naini-Seni (Pithoragarh), Gauchar (Chamoli) and Chinyalisaur (Uttarkashi) are under construction. Pawan Hans Ltd. is also operating helicopter service from Rudraprayag to Kedarnath for pilgrims.

Festivals

The world-famous *Kumbh Mela/Ardh Kumbh Mela* is held at Haridwar at every twelfth/sixth year interval. Other prominent fairs/festivals are *Devidhura Mela* (Champawat), *Purnagiri Mela* (Champawat), *Nanda Devi Mela* (Almora), *Gauchar Mela* (Chamoli), *Baisakhi* (Uttarkashi), *Magha Mela* (Uttarkashi), *Uttaraini Mela* (Bageshwar), *Vishu Mela* (Jaunsar Bhabar), *Peerane-Kaliyar* (Roorkee), and Nanda Devi Raj Jat Yatra held every twelfth year.

Tourist Centres

Prominent places of pilgrimage/tourist interests are Gangotri, Yamunotri, Badrinath, Kedarnath, Haridwar, Rishikesh, Hemkund Sahib, Nanakmatta, etc. Kailash Mansarovar Yatra can be performed through Kumaon region. The world-famous Valley of Flowers, Pindari Glacier, Roop Kund, Dayara Bugyal, Auli and hill stations like Mussoorie, Dehradun, Chakrata, Nainital, Ranikhet, Bageshwar, Bhimtal, Kausani, Lansdowne, etc. are the other tourist destinations.

Relevant Website : www.uk.gov.in

Government

Governor	: Baby Rani Maurya	*Chief Secretary*	: Utpal Kumar Singh
Chief Minister	: Trivendra Singh Rawat	*Jurisdiction of High Court*	: Uttarakhand

Uttar Pradesh

Area	: 2,36,286 sq km	*Population*	:	19.98 crore (prov. census 2011)
Capital	: Lucknow	*Principal Languages*	:	Hindi and Urdu

History

The history of Uttar Pradesh is very ancient and interesting. It is recognised in the later Vedic Age as Brahmarshi Desha or Madhya Desha. Many great sages of the Vedic times like Bhardwaja, Gautam, Yagyavalkaya, Vashishtha, Vishwamitra and Valmiki flourished in this state. Several sacred books of the Aryans were also composed here. In the sixth century BC Uttar Pradesh was associated with two new religions—Jainism and Buddhism. It was at Sarnath that Buddha preached his first sermon and laid the foundations of his order and it was in Kushinagar in Uttar Pradesh where Buddha breathed his last. Several centres in Uttar Pradesh like Ayodhya, Prayag, Varanasi and Mathura became reputed centres of learning. In the medieval period Uttar Pradesh passed under Muslim rule and led the way to new synthesis of Hindu and Islamic cultures. Ramananda and his Muslim disciple Kabir, Tulsidas, Surdas and many other intellectuals contributed to the growth of Hindi and other languages.

Uttar Pradesh preserved its intellectual excellence even under the British administration. The British combined Agra and Oudh into one province and called it United Provinces of Agra and Oudh. The name was shortened to the United Provinces in 1935. In January 1950, the United Provinces was renamed as Uttar Pradesh. The state is bounded by Uttarakhand and Himachal Pradesh in the north, Haryana in the west, Madhya Pradesh in the south and Bihar in the east. Uttar Pradesh can be divided into two distinct regions (i) Southern Hills and (ii) Gangetic Plains.

Agriculture

Agriculture is the main occupation of 66 per cent of the population. The net cultivated area is 164.17 lakh hectare.

Industry and Minerals

There were 6,12,338 small scale industries involving a total investment of 7172 crores. Under the public sector, mining of limestone, magnesite, coal, rock phosphate, dolomite and silicon-sand is carried out. The bulk production of minor and some of the major minerals like limestone, silica-sand, magnesite, pyrophyllite and diaspora is mostly with the private sector. Important mineral based industries include large cement plants in Sonebhadra.

Irrigation and Power

UP Power Corporation, UP State Power Generation and UP Hydel Power Corporation had been formed by reorganising UP State Electricity Board. Power is an important input to accelerate the process of economic growth.

Transport

Roads : The total road length of PWD is 146728 km. This includes 3820 km of national highways, 8391 km of state highways, 119726 of other district roads and 134517 km of rural roads.

Railways : Lucknow is the main junction of the northern network. Other important railway junctions are Agra, Kanpur, Prayagraj, Mughalsarai, Jhansi, Moradabad, Varanasi, Tundla, Gorakhpur, Gonda, Faizabad, Bareilly and Sitapur.

Aviation : There are airports at Lucknow, Kanpur, Varanasi, Prayagraj, Agra, Jhansi, Bareilly, Hindon (Ghaziabad), Gorakhpur, Sarsawa (Saharanpur) and Fursatganj (Raebarelli).

Festivals

The biggest congregation, perhaps of the world, *Kumbha Mela* is held at Prayagraj every twelfth year and *Ardh Kumbh Mela* every sixth year. *Magh Mela* is also held at Prayagraj in January when the people come in large numbers to have a dip in the holy Sangam. Among other fairs is the fortnight long *Jhoola* fair of Mathura, Vrindavan and Ayodhya, when dolls are placed in gold and silver *jhoolas* or cradles. A dip in the Ganga on Kartik Poornamasi is supposed to be the holiest and there are big congregations at Garhmukteshwar, Soran, Rajghat, Kakora, Bithur, Kanpur, Prayagraj, Varanasi and Ayodhya. A famous cattle fair is held at Bateswar in Agra district. Dewa in Barabanki district has become famous because of the Muslim saint Waris Ali Shah. Besides, important festivals of the Hindus, Muslims, etc., are widely celebrated in the state.

Tourist Centres

Besides ancient places of pilgrimage like Varanasi, Vindhyachal, Ayodhya, Chitrakoot, Prayag, Naimisharanya, Mathura, Vrindavan, Dewa Sharief, Dargah of Sheikh Saleem Chisti in Fatehpur Sikri, Sarnath, Shravasti, Kushinagar, Sankisa, Kampil, Piprahwa and Kaushambi, places like Agra, Ayodhya, Sarnath, Varanasi, Lucknow, Jhansi, Gorakhpur, Jaunpur, Kannauj, Mahoba, Devgarh, Bithur, and Vindhyachal have rich treasures of Hindu and Islamic architecture and culture.

Relevant Website : www.up.gov.in

Government

Governor	:	Ram Naik	*Chief Secretary*	:	Anup Chandra Pandey
Chief Minister	:	Yogi Aditya Nath	*Jurisdiction of High Court*	:	Allahabad High Court

West Bengal

Area	:	88,752 sq km	Population	:	9.13 crore (prov. census 2011)
Capital	:	Kolkata	Principal Language	:	Bangla

History

The name of Bengal or *Bangla* is derived from the ancient kingdom of Vanga, or Banga. However, Stone Age tools dating back 20,000 years have been excavated in the state. The region was settled by Dravidian, Tibet-Burman, and Austro-Asiatic peoples and was a part of the Vanga kingdom of ancient India. It was a part of Magadha empire. It was one of the four main kingdoms of India during the times of Mahaveera and Buddha, and consisted of several *Janapadas*. Bengal was referred to as Gangaridai by the ancient Greeks around 100 BC, meaning, speculatively, a land with the river Ganga in its heart. The first recorded independent King of Bengal was Shashanka, reigning around the early 7th century. After a period of anarchy, the Buddhist Pala dynasty ruled the region for four hundred years, followed by a shorter region of the Hindu Sena dynasty.

Islam came to Bengal in 12th century by Sufi missionaries. Later, occasional Muslim raiders reinforced the process of conversion by building mosques, madrassas and Sufi Khanqahh. Bengal was ruled by various Muslim rulers and governors till the Mughal period in the 16th century.

History of modern Bengal begins with the advent of Europeans, more precisely, with the English trading companies. The Battle of Plassey in 1757 changed the course of history when the English first gained a strong foothold in Bengal and India as well. Bengal was partitioned in 1905 to achieve some political returns. The land frontiers touch Bangladesh in the east and are separated from Nepal in the west, Bhutan lies in the north-east, while Sikkim is on the north. On the west are the states of Bihar and Jharkhand, while in the south lies Odisha and the Bay of Bengal washes its southern frontiers.

Agriculture

Agriculture is the main source of income for about 70 per cent of the population. Jute and rice are the principal crops grown in the state, along with tea, maize, tobacco and sugarcane.

Industry

The state policy on industrial promotion and economic development welcomes foreign technology and investment, private sector investment in power generation, improvement and upgradation of industrial infrastructure. The thrust areas are petrochemicals and downstream industries, electronics and information technology, iron and steel, metallurgical and engineering, textile, leather and leather products, food processing, medicinal plants, edible oil, vegetable processing and aquaculture.

Power and Irrigation

Provision of electricity is vital for the socio-economic development as it accelerates economic growth, generates employment, eliminates poverty and is an essential input for human development. The power sector in West Bengal is predominantly thermal in view of the easy and cheaper availability of cost; the state has an adverse hydel-thermal power mix of 3:97. Significant ground has been broken in the renewable energy sector. WBREDA, the nodal agency for implementation of technology demonstration projects in the state, have benefited a large number of remote villages in the Sundarbans, parts of West Midnapur and Bankura and areas of Malda, Murshidabad.

Transport

Transport Department is primarily responsible for providing better transportation facilities both for passengers and goods by way of formulation and implementation of policies and creation of transport oriented infrastructures. The state transport undertakings are playing a pivotal role in social commitment. The Department has taken some initiatives to improve the scenario like, computerization of motor vehicles department, road safety schemes, bus stand schemes, TOIP schemes, pollution control, replacement of existing 2-stroke auto rickshaws by 4-stroke auto rickshaws to reduce automobile pollution, replacement of buses of more than 15 years old, etc.

Festivals

The state celebrates myriad festivals like the Durga Puja, Poila Baishakh (the Bengali New Year), Rathayatra, Dolyatra or Basanta-Ursab. From christmas Carnivals to Eid ul-Fitr and Muharram; from Buddha Purnima to the legendary Ganga Sagar Yatra, all celebtrated with great zeal.

Tourism

West Bangal boasts of artisanal excellence with its extraordinary terracotta work, handloom weaves, heritage sarees and various other unique handicrafts. The state offers an astounding variety of religious places such as the most number of Shaktipeeths in the likes of Kalighat Temple and Tarapith; magnificent temples like Belur Math, Mayapur ISKCON Temple, Hangseshwari Temple and Tarakeshwar Temple; opulent mosques like the Nizamat Imambara and Katra Mosque in Murshidabad, Furfura Sharif and Tipu Sultan Shahi Mosque in Kolkata; Gurdwaras and majestic churches like the Basilica of the Holy Rosary in Bandel, St. John's Church, Lt. Jame's Church (Jora Girja), St. Paul's Cathedral and Church of the Lord Jesus and spectacular Buddhist monasteries of Ghoom, Bhutia Busty, Mag-Dhog Yolmowa, Tharpa Choling, Zang Dhok Palri Phodang among others.

The state has no dearth of adventure attractions. From the dense mangroves of Sunderbans for waterway rides to spot a staggering variety of flora and fauna including the famed Royal Bengal Tiger, trek the Himalayan Mountains; or enjoy a safari in the misty forests of Jaldapara, Chilapata.

Relevant Website : www.westbengal.gov.in

Government

Governor	: Keshari Nath Tripathi	*Chief Secretary*	: Malay Kumar De
Chief Minister	: Mamata Banerjee	*Jurisdiction of High Court*	: Calcutta High Court

Andaman and Nicobar Islands

Area	: 8,249 sq km	*Population*	:	3,79,944 (2001 census)
Capital	: Port Blair	*Principal Languages*	:	Hindi, Nicobarese, Bengali, Tamil, Malayalam, Telugu

History and Geography

The union territory of the Andaman and Nicobar Islands is situated between 6° and 14° latitude and 92° and 94° longitude. The Islands located north of 10° north latitude are known as Andaman Group of Islands while islands located south of 10° north latitude are called Nicobar Group of Islands. The climate of the Islands can be defined as humid, tropical coastal climate. The Islands receive rainfall from both the south-west and north-east monsoons and maximum precipitation is between May and December.

The original inhabitants of Islands lived in the forests on hunting and fishing. There are four Negrito tribes, viz., Great Andamanese, Onge, Jarawa and Sentinalese in the Andaman Group of Islands and two Mongoloid tribes, viz., Nicobarese and Shompens in the Nicobar Group of Islands.

Agriculture

Out of the geographical area of 8249 sq.km only 6 per cent i.e., around 50,000 ha which has been reduced to 47,000 ha (of the Tsunami 2004) is at present under agriculture. Paddy, the main food crop, is mostly cultivated in Andaman Group of Islands, whereas coconut and arecanut are the cash crops of Nicobar Group of Islands. Field crops, namely, pulses, oilseeds and vegetables are grown followed by paddy during rabi season. Different kinds of fruits such as mango, sapota, orange, banana, papaya, pineapple and root crops are grown on hilly land. Spices, viz. pepper, clove, nutmeg and cinnamon are grown under multi-tier cropping system. Rubber, red oil, palm and cashew are grown on a limited scale in these Islands.

Forests

Recorded forest is 7,171 sq km of the total geographical area of the Islands. Many types of forests are found, such as tropical wet evergreen, tropical semi-evergreen, moist deciduous, littoral mangrove and swamp forests. A large variety of timbers are also found. The most valuable timbers are padauk and gurjan. These species are not found in Nicobar.

Wildlife

There are 96 wildlife sanctuaries, 9 national parks and 1 biosphere reserve in these Islands. Mammals—out of 55 terrestrial and 7 marine mammal species reported so far, 32 species are endemic. Birds—as many as 246 species and sub -species of birds are reported to inhabit these Islands and of these 99 species and sub-species are endemic. Reptiles - there are 76 terrestrial reptiles found here, of these, 24 species are endemic. Marine Life - Islands harbour more than

1,200 species of fish, 359 species of echinoderms, 1067 species of molusscs and many more lower forms of life. Among vertebrates dugongs, dolphins, whales, salt water crocodiles, sea turtles, sea snakes, etc., are common. Reefs are mostly fringing type on eastern coast and barrier type on the western coast.

Industry

There are 1833 registered MSMEs and handicrafts units. Two units are 100 per cent export oriented in the line of fish/prawn processing activity. Apart from this, there are shells and wood based handicraft units. SSI units are engaged in the production of paints and varnishes, mini flour mills, soft drinks and beverages, steel furniture and fixtures, readymade garments, steel gate grills and structures. MSMEs handicraft units are also engaged in shell crafts, bakery products, rice-milling, furniture-making, etc. The Andaman and Nicobar Islands Integrated Development Corporation in the public sector has spread its wings in the field of tourism, fisheries, industries and industrial financing and functions as authorized agents.

Transport

The Motor Transport Department operates from 14 stations in northern and southern Islands. The Department has a fleet of 264 buses in operation mainly in rural area. Computerized advanced ticketing for ATR express service is in operation since 2007 where advance tickets can be obtained.

Tourism

Andaman and Nicobar Islands have been recognised as an eco-friendly tourist's destination. As a tourist paradise, these Islands have something very special to offer like historic Cellular Jail, Ross and Havelock Islands. The Andaman tropical evergreen rain forests, beautiful silver sandy beaches, serpentine mangrove-lined creeks, marine life abounding in rare species of plants, animals, corals, etc. provide a memorable experience to the tourists. There is a tremendous scope for enjoying nature in the beach resorts, water sports and adventure water sports, adventure tourism like trekking, island camping, nature trail, scuba diving, etc.

Tourism Department runs guest houses in various parts for comfortable accommodation. The important places of tourist interest are Anthropological Museum, Marine Museum, Water Sports Complex, Gandhi Park, North Bay, Viper Island, Ross Island, Chidiya Tapu, (Bird watching), Red Skin Island, Corbyn's Cove Beach, Islands like Neil Island, Havelock Island, Cinque, Little Andaman, Diglipur (Ross and Smith), etc.

The Islands are well connected to the mainland by air and sea. Air Deccan, Jetlite, Air India operate to Port Blair from Kolkata and Chennai. There are regular passengership services from Chennai, Kolkata and Vishakhapatnam.

Relevant Website : www.and.nic.in

Government

Lt. Governor	:	Admiral D. K. Joshi	*Chief Secretary*	:	Anindo Majumdar
			Jurisdiction of High Court	:	Falls under the jurisdiction of Calcutta High Court

Chandigarh

Area	:	114 sq km	*Population*	:	10.55 lakh (census 2011)
Capital	:	Chandigarh	*Languages*	:	Hindi, Punjabi

History and Geography

Chandigarh is a fully grown town of most modern architectural splendour. The city nestles in a picturesque setting in the foothills of Shivalik hills and enjoys the popular epithet the "City Beautiful". Representative of modern architecture and town planning, the city is a creation of the French architect, Le Corbusier. Chandigarh and the area surrounding it, were constituted as a Union Territory on 1 November 1966. It serves as the joint capital of both Punjab and Haryana states. It shares its boundary on north and west by Punjab and on the east and south by Haryana.

Transport

Chandigarh administration comprehending the need for a user-friendly transport system has decided to launch a Mass Rapid Transport System shortly. The UT administration and the state governments of Punjab and Haryana have come together for implementation of the project.

CTU has computerized 70 per cent of its working and is in the process of further computerization. The undertaking will also install a Global Positioning System to monitor its fleet in a phased manner.

Rural Development

In order to sensitize the poor and weaker sections of the society about the rights and different benefits being extended to them by the State Legal Services Authority, 14 legal awareness seminars have already been organized in different villages of the UT.

Cement concrete paving and underground drains in village Kajheri and Palsora have been completed. 70 per cent work in village Mauli Jagran has been completed.

Information Technology

Chandigarh has become a role model in using Information Technology to provide fast and user friendly services to the masses. Under the e-Governance initiatives of the Department, seven more Gram Sampark Centres have been set up in the villages of Dhanas, Khudda Jassu, Kaimbwala, Raipur Khurd, Raipur Kalan, Makhan Majra and Bahlana. Gram Sampark Centres in villages

Palsora, Dadu Majra, Hallo Majra, Khuda Alisher, Daria, Mauli Jagran and Maloya are operative. The administration is working on energy conservation. A work order has been issued to the Tata BP Solar Ltd. for commissioning the Energy Park at the Botanical Garden. Under the solar lighting initiative, all street lights in the villages would be replaced with solar based street lights.

Industries

The administration is developing the Phase-III of the industrial area at the revenue estate of village Mauli Jagran.

Tourism

Administration has taken many innovative and novel measures like Wedding Tourism. With the focus on extending efficient medical, educational and entertainment oriented facilities, administration is promoting cinematic tourism, sports tourism and medical tourism in a big way.

Power

Provision of sufficient electricity to all the residents is also getting attention of the administration. To improve the voltage profile and to reduce the load on the power distribution network the electricity wing had planned to add 80 MVAR automatic capacitor banks at various existing 66 KV grid sub-stations located at different points in the periphery of UT. Use of CFL is mandatory in all government buildings. Similarly, all institutional buildings will have to provide solar lighting in their parking spaces within their complexes.

Relevant Website : www.chandigarh.gov.in

Government

Administrator	:	V.P. Singh Badnore
Advisor to the Administrator	:	Manoj Kumar Parida

Dadra and Nagar Haveli

Area	:	491 sq km	*Population*	:	3. 44 lakh
Capital	:	Silvassa	*Principal Languages*	:	Gujarati, Hindi, English

History and Geography

The Portuguese ruled this territory until its liberation by the people in 1954. From 1954 till 1961 the territory functioned almost independently by what was known as "Free Dadra and Nagar Haveli Administration". However, the territory was merged with the Indian Union in 1961 and since then is being administered by the Government of India as a Union Territory. After liberation from the Portuguese rule, a *Varishtha Panchayat* was working as an advisory body of the administration. This was dissolved in August 1989 and a Pradesh

Council for Dadra and Nagar Haveli District Panchayat and 11 Village Panchayats were constituted as per constitutional amendments. Dadra and Nagar Haveli has an area of 491 sq km and it is surrounded by Gujarat and Maharashtra. It consists of two pockets, namely, Dadra and Nagar Haveli. The nearest railway station is at Vapi which is 18 km from Silvassa, which is also the capital of this UT. Silvassa Municipal Council came in existence in 2006 and is formed of two towns namely– Silvassa and Amli. Another five villages viz., Dadra, Naroli, Samarvani, Mast and Rakholi are treated as non-statutory census towns in population census 2011.

Agriculture

Dadra and Nagar Haveli is a predominantly rural area with about 79 per cent tribal population. It has about 21,115 hectare land under cultivation. Major crop is paddy (*Kharif*) while *Nagli* and hill millets are the other crops of the area. Among fruits mango, chiku, banana, etc., are also produced. Forests cover 40 per cent of the total geographical area. Sugarcane cultivation has also been taken up in a big way in the UT. Efforts are afoot to adopt a multiple cropping system in assured irrigated areas. The Wadi Development programme in the tribal area of both Dadra and Nagar Haveli is being implemented by the Bhartiya Agro Industries Foundation (BAIF) an NGO with the financial allocation from NABARD.

Industry

Prior to 1965-66 there was no industry. There were a few traditional craftsmen who used to make pots, leather items, viz., chappals, shoes and some other items of bamboo. Industrial development started on a low-key during 1967-68 with the establishment of an industrial estate under the cooperative sector by Dan Udyog Sahakari Sangh Ltd. Thereafter, three government industrial estates were developed at Silvassa, Masat and Khadoli. With the inception of the economic liberalization policy, a real boost in industrial development was seen. There are 1863 small sector industrial units and 430 MSI/LSI units functioning in the Union Territory providing gainful employment to over 46,000 people.

Irrigation and Power

Prior to liberation of the territory, there was no irrigation facility and cultivators had to fully depend upon rainfall. After the merger of the territory with the Indian Union, adequate steps were taken under minor irrigation sector. So far 128 lift irrigation schemes have been completed creating an additional irrigation potential of 1,851 hectare. Under medium irrigation project viz. Damanganga Reservoir Project, about 115 km of minor canals and distributaries are falling in the union territory. Development works have been completed in field channels in all respects in 4,300 hectare and testing is done in 4,049 hectare.

Transport

The Union Territory depends heavily on Maharashtra and Gujarat road network as the territory can be accessed only after crossing these two states from Mumbai. At present road length is about 635 km out of which 570 km is surfaced. Almost all villages are connected with all-weather roads. The rail route from Mumbai to Ahmedabad links Vapi also. Mumbai is the nearest airport. Recently, the work of widening of roads has been taken up to meet the requirement of increasing vehicular traffic. To meet the need of rapid industrialisation, four-lane work has been taken up in Silvassa and adjoining areas, besides other spillover works.

Tourism

Tourism sector has been assigned high priority, keeping in view the dense forest area and favourable climate.

The prominent places of tourist interest are Tadekeshwar Shiva Mandir, Bindrabin, Deer Park at Khanvel, Vanganga Lake and Island Garden, Dadra, and Vanvihar Udhyan, Mini Zoo, Bal Udhyan, Tribal Museum and Hirvavan Garden at Silvassa. To attract tourists, annual celebration of festivals like Tarpa and World Tourism Day is a regular event.

Festivals

Normally all festivals of Hindus, Muslims and Christians are celebrated in the territory, while tribals celebrate their own festivals. *Diwaso* is celebrated by Dhodia and Varli tribes and *Raksha Bandhan* is celebrated by Dhodia tribe. Other festivals include *Bhawada* amongst Varlis, Koli tribes and *Khali* Puja by all tribes after harvesting of crops and Gram Devi before harvesting of crops.

Relevant Website : www.dnh.nic.in

Government

Administrator	:	Praful Khoda Patel
Jurisdiction of High Court	:	Falls under Bombay High Court

Daman and Diu

Area	:	111 sq km	*Population*	:	2,42,911 (prov. census 2011)
Capital	:	Daman	*Principal Language*	:	Gujarati

History and Geography

Daman and Diu along with Goa was a colony held by the Portuguese even after Independence. In 1961, it was made an integral part of India. After Goa was conferred statehood on 30 May 1987, Daman and Diu was made a separate Union Territory. Daman lies about 193 km away from Mumbai. It is bound on the east by Gujarat, on the west by the Arabian Sea, on the north by the Kolak river and on the south by Kalai river. The neighbouring district of Daman is Valsad in Gujarat. Diu is an island connected by two bridges. The neighbouring district of Diu is Junagadh of Gujarat.

Agriculture and Irrigation

Total irrigated area is 393.93 ha and unirrigated is 3304.73 ha. Important field and garden crops are paddy, ragi, bajra, jowar, groundnut, pulses and beans, wheat, banana, sapota, mango, coconut and sugarcane. There are no major forests in the territory.

Industry and Power

There are 2930 small-scale and medium-scale industries in Daman and Diu. Two industrial areas have been developed by Omnibus Industrial Development Corporation at Daman. The other industrial areas are Dabhel, Bhimpore, Kachigam and Kadaiya.

All villages have been electrified. Daman and Diu have got adequate power allocation from central sector power stations in western region.

Transport

Roads : The total length of roads is 191 km and 78 km respectively.

Railways : There is no railway link with Daman and Diu. The nearest railway station from Daman is Vapi on western railway on Mumbai-Delhi route. The nearest railway station from Diu is Delvada on metre-gauge.

Aviation : There are airports both in Daman and Diu. Diu is connected by air and there is regular air service from Mumbai.

Tourist Places

Important tourist places in Daman are Bom Jesus Church; Our Lady of Sea Church; Our Lady of Remedios Church; Forts of Moti Daman and Nani Daman; Jampore and Devka Beaches; Public Garden at Nani Daman and Moti Daman Jetty; Pergola Garden; Moti Daman; Amusement Park, Devka; Damanganga Tourist Complex, Kachigam; Satya Sagar Udyan; Mirasol Garden; Mirasol Water Park.

In Diu, St. Paul's Church; Diu Fort and Panikota Fort; Nagoa and Chakratirth and Children's Park at Ghoghla and Summer House are worth seeing.

Relevant Website : www.daman.nic.in

Government

Administrator	:	Praful Khoda Patel
Jurisdiction of High Court	:	Falls under Bombay High Court

Delhi

Area	: 1,483 sq km	*Population*	:	1.68 crore (as per census 2011)
Capital	: Delhi	*Principal Languages*	:	Hindi, Punjabi, Urdu and English

History and Geography

Delhi finds prominent reference right from the times of the epic *Mahabharata*. Its control passed from one ruler/dynasty to another, beginning with the Mauryas, Pallavas, Guptas of Central India and then going on to the Turks of Afghan during the 13th to 15th centuries, and finally to the Mughals in the 16th century. In the latter half of the 18th century and early 19th century, British rule was established in Delhi. In 1911, Delhi became the centre of all activities after the capital was shifted from Kolkata (Calcutta). It was made a Union Territory in 1956. Lying in the northern part of the country, Delhi is surrounded by Haryana on all sides except the east where it borders with Uttar Pradesh. The 69th constitutional amendment is a milestone in Delhi's history as it got a Legislative Assembly with the enactment of the National Capital Territory Act, 1991.

Agriculture

The principal food crops are wheat, bajra, jowar, gram and maize. However, emphasis has now shifted from food crops to vegetables and fruit crops, dairy and poultry farming, floriculture, etc., as these are more remunerative than food crops in the territory.

Industry

Delhi is not only the largest commercial centre in northern India, but also the largest centre of small industries. These units manufacture a wide variety of items like television, tape recorders, light engineering machines and automobile parts, sports goods, bicycles and PVC goods including footwear, textiles, fertilizers, medicines, hosiery, leather goods, software, etc.

Irrigation and Power

Due to fast urbanisation of the rural areas of Delhi, cultivable command area under irrigation is getting reduced day by day. Two schemes, namely, "Keshopur Effluent Irrigation Scheme Phase-III" and "Improvement and Extension of Effluent Irrigation System from Coronation Treatment Plant" are under execution. Irrigation of about 350 hectare with state tube-wells and 1,376 hectare from effluent water is being provided in the rural area of NCT of Delhi. In addition about 4,900 hectare of land is being irrigated from western Yamuna canal network.

The availability of power for Delhi from its own generating units at Rajghat Power Houses, IP Station and Gas Turbines including Badarpur Thermal Station is of the order of 850-900 MW. The remaining power is drawn from Northern Regional Grid. Delhi has also envisaged a number of generating projects to be taken up. Pragati Combined Cycle Power Project has been established at Indraprastha Estate. A 330 MW Pragati Power Project under construction is scheduled to be commissioned soon. To streamline the distribution of power, DVB has been privatised and Delhi is now served by two of the best electric utilities in India, BSES and Tata Power (NDPL).

Transport

Delhi is well connected by roads, rail and air with all parts of India. It has three airports—Indira Gandhi International Airport for the international flights, Palam Airport for domestic air services and Safdarjung Airport for training purposes. It has five important railway stations — Delhi Junction, New Delhi Railway Station Nizamuddin Railway Station, Anand Vihar Railway Station and Sarai Rohilla Railway Station. Delhi has three interstate bus terminals at Kashmere Gate, Sarai Kale Khan and Anand Vihar.

Keeping in view the rising vehicular pollution and chaotic traffic condition in the city of Delhi, it has been decided to start Mass Rapid Transit System (MRTS) in Delhi. The project is under implementation and it uses the state-of-the-art modern technology. The metro rail project runs in Delhi. Now Delhi Metro comprises six lines.

Festivals

Being a cosmopolitan city, all major festivals of India are celebrated here. Moreover, some tourism festivals have become regular annual events of Delhi. Delhi Tourism and Transportation Development Corporation organises Roshnara Festival, Shalimar Festival, Qutab Festival, Winter Carnival, Garden Tourism Festival, Jahan-e-Khusrao Festival and Mango Festival every year.

Tourist Places

Important tourist places are Lal Quila (Red Fort), Jama Masjid, Qutab Minar, India Gate, Laxmi Narain Mandir (Birla Mandir), Humayun's Tomb, Lotus Temple, Akshardham, etc. Delhi Tourism and Transportation Development Corporation Limited conducts city sight-seeing and excursion tours. The Corporation has also introduced adventure tourism activities such as para-sailing, rock-climbing and boating in Delhi. The Corporation has also developed two Delhi Haats where beverages and food items of different states are available at one place. More such Haats are planned in different parts of Delhi. The Corporation is also running Coffee Homes in different parts of Delhi. The "Garden of Five Senses" has also been opened in the South District of Delhi, which attracts a lot of tourists visiting Delhi.

Relevant Website : www.delhi.gov.in

Government

Lt. Governor	:	Anil Baijal	*Chief Secretary*	:	Vijay Kumar Dev
Chief Minister	:	Arvind Kejriwal	*Jurisdiction of High Court*	:	Delhi

Lakshadweep

Area	:	30 sq km	*Population*	:	64 thousand (census 2011)
Capital	:	Kavaratti	*Principal Languages*	:	Malyalam, Dhivehi (language of Maldives)

History and Geography

Not much is known of the early history of these Islands. The Islands supposed to have been inhabited first by Amini, Andrott, Kavaratti and Agatti. It was earlier believed that the islanders were originally Hindus and later converted to Islam under the influence of Arab traders sometime in the 14th century. But archaeological evidences unearthed indicate that there were Buddhist settlements around the 6th or 7th century. Earliest Muslim converts or settlers pre-date the year 139 AH of the Hijri year (eighth century) of which period grave stones have recently been discovered in Agatti. This would tend to bear out the traditional belief that Islam was brought to the Island by Arab Saint, Ubaidulla in 41 AH.

Probably independent till 16th century the Islands were driven to seek the assistance of Raja of Chirakal to help them avert establishment of Portuguese domination. This enabled him to establish his authority and, later, the Islands were transferred in jaggeer to Ali Raja, head of Moplah community in Cannanore, who later became an independent ruler himself. The Arakkal rule was not popular and in 1787, Tipu Sultan acceded to the petitions of the Northern Islands to annex these Islands. After the fall of Tipu Sultan, the Islands were passed to East India Company but continued to be ruled de facto by the rulers of Cannanore till their ultimate annexation by the British in the early 20th century. In 1956, the Islands were constituted into a single territory and since then, have been directly administered by the Union Government through an administrator. The Laccadives, Minicoy and Amindivi Group of Islands were renamed Lakshadweep in 1973. Lakshadweep, a Group of Coral Islands, consists of 11 inhabited Islands, 16 uninhabited Islands, 3 reefs and 6 submerged sand banks. These lie scattered in the Arabian Sea about 280 km off Kerala coast between 8° and 12° 3′ North Latitude and 71° and 74° East Longitude.

Agriculture

Coconut is the only major crop with a production of 60 million nuts per year. The area under cultivation is about 2,689 hectare. Lakshadweep coconut is branded as an organic product. In India, Lakshadweep stands first in coconut production and productivity per hectare is 20,600 and average yield per palm per year is 82 coconuts. The Lakshadweep coconuts are the highest oil content nuts in the world (82 per cent).

Fisheries

Fishing is another major activity. The sea around the Islands is highly productive. The Islands stand first in the country in per capita availability of fish.

Industries

Coconut fibre extraction and conversion into fibre products is the main industry in the Islands. Under Government Sector, there are 7 coir fibre factories, 5 coir production-cum-demonstration centres and 7 fibre curling units, functioning under coir sector. These units produced coir fibre and coir yarn in addition to other coir products like curled fibre, corridor mat, mat and mattings. A few coir twisting units also function in private sector.

Transport

At present M.V. Kavaratti, M.V. Arabian Sea, M.V. Lakshadweep Sea, M.V. Bharat Seema, M.V. Amindivi and M.V. Minicoy accommodate the passenger traffic in mainland-islands and inter-island sector. Further three 150 Passenger High Speed Vessels (HSC Parali, HSC Valiyapani and HSC Cheryapani), three 50 Passenger High Speed Vessels (HSC Skip Jack, Hsc Blue Marlin and HSC Black Marlin), one 15 Passenger High Speed Vessel HSC Viringili and two 100 passenger Ferry Vessels (M.V. Kadeeja Beevi and M.V. Hameedath Bee) provides connectivity between inter-island sectors. Moreover three 150 Passenger HSCs also connect island and mainland depending upon the requirements. The cargo transportation from mainland to islands are handled with four cargo barges, MV Ubaidulla, M.V. Thinnakara, MV. Laccadives and M.V. Cheriyam.

The administration operates two Pawan Hans helicopters on charter for the inter-Island service and evacuation of patients from Islands to Kavaratti/ Agatti and mainland. Besides connectivity is maintained by Indian Airlines between Agatti and Kochi except on Sundays.

Tourist Centres

Tourism is developing into an important industry. Important tourist places are Agatti, Bangaram, Kalpeni, Kadmat, Kavaratti and Minicoy, etc.

Relevant Website : www.lakshadweep.gov.in

Government

Administrator	:	Farooq Khan
Collector and Development Commissioner		
Jurisdiction of High Court	:	Falls under Jurisdiction of Kerala High Court

Puducherry

Area	:	490 sq km	*Population*	:	12.47, 953 (2011 census)
Capital	:	Puducherry	*Principal Languages*	:	Tamil, Telugu, Malayalam, English and French

History and Geography

The Union Territory of Puducherry, an ex-French enclave, comprises four isolated region of Puducherry, Karaikal, Mahe and Yanam. Puducherry, the capital of the territory was once the original headquarters of the French

Government in India. The French Government handed over the administration of their territories in November 1954. The territories thus handed over were constituted into the Union Territory of Puducherry. Puducherry region is bounded on the east by the Bay of Bengal and on the three sides by Tamil Nadu as a conclave of Cuddalore and Villupuram districts of Tamil Nadu.

Agriculture

In order to enhance the area under pandal cultivation and to improve the production potential the formers are encouraged for cultivation of gourd vegetables by providing monetary assistance for erecting permanent pandal structures which remained as a constraint for the farmers due to high initial investment cost. Assistance of 50 per cent subsidy to a maximum of 1 lakh per acre is being provided. It offers viable option for the vegetable growers to get increased and stable income per unit area.

Industry

The union territory has a total area of 479 sq.km with a total population of 12.44 lakh as per last census. With its reputation of being an investor-friendly, the union territory having proven track record of attracting surplus investment and has witnessed vibrant industrial growth over the years. Even though there was some industrial slow down for a few years because of the general down turn in the economy, the growth continues. Puducherry has nearly 77 large and 9,067 micro, small and medium enterprises (MSMEs) and with an investment of ₹ 2909 cores, these industries are deemed to be the life blood of economy providing employment to about one lakh persons.

Tourism

The old part of the UT is known as Boulevard Town since it is bounded by four boulevards that once constituted the outer limits of the city's fortification. The Boulevard Town presents two distinct architectural styles in the Tamil and French Quarters, which are separated by a canal and unified by a rectilinear grid plan.There are few monumental buildings, and the architectural character of the town is the result of hundreds of traditional-style houses (both in Tamil and French Quarters) that form the unique streetscapes so distinctive of Puucherry. Some must-see sights include Arikanmedu, a famous historical site that was discovered by the Romans in 200 B.C and is being excavated, Aayi Mandapam, a monument built during the reign of Napoleon III, Eglise De Sacre Coeur De Jesus or Church of Sacred Heart of Jesus, known for its Gothic architecture and the Mansion of Ananda Rangapillai, a fine specimen of Indo-French architecture that was built in 1773.

Electricity

The present power requirement of the union territory is met from the power allocations made by the Government of India in various Central

Generating Stations (CGS) and from purchase of power from neighbouring State Electricity Boards (TANGEDCO & KSEB). There is a gas based power plant of capacity 32.5 MW at Karaikal region owned by the Puducherry Power Corporation Limited to meet the partial requirement of Karaikal region.

Government

Lieutenant Governor	:	Dr. Kiran Bedi I.P.S. (Retd.)
Chief Minister	:	V. Narayanasamy
Chief Secretary	:	Ashwini Kumar
Jurisdiction of High Court	:	Falls under jurisdiction of Madras High Court

31 Diary of National Events

January 1, 2018—December 31, 2018

January, 2018

- Assamese and Manipuri versions of Prime Minister's Official Website launched.
- The Union Cabinet approves establishment of new AIIMS in Bilaspur (Himachal Pradesh) under the Pradhan Mantri Swasthya Suraksha Yojana (PMSSY).
- The Cabinet Committee on Economic Affairs, has approved the implementation of the Jal Marg Vikas Project (JMVP) for capacity augmentation of navigation on National Waterway-1 (NW-1) at a cost of ₹ 5,369.18 crore with the technical assistance and investment support of the World Bank.
- The Cabinet Committee on Economic Affairs, has given its approval to the construction, operation and maintenance of 2-lane bi-directional Zojila Tunnel with Parallel Escape (Egress) Tunnel excluding approaches on Srinagar-Leh section connecting NH-1A at km 95.00 and at km 118.00 in Jammu & Kashmir on Engineering, Procurement and Construction (EPCJ mode.
- The Central Government notified the Companies (Amendment) Act, 2017 (Amendment Act).
- First PlO-Parliamentarian Conference held in New Delhi.
- The Cell for IPR Promotion and Management (CIPAM), Department of Industrial Policy and Promotion (DIPP), in collaboration with ASSOCHAM and ERICSSON India, has launched a one of its kind Intellectual Property (IP) Competition 'IPrism' for college and university students.
- The International Workshop on Disaster Resilient Infrastructure (IWDRI) inaugurated.
- In an endeavor to encourage mass participation and promote excellence in sports, the Ministry of Youth Affairs and Sports unveiled the Khelo India Anthem. Commencing on January 31, 2018, the Khelo India School Games will be the first programme to mark the beginning of Khelo India, a category defining, holistic sports development programme.
- The President of India, presented the Sangeet Natak Akademi's Fellowships (Akademi Ratna) and Sangeet Natak Akademi Awards (Akademi Puraskar) for 2016.

- Long Range Surface-to-Surface Ballistic Missile, Agni-5, was successfully flight tested for its full range from Dr Abdul Kalam Island, Odisha. This was the fifth test of the Missile and the third consecutive one from a canister on a road mobile launcher. All the five missions have been successful.
- Shri Om Prakash Rawat appointed as the Chief Election Commissioner.
- The 'Bharat Parv' event organized by the Government of India at the Red Fort, Delhi from 26th to 31st January, 2018 as part of the Republic Day 2018 celebrations.
- Finance Minister presents Economic Survey 2017-18 in Parliament. The Survey predicts 7-7.5 per cent growth in 2018-19.

February, 2018

- Finance Minister presents General Budget 2018-19 in Parliament.
- The Union Minister for Finance and Corporate Affairs launched CriSidEx, India's first sentiment index for micro and small enterprises (MSEs) developed jointly by CRISIL and SIDBI.
- The Union Cabinet has approved the proposal for ratification of Minamata Convention on mercury and depositing the instrument of ratification enabling India to become a Party of the Convention.
- The Union Cabinet has given its approval for signing and ratification of protocol amending the Agreement between India and China for the avoidance of double taxation and the prevention of fiscal evasion with respect to taxes on income.
- The Union Cabinet has approved the proposal for closure of Autonomous Bodies, namely, Rashtriya Arogya Nidhi (RAN) and Jansankhya Sthirata Kosh (JSK) and the functions are proposed to be vested in Department of Health & Family Welfare (DoHFW).
- The Union Cabinet approved implementation of 'Prime Minister's Research Fellows (PMRF)' scheme at a cost of ₹ 1,650 crore for a period of seven years beginning 2018-19.
- NITI Aayog launches the 'Healthy States, Progressive India Report'. Kerala, Punjab and Tamil Nadu have ranked top among the larger states in terms of overall performance.
- Prime Minister Narendra Modi conferred with Palestine's highest award "Grand Collar of State of Palestine" for promoting bilateral relations.
- The Ministry of Agriculture & Farmers Welfare (MoA&FW) organizes a national conference "Agriculture 2022 - Doubling Farmers' Income" at National Agriculture Science Complex (NASC), Pusa, New Delhi.
- The Union Government sets up the 'Niti Forum for North-East'. The Forum will be co-chaired by the Vice-Chairman of NITI Aayog and Minister of State (I/C), Ministry of Development of Northeastern Region (DoNER).The forum will have its Secretariat in the Ministry of DoNER.

- Bureau of Indian Standards (BIS), the National Standards Body of India, in association with Data Science Foundation organized the fifth international data science summit in New Delhi.
- DRDO successfully flew its Rustom 2 at its Aeronautical Test Range at Chitradurga.
- The Department of Administrative Reforms and Public Grievances (DARPG), Government of India, along with the Ministry of Electronics & Information Technology, Government of India in association with Government of Telangana organises the 2 lst National Conference on e-Governance.
- Anti Tank Guided Missiles (ATOM) NAG were successfully flight-tested in desert conditions against two tank targets at different ranges and timings.

March, 2018

- The Union Cabinet has approved the proposal for establishment of National Financial Reporting Authority (NFRA). The decision aims at establishment of NFRA as an independent regulator for the auditing profession which is one of the key changes brought in by the Companies Act, 2013.
- The Union Cabinet has approved the signing of Migration and Mobility Partnership Agreement between India and France.
- Union Minister for Chemicals & Fertilizers and Parliamentary Affairs launches 'Suvidha', the 100 per cent oxo-biodegradable sanitary napkin, under the Pradhan Manrri Bhartiya Janaushadhi Pariyojana (PMBJP).
- "I-METROS" an association of all Indian Metro Rail companies launched.
- Government has approved setting up of 9 Research Parks one each at IIT Madras, IIT Kharagpur, IIT Bombay, IIT Gandhinagar, IIT Delhi, IIT Guwahati, IIT Kanpur, IIT Hyderabad, and IISc Bangalore.
- On the occasion of International Women's Day, March 8,the Ministry of Micro, Small and Medium Enterprises(MSME) launched a portal for women entrepreneursof India: www.udyamsakhi.org.
- On the occasion of International Women's Day, the Prime Minister, launched the National Nutrition Mission and Pan India Expansion of Beti Bachao Beti Padhao (BBBP) covering all 640 districts of the country.
- India awarded Best Exhibitor Award for Australia and Oceania category at the world's Tourism exhibition at lnternationale Tourismus Borse (ITB) 2018.
- The Union Cabinet has approved an Agreement for the avoidance of double taxation and the prevention of fiscal evasion with respect to taxes on income between India and Iran.
- The National Crime Records Bureau (NCRB) celebrated its 33rd Inception Day and released Citizen Services Mobile App.

- Prime Minister and French President inaugurated Uttar Pradesh's biggest solar power plant of 75 MW (101DC) capacity in Mirzapur. Built at a cost of around ₹ 528 crores, the 75 MW solar plant at Vijaypur village in Mirzapur, will generate 13 crore units of electricity per annum.
- The Prime Minister, launched development projects worth ₹ 750 crore in Manipur.
- Union Minister of Road Transport and Highways, Shipping and Water Resources, River Development and Ganga Rejuvenation inaugurated the inland ferry services in the port city of Vasco in Goa.
- The Union Cabinet has approved the opening of 18 new Indian Missions in Africa over a four year period from 2018-2021.
- The Cabinet Committee on Economic Affairs has approved continuation of centrally sponsored scheme of Rashtriya Uchchatar Shiksha Abhiyan (RUSA) from 1.04.2017 to 31.03.2020.
- The Union Cabinet has approved the launch of a new centrally sponsored Ayushman Bharat -National Health Protection Mission (AB-NHPM) having central sector component under Ayushman Bharat Mission anchored in the MoHFW.
- India's Geosynchronous Satellite Launch Vehicle (GSLV-F08) successfully launched GSAT-6A Satellite into Geosynchronous Transfer Orbit (GTO).

April, 2018

- The Union Minister of Human Resource Development, released the NIRF India Rankings 2018 in various categories on the basis of performance of Higher Educational Institutions.
- The Union Cabinet has approved the closure of Burn Standard Company Ltd (BSCL) - a Central Public Sector Enterprise (CPSE) under Ministry of Railways.
- The Union Cabinet has approved the revision of pay and allowances of Lieutenant Governors of Union Territories. It will bring the pay and allowances of LGs at par with that of the Secretary to the Government of India.
- In its forty third flight, ISRO's Polar Satellite Launch Vehicle PSLV-C41 successfully launched the 1,425 kg IRNSS-11 navigation satellite from Satish Dhawan Space Centre SHAR, Sriharikota.
- Prime Minister inaugurated Dr. Ambedkar National Memorial.
- The Union Home Minister launched the web-based application 'e- FRRO' (e-Foreigners Regional Registration Office).
- Department of Posts has launched Digital Advancement of Rural Post Office for a New India (DARPAN), Project, which aims to connect all 1.29 lakh rural branch post offices in the country, to enable them to do online postal and financial transactions.

- Study in India programme of HRD Ministry launched with the launch of 'Study in India Portal'.
- Cabinet Committee on Economic Affairs approves increase in minimum support price for raw jute by ₹ 200 for 2018-19 season; also gives nod to restructured National Bamboo Mission.
- Light Combat Aircraft Tejas hassuccessfully fired an air-to-air beyond visual range (BVR) missile.
- The Cabinet Committee on Economic Affairs, approved continuation of Umbrella Scheme Green Revolution - Krishonnati Yojana' in agriculture sector.

May, 2018

- Cabinet approves doubling of investment limit for senior citizens from ₹ 5 lakh under Pradhan Mantri VayaVandan,Yojana (PMVVY).
- The Cabinet Committee on Economic Affairs, has given its approval for Green Revolution -Krishonnati Yojana in agriculture beyond 12th Five Year Plan for the period 2017-18 to 2019-20.
- The Union Cabinet has given its approval for continuation of Pradhan Mantri Swasthya SurakshaYojana (PMSSY) beyond 12th Five Year Plan for a period 2017-18 to 2019-20.
- The Ministry of Human Resource Development has launched a major and unique initiative of online professional development of 1.5 million higher education faculty using the MOOCs platform SWAYAM.
- The Government of India carried out an amendment to the Government of India (Allocation of Business) Rules, 1961 substituting Directorate General of Trade Remedies in place of Directorate General of Anti-Dumping and Allied Duties in Department of Commerce. This has paved way for creation of an integrated single umbrella national authority to be called the Directorate General of Trade Remedies (DGTR) for providing comprehensive and swift trade defence mechanism in India.
- The Union Cabinet, has approved National Policy on Biofuels - 2018.
- The Union Cabinet has approved setting up of a new All India Institute of Medical Sciences in Deoghar, Jharkhand under the Pradhan Mantri Swasthya Suraksha Yojana (PMSSY).
- The Union Cabinet has approved the establishment of National Institute of Mental Health Rehabilitation (NIMHR) at Bhopal as a Society under the Societies Registration Act, 1860 under the aegis of the Department of Empowerment of Persons with Disabilities.
- Prime Minister inaugurated Kishanganga hydroelectric project and laid the foundation stone of the Pakal Dul Power Project in Jammu & Kashmir.
- BrahMos, supersonic cruise missile was successfully test fired from the Integrated Test Range (ITR) in Balasore, Odisha as part of service life extension programme.

- Indian Naval Sailing Vessel Tarini (INSV Tarini) entered Goa harbour and came alongside the INS Mandovi jetty on completion of a historic global circum-navigation voyage.
- In a landmark reform in higher education, University Grants Commission has approved UGC (Online Courses) Regulations, 2018.
- A Web portal and an App namely PRAAPTI (Payment Ratification and Analysis in Power procurement for bringing transparency in invoicing of generators), www.praapti.in is launched.

June, 2018

- The long range ballistic missile Agni 5 is successfully flight tested from Dr APJ Abdul Kalam Island (Wheeler Island).
- Election Commission of India launches its online RTI portal.
- In a major step for the welfare of sportspersons, upward revision of pension to meritorious sportspersons has been apporved. Under the revision, the rate of pension has been doubled of the existing rate on winning medals in international events.
- The Ministry of Women and Child Development has launched Yoga for 9 to 5: A contest focused on generating awareness regarding benefits of yoga at workplace for women.
- The new digital initiative of HRD Ministry, National Digital Library of India launched on the occasion of National Reading Day.
- The Prime Minister laid the foundation stone of the National Centre for Ageing at AIIMS.

July, 2018

- Election Commission of India launches Mobile App "cVIGIL" to enable citizens to report on violation of election code of conduct.
- The Ministry of Drinking Water and Sanitation launches the Swachh Survekshan Grameen 2018.

August, 2018

- DRDO conducted the successful test of the Ballistic Missile Interceptor Advanced Area Defence (AAD) from Abdul Kalam Island, Odisha.
- Government of India launched a Swachh Bharat Summer Internship-100 hours of Swachhta programme for the students of universities and higher education institutions.

September, 2018

- The Union Cabinet has approved the establishement and operationalization of permanent campus of seven new Indian Institutes or Management (IIMs) at Amritsar, Bodh Gaya, Nagpur, Sambalpur, Sirmaur, Vishakhapatnam and Jammu.

- The Cabinet Committee on Economic Affairs, approved enhancement of honorarium to Anganwadi Workers/Anganwadi helpers and performance linked incentive to AWHs {Umbrella Integrated Child Development Services (ICDS) Scheme}.
- The Pakyong Airport in Sikkim is inaugurated. This is the first airport in the Himalayan state, and the 100th airport in the country.

October, 2018

- India International Science Festival (IISF-2018) begins in Lucknow.
- Air Quality Early Warning System for Delhi launched in Delhi.
- World's tallest statue, the Statue of Unity is dedicated to the nation. The 182 meter statue of Sardar Vallabhbhai Patel was dedicated on his birth anniversary, at Kevadiya in Narmada district of Gujarat.

November, 2018

- The Ministry of Drinking Water and Sanitation announced the Swachh Bharat World Toilet Day Contests for districts and states.
- Former Prime Minister and Bharat Ratna Atal Bihari Vajpayee passes away.
- The Indian Space Research Organisation's (ISRO) Polar Satelite Launch Vehicle (PSLV-C43) successfully launched 31 satelites from Satish Dhawan Space Centre (SDSC), Sriharikota.
- 49th edition of International Film Festival of India (IFFI) 2018 gets underway in Panaji, Goa. The opening ceremony also saw the launch of the web portal of Film Facilitation Office. Israeli master craftsman Dan Wolman was honoured with the Lifetime Achievement Award at the ceremony.
- International Film Festival comes to a close in Goa. The nine day long festival of quality cinema concludes with the world premier of German Film *Sealed Lips*. Various prestigious awards including Golden Peacock, Silver Peacock, Lifetime Achievement Award were conferred in the festival.

December, 2018

- Indian Space Research Organisation's (ISRO) heaviest and most-advanced high throughput communication satellite GSAT-11 was successfully launched from the Spaceport in French Guiana.
- Digital Sky Platform is launched – India to start registration of drones, pilots, and operators; Registration portal for online permission is also launched .
- Sunil Arora takes over as new Chief Election Commissioner of India. Shri Arora takes over as the 23rd Chief Election Commissioner of India succeeding O. P. Rawat.
- To connect with Direct Benefit Transfer, an online portal "Ensure" has been launched to provide a very simple, useful and transparent system to the beneficiary.

- The Agriculture Export Policy, 2018 is approved.
- The National Mission on Interdisciplinary Cyber-Physical Systems to be implemented by Department of Science and Technology is approved.
- A new airport complex, and an Integrated Command and Control Centre for the Kumbh Mela, is inaugurated at Prayagraj.
- Ashok Gehlot, Kamal Nath and Bhupesh Baghel take over as new chief ministers of Rajasthan, Madhya Pardesh and Chhatisgarh respectively.
- The Union Cabinet approves the establishment of two new All India Institute of Medical Sciences at Madurai, Tamil Nadu.
- "The Republican Ethic" and "Loktantra Ke Swar" - select speeches of President released.
- The Ministry of Environment, Forest and Climate Change has launched the "Asiatic Lion Conservation Project" with an aim to protect and conserve the world's last ranging free population of Asiatic Lion and its associated ecosystem.
- International Centre for Automotive Technology has launched the Certification with high security features in order to prevent forgery.
- The Bogibeel bridge in Assam, is inaugurated. The bridge is a combined road and rail bridge over the Brahmaputra river between Dhemaji and Dibrugarh districts.
- Cabinet approves Indian Human Spaceflight Initiative: Gaganyaan Programme. Two unmanned and one manned flights are planned.

32 General Information

Table of Precedence

The Table, with respect to the rank and precedence of the persons named therein as approved by the President, is given as under :

1. President
2. Vice-President
3. Prime Minister
4. Governors of States within their respective States
5. Former Presidents

5A. Deputy Prime Minister

6. Chief Justice of India
   Speaker of Lok Sabha
7. Cabinet Ministers of the Union
   Chief Ministers of States within their respective States
   Deputy Chairman, NITI Aayog
   Former Prime Ministers
   Leaders of Opposition in Rajya Sabha and Lok Sabha

7A. Holders of Bharat Ratna Decoration

8. Ambassadors Extraordinary and Plenipotentiary and High Commissioners of Commonwealth Countries accredited to India
   Chief Ministers of States outside their respective States
   Governors of States outside their respective States
9. Judges of Supreme Court

9A. Chairperson, Union Public Service Commission
   Chief Election Commissioner
   Comptroller & Auditor General of India

10. Deputy Chairman, Rajya Sabha
    Deputy Chief Ministers of States
    Deputy Speaker, Lok Sabha
    Members of the NITI Aayog
    Ministers of State of the Union (and any other Minister in the Ministry of Defence for defence matters)
11. Attorney General of India
    Cabinet Secretary
    Lieutenant Governors within their respective Union Territories
12. Chiefs of Staff holding the rank of full General or equivalent rank

---

1. Source : mha.nic.in/sites/upload_files/mha files/table_of_precedence.pdf

13. Envoys Extraordinary and Ministers Plenipotentiary accredited to India.
14. Chairmen and Speakers of State Legislatures within their respective States.
    Chief Justices of High Courts within their respective jurisdictions
15. Cabinet Ministers in States within their respective States
    Chief Ministers of Union Territories and Chief Executive Councillor, Delhi within their respective Union Territories
    Deputy Ministers of the Union
16. Officiating Chiefs of Staff holding the rank of Lieutenant General or equivalent rank
17. Chairman, Central Administrative Tribunal
    Chairman, Minorities Commission
    Chairperson, National Commission for Scheduled Castes
    Chairperson, National Commission for Scheduled Tribes
    Chief Justices of High Courts outside their respective jurisdictions
    Puisne Judges of High Courts within their respective jurisdictions
18. Cabinet Ministers in States outside their respective States
    Chairmen and Speakers of State Legislatures outside their respective States
    Chairman, Monopolies and Restrictive Trade Practices Commission
    Deputy Chairmen and Deputy Speakers of State Legislatures within their respective States
    Ministers of State in States within their respective States
    Ministers of Union Territories and Executive Councillors, Delhi, within their respective Union Territories
    Speakers of Legislative Assemblies in Union Territories and Chairman of Delhi Metropolitan Council within their respective Union Territories
19. Chief Commissioners of Union Territories not having Councils of Ministers, within their respective Union Territories
    Deputy Ministers in States within their respective States
    Deputy Speakers of Legislative Assemblies in Union Territories and Deputy Chairman of Metropolitan Council, Delhi, within their respective Union Territories
20. Deputy Chairman and Deputy Speakers of State Legislatures, outside their respective States
    Ministers of State in States outside their respective States
    Puisne Judges of High Courts outside their respective jurisdictions
21. Members of Parliament
22. Deputy Ministers in States outside their respective States
23. Army Commanders/Vice-Chief of the Army Staff or equivalent in other services
    Chief Secretaries to State governments within their respective States
    Commissioner for Linguistic Minorities
    Commissioner for Scheduled Castes and Scheduled Tribes
    Members, Minorities Commission
    Members, National Commission for Scheduled Castes and Scheduled Tribes
    Officers of the rank of full General or equivalent rank

Secretaries to the Government of India (including officers holding this office ex-officio)
Secretary, Minorities Commission
Secretary, Scheduled Castes and Scheduled Tribes Commission
Secretary to the President
Secretary to the Prime Minister
Secretary, Rajya Sabha/Lok Sabha
Solicitor General
Vice-Chairman, Central Administrative Tribunal

24. Officers of the rank of Lieutenant General or equivalent rank

25. Additional Secretaries to the Government of India
Additional Solicitor General
Advocate Generals of States
Chairman, Tariff Commission
Chargê d'affaires and Acting High Commissioners *en-pied* and *ad interim*
Chief Ministers of Union Territories and Chief Executive Councillor, Delhi outside their respective Union Territories
Chief Secretaries of State Governments outside their respective States
Deputy Comptroller and Auditor General, Deputy Speakers of Legislative Assemblies in Union Territories and Deputy Chairman, Delhi Metropolitan Council, outside their respective Union Territories
Director, Central Bureau of Investigation
Director General, Border Security Force
Director General, Central Reserve Police Force
Director, Intelligence Bureau
Lieutenant Governors outside their respective Union Territories
Members, Central Administrative Tribunal
Members, Monopolies and Restrictive Trade Practices Commission
Members, Union Public Service Commission
Ministers of Union Territories and Executive Councillors, Delhi, outside their respective Union Territories
Principal Staff Officers of the Armed Forces of the rank of Major General or equivalent rank
Speakers of Legislative Assemblies in Union Territories and Chairman of Delhi Metropolitan Council, outside their respective Union Territories

26. Joint Secretaries to the Government of India and officers of equivalent rank
Officers of the rank of Major-General or equivalent rank

NOTES

Note 1 The order in this Table of Precedence is meant for State and Ceremonial occasions and has no application in the day-to-day business of Government.

Note 2 Persons in the Table of Precedence will take rank in order of the number of the articles. The entries in the same article are arranged alphabetically. Those included in the same article will take precedence *inter se* according to date of entry into that article. However, where the dignitaries of different States and Union Territories included in the same article are present at a function outside their States or Union Territories and there is difficulty in ascertaining their dates of entry, they may be assigned precedence *inter se* in the alphabetical order of the name of States and Union Territories concerned after those whose precedence is determined according to date of entry into that article.

Note 3 In Article 7, former Prime Ministers will take precedence over the Cabinet Ministers of the Union and the Leaders of Opposition in the Rajya Sabha and the Lok Sabha. The Chief Ministers of States within their respective States will take precedence over the Cabinet Ministers of the Union in official functions held in the respective States.

Note 4 In Article 8 :

(a) Ambassadors Extraordinary and Plenipotentiary and High Commissioners of Commonwealth countries accredited to India will *en bloc* rank above Governors of States outside their respective States.

(b) Governors of States outside their respective States will en bloc rank above Chief Ministers of States outside their respective States.

Note 5 The Ministry of External Affairs may assign appropriate ranks to foreign dignitaries and Indian Ambassadors, High Commissioners and Ministers Plenipotentiary during their visit to India.

Note 6 Notwithstanding the procedure laid down in Note 2, the rank *inter se* and precedence of the persons in Article 10 shall be assigned in the following order :

(1) Deputy Chairman, Rajya Sabha

(2) Deputy Speaker, Lok Sabha

(3) Ministers of State of the Union and any other Minister in the Ministry of Defence for defence matters

(4) Deputy Chief Ministers of States

(5) Members of NITI Aayog.

However, the Deputy Chief Ministers of States outside their respective States will always rank below all other dignitaries figuring in this article.

Note 7 The Chairman of State Legislative Councils will rank above the Speakers of Legislative Assemblies in cases where they were elected on the same date.

Note 8 When Members of Parliament are invited *en bloc* to major State functions, the enclosures reserved for them should be next to the Chief Justice, Speaker of the Lok Sabha, Ambassadors, etc.

Note 9 Speakers of Legislative Assemblies in Union Territories and Chairman of the Delhi Metropolitan Council, Delhi, will take precedence over Ministers and Executive Councillors, included in the same article.

Note 10 In Article 23 :

(a) Secretaries in the Ministry of External Affairs other than the Foreign Secretary, between themselves, will take precedence in the order to their seniority in Grade-I of the Indian Foreign Service and both of them will take precedence after the Foreign Secretary.

(b) Members of the Minorities Commission and the Scheduled Castes and Schedule Tribes Commission will always take precedence over the Secretaries of these Commissions.

(c) In official functions held at Delhi/New Delhi, Army Commanders/Vice Chief of the Army Staff or equivalent in other Services will always rank after Secretaries to the Government of India.

Note 11 In Article 25 :

(a) Additional Secretaries in the Ministry of External Affairs, among themselves, will take procedence in the order of their seniority in Grade-II of the Indian Foreign Service;

(b) Additional Solicitor General will take precedence above the Advocate General of States.

PRESIDENTS OF INDIA[2]

Name	Tenure
Dr Rajendra Prasad (1884-1963)	January 26, 1950-May 13, 1962
Dr Sarvepalli Radhakrishnan (1888-1975)	May 13, 1962-May 13, 1967
Dr Zakir Husain (1897-1969)	May 13, 1967-May 03, 1969
Varahagiri Venkata Giri (1894-1980)	May 03, 1969-July 20, 1969 (Acting)
Justice Muhammad Hidayatullah (1905-1992)	July 20, 1969-August 24, 1969 (Acting)
Varahagiri Venkata Giri (1894-1980)	August 24, 1969-August 24, 1974
Dr. Fakhruddin Ali Ahmed (1905-1977)	August 24, 1974-February 11, 1977
B.D. Jatti (1912-2002)	February 11, 1977-July 25, 1977 (Acting)
Neelam Sanjiva Reddy (1913-1996)	July 25, 1977-July 25, 1982
Giani Zail Singh (1916-1994)	July 25, 1982-July 25, 1987
R. Venkataraman (1910-2009)	July 25, 1987-July 25, 1992
Dr Shankar Dayal Sharma (1918-1999)	July 25, 1992-July 25, 1997
K.R. Narayanan (1920-2005)	July 25, 1997-July 25, 2002
Dr. A.P.J. Abdul Kalam (1931-2015)	July 25, 2002-July 25, 2007
Pratibha Devisingh Patil (b-1934)	July 25, 2007-July 25, 2012
Pranab Mukherjee (b-1935)	July 25, 2012-July 25, 2017
Ram Nath Kovind (b-1945)	July 25, 2017-till date

VICE-PRESIDENTS OF INDIA[3]

Name	Tenure
Dr Sarvepalli Radhakrishnan (1888-1975)	May 13, 1952-May 12, 1962
Dr Zakir Hussain (1897-1969)	May 13, 1962-May 12, 1967
Varahagiri Venkata Giri (1894-1980)	May 13, 1967-May 03, 1969
Gopal Swarup Pathak (1896-1982)	August 31, 1969-August 30, 1974
B.D. Jatti (1912-2002)	August 31, 1974-August 30, 1979
Justice Muhammad Hidayatullah (1905-1992)	August 31, 1979-August 30, 1984
R. Venkataraman (1910-2009)	August 31, 1984-July 24, 1987
Dr. Shankar Dayal Sharma (1918-1999)	September 03, 1987-July 24, 1992
K.R. Narayanan (1920-2005)	August 21, 1992-July 24, 1997
Krishan Kant (1927-2002)	August 21, 1997-July 21, 2002

2. Source : President of India website http://presidentofindia.nic.in
3. Source : Vice President of India website http://vicepresidentofindia.nic.in

Bhairon Singh Shekhawat (1923-2010)	August 19, 2002-July 21, 2007
Mohammad Hamid Ansari (b-1937)	August 11, 2007-August 10, 2017
M. Venkaiah Naidu (b-1949)	August 11, 2017-till date

PRIME MINISTERS OF INDIA[4]

Name	Tenure
Jawaharlal Nehru (1889-1964)	August 15, 1947-May 27, 1964
Gulzari Lal Nanda (1898-1998)	May 27, 1964-June 09, 1964 (Acting)
Lal Bahadur Shastri (1904-1966)	June 09, 1964-January 11, 1966
Gulzari Lal Nanda (1898-1998)	January 11, 1966-January 24, 1966 (Acting)
Indira Gandhi (1917-1984)	January 24, 1966-March 24, 1977
Morarji Desai (1896-1995)	March 24, 1977-July 28, 1979
Charan Singh (1902-1987)	July 28, 1979-January 14, 1980
Indira Gandhi (1917-1984)	January 14, 1980-October 31, 1984
Rajiv Gandhi (1944-1991)	October 31, 1984-December 02, 1989
Vishwanath Pratap Singh (1931-2008)	December 02, 1989-November 10, 1990
Chandra Shekhar (1927-2007)	November 10, 1990-June 21, 1991
P.V. Narasimha Rao (1921-2004)	June 21, 1991-May 16, 1996
Atal Bihari Vajpayee (b-1924)	May 16, 1996-June 01, 1996
H.D. Deve Gowda (b-1933)	June 01, 1996-April 21, 1997
I.K. Gujral (1919-2012)	April 21, 1997-March 19, 1998
Atal Bihari Vajpayee (b-1924)	March 19, 1998 -May 22, 2004
Dr. Manmohan Singh (b-1932)	May 22, 2004-May 26, 2014
Narendra Modi (b-1950)	May 26, 2014 - till date

CHIEF JUSTICES OF INDIA[5]

Name	Tenure
Harilal J. Kania	January 26, 1950—November 06, 1951
M. Patanjali Sastri	November 07, 1951—January 03, 1954
Mehr Chand Mahajan	January 04, 1954—December 22, 1954
B.K. Mukherjea	December 23, 1954—January 31, 1956
S.R. Das	February 01, 1956—September 30, 1959
Bhuvneshwar Prasad Sinha	October 01, 1959—January 31, 1964
P.B. Gajendragadkar	February 01, 1964—March 15, 1966
A.K. Sarkar	March 16, 1966—June 29, 1966
K. Subba Rao	June 30, 1966—April 11, 1967

4. Source : Prime Minister's office website http://pmindia.nic.in
5. Source : Supreme Court of of India website http://www.supremecourtofindia.nic.in.

K.N. Wanchoo	April 12, 1967—February 24, 1968
M. Hidayatullah	February 25, 1968—December 16, 1970
J.C. Shah	December 17, 1970—January 21, 1971
S.M. Sikri	January 22, 1971—April 25, 1973
A.N. Ray	April 26, 1973—January 28, 1977
M.H. Beg	January 29, 1977—February 21, 1978
Y.V. Chandrachud	February 22, 1978—July 11, 1985
P .N. Bhagwati	July 12, 1985—December 20, 1986
R.S. Pathak	December 21, 1986—June 18, 1989
E.S. Venkataramiah	June 19, 1989—December 17, 1989
S. Mukherjee	December 18, 1989—September 25, 1990
Ranganath Misra	September 25, 1990—November 24, 1991
K.N. Singh	November 25, 1991—December 12, 1991
M.H. Kania	December 13, 1991—November 17, 1992
L.M. Sharma	November 18, 1992—February 11, 1993
M.N. Venkatachaliah	February 12, 1993—October 24, 1994
A.M. Ahmadi	October 25, 1994—March 24, 1997
J.S. Verma	March 25, 1997—January 17, 1998
M.M. Punchhi	January 18, 1998—October 09, 1998
A.S. Anand	October 10, 1998—October 31, 2001
S.P. Bharucha	November 01, 2001—May 05, 2002
B.N. Kirpal	May 06, 2002—November 07, 2002
G.B. Pattanaik	November 08, 2002—December 18, 2002
V. N. Khare	December 19, 2002—May 01, 2004
S. Rajendra Babu	May 02, 2004—May 31, 2004
R.C. Lahoti	June 01, 2004—October 31, 2005
Y.K. Sabharwal	November 01, 2005—January 13, 2007
K.G. Balakrishnan	January 14, 2007—May 11, 2010
S.H. Kapadia	May 12, 2010—September 28, 2012
Altamas Kabir	September 29, 2012—July 18, 2013
P. Sathasivam	July 19, 2013—April 26, 2014
R.M. Lodha	April 27, 2014—September 27, 2014
H.L. Dattu	September 28, 2014—December 02, 2015
T.S. Thakur	December 03, 2015—January 03, 2017
Jagdish Singh Khehar	January 04, 2017—August 27, 2017
Dipak Mishra	August 28, 2017—October 02, 2018
Ranjan Gogoi	October 03, 2018—till date

CHIEF ELECTION COMMISSIONERS OF INDIA[6]

Name	Tenure
Sukumar Sen	March 21, 1950—December 19, 1958
K.V. K. Sundaram	December 20, 1958—September 30, 1967
S.P. Sen Verma	October 01, 1967—September 30, 1972
Dr Nagendra Singh	October 01, 1972—February 06, 1973
T. Swaminathan	February 07, 1973—June 17, 1977
S.L. Shakdhar	June 18, 1977—June 17, 1982
R.K. Trivedi	June 18, 1982—December 31, 1985
R.V. S. Peri Sastri	January 01, 1986—November 25, 1990
Smt V. S. Ramadevi	November 26, 1990—December 11, 1990
T.N. Seshan	December 12, 1990—December 11, 1996
M.S. Gill	December 12, 1996—June 13, 2001
J.M. Lyngdoh	June 14, 2001—February 07, 2004
T.S. Krishna Murthy	February 08, 2004—May 15, 2005
B.B. Tandon	May 16, 2005—June 29, 2006
N. Gopalaswami	June 30, 2006—April 20, 2009
Navin B. Chawla	April 21, 2009—July 29, 2010
S.Y. Quraishi	July 30, 2010—June 10, 2012
V.S. Sampath	June 11, 2012—January 15, 2015
H.S. Brahma	January 16, 2015—April 18, 2015
Nasim Zaidi	April 19, 2015—July 05, 2017
Achal Kumar Joti	July 06, 2017—January 22, 2018
Om Parkash Rawat	January 23, 2018—December 1, 2018
Sunil Arora	December 2, 2018—till date

CABINET SECRETARIES[7]

Cabinet Secretary	From	To
N.R. Pillai	06-02-1950	13-05-1953
Y.N. Sukthankar	14-05-1953	31-07-1957
M.K. Vellodi	01-08-1957	04-06-1958
Vishnu Sahay	01-07-1958	10-11-1960
B.N. Jha	10-11-1960	08-03-1961
Vishnu Sahay	09-03-1961	15-04-1962
S.S. Khera	15-04-1962	18-11-1964
Dharam Vira	18-11-1964	27-06-1966
D.S. Joshi	27-06-1966	31-12-1968
B. Sivaraman	01-01-1969	30-11-1970
T. Swaminathan	01-12-1970	02-11-1972
B.D. Pande	02-11-1972	31-03-1977

6. Source : Website of Election Commission of India http://eci.nic.in
7. Source : Cabinet Secretariat Website http://cabsec.nic.in

N.K. Mukarji	31-03-1977	31-03-1980
S.S. Grewal	02-04-1980	30-04-1981
C.R. Krishnaswamy Rao	30-04-1981	08-02-1985
P.K. Kaul	08-02-1985	22-08-1986
B.G. Deshmukh	23-08-1986	27-03-1989
T.N. Seshan	27-03-1989	23-12-1989
V.C. Pande	23-12-1989	11-12-1990
Naresh Chandra	11-12-1990	31-07-1992
S. Rajgopal	01-08-1992	31-07-1993
Zafar Saifullah	31-07-1993	31-07-1994
Surendra Singh	01-08-1994	31-07-1996
T.S.R. Subramanian	01-08-1996	31-03-1998
Prabhat Kumar	01-04-1998	31-10-2000
T.R. Prasad	01-11-2000	31-10-2002
Kamal Pande	01-11-2002	14-06-2004
B.K. Chaturvedi	14-06-2004	13-06-2007
K.M. Chandrasekhar	14-06-2007	13-06-2011
Ajit Kumar Seth	14-06-2011	13-06.2015
Pradeep Kumar Sinha	13-06-2015	till date

CIVILIAN AWARDS

Bharat Ratna Award

Bharat Ratna is the highest civilian award. It is given in recognition of exceptional service/ performance of the highest order in any field of human endeavour. Since its inception in 1954, 45 persons have been decorated with Bharat Ratna so far. In 2015, the President of India conferred the award on Pandit Madan Mohan Malaviya (Posthumous) and Shri Atal Bihari Vajpayee.

RECIPIENTS OF BHARAT RATNA

S. No.	Name	Awarded in
1.	Chakravarti Rajagopalachari (1878-1972)	1954
2.	Dr Sarvepalli Radhakrishnan (1888-1975)	1954
3.	Dr Chandrasekhara Venkata Raman (1888-1970)	1954
4.	Dr Bhagwan Das (1869-1958)	1955
5.	Dr Mokshagundam Visvesvaraya (1861-1962)	1955
6.	Pt. Jawaharlal Nehru (1889-1964)	1955
7.	Pt. Govind Ballabh Pant (1887-1961)	1957
8.	Dr Dhondo Keshav Karve (1858-1962)	1958
9.	Dr Bidhan Chandra Roy (1882-1962)	1961
10.	Purushottam Das Tandon (1882-1962)	1961

11.	Dr Rajendra Prasad (1884-1963)	1962
12.	Dr Zakir Hussain (1897-1969)	1963
13.	Dr Pandurang Vaman Kane (1880-1972)	1963
14.	Lal Bahadur Shastri (Posthumous) (1904-1966)	1966
15.	Smt. Indira Gandhi (1917-1984)	1971
16.	Varahagiri Venkata Giri (1894-1980)	1975
17.	Kumaraswamy Kamraj (Posthumous) (1903-1975)	1976
18.	Mother Mary Teresa Bojaxhiu (Mother Teresa) (1910-1997)	1980
19.	Acharya Vinoba Bhave (Posthumous) (1895-1982)	1983
20.	Khan Abdul Ghaffar Khan (1890-1988)	1987
21.	Marudur Gopalan Ramachandran (Posthumous)(1917-1987)	1988
22.	Dr Bhimrao Ramji Ambedkar (Posthumous) (1891-1956)	1990
23.	Dr Nelson Rolihlahla Mandela (1918-2013)	1990
24.	Rajiv Gandhi (Posthumous) (1944-1991)	1991
25.	Sardar Vallabhbhai Patel (Posthumous) (1875-1950)	1991
26.	Morarji Ranchhodji Desai (1896-1995)	1991
27.	Maulana Abul Kalam Azad (Posthumous) (1888-1958)	1992
28.	Jehangir Ratanji Dadabhai Tata (1904-1993)	1992
29.	Satyajit Ray (Posthumous) (1922-1992)	1992
30.	Gulzari Lal Nanda (Posthumous) (1898-1998)	1997
31.	Smt. Aruna Asaf Ali (Posthumous) (1909-1996)	1997
32.	Dr A.P.J. Abdul Kalam (1931-2015)	1997
33.	Smt. Madurai Shanmukhavadivu Subbulakshmi (1916-2005)	1998
34.	Chidambaram Subramaniam (1910-2000)	1998
35.	Loknayak Jayaprakash Narayan (Posthumous) (1902-1979)	1999
36.	Professor Amartya Sen (b-1933)	1999
37.	Lokpriya Gopinath Bordoloi (Posthumous) (1890-1950)	1999
38.	Pandit Ravi Shankar (1920-2012)	1999
39.	Sushil Lata Dinanath Mangeshkar (b-1929)	2001
40.	Ustad Bismillah Khan (1916-2006)	2001
41.	Pandit Bhimsen Gururaj Joshi (b-1922-2011)	2009
42.	Prof. C.N.R. Rao (1934)	2014
43.	Sachin Ramesh Tendulkar (b-1973)	2014
44.	Pandit Madan Mohan Malaviya (Posthumous) (1861-1946)	2015
45.	Atal Behari Vajpayee (1924-2018)	2015

PADMA AWARDS ANNOUNCED ON REPUBLIC DAY 2018

Padma Awards

Padma Awards are amongst the highest civilian awards of the country. There are three categories of Padma Awards- 'Padma Vibhushan', 'Padma Bhushan' and 'Padma Shri'. These are given for distinguished service in any fieid including art, literature and education, science, engineering, sports, medicine, etc. Padma Awards are announced on the eve of the Republic Day every year. In 2017, the President of India conferred 88 Padma Awards as listed below. The list comprises 7 Padma Vibhushan, 7 Padma Bhushan and 74 Padma Shri awardees. 19 of the awardees are women and the list also includes 10 persons from the category of foreigners, NRls, PIOs and Posthumous Awardees.

Padma Vibhushan Recipients : Ilaiyaraaja
: Ustad Ghulam Mustafa Khan
: P. Parameswaran

Padma Bhushan Recipients : Pankaj Advani
: Most Rev. Dr. Philipose Mar Chrysostom Mar Thoma Valiya Metropolitan
: Mahendra Singh Dhoni
: His Excellency Alexander Kadakin (Foreigner/Posthumous)
: Dr. Ramachandran Nagaswamy
: Prof. Ved Prakash Nanda (OCI)
: Laxman Pai
: Pandit Arvind Parikh
: Dr. Sharda Sinha

Padma Recipients : Abhay Bang (Duo)
: Rani Bang (Duo)
: Damodar Ganesh Bapat
: Prafulla Govinda Baruah
: Mohan Swaroop Bhatia
: Sudhanshu Biswas
: Saikhom Mirabai Chanu
: Pandit Shyamlal Chaturvedi

: Jose Ma Joey Concepcion (Foreigner)

: Langpoklakpam Subadani Devi

: Somdev Kishore Devvarman

: Dr. Yeshi Dhonden

: Arup Kumar Dutta

: Dr. Dodda Range Gowda

: Arvind Kumar Gupta

: Prof. Digamber Hansda

: Datuk Ramli Ibrahim (Foreigner)

: Anwar Ahmad (Anwar Jalalpuri) (Posthumous)

: M. Piyongtemjen Jamir

: Sitavva Dundappa Jodatti

: Malti Joshi

: Manoj Navneet Joshi

: Rameshwarlal Kabra

: Pran Kishore Kaul

: Bounlap Keokangna (Foreigner)

: Vijay Kumar Kichlu

: Prof. Tommy Koh (Foreigner)

: Lekshmikutty

: Joyshree Goswami Mahanta

: Narayan Das Maharaj

: Pravakar Maharana

: His Excellency Hun Many (Foreigner)

: Nouf Marwaai (Foreigner)

: Zaverilal Dalpatram Mehta

: Dr. Krishna Bihari Mishra

: Sissir Purushottam Mishra

: Subasini Mistry

: Prof. Tomio Mizokami (Foreigner)

: His Holiness Sorndet Phra Ariyawongsakhottayan Somdet Phra Sangharaja Sakalamahasangha Parinayaka (Foreigner)

: Dr. Keshav Rao Sadashiv Shastri Musalgaonkar (Foreigner)

: V Nanammal

: Dr. Sulagitti Narasamma

: Vijayalakshmi Navaneethakrishnan

: I Nyoman Nuarta (Foreigner)

: Malai Haji Abdullah Bin Malai Haji Othman (Foreigner)

: Gobardhan Panika

: Bhabani Charan Pattanaik

: Murlikant Rajaram Petkar

: Prof. Habibullo Rajabov (Foreigner)

: Dr. M R Rajagopal

: Sampat Tukaram Ramteke (Posthumous)

: Chandra Sekhar Rath (Posthumous)

: Satyanarayansingh Shivsinghji Rathore

: Amitava Roy

: Sanduk Ruit (Foreigner)

: R Sathyanarayana

: Dr. Pankaj Manubhai Shah

: Bhajju Shyam

: Maharao Raghuveer Singh Sirohi

: Kidambi Srikanth

: Ibrahim Nabisaheb Sutar

: Lentina Ao Thakkar

: Dr. Vikrarn Chandra Thakur

: Dr. Rudrapatnam Narayanaswamy Tharanathan (Duo)

: Rudrapatnam Narayanaswamy Thyagarajan (Duo)

: Most Venerable Thicn Due Thien (Foreigner)

: Prof. Bhagirath Prasad Tripathi 'Vagish Shastri'

: Prof. Rajagopalan Vasudevan

: Manas Bihari Verma

: Panatawane Gangadhar Vithobaji

: Romulus Whitaker

: Yogendra

: A Zakia

JEEVAN RAKSHA PADAK SERIES OF AWARDS

Jeevan Raksha Padak series of awards are given for courage and promptitude under circumstances of great danger to the life or bodily injury of the rescuer, displayed in an act or a series of acts of humane nature, in saving the life of a person from drowning, fire, rescue operations in mines, etc. There are three categories of Jeevan Raksha Padak awards, viz., Sarvottam Jeevan Raksha Padak, Uttam Jeevan Raksha Padak and Jeevan Raksha Padak. Recommendations for Jeevan Raksha Padak series of awards are received from the State Governments/Union Territory Administrations and Ministries /Departments of the Government of India. On the basis of the recommendations of the Awards Committee, the President conferred the award of Sarvotttam Jeevan Raksha Padak to 5 persons, Uttam Jeevan Raksha Padak to 8 persons and Jeevan Raksha Padak to 23 persons, for the year 2016.

Sarvottam Jeevan Raksha Padak (7)

1. F. Lalchhandama (Posthumous), Mizoram
2. Bablu Martin (Posthumous), Madhya Pradesh
3. K. Pugazendy (Posthumous), Puducherry
4. Supreet Rathi (Posthumous), Delhi
5. Deepak Sahu (Posthumous), Madhya Pradesh
6. Satyavir (Posthumous), Delhi
7. Basant Verma (Posthumous), Madhya Pradesh

Uttam Jeevan Raksha Padak (13)

1. Sheikh Salim Gafur, Gujarat
2. Ravi Gorle, Andhra Pradesh
3. Rajendra Tukaram Gurav, Maharashtra
4. Dr. Suneem Ahmad Khan, Jammu & Kashmir
5. B. Laltlanthanga, Mizoram
6. Lianhmingthanga, Mizoram
7. Pankaj Mahanta, Odisha
8. Ameen Muhammed, Kerala
9. Bhanu Chandra Pandey, Maharashtra
10. Reena Patel, Madhya Pradesh
11. Sujan Singh, Himachal Pradesh
12. Satyen Singh, Karnataka
13. Zonuntluanga, Mizoram

Jeevan Raksha Padak (24)

1. Hariom Singh Bais, Madhya Pradesh
2. Abin Chacko, Kerala
3. Mamata Dalai, Odisha
4. Abhay Das, Kerala
5. Chirayu Gupta, Uttar Pradesh
6. Gaius James, Andaman and Nicobar
7. Stephen Joseph, Kerala
8. Hareesh K.H., Kerala
9. Nishanth K.U., Karnataka
10. Pradeep Kumar, Delhi
11. Sachin Kumar, Uttar Pradesh
12. John Lalditsak, Manipur
13. Pravin Kumar Mishra, Madhya Pradesh
14. Madan Mohan, Punjab
15. Rajasree R. Nair, Kerala
16. Narender, Madhya Pradesh
17. Tambe Pranay Rahul, Maharashtra
18. Sourabh Singh Rajput, Madhya Pradesh
19. Nimma Veera Venkata Ramana, Andhra Pradesh

20. Yamini Sahu, Chhattisgarh
21. Prabhakar Gangadhar Sathe, Maharashtra
22. Surendra Sharma, Madhya Pradesh
23. Puran Mal Verma, West Bengal
24. Zairemtluanga, Mizoram

NOBEL LAUREATES

KAILASH SATYARTHI (b. 1954): The Nobel Peace Prize of 2014 was awarded to Kailash Satyarthi for struggle against the suppression of children and young people and for the right of all children to education. Satyarthi was born in Vidisha, Madhya Pradesh. He completed his degree in electrical engineering and a post-graduate degree in high voltage engineering. In 1980, he left his career as an electrical engineer to set up Bachpan Bachao Andolan (Save Childhood Movement). He also heads the Global March Against Child Labour, a movement to mobilise worldwise efforts to protect and promote the rights of all children.

VENKATRAMAN RAMAKRISHNAN (b. 1952) : Venkatraman Ramakrishnan was awarded the Nobel Prize for Chemistry in 2009 for studies of the structure and function of the ribosome, molecular machine that makes protein. He was born in Chidambaram, Tamil Nadu. Dr. Ramakrishnan earned his B.Sc. in Physics (1971) from M. S. University in Baroda, Gujarat and Ph.D. (1976) in Physics from Ohio University in the USA. Making a transition from physics to biology, he studied a molecule called rhodopsin, as a graduate student in biology at the University of California, San Diego, from 1976 to 1978.

AMARTYA SEN (b-1933) : Prof. Amartya Sen is the recipient of the Nobel Prize for Economics for the year 1998, becoming the first Asian to have been honoured with the award. The Santiniketan-born economist who is a pioneer in Welfare Economics has to his credit several books and papers on aspects of welfare and development. An economist with a difference, Prof. Sen is a humanist. He has distinguished himself with his outstanding writings on famine, poverty, democracy, gender and social issues. The 'impossibility theorem' suggested earlier by Kenneth Arrow states that it was not possible to aggregate individual choices into a satisfactory choice for society as a whole. Prof. Sen showed mathematically that societies could find ways to alleviate such a poor outcome.

SUBRAMANIAN CHANDRASHEKHAR (1910-1995) : The Nobel Prize for Physics in 1983 was awarded to Dr S. Chandrashekhar, an Indian-born astrophysicist. Educated in Presidency College, Chennai, Dr Chandrashekhar happened to be the nephew of his Nobel forbear, Sir C.V. Raman. He later migrated to the United States where he authored several books on Astrophysics and Stellar Dynamics. He developed a theory on white dwarf stars which posts a limit of mass of dwarf stars known also as Chandrashekhar Limit. His theory explains the final stages of stellar evolution.

MOTHER TERESA (1910-1997) : The Nobel Peace Prize was awarded to Mother Teresa in 1979. Of Albanian parentage, Agnes Gonxha Bojaxhiu was born at Skopje, now in Yogoslavia. She joined the Irish order of the Sisters of Loretto at Dublin in 1928 and came to Kolkata in 1929 as a missionary, only to find the misery of the abandoned and the destitute. Concern for the poor and the sick prompted her to found a new congregation, Missionaries of Charity. Having become an Indian citizen, Mother Teresa served the cause of dying destitutes, lepers and drug addicts, through *Nirmal Hriday* (meaning Pure Heart), the main centre of her activity. Her selfless service and unique devotion, not only to helpless fellow-Indians but also to the cause of world peace, earned her and India the first Nobel Peace Prize.

HARGOBIND KHORANA (b. 1922-2011) : Hargobind Khorana was awarded the Nobel Prize for Medicine in 1968. Of Indian origin, Dr Khorana was born in Raipur, Punjab (now in Pakistan). He took his doctoral degree in Chemistry from Liverpool University and joined the University of Wisconsin as a Faculty Member in 1960. His major breakthrough in the field of Medicine —interpreting the genetic code and analysing its function in protein synthesis — fetched him the Nobel Prize.

CHANDRASEKHARA VENKATA RAMAN (1888-1970) : India's first Nobel Prize for Physics was claimed in 1930 by the renowned physicist Sir C.V. Raman. Born at Thiruvanaikkaval near Tiruchirapalli in Tamilnadu, Raman studied at Presidency College, Chennai. Later, he served as Professor of Physics at Calcutta University. Recipient of many honours and awards, including the title of 'Sir', Sir C.V. Raman received the Nobel Prize for an important optics research, in which he discovered that diffused light contained rays of other wavelengths—what is now popularly known as Raman Effect. His theory discovered in 1928 explains the change in the frequency of light passing through a transparent medium.

RABINDRANATH TAGORE (1861-1941) : Rabindranath Tagore was the first Indian ever to receive a Nobel Prize. Popularly known as *Gurudev*, India's Poet Laureate Tagore was born on May 07, 1861 in Kolkata. He was awarded the Nobel Prize for Literature in recognition of his work *Geetanjali*, a collection of poems, in 1913. Tagore wrote many love lyrics. *Geetanjali* and *Sadhana* are among his important works. The poet, dramatist and novelist is also the author of India's National Anthem. In 1901, he founded the famous Santiniketan which later came to be known as Vishwabharati University.

COMMANDERS-IN-CHIEF

Name	Tenure
General Sir Rob Lockhart	August 15, 1947-December 31, 1947
General Sir Roy Bucher	January 01, 1948-January 14, 1949
General (Late Field Marshal) K.M. Cariappa	January 15, 1949-January 14, 1953
General Maharaj Rajendra Sinhji	January 15, 1953-March 31, 1955

CHIEFS OF ARMY STAFF

Name	Tenure
General Maharaj Rajendra Sinhji	January 15, 1953-May 14, 1955

General S.M. Srinagesh	May 15, 1955-May 07, 1957
General K.S. Thimayya	May 08, 1957-May 07, 1961
General P.N. Thapar	May 08, 1961-November 19, 1962
General J.N. Choudhuri	November 20, 1962-June 07, 1966
General P.P. Kumaramangalam	June 08, 1966-June 07, 1969
Field Marshal S.H.F.J. Manekshaw	08 June 1969-15 January 1973
General G.G. Bewoor	January 16, 1973-May 31, 1975
General T.N. Raina	June 01, 1975-May 31, 1978
General O.P. Malhotra	June 01, 1978-May 31, 1981
General K.V. Krishna Rao	June 01, 1981-July 31, 1983
General A.S. Vaidya	August 01, 1983-January 31, 1985
General K. Sundarji	February 01, 1985-May 31, 1988
General V.N. Sharma	June 01, 1988-June 30, 1990
General S.F. Rodrigues	July 01, 1990-June 30, 1993
General B.C. Joshi	July 01, 1993-November 19, 1994
General S. Roychowdhury	November 20, 1994-September 30, 1997
General V.P. Malik	October 01, 1997-September 30, 2000
General S. Padmanabhan	October 01, 2000-December 30, 2002
General N.C. Vij	December 31, 2002-January 31, 2005
General J.J. Singh	February 01, 2005 -September 30, 2007
General Deepak Kapoor	September 30, 2007-March 30, 2010
General V.K. Singh	March 31, 2010 - May 31, 2012
General Bikram Singh	June 01, 2012 - July 31, 2014
General Dalbir Singh	August 01, 2014 - December 31, 2016
General Bipin Rawat	January 01, 2017 - till date

Source : indianarmy.nic.in

CHIEFS OF NAVAL STAFF

Name	Tenure
Rear Admiral J.T.S. Hall	August 15, 1947-August 14, 1948
Admiral Sir Edward Parry	August 14, 1948-October 13, 1951
Admiral Sir Mark Pizey	October 13, 1951-July 21, 1955
Vice Admiral Sir Stephen Carlill	July 21, 1955-April 21, 1958
Vice Admiral R.D. Katari	April 22, 1958-June 04, 1962
Vice Admiral B.S. Soman	June 04, 1962-March 03, 1966

Admiral A.K. Chatterjee	March 03, 1966-February 27, 1970
Admiral S.M. Nanda	February 28, 1970-February 28, 1973
Admiral S.N. Kohli	February 28, 1973-February 28, 1976
Admiral J.L. Cursetji	February 29, 1976-February 28, 1979
Admiral R.L. Pereira	February 28, 1979-February 28, 1982
Admiral O.S. Dawson	February 28, 1982-November 30, 1984
Admiral R.H. Tahiliani	November 30, 1984-November 30, 1987
Admiral J.G. Nadkarni	November 30, 1987-November 30, 1990
Admiral L. Ramdas	November 30, 1990-September 30, 1993
Admiral V.S. Shekhawat	September 30, 1993-September 30, 1996
Admiral Vishnu Bhagwat	September 30, 1996-December 30, 1998
Admiral Sushil Kumar	December 30, 1998 -December 29, 2001
Admiral Madhvendra Singh	December 29, 2001 -July 31, 2004
Admiral Arun Prakash	July 31, 2004 -October 30, 2006
Admiral Sureesh Mehta	October 31, 2006 -August 31, 2009
Admiral Nirmal Verma	August 31, 2009 -August 31, 2012
Admiral D.K. Joshi	August 31, 2012 - April 16, 2014
Admiral Robin K. Dhawan	April 17, 2014 -May 31, 2016
Admiral Sunil Lanba	June 01, 2016 - till date

Source : india.gov.in

CHIEFS OF AIR STAFF

Name	Tenure
Air Marshal Sir Thomas W. Elmhirst	August 15, 1947-February 21, 1950
Air Marshal Sir Ronald I. Chapman	February 22, 1950-December 09, 1951
Air Marshal Sir Gerald E. Gibbs	December 10, 1951-March 31, 1954
Air Marshal S. Mukherjee	April 01, 1954-November 08, 1960
Air Marshal A.M. Engineer	December 01, 1960-July 31, 1964
Air Chief Marshal Arjan Singh	August 01, 1964- July 15, 1969
Air Chief Marshal P.C. Lal	July 16, 1969-January 15, 1973
Air Chief Marshal O.P. Mehra	January 16, 1973-January 31, 1976
Air Chief Marshal H. Moolgavkar	February 01, 1976-August 31, 1978
Air Chief Marshal I.H. Latif	September 01, 1978-August 31, 1981
Air Chief Marshal Dilbagh Singh	September 01, 1981-September 03, 1984
Air Chief Marshal L.M. Katre	September 04, 1984-July 01, 1985

Air Chief Marshal D.A. La Fontaine	July 03, 1985-July 31, 1988
Air Chief Marshal S.K. Mehra	August 01, 1988-July 31, 1991
Air Chief Marshal N.C. Suri	July 31, 1991-July 31, 1993
Air Chief Marshal S.K. Kaul	August 01, 1993- December 31, 1995
Air Chief Marshal S.K. Sareen	December 31, 1995-December 31, 1998
Air Chief Marshal A.Y. Tipnis	December 31, 1998-December 31, 2001
Air Chief Marshal S. Krishnaswamy	December 31, 2001-December 31, 2004
Air Chief Marshal S. P. Tyagi	December 31, 2004-March 31, 2007
Air Chief Marshal F. H. Major	March 31, 2007-May 31, 2009
Air Chief Marshal P. V. Naik	May 31, 2009-July 31, 2011
Air Chief Marshal N.A.K. Browne	July 31, 2011-December 31, 2013
Air Chief Marshal Aroop Raha	January 01, 2014-December 31, 2016
Air Chief Marshal B. S. Dhanoa	January 01, 2017-till date

Source : indianairforce.nic.in

WINNERS OF PARAM VIR CHAKRA

Major Som Nath Sharma, Kumaon Regiment
Posthumous-November 1947 (Kashmir Operations 1947-48)

2nd Lt. R.R. Rane, Corps of Engineers
April 1948 (Kashmir Operations 1947-48)

Company Havaldar Major Piru Singh, Rajputana Rifles
Posthumous-July 1948 (Kashmir Operations 1947-48)

L/NK Karam Singh, Sikh Regiment
October 1948 (Kashmir Operations 1947-48)

Naik Jadunath Singh, Rajput Regiment
Posthumous-February 1948 (Kashmir Operations 1947-48)

Captain Gurbachan Singh Salaria, Gorkha Rifles
Posthumous-December 1961 (Congo)

Major Dhan Singh Thapa, Gorkha Rifles
October 1962 (Ladakh)

Subedar Joginder Singh, Sikh Regiment
Posthumous-October 1962 (NEFA)

Major Shaitan Singh, Kumaon Regiment
Posthumous-November 1962 (Ladakh)

CQMH Abdul Hamid, Grenadiers
Posthumous-September 1965 (Operation against Pakistan)

Lt. Col. A.B. Tarapore, Poona Horse
Posthumous-October 1965 (Operation against Pakistan)

Flg. Officer Nirmal Jit Singh Sekhon, Flg. Pilot
Posthumous-December 1971 (Indo-Pakistan conflict)

Major Hoshiar Singh, Grenadiers

December 1971 (Indo-Pakistan conflict)

2nd Lt. Arun Khetarpal, 17 Poona Horse
Posthumous-December 1971 (Indo-Pakistan conflict)

L/NK Albert Ekka, Brigade of Guards
Posthumous-December 1971 (Indo-Pakistan conflict)

Naib Subedar Bana Singh, J & K Light Infantry
June 1987 (Operations in Siachen Glacier)

Major Ramaswamy Parameswaran, Mahar Regiment,
Posthumous-November 1987 (IPKF Operations in Sri Lanka)

Capt Vikram Batra, 13 J & K Rifles
Posthumous-June 1999 (OP Vijay in Kargil)

Lt Manoj Kumar Pandey, 11th Gorkha Rifles
Posthumous-July 1999 (OP Vijay in Kargil)

Rifleman Sanjay Kumar, 13 J&K Rifles
July1999 (OP Vijay in Kargil)

Gdr Yogender Singh Yadav, 18 Grenadiers
July 1999 (OP Vijay in Kargil)

GALLANTRY AWARDS

The following Gallantry Awards were announced on Independence Day, 2018:

Award	Total	Posthumous
Kirti Chakra	01	01
Shaurya Chakra	14	02
Sena Medal (Gallantry)	96	08
Mention-in-Despatches	27	04

SAHITYA AKADEMI AWARDS 2017

Language	Title and Genre	Author
Assamese	Moriahola (Novel)	Jayanta Madhab Bora
Bengali	Sei Nikhonj Manusta (Novel)	Afsar Ahmed
Bodo	Thwisam (Novel)	Rita Boro
Dogri	Banna (Short Stories)	Shiv Mehta
English	The Black Hill (Novel)	Mamang Dai
Gujarati	Gujarati Vyakaranna Baso Varsh (Criticism)	Urmi Ghanshyam Desai

Hindi	Vishw Mithak Sarit Sagar (Literary Criticism)	Ramesh Kuntal Megh
Kannada	Kathana Bharathi (Literary Criticism)	T.P. Ashoka
Kashmiri	Yeli Parda Woth (Short Stories)	Autar Krishen Rahbar
Konkani	Khand Ani Her Katha (Short Stories)	Gajanan Jog
Maithili	Jahalak Diary (Poetry)	Udaya Narayana Singh 'Nachiketa'
Malayalam	Daivathinte Pusthakam (Novel)	K.P. Ramanunni
Manipuri	Chahee Taret Khuntakpa (Play)	Rajen Toijamba
Marathi	Bolave Te Amhi (Poetry)	Shrikant Deshmukh
Nepali	Kriti Vimarsha (Literary Criticism)	Bina Hangkhim
Odia	Etavatira Shilpi (Short Stories)	Gayatri Saraf
Punjabi	Slow Down (Novel)	Nachhattar
Rajasthani	Bina Hasal Pai (Criticism)	Neeraj Daiya
Sanskrit	Gangaputravadanam (Poetry)	Niranjan Mishra
Santhali	Tahena.n Tangi re (Poetry)	Bhujanga Tudu
Sindhi	Aachhende Laja Maraan (Essays)	Jagdish Lachhani
Tamil	Kaandhal Naatkal (Poetry)	(Late) Inqulab
Telugu	Gaali Rangu (Poetry)	Devipriya
Urdu	Dakhma (Short Stories)	Baig Ehsas

National Sports and Adventure Awards

The Rajiv Gandhi Khel Ratna, officially known as Rajiv Gandhi Khel Ratna Award in Sports and Games is the highest sporting honour of the country. It is awarded annually by the Ministry of Youth Affairs and Sports. The recipient(s) is/are selected and honoured for their "spectacular and most outstanding performance in the field of sports over a period of four years" at international level.

The Dronacharya Award for Outstanding Coaches in Sports and Games, is sports coaching honour of the country. It is awarded annually to selected people for "outstanding and meritorious work on a consistent basis and enabled sportspersons to excel in international events" over a period of four years.

The Arjuna Awards are given to recognize outstanding achievement in sports.

The Dhyan Chand Award is the lifetime achievement sporting honour of the country.

The Rashtriya Khel Protsahan Puruskar is conferred in four categories: (a) Identification and nurturing of budding/young talent; (b) Encouragement to sports through Corporate Social Responsibility; (c) Employment of sports persons and sports welfare measures ; and (d) Sports for Development.

The Tenzing Norgay National Adventure Award is the highest national recognition for outstanding achievements in the field of adventure on land, sea and air. It is at par with the Arjuna Award for sporting excellence.

Maulana Abul Kalam Azad Trophy is a running trophy by the Ministry of Education and awarded each year to a University which has all round best performance in sports at inter-university, national and international competitions.

Rajiv Gandhi Khel Ratna Awards 2018

S. Mirabai Chanu; Virat Kohli

Dronacharya Awards 2018

Subedar Chenanda Achaiah Kuttappa; Vijay Sharma; A. Srinivasa Rao; Sukhdev Singh Pannu; Clarence Lobo; Tarak Sinha; Jiwan Kumar Sharma; and V. R. Beedu.

Arjuna Awards 2018

Neeraj Chopra; Naib Subedar Jinson Johnson; Hima Das; Nelakurthi Sikki Reddy; Subedar Satish Kumar; Smriti Mandhana; Shubhankar Sharma; Manpreet Singh; Savita; Col. Ravi Rathore; Rahi Sarnobat; Ankur Mittal; Shreyasi Singh; Manika Batra; G. Sathiyan; Rohan Bopanna; Sumit; Pooja Kadian; Ankur Dhama; and Manoj Sarkar.

Dhyan Chand Awards 2018

Satyadev Prasad; Bharat Kumar Chetri; Bobby Aloysius; and Chougale Dadu Dattatray.

Rashtriya Khel Protsahan Puruskar 2018

Identification and Nurturing of Budding and Young Talent: Rahstriya Ispat Nigam Limited; Encouragement to Sports through Corporate Social Responisibility: JSW Sports; Sports for Development: Isha Outreach.

Tenzing Norgay National Adventure Awards, 2017

Dr. Anshu Jamsenpa; Late Shri Ravi Kumar; Lt Cdr Vartika Joshi; Lt Cdr Pratibha Jamwal; Lt Cdr Patarlapalli Swathi; Lt Cdr Shougrakpam Vijaya Devi; Lt Cdr Aishwarya Boddapati; Lt Payal Gupta; Capt Udit Thapar; and Sonam Wangyal.

Guru Nanak Dev University, Amritsar was conferred **Maulana Abul Kalam Azad (MAKA) Trophy 2017-18.**

LIST OF STATE-WISE NATIONAL HIGHWAYS IN THE COUNTRY

Sl. No.	Name of State	National Highway No.	Total Length (in km)
1	Andhra Pradesh	16 G.Q., 216, 216A, 716,26, 326, 326A, 30,40, 140,42,44 N.S., 65, 165, 365 BB, 565, 67, 69, 71, 75, 340, 765, 340C, 516D, 544D, 167, 167B, 167A, 516E, 544DD, 544E, 65&5 - All new numbers	6,286

2	Arunachal Pradesh	13, 15, 115,215,315,415, 515, 315A, 113, 313, 513, 713, 713A - All new numbers	2,537
3	Assam	31, 31B, 31C, 36, 37, 37A, 38, 39, 44, 51, 52, 52A, 52B, 53, 54, 61, 62, 117A New, 127B New, 127E New, 151,152, 153, 154, 315A New, 127C New & 127D New, 208A New, 329 New, 329A New, 427 New, 627 New, 702 New, 702C New, 702D New, 7I5A New	3,845
4	Bihar	2,2C, 19,28,28A, 28B, 30, 30A, 31, 57, 57A, 77, 80, 81, 82, 83, 84, 85,98,99,101, 102, 103, 104, 105,106, 107, 110, 120 New, 122ANew, 131ANew, 133 New, 133B New, 219 New, 227 A New, 327A New, 327 Ext. New, 333 New, 333 A New, 333B New, 527A New, 527C New, 727 A New, 120 New	4,839
5	Chandigarh	5 New	15
6	Chhattisgarh	6, 12A, 16,43,45ExtNew,78, 111, 130A New, 130BNew, 130CNew, 130DNew, 149B New, 163A New, 200, 202, 216, 217, 221, 343 New, 930New	3,232
7	Delhi	9, 19, 44, 48, 148A, 248BB - All new numbers	79
8	Goa	748, 66, 366, 566 - All new numbers	262
9	Gujarat	NE-1 ,53 New, 48 New, 47 New, 41 New, 27 New, 147 New, 151 New, 51 New, 68 New, 56 New, 64 New, 58 New, 848 New, 848A New, 848 B New, 251 New, 753 B New, 341 New, 351 New, 953 New, 927D New, 168-A New, 168 New	5,017
10	Haryana	1, 2, 8, 10, 11 New, 21A, 22, 54 New, 64, 65, 71, 71 A, 72, 73, 73A , 71B, 148B New, 236, 248 A New, 254 New, 334B New, 352A, 444A New, 703 New, 709 Ext New, 709A New, NE-II	2,641
11	Himachal Pradesh	1A, 3 New, 20, 20A, 21, 21 A, 22, 70, 72, 72B, 88, 73A , 154A New, 305 New, 503 New, 503A New, 503 Ext. New, 505 New, 505A New, 705 New, 907 A New	2,642
12	Jammu & Kashmir	1A, IB, 1C, ID, 3 New, 144 New, 144A New, 301 New, 444 New, 501 New, 701 New, 244 New	2,601
13	Jharkhand	2, 6, 23, 31, 32, 33, 43 New, 75, 78, 80, 98, 99, 100, 114A New, 133 New, 133A New, 133BNew, 143A New, 220 New, 333 New, 333A New, 343 New & 419 New	2,661
14	Karnataka	4, 4A, 7, 9, 13, 17, 48, 50 New, 63, 67, 67 New, 150 New, 150 Ext. New, 150A New, 160 New, 161A,161 New, 166E New 167 New, 169A New, 173 New, 206, 207, 209, 212, 218, 234, 275 New, 367 New, 544 DD New, 544E New, 548B New, 561 A New, 752K New, 766C New	6,791
15	Kerala	66, 85, 183, 185, 544, 744, 766, 966, 183A, 966A, 966B - All new numbers	1,782
16	Madhya Pradesh	3, 7, 12, 12A, 25, 26, 26A, 26B, 27, 34 New, 43Ext. New, 45 Ext. New, 56 New, 59, 59A, 69, 69A, 75, 76, 78, 86,92,135B New, 146BNew, 161GNew,339B New, 346 New, 347A New, 347B New, 347C New, 543 New, 548C New,	7,854

		552Ext. New, 752B New, 752C New, 752G New, 753L New, 927A New, 943 New	
17	Maharashtra	3, 4, 6, 7, 8, 9, 13, 16, 17, 26B, 50, 50 New, 63 New, 69, 130D New, 150 Ext. New, 161 New, 161A New, 161ENew, 161GNew, 161H New, 204, 211, 222, 247 New, 848 New, 160 New, 166 New, 166A New, 166E New, 266 New, 347A New, 347C New, 348 New, 348A New, 353B New, 353C New, 353D New, 353E New, 353I New, 353J New, 353K New, 361 New, 361B New, 361C New, 361H New, 543 New, 547E New, 548 New, 548A New, 548B New, 548C New, 548CC New, 548D New, 548E New, 561 New, 561A New, 752E New, 752G New, 752H New, 752I New, 752K New, 753 New, 753A New, 753B New, 753E New, 753F New, 753J New, 753L New, 753M New, 848A New, 930 New, 930D New, 953 New, 965 New, 965C New, 965G New	15,436
18	Manipur	39, 53, 102A New, 102B New, 102 C New, 129A New, 108A New, 129 New, 137 New, 137ANew, 150, 155, 702ANew	1,746
19	Meghalaya	40, 44, 217 New & 127B New	1,204
20	Mizoram	2, 6, 108, 302, 502A, 306A, 102B, 306, 502 - All new numbers	1,422
21	Nagaland	36, 39, 61, 150, 155, 129A New, 229 New, 329A New, 702 New, 702A New, 702B New, 702D New	1,547
22	Odisha	5, 5A, 6, 20 New, 23, 43, 55 New, 57 New, 60, 130C New, 153B New, 157 New, 200, 201, 203, 203A, 215, 217, 220 New, 326 New, 326A New	4,838
23	Puducherry	45A & 66 - All New numbers	64
24	Punjab	1, 1A, 10, 15, 20, 21, 22, 64, 70, 71, 72, 95, 103 A New, 154A New, 205A New, 254 New, 344A New, 344B New, 503 Ext. New, 503A New, 703 New, 703A New, 754 New &148B New	2,769
25	Rajasthan	3, 11New, 123 New, 8, 11, 11 A, 11B, 11C, 12, 14, 15, 25 Ext. New, 54 New, 65, 458New, 71B, 76, 58 Ext New, 758 New, 79, 79A, 89,90,113,112,114 ,116,148B New,148D New, 158 New, 162A New, 162 Ext. New, 168 New, 168A New, 248A New, 325 New, 709 Ext. New, 927A New	7,906
26	Sikkim	10, 310, 310A, 510, 710, 717A, 717B - All new numbers	463
27	Tamil Nadu	32 , 36 , 38 ,40 ,42 , 66 ,75 ,77 , 79 , 81 , 83 , 85 , 87 , 132 ,136 , 138 , 181 , 183 , 332 , 336 , 381 , 532 , 536 , 544 , 648 , 716 , 744 , 944 , 948 ,16 G.Q., 44 N.S., 48 G.Q., 544H, 136 , 179A - All new numbers	5,381
28	Telangana	30, 44, 61, 161,161B, 63, 163, 163 extn., 63 extn., 363, 563, 65, 365, 365B, 365BB, 565, 765, 150, 167, 353C, 365A, 167 extn., 353B, 765D, 161AA, 161BB, 248BB - All new numbers	3,786
29	Tripura	8, 108, 108A, 208, 208A, 108B - All new numbers	854
30	Uttar Pradesh	2,2A, 3,123 New (3A Old), 7,11,12A, 19,21 New, 24,24A, 24B, 25,25A, 26,27, 28, 28B, 28C, 29, 56, 56A, 56B, 58, 72A,	8,711

		73, 74, 75, 76, 86, 87, 91,91 A, 92,93 ,96, 97, 119, 135BNew, 219 New, 227 ANew, 231,232, 232A, 233, 235, 330 New, 330A New, 330 B New, 334B New, 334C New, 552 Ext. New, 709 A New, 727 A New, 730 New, 730A New, 731 A New, 931 New, 931A New & NE-II	
31	Uttarakhand	9 New, 58, 72, 72A, 72B, 73, 74, 87, 94,107ANew, 108, 109, 123, 119, 121 , 125, 309ANew, 309B New, 334A, 707ANew	2,842
32	West Bengal	2,2B,6,10 New, 31, 31A, 31C, 31D, 32,34,35,41, 55,60,60A, 80, 81,114ANew,116BNew,117,131ANew,133ANew, 317ANew,327BNew,419New,512New, 717 New, 717ANew	2,998
33	Andaman & Nicobar	4 New	331
34	Dadra & Nagar Haveli	848A New	31
35	Daman and Diu	848B New, 251 New	22
		Total	115,435

Sources: Ministry of Road Transport & Highways http://morth.nic.in

AMENDMENTS TO THE CONSTITUTION

1. *The Constitution (First Amendment) Act, 1950*—This amendment provided for several new grounds of restrictions to the right to freedom of speech and expression and the right to practise any profession or to carry on any trade or business as contained in Article 19 of the Constitution. These restrictions related to public order, friendly relations with foreign States or incitement to an offence in relation to the right to freedom of speech, and to the prescribing of professional or technical qualifications or the carrying on by the State, etc., of any trade, business, industry or service in relation to the right to carry on any trade or business. The amendment also inserted two new Articles, 31A and 31B and the Ninth Schedule to give protection from challenge to land reform laws.

2. *The Constitution (Second Amendment) Act, 1952*—By this amendment, the scale or representation for election to the Lok Sabha was readjusted.

3. *The Constitution (Third Amendment) Act, 1954*—This amendment substituted entry 33 of List III (Concurrent List) of the Seventh Schedule to make it correspond to Article 369.

4. *The Constitution (Fourth Amendment) Act, 1955*—Article 31 (2) of the Constitution was amended to re-state more precisely the State's power of compulsory acquisition and requisitioning of private property and distinguish it from cases where the operation of regulatory or prohibitory laws of the States results in "deprivation of property". Article 31A of the Constitution was also amended to extend its scope to cover categories of essential welfare legislation like abolition of zamindaris, proper planning of urban and rural areas and for effecting a full control over the mineral and oil resources of the country, etc. Six Acts were also included in the Ninth Schedule. Article 305 was also amended to save certain laws providing of State Monopolies.

5. *The Constitution (Fifth Amendment) Act, 1955*—This amendment made a change in Article 3 so as to empower President to specify a time limit for state legislatures to convey their views on the proposed Central laws affecting areas, boundaries, etc., of their states.

6. *The Constitution (Sixth Amendment) Act, 1956*—This amendment made some changes in Articles 269 and 286 relating to taxes on sale and purchase of goods in the course of inter-state trade and commerce. A new entry 92 A was added to the Union List of the Seventh Schedule to the Constitution.

7. *The Constitution (Seventh Amendment) Act, 1956*—This amendment purported to give effect to the recommendations of the State Reorganisation Commission and the necessary consequential changes. Broadly, the then existing states and territories were changed to have two-fold classification

of states and union territories. The amendment also provided for composition of the House of the People, re-adjustment after every census, provisions regarding the establishment of new High Courts, High Court Judges, etc.

8. *The Constitution (Eighth Amendment) Act, 1960*—Article 334 was amended with a view to extending the period of reservation of seats for Scheduled Castes and Scheduled Tribes and to the Anglo-Indian community by nomination in Parliament and in the State Legislatures for a further period of ten years.

9. *The Constitution (Ninth Amendment) Act, 1960*—The purpose of this amendment is to give effect to the transfer of certain territories to Pakistan in pursuance of the agreement entered into between Governments of India and Pakistan. This amendment was necessitated in view of the Judgement of Supreme Court in *In Re Berubari Union* by which it was held that any agreement to cede a territory to another country could not be implemented by a law made under Article 3 but would only be implemented by an amendment of the Constitution.

10. *The Constitution (Tenth Amendment) Act, 1961*—This Act amended Article 240 and the First Schedule in order to include areas of Dadra and Nagar Haveli as a Union Territory and to provide for its administration under the regulation making powers of President.

11. *The Constitution (Eleventh Amendment) Act, 1961*—The purpose of this amendment was to amend Articles 66 and 71 of the Constitution to provide that the election of President or Vice President could not be challenged on the ground of any vacancy in the appropriate electoral college.

12. *The Constitution (Twelfth Amendment) Act, 1962*—This amendment sought to include Goa, Daman and Diu as a Union Territory and to amend Article 240 for the purpose.

13. *The Constitution (Thirteenth Amendment) Act, 1962*—By this amendment, a new Article 371A was added to make special provisions with respect to state of Nagaland in pursuance of an agreement between Government of India and Naga People's Convention.

14. *The Constitution (Fourteenth Amendment) Act, 1962*—By this Act, Pondicherry was included in the First Schedule as a Union Territory, and this Act has also enabled the creation of Legislature by Parliamentary law for Himachal Pradesh, Manipur, Tripura, Goa, Daman and Diu and Pondicherry.

15. *The Constitution (Fifteenth Amendment) Act, 1963*—This amendment provided for increase in the age of retirement of High Court Judges and for the provision of compensatory allowance to judges who are transferred from one High Court to another. The Act also provided for appointment of retired judges to act as judges of High Court. Article 226 was also enlarged to empower High Court to issue direction, orders or writs to any Government authority, etc., if the cause of action for the exercise of such power arose in the territories wherein the High Court exercise jurisdiction notwithstanding that seat of such Government authority is not within those territories. The Act also provided for the exercise of powers of Chairman of the Service Commissions, in their absence, by one of their Members.

16. *The Constitution (Sixteenth Amendment) Act, 1963*—Article 19 was amended by this Act to impose further restriction on the rights to freedom of speech and expression, to assemble peaceably and without arms and to form associations in the interests of sovereignty and integrity of India. The oath of affirmation to be subscribed by candidates seeking election to Parliament and State Legislatures have been amended to include as one of the conditions that they will uphold the sovereignty and integrity of India. The amendments are intended to promote national integration.

17. *The Constitution (Seventeenth Amendment) Act, 1964*—Article 31A was further amended to prohibit the acquisition of land under personal cultivation unless the market value of the land is paid as compensation and the definition of "estate" as contained in that Article had also been enlarged with retrospective effect. The Ninth Schedule had also been amended to include 44 more Acts.

18. *The Constitution (Eighteenth Amendment) Act, 1966*—Article 3 was amended by this Act to specify that the expression "State" will include a union territory also and to make it clear that the power to form a new state under this Article includes a power to form a new state or union territory by uniting a part of a state or a union territory to another state or union territory.

19. *The Constitution (Nineteenth Amendment) Act, 1966*—Article 324 was amended to effect a consequential change as a result of the decision to abolish Election Tribunals and to hear election petitions by High Courts.

20. *The Constitution (Twentieth Amendment) Act, 1966*—This amendment was necessitated by the decision of the Supreme Courts in Chandramohan vs. State of Uttar Pradesh in which certain appointments of District Judges in State of Uttar Pradesh were declared void by Supreme Court. A new Article 233A was added and the appointments made by Governor were validated.

21. *The Constitution (Twenty-first Amendment) Act, 1967*—By this amendment, Sindhi Language was included in the Eighth Schedule.

22. *The Constitution (Twenty-second Amendment) Act, 1969*—This act was enacted to facilitate the formation of a new autonomous state of Meghalaya within state of Assam.

23. *The Constitution (Twenty-third Amendment) Act, 1969*—Article 334 was amended so as to extend the safeguards in respect of reservation of seats in Parliament and State Legislatures for Schedules Castes and Scheduled Tribes as well as for Anglo-Indians for a further period of ten years.

24. *The Constitution (Twenty-fourth Amendment) Act, 1971*—This amendment was passed in the context of a situation that emerged with the verdict in Golaknath's case by Supreme Court. Accordingly, this Act amended Article 13 and Article 368 to remove all doubts regarding the power of Parliament to amend the Constitution including the Fundamental Rights.

25. *The Constitution (Twenty-fifth Amendment) Act, 1971*—This amendment further amended Article 31 in the wake of the Bank Nationalisation case. The word 'amount' was substituted in place of 'compensation' in the light of the judicial interpretation of the word 'compensation' meaning 'adequate compensation'.

26. *The Constitution (Twenty-sixth Amendment) Act, 1971*—By this amendment, the privy and privileges of the former rulers of Indian states were abolished. This amendment was passed as a result of Supreme Court decision in Madhav Rao's case.

27. *The Constitution (Twenty-seventh Amendment) Act, 1971*—This amendment was passed to provide for certain matters necessitated by the reorganisation of north-eastern states. A new Article 239B was inserted which enabled the promulgation of Ordinances by Administrators of certain union territories.

28. *The Constitution (Twenty-eighth Amendment) Act, 1972*—The amendment was enacted to abolish the special privileges of the members of Indian Civil Services in matters of leave, pension and rights as regard to disciplinary matters.

29. *The Constitution (Twenty-ninth Amendment) Act, 1972*—The Ninth Schedule to the Constitution was amended to include therein two Kerala Acts on land reforms.

30. *The Constitution (Thirtieth Amendment) Act, 1972*—The purpose of the amendment was to amend Article 133 in order to do away with the valuation test of Rs 20,000 as fixed therein, and to provide instead for an appeal to Supreme Court in Civil proceedings only on a certificate issued by High Court that the case involves a substantial question of law of general importance and that in opinion of High Court, the question needs to be decided by Supreme Court.

31. *The Constitution (Thirty-first Amendment) Act, 1973*—This Act, *inter alia*, raises the upper limit for the representation of states in the Lok Sabha from 500 to 525 and reducing the upper limit for the representation of union territories from 25 members to 20.

32. *The Constitution (Thirty-second Amendment) Act, 1973*—This Act provided the necessary constitutional authority for giving effect to the provision of equal opportunities to different areas of the State of Andhra Pradesh and for the constitution of an Administrative Tribunal with jurisdiction to deal with grievances relating to public services. It also empowered Parliament to legislate for the establishment of a Central University in the State.

33. *The Constitution (Thirty-third Amendment) Act, 1974*—By this amendment, Articles 101 and

190 were amended in order to streamline the procedure for resignation of Members of Parliament and State Legislatures.

34. *The Constitution (Thirty-fourth Amendment) Act, 1974*—By this Act, twenty more land tenure and land reforms laws enacted by various State Legislatures were included in the Ninth Schedule.

35. *The Constitution (Thirty-fifth Amendment) Act, 1974*—By this Act a new Article 2A was added thereby conferring on Sikkim the status of an associate State of Indian Union. Consequent amendments were made to Articles 80 and 81. A new schedule, *i.e.,* Tenth Schedule, was added laying down terms and conditions of association of Sikkim with the Union.

36. *The Constitution (Thirty-sixth Amendment) Act, 1975*—This was enacted to make Sikkim a full-fledged State of Indian Union and to include it in the First Schedule to the Constitution and to allot to Sikkim one seat each in the Council of States and in the House of the People. Article 2A and the Tenth Schedule inserted by the Constitution (Thirty-fifth Amendment) Act were omitted and Articles 80 and 81 were suitably amended.

37. *The Constitution (Thirty-seventh Amendment) Act, 1975*—By this Act, Union Territory of Arunachal Pradesh was provided with a Legislative Assembly. Article 240 of the Constitution was also amended to provide that as in the case of other union territories with Legislatures, the power of President to make regulations for the Union Territory of Arunachal Pradesh may be exercised only when the assembly is either dissolved or its functions remain suspended.

38. *The Constitution (Thirty-eighth Amendment) Act, 1975*—This Act amended Articles 123, 213 and 352 of the Constitution to provide that the satisfaction of President or Governor contained in these Articles would be called in question in any court of law.

39. *The Constitution (Thirty-ninth Amendment)* Act, 1975—By this Act, disputes relating to the election of President, Vice-President, Prime Minister and Speaker are to be determined by such authority as may be determined by Parliamentary Law. Certain Central enactments were also included in the Ninth Schedule by this Act.

40. *The Constitution (Fortieth Amendment) Act, 1976*—This act provided for vesting in the Union of all mines, minerals and other things of value lying in the ocean within the territorial waters or the continental shelf or the exclusive economic zone of India. It further provided that all other resources of the exclusive economic zone of India shall also vest in the Union. This act also provided that the limits of the territorial waters, the continental shelf, the exclusive economic zone and the maritime zones of India shall be as specified from time to time by or under any law made by Parliament. Also some more Acts were added to the Ninth Schedule.

41. *The Constitution (Forty-first Amendment) Act, 1976*—By this Act, Article 316 was amended to raise the retirement age of Members of State Public Service Commissions and Joint Public Service Commissions from 60 to 62 years.

42. *The Constitution (Forty-second Amendment) Act, 1976*—This act made a number of important amendments in the Constitution. These amendments were mainly for purpose of giving effect to the recommendations of Swaran Singh Committee.

Some of the important amendments made are for the purpose of spelling out expressly the high ideals of socialism, secularism and the integrity of the nation, to make the Directive Principles more comprehensive and giving them precedence over those Fundamental Rights which have been allowed to be relied upon to frustrate socio-economic reforms. The amendment Act also inserted a new chapter on the Fundamental Duties of citizens and made special provisions for dealing with anti-national activities, whether by individuals or by associations. The judiciary provisions were also amended by providing for a requirement as to the minimum number of judges for determining question as to the constitutional validity of law and for a special majority of not less than two-third for declaring any law to be constitutionally invalid.

To reduce the mounting arrears in High Courts and to secure the speedy disposal of service matters, revenue matters and certain other matters of special importance in the context of socio-economic development and progress, this amendment Act provided for the creation of

Administrative and other tribunals for dealing with such matters while preserving the jurisdiction of the Supreme Court in regard to such matters under Article 136 of the Constitution. Certain modifications in the writ jurisdiction of High Courts under Article 226 were also made.

43. *The Constitution (Forty-third Amendment) Act, 1977*—This Act, *inter alia*, provided for the restoration of the jurisdiction of the Supreme Court and High Courts, curtailed by the enactment of the Constitution (Forty-second Amendment) Act, 1976 and accordingly Articles 32A, 131A, 144A, 226A and 228A included in the Constitution by the said amendment, were omitted by this Act. The Act also provided for the omission of Article 31 which conferred special powers on Parliament to enact certain laws in respect of anti-national activities.

44. *The Constitution (Forty-fourth Amendment) Act, 1978*—The right to property which had been the occasion for more than one amendment of Constitution was omitted as a Fundamental Right and it was made only as a legal right. It was, however, ensured that the removal of the right to property from the list of Fundamental Rights would not affect the right of minorities to establish and administer educational institutions of their choice. Article 352 of the Constitution was amended to provide "armed rebellion" as one of the circumstances for declaration of emergency. Internal disturbance not amounting to armed rebellion would not be a ground for the issuance of a Proclamation. The right to personal liberty as contained in Articles 21 and 22 is further strengthened by the provision that a law for preventive detention cannot authorise, in any case, detention for a longer period than two months unless an Advisory Board has reported that there is sufficient cause for such detention. The additional safeguard has also been provided by the requirements that Chairman of an Advisory Board shall be a serving Judge of the appropriate High Court and that the Board shall be constituted in accordance with the recommendations of the Chief Justice of that High Court.

With a view to avoid delays, Articles 132 and 134 were amended and a new Article 134A was inserted to provide that a High Court should consider the question of granting a certificate for appeal to Supreme Court immediately after the delivery of the judgement, final order or sentence concerned on the basis of an oral application by a party or, if the High Court deems it so to do, on its own. The other amendments made by the Act are mainly for removing or correcting the distortions which came into the Constitution by reason of the amendment initiated during the period of internal emergency.

45. *The Constitution (Forty-fifth Amendment) Act, 1980*—This was passed to extend safeguards in respect of reservation of seats in Parliament and State Assemblies for Scheduled Castes, Scheduled Tribes as well as for Anglo-Indians for a further period of ten years.

46. *The Constitution (Forty-sixth Amendment) Act, 1982*—Article 269 was amended so that the tax levied on the consignment of goods in the course of inter-state or commerce shall be assigned to the states. This Article was also amended to enable Parliament to formulate by law principle for determining when a consignment of goods takes place in the course of inter-state trade or commerce. A new entry 92B was also inserted in the Union List to enable the levy of tax on the consignment of goods where such consignment takes place in the course of inter-state trade or commerce.

Clause (3) of Article 286 was amended to enable Parliament to specify, by law, restrictions and conditions in regard to the system of levy rates and other incidence of tax on the transfer of goods involved in the execution of a works contract, on the delivery of goods on hire-purchase or any system of payment of instalments, etc.

Article 366 was also suitably amended to insert a definition of "tax on the sale or purchase of goods" to include transfer for consideration of controlled commodities, transfer of property in goods involved in the execution of a works contract, delivery of goods on hire-purchase or any system of payment by instalments, etc.

47. *The Constitution (Forty-seventh Amendment) Act, 1984*—This amendment is intended to provide for the inclusion of certain land Reforms Acts in the Ninth Schedule to the Constitution with a view to obviating the scope of litigation hampering the implementation process of those Acts.

48. *The Constitution (Forty-eighth Amendment) Act, 1984*—The Proclamation issued by President

under Article 356 of the Constitution with respect to the State of Punjab cannot be continued in force for more than one year unless the special conditions mentioned in clause (5) of the said Article are satisfied. As it is felt that the continued force of the said Proclamation is necessary, therefore, the present amendment had been effected so as to make the conditions mentioned in clause (5) of Article 356 inapplicable in the instant case.

49. *The Constitution (Forty-ninth Amendment) Act, 1984*—Tripura Government recommended that the provisions of the Sixth Schedule to the Constitution may be made applicable to tribal areas of that State. The amendment involved in this Act is intended to give a constitutional security to the autonomous District Council functioning in the State.

50. *The Constitution (Fiftieth Amendment) Act, 1984*—By Article 33 of the constitution, Parliament is empowered to enact laws determining to what extent any of the rights conferred by Part III of the constitution shall, in their application to the members of the armed forces or the forces charged with the maintenance of public order, be restricted or abrogated so as to ensure proper discharge of their duties and maintenance of discipline among them.

It was proposed to amend Article 33 so as to bring within its ambit:

(i) the members of the Force charged with the protection of property belonging to or in the charge or possession of the state; or

(ii) persons employed in any bureau or other organisation established by the state for purposes of intelligence or counter-intelligence; or

(iii) persons employed in or in connection with the telecommunication systems set up for the purposes of any Force, bureau or organisation.

Experience has revealed that the need for ensuring proper discharge of their duties and maintenance of discipline among them is of paramount importance in the national interest.

51. *The Constitution (Fifty-first Amendment) Act, 1984*—Article 330 has been amended by this Act for providing reservation of seats for Scheduled Tribes in Meghalaya, Nagaland, Arunachal Pradesh and Mizoram in Parliament and Article 332 has been amended to provide similar reservation in the Legislative Assemblies of Nagaland and Meghalaya to meet the aspirations of local tribal population.

52. *The Constitution (Fifty-second Amendment) Act, 1985*—It amends the Constitution to provide that a Member of Parliament or a State Legislature who defects or is expelled from the party which set him up as a candidate in the election or if an independent member of the House joins a political party after expiry of six months from the date on which he takes seat in the House shall be disqualified to remain a member of the House. The Act also makes suitable provisions with respect to splits in and merger of political parties.

53. *The Constitution (Fifty-third Amendment) Act, 1986*—This has been enacted to give effect to the Memorandum of Settlement of Mizoram which was signed by Government of India and Mizoram Government with Mizoram National Front on 30th June 1986. For this purpose, a new Article 371G has been inserted in the Constitution *inter alia* preventing application of any Act of Parliament in Mizoram in respect of religious or social practices of Mizos, Mizos' customary law and procedure, administration of civil and criminal practice involving decisions according to Mizos' customary law and ownership and transfer of land unless a resolution is passed in the Legislative Assembly to that effect. This, however, will not apply to any Central Act already in force in Mizoram before the commencement of this amendment. The new Article also provides that the Legislative Assembly of Mizoram shall consist of not less than 40 members.

54. *The Constitution (Fifty-fourth Amendment) Act, 1986*—This Act increases the salaries of Supreme Court and High Court judges as follows :

Chief Justice of India	₹ 10,000 per month
Judges of Supreme Court	₹ 9,000 per month

Chief Justice of High Court	₹ 9,000 per month
Judges of High Court	₹ 8,000 per month

This Act amended Part 'D' of the Second Schedule to the Constitution to give effect to the above increases in the salaries of judges and to make an enabling provision in Articles 125 and 221 to provide for changes in the salaries of judges in future by Parliament by law.

55. *The Constitution (Fifty-fifth Amendment) Act, 1986*—This Act seeks to give effect to the proposal of Government of India to confer statehood on the Union Territory of Arunachal Pradesh and for this purpose, a new Article 371H has been inserted which, *inter alia,* confers, having regard to the sensitive location of Arunachal Pradesh to vest special responsibility on Governor of the new State of Arunachal Pradesh with respect to law and order in the State and in the discharge of his functions, the Governor shall after consulting the Council of Ministers, exercise his individual judgement, as to the action to be taken and this responsibility shall cease when President so directs. The new Article also provides that the new Legislative Assembly of the new State of Arunachal Pradesh, shall consist of not less than thirty members.

56. *The Constitution (Fifty-sixth Amendment) Act, 1987*—Government of India has proposed to constitute the territories comprised in Goa District of the Union Territory of Goa, Daman and Diu as the State of Goa and the territories comprised in Daman and Diu districts of that Union Territory as a new Union Territory of Daman and Diu. In this context, it was proposed that the Legislative Assembly of the new State of Goa shall consist of 40 members. The existing Legislative Assembly of the Union Territory of Goa, Daman and Diu has 30 elected members and three nominated members. It was intended to make this Assembly with the exclusion of two members representing Daman and Diu districts the provisional Legislative Assembly for the new State of Goa until elections are held on the expiry of the five year terms of the existing Assembly. It was, therefore, decided to provide that the Legislative Assembly of the new State of Goa shall consist of not less than 30 members. The special provision required to be made to give effect to this proposal is carried out by this amendment.

57. *The Constitution (Fifty-seventh amendment) Act, 1987*—The Constitution (Fifty-first Amendment) Act, 1984 was enacted to provide for reservation of seats in the house of the people for scheduled tribes in Nagaland, Meghalaya, Mizoram and Arunachal Pradesh and also for reservation of seats for scheduled tribes in the legislative assemblies of Nagaland and Meghalaya by suitably amending articles 330 and 332. Even though these states are predominantly tribal, the underlying objective of the aforesaid act was to ensure that the members of scheduled tribes in these areas do not fail to secure a minimal representation because of their inability to compete with the advanced sections of the people. The Constitution (fifty-first amendment) Act, though formally enforced, could not be fully implemented unless parallel action is taken to determine the seats which are to be reserved for Scheduled tribes in these areas. The number of seats reserved for Schedule Castes and Schedule Tribes in the Legislative Assembly of any State under article 332 of the constitution will have to be determined having regard to the provisions of article 332 (3) of the Constitution. However, in view of the historical background with respect to the areas comprised in north-eastern states, the circumstances obtaining in these areas in the State of development of Scheduled Tribes and other relevant considerations, it was considered necessary to provide for special arrangements with regard to the reservation for Scheduled Tribes in these areas for a temporary period so as to facilitate easy transition of these areas to the normal arrangements as envisaged in the Constitution. Article 332 of the Constitution was further amended for making a temporary provision, until the re-adjustment of seats on the basis of first census after the year 2000 under article 170 of the Constitution for these states, for the determination of the number of seats reserved for Scheduled Tribes. This amendment seeks to provide that if all the seats in the Legislative Assembly of such States in existence on the date of coming into force of this constitution amendment act are held by the members of Scheduled Tribes, all the seats except one shall be reserved for scheduled tribes and in any other case such number of seats as bears to the total number of seats a proportion not less than the number of members belonging to Scheduled Tribes in the existing assembly bears to the total number of seats in the existing assembly. The Act achieves these objectives.

58. *The Constitution (Fifty-eighth Amendment) Act, 1987*—There has been general demand for the publication of authoritative text of the Constitution in Hindi. It is imperative to have an authoritative text of the Constitution for facilitating its use in the legal process. Any Hindi version of the Constitution should not only conform to the Hindi translation published by the Constituent Assembly, but should be in conformity, with the language style and terminology adopted in the authoritative texts of Central Acts in Hindi. The Constitution has been amended to empower President of India to publish under his authority the translation of the Constitution in Hindi signed by the Members of the Constituent Assembly with such modification as may be necessary to bring it in conformity with the language, style and terminology adopted in the authoritative texts of Central Acts in Hindi language. President has also been authorised to publish the translation in Hindi of every amendment of the Constitution made in English.

59. *The Constitution (Fifty-ninth Amendment) Act, 1988*—The Act amends Article 365 (5) of the Constitution so as to facilitate the extension of a Presidential Proclamation issued under clause (1) of Article 356 beyond a period of one year, if necessary upto a period of three years, as permissible under clause (4) of Article 356 with respect to the State of Punjab because of the continued disturbed situation there. The Act also amends Article 352 of the Constitution pertaining to the Proclamation of Emergency in its application to the State of Punjab and includes internal disturbance as one of the grounds for making a Proclamation in respect of the State of Punjab only. As a consequence of amendment in Article 352, Articles 358 and 359 in relation to the State of Punjab will be operative only for a period of two years from 30 March 1988, which is the date of commencement of the amendment.

60. *The Constitution (Sixtieth Amendment) Act, 1988*—The Act amends clause (2) of Article 276 of the Constitution so as to increase the ceiling of taxes on professions, trades, callings and employment from Rs 250 per annum to Rs 2,500 per annum. The upward revision of this tax will help state governments in raising additional resources. The proviso to clause (2) has been omitted.

61. *The Constitution (Sixty-first Amendment) Act, 1989*—The Act provides for reducing voting age from 21 to 18 years by amending Article 326 of the Constitution to provide to the unrepresented youth of the country an opportunity to give vent to their feelings and help them become a part of political process.

62. *The Constitution (Sixty-second Amendment) Act, 1989*—Article 334 of the Constitution lays down that the provisions of the Constitution relating to the reservation of seats for the Scheduled Castes and the Scheduled Tribes and the representation of the Anglo-Indian community by nomination in the Lok Sabha and in the Legislative Assemblies of the States shall cease to have effect on the expiry of a period of 40 years from the commencement of the Constitution. Although the Scheduled Castes and the Scheduled Tribes have made considerable progress in the last 40 years, the reasons which weighed with the Constituent Assembly in making provisions with regard to the aforesaid reservation of seats and nomination of members, have not ceased to exist. The Act amends Article 334 of the Constitution to continue the reservation for the Scheduled Castes and the Scheduled Tribes and the representation of the Anglo-Indians by nomination for a further period of 10 years.

63. *The Constitution (Sixty-third Amendment) Act, 1989*—The Constitution (Fifty-ninth Amendment) Act, 1988 was enacted in March 1988 making certain changes in regard to making a Proclamation of Emergency in Punjab and to the duration of President's rule in State. On reconsideration, the Government decided that the special powers in regard to the Proclamation of Emergency in Punjab as envisaged in the said amendment is no longer required. Accordingly the provision to clause (5) of Article 356 and Article 359A of the Constitution have been omitted.

64. *The Constitution (Sixty-fourth Amendment) Act, 1990*—This Act amends clauses (4) and (5) of Article 356 of the Constitution with a view to facilitate the extension of the proclamation issued under clause (1) of Article 356 of the Constitution on 11th May 1987 upto a total period of three years and six months in relation to the State of Punjab.

65. *The Constitution (Sixty-fifth Amendment) Act, 1990*—Article 338 of the Constitution provides for a Special Officer for the Scheduled Castes and Scheduled Tribes to investigate all matters relating

to the safeguards provided for the Scheduled Castes and Scheduled Tribes under the Constitution and to report to the President on their working. The Article has been amended for the constitution of a National Commission for Scheduled Castes and Scheduled Tribes consisting of a Chairperson, Vice Chairperson and five other Members who shall be appointed by the President by warrant under his hand and seal. The amended Article elaborates the duties of the said Commission and covers measures that should be taken by the Union or any state for the effective implementation of the reports presented by the Commission. It also provides that the Commission shall, while investigating any matter or inquiring into any complaint have all the powers of a Civil Court trying a suit and the reports of the said Commission shall be laid before Parliament and the Legislature of the states.

66. *The Constitution (Sixty-sixth Amendment) Act, 1990*—The Act protects 55 State Acts relating to land reforms and ceiling on agricultural land holdings enacted by States of Andhra Pradesh, Bihar, Gujarat, Himachal Pradesh, Karnataka, Kerala, Madhya Pradesh, Maharashtra, Orissa, Rajasthan,Tamilnadu, Uttar Pradesh, West Bengal and administration of the Union Territory of Puducherry, from challenge in courts, by including them in the Ninth Schedule to the Constitution.

67. *The Constitution (Sixty-seventh Amendment) Act, 1990*—The three year period in the case of proclamation issued on 11th May 1987 with respect to the State of Punjab was extended to three years and six months by the Constitution (Sixty-fourth Amendment) Act, 1990. This Act further amends clause (4) of Article 356 so as to further extend the period upto a total period of four years.

68. *The Constitution (Sixty-eighth Amendment) Act, 1991*—The three year period in the case of proclamation issued on 17th May 1987 with respect to the State of Punjab was earlier extended to four years by the Constitution (sixty-seventh Amendment) Act, 1990. This Act further amends clause (4) of Article 356 so as to further extend the period upto a total period of five years.

69. *The Constitution (Sixty-ninth Amendment) Act, 1991*—The Government of India appointed on 24th December 1987 a Committee to go into various issues connected with the administration of Delhi and to recommend measures, *inter alia,* for the streamlining of the administrative set up. After detailed inquiry and examination, it recommended that Delhi should continue to be a union territory and may be provided with a Legislative Assembly and a Council of Ministers responsible to such assembly with appropriate powers to deal with matters of concern to the common man. The Committee also recommended that with a view to ensuring stability and permanence, arrangements should be incorporated in the constitution to give the national capital a special status among the union territories. This act has been passed to give effect to the above recommendations.

70. *The Constitution (Seventieth Amendment) Act, 1992*—While considering the (Seventy-fourth Amendment) Bill, 1991 and the Government of National Capital Territory Bill, 1991 views were expressed in both the Houses of Parliament in favour of including also the elected members of the legislative assemblies of union territories in the electoral college for the election of the President under Article 54 of the Constitution.

At present Article 54 relating to the election of the President provides for an electoral college consisting of only the elected Members of Parliament as well as the legislative assemblies of the states (not of union territories). Similarly, Article 55 providing for the manner of such election also speaks of legislative assemblies of states.

Accordingly, an Explanation was inserted in Article 54 to provide that reference to 'State' in Article 54 and 55 would include the National Capital Territory of Delhi and the Union Territory of Puducherry for constituting the electoral college for election of the President. This would enable the elected members of the Legislative Assembly created for the Union Territory of Puducherry under the provisions of Article 239A and of the proposed Legislative Assembly of the National Capital Territory of Delhi under Article 239AA to be included in the electoral college.

71. *The Constitution (Seventy-first Amendment) Act, 1992*—There have been demands for inclusion of certain languages in the Eighth Schedule to the Constitution. This Act amends the Eighth Schedule

to the Constitution to include Konkani, Manipuri and Nepali languages in the Eighth Schedule to the Constitution.

72. *The Constitution (Seventy-second Amendment) Act, 1992*—For restoring peace and harmony in the areas of the State of Tripura where disturbed conditions prevailed, a Memorandum of Settlement was signed by the Government of India with Tripura National Volunteers on 12 August 1988.

In order to implement the said Memorandum, Article 332 of the Constitution has been amended by the Constitution (Seventy-second Amendment) Act, 1992 for making a temporary provision for the determination of the number of seats reserved for the Scheduled Tribes in the State Assembly of Tripura, until the re-adjustment of seats is made on the basis of the first Census after the year 2000 under Article 170 of the Constitution.

73. *The Constitution (Seventy-third Amendment) Act, 1993*—Article 40 of the Constitution which enshrines one of the Directive Principles of State Policy lays down that the State shall take steps to organise village *panchayats* and endow them with such powers and authority as may be necessary to enable them to function as units of self-government.

In the light of the above, a new Part IX relating to the Panchayats has been inserted in the Constitution to provide for among other things, *Gram Sabha* in a village or group of villages; constitution of *Panchayats* at village and other level or levels; direct elections to all seats in Panchayats at the village and intermediate level, if any and to the offices of Chairpersons of Panchayats at such levels; reservation of seats for the Scheduled Castes and Scheduled Tribes in proportion to their population for membership of Panchayats and office of Chairpersons in Panchayats at each level; reservation of not less than one-third of the seats for women; fixing tenure of five years for Panchayats and holding elections within a period of six months in the event of supersession of any Panchayat.

74. *The Constitution (Seventy-fourth Amendment) Act, 1993*—In many states local bodies have become weak and ineffective on account of a variety of reasons, including the failure to hold regular elections, prolonged supersession and inadequate devolutions of powers and functions. As a result, Urban Local Bodies are not able to perform effectively as vibrant democratic units of self-government.

Having regard to these inadequacies a new part IX-A relating to the Municipalities has been incorporated in the Constitution to provide for among other things, constitution of three types of Municipalities, *i.e., Nagar Panchayats* for areas in transition from a rural area to urban area, Municipal Councils for smaller urban areas and Municipal Corporations for larger urban areas.

75. *The Constitution (Seventy-fifth Amendment) Act, 1994*—The operation of the Rent Control Legislations, as are today in various states, suffers from major weaknesses and has led to various unintended consequences. Some of the deleterious legal consequences include mounting and mending litigation, inability of the courts to provide timely justice, evolution of practices and systems to bypass the operations of rent legislations and steady shrinkage of rental housing market.

The Supreme Court taking note of the precarious state of rent litigation in the country in case of Prabhakaran Nair and others vs. State of Tamilnadu (Civil Writ Petition 506 of 1986) and other writs observed that the Supreme Court and the High Courts should be relieved of the heavy burden of rent litigation. Tiers of appeals should be curtailed. Laws should be simple, rational and clear, litigations must come to end quickly.

Therefore, this Act amends Article 323B in Part XIVA of the Constitution so as to give timely relief to the rent litigants by providing for setting up of state-level Rent Tribunals in order to reduce the tiers of appeals and to exclude the jurisdiction of all courts, except that of the Supreme Court, under Article 136 of the Constitution.

76. *The Constitution (Seventy-sixth Amendment) Act, 1994*—The policy of reservation of seats in educational institutions and reservation of appointments or posts in public services for Backward Classes, Scheduled Castes and Scheduled Tribes has had a long history in Tamilnadu dating back

to the year 1921. The extent of reservation has been increased by the State Government from time to time, consistent with the needs of the majority of the people and it has now reached the level of 69 per cent (18 per cent Scheduled Castes, one per cent Scheduled Tribes and 50 per cent Other Backward Classes).

The Supreme Court in Indira Sawhney and others vs. Union of India and others (AIR, 1993 SC 477) on 16th November 1992 ruled that the total reservations under Article 16(4) should not exceed 50 per cent.

The Tamilnadu Government enacted a legislation, namely, Tamilnadu Backward Classes, Scheduled Castes and Scheduled Tribes (Reservation of Seats in Educational Institution and of appointments or posts in the Services under the State) Bill, 1993 and forwarded it to the Government of India for consideration of the President of India in terms of Article 31-C of the Constitution. The Government of India supported the provision of the State legislation by giving the President's assent to the Tamilnadu Bill. As a corollary to this decision, it was necessary that the Tamilnadu Act 45 of 1994 was brought within the purview of the Ninth Schedule to the Constitution so that it could get protection under Article 31B of the Constitution with regard to the judicial review.

77. *The Constitution (Seventy-seventh Amendment) Act, 1995*—The Schedule Castes and the scheduled tribes have been enjoying the facility of reservation in promotion since 1955. The Supreme Court in its judgment dated 16th November 1992 in the case of Indira Sawhney and others vs. Union of India and others, however, observed that reservation of appointments or posts under Article 16(4) of the Constitution is confined to initial appointment and cannot extend to reservation in the matter of promotion. This ruling of the Supreme Court will adversely affect the interests of the Scheduled Castes and the Scheduled Tribes. Since the representation of the Scheduled Castes and the Scheduled Tribes in services in the States have not reached the required level, it is necessary to continue the existing dispensation of providing reservation in promotion in the case of the Scheduled Castes and the Scheduled Tribes. In view of the commitment of the Government to protect the interests of the Scheduled Castes and the Scheduled Tribes, the Government have decided to continue the existing policy of reservation in promotion for the Scheduled Castes and the Scheduled Tribes. To carry out this, it was necessary to amend Article 16 of the Constitution by inserting a new clause (4A) in the said Article to provide for reservation in promotion for the Scheduled Castes and the Scheduled Tribes.

78. *The Constitution (Seventy-eighth Amendment) Act, 1995*—Article 31B of the Constitution confers on the enactments included in the Ninth Schedule to the Constitution immunity from legal challenge on the ground that they violate the fundamental rights enshrined in Part III of the Constitution. The Schedule consists of list of laws enacted by various State Governments and Central Government which, *inter alia*, affect rights and interest in property including land.

In the past, whenever, it was found that progressive legislation conceived in the interest of the public was imperilled by litigation, recourse was taken to the Ninth Schedule. Accordingly, several State enactments relating to land reforms and ceiling on agricultural land holdings have already been included in the Ninth Schedule. Since, the Government is committed to give importance to land reforms, it was decided to include land reform laws in the Ninth Schedule so that they are not challenged before the courts. The State Governments of Bihar, Karnataka, Kerala, Orissa, Rajasthan, Tamilnadu and West Bengal had suggested the inclusion of some of their Acts relating to land reforms in the Ninth Schedule.

Since the amendment to Acts which are already placed in the Ninth Schedule are not automatically immunised from legal challenge, a number of amending Acts along with a few principal Acts have been included in the Ninth Schedule so as to ensure that implementation of these Acts is not adversely affected by litigation.

79. *The Constitution (Seventy-ninth Amendment) Act, 1999*—By this Act the Government has extended the reservations of seats for the Scheduled Castes and the Scheduled Tribes as well as for the Anglo-Indians in the House of the People and in the Legislative Assemblies of the States for another ten years.

80. *The Constitution (Eightieth Amendment) Act, 2000*—Based on the recommendations of the Tenth Finance Commission, an alternative scheme for sharing taxes between the Union and the

States has been enacted by the Constitution (Eightieth Amendment) Act, 2000. Under the new scheme of devolution of revenue between Union and the States, 26 per cent out of gross proceeds of Union taxes and duties is to be assigned to the States in lieu of their existing share in the income-tax, excise duties, special excise duties and grants in lieu of tax on railway passenger fares.

81. *The Constitution (Eighty-first Amendment) Act, 2000*—By this amendment the unfilled vacancies of a year which were reserved for the Scheduled Castes and the Scheduled Tribes for being filled up in that year in accordance with any provision for reservations made under Article 16 of the Constitution, shall be considered as a separate class of vacancies to be filled up in any succeeding year or years, and such class of vacancies shall not be considered together with the vacancies of the year in which they were filled up for determining the ceiling of fifty per cent reservation against total number of vacancies of that year.

82. *The Constitution (Eighty-second Amendment) Act, 2000*—The amendment provides that nothing in Article 335 shall prevent the State from making any provision in favour of the members of the Scheduled Castes and the Scheduled Tribes for relaxation in qualifying marks in any examination or lowering the standards of evaluation for reservation in matters of promotion to any class or classes of services or posts in connection with affairs of the Union or of a State.

83. *The Constitution (Eighty-third Amendment) Act, 2000*—The Act amended Acticle 243M of the Constitution to provide that no reservation in Panchayats need be made in favour of the Scheduled Castes in Arunachal Pradesh wholly inhabited by tribal population.

84. *The Constitution (Eighty-fourth Amendment) Act, 2001*—The Act amended provisos to articles 82 and 170(3) of the Constitution to readjust and rationalise the territorial constitutencies in the States, without altering the number of seats allotted to each State in House of People and Legislative Assemblies of the States, including the Scheduled Castes and Scheduled Tribes constituencies, on the basis of the population ascertained at the census for the year 1991 so as to remove the imbalance caused due to uneven growth of population/electorate in different constituencies. It is also to refix the number of seats reserved for the Scheduled Castes and the Scheduled Tribes in the House of the People and the Legislative Assemblies of the States on the basis of the population ascertained at the census for the year 1991 so as to remove the imbalance caused due to uneven growth of population/electorate in different constituencies. It is also to refix the number of seats reserved for Scheduled Castes and the Scheduled Tribes in the House of the People and the Legislative Assemblies of the States on the basis of the population ascertained at the census for the year 1991.

85. *The Constitution (Eighty-fifth Amendment) Act, 2001*—This Act amended article 16(4A) of the Constitution to provide for consequential seniority in the case of promotion by virtue of rule of reservation for the Government servants belonging to the Scheduled Castes and the Scheduled Tribes. It also provides retrospective effect from 17th day of June 1995.

86. *The Constitution (Eighty-sixth Amendment) Act, 2002*—The Act deals with insertion of a new article 21A after article 21. The new article 21A deals with Right to Education—"The State shall provide free and compulsory education to all children of the age of six to fourteen years in such manner as the State may, by law, determine".

Substitution of new Article for Article 45. For Article 45 of the Constitution, the following article shall be substituted, namely, Provision for early childhood care and education to children below the age of six years. Article 45: "The State shall endeavour to provide early childhood care and education for all children until they complete the age of six years."

Article 51A of the Constitution was amended and a new clause (k) was added after clause (j), namely, "(k) who is a parent or guardian to provide opportunities for education to his child or, as the case may be, ward between the age of six and fourteen years."

87. *The Constitution (Eighty-seventh Amendment) Act, 2003* - In Article 81 of the Constitution, in clause (3), in the proviso, in clause (ii), for the figures "1991", the figures "2001" shall be substituted.

In Article 82 of the Constitution, in the third proviso, in clause (ii), for the figures "1991", the figures "2001" shall be substituted.

In Article 170 of the Constitution, - (i) in clause (2), in the Explanation, in the proviso, for the figures "1991", the figures "2001" shall be substituted; (ii) in clause (3), in the Explanation, in the third proviso, for the figures "1991", the figures "2001" shall be substituted.

In Article 330 of the Constitution, in the Explanation, in the proviso, for the figures "1991", the figures "2001" shall be substituted.

88. *The Constitution (Eighty-eighth Amendment) Act, 2003* - It shall come into force on such date as the Central Government may, by notification in the Official Gazette, appoint.

After Article 268 of the Constitution, the following article shall be inserted, namely :

"268A. (1) Taxes on services shall be levied by the Government of India and such tax shall be collected and appropriated by the Government of India and the States in the manner provided in clause (2).

(2) The proceeds in any financial year of any such tax levied in accordance with the provisions of clause (1) shall be - (a) collected by the Government of India and the States; (b) appropriated by the Government of India and the States, in accordance with such principles of collection and appropriation as may be formulated by Parliament by law".

In Article 270 of the constitution, in clause(1), for the words and figures "Article 268 and 269", the words, figures and letter "Articles 268, 268A and 269" shall be substituted.

In the Seventh Schedule to the Constitution, in **List I-Union List,** after entry 9.2B, the following entry shall be inserted, namely : "92C. Taxes on services".

89 *The Constitution (Eighty-ninth Amendment) Act, 2003*-It shall come into force on such date as the Central Government may, by notification in the Official Gazette, appoint.

In Article 338 of the Constitution, - (a) for the marginal heading, the following marginal heading shall be substituted, namely :

"National Commission for : Scheduled Castes";

(b) for clauses (1) and (2), the following clauses shall be substituted, namely:

"(1) There shall be a Commission for the Scheduled Castes to be known as the National Commission for the Scheduled Castes.

(2) Subject to the provisions of any law made in this behalf by Parliament, the Commission shall consist of a Chairperson, Vice-Chairperson and three other Members and the conditions of service and tenure of office of the Chairperson, Vice-Chairperson and other Members so appointed shall be such as the President may by rule determine";

(c) in clauses (5), (9) and (10), the words "and Scheduled Tribes", wherever they occur, shall be omitted.

After Article 338 of the Constitution, the following article shall be inserted, namely:

"338A. (1) There shall be a Commission for the Scheduled Tribes to be known as the National Commission for the Scheduled Tribes.

(2) Subject to the provisions of any law made in this behalf by Parliament, the Commission shall consist of a Chairperson, Vice-Chairperson and three other Members and the conditions of service and tenure of office of the Chairperson, Vice-Chairperson and other Members so appointed shall be such as the President may by rule determine.

(3) The Chairperson, Vice-Chairperson and other Members of the Commission shall be appointed by the President by warrant under his hand and seal.

(4) The Commission shall have the power to regulate its own procedure.

(5) It shall be the duty of the Commission - (a) to investigate and monitor all matters relating to the safeguards provided for the Scheduled Tribes under this Constitution or under any other law for the time being in force or under any order of the Government and to evaluate the

working of such safeguards; (b) to inquire into specific complaints with respect to the deprivation of rights and safeguards of the Scheduled Tribes; (c) to participate and advise on the planning process of socio-economic development of the Scheduled Tribes and to evaluate the progress of their development under the Union and any State; (d) to present to the President, annually and at such other times as the Commission may deem fit, reports upon the working of those safeguards; (e) to make in such reports recommendations as to the measures that should be taken by the Union or any State for the effective implementation of those safeguards and other measures for the protection, welfare and socio-economic development of the Scheduled Tribes; and (f) to discharge such other functions in relation to the protection, welfare and development and advancement of the Scheduled Tribes as the President may, subject to the provisions of any law made by Parliament, by rule specify.

(6) The President shall cause all such reports to be laid before each House of Parliament along with a memorandum explaining the action taken or proposed to be taken on the recommendations relating to the Union and the reasons for the non-acceptance, if any, of any of such recommendations.

(7) Where any such report, or any part thereof, relates to any matter with which any State Government is concerned, a copy of such report shall be forwarded to the Governor of the State who shall cause it to be laid before the Legislature of the State along with a memorandum explaining the action taken or proposed to be taken on the recommendations relating to the State and reasons for the non-acceptance, if any, of any of such recommendations.

(8) The Commission shall, while investigating any matter referred to in sub-clause(a) or inquiring into any complaint referred to in sub-clause (b) of clause (5), have all the powers of a civil court trying a suit and in particular in respect of the following matters, namely:

(a) summoning and enforcing the attendance of any person from any part of India and examining him on oath; (b) requiring the discovery and production of any document; (c) receiving evidence on affidavits; (d) requisitioning any public record or copy thereof from any court or office; (e) issuing commissions for the examination of witnesses and documents; (f) any other matter which the President may, by rule, determine.

(9) The Union and every State Government shall consult the Commission on all major policy matters affecting Scheduled Tribes".

90. *The Constitution (Ninetieth Amendment) Act, 2003*-In Article 332 of the Consitution, in clause (6), the following proviso shall be inserted, namely :

"Provided that for elections to the Legislative Assembly of the State of Assam, the representation of the Scheduled Tribes and non-Scheduled Tribes in the constituencies included in the Bodoland Territorial Areas District, so notified, and existing prior to the constitution of the Bodoland Territorial Areas District, shall be maintained".

91. *The Constitution (Ninety-first Amendment), Act, 2003* - In Article 75 of the Constitution, after clause (1), the following clauses shall be inserted, namely :

"(1A) The total number of Ministers, including the Prime Minister, in the Council of Ministers shall not exceed fifteen per cent of the total number of members of the House of the People.

(1B) A member of either House of Parliament belonging to any political party who is disqualified for being a member of that House under paragraph 2 of the Tenth Schedule shall also be disqualified to be appointed as a Minister under clause (1) for duration of the period commencing from the date of his disqualification till the date on which the term of his office as such member would expire or where he contests any election to either House of Parliament before the expiry of such period, till the date on which he is declared elected, whichever is earlier"

In Article 164 of the Constitution, after clause (i), the following clauses shall be inserted, namely:

"(1A) the total number of Ministers, including the Chief Minister, in the Council of Ministers in a State sall not exceed fifteen per cent of the total number of members of the Legislative Assembly of that State :

Provided that the number of Ministers, including the Chief Minister, in a State shall not be less than twelve:

Provided further that where the total number of Ministers, including the Chief Minister, in the Council of Ministers in any State at the commencement of the Constitution (Ninety-first Amendment) Act, 2003 exceeds the said fifteen per cent or the number specified in the first proviso, as the case may be, then, the total number of Ministers in that State shall be brought in conformity with the provisions of this clause within six months from such date as the President may by public notification appoint.

(1B) A member of the Legislative Assembly of a State or either House of the Legislature of a State having Legislative Council beloging to any poitical party who is disqualified for being a member of that House under paragraph 2 of the Tenth Schedule shall also be disqualified to be appointed as a Minister under clause (1) for duration of the period commencing from the date of his disqualification till the date on which the term of his office as such member would expire or where he contests any election to the Legislative Assembly of a State or either House of the Legislature of a State having Legislative Council, as the case may be, before the expiry of such period, till the date on which he is declared elected, whichever is earlier"

After Article 361A of the Constitution, the following article shall be inserted, namely :

316B. A member of a House belonging to any political party who is disqualified for being a member of the House under paragraph 2 of the Tenth Schedule shall also be disqualified to hold any remunerative political post for duration of the period commencing from the date of his disqualification till the date on which the term of his office as such member would expire or till the date on which he contests an election to a House and is declared elected, whichever is earlier.

Explanation : For the purposes of this Article,—

(a) the expression "House" has the meaning assigned to it in clause (a) of paragraph 1 of the Tenth Schedule :

(b) the expression "remunerative political post" means any office—(i) under the Government of India or the Government of a State where the salary or remuneration for such office is paid out of the public revenue of the Government of India or the Government of the State, as the case may be, or (ii) under a body, whether incorporated or not, which is wholly or partially owned by the Government of India or the Government of a State and the salary or remuneration for such office is paid by such body, except where such salary or remuneration paid is compensatory in nature'.

In the Tenth Schedule to the Constitution,—(a) in paragraph, 1, in clause (b), the words and figure "paragraph 3 or, as the case may be," shall be omitted; (b) in paragraph 2, in sub-paragraph (1), for the words and figures "paragraphs 3, 4 and 5", the words and figures "paragraphs 4 and 5" shall be substituted; (c) paragraph 3 shall be omitted.

92. *The Constitution (Ninety-second Amendment) Act, 2003*—In the Eighth Schedule to the Constitution,—(a) existing entry 3 shall be re-numbered as entry 5, and before entry 5 as so re-numbered, the following entries shall be inserted, namely:

"3. Bodo;

4. Dogri".

(b) existing 4 to 7 shall respectively be re-numbered as entries 6 to 9; (c) existing entry 8 shall be re-numbered as entry 11 and before entry 11 as so renumbered, the following entry shall be inserted, namely:

"10. Maithili".

(d) existing entries 9 to 14 shall respectively be re-numbered as entries 12 to 17;

(e) existing entry 15 shall be re-numbered as entry 19 and before entry 19 as so re-numbered, the following entry shall be inserted, namely :

"18. Santhali".

(f) existing entries 16 to 18 shall respectively be re-numbered as entries 20 to 22.

93. *The Constitution (Ninety-third amendment) Act, 2006*—Greater access to higher education including professional education, is of great importance to a large number of students belonging to the Scheduled Castes, the Scheduled Tribes and other socially and educationally backward classes of citizens. The reservation of seats for the Scheduled Castes, the Scheduled Tribes and the Other Backward Classes of citizens in admission to educational institution is derived from the provisions of clause (4) of articles 15 of the constitution. At present, the number of seats available in aided or State maintained institutions, particularly in respect of professional education, is limited, in comparison to those in private unaided institutions.

Clause (i) of article 30 of the Constitution provides the right to all minorities to establish and administer educational institutions of their choice. It is essential that the rights available to minorities are protected in regard to institutions established and administered by them. Accordingly, institutions declared by the State to be minority institutions under clause (1) of article 30 are excluded from the operation of this enactment.

To promote the educational advancement of the socially and educationally backward classes of citizens, i.e., the Other Backward Classes or of the Scheduled Castes and the Scheduled Tribes in matters of admission of students belonging to these categories in unaided educational institutions, other than the minority educational institutions referred to in clause (1) of article 30, the provisions of article 15 were amplified. The new clause (5) of said article 15 shall enable the Parliament as well as the State Legislatures to make appropriate laws for the above mentioned purpose.

94. *The Constitution (Ninety-fourth amendment) Act, 2006*—In Article 164 of the Constitution, in Clause (I), in the proviso, for the word "Bihar", the words "Chhattisgarh, Jharkhand" shall be substituted.

95. *The Constitution (Ninety-fifth amendment) Act, 2009*—In Article 334, Extended the reservation of the seats for SCs and STs in the Lok Sabha and State Assemblies from Sixty Years to Seventy Years.

96. *The Constitution (Ninety-Sixth Amendment) Act, 2011*—In Schedule 8 of the Constitution, Substituted "Odia" for "Oriya".

97. *The Constitutions (Ninety-Seventh Amendment) Act, 2011*—Added the words "Or Co-operative Societies" after the world "Or Unions" in Article 19(i)(c) and insertion of article 43B, i.e., Promotion of Co-operative Societies and added Part 1x8, i.e. The Co-operative Societies.

98. *The Constitution (Ninety-Eighth Amendment) Act, 2012*—Inserted Article 371J in the constitution. The objective was to empower the Governor of Karnataka to take steps to develop the Hyderabad-Karnataka region.

99. The Constitution (*Ninety-Ninth Amendment*) Act, 2014–Inserted new articles-124 A, 124B and 124C after article 124 of the constitution. The Act also provided for the composition and the functions of the proposed National Judicial Appointments Commission.

100. The Constitution (*One Hundredth Amendment*) Act, 2015—amended the First Schedule of the Constitution, for the purpose of giving effect to the acquiring of territories by India and transfer of territories to Bangladesh through retaining of adverse possession and exchange of enclaves, in pursuance of the Agreement between India and Bangladesh concerning the demarcation of the land boundary, signed on 16th May 1974 and its Protocal, signed on 6th September, 2011.

101. The Constitution (*One Hundred and First Amendment*) Act, 2016—The act amends the constitution to introduce "The Goods and Services Tax (GST)". It amended the articles 248, 249, 250, 268, 269, 270, 271, 286, 366 & 368. Amended the Sixth & Seventh Schedules. Omitted article 268A. Inserted new articles 246A (Special provision with respect to goods and services tax), 269A (Levy and collection of goods and services tax in course of inter-State trade or commerce) and 279A (Goods and Services Tax Council). The act also provided for compensation to States for loss of revenue on account of introduction of goods and services tax.

Source : http/indiacode.nic.in

Appendices

GOVERNMENT OF INDIA

Shri Ram Nath Kovind—President

Shri M. Venkaiah Naidu—Vice-President

COUNCIL OF MINISTERS

(As on December 31, 2018)[1]

Shri Narendra Modi	Prime Minister and also in-charge of: Ministry of Personnel, Public Grievances and Pensions; Department of Atomic Energy; Department of Space; and All important policy issues and all other portfolios not allocated to any Minister

CABINET MINISTERS

Shri Raj Nath Singh	Minister of Home Affairs
Smt. Sushma Swaraj	Minister of External Affairs
Shri Arun Jaitley	Minister of Finance; and Minister of Corporate Affairs
Shri Nitin Jairam Gadkari	Minister of Road Transport and Highways; Minister of Shipping; and Minister of Water Resources, River Development and Ganga Rejuvenation
Shri Suresh Prabhu	Minister of Commerce and Industry; and Minister of Civil Aviation
Shri D.V. Sadananda Gowda	Minister of Statistics and Programme Implementation; and Minister of Chemical and Fertilizers
Sushri Uma Bharati	Minister of Drinking Water and Sanitation
Shri Ramvilas Paswan	Minister of Consumer Affairs, Food and Public Distribution
Smt. Maneka Sanjay Gandhi	Minister of Women and Child Development
Shri Ravi Shankar Prasad	Minister of Law and Justice; and Minister of Electronics and Information Technology

1. Source : Cabinet Secretariat website http://cabsec.gov.in

Shri Jagat Prakash Nadda	Minister of Health and Family Welfare
Shri Anant Geete	Minister of Heavy Industries and Public Enterprises
Smt. Harsimrat Kaur Badal	Minister of Food Processing Industries
Shri Narendra Singh Tomar	Minister of Rural Development; Minister of Panchayati Raj; Minister of Mines; and Minister of Parliamentary Affairs
Shri Chaudhary Birender Singh	Minister of Steel
Shri Jual Oram	Minister of Tribal Affairs
Shri Radha Mohan Singh	Minister of Agriculture and Farmers Welfare
Shri Thaawar Chand Gehlot	Minister of Social Justice and Empowerment
Smt. Smriti Zubin Irani	Minister of Textiles
Dr. Harsh Vardhan	Minister of Science and Technology; Minister of Earth Sciences; and Minister of Environment, Forest and Climate Change
Shri Prakash Javadekar	Minister of Human Resource Development
Shri Dharmendra Pradhan	Minister of Petroleum and Natural Gas; and Minister of Skill Development and Entrepreneurship
Shri Piyush Goyal	Minister of Railways; and Minister of Coal
Smt. Nirmala Sitharaman	Minister of Defence
Shri Mukhtar Abbas Naqvi	Minister of Minority Affairs

MINISTERS OF STATE (Independent Charge)

Rao Inderjit Singh	Minister of State (Independent Charge) of the Ministry of Planning; and Minister of State in the Ministry of Chemicals and Fertilizers
Shri Santosh Kumar Gangwar	Minister of State (Independent Charge) of the Ministry of Labour and Employment
Shri Shripad Yesso Naik	Minister of State (Independent Charge) of the Ministry of Ayurveda, Yoga and Naturopathy, Unani, Siddha and Homoeopathy (AYUSH)
Dr. Jitendra Singh	Minister of State (Independent Charge) of the Ministry of Development of North Eastern Region; Minister of State in the Prime Minister's Office; Minister of State in the Ministry of Personnel, Public Grievances and Pensions;

	Minister of State in the Department of Atomic Energy; and Minister of State in the Department of Space
Dr. Mahesh Sharma	Minister of State (Independent Charge) of the Ministry of Culture; and Minister of State in the Ministry of Environment, Forest and Climate Change
Shri Giriraj Singh	Minister of State (Independent Charge) of the Ministry of Micro, Small and Medium Enterprises
Shri Manoj Sinha	Minister of State (Independent Charge) of the Ministry of Communications; and Minister of State in the Ministry of Railways
Col. Rajyavardhan Singh Rathore	Minister of State (Independent Charge) of the Ministry of Youth Affairs and Sports; and Minister of State (Independent Charge) of the Ministry of Information and Broadcasting
Shri Raj Kumar Singh	Minister of State (Independent Charge) of the Ministry of Power; and Minister of State (Independent Charge) of the Ministry of New and Renewable Energy
Shri Hardeep Singh Puri	Minister of State (Independent Charge) of the Ministry of Housing and Urban Affairs
Shri Alphons Kannanthanam	Minister of State (Independent Charge) of the Ministry of Tourism

MINISTERS OF STATE

Shri Vijay Goel	Minister of State in the Ministry of Parliamentary Affairs; and Minister of State in the Ministry of Statistics and Programme Implementation
Shri Radhakrishnan P.	Minister of State in the Ministry of Finance; and Minister of State in the Ministry of Shipping
Shri S. S. Ahluwalia	Minister of State in the Ministry of Electronics and Information Technology
Shri Ramesh Chandappa Jigajinagi	Minister of State in the Ministry of Drinking Water and Sanitation
Shri Ramdas Athawale	Minister of State in the Ministry of Social Justice and Empowerment

Shri Vishnu Deo Sai	Minister of State in the Ministry of Steel
Shri Ram Kripal Yadav	Minister of State in the Ministry of Rural Development
Shri Hansraj Gangaram Ahir	Minister of State in the Ministry of Home Affairs
Shri Haribhai Parthibhai Chaudhary	Minister of State in the Ministry of Mines; and Minister of State in the Ministry of Coal
Shri Rajen Gohain	Minister of State in the Ministry of Railways
General (Retd.) V.K. Singh	Minister of State in the Ministry of External Affairs
Shri Parshottam Rupala	Minister of State in the Ministry of Agriculture and Farmers Welfare; and Minister of State in the Ministry of Panchayati Raj
Shri Krishan Pal	Minister of State in the Ministry of Social Justice and Empowerment
Shri Jaswantsinh Sumanbhai Bhabhor	Minister of State in the Ministry of Tribal Affairs
Shri Shiv Pratap Shukla	Minister of State in the Ministry of Finance
Shri Ashwani Kumar Choubey	Minister of State in the Ministry of Health and Family Welfare
Shri Sudarshan Bhagat	Minister of State in the Ministry of Tribal Affairs
Shri Kiren Rijiju	Minister of State in the Ministry of Home Affairs
Dr. Virender Kumar	Minister of State in the Ministry of Women and Child Development; and Minister of State in the Ministry of Minority Affairs
Shri Anantkumar Hegde	Minister of State in the Ministry of Skill Development and Entrepreneurship
Sadhvi Niranjan Jyoti	Minister of State in the Ministry of Food Processing Industries
Shri Jayant Sinha	Minister of State in the Ministry of Civil Aviation
Shri Babul Supriyo	Minister of State in the Ministry of Heavy Industries and Public Enterprises
Shri Vijay Sampla	Minister of State in the Ministry of Social Justice and Empowerment

Shri Arjun Ram Meghwal	Minister of State in the Ministry of Parliamentary Affairs; and Minister of State in the Ministry of Water Resources, River Development and Ganga Rejuvenation
Shri Ajay Tamta	Minister of State in the Ministry of Textiles
Smt. Krishna Raj	Minister of State in the Ministry of Agriculture and Farmers Welfare
Shri Mansukh L. Mandaviya	Minister of State in the Ministry of Road Transport and Highways; Minister of State in the Ministry of Shipping; and Minister of State in the Ministry of Chemicals and Fertilizers
Smt. Anupriya Patel	Minister of State in the Ministry of Health and Family Welfare
Shri C. R. Chaudhary	Minister of State in the Ministry of Consumer Affairs, Food and Public Distribution; and Minister of State in the Ministry of Commerce and Industry
Shri P. P. Chaudhary	Minister of State in the Ministry of Law and Justice; and Minister of State in the Ministry of Corporate Affairs
Dr. Subhash Ramrao Bhamre	Minister of State in the Ministry of Defence
Shri Gajendra Singh Shekhawat	Minister of State in the Ministry of Agriculture and Farmers Welfare
Dr. Satya Pal Singh	Minister of State in the Ministry of Human Resource Development; and Minister of State in the Ministry of Water Resources, River Development and Ganga Rejuvenation

MEMBERS OF PARLIAMENT

RAJYA SABHA (Statewise List as on December 31, 2018)

Chairman — **Shri M Venkaiah Naidu**
Deputy Chairman — **Harivansh Naryan Singh**

Name	Party/Group
STATES	
ANDHRA PRADESH (11)	
1. Reddy, Dr. T. Subbarami	INC
2. Rao, Dr. K. Keshava	TRS
3. Khan, Shri Mohd. Ali	INC
4. Chowdary, Shri Y. S.	TDP
5. Ramesh, Shri C.M.	TDP
6. Seetharama Lakshmi, Smt. Thota	TDP
7. Prabhu, Shri Suresh	BJP
8. Venkatesh, Shri T.G.	TDP
9. Reddy, Shri V. Vijayasai	YSRCP
10. Vemireddy, Shri Prabhakar Reddy	YSRCP
11. Kanakamedala Ravindra Kumar, Shri	TDP
ARUNACHAL PRADESH (1)	
12. Mukut Mithi, Shri	INC
ASSAM (7)	
13. Daimary, Shri Biswajit	BPF
14. Kalita, Shri Bhubaneswar	INC
15. Sinh, Dr. Sanjay	INC
16. Singh, Dr. Manmohan	INC
17. Narah, Smt. Ranee	INC
18. Bora, Shri Ripun	INC
19. Kujur, Shri Santiuse	INC
BIHAR (16)	
20. Sinha, Shri R. K.	BJP
21. Thakur, Shri Ram Nath	JD (U)
22. Harivansh, Shri	JD (U)

website http://rajyasabha.nic.in

23.	Perween, Smt. Kahkashan	JD (U)
24.	Jethmalani, Shri Ram	RJD
25.	Mahendra Prasad, Dr.	JD (U)
26.	Prasad, Shri Ravi Shankar	BJP
27.	Singh, Shri Bashistha Narain	JD (U)
28.	Singh, Shri Ram Chandra Prasad	JD (U)
29.	Thakur, Dr. C.P.	BJP
30.	Singh, Shri Akhilesh Prasad	INC
31.	Karim, Shri Ahmad Ashfaque	RJD
32.	Jha, Prof. Manoj Kumar	RJD
33.	Singh, Shri Gopal Narayan	BJP
34.	Bharti, Smt. Misha	RJD
35.	Vacant	

CHHATTISGARH (5)

36.	Verma, Smt. Chhaya	INC
37.	Netam, Shri Ram Vichar	BJP
38.	Pandey, Ms. Saroj	BJP
39.	Vora, Shri Motilal	INC
40.	Judev, Shri Ranvijay Singh	BJP

GOA (1)

41.	Tendulkar, Shri Vinay Dinu	BJP

GUJARAT (11)

42.	Yajnik, Dr. Amee	INC
43.	Rathwa, Shri Naranbhai J.	INC
44.	Shah, Shri Amit Anil Chandra	BJP
45.	Gohel, Shri Chunibhai Kanjibhai	BJP
46.	Tundiya, Mahant Shambhuprasadji	BJP
47.	Vadodia, Shri Lal Sinh	BJP
48.	Mistry, Shri Madhusudan	INC
49.	Mandaviya, Shri Mansukh	BJP
50.	Patel, Shri Ahmed	INC
51.	Rupala, Shri Parshottam	BJP
52.	Irani, Smt. Smriti Zubin	BJP

HARYANA (5)

53.	Selja, Kumari	INC

54.	Kashyap, Shri Ram Kumar	INLD
55.	Singh, Chaudhary Birender	BJP
56.	Vats, Dr. D. P.	BJP
57.	Subhash Chandra, Dr.	IND

HIMACHAL PRADESH (3)

58.	Thakur, Smt. Viplove	INC
59.	Anand Sharma, Shri	INC
60.	Nadda, Shri Jagat Prakash	BJP

JAMMU AND KASHMIR (4)

61.	Azad, Shri Ghulam Nabi	INC
62.	Manhas, Shri Shamsher Singh	BJP
63.	Fayaz, Mir Mohammad	J&K PDP
64.	Laway, Shri Nazir Ahmed	J&K PDP

JHARKHAND (6)

65.	Gupta, Shri Prem Chand	RJD
66.	Naqvi, Shri Mukhtar Abbas	BJP
67.	Sahu, Shri Dhiraj Prasad	INC
68.	Nathwani, Shri Parimal	IND
69.	Poddar, Shri Mahesh	BJP
70.	Oraon, Shri Samir	BJP

KARNATAKA (12)

71.	Ramamurthy, Shri K. C.	INC
72.	Chandrashekhar, Shri G.C.	INC
73.	Hanumanthaiah, Dr. L.	INC
74.	Hussain, Shri Syed Nasir	INC
75.	Chandrasekhar, Shri Rajeev	BJP
76.	Ramesh, Shri Jairam	INC
77.	Hariprasad, Shri B.K.	INC
78.	Kore, Dr. Prabhakar	BJP
79.	Fernandes, Shri Oscar	INC
80.	Nirmala Sitharaman, Smt.	BJP
81.	Reddy, Shri D. Kupendra	JD (S)
82.	Gowda, Prof. M.V. Rajeev	INC

KERALA (9)

83.	Ragesh, Shri K.K.	CPI (M)

84. Veerendra Kumar, Shri M.P.	IND
85. Somaprasad, Shri K.	CPI (M)
86. Antony, Shri A.K.	INC
87. Ravi, Shri Vayalar	INC
88. Abdul Wahab, Shri	IUML
89. Viswam, Shri Binoy	CPI
90. Kareem, Shri Elamaram	CPI (M)
91. Mani, Shri Jose K.	KC (M)

MADHYA PRADESH (11)

92. Uikey, Smt. Sampatiya	BJP
93. Singh, Shri Ajay Pratap	BJP
94. Soni, Shri Kailash	BJP
95. Patel, Shri Rajmani	INC
96. Tankha, Shri Vivek K.	INC
97. Jha, Shri Prabhat	BJP
98. Akbar, Shri M.J.	BJP
99. Gehlot, Shri Thaawarchand	BJP
100. Pradhan, Shri Dharmendra	BJP
101. Jatiya, Dr. Satyanarayan	BJP
102. Singh, Shri Digvijaya	INC

MAHARASHTRA (19)

103. Chavan, Smt. Vandana	NCP
104. Desai, Shri Anil	SS
105. Athawale, Shri Ramdas	RPI(A)
106. Kakade, Shri Sanjay Dattatraya	IND
107. Memon, Shri Majeed	NCP
108. Pawar, Shri Sharad	NCP
109. Sable, Shri Amar Shankar	BJP
110. Dhoot, Shri Rajkumar	SS
111. Javadekar, Shri Prakash	BJP
112. Goyal, Shri Piyush	BJP
113. Dalwai, Shri Husain	INC
114. Patel, Shri Praful	NCP
115. Raut, Shri Sanjay	SS

116. Ketkar, Shri Kumar	INC
117. Rane, Shri Narayan	BJP
118. Muraleedharan, Shri V.	BJP
119. Chidambaram, Shri P.	INC
120. Mahatme, Dr. Vikas	BJP
121. Sahasrabuddhe, Dr. Vinay P.	BJP

MANIPUR (1)

122. Singh, Shri K. Bhabananda	BJP

MEGHALAYA (1)

123. Syiem, Smt. Wansuk	INC

MIZORAM (1)

124. Tlau, Shri Ronald Sapa	INC

NAGALAND (1)

125. Kenye, Shri K. G.	NPF

NATIONAL CAPITAL TERRITORY OF DELHI (3)

126. Singh, Shri Sanjay	AAP
127. Gupta, Shri Sushil Kumar	AAP
128. Gupta, Shri Narain Dass	AAP

ODISHA (10)

129. Samanta, Shri Achyutananda	BJD
130. Nanda, Shri Prashanta	BJD
131. Patnaik, Shri Soumya R.	BJD
132. Nekkanti, Shri Bhaskar Rao	BJD
133. Acharya, Shri Prasanna	BJD
134. Swain, Shri Narendra Kumar	BJD
135. Deb, Shri Pratap Keshari	BJD
136. Mohanty, Shri Anubhav	BJD
137. Hembram, Smt. Sarojini	BJD
138. Biswal, Shri Ranjib	INC

PUDUCHERRY (1)

139.	Gokulakrishnan, Shri N.	AIADMK

PUNJAB (7)

140.	Bajwa, Shri Pratap Singh	INC
141.	Malik, Shri Shwait	BJP
142.	Dullo, Shri Shamsher Singh	INC
143.	Bhunder, Sardar Balwinder Singh	SAD
144.	Dhindsa, Sardar Sukhdev Singh	SAD
145.	Soni, Smt. Ambika	INC
146.	Gujral, Shri Naresh	SAD

RAJASTHAN (10)

147.	Yadav, Shri Bhupender	BJP
148.	Goel, Shri Vijay	BJP
149.	Dudi, Shri Ram Narain	BJP
150.	Panchariya, Shri Narayan Lal	BJP
151.	Mathur, Shri Om Prakash	BJP
152.	Alphons, Shri K. J.	BJP
153.	Verma, Shri Ramkumar	BJP
154.	Dungarpur, Shri Harshvardhan Singh	BJP
155.	Meena, Dr. Kirodi Lal	BJP
156.	Saini, Shri Madanlal	BJP

SIKKIM (1)

157.	Lachungpa, Shri Hishey	SDF

TAMIL NADU (18)

158.	Vaithilingam, Shri R.	AIADMK
159.	Vijayakumar, Shri A.	AIADMK
160.	Balasubramoniyan, Shri S.R.	AIADMK
161.	Elangovan, Shri T.K.S.	DMK
162.	Bharathi, Shri R.S.	DMK
163.	Arjunan, Shri K. R.	AIADMK
164.	Lakshmanan, Dr. R.	AIADMK

165.	Rathinavel, Shri T.	AIADMK
166.	Navaneethakrishnan, Shri A.	AIADMK
167.	Selvaraj, Shri A. K.	AIADMK
168.	Ramaswamy, Dr. Sasikala Pushpa	AIADMK
169.	Vijila Sathyananth, Smt.	AIADMK
170.	Muthukaruppan, Shri S.	AIADMK
171.	Rangarajan, Shri T.K.	CPI(M)
172.	Kanimozhi, Smt.	DMK
173.	Raja, Shri D.	CPI
174.	Siva, Shri Tiruchi	DMK
175.	Maitreyan, Dr. V.	AIADMK

TELANGANA (7)

176.	Rao, Dr. K.V.P. Ramachandra	INC
177.	Rao, Shri Garikapati Mohan	TDP
178.	Rao, Shri V. Lakshmikantha	TRS
179.	Srinivas, Shri Dharmapuri	TRS
180.	Banda Prakash, Dr.	TRS
181.	Yadav, Shri B. Lingaiah	TRS
182.	Joginipally Santosh Kumar, Shri	TRS

TRIPURA (1)

183.	Baidya, Smt. Jharna Das	CPI(M)

UTTAR PRADESH (31)

184.	Rajaram, Shri	BSP
185.	Bachchan, Smt. Jaya	SP
186.	Misra, Shri Satish Chandra	BSP
187.	Singh, Shri Veer	BSP
188.	Yadav, Prof. Ram Gopal	SP
189.	Jaitley, Shri Arun	BJP
190.	Singh, Shri Amar	IND
191.	Sibal, Shri Kapil	INC
192.	Nishad, Shri Vishambhar Prasad	SP

193.	Yadav, Dr. Chandrapal Singh	SP
194.	Khan, Shri Javed Ali	SP
195.	Tazeen Fatma, Dr.	SP
196.	Shekhar, Shri Neeraj	SP
197.	Punia, Shri P.L.	INC
198.	Verma, Shri Ravi Prakash	SP
199.	Ashok Siddharth, Shri	BSP
200.	Verma, Shri Beni Prasad	SP
201.	Singh, Shri Rewati Raman	SP
202.	Shukla, Shri Shiv Pratap	BJP
203.	Seth, Shri Sanjay	SP
204.	Yadav, Ch. Sukhram Singh	SP
205.	Nagar, Shri Surendra Singh	SP
206.	Agrawal, Dr. Anil	BJP
207.	Jain, Dr. Anil	BJP
208.	Bajpai, Dr. Ashok	BJP
209.	Kardam, Smt. Kanta	BJP
210.	Rao, Shri G.V.L. Narasimha	BJP
211.	Tomar, Shri Vijay Pal Singh	BJP
212.	Rajbhar, Shri Sakaldeep	BJP
213.	Yadav, Shri Harnath Singh	BJP
214.	Puri, Shri Hardeep Singh	BJP

UTTARAKHAND (3)

215.	Baluni, Shri Anil	BJP
216.	Tamta, Shri Pradeep	INC
217.	Babbar, Shri Raj	INC

WEST BENGAL (16)

218.	Singh, Dr. Kanwar Deep	AITC
219.	Haque, Shri Md. Nadimul	AITC
220.	O Brien, Shri Derek	AITC
221.	Bhattacharya, Shri P.	INC
222.	Ray, Shri Sukhendu Sekhar	AITC
223.	Singhvi, Dr. Abhishek Manu	INC

224.	Sen, Ms. Dola	AITC
225.	Chowdhury, Prof. Jogen	AITC
226.	Hassan, Shri Ahamed	AITC
227.	Banerjee, Shri Ritabrata	IND
228.	Gupta, Shri Manish	AITC
229.	Chakraborty, Shri Subhasish	AITC
230.	Biswas, Shri Abir Ranjan	AITC
231.	Sen Dr. Santanu	AITC
232.	Chhetri, Smt. Shanta	AITC
233.	Bhunia, Shri Manas Ranjan	AITC

NOMINATED (12)

234.	Chhatrapati, Shri Sambhaji	BJP
235.	Dasgupta, Shri Swapan	NOM
236.	Ganguly, Smt. Roopa	BJP
237.	Jadhav, Dr. Narendra	NOM
238.	Kom, Smt. M.C. Mary	NOM
239.	Mansingh, Dr. Sonal	BJP
240.	Mohapatra, Dr. Raghunath	BJP
241.	Ram Shakal, Shri	BJP
242.	Sinha, Shri Rakesh	BJP
243.	Suresh Gopi, Shri	BJP
244.	Swamy, Dr. Subramanian	BJP
245.	Tulsi, Shri K.T.S.	NOM

LOK SABHA (Statewise List as on December 31, 2018)

Speaker : Smt. Sumitra Mahajan

Deputy Speaker : Dr. M. Thambidurai

S. No.	State/Constituency	Name of the Member	Party/ Group
ANDHRA PRADESH (25)			
1.	Amalapuram (SC)	Pandula, Dr. Ravindra Babu	TDP
2.	Anakapalle	Rao (Avanthi), Shri Muthamsetti Srinivasa	TDP
3.	Anantapur	Reddy, Shri J.C. Divakar	TDP

website http://loksabha.nic.in

4.	Araku (ST)	Kothapalli, Smt. Geetha	YSR (CP)
5.	Bapatla (SC)	Malyadri, Shri Sriram	TDP
6.	Chittoor (SC)	Sivaprasad, Dr. Naramalli	TDP
7.	Eluru	Magantti, Shri Venkateswara Rao (Babu)	TDP
8.	Guntur	Galla, Shri Jayadev	TDP
9.	Hindupur	Nimmala, Shri Kristappa	TDP
10.	Kakinada	Thota, Shri Narasimham	TDP
11.	Kurnool	Butta, Smt. Renuka	YSR (CP)
12.	Machilipatnam	Rao, Shri Konakalla Narayana	TDP
13.	Nandyal	Reddy, Shri S.P.Y.	YSR (CP)
14.	Narasaraopet	Rao, Shri Rayapati Sambasiva	TDP
15.	Narsapuram	Raju, Shri Gokaraju Ganga	BJP
16.	Rajahmundry	Maganti, Shri Murali Mohan	TDP
17.	Srikakulam	Ram Mohan Naidu, Shri Kinjarapu	TDP
18.	Vijayawada	Kesineni, Shri Srinivas	TDP
19.	Visakhapatnam	Kambhampati, Dr. Hari Babu	BJP
20.	Vizianagaram	Pusapati, Shri Ashok Gajapathi Raju	TDP
21.	Kadapa	Vacant	
22.	Nellore	Vacant	
23.	Ongole	Vacant	
24.	Rajampet	Vacant	
25.	Tirupati	Vacant	

ARUNACHAL PRADESH (2)

26.	Arunachal East	Ering, Shri Ninong	INC
27.	Arunachal West	Rijiju, Shri Kiren	BJP

ASSAM (14)

28.	Autonomous District (ST)	Engti, Shri Biren Singh	INC
29.	Barpeta	Ajmal, Shri Sirajuddin	AIUDF
30.	Dhubri	Ajmal, Maulana Badruddin	AIUDF
31.	Dibrugarh	Teli, Shri Rameswar	BJP
32.	Gauhati	Chakravarty, Smt. Bijoya	BJP
33.	Jorhat	Tasa, Shri Kamakhya Prasad	BJP
34.	Kaliabor	Gogoi, Shri Gaurav	INC
35.	Karimganj (SC)	Biswas, Shri Radheshyam	AIUDF
36.	Kokrajhar (ST)	Sarania, Shri Naba (Hira) Kumar	IND
37.	Lakhimpur	Baruah, Shri Pradan	BJP

38. Mangaldoi	Deka, Shri Ramen	BJP
39. Nawgong	Gohain, Shri Rajen	BJP
40. Silchar	Dev, Km. Sushmita	INC
41. Tezpur	Sarmah, Shri Ram Prasad	BJP

BIHAR (40)

42. Araria	Alam, Shri Sarfaraz	RJD
43. Arrah	Singh, Shri Raj Kumar	BJP
44. Aurangabad	Singh, Shri Sushil Kumar	BJP
45. Banka	Yadav, Shri Jay Prakash Narayan	RJD
46. Bhagalpur	Kumar, Shri Shailesh (Bulo Mandal)	RJD
47. Buxar	Choubey, Shri Ashwini Kumar	BJP
48. Darbhanga	Azad, Shri Kirti (JHA)	BJP
49. Gaya (SC)	Manjhi, Shri Hari	BJP
50. Gopalganj (SC)	Ram, Shri Janak	BJP
51. Hajipur (SC)	Paswan, Shri Ram Vilas	LJSP
52. Jahanabad	Kumar, Dr. Arun	RLSP
53. Jamui (SC)	Paswan, Shri Chirag	LJSP
54. Jhanjharpur	Chaudhary, Shri Birendra Kumar	BJP
55. Karakat	Kushwaha, Shri Upendra	RLSP
56. Katihar	Anwar, Shri Tariq	NCP
57. Khagaria	Kaiser, Choudhary Mehboob Ali	LJSP
58. Kishanganj	Mohammad, Shri Asrarul Haque	INC
59. Madhepura	Ranjan (Pappu Yadav), Shri Rajesh	RJD
60. Madhubani	Yadav, Shri Hukmdev Narayan	BJP
61. Maharajganj	Sigriwal, Shri Janardan Singh	BJP
62. Munger	Devi, Smt. Veena	LJSP
63. Muzaffarpur	Nishad, Shri Ajay	BJP
64. Nalanda	Kumar, Shri Kaushalendra	JD (U)
65. Nawada	Singh, Shri Giriraj	BJP
66. Paschim Champaran	Jaiswal, Dr. Sanjay	BJP
67. Pataliputra	Yadav, Shri Ram Kripal	BJP
68. Patna Sahib	Sinha, Shri Shatrughan Prasad	BJP
69. Purnia	Kumar, Shri Santosh	JD (U)
70. Purvi Champaran	Singh, Shri Radha Mohan	BJP
71. Samastipur (SC)	Paswan, Shri Ramchandra	LJSP

72. Saran	Rudy, Shri Rajiv Pratap	BJP
73. Sasaram (SC)	Paswan, Shri Chhedi	BJP
74. Sheohar	Devi, Smt. Rama	BJP
75. Sitamarhi	Sharma, Shri Ram Kumar	RLSP
76. Siwan	Yadav, Shri Om Prakash	BJP
77. Supaul	Ranjan, Smt. Ranjeet	INC
78. Ujiarpur	Rai, Shri Nityanand	BJP
79. Vaishali	Singh, Shri Rama Kishore	LJSP
80. Valmiki Nagar	Dubey, Shri Satish Chandra	BJP
81. Begusarai	Vacant	

CHHATTISGARH (11)

82. Bastar (ST)	Kashyap, Shri Dinesh	BJP
83. Bilaspur	Sahu, Shri Lakhan Lal	BJP
84. Durg	Sahu, Shri Tamradhwaj	INC
85. Janjgir-Champa (SC)	Patle, Smt. Kamla Devi	BJP
86. Kanker(ST)	Usendi, Shri Vikram	BJP
87. Korba	Mahto, Dr. Banshilal	BJP
88. Mahasamund	Sahu, Shri Chandu Lal	BJP
89. Raigarh (ST)	Sai, Shri Vishnu Deo	BJP
90. Raipur	Bais, Shri Ramesh	BJP
91. Rajnandgaon	Singh, Shri Abhishek	BJP
92. Surguja (ST)	Marabi, Shri Kamalbhan Singh	BJP

GOA (2)

93. North Goa	Naik, Shri Shripad Yesso	BJP
94. South Goa	Sawaikar, Advocate Shri Narendra Keshav	BJP

GUJARAT (26)

95. Ahmedabad East	Rawal, Shri Paresh	BJP
96. Ahmedabad West	Solanki, Dr. (Prof.) Kirit Premjibhai	BJP
97. Amreli	Kachhadiya, Shri Naranbhai Bhikhabhai	BJP
98. Anand	Patel, Shri Dilip M.	BJP
99. Banaskantha	Chaudhary, Shri Haribhai Parthibhai	BJP
100. Bardoli	Vasava, Shri Parbhubhai Nagarbhai	BJP
101. Bharuch	Vasava, Shri Mansukhbhai Dhanjibhai	BJP
102. Bhavnagar	Shyal, Dr. Bharati Dhirubhai	BJP
103. Chhota Udaipur	Rathwa, Shri Ramsinh Patalayabhai	BJP
104. Dahod	Bhabhor, Shri Jaswantsinh Sumanbhai	BJP

105. Gandhinagar	Advani, Shri Lal Krishna	BJP
106. Jamnagar	Maadam, Smt. Poonamben Hematbhai	BJP
107. Junagadh	Chudasama, Shri Rajeshbhai Naranbhai	BJP
108. Kachchh (SC)	Chavda, Shri Vinod	BJP
109. Kheda	Chauhan, Shri Devusinh Jesingbhai	BJP
110. Mehsana	Patel, Smt. Jayshreeben	BJP
111. Navsari	Patil, Shri C. R.	BJP
112. Panchmahal	Chauhan, Shri Prabhatsinh Pratapsinh	BJP
113. Patan	Vaghela, Shri Liladharbhai Khodaji	BJP
114. Porbandar	Radadiya, Shri Vitthalbhai Hansrajbhai	BJP
115. Rajkot	Kundariya, Shri Mohanbhai Kalyanji	BJP
116. Sabarkantha	Rathod, Shri Dipsinh Shankarsinh	BJP
117. Surat	Jardosh, Smt. Darshana Vikram	BJP
118. Surendranagar	Fatepara, Shri Devajibhai Govindbhai	BJP
119. Vadodara	Bhatt, Smt. Ranjanben Dhananjay	BJP
120. Valsad(ST)	Patel, Dr. K. C.	BJP

HARYANA (10)

121. Ambala (SC)	Kataria, Shri Rattan Lal	BJP
122. Bhiwani-Mahendragarh	Dharambir Singh, Shri	BJP
123. Faridabad	Gurjar, Shri Krishan Pal	BJP
124. Gurgaon	Rao, Inderjit Singh	BJP
125. Hisar	Chautala, Shri Dushyant	INLD
126. Karnal	Ashwini Kumar, Shri	BJP
127. Kurukshetra	Saini, Shri Raj Kumar	BJP
128. Rohtak	Hooda, Shri Deepender Singh	INC
129. Sirsa (SC)	Rori, Shri Charanjeet Singh	INLD
130. Sonipat	Kaushik, Shri Ramesh Chander	BJP

HIMACHAL PRADESH (4)

131. Hamirpur	Thakur, Shri Anurag Singh	BJP
132. Kangra	Kumar, Shri Shanta	BJP
133. Mandi	Sharma, Shri Ram Swaroop	BJP
134. Shimla (SC)	Kashyap, Shri Virender	BJP

JAMMU AND KASHMIR (6)

135. Baramulla	Baig, Shri Muzaffar Hussain	J&K PDP
136. Jammu	Sharma, Shri Jugal Kishore	BJP
137. Ladakh	Chhewang, Shri Thupstan	BJP

138. Srinagar	Abdullah, Dr. Farooq	J&K NC
139. Udhampur	Singh, Dr. Jitendra	BJP
140. Anantnag	Vacant	

JHARKHAND (14)

141. Chatra	Singh, Shri Sunil Kumar	BJP
142. Dhanbad	Singh, Shri Pashupati Nath	BJP
143. Dumka (ST)	Soren, Shri Shibu	JMM
144. Giridih	Pandey, Shri Ravindra Kumar	BJP
145. Godda	Dubey, Shri Nishikant	BJP
146. Hazaribagh	Sinha, Shri Jayant	BJP
147. Jamshedpur	Mahato, Shri Bidyut Baran	BJP
148. Khunti (ST)	Munda, Shri Kariya	BJP
149. Kodarma	Ray, Dr. Ravindra Kumar	BJP
150. Lohardaga (ST)	Bhagat, Shri Sudarshan	BJP
151. Palamu (SC)	Ram, Shri Vishnu Dayal	BJP
152. Rajmahal (ST)	Hansdak, Shri Vijay Kumar	JMM
153. Ranchi	Choudhary, Shri Ram Tahal	BJP
154. Singhbhum (ST)	Giluwa, Shri Laxman	BJP

KARNATAKA (28)

155. Gaddigoudar, Shri Parvatagouda Chandanagouda		BJP
156. Bangalore Central	Mohan, Shri P. C.	BJP
157. Bangalore North	Gowda, Shri D.V. Sadananda	BJP
158. Bangalore Rural	Suresh, Shri Doddaalahalli Kempegowda	INC
159. Belgaum	Angadi, Shri Suresh Chanabasappa	BJP
160. Bidar	Khuba, Shri Bhagwanth	BJP
161. Bijapur (SC)	Jigajinagi, Shri Ramesh Chandappa	BJP
162. Chamrajanagar	Dhruvanarayana, Shri R.	INC
163. Chikkballapur	Moily, Dr. M. Veerappa	INC
164. Chikkodi	Hukkeri, Shri Prakash Babanna	INC
165. Chitradurga (SC)	Chandrappa, Shri B.N.	INC
166. Dakshina Kannada	Kateel, Shri Nalin Kumar	BJP
167. Davanagere	Siddeshwara, Shri Gowdar Mallikarjunappa	BJP
168. Dharwad	Joshi, Shri Pralhad Venkatesh	BJP
169. Gulbarga (SC)	Kharge, Shri Mallikarjun	INC
170. Hassan	Devegowda, Shri H.D.	JD(S)
171. Haveri	Udasi, Shri Shivkumar Chanabasappa	BJP

172. Kolar	Muniyappa, Dr. K.H.	INC
173. Koppal	Karadi, Shri Sanganna Amarappa	BJP
174. Mysore	Simha, Shri Prathap	BJP
175. Raichur	Naik,Shri B.V.	INC
176. Tumkur	Muddahanumegowda, Shri S.P.	INC
177. Udupi Chikmagalur	Karandlaje, Km. Shobha	BJP
178. Uttara Kannada	Hegde, Shri Anantkumar	BJP
179. Bellary (ST)	Vacant	
180. Mandya	Vacant	
181. Shimoga	Vacant	
182. Bangalore South	Vacant	

KERALA (20)

183. Alappuzha	Venugopal, Shri K. C.	INC
184. Alathur	Biju, Dr. Parayamparambil Kuttappan	CPI(M)
185. Attingal	Sampath, Dr. Anirudhan	CPI(M)
186. Chalakudy	Innocent, Shri	IND
187. Ernakulam	Thomas, Prof. Kuruppassery Varkey	INC
188. Idukki	George, Shri (Adv.) Joice	IND
189. Kannur	Teacher, Smt. P.K. Sreemathi	CPI(M)
190. Kasaragod	Karunakaran, Shri P.	CPI(M)
191. Kollam	Premachandran, Shri N.K.	RSP
192. Kozhikode	Raghavan, Shri M. K.	INC
193. Malappuram	P.K. , Shri Kunhalikutty	IUML
194. Mavelikkara	Kodikunnil, Shri Suresh	INC
195. Palakkad	Rajesh, Shri M. B.	CPI(M)
196. Pathanamthitta	Antony, Shri Anto	INC
197. Ponnani	Basheer, Shri E. T. Mohammed	IUML
198. Thiruvananthapuram	Tharoor, Dr. Shashi	INC
199. Thrissur	Jayadevan, Shri C. N.	CPI
200. Vadakara	Mullappally, Shri Ramachandran	INC
201. Wayanad	Shanavas, Shri M. I.	INC
202. Kottayam	Vacant	

MADHYA PRADESH (29)

203. Balaghat	Bhagat, Shri Bodhsingh	BJP
204. Betul (ST)	Dhurve, Smt. Jyoti	BJP
205. Bhind (SC)	Prasad, Dr. Bhagirath	BJP
206. Bhopal	Sanjar, Shri Alok	BJP
207. Chhindwara	Kamal Nath, Shri	INC

208. Damoh	Patel, Shri Prahlad Singh	BJP
209. Dewas	Utawal, Shri Manohar	BJP
210. Dhar (ST)	Thakur, Smt. Savitri	BJP
211. Guna	Scindia, Shri Jyotiraditya Madhavrao	INC
212. Gwalior	Tomar, Shri Narendra Singh	BJP
213. Hoshangabad	Singh, Shri Uday Pratap	BJP
214. Indore	Mahajan (Tai), Sumitra	BJP
215. Jabalpur	Singh, Shri Rakesh	BJP
216. Khajuraho	Singh, Shri Nagendra	BJP
217. Khandwa	Chauhan, Shri Nand Kumar Singh	BJP
218. Khargone (ST)	Patel, Shri Subhash	BJP
219. Mandla (ST)	Kulaste, Shri Faggan Singh	BJP
220. Mandsour	Gupta, Shri Sudheer	BJP
221. Morena	Mishra, Shri Anoop	BJP
222. Rajgarh	Nagar, Shri Rodmal	BJP
223. Ratlam (ST)	Bhuria, Shri Kantilal	INC
224. Rewa	Mishra, Shri Janardan	BJP
225. Sagar	Yadav, Shri Laxmi Narayan	BJP
226. Satna	Singh, Shri Ganesh	BJP
227. Shahdol (ST)	Singh, Shri Gyan	BJP
228. Sidhi	Pathak, Smt. Riti	BJP
229. Tikamgarh (SC)	Kumar, Dr. Virendra	BJP
230. Ujjain (SC)	Malviya, Prof. Chintamani	BJP
231. Vidisha	Swaraj, Smt. Sushma	BJP

MAHARASHTRA (48)

232. Ahmednagar	Gandhi, Shri Dilip Kumar Mansukhlal	BJP
233. Akola	Dhotre, Shri Sanjay Shamrao	BJP
234. Amravati	Adsul, Shri Anandrao	SS
235. Aurangabad	Khaire, Shri Chandrakant Bhaurao	SS
236. Baramati	Sule, Smt. Supriya Sadanand	NCP
237. Beed	Munde, Dr. Pritam Gopinath	BJP
238. Bhandara-Gondiya	Kukde, Shri Madhukarrao Yashwantrao	NCP
239. Bhiwandi	Patil, Shri Kapil Moreshwar	BJP
240. Buldhana	Jadhav, Shri Prataprao	SS
241. Chandrapur	Ahir, Shri Hansraj Gangaram	BJP
242. Dhule	Bhamre, Dr. Subhash Ramrao	BJP
243. Dindori (ST)	Chavan, Shri Harishchandra Deoram	BJP

244. Gadchiroli-Chimur (ST)	Nete, Shri Ashok Mahadeorao	BJP
245. Hatkanangle	Shetti, Shri Raju alias Devappa Anna	SWP
246. Hingoli	Satav, Shri Rajeev Shankarrao	INC
247. Jalgaon	Patil, Shri A.T. (Nana)	BJP
248. Jalna	Danve, Shri Raosaheb Patil	BJP
249. Kalyan	Shinde, Dr. Shrikant Eknath	SS
250. Kolhapur	Mahadik, Shri Dhananjay Bhimrao	NCP
251. Latur (SC)	Gaikwad, Dr. Sunil Baliram	BJP
252. Madha	Patil, Shri Vijaysinh Mohite	NCP
253. Maval	Barne, Shri Shrirang Appa	SS
254. Mumbai-South-Central	Shewale, Shri Rahul Ramesh	SS
255. Mumbai-North	Shetty, Shri Gopal Chinayya	BJP
256. Mumbai-North-Central	Mahajan, Smt. Poonam	BJP
257. Mumbai-North-East	Somaiya, Dr. Kirit	BJP
258. Mumbai-North-West	Kirtikar, Shri Gajanan Chandrakant	SS
259. Mumbai-South	Sawant, Shri Arvind Ganpat	SS
260. Nagpur	Gadkari, Shri Nitin Jairam	BJP
261. Nanded	Chavan, Shri Ashok Shankarrao	INC
262. Nandurbar (ST)	Gavit, Dr. Heena Vijaykumar	BJP
263. Nashik	Godse, Shri Hemant Tukaram	SS
264. Osmanabad	Gaikwad, Prof. Ravindra Vishwanath	SS
265. Palghar	Gavit, Shri Rajendra Dhedya	BJP
266. Parbhani	Jadhav, Shri Sanjay Haribhau	SS
267. Pune	Anil (alias Padmakar) Gulabrao, Shirole, Shri	BJP
268. Raigad	Geete, Shri Anant Gangaram	SS
269. Ramtek (SC)	Tumane, Shri Krupal Balaji	SS
270. Ratnagiri-Sindhudurg	Raut, Shri Vinayak Bhaurao	SS
271. Raver	Khadse, Smt. Raksha Nikhil	BJP
272. Sangli	Patil, Shri Sanjay (Kaka) Ramchandra	BJP
273. Satara	Bhonsle, Shri Udayanraje Pratapsingh	NCP
274. Shirdi (SC)	Lokhande, Shri Sadashiv Kisan	SS
275. Shirur	Adhalrao Patil, Shri Shivaji	SS
276. Solapur (SC)	Bansode, Shri Sharadkumar Maruti	BJP
277. Thane	Vichare, Shri Rajan Baburao	SS
278. Wardha	Tadas, Shri Ramdas Chandrabhanji	BJP
279. Yavatmal-Washim	Bhawana Gawali (Patil), Ms.	SS

MANIPUR (2)

280. Inner Manipur	Meinya, Dr. Thokchom	INC
281. Outer Manipur (ST)	Baite, Shri Thangso	INC

MEGHALAYA (2)

282. Shillong (ST)	Pala, Shri Vincent H	INC
283. Tura	Vacant	

MIZORAM (1)

284. Mizoram (ST)	Ruala, Shri C. L.	INC

NAGALAND (1)

285. Nagaland	Tokheho, Shri	NDPP

ODISHA (21)

286. Aska	Swain, Shri Ladu Kishore	BJD
287. Balasore	Jena, Shri Rabindra Kumar	BJD
288. Bargarh	Singh, Dr. Prabhas Kumar	BJD
289. Berhampur	Mohapatra, Shri Sidhant	BJD
290. Bhadrak (SC)	Sethi, Shri Arjun Charan	BJD
291. Bhubaneswar	Patasani, Dr. (Prof.) Prasanna Kumar	BJD
292. Bolangir	Singh Deo, Shri Kalikesh Narayan	BJD
293. Cuttack	Mahtab, Shri Bhartruhari	BJD
294. Dhenkanal	Satpathy, Shri Tathagata	BJD
295. Jagatsinghpur (SC)	Samal, Dr. Kulamani	BJD
296. Jajpur (SC)	Tarai, Smt. Rita	BJD
297. Kalahandi	Deo, Shri Arka Keshari	BJD
298. Kandhamal	Singh, Smt. Pratyusha Rajeshwari	BJD
299. Keonjhar (ST)	Laguri, Smt. Sakuntala	BJD
300. Koraput (ST)	Hikaka, Shri Jhina	BJD
301. Mayurbhanj (ST)	Hansdah, Shri Rama Chandra	BJD
302. Nabarangpur (ST)	Majhi, Shri Balabhadra	BJD
303. Puri	Misra, Shri Pinaki	BJD
304. Sambalpur	Pradhan, Shri Nagendra Kumar	BJD
305. Sundargarh (ST)	Oram, Shri Jual	BJP
306. Kendrapara	Vacant	

PUNJAB (13)

307. Amritsar	Aujila, Shri Gurjeet Singh	INC
308. Anandpur Sahib	Chandumajra, Shri Prem Singh	SAD
309. Bathinda	Badal, Smt. Harsimrat Kaur	SAD
310. Faridkot (SC)	Singh, Prof. Sadhu	AAP
311. Fatehgarh Sahib (SC)	Khalsa, Shri Harinder Singh	AAP
312. Ferozpur	Ghubaya, Shri Sher Singh	SAD
313. Gurdaspur	Jakhar, Shri Sunil Kumar	INC
314. Hoshiarpur (SC)	Sampla, Shri Vijay	BJP
315. Jalandhar	Chaudhary, Shri Santokh Singh	INC
316. Khadoor Sahib	Brahmpura, Shri Ranjit Singh	SAD
317. Ludhiana	Singh, Shri Ravneet	INC
318. Patiala	Gandhi, Dr. Dharam Vira	AAP
319. Sangrur	Mann, Shri Bhagwant	AAP

RAJASTHAN (25)

320. Ajmer	Sharma, Dr. Raghu	INC
321. Alwar	Yadav, Dr. Karan Singh	INC
322. Banswara (ST)	Ninama, Shri Manshankar	BJP
323. Barmer	Col. Choudhary, Sona Ram, VSM (Retd.)	BJP
324. Bharatpur (SC)	Koli, Shri Bahadur Singh	BJP
325. Bhilwara	Baheria, Shri Subhash Chandra	BJP
326. Bikaner (SC)	Meghwal, Shri Arjun Ram	BJP
327. Chittorgarh	Joshi, Shri C. P.	BJP
328. Churu	Kaswan, Shri Rahul	BJP
329. Dausa (ST)	Meena, Shri Harish Chandra	BJP
330. Ganganagar (SC)	Chauhan, Shri Nihal Chand	BJP
331. Jaipur	Bohra, Shri Ramcharan	BJP
332. Jaipur Rural	Rathore, Col. Rajyavardhan Singh	BJP
333. Jalore	Patel, Shri Devji Mansingram	BJP
334. Jhalawar-Baran	Singh, Shri Dushyant	BJP
335. Jhunjhunu	Ahlawat, Smt. Santosh	BJP
336. Jodhpur	Shekhawat, Shri Gajendra Singh	BJP
337. Karauli-Dholpur (SC)	Rajoria, Dr. Manoj	BJP
338. Kota	Birla, Shri Om	BJP
339. Nagaur	Chaudhary, Shri C.R.	BJP
340. Pali	Chaudhary, Shri P.P.	BJP
341. Rajsamand	Rathore, Shri Hariom Singh	BJP

342. Sikar	Saraswati, Shri Sumedhanand	BJP
343. Tonk-Sawai Madhopur	Jaunapuria, Shri Sukhbir Singh	BJP
344. Udaipur	Meena, Shri Arjunlal	BJP

SIKKIM (1)

345. Sikkim	Rai, Shri Prem Das	SDF

TAMIL NADU (39)

346. Arakkonam	Hari, Shri G.	AIADMK
347. Arani	V., Shri Elumalai	AIADMK
348. Chennai Central	S.R., Shri Vijayakumar	AIADMK
349. Chennai North	Venkatesh Babu, Shri T.G.	AIADMK
350. Chennai South	Jayavardhan, Dr. Jayakumar	AIADMK
351. Chidambaram (SC)	Chandrakasi, Shri M.	AIADMK
352. Coimbatore	P., Shri Nagarajan	AIADMK
353. Cuddalore	Arunmozhithevan, Shri A.	AIADMK
354. Dharmapuri	Ramadoss, Dr. Anbumani	PMK
355. Dindigul	Udhayakumar, Shri M.	AIADMK
356. Erode	Selvakumarachinnayan, Shri S.	AIADMK
357. Kallakurichi	Kamaraj, Dr. K.	AIADMK
358. Kancheepuram(SC)	Maragatham, Smt. K.	AIADMK
359. Kanniyakumari	Radhakrishnan, Shri Pon	BJP
360. Karur	Thambi Durai, Dr. M.	AIADMK
361. Krishnagiri	Ashokkumar, Shri K.	AIADMK
362. Madurai	Gopalakrishnan, Shri R.	AIADMK
363. Mayiladuthurai	Bharathimohan, Shri R.K.	AIADMK
364. Nagapattinam (SC)	Gopal, Dr. K.	AIADMK
365. Namakkal	Sundaram, Shri P.R.	AIADMK
366. Nilgiris (SC)	Chinnaraj, Shri Gopalakrishnan	AIADMK
367. Perambalur	Marutharajaa, Shri R.P.	AIADMK
368. Pollachi	Mahendran, Shri C.	AIADMK
369. Ramanathapuram	Raajhaa, Shri A. Anwhar	AIADMK
370. Salem	Selvam, Shri V. Panneer	AIADMK
371. Sivaganga	Senthilnathan, Shri P.R.	AIADMK
372. Sriperumbudur	Ramachandran, Shri Krishnan Narayanasamy	AIADMK
373. Tenkasi (SC)	M., Smt. Vasanthi	AIADMK
374. Thanjavur	K., Shri Parasuraman	AIADMK
375. Theni	Parthipan, Shri R.	AIADMK
376. Thoothukkudi	Natterjee, Advocate Jayasingh Thiyagaraj	AIADMK

377. Tiruchirappalli	Kumar, Shri P.	AIADMK
378. Tirunelveli	Prabakaran, Shri K.R.P.	AIADMK
379. Tiruppur	Sathyabama, Smt. V.	AIADMK
380. Tiruvallur (SC)	Venugopal, Dr. Ponnusamy	AIADMK
381. Tiruvannamalai	Vanaroja, Smt. R.	AIADMK
382. Vellore	Senguttuvan, Shri B.	AIADMK
383. Viluppuram (SC)	Rajendran, Shri S.	AIADMK
384. Virudhunagar	Radhakrishnan, Shri T.	AIADMK

TELANGANA (17)

385. Adilabad (ST)	Godam, Shri Nagesh	TRS
386. Bhongir	Goud, Dr. Boora Narsaiah	TRS
387. Chevella	Reddy, Shri Konda Vishweshwar	TRS
388. Hyderabad	Owaisi, Shri Asaduddin	AIMIM
389. Karimnagar	Boianapalli, Shri Vinod Kumar	TRS
390. Khammam	Reddy, Shri Ponguleti Srinivasa	YSR (CP)
391. Mahabubabad	Naik, Dr. (Prof.) Azmeera Seetaram	TRS
392. Mahabubnagar	Reddy, Shri A.P. Jithender	TRS
393. Malkajgiri	Reddy, Shri Ch. Malla	TDP
394. Medak	Reddy, Shri Kotha Prabhakar	TRS
395. Nagarkurnool (SC)	Yellaiah, Shri Nandi	INC
396. Nalgonda	Gutha, Shri Sukender Reddy	INC
397. Nizamabad	Kalvakuntla, Smt. Kavitha	TRS
398. Peddapalle (SC)	Suman, Shri Balka	TRS
399. Secunderabad	Dattatreya, Shri Bandaru	BJP
400. Warangal	Pasunoori, Shri Dayakar	TRS
401. Zahirabad	Patil, Shri Bheemrao Baswanthrao	TRS

TRIPURA (2)

402. Tripura East (ST)	Chaudhury, Shri Jitendra	CPI(M)
403. Tripura West	Datta, Shri Sankar Prasad	CPI(M)

UTTAR PRADESH (80)

404. Agra	Ram Shankar, Prof. (Dr.)	BJP
405. Akbarpur	Singh, Shri Devendra (Alias) Bhole Singh	BJP
406. Aligarh	Gautam, Shri Satish Kumar	BJP
407. Allahabad	Gupta, Shri Shyama Charan	BJP
408. Ambedkar Nagar	Pandey, Shri Hari Om	BJP
409. Amethi	Gandhi, Shri Rahul	INC

410. Amroha	Tanwar, Shri Kanwar Singh	BJP
411. Aonla	Kumar, Shri Dharmendra	BJP
412. Azamgarh	Yadav, Shri Mulayam Singh	SP
413. Badaun	Yadav, Shri Dharmendra	SP
414. Baghpat	Singh, Dr. Satya Pal	BJP
415. Bahraich (SC)	Phoole, Sushree Sadhvi Savitri Bai	BJP
416. Ballia	Singh, Shri Bharat	BJP
417. Banda	Mishra, Shri Bhairon Prasad	BJP
418. Bansgaon (SC)	Paswan, Shri Kamlesh	BJP
419. Barabanki (SC)	Rawat, Smt. Priyanka Singh	BJP
420. Bareilly	Gangwar, Shri Santosh Kumar	BJP
421. Basti	Dwivedi, Shri Harish	BJP
422. Bhadohi	Singh, Shri Virendra	BJP
423. Bijnor	Singh, Kunwar Bharatendra	BJP
424. Bulandshahr	Singh, Shri Bhola	BJP
425. Chandauli	Pandey, Dr. Mahendra Nath	BJP
426. Deoria	Mishra, Shri Kalraj	BJP
427. Dhaurahra	Verma, Smt. Rekha Arun	BJP
428. Domariyaganj	Pal, Shri Jagdambika	BJP
429. Etah	Singh, Shri Rajveer (Raju Bhaiya)	BJP
430. Etawah (SC)	Dohrey, Shri Ashok Kumar	BJP
431. Faizabad	Singh, Shri Lallu	BJP
432. Farrukhabad	Rajput, Shri Mukesh	BJP
433. Fatehpur	Jyoti, Sadhvi Niranjan	BJP
434. Fatehpur Sikri	Chaudhary, Shri Babulal	BJP
435. Firozabad	Yadav, Shri Akshay	SP
436. Gautam Buddha Nagar	Sharma, Dr. Mahesh	BJP
437. Ghaziabad	General (Dr.) Vijay Kumar Singh (Retd.)	BJP
438. Ghazipur	Sinha, Shri Manoj Kumar	BJP
439. Ghosi	Rajbhar, Shri Hari Narayan	BJP
440. Gonda	Singh, Shri Kirti Vardhan	BJP
441. Gorakhpur	Nishad, Shri Praveen Kumar	SP
442. Hamirpur	Chandel, Kunwar Pushpendra Singh	BJP
443. Hardoi (SC)	Verma, Shri Anshul	BJP
444. Hathras (SC)	Diwakar, Shri Rajesh Kumar	BJP
445. Jalaun (SC)	Verma, Shri Bhanu Pratap Singh	BJP
446. Jaunpur	Singh, Dr. Krishna Pratap	BJP
447. Jhansi	Sushree, Uma Bharati	BJP

448. Kairana	Hasan, Begum Tabassum	RLD
449. Kaiserganj	Singh, Shri Brijbhushan Sharan	BJP
450. Kannauj	Yadav, Smt. Dimple	SP
451. Kanpur	Joshi, Dr. Murli Manohar	BJP
452. Kaushambi (SC)	Sonkar, Shri Vinod Kumar	BJP
453. Kheri	Misra, Shri Ajay (Teni)	BJP
454. Kushi Nagar	Pandey, Shri Rajesh	BJP
455. Lalganj (SC)	Sonker, Smt. Neelam	BJP
456. Lucknow	Singh, Shri Rajnath	BJP
457. Machhlishahr	Ram Charitra Nishad, Shri	BJP
458. Maharajganj	Chowdhary, Shri Pankaj	BJP
459. Mainpuri	Yadav, Shri Tejpratap Singh	SP
460. Mathura	Hema Malini, Smt.	BJP
461. Meerut	Agrawal, Shri Rajendra	BJP
462. Mirzapur	Patel, Smt. Anupriya	Apna Dal
463. Misrikh (SC)	Bala, Smt. Anju	BJP
464. Mohanlalganj (SC)	Kishore, Shri Kaushal	BJP
465. Moradabad	Kumar, Shri Kunwar Sarvesh	BJP
466. Muzaffarnagar	Balyan, Dr. Sanjeev Kumar	BJP
467. Nagina (SC)	Singh, Dr. Yashwant	BJP
468. Phulpur	Patel, Shri Nagendra Pratap Singh	SP
469. Pilibhit	Gandhi, Smt. Maneka Sanjay	BJP
470. Pratapgarh	Singh, Shri Kunwar Haribansh	Apna Dal
471. Rae Bareli	Gandhi, Smt. Sonia	INC
472. Rampur	Singh, Dr. Nepal	BJP
473. Robertsganj (SC)	Chhotelal, Shri	BJP
474. Saharanpur	Lakhanpal, Shri Raghav	BJP
475. Salempur	Kushawaha, Shri Ravindra	BJP
476. Sambhal	Singh, Shri Satya Pal	BJP
477. Sant Kabir Nagar	Tripathi, Shri Sharad	BJP
478. Shahjahanpur (SC)	Raj, Smt. Krishna	BJP
479. Shrawasti	Mishra, Shri Daddan	BJP
480. Sitapur	Verma, Shri Rajesh	BJP
481. Sultanpur	Gandhi, Shri Feroze Varun	BJP
482. Unnao	Swami Maharaj, Dr. Sakshi Ji	BJP
483. Varanasi	Modi, Shri Narendra	BJP

UTTARAKHAND (5)

484. Almora (SC)	Tamta, Shri Ajay	BJP
485. Garhwal	Khanduri, Maj Gen Bhuwan Chandra AVSM (Retd.)	BJP
486. Hardwar	Nishank, Dr. Ramesh Pokhriyal	BJP
487. Nainital-Udhamsingh Nagar	Koshyari, Shri Bhagat Singh	BJP
488. Tehri Garhwal	Shah, Smt. Mala Rajya Laxmi	BJP

WEST BENGAL (42)

489. Alipurduars (ST)	Tirkey, Shri Dasrath	AITC
490. Arambagh (SC)	Poddar, Smt. Aparupa	AITC
491. Asansol	Babul Supriyo, Shri	BJP
492. Baharampur	Chowdhury, Shri Adhir Ranjan	INC
493. Balurghat	Ghosh, Ms. Arpita	AITC
494. Bangaon (SC)	Thakur, Smt. Mamata	AITC
495. Bankura	Varma, Smt. Dev (Moon Moon Sen)	AITC
496. Barasat	Dastidar, Dr. (Smt.) Kakoli Ghosh	AITC
497. Bardhaman Purba (SC)	Mondal, Shri Sunil Kumar	AITC
498. Bardhaman-Durgapur	Sanghamita, Prof. (Dr.) Mamtaz	AITC
499. Barrackpur	Trivedi, Shri Dinesh	AITC
500. Basirhat	Ali, Shri Idris	AITC
501. Birbhum	Roy (Banerjee), Smt. Satabdi	AITC
502. Bishnupur (SC)	Khan, Shri Saumitra	AITC
503. Bolpur (SC)	Hazra, Dr. Anupam	AITC
504. Coochbehar	Ray, Shri Partha Pratim	AITC
505. Darjeeling	Ahluwalia, Shri S.S.	BJP
506. Diamond Harbour	Banerjee, Shri Abhishek	AITC
507. Dum Dum	Roy, Prof. Saugata	AITC
508. Ghatal	Adhikari, Shri Deepak (Dev)	AITC
509. Hooghly	De (Nag), Dr. (Smt.) Ratna	AITC
510. Howrah	Banerjee, Shri Prasun	AITC
511. Jadavpur	Bose, Prof. Sugata	AITC
512. Jalpaiguri (SC)	Barman, Shri Bijoy Chandra	AITC
513. Jangipur	Mukherjee, Dr. Abhijit	INC
514. Jaynagar (SC)	Mondal, Smt. Pratima	AITC

515. Jhargram (ST)	Saren, Dr. Uma	AITC
516. Kanthi	Adhikari, Shri Sisir Kumar	AITC
517. Kolkata Dakshin	Bakshi, Shri Subrata	AITC
518. Kolkata Uttar	Bandyopadhyay, Shri Sudip	AITC
519. Krishnanagar	Paul, Shri Tapas	AITC
520. Maldaha Dakshin	Choudhury, Shri Abu Hasem Khan	INC
521. Maldaha Uttar	Noor, Smt. Mausam	INC
522. Mathurapur (SC)	Jatua, Shri Choudhury Mohan	AITC
523. Medinipur	Roy, Smt. Sandhya	AITC
524. Murshidabad	Khan, Shri Md. Badaruddoza	CPI(M)
525. Purulia	Mahato, Dr. Mriganka	AITC
526. Raiganj	Salim, Shri Mohammad	CPI(M)
527. Ranaghat (SC)	Mandal, Dr. Tapas	AITC
528. Serampore	Banerjee, Shri Kalyan	AITC
529. Tamluk	Adhikari, Shri Dibyendu	AITC
530. Uluberia	Ahmed, Smt. Sajda	AITC

ANDAMAN AND NICOBAR ISLANDS (1)

531. Andaman and Nicobar Islands	Ray, Shri Bishnu Pada	BJP

CHANDIGARH (1)

532. Chandigarh	Kher, Smt. Kirron Anupam	BJP

DADRA AND NAGAR HAVELI (1)

533. Dadra and Nagar Haveli (ST)	Patel, Shri Natubhai Gomanbhai	BJP

DAMAN AND DIU (1)

534. Daman and Diu	Patel, Shri Lalubhai Babubhai	BJP

NATIONAL CAPITAL TERRITORY OF DELHI (7)

535. Chandni Chowk	Harsh Vardhan, Dr.	BJP
536. East Delhi	Girri, Shri Maheish	BJP
537. New Delhi	Lekhi, Smt. Meenakashi	BJP
538. North East Delhi	Tiwari, Shri Manoj Kumar	BJP
539. North West Delhi (SC)	Raj, Dr. Udit	BJP

540. South Delhi	Bidhuri, Shri Ramesh	BJP
541. West Delhi	Singh, Shri Parvesh Sahib	BJP

LAKSHADWEEP (1)

542. Lakshadweep (ST)	Mohammed, Shri Faizal P. P.	NCP

PUDUCHERRY (1)

543. Puducherry	Radhakrishnan, Shri R.	AINRC

NOMINATED (2)

544. Baker, Shri George	Nominated Anglo-Indian (West Bengal)	BJP
545. Hay, Prof. Richard	Nominated Anglo-Indian (Kerala)	BJP

Abbreviations used for Parties : All India Forward Bloc - AIFB; All India Majlis-e-Ittehadul Muslimeen - AIMEIM; All India Namathu Rajiyam (Our Kingdom Congress - AINR Congress; All India Trinamool Congress -AITC; Asom Gana Parishad - AGP; Bahujan Samaj Party - BSP; Bharatiya Janata Party- BJP; Bharatiya Navshakti Party - BNP; Biju Janata Dal - BJD; Communist Party of India - CPI; Communist Party of India (Marxist) - CPI(M); Dravida Munnetra Kazhagam - DMK; Indian National Congress - INC; Jammu & Kashmir National Conference - J&KNC; Janata Dal (Secular) - JD (S); Janata Dal (United) - JD (U); Jharkhand Mukti Morcha - JMM; Kerala Congress - KC; Lok Jan Shakti Party - LJSP; Marumalarchi Dravida Munnetra Kazhagam - MDMK; Mizo National Front - MNF; Muslim League - ML; Nagaland Peoples Front - NPF; Nationalist Congress Party - NCP; National Democratic Progressive Party - NDPP; Pattali Makkal Katchi - PMK; Jammu and Kashmir Peoples Democratic Party - J&K PDP; Rashtriya Janata Dal - RJD; Rashtriya Lok Dal - RLD; Republican Party of India (A) - RPI (A); Revolutionary Socialist Party - RSP; Samajwadi Janata Party (Rashtriya) - SJP (R); Samajwadi Party - SP; Shiromani Akali Dal - SAD; Shiv Sena - SS; Sikkim Democratic Front - SDF; Swabhimani Rpaksha Party - SWP; Telangana Rashtra Samithi - TRS; Telugu Desam Party - TDP; Viduthalai Chiruthaigal Katchi - VCK; Independent - IND.

लोकतंत्र के स्वर
राष्ट्रपति राम नाथ कोविन्द
The Republican Ethic
President Ram Nath Kovind
2500 YEARS OF BUDDHISM
आधुनिक भारत के निर्माता
सरदार वल्लभभाई पटेल
BUILDERS OF MODERN INDIA
Pandit Deendayal Upadhyaya
हमारे समय में उपनिषद्
CHILDREN'S VIVEKANANDA
WOMEN
PORTRAITS OF STRENGTH
शेखावाटी की लोकसंस्कृति
वेद-गाथा
SARAL PANCHATANTRA
हार की खुशी
बादल की सैर
मां का जन्मदिन
रंग-बिरंगी कहानियां
बाल महाभारत

INDIA's LEADING INSTITUTE FOR IAS / IFoS EXAMINATIONS
Website: www.diasindia.com
E-Mail: diasindia123@gmail.com
DIAS
Delhi Institute For Administrative Services
(M): 09350934622
011-40079000
ALMOST ALL SELECTIONS FROM SCIENCE OPTIONALS IN IAS 2018 HAVE BEEN OUR STUDENTS
ABHISHEK SURANA RANK 10 PHYSICS (327)
SAGAR KUMAR RANK 13 MATHS (299)
VARJIT WALIA RANK 21 PHYSICS (314)
ABHISHEK CHAUDHARY RANK 37 PHYSICS (302)
VIDEH KHARE RANK 99 CHEMISTRY (292)
AKASH BANSAL RANK 130 CHEMISTRY (255)
ARCHIT CHANDAK RANK 184 MATHS (307)
DEEPESH KEDIA RANK 221 CHEMISTRY (314)
K. VARUN REDDY RANK 225 MATHS (330)
ABHISHREE RANK 297 PHYSICS (306)
SAHIL SANGWAN RANK 336 CHEMISTRY (318)
PUNEET K. SINGH RANK 353 PHYSICS (315)
GS / Essay by DIAS Team
DIAS OPTIONALS
PHYSICS
By Renowned D.P.Vajpayee
Online classes also available.
CHEMISTRY
By Dr. R.K Singh
MATHEMATICS
By Shukla & Vajpayee Sir
LAW
By H. Kaushik
Courses Offered at our Lucknow Centre
1. G.S. by DIAS Team
2. History by Dr. Anshul Bajpai
3. Pub. Admn. by Gaurav/Srivastav Sir
Batches start 5 times in a year
DIAS is having its own hostel in Delhi for the benefit of outstation candidates
DELHI INSTITUTE FOR ADMINISTRATIVE SERVICES
DIAS
Delhi Institute For Administrative Services
DIAS INDIA EDUTECH (PVT) LTD
Head Off.: 26/3 & 18/1, 2nd Floor, Old Rajinder Nagar, New Delhi - 60.
Lucknow Centre: MS-141, Aliganj Sec.D, Near Puraniya Railway Crossing
Tel.: 011-40079000, Mob.: 9350934622